The Three Pillars of Zion

Larry Barkdull

SERIES TITLES

Book 1: *Zion—Our Origin and Our Destiny*

Book 2: *The First Pillar of Zion—The New and Everlasting Covenant*

Book 3: *The Second Pillar of Zion—The Oath and Covenant of the Priesthood*

Book 4: *The Third Pillar of Zion—The Law of Consecration*

Book 5: *The Pure in Heart*

Pillars of Zion Publishing
Orem, Utah

Copyright and Permission

Copyright © 2009 Barkdull Publishing LLC
Publishing Imprint: *Pillars of Zion Publishing,* a division of Barkdull Marketing Inc.
Sole Selling Agent: Barkdull Marketing Inc.
All Rights Reserved. No part of this book may be reproduced in any format or in any medium without the written consent of the publisher, Pillars of Zion Publishing.

Contact

Contact us at Info@PillarsOfZion.com
Visit our Website at www.PillarsOfZion.com

Disclaimer

This series is heavily documented with over 3,800 references and 242 works cited. Every effort has been made to achieve accuracy, nevertheless, this work is not an official publication of the Church of Jesus Christ of Latter-day Saints, and the views expressed within this work are the sole responsibility of the author and do not necessarily reflect the position of The Church of Jesus Christ of Latter-day Saints or any other entity.

Library of Congress Cataloging Publication Data is on file at the Library of Congress.
ISBN: 978-0-9824904-7-1

Dedication

To Elizabeth Barkdull
Ron and Bonnie McMillan
David and Loralea Anderson
Randall and Marla Vaughan
Paul and Sharon Meyers

Acknowledgments

My wife, Elizabeth, and I would like to acknowledge a number of people, who, in one way or another, lent their support for the creation of this project.

Lawrence and Georgia Shaw
Lance and Jozet Richardson
Blaine Yorgason
Scot and Maurine Proctor
Clay Gorton
Ted Gibbons
Grover Cardon
Gary and Bonnie Leavitt
David and Bianca Lisonbee
Max and Peggy Park
Bud and Barbara Poduska
Dee Jay Bawden
Steve Glenn
Gavon and Tanya Barkdull

Production Staff

Editor—Jay A. Parry
Graphic Artist—Ryan Davis (www.RybreadStudio.com)
Typesetter—Paul Meyers
Website Development—Sebo Marketing (www.sebomarketing.com)

Pagination Note

Because this work is serialized, the pagination and footnoting between books are continuous.

Table of Contents

BOOK 1: ZION—OUR ORIGIN AND OUR DESTINY	1
INTRODUCTION	3
Parallels between the Third Nephi Saints and the Latter-day Saints	3
An Important Key to Establishing Zion	4
Enoch's Dispensation Is a Pattern	4
The Three Pillars of Zion	5
SECTION 1	6
ZION—WHAT DO WE KNOW OF IT?	6
Zion Is Our Ideal	7
The Celestial Order	8
Zion and Babylon—Exact Opposites	8
Becoming a Zion Person	9
SECTION 2	10
OVERVIEW OF ZION PEOPLES	10
Fall from Zion	10
The Way Back to Zion Revealed	11
Zion—A New Way of Life	12
Surety of a Better World	13
Adam's Zion	13
Enos's Zion	13
Enoch's Zion	14
Methuselah and Noah's Zion	14
Melchizedek's Zion	15
Abraham's Zion	16
Moses' Attempt at Zion	17
Alma the Elder's Zion	19
King Benjamin's Zion	19
Alma the Younger's Zion	25
The Apostles' Zion	26
The Nephites' Zion	26
Joseph Smith's Zion	29
Latter-day Zion	33
Summary and Conclusion	34
SECTION 3	35
WE WERE PREPARED TO BECOME LATTER-DAY ZION PEOPLE	35
Divine Appointment	36
Special Spirits of the Royal Generation	37
Perspective on the Cosmic War	39
Preparation in the "First Place"	40
Summary and Conclusion	41

SECTION 4	44
BABYLON THE GREAT	44
Anti-Christ Philosophy	45
Cain	45
Nimrod	47
Sodom and Gomorrah	49
Descriptions of Babylon	51
Babylon As a Religion	53
The "Great Church" of the Devil	54
Babylon As a Temple	56
Nephi's Description of Babylon	56
Spiritual Babylon	64
Competition	66
Hypocrites	68
False Philosophies	69
Popularity	71
Latter-day Babylon—Prophetic Description of Our Time	72
Babylon Today Compared to the Days of Noah	73
Paul's Prophecy	75
Inverting the Truth	76
Moroni's Prophecy	77
The Fall of Babylon	78
Samuel the Lamanite's Parallel Denunciation of Babylon	80
Go Ye Out from Babylon	84
Summary and Conclusion	85
Postlude	87
BOOK 2: THE FIRST PILLAR OF ZION—THE NEW AND EVERLASTING COVENANT	89
INTRODUCTION	90
SECTION 5	92
PREFACE TO THE NEW AND EVERLASTING COVENANT	92
The Plan of Happiness	93
The Covenant of the Gods	93
Happiness Encompasses All That Is Good	94
Balancing Justice and Mercy	94
Placed beyond Our Enemies	95
How Mercy Appeases Justice	95
Experiencing Contrasts Leads to Happiness	96
Overview of the New and Everlasting Covenant	97
The Covenant of Justice	98
Who Are the Just, and How Are They Justified?	98
Justification and Agency	100
Celestial Law	101
Preserved, Perfected, and Sanctified by the Laws of God	101
Blessed As If We Understood	102
The Covenant of Mercy	102

Mercy and Grace	103
Justification	104
Purification	104
Sanctification	106
Our Responsibility	106
The Crucible—the Baptism of Fire	107
Purified and Sanctified to Make an Offering	107
Oneness or Unification	108
Oneness and the Law of Restoration	110
Restoration and Resurrection	110
Hundredfold Restoration	111
Oneness and Deliverance	112
Summary and Conclusion	112

Section 6

The New and Everlasting Covenant: 115

The First Pillar of Zion 115

The Structure of the Covenant	116
The New and Everlasting Covenant As an Agreement	117
1. Introduction	117
2. The Covenant of Justice	118
3. The Covenant of Mercy	118
4. The Covenant of Baptism	119
4a) Agreement to Renew and Abide in the Covenant of Baptism	120
4b) Agreement to Live the Law of the Sabbath Day	121
5. Agreement to Receive the Covenant of the Priesthood	123
5a) Worthy Men Agree to Be Ordained	123
5b) Ordained Men Agree to Magnify Their Calling	125
5c) Ordained Men Agree to Continued Faithfulness	125
6. Abide in the Covenant to the End	126
The Father's Guarantee	127
Effective Signatures	127

Section 7 128

Abide in the Covenant 128

The Leavening Power of the Doctrine of the Covenant	129
The Covenant Separates Us from Babylon, or the World	130
Zion People Are Distinguished by Observing the Sabbath Day	131
Power in the Covenant	131
Other Powers Manifested in the Covenant	133
Safety in the Covenant	133
Safety through Consecration in the Covenant	135
The Great Discovery	136
Examples of Safety in the Covenant	136
Progressing in the Covenant	138
Discovering the Relationship through Progression	139
Order in the Covenant	140

Order and Ordinances	141
Order and Consecration	142
Abide in the Covenant	142
Abiding in the Covenant Summons Divine Love	143
Abiding in the Covenant through the Sacrament	144
Summary and Conclusion	145

SECTION 8 — 147

THE NEW AND EVERLASTING COVENANT—THE HOLY MARRIAGE — 147

Born to Marry	148
The Parents' Responsibility and the Bride's Choice	149
Requirements to Legalize the Covenant	149
Initiating the Marriage Proposal	150
Entering into the Covenant	151
Bought with a Price	151
The Marriage Contract	152
The Gift of Value	154
The Pledge	155
The Cup to Seal the Covenant	155
The Covenantal Feast	156
The Father's Announcement	157
The Bride's Veil	157
The Friend of the Bridegroom	158
Preparing for Each Other	159
The Serious Nature of Preparing	161
The Bride's Final Preparations	162
Invitation to the Wedding	164
The Wedding Processional	165
Claiming the Bride	165
The Wedding	166
The Bridegroom's Plea	168
Postlude	170

BOOK 3: THE SECOND PILLAR OF ZION—THE OATH AND COVENANT OF THE PRIESTHOOD — 171

INTRODUCTION — 172

SECTION 9 — 174

THE HOLY PRIESTHOOD AFTER THE ORDER OF THE SON OF GOD — 174

The Doctrines of the Priesthood As They Apply to Men and Women	175
Melchizedek, the Title and the Man	175
King Benjamin, a Type of Melchizedek	177
The Restoration of the Priesthood	181
Elijah Restores the Sealing Keys of the Patriarchal Order of the Priesthood	182
Elijah Restores the Fulness of the Priesthood	183
Moses Restores Priesthood Keys of Family Gathering	183
Elias Restores Priesthood Keys	183
The Joint Missions of Elias and Elijah	184
Building One Priesthood Power upon Another	185

Rescuing This Generation	185
Eternal Principle of Power	186
Premortal Qualification for the Priesthood	186
The Obligation of Zion Priesthood Holders	187
Our Priesthood Work Then and Now	188
The Covenant of the Priesthood	189
The Lesser and Greater Portions	189
The Patriarchal Order	190
Differing Purposes and Powers	190
Grand Purposes of the Priesthood	191
Priesthood Blessings	191
The Blessings of Adam	192
The Blessings of Abraham	193
Abraham's Qualifications and Desire	194
Blessings of the Priesthood	195
The Prize Is Worth the Price	196
The Authority and Keys of the Priesthood	197
Doctrine of the Priesthood	198
"As My Father Hath Sent Me, Even So Send I You"	199
Summary and Conclusion	200

SECTION 10 — 202

THE OATH AND COVENANT OF THE PRIESTHOOD: — 202

OUR AGREEMENTS — 202

If We Are Faithful . . .	203
If We Obtain the Aaronic and the Melchizedek Priesthoods . . .	204
If We Magnify Our *Calling* . . .	205
Magnifying the *Calling* and *Callings*	206
Three Ways to Magnify Our Calling	208
Obtaining Gospel Knowledge	208
Personal Righteousness	208
Dedicated Service	212
Grace *to* Grace by Grace *for* Grace	213
If Any of You Lack	214
Magnifying Our Priesthood Calling by Bearing Testimony	215
The Ultimate Magnification of Our *Calling*	217
The Three Stages of the Priesthood Covenant	218
Summary and Conclusion	219

SECTION 11 — 221

THE OATH AND COVENANT OF THE PRIESTHOOD: — 221

THE FATHER'S OATH, INSTRUCTIONS, AND PROMISES — 221

The Father's Two Oaths Guaranteeing Us the Blessings of Abraham	222
Sanctification by the Spirit unto the Renewing of Our Bodies	224
The Progression of the Renewing of Our Bodies	225
Power Given to the Renewed and Sanctified	226
Blessings Given to the Renewed and Sanctified	227

"I Sanctify Myself, That They Also Might Be Sanctified"	230
The Sons of Moses and of Aaron	231
The Seed of Abraham	233
The Church and Kingdom of God	234
The Elect of God	234
Calling and Election Made Sure	236
Receiving Christ and the Father	238
"All That My Father Hath"	241
Ministering and Protection of Angels	242
The Father's Instructions: *Be Careful and Be Diligent*	245
"And the Father Teacheth Him of the Covenant"	246
The Promise of Eternal Life	248
Penalties for Neglecting or Rejecting the Covenant of the Priesthood	251
Summary and Conclusion	252

Section 12

The Constitution of the Priesthood:

Why Many Are Called, but Not Chosen

	255
	255
	255
Two Groups	256
A Satanic Strategy	256
A Test of Loyalties	257
Restoration of the Constitution of the Priesthood	258
The Marriage of the King's Son	258
"Many Will Say to Me in That Day"	260
Called and Chosen for Eternal Life	261
Abiding Zion's Celestial Law in Babylon's Telestial Setting	262
The End-Purpose of Our Calling	263
Distinctions between Those Who Are Called and Chosen	264
Building a Sure House	265
Mortal Tests That Challenge Our Calling	265
The Daunting Test of Riches	266
Safety and Perfection in Consecration	267
The Sacrifice of All Things—a "Hard Thing"	268
Safety in the "Royal Law"	268
The Dangers of Rationalization and Postponement	269
The Law of Restitution—an *Hundredfold* Reward	270
Babylon among Us	271
Walking in Darkness at Noon-day	273
The Test of Praise	274
"Rights of the Priesthood"	275
"Inseparably Connected"—Righteousness and Priesthood Power	276
Connecting to the True Vine	277
Amen to the Priesthood	278
Summary and Conclusion	279

Section 13— — 283

The Constitution of the Priesthood: — 283

Instructing the Chosen Few — 283

- Stages of Progression within the Covenant — 284
- No Power or Influence Can or Ought to Be Maintained by Virtue of the Priesthood — 284
- Zion's Approach to Agency — 285
- Persuasion vs. Babylon's Counterparts — 286
- Zion's Patient Persuasion — 286
- Patience and Long-suffering — 286
- Patience — 287
- Long-suffering — 289
- Gentleness and Meekness — 290
- Feigned and Unfeigned Love — 291
- Love Unfeigned — 292
- What Is "True Love?" — 293
- To Love First — 294
- Love Perfected — 294
- No Fear in Love — 295
- Love—the Greatest Power — 295
- Kindness — 295
- Pure Knowledge vs. False Knowledge — 296
- Zion's Approach to "Pure Knowledge" — 299
- Wisdom and "Pure Knowledge" — 301
- Reproving the Lord's Way — 302
- Reproving with Love — 303
- Cords of Death and Bonds of Love — 304
- Charity toward All Men and the Household of God — 304
- Let Virtue Garnish Thy Thoughts Unceasingly — 305
- Garnishing Our Thoughts with Virtue — 306
- Summary and Conclusion — 307

Section 14 — 308

The Constitution of the Priesthood: — 308

The Rewards for the Chosen Few — 308

- The Rewards — 309
- "Then Shall Thy Confidence Wax Strong in the Presence of God" — 309
- Now Is the Time — 310
- A Change of Paradigm — 311
- Turning the *Key* — 311
- Obtaining, at Last, a Perfect Knowledge of the Savior — 312
- Receiving the Greatest Comfort — 313
- Regaining the Presence of God—the End-Purpose of the Priesthood — 314
- The Revealed Process for Standing in the Presence of God — 314
- The Priesthood Is the Power to Stand in God's Presence — 315
- "The Doctrine of the Priesthood Shall Distil upon Thy Soul" — 315
- The Rights and the Doctrine of the Priesthood — 317

The Doctrine of the Priesthood and the Law of Asking	317
Lesser and Greater Portions of the Doctrine of the Priesthood	319
The Necessity and Power of Priesthood Ordinances	319
The Doctrine of the Priesthood and Revelatory "Keys"	321
"The Holy Ghost Shall Be Thy Constant Companion"	322
The Holy Spirit of Promise	323
Scepters and Dominions—the Holy Interview	323
Priests and Kings, Priestesses and Queens	325
Becoming Members of the Church of the Firstborn	327
Angelic Ministers from the Church of the Firstborn	329
The Order of the Son of God	330
The Order of the Son of God and Marriage	332
The Fulness of the Priesthood	333
Power in the Priesthood	334
"Without Compulsory Means It Shall Flow unto Thee Forever"	335
Summary and Conclusion	336
Postlude	338

BOOK 4: THE THIRD PILLAR OF ZION—THE LAW OF CONSECRATION	340
INTRODUCTION	341
SECTION 15	343

WHAT IS THE LAW OF CONSECRATION?	343
Consecration—the Principle of Exaltation	343
The Condition of Babylon	345
The Greatest Desire	345
Definition of Consecration	346
The Law We Must Live to Achieve the Celestial Kingdom	347
Consecrating the Good and the Bad	347
Premise of Consecration	348
Consecration Is Nonnegotiable	348
Restoration of the Law of Consecration	349
Consecrating Tithes and Offerings	351
Modern Applications of Consecration	351
Learning to Better Live the Law of Consecration	352
Sanctified by Consecration: The Law of the Celestial Kingdom	352
Familiarity	353
Ultimate Consecration—to Sacrifice a Prepared and Purified Heart	353
Live Consecration or Lose Eternal Life	354
Laying Everything on the Altar	355
Consecration and the Atonement	356
Consecration—A Temporal Law with Spiritual Implications	357
Consecration—A Law That Makes Us Independent from the World	358
Consecration—An Order That Orders Our Lives	361
What Consecration Is Not	363
Temporal and Spiritual Salvation	363
Summary and Conclusion	364

SECTION 16 — 367

CONSECRATION RESULTS IN EQUALITY AND UNITY — 367

- Equality—"In Mine Own Way" — 368
  - Equality and the Law of Prosperity — 368
  - New Math — 369
  - Esteeming All Flesh in One — 370
  - Seven Points of Equality — 371
  - Taking Equal Responsibility for the Cause of Zion — 372
- Unity — 373
  - The Unifying Power of the At-one-ment — 374
  - Oneness and Synergy — 375
  - Antagonism—the Opposite of Synergy — 377
  - Unity and Prayer — 377
  - How We Achieve Unity — 379
  - The End Result of Unity — 379
- All Things Common among Them — 379
- Consecration and the Law of Offense — 380
- Law of Common Consent — 381
- Connecting Consecration with the Law of the Gospel and the Law of Sacrifice — 381
- Love Leads Us to Eternal Life — 382
- Is Baptism Sufficient for Exaltation? — 383
- Two Purposes of the Law of the Gospel — 383
- No Other Way — 384
- The Interwoven Covenants — 384
- The Law of Sacrifice — 385
- Sacrifice and love — 386
- Sacrifice—Our Contribution to Our Salvation — 386
- Summary and Conclusion — 387

SECTION 17 — 391

THE GUIDING PRINCIPLES OF CONSECRATION — 391

- Guiding Principles of Consecration — 392
- Agency — 392
  - Agency and Truth — 392
  - Agency—a Gift Assured and Protected by the Savior — 393
  - The Body—the Vehicle for Moral Agency — 393
  - Our Eternal Destiny Lies within Our Body — 394
  - Agency and Agents — 395
  - Agency and Self-reliance — 396
  - Agency Fueled by Opposites — 397
- Stewardship — 397
  - The Riches of the Earth Are the Lord's — 397
  - God Becomes Our Paymaster — 399
  - Never Turn Back — 400
  - The Law of Stewardship and the Oath and Covenant of the Priesthood — 400
  - Stewardship and Equality — 401
  - Stewardships in the Scriptures — 402
  - Understanding the Order of the Law of Stewardship — 403

Spiritual Gifts Are Stewardships to Bless Others	404
Profitable and Unprofitable Servants	405
Stewardships Prepare Us for Eternal Life	407
Accountability	407
Accounting in Time and Eternity	408
Accountability and Agency	409
Labor	409
Idleness Condemned	410
The Idle Poor	410
The Idle Rich	411
The Virtue of Labor	412
Labor for What?	413
Augmenting the Effect of Labor	414
Labor and Judgment	415
Summary and Conclusion	416

Section 18   418

The Ultimate Test: God or Mammon	418
The Test of Riches	419
Only the Pure in Heart Can Pass This Test	419
The Lord's Willingness to Be Tested	420
Consecration Is All about Love	421
A Change of Orders	422
Love of Money Is the Root of *All* Evil	422
Covetousness—the Last Law	424
The Higher and Lower Laws of Prosperity	424
The More Weighty Matters	425
Trying to Mix Mammon and Zion	426
Warnings against Compromise	428
Making Mammon Holy	428
Mormon's View of the Last Days	429
The First Commandments of This Dispensation	430
No Security in Mammon	431
Slippery Treasures	432
Lazarus and the Rich Man	433
Nothing Compares to the Danger	434
Lessons in the Scriptures Concerning Wealth	435
Scriptural Description of the Last Days	437
Scriptures about Idolatry and Wealth	437
Scriptures about Seeking Wealth and Forgetting God	438
Scriptures about Mammon, Inequality, and Divisiveness	438
Scriptural Evidence That the Lord Despises the Selfish Rich	440
Persecuting the Poor	441
Wo unto the Rich Who Despise the Poor	441
They Rob the Poor	442
Building Sanctuaries	442
Wealth-Seeking—The Sin That Hinders and Destroys the Church	443
The Ugliness of Inequality Contrasted with the Beautiful Work of Angels	444

- Withholding from and Judging the Poor Harshly ... 445
- The Evil of the Age: Life for Money ... 445
- A Curse on the Daughters of Zion ... 446
- Blessings for Those Who Rescue the Poor ... 447
- The Poor of the Lord's People Shall Trust in Zion ... 448
- Consequences of Seeking Wealth and Persecuting the Poor ... 449
  - Loss of the Providences of Heaven ... 450
  - Loss of Priesthood Power and Exaltation ... 450
  - Loss of the Spirit ... 450
  - Loss of Revelation ... 450
  - Loss of Happy Family Life and Spiritual Commitment ... 451
  - Loss of the Lord's Help ... 451
  - Loss of True Worship ... 451
  - Failure in Our Mission ... 452
  - Loss of Peace ... 452
  - Loss of National Security ... 454
- Who Shall Enter? ... 455
- What Doth It Profit? ... 455
- The Voice of Seven Thunders ... 456
- Choosing God over Mammon ... 457
- Obtaining a Hope in Christ ... 458
- Freely Ye Have Received, Freely Give ... 459
- Feeding the Lord's Lambs ... 460
- Choosing God's Marvelous Work over Babylon's Charms ... 460
- Invoking the Law of Asking to Receive ... 461
- Summary and Conclusion ... 461

SECTION 19 ... 468

THE ROYAL LAW ... 468
- The Royal Law Explains the Principles of Consecration ... 469
- Doctrine and Covenants 42—The Cornerstones of the Law of Consecration ... 470
- Mutual Assistance ... 470
- Faith and the Proper Use of the Priesthood ... 471
- Announcing the Kingdom of Heaven through Administrations ... 472
- Consecrating a Sickness and a Life to the Lord ... 472
- Administration and Forgiveness of Sins ... 473
- Consecration Requires Faith ... 474
- Reciprocal Love ... 475
- Charity—the Pure Love of Christ ... 476
- Charity Emerges from Faith and Hope ... 477
- Charity Transforms the Heart ... 478
- Charity Defines Discipleship ... 479
- Keeping and Feeding—the Two Tests of Charity ... 480
- Charity—the Life Blood of Zion ... 481
- Charity Is Defined by Service ... 482
- Charitable Service Saves and Exalts ... 484
- Moroni's Prayer for Latter-day Charity ... 484
- Charitable Service Protects the Giver ... 485

Charitable Service Prospers the Giver	486
Patience and Charity	487
Charity and Virtue—Essential Elements of Priesthood Power	488
Charity Draws the Lord Near	488
Charity Is an Absolute	490
Charity Is a Gift—the Greatest Gift	490
Summary and Conclusion	490
Postlude	493

BOOK 5: THE PURE IN HEART — 495

INTRODUCTION — 496

SECTION 20 — 500

COME TO ZION: THE UNIVERSAL JOURNEY TO THE LAND OF PROMISE — 500

Zion Is Our Heritage	501
The Fall	503
The Wilderness of Sin	505
The Awakening	506
The Cry for Help	507
The Lord's Wilderness	509
Experiencing Opposites	509
Strangers and Pilgrims	510
Separation from Babylon	510
Fleeing for Safety	512
The Crucible	513
The Tragedy of Murmuring	516
Finding Joy in the Journey	517
Conditions of the Lord's Wilderness	520
Living by Manna	520
Hard Work	521
Traveling by Revelation	522
Journeying According to the Lord's Will	523
Angels Attend Us	523
Safety and Security	525
Deliverance Experiences	526
The Fourth Watch	527
Lessons to Be Learned in the Lord's Wilderness	528
Preparation to Live the Higher Law	529
Putting Off the Natural Man	530
Learning the Formula of Obedience	532
Learning to Trust God: The Universal Lesson	534
Bountiful—a Reprieve	538
Confronting Satan	539
The Abrahamic Test	541
Taking upon Us the Name of Jesus Christ	543
Taking upon Us the Name of Christ through Baptism and the Sacrament	544
Common Ways of Taking upon Ourselves the Name of Christ	544
Born of God—the Mystery of Spiritual Rebirth	545

Fully Taking upon Us the Name of Jesus Christ	546
The Temple and the Name of Christ	547
The Name of Christ and Coronation	548
Coming to Christ	549
Deliverance	551
Giving Ourselves Free	552
Restoration and Exaltation	554
Sent Back as an Emissary of Zion	556
Summary and Conclusion	556

SECTION 21 — 559

THE PURE IN HEART — 559

Blessings for the Pure in Heart	559
Commanded to Seek the Lord's Face	560
Purification	561
Sanctification	561
Who May Seek the Lord's Face?	562
How Do We Come into the Presence of the Lord?	563
Knowing and Living the Correct Process	563
Knowing and Living the Higher Law and Its Principles of Progression	563
Receiving Power from on High	564
Receiving More Doctrine	564
Receiving More Doctrine by Choice	565
Receiving More Doctrine by Desire	565
Receiving More Doctrine by Faith	566
Receiving More Doctrine by Persistence and Improvement	566
Receiving More Doctrine by Service	566
Receiving More Doctrine by Seeking	566
Receiving More Doctrine by Treasuring Up	567
The Significance of the Temple Recommend	567
By What Power Might We Seek the Lord's Face?	568
Holiness to the Lord	570
A New Commitment	571
"It Is High Time to Establish Zion"	572
Priesthood Holders Must Set the Example	574
A Few Could Form the Foundation of Zion	575
According to Revelation	576
Our Duty to Individually Become Zion	577
Third Nephi—Latter-day Guide to Establishing Zion	578
"Which We Might Have Received in One Year"	582
The Pure in Heart *Shall* See God	586
The Father's Testimony	586
The Savior's Testimony	586
Coming Forth to See and Know	587
Receiving an Endowment of Knowledge	588
Healing	588
The Savior's Prayer for Us and Our Prayer to Him	589
Encircled about by Angels	591

Partaking of the Lord's Supper in His Presence	592
Receiving a Greater Endowment of the Holy Ghost	592
The Hundredfold Law	593
Revelations, Prophecies, and Explanations	593
Greater Commandments	594
The Greater Commandment to Pray Always	594
The Greater Commandment to Have All Things in Common	596
The Greater Commandment to Be "Even As the Lord Is"	597
Receiving a Special Gift	598
Beautiful Zion	600
Blessings for the Beautiful Ones	603
Summary and Conclusion—The Three Pillars of Zion	604
BIBLIOGRAPHY	610
CONCORDANCE	617
ABOUT THE AUTHOR	630

BOOK 1:

ZION—OUR ORIGIN AND OUR DESTINY

INTRODUCTION

In the beginning of the thirty-fourth year of the Nephite calendar,[1] a remarkable event occurred, one that is of critical importance to us today. According to Mormon, on the fourth day of the first month of the year, the Nephite nation collapsed under the weight of its own depravity. The fall was on the scale of the cataclysms of the Flood and Sodom and Gomorrah. Only a small group of Christians survived. Suddenly, above the darkness that had choked out any semblance of light, the voice of Christ was heard announcing his identity and the fulfillment of his mission; he declared the destruction of the wicked, lamented the evils of his people, and invited the remnant to come unto him with full purpose of heart.

Then the record goes silent. Mormon picks up the account "in the *ending* of the thirty and fourth year,"[2] nearly twelve months later. What happened in the lives of the surviving Nephites during that year? Mormon only hints at what the people did with Jesus' message; but when we piece together the account, we discover one of the great sermons of the Book of Mormon—a sermon that is of utmost importance to those of us who would become Zionlike.

Parallels between the Third Nephi Saints and the Latter-day Saints

We should keep in mind that these people were not unlike many of us: either they were new members or they were good people who were trying to live the gospel as best they could. Perhaps some were lukewarm; maybe others were sitting atop spiritual plateaus and lacking the motivation to keep climbing. Whatever their condition, we do know this: The Lord declared that they had escaped the destructions only because they were "more righteous" than the ones who had perished. We are left to speculate as to their degree of righteousness, but as we shall see, they needed time to change some things. The Savior was also quick to point out that they needed to change. Therefore, he called them to repentance and bade them strive to become truly converted so he could heal them.[3]

Why is this account important to us? To answer that question, we must first remember that from the outset of the Book of Mormon, Moroni testifies that the book was written for us.[4] Then, within the first pages of the Book of Mormon, Nephi instructs us to read the book by *likening* the scriptures unto ourselves.[5] Armed with those two pieces of information, we might envision ourselves as members of that small group of Nephite survivors. Somehow these people, who had escaped the annihilation, had taken to heart his commandment and invitation and had changed their lives so that within twelve months they achieved Zion.

---

[1] 3 Nephi 8:5.
[2] 3 Nephi 10:18.
[3] 3 Nephi 9:13.
[4] Book of Mormon title page.
[5] 1 Nephi 19:24; 2 Nephi 11:8.

How did they do it? How can we do it?

Mormon seems to have wanted us to dig for the answer, as one would mine for a pearl of great price. A careful reading of the books of Third and Fourth Nephi, which include the Savior's directives and Mormon's description of the achievement of Zion by the Nephite people, fill in the twelve-month gap and show us what we must do to rise to such a lofty ideal. This book explores the Lord's call to us to likewise repent, become converted, and come to Jesus with full purpose of heart so that he might heal us too and establish us as Zion people.

An Important Key to Establishing Zion

In the latter days, a key to establishing Zion in our lives is found in Doctrine and Covenants 42, the revelation called, "the law of the Church,"[6] which comprises the law of Zion. In one sentence, the Lord prophesied that he would give us three significant covenants that had the power to make us Zion individuals: "And ye shall hereafter receive church covenants, such as shall be sufficient to establish you, both here and in the New Jerusalem."[7] The references in this scripture lead to what we are calling in this series *The Three Pillars of Zion*:

1. The New and Everlasting Covenant (D&C 132:4–7).
2. The Oath and Covenant of the Priesthood (D&C 84:33–44).
3. The Law of Consecration (D&C 82:11–15).

These three covenants (pillars) are sufficient to establish Zionlike qualities in our individual lives and in our marriages, families, and other groups under the direction of the priesthood. Understanding that this is the Lord's way of establishing Zion, we are left without excuse. Clearly, we have been given all that we need. To become the pure in heart, which is the definition of Zion people,[8] we simply must better understand our covenants, and then live up to our privileges.

This book explores the contrast between Zion and Babylon, the three covenants or pillars upon which Zion lives are built, the elements of the journey to achieve a Zionlike life, and a portrait of the pure in heart.

Enoch's Dispensation Is a Pattern

The scriptures that describe Enoch's Zion provide us a model for establishing Zion in our lives. For example, both Enoch and Joseph Smith were commanded to:

Preach the gospel of Jesus Christ (Moses 6:37; 7:19; D&C 19:21, 31; 38:41)
Gather the Saints to places of safety (Moses 7:17–19; D&C 33:6; 45:69, 71; 115:6)
Attain unity and righteousness (Moses 7:18; D&C 21:4–7; 38:27)
Become "pure in heart" (Moses 7:18; D&C 97:21)
Care for the poor and needy (Moses 7:18; D&C 38:35; 42:30)
Build a "City of Holiness" (Moses 7:19; D&C 45:66–70)[9]

"Zion is the ensign to the nations. 'I intend to lay a foundation,' Joseph Smith boldly declared, 'that will revolutionize the whole world.' And then, emphasizing the source of this

---

[6] D&C 42 head note.
[7] D&C 42:67.
[8] D&C 97:21.
[9] "Enoch and His Message for Latter Days," *LDS Church News*, Feb. 5, 1994.

revolutionary movement, he added, 'It will not be by sword or gun that this kingdom will roll on: the power of truth is such that all nations will be under the necessity of obeying the Gospel.'"[10]

THE THREE PILLARS OF ZION

With very few exceptions, this series does *not* attempt to describe what the latter-day "priesthood society"[11] of Zion will look like. That is the prerogative of the President of the Church. What this book series does attempt to describe is Zion people, those individuals who become Zionlike now and who will one day make up the latter-day Zion priesthood society. Therefore, when the word *Zion* is used in this set, it is almost exclusively meant to refer to a Zionlike person.

We must keep in mind that the term *Zion* is described in the scriptures and by prophets in a variety of ways. Zion is a location, a group of followers, a journey, and a destination.[12] It is always a condition of the heart.[13] Zion can be manifested in a telestial setting and an Edenic terrestrial setting—and, of course, its ultimate manifestation is in a celestial setting.

Despite our best efforts, without divine help we cannot establish Zion in our lives, marriages, families, or a priesthood society. Only the Lord can establish Zion.[14] The Saints in Third Nephi are a case in point. They did all that they could do, but in the end the ideal of Zion was created because the Lord came to help them complete their journey. Were they Zion people before his appearance? Of course; but they had not yet achieved the ideal. That step required the Lord's intervention. Can we similarly qualify as Zion people without having achieved the ideal? Most assuredly. As we journey toward Zion and earnestly strive to assimilate Zionlike attributes in our lives, we are Zion. We simply must keep our eye single to the ideal of Zion and move forward with the Lord's grace compensating for those attributes that we have not yet acquired. Thus, in these books, when we discuss Zion and its various manifestations, we will typically be describing the ideal that should be our goal.

Striving to become Zion people is as important as arriving. Enoch's people achieved their ideal of Zion "in the process of time."[15] Neither Enoch's people nor Melchizedek's people nor the Nephites who were visited by Christ achieved the ideal of Zion overnight. As far as we can tell, they were much like us, people who made covenants with the Lord and did their best to understand and live those covenants. Their prophets, like ours, held the ideal of Zion before them, and they rose to the occasion. According to prophecy, we will do likewise in the latter-days. In writing these books, my only desire was to promote the cause of Zion and to urge us to gain a greater appreciation of our covenants, which have the power to make us the pure in heart.

In these books, I made every effort to research and document statements. Combined, the set includes more than 3,800 references. When I presented an opinion, I attempted to use qualifying language so as not to advance a doctrine or interpretation. I tried to assume the position of *guide*, allowing prophets and well-respected gospel writers to state or clarify doctrine, offer explanations, or paint descriptions. In the end, however, this work is uniquely mine and not an official statement of The Church of Jesus Christ of Latter-day Saints.

---

[10] "Enoch and His Message for Latter Days," *LDS Church News*, Feb. 5, 1994, quoting Smith, *Teachings of the Prophet Joseph Smith*, 366.

[11] President Spencer W. Kimball called Zion a "priesthood society" in his address, "Welfare Services: The Gospel in Action," 77–78.

[12] *Encyclopedia of Mormonism*, 1624–26.

[13] Young, *Discourses of Brigham Young*, 118.

[14] Nibley, *Approaching Zion*, 6–7.

[15] JST Genesis 7:27.

Section 1

Zion—What Do We Know of It?

We speak of Zion, sing of Zion, covenant to promote the establishment of Zion, and long for Zion—but what is Zion? Latter-day Saints ought to know. We have more scriptures and prophets' statements about it than any other people. One could hardly read a page from the Book of Mormon, Doctrine and Covenants, or Pearl of Great Price and not bump into the term or its principles. Why? Because we have the singular charge to become Zion individually, and we have the charge to prepare for the collective establishment of the Lord's Zion. Consequently, we—all of us—are (or should be) more identified with Zion than any other generation.

Moreover, the fact that we have the additional responsibility to call God's children to Zion suggests that we, individually, must first become Zion people: "Verily I say unto you all: Arise and shine forth, that thy light may be a standard for the nations."[16] Hugh Nibley reminded us that a primary purpose of the Church [the kingdom of God] is to prepare a people to become Zion: "[We] work for the building up the Kingdom of God on earth and the establishment of Zion. *The first step makes the second possible.*"[17] At the outset of this last dispensation—the dispensation of Zion—Joseph Smith said, "We ought to have the building up of Zion as our greatest object."[18] If we were to conduct a survey, would the building up of Zion be our greatest object? Regardless of how we might answer, we nevertheless are fond of defending Zion as uniquely *us*, and we are not timid about claiming the blessings of Zion as our birthright. Nevertheless, many of us are hard-pressed to describe or envision Zion, let alone live its principles.

What can we do about this dilemma?

---

[16] D&C 115:5.
[17] Nibley, *Approaching Zion*, 25; emphasis added.
[18] Smith, *Teachings of the Prophet Joseph Smith*, 160.

Brigham Young had the answer: "[Zion] commences in the heart of each person."[19] That is, Zion, the priesthood society, is made up of Zion, individual people. Beyond the typical uses of the word *Zion*—as a location or a society—Zion is a person whose heart is pure; therefore, that person "shall see God"[20]—in other words, to stand in and regain his presence. President John Taylor said, "The Zion of God. What does it mean? The pure in heart in the first place. In the second place . . . the pure in heart who are governed by the law of God."[21] Elder Matthew Cowley added, "And to you whose lives are committed to righteousness, I say unto you, You are Zion."[22] If we will fully embrace these statements, a vast library of Zion material will open to our view. We suddenly realize that by *likening* the scriptures concerning Zion to ourselves,[23] many of the descriptions of that ideal priesthood society are also descriptions of individual Zionlike people, who are comprised of the same attributes. Therefore, none of us is exempt. Zion is a vibrant, current idea that we must embrace. Zion is now; we are Zion!

ZION IS OUR IDEAL

Although there are a number of usages of the word *Zion*, we will examine it in its ultimate sense—a person who is striving to become pure in heart and who is in the process of qualifying to stand in the presence of God. As we stated in the introduction, the term *Zion* is described in the scriptures and by prophets in a variety of ways. Zion is a process, a people, and a place.[24] It is always a condition of the heart.[25] Zion can be manifested in a variety of settings, from telestial to terrestrial to, ultimately, celestial. We qualify as Zion people by remaining on the path to Zion. As we journey toward the ideal of Zion and strive to assimilate Zionlike attributes in our lives, we are Zion. We simply must keep our eye single and move forward with the Lord's grace compensating for those Zionlike attributes we have not yet acquired.

The ideal of Zion, we will learn, is the end purpose of the new and everlasting covenant, the oath and covenant of the priesthood, and every saving covenant and ordinance of the gospel. Therefore, if we do not have becoming Zionlike in mind, the gospel plan has little meaning or power in our lives. To become a Zion person or to have a Zion marriage or a Zion family should be our *only* aims in the gospel of Jesus Christ. Every program, every function, every activity is (or ought to be) designed with Zion in mind. We can become distracted and caught up in extraneous details, but in the end we will only postpone or forfeit our blessings. Because the celestial world and law are the ultimate manifestations of Zion, our origin is Zion, Zion is our earthly birthright,[26] and it can be our destiny. Very literally, we are children of Zion.

Zion people take their covenants seriously and literally. They have a feeling of urgency and a longing that drives them to establish Zion in their hearts. The day will come when Zion individuals will receive their inheritance in the priesthood society of Zion. But until that day, each of us is commanded to become individually Zion. President Benson handed each covenant person the responsibility for becoming Zionlike. Zion, the priesthood society, he said, can be brought about only by Zion people. As more and more of us decide to embrace the principles of Zion, the celestial order will finally exist among us and we, individually and collectively, will be prepared to

---

[19] Young, *Discourses of Brigham Young*, 118.
[20] JST Matthew 5:10; 3 Nephi 12:8.
[21] Taylor, *The Gospel Kingdom*, 245.
[22] Cowley, *Matthew Cowley Speaks*, 30.
[23] 1 Nephi 19:23–24.
[24] *Encyclopedia of Mormonism*, 1624–26.
[25] Young, *Discourses of Brigham Young*, 118.
[26] Every person descends from Enoch, and a high percentage of the world descends from Abraham.

receive the Lord.[27] We recall that Enoch built his city of Zion *after* his people had individually qualified as Zion people (notice the sequence); just so, we will gather to build latter-day Zion when our hearts are pure, and then only under the direction of the prophet.[28] President Spencer W. Kimball was another prophet who laid the responsibility for becoming and establishing Zion squarely upon our shoulders. How well we incorporate the new and everlasting covenant (*the Covenant*[29]) in our lives directly determines the time required to "accomplish all things pertaining to Zion."[30]

THE CELESTIAL ORDER

Zion is the standard among celestial and celestial-seeking beings.[31] We can measure substantially any situation, institution, person, group, philosophy, theory, or motivation against the standard of Zion. Hugh Nibley explained that three orders exist on the earth, just as they exist in the universe: The order of Zion is celestial; the order of Eden is terrestrial; and the order of Babylon is telestial.[32] Discernment is a gift of the Spirit,[33] and freedom of choice is inherent in the spirit of man.[34] How we choose among these orders determines where our hearts are now and where they will be in eternity.[35] This life is uniquely and strategically designed so that the three orders are ever before us. We must learn to discern between them and make our choices consistently with our eternal desires.

ZION AND BABYLON—EXACT OPPOSITES

Wherever there exists anything or anyone that is celestial, there exists Zion. It is in every way the exact opposite of the telestial order of Babylon,[36] making the two as incompatible and mutually resistant as positive and negative poles. President Gordon B. Hinckley said that compromising the revealed doctrines of the Covenant is never an option.[37] Like Jesus and Satan, celestial and telestial things cannot compromise in any degree. When a person attempts to straddle Babylon and Zion, he will eventually be pulled into Babylon. It is unavoidable.

When we attempt to mix celestial Zion with telestial Babylon (often called the *world*), Zion simply flees to its eternal lofty location. Thus the saying, "Zion is fled."[38] Why? Because Zion is a constant that never changes despite the inconsistency of her children: "Zion shall not be moved out of her place, notwithstanding her children are scattered." Our covenantal responsibility, then, is to conform to Zion rather than insisting that Zion conform to us: "They that remain, and are pure in heart, shall return, and come to their inheritances, they and their children, with songs of everlasting joy, to build up the waste places of Zion."[39] If we choose otherwise or if we lack courage and commitment, we will be left to ourselves to languish in this telestial world and its order. Referencing Elder John A. Widtsoe, Elder Ezra Taft Benson said, "The troubles of the

---

[27] Benson, "Jesus Christ—Gifts and Expectations," 16.
[28] Moses 7:19.
[29] Note: In this book we will refer to the new and everlasting covenant as the *Covenant*.
[30] Kimball, "Becoming the Pure in Heart," quoting D&C 105:37.
[31] D&C 105:5.
[32] Nibley, *Approaching Zion*, xv.
[33] D&C 50:23–24; 1 Corinthians 2:11.
[34] McKay, *Gospel Ideals*, 299.
[35] Matthew 6:21; Luke 12:34; 3 Nephi 13:21.
[36] Nibley, *Approaching Zion*, 30.
[37] Hinckley, "The Dawning of a Brighter Day," 81.
[38] Moses 7:69.
[39] D&C 101:17–18.

world may largely be laid at the doors of those who are neither hot nor cold; who always follow the line of least resistance; whose timid hearts flutter at taking sides for truth. As in the great Council in the heavens, so in the Church of Christ on earth, there can be no neutrality."[40] Therefore, either we are Zion or we are not. There is no compromising or mingling of Zion and Babylon. Hugh Nibley explained: "Zion is pure, which means 'not mixed with any impurities, unalloyed'; it is all Zion and nothing else."[41]

BECOMING A ZION PERSON

If we truly long for Zion, to become that kind of person and to enjoy Zion's unique privileges, we must first make and keep the foundational covenant of Zion—*The New and Everlasting Covenant*. This Covenant is *not* the covenant that will someday be required of Zion people when they are invited into that order; that future covenant will be an appendage to the new and everlasting covenant, which is the totality of all saving covenants, ordinances, and commandments. The new and everlasting covenant prepares us to become Zion in our hearts and to someday gain an inheritance in the heavenly society of Zion. The new and everlasting covenant that we embrace with all our hearts walls out Babylon and welds us irrevocably to Zion and her King. The pure in heart become "all Zion and nothing else."

This, then, is what we know of Zion. She is our origin, our birthright, and our destiny. She is our ideal. Her establishment should be our greatest desire. As part of the latter-day dispensation, we are under covenant to build up the kingdom of God for the purpose of establishing Zion. To accomplish that feat, and to ensure our salvation and exaltation, we enter into the new and everlasting covenant. By this act, we specify that we have made a choice between Zion and Babylon and that forevermore we will not attempt to mix the two. We will follow the Covenant to its perfect conclusion: to snatch us from Babylon, to single us out, to purify our hearts, to prepare us in every way to regain the presence of God, and to obtain our inheritance and our crown. "This is Zion: THE PURE IN HEART."[42]

---

[40] Benson, *God, Family, Country*, 359.
[41] Nibley, *Approaching Zion*, 26.
[42] D&C 97:21.

Section 2

Overview of Zion Peoples

When God completed the creation of the earth, he looked upon his work and pronounced it "good."[43] Then when he placed Adam and Eve in the garden of the earth, he pronounced the creation "very good."[44] The term seems more than a convenient modifier. Once a young man saluted Jesus as "Good Master." Jesus quickly challenged him: "Why callest thou me good? There is none good but one, that is, God."[45] That Jesus would equate *good* with God is telling. Moreover, that God would pronounce his creation with Adam and Eve on it as "very good" seems to suggest that he considered the end-result *Godlike*. Why would that be? Perhaps the answer lies in the fact that Heavenly Father patterned this creation after our heavenly home—*Zion*.[46] Certainly heaven is a "very good" and *Godlike* place. Could we expect anything less from a perfect being?

Interestingly, "the word *Zion* may derive from the Hebrew root *tsayan*, meaning 'perfection,' which is also a meaning of the former city name Salem or Shalem, 'city of perfection.'"[47] Therefore, from the outset of human history, Adam and Eve were placed in a condition that was preeminently *good*—that "very good" Zionlike place that pointed our first parents and all of humanity toward the ideal of Zion.

Fall from Zion

Adam and Eve's *fall* from Eden's Zionlike state shot cataclysmic changes through their bodies and all creation. This earth has likely never before nor since experienced such a violent change. Where there had been unity, equality, peace, abundant health, eternal life, spontaneously growing fruits and flowers, incorruption, and the presence of God, there now existed discord, competition, enmity, illness, death, tormenting thorns, briars, and noxious weeds, and worst of all, separation from God.

---

[43] Genesis 1:25.
[44] Genesis 1:31.
[45] Mark 10:17–18.
[46] D&C 77:2; Moses 6:63.
[47] Galbraith, Ogden, and Skinner, *Jerusalem: The Eternal City*, 41.

Adam and Eve had just entered the telestial world, which would be corrupted by Lucifer and become Babylon! The profound differences between Zion and Babylon were as opposite as day and night. Adam and Eve's immediate reaction was to find a way out, and they knew that there was only one Person who knew the way. Therefore, they built an altar and prayed. The answer that they received became the universal answer for all of us who came after them; that answer was and is the Covenant—*The New and Everlasting Covenant.*

> And after many days an angel of the Lord appeared unto Adam, saying: Why dost thou offer sacrifices unto the Lord?
>
> And Adam said unto him: I know not, save the Lord commanded me. And then the angel spake, saying: This thing is a similitude of the sacrifice of the Only Begotten of the Father, which is full of grace and truth. *Wherefore, thou shalt do all that thou doest in the name of the Son, and thou shalt repent and call upon God in the name of the Son forevermore.*
>
> And in that day the Holy Ghost fell upon Adam, which beareth record of the Father and the Son, saying: I am the Only Begotten of the Father from the beginning, henceforth and forever, that as thou hast fallen thou mayest be redeemed, and all mankind, even as many as will.
>
> And in that day Adam blessed God and was filled, and began to prophesy concerning all the families of the earth, saying: Blessed be the name of God, for because of my transgression my eyes are opened, *and in this life I shall have joy, and again in the flesh I shall see God.*
>
> And Eve, his wife, heard all these things and was glad, saying: Were it not for our transgression we never should have had seed, and never should have known good and evil, and the joy of our redemption, and the eternal life which God giveth unto all the obedient.[48]

THE WAY BACK TO ZION REVEALED

Adam and Eve were going home! By entering into the Covenant that God offered them, they could once again enjoy the happiness of heaven and experience the presence of God—*in this life!* That was *good* news—*God's* news.

The new and everlasting covenant is "the fulness of the gospel (D&C 39:11; 45:9; 66:2; 133:57)," said Elder Bruce R. McConkie. "When men accept the gospel, they thereby agree or covenant to keep the commandments of God, and he promises or covenants to give them salvation in his kingdom. The gospel is the *everlasting* covenant because it is ordained by Him who is Everlasting and also because it is everlastingly the same.... Each time this everlasting covenant is revealed it is *new* to those of that dispensation. Hence the gospel is the *new and everlasting covenant.*"[49] Immediately, Adam and Eve entered into the new and everlasting covenant by accepting the ordinance of baptism and receiving the gift of the Holy Ghost. Upon Adam's doing so, God declared that those ordinances had been simultaneously recorded in heaven; thus they were valid "henceforth and forever."[50] Clearly,

---

[48] Moses 5:6–12; emphasis added.
[49] McConkie, *Mormon Doctrine*, 529.
[50] Moses 6:64–66.

if our desire is to become Zionlike, as were our first parents, we must likewise enter into the new and everlasting covenant.

But there is more. No one can make the journey to Zion alone; we must take others with us. Hence, Adam received the authority of God to administer the Covenant to his children, that they might also escape Babylon and come home to Zion. That is the pattern: the redeemed of Zion are sent back into the world to bring others to the redemption of Zion. Something marvelous happened when Adam was ordained to the priesthood: He was inducted into the order of Jesus Christ, receiving from him the authority to administer the Covenant and thus become a savior in the similitude of the Savior. The Lord said to Adam, "And thou art after the order [priesthood] of him who was without beginning of days or end of years, from all eternity to all eternity. Behold, thou art one in me, a son of God; and thus [by receiving the holy priesthood] may all become my sons. Amen."[51] Again, we see the pattern; we become sons of God in the order of Jesus Christ in the same way Adam became a son of God in the order of Jesus Christ.

How grand is the Covenant! Fallen Adam could become redeemed, saved, and exalted Adam. Doomed Adam could be rescued and reconciled with God. He could become one with God in knowledge, might, dominion, and lifestyle, and he could become heir to all that the Father has. Furthermore, Adam received God's authority and thereby became a son of God[52] in the similitude of *the* Son of God.[53] He was empowered to become a savior to his family[54] like *the* Savior was to the family of God.

Only the Atonement of Jesus Christ makes the Covenant possible; and we accept the Atonement by means of the Covenant. By our accepting the terms of the Atonement and enduring in the Covenant to the end, we are delivered from Babylon (redeemed), we are provided the Savior's grace to become Zion people and return home to Zion (saved), and we are blessed to become like God (exalted).

Zion—A New Way of Life

Of course, the Fall brought with it a new set of realities. For one thing, Adam had to work for his support. Nevertheless, even his definition of work changed when he received the Covenant and the priesthood. Now he would redefine his work as the work of God. That mindset and reprioritization is essential to becoming a Zion person. Although Adam would continue to work to support his family, he would adopt as his real work the teaching, preaching and administering of the Covenant to all the souls of men. And Eve was his helpmeet in all his labors: "And Adam and Eve blessed the name of God, and they made all things known unto their sons and their daughters."[55] How, then, do we, the children of Adam and Eve, likewise flee Babylon and find our way back to Zion? Follow the example of our first parents: receive and keep the Covenant, and bring others to Zion with us.

If the definition of Zion is "perfection," as well as "reaching for perfection," as we have said, then the definition of a Zion person is someone who receives the Covenant for the purpose of becoming perfect and entering into a perfect priesthood society. A Zion person will strive to become pure in heart and become one with God. Such a person will certainly find his or her way home.

---

[51] Moses 6:68.
[52] D&C 45:8; Abraham 1:18.
[53] Moses 1:6, 13, 16.
[54] Petersen, Conference Report, Oct. 1959, 14.
[55] Moses 5:12.

Surety of a Better World

Making and keeping the Covenant are worth the effort. The Book of Mormon prophet Ether said, "Wherefore, whoso believeth in God might with surety hope for a better world."[56] That better world is Zion, a place devoid of pettiness, selfishness, and wickedness, a place of abundance and no lack, a place of oneness, equality, and righteousness—a place described by Mormon as consummately happy: "And surely there could not be a happier people among all the people who had been created by the hand of God."[57] In this better world, the Savior reigns as the King of Zion.[58] The scriptures state that Zion is his habitation.[59] But that better world begins in each person's heart,[60] which also is ruled by the Lord as his holy habitation. Such a heart, then, must be changed, purified, and prepared for Zion by the Atonement of Jesus Christ, and that process occurs by entering and abiding in the Covenant.

The better world of Zion has always been the goal of people of the Covenant, and many have achieved it. Certainly achieving Zion is possible for us as well. Elder Neal A. Maxwell said, "Those who look forward to a next and better world are usually 'anxiously engaged' in improving this one, for they 'always abound in good works' (D&C 58:27; Alma 7:24)."[61]

The following is a brief overview of people who responded to the Covenant and became Zion people. This is not an exhaustive list. We expect that other groups, such as the Brother of Jared and his people, and the Ten Tribes, who were visited by the resurrected Savior, also achieved Zion.

Adam's Zion

Beginning with Adam, the Lord, "the Holy One of Zion . . . established the foundations of Adam-ondi-Ahman."[62] In the hymn, "Glorious Things Are Sung of Zion," William W. Phelps preserved the doctrine: "In Adam-ondi-Ahman, Zion rose where Eden was."[63] In another hymn, "Adam-ondi-Ahman," Phelps wrote, "This earth was once a garden place, / With all her glories common, / And men did live a holy race, / And worship Jesus face to face, / In Adam-ondi-Ahman."[64]

When Adam and Eve lost the Garden of Eden, the first Zion, the Lord again established Zion in the hearts of the people, who gathered to Adam-ondi-Ahman. This new Zion society became the model for all subsequent Zion societies, and Adam and Eve became the models for all Zion people. Having experienced "the joy of [their] redemption and the eternal life which God giveth unto all the obedient," they "blessed the name of God, and they made all things known unto their sons and daughters."[65] Thus, beginning at Adam-ondi-Ahman, Zion was established in the hearts of the righteous.

Enos's Zion

At the rebellion of Cain, who created spiritual Babylon under the direction of Satan, a crisis arose in the earth. In response, a group of people under the leadership of Adam's grandson, Enos, fled the wicked land of Shulon and established *Cainan*,[66] named after Enos's son. The land of Cainan became a new Zion with a new Zion people.

---

[56] Ether 12:4.
[57] 4 Nephi 1:16; see Moses 7:18.
[58] Moses 7:53.
[59] Psalms 132:13.
[60] Young, *Discourses of Brigham Young*, 118.
[61] Maxwell, *The Neal A. Maxwell Quote Book*, 265.
[62] D&C 78:15.
[63] "Glorious Things Are Sung of Zion," *Hymns*, no. 48.
[64] "Adam-ondi-Ahman," *Hymns*, no. 40.
[65] Moses 5:11–12.
[66] Moses 6:17.

Cainan may have been the longest-lived Zion in history, perhaps even longer than Enoch's Zion. Four generations later, Enoch was born there. His father, Jared, "taught Enoch in all the ways of God,"[67] which is a significant key to establishing Zion in a family. From the land of Cainan, Enoch and other righteous priesthood brethren went out into the world to teach the Covenant and draw people to Zion. "They were preachers of righteousness, and spake and prophesied, and called upon all men, everywhere, to repent; and faith was taught unto the children of men."[68]

ENOCH'S ZION

Enoch experienced amazing success. Many people received the Covenant under his hands. Wherever they lived, "upon the mountains and upon the high places, [Zion] did flourish."[69] In these pockets of Christianity, "the glory of the Lord . . . was upon his people. And the Lord blessed the land, and they were blessed. . . . And the Lord called his people ZION, because they were of one heart and one mind, and dwelt in righteousness; and there was no poor among them."[70] Of significance, "the Lord came and dwelt with his people, and they dwelt in righteousness."[71]

Eventually, when the world was filled with violence and wickedness, Enoch's pure-hearted people gathered to build a "city that was called the City of Holiness, even ZION,"[72] which, "in process of time, was taken up into heaven."[73]

We see a pattern here. Zion people precede the Zion priesthood society. They gather into local groups; in our day, these groups are called wards and stakes. Then, when the world grows incredibly wicked and dangerous, Zion people gather to one or more central locations for protection and unity. If we knew more about the gathering of Enoch's people, we would likely discover that they gathered to build a temple. That is always the reason why Zion people gather together. They desire to worship God and come into his presence, and the temple is the only way.

METHUSELAH AND NOAH'S ZION

After Enoch's Zion had "fled,"[74] Enoch's son, Methuselah remained to perpetuate the chosen bloodline and to continue the missionary effort.[75] When Methuselah was 269 years old, his grandson, Noah, was born.[76] Together, as suggested by Joseph Fielding Smith,[77] Methuselah and Noah, and possibly three of Noah's sons, declared the "Gospel unto the children of men, even as it was given unto Enoch."[78] Contrary to popular opinion, these men had tremendous success in teaching and preaching the Covenant and perpetuating the cause of Zion. Enoch foresaw their success. In vision, he noted that, before the Flood, "many would be caught up by the powers of heaven into Zion."[79] We can't know for certain, but it seems reasonable that the converts of Noah and his family formed a Zion society before they were caught up to the heavenly Zion.

---

[67] Moses 6:21.
[68] Moses 6:23.
[69] Moses 7:16.
[70] Moses 7:17–18.
[71] Moses 7:16.
[72] Moses 7:19.
[73] Moses 7:21.
[74] Moses 7:69.
[75] Moses 8:2.
[76] Moses 8:8–9.
[77] Smith, *Doctrines of Salvation*, 3:204.
[78] Moses 8:19; see Moses 8:27.
[79] Moses 7:27.

Noah received a promise from the Lord regarding latter-day Zion. This promise was a renewal of the promise the Lord had made earlier to Enoch. The sign of that promise or covenant was the rainbow. The promise was twofold: (1) God promised never again to destroy the wicked with a universal flood, (2) Zion would be established in the last days and be joined by Enoch's Zion: "When men should keep all my commandments, Zion should again come on the earth, the city of Enoch which I have caught up unto myself. And this is mine everlasting covenant, that when thy [Noah's] posterity shall embrace the truth, and look upward, then shall Zion look downward, and all the heavens shall shake with gladness, and the earth shall tremble with joy; and the general assembly of the church of the firstborn shall come down out of heaven, and possess the earth, and shall have place until the end come. And this is mine everlasting covenant, which I made with thy father Enoch."[80]

Regarding the rainbow as the physical sign of this promise made to Enoch and Noah, Joseph Smith said, "The Lord hath set the bow in the cloud for a sign that while it shall be seen, seed time and harvest, summer and winter shall not fail; but when it shall disappear, woe to that generation, for behold the end cometh quickly."[81] Commenting, gospel writers Jay A. Parry and Donald W. Parry stated: "The rainbow . . . also suggests the Lord's covenant with Noah, signified by a rainbow, that He would again bring Zion to the earth (JST Gen. 9:21–23)."[82]

The absence of the rainbow in a coming year will be bad news for the wicked and good news for the pure in heart. For the righteous, an event rivaled only by the coming of the Lord will occur. Heavenly Zion will descend to meet earthly Zion. The Lord prophesied: "I shall prepare an Holy City that my people may gird up their loins, and be looking forth for the time of my coming; for there shall be my tabernacle, and it shall be called Zion, a New Jerusalem. And the Lord said unto Enoch: Then shalt thou and all thy city meet them there, and we will receive them into our bosom, and they shall see us; and we will fall upon their necks, and they shall fall upon our necks, and we will kiss each other; and there shall be mine abode, and it shall be Zion, which shall come forth out of all the creations which I have made; and for the space of a thousand years the earth shall rest."[83]

MELCHIZEDEK'S ZION

The next Zion people of record were those to whom Melchizedek preached and administered the Covenant. This man's name is also actually a title. In Hebrew, *Melchizedek* is a combination of "king" and "righteousness." Therefore, Melchizedek was the *King of Righteousness*, a fitting title for all those who would receive the priesthood after him.[84] Melchizedek "represents the scriptural ideal of one who obtains the power of God through faith, repentance, and sacred ordinances, for the purpose of inspiring and blessing his fellow beings."[85]

Alma gave us insight into Melchizedek's ministry: "Now this Melchizedek was a king over the land of Salem [meaning "city of perfection"[86] or "righteousness and peace,"[87] the forerunner of Jerusalem[88]]; and his people had waxed strong in iniquity and abomination; yea, they had all gone astray; they were full of all manner of wickedness; but Melchizedek having exercised mighty faith, and received the office of the high priesthood according to the holy order of God, did preach repentance unto his people. And behold, they did repent; and Melchizedek did establish peace in the land in his

---

[80] JST Genesis 9:21–23.
[81] Smith, *Teachings of the Prophet Joseph Smith*, 305.
[82] Parry and Parry, *Understanding the Book of Revelation*, 126.
[83] Moses 7:62–64; emphasis added.
[84] D&C 107:2–4.
[85] *Encyclopedia of Mormonism*, 879–80.
[86] Galbraith, Ogden, and Skinner, *Jerusalem: The Eternal City*, 41.
[87] Smith, *Teachings of the Prophet Joseph Smith*, 321.
[88] McConkie, *Mormon Doctrine*, 531.

days; therefore he was called the prince of peace, for he was the king of Salem; and he did reign under his father."[89]

Melchizedek, like Enoch, was enormously successful in establishing Zion in the hearts of his people: "And his people wrought righteousness, and obtained heaven, and sought for the city of Enoch [they were likewise translated]."[90] Of note, Melchizedek became Abraham's spiritual tutor,[91] the one who ordained Abraham to the Holy Priesthood,[92] and the one, we assume, who "blessed" or administered the Covenant to Abraham.[93] None of these blessings could have been possible without the higher ordinances, of course. We thank the Jewish historian, Josephus, for preserving the fact that Melchizedek built in Salem a temple,[94] around which such edifices Zion people always gather.

ABRAHAM'S ZION

When Melchizedek and his Zion people were translated and taken into heaven to join with the City of Enoch, Abraham remained on the earth, the only man, who held "all the priesthood and authority of his predecessors," and the remaining Zion person.[95] Like Methuselah and Noah, Abraham became the primal father of the covenant people, and for the remainder of his days, Abraham sought to reestablish Zion. In his monumental work, *The Blessings of Abraham—Becoming a Zion People*, E. Douglas Clark writes, "It was Abraham's right [by lineage] . . . to be ordained to the patriarchal priesthood to establish and preside over Zion for the benefit of all mankind."[96]

The Lord, through his servant Melchizedek, gave Abraham the fulness of the new and everlasting covenant, and he blessed Abraham to be associated with the Covenant eternally. From that point forward the Covenant would also be known as the Abrahamic covenant, and, as mentioned above, Abraham would be known as the father of the covenant people. The Abrahamic covenant emphasizes several important promises that flow to each person who chooses to receive it: (1) a covenant person's posterity has the right by lineage to receive all the blessings of the gospel and priesthood; (2) a covenant person will have an inheritance in the promised land of Zion both now and in eternity; (3) a covenant person will be blessed with "eternal lives,"[97] meaning eternal marriage and infinite and endless posterity.

Abraham received the Melchizedek Priesthood from the man Melchizedek,[98] and we assume that he received from Melchizedek the keys of the priesthood as well. When Melchizedek and his people were translated, Abraham was left as the sole administrator.

The advent of Abraham marked a new gospel dispensation. From that point forward, as is evidenced in the scriptures, priesthood keys would be held by a prophet, a high priest in the Melchizedek Priesthood, a worthy man called of God and not necessarily entitled to presidency because of his lineage, a man who would have the right to preside over the covenant people, administer the Covenant to God's children, and ordain worthy men to the priesthood, regardless of their bloodline.[99] These priesthood keys are highly important. Only by them can the ordinances of salvation and exaltation be bound or validated for eternity.[100]

---

[89] Alma 13:17–18.
[90] JST Genesis 14:34.
[91] Alma 13:15; JST Genesis 14:37–40.
[92] D&C 84:14.
[93] JST Genesis 14:40.
[94] Josephus, "The Wars," *Complete Works*, 6.10.1.
[95] Clark, *The Blessings of Abraham*, 140.
[96] Clark, *The Blessings of Abraham*, 79.
[97] D&C 132:24.
[98] D&C 84:14.
[99] D&C 81:2; 107:8–9.
[100] Packer, "Restoration," 2.

Abraham's family was given the responsibility to teach and bless all other families of the earth with the Covenant.[101] Thus authorized with the Melchizedek Priesthood, Abraham set out to establish Zion by preaching the Covenant to all the world. According to E. Douglas Clark, Abraham's success was legendary. Everywhere he went, from Ur to Haran to Canaan to Egypt and back to Canaan, he taught and administered the Covenant and introduced many souls to the principles of Zion.[102]

Abraham set the example of Zion for all who would follow him. For example, we read that he paid tithes to Melchizedek, because Melchizedek was "the high priest, and the keeper of the storehouse of God."[103] Additionally, he paid generous offerings of "all the riches which he possessed, which God had given him *more than that which he had need.*"[104] That is, he lived the law of consecration and paid offerings of his excess. The result of Abraham's being true to the Covenant and living the law of Zion was the Lord's pouring out upon him unimaginable riches: "And it came to pass, that God blessed Abram, *and gave unto him riches, and lands* for an everlasting possession, *according to the covenant which he had made,* and according to the blessing wherewith Melchizedek had blessed him."[105]

We see in Abraham's example Zion's celestial law of prosperity in contrast to Babylon's telestial law of wealth building. For Zion people such as Abraham, God himself becomes the Paymaster. How many times, especially in the Book of Mormon, do we read that the Lord rewards obedience to the Covenant with great prosperity and a multitude of blessings? Like Abraham, Zion people pay tithing on their increase, and additionally, they pay generous offerings of "more than that which [they have] need." As a reward for their obedience and sacrifice, God gives unto them "riches . . . and lands for an everlasting possession; according to the covenant which [they have] made, and according to the blessing wherewith [they have been blessed in the temple of God by the Melchizedek Priesthood]."[106]

If Father Abraham had written a book called *How to Become Rich*, he might have recommended that we have faith in the Covenant that we have made and give our surplus to the bishop, "the keeper of the storehouse," who shoulders the responsibility to care for the poor. It is by means of consecrating who we are and what we have to the Lord that abundance flows. Abraham might have reminded us that whereas tithing is a defined sum, offerings are not. The faith required to pay generous offerings is greater than the faith required to pay tithing, and the greater the faith and sacrifice, the greater the blessings. Therefore, our opportunity for growth and blessings lies in our paying offerings.

Abraham's Zion set the stage for latter-day Zion. Because the latter-day Church is either made up of Abraham's children or people who are adopted into the family of Abraham, we all share the responsibility of extending the blessings of Abraham, including the blessings of Zion, to all people.

Moses' Attempt at Zion

Moses led the children of Israel out of Egypt—which has represented Babylon, the wicked world, ever since[107]—with an overwhelming display of power. The Israelites experienced the power of Jehovah and the grandeur of his Covenant with unmistakable signs, wonders and symbolic representations: such as deliverance by the blood of the lamb, escaping their lives as captives, entering their new life by passing through the water, and so forth. By the power of the priesthood, six hundred thousand men, plus women and children,[108] united as one, and left behind the fleshpots of Egypt to go forth into an

---

[101] Abraham 2:11.
[102] Abraham 2:4, 15; Clark, *The Blessings of Abraham*, 85-87.
[103] JST Genesis 14:37.
[104] JST Genesis 14:39; emphasis added.
[105] JST Genesis 14:40; emphasis added.
[106] JST Genesis 14:40; emphasis added.
[107] "The 'Hymn of the Pearl,'" 129-31.
[108] Exodus 12:37.

unknown wilderness with the purpose of becoming "a holy community, a nation of priests, God's own people (see Exodus 19:6)."[109] Moses had one intention: to return Israel to its inheritance—Zion. To that end he built a tabernacle where the ordinances of the priesthood could be administered and where the Lord could visit his people.

Moses wore out his life teaching and administering the Covenant of the fathers to their children. This covenant was the Abrahamic covenant, the same covenant that Adam, Enos, Enoch, Methuselah, Noah, and Melchizedek had embraced to establish their Zions. Moses taught his people that the Melchizedek Priesthood "administereth the gospel and holdeth the key of the mysteries of the kingdom, even the key of the knowledge of God." Moreover, he taught them that in the ordinances of the Melchizedek Priesthood "the power of godliness is manifest," and by means of these ordinances a "man can see the face of God, even the Father, and live."[110] Tragically, of the millions of Israelites, only "Moses, and Aaron, Nadab, and Abihu, and seventy of the elders of Israel"[111] accepted Moses' invitation to become Zionlike and receive Zion's blessings. This failing was a terrible indictment of the children of Abraham, Isaac, and Jacob. Moses had done his best to "plainly" teach the principles of Zion "to the children of Israel in the wilderness, and [he] sought diligently to sanctify his people that they might behold the face of God; but they hardened their hearts and could not endure his presence; therefore, the Lord in his wrath, for his anger was kindled against them, swore that they should not enter into his rest while in the wilderness, which rest is the fulness of his glory."[112]

Substantially all of the Israelites rejected their heritage—Zion! The disappointing result recalls the impact of the fall of Adam and Eve: "Therefore, he took Moses out of their midst, and the Holy Priesthood also."[113] Or in an Enochian term, "Zion is fled!"[114] Moses was removed, and the balance of the people remained. When people reject the Covenant and the invitation to establish Zion, the pure in heart are separated and either taken into heaven or a heavenly setting. Those who are left behind are the weak and the rebellious, who continue to struggle in Babylon. In that situation, depending on the hearts of the remaining people, the Lord does one of two things: either he destroys the people because of their wickedness, or he reaches out to them with a preparatory gospel. In the case of the ancient Israelites, the Lord provided the lesser priesthood to administer the preparatory gospel, because the higher priesthood is the priesthood of Zion. Now angels would minister to them, while Zion people enjoy the presence of God. Their preparatory gospel was limited to faith, repentance, baptism, the remission of sins, and the law of carnal commandments,[115] while the higher commandments and ordinances, which pertain to Zion, are administered by the Melchizedek Priesthood and received in the temple.

This preparatory gospel, called the law of Moses, was intended to point the hearts of the Israelites toward Zion, and in fact it succeeded in its purpose among the people of Alma the Elder,[116] the people of King Benjamin,[117] and the people of Alma the Younger.[118] But the full realization of the law of Moses[119] was not complete until the Savior established Zion after his resurrection among the Jews and the Nephites.[120]

---

[109] Smith, *Church History and Modern Revelation*, 1:58.
[110] D&C 84:19–22.
[111] Exodus 24:9–10.
[112] D&C 84:23–24.
[113] D&C 84:25.
[114] Moses 7:69.
[115] D&C 84:26–27.
[116] Mosiah 18:21, 27–30.
[117] Mosiah 2–5; see Mosiah 5:5–12.
[118] Alma 1:25–32.
[119] Matthew 5:17–18.
[120] Acts 4:32–35; 4 Nephi 1:2–3, 15–18.

Alma the Elder's Zion

Upon organizing the Church among the Nephites, Alma the Elder administered the Covenant to his people and immediately encouraged them to adopt the principles of Zion: no contention, true unity, love of God and neighbor, equality, consecration, freewill offerings, obedience, sacrifice, and blessedness.

> And he commanded them that there should be no contention one with another, but that they should look forward with one eye, having one faith and one baptism, having their hearts knit together in unity and in love one towards another. . . . And thus they became the children of God. . . . And again Alma commanded that the people of the church should impart of their substance, every one according to that which he had; if he have more abundantly he should impart more abundantly; and of him that he had but little, but little should be required; and to him that had not should be given. And thus they should impart of their substance of their own free will and good desires towards God, and to those priests that stood in need, yea, and to every needy, naked soul. And this he said unto them, having been commanded of God; and they did walk uprightly before God, imparting to one another both temporally and spiritually according to their needs and their wants. And . . . how beautiful are they to the eyes of them who there came to the knowledge of their Redeemer; yea, and how blessed are they, for they shall sing to his praise forever.[121]

King Benjamin's Zion

In an event that defined the Nephite nation ever after, the prophet-king Benjamin taught his people the Covenant and introduced them to the principles of Zion. In doing so, he applied the principle of gathering "to raise up a committed society of 'pure people' who will 'serve [God] in righteousness.'"[122] Gathering always is associated with Zion. When Benjamin, who had been called and consecrated to his holy office[123] and whose right it was to call such a gathering, had assembled his people, he stood before them and taught one of the greatest sermons on Zion ever delivered. He began by explaining that he had never exacted money for his service, a restatement of Nephi's principle: "The laborer in Zion shall labor for Zion; for if they labor for money they shall perish."[124] Furthermore, Benjamin said that he had always sought to maintain a people free from sin.[125] He also had tried to set an example of service—service to God and to God's children, which is the essence of "the law and the prophets."[126] Service was the sermon of his life, and he exhorted his people to follow his example.[127] Remarkably, giving service to one of God's children is counted as giving service to God.[128]

---

[121] Mosiah 18:21–30.
[122] *Encyclopedia of Mormonism*, 1625; D&C 100:13, 16.
[123] Mosiah 2:11–12.
[124] 2 Nephi 26:31.
[125] Mosiah 2:13.
[126] Matthew 22:40.
[127] Mosiah 2:16–19.
[128] Mosiah 2:17.

King Benjamin bid them to be grateful for their blessings[129] and to become profoundly aware of their continual dependence on the Lord. This doctrine stands in stark contrast to Babylon's anti-Christ doctrine of self-dependency: "every man fared in this life according to the management of the creature . . . prospered according to his genius, and . . . every man conquered according to his strength."[130] Benjamin explained that pride claims that we, without God, are independently "profitable," a satanical notion. When we take into account that our very creation, including our "every breath,"[131] comes from God, we realize that we consume more than we produce—unprofitable indeed! Therefore, Benjamin explained, we are ever in debt to God, implying that he is never in debt to anyone.[132] As an example of the ledger of indebtedness, when we obey him, he "doth immediately bless you; and therefore he hath paid you. And ye are still indebted unto him, and are, and will be, forever and ever."[133]

King Benjamin taught his people the Zion principle of equality: "And I, even I, whom ye call your king, am no better than ye yourselves are."[134] Equality and service allow us to walk "with a clear conscience before God . . . [and] be found blameless . . . when [we] shall stand to be judged of God."[135] He reminded his people that prosperity and protection follow obedience to God's commandments: "Ye shall prosper in the land, and your enemies shall have no power over you."[136]

King Benjamin singled out the danger of contention, which is a condition of Babylon and therefore a device of the devil.[137] Contention results from listening to and obeying "the evil spirit,"[138] he said. Moreover, contention draws from God a "wo" upon the contender. A wo (woe) is a condition of "calamity, wretchedness, deep distress, misery and grief."[139] That person who listens to and obeys Satan, "and remaineth and dieth in his sins, the same drinketh damnation to his own soul."[140] Where Zion exists contention does not.[141]

King Benjamin taught his people the law of consecration: a person must render all that he has and is to God.[142]

King Benjamin spoke of our obligation regarding the revealed word of God. Because we are the covenant people, we are under covenant to study and obey the word of God or face severe and eternal consequences.[143] If a person lives contrary to the scriptures and thereby rejects the Covenant, he has abandoned Zion and defected to Babylon. He has come "out in open rebellion against God . . . and [become] an enemy to all righteousness; therefore, the Lord has no place in him, for he dwelleth not in unholy temples. Therefore, if that man repenteth not, and remaineth and dieth an enemy to God, the demands of divine justice do awaken his immortal soul to a lively sense of his own guilt, which doth cause him to shrink from the presence of the Lord, and doth fill his breast with guilt, and pain, and anguish, which is like an unquenchable fire, whose flame ascendeth up forever and ever."[144] Then

---

[129] Mosiah 2:19–21.
[130] Alma 30:17.
[131] Mosiah 2:21, 23.
[132] Mosiah 2:23.
[133] Mosiah 2:24.
[134] Mosiah 2:26.
[135] Mosiah 2:27.
[136] Mosiah 2:31.
[137] 3 Nephi 11:29.
[138] Mosiah 2:32.
[139] *American Heritage Dictionary*, s.v. "woe."
[140] Mosiah 2:33.
[141] 4 Nephi 1:2, 15.
[142] Mosiah 2:34.
[143] Mosiah 2:9, 36.
[144] Mosiah 2:37–38.

the words of the prophets and the scriptures "shall stand as a bright testimony against this people, at the judgment day; whereof they shall be judged, every man according to his works, whether they be good, or whether they be evil."[145] On the other hand, embracing the word of God and abiding in the Covenant result in safety, prosperity, and eternal happiness.[146]

King Benjamin explained the mission of the Savior and how we must embrace the Atonement, if we ever hope to escape Babylon. Otherwise our path leads to eternal damnation.[147] Benjamin explained that this message corresponds with the universal message of all the prophets that is sent to "every kindred, nation, and tongue, that thereby whosoever should believe that Christ should come, the same might receive remission of their sins, and rejoice with exceedingly great joy."[148] The Atonement of Jesus Christ is far-reaching, King Benjamin said; little children who die before the age of accountability will be saved and exalted.[149]

With reference to the atoning Savior, the name *Jesus Christ* is both the identity of the great atoning God and the name of salvational power. King Benjamin explained that only *by* Jesus Christ and *in the name of* Jesus Christ can salvation "come unto the children of men."[150] Furthermore, an unavoidable reality lies in every person's future; that event is the Judgment, when each of us must stand before Jesus Christ, the Lord Omnipotent to be judged by him. Then we will have no excuse, for the Lord's judgment will be just.[151] King Benjamin prophesied that "the time shall come when the knowledge of a Savior shall spread throughout every nation, kindred, tongue, and people,"[152] and when that time comes, everyone will be held accountable for his actions.[153] Judgment can be just only on the principles of total knowledge and unrestricted agency. Neither will we be condemned for another's actions, nor will we be convicted if we are victims of deception.

King Benjamin drew a stark contrast between Babylon's "natural man," who "is an enemy to God," and Zion's "saint," who embraces "the Atonement of Christ the Lord." A sign of this transformation is our willingness to "[yield] to the enticings of the Holy Spirit, and [put] off the natural man . . . [becoming] as a child, submissive, meek, humble, patient, full of love, willing to submit to all things which the Lord seeth fit to inflict upon him, even as a child doth submit to his father."[154]

King Benjamin successfully laid out the two universal philosophies: Zion and Babylon, or Christ and Satan. He showed his people that one philosophy leads to immeasurable blessings, while the other leads to immeasurable misery. The people could no longer "halt between two opinions."[155] Having received their prophet/king's words, which he had borne "down in pure testimony,"[156] he constrained them to choose immediately. Either they were for Zion or they were for Babylon, but they could no longer straddle the two.

King Benjamin's people were shocked. These were good people, members of the Church who by and large obeyed the commandments and were trying to do what was right. Yet Babylon had crept in among them. Now their astonishment overwhelmed them. They may have thought that they had been Zion people, but they were not. Not yet. They may have thought that all was well in Zion and

---

[145] Mosiah 3:24.
[146] Mosiah 2:41.
[147] Mosiah 3:1–12.
[148] Mosiah 3:13.
[149] Mosiah 3:16, 18.
[150] Mosiah 3:17, 18.
[151] Mosiah 3:18.
[152] Mosiah 3:20.
[153] Mosiah 3:21.
[154] Mosiah 3:19.
[155] 1 Kings 18:21.
[156] Alma 4:19.

that Zion was prospering, but now they saw themselves as lacking. Their reaction was astonishing: they collapsed "to the earth, for the fear of the Lord had come upon them. And they had viewed themselves in their own carnal state, even less than the dust of the earth."[157] What could they do to shed Babylon and fully embrace Zion?

King Benjamin had given them the answer: The Atonement. "And they all cried aloud with one voice, saying: O have mercy, and apply the atoning blood of Christ that we may receive forgiveness of our sins, and our hearts may be purified; for we believe in Jesus Christ, the Son of God."[158] Their declaration had the effect of renewing their Covenant, which they had made at baptism, and renewing their allegiance to Christ and his Zion. Such renewal brought them joy, remission of sins, and peace of conscience,[159] all attributes of Zion people.

Now that they had made a choice, King Benjamin was able to teach them the foundational points of the law of Zion. First, he said, we must always remember that we are wholly dependent upon and beholden to God, who is infinitely good, and matchless in his power, wisdom, patience, and long-suffering. Because of his love for us, he provided the Atonement to rescue us from Babylon, reconcile us to him, and bring us back to his presence—Zion. The journey to Zion is made possible by believing that God exists, that he is a being comprised of a perfection of attributes, and that therefore we can trust him. Zion is achieved by repenting and forsaking sin, humbling ourselves, asking forgiveness, diligently keeping the commandments, and abiding in the Covenant to the end. Such a person "receiveth salvation."[160] There is no other way.[161]

King Benjamin taught that our prayers must be continual and humble, so that they might anchor us to Jesus Christ and his Atonement. If we do this, we shall: (1) always rejoice, (2) be filled with the love of God, (3) always retain a remission of our sins, and (4) grow in the knowledge of God and that which is just and true.[162] The benefits of humble prayer are many, he said. We abandon Babylon's disposition to injure other people, and we embrace Zion's disposition to live peaceably and to treat people fairly and as equals.[163] Through humble prayer our families become Zionlike. Parents labor to support their children, as is required by the law of God. They teach their children the commandments and correct them when they transgress. They check contention when it enters into the family, so that the devil can never gain a foothold. They teach their children "to walk in the ways of truth and soberness . . . to love one another, and to serve one another."[164] Clearly, Zion principles must be learned first in the home.

A hallmark of Zion is to have no poor of any kind among us.[165] Reminding his people that all of us are poor and therefore in a constant state of begging for the Lord's assistance, King Benjamin commanded his people to succor (help) "those that stand in need of your succor; . . . to administer of your substance unto him that standeth in need; and . . . to respond to "the beggar [who] putteth up his petition to you."[166] And they were required do all of this without judgment or prejudice! For "whosoever doeth this the same hath great cause to repent; and except he repenteth of that which he hath done *he perisheth forever, and hath no interest in the kingdom of God.*"[167] Therefore, we are left without excuse. If God is willing to respond to our pleas for help, if he has blessed us with resources

---

[157] Mosiah 4:1–2.
[158] Mosiah 4:2.
[159] Mosiah 4:3.
[160] Mosiah 4:5–10.
[161] Mosiah 4:8.
[162] Mosiah 4:11–12.
[163] Mosiah 4:13.
[164] Mosiah 4:14–15.
[165] Moses 7:18.
[166] Mosiah 4:16.
[167] Mosiah 4:18; emphasis added.

and abundance, which the Covenant defines as belonging to him, how can we, the Lord's stewards, withhold the Lord's goods from one of his needy children? What right do we have to judge harshly, treat the beggar as an inferior, or consider our property as our own? If we claim to desire to become like God, should we not strive to act as unselfishly as he does? King Benjamin thought so.[168] He could not abide the Babylonian attitude of selfishness. He said, "Wo be unto that man, for his substance shall perish with him."[169]

The mindset of a Zion people is opposite that of the people of Babylon. Zion pivots on the absence or existence of pride. Neither the rich nor the poor are exempt from pride, Benjamin said. President Ezra Taft Benson concurred, warning that pride retards the establishment of Zion.[170] The rich are under covenant not to withhold, and the poor are under covenant not to covet. Neither attribute is Zionlike. The antidote for pride is humility. Even the poor Zionlike person humbly assumes a giving attitude: "I give not because I have not, but if I had I would give."[171] King Benjamin stated a powerful principle that forms the foundation of selfless giving and service: obtaining a remission of sins and retaining a guiltless life are dependent upon charity: "For the sake of retaining a remission of your sins from day to day, that ye may walk guiltless before God—I would that ye should impart of your substance to the poor, every man according to that which he hath, such as feeding the hungry, clothing the naked, visiting the sick and administering to their relief, both spiritually and temporally, according to their wants." As we extend charitable service, we should follow Benjamin's counsel to do so with wisdom, order, and temperance: "for it is not requisite that a man should run faster than he has strength." But this counsel is not to be an excuse for noncompliance. Diligence, he said, enables us to "win the prize; therefore, all things must be done in order."[172]

Finally, a Zion person is fair and honest in his dealings.

Now that King Benjamin had clearly described a Zion person, his people recognized that despite their perception, they had allied themselves with various philosophies of Babylon. Evidently they were horrified and cried out for deliverance. Then the compassionate Lord responded, and the "Spirit of the Lord came upon them, and they were filled with joy, having received a remission of their sins, and having peace of conscience."[173] Now they were ready to be presented with the Covenant,[174] which would formalize their commitment and give them power to become Zion. But first, King Benjamin needed to ascertain their level of belief and judge the condition of their hearts, for Zion is the pure in heart.[175]

> And now, it came to pass that when king Benjamin had thus spoken to his people, he sent among them, desiring to know of his people if they believed the words which he had spoken unto them. And they all cried with one voice, saying: Yea, we believe all the words which thou hast spoken unto us; and also, we know of their surety and truth, because of the Spirit of the Lord Omnipotent, which has wrought a mighty change in us, or in our hearts, that we have no more disposition to do evil, but to do good continually.[176]

---

[168] Mosiah 4:19–22.
[169] Mosiah 4:23.
[170] Benson, "Beware of Pride," 4.
[171] Mosiah 4:24.
[172] Mosiah 4:26–27.
[173] Mosiah 4:3.
[174] Note: This occasion may have been one renewing the Covenant.
[175] D&C 97:21.
[176] Mosiah 5:1–2.

Note that the state of a changed heart is defined as "no more disposition to do evil, but to do good continually." That the people bore testimony of the miracle of a changed heart is significant. Sincere testimony becomes part of the record of heaven; it is "recorded in heaven for the angels to look upon; and they rejoice over you, *and your sins are forgiven you.*"[177] Bearing testimony purifies the heart!

Suddenly the people began to enjoy Zion's abundance: "the infinite goodness of God, and the manifestations of his Spirit." Revelation poured into their minds and hearts. With astonishment, they cried, "[We] have great views of that which is to come; and were it expedient, we could prophesy of all things."[178] Their faith increased exponentially, resulting in extraordinary knowledge, rejoicing, and "exceedingly great joy."[179] What did they want then? The Covenant! They wanted to enter into an agreement with God that he would bring them out of Babylon and back into Zion.

> And we are willing to enter into a covenant with our God to do his will, and to be obedient to his commandments in all things that he shall command us, all the remainder of our days, that we may not bring upon ourselves a never-ending torment, as has been spoken by the angel, that we may not drink out of the cup of the wrath of God.[180]

King Benjamin, because he had the keys of authority, was in a position to administer this Covenant to the people:

> And now, these are the words which king Benjamin desired of them; and therefore he said unto them: Ye have spoken the words that I desired; and the covenant which ye have made is a righteous covenant. And now, because of the covenant which ye have made ye shall be called the children of Christ, his sons, and his daughters; for behold, this day he hath spiritually begotten you; for ye say that your hearts are changed through faith on his name; therefore, ye are born of him and have become his sons and his daughters.[181]

A Zion person receives a new family and a new name; that name is *Jesus Christ.* Suddenly empowered with the name of Jesus Christ and armed with the Covenant, we are free—free from Babylon, its sins, its philosophies, its trappings, its enticements and follies. We can leave Babylon with the full assurance that we will be safe in Christ's Zion—safe, because we are holding fast to the Covenant in the family of Christ and because we are bearing the Lord's name with dignity. Now we are in a position to receive an inheritance in Zion in this life and in eternity.[182] Ultimately, the Lord will seal us his, which is the Lord's absolute guarantee of eternal life.[183] There are no greater blessings than those associated with the Covenant. Hence, King Mosiah admonished his people to stay put in the Covenant: "Therefore, I would that ye should be steadfast and immovable, always abounding in good works, that Christ, the Lord God Omnipotent, may seal you his, that you may be brought to heaven, that ye may have everlasting salvation and eternal life, through the wisdom, and power, and

---

[177] D&C 62:3.
[178] Mosiah 5:3.
[179] Mosiah 5:4.
[180] Mosiah 5:5.
[181] Mosiah 5:6–7.
[182] Mosiah 5:8–12.
[183] Smith, *Teachings of the Prophet Joseph Smith,* 149–51; see D&C 131:5.

justice, and mercy of him who created all things, in heaven and in earth, who is God above all. Amen."[184]

ALMA THE YOUNGER'S ZION

Under King Mosiah, King Benjamin's son, a major shift in the Nephite government occurred. The people adopted a constitution of elected representation, and Alma the Younger became the nation's first chief judge. To compound his responsibilities, he also had been called of God to lead the Church as its presiding high priest.[185]

In the first year of the constitution, a wicked man named Nehor introduced priestcraft to the people, challenging both the laws of the land and of the Church. Because priestcraft makes "merchandise" of men's souls,[186] it stands opposite to charity.

"Priestcrafts are that men preach and set themselves up for a light unto the world, that they may get gain and the praise of the world; *but they seek not the welfare of Zion.* Behold, the Lord hath forbidden this thing; wherefore, the Lord God hath given a commandment that *all men should have charity,* which charity is love."[187]

The introduction of priestcraft set off a series of events that sent both the country and the Church into a freefall. Alma did all he could to check the downslide, but after several years, he realized that he could no longer occupy both positions effectively. His choice between his two occupations is an indication of Zion principles in action: the work of God trumps every other labor. Understanding the greater work, Alma, a Zion person, resigned as Chief Judge, the most powerful political position in the land; he gave up all of the job's benefits, prestige and protections, and he became a servant, devoting himself fully to the work of God. For the rest of his life, his labor would focus on teaching, preaching and administering the Covenant. We are forever grateful for his choice.

Under Alma's leadership, and in response to the threat of ongoing priestcrafts, the Saints gathered around the Covenant and Zion principles, and found safety and prosperity amid the storms of apostasy and persecution that raged about them. Consider the descriptive language that reminds us of Zion:

> They were *steadfast and immovable* in keeping the commandments of God.
> They bore with *patience* the persecution which was heaped upon them.
> They were all *equal.*
> They did all *labor,* every man according to his strength.
> They did *impart of their substance,* every man according to that which he had, to the poor, and the needy, and the sick, and the afflicted.
> They did not wear *costly apparel,* yet they were neat and comely.
> They began to have *continual peace* again, notwithstanding all their persecutions.
> And now, because of the *steadiness* of the church they began to be *exceedingly rich, having abundance of all things whatsoever they stood in need*—an abundance of flocks and herds, and fatlings of every kind, and also abundance of grain, and of gold, and of silver, and of precious things, and abundance of silk and fine-twined linen, and all manner of good homely cloth.[188]

Abundance and wealth always describe Zion people. Because Alma's people were willing to abide in the Covenant, the Lord prospered them.

---

[184] Mosiah 5:15.
[185] Mosiah 29:42.
[186] 2 Peter 2:3.
[187] 2 Nephi 26:29–30.
[188] Alma 1:25–29.

Central to the Covenant is the law of consecration, which makes a Zion person the Lord's conduit through which he can funnel resources to bless the poor: "And thus, in their prosperous circumstances, they did not send away any who were naked, or that were hungry, or that were athirst, or that were sick, or that had not been nourished; and they did not set their hearts upon riches; therefore they were liberal to all, both old and young, both bond and free, both male and female, whether out of the church or in the church, having no respect to persons as to those who stood in need."[189]

The result drew a stark contrast between Zion and Babylon: "And thus they did prosper and become *far more wealthy* than those who did not belong to their church."[190] To drive home the point, Mormon, who is recounting the story, painted a frightening picture of the condition of the people remaining in Babylon: "For those who did not belong to their church did indulge themselves in sorceries, and in idolatry or idleness, and in babblings, and in envyings and strife; wearing costly apparel; being lifted up in the pride of their own eyes; persecuting, lying, thieving, robbing, committing whoredoms, and murdering, and all manner of wickedness."[191] With such a clear portrayal of the two ways of life, we are left to wonder why people would choose Babylon over Zion.

THE APOSTLES' ZION

After the resurrection and ascension of Christ, the apostles assumed the leadership of the Church and began to experience great success. As they administered the Covenant, they implemented the principles of Zion.

> And the multitude of them that believed were of one heart and of one soul: neither said any that [any] of the things which he possessed was his own; but they had all things common. And with great power gave the apostles witness of the resurrection of the Lord Jesus: and great grace was upon them all. Neither was there any among them that lacked: for as many as were possessors of lands or houses sold them, and brought the prices of the things that were sold, and laid them down at the apostles' feet: and distribution was made unto every man according as he had need.[192]

As mentioned, the m's mission was to fulfill the law of Moses,[193] which had been given to the Israelites to prepare them for the fulness of the gospel and the law of Zion, which their fathers had rejected.[194] Therefore, when the Lord finally established Zion among the Jews, the law of Moses had completely fulfilled its purpose and was dismantled. Now the apostles, clothed in the authority of the Melchizedek Priesthood, administered the fulness of the new and everlasting covenant and advanced the cause of Zion.

THE NEPHITES' ZION

To fulfill the law of Moses among the Nephites in the western hemisphere, the resurrected Savior administered to them the Covenant and taught them the principles of Zion. The account is found in the book of 3 Nephi, and the occasion was the Sermon at the Temple. Remarkably, the principles

---

[189] Alma 1:30.
[190] Alma 1:31; emphasis added.
[191] Alma 1:32.
[192] Acts 4:32–35.
[193] Matthew 5:17–18.
[194] D&C 84:23–26.

taught in this sermon are so universal and weighty that he repeated to the Nephites almost word for word what he had originally given to the Jews in what we call the Sermon on the Mount. According to President Harold B. Lee, this sermon contains "the constitution for a perfect life,"[195] specifying the Zion principles of *blessedness,* which we call the *Beatitudes.*

Jesus began by gathering the Nephites together. The process of gathering, we have learned, always precedes the establishment of Zion.[196] A year earlier, when he had spoken to them through the mist of darkness, he had chastised them for their historical unwillingness to gather to him "with full purpose of heart."[197] Now they gathered without reservation. He taught the Nephites precepts that echoed principles associated with Zion. For instance:

- avoid contention[198]
- become selfless[199]
- love our neighbor[200]
- give to the poor for the right reasons[201]
- establish our treasure according to Zion standards[202]
- become an ambassador of Zion[203]
- decide between Mammon and God (Babylon and Zion)[204]
- embrace the Lord's offer of safety and security[205]
- set in order our priorities: first, the kingdom of God, *then* all things will be added[206]
- draw upon the resources of heaven by asking for what we need, seeking for knowledge, and knocking to come into the presence of God.[207]

Jesus expounded the reciprocal law of service: We receive in proportion to how well we serve.[208] He promised the people that their latter-day posterity would be blessed with Zion.[209] He taught them to selflessly draw others into their circle and strive for equality.[210]

Amazingly, the Savior's visitation seems to have suspended telestial laws. Apparently, time was no longer a factor. In the period of one earth day, he managed to invite some 2,500 people to come and touch his wounds; he organized the Quorum of Twelve Apostles; he taught major sermons; he instructed the people on prayer, explained his mission pertaining to the house of Israel, and prophesied of critical future events; he invited all 2,500 to bring their sick to him to be healed; he prayed for the people; he blessed their children with angelic ministrations; he instituted the sacrament; he gave the apostles power to confer the Holy Ghost—all in a time frame that would seem

---

[195] Lee, *Decisions for Successful Living,* 56–57.
[196] 3 Nephi 11:1.
[197] 3 Nephi 10:6.
[198] 3 Nephi 12:23–24, 39–40; 13:14–15.
[199] 3 Nephi 12:42.
[200] 3 Nephi 12:43–45.
[201] 3 Nephi 13:1–4.
[202] 3 Nephi 13:19–21.
[203] 3 Nephi 12:13–16; 18:24–24.
[204] 3 Nephi 13:24.
[205] 3 Nephi 13:25–34.
[206] 3 Nephi 13:33.
[207] 3 Nephi 14:7–11.
[208] 3 Nephi 14:12.
[209] 3 Nephi 16:17–18.
[210] 3 Nephi 18:22–23, 25, 32.

impossible in a telestial setting.[211] Perhaps only in the celestial condition of Zion could an abundance of love, resources, spiritual gifts, and *time* be possible.

Within the pages of 3 Nephi, we glimpse the wonders of Zion: angels ascending and blessing spontaneously, children prophesying, protective fire from heaven, widespread healings, transfigurations, Christ himself ministering to his people, the books of heaven open so that revelation flows freely, and boundless and unequalled miracles.

Throughout the course of his visitation, Jesus continually taught of Zion, particularly when he quoted Isaiah concerning the latter-day redemption and glory of Zion.[212] The result was immediate and dramatic. Individually and collectively, the people embraced this new culture: "And they taught, and did minister one to another; and they had all things common among them, every man dealing justly, one with another."[213]

They became unified, as is required by Zion.[214]

With Christ's visit, the definition of labor changed. Without interrupting the command to work for their support, Jesus focused the Nephites' attention on the need to reprioritize their efforts by adopting Christ's work as their own and placing it first, with the promise that all else would be added unto them.[215]

The results of Christ's teachings and the people's implementing them were amazing. Within two years of intense missionary effort, all people in the land were converted and became Zion people.[216] Mormon gives a description: No contentions or disputations; every man dealing justly one with another; all things in common; no rich or poor; no one in bondage; peace in the land; prosperity enjoyed by all; a love of God in the hearts of the people; no envyings, strifes, tumults, whoredoms, lyings, murders, or lasciviousness; no robbers, murderers, or any "-ites."[217] Widespread healings and mighty miracles abounded.[218] "The Lord did prosper them exceedingly,"[219] and "the people of Nephi did wax strong, and did multiply exceedingly fast, and became an exceedingly fair and delightsome people."[220] "There could not have been a happier people among all the people who had been created by the hand of God. . . . And how blessed were they! For the Lord did bless them in all their doings."[221]

All of these blessings were preceded by a decision to once and for all receive and live the new and everlasting covenant. In the course of his sermon, the Lord warned the people about refusing to make or choosing to break this Covenant: "Wo unto him that spurneth at the doings of the Lord; yea, wo unto him that shall deny the Christ and his works! Yea, wo unto him that shall deny the revelations of the Lord, and that shall say the Lord no longer worketh by revelation, or by prophecy, or by gifts, or by tongues, or by healings, or by the power of the Holy Ghost! Yea, and wo unto him that shall say at that day, to get gain, that there can be no miracle wrought by Jesus Christ; for he that doeth this shall become like unto the son of perdition, for whom there was no mercy, according to the word of Christ!"[222] One need only read the remainder of the Book of Mormon to realize the tragedy of rejecting the Covenant.

---

[211] 3 Nephi 12–17.
[212] 3 Nephi 20–23.
[213] 3 Nephi 26:19.
[214] 3 Nephi 27:1.
[215] 3 Nephi 27:21; 13:3.
[216] 4 Nephi 1:2.
[217] 4 Nephi 1:15–17.
[218] 4 Nephi 1:5.
[219] 4 Nephi 1:7.
[220] 4 Nephi 1:10.
[221] 4 Nephi 1:16, 18.
[222] 3 Nephi 29:5–7.

Joseph Smith's Zion

The subject of Zion was ever on the Prophet's mind. One of the first recorded commandments in this dispensation regarded Zion: "Seek to bring forth and establish the cause of Zion." Then followed the sister commandment, which set in place the foundation upon which all subsequent Zion relationships would arise: "Seek not for riches but for wisdom."[223] Clearly, the Restoration was establishing a culture diverse from Babylon.

A year later, on the day that the Church was organized, the subject of Zion once again was advanced as the predominant goal of the Restoration. The Lord announced, "[Joseph Smith] have I inspired to move the cause of Zion in mighty power for good, and his diligence I know, and his prayers I have heard. Yea, his weeping for Zion I have seen, and I will cause that he shall mourn for her no longer; for his days of rejoicing are come."[224] The time for the glorious latter-day Zion had come at last!

On April 6, 1830, much of the new and everlasting covenant had already been restored, including the Melchizedek Priesthood, but an essential element was missing for Zion to be built up "by the principles of the law of the Celestial Kingdom."[225] That missing element was the "revelation of the priesthood," that is, the temple covenants and ordinances. Those who would call themselves Zion people needed to be endowed with "power from on high,"[226] for the purpose "that they themselves may be prepared, and that my people may be taught more perfectly, and have experience, and know more perfectly concerning their duty, and the things which I require at their hands."[227]

This endowment of knowledge and power had been promised years earlier, when Moroni had first appeared to the young Prophet. On the night of September 21, 1823, Moroni announced that the day would soon come when Elijah the prophet would come to *reveal* the Priesthood.[228] (Note: When *Priesthood* is capitalized in this work, it refers to the patriarchal order of the Melchizedek Priesthood, which is entered into by husbands and wives when they are sealed by the keys of Elijah in the temple.) The *revelation* of the Priesthood would complete the *restoration* of the priesthood, which included the visitations of John the Baptist and Peter, James, and John.

The revelation of the Priesthood—the initiatory ordinances, the endowment covenants and ordinances, and the sealing covenant and ordinance—is central to the establishment of Zion. Zion people must receive this revelation in a most holy place: a temple, "the earthly type of Zion."[229] Therefore, for the purpose of establishing Zion and exalting his people, the Lord commanded the Saints to build a house of God to endow them with power from on high.[230] This endowment of knowledge and power would include the sacred ordinances of the Melchizedek Priesthood by which "the power of godliness is manifest. And without the ordinances thereof, and the authority of the priesthood, the power of godliness is not manifest unto men in the flesh; for without this [the ordinances and authority of the priesthood and the power of godliness] no man can see the face of God, even the Father, and live."[231]

We recall that Moses had attempted to endow his people with the revelation of the Priesthood, to make of them a Zion people, and to bring them into the presence God, but they refused.[232] Now

---

[223] D&C 6:6–7.
[224] D&C 21:7–8.
[225] D&C 105:5.
[226] D&C 38:32, 38; 95:8; 105:11.
[227] D&C 105:10.
[228] D&C 2:1.
[229] Nibley, *Approaching Zion*, 27.
[230] D&C 95:8; emphasis added.
[231] D&C 84:20–22.
[232] D&C 84:23–24.

Joseph Smith, the latter-day Moses,[233] whose code name, interestingly, was *Enoch*,[234] shouldered the same responsibility to administer the Covenant to his people that thereby we might be cleansed, sanctified, endowed with knowledge and power, sealed into the patriarchal chain, and prepared in every way to become Zion people. In preparation for the revelation of the Priesthood, the Lord had earlier revealed the law of Zion,[235] and shortly thereafter, he had revealed the oath and covenant of the priesthood.[236] Now, the new and everlasting covenant was nearly complete, lacking only the revelation on eternal marriage, which had been revealed to the Prophet as early as 1831 but had not been made public.[237] When that revelation was finally recorded in 1843, the Covenant now embodied all the principles, laws, covenants, and ordinances for the individual and collective building up of the kingdom of God on the earth and the establishment of Zion. Now to become Zion individuals, marriages, families, and a Zion church, all the Saints had to do was implement the Covenant. That single act had the power to purify their hearts and make them individually Zion.

Would they live up to their privileges? Or would they, like the children of Israel, reject Zion and be relegated to a lesser, preparatory law that would merely point them toward Zion?

Blaine M. Yorgason writes:

> With the dedication of the Kirtland Temple, Joseph's lofty desire of establishing a Zion for this priesthood generation of the last days had begun its fulfillment. Truly had the Lord blessed His people as they struggled and sacrificed to expand their city, construct a temple to the Most High God, and become a holy people like the ancient Saints of Enoch. Like Enoch's people, these Latter-day Saints were led by a mighty prophet to whom the Lord revealed His will and who had also been given keys . . . powerful enough to open the heavens. These keys Joseph freely passed on to the Lord's people through what the Lord termed the "endowment," thus giving all, who were so blessed, power to bring themselves back into His presence. And like Enoch's people, a remarkable number in this generation did so, seeing and hearing glorious heavenly manifestations during that season of rejoicing.[238]

The spiritual manifestations surrounding the dedication of the Kirtland Temple were reminiscent of Christ's visit to the Nephites in America and the day of Pentecost in Jerusalem. On all three occasions, the people experienced great spiritual outpourings of the magnitude that we might expect of Zion.[239] "For a period of weeks," Elder McConkie writes, "the visions of eternity were opened to many, angels visited in the congregations of the saints, the Lord himself was seen by many, and tongues and prophecy were multiplied."[240] In Kirtland, many of the pure in heart truly achieved and experienced the condition of Zion. But sadly, many of the Latter-day Saints, like the Nephites, could not contend with the subsequent opposition, and, worse, they could not contain their desire for the

---

[233] D&C 28:2.

[234] Note: In earlier versions of the Doctrine and Covenants, Joseph Smith and other brethren occasionally used code names for their protection. For example, see D&C 78:1 in the 1969 edition of the Doctrine and Covenants.

[235] D&C 42.

[236] D&C 84:33–44.

[237] D&C 132 Preface.

[238] Yorgason, *I Need Thee Every Hour*, 49–50.

[239] Acts 2:1–17.

[240] McConkie, *Mormon Doctrine*, 181–82.

things of this world. They looked back longingly at Babylon, as did Lot's wife,[241] and when they chose Babylon over Zion, they quickly lost their privileges.

> Sadly, a period of great apostasy followed immediately thereafter, and many of the Saints succumbed to the enticements of Satan and the cares of the world.... Between November 1837 and June 1838, possibly two or three hundred Saints withdrew from the Church in Kirtland, and a significant number also left the Church in Missouri. In that nine-month period, the Three Witnesses, a member of the First Presidency (Frederick G. Williams), four members of the Twelve Apostles, and several members of the First Quorum of Seventy left the Church.... On both continents Jesus taught: "No man can serve two masters: for either he will hate the one, and love the other; or else he will hold to the one, and despise the other. Ye cannot serve God and mammon" (Matthew 6:24; 3 Nephi 13:24). And Hugh Nibley adds: "The first commandment given to the Saints . . . was an ominous warning: 'Seek not for riches but for wisdom' (D&C 6:7)—all in one brief mandate that does not allow compromise. Why start out on such a negative note? The Lord knew well that the great obstacle to the work would be what it always had been in the past. The warning is repeated throughout the Doctrine and Covenants and the Book of Mormon again and again. The positive and negative are here side by side and back to back, making it clear, as the scriptures often do, that the two quests are mutually exclusive—you cannot go after both, you cannot serve both God and Mammon, even if you should be foolish enough to try" (Hugh Nibley, *Approaching Zion* [Provo and Salt Lake City: Foundation for Ancient Research and Mormon Studies and Deseret Book Company, 1989], 343)."[242]

Like the Israelites in the days of Moses, the Latter-day Saints rejected Zion and shifted "their allegiance from God to mammon, or the things of the world. Eliza R. Snow apparently understood the cause of the spiritual decline of the Saints perfectly, for she said that many members felt that 'prosperity was dawning upon them . . . and many who had been humble and faithful . . . were getting haughty in their spirits, and lifted up in the pride of their hearts. As the Saints drank in the love and spirit of the world, the Spirit of the Lord withdrew from their hearts, and they were filled with pride and hatred toward those who maintained their integrity' (*History of the Church*, 2:487–88, footnotes)."[243]

Hugh Nibley wrote, "Then came the crash of 1837, brought on by those same shrewd, hardheaded businessmen. 'During this time,' [Heber C.] Kimball recalled, 'I had many days of sorrow and mourning, for my heart sickened to see the awful extent that things were getting to.' Many apostatized and 'also entered into combinations to obtain wealth by fraud and every means that was evil.' Later, Kimball returned to Kirtland again after a mission to England: 'The Church had suffered terribly from the ravages of apostasy.' Looking back over many years, he recalled that 'the Ohio mobbings, the Missouri persecutions, the martyrdom, the exodus, nor all that Zion's cause has suffered

---

[241] Genesis 19:26.
[242] Yorgason, *I Need Thee Every Hour*, 49–52.
[243] Yorgason, *I Need Thee Every Hour*, 52.

since, have imperiled it half so much as when mammon and the love of God strove for supremacy in the hearts of His people.' Note that they were torn between God and Mammon, and 'no man can serve both!'"[244]

Continuing, Nibley wrote, "Every step in the direction of increasing one's personal holdings is a step away from Zion, which is another way of saying, as the Lord has proclaimed in various ways, that one cannot serve two masters: to the degree in which he loves the one he will hate the other, and so it is with God and business, for mammon is simply the standard Hebrew word for any kind of financial dealing."[245]

The result? Beautiful Zion returned to its heavenly home, so to speak, and the Saints in Kirtland and Missouri, like their fathers of old, were left in Babylon to live a preparatory law, which financially was marked by *tithing*.[246] We should note here that the law of tithing was not a step down; tithing is an essential part of the law of consecration, and a "standing law . . . forever."[247] Nevertheless, tithing is not the fulness of consecration, and therefore, as magnificent as is tithing, it does not offer the Saints the same weight of blessings as does consecration. Gratefully, the Lord left in place the law of *offerings*, which allowed the Saints the individual choice to better live the law of consecration and receive its blessings. But because many of the Saints in Kirtland and Missouri rejected the Covenant, they forfeited the supernal blessings of Zion.

They had recently tasted the wonderful fruit of Zion—how could they have fallen so far in such a short period of time? Blaine Yorgason describes the tragedy of the Saints' abandoning their covenant to establish Zion in their hearts and as a people.

> Once the Saints were no longer sacrificing their all for the building of the temple in Kirtland, many of them bowed down to the god of mammon. They began looking to themselves, and soon their personal religion was no longer a religion of spiritual power and progression. . . . [It became] a gospel of convenience, [and as it] increased its hold in the hearts and minds of Latter-day Saints, fewer and fewer of them had power to bring to pass and enjoy such spiritual experiences as had occurred in Kirtland—and this despite the fact that they had been endowed with that power from on high. Truly, had their spiritual progression been slowed or in some cases even stopped altogether. The next step, of course, was that angelic ministrations and other manifestations of the Lord's Spirit quite literally went out of fashion. Those who continued to seek and enjoy such rich spiritual blessings hesitated to discuss them or bear witness of them for fear of ridicule and outright scorn, and so their numbers grew fewer and fewer. And the scorners? Besides the apostates and the anti-Christs, they grew to include good, well-meaning people, especially members of the Church, who had never sought such transcendent experiences, had never sacrificed the things of the world in order to experience them, and who doubted that ordinary people such as themselves could ever see, hear, feel, and know such things. And so they mocked and scorned or shook their heads in

---

[244] Nibley, *Approaching Zion*, 347.
[245] Nibley, *Approaching Zion*, 37.
[246] *Encyclopedia of Mormonism*, 313; see 1481–82.
[247] D&C 119:4.

sorrow and pity that so-and-so could be so deluded as to think he or she had actually seen and spoken with an angel.[248]

Latter-day Zion

The Lord told Noah, "When men should keep all my commandments, Zion should again come on the earth, the city of Enoch which I have caught up unto myself. And this is mine everlasting covenant, that when thy posterity shall embrace the truth, and look upward, then shall Zion look downward, and all the heavens shall shake with gladness, and the earth shall tremble with joy; and the general assembly of the church of the firstborn shall come down out of heaven, and possess the earth, and shall have place until the end come. And this is mine everlasting covenant, which I made with thy father Enoch."[249]

Zion has always been our destiny!

Zion's day of redemption shall come with power. Quoting the revelation, Elder McConkie wrote: "'Behold, I do not require at their hands'—the hands of mine elders—'to fight the battles of Zion; for, as I said in a former commandment, even so will I fulfill—I will fight your battles.' [D&C 105:14.] We need not suppose our swords must slay the enemies of God, or that any mortal power must cleanse the land and make it available for the Saints. The building of the New Jerusalem is the Lord's work, and he will prepare the way for his people when that people have prepared themselves to perform the heaven-given labors."[250]

How will the Lord do this? Again, quoting the revelation, Elder McConkie stated: "'Behold, the destroyer I have sent forth to destroy and lay waste mine enemies.' [D&C 105:15.] Destructions, wars, calamities, the violence of nature—those things that men call 'acts of God'—shall sweep over the land. 'And not many years hence'—the 'little season' shall last for years—'they shall not be left to pollute mine heritage, and to blaspheme my name upon the lands which I have consecrated for the gathering together of my saints.' [D&C 105:15.] We are thus left to conclude that the wicked will slay the wicked, and the God of Nature will loose the forces of nature to destroy those who oppose the manifest destiny of his saints."[251]

The redemption of Zion is a sacred subject not to be discussed with the world: "The Lord then counsels his people to be wise and discreet and not stir up opposition as they gather together. 'Talk not of judgments, neither boast of faith nor of mighty works,' they are commanded, 'but carefully gather together, as much in one region as can be, consistently with the feelings of the people.' [D&C 105:24.] They are to seek 'favor in the eyes of the people, until the army of Israel becomes very great.' [D&C 105:26.]"[252] Zion is not a threat to the world; rather, Zion is the world's salvation. To become so, Zion's "army"—its people—must become holy, a pure-hearted people who are capable of living the celestial law: "And let it [the army of the Lord] be sanctified before me, that it may become fair as the sun, and clear as the moon, and that her banners may be terrible unto all nations; that the kingdoms of this world may be constrained to acknowledge that the kingdom of Zion is in very deed the kingdom of our God and his Christ; therefore, let us become subject unto her laws."[253]

Each of us must individually become Zion. Elder McConkie wrote: "Again the word is this: The worthiness of the Lord's people, their sanctified state, their purity and uprightness before him—these are the things that will enable them to build the New Jerusalem, for Zion is the City of Holiness. When it is built, as it was in Enoch's day, its grandeur and glory and power must be such that those in

---

[248] Yorgason, *I Need Thee Every Hour*, 54–55.
[249] JST Genesis 9:21–23.
[250] McConkie, *A New Witness for the Articles of Faith*, 616.
[251] McConkie, *A New Witness for the Articles of Faith*, 617.
[252] McConkie, *A New Witness for the Articles of Faith*, 617.
[253] D&C 105:31–32.

all nations, from one end of the earth to the other, standing in awe, will feel inclined to be subject to such a mighty city, whence comes such a perfect law. The day in which the latter-day Zion will have such renown and be held in such unlimited awe is clearly Millennial."[254]

SUMMARY AND CONCLUSION

Today, we still are awaiting the promised redemption of Zion.[255] But if we are waiting to become Zion individuals in response to a Zion program issued from Church headquarters, we are being deceived and irresponsible. *Zion is us!*[256] Right now—today! Every person who has entered into the new and everlasting covenant has the immediate responsibility to live the Covenant—*all of it!*

We might ask ourselves, what part of the Covenant has ever required a program? Baptism? Sabbath-day observance? Temple worship? Eternal marriage? Why, then, should we consider parts of the Covenant futuristic, including consecration? If we have accepted the Covenant, which is intended to make of us Zion people, what stops us from becoming such? If the answer is lack of understanding and fear, we might be served by striving for a clearer comprehension of the Covenant, so that we might gain the courage to break loose from Babylon's hold on us.

Gratefully, the Lord has given us the law of tithes and offerings to prepare our minds and hearts to live the higher manifestation of the Covenant. No one who has faithfully lived the preparatory law of tithes and offerings can deny that the law foreshadows Zion's power, safety, security, and prosperity. No one has ended up with less by living the law. Therefore, armed with that knowledge, we might, with confidence, press past our fears and embrace Zion's principles entirely, as we covenanted to do.

Perhaps in the spirit of allaying our fears, the Lord encouraged us to consider the fowls in the air and the lilies of the field.[257] Most certainly, if he is willing to take care of them that have made no covenant, he will take care of us, his covenant children. To the end that we become such, the Lord gave us the Book of Mormon, the textbook on becoming Zion people. We are without excuse. President Spencer W. Kimball laid the responsibility for becoming and establishing Zion squarely on our shoulders.[258] How well we incorporate the Covenant in our lives, he said, will determine the required time to "accomplish all things pertaining to Zion."[259]

---

[254] McConkie, *A New Witness for the Articles of Faith*, 618; emphasis added.
[255] D&C section 101; 103:15, 18; 105:9, 13.
[256] Taylor, *The Gospel Kingdom*, 245.
[257] Matthew 6:28–29; 3 Nephi 13:28–29.
[258] Kimball, "Becoming the Pure in Heart," 79.
[259] D&C 105:37.

Section 3

We Were Prepared to Become

Latter-day Zion People

Neither the telestial world nor Babylon is our home. They are as foreign to us as would be slavery to a free person. We are strangers here.[260] We have fallen into a state that is completely alien to us. We cannot comprehend the Fall's depth and distance. We fell physically, spiritually, and emotionally into a condition described by President Joseph F. Smith as "below all things,"[261] and Babylon compounds the circumstances of the Fall. Nevertheless, this experience is evidently essential to our eventually achieving the condition of the heart called *Zion*.

The Savior is our Exemplar: as he descended below all things so that he could ascend above all things, so we, in like manner, must "follow him below." "If with our Lord, we would be heirs," we sing, we must "in his footsteps tread."[262] The universal law of opposites[263] states that rising above depends on descending below, to the end that we might comprehend all things, and thereby gain the ability to become as the gods, who are above and in and through all things.[264] Brigham Young said, "It seems to be absolutely necessary in the providence of him who created us, and who organized and fashioned all things according to his wisdom, that man must descend below all things. It is written of the Savior in the Bible that he descended below all things that he might ascend above all. Is it not so with every man? Certainly it is. It is fit, then, that we should descend below all things and come up gradually, and learn a little now and again, receive 'line upon line, precept upon precept, here a little and there a

---

[260] Cook, "Home and Family: A Divine Eternal Pattern," 30.
[261] Smith, *Gospel Doctrine*, 13.
[262] "Come Follow Me," *Hymns*, no. 116.
[263] 2 Nephi 2:10.
[264] D&C 88:6.

little.'"²⁶⁵ For reasons that we do not completely understand, this process is the only way to become Zionlike and achieve exaltation.

We cannot fathom the range of emotions that must have barraged us as we contemplated our descent from the celestial condition of the Zion of premortality into the telestial condition of the Babylon of the world. Nevertheless, this mortal experience was what we had fought for. Mortality would provide us at least three essential blessings that we could not obtain in any other environment: a physical body, experience with good and evil, and establishment in our own eternal kingdom: *marriage and family*. We vigorously defended the Father's plan for the possibility of receiving those blessings—and to sustain God and his Son—and we shouted for joy at the expectation.²⁶⁶ In that premortal setting, we dedicated our lives to Jesus Christ, who was to become our Savior and the central figure of the plan. But despite the glorious possibilities, we must have been horrified at the prospects of living in Babylon and most assuredly succumbing to sin.

Brigham Young University professor M. Catherine Thomas wrote: "The period of descent was surely seen by the righteous premortal spirits as a great sacrifice. The most righteous did not want to sin. They knew the truth about sin. A veil was necessary so that they would make the descent . . . into spiritual darkness."²⁶⁷ Only profound faith in Christ could have persuaded us to step off the celestial ledge and, by choice—for agency demands that no one is forced—fall into this dark telestial world, armed only with the Light of Christ. Our hope lay in the transcendent possibilities of eternal life. We knew that everything depended on keeping our Second Estate,²⁶⁸ and that feat required our having experience with Babylon, completely rejecting it, and rediscovering and embracing Zion. Therefore, it was with "trailing clouds of glory"²⁶⁹ and commissioned with a divine purpose that we willingly fell into this benighted orb to finally, after untold eons of preparing, claim our eternal inheritance in Zion by working out our salvation with "fear and trembling."²⁷⁰

Divine Appointment

We are not here by accident; rather we qualified in the premortal life.²⁷¹ With humble acknowledgment, we concede that we were among the most capable and qualified spirits. That we have emerged at this place and time signals that Zion is at hand. President Wilford Woodruff said, "I want to say to my brethren and sisters, that we are placed upon the earth to build up Zion."²⁷² Our specific commission could not be clearer: we Latter-day Saints have the mandate to build up the kingdom of God on the earth for the establishment of Zion.

Elder Neal A. Maxwell taught that we were placed here by *divine appointment* according to God's intimate knowledge our unique abilities.²⁷³ Heavenly Father's house is a house of order;²⁷⁴ we are not here by a cosmic roll of the dice. In the premortal world we certainly had proven ourselves by consecrating our all to the Lord. Evidently, the Lord extended to us the call to come in this generation to become Zion people and help to establish latter-day Zion. By our choice, we must have accepted the call and perhaps even requested to come in this day of wickedness and promise.

---

²⁶⁵ Young, *Discourses of Brigham Young*, 60.
²⁶⁶ Job 38:7.
²⁶⁷ Thomas, "Alma the Younger, Part 1," n.p.
²⁶⁸ Abraham 3:26.
²⁶⁹ Wordsworth, "Ode on Intimations of Immortality," in *Narcissism and the Text*, 116–29.
²⁷⁰ Mormon 9:27.
²⁷¹ Larsen, "A Royal Generation," 33.
²⁷² Woodruff, *Journal of Discourses*, 22:334.
²⁷³ Maxwell, "These Are Your Days," 4.
²⁷⁴ D&C 132:8.

Therefore, we assume, the Lord strategically positioned us to combat Babylon, champion Zion, and prepare the world for the Savior's Second Coming.

Our importance to the Lord and the magnitude of our missions cannot be overstated. President Ezra Taft Benson referred to us as a generation marked for greatness, with more expected of us than any other generation. And we have very little time to accomplish our work.[275] There is no boasting here, only a humble owning of truth and our recognizing that we have been "given much," so "much is required"; and if we sin "against the greater light," we "shall receive the greater condemnation."[276] Clearly, our responsibility is equal to our privileges. We must rise to the level of our true character and special commission by accomplishing our mission or face the eternal consequences for our disregard.

To be purposely and divinely placed at this crucial time and place, each person of the Covenant must have proven exceedingly righteous. Joseph Smith taught, "There is a time appointed for every man, according as his works shall be."[277] Paul explained that this "time appointed" would be especially true of the Latter-day Saints; we would be specifically singled out and strategically placed because premortally we had "to be conformed [made similar] to the image of [God's] Son."[278] Therefore, God had taken careful note of our potential to do good and deigned to position us in an era and circumstance that was best suited to our abilities. Elder Erastus Snow explained that the premortal ministry of God's "peculiar people," destined us to assume important mortal assignments and obtain our exaltation:

> For he has had his eye upon the chosen spirits that have come upon the earth in the various ages from the beginning of the world up to this time. . . . The Lord has sent those noble spirits into the world to perform a special work, and appointed their times . . . , *and their future glory and exaltation is secured unto them;* and that is what I understand by the doctrine of election spoken of by the Apostle Paul and other sacred writers: "For whom he did foreknow, he also did predestinate to be conformed to the image of His Son, that he might be the first-born among many brethren." Such were called and chosen and elected of God to perform a certain work at a certain time of the world's history and in due time he fitted them for that work.[279]

This is an amazing promise, one that should give us humble pause as we consider our true identity. Only by embracing the Covenant can we rise to the stature of our premortal greatness and accomplish the latter-day work of Zion.

Special Spirits of the Royal Generation

Pursuant to the perfect foreknowledge of God, we may well have been assigned family placement, birth time, location, and mortal opportunities according to our strengths and weaknesses. We—*all of us*[280]—are part of the group that the prophets have referred as the "royal generation" of very special spirits.[281]

---

[275] Benson, "In His Steps," 2.
[276] D&C 82:3.
[277] D&C 121:25.
[278] Romans 8:29.
[279] Erastus Snow, *Journal of Discourses*, 23:186–87; emphasis added.
[280] Peterson, "Your Special Purpose," 34.
[281] Kimball, "In Love and Power and without Fear," 8.

Clearly, we were "good," and that goodness needed expression at the right time and place. Our divine positioning allowed us to continue our premortal work—advancing the Atonement of Jesus Christ and offering the Covenant to God's children. We had adopted God's work as our eternal work. In the celestial world, the work of redemption is not *a* work of God, it is *the* work of God, and therefore it is the preeminent work of all celestial beings. M. Catherine Thomas wrote:

> Out of all of Heavenly Father's spirit children, a smaller group distinguished itself by its exceeding faith in the Lord Jesus Christ during the conflicts that occurred incident to the war in heaven. Those who were valiant in these conflicts, and in other ways also, demonstrated both their abilities and their desires to become actively involved in the cosmic work of redemption through the great Atonement of the Lord Jesus Christ. The thing that characterizes the Gods and those who aspire to godhood is the love of the work of redemption; that is, nurturing spirit children through the first estate of premortality, then leading them through a mortal probation, and finally raising them to the level of their parent gods. . . . The great work of the gods is family work—the raising and nurturing of children and the redemption of families to be sealed together for all eternity. We cannot comprehend the cosmic proportions of the love and the infinite investment of labor and grace that go into this magnificent work. You and I, as members of the literal house of Israel and of the Church of Jesus Christ, were called in the premortal world to participate in that work, everything else being trivial in comparison. Redemption is not just one of the things going on in the universe; it is *the* thing. That work of redemption is *the* work to which the premortal covenant people, the house of Israel, were called, and it was to take precedence over all other work and to subordinate all other work to itself.[282]

Because we tried in every way to become like the Savior, we became *savior-like*—saviors on Mount Zion.[283] In vision, Nephi saw that our numbers would be few.[284] In proportion to the world's present population, each Latter-day Saint represents 1 in 508.[285] In proportion to all the people who have ever lived, each Latter-day Saint is 1 in 7,692.[286] Because we have always been in the minority, our accomplishing our premortal calling is highly important. As we have mentioned, our latter-day charge is singular: to offer the Covenant to all of God's children since the world began, and to gather those who will to Zion.[287] We are the heralds of Zion, the Lord's "very great" army,[288] the might of which is unparalleled in the earth's history. Our influence will circumscribe the globe, and the amount of good that we will accomplish will be incalculable.[289]

Because the redemptive work of Zion is so essential, and because the laborers who can effectively do the work are few, God, in order to save his children, in the beginning divided his family according

---

[282] Thomas, "Alma the Younger, Part 1," n.p.
[283] Petersen, Conference Report, Oct. 1959, 14.
[284] 1 Nephi 14:12.
[285] Church membership at the end of 2008 was about 13 million, and world population was 6.6 billion.
[286] Estimated human population across history is about 100 billion.
[287] D&C 128:22–24.
[288] D&C 105:31.
[289] Cook, "The Seat Next to You," 4.

to the number of the "special spirits," whom he called "Israel."[290] These are faithful individuals who are *becoming like God* or *prevailing with God*.[291] When we consider the proportionately small number of Israelites who have been born or adopted into the Church, we wonder at our apparent premortal stature and our weighty responsibility. Clearly, without becoming egotistical, each of us is one covenant person among thousands of non-covenant people.

Perspective on the Cosmic War

We have come to earth at this time and place to fight for Zion and vanquish Babylon. We can neither fathom the length of time that we were engaged in the work of redemption nor imagine our potential to bring other people to Christ. To gain perspective, let us review some truths.

We have been told that we are ancient souls, who practiced righteousness and did the work of redemption over vast eons in the premortal life. For how long, we do not know. The scriptures indicate that before the world was created, we existed as spirits.[292] If the current scientific estimate of the earth's age—4.55 billion years[293]—is accurate, our spirits have existed for a long time. During that enormous duration, we lived in the celestial atmosphere of Zion. The focus of our attention was to become like our heavenly parents; therefore, we needed to come to earth and gain a body, experience mortality, choose good over evil, enter into the new and everlasting covenant and follow it to its perfect conclusion, die and achieve a glorious resurrection, and earn exaltation.

We brought with us mature gospel knowledge. For the moment, it might be buried deep in our souls, but it is there just the same. The Fall might have caused us temporary amnesia, but God has not forgotten who we are or what we did.

Of course, neither has Satan forgotten us. We are the ones who helped Michael cast out the devil and his angels from heaven, causing Satan to swear in his wrath that he would attempt to destroy us in the flesh. And for good reason. Satan knew if we were allowed to continue our premortal work, we would conquer him again and help to cast him into outer darkness forever. Therefore, we are and have been enemies. The war in heaven goes on, and this earth is its frontline. The adversary treats us differently. While he merely tempts the people of Babylon,[294] he viciously attacks us.[295] Why are we so ruthlessly confronted? Brigham Young had the answer:

> God never bestows upon his people, or upon an individual, superior blessings without a severe trial to prove them, to prove that individual, or that people, to see whether they will keep their covenants with him, and keep in remembrance what he has shown them. Then the greater the vision [or blessings], the greater the display of the power of the enemy. So when individuals are blessed with visions, revelations, and great manifestations, look out, then the Devil is nigh you, and you will be tempted in proportion to the visions, revelations, or manifestations you have received.[296]

Our premortal nobility, righteousness, and exceedingly good works surely warranted extraordinary blessings and opportunities in this life—royal birth, immediate access to gospel

---

[290] McConkie, *A New Witness for the Articles of Faith*, 510.
[291] Brickey, BYU Education Week address, 2006; see Genesis 32:28.
[292] Job 38:7; Alma 13:3; Abraham 3:22.
[293] Dalrymple, *The Age of the Earth*, 492.
[294] D&C 29:39.
[295] D&C 76:28–29.
[296] Young, *Discourses of Brigham Young*, 338.

blessings, the privileges of Zion, and so forth. But these blessings carry a price. The adversary attacks us in proportion to our blessings, and our seemingly invincible premortal souls, now weakened by the Fall, are more susceptible to Satan's attacks.

Nevertheless, we were prepared.

Preparation in the "First Place"

The Prophet Joseph said: "Every man who has a calling—*every man or woman*—to minister to the inhabitants of the world was ordained to that very purpose in the grand council of heaven before this world was."[297] Virtually every prophet has echoed these words. In the premortal world, reasoned President J. Reuben Clark Jr., we accepted placement in the last days and were empowered and trained for our individual assignments to build up God's kingdom for the establishment of Zion.[298]

Alma spoke in depth about our stature and preparation in the premortal world or the "first place."[299] In that setting, as Catherine Thomas explained, a select group of people received a special calling into the *holy order*[300] because they were "conformed to the image of [God's] Son."[301] That premortal holy order was comprised of righteous men who were ordained to the priesthood, and also righteous women who were worthy of the blessings of the priesthood. We, who now hold the priesthood and enjoy the blessings of the temple, were likely included in that select group. We had "demonstrated [our] abilities and desires to become actively involved in the cosmic work of redemption through the Atonement of Jesus Christ,"[302] which is that "mighty power that can take a lost and fallen person and work a miraculous transformation."[303] In other words, in the premortal world we loved Zion and the work of redemption so much that we dedicated ourselves to the cause by nurturing the weaker spirits and bringing them to Christ. In the process we became Christlike, or "types of Christ,"[304] "that thereby [other premortal spirits] might look forward on the Son of God, . . . that they might look forward to him for a remission of their sins, that they might enter into the rest of the Lord."[305]

There, in that "first place," we of the holy order "elected to become gods," to "come to earth and learn the work of redemption in apprenticeship to the Lord Jesus Christ." The Lord promised us that if we continued to embrace the principles of Zion and do the work of redemption on the earth, we would someday "qualify to live with the Gods in the eternal worlds"[306] and be blessed to live in Zion and do the work of redemption forever. Here in mortality we would be called "Saviors on Mount Zion"[307] because we would try to emulate the Lord in every way,[308] as we had done in the premortal world. Such emulation transcends admiring Jesus' teachings and striving to adopt his attributes; true emulation includes doing his work—the work of redemption. Elder John A. Widtsoe gave us an important insight into our premortal preparation for our life's missions. He said that we made a contractual agreement with God concerning the eternal welfare of all of his children. Each of us,

---

[297] Smith, *Teachings of the Prophet Joseph Smith*, 365.
[298] Clark, Conference Report, Oct. 1950, 169–71.
[299] Alma 13:3.
[300] Alma 13:1.
[301] Romans 8:29.
[302] Thomas, "Alma the Younger, Part 1," n.p.
[303] Thomas, "Alma the Younger, Part 2," n.p.
[304] Thomas, "Alma the Younger, Part 1," n.p.
[305] Alma 13:16.
[306] Thomas, "Alma the Younger, Part 1," n.p.
[307] JST Obadiah 1:21.
[308] 3 Nephi 27:27.

whether we are weak or strong, became partners with the Lord to become saviors for the entire family of Adam to bless them with the Covenant and bring them to Zion.[309]

As mentioned, we who formed the holy order in premortality became known by the family name *Israel*. In mortality, our founding fathers would be Abraham, Isaac, and Jacob (or *Israel*). Elder Bruce R. McConkie wrote: "Israel is an eternal people. She came into being as a chosen and separate congregation before the foundations of the earth were laid; she was a distinct and a peculiar people in preexistence, even as she is in this sphere."[310] As Israelites, by blood or by adoption, we, like our father Abraham, desired to come to earth and teach the gospel, administer the ordinances of salvation, and become a "father [or mother] of many nations and a prince [or princess[311]] of peace."[312] This is the desire and attitude of Zion people. Moreover, righteous men, who were premortally ordained "High Priests of God,"[313] having proved themselves by choosing good over evil and endorsing Zion in the conflict in heaven, had "undoubtedly labored among the spirits in the premortal world and were ordained and prepared to descend to earth and be leaders in the Lord's redeeming work here."[314] Additionally, said President Kimball, righteous women were given special assignments and prepared for those responsibilities.[315]

The power to redeem, bless, heal, and save is possibly "the most coveted power among enlightened beings."[316] Those who will persist in learning and perfecting that power will be exalted to the stature of their parent Gods. Is it any wonder, then, that God places so much weight on our learning the principles of redemption? Clearly, we who lived in Zion in the "first place" were pure-hearted, and apparently we were assigned missions, trained, and strategically positioned to come to earth at this time to become the pure in heart again and do the work of redemption among God's children for the establishment of latter-day Zion. We are, perhaps, the greatest army of Zion people to ever have inhabited the globe.

Summary and Conclusion

We began this book by quoting the Prophet Joseph Smith: "We ought to have the building up of Zion as our greatest object."[317] Brigham Young laid the responsibility of Zion upon each of us individually, saying, "[Zion] commences in the heart of each person,"[318] and Elder Matthew Cowley stated unequivocally that individually, we are Zion.[319] We cannot read the scriptures, especially latter-day scriptures, and avoid personal responsibility for becoming Zion people. Without reservation, our obligation is to accept every revealed Zion principle and put it into practice. To that end, President Benson laid the responsibility of becoming Zion squarely on our shoulders. Zion, the priesthood society, he said, can be brought about only by Zion people. As more and more of us decide to embrace the principles of Zion, the celestial order will finally exist among us; then we, individually and collectively, will be prepared to receive the Lord.[320]

---

[309] Widtsoe, *Utah Genealogical and Historical Magazine*, Oct. 1934, 189.

[310] McConkie, *A New Witness for the Articles of Faith*, 510.

[311] Note: Jacob or Israel was called a *prince* (Genesis 32:28), and the name Sarah means *princess* (Genesis 17:15 footnote).

[312] Abraham 1:2.

[313] Alma 13:1–2, 10.

[314] Thomas, "Alma the Younger, Part 1," n.p.

[315] Kimball, "The Role of Righteous Women," 102.

[316] Thomas, "Alma the Younger, Part 1," n.p.

[317] Smith, *Teachings of the Prophet Joseph Smith*, 60.

[318] Young, *Discourses of Brigham Young*, 118.

[319] Cowley, *Matthew Cowley Speaks*, 30.

[320] Benson, "Jesus Christ—Gifts and Expectations," 16.

Zion is the standard among celestial and celestial-seeking beings.[321] The celestial condition of Zion is the exact opposite of the telestial condition of Babylon;[322] therefore, we are constantly faced with choosing between the two. We cannot have it both ways. Alma reminded us that that which is good comes from God, and that which is evil comes from the devil.[323] Nothing good has ever come from attempting to mix Zion with Babylon. Moreover, it is impossible. No one has ever made it work, although there seems to be a universal effort to prove this eternal verity wrong.[324]

In the "first place," or the premortal world, we lived in the celestial atmosphere of Zion. We, who were among a select group called *Israel,* fully internalized the principles of Zion and became ambassadors for the virtues of Zion to weaker spirits. We took as our example the Lord Jesus Christ and desired to become, like him, saviors to our fellow beings. To further our work, we entered into the *holy order* of the priesthood, which gave us the power of redemption under the direction of Jesus Christ. His work became our work: to preach and teach the virtue of the new and everlasting covenant for the purpose of establishing Zion. By *divine appointment,* and with intense preparation, we qualified for the blessings of Abraham, Isaac, and Jacob and were assigned mortal missions to come into this life and continue with our premortal work. Here, we were to receive the Covenant, fully incorporate it into our lives, and then take it to family, friends, and the children of God within our influence. As heirs of Zion, we were to become Zion, and then invite all people to likewise become Zion.

Mortality is the testing ground that determines our genuine desires and the quality of our hearts; therefore, embracing Zion principles in this life ensures our inheritance in Zion in the eternal world. If we truly seek Zion, we must choose Zion here and now. The scriptures are filled with tragic examples of people who made the Covenant, then became lukewarm to it or rejected it altogether. That the latter-day Church is prospering does not necessarily mean that all is well in the lives of the people who call themselves Zion. Nephi clearly warned that adopting this philosophy is a one-way ticket to hell.[325]

For Latter-day Saints, the subject of Zion should be familiar and delightsome. Zion is our heritage, and it will be our destiny. Zion was and is heaven, the habitation of Deity, the presence of God. Zion was introduced to Adam and Eve in the Garden, a place that was preeminently *good,* or "perfect," for one meaning of the word Zion is "perfection."[326] Our first parents' subsequent *fall* from Zion created cataclysmic changes in their bodies that effected all Creation. Suddenly everything became mortal and telestial, and eventually that situation opened the door for a fallen condition of the heart called *Babylon.* Adam and Eve's immediate reaction to discovering themselves in the lone and dreary world[327] was to find a way out and return to Zion, which represented a return to the presence of God. Theirs is an example for all of us. God the Father provided the answer for their return: His Beloved Son would atone for every sin that they committed and break down every obstacle that stood between them and the celestial state of Zion. The vehicle by which Adam and Eve could embrace the Atonement and reap its benefits was the new and everlasting covenant. This Covenant is an agreement of salvation, which Jesus Christ offers to each of us. We simply need to agree to the Covenant's stipulations and abide in it to the end.[328] The Covenant is a product of the Atonement, with power to rescue us from Babylon and return us to Zion.

---

[321] D&C 105:5.
[322] Nibley, *Approaching Zion,* 30.
[323] Alma 5:40.
[324] Faust, "The Devil's Throat," 51.
[325] 2 Nephi 28:21.
[326] Galbraith, Ogden, and Skinner, *Jerusalem: The Eternal City,* 41.
[327] Holland and Holland, *On Earth As It Is in Heaven,* 62.
[328] D&C 98:14–15; 132:4.

The new and everlasting covenant is the most glorious doctrine ever revealed. It comprises the totality of the gospel of Jesus Christ, the authority and power of the priesthood, and all of the covenants and ordinances of salvation and exaltation.[329] When we fully receive and live the Covenant, we can escape the captivity and misery of Babylon and enter the embrace and glory of Zion. Our obedience to the Covenant has the power to bind the Lord and guarantee eternal blessings.[330] The Covenant cleanses us and sets us apart for a holy purpose; it endows us with knowledge and power to think, feel, see, hear, and act like and become like God in every way. It empowers us to do work that only God can do. When we enter into the Covenant, we are immediately separated for salvation; that is, we are "called" and become candidates for celestial glory. Then by abiding (staying put) in the Covenant, we qualify for "election" in the celestial kingdom. That is, we are *selected*[331] for eternal life. If we receive the Covenant with full purpose of heart and follow it through to its perfect conclusion, we will become pure in heart and in every way like God.

The more deeply we dig into scriptures, the more we learn that the Covenant has everything to do with our relationship with God. Our journey to Zion, therefore, involves discovering that relationship and following it until we come face to face with our Maker. All of the prophets, from Adam to Joseph Smith, including the latter-day prophets, set the example by making the Covenant and then embracing the resulting relationship with the Lord. When they understood and laid hold of the benefits of the Covenant, they wore out their lives preaching, teaching, and offering the Covenant to all the children of God. Some of the greatest moments in history were when they succeeded in administering the Covenant to people who responded. Those people became Zion. They escaped Babylon and entered into the rest of the Lord.

That is the destiny of every person who will forsake Babylon and come to and become Zion.

---

[329] D&C 132:5–7.
[330] D&C 82:10.
[331] *LDS Bible Dictionary*, "Election," 662–63.

Section 4

Babylon the Great

The antithesis of Zion is Babylon. The two systems are reverse orders, contrary programs, opposed and inverse in every way. They are like day and night or opposite poles on a compass. The king of Zion is Jesus Christ;[332] the king of Babylon is the anti-Christ, Satan. The work of the king of Zion is "to bring to pass the immortality and eternal life of man,"[333] that we might have "fulness of joy."[334] The work of the king of Babylon is captivity and death, that we might become miserable like him.[335]

There can be no greater fall than from Zion to Babylon. An example is the Nephites. Within two hundred years of the coming of Christ, they plummeted from Zion (described as a condition with no contentions or disputations; every man dealing justly one with another; having all things common among them; no rich or poor; widespread freedom; great and marvelous spiritual outpourings and miracles; incredible prosperity; the love of God felt in the hearts of the people; no envyings, strifes, tumults, whoredoms, lyings, murders, or any manner of lasciviousness; no robbers or murderers; no separate classes of people; true equality and oneness; all people qualifying as the children of Christ and heirs to the kingdom of God; the happiest people ever created by God, and blessed in all their doings[336]) to Babylon (described as being lifted up in pride, with hearts set upon costly apparel, expensive jewelry, and the fine things of the world; the people ceased to have all things in common, divided into classes, built up churches and manmade philosophies to get gain, denied the true church of Christ and the more parts of his gospel, participated in all manner of wickedness, exercised power and authority over each other, hardened their hearts against God, willfully rebelled against the gospel,

---

[332] Moses 7:53.
[333] Moses 1:39.
[334] 3 Nephi 28:10.
[335] 2 Nephi 2:27.
[336] 4 Nephi 1:1–18.

taught their children to not believe, reestablished secret combinations, sought after and horded gold and silver, and did traffic in all manner of merchandising—the economy became their preoccupation and their god[337]).

The downfall of the Nephite nation can be traced back to their abandoning Zion and embracing Babylon.

Anti-Christ Philosophy

According to Blaine Yorgason, Satan's first two articles of faith are that "we can buy anything in this world with money, and . . . we can buy it now and pay for it later on."[338] The philosophy of Babylon is anti-Christ. Godlessness, selfishness, and competition are its hallmarks.[339] The anti-Christ doctrine states that people fare "according to the management of the creature," prosper according to their genius, and conquer according to their strength. Because they assume no accountability to God, they believe that they can act without moral consequences. In Babylon, people succeed or fail on their own merits; they are totally alone. They pretend a form of godliness, but deny the power that comes from and makes godliness possible. They eschew hope in and dependency upon Jesus Christ; they trample the plan of salvation and reject the holy priesthood and the gifts of the Spirit; they judge the humble followers of Christ as having frenzied minds and being held captive by what they call the false traditions of the gospel.[340]

In a general conference address, Elder Mark E. Petersen said, "Every force now corrupting America is a form of anti-Christ. Criminality is anti-Christ. Immorality is anti-Christ. Drunkenness is anti-Christ. Rioting, pillaging, and anarchy likewise are anti-Christ. Robbery, assault, and murder are all anti-Christ. Deception, duplicity, perjury, and covetousness are anti-Christ. The distribution of pornographic material that corrupts the morals of young and old alike is anti-Christ. And so is every other force destructive of the high principles that have made America great. . . . Oh, America—wake up to the peril that confronts you. Arouse yourself from this delirium in which you find yourself. Realize that this Christian nation can never survive on the principles of anti-Christ."[341]

Frighteningly, the anti-Christ philosophy forms a type of sinister worship. Hugh Nibley wrote: "This is the great voice of the economy of Babylon. It does not renounce its religious pretensions for a minute. Many in it think they are identical with a pious life."[342] We shall discuss Babylon as a religion hereafter. Suffice it to say that the anti-Christ philosophy always results in the downfall of those who subscribe to any part of it. We recall the dismal demises of Sherem and Korihor,[343] and we have the testimonies of the once-mighty Jaredite and Nephite nations. Clearly, there is no safety in Babylon. Satan will not support his children;[344] his only aim is to captivate them, make them miserable, and destroy them.[345]

Cain

We can thank Cain and his descendant Nimrod for creating Babylon and perpetuating the anti-Christ philosophy that has enslaved the world and engulfed it in incarcerating misery.

---

[337] 4 Nephi 1:24–46.
[338] Yorgason, *I Need Thee Every Hour*, 200.
[339] Alma 30:12.
[340] Alma 30:12–18.
[341] Petersen, Conference Report, Oct. 1967, 67–68.
[342] Nibley, *Approaching Zion*, 334.
[343] Jacob 7:13–20; Alma 30:49–60.
[344] Alma 30:60.
[345] 2 Nephi 2:27.

From the dawn of history, Satan, the "father of lies"[346] and the would-be usurper of the Father and the Son's power, glory, and missions,[347] endeavored to gain a foothold in this world and build a kingdom here. He devised a "cunning plan" to make men miserable by means of deceptions and false revelations, which things would be "particularly effective against those who struggle with vanity and pride (2 Nephi 9:28). . . . His goal is to destroy the world (Moses 4:6) . . . [and] to separate what God has joined together and unite what God has separated."[348]

Failing to indoctrinate Adam and Eve with the anti-Christ doctrine, he found a willing apprentice in Cain. The two became inseparable, literally the inverse of the Father and the Son. Moses reports: "And Cain loved Satan more than God." This perverted affection allowed Satan to drive a wedge between Cain and God. To bring Cain to the point of decision, he told him to "make an offering unto the Lord." Of course, offerings ordered by Satan are rejected out of hand by God. It is God alone who mandates offerings; such offerings must be accomplished by proper priesthood authority through a specific ordinance. No wonder, then, that the Lord had no respect for Cain's offering. "Now Satan knew this, and it pleased him. And Cain was very wroth, and his countenance fell." We know the result. The Lord warned Cain of the consequences of following his course of action, but Cain had made his choice.[349] Thereafter, the Lord would call him "Perdition," which means entirely lost or ruined.[350]

On the other hand, Satan called Cain "Master Mahan," which suggests that Satan had given Cain a "new name"[351] within the order of his priestcraft (not *priesthood*), which name suggests a high level of authority in the demonic craft and extraordinary expertise. Now fully willing to establish the foundation of Satan's benighted kingdom, which would become known as Babylon, Cain learned from Satan the signs, tokens, and oaths of the devil's priestcraft, which were calculated to deliver power into his hands so that he could gain control and dominate the people of the earth.[352] The success of this diabolical father-and-son team was so great that their *religion* soon enslaved and degraded the whole world until the Lord had no choice except to destroy it by flood.

Hugh Nibley explained:

> [Satan] boasts just how he plans to put the world under his bloody and horrible misrule: He will control the world economy by claiming possession of the earth's resources; and by manipulation of its currency—gold and silver—he will buy up the political, military, and ecclesiastical complex and run everything his way. We see him putting his plan into operation when he lays legal claim to the whole earth as his estate, accusing others of trespass, but putting everything up for sale to anyone who has the money. And how will they get the money? By going to work for him. He not only offers employment but a course of instruction in how the whole thing works, teaching the ultimate secret: "That great secret" (Moses 5:49–50) of converting life into property. Cain got the degree of Master Mahan, tried the system out on his brother, and gloried in its brilliant success,

---

[346] 2 Nephi 9:9.
[347] Moses 4:3; Isaiah 14:12–17.
[348] Yorgason, *I Need Thee Every Hour*, 326.
[349] Moses 5:18, 21–26.
[350] *Webster's New World Dictionary*, s.v. "perdition."
[351] D&C 130:11.
[352] Moses 5:16–34.

declaring that at last he could be free, as only property makes free, and that Abel had been a loser in a free competition.

The discipline was handed down through Lamech and finally became the pattern of the world's economy (Moses 5:55–56). . . . Cain slew "his brother Abel for the sake of getting gain" (Moses 5:50)—not in a fit of pique but by careful business planning, "by the conspiracy" (D&C 84:16). The great secret he learned from Satan was the art of converting life into property—all life, even eternal life! The exchange of eternal life for worldly success is in fact the essence of the classic Pact with the Devil, in which the hero (Faust, Jabez Stone, even Jesus) is offered everything that the wealth of the earth [...] an hereafter. There is no [...] cannot serve two masters" [...] mmon; if you try to have it [...] ment, says Amulek, "the Spirit [...] and has no place in you, and [...] na 34:35).[353]

NIMROD

The [...] as not to be denied. The principles of Babylon are a[...] evealing to a new Babylonian "prophet" in a new [...] s Nimrod, a descendant of Cain through Ham'[...] ct descendant and therefore that he posse[...] ot be overlooked. Nimrod, Cain's legal heir, who i[...] ried to take the life of Abraham, the rightful heir t[o ...]

[...] tial apostates in the [...], who was the son of Cush, [...] y hunter and hero. He [...] cad (Shinar). Josephus tells [...] pt of God. He persuaded [...] imself instead of God. "He [...], seeing no other way of [...] ring them into a constant [...] he would avenge himself [...] urthermore, Josephus [...] m through rapine, murder, [...] ws, Book I, chap. 4.) He [...] of Shem and cleave to [...] nmentary, Vol. I, p. 84.) [...] erors and in time the [...] cteristic of heathen [...] Egypt, Babylon, Greece, Rome, China, and India. He also

---

[353] Nibley, *Approaching Zion*, 166–67.
[354] Nibley, *Abraham in Egypt*, 61–66.
[355] Clark, *The Blessings of Abraham*, 35.

introduced animal worship. Idolatry and adultery ("institutionalized immorality") became common religious rites. Even human sacrifices were instituted.[356]

The philosophies of Babylon were championed by Cain, but Babylon became an institution under Nimrod. Adjacent to the Euphrates River, Nimrod built a city (*Babel*), which over time became "one of the wonders of the ancient world, with its ziggurat and many miles of hanging (terraced) gardens."[357] Babel (later Babylon) became known for supplying its citizens every luxury that the world had to offer. Later, under Nebuchadnezzar, Babylon grew into an enormous city spreading fifty-six miles in circumference; it had massive walls and elegant parks and gardens.[358] We can immediately see the trappings and dangers of Babylon. From Cain to Nimrod to Nebuchadnezzar to Caesar to the latter days, Babylon has been a place or state of mind defined by excesses, self-indulgence, wanton sin, and contempt of God. Babylon has always been the nemesis of Zion.

Elder McConkie wrote: "As the seat of world empire, Babylon was the persistent persecutor and enemy of the Lord's people. . . . To the Lord's people anciently, Babylon was known as the center of iniquity, carnality, and worldliness. Everything connected with it was in opposition to all righteousness and had the effect of leading men downward to the destruction of their souls. It was natural, therefore, for the apostles and inspired men of New Testament times to apply the name Babylon to the forces organized to spread confusion and darkness in the realm of spiritual things. (Rev. 17; 18; D&C 29:21; Ezek. 38; 39.) In a general sense, the wickedness of the world generally is Babylon. (D&C 1:16; 35:11; 64:24; 133:14)."[359]

Nimrod sought to dominate the world from his capital city, Babel, and, according to M. Catherine Thomas, Nimrod, like his spiritual father, Satan, "sought to dethrone God by bringing men into constant dependence on his, Nimrod's, power." Nimrod was very successful. "A multitude followed Nimrod, persuaded that it was cowardice to submit to God. The people began to build the tower, apparently some type of temple, as their objective was to reach heaven by means of the tower. God's response was to break up their evil combination by scrambling their languages, thus depriving them of the powerful Adamic language. The name *babel* means, in Akkadian, 'gate of God' and is a play on the Hebrew *balal*, meaning 'to mix or confound.' It is apparent then that the tower of Babel was a counterfeit gate of God, or temple, that Ham's priesthood-deprived descendants built in rebellion against God. Jared and his family and friends rejected this temple and were spared the Lord's punishments."[360]

Nimrod's Babel became Babylon, the world order, philosophy, and religion that would dominate the hearts of people throughout the millennia. Elder McConkie explained: "The name Babylon means many things to many people. The Hebrew word (*bbel*) goes back to a kingdom Nimrod founded, where the ancients built the tower of Babel, or Babylon (Genesis 10:9–10; 11:1–9). This kingdom evolved into an idolatrous materialistic civilization that reached a zenith in the powerful neo-Babylonian empire of Nebuchadnezzar (cf. Daniel 2:37–38). The prophet Isaiah identifies Babylon typologically as both a people and a place: the sinners and the wicked; the earth and the world (Isaiah 13:1, 9, 11). He predicts latter-day Babylon will suffer the fate of Sodom and Gomorrah, thus likening the world's desolation to a fiery cataclysm falling upon the wicked (Isaiah 13:4–19)."[361]

---

[356] Yarn, *The Gospel: God, Man, and Truth*, 127–28.
[357] Galbraith, Ogden, and Skinner, *Jerusalem: The Eternal City*, 103–4.
[358] *LDS Bible Dictionary*, "Babylon or Babel," 618.
[359] McConkie, *Mormon Doctrine*, 69.
[360] Parry, *Temples of the Ancient World*, 389–90.
[361] Lundquist and Ricks, *By Study and Also by Faith*, 2:384.

Nimrod and his people rebelled against God, and their religion of choice became idolatry, the worship of nature, images or false gods—all defined by covetousness.[362] E. Douglas Clark writes: "An early Christian source reported . . . , 'The whole world was again overspread with errors, and . . . for the hideousness of its crimes destruction was ready for it, this time not by water, but fire, and . . . already the scourge was hanging over the whole earth.' Never in the troubled history of mankind had there been greater darkness and depravity. It was a world as far from Zion as possible."

Clark continues by quoting from the book of Jubilees:

> Noah's children began to fight one another, to take captive, and to kill one another; to shed human blood on the earth, to consume blood; to build fortified cities, walls, and towers; men to elevate themselves over peoples, to set up the first kingdoms; to go to war—people against people, nations against nations, city against city; and everyone to do evil, to acquire weapons, and to teach warfare to their sons. City began to capture city and to sell male and female slaves. . . . They made molten images for themselves. Each one would worship the idol which he had made as his own molten image. They began to make statues, images, and unclean things; the spirits of the savage ones were helping and misleading them so that they would commit sins, impurities, and transgressions. Prince Mastema [Satan] was exerting his power in effecting all these actions and, by means of the spirits, he was sending to those who were placed in his control the ability to commit every kind of error and sin and every kind of transgression; to corrupt, to destroy, and to shed blood on the earth.[363]

This description reads like a how-to book for Babylon—or the morning newspaper.

Nimrod succeeded in contaminating the entire world with his Babylonian practices. Thereafter, Satan's great chain once again veiled the earth in darkness, as it had in the days preceding the Flood. "And he looked up and laughed, and his angels rejoiced."[364] That same chain binds down the people of the latter days. Enoch foresaw our day and recorded that "a veil of darkness shall cover the earth."[365]

SODOM AND GOMORRAH

President Spencer W. Kimball spoke of "the rise and fall of great civilizations, such as Babylon, Ninevah, Jerusalem, Egypt, Greece, Rome, and numerous others which have flared like an arc-light, then dimmed even to candlelight proportions, or to be extinguished."[366] Sodom and Gomorrah, too, had their day and likewise perished. These cities, now covered by the Dead Sea, were in the image of Babylon. Because the latter days have been compared to Sodom and Gomorrah, we would do well to examine the characteristics that brought about their downfall.

Quoting Rabbi Eliezer, Hugh Nibley wrote:

---

[362] Colossians 3:5; Ephesians 5:5; Philippians 3:19; see also *LDS Bible Dictionary*, "Idol," 706.
[363] Clark, *The Blessings of Abraham*, 31, quoting Jubilees 11:2–5.
[364] Moses 7:26.
[365] Moses 7:61.
[366] Kimball, *Faith Precedes the Miracle*, 51.

> The men of Sodom were the wealthy men of prosperity, on account of the good and fruitful land whereon they dwelt. For every need which the world requires, they obtained therefrom.... But they did not trust in the shadow of their Creator, but [they trusted] in the multitude of their wealth, for wealth thrusts aside its owners from the fear of Heaven.... The men of Sodom had no consideration for the honour of their Owner by (not) distributing food to the wayfarer and the stranger.... They [even] fenced in all their trees on top above their fruit so that they should not be seized; [not] even by the bird of heaven.... These were the crimes of Sodom and Gomorrah. At the time of Abraham, the people elected leaders "of falsehood and wickedness, who mocked justice and equity and committed evil deeds"... the wicked oppressed the weak and gave power to the strong. Inside the city was tyranny and the receiving of bribes. Every day, without fail, they plundered each others' goods. The son cursed his father in the streets, the slave his master. They put an end to the offerings and entered into conspiracy.... It's not surprising, the records tell, that travelers and birds alike learned to avoid the rich cities of the plain, while the poor emigrated to other parts. "If a stranger merchant passed through their territory, he was besieged by them all, big and little alike, and robbed of whatever he possessed."... This was a world in which every man was for himself. What a terrible state of things.[367]

Elsewhere, Ezekiel and Jude describe Sodom and Gomorrah's sins as:

1. pride
2. "fulness of bread" (luxuriant living)
3. abundant idleness
4. failure to care for poor and needy
5. idolatry (worshipping anything else instead of God)
6. contempt for others
7. fornication
8. "going after strange flesh" (homosexuality)[368]

We know the fate of these offshoots of Babylon. The Lord obliterated them with fire from heaven;[369] then he hid Sodom and Gomorrah from his face by covering them with the waters of the Dead Sea.[370]

Our leaders have compared the conditions of the last days to the evils of Sodom and Gomorrah. They have stated that they know of no time in the history of the earth when there was greater spiritual danger from evil that permeates the world in epidemic proportions, not even in the time of Sodom and Gomorrah. At no time has wickedness been so widely accepted. Whereas evil was localized in Sodom and Gomorrah, our leaders have pointed out, now it has spread across the world.[371]

---

[367] Nibley, *Approaching Zion*, 322–23.
[368] Ezekiel 16:49–50; Jude 1:7.
[369] Genesis 19:24.
[370] "Map: Old Testament Stories: Part Two," *LDS Church News*, Jan. 8, 1994.
[371] Packer, "One Pure Defense," Feb. 6, 2004.

Descriptions of Babylon

When we read the descriptions of Babylon, we wonder why anyone would want to live there, and yet all of us, to one degree or another, shop in her stores, partake of her delicacies, and participate in her wickedness. Raising a voice of warning, Jesus prophesied that even the very elect of the latter-day Church would be deceived.[372] Babylon is simply so pervasive in our world that avoiding her requires divine intervention and dogged determination.

Paul explained that Babylon focuses on "the works of the flesh," which are "adultery, fornication, uncleanness [pursuing that which is unholy], lasciviousness [an unseemly focus on sex], idolatry [worshipping anything other than the true God], witchcraft, hatred, variance [disputations], emulations [trying to equal or surpass someone else], wrath [anger and revenge], strife [bitter conflict], seditions [to incite rebellion], heresies [contradicting the truth], envying [covetousness], murders, drunkenness, revellings [uproarious partying], and such like." Then, in damning language, he informs us, "They which do such things shall not inherit the kingdom of God."[373]

Satan is the founder of Babylon. From the beginning, Hugh Nibley said, Satan "taught men how to make knives, weapons, shields, and breastplates, the trade secrets, and showed them the various metals and how to work them, and bracelets, jewelry, makeup, and eyepaint, and all kind of precious stones and hairdos." Then quoting from another ancient document, he says Satan's primary weapon was "all the treasures of the earth. And there were great wickedness and whoredoms [sexual perversions], and they all became perverted and lost in all their ways. And he taught them spells, drugs and quackery." How similar this sounds to Satan's attacks on our youth. Over the millennia, his strategy has not changed much. To the ancients, Satan introduced the science of astrology, a counterfeit for seeking the words of true prophets, which science contributed in a major way to the people's downfall: "And Araqil [Satan] taught them astrology, the interpretation of signs, the observations of signs, and the series of the moon. They maliciously brought them gold and silver and copper and all manner of metals; and this was what finally completed their ruin, and established their perennial earthly order of human society, which persists to this day."[374]

Once Satan can get a person to buy into the philosophy of Babylon, he can have a heyday. He is capable of taking our fears, insecurities, appetites, and passions and transforming them to his advantage. Continuing, Nibley wrote:

> The Abraham literature includes the Old Testament, which also makes it clear that the people he dealt with were scoundrels—mean and inhospitable. The nature of their economy is fully set forth: their one guiding principle was the maximizing of profits. After the flood, the Jewish writings explain, the people were haunted by an understandable feeling of insecurity. To overcome it, they undertook tremendous engineering projects and became very knowledgeable in fire, flood, earthquake, and other potential disasters. A great economic boom and commercial expansion enabled them to undertake all kinds of engineering projects for controlling a dangerous nature. . . . And the Nimrod legends are full of the great scientific understanding of Abraham's day of which a good deal is made in the time of Enoch. The people had a great deal of sophistication and know-how. It was a world of unrest and insecurity,

---

[372] Matthew 24:24.
[373] Galatians 5:19–21.
[374] Nibley, *Approaching Zion*, 321–22.

> and the people were mean and short-tempered.... The fabulous prosperity of the cities of the plain turned them into little Babylons. The record describes their ways of doing things, how they dealt with all strangers, taking away possessions by force; then the wrath of the Lord came upon them.... [Abraham] found the same hostility elsewhere. There was world-wide cruelty, inhospitality, insecurity, suspicion wherever he went.[375]

Do we not see the same in our day?

John the Revelator described Babylon as "the great whore that sitteth upon many waters: With whom the kings of the earth have committed fornication, and the inhabitants of the earth have been made drunk with the wine of her fornication."[376] The reference to universal domination is terrifying. Perhaps worse is the mention of sexual intercourse with a whore; that is, intimacy that is unlawful and unholy; selfish, lustful, wanton, immoral gratification with no accountability to one's spouse or to the Lord; the buying and selling for money of the power of creation given by God to man. Who is this whore, who lures us in with her charms, who is "full of names of blasphemy" and "arrayed in purple and scarlet colour, and decked with gold and precious stones and pearls, having a golden cup in her hand full of abominations and filthiness of her fornication"? John identifies her: "MYSTERY, BABYLON THE GREAT, THE MOTHER OF HARLOTS AND ABOMINATIONS OF THE EARTH." Babylon is the great seducer of the world and the persecutor of the Saints: "And I saw the woman drunken with the blood of the saints, and with the blood of the martyrs of Jesus: and when I saw her, I wondered with great admiration."[377] Nephi's brother, Jacob, adds that the whore of all the earth is anyone who "fighteth against Zion, both Jew and Gentile, both bond and free, both male and female, [and they] shall perish; for they are they who are the whore of all the earth; for they who are not for me are against me, saith our God."[378]

In Section 1 of the Doctrine and Covenants, the Lord describes Babylon as the world itself and the people who in any degree worship or partake of the things of the world: "They seek not the Lord to establish his righteousness, but every man walketh in his own way, and after the image of his own god, whose image is in the likeness of the world, and whose substance is that of an idol, which waxeth old and shall perish in Babylon, even Babylon the great, which shall fall."[379] Such people define their priorities and relationships in terms of money and property, "preach[ing] up unto themselves their own wisdom and their own learning, that they might get gain and grind upon the face of the poor."[380] This attitude of idolatry, pride, wealth-seeking, and selfishness is not exempted from the Latter-day Saints.

The fact that mortal men are by nature carnal, sensual, and devilish[381] plays to Satan's advantage in establishing Babylon among them. Carnal, sensual, and devilish seems to form a downward, spiraling cycle. To be carnal is to be of the flesh; that is, we naturally pamper the physical body and are inclined to succumb to its passions and appetites. Both the apostle Paul and Nephi's brother, Jacob, state that "to be carnally-minded is death."[382] That is, if we give in to carnality, we will eventually submit to sensuality by seeking more and more physical and sexual pleasures. Lying goes

---

[375] Nibley, *Approaching Zion*, 321–22.
[376] Revelation 17:1–2.
[377] Revelation 17:1–6.
[378] 2 Nephi 10:16.
[379] D&C 1:16.
[380] 2 Nephi 26:20.
[381] Alma 42:10.
[382] Romans 8:6; 2 Nephi 9:39.

hand-in-hand with sensuality, as does a damaged testimony. The carnally minded who become sensual will stop believing and begin seeking physical evidence and signs to bolster their faith.[383] This is death. Such behavior weakens us to the point that Satan can take control of our bodies and we become devilish. Our behavior begins to mirror that of Satan; we become sexually perverted, sinister, cruel, scheming, deceitful, mischievous, and in every way like the demons who prod us to be like them. The carnal, sensual, and devilish cycle inevitably leads to apostasy. Breaking the new and everlasting covenant[384] is inevitable, and that tragedy summons the judgment of God and the damnation of the soul.[385]

Clearly, Babylon is designed to make us miserable and to destroy us. It waves the flag of safety and security, but when hard times come—and they always do in this benighted condition—Babylon will leave us flat. Thus, we read, there is a natural curse placed upon those who place their trust in the "arm of flesh" rather than in the arm of the Lord.[386] There is neither safety nor security in Babylon.

Babylon As a Religion

Nephi speaks of a false religion that shall be set up among the latter-day Gentiles. That he casts Babylon in terms of a church is chilling. At once we see Satan declaring himself as the god of this world and advancing philosophies that his followers worship, as if they were holy.

Because this religion's founder is the devil, it can neither endure nor remain unified. Therefore, Nephi describes this false religion as "many churches" whose goal is to destroy the one true church of God. In the process, this demonic religion will strive to cause as much misery as possible, especially among the weak and vulnerable. Here is Nephi's description of Babylon as a false religion:

> And the Gentiles are lifted up in the pride of their eyes, and
> have stumbled, because of the greatness of their stumbling block,
> that they have built up many churches; nevertheless, they put down
> the power and miracles of God, and preach up unto themselves their
> own wisdom and their own learning, that they may get gain and grind
> upon the face of the poor.
> And there are many churches built up which cause envyings,
> and strifes, and malice.
> And there are also secret combinations, even as in times of old,
> according to the combinations of the devil, for he is the founder of all
> these things; yea, the founder of murder, and works of darkness; yea,
> and he leadeth them by the neck with a flaxen cord, until he bindeth
> them with his strong cords forever.[387]

Note that this religion consists of doctrines that run counter to the doctrines of Zion. In fact, they discount God, his power, and miracles, and replace them with intellectualism, which is a powerful counterfeit philosophy promoted by Babylon. Intellectualism and other false doctrines cause envy, strife, malice, and poverty. Interestingly, because Nephi describes Babylon in religious terms, he seems to suggest that the false religion's precepts are preached as if they were holy principles; he states categorically that they "put down the power and miracles of God." The people of Babylon worship

---

[383] Matthew 12:39; 16:4.
[384] D&C 1:15; Isaiah 24:5.
[385] D&C 76:101; 132:5, 15–27; see 41:1; 82:2; 132:27.
[386] 2 Nephi 4:34; 28:31.
[387] 2 Nephi 26:20–22.

these doctrines as if they had issued from the mouth of their god. Nevertheless, however one wishes to define it, Babylon as a religion is pure and simple idolatry and anti-Christ.

Moroni ends the Book of Mormon with an ominous warning to us who live in the latter days: "Wherefore I would exhort you that ye deny not the power of God; for he worketh by power, according to the faith of the children of men, the same today and tomorrow, and forever."[388] Both Moroni and Nephi foresaw the formation of this false religion that would limit or outright deny the power of God and his miracles and replace them with intellectualism, wealth-building, oppressive selfishness, and other counter-doctrines to Zion. Our adherence to these Babylonian philosophies in any degree makes us proponents of that false religion. Moreover, our adopting these doctrines in any degree serves to increase our pride and pave the way for envy, strife, and malice, and ultimately we will persecute and withhold from the poor.

THE "GREAT CHURCH" OF THE DEVIL

The false religion is also described as a false church or the "great church" of the devil.[389] In every way, Satan seeks to duplicate and counterfeit God and his works. If God has a beloved Son, Satan will have a beloved son (Cain, and later Nimrod); if God has a church, Satan will have a church; if God has priesthood power, Satan will have priestcraft power; if God has a religion with saving covenants and ordinances, Satan will have a religion with damning covenants and ordinances (secret combinations); if God has *mysteries* that can be learned only by revelation from God, Satan will have *secrets* that can be learned only by revelation from Satan; if God has a capital city (Jerusalem and New Jerusalem), Satan will have a capital city (Babylon); if God has a temple, Satan will have a temple (Tower of Babel, great and spacious building, etc.).

Nephi was shown in vision that "there are save two churches only; the one is the church of the Lamb of God, and the other is the church of the devil; wherefore, whoso belongeth not to the church of the Lamb of God belongeth to that great church, which is the mother of abominations; and she is the whore of all the earth."[390] There are only two ways, two religions, two churches, and they are exact opposites that take us in conflicting directions. We are incapable of standing still. We are either going one way or the other; we believe one philosophy or the other; we belong to one church or the other. There is no neutrality. Quoting Elder John A. Widtsoe, Elder Ezra Taft Benson wrote: "'The troubles of the world may largely be laid at the doors of those who are neither hot nor cold; who always follow the line of least resistance; whose timid hearts flutter at taking sides for truth. As in the great Council in the heavens, so in the Church of Christ on earth, there can be no neutrality.'"[391]

We are presented with the two churches and we must choose, but we cannot choose both. The purpose of the church of the Lamb of God is to preserve agency and save souls; the purpose of the church of the devil is to dominate and destroy souls.[392] Which we claim membership in is our choice.

Nephi casts the church of the devil as an unfaithful woman, reminiscent of Hosea's imagery of the unfaithful wife who becomes a prostitute.[393] Nephi's term, "mother of abominations," summons the image of a mother giving birth to wicked children. Clearly, the devil's church spawns evil in every variety. Nephi also uses the term "whore" to describe this church. The suggestion seems to be one of an illegitimate relationship, broken covenants, and carnal gratification. In another place, Nephi describes the members of the church of the devil as those who commit "whoredoms,"[394] that is, sexual

---

[388] Moroni 10:7.
[389] 1 Nephi 14:10.
[390] 1 Nephi 14:10.
[391] Benson, *God, Family, Country*, 359.
[392] 1 Nephi 14:9–13.
[393] Hosea 1–3.
[394] 2 Nephi 28:14.

sins of every kind. He calls such people "harlots,"[395] a genderless term suggesting those who engage in illicit sexual activity, which is a central doctrine of the church of the devil.

According to Nephi, the devil's church is the "most abominable" institution on the earth. It "slayeth the saints of God, yea, and tortureth them and bindeth them down, and yoketh them with a yoke of iron, and bringeth them down into captivity."[396] Nephi's adopting the language of war should strike horror in our hearts. Beyond enslaving the people of the earth and causing widespread misery, the church of the devil specifically singles out the Saints of God to inflict upon them intense pain and anguish by twisting and contorting us to the boundaries of endurance. The devil's ultimate intent is to murder us both physically and spiritually. To that end, he employs every evil device to load us with heavy burdens and to subjugate and press us into his servitude. What is the devil's strategy? Nephi says it is four-fold:

1. The pursuit of wealth—"gold and silver"
2. Fashion and materialism—"silks and scarlets and fine-twined linen, and all manner of precious clothing"
3. Sexual sin of every variety—"many harlots"
4. Peer acceptance and popularity or recognition—"praise of the world."

According to the angel who instructed Nephi, these four things are the primary "desires of this great and abominable church."[397] One need only survey the membership of the Latter-day Saints to observe the devil's success in luring us away from the true Church and into his church with these four strategies. As the angel predicted, the result is always heavy burdens, loss of freedom, confinement, torment, suffering, and death. And with every success, Satan and his followers rejoice. Their triumph in destroying the Saints of God and bringing them down into captivity garners them and their adherents "the praise of the world,"[398] the perfect prize for the great and abominable church of the devil.

Satan's strategy to deceive and destroy even the very elect[399] is working. He has made us to "bow down with grief, sorrow, and care, under the most damning hand of murder, tyranny, and oppression." He has "strongly riveted the creeds of the fathers, who have inherited lies, upon the hearts of the children, and filled the world with confusion." This multigenerational oppression forms the foundation of our culture, and we are hard-pressed to imagine life any other way. Frighteningly, this deep-seated culture of wickedness and confusion has been "growing stronger and stronger, and is now the very mainspring of all corruption, and the whole earth groans under the weight of its iniquity." As a society, we live in a condition of bondage to the church of the devil. "It is an iron yoke, it is a strong band; they are the very handcuffs, and chains, and shackles, and fetters of hell." Satan has been so successful in establishing his church that even he is horrified. His "dark and blackening deeds are enough to make hell itself shudder, and to stand aghast and pale, and the hands of the very devil to tremble and palsy."[400]

To establish his diabolical church, Satan must have a set of scriptures. To accomplish this feat, he simply wrested troublesome doctrines from the true scriptures and reassembled the remaining parts so that they could seem mystifying. Yes, the Bible has beautiful language and contains much important truth—but some of the most vital truths have been removed. Nephi says, "[He has] taken

---

[395] 1 Nephi 13:8.
[396] 1 Nephi 13:5.
[397] 1 Nephi 13:8.
[398] 1 Nephi 13:9.
[399] Matthew 24:24.
[400] D&C 123:7–10.

away from the gospel of the Lamb many parts which are plain and most precious; and also many covenants of the Lord [has he] taken away. And all this [has he] done that [he] might pervert the right ways of the Lord, that [he] might blind the eyes and harden the hearts of the children of men."[401] It is a sinister plot to tamper with the words of God and make that which was once "plain and precious" mystifying and dangerous.

To further deceive the Latter-day Saints, Satan will resort to such strategies as intellectualism, rumor, apathy, conjecture, criticism of the Lord's anointed, seeking counsel from external sources that are separate from and nonsupportive of those with s keys, pursuing gospel hobbies, and the "private interpretation" of the scriptures.[402] It all has the same effect. The true scriptures are displaced or whittled down by these philosophies or practices, and our attention shifts to the doctrines of the great church of the devil.

Babylon As a Temple

Perhaps one of the most detailed descriptions of latter-day Babylon comes from the father-son team of Lehi and Nephi. Lehi began his description by viewing a "great and spacious building" that "stood as it were in the air, high above the earth." Immediately, we note that the building has no foundation and it is elevated high in the air by its pride. Lehi observed that multitudes of people of every age, gender and class occupied this building. These people had two identifying characteristics: "their manner of dress was exceedingly fine, and they were in the attitude of mocking." Commenting, Nephi described this building as "strange," that is, unnatural, difficult to understand, something that Nephi was not acquainted with. Those who migrated to this building after they had tasted of the fruit of the tree of life (and thus by definition were members of the true Church), then fell away from the love of God and departed from the truth because they felt shame.[403]

We might assume that this building was indeed Babylon's temple, where the malevolent doctrines, covenants, and ordinances of the false religion are disseminated. These doctrines are pursuit of wealth, fashion, materialism, and sexual sin of every variety; seeking peer acceptance, recognition, and popularity; embracing priestcrafts and combinations; and delving into secrets. Nephi described this false temple and its doctrines as "the world and the wisdom thereof," "the pride of the world," and the "vain imaginations and pride of the children of men." The purpose of this false temple was to "fight against the twelve apostles of the Lamb." When the false temple finally fell, "the fall thereof was exceedingly great."[404] Speaking futuristically, Nephi says Babylon will be destroyed "speedily . . . : It shall be at an instant, suddenly."[405]

Nephi's Description of Babylon

We can thank Nephi for detecting and detailing the characteristics of Babylon. He portrays Babylon so plainly that we are left without excuse if we fail to distinguish her. In plain language, Nephi gives us the keys that expose Babylon. For example, anytime we perceive people seeking material wealth for their own purposes, when we observe people dominating or manipulating others, when we see people striving for recognition and popularity or indulging in the lusts of the flesh, we see Babylon. Nephi warns that such people "need fear, and tremble, and quake; they are those who must be brought low in the dust; they are those who must be consumed as stubble."[406]

In an effort to help us detect and steer clear of Babylon, Nephi lists at least ten indicators:

---

[401] 1 Nephi 13:26–27.
[402] 1 Peter 1:20.
[403] 1 Nephi 8:25–28, 31–34.
[404] 1 Nephi 11:35–36; 12:18.
[405] 2 Nephi 26:18.
[406] 1 Nephi 22:23.

1. **Contention.** Foremost, is contention.[407] The trouble with contention is one of the predominant themes of the Book of Mormon. The resurrected Savior told the Nephites: "For verily, verily I say unto you, he that hath the spirit of contention is not of me, but is of the devil, who is the father of contention, and he stirreth up the hearts of men to contend with anger, one with another."[408] Where there is contention and anger, there is Babylon.

2. **Man's wisdom.** People who espouse the doctrine of Babylon "teach with their learning and deny the Holy Ghost, which giveth utterance."[409] This statement hearkens to one of the first things Jesus told young Joseph Smith about the despicable condition of the last days: "I was answered that I must join none of [the churches], for they were all wrong; and the Personage who addressed me said that all their creeds were an abomination in his sight; that those professors were all corrupt; that: 'they draw near to me with their lips, but their hearts are far from me, they teach for doctrines the commandments of men, having a form of godliness, but they deny the power thereof.'"[410]

    The creeds of Babylon rely on the learning of man, but Nephi pronounces a wo on those who depend on man's wisdom. The Holy Ghost is the source of the power of God for man and the conveyor of pure knowledge. Whereas Zion people look to God for intelligence, Babylon people look to man while simultaneously limiting or discounting God's words to safeguard Babylon's position: "Yea, wo be unto him that saith: We have received, and we need no more!" The foundation of man's knowledge is at best a "sandy foundation," says Nephi. Nevertheless, Babylonians tenaciously build their foundation upon the sand and tremble when their precepts are threatened by the word of God; they even react violently toward the truth in order to protect the precepts of men: "Wo unto all those who tremble, and are angry because of the truth of God!" To maintain some semblance of piety, Babylonians will tolerate a smattering of the word of God, carefully extracted from the whole to bolster their position—but they will only put up with so much: "Wo be unto him that shall say: We have received the word of God, and we need no more of the word of God, for we have enough!" What will be the fate of the people of Babylon? "From them shall be taken away even that which they have."[411] Satan intends to keep the people of Babylon off balance and in the dark.

3. **Denying the power of God.** Babylon denies "the power of God, the Holy One of Israel."[412] All the dominoes begin to fall when we ignore, discount, or deny the power of Christ. Not only do miracles cease, but we begin to doubt the reality of the Lord's perfections, upon which the scaffolding of faith is constructed—power, knowledge, love, consistency, justice, and truth.[413] Nephi explains that marginalizing the power of God leads to at least four false premises, which are calculated to retard our progress, empower men, enthrone self-reliance and personal wisdom, and discount modern-day miracles, God's consistency, and his treating his children with equal regard: (1) "there is no God today," (2) "the Lord and the Redeemer hath done his work," (3) "he hath given his power unto men," and (4) "if they shall say there

---

[407] 2 Nephi 28:4.
[408] 3 Nephi 11:29.
[409] 2 Nephi 28:4.
[410] JS–H 1:19.
[411] 2 Nephi 28:26–30.
[412] 2 Nephi 28:5.
[413] Smith, *Lectures on Faith*, 3.

is a miracle wrought by the hand of the Lord, believe it not; for this day he is not a God of miracles; he hath done his work."[414]

Need we be reminded that Babylon's doctrine is exactly opposite that of Zion's? If we marginalize the power of God, we simultaneously deny the spirit of revelation and question whether God can or will intervene in our lives. Then we embrace scientific theories over faith; we look to man as the source of all knowledge and help; we disregard the justice of God; and we reduce to the level of myth the resurrection and the Atonement.

4. **Eat, drink, and be merry.** Babylon would like to portray life as a time to get, accumulate, indulge, and seek pleasure. Zion's goals of *giving* and *becoming* are foreign in Babylon, unless *giving* is done to get something better in return or *becoming* is done to become rich, popular, supposedly wise, or influential.[415] To eat, drink, and be merry is more than a decadent lifestyle; it is a wasted life, as life pertains to eternity; it is a life without accountability to God. Such a life is telestial and therefore Babylonian.

Nephi reveals that Babylon's philosophy of eat, drink, and be merry is one that telestial people worship. It is a perverse creed, and when it becomes life's goal it leads to all sorts of mischief. For example, the people of Babylon believe that they can either change the definition of sin or justify a little wrongdoing: "Yea, lie a little, take the advantage of one because of his words, dig a pit for thy neighbor; there is no harm in this." Living for today while taking no thought for eternity is Babylon's motto: "and do all these things, for tomorrow we die."

All of these follies lead to lack of accountability for one's actions, the prideful attitude of putting words in God's mouth and inventing a private interpretation of justice and mercy: "and if it so be that we are guilty, God will beat us with a few stripes, and at last we shall be saved in the kingdom of God."[416] There is no evidence that God ever said such a thing. Satan invented this lie; it is his doctrine, and God had nothing to do with it. Nevertheless, in Babylon, "there shall be many which shall teach after this manner, false and vain and foolish doctrines."[417]

5. **Pride.** Nephi cannot say enough about this damning characteristic of Babylon. He says that Babylonians are "puffed up in their hearts." "Because of pride, and because of false teachers, and false doctrine, their churches have become corrupted, and their churches are lifted up; because of pride they are puffed up." Once again, we read the word "church" as a descriptor of Babylon. The people of Babylon worship their culture and practices as if they were holy. These people are elitists; they feel entitled; they indulge in every form of evil, with sex as the common denominator: "They wear stiff necks and high heads; yea, and because of pride, and wickedness, and abominations, and whoredoms, they have all gone astray save it be a few, who are the humble followers of Christ."[418]

Where does their pride lead them? As far from Zion as possible: "They rob the poor because of their fine sanctuaries [the monuments they build to themselves where they can worship the things of the world and practice the doctrines of Babylon]; they rob the poor because of their fine clothing; and they persecute the meek and the poor in heart, because in

---

[414] 2 Nephi 28:5–6.
[415] Wickman, "Today," 103–5.
[416] 2 Nephi 28:7–8.
[417] 2 Nephi 28:9.
[418] 2 Nephi 28:9, 12, 14.

their pride they are puffed up."[419] Sadly, they could choose to help the poor with their money, but instead they selfishly accumulate riches, build elaborate houses that they adore, and wear elegant clothing—during all of which they persecute and rob the less fortunate. *Pride!*

Pride is death to Zion. We are not to build up ourselves. "God has commanded the Saints to 'seek to bring forth and establish the cause of Zion' (D&C 6:6). When Zion is established, its people will be 'of one heart and one mind' and will dwell together in righteousness (Moses 7:18). But 'pride is the great stumbling block to Zion' (Benson, 1989, p. 7). Pride leads people to diminish others in the attempt to elevate themselves, resulting in selfishness and contention."[420] President Ezra Taft Benson taught, "We must prepare to redeem Zion. It was essentially the sin of pride that kept us from establishing Zion in the days of the Prophet Joseph Smith. It was the same sin of pride that brought consecration to an end among the Nephites. (See 4 Ne. 1:24–25)."[421]

"President Benson brings the . . . message to our doorstep with the warning that 'pride is the great stumbling block to Zion. I repeat: Pride is the great stumbling block to Zion.' Our modern-day prophet said further: 'The central feature of pride is enmity—enmity toward God and enmity toward our fellowmen. Enmity means 'hatred toward, hostility to, or a state of opposition.' It is the power by which Satan wishes to reign over us. . . . Our enmity toward God takes on many labels, such as rebellion, hardheartedness, stiffneckedness, unrepentant, puffed up, easily offended, and sign seekers.'"[422]

Commenting on the proud of Babylon, Robert L. Millet writes: "They are proud, overly competitive, reactionary, and externally driven. Natural men and women—be they the irreverent and ungodly or the well-meaning but spiritually unregenerate—are preoccupied with self and obsessed with personal aggrandizement. Their lives are keyed to the rewards of this ephemeral sphere; their values derive solely from pragmatism and utility. They take their cues from the world and the worldly. The central feature of pride, as President Ezra Taft Benson warned the Latter-day Saints, is enmity—enmity toward God and enmity toward man. The look of natural men and women is neither up (to God) nor over (to their fellow humans), except as the horizontal glance allows them to maintain a distance from others. 'Pride is essentially competitive in nature,' President Benson explained. 'We pit our will against God's. When we direct our pride toward God, it is in the spirit of 'my will and not thine be done.' . . . The proud cannot accept the authority of God giving direction to their lives. . . . The proud wish God would agree with them. They aren't interested in changing their opinions to agree with God's.' With regard to other people, the proud 'are tempted daily to elevate [themselves] above others and diminish them.' There is no pleasure, as C. S. Lewis says, in 'having something,' only in 'having more of it than the next man.' In short, 'Pride is the universal sin, the great vice. . . . [It] is the great stumbling block to Zion.'"[423]

Explaining how pride brought down the Zion of the Nephites and caused the destruction of their society, Monte S. Nyman and Charles D. Tate Jr. write: "Mormon explicitly links apostasy and priestcraft with two other evils profoundly detrimental to the maintenance of a Zion society. These are pride and social stratification, which began to appear in A.D. 201—less than a decade after the initial cracks in the solidarity of the society were first noted by Mormon. The prosperity of the people of Nephi, owing to their faith in Christ, had produced great wealth among the populace. Unfortunately, this, in turn, led to

---

[419] 2 Nephi 28:13.
[420] *Encyclopedia of Mormonism*, 1132.
[421] Benson, *The Teachings of Ezra Taft Benson*, 7.
[422] Van Orden and Top, "Doctrines of the Book of Mormon," 16–17.
[423] Millet, *The Power of the Word*, 77.

pride and materialism as the people forgot the source of their strength. The result was that 'from that time forth they did have their goods and their substance no more in common among them' (4 Nephi 1:25).

"Here the insidious nature of pride is laid bare, and its destructive effects on Zion seen in an unmistakable way. Pride destroys unity and promotes selfishness. . . . Pride seeks to create divisions among people purely for the sake of self-interest, so that some may place themselves above others and exploit them. . . . Pride was the cause of social stratification among the people of 4 Nephi."[424] What is the destiny of the proud people of Babylon? "O the wise, and the learned, and the rich, that are puffed up in the pride of their hearts, and all those who preach false doctrines, and all those who commit whoredoms, and pervert the right way of the Lord, wo, wo, wo be unto them, saith the Lord God Almighty, for they shall be thrust down to hell!"[425] It is rare indeed for the Lord to pronounce three woes, but for the proud of Babylon he does not hesitate.

6. **Secrecy.** Babylon thrives in darkness. Babylonians "seek deep to hide their counsels from the Lord, and their works shall be in the dark."[426] Babylon is a brave sinner when she is not known, but shine a light on her and she shudders and runs for cover. The church of the devil promotes a secret double life: the first life is outwardly proper and pious, and the second is that of the secret sinner. Of necessity, the sinner in Babylon must learn the art of telling and living a lie. This is part of the "great secret" or Mahan doctrine that Satan taught Cain. "And Satan said unto Cain: Swear unto me by thy throat, and if thou tell it thou shalt die; and swear thy brethren by their heads, and by the living God, that they tell it not; for if they tell it, they shall surely die; and this that thy father may not know it; and this day I will deliver thy brother Abel into thine hands. And Satan sware unto Cain that he would do according to his commands. And all these things were done in secret. And Cain said: Truly I am Mahan, the master of this great secret, that I may murder and get gain. Wherefore Cain was called Master Mahan, and he gloried in his wickedness."[427]

Whether Babylon is a secret combination of willing participants who counsel and covenant to commit a crime, or an individual who rationalizes living a secret sinful life, the result is the absence of remorse for the dark behavior. Why would Babylon be sorry for embracing its own doctrine? No, Babylon, like Cain, loves her wickedness and glories in it. She proclaims, "This is normal worldly behavior; everyone does it." Babylon acts in secrecy as a declaration of freedom: "And Cain gloried in that which he had done, saying: I am free; surely the flocks of my brother falleth into my hands."[428]

Babylon lurks in the shadows, deceiving herself into thinking that no one knows of her sinning, not even God. "All these things were done in secret." Over time, Babylon learns to secretly sin so well that she achieves a degree in wickedness—"Master Mahan, master of that great secret." Babylon becomes so arrogant in thinking that "none seeth me" that in her wickedness she begins to place her trust only in herself, saying, "I am, and none else beside me."[429] But what Zion people understand, which Babylonians will eventually discover, is that God knows; in fact, he knows in detail: "These things are not hid from the Lord."[430] Those

---

[424] Nyman and Tate, *Fourth Nephi through Moroni*, 298.
[425] 2 Nephi 28:15.
[426] 2 Nephi 28:9.
[427] Moses 5:29–31.
[428] Moses 5:33.
[429] Isaiah 47:10.
[430] Moses 5:39.

people who sin in secret receive the Lord's curse: "And wo unto them that seek deep to hide their counsel from the Lord! And their works are in the dark; and they say: Who seeth us, and who knoweth us?.... But behold, I will show unto them, saith the Lord of Hosts, that I know all their works."[431]

7. **Reviling against anything good.** Babylon is not content simply with deceiving us. She might start out with that tactic, but her intent from the outset is our destruction by means of all-out war. Babylon will make a fierce, abusive, and insulting attack on each true doctrine, principle, sacred institution, and everything else that is just and holy. Babylon will cast the things of God as outdated, frivolous, unfair, limiting, foolish, vain, unscientific, ludicrous, cultish, unnatural, and even immoral.

    Nephi pronounces a wo on those who "turn aside the just for a thing of naught and revile against that which is good, and say that it is of no worth!" Their opposition to Zion lands them on dangerous ground, and if they do not repent, their days are numbered: "For the day shall come that the Lord God will speedily visit the inhabitants of the earth; and in that day that they are fully ripe in iniquity they shall perish."[432]

8. **Carnal security.** With apostolic authority, Paul identified the love of money as the root of all evil.[433] This is an astounding revelation. Somewhere in the spectrum of wrongdoing, the accumulation, adoration, or envy of money seems to contribute to every sin. If Satan can convince us to covet, he can lead us into all sorts of mischief.

    The love of money is a powerful Babylonian lure, and if we step into the devil's trap, there is little hope of escape. Paul says, "But they that will be rich fall into temptation and a snare, and into many foolish and hurtful lusts, which drown men in destruction and perdition."[434]

    Nephi foresaw a latter-day epidemic of money loving, and he specifically identified the Saints who flirt with Babylon as Satan's target: "And others [of the Latter-day Saints] will he pacify, and lull them away into carnal security, that they will say: All is well in Zion; yea, Zion prospereth, all is well—and thus the devil cheateth their souls, and leadeth them away carefully down to hell."[435] Clearly, Nephi is talking about us, the only people who would be interested in Zion's welfare. Paul agrees. He condemns the Saints who persist in pursuing wealth as having "erred from the faith, and pierced themselves through with many sorrows."[436] Such a money-loving attitude is vintage Babylon and anti-Zion.

    The Book of Mormon prophet Jacob listed the love of money as one of the foremost offenses against God. Hugh Nibley wrote: "It is at the climax of his great discourse on the Atonement that Jacob cries out, 'But wo unto the rich, who are rich as to the things of the world. For because they are rich they despise the poor.' This is a very important statement, setting down as a general principle that the rich as a matter of course despise the poor, for 'their hearts are upon their treasures; wherefore, their treasure is their God. And behold, their treasure shall perish with them also' (2 Nephi 9:30). Why does Jacob make this number one in his explicit list of offenses against God? Because it is the number-one device among the enticings of 'that cunning one' (2 Nephi 9:39), who knows that riches are his most effective

---

[431] 2 Nephi 27:32.
[432] 2 Nephi 28:16.
[433] 1 Timothy 6:10.
[434] 1 Timothy 6:9.
[435] 2 Nephi 28:21.
[436] 1 Timothy 6:10.

weapon in leading men astray. You must choose between being at one with God or with Mammon, not both; the one promises everything in this world for money, the other a place in the kingdom after you have 'endured the crosses of the world, and despised the shame of it,' for only so can you 'inherit the kingdom of God, which was prepared for them from the foundation of the world,' and where your 'joy shall be full forever' (2 Nephi 9:18). Need we point out that the main reason for having money is precisely to avoid 'the crosses of the world, and . . . the shame of it'?"[437]

President Anthon H. Lund taught, "The riches of eternal life we ought to seek, not the riches of the world. There is a raging thirst for riches in this land. The love of money is growing, even in our midst. We do not look upon wealth in itself as a curse. We believe that those who can handle means rightly can do much to bless their fellows. But he who is ruled by the love of money is tempted to commit sin. The love of money is the root of all evil. *There is hardly a commandment but is violated through this seeking for riches.*"[438]

In the contest between mammon and God, mammon most often wins. But the stakes are high in making this choice. Jesus told his disciples, "How hard is it for them that trust in riches to enter into the kingdom of God!"[439] A scan of history shows us that there is no lasting security in mammon. Moreover, those who trust in riches receive the Lord's curse and risk losing everything: "And the day shall come that they shall hide up their treasures, because they have set their hearts upon riches; and because they have set their hearts upon their riches, and will hide up their treasures when they shall flee before their enemies; because they will not hide them up unto me, cursed be they and also their treasures; and in that day shall they be smitten, saith the Lord . . . ye are cursed because of your riches, and also are your riches cursed because ye have set your hearts upon them, and have not hearkened unto the words of him who gave them unto you."[440]

To the people of Babylon, however, such warnings are taken lightly. The love of money is a heady narcotic. In Babylon, making money is the fulfillment of one's existence, says Hugh Nibley; "he who has made money has already fulfilled his calling and has no further obligation—in fact, the whole virtue of money is that it frees one from any feeling of obligation to anyone . . . the worst thing is for a businessman to feel responsible for society."[441] We recall that Cain raised a jubilant shout of freedom after he had slain Abel to obtain his brother's flocks.[442] He supposed that his newly gotten wealth had liberated him and made him independent, even from accountability to God.

Trusting in riches is akin to another Babylonian doctrine: trusting in the arm of flesh—*man*. Nephi reveals that there is a curse on those who succumb to such a folly: "Cursed is he that putteth his trust in man, or maketh flesh his arm."[443] The *Encyclopedia of Mormonism* defines cursings as "the opposite of blessings."[444] To the degree that we look to man for strength, counsel, security or safety, we cease depending on the Savior, "the Mighty One of Jacob,"[445] and we are left to the whims, devices and frailties of weak, imperfect human beings. We are therefore "cursed." When we choose man over God, God willingly steps aside

---

[437] Nibley, *Approaching Zion*, 592–93.
[438] Lund, Conference Report, April 1903, 24; emphasis added.
[439] Mark 10:24.
[440] Helaman 13:20–21.
[441] Nibley, *Approaching Zion*, 459–60.
[442] Moses 5:33.
[443] 2 Nephi 28:31.
[444] *Encyclopedia of Mormonism*, 352.
[445] 2 Nephi 6:18.

and allows us the consequences of our choice. As much as we cannot mix Zion and Babylon, we cannot choose or be supported by both God and man. We must decide, but as we do we should remember that the one choice will bring blessings while the other will bring a cursing.

9. **Flattery.** Joseph Smith said, "Flattery is a deadly poison."[446] Elder McConkie writes: "Flattery is the act of ingratiating oneself into another's confidence by excessive praise, or by insincere speech and acts. It includes the raising of false and unfounded hopes; there is always an element of dishonesty attending it."[447] We need only survey Babylon's long history to view lost fortunes, broken marriages, secret intrigues, lies, deceptions, and a host of other destructive conditions, all of which were perpetrated by flattering language.

    The *Encarta Dictionary* defines flattery "an act or instance of complimenting somebody, often excessively or insincerely, especially in order to gain an advantage." This definition goes along with Nephi's depiction of Satan, whose tactic is to sweet-talk us down to hell: "And behold, others he flattereth away."[448] The devil's strategy is to ease into our lives by making us feel so good about ourselves that he can tell us almost anything and we will believe it. Over time, we become used to his silky voice, and because he butters us up whenever he speaks to us, we cannot wait for the next communication. Now we are in a position for Satan to easily feed us lies and false doctrine that have the ring of truth. Nephi says, he "telleth them there is no hell; and he saith unto them: I am no devil, for there is none—and thus he whispereth in their ears, until he grasps them with his awful chains, from whence there is no deliverance."

    If we listen long enough to Satan, we will contemplate then believe and finally act on his flattering message. Now Satan has us trapped, and we are doomed: "Yea, they are grasped with death, and hell; and death, and hell, and the devil, and all that have been seized therewith must stand before the throne of God, and be judged according to their works, from whence they must go into the place prepared for them, even a lake of fire and brimstone, which is endless torment."[449]

    Babylon is awash in flattery. One can hardly get ahead in Babylon without employing this diabolical art of language. Satan tutors eager students how flattery can be used as an effective means to a sinister end: "Yea, he saith unto them: Deceive and lie in wait to catch, that ye may destroy; behold, this is no harm. And thus he flattereth them, and telleth them that it is no sin to lie that they may catch a man in a lie, that they may destroy him." He even teaches his pupils to flatter, lie and deceive so that they might trump other flatterers, liars, and deceivers: "Verily, verily, I say unto you, wo be unto him that lieth to deceive because he supposeth that another lieth to deceive, for such are not exempt from the justice of God." Satan's goal is not to help his students, but rather to destroy them: "And thus he flattereth them, and leadeth them along until he draggeth their souls down to hell; and thus he causeth them to catch themselves in their own snare. And thus he goeth up and down, to and fro in the earth, seeking to destroy the souls of men."[450]

10. **Taking and giving offense.** Babylon is a place and condition of discouragement and offense. Describing Babylon in the last days, Jesus said, "And then shall many be offended, and shall

---

[446] Smith, *Teachings of the Prophet Joseph Smith*, 137.
[447] McConkie, *Mormon Doctrine*, 287.
[448] 2 Nephi 28:22.
[449] 2 Nephi 28:22–23.
[450] D&C 10:25–28.

betray one another, and shall hate one another."[451] It is characteristic of Babylon to take offense at little things—to "make a man an offender for a word." Then the cycle of offense begins with the offended viciously turning on their offenders, laying snares for them, and discounting any good thing that their offenders might do "for a thing of naught."[452]

Both those who offend and take offense are cursed by the Lord: "Woe unto the world because of offences! for it must needs be that offences come; but woe to that man by whom the offence cometh!"[453] As much as Babylon is identified by people who take offense, she can also be detected by people who offend. Paul had no patience for offenders; to him they were divisive and selfish and individuals who deserved to be avoided: "Now I beseech you, brethren, mark them which cause divisions and offences contrary to the doctrine which ye have learned; and avoid them. For they that are such serve not our Lord Jesus Christ, but their own belly."[454] Jesus was equally indignant when it came to offenders: "But whoso shall offend one of these little ones which believe in me, it were better for him that a millstone were hanged about his neck, and that he were drowned in the depth of the sea."[455] Neither taking nor giving offense is a trait of Zion people; but such characteristics are readily evident in the people of Babylon.

Some people choose to take offense "because of the strictness of the word [of God]."[456] They would be more comfortable with extra latitude in the commandments and a more relaxed gospel. If Satan persuade us to collide with a troublesome doctrine, historical point, or someone else's actions or example, he can easily drag us down to his level. Worse, we become enemies with God—"angry because of the truth of God."[457] We recall that at the Lord's rebuke, Cain's countenance fell and that sealed his fate. Taking offense was the final stride in Cain's gallop to hell. "And Cain was wroth, and listened not any more to the voice of the Lord."[458]

Spiritual Babylon

Babylon exists both physically and spiritually; it is the physical environs of the world and the evil that exists therein. The Lord's continual cry to his people is: "Go ye out from Babylon. Be ye clean that bear the vessels of the Lord. . . . Go ye out from among the nations, even from Babylon, *from the midst of wickedness, which is spiritual Babylon.*"[459]

Occasionally, the Lord has removed his Saints from physical Babylon for their own safety. Enoch, Abraham, Moses, Lehi, the brother of Jared, and the Mormon pioneers are examples. But if we are to leave Babylon physically, it will be the Lord's prerogative. Unless he commands otherwise, our assignment is to live in the world without partaking of the things that characterize the world. For the present, the commandment is that we leave Babylon only spiritually. The Lord gives the reason for our remaining in physical Babylon. We are to minister among the people of the world and call them out of Babylon to the new and everlasting covenant associated with Zion, by which they might prepare for the coming of Christ:

---

[451] Matthew 24:10.
[452] 2 Nephi 27:22.
[453] Matthew 18:7.
[454] Romans 16:17–18.
[455] Matthew 18:6.
[456] Alma 35:15.
[457] 2 Nephi 28:28.
[458] Moses 5:21–26.
[459] D&C 133:5, 14.

> Send forth the elders of my church unto the nations which are afar off; unto the islands of the sea; send forth unto foreign lands; call upon all nations, first upon the Gentiles, and then upon the Jews. And behold, and lo, this shall be their cry, and the voice of the Lord unto all people: Go ye forth unto the land of Zion, that the borders of my people may be enlarged, and that her stakes may be strengthened, and that Zion may go forth unto the regions round about. Yea, let the cry go forth among all people: Awake and arise and go forth to meet the Bridegroom; behold and lo, the Bridegroom cometh; go ye out to meet him. Prepare yourselves for the great day of the Lord. . . . Let them, therefore, who are among the Gentiles flee unto Zion. And let them who be of Judah flee unto Jerusalem, unto the mountains of the Lord's house."[460]

Blaine Yorgason writes: "Where or what, therefore, is this spiritual Babylon that we are commanded to leave? Two days before giving [D&C 133], the Lord had given another revelation (section 1) wherein He answered our question: 'And the anger of the Lord is kindled, and his sword is bathed in heaven, and it shall fall upon the inhabitants of the earth. And the arm of the Lord shall be revealed; and the day cometh that they who will not hear the voice of the Lord, neither the voice of his servants, neither give heed to the words of the prophets and apostles, shall be cut off from among the people; for they have strayed from mine ordinances, and have broken mine everlasting covenant; they seek not the Lord to establish his righteousness, but every man walketh in his own way, and after the image of his own god, *whose image is in the likeness of the world, and whose substance is that of an idol, which waxeth old and shall perish in Babylon, even Babylon the great, which shall fall* (D&C 1:13–16; italics mine).'"[461] The spiritual Babylon that we are to leave, therefore, is the wickedness, idolatry and man-made philosophies of the world.

Of interest, Elder McConkie reminds us that the name *Babylon* "is the Greek form of *Babel* and means *confusion*." Babylon is awash in confusion, wickedness and forbidden things that we term *worldliness*.[462] Money is at the root of Babylon's desires and indulgences. Commenting on John's revelation of condition of spiritual Babylon, Hugh Nibley says everything in the world is defined by business and the economy. Money, merchandising and profiteering occupy our thought and confuse the more weighty issues of God. Nibley reminds us that money can buy anything in Babylon: relationships, loyalties, recognition, influence, health, education, luxuriant clothing, leisure, mansions, military might, everything that men need to enrich themselves while impoverishing others—and love of money is always cast against the backdrop of the ever-prevalent preoccupation with sex:

> Babylon is a state of mind, as Zion is, with its appropriate environment. . . . The great world center of commerce and business, "the kings of the earth have committed fornication with her, and the merchants of the earth are waxed rich through the abundance of her delicacies" (Revelation 18:3). Indeed, "thy merchants were the great men of the earth; for by thy sorceries were all nations deceived" (Revelation 18:23). Babylon's economy is built on deceptions. Babylon is described fully in Revelation 18: She is rich, luxurious, immoral, full of fornications, merchants, riches, delicacies, sins,

---

[460] D&C 133:8–10, 12–13.
[461] Yorgason, *I Need Thee Every Hour*, 14, quoting D&C 1:13–16.
[462] McConkie, *Mormon Doctrine*, 68–69.

merchandise, gold, silver, precious stones, pearls, fine linens, purples, silks, scarlets, thyine wood, all manner of vessels, ivory, precious wood, brass, iron, marble, and so on. She is a giant delicatessen, full of wine, oil, fine flour, wheat; a perfume counter with cinnamon, odors, ointments, and frankincense; a market with beasts and sheep. It reads like a savings stamp catalog or a guide to a modern supermarket or department store. Horses and chariots and all manner of services are available; slaves in the souls of men. These are "the fruits thy soul lusted after . . . and all things which were dainty and goodly" (Revelation 18:14). And it is all for sale.[463]

Summing up spiritual Babylon, Blaine Yorgason writes: "These worldly things, then,—habits, practices, policies, pleasures, possessions, entertainments, conversations, trappings, attitudes, and so forth—are described as unclean and having the substance of an idol, and they divert the children of God from hearing the apostles and prophets, seeking the Lord's ordinances, and keeping His everlasting covenant. It doesn't matter where we find these Babylonian 'things' or even what they are; in subtle and not so subtle ways they distract or divert us from diligently coming unto Christ and seeking His face, or of praying for charity, or His pure i. That is why, just four months after the Church was organized, the Lord declared, 'Thou shalt lay aside the things of this world and seek for the things of a better' (D&C 25:10). Why? Because worldly things are not Godly things, and we are commanded to leave them behind!"[464]

Competition

Zion is distinguished by cooperation while Babylon is characterized by competition. Whereas cooperation ensures that no one loses, competition is structured so that everyone loses but one. While the winner rejoices, having defeated his opponent(s), the loser(s) are miserable. Neither equality nor unity nor charity can exist in such an atmosphere. Therefore, we might say with some certainty that competition does not exist in Zion—competition is wholly a phenomenon of Babylon.

Hugh Nibley states, "Competitiveness always rests on the assumption of a life-and-death struggle: 'There is no free lunch' is the clarion cry. The name of the game is survival. . . . It means to still be on the scene after everyone else has been wiped out. . . . If you're going to be successful, you can't let any person stand in the way. . . . In the end you are competing with everyone, or as everyone was saying when I was young, 'Self-preservation is the first law of nature,' a doctrine that justifies the commission of any possible crime in the name of survival. Nobody loves the rat race, but nobody can think of anything else—Satan has us just where he wants us."[465]

Nibley traces competition back to the Garden of Eden:

> Just as the order of Zion began with Adam in the garden, the rival system is just as old. It, too, was proposed to Adam, and he rejected it, while his son Cain accepted it. The plan Satan proposed to Adam was to put everything in this glorious and beautiful world up for sale. You could have anything in this world for money, but you had to have money. This launched a scramble that has gone on ever since Cain slew Abel, his brother, for gain; and he, says the Pearl of Great Price, "gloried in that which he had done, saying: I am free;

---

[463] Nibley, *Approaching Zion*, 14.
[464] Yorgason, *I Need Thee Every Hour*, 199.
[465] Nibley, *Approaching Zion*, 460.

surely the flocks of my brother falleth into my hands" (Moses 5:33). And this vigorous competition has imparted an air of dynamism and excitement to the scene that some find most attractive. What would the human drama be to us without an element of conflict and competition? We would find it insufferably dull. Who would exchange this for the pale and bloodless activities of Eden? In the Book of Mormon, the Nephites, the Jaredites, and the Jews at Jerusalem all walked straight to their certain destruction because they were helpless to conceive of acting in any other way. They were so completely captivated by one way of life that they could not conceive of any other.[466]

What would life be like without pinewood derbies, increasing market share, or moving up the ladder of success at the expense of others? We are so entrenched in competition that we can hardly imagine a viable world without it. We equate progress with competition. Advancement, improvement, strength, ingenuity, success—all of these are supposedly products of competition and can be had in no other way. In society as we know it, we wink at competitive game playing as innocent fun, when in fact we know that it feeds the need of the natural man to conquer and ascend. Without debating the wisdom of engaging in lesser forms of competition, we simply note that the practice permeates our culture to such a degree that we believe that it must be the natural order of things and therefore must exist in eternity. Surely heaven must be filled with stadiums, and gods must mount from one exaltation to another by proving themselves better than lesser gods. Have we forgotten that the war in heaven was caused by a competitor who pitted his will against the Father's?

Do we have the courage to admit that competition—every form of it—is an invention of Satan, and that he sensitizes us to it in playful forms? Then, when he has converted us as competitors, he sets out to teach us the finer points of competition. For example, we must never show that losing makes us miserable. That is bad sportsmanship. We have to pretend to feel good about being crushed by an opponent; we have to learn how to congratulate him for besting us. Moreover, we have to learn how to tell ourselves that being beaten does not matter; our damaged self-image will recover, we say; we will follow the rules of the defeated: lick our wounds, regroup, and hone our skills so we can come off conqueror next time. It is insanity! This attitude invades classrooms, businesses, marriages, and families with devastating effects. Where are charity, cooperation, unity, equality, and service in competition? Where is Zion in this practice? President Lorenzo Snow said, "It is high time to establish Zion.... It is more pleasant and agreeable for the Latter-day Saints to enter into this work and build up Zion, than to build up ourselves and have this great competition which is destroying us.... There should be no unjust competition in matters that belong to the Latter-day Saints. That which creates division among us pertaining to our temporal interests should not be."[467]

In Babylon, commerce, invention, and economic expansion all depend on competition—and we are blind to see that there is another way. Hugh Nibley writes: "The doctrine as we hear it on every side is that if we do not grow, we must perish. It is not enough for the economy to hold its own, the Gross National Product must constantly increase, which means manufacturing must expand and consumption increase, demand must increase, nothing must relax lest everything contract and collapse."[468] When we finally arrive in Zion, will we be shocked at its stability, uniformity, and ability to rapidly progress *without* competition? Or will we be bored to death and retreat to Babylon where self-image is measured by wins and losses; husbands and wives pit their wills against each other and

---

[466] Nibley, *Approaching Zion*, 17–18.
[467] Snow, *The Teachings of Lorenzo Snow*, 181.
[468] Nibley, *Approaching Zion*, 448.

fracture love; siblings vie for attention, position, and privilege; educational prizes go to the few; quarterbacks get the cheerleaders; co-workers stab each other in the back to obtain the better job; nations dispute borders and treasures; and the economy spikes and plummets, and fortunes are made and lost by the world's most skilled competitors?

Perhaps this might sound like heresy. Some might cry, "Treason! Socialism! Our beloved competition is as American as apple pie and therefore holy." Not true. Search the scriptures. Competition is Babylonian, and cooperation is Zion. Nevertheless, we are wont to lump competition alongside constitutional freedom. We say, "We are a free people, and thus we are free to compete." This perverse definition of freedom, which promotes the idea that *winners are made free by defeating all others*, is completely Babylonian and hearkens back, as we have learned, to Cain, who competed with Abel and slew his brother "for the sake of getting gain." Need we be reminded that Cain gloried in his newly found freedom?[469] Thus competition became the anchor of the "great secret" that Satan taught Cain: "the Mahan principle . . . the exchange of life for property." This is *competition!*

Cain was not bothered by his action. Competitors cannot allow themselves to lapse into empathy or compassion. Hugh Nibley explains, "Thus when the Lord asked him, 'Where is your brother Abel?' Cain said, 'That is none of my business; he can take care of himself. If not, that is just too bad for him—he deserves what he gets' (cf. Moses 5:34). It's a dog-eat-dog world, says the entrepreneur who comforts his ruined investors with the magnanimous submission that life is unfair after all." Thus competition thrives on ruined losers and the winner's "descending scale of accountability."[470]

The doctrine of competitive enterprise reads like a chapter from the book of Korihor, the anti-Christ: "Every man prospered according to his genius, and . . . every man conquered according to his strength; and whatsoever a man did was no crime."[471] In a competitive world there are myriad losers and a handful of winners. Moreover, competition classifies and stratifies people. It guarantees that there will always be poor among us, and it ensures that the poor will likely remain at their level. Competition wants to conquer, not to help. It makes opponents of otherwise friendly people and engenders hatred, depression, feelings of inferiority, contention, selfishness, and entitlement for the winners. By competitive action, we elevate our wants over others' needs and judge ours as more important. Competition makes for vertical rather than horizontal relationships—we are on the top and others are beneath us. Competition is propelled by the false assumption of scarcity, when the Lord has plainly stated that there is enough and to spare,[472] that is, unless we hoard. Competition leads to a variety of sins, including lying, stealing, coveting, committing fornication and adultery; and taken to extremes, competition causes murder and war.

If we are competitive by nature, we are not Zion. Of course, competition in this telestial world can offer healthy advantages, allowing us to enjoy affordable products and services that enhance our well-being. Nevertheless, if we espouse competition as a way of life, we had better get our fill of it now. Competition simply does not exist in Zion. To become Zionlike, we must abandon this destructive tendency, and learn to become cooperative.

Hypocrites

A prevalent practice in Babylon is that of hypocrisy. A hypocrite is "a person who pretends to be what he is not; one who pretends to be better than he really is, or to be pious, virtuous, etc., without really being so."[473] Explaining, Elder McConkie writes: "Thus if a person knows what is right and makes open profession of conforming thereto and yet does not in reality live the gospel law, he is a hypocrite.

---

[469] Moses 5:33, 50.
[470] Nibley, *Approaching Zion*, 436.
[471] Alma 30:17.
[472] D&C 104:17.
[473] *Webster's New World Dictionary*, s.v. "hypocrite."

Hypocrisy is to profess religion and not practice it. If a teacher advocates the payment of tithing, but does not himself pay an honest tithing, he is a hypocrite. If a person prays and seeks temporal and spiritual blessings from the Lord, and then turns away the naked and needy and fails to visit the sick and afflicted, he is a hypocrite. He has professed religion, but not practiced it."[474]

Amulek taught that prayer without the action of charity is hypocritical: "And now behold, my beloved brethren, I say unto you, do not suppose that this is all; for after ye have done all these things, if ye turn away the needy, and the naked, and visit not the sick and afflicted, and impart of your substance, if ye have, to those who stand in need—I say unto you, if ye do not any of these things, behold, your prayer is vain, and availeth you nothing, and ye are as hypocrites who do deny the faith."[475] It makes sense. How is it that on the one hand we feel justified to pray for our needs while on the other hand we ignore the needs of others?

Hugh Nibley wrote: "The worst sinners, according to Jesus, are not the harlots and publicans, but the religious leaders with their insistence on proper dress and grooming, their careful observance of all the rules, their precious concern for status symbols, their strict legality, their pious patriotism. . . . Babylon is . . . rich, respectable, immovable, with its granite walls and steel vaults, its bronze gates, its onyx trimmings and marble floors . . . and its bullet-proof glass—the awesome symbols of total security. Keeping her orgies decently private, she presents a front of unalterable propriety to all."[476] Wherever hypocrisy rears its ugly head, there is Babylon.

FALSE PHILOSOPHIES

Babylon is always promoting a new philosophy to replace God or ascribe his power to phenomena of nature or the mind of man. These pseudo religions come and go like flavors of the month, but they are damning to those who believe and practice them. One popular philosophy states that the universe itself is capable of delivering benefits to those who cast their thoughts "out there," and then, by simply maintaining a positive attitude, those thoughts will return with a caravan of blessings. God is never mentioned in the equation.

The ancient practice of astrology pretends to be a science to predict the future. This abominable craft has ensnared countless people over time, according to Elder McConkie.[477] He wrote: "A form of divination and fortune telling akin to sorcery, astrology is a pseudo science that pretends to divulge the influence of the stars upon human affairs; it is a false science that claims to foretell earthly events by means of the positions and aspects of these heavenly luminaries. It is, of course, one of Satan's substitutes for the true science of astronomy and for the true principle of receiving revelation of future events from divine sources."[478] Modern-day computers have added an element of scientific legitimacy to astrology, and therefore have made the practice appear credible. But the underlying philosophy and motive can be traced back to Satan, who continues to decoy gullible people by shifting their focus away from the true source of revelation and prophecy.

Another equally damaging Babylonian philosophy is humanism, a "rationalist movement that holds that man is capable of self-fulfillment, ethical conduct, etc., without recourse to [God]."[479] Rationalism is the doctrine that human reason alone is the supreme authority and source of knowledge, and that "reason, unaided by divine revelation, is an adequate or the sole guide to all attainable religious truth."[480] President Joseph Fielding Smith quoted prominent rationalists as

---

[474] McConkie, *Mormon Doctrine*, 371.
[475] Alma 34:28.
[476] Nibley, *Approaching Zion*, 53–54.
[477] Isaiah 47; Daniel 1:20; 2:27; 4:7; 5:7.
[478] McConkie, *Mormon Doctrine*, 56.
[479] *Webster's New World Dictionary*, s.v. "humanism."
[480] *Webster's New World Dictionary*, s.v. "rationalism."

declaring, "'The religious forms and ideas of our fathers are no longer adequate.'" Then President Smith commented, "As a substitute they offer 'humanism,' and give an explanation of their 'faith' in 15 points. . . . Let it suffice to say that they maintain that Christianity has failed, and that 'religion must formulate its hopes and plans in the light of the scientific spirit and method.' They say the distinction between the sacred and the secular cannot be maintained, that worship of the supreme ruler and religious prayer to him are futile. Men must find expression to their emotions in 'a higher sense of personal life and in a cooperative effort to promote social well being.' To these 'worshipers' the universe is self-existing—it had no creator; Dr. Charles E. Schofield, in his book, *The Adventurous God*, says, 'The major trend of unbelief today seems to be more and more towards the position that we very much need a religion, but it must be a religion without a God.'"[481]

Humanism itself or humanistic trends account for all sorts of philosophies that approach but reside just outside the boundaries of atheism. Each of these philosophies discounts or limits God, while enthroning the human mind. Intellectualism is an example. Like humanism, intellectualism is devotion to intellectual pursuits. It places excessive emphasis on the mind of man as the summit of genius, and therefore that to which we should pay homage. Both intellectualism and humanism are agnostic and an affront to God.

President Harold B. Lee wrote: "Humanism is a threat to the work of the Lord. One of the greatest threats to the work of the Lord today comes from false educational ideas. There is a growing tendency of teachers within and without the Church to make academic interpretations of gospel teachings—to read, as a prophet-leader has said, 'by the lamp of their own conceit.' Unfortunately, much in the sciences, the arts, politics, and the entertainment field, as has been well said by an eminent scholar, is 'all dominated by this humanistic approach which ignores God and His word as revealed through the prophets.' This kind of worldly system apparently hopes to draw men away from God by making man the 'measure of all things,' as some worldly philosophers have said."[482]

Relativism promotes tolerance as the ultimate human virtue. This philosophy is a plague of the latter days. Relativism preaches open-mindedness to other people's lifestyles and values regardless of traditional ethics. At the foundation of relativism is the falsehood that there is no universal standard to measure the truth of an ethical proposition, so lifestyle becomes a matter of individual choice, which is made relative to one's conscience. Moreover, to relativists, conscience itself is the product of a person's environment or preferences; therefore, one person's morals are no better or worse than another's. To relativists, good and bad are relative and not absolute but rather subjective; therefore, we ought to be tolerant.

The number of "-isms" that Babylon promotes is dizzying. For example, universalism holds that all persons will be reconciled to God, regardless of church affiliation. A universalistic organization would teach the common tenets held by most religions while accepting other religions inclusively. In the end, they say, it does not matter, because there looms universal reconciliation between God and mankind.

Monism holds that in a given field, everything comes down to one thing and only one correct opinion. Monistic theologians support the view that there is one God, who can manifest himself in any number of religions.

Subjectivism is the view that people can know only what they experience directly; everything else is subjective. Like relativism, subjectivism states that the only moral standard is the one that emerges from one's own conscience; therefore, moral codes that are held by society are invalid.

Fundamentalism is another Babylonian philosophy that retards man's progress and diminishes God. Fundamentalism mixes man's philosophies with the scriptures to give them an air of legitimacy. This clever philosophy "stresses the infallibility of the Bible, not only in matters of faith and morals,

---

[481] Smith, *Doctrines of Salvation*, 3:275.
[482] Lee, *The Teachings of Harold B. Lee*, 342.

but also as a literal historical record." Of course, this means that there can be no revelation outside the Bible. The fundamentalist movement arose in American Protestantism in the early part of the twentieth century in reaction to Modernism,[483] which was comprised of various attempts to "redefine Biblical and Christian dogma and traditional teachings in light of modern science, historical and critical research."[484]

Considering this maze of "-isms," we could go crazy trying to find the truth. Clearly, Satan does not care which doctrine we believe as long as it is not the true one. Taking advantage of our natural tendency to search for truth, he keeps us off-balance by bouncing us from one philosophical room to another in a house that can be escaped only by burning it down. In the 1950 October general conference, Elder Albert E. Bowen of the Quorum of the Twelve taught: "Under the impact of agnosticism, atheism, and the extreme humanism which denies God and makes man the source of all meaning, the Christian church as a body has compromised its basic doctrines to make its teachings more harmonious with the current of popular opinion. And where has it got itself? It has lost its saving faith, weakened its influence, and almost forfeited its moral leadership. In consequence, men are floundering about in confusion, not knowing what they ought to do, but well-assured that the fair promises of irreligion and unbelief and human sufficiency have failed them, and they are casting about for anchorage. That is the sorry plight of man in this age."[485] Since the time that Elder Bowen issued his denunciation of "-isms," they have only increased in number and followers.

False, man-made philosophies permeate Babylon and run counter to the gospel truth that everything—*absolutely everything*—that is good comes from God.[486] President James E. Faust taught that while advances in science and technology are wonderful and provide amazing opportunities, they can also be fraught with hazard. Satan can use them to titillate the human ego and point gullible people to man's genius as the source of good things. The future holds great challenges, President Faust said, and we will be able to survive those challenges only by our compensating the expansion of secular knowledge with proportionate virtues of faith, judgment, honesty, decency, self-control, and character.[487]

The people of Babylon who embrace the philosophies of men will share the doom of that fallen system. Nephi wrote: "O that cunning plan of the evil one! O the vainness, and the frailties, and the foolishness of men! When they are learned they think they are wise, and they hearken not unto the counsel of God, for they set it aside, supposing they know of themselves, wherefore, their wisdom is foolishness and it profiteth them not. And they shall perish. . . . And the wise, and the learned, and they that are rich, who are puffed up because of their learning, and their wisdom, and their riches—yea, they are they whom he despiseth; and save they shall cast these things away, and consider themselves fools before God, and come down in the depths of humility, he will not open unto them."[488]

Popularity

Nehor, the anti-Christ, taught "the people that every priest and teacher ought to become popular; and they ought not to labor with their hands, but that they ought to be supported by the people."[489] Because Nehor was promoting a *priestcraft*—a false religion—his inference was that recognition or

---

[483] Dr. Frederick J. Pack, "Was the Earth Created in Six Days of Twenty-Four Hours Each?"
[484] *Webster's New World Dictionary*, s.v. "modernism."
[485] Bowen, *Conference Report*, Oct. 1950, 71.
[486] Omni 1:25.
[487] Faust, "The Shield of Faith," 17.
[488] 2 Nephi 9:28, 42.
[489] Alma 1:3.

influence should be worshipped and that it could be bought or sold for money. This attitude is a mainstay of Babylon.

To be popular is to be liked and accepted by most people. But Babylon places a demonic twist of popularity. In Babylon the goal of popularity is to seek recognition to obtain money, power, rank, and influence. According to Nehor, popular people are in a position to cease laboring with their hands and to be supported by the people. Is this not a primary goal of wealth and popularity today?

Flattering words are an avenue to popularity. Likewise, to pleasingly, and often falsely, present one's self in public promotes popularity. Other tools to become popular are the deft use of fashion, exploiting one's beauty or intelligence, offering vacant promises, and applying the skill of rhetoric. Nephi lumps the popular in with the wealth seekers, power brokers, the lustful, and the sinful—and he predicts a swift collapse of those people and institutions: "For the time speedily shall come that all churches [or individuals and institutions] which are built up to get gain, and all those who are built up to get power over the flesh, and those who are built up to become popular in the eyes of the world, and those who seek the lusts of the flesh and the things of the world, and to do all manner of iniquity; yea, in fine, all those who belong to the kingdom of the devil are they who need fear, and tremble, and quake; they are those who must be brought low in the dust; they are those who must be consumed as stubble; and this is according to the words of the prophet."[490]

In Zion, prominent people deflect popularity. They do not seek it, but if recognition comes, they are quick to use it to bless others.

LATTER-DAY BABYLON—PROPHETIC DESCRIPTION OF OUR TIME

Through the eyes of a prophet and seer, President Kimball looked upon the condition of Babylon and said that he was appalled and frightened. Three things in particular distressed him: (1) *The abuse of the environment:* allowing filth and contaminants to pollute our minds, bodies, and surroundings; (2) *The pursuit of personal affluence:* transferring our trust in God to a trust in material things in an effort to assure security and happiness for the remainder of our life; (3) *Trust in military security:* expending enormous resources to purchase and develop armaments with the intention of depending upon them for protection, rather than depending upon God. "When threatened, we become anti-enemy instead of pro-kingdom of God; we train a man in the art of war and call him a patriot, thus, in the manner of Satan's counterfeit of true patriotism, perverting the Savior's teaching: 'Love your enemies, bless them that curse you, do good to them that hate you, and pray for them which despitefully use you, and persecute you.'"

President Kimball was unabashedly pro-Zion. Certainly Babylon would have considered him idealistic and detached from reality. Babylon would teach us to flex our military muscle and destroy our enemy, but President Kimball taught: "We forget that if we are righteous the Lord will either not suffer our enemies to come upon us—and this is the special promise to the inhabitants of the land of the Americas—or he will fight our battles for us. . . . What are we to fear when the Lord is with us?"[491]

As we have mentioned, Jesus, looking forward to our day, foretold that many of the "very elect" would be deceived.[492] Our leaders have referred to the parable of the Ten Virgins, warning us about the arithmetic of this parable. Of the ten, who were obviously Latter-day Saints, only five actually prepared themselves to attend the marriage of the Bridegroom.[493] To decoy the unprepared five virgins in the last days, Babylon will dish up a menu of evils and deceptions that exceed the wickedness of former generations. Some of these deceptions will come from a preponderance of anti-Christs and false prophets (seducers, imposters, alarmists, promoters of new doctrines and

---

[490] 1 Nephi 22:23.
[491] Kimball, *The Teachings of Spencer W. Kimball*, 417.
[492] Matthew 24:24.
[493] Oaks, "Preparation for the Second Coming," *Ensign*, May 2004, 7; see Matthew 25:1–13.

philosophies), whom we deify and follow because of their titillating ideas and predictions. These things, however, are nothing more or less than a manifestation of priestcraft, which is motivated by money, influence, and popularity. The latter-day anti-Christs and false prophets build their professions and practices upon the anti-Christ doctrine and manage to mislead many. Some of these anti-Christs and false prophets come from the ranks of the Saints. They are people who zero in on a gospel topic and promote it as an essential issue. They *prophesy* of future events and call people to action without priesthood keys or the mantle of a prophet. They are extremists, dooms-dayers, catastrophists, and conspiracy promoters, those whom the Savior predicted would spread "rumors of wars." These anti-Christs and false prophets can frighten and deceive even the very elect. They can be detected by their enthusiastic embracing of a gospel subject, while neglecting the more weighty parts of the true gospel or by stepping in front of the Lord's prophet and leaders.

Jesus prophesied that latter-day Babylon would become an environment of continual unrest, disobedience, contention, and war, which conditions would escalate and increasingly torment and devastate the earth until he came. Moreover, latter-day Babylon would be a place of widespread hunger caused by natural and man-made pestilences. Babylon would be characterized by persecution, anger, hatred, and betrayal. Her people would become easily offended, and "because iniquity shall abound, the love of many shall wax cold."[494]

Babylon in the latter days is a time when "darkness covereth the earth, and gross darkness the minds of the people, and all flesh has become corrupt before my face."[495] Well did Jeremiah say that "Babylon hath . . . made all the earth drunken: the nations have drunken of her wine; therefore the nations are mad."[496] As it was in the days of the wicked Nephites before the resurrected Lord appeared, so it will be in latter-day Babylon: "disputings among the people," many being "lifted up unto pride and boastings because of their exceedingly great riches," "great persecutions," "many merchants, lawyers, and officers," people being "distinguished by ranks, according to their riches and their chances for learning," widespread ignorance and poverty, preferential educational opportunities proffered to the rich. Moreover, people will return "railing for railing," and there will be "great inequality in all the land," which condition, in the days of the Nephites, infiltrated the Church and gave Satan "great power unto the stirring up of the people to do all manner of iniquity, and to the puffing them up with pride, tempting them to seek for power, and authority, and riches, and the vain things of the world."

We have been warned! The people of Babylon, whether inside or outside the Church, were carried about by the temptations of the devil whithersoever he listed to carry them. Without much resistance, he managed to convince them to do whatsoever iniquity he desired—and thus "they were in a state of awful wickedness." Babylon leads people to destruction by initially deceiving them into sinning; but eventually the people sin because they like it: "Now they did not sin ignorantly, for they knew the will of God concerning them, for it had been taught unto them; therefore they did wilfully rebel against God."[497]

Babylon Today Compared to the Days of Noah

We remain in Babylon as though we had no other option. Often we feel paralyzed, and therefore make no attempt to flee or cease partaking of her lifestyle and philosophies. We assume that this is just the way life is, and we are powerless to change things. The people in Noah's and Lot's days held similar views and were caught up in the destructions. The Lord's words hang over us heavily: "And as it was in the days of [Noah], so shall it be also in the days of the Son of man. They did eat, they drank,

---

[494] Matthew 24:5–24.
[495] D&C 112:24.
[496] Jeremiah 51:7.
[497] 3 Nephi 6:10–18.

they married wives, they were given in marriage, until the day that [Noah] entered into the ark, and the flood came, and destroyed them all. Likewise also as it was in the days of Lot; they did eat, they drank, they bought, they sold, they planted, they builded; but the same day that Lot went out of Sodom it rained fire and brimstone from heaven, and destroyed them all. Even thus shall it be in the day when the Son of man is revealed."[498]

What was it like in former days when Babylon was destroyed? The Pearl of Great Price describes the world of Enoch and Noah as wicked beyond anything that had been created by God, which, in this context, suggests wickedness beyond anything that God had created in the *universe*. Of those wicked people, the Lord said, "Satan shall be their father, and misery shall be their doom; and the *whole* heaven shall weep over them, even *all* the workmanship of mine hands."[499] We would do well to consider the descriptions of the evil in that day. We are told that our generation's wickedness is equal to or exceeds that of Noah's generation, and because of that level of wickedness, Noah's generation was completely obliterated.

Noah's generation was an extension of Enoch's generation. Moses, who wrote the account, explained that Enoch's people were pursued by their enemies from place to place, but they were always protected by God and his prophet.[500] We could say the same today. In the days of Enoch, the enemies of the people of God turned against each other, "and from that time forth there were wars and bloodshed among them."[501] This statement gives a key to how we might be protected in the last days: to align ourselves with the true God and his anointed prophets. War and violence continued to define ancient Babylon: "The earth was corrupt before God, and it was filled with violence."[502] Moreover, the world of Enoch and Noah was filled with men of "great renown,"[503] popular people of influence, who swayed the populace to commit evil. Consequently, the majority of the people rejected the gospel and the prophets.[504]

Of all the words that Moses could have used to describe that ancient world, he chose *corrupt*: "And God looked upon the earth, and, behold, it was corrupt, for all flesh had corrupted its way upon the earth."[505] The word *corrupt* has a variety of meanings: "changed from a sound condition to an unsound one; spoiled; contaminated; rotten; deteriorated from the normal or standard; morally unsound or debased; perverted; evil; depraved."[506] The widespread corruption retarded the people's ability to show love, and corruption attacked their marriages and families: "Behold, they are without affection, and they hate their own blood."[507] Their corruption made them wicked and immoral beings; evil pervaded their minds constantly: "And God saw that the wickedness of men had become great in the earth; and every man was lifted up in the imagination of the thoughts of his heart, being only evil continually."[508] Even the most righteous parents could not hold back wickedness and immorality from infiltrating their homes: "And the Lord said unto Noah: The daughters of thy sons have sold themselves; for behold mine anger is kindled against the sons of men, for they will not hearken to my voice."[509]

---

[498] Luke 17:26–30.
[499] Moses 7:36–37; emphasis added.
[500] Moses 7:14–15; see Moses 8:18.
[501] Moses 7:16.
[502] Moses 8:28.
[503] Moses 8:21.
[504] Moses 8:19–20, 24.
[505] Moses 8:29.
[506] *Webster's New World Dictionary*, s.v. "corrupt."
[507] Moses 7:33.
[508] Moses 8:22.
[509] Moses 8:15.

Moses' description reads like the evening news. These people were suddenly swept off the planet and sent to a hellish place: "Behold, I will shut them up; a prison have I prepared for them. . . . And until that day [Christ's resurrection] they shall be in torment; . . . wherefore Enoch knew, and looked upon their wickedness, and misery, and wept."[510]

Why do we remain in Babylon? Does the example of these ancient people mean nothing to us?

Paul's Prophecy

Paul's description of Babylon in the last days confirms Moses' portrayal. With apostolic boldness, he declared: "in the last days perilous times shall come." Paul's statement runs counter to Babylon's assertion that her institutions are sound and secure. What is the source of the peril? Paul answers with a terrifying depiction of pervasive personal wickedness:

"Lovers of their own selves"—those who are self-centered, conceited

"Covetous"—those who are easily distracted from spiritual things; those who set their hearts on something other than God; those who are idolatrous and adulterous; those who are completely unfaithful

"Boasters"—those braggers who strut and gloat in their accomplishments, who think they are great in their own eyes, and who glory in their wickedness

"Proud"—those who have an exaggerated opinion of themselves and who selfishly pit their will against God's

"Blasphemers"—those who insult God or treat him and sacred things with contempt

"Disobedient to parents"—those who compete with their parents so as to cause contention; those who exhibit willful rebellion against righteous parental authority

"Unthankful"—those who are spoiled and feel entitled; those who offend God by not confessing his hand in all things (see D&C 59:21)

"Unholy"—those who are deliberately defiant, intentionally evil, profane, and ungodly; those who reject or neglect the sacred gospel ordinances that assure holiness

"Without natural affection"—those who are hard-hearted, whose actions break apart marriages, families, and friendships; those whose affections divert to alternative lifestyles

"Trucebreakers"—these are the opposite of peacemakers: those who would make a pact of peace with no intention of keeping it; those who have not the discipline to keep the peace; or those would make a pact of peace to gain an advantage and then break it

"False accusers"—those who are slanderers; they who would criticize to destroy another person while elevating themselves, or those who would accuse while knowing that their accusation is a lie

"Incontinent"—those people who are without self-restraint, especially with regard to sexual activity, or those who are incapable of keeping a trust or promise or holding to a virtue

"Fierce"—those who are violently cruel or aggressively, intensely, or uncontrollably angry

"Despisers of those that are good"—those who are scorners, who mock and show contempt for the children and things of God

"Traitors"—those who are disloyal to vows; these people can be treacherous and for selfish reasons will betray causes, friends, and family

"Heady"—those who are impetuous, rash, and willful, especially when following impulses to gratify their senses

"Highminded"—those who are proud and conceited and show an excessively high opinion of themselves

"Lovers of pleasures more than lovers of God"—those who are carnal, sensual and devilish; like the heady, these people seek to gratify their senses without thought to spiritual consequences, accountability, and realities

---

[510] Moses 7:38–41.

"Having a form of godliness, but denying the power thereof"—these people appear godly and go through the motions of religiosity, but they reject the idea of saving covenants and ordinances that must be performed by proper authority; their pseudo religions and teachings are man-made and based on selected scriptures, which they interpret to suit their philosophies and desires

"They which creep into houses, and lead captive silly women laden with sins, led away with divers lusts"—those who are overly enthusiastic about pleasing and satisfying their multiple carnal and sensual desires, especially gratifying their desire to have sexual relations without feelings of love and affection for their partner; these people practice their works of evil in the darkness of secrecy

"Ever learning but never able to come to a knowledge of the truth"—those people who immerse themselves in the knowledge of man without giving credit to God as the source of true knowledge; these people "resist the truth;" they have "corrupt minds," and are "reprobate concerning the faith"; they congratulate, worship, and deify man's genius. Of such people, Paul prophesies, "For the time will come when they will not endure sound doctrine; but after their own lusts shall they heap to themselves teachers, having itching ears; and they shall turn away their ears from the truth, and shall be turned unto fables."[511]

INVERTING THE TRUTH

One neat trick of Babylon is to confuse and reverse the order of good and bad. Those in Babylon all too frequently "call evil good, and good evil, . . . put darkness for light, and light for darkness, [and] put bitter for sweet, and sweet for bitter!"[512] Hugh Nibley explains how Satan manages this deception:

> In order to reconcile the ways of Babylon with the ways of Zion, it has been necessary to circumvent the inconvenient barriers of scripture and conscience by the use of the tried and true device of *rhetoric*, defined by Plato as the art of making true things seem false and false things seem true by the use of words. This invaluable art has, since the time of Cain, invested the ways of Babylon with an air of high purpose, solid virtue, and impeccable respectability. "The servants of sin should appear polished and pious, . . . able to call to their assistance . . . the subtle, persuasive power of rhetoric." "The devil is an orator; he is powerful; . . . he can tempt all classes."[513] . . . [We have, for example, the philosophy stating that] "Rome was great because Rome was good, giving expression to the old Roman belief in the close association between piety and success." This was the rhetoric of wealth, and it was inevitable—it always follows in such a situation, because people simply can't live virtuously and viciously at the same time. Yet they want to be good and rich at the same time, and so they reach a compromise called respectability, which is nothing less than Babylon masquerading as Zion. . . . It is not enough for the wicked to make excuses or explanations; in order to live with themselves and succeed in their undertakings, they must stand forth and be counted as pillars of righteousness, raising a hue and cry with practiced skill against those who would jeopardize their position, demonstrating, usually with the aid of paid rhetoricians, ministers,

---

[511] 2 Timothy 3:1–8; 4:3–4.
[512] 2 Nephi 15:20; see also Isaiah 5:20.
[513] Nibley, *Approaching Zion*, 45, quoting Brigham Young, *Journal of Discourses*, 11:234–35; quoting Smith, *Teachings of the Prophet Joseph Smith*, 162.

and lawyers, that it is not they but their opponents who are wicked.[514]

Hence, by the clever use of language and appealing to a sense of morality, Babylon manages to murder unborn children under the rhetoric of *pro-choice, individual liberty, reproductive freedom,* and *reproductive rights,* and Babylon redefines marriage by waving the flag of *tolerance.* A comparison of gospel beliefs—such as the purposes of money, relationships, education, health, personal management, religious beliefs, and so forth—against the issues and doctrines of Babylon reveals a host of inversions of the truth. With certainty, in Babylon we can expect to find a falsehood wherever we find a truth, and that falsehood will be upheld by rhetoric.

Moroni's Prophecy

Through eyes of a seer, Moroni gazed into the future and saw our day in detail. He wrote, "Behold, I speak unto you as if ye were present, and yet ye are not. But behold, Jesus Christ hath shown you unto me, and I know your doing." Then Moroni described latter-day Babylon as if he were a modern-day journalist: "And I know that ye do walk in the pride of your hearts; and there are none save a few only who do not lift themselves up in the pride of their hearts, unto the wearing of very fine apparel, unto envying, and strifes, and malice, and persecutions, and all manner of iniquities; and your churches, yea, even every one, have become polluted because of the pride of your hearts. For behold, ye do love money, and your substance, and your fine apparel, and the adorning of your churches, more than ye love the poor and the needy, the sick and the afflicted."[515]

Moroni's vision was essentially the same vision as that seen by Jesus, Paul, and John the Revelator. He foresaw pervasive pride, attention to fashion, envy, strife, malice, persecution, iniquity, and polluted churches, which are actual religious institutions and the philosophies of men, all of which are worshipped and followed devoutly. Sadly, Moroni reported, these conditions would exist among the Saints, whose affiliation with Babylon would defile the holy church of God: "O ye pollutions, ye hypocrites, ye teachers, who sell yourselves for that which will canker, *why have ye polluted the holy church of God?* Why are ye ashamed to take upon you the name of Christ? Why do ye not think that greater is the value of an endless happiness than that misery which never dies—because of the praise of the world?" Moreover, Moroni said that our embracing Babylon while professing Zion would serve to persecute, rank, alienate, and maltreat the less fortunate among us: "Why do ye adorn yourselves with that which hath no life, and yet suffer the hungry, and the needy, and the naked, and the sick and the afflicted to pass by you, and notice them not?"

Frighteningly, he noted that some Saints would adopt Babylon's strategy of sinful secret dealings to get rich. Once again, our selfish attitude toward money holds the vulnerable and poor in captivity: "Yea, why do ye build up your secret abominations to get gain, and cause that widows should mourn before the Lord, and also orphans to mourn before the Lord, and also the blood of their fathers and their husbands to cry unto the Lord from the ground, for vengeance upon your heads?" Unless we Saints repent and flee Babylon, we will suffer her fate: "Behold, the sword of vengeance hangeth over you; and the time soon cometh that he avengeth the blood of the saints upon you, for he will not suffer their cries any longer."[516]

Moroni describes latter-day Babylon as "a day when the blood of saints shall cry unto the Lord, because of secret combinations and the works of darkness. Yea, it shall come in a day when the power of God shall be denied, and churches become defiled and be lifted up in the pride of their hearts; yea,

---

[514] Nibley, *Approaching Zion*, 45–46.
[515] Mormon 8:35–37.
[516] Mormon 8:38–41; emphasis added.

even in a day when leaders of churches and teachers shall rise in the pride of their hearts, even to the envying of them who belong to their churches."

Beyond the preponderance of latter-day secret combinations, denials of the power of God, and myriad competing churches and man-made philosophies that are built up to get gain, Babylon boasts one continual scene of natural disasters and war: "Yea, it shall come in a day when there shall be heard of fires, and tempests, and vapors of smoke in foreign lands; and there shall also be heard of wars, rumors of wars, and earthquakes in divers places." Moreover, Babylon is a place and condition of "great pollutions," both physical and spiritual: "Yea, it shall come in a day when there shall be great pollutions upon the face of the earth." Every conceivable sin abounds: "There shall be murders, and robbing, and lying, and deceivings, and whoredoms [every form of sexual sin], and all manner of abominations." Babylon is a place and condition of apathy and lack of accountability to God: "Many . . . will say, Do this, or do that, and it mattereth not, for the Lord will uphold such at the last day. But wo unto such, for they are in the gall of bitterness and in the bonds of iniquity."[517]

As we recall, the word *church*, in Babylonian terms, means both a religious institution and a worshipped philosophy of man, anything that we worship other than God, whose leaders and teachers are those to whom we give our allegiance in place of God. Therefore, for example, Moroni prophesies: "Yea, it shall come in a day when there shall be churches built up that shall say: Come unto me, and for your money you shall be forgiven of your sins."[518]

Beyond spawning many corrupt religious institutions and man-made philosophies, Babylon promotes the attitude of entitlement, the doctrines that having money equals personal goodness, and that money exalts its owner above those of lesser fortunes. In the process, Zion's equality, unity, and oneness become nonexistent. To achieve her goals, Babylon first focuses her people on seeking riches for self-serving purposes; then she soothes their consciences with the lie that God will favor or at least wink at the rich (they must be good because they are rich), and eventually usher them into heaven where more riches await. This is false doctrine. Hugh Nibley notes, "God recognizes only one justification for seeking wealth, and that is with the express intent of helping the poor (Jacob 2:19)."[519] Moroni holds out no comfort to those who espouse such Babylonian attitudes: "O ye wicked and perverse and stiffnecked people, why have ye built up churches [worshipped philosophies] unto yourselves to get gain? Why have ye transfigured [reinvented] the holy word of God, that ye might bring damnation upon your souls?"[520] Clearly, Babylon wants money so badly that she will ignore or wrest the scriptures to justify her actions.

THE FALL OF BABYLON

Babylon is like a cancer: her presence is destructive to the system. She is an unwelcomed intruder that must be excised completely, or she will overwhelm and kill her host. Babylon can be neither converted nor saved. Total annihilation is the only answer. "We would have healed Babylon, but she is not healed: forsake her, and let us go every one into his own country: for her judgment reacheth unto heaven, and is lifted up even to the skies."[521] The future of Babylon is absolute destruction: "Behold, that great and abominable church, the whore of all the earth, must tumble to the earth, and great must be the fall thereof. For the kingdom of the devil must shake, and they which belong to it must needs be stirred up unto repentance, or the devil will grasp them with his everlasting chains, and

---

[517] Mormon 8:27–31.
[518] Mormon 8:32.
[519] Nibley, *Approaching Zion*, 53.
[520] Mormon 8:33.
[521] Jeremiah 51:9.

they be stirred up to anger, and perish."[522] Unfortunately, many people who are aware of these scriptures will still choose to wait it out, then try to jump ship to Zion at the very last minute.

We should take to heart these prophecies. Babylon and Zion do not mix. Zion merged with even a little bit of Babylon is no longer Zion. For Zion to be Zion—a Zion person, a Zion family, or a Zion priesthood community—there can be no hint of Babylon. Hugh Nibley writes: "Zion is pure, which means 'not mixed with any impurities, unalloyed'; it is all Zion and nothing else. . . . It is all pure—it is a society, a community, and an environment into which no unclean thing can enter. 'Henceforth there shall no more come into thee the uncircumcised and the unclean' (3 Nephi 20:36). It is not even pure people in a dirty environment, or pure people with a few impure ones among them; it is the perfectly pure in a perfectly pure environment."[523] If we partake of Babylon or embrace her teachings in any degree, we are not Zion, and we will suffer Babylon's fate.

In the revelation of John, the apostle saw a powerful angel descend from heaven, "and the earth was lightened with his glory. And he cried mightily with a strong voice, saying, Babylon the great is fallen, is fallen, and is become the habitation of devils."[524] John lists five reasons for Babylon's fall: (1) illicit relationships, interactions, and transactions that bring power and wealth. Described as "fornication," these universally accepted things stand contrary to the Covenant; (2) the intolerable sin of wealth-seeking: "and the merchants of the earth are waxed rich through the abundance of her delicacies"; (3) Pride: "How much she hath glorified herself"; (4) Excess and selfishness: "[Babylon] lived deliciously"; (5) Ignoring the underprivileged: "I sit a queen, and am no widow, and shall see no sorrow." But enough is too much: "her sins have reached unto heaven, and God hath remembered her iniquities."

The first angel's voice is now joined by a voice from heaven, which is directed at the Saints: "And I heard another voice from heaven, saying, Come out of her, my people, that ye be not partakers of her sins, and that ye receive not of her plagues." This merciful warning is dire; the Lord has undertaken to judge Babylon, and neither she nor the people who remain in her will be able to withstand his judgment: "Therefore shall her plagues come in one day, death, and mourning, and famine; and she shall be utterly burned with fire: for strong is the Lord God who judgeth her."

The reference to a sudden and astonishing fall is repeated throughout the prophecy: "in one day"; "Alas, alas, that great city Babylon, that mighty city! for in one hour is thy judgment come"; "For in one hour so great riches is come to nought"; "in one hour is she made desolate." Babylon's fall will be violent and permanent: "Thus with violence shall that great city Babylon be thrown down, and shall be found no more at all."

The wicked, who have loved Babylon, will greatly miss her; their reaction will be widespread mourning: "And the kings of the earth, who have committed fornication and lived deliciously with her, shall bewail her, and lament for her, when they shall see the smoke of her burning, standing afar off for the fear of her torment."

The world's economy will collapse, and those who have bought and sold will never recover: "And the merchants of the earth shall weep and mourn over her; for no man buyeth their merchandise any more." John then records the words of a voice from heaven, as if it were speaking directly to Babylon, saying, "All things which were dainty and goodly are departed from thee, and thou shalt find them no more at all." Then viewing the merchants, the voice adds, "The merchants of these things, which were made rich by her, shall stand afar off for the fear of her torment, weeping and wailing, and saying, Alas, alas." But the merchants are not the only ones to mourn. The fall of Babylon is lamented by everyone who has remained within her precincts: "And every shipmaster, and all the company in ships, and sailors, and as many as trade by sea, stood afar off, and cried when they saw the smoke of

---

[522] 2 Nephi 28:18–19.
[523] Nibley, *Approaching Zion*, 26–27.
[524] Revelation 18:1–2.

her burning, saying, What [city is] like unto this great city! And they cast dust on their heads, and cried, weeping and wailing, saying, Alas, alas, that great city, wherein were made rich all that had ships in the sea by reason of her costliness! for in one hour is she made desolate."

Then a mighty angel assesses the extent of the destruction: "And the voice of harpers, and musicians, and of pipers, and trumpeters, shall be heard no more at all in thee; and no craftsman, of whatsoever craft he be, shall be found any more in thee; and the sound of a millstone shall be heard no more at all in thee; and the light of a candle shall shine no more at all in thee." No more of the world's music and art; no more worldly crafts; no more worldly manufacturing. Babylon's light has been snuffed out forever, and the world mourns, "For thy merchants were the great men of the earth; for by thy sorceries were all nations deceived. And in her was found the blood of prophets, and of saints, and of all that were slain upon the earth."

But Zion's hour has come at last. While the people of Babylon mourn, the people of Zion rejoice. "Rejoice over her, thou heaven, and ye holy apostles and prophets; for God hath avenged you on her." We have a choice: we can remain in Babylon, suffer her plagues and mourn, or we can come to Zion, obtain safety in the Covenant, and rejoice.

According to Nephi, the fall of Babylon will be "exceedingly great."[525] Babylon will be destroyed "speedily; . . . it shall be at an instant, suddenly."[526] Lehi's foundationless "great and spacious building" that "stood as it were in the air, high above the earth" will collapse, to the astonishment and fear of the world. Then a voice from heaven will be heard: "Babylon the great is fallen, is fallen, and is become the habitation of devils, and the hold of every foul spirit."[527] Moreover, when Babylon, "the glory of kingdoms," falls, it "shall be as when God overthrew Sodom and Gomorrah." That is, Babylon will be so fully eradicated that "it shall never be inhabited, neither shall it be dwelt in from generation to generation; . . . her time is near to come, and her day shall not be prolonged. For I will destroy her speedily; yea, for I will be merciful unto my people, but the wicked shall perish."[528]

Speaking to the Prophet Joseph Smith, the Lord said, "Behold, vengeance cometh speedily upon the inhabitants of the earth, a day of wrath, a day of burning, a day of desolation, of weeping, of mourning, and of lamentation; and as a whirlwind it shall come upon all the face of the earth, saith the Lord. *And upon my house shall it begin,* and from my house shall it go forth, saith the Lord; first among those among you, saith the Lord, who have professed to know my name and have not known me, and have blasphemed against me in the midst of my house, saith the Lord."[529] The Saints are not exempt. Those Saints who hold to Babylon and its philosophies will suffer the consequences of Babylon's fall. Either we must decide to be safe in Zion or defenseless in Babylon. To the extent that we dabble with Babylon we are vulnerable.

SAMUEL THE LAMANITE'S PARALLEL DENUNCIATION OF BABYLON

A few years before the birth of Christ, Samuel, a Lamanite prophet, entered the land of the Nephites to warn the people, cry repentance, and prophesy of simultaneously glorious and catastrophic events. That Mormon would record Samuel's words in such detail should signal to us their latter-day import. Furthermore, that Samuel delivered his message only years before the advent of the Savior, with the advent's attendant destructions, should add more weight to our latter-day consideration. The fact that the resurrected Jesus drew attention to Samuel's prophecies and insisted that they be added to the Nephite record in detail should further signal their importance to us in the latter days.[530]

---

[525] 1 Nephi 11:35–36; 12:18.
[526] 2 Nephi 26:18.
[527] Revelation 18:2.
[528] 2 Nephi 23:19–22.
[529] D&C 112:24–26.
[530] 3 Nephi 23:7–14.

Let us consider Samuel's denunciation of the Nephites' Babylon as that denunciation parallels Babylon today.

To set the stage, Mormon describes the Nephite world as one of "great wickedness." Only a few "did observe strictly to keep the commandments of God." The Nephites' reaction to the prophet's preaching ranged from disregard to violence.[531] Immediately, we see our latter-day condition mirroring that of the Nephites.

Frighteningly, Samuel warned that "the sword of justice hangeth over this people. . . . Yea, heavy destruction awaiteth this people, and it surely cometh unto this people, and nothing can save this people save it be repentance and faith on the Lord Jesus Christ." The Nephites' condition had resulted from "the hardness of the hearts of the people." That hardness of heart was being manifested in a variety of ways:

- Misusing the money the Lord had given them.
- Setting their hearts on acquiring riches.
- Not hearkening unto the Lord or his words.
- Neither remembering the Lord or his blessings nor thanking him for them.
- Always thinking about their riches and how to acquire more of them.
- Not allowing their hearts to be "drawn out unto the Lord."
- Giving themselves over to "great pride, unto boasting, and unto great swelling, envyings, strifes, malice, persecutions, and murders, and all manner of iniquities."
- Mocking and rejecting the prophets.[532]

Another sinful condition of the Nephites was their willingness to follow, idolize, and uphold people who flattered their egos— Samuel called these deceivers "blind guides."[533] The Nephites were more interested in the philosophies of these smooth-tongued "guides" than the prophets. They would enrich these people and canonize their words as if they were scripture.

> But behold, if a man shall come among you and shall say: Do this, and there is no iniquity; do that and ye shall not suffer; yea, he will say: Walk after the pride of your own hearts; yea, walk after the pride of your eyes, and do whatsoever your heart desireth—and if a man shall come among you and say this, ye will receive him, and say that he is a prophet. Yea, ye will lift him up, and ye will give unto him of your substance; ye will give unto him of your gold, and of your silver, and ye will clothe him with costly apparel; and because he speaketh flattering words unto you, and he saith that all is well, then ye will not find fault with him.[534]

"Blind guides" are those people who receive our support and adoration for flattering us with their mouth, but more often with their life-style. We give them riches not for what they produce or contribute; we give them riches for being famous. They are famous for being famous. They flatter us by parading before us the rewards that come with a lifestyle that glamorizes Babylon, and we applaud them for their having legitimized a life of wealth, self-indulgence, power, recognition, and excess.

---

[531] Helaman 13:1–2.
[532] Helaman 13:19–24.
[533] Helaman 13:29.
[534] Helaman 13:27–28.

The Lord's Spirit cannot abide in such wickedness. In Samuel's day, only the presence of a few righteous individuals was holding back the judgments. But the clock was ticking. The gathering of the righteous was taking place. Soon the faithful few would be called out (or cast out), and only the repentant would be spared. Then the wicked would be ripe for destruction.[535] A fruit that is ripe will fall from the tree, an interesting analogy of separating one's self from the Tree of Life. In its insistence for a sinful, independent life from the tree, the ripe and fallen fruit can ultimately do nothing on its own except lie on the ground and rot.

Speaking for the Lord, Samuel pronounced a series of curses: (1) "I will take away my word from them"; (2) "I will withdraw my spirit"; (3) "I will suffer them no longer," that is, *I will not allow them to continue living this way;* (4) "I will turn the hearts of their [enemies] against them"; (5) "I will cause that they shall be smitten . . . with the sword and with famine and with pestilence. . . . I will visit them in my fierce anger"; and (6) "Whoso shall hide up treasures in the earth shall find them no more . . . save he be a righteous man."[536]

If the people cared little about the first five curses, the last one was sure to get their attention. This curse was aimed at what they loved most: their treasures. The curse stipulated that a righteous person was exempt; he could "hide up" his treasure unto the Lord—that is, he could consecrate it—and it would remain safe. But a wicked person or a good person who still trusted in Babylon would not be so fortunate. Because he was in the selfish habit of hiding his treasure unto himself and not the Lord, he would discover that his treasure had become "slippery."[537] Consequently, the fortunes of those who were wicked or those good people who trusted in Babylon would slip away from them; the economy would collapse, and financial ruin would result. "And behold, the time cometh that he curseth your riches, that they become slippery, that ye cannot hold them; and in the days of your poverty ye cannot retain them."[538]

Then things would go from bad to worse. In the people's impoverished situation, they would be vulnerable to attack from their enemies, particularly those enemies who constitute secret combinations. We note that Samuel's prophecies were followed by the near destruction of the nation by the Gadianton robbers.[539] Samuel foretold that the people would "flee before their enemies" following the economic collapse.[540] Their lamentations should strike fear in every person who trusts in his riches and adores Babylon:

> And in the days of your poverty ye shall cry unto the Lord; and in vain shall ye cry, for your desolation is already come upon you, and your destruction is made sure; and then shall ye weep and howl in that day, saith the Lord of Hosts. And then shall ye lament, and say:
>
> O that I had repented, and had not killed the prophets, and stoned them, and cast them out. Yea, in that day ye shall say: O that we had remembered the Lord our God in the day that he gave us our riches, and then they would not have become slippery that we should lose them; for behold, our riches are gone from us.
>
> Behold, we lay a tool here and on the morrow it is gone; and behold, our swords are taken from us in the day we have sought them for battle.

---

[535] Helaman 13:12–14.
[536] Helaman 13:8–10, 18.
[537] Helaman 13:18–19, 31, 33, 36.
[538] Helaman 13:31.
[539] 3 Nephi 1–4.
[540] Helaman 13:20.

> Yea, we have hid up our treasures and they have slipped away from us, because of the curse of the land.
>
> O that we had repented in the day that the word of the Lord came unto us; for behold the land is cursed, and all things are become slippery, and we cannot hold them.
>
> Behold, we are surrounded by demons, yea, we are encircled about by the angels of him who hath sought to destroy our souls. Behold, our iniquities are great. O Lord, canst thou not turn away thine anger from us? And this shall be your language in those days.
>
> But behold, your days of probation are past; ye have procrastinated the day of your salvation until it is everlastingly too late, and your destruction is made sure; yea, for ye have sought all the days of your lives for that which ye could not obtain; and ye have sought for happiness in doing iniquity, which thing is contrary to the nature of that righteousness which is in our great and Eternal Head.
>
> O ye people of the land, that ye would hear my words! And I pray that the anger of the Lord be turned away from you, and that ye would repent and be saved.[541]

Samuel's prophecies began to be fulfilled, but the Nephites did not repent. Mormon reported that "there was but little alteration in the affairs of the people, save it were the people began to be more hardened in iniquity." Even when "great signs [were] given unto the people, and wonders; and the words of the prophets began to be fulfilled," the Nephites hardened their hearts.[542] They simply would not believe the signs or respond to the Lord's invitation to repent, which invitation he offered by means of cataclysmic events. Mormon identified four reasons why the people did not repent:

1. Prophecies are nothing more than good guesses: "Some things they [the prophets] may have guessed right, among so many; but behold, we know that all these great and marvelous works cannot come to pass, of which has been spoken."
2. Prophecies do not make sense: "And they began to reason and to contend among themselves, saying: That it is not reasonable that such a being as a Christ shall come.
3. Prophecies are false traditions: "But behold, we know that this is a wicked tradition, which has been handed down unto us by our fathers, to cause us that we should believe in some great and marvelous thing which should come to pass . . . ; therefore they can keep us in ignorance."
4. Prophets deceive us to keep us bound to them: "And they [the prophets] will, by the cunning and the mysterious arts of the evil one, work some great mystery which we cannot understand, which will keep us down to be servants to their words, and also servants unto them, for we depend upon them to teach us the word; and thus will they keep us in ignorance if we will yield ourselves unto them, all the days of our lives."

Mormon informed us that the Nephites "began to depend upon their own strength and upon their own wisdom." They "imagine[d] up in their hearts" "many more things" "which were foolish and vain." Mormon said that the people "were much disturbed, for Satan did stir them up to do iniquity continually; yea, he did go about spreading rumors and contentions upon all the face of the land, that he might harden the hearts of the people against that which was good and against that which should

---

[541] Helaman 13:32–39.
[542] Helaman 16:12–15.

come. And notwithstanding the signs and the wonders which were wrought among the people of the Lord, and the many miracles which they did, Satan did get great hold upon the hearts of the people upon all the face of the land."[543]

It is difficult to read this account and not see the condition of Babylon today. Clearly, we are mere years away from the Savior's advent. The prophets are widely mocked, ignored, and often soundly rejected. Only a few Zion people practice righteousness, and for the sake of those few the Lord is holding back the destructions. The condition of Babylon's people is defined by hardness of heart. They love their money and selfishly misuse it; they always think about their riches and how to acquire more. They will not hearken unto the Lord or his words; they will not remember or thank him for their blessings. Their hearts are not "drawn out unto the Lord." Their lives are marked with "great pride," boastings, envyings, strifes, malice, persecutions, and murders, and all manner of iniquities." They follow "blind guides," who use flattering words to stroke their egos and legitimize a lifestyle that glamorizes wealth, self-indulgence, popularity, power, and excess.

Now the curses of the Lord are becoming apparent. Personal treasures are becoming slippery; economies are lying in ruins. In this condition, the people of Babylon are vulnerable to their enemies, especially those of secret combinations. Despite cataclysmic events, they will not repent and return to the Lord. Rather, they find all sorts of reasons not to repent, and they grow in wickedness. Samuel might as well have been warning and prophesying to us.

Go Ye Out from Babylon

Knowing the condition and future of Babylon, why do we try so hard to stay here? The Lord has instructed us implicitly: "Go ye out from Babylon. Be ye clean that bear the vessels of the Lord. . . . Yea, verily I say unto you again, the time has come when the voice of the Lord is unto you: Go ye out of Babylon; gather ye out from among the nations, from the four winds, from one end of heaven to the other. . . . Go ye out from among the nations, even from Babylon, from the midst of wickedness, which is spiritual Babylon."[544]

As we have learned, Babylon is simultaneously a location, the sum of false philosophies and doctrines, and a condition of the heart. While our present circumstances might not involve moving away from physical Babylon, we nevertheless must flee from spiritual Babylon. In unmistakable language, the Lord has commanded us to "forsake the world,"[545] and "lay aside the things of this world, and seek for the things of a better."[546] He charges us to escape for our own safety: "For after today cometh the burning—this is speaking after the manner of the Lord—for verily I say, tomorrow all the proud and they that do wickedly shall be as stubble; and I will burn them up, for I am the Lord of Hosts; and I will not spare any that remain in Babylon."[547] If we choose to remain in spiritual Babylon, we do so at our own risk. Most certainly, we will be caught up in the destructions: "That great whore, who hath perverted the right ways of the Lord, yea, that great and abominable church, shall tumble to the dust and great shall be the fall of it."[548]

The Lord's command to leave Babylon is also an invitation to come to Zion, with the Lord's offer to help us. Still, there is nothing easy about leaving Babylon and converting to a Zionlike way of life founded on its celestial doctrines. Occasionally, we must be "stirred up" so that we might see the truth about Babylon and decide once and for all to leave. Blaine Yorgason writes:

---

[543] Helaman 16:15, 22–24.
[544] D&C 133:5, 7, 14.
[545] D&C 53:2.
[546] D&C 25:10.
[547] D&C 64:24.
[548] 1 Nephi 22:14.

> Whether we think we need to give up [the things of Babylon] or not, it seems that the Lord is frequently willing to help us in the giving up of worldly things. He might do this by allowing financial reversals to occur, bringing loss of homes, cars, boats, and incomes; personal or corporate bankruptcy; and so forth. We might also experience a severe loss of health or death of a loved one, which can do the same thing by making worldly things unattractive or meaningless. . . . This is called being stirred up unto repentance. In this case, however, I will substitute the word *humility*, which always strikes at the heart of pride, vanity, and worldliness! "Behold, the world is ripening in iniquity; and it must needs be that the children of men are stirred up unto *humility*, both the Gentiles and also the house of Israel" (D&C 18:6); and, "The kingdom of the devil must shake, and they which belong to it must needs be stirred up unto repentance, or the devil will grasp them with his everlasting chains, and they . . . perish" (2 Nephi 28:19).
>
> When we experience this divine assistance in leaving behind the things of the world—and to some degree we will all experience it—then above all else we ought to be filled with joy and rejoicing in the Lord's goodness and mercy (D&C 52:43).[549]

Summary and Conclusion

Babylon is the inverse of Zion. Wherever we detect any of the loathsome things that we have discussed in this section (and this section is not exhaustive), we find Babylon. If we desire to become Zionlike, we must not partake of or participate in anything that Babylon does, believes or promotes; otherwise, we will suffer her fate. To the degree that we embrace Babylon, we reject Zion. Only when we make a clean break from Babylon and never turn back will we finally qualify as Zion people. There are only two choices.

The process of leaving Babylon and coming to Zion begins with the discovery that we are not home; we have fallen into a lone and dreary world that is as foreign to heaven as is hell. From that moment of discovery for the rest of our lives, our direction must be away and up.

This earth began as Zion but was soon infiltrated by a being who determined to wrest ownership from its Creator and reign as the god of this world. That being was Satan, who systematically reversed every Zion doctrine and replaced it with his anti-Christ philosophy, which he designed to appear so reasonable and close to the truth that it could deceive even the very elect. Attempting to imitate God the Father, Satan searched for a *son* to champion his anti-Christ *gospel*. He found a willing candidate in Cain, who advanced a doctrine so damning that the entire antediluvian world became irretrievably corrupt, and in the days of Noah, it eventually warranted annihilation.

After the Flood, Cain's descendant, Nimrod, became heir to Cain's diabolical throne, and a new anti-Christ *dispensation* began. Nimrod advanced what Cain had started by conquering much of the world and building a capital with a tower or *temple* to attempt to ascend illegitimately into heaven. Nimrod's temple city was called Babel, or Babylon. Forevermore, *Babylon* would be the code name by which the prophets of God would identify and describe the Satanic kingdom, culture, and doctrines that always led people to individual damnation and collective destruction. Sodom and Gomorrah are examples.

---

[549] Yorgason, *I Need Thee Every Hour*, 206–7.

Today, the anti-Christ philosophy dominates the earth. Both figuratively and literally, it "slayeth the saints of God, yea, and tortureth them and bindeth them down, and yoketh them with a yoke of iron, and bringeth them down into captivity."[550]

In one way or another we have all partaken of Babylon, and when we become sufficiently sick, we seek heavenly help to get out and go home. To make a clean break from Babylon requires making the new and everlasting covenant, receiving priesthood authority by ordination with the Father's oath and our covenant, receiving priesthood power by means of temple ordinances and righteous living, being endowed with knowledge from on high, and of course enduring in the Covenant to the end and its perfect conclusion. For a season, we might react like Laman and Lemuel, constantly looking back and longing for life in Babylon; but at some point we will realize that Zion and Babylon cannot co-exist, and therefore we have to make a choice. We can only straddle the gulf between Zion and Babylon for so long; because the two go in opposite directions, we will eventually be forced to jump to one side or another. Nephi gives us the key to escape Babylon and come to Zion: "We heeded [Babylon] not."[551]

Babylon is so diverse, pervasive, and disgusting that the prophets seem to struggle to find adequate language to describe her. Babylon is often called "the world," but that term usually gives way to more graphic descriptors that focus us on Babylon's central elements: *"whore"* to portray her many sexual perversions; *"The Mother of Harlots and Abominations of the Earth"* to illustrate her continually spawning, myriad seductive evils; *"carnal, sensual, and devilish"* to depict her ability to exploit human nature and to tempt us to gratify our senses, which will cause us to become like the devil; *"Great and Abominable Church"* to illustrate that she is full of idolatry, envy, and covetousness, and that her vile desires and philosophies are worshipped by her adherents; and *"great and spacious building"* to express her excessive pride and the scope of her influence. By whatever name, Babylon's aim is to trap and destroy us.

Babylon's four-fold strategy to torture and "murder" us centers on the pursuits of money, power, recognition, and selfishness and self-indulgence. According to Nephi, these pursuits are facilitated by:

1. The desire for wealth.
2. Fashion and materialism.
3. Sexual sins.
4. Peer acceptance, recognition and popularity.[552]

This strategy is so successful that even Satan is taken aback by Babylon's "dark and blackening deeds [which] are enough to make hell itself shudder, and to stand aghast and pale, and the hands of the very devil to tremble and palsy."[553] Babylon has made us to "bow down with grief, sorrow, and care, under the most damning hand of murder, tyranny, and oppression."[554]

Nephi describes Babylon in terms of the extent of her detestable deeds and the depth her corruption. His list includes contention; man's wisdom replacing God's wisdom; denying the power of God; "eat, drink and be merry" as a way of life; pride; secret sinning; reviling against that which is good; placing trust in carnal security; flattery; and taking and giving offense.[555] These items and more define Babylon as a physical location and a spiritual condition, which condition includes false philosophies and doctrines and a corruption of the heart.

---

[550] 1 Nephi 13:5.
[551] 1 Nephi 8:33.
[552] 1 Nephi 13:5–9.
[553] D&C 123:10.
[554] D&C 123:7.
[555] 2 Nephi 28:4–16, 26–30.

In Babylon, competition rather than cooperation is the name of the game. In Babylon, competitive enterprise is the primary engine that drives progress. Competition, however, spawns more losers than winners, and therefore it is the cause of widespread misery. Competition accounts for social classes, educational disparity, poverty, oppression, dishonesty, murder, and war.

Babylon is filled with hypocrites, whom Jesus labeled the worst sinners—those people who pretend to be what they are not, to seem better than they really are, or to appear pious and virtuous when they are not.

Babylon bounces her adherents from one false philosophy to another, always keeping them off balance so that they will never find the truth. These man-made philosophies are embraced by the people of Babylon as pseudo religions; humanism, intellectualism, atheism, fundamentalism, relativism, universalism, monism, subjectivism, and modernism are a few. All of these are designed to limit or remove God from our consciousness and to enthrone man and his genius.

Prophets have compared modern Babylon to the days of Noah and Lot, whose worlds, along with the societies of Sodom and Gomorrah, were completely obliterated as punishment for their sins. To help us negotiate through Babylon's filthiness in the last days, the Lord has given us the Book of Mormon. This book of scripture contains two accounts of once-mighty nations that imploded by their embracing Babylonian ideals. Do we really believe we are immune? President Kimball stated that latter-day Babylon would deceive even the very elect—as many as half the Saints, according to the parable of the Ten Virgins. He had three primary concerns: (1) *The abuse of the environment:* filth and contaminants that pollute our minds, bodies, and our surroundings; (2) *The pursuit of personal affluence:* a transfer of trust in God to a trust in material things in an effort to assure security and happiness for the remainder of our life; (3) *Trust in military security:* the expenditure of enormous resources to purchase and develop armaments with the intention of depending upon them for protection, rather than depending upon God.

Jesus, John, Paul, and Moroni join Nephi and other prophets who foresaw Babylon's latter-day dominance. Their descriptions are chilling, and yet many of us still make no attempt to flee. Jesus portrayed our day as a time when "darkness covereth the earth, and gross darkness the minds of the people, and all flesh has become corrupt before my face."[556] We live in physical Babylon and partake of spiritual Babylon as though we had no option. At times, we seem powerless to cease partaking of her lifestyle and philosophies. We assume that this is just the way life is and that we are helpless to change things. The people in Noah's and Lot's day held similar views and were caught up in the destructions: "And as it was in the days of [Noah], so shall it be also in the days of the Son of man. They did eat, they drank, they married wives, they were given in marriage, until the day that [Noah] entered into the ark, and the flood came, and destroyed them all. Likewise also as it was in the days of Lot; they did eat, they drank, they bought, they sold, they planted, they builded; but the same day that Lot went out of Sodom it rained fire and brimstone from heaven, and destroyed them all. Even thus shall it be in the day when the Son of man is revealed."[557]

Babylon will fall again. Can there be any doubt? From the days of Enoch to the present, Babylon's fall has been prophesied repeatedly. Moreover, there are countless prophetic descriptions of Babylon and authoritative declarations concerning why she must be destroyed once and for all. When we consider Babylon's characteristics, we are astonished that anyone would want to stay. The one and only solution for safety and security in a world gone mad is to flee to Zion.

Postlude

Zion was our origin, our birthright, and Zion will be our destiny. She is our ideal. Her establishment should be our greatest desire. Joseph Smith said, "We ought to have the building up of Zion as our

---

[556] D&C 112:24.
[557] Luke 17:26–30.

greatest object."558 Brigham Young laid the responsibility of Zion upon each of us individually: "[Zion] commences in the heart of each person."559 We cannot read the scriptures, especially latter-day scriptures, and avoid personal responsibility for becoming Zion people. Without reservation, our obligation is to accept every revealed Zion principle and put it into practice.

Zion is the standard among celestial and celestial-seeking beings.560 The celestial condition of Zion is the exact opposite of the telestial condition of Babylon;561 therefore, we are constantly faced with choosing between the two. We cannot have it both ways. Nothing good has ever come from attempting to mix Zion with Babylon.

As members of the dispensation of the fulness of times, we are under covenant to build up the kingdom of God for the purpose of establishing Zion. A key to establishing Zion in our lives is found in Doctrine and Covenants 42, the revelation called, "the Law of the Church,"562 which comprises the law of Zion. In one sentence, the Lord prophesies of three significant events that will make us Zion individuals: "And ye shall hereafter receive church covenants, such as shall be sufficient to establish you, both here and in the New Jerusalem."563 The references in this scripture lead to what we are calling in this book *The Three Pillars of Zion*:

The New and Everlasting Covenant (D&C 132:4–7)
The Oath and Covenant of the Priesthood (D&C 84:33–44)
The Law of Consecration (D&C 82:11–15)

These three covenants (pillars) are sufficient to establish Zionlike qualities in our individual lives, as well as in our marriages, families, or other groups of people under the direction of the priesthood.

Therefore, to become Zionlike and thus ensure our salvation and exaltation, we enter into the new and everlasting covenant. By this act, we specify that we have made a choice between Zion and Babylon and that forevermore we will not attempt to mix the two. We agree to follow the Covenant to its perfect conclusion: to snatch us from Babylon, to single us out, to purify and sanctify our hearts, to prepare us in every way to regain the presence of God, and to obtain our inheritance and our crown. "This is Zion: THE PURE IN HEART."564

---

558 Smith, *Teachings of the Prophet Joseph Smith*, 60.
559 Young, *Discourses of Brigham Young*, 118.
560 D&C 105:5.
561 Nibley, *Approaching Zion*, 30.
562 D&C 42 head note.
563 D&C 42:67.
564 D&C 97:21.

Book 2:

The First Pillar of Zion—The New and Everlasting Covenant

Introduction

In this second book of *The Three Pillars of Zion* series, we will examine in depth the first pillar of Zion: *The New and Everlasting Covenant*. We recall that the "Law of the Church" (D&C 42) states that three covenants are sufficient to establish us as Zion people: "And ye shall hereafter receive church covenants, such as shall be sufficient to establish you, both here and in the New Jerusalem."[565] These covenants are:

1. The New and Everlasting Covenant (D&C 132:4–7).
2. The Oath and Covenant of the Priesthood (D&C 84:33–44).
3. The Law of Consecration (D&C 82:11–15).

In Book 1, we learned that Zion was our origin and will be our destiny. She is our ideal, and she is also the antithesis of Babylon. Zion is the standard among celestial and celestial-seeking people.[566] Joseph Smith declared that the establishment of Zion should be our greatest desire: "We ought to have the building up of Zion as our greatest object."[567] Brigham Young taught that "[Zion] commences in the heart of each person."[568] Clearly, the responsibility to become a Zion people rests upon each of us individually. Our obligation is to accept every revealed Zion principle and put it into practice.

That obligation begins with formally accepting the Atonement of Jesus Christ by receiving the new and everlasting covenant. Widely misunderstood, this covenant is the *umbrella covenant* under which all other gospel covenants exist. The new and everlasting covenant is not only the product of the Atonement, but it is the vehicle by which we can access the Atonement's power to save and exalt us.

The new and everlasting covenant consists of two primary covenants: the covenant of baptism, and the oath and covenant of the priesthood. The fulness of the priesthood covenant includes (1) ordination for worthy men; (2) temple covenants and ordinances for worthy men and women; (3) the temple sealing covenant, which is called the Covenant of Exaltation,[569] for worthy men and women.

---

[565] D&C 42:67.
[566] D&C 105:5.
[567] Smith, *Teachings of the Prophet Joseph Smith*, 60.
[568] Young, *Discourses of Brigham Young*, 118.
[569] See Nelson, *The Power within Us*, 136; Smith, *Doctrines of Salvation*, 2:58. Note: Elder Bruce R. McConkie stated that men make a covenant of exaltation twice: once upon ordination to the Melchizedek Priesthood and again at the time of the marriage sealing: "Ordination to office in the Melchizedek priesthood

INTRODUCTION

The new and everlasting covenant, along with its supporting covenants, serves to cleanse us, separate us from the world, prepare us for coronation, and protect us from Satan. These covenants endow us with keys to the knowledge and power of God, and they establish us in our eternal kingdoms. Collectively, these covenants and the laws of God are enveloped by the new and everlasting covenant.[570] This Covenant is also a contract, which, remarkably, is agreed to by each member of the Godhead: the Father, the Son, and the Holy Ghost, a contract which is described as a marriage, the most intimate of relationships. Love is the single most motivating factor of the Covenant.

To become Zion people and thus ensure our salvation and exaltation, we must enter into the new and everlasting covenant and abide in it forevermore. By this, we witness that we have made a choice between Zion and Babylon. Furthermore, we witness that we agree to follow the Covenant to its perfect conclusion: to snatch us from Babylon, to single us out, to purify and sanctify our hearts, to prepare us in every way to regain the presence of God, and to obtain our inheritance and our crown. "This is Zion: THE PURE IN HEART."[571]

---

and entering into that 'order of the priesthood' named 'the new and everlasting covenant of marriage' are both occasions when men make the covenant of exaltation, being promised through their faithfulness all that the Father hath (D&C 131:1–4; 84:39–41; 132; Num. 25:13)." (*Mormon Doctrine*, 167.) Note that in this series the first time we mention a covenant or distinctive part of the Father's plan, we will put the name of the covenant or doctrine in capital letters to emphasize it, but thereafter we will put the name in lowercase. One exception: when we refer to the new and everlasting covenant by the shortened title of "Covenant," we will capitalize it to distinguish it from the other covenants discussed herein.

[570] See McConkie, *Mormon Doctrine*, 529–30.
[571] D&C 97:21.

Section 5

Preface to the New and Everlasting Covenant

Note: Because this series is a sequential work, one concept building upon another, the section numbers pick up where the last book ended. Thus, this book begins with Section 5.

On January 2, 1831, the Lord promised the Prophet Joseph Smith that he would reveal to him "the law," which was the law of Zion, that would open the door to an endowment of "power from on high."[572] In obedience to the Lord's commandment, the Prophet traveled to Kirtland, Ohio, and on February 9, 1831, he received the "law of the Church," known as section 42 of the Doctrine and Covenants. Within that revelation, the Lord promised to reveal "church covenants, such as shall be sufficient to establish you, both here and in the New Jerusalem."[573] That is, the Lord was going to reveal to the Prophet the foundational covenants and laws of Zion. Significantly, the cross references for Doctrine and Covenants 42:67 lead to:

1. The New and Everlasting Covenant (D&C 132:4–7).
2. The Oath and Covenant of the Priesthood (D&C 84:33–44).
3. The Law of Consecration (D&C 82:11–15).

These three covenants are the Pillars of Zion that arise from the foundation of the Atonement. Because all gospel covenants and laws are included in the new and everlasting covenant, we will examine this covenant first.

Perhaps no discovery is more astonishing or humbling than the realization that the Father, the Son, and the Holy Ghost have invited us to become *one* with them. To be beckoned into their inner circle and to be offered all that they are and have constitute unparalleled blessings that speak to their generosity and love. In his address entitled "The New and Everlasting Covenant," BYU professor Chauncey C. Riddle explained: "To be invited to join them by hearing the gospel of Jesus Christ is to receive *the greatest message in the universe;* to be enabled to join them by receiving the new and everlasting covenant is to have *the greatest opportunity in the universe;* to be joined with them is *the greatest gift in the universe,* which gift is life eternal, sharing with them all the good they have and are (D&C 14:7)."[574]

---

[572] D&C 38:32.
[573] D&C 42:67.
[574] Riddle, "The New and Everlasting Covenant," 224–25; emphasis added.

Perhaps equally humbling is the realization that their primary purpose for doing all that they do is to offer us the greatest degree of happiness.

THE PLAN OF HAPPINESS

The Plan of Happiness is central to becoming a Zion person. Happiness is always associated with Zion: "and surely there could not be a happier people among all the people who had been created by the hand of God."[575] The end purpose of our creation is happiness: "men are that they might have joy."[576] The ultimate definition of happiness is to be like God; the more we approach the stature of God in attributes, knowledge, power, and dominion, the happier we are. Conversely, the definition of misery is to be like Satan. Misery is always associated with Babylon.

To become like God and experience his level of happiness rests on two criteria: (1) Justice—the system of celestial laws that make God who he is and provide him what he has; that is, God's power and quality of life derive from his obedience to celestial laws. (2) Mercy—the Lord's love, grace, forbearance, clemency, and pity on us lesser beings, as he patiently works with us to help us to become like him. To a great extent our happiness depends upon God's merciful interaction with us and our extending mercy to others.[577]

THE COVENANT OF THE GODS

In a premortal council of the Gods[578] (which preceded the Council in Heaven that we attended), the Father, the Son, and the Holy Ghost entered into a covenant to work together for the happiness, salvation, and exaltation of the Father's children. Joseph Smith taught that an "everlasting covenant was made between three personages before the organization of this earth, and relates to their dispensation of things to men on the earth; these personages, according to Abraham's record, are called God the first, the Creator; God the second, the Redeemer; and God the third, the witness or Testator."[579] Our interaction with these three Gods began before the world was created, continues here, and will endure into eternity. Every aspect of our interaction with them has to do with our present redemption and our eternal happiness.

Too often we miss the fact that the Father, the Son, and the Holy Ghost define their dealings with us in terms of *relationship*. Each one of us is dearer to them than we can comprehend. Motivated solely by their relationship with us, they initiated the plan of happiness.[580]

In the premortal world, when the Father announced the plan of happiness, we shouted for joy, perhaps because the plan's far-reaching benefits were so extraordinary.[581] In that supreme act of love, Heavenly Father offered us the opportunity to become what he is. He held nothing back. His package included indivisible access to and inheritance of the totality of his kingdom, the fulness of his power, the keys to the library of everything he knows, and the ability to become like him in perfections, characteristic, and attributes. His offer included the quintessential gift of a physical body, and a tabernacle of flesh and bones for our immortal spirits to eternally "act upon."[582] He also offered us the invaluable gift of divine education: the opportunity to experience good and evil and the unrestricted

---

[575] 4 Nephi 1:16.
[576] 2 Nephi 2:25.
[577] See Alma 42:15.
[578] Smith, *Teachings of the Prophet Joseph Smith*, 349.
[579] Smith, *Teachings of the Prophet Joseph Smith*, 190.
[580] Alma 42:1–26.
[581] Job 38:7.
[582] 2 Nephi 2:13–14.

gift of agency to choose between them. Finally, he offered us the opportunity to enjoy his lifestyle—*eternal marriage and family*—with the promise of eternal posterity.[583]

Happiness Encompasses All That Is Good

Clearly, the plan of happiness offered us all that was *good,* which is called *righteousness.* Righteousness, according to Chauncey Riddle, is "that necessary order of social relationships in which beings of knowledge and power must bind themselves in order to live together in accomplishment and happiness for eternity."[584] Happiness is wholly dependent upon righteousness, and it is in righteousness that Zion people weld themselves together by solemn covenants so that they become "predictable, dependable, and united so that they can be trusted. They bind themselves to be honest, true, chaste, and benevolent so that they can do good for all other beings, which good they do by personal sacrifice to fulfill all righteousness."[585] Thus, being and doing *good* and being and doing *righteousness* are synonymous terms; *goodness* and *righteousness* are unifying, perfecting, selfless principles that produce happiness. On the other hand, *evil,* the opposite of *goodness* and *righteousness,* is without discipline, a law unto itself,[586] a corrupting and self-serving principle that produces misery. Evil defines Babylon.

Heavenly Father structured the plan of happiness so as to mercifully wrest us from Babylon, from our complacency, from our evil tendencies, and from the effects of the Fall. Heavenly Father built into the plan of happiness his promise that he would endow us with the Light of Christ, which is an agent employed by the Holy Ghost to "feel after"[587] us and draw us out of Babylon and into Zion. By means of that light, the Holy Ghost would continually offer us opportunities to view ourselves in our "awful state,"[588] for the purpose of shaking us loose from Babylon. Moreover, the Father promised that he would offer each of us an unmistakable witness of the truth by the power of the Holy Ghost, so that we might reconsider our destructive path, repent of evil, and embrace "the godly order of good."[589] Clearly, the Father makes every effort to offer us happiness.

Balancing Justice and Mercy

To make the plan of happiness operational, the Father first instigated the covenant of justice,[590] that system of laws that he obeyed in order to become who he is and enjoy what he has. That is, by obedience to celestial law he was justified to enjoy the blessings associated with those laws. By living those laws, we, God's children, can progress and become like him in every way. That is the process that leads to true happiness.

Knowing that his children would break the celestial laws while they struggled to assimilate them in their lives, and knowing that those broken laws would consign his children "forever to be cut off from his presence,"[591] the Father decreed a second law, which would have the power to override the consequences of broken celestial laws and to thereby save his children. That new law is called the covenant of mercy.[592] We know this law by another name: the new and everlasting covenant.

---

[583] D&C 132:24, 55.
[584] Riddle, "The New and Everlasting Covenant," 225.
[585] Riddle, "The New and Everlasting Covenant," 225.
[586] D&C 88:21–35.
[587] D&C 112:13.
[588] Ether 4:15.
[589] Riddle, "The New and Everlasting Covenant," 225.
[590] Alma 42:13–15.
[591] Alma 42:14.
[592] See Alma 42:13–15.

The covenant of mercy called for the Father to provide an atoning Savior to balance the demands of justice against the purposes of mercy: "And now, the plan of mercy could not be brought about except an atonement should be made; therefore God himself [Jesus Christ] atoneth for the sins of the world, to bring about the plan of mercy, to appease the demands of justice, that God might be a perfect, just God, and a merciful God also."[593] Mercy would also allow the children of God to receive physical bodies like their Father's, with the assurance that these eternal gifts would not be cancelled out by death. The Savior's merciful universal resurrection would make that possible.[594]

Accessing the benefits of mercy through the Atonement was decreed to be a matter of individual choice. To facilitate that choice, the Father instigated a covenant that we could choose to embrace if we desired to access the Atonement, draw upon its mercy, receive shelter from the demands of justice, and be placed beyond the reach of our enemies. This covenant is called the new and everlasting covenant, and we enter it by our individual agency.

Placed beyond Our Enemies

The Atonement makes goodness, righteousness, happiness, and salvation possible. According to Joseph Smith, salvation is the power to be placed beyond the reach of one's enemies.[595] The specific enemy he spoke of was death, but, as Brother Riddle says, "The great enemy of each human being is himself, for in our weakness and selfishness we are and do evil."[596] We, alone, can neither save ourselves nor fully overcome our weakness or selfishness.

Overcoming our natural selves and our enemies is made possible "only if we fully cooperate with Jesus Christ."[597] He has the ability to cleanse us completely of the stains of our evildoing and to transform us into righteous individuals who have no more desires to do evil.[598] This process leads to progressively higher levels of happiness. By entering into the new and everlasting covenant for the purpose of accepting the Atonement of Jesus Christ, a repentant person can be "rescued from being and doing evil" through the "merits and mercy of the Son of God."[599]

How Mercy Appeases Justice

That mercy is a covenant is an essential truth. Every covenant or law of God is obeyed or disobeyed by individual choice. Specific blessings and consequences are associated with that choice, and either misery or happiness results. If we desire mercy, we must live the covenant associated with mercy. As we have learned, that covenant is the new and everlasting covenant, which we are required to receive in order to accept Jesus Christ and his Atonement. It is a truth that this Covenant springs from the Atonement and is the instrument by which we are justified to receive the Lord's mercy and by which the plan of happiness is realized.

Clearly, the new and everlasting covenant activates the plan of redemption. By means of this Covenant, the Father's children can receive celestial laws and experiment with them without being destroyed by them. By means of the Covenant, the children of God can lay hold on the blessings of the Atonement by choosing to repent, progress, obtain salvation, become like God, and inherit all that he has. This is the ultimate condition of Zion people. The new and everlasting covenant also sets us on the defined path that leads to eternal life, gives us the authority of God, places in our hands the *keys* (not priesthood administrative keys) to God's knowledge and power, and sets us up in our

---

[593] Alma 42:15.
[594] See Alma 11:44.
[595] Smith, *Teachings of the Prophet Joseph Smith*, 305.
[596] Acts 4:12.
[597] Riddle, "The New and Everlasting Covenant," 225–26.
[598] Alma 19:33.
[599] Riddle, "The New and Everlasting Covenant," 225.

individual eternal kingdoms. Only the Atonement itself exceeds in glory the magnificence of the new and everlasting covenant. The two are inseparable, and both answer the end-purpose of the Father's plan of mercy: *our happiness.*

Experiencing Contrasts Leads to Happiness

To lay hold on the plan of happiness, we must be presented with two contrasting revelations: (1) God and his goodness, and (2) our fallen situation. Because agency is crucial, the Lord uses contrast to motivate us to choose between these opposites.

As we have noted, there are good and bad consequences attached to God's laws. Breaking his commandments always results in being "cut off both temporally and spiritually from the presence of the Lord."[600] This is misery, which Alma described as "the gall of bitterness," and being "encircled about by the everlasting chains of death."[601] On the other hand, happiness always results from being brought, through our obedience, into "the marvelous light of God."[602] For instance, after Alma had been "racked with eternal torment" for his sins and "harrowed to the greatest degree,"[603] he appealed to the Savior and suddenly swung from misery to happiness. He moved from "inexpressible horror" to "exquisite and sweet"[604] joy, from the "pains of a damned soul" to experiencing redemption and seeing "God sitting upon his throne, surrounded with numberless concourses of angels," with his soul longing to be there.[605] He exulted, "Oh, what joy, and what marvelous light I did behold." Then describing the contrast, "My soul was filled with joy as exceeding as was my pain."[606]

Clearly, seeing the contrast between good and evil motivates us toward happiness. After the Lord appeared to Moses, he left him to himself and he was tempted by Satan. That contrast allowed Moses to experience the distinct difference between having the Lord and not having the Lord with him: "Now, for this cause I know that man is nothing, which thing I never had supposed." Moses also perceived the contrasting differences in glory between the Lord and Satan: "Moses looked upon Satan and said: . . . where is thy glory that I should worship thee?"[607] Now that Moses had experienced these contrasting visions, he was empowered to choose between misery and happiness. He said, "Depart from me, Satan, for this one God only will I worship, which is the God of glory."[608]

Similarly, but in reverse order, King Benjamin's people literally collapsed when they "viewed themselves in their own carnal state, even less than the dust of the earth." Then, after they cried out to the Lord for mercy, "the Spirit of the Lord came upon them, and they were filled with joy, having received a remission of their sins, and having peace of conscience."[609] Happiness came only after they experienced the contrast.

Similarly, and in a unique way, the Lord will offer us happiness by helping us understand who he is and showing us who and where we are. Then we, like King Benjamin's people, might be so astonished that we cry out for mercy and deliverance. Hopefully, when we are offered deliverance, we will choose to embrace it with all our hearts. The account of King Benjamin and his people teach us the truth that mercy, deliverance, and eternal happiness are available to us only through the new and everlasting covenant. We note that King Benjamin's people were willing "to enter into a covenant

---

[600] Alma 42:7.
[601] Alma 36:18.
[602] Mosiah 27:29.
[603] Alma 36:12.
[604] Alma 36:14, 21.
[605] Alma 36:16, 19–22.
[606] Alma 36:20.
[607] Moses 1:10, 13.
[608] Moses 1:20.
[609] Mosiah 4:12–13.

with [their] God to do his will, and to be obedient to his commandments in all things that he [would] command [them], all the remainder of [their] days."[610]

Covenant-making leads to deliverance, which leads to happiness. After we have made a covenant and experienced deliverance and happiness, we will never want to return to our miserable past. Our desire now centers on the Lord sending the Holy Ghost to transform us into new creatures with new hearts. Because that process is beyond our ability, we look to Christ. To achieve a change of heart, we must first accept Jesus Christ and his Atonement, enter into a covenant of salvation with him, and cooperate with him to the fullest extent.[611] Moreover, we must fully submit to his incomparable power and trust him as he remakes us into new creatures by planting the seeds of salvation and happiness into our souls.[612] "Thus human beings may become good and may become gods."[613]

To summarize, the Father, the Son, and the Holy Ghost entered into a premortal covenant to save and exalt the Father's children. A primary purpose of that covenant was that the children achieve ultimate happiness. Therefore, the Gods initiated the plan of happiness, which called for the Father to reveal the system of celestial laws that made him who he is and gave him what he has. The Gods knew that in the process of our learning those laws, we, God's children, would inevitably break the laws and become liable to pay severe penalties. Therefore, to mitigate the adverse effects of broken laws, the Gods initiated the Plan of Redemption, or the Plan of Mercy. That plan called for the Father to provide a Savior to rescue us from death and to atone for the consequences of broken celestial laws. The blessings of mercy through this plan could be accessed only by law and by choice; therefore, the Father established the new and everlasting covenant. Now his children could agree to obey this new law that would provide mercy, and God in turn would agree to set aside "the demands of justice."[614] Thus, justice could be satisfied, mercy could rescue and claim her own, and the children of God could progress in the Covenant until they achieved salvation, exaltation, and ultimate happiness, as the Gods had planned in the beginning.

Overview of the New and Everlasting Covenant

The new and everlasting covenant consists of two primary covenants: the covenant of baptism, and the oath and covenant of the priesthood.

The fulness of the priesthood covenant comes through (1) ordination for worthy men; (2) temple covenants and ordinances for worthy men and women; (3) the temple sealing covenant, which is called the covenant of exaltation,[615] for worthy men and women.

Combined, the new and everlasting covenant and its supporting covenants serve to cleanse us, separate us from the world, prepare us for coronation, and protect us from Satan. They endow us with keys to the knowledge and power of God, and they establish us in our eternal kingdoms. Collectively, these covenants and the laws of God embrace the new and everlasting covenant.[616] When we enter

---

[610] Mosiah 5:5.

[611] 2 Nephi 25:28.

[612] 2 Corinthians 5:17.

[613] Riddle, "The New and Everlasting Covenant," 226.

[614] Alma 42:15.

[615] See Nelson, *The Power within Us*, 136; Smith, *Doctrines of Salvation*, 2:58. Note: Elder McConkie stated that men make a covenant of exaltation twice: once upon ordination to the Melchizedek Priesthood and again at the time of the marriage sealing: "Ordination to office in the Melchizedek priesthood and entering into that 'order of the priesthood' named 'the new and everlasting covenant of marriage' are both occasions when men make the covenant of exaltation, being promised through their faithfulness all that the Father hath (D&C 131:1–4; 84:39–41; 132; Num. 25:13)." (*Mormon Doctrine*, 167.)

[616] McConkie, *Mormon Doctrine*, 529–30.

into the new and everlasting covenant, the Atonement satisfies the demands of justice that we cannot pay and encircles us in mercy's "arms of safety."[617]

THE COVENANT OF JUSTICE

Let us examine in depth the covenants of justice and mercy.

As we learned, the covenant of justice grew out of the premortal covenant of the Gods to provide the Father's children with consummate happiness. That could not happen unless the children were presented with the laws that the Father had obeyed that resulted in his exalted status. Therefore, to fulfill that premortal covenant, the Father revealed to us the pattern of his lifestyle, which pattern allows him to be both perfect and perfectly *just*. This pattern consists of obeying the immutable laws that govern him and all celestial beings. The purpose of the Father's revelation of these laws was to provide us the roadmap to follow to become just in the way that the Father is just. This purpose is central to the covenant of justice. Joseph Smith taught that "God Himself found Himself in the midst of spirits and glory. Because He was greater He saw proper to institute laws whereby the rest, who were less in intelligence, could have a privilege to advance like Himself and be exalted with Him, so that they might have one glory upon another in all that knowledge, power, and glory. So He took in hand to save the world of spirits."[618]

To that end, the Father decreed a single *umbrella law* that would govern all other laws: "There is *a law*, irrevocably decreed in heaven before the foundations of this world, upon which all blessings are predicated."[619] That is, atop the covenant of justice stands the supreme umbrella law, under which *every other* law of God exists; each of God's laws must be comprised of two things: immutable blessings ("when we obtain any blessing from God, it is by obedience to that law upon which it is predicated"[620]), and immutable punishments ("all mankind . . . were in the grasp of justice . . . which consigned them forever to be cut off from his presence"[621]).

WHO ARE THE JUST, AND HOW ARE THEY JUSTIFIED?

We read of an early manifestation of the covenant of justice, including its blessings and punishments, when the Gods stated their purpose for creating the world: "And we will prove them herewith, to see if they will do all things whatsoever the Lord their God shall command them; and they who keep their first estate shall be added upon; and they who keep not their first estate shall not have glory in the same kingdom with those who keep their first estate; and they who keep their second estate shall have glory added upon their heads for ever and ever."[622] Those who keep their second estate and receive eternal glory are called "the just," an appellation that seems to suggest that they are in the process of being fashioned in the similitude of God, who is fully just. They are those who: (1) have been "faithful in the testimony of Jesus while they lived in mortality," (2) have "offered sacrifice in the similitude of the great sacrifice of the Son of God," and (3) have "suffered tribulation in their Redeemer's name."[623] That is, faithfulness, willingness to sacrifice, and suffering tribulation while remaining true describe the just. Clearly, those who are "just" *chose* to become just by obeying celestial laws in the same way God obeyed them. Therefore, according to the covenant of justice, they are *justified* in receiving the blessings associated with obeyed laws.

The Lord describes the just and their blessings this way:

---

[617] Alma 34:16.
[618] Larson, "The King Follett Discourse," 204.
[619] D&C 130:20.
[620] D&C 130:21.
[621] D&C 1:31.
[622] Abraham 3:25–26.
[623] D&C 138:12–13.

They are they who received the testimony of Jesus, and believed on his name and were baptized after the manner of his burial, being buried in the water in his name, and this according to the commandment which he has given—

That by keeping the commandments they might be washed and cleansed from all their sins, and receive the Holy Spirit by the laying on of the hands of him who is ordained and sealed unto this power;

And who overcome by faith, and are sealed by the Holy Spirit of promise, which the Father sheds forth upon all those who are just and true.

They are they who are the church of the Firstborn.

They are they into whose hands the Father has given all things—

They are they who are priests and kings, who have received of his fulness, and of his glory;

And are priests of the Most High, after the order of Melchizedek, which was after the order of Enoch, which was after the order of the Only Begotten Son.

Wherefore, as it is written, they are gods, even the sons of God—

Wherefore, all things are theirs, whether life or death, or things present, or things to come, all are theirs and they are Christ's, and Christ is God's.

And they shall overcome all things.

Wherefore, let no man glory in man, but rather let him glory in God, who shall subdue all enemies under his feet.

These shall dwell in the presence of God and his Christ forever and ever.

These are they whom he shall bring with him, when he shall come in the clouds of heaven to reign on the earth over his people.

These are they who shall have part in the first resurrection.

These are they who shall come forth in the resurrection of the just.

These are they who are come unto Mount Zion, and unto the city of the living God, the heavenly place, the holiest of all.

These are they who have come to an innumerable company of angels, to the general assembly and church of Enoch, and of the Firstborn.

These are they whose names are written in heaven, where God and Christ are the judge of all.

These are they who are just men made perfect through Jesus the mediator of the new covenant, who wrought out this perfect atonement through the shedding of his own blood.

These are they whose bodies are celestial, whose glory is that of the sun, even the glory of God, the highest of all, whose glory the sun of the firmament is written of as being typical.[624]

---

[624] D&C 76:51–70.

Justification and Agency

The covenant of justice could not function without agency. It was to be by choice that we could become just and justified for the highest blessings. Our choice would translate into obedience to God's laws, which we would be required to obey by sacrifice.[625] That is, in the process of obeying a law, we are always faced with alternatives, and thus we must sacrifice all other choices in favor of choosing one course of action. Thus it was determined in the beginning that obedience to God's laws would be proven by sacrifice, and that the combination of obedience and sacrifice would justify us for blessings. That is, we would be exalted in proportion to our obedience and sacrifice. Let us note here that we are attempting to explore the law of justice more deeply than is typically understood.

The Fall became the perfect environment in which obedience and sacrifice could be best demonstrated. Clearly, to choose to obey by sacrifice without memory of our premortal existence with Heavenly Father defines the desires of heart. The Fall provided an atmosphere in which each person could "see for himself if he [would] choose good or evil."[626] Here in mortality it is decided once and for all if we can be forever trusted with the Father's unlimited knowledge and power.

Brother Riddle explains the covenant of justice this way:

> The conditions of the first covenant, the covenant of justice, were these: 1. Father would give his children instruction and commandments. 2. Any child who would believe Father and obey his every commandment, without exception, would in that obedience grow to attain and maintain all the good that Father is and does, which is exaltation. 3. Any child who disobeyed any single commandment of Father, would, without exception, immediately die spiritually, which spiritual death is to be cut off from Father's presence, no longer to be able to grow in his order of good (Alma 42:14). 4. For every transgression of a commandment of Father, the offender must suffer for that sin and make full restitution for that sin, this suffering and restitution being at least equal to the suffering and loss caused to the person(s) against whom the transgression was committed (Alma 42:22–28).[627]

Why is justice termed a *covenant* here? Because every person who desired to progress and become like God had to agree that: (1) God is the supreme lawgiver; (2) his laws are just; and (3) we would accept the consequences of his laws, which would either qualify us for immutable blessings or condemn us to eternal punishments. Perhaps a reason why Satan's followers were cast out of heaven[628] was that they refused to enter into the covenant of justice. When they rejected God and his covenant, they suffered the law's eternal consequences. The important point is this: Each one of us voluntarily entered into the covenant of justice and agreed to its terms; otherwise we would not be here. This was the covenant by which we gained a physical body, earned the privilege of experiencing mortality, and received the opportunity to choose eternal life and exaltation.

---

[625] D&C 97:8.
[626] Riddle, "The New and Everlasting Covenant," 227.
[627] Riddle, "The New and Everlasting Covenant," 228.
[628] See Moses 4:1–2; Revelation 12:7–11.

Celestial Law

The covenant of justice is comprised of laws that qualify us for celestial glory. Often stated in the singular, these laws are called the *Celestial Law,* or the *Law of Christ,* or the *Law of the Celestial Kingdom,* or the *Law of the Gospel.* The celestial law, according to Elder McConkie, is "that law by obedience to which men gain an inheritance in the Kingdom of God. . . . It is the law of the gospel [that] qualifies men for admission to the Celestial Kingdom."[629] "And they who are not sanctified through the law which I have given unto you, even the *law of Christ* [or the celestial law], must inherit another kingdom, even that of a terrestrial kingdom, or that of a telestial kingdom. For he who is not able to abide the law of a celestial kingdom cannot abide a celestial glory."[630] Elder McConkie ties the celestial law or the law of Christ to Zion people: "Those who have the companionship of the Holy Ghost and are guided thereby in their lives are 'able to abide the law of a Celestial Kingdom,' including the Law of Consecration or anything else the Lord might ask of them. They are the ones who—'united according to the union required by the law of the celestial kingdom' (D&C 105:1–5)—will build up Zion in the last days."[631]

If we desire to achieve the celestial kingdom, we must set our sights higher than the telestial world in which we live; we must look beyond the telestial laws that govern such a world. That is not easy. Whenever we encounter any celestial law, we are hard-pressed to explain it. We often suffer culture shock when something celestial is manifested in our telestial environment.

God's celestial laws do not make much sense here. For instance, how can God travel at the speed of *thought* when science claims that nothing can exceed the speed of light? Or how can God know every detail of the future as if he were viewing it in present time? Or how is he able to be with each person individually when there are billions of us pleading for his attention at any given moment? The questions continue. For instance, how could water sustain the weight of a man and allow him to walk upon it as though it were solid pavement? And, speaking of water, how could it be instantly transformed into wine that had the taste of vintage aging? Moreover, how could a few fishes and loaves of bread feed thousands *until they were filled* and the quantity of the remnants exceed the original resource? How could the resurrected Savior invite some 2,500 people to step forward one by one and touch his wounds, organize the apostles, teach major sermons, instruct the people on prayer, explain his mission concerning the entire house of Israel, prophesy, invite all 2,500 to come to him again and this time bring their sick to be healed, then pray for the people, bless the children with angelic ministrations, instruct them concerning the sacrament, give the apostles power to confer the Holy Ghost—*and do this during the daylight hours of a single day?*[632] Or, on a more personal basis, how can a newly ordained elder become the agent of healing by simply speaking words? How can paying 10 percent result in an amount greater than the original principal? How can the consecration of time, talents, and resources result in prosperity rather than poverty? Clearly, celestial laws are foreign here, but, nevertheless, we must embrace them if we ever hope to become Zion people.

Preserved, Perfected, and Sanctified by the Laws of God

Flight is a complicated process wholly dependent upon adherence to the laws of aerodynamics. By obeying these laws, gravitation works for us rather than against us. To achieve flight, the wing of a plane must be thick and rounded on the upper surface and flat on the lower surface. Thus, the air that flows over the wing accelerates and becomes thinner than the air that flows under the wing. The difference in air density over and under the wing gives the airplane lift. The aircraft suddenly becomes

---

[629] McConkie, *Mormon Doctrine,* 117.
[630] D&C 88:21–22; emphasis added.
[631] McConkie, *Mormon Doctrine,* 117.
[632] 3 Nephi 12–17.

buoyant like a boat floating on water; it is as though the plane is floating on air. Without interrupting the laws of gravitation, volume, mass, and velocity, but rather by applying them and causing them to work together, flight becomes possible.

So it is with the celestial laws of God. Obeyed, they result in a level of safety, security, power, and exaltation that otherwise would not be achievable. Broken, they result in danger, instability, helplessness, and damnation. Renowned filmmaker Cecil B. DeMille said, "We cannot break the Ten Commandments. We can only break ourselves against them."[633]

The Lord revealed to Joseph Smith the power of obedience to the celestial law: "And again, verily I say unto you, *that which is governed by law is also preserved by law and perfected and sanctified by the same.* That which breaketh a law, and abideth not by law, but seeketh to become a law unto itself, and willeth to abide in sin, and altogether abideth in sin, cannot be sanctified by law, neither by mercy, justice, nor judgment. Therefore, they must remain filthy still."[634] If a person insists on becoming a law unto himself, he will earn the telestial kingdom, where he can never hope to be preserved by the celestial law. Prisons are filled with people who reject law, and cemeteries contain the remains of many who broke themselves against the laws.

With regard to obeying the celestial law, we have a choice: we can remain forever telestially earthbound, or we can apply the laws of celestial flight and soar. "All kingdoms have a law given," the Lord said. "And unto every kingdom is given a law; and unto every law there are certain bounds also and conditions. All beings who abide not in those conditions are not justified."[635] We cannot expect to live a telestial law and achieve celestial benefits. If the celestial kingdom is our goal, we must learn and embrace the celestial law. This law alone will *preserve, perfect, and sanctify* us in that exalted kingdom.

Blessed As If We Understood

Amazingly, our obeying a law that we do not fully understand will still result in our receiving that law's benefits. Without our fully comprehending the laws of aerodynamics, we are still willing to board airplanes and fly from one destination to another. Our faith is in the laws that make flight possible. We believe that they are constant and will not fail; therefore, most of us climb aboard planes in faith rather than by knowledge.

Our obeying celestial law "as a child, submissive, meek, humble, patient,"[636] results in our receiving the law's blessings *as if we fully understood*. Over time, as we have more experience with the laws of God, we receive more understanding and our faith is quickened; that understanding will increase until we know all that God knows. Until then we progress in the safety, and the preserving, perfecting, and sanctifying power of the celestial law, with faith that the purpose of the law is to make of us Saints "through the atonement of Jesus Christ."[637] The end-purpose of celestial law, of course, is to make of us celestial people, who, by definition, are people of Zion.

The Covenant of Mercy

The Father knew that once we had a physical body and began to encounter good and evil, we would inevitably sometimes choose wrong. Broken laws of God carry severe consequences. In addition to specific penalties, the covenant of justice universally demands that each divine broken law carry the penalty of *spiritual death*,[638] the consequence that means we are cut off from God forever.[639] No more

---

[633] DeMille, *BYU Speeches of the Year*, May 31, 1957, 6.
[634] D&C 88:34–35.
[635] D&C 88:36, 38–39.
[636] Mosiah 3:19.
[637] Mosiah 3:19.
[638] 2 Nephi 9:12.

are we fit for the celestial kingdom; the condition of having or being in the presence of God is one of perfection: "Wherefore . . . all men, everywhere, must repent, or they can in nowise inherit the kingdom of God, for no unclean thing can dwell there, or dwell in his presence."[640] We immediately see the harshness of justice and the necessity of mercy. Because all of us have fallen short and are separated from God by the demands of justice, we are, and would be forever, subject to Satan, and therefore miserable, were it not for the Lord's merciful intervention.

So that we could learn from our mistakes without being destroyed by them, God established a second covenant, the covenant of mercy. From the beginning, the Father's plan determined that the Atonement would serve as the foundation of the covenant of mercy. Without the Atonement, our agency would prove irreparably fatal. "And thus we see that all mankind were fallen, and they were in the grasp of justice; yea, the justice of God, which consigned them forever to be cut off from his presence."[641]

According to professor Chauncey C. Riddle, the covenant of mercy is called the new and everlasting covenant. It is *new* "because it is the second covenant (see Moses 6:56)," meaning that it follows the first covenant, which is the covenant of justice.[642] The covenant of mercy is also new because it is "revealed *new*"[643] to each person who receives it. The covenant is everlasting in that "the gospel is the everlasting covenant because it is ordained by Him who is Everlasting and also because it is everlastingly the same."[644] If we obey the terms of the covenant of mercy (which will be explained later), we gain access to the Atonement, which has power to pay the price of our sins, and encircle us in the arms of safety.[645]

Mercy and Grace

The Atonement provides us with the Savior's grace or enabling power, so that we might grow and learn from our mistakes while we try to adopt the celestial laws as a way of life. We access the Atonement by the new and everlasting covenant. The Atonement rescues us from physical and spiritual death, the negative effects of the Fall, the demands of justice, and the chains of Satan. The merciful Atonement of Jesus Christ recompenses every wrong perpetrated upon or suffered by us, reconciles us to God, and transforms us into celestial beings. "And now, the plan of mercy could not be brought about except an atonement should be made; therefore God himself [Jesus Christ] atoneth for the sins of the world, to bring about the plan of mercy, to appease the demands of justice, that God [the Father] might be a perfect, just God, and a merciful God also."[646] By means of the Atonement of Jesus Christ and on the condition of repentance, every obstacle that stands between us and exaltation is eliminated.

By God's grace, mercy rehabilitates the sinner. Mercy does not call for us to recompense the Savior for his redeeming efforts; mercy does, however, ask that we repent and change so that we become more Christlike.[647]

Every person who has inhabited or will inhabit this earth chose the Father's plan over Satan's plan by accepting the Father's covenants of justice and mercy. Moreover, each member of the human race, from the worst to the best, covenanted in the premortal world to reject Satan and accept Jesus

---

[639] Alma 42:14.
[640] Moses 6:57.
[641] Alma 42:14.
[642] Riddle, "The New and Everlasting Covenant," 226, 228.
[643] McConkie, *Mormon Doctrine*, 530.
[644] McConkie, *Mormon Doctrine*, 529.
[645] Alma 34:16.
[646] Alma 42:15.
[647] See *Encyclopedia of Mormonism*, 776.

Christ as his or her personal Savior; otherwise we would not be here.[648] There was no other way to gain a physical body and receive the opportunity of mortality.

JUSTIFICATION

Within the new and everlasting covenant, the covenants of justice and mercy work hand in hand to make of us Zion people and propel us toward eternal life—to make us *just* or *justified*. We often think of justice in terms of inflicting penalties for sin, but justice also rewards us for obedience to God's eternal laws. Mercy assures that those rewards are given according to our best—not perfect—effort. As we have mentioned, this is a manifestation of *grace*—we do all that we can and Jesus Christ makes up the difference.[649] Thus, by obedience and grace, a child might be justified to receive the same reward for obedience as an apostle, as evidenced in the account of Third Nephi, when both the children and the apostles were equally blessed with access to the Savior, his teachings, healing, and heavenly ministrations. Justification, therefore, means to be judged worthy of the blessings that are specified by the laws of God on the basis of our best efforts. In the end, of course, we understand that all blessings come to us by the merits of Jesus Christ.[650] We cannot obtain any blessing from God, become just, attain to Zion, or obtain inheritance in the celestial kingdom without being justified by obeying God's laws and by applying the grace that is available through the mercy of Jesus Christ.

The Holy Ghost is the Savior's *justifying* agent. Elder McConkie wrote: "What then is the law of justification? It is simply this: 'All covenants, contracts, bonds, obligations, oaths, vows, performances, connections, associations, or expectations' (D&C 132:7), in which men must abide to be saved and exalted, must be entered into and performed in righteousness so that the Holy Spirit can justify the candidate for salvation in what has been done. (1 Ne. 16:2; Jac. 2:13–14; Alma 41:15; D. & C. 98; 132:1, 62.) *An act that is justified by the Spirit is one that is sealed by the Holy Spirit of Promise, or in other words, ratified and approved by the Holy Ghost.*"[651]

Some of the most definitive statements on justification are found in the Sermon on the Mount and the Sermon at the Nephite Temple.[652] Brother Riddle says, "The Book of Mormon is the scripture that lays out with great clarity justification both as a process and a product [see Alma 5]."[653] Only by entering into the new and everlasting covenant can we exercise faith in Jesus Christ unto repentance, be cleansed from his sins through baptism, then live obediently by sacrifice so that the Holy Ghost can justify us to receive the prescribed blessings affixed to the laws of God. By this process, and by this only, can we truly become just.

PURIFICATION

Purification and sanctification are words that are often interchanged. That they are closely associated is evident. In this book, we will define *purification* as extracting any impurities that would stand between us and perfection; we will define *sanctification* as changing the purpose of something. (These will be explained more fully shortly.) We enter the new and everlasting covenant to draw upon the Atonement and become pure and therefore Zionlike.

Zion people are purified people; they are the "pure in heart."[654] Quoting Brother Riddle: "[The Atonement of Jesus Christ has the power to] reach into our bosom and give each of us a new

---

[648] McConkie, *Mormon Doctrine*, 828.
[649] *LDS Bible Dictionary*, "Grace," 697.
[650] 2 Nephi 31:19; Moroni 6:4.
[651] McConkie, *Mormon Doctrine*, 408; emphasis added.
[652] Matthew 5–7; 3 Nephi 12–14.
[653] Riddle, "The New and Everlasting Covenant," 234.
[654] D&C 97:21.

heart."[655] Purification flows from the covenant of mercy; by covenant we agree to allow the Lord to extract from our lives all impurities and pollutions that would stand between us and the celestial kingdom. This is necessary because, ultimately, our desire to become Zionlike will require divine intervention: "To pour light and truth into the human vessel is not enough. As a child of Christ attempts to love the light and truth . . . each becomes aware of an alarming fact: having light and truth is no guarantee of being able to do what is right."[656] Only the Atonement can purify a heart.

Purification is dependent upon two factors: (1) our complete effort to change and make amends, and (2) the grace of Jesus Christ to do for us what lies beyond our ability to do. The Savior is the Purifier, but the agent for the purification process is the Holy Ghost: "The Holy Ghost is also a Purifier in that, because of Christ and the Atonement, this Spirit member of the Godhead has power given him to cleanse, sanctify, and purify the human soul. (3 Ne. 27:19–21.)"[657] The process of purification is often called the baptism of fire.[658] We are fully immersed in the heat of the Lord's furnace to burn out of us all impurities. The Holy Ghost will persist in the process until he can commend us to God as being pure, that is, "true and faithful in all things" in the similitude of "Him whose very name is 'Faithful and True.'"[659]

We must do our part to purify ourselves, but in the end we will need the Holy Ghost and the Savior to make us completely pure. Brother Riddle said:

> If we have repented of every sin we can repent of, have made fourfold restitution as far as we are able [D&C 98:44; Luke 19:8], and have been reconciled to our brother [Matthew 5:23–24], we may present ourselves at the altar with a broken heart and a contrite spirit [2 Nephi 2:7] and plead in mighty prayer for this change of heart [Mormon 7:48; Mosiah 4:2]. Then and only then will our Savior reach in and give us a new heart. The new heart will be a pure heart, one that has no selfish desires, one that is willing to do the right thing. It will choose to do the will of God at all times and places, no matter what the opposition or the sacrifice involved.
>
> This new heart is made in the image of Jesus Christ, that same heart that enabled our Savior to say, "Father, not my will, but thine be done," that same heart that enabled him to live a sinless life, that same heart for which he was chosen to be the Firstborn and to be the Only Begotten. To be purified is to become literally a new creature in Christ, to die as to the old person that we were, literally to become of the heart and mind of [Christ]. The scriptures promise great rewards for those who qualify and take this step. The scriptural name for this new heart is "charity." Charity is to have a heart that loves with the pure love of Christ.[660]

---

[655] Riddle, "The New and Everlasting Covenant," 236.
[656] Riddle, "The New and Everlasting Covenant," 236.
[657] McConkie, *Mormon Doctrine*, 612.
[658] 2 Nephi 31:13–14; D&C 20:41; 33:11; 39:6.
[659] McConkie, *A New Witness for the Articles of Faith*, 316.
[660] Riddle, "The New and Everlasting Covenant," 236–37.

Sanctification

Like purification, sanctification also flows from the covenant of mercy, which is the new and everlasting covenant. As much as we enter the Covenant to receive the blessings of the Atonement and become purified, we also enter the Covenant to be sanctified.

Sanctification is the *result* of being purified. When the contaminants, pollutions, and alloys have been burned from our souls, we emerge from the furnace sanctified; that is, we now have a new purpose. Let us examine, for example, the sacrament prayer, in which the priests bless and sanctify "profane" bread and, by the priesthood, change its purpose to calling us to remembrance of the body of Jesus Christ,[661] the Bread of Life.[662] Now blessed and sanctified (or "made holy"), the bread's purpose has changed from sustaining physical life to sustaining spiritual life. Likewise, a pile of stones can, by the priesthood, be changed in purpose to become an altar: "And thou shalt anoint the altar of the burnt offering, and all his vessels, and sanctify the altar: and it shall be an altar most holy."[663] Or a natural man can be purified of sin, then sanctified by the Holy Ghost, so that his purpose now becomes that of service to God: "And thou shalt put them upon Aaron thy brother, and his sons with him; and shalt anoint them, and consecrate them, and sanctify them, that they may minister unto me in the priest's office."[664]

The Savior sanctifies us through the Atonement, but the Holy Ghost is the agent of sanctification,[665] just as he is the agent of purification.[666] The Holy Ghost rids us of impurities so that he might change our purpose. This is purification and sanctification. We have a responsibility in receiving these blessings. We must actively participate in the process as the Savior and the Holy Ghost purify and sanctify us. The Lord commanded: "Sanctify yourselves; yea purify your hearts, and cleanse your hands and your feet before me, that I may make you clean."[667] None of this is possible outside the Covenant.

Our Responsibility

Our part of the sanctifying process requires that we separate ourselves from Babylon and all that is profane, unholy, and ungodly. To accomplish this, wrote *Mormon Times* editor Joseph A. Cannon, "We fast and pray, we 'wax stronger' in our humility and become 'firmer in the faith of Christ . . . even to the purifying and the sanctification of [our] hearts, which sanctification cometh because of [our] yielding [our] hearts unto God' (Helaman 3:35). If we 'come unto Christ' and 'deny [our]selves of all ungodliness' and yield our hearts to God, then we are 'sanctified in Christ by the grace of God through the shedding of the blood of Christ.' It is through this [process] that we can 'become holy [sanctified] without spot.' (Moroni 10:32–33)."[668] Thus each of us is commanded: "sanctify yourselves that your minds become single to God."[669]

Our effort to purify and sanctify ourselves begins with faith in Jesus Christ; we must believe that he has the power to cleanse and transform us, and we must trust in his methods and his timing. Faith in Jesus Christ—*true faith*—always leads to repentance; we must eliminate the impurities from our souls and change our purpose. Repentance leads to covenant-making; we desire to legitimize our resolve by entering into an agreement with the Lord for him to purify, sanctify, and make us in every

---

[661] D&C 20:77.
[662] John 6:35.
[663] Exodus 40:10.
[664] Exodus 28:41.
[665] McConkie, *The Mortal Messiah*, 4:114.
[666] Alma 13:11–12; 3 Nephi 27:19–21; D&C 84:33.
[667] D&C 88:74.
[668] Cannon, *Mormon Times*, June 12, 2008.
[669] D&C 88:68.

way fit for the celestial kingdom. That agreement is called the new and everlasting covenant, and we enter that Covenant by the covenant of baptism. Now we are pronounced clean, but we are not yet pure and sanctified. For that reason, we receive a special gift: the gift of the consummate purifying and sanctifying agent, the Holy Ghost.[670]

Reception of the gift of the Holy Ghost is the baptism of fire spoken of in the scriptures.[671] When a person enters into the new and everlasting covenant, he does so for the purposes of receiving relief from his sins and starting down the path to becoming like God. That process of transformation requires burning out of him the impurities that made him a sinful "natural man,"[672] then molding him into a new creature,[673] a Saint,[674] to assume the image of God.[675]

The Crucible—The Baptism of Fire

A common metaphor for this sanctification process is the making of steel. When raw ore is placed in a crucible and heated in a furnace, the substance becomes molten and the properties separate. At that point, a skilled metallurgist can divide out the impurities from the pure, refined iron. An alloying process ensues, whereby the metallurgist carefully combines select elements in perfect proportion with the pure iron. The result is steel. But the process is not yet complete. For steel to become strong and not brittle, it must be subjected to reheating in the furnace, which is followed by pounding to align the molecules into their strongest position. The process of being thrust into the furnace and beaten is repeated multiple times until the steel is free from impurities and aligned so that it cannot be broken. At some point, the metallurgist pours the steel into a mold to change its purpose, and as a final step he polishes it. The finished product is incredibly strong and beautiful and it will remain so indefinitely.

In a similar manner, we are immersed in the crucibles attendant to the mortal experience, those fiery trials that heat, pound, mold, and polish us so that we might be purified, sanctified, and conformed to the image of God.[676] The Lord has every right to do this. We agreed to it when we entered into the new and everlasting covenant. John Taylor wrote: "I heard the Prophet Joseph say, in speaking to the Twelve on one occasion: 'You will have all kinds of trials to pass through. And it is quite as necessary for you to be tried as it was for Abraham and other men of God, and (said he) God will feel after you, and He will take hold of you and wrench your very heart strings, and if you cannot stand it you will not be fit for an inheritance in the Celestial Kingdom of God.'"[677]

Purified and Sanctified to Make an Offering

When we entered into the new and everlasting covenant, we agreed to submit to the Lord's crucible and allow him to make of us what we could not make of ourselves, and we also agreed to make an offering in righteousness. We read: "And he shall sit as a refiner and purifier of silver; and he shall purify the sons of Levi, and purge them as gold and silver, that they may offer unto the Lord an offering in righteousness."[678] We qualify as the sons of Levi. When we enter into the Melchizedek Priesthood, we become the sons of Aaron—who was the son of Levi—and the sons of Moses.[679] The offerings required of us are twofold: (1) a broken heart and a contrite spirit—"And ye shall offer for a

---

[670] 2 Nephi 27:19–21.
[671] See 2 Nephi 31:13–14; D&C 20:41; 33:11; 39:6.
[672] Mosiah 3:19.
[673] JST 2 Corinthians 5:17.
[674] Mosiah 3:19.
[675] Alma 5:19.
[676] Romans 8:29.
[677] Taylor, *Journal of Discourses*, 24:197.
[678] 3 Nephi 24:3; D&C 128:24.
[679] D&C 84:31–34.

sacrifice unto me a broken heart and a contrite spirit. And whoso cometh unto me with a broken heart and a contrite spirit, him will I baptize with fire and with the Holy Ghost"[680]—and (2) "a book containing the records of our dead."[681]

Job understood the process and submitted to the Lord's crucible: "When he hath tried me, I shall come forth as gold."[682] Sometimes this process is called trying or chastisement, and we must endure it or forfeit our eternal inheritance: "My people must be tried in all things, that they may be prepared to receive the glory that I have for them, even the glory of Zion; and he that will not bear chastisement is not worthy of my kingdom."[683] Interestingly, the word *chastise* means more than to punish; it also means "to make chaste,"[684] or to purify. Job patiently endured the Lord's chastisement without murmuring. To murmur is to believe in God while simultaneously complaining about how he is managing the affairs of one's life. Job, by contrast, waited confidently on the Lord's deliverance from the crucible he was in. He followed the same admonition that Joseph Smith gave to the Saints: "Therefore, dearly beloved brethren, let us cheerfully do all things that lie in our power; and then may we stand still, with the utmost assurance, to see the salvation of God, and for his arm to be revealed."[685] Whereas murmuring postpones or cancels out blessings, cheerfully submitting in patience summons the Lord's deliverance.

Only the grace of Jesus Christ enables us to endure the heat of the purifying and sanctifying procedure while trusting him in the process. The Lord will strengthen us and uphold us until we can make an offering unto him in righteousness, which offering brings us finally to where we desired to be someday when we entered into the new and everlasting covenant. Only the Lord's grace can expunge us of all impurities; only his grace can transform us and give us a new purpose. The promises to those who are purified and sanctified are unequalled: "And unto him that repenteth and sanctifieth himself before the Lord shall be given eternal life."[686]

ONENESS OR UNIFICATION

A significant goal of the new and everlasting covenant is to make us *one*—one with the Father, the Son, and the Holy Ghost, one with our spouse, one with our family, one with the children of Zion. Oneness and separation are opposites. Whereas separation causes misery, oneness or unity results in joy. The Atonement restores that which was lost and reunites that which was separated: "The literal meaning of the word 'Atonement' is self-evident: At-one-ment, the act of unifying or bringing together what has been separated and estranged."[687] In the Atonement, we can readily see the principle of *oneness* as a central feature of the covenant of mercy or the new and everlasting covenant. Zion people are "of one heart and one mind"[688]; they are *one*.

The Atonement of Jesus Christ makes us whole, reconciled, and *one*. Alma referred to this condition of oneness as *restoration*.[689] Because the covenant of justice demands the separation of the sinner from God, because the condition of this telestial world is continual decay, deterioration, entropy, and corruption, and because physical death is the inevitable end of every mortal life form, the Father, in order to be just, established the Plan of Restoration as a manifestation of his mercy to

---

[680] 3 Nephi 9:20.
[681] D&C 128:24.
[682] Job 23:10.
[683] D&C 136:31.
[684] *Encyclopedia of Mormonism*, 264.
[685] D&C 123:17.
[686] D&C 133:62.
[687] *Encyclopedia of Mormonism*, 83.
[688] Moses 7:18.
[689] Alma 40–41.

restore everything to its proper order. Alma taught: "The plan of restoration is requisite with the justice of God; for it is requisite that all things should be restored to their proper order."[690] Furthermore, the Prophet Joseph Smith said, God glorifies himself "by saving [restoring] all that His hands had made, whether beasts, fowls, fishes or men."[691]

In gospel terms, *separation* is another term for *death*. The separation of a sinner from God is *spiritual death;* the separation of the physical body from the spirit is *physical death*. Our fallen condition is, by definition, a *death,* a separation from God that causes misery, and is, therefore, in need of the Lord's immediate attention and restoration: "All men that are in a state of nature, or I would say, in a carnal state, are in the gall of bitterness and in the bonds of iniquity; they are without God in the world, and they have gone contrary to the nature of God; therefore, they are in a state contrary to the nature of happiness."[692]

Death can take other forms. For example, husbands and wives can experience a kind of emotional death when they are separated by oppression, distance, time, lack of affection, indifference, neglect, abuse, unkind worlds, and physical death. Likewise, a type of death can be experienced in cases of the separation of children from parents, friends from friends, Saints from the Church, the gospel from the earth, people from their true identity and birthright, or individuals separated from their health, youth, innocence, rights, and possessions. When any estrangement or breach occurs, misery inevitably follows, and it can feel like a death; but when all is restored, joy and peace ensue.

As we have said, restoration to oneness and unity is a central purpose of the *At-one-ment*. By the Atonement, the spirit becomes *at one* with the body; the husband and the wife become *at one* with each other; children become *at one* with their parents; friends become *at one* with each other; Saints become *at one* with the Church and its doctrines; individuals become *at one* with or restored to their health, youth, innocence, rights, and possessions, and we become *at one* with God and his children. How is this done? When we enter into the new and everlasting covenant, the Savior wraps us in his atoning mercy, which is the power to repair every breach, overcome every form of death, restore all that was lost to its perfect order, return us to God, and make us *one* with him. The power of the Atonement is to make all things *at one* and to seal them together in a form that can attain to perfection. In that condition, the creation can eventually achieve a fulness of joy. The Lord's restoration is complete and perfect: "And not one hair, neither mote, shall be lost, for it is the workmanship of mine hand."[693]

But we must beware: The law of restoration functions according to our actions and our desires. Alma taught:

> If their works were good in this life, and the desires of their hearts were good, . . . they should also, at the last day, be restored unto that which is good. And if their works are evil they shall be restored unto them for evil. Therefore, all things shall be restored to their proper order, . . . the one raised to happiness according to his desires of happiness, or good according to his desires of good; and the other to evil according to his desires of evil; for as he has desired to do evil all the day long even so shall he have his reward of evil when the night cometh. And so it is on the other hand. If he hath repented of his sins, and desired righteousness until the end of his days, even

---

[690] Alma 41:2.
[691] Smith, *Teachings of the Prophet Joseph Smith,* 291.
[692] Alma 41:11.
[693] D&C 29:25.

so he shall be rewarded unto righteousness. . . . For that which ye do
send out shall return unto you again, and be restored.[694]

Oneness and the Law of Restoration

The law of restoration follows natural laws. Amoeba are not restored as fish; fish are not restored as apes; apes are not restored as humans; and wicked individuals are not restored as righteous people: "And now behold, is the meaning of the word restoration to take a thing of a natural state and place it in an unnatural state, or to place it in a state opposite to its nature? O, my son, this is not the case; but the meaning of the word restoration is to bring back again evil for evil, or carnal for carnal, or devilish for devilish—good for that which is good; righteous for that which is righteous; just for that which is just; merciful for that which is merciful. . . . Do not suppose, because it has been spoken concerning restoration, that ye shall be restored from sin to happiness. Behold, I say unto you, wickedness never was happiness."[695]

What has this to do with becoming a Zion person? Zion is always described in terms of perfection, beauty, unity, and oneness; furthermore, Zion is described as a condition of no lack—things that have been divided from us are now restored, and we experience abundance. This is the condition of Zion people. The Atonement and the Covenant are always drawing us toward these ideals. Therefore, the more we align ourselves with the purifying, sanctifying, and unifying motions of the Atonement, and the more we abide in the Covenant, the more Zionlike we become; the more *at one* we become with God and his children.

Restoration and Resurrection

The law of restoration becomes operational when we enter into the new and everlasting covenant, and the law reaches its zenith in the resurrection. Beyond being a victory over death and the eternal restoration of the body and spirit in "perfect form,"[696] the resurrection is the consummate event wherein everything that we have lost or been denied by reason of the Fall is restored. Joseph Smith said, "All your losses will be made up to you in the resurrection, provided you continue faithful."[697] As much as the Fall renders us temporarily but significantly impotent, as compared with our former stature, and exposes us to evil and unclean spirits, pain, illness, hunger, aging, and other kinds of physical distress, the resurrection restores to us every loss that we have experienced and repairs each defeat. It is almost an understatement when we read that "the Lamb . . . shall feed them, and shall lead them unto living fountains of waters: and God shall wipe away all tears from their eyes."[698] To the degree that we have suffered or been opposed or denied, we shall be restored to happiness. In fact, the Lord promised that we would be restored *an hundredfold*: "And every one that hath forsaken houses, or brethren, or sisters, or father, or mother, or wife, or children, or lands, for my name's sake, shall receive *an hundredfold,* and shall inherit everlasting life."[699]

The scriptures state that resurrection is a free gift given to all people through the grace and mercy of Jesus Christ,[700] but the quality of our resurrected glory is wholly dependent upon our works and desires.[701] For example, only celestial resurrection provides us a fulness of joy.[702] Only the eternal

---

[694] Alma 41:3–6, 15.
[695] Alma 41:12–13, 10.
[696] Alma 11:43–44; 40:23–26.
[697] Smith, *Teachings of the Prophet Joseph Smith,* 296.
[698] Revelation 7:17.
[699] Matthew 19:29.
[700] Alma 11:43–44.
[701] Alma 41:3–5.
[702] D&C 93:33–34; 138:17.

sealings of husbands to wives and children to parents can be fully realized in the resurrection. Only celestial resurrection in the highest degree of glory provides righteous individuals the divine power of procreation.[703] Only celestial resurrection carries the possibility of exaltation, which includes obtaining the fulness of God's power and glory, and receiving dominion over the angels.[704] Brother Riddle said, "Thus, after all probation has been extended, after each human creature has chosen the law by which he desires to be governed, after all things are set in order and there is no further need of the special change known as repentance, then our Savior extends the opportunity of resurrection to each human being through his priesthood order. Every soul will receive again a tabernacle of flesh and bone, nevermore to die. [Christ's] righteous children receive a tabernacle of *his own order*, a celestial body, having the same powers that he inherited from his Father in becoming the Only Begotten. Thus our Savior draws us into the same order of flesh and bone as that which he and Father enjoy."[705]

Joseph Smith taught that the resurrection gives us power over all spirits[706]; it places us beyond all of our enemies and every opposition. Chauncey Riddle wrote: "Because of the circumstances in which Adam fell, he became subject to Satan, and that subjection would have been complete and final had not the Savior [provided the Atonement and resurrection. But Jesus] by dying voluntarily . . . performed the sacrifice of the Atonement, *and by that sacrifice seized the keys of death and hell from Satan, who had gained them in the Fall,* and thus prepared the way for the resurrection of all mankind."[707] In other words, by the Atonement and by the resurrection, Jesus Christ places us beyond the reach of our worst enemies, death and hell, and makes us free.

As noted above, although these descriptions appear on the surface to have little to do with Zion, they have everything to do with it. Zion is a condition of no lack and of abundance; it is beauty, perfection, and protection from enemies. Zion is the eternal habitation of God. Zion people move toward this ideal in this life and fully realize it in the resurrection. Then they, as Zion people, remain as Zion people and abide in the celestial Zion society forever.

Hundredfold Restoration

As we have learned, the covenant of mercy called for an Atonement that would recompense our losses and afflictions "an hundredfold." The idea of a "hundredfold restoration" is repeated so often in the scriptures that we are obligated to give it consideration. For example, "But he shall receive an hundredfold now in this time, houses, and brethren, and sisters, and mothers, and children, and lands, . . . and in the world to come eternal life."[708] The Apostle Paul wrote, "Eye hath not seen, nor ear heard, neither have entered into the heart of man, the things which God hath prepared for them that love him."[709] Imagine experiencing the unjust loss of $10,000. The pain of that loss might be overwhelming. But suppose that the Lord were to restore to us $1,000,000. Suddenly, the $10,000 loss would fade away as a nonissue. We are redeemed by compensation that exceeds the debt—by a hundredfold, the promise of an overabundance or perhaps an amount beyond measurement.

Or imagine this scenario: Let us say that we had committed a crime against another person, who sued us and received a $10,000 judgment, which we could not pay. Now, let us imagine that a benevolent friend stepped forward to rectify the situation by offering the offended person the $10,000, plus another $990,000 for damages. Could the offended person ever claim that he had not been treated justly? Clearly, the Lord's restoration is a manifestation of his mercy, "which overpowereth

---

[703] D&C 132:19.
[704] D&C 132:20.
[705] Riddle, "The New and Everlasting Covenant," 239.
[706] Smith, *Teachings of the Prophet Joseph Smith*, 190; 2 Nephi 9:8.
[707] Riddle, "The New and Everlasting Covenant," 237–38; emphasis added.
[708] Mark 10:30.
[709] 1 Corinthians 2:9.

justice . . . and encircles them in the arms of safety, while he that exercises no faith unto repentance is exposed to the whole law of the demands of justice."[710] Clearly, in the resurrection all losses and debts are restored to the extent that justice can never again make a claim—*an hundredfold!*

Oneness and Deliverance

At the heart of the Atonement are the issues of happiness, balancing justice and mercy, purifying and sanctifying us, justifying us for blessings based on the merits of Jesus Christ, bringing us into *oneness* with God and his children, and restoring us to a condition of perfection that is indicative of Zion. The Atonement allows us to become one in the Covenant, and oneness is made possible by redemption. What we do with that redemption determines whether or not we become Zion people. Unless we are drawn into unity, we are nothing and cannot fill the measure of our creation.[711]

Oneness or unity is characteristic of Zion, and thus of the celestial kingdom. There is inherent power in unity. Joseph Smith said, "The greatest temporal and spiritual blessings which always come from faithfulness and concentrated effort, *never attended individual exertion or enterprise.*"[712] President Gordon B. Hinckley taught, "When you are united, your power is limitless. You can accomplish anything you wish to accomplish."[713] We become one and unified by covenant.

The Lord said, "I say unto you, be one; and if ye are not one ye are not mine."[714] Inasmuch as the Godhead are one,[715] so Zion people must likewise become one with each other and with the Father and with Jesus: "That they all may be one; as thou, Father, art in me, and I in thee, that they also may be one in us . . . ; that they may be one, even as we are one: I in them, and thou in me, that they may be made perfect in one."[716] We cannot fully accept the Atonement without becoming one with the Father and the Son and with each other by means of the Covenant. Whereas divisiveness is of the devil[717] and therefore characteristic of Babylon, *oneness* is of God and therefore characteristic of Zion: "And the Lord called his people ZION, because they were of one heart and one mind, and dwelt in righteousness; and there was no poor among them."[718]

Summary and Conclusion

God the Father in a premortal council of the Gods instituted the first covenant, called the covenant of justice, for the purpose of allowing his children the highest level of happiness. The purpose of the covenant of justice was to reveal the celestial laws by which the Father had become God, and by which his children could advance and become gods like him. The terms of the covenant of justice are: (1) God is the supreme lawgiver; (2) his laws are just; (3) all laws have immutable blessings and punishments that follow obedience and disobedience. Essential to the covenant of justice is agency; we rise or fall by personal choice. Agency was a central issue of the war in heaven. In that premortal setting, every person who has or would receive a physical body and thus have the potential to become like God chose to accept the covenant of justice.

The first covenant, the covenant of justice, was followed by the Father's establishing a second covenant: the covenant of mercy. The agent of mercy was Jesus Christ, and the vehicle of mercy was the Atonement. The way that we could begin to receive the purifying and sanctifying benefits of the

---

[710] Alma 34:15–16.
[711] D&C 49:17; 88:19, 25.
[712] Kimball, "Becoming the Pure in Heart," quoting Smith, *Teachings of the Prophet Joseph Smith*, 183.
[713] Hinckley, "Your Greatest Challenge, Mother," 97.
[714] D&C 38:27.
[715] 3 Nephi 11:36.
[716] John 17:21–23.
[717] 3 Nephi 11:29.
[718] Moses 7:18.

Atonement was to enter into the new and everlasting covenant by the covenant and ordinance of baptism. Because the foundation of the covenant of mercy is the Atonement, and because key aspects of the Atonement are accessed by the new and everlasting covenant, the covenant of mercy and the new and everlasting covenant are synonymous.

The covenant of mercy called for the Father to provide us a Savior to assure that the purposes of the covenant of justice, including the preservation of agency, justification for blessings, and advancement based on obedience, would remain intact. Moreover, the covenant of mercy provides that the demands of justice and the purposes of mercy can remain perfectly in balance so that God can be simultaneously just and merciful.[719] The covenant of mercy also provides a number of other blessings. For example, the merciful Atonement rescues us from the effects of the Fall and the consequences of our bad choices. Mercy also provides a means of payment of the debts for our sins, after our best efforts. Furthermore, the merciful Atonement allows the Holy Ghost to justify us to receive blessings for obeyed laws, even when we are not yet perfect.

By means of the Atonement and through the Holy Ghost, the covenant of mercy makes us just by progressively purifying our hearts; that is, the Holy Ghost expunges from us the impurities, contaminants, and pollutions that differentiate us from God and keep us from receiving his blessings. Similarly, the merciful Atonement allows the Holy Ghost to sanctify us, that is, to change our carnal, sensual, and devilish natures to the heart and nature of God. Finally, the merciful Atonement enacts the law of restoration and brings *oneness* where there has been loss or separation due to the Fall or transgression. Mercy restores everything in our lives to its perfect form—everything that had been lost by reason of separation or *death*, and makes *an hundredfold* recompense. Mercy, through the Atonement and by means of the new and everlasting covenant, makes us *one*, with our true selves, with God, and with each other. This process of becoming *one* begins when we enter the covenant of mercy or the new and everlasting covenant, and the process reaches its perfection in the resurrection.

Central to the power of the merciful Atonement is the saving grace of Jesus Christ. We cannot rescue ourselves from the Fall or from the consequences of sin; make ourselves clean and purified so that we might be justified to receive blessings; make ourselves sanctified so that our nature and purpose changes; free ourselves from Satan's grasp; make ourselves one with God, our spouse, family, and the Saints of God; or, in terms our approaching our ideal self, we become one in health, youth, and in eternal union of body and spirit—these things are totally beyond our capability without the Lord's grace. Such miraculous events are the work of God; we are completely dependent upon the Savior to accomplish these things in our behalf. His grace is that enabling power that allows us to do all that we can do with the faith that he will make up the difference where we fall short;[720] grace is the power that justifies imperfect beings to receive blessings that otherwise would be outside of our reach, were it not for the merits of Jesus Christ.[721]

When we bind ourselves to Jesus Christ in the new and everlasting covenant, he assigns his agent, the Holy Ghost, to transform us into a God, like our Father. We cannot become truly righteous by our own efforts; we need the Lord's grace. Chauncey Riddle said:

> Only in him and by him are [we] able to do any good thing. The righteous acts [we] do are not strictly [our] own acts; therefore [we] take no credit for them. Rather do [we] give the glory to God. [We] know that [our] righteous acts are acts of Christ, chosen by the pure heart given by Christ, understood by the just mind given by Christ, carried out by the new strength given by Christ, redounding to the

---

[719] Alma 42:13–15.
[720] LDS Bible Dictionary, "Grace," 697.
[721] Alma 24:10; Moroni 6:4.

> blessing of others in the priesthood might of Christ. Thus in Christ the righteous move, and live, and have their being (Acts 17:28).... When we endure to the end in the New and Everlasting Covenant, we will be literally transformed into the stature of Christ in heart, might, mind, and strength.... Thus the purpose of the new and everlasting covenant is to provide a means whereby every human being may come to be able to fulfill the first covenant [the covenant of justice].[722]

Now we understand what John meant when he said, "Beloved, now are we the sons of God, and it doth not yet appear what we shall be: but we know that, when he shall appear, we shall be like him; for we shall see him as he is."[723]

Such are the blessings of the covenant of mercy, the new and everlasting covenant, the magnificent plan that is founded on the Atonement and offered by the Father through his Only Begotten Son. This is the Covenant to which the Father, the Son, and the Holy Ghost effectively affix their names and place their godhood on the line to uphold, provided that we keep the terms of the Covenant. Truly, the new and everlasting covenant is the most glorious doctrine ever revealed. It contains the greatest hope and the most impressive promises of anything found on earth or in the far reaches of the universe. By abiding by its precepts, we can escape Babylon, flee to Zion, and forever abide safely in the embrace of our Eternal Father.

---

[722] Riddle, "The New and Everlasting Covenant," 241–42.
[723] 1 John 3:2.

SECTION 6

THE NEW AND EVERLASTING COVENANT:

THE FIRST PILLAR OF ZION

Joseph Smith said, "For a man to be great, he must not dwell on small things."[724]

The first pillar of Zion is the *New and Everlasting Covenant*.[725] This Covenant is made possible by the Atonement of Jesus Christ and is the vehicle by which the Atonement becomes operative in our lives. Infinite and eternal in scope, the Covenant has the power to save men and women and transform them into the image of God. We are saved to the degree that we receive and conform to this Covenant. If we become complacent about the Covenant, we risk forfeiture of our privileges. Zion people build their lives upon the bedrock of the Atonement by entering into the new and everlasting covenant.

The new and everlasting covenant is the sum of all gospel covenants, ordinances, and commandments[726]—"the fulness of the gospel."[727] The purposes of entering into the Covenant are: (1) to obtain knowledge and power for personal salvation, and (2) to obtain knowledge and power to help save other people by teaching them of the Atonement and administering to them the Covenant.

God sets the terms of the Covenant and of every other saving covenant within the Covenant, and he invites us to accept those terms. Our *signature*, which signifies our agreement to the terms of the covenants, is the ordinance that is associated with that covenant. For example, we affix our "signature" of agreement to the new and everlasting covenant by the ordinance of baptism. Each covenant associated with the new and everlasting covenant is also "*a* new and *an* everlasting

---

[724] Smith, *History of the Church*, 5:298.
[725] D&C 42:67.
[726] D&C 22; 132:6–7.
[727] D&C 39:11; 45:9; 66:2; 133:57.

covenant"[728] because all such covenants are revealed anew to each recipient, and because they are everlasting in nature.

Enos was one who entered into the new and everlasting covenant and thereafter exemplified the Covenant's two purposes. First, Enos obtained the assurance of his personal salvation; then he sought to bring his family into the Covenant; and finally he sought to bring other people into the Covenant.[729] Thereafter, the Lord told him that his response to the Covenant was both a proper and a universal response shared by other faithful souls: "And the Lord said unto me: Thy fathers have also required of me this thing; and it shall be done unto them according to their faith; for their faith was like unto thine."[730] Clearly, we see Zion in his life: the attributes of making saving covenants, being purified and sanctified by the covenants, and inviting other people to also make the covenants.

Centuries earlier, Abraham's response to the Covenant was similar. He also wanted to move beyond personal salvation and seek to administer the Covenant to other people so as to invite them into the lifestyle of Zion. For that reason, he sought for his "appointment unto the Priesthood." After listing a number of supernal blessings that the priesthood had to offer, Abraham exulted that he desired to possess this authority so that he could "administer the same."[731] That is, he wanted to administer the Covenant and the priesthood to other people so that they, too, could gain their salvation. Throughout the scriptures, we read of other righteous individuals who followed the twofold purpose of the Covenant. They sought to enter it for their personal redemption, and once they had experienced redemption, they sought to introduce others to the Covenant for their redemption. Their hearts were changed, and they were transformed from naturally selfish people into selfless saviors on Mount Zion.

The Structure of the Covenant

The Father instituted the covenant of mercy to rescue and exalt his children. The agent of salvation is Jesus Christ; the vehicle of salvation is the Atonement, which establishes the foundation of the covenant of mercy. Upon that foundation, the new and everlasting covenant rises and forms the framework of our new life in Christ. Helaman explains, "And now, my sons, remember, remember that it is upon the rock of our Redeemer, who is Christ, the Son of God, that ye must build your foundation; that when the devil shall send forth his mighty winds, yea, his shafts in the whirlwind, yea, when all his hail and his mighty storm shall beat upon you, it shall have no power over you to drag you down to the gulf of misery and endless wo, because of the rock upon which ye are built, which is a sure foundation, a foundation whereon if men build they cannot fall."[732]

Our new life is like a temple. As that new structure rises, other covenants are added. If we were to attempt to outline the new and everlasting covenant, it might look like this:

New and Everlasting Covenant
1. Covenant of Baptism
2. Oath and Covenant of the Priesthood
    a. Ordination (men)
    b. Temple covenants (men and women)
    c. Eternal marriage covenant (men and women)

---

[728] *Encyclopedia of Mormonism*, 1008; D&C 22; 132:4.
[729] Enos 1:4–17.
[730] Enos 1:18.
[731] Abraham 1:2–4.
[732] Helaman 5:12.

Of profound importance is the fact that we make the new and everlasting covenant at the time of baptism with the Father, the Son, and the Holy Ghost. All three members of the Godhead effectively "affix" their names to the agreement with a covenant to save and exalt us. This is the purpose of the new and everlasting covenant. Each member of the Godhead now takes a part in our advancement and transformation, although "we receive all of the blessings of this covenant through the Son, who is Everlasting."[733] Forming a bookend with the new and everlasting covenant is the other covenant to which the Father, the Son, and the Holy Ghost "affix" their names: the covenant of eternal marriage. Now the new and everlasting covenant is complete. Clearly, we become Zion people by means of the Covenant—a combination of our best efforts and the best efforts of the Father, the Son, and the Holy Ghost.

THE NEW AND EVERLASTING COVENANT AS AN AGREEMENT

Imagine the Covenant as a traditional contract. By taking some liberties, let us take what we have learned about the Covenant and cast it in the form of an agreement. Much of what we note in this contract has been said before, but it may be helpful to view it in this context.

1. INTRODUCTION

The purposes of the new and everlasting covenant are to save us from the effects of the Fall and from the consequences of our sins; to turn our weaknesses into strengths; to place us beyond all our enemies and every adversity; to transform us from natural men, who are carnal, sensual, and devilish, to Saints, who are justified to receive blessings by obedience to God's laws; to make our hearts pure; to sanctify, exalt, and bless us with the fulness of God's glory;[734] and to make us all that the Father is and give us all that he has.

> The Father sets the terms of the Covenant; the Son presides over, administers, and makes the Covenant operational; the Holy Ghost instructs us regarding the Covenant, makes and judges us worthy of the Covenant's blessings, and ratifies and seals the terms of the Covenant so that these blessings endure eternally. Because God's "house is a house of order . . . and not a house of confusion,"[735] he stipulates that "all covenants, contracts, bonds, obligations, oaths, vows, performances, connections, associations, or expectations," in the new and everlasting covenant must be "entered into and sealed by the Holy Spirit of promise [the Holy Ghost]." This sealing is done by means of the priesthood keys residing in the Lord's anointed servant, the President of the Church, who holds the exclusive right to bind in heaven what is done on earth. Otherwise, without the authority of the priesthood and the subsequent ratification of the Holy Ghost, no covenant is binding "after the resurrection from the dead; for all contracts that are not made unto this end have an end when men are dead."[736]

> Through delegation of those priesthood keys, we enter the Covenant by baptism at the hands of one of Jesus Christ's servants. Because this servant holds the priesthood, he is authorized to perform the ordinance as if he were Jesus Christ: "whether by mine own voice or by the voice of my servants, it is the same."[737] This servant also has the authority to effectively "affix" the names of the three members of the Godhead—the Father, the Son, and the Holy Ghost—to this agreement: "Having been commissioned of Jesus Christ, I baptize you in the

---

[733] Riddle, "The New and Everlasting Covenant," 228.
[734] D&C 132:6.
[735] D&C 132:8.
[736] D&C 132:7.
[737] D&C 1:38.

name of the Father, and of the Son, and of the Holy Ghost. Amen."[738] Our "signature," signifying our agreeing to the terms of the Covenant, is symbolized by our receiving the associated ordinance (baptism). Receiving any covenant's associated ordinance to signify our agreement becomes the pattern for our making all other saving covenants within the new and everlasting covenant. Fulfilling the terms of any covenant justifies us for that covenant's attendant blessings.

The new and everlasting covenant is the Father's response to the demands of justice. To rescue and protect us from the consequences of broken celestial laws, and to allow us to progress, regain our bodies, and be preserved by obedience to celestial law, the Father provides the covenant of mercy. Mercy calls for a Savior to atone for us. The new and everlasting covenant is the agreement we make with the Father to access the blessings of the Atonement. The new and everlasting covenant consists of two major covenants: the covenant of baptism, and the oath and covenant of the priesthood. The priesthood covenant, which is initially made by worthy men at the time of ordination, expands to eventually include both men and women. These additional priesthood covenants are those taken by worthy men and women in the temple, culminating with the covenant of eternal marriage.

2. The Covenant of Justice

The covenant of justice provides that the Father will reveal to us the immutable laws that govern him and all celestial beings. These laws comprise the pattern of his lifestyle, which set of laws allows him to be both perfect and perfectly *just*. By obeying these same laws we adopt his lifestyle and can become like him.

The Father has decreed an *umbrella law* to govern all other laws. This law provides that all laws of God must contain two things: immutable blessings and immutable punishments. By accepting the covenant of justice, we agree that God: (1) is the supreme lawgiver; (2) his laws are just; (3) we will accept the consequences of obedience or disobedience to his laws.

The covenant of justice functions on the principle of agency. By choice we demonstrate our obedience, which is likewise demonstrated by our willingness to sacrifice in order to obey. It is by choice, therefore, that we become both just and justified for blessings.

Blessings for Obedience

The covenant of justice is harsh when disobeyed but glorious when obeyed. By obedience to any law of God, we are justified to receive the blessing associated with that law. Moreover, we are preserved, perfected, and sanctified by obedience to God's law.[739] This is the covenant by which men and women are justified to "gain an inheritance in the Kingdom of God."[740]

3. The Covenant of Mercy

The covenant of mercy or the new and everlasting covenant was established by the Father in response to the demands made by the covenant of justice. The covenant of mercy is the law of God that has the power to "appease the demands of justice,"[741] if obeyed. The primary stipulations associated with the covenant of mercy are these: (1) We agree to accept Jesus Christ and his Atonement by exercising faith in Jesus Christ; (2) We agree to repent and change our lives; (3) We agree to enter into the new and everlasting covenant through baptism, and thereafter to make all other saving covenants; (4) We agree to receive the Holy

---

[738] D&C 20:73.
[739] D&C 88:34–35.
[740] McConkie, *Mormon Doctrine*, 117.
[741] Alma 42:15.

Ghost and yield to his efforts to purify us, sanctify us, and to make us fit in every way for celestial glory.

BLESSINGS FOR OBEDIENCE

Because we desire deliverance from the world and rescue from the effects of our sinful choices, we seek mercy. The only source of that mercy is Jesus Christ. Like all laws of God, the covenant of mercy contains both a blessing and a punishment. If we obey the laws associated with this covenant, we receive forgiveness of sins, reconciliation to God, and inheritance in his kingdom, which includes all that he has and is. If we disobey the law associated with this covenant, we receive damnation and must pay the price of our sins alone.[742]

The covenant of mercy allows us to embrace the covenant of justice without being destroyed by the laws of God that we break. Therefore, the covenant of mercy provides a Savior to atone for us. The Atonement of Jesus Christ provides us a sure foundation upon which we can build a new life that will become worthy of God's presence and inheritance in his kingdom.

Upon our accepting the Atonement and entering into the new and everlasting covenant by baptism, the Savior meets the demands of justice for every sin that we have committed or will commit. He provides us the supernal gift of the Holy Ghost to purify, sanctify, and justify us, and to transform us into perfect beings like our Father. The Savior provides us his grace to make up for what our best effort will not cover. Additionally, he reconciles us to God so that nothing stands between us and the Father and so that we can one day appear before God without guilt, shame, spot, or blemish.

The covenant of mercy, or the new and everlasting covenant, forms the defined path that leads to eternal life, places in our hands the authority of God, gives us access to God's knowledge and power, and establishes us in our eternal kingdom. To accomplish these objectives, the covenant of mercy provides us two additional primary covenants: the covenant of baptism, and the oath and covenant of the priesthood.

4. THE COVENANT OF BAPTISM

To receive power to leave behind our lives in Babylon, and to "fulfill all righteousness"[743] by being born again into a new life, we agree to exercise faith in Jesus Christ, repent of our sins, and follow the Savior's example of entering into the new and everlasting covenant by means of the ordinance of baptism by immersion.[744]

By baptism, we signify our agreement to become an adopted son or daughter of Jesus Christ, spiritually begotten[745] of him to become part of his family. We agree to take upon ourselves the name of Jesus Christ, our new spiritual father. We agree to always remember him and to keep his commandments, including every word that proceeds from the mouth of God.[746] We agree to become active, sustaining members of Christ's family, the earthly name of which is The Church of Jesus Christ of Latter-day Saints. This family or Church is God's kingdom on earth. Furthermore, we agree to stand as witnesses of God, to bear one another's burdens, to mourn with those who mourn, to comfort those who stand in need of comfort, to manifest a determination to serve God to the end, and to receive the Holy Ghost to facilitate

---

[742] D&C 19:15–20.
[743] Matthew 3:15.
[744] Articles of Faith 1:4.
[745] Mosiah 5:7.
[746] D&C 20:77; 84:44.

the process by which we are purified of our sins. We agree to submit to the Holy Ghost's purifying and sanctifying efforts to transform us into new creatures.[747] We agree to renew our baptismal covenant by making the covenant associated with the sacrament.

BLESSINGS FOR OBEDIENCE

Baptism provides us an initial and immediate remission of our sins.[748] We are *born again*[749] into the family of Jesus Christ. We entered physical life by the breaking of the birth water, the entrance of our spirits into our bodies, and the issue of blood; by baptism we are born again by the water (baptism), of the spirit (Holy Ghost), and of the blood (the Atonement of Jesus Christ).[750] We become members of Jesus Christ's family (The Church of Jesus Christ of Latter-day Saints), and receive him as our adopted spiritual father.[751]

Thereafter, by a holy ordinance (confirmation), our membership in our new family is *confirmed* or made sure.[752] As part of the confirmation ordinance, we are commanded to receive the Holy Ghost. This is the Spirit that enters our new "selves" and makes us "alive in Christ."[753] As long as we remain worthy, the Holy Ghost will be our guide, comforter, companion, testator, revelator, justifier, purifier, and sanctifier. The Holy Ghost will teach us the truth of all things[754] and give us power to keep the terms of the Covenant and every covenant within the Covenant. He will burn out of us, as if by fire, all iniquity, carnality, sensuality, and every evil thing, so that we might become perfectly fit for eternal life.[755] The Holy Ghost will make of us a new being capable of standing spotless before God in the day of judgment.[756]

By baptism, we enter in at the gate, where Jesus is the gatekeeper,[757] which gate opens onto the path called *strait and narrow*.[758] This path leads to the celestial kingdom. If we endure in faithfulness in the new and everlasting covenant, we will experience the highest manifestation of salvation:[759] eternal life and exaltation.[760] By continuing obedience to terms of the covenant of baptism, we will become the "redeemed of God, . . . numbered with those of the first [celestial] resurrection" and "have eternal life."[761]

4A) AGREEMENT TO RENEW AND ABIDE IN THE COVENANT OF BAPTISM

To "retain a remission of sins,"[762] we agree to "remember, and always retain in remembrance, the greatness of God."[763] We agree to always remember Jesus Christ, specifically his sacrificed

---

[747] Mosiah 5:7; 18:7–10; 27:24–26.
[748] D&C 13.
[749] John 3:3, 7.
[750] Moses 6:59–60.
[751] Mosiah 5:7.
[752] *LDS Bible Dictionary*, "Confirmation," 649.
[753] 2 Nephi 25:25.
[754] Moroni 10:5.
[755] 3 Nephi 27:24–26.
[756] 3 Nephi 27:20.
[757] 2 Nephi 9:41.
[758] McConkie, Conference Report, Oct. 1955, 12; 2 Nephi 31:18.
[759] 2 Nephi 9:23–24; 31:13–21.
[760] 2 Nephi 31:20.
[761] Mosiah 18:9.
[762] Mosiah 4:12; JST Matthew 26:22–25; JST Mark 14:20–25; JST Luke 22:17–20.
[763] Mosiah 4:12.

body and his blood that he gave to redeem us.[764] The sacrament is the ordinance that signifies this remembrance.

By this ordinance, we renew our covenant of baptism, which is at the same time a renewal of the new and everlasting covenant. To that end, we agree to worthily and willingly partake of "the emblems of the flesh and blood of Christ"[765] as the priests administer them. We agree to (1) again take upon us the name of Christ; (2) always remember Jesus, his broken body, sacrificed blood, teachings, example, and his love for us; and (3) renew and keep the agreements that we made at baptism.

To retain a remission of our sins, we agree to walk in all humility, remembering our own nothingness and the Lord's goodness and long-suffering towards us; we agree to call upon the name of the Lord daily, and to stand steadfastly "in the faith of that which has been wrought for us by the Atonement of Jesus Christ."[766]

BLESSINGS FOR OBEDIENCE

The sacrament is the ordinance that renews the terms of the baptismal covenant, which is the entrance covenant into the new and everlasting covenant. Moreover, the sacrament is the ordinance that assures us of retaining the gift of the Holy Ghost. By obedience to the sacramental covenant, we qualify to always have the Lord's Spirit—the Holy Ghost—to be with us. Therefore, the presence of the Holy Ghost in our lives is given to us as a special sign that we are yet retaining a remission of sins by the merits and grace of Jesus Christ.[767] This allows us to progress in the Covenant toward perfection and receive blessings without having yet achieved perfection. In the sacramental covenant, the Lord blesses us that in due course we shall inherit eternal life.[768]

We receive the blessing of receiving the Lord's gifts. Symbolically, we come to the sacramental table to exchange gifts: we offer the Lord our hearts, and he offers us emblems, or tokens, that represent the sacrifice that he made for us. By worthily partaking of the sacrament, the Lord blesses us with the fruits[769] and gifts of the Spirit.[770]

4B) AGREEMENT TO LIVE THE LAW OF THE SABBATH DAY

As a special sign that we have entered into the new and everlasting covenant by baptism, we agree to "remember the Sabbath day, to keep it holy."[771] This law has always been associated with covenant people. By keeping this law, we indicate that we are separate, distinct, and known to the world as covenant people.[772] By living this law, we keep ourselves more unspotted from the world.[773]

We agree to acknowledge that the Sabbath day is the Lord's day,[774] which he has hallowed.[775] The law of the Sabbath day requires that we labor six days for our temporal sustenance; then on the Sabbath day we rest from that work and completely devote ourselves

---

[764] D&C 20:40, 77, 79.
[765] D&C 20:40.
[766] Mosiah 4:11.
[767] 2 Nephi 31:19; Moroni 6:4; D&C 3:20.
[768] John 6:5–4; McConkie, *Mormon Doctrine*, 660.
[769] Galatians 5:22.
[770] D&C 46.
[771] Exodus 20:8–11.
[772] Nehemiah 13:15–22; Isaiah 56:1–8; Jeremiah 17:19–27; Ezekiel 46:1–7.
[773] D&C 59:9.
[774] D&C 59:12.
[775] Exodus 20:8–11.

to the Lord's work and to worshipping Him. Therefore, we agree to consecrate the Sabbath day to the Lord, and use that day to chart a course leading to eternal life.[776]

Because we have been commanded to "thank the Lord thy God in all things," and to "offer a sacrifice unto the Lord thy God in righteousness, even that of a broken heart and a contrite spirit,"[777] we agree to go to the house of prayer on the Sabbath day and there offer up our sacraments, meaning our personal promises to forsake our sins and failings, with the faith that if we do so, the Lord will forgive and bless us.[778] We agree to pay, on the Sabbath day, our personal and spiritual devotions and oblations unto the Lord—that is, our worship, thanks, and temporal and spiritual offerings. An oblation is an offering. "The Hebrew word . . . is to come near. The person bringing the offering does so in order to come closer to God. . . . It is in sacrament meeting as we contemplate the sacramental altar that our offering of a broken heart and a contrite spirit brings us nearer to the altar of sacrifice and reminds us of our complete dependence upon the Atonement of the Savior."[779]

On the Sabbath day, we confess "our sins unto [our] brethren, and before the Lord."[780] Partaking of the sacrament and confessing to the bishop, when necessary, qualify as two ways to fulfill this stipulation. The Sabbath day is a day to fast and bear witness of the Lord.[781] On this day, we agree to rest, that is, to enter into the Lord's rest, meaning his glory,[782] whereby we might commune with him.

BLESSINGS FOR OBEDIENCE

For keeping the Sabbath day holy, the Lord will bless and prosper us beyond our comprehension.[783] He will establish and preserve our kingdom forever.[784] He will send us rain in due season. He will help us overcome our enemies, which include our weaknesses and adversities. He will bless us with peace, multiply us, and establish the Covenant with us and our succeeding generations.[785] He promises: "I will walk among you; and will be your God, and ye will be my people."[786] By obedience to the law of the Sabbath day, the Lord swears to the world that we are his chosen people and that we have entered into the everlasting Covenant.[787]

Inasmuch as we keep the law of the Sabbath day, the earth will yield up its bounty to us: "The fulness of the earth is yours, the beasts of the field and the fowls of the air, and that which climbeth upon the trees and walketh upon the earth; yea, and the herb, and the good things which come of the earth, whether for food or for raiment, or for houses, or for barns, or for orchards, or for gardens, or for vineyards; yea, all things which come of the earth, in the season thereof, are made for the benefit and the use of man, both to please the eye and to gladden the heart; yea, for food and for raiment, for taste and for smell, to strengthen the body and to enliven the soul."[788]

---

[776] McConkie, *A New Witness for the Articles of Faith*, 301.
[777] D&C 59:8.
[778] McConkie, *A New Witness for the Articles of Faith*, 301–2.
[779] Cannon, "Oblation," *Mormon Times*, Feb. 5, 2009.
[780] D&C 59:12.
[781] D&C 59:7–13.
[782] D&C 84:24.
[783] McConkie, *A New Witness for the Articles of Faith*, 301.
[784] Jeremiah 17:20–27.
[785] Leviticus 26:2–9.
[786] Isaiah 58:13–14.
[787] Nehemiah 13:15–22; Isaiah 56:1–8; Jeremiah 17:19–17; Ezekiel 31:12–17.
[788] D&C 59:16–19.

The First Pillar of Zion

As we partake of the sacrament on the Sabbath day, the Lord will count our sacrifice of a broken heart and a contrite spirit as though we had placed all things on the altar. He will forgive us of our sins, and he will help us face and overcome our weaknesses.[789] Ultimately, he will bless us to enter into his rest.[790]

5. Agreement to Receive the Covenant of the Priesthood

When we have experienced personal salvation, we (a man or a woman) agree to become saviors on Mount Zion[791] and help save both the living and the dead. To do this redemptive work, we agree to receive the blessings of the priesthood "for your sake, and not for your sake only, but for the sake of the whole world."[792]

Only worthy men receive ordination to the priesthood. When men are ordained to the Melchizedek Priesthood, they receive it by covenant and with the Father's oath. Men agree to magnify their calling, and the first way is through ordination, which carries with it the charge to serve others and accept and diligently fulfill other assignments and callings in the Church. The second and third ways involve both men and women.[793] These ways are receiving the temple initiatory ordinances and the priesthood endowment, and finally to receive celestial marriage and thereby enter into the patriarchal order of the priesthood.

5A) Worthy Men Agree to Be Ordained

Men agree to make themselves worthy to receive both the Aaronic and Melchizedek priesthoods, and thereby be called the sons of Aaron and of Moses.[794] When men are ordained to the Melchizedek Priesthood, Jesus Christ will place upon them his name,[795] allowing those men to minister as if they were Jesus Christ.

Ordained men agree to remember that "the rights of the priesthood are inseparably connected with the powers of heaven, and that the powers of heaven cannot be controlled nor handled only upon the principles of righteousness." Therefore, they agree not to set their hearts upon the things of this world; neither will they undertake to cover their sins, to gratify their pride, their vain ambition, nor to exercise control or dominion or compulsion upon the souls of the children of men, in any degree of unrighteousness. Rather, as the Lord's authorized servants and thus representing him, ordained men agree to exercise gentle persuasion, long-suffering, gentleness, meekness, love unfeigned, kindness, and pure knowledge, which greatly enlarges the soul without hypocrisy or guile. When ordained men need to occasionally reprove with sharpness, they agree to do so only when moved upon by the Holy Ghost, and then showing forth afterwards an increase of love toward him whom they have reproved. Ordained men agree to extend charity towards all people, to their own families, and to the household of faith, who are the members of the Church, the family of Jesus Christ.

---

[789] McConkie, *A New Witness for the Articles of Faith*, 301–2.

[790] D&C 84:24.

[791] Obadiah 1:21.

[792] D&C 84:48.

[793] "Now, *as far as the Church of Christ is concerned*, this oath and covenant is made first in baptism, when the Holy Ghost is given, and more especially when the Priesthood is conferred. It is, secondly, repeated by partaking of the Sacrament, and by entering into special covenants in holy places [the temple]." (Editor's Table, "The Bondage of Sin," *Improvement Era*, Feb. 1923; emphasis added.) Also: "This covenant, made when the priesthood is received, is renewed when the recipient enters the order of eternal marriage." (McConkie, *A New Witness for the Articles of Faith*, 313.)

[794] D&C 84:34.

[795] Abraham 1:18.

They agree to let virtue garnish their thoughts unceasingly.[796]

BLESSINGS FOR OBEDIENCE

Worthy ordained men become "priest[s] of the Most High . . . after the order of Melchizedek."[797] They receive the right, when called upon, to preside in the offices of the Aaronic and the Melchizedek priesthoods. They are blessed to have Jesus Christ place upon them his own name[798] and his authority, which is the right to act in his name under the direction of priesthood leaders who hold the keys to this authority. They receive the "power of God to act in all things for the benefit of mankind, both in and out of the world."[799]

Holding the Aaronic Priesthood, ordained men have the authority to administer in the outward ordinances,[800] including baptism, the sacrament; to teach, expound, exhort, and watch over the Church always, being with and strengthening members, seeing that there is no iniquity or hardness with each other, no lying, backbiting, or evil-speaking; to see that the Church meets together often and that the members attend to their duties; to assist the higher priesthood, and take the lead when no elder is present.[801] They are entitled to the ministering of angels.[802]

Holding the Melchizedek Priesthood, ordained men are now empowered to resume their premortal work, which Catherine Thomas said was the work of redemption,[803] and thereafter to continue on with that work in eternity, being kings and priests unto God forever.[804] They have the right of presidency, should they be called upon, because this higher priesthood has authority over all the offices in the Church. Being Melchizedek Priesthood holders, they have authority to administer the "spiritual blessings of the church."[805] This high priesthood has the power to administer "endless lives to the sons and daughters of Adam."[806]

Ordained men have the authority to confirm the children of God members of the Church of Jesus Christ and to confer upon them the gift of the Holy Ghost. Additionally, they have the authority, under the direction of priesthood leaders, to take the lead in meetings of the Church, and to ordain other worthy men to offices in the priesthood.[807]

By giving diligence to their ordination, their confidence will wax strong in God's presence; and the doctrine of the priesthood shall distill upon their souls like the dews from heaven. The Holy Ghost shall be their constant companion, and their scepter shall be an unchanging scepter of righteousness and truth. Their celestial dominion shall be everlasting, and without compulsory means it shall flow unto them forever and ever.[808]

Ordained men are empowered to become as the Father and the Son are—gods, in their own right. They can achieve this exalted status upon the same principle that the Father and the Son gained their exaltation: by receiving the same oath and keeping this same covenant.

---

[796] D&C 121:35–37, 41–45.
[797] D&C 76:57–58.
[798] Abraham 1:18.
[799] *Encyclopedia of Mormonism*, 1134.
[800] D&C 107:13–14.
[801] D&C 20:46–56.
[802] D&C 84:26.
[803] Thomas, "Alma the Younger, Part 1," n.p.
[804] D&C 76:56–57; 138:57.
[805] D&C 107:8, 10.
[806] Smith, *Teachings of the Prophet Joseph Smith*, 322.
[807] D&C 20:39–45.
[808] D&C 121:45–46.

The First Pillar of Zion

5b) Ordained Men Agree to Magnify Their Calling

Melchizedek Priesthood holders agree to magnify their calling in the kingdom of God by taking their responsibilities seriously, making those responsibilities honorable in the eyes of God's children, and glorious to God.[809] They agree to function faithfully under the guidance of priesthood leadership and the instruction of the Holy Ghost.[810]

Because the primary *calling* is the call to eternal life, they agree to become like God. They agree to accomplish this by going to the temple to be cleansed, purified, set apart, and prepared for that purpose so that they might be initiated into the order of the gods. They continue by being endowed with keys to God's knowledge and power. Then they agree to receive the crowning event to become like God: entering into eternal marriage. These steps facilitate the fulfillment of their calling, and they magnify that calling by obedience and diligence.

Blessings for Obedience

If ordained men magnify their *calling* faithfully, they will be given progressively greater authority and power, and they will shoulder increasing responsibility in their stewardships, which might or might not by manifested in Church positions.[811]

Because the *calling* of an ordained Melchizedek Priesthood holder is to be "*called* into the fellowship of Jesus Christ,"[812] and because such men were "*called* and prepared from the foundation of the world according to the foreknowledge of God, on account of their exceeding faith and good works,"[813] if they continue faithful they receive the blessing on earth to be *called* and elected (selected) for eternal life. For that purpose, they are blessed to go to the holy temple and receive sanctifying ordinances. These include being cleansed, purified, set apart, prepared, and initiated into the order of the gods. Additionally, they are endowed with keys to the knowledge and power of God,[814] and they are established in their eternal kingdoms by entering into the highest order of the priesthood—the patriarchal order—which is the new and everlasting covenant of marriage.[815]

5c) Ordained Men Agree to Continued Faithfulness

Ordained men agree to "keep the commandments of God, to live by every word that proceedeth forth from the mouth of Deity, and to walk in paths of righteousness and virtue."[816]

Blessings for Obedience

Worthy ordained men (and worthy women) make up "the church and kingdom, and the elect of God,"[817] having premortally received the "election of grace."[818] This means that in premortality they qualified to be selected in this life to receive the new and everlasting covenant for their own salvation, and that they were selected to administer the Covenant to

---

[809] *Encyclopedia of Mormonism*, 850.
[810] Riddle, "The New and Everlasting Covenant," 232.
[811] Riddle, "The New and Everlasting Covenant," 232; Matthew 25:14–30.
[812] 1 Corinthians 1:9, 26–27; Hebrews 3:1.
[813] Alma 13:3–5.
[814] D&C 95:8.
[815] D&C 131:1–4.
[816] McConkie, *Mormon Doctrine*, 480.
[817] D&C 84:34.
[818] D&C 84:98–102; Romans 11:1–5.

others so that they, too, could be saved.[819] To that end, they become "the seed of Abraham,"[820] and are thus entitled to all the blessings of Abraham, Isaac, and Jacob. These blessings include the right for their posterity to become "lawful heirs" to the fulness of priesthood and gospel blessings "according to the flesh."[821]

The Holy Ghost will purify and sanctify worthy ordained men unto the renewing of their bodies,[822] thus enlivening and strengthening them so that they might administer the Covenant to other people.[823] Furthermore, they are renewed by being married for eternity and by means of the posterity born to them in the Covenant. Worthy ordained men will enter into the Lord's *rest*, which is "the fulness of his glory."[824] They will receive the Father's kingdom, and thus all that he has and is shall be theirs.[825]

During their sojourn on this earth, ordained men are entitled to revelation for their personal lives and for their stewardships.[826] They are entitled "to have the privilege of receiving the mysteries of the kingdom of heaven, to have the heavens opened unto them, to commune with the general assembly and church of the Firstborn, and to enjoy the communion and presence of God the Father, and Jesus the mediator of the new covenant."[827] Moreover, they are entitled to the ministering of angels for guidance, protection and instruction.[828]

6. Abide in the Covenant to the End

Now that we have made the covenants of baptism and the priesthood, we agree to abide in the new and everlasting covenant to the end, and to give strict diligence to making our calling and election sure. We agree to be perfect as the Father is perfect;[829] that is, we agree to abide in the Covenant with as much diligence as does the Father, "even unto death, that you may be found worthy."[830] We agree to fiercely pursue the "strait and narrow path" "with unshaken faith in [Christ], relying wholly upon the merits of him who is mighty to save." We agree to "press forward with a steadfastness in Christ, having a perfect brightness of hope, and a love of God and of all men." The Father has decreed that "this is the way; and there is none other way nor name given under heaven whereby man can be saved in the kingdom of God." Furthermore, "this is the doctrine of Christ, and the only and true doctrine of the Father, and of the Son, and of the Holy Ghost, which is one God, without end."[831]

Blessings for Enduring to the End

If we keep all the terms of the new and everlasting covenant, including all of the Lord's commandments, and if we receive and obey all the ordinances of the House of the Lord, we will receive a "fulness of the priesthood" and become heirs of God and joint-heirs with Jesus

---

[819] Romans 9:11; 11:5, 7, 28.
[820] D&C 84:34.
[821] D&C 86:8–11; 113:6.
[822] D&C 84:33.
[823] *Encyclopedia of Mormonism*, 1019.
[824] D&C 84:24.
[825] D&C 84:35–38.
[826] D&C 84:44.
[827] D&C 107:19.
[828] D&C 84:42.
[829] Matthew 5:48.
[830] D&C 98:14.
[831] 2 Nephi 31:17–21.

Christ.[832] "Those holding the fulness of the Melchizedek Priesthood are kings and priests [women are queens and priestesses] of the Most High God, holding the keys of power and blessing."[833] If we will do this, "feasting upon the word of Christ, and endure to the end, behold, thus saith the Father: Ye shall have eternal life."[834]

THE FATHER'S GUARANTEE

If we will abide in the new and everlasting covenant, the Father promises by his own name, putting his own Godhood on the line,[835] that, upon our faithfulness, he will fulfill every promise that he has made herein: "I, the Lord, am bound when ye do what I say; but when ye do not what I say, ye have no promise."[836] Therefore, he can unequivocally promise that if we do our part, we shall have eternal life.[837]

EFFECTIVE SIGNATURES

We agree to the terms of the new and everlasting covenant by receiving the ordinance of baptism. The Father, the Son, and the Holy Ghost effectively affix their names to the Covenant when the officiating priesthood holder invokes their names in the baptismal ordinance.[838]

The foregoing was an attempt to visualize the new and everlasting covenant as an agreement. Without the Atonement of Jesus Christ, the Covenant would be meaningless; but built upon that sure foundation, the Covenant has the power to transform, save, and exalt God's children.

We must keep in mind that learning of the Covenant and living it are a process. Because we have listed the elements of the Covenant in superlative terms that define the ideal, we might become tempted to become discouraged because of our present location on the path. But we must remember that the Lord's mercy includes his grace. Therefore, our forward movement is more important than whether or not we have arrived yet. Blessings come by trying and improving; we are rewarded by grace as though we had achieved the ideal—and we likewise receive grace to help us in our efforts to improve along the way. "For behold, thus saith the Lord God: I will give unto the children of men line upon line, precept upon precept, here a little and there a little; and blessed are those who hearken unto my precepts, and lend an ear unto my counsel, for they shall learn wisdom; for unto him that receiveth I will give more."[839] Hence, regardless of our present situation, Zion is ever within our grasp.

---

[832] Smith, *Teachings of the Prophet Joseph Smith*, 308–9.
[833] Smith, *Teachings of the Prophet Joseph Smith*, 322.
[834] 2 Nephi 31:20.
[835] McConkie, *A New Witness for the Articles of Faith*, 317.
[836] D&C 82:10.
[837] 2 Nephi 31:20.
[838] Articles of Faith 1:5.
[839] 2 Nephi 28:30.

Section 7

Abide in the Covenant

Of unparalleled significance is the fact that the Father created the new and everlasting covenant.[840] He established it for the salvation of his children, and to that end he set the unalterable terms that result in the absolute promise of exaltation: "And as pertaining to the new and everlasting covenant, it was instituted for the fulness of my glory; and he that receiveth a fulness thereof must and shall abide the law."[841] No one having received the Covenant can thereafter deny or reject it without experiencing serious and eternal consequences: "I reveal unto you a new and an everlasting covenant; and if ye abide not that covenant, then are ye damned; for no one can reject this covenant and be permitted to enter into my glory."[842] Our ability to become Zion people and our eternal future hinge upon our diligence in keeping the terms of the new and everlasting covenant: "I have decreed in my heart, saith the Lord, that I will prove you in all things, whether you will abide in my covenant, even unto death, that you may be found worthy. For if ye will not abide in my covenant ye are not worthy of me."[843]

An additional thought-provoking verity is found in the oath and covenant of the priesthood: if we will abide ("remain in a place, and continue to be sure or firm"[844]) in the Covenant, the Father himself will teach us regarding it.[845] This astonishing idea speaks to the importance that the Father places on the new and everlasting covenant. Truly, it is by this Covenant that he accomplishes his work that glorifies him.[846]

The deeper we dig into the doctrine of the Covenant, the more we discover a loving relationship. A caring Father is offering us all that he has and is. To that end, he reveals the laws by which he lives, which are the commandments that he gives us, and he offers us the same eternal covenants of

---

[840] 3 Nephi 16:5; 20:12, 25, 27, 29, 46; 21:4, 7; 29:1; Mormon 5:14; 9:47; Ether 4:15; Moroni 10:33; D&C 84:40.
[841] D&C 132:6.
[842] D&C 132:4; see also verse 6.
[843] D&C 98:14–15.
[844] *American Heritage Dictionary*, s.v. "abide."
[845] D&C 84:48.
[846] Moses 1:39.

progression and exaltation that made him who he is. He knows that the Covenant will help us grow from dependence to independence. For all these reasons, he invites us into a covenantal relationship, whereby we, together with him, share his order of life and his pattern of celestial living. This is Zion!

Most certainly, Heavenly Father fully dedicates himself to offering us the Covenant, teaching us its intricacies, and walking with us step by step toward the Covenant's stated purpose: immortality and eternal life.[847] At each significant event along the way, "to fulfill all righteousness,"[848] we meet with him, often at an altar, of our own free will, to exchange vows and gifts. We promise and give our hearts, and he promises and gives us tokens and emblems, *treasures* that help us to remember his gift of a Savior and to retain in our remembrance the infinite price that was paid by the Father and the Son to make the Covenant possible. Moreover, by the Covenant we become *his* "peculiar treasures"[849] by treasuring up the words of eternal life[850] for the everlasting salvation of our souls in the kingdom of God.[851] By the Covenant, he *calls* us out of the world and separates us for a holy purpose, so that one day he might elect (select) us for the highest manifestation of salvation called eternal life.

Clearly, the Covenant is all about *relationship*. Broadly, the relationship is called *Zion*, a celestial condition and an order of pure-hearted individuals who live in eternal marriages and families. The members of such families are pure, happy, and unselfish. They increase in number and joy forever. To make those relationships sure, and to confirm, or "make sure" the terms of the Covenant, three distinct offerings must be made:

1. The Father offers to share with us the supernal blessings of the Covenant.
2. The Son offers to cover the infinite expenses of the Covenant that we cannot meet.
3. We offer our hearts.

Yielding our hearts to God allows us to be assimilated into the celestial order. We do this by living the celestial laws of Zion in a telestial world, adopting the Father's work of redemption as our own, and becoming experts at serving and saving his children. As covenant people, our responsibility is to draw the Father's children into a holy circle of oneness that is indicative of Zion: safe, secure, peaceful, cooperative, merciful, charitable, 4, and unified.

THE LEAVENING POWER OF THE DOCTRINE OF THE COVENANT

After yet another run-in with the Pharisees, Jesus and the disciples entered into a boat to depart to the other side of the Sea of Galilee. This incident had been preceded by the Savior's feeding four thousand men and their wives and families, the second time that he had miraculously fed thousands with very few resources. As the disciples were sailing to the other side, they discovered that they had taken with them only a single loaf of bread, hardly enough to feed thirteen men. Jesus seized the teaching opportunity by connecting an ingredient of the bread with the doctrine of the Pharisees, whom they had just left: "And he charged them, saying, Take heed, beware of the leaven of the Pharisees, and of the leaven of Herod." Of course, leaven is yeast, the ingredient that expands quickly throughout the bread dough, making it rise. The connection of leaven to the Pharisees' doctrine escaped the disciples, "and they reasoned among themselves, saying, It is because we have no bread."

We can hear some frustration in Jesus' reply to their inability to see past their hunger: "Why reason ye, because ye have no bread? perceive ye not yet, neither understand? have ye your heart yet hardened? Having eyes, see ye not? and having ears, hear ye not? and do ye not remember?"

---

[847] Moses 1:39.
[848] Matthew 3:15.
[849] Exodus 19:5; Psalms 135:4.
[850] D&C 6:20; 84:5.
[851] D&C 11:3; 12:3; 14:3.

Then came the lesson.

"When I brake the five loaves among five thousand, how many baskets full of fragments took ye up? They say unto him, Twelve. And when the seven among four thousand, how many baskets full of fragments took ye up? And they said, Seven. And he said unto them, How is it that ye do not understand?"[852]

The lesson might escape us, too, if it were not for Matthew's account of the incident: "How is it that ye do not understand that I spake it not to you concerning bread, that ye should beware of the leaven of the Pharisees and of the Sadducees? Then understood they how that he bade them not beware of the leaven of bread, but of the doctrine of the Pharisees and of the Sadducees."[853]

Words are like leaven! Once planted in the soul, they grow. Leaven is like that good seed that Alma describes; if nourished, the seed will begin to swell, then to sprout, and eventually to grow into a bearing tree with delicious fruit.[854] Both leaven and the seed are little things that become great things. On the other hand, if the words of Satan are planted and remain in the soul, they will take root and grow into a briar-like tangle that becomes very destructive.

Once the doctrine of the Covenant takes hold in the fertile ground of a receptive soul, the Father will come and teach us its sublime intricacies[855] and empower us to abide in its precepts. More and more, the Covenant becomes a part of us, until we are totally "leavened" by it. Given a chance to grow, the Covenant will make of us Zion people. As we become Zion people by the leavening power of the Covenant, we feel no urge to be drawn back to the great and spacious building or the filthy river or the mists of darkness, which also describe the church of the devil and Babylon. Zion simply looks and feels better than anything Babylon has to offer.

THE COVENANT SEPARATES US FROM BABYLON, OR THE WORLD

When we enter into the new and everlasting covenant by baptism, we are *born again* into a new life.[856] That life is a Zion life. Baptism symbolizes death and rebirth or resurrection.[857] That is, we *die* to our old life and are born into a new life with a new spiritual father, Jesus Christ, and a new family, the Church of Jesus Christ.[858] We are, and must remain forever, separate and unique, the Lord's peculiar treasure[859] and his covenant people. Alma taught, "And now I say unto you, all you that are desirous to follow the voice of the good shepherd, come ye out from the wicked, and be ye separate, and touch not their unclean things; and behold, their names shall be blotted out, that the names of the wicked shall not be numbered among the names of the righteous, that the word of God may be fulfilled, which saith: The names of the wicked shall not be mingled with the names of my people."[860]

In our former, "natural man" life, we were identified with Babylon, but in our new life, we must never be identified with Babylon again. We are Zion now, separate and distinct. The kingdom of which we are now a part is "not of this world."[861] We, like Jesus, our spiritual father, must overcome the world "by valuing spiritual wealth and eternal treasure above earthly goods and attainments."[862] Whereas Babylon people are distinguished by "works of the flesh," such as "adultery, fornication,

---

[852] Mark 8:10–21.
[853] Matthew 16:11–12.
[854] Alma 32:28–41.
[855] D&C 84:48.
[856] Mosiah 27:25; Alma 7:14; Moses 6:59; John 3:3–7.
[857] *Encyclopedia of Mormonism*, 93.
[858] Moses 5:7.
[859] Exodus 19:5; Psalms 135:4.
[860] Alma 5:57.
[861] John 18:36.
[862] *Encyclopedia of Mormonism*, 1587.

uncleanness, lasciviousness, idolatry, witchcraft, hatred, variance, emulations, wrath, strife, seditions, heresies, envyings, murders, drunkenness, revellings, and such," Zion people are distinguished by the fruits of the Spirit: "love, joy, peace, longsuffering, gentleness, goodness, faith, meekness, temperance."[863]

Zion people are commissioned to invite others out of Babylon and into Zion so that they, too, might partake of the Covenant and be saved. Just as the Father sent his Son into the world to offer the Covenant to the people of the world, so Jesus (beginning with his apostles) sends us into the world to offer the Covenant.[864] We have no business being seduced or drawn back to Babylon in any degree. By doing so, we abandon our Covenant and commit treason against Zion.[865]

ZION PEOPLE ARE DISTINGUISHED BY OBSERVING THE SABBATH DAY

As mentioned, the Sabbath day is a *sign* that distinguishes and identifies us as people of the Covenant. By keeping the law of the Sabbath day, we signify among other things that we have abandoned Babylon in favor of Zion and that we intend to remain separate and distinct from the world. We have no desire to be "spotted" or contaminated by associating with the world.[866] Moreover, we live Zion's law of consecration in part by consecrating this day—the Lord's day[867]—to him to do his work and no other. This is a concept completely foreign to Babylon, whose philosophy is to make profit, seek pleasure, and indulge in self-serving activities twenty-four hours a day, every day, including the Sabbath day. On the Sabbath, Zion people worship their God, while Babylon people worship the idols of moneymaking ventures and pleasure.

On the Sabbath day, Zion people go to the house of God to express gratitude to him, to offer to him the sacrifice of a broken heart and a contrite spirit, to confess to him their sins, to fast and bear testimony of God, and thereby to enter into his rest.

Conversely, Babylon people serve a different god on the Sabbath day. Babylon people cheer for the home team, indulge, play, shop, camp, and barbeque; they worship their boats, go rock climbing, escape into nature, watch television, go to movies, and do anything to gratify themselves. On the Sabbath day, Babylon people lounge or sleep, whereas Zion people *rest*.

For the obedience of the people of Zion, the Lord blesses them with rain in due season and with protection from their enemies and from adversity; he blesses them with peace and with abundance in family and in the good things of the earth; he will grant their posterity the right to the blessings of the Covenant; he will bless them with his presence and call them his *chosen*. The earth will yield up its bounty to Zion people who live the law of the Sabbath day.

On the other hand, by mocking the Sabbath day Babylon receives the Lord's curse and spiritual death.

POWER IN THE COVENANT

In a sweeping vision of the last days, Nephi saw us, the latter-day followers of the Lamb of God, as the objects of Satan's wrath. Our righteousness became our defense, righteousness which summoned the power of God and in turn empowered us to withstand the adversary so that we might go forth and accomplish our missions. "And it came to pass that I beheld that the great mother of abominations did gather together multitudes upon the face of all the earth, among all the nations of the Gentiles, to fight against the Lamb of God. And it came to pass that I, Nephi, beheld the power of the Lamb of God, that it descended upon the saints of the church of the Lamb, and upon the covenant people of

---

[863] Galatians 5:19–23.
[864] John 17:18.
[865] Smith, *Teachings of the Prophet Joseph Smith*, 348–49.
[866] D&C 59:9.
[867] D&C 59:12.

the Lord, who were scattered upon all the face of the earth; and *they were armed with righteousness and with the power of God in great glory.*"[868]

Zion people derive their power from abiding in the Covenant!

Drawing upon the perspective of his experiences in escaping from Jerusalem (Babylon), his wilderness journey, and inheriting the promised land (Zion), Nephi recorded this profound insight: "I, Nephi, will show unto you that the tender mercies of the Lord are over all those whom he hath chosen, *because of their faith, to make them mighty even unto the power of deliverance.*"[869] Thereafter, he narrates incident after incident in which the power of his covenant with the Lord saved him and his family. The Book of Mormon is a textbook on power in the Covenant.

Alma and Amulek experienced the power of the Covenant as they went forth in faith to minister among the people. When they had been cast into prison and suffered exceedingly for the sake of Christ, Alma cried unto the Lord for the power of deliverance, a power available because he had made the Covenant, remained faithful to it, and exercised faith in Christ. In an astonishing turn of events, Alma and Amulek broke the cords that bound them—in the same way that Nephi broke his cords[870]—and the earth shook until the prison fell and killed the abusers. "And Alma and Amulek came forth out of the prison, and they were not hurt; *for the Lord had granted unto them power, according to their faith which was in Christ.*"[871] Of their ministry, Mormon wrote, "And they had power given unto them, insomuch that they could not be confined in dungeons; neither was it possible that any man could slay them."[872]

Zion people obtain the power of deliverance by abiding in the Covenant!

When Alma had served as leader of the Church for many years and now was instructing his son, Helaman, in the doctrine of the Covenant, he made this observation: "I have been supported under trials and troubles of every kind, yea, and in all manner of afflictions; yea, God has delivered me from prison, and from bonds, and from death; yea, and I do put my trust in him, and he will still deliver me."[873] With perspective, we, too, can look back and point to constant demonstrations of God's power in our lives. Because he and we abide in the Covenant together, we, by our righteousness, are ever in a position to draw upon his power to mitigate life's difficulties. Like the ancient Israelites, we, too, can point to times when we have been delivered from bondage and captivity, and our enemies have been neutralized or destroyed. Like Lehi and his family, we, too, by God's everlasting power, have been called out of a wicked environment, and he has delivered us from time to time even down to the present day.[874]

When the circumstances of our lives bind us with seemingly unbreakable bands that only God can break, we, like Alma, should retain in our remembrance our former experiences with the power of God. Because God never changes and because he keeps the Covenant, he will likewise intervene now and in the future, as he has intervened in the past, to help us to face our challenges.[875] Our access to his power is a combination of our righteousness and our faith in Christ. We have confidence that he will not leave us forever bound in cords or held in prison or beaten or despised. We believe that our abiding in the Covenant has summoned his power many times, and our continuing to abide in the Covenant will summon his power of deliverance in the future. Then we, like Alma, can declare that we have been supported under trials and troubles of every kind, and in all manner of afflictions, and

---

[868] 1 Nephi 14:14; emphasis added.
[869] 1 Nephi 1:20; emphasis added.
[870] 1 Nephi 8:16–18.
[871] Alma 14:26–28; emphasis added.
[872] Alma 8:31.
[873] Alma 36:27.
[874] Alma 36:29.
[875] Alma 36:28–29.

that God will yet deliver us from prison, and from bonds, and from death. Therefore, we abide in the Covenant with the assurance that if we continue to put our trust in God, he will manifest his power and deliver us.

Other Powers Manifested in the Covenant

Power in the Covenant is manifested in other ways. For example, we enter the Covenant through the ordinance of baptism, which places upon us a name of power—*Jesus Christ*. The power of the name of Jesus Christ is unequaled. During His mortal ministry, Jesus ordained the seventy, gave them power to use his name, and then sent them on missions. He instructed them: "Heal the sick therein, and say unto them, The kingdom of heaven is come nigh unto you [i.e., *We have come with power as authorized servants from the kingdom of heaven and have authority to use the name of Jesus Christ to bless you.*]." When the seventy returned from their missions, they were astonished at the power of the name of Jesus Christ: "And the seventy returned again with joy, saying, Lord, even the devils are subject unto us *through thy name.*"[876] Clearly, the name of Christ is "that ultimate statement of authority."[877]

Concerning the importance of the name of Jesus Christ, the Lord commanded us as Zion people to "take upon you *the name of Christ*. . . . Behold, *Jesus Christ is the name* which is given of the Father, and there is none other name given whereby man can be saved [now or in the future]; . . . for in that name [*Jesus Christ*] shall they be called at the last day."[878] The name of Jesus Christ is a blessing that we often overlook. Given to us at baptism, the name of Jesus Christ opens the door to prayer and access to the Father. This power to ask for and receive blessings is one of the supernal powers of the Covenant. Prayer is perhaps most efficacious when it is preceded by sacrifice. Because the vicarious sacrifices that we offer in the temple are some of the most Christlike sacrifices—sacrificing for the sake of someone who could not otherwise achieve redemption—our subsequent prayers that we offer in the temple often carry added spiritual weight. We cannot quantify the power of prayers offered in the holy temple.

Prayer in the name of Jesus Christ speaks eloquently regarding our relationship with the Lord as it exists in the Covenant. If we would more readily respond to a request from a friend or a family member than we would from a stranger, would not Heavenly Father readily respond to us because we are in the Covenant with him and a member of the family of Jesus Christ? Moreover, if we were to ask a friend or a family member for help in assisting someone of our acquaintance, would they not be willing to respond favorably because of their relationship to us? In like manner, when Zion people, who are of the Covenant, ask Heavenly Father in the name of Jesus Christ to bless people of their acquaintance, he will respond to their request because of their covenant relationship. Because the law of heaven requires asking in the name of Jesus Christ to receive blessings, someone must ask.[879] We believe that it is because of our loving covenantal relationship with the Father that we can ask and he will respond—*because we are family*.

That is the power of the Covenant!

Safety in the Covenant

Despite its propaganda, Babylon is neither a safe nor a nice place or condition. Those who are foolish enough to reside in Babylon are prone to dangers and adversities without the benefit of armor. The Apostle John calls Babylon a "hold" and a "cage," that is, a prison.[880]

---

[876] Luke 10:9, 17; emphasis added.
[877] Packer, "An Evening with President Boyd K. Packer," Feb. 29, 2008.
[878] D&C 18:21–24; emphasis added.
[879] Packer, "Personal Revelation," 59–62.
[880] Revelation 18:2.

In Babylon, idolatrous people worship other gods, so when trouble strikes, they are left alone to suffer and face overwhelming challenges. The harsh philosophy of Babylon is one that is godless, self-serving, competitive, and lonesome—*anti-Christ*.[881] People in Babylon fare "according to the management of the creature," prosper according to their genius, and conquer according to their strength. They assume no accountability to God; therefore they feel that they can do whatever they please without consequence. In Babylon, they succeed or fail alone. They have a form of godliness but deny the power thereof (the power of hope in Jesus Christ, the plan of salvation, the holy priesthood, and gifts of the Spirit), and they label the humble followers of Christ as frenzied captives bound by false traditions (ironically, it is the inhabitants of Babylon that are the "frenzied captives"!).[882] When the people of Babylon are faced with trouble, they receive neither aid from Babylon nor respite from her unmerciful and unrelenting attacks. Amazingly, many people insist on living in Babylon and embracing that lifestyle, all the while considering themselves safe.

A scan of the scriptures proves otherwise—in every case! Safety is found *only* in the Covenant. Does that mean a person of the Covenant will not suffer? Of course not. Suffering is part of the testing process for every mortal being. But by abiding in the Covenant, we understand that our afflictions are consecrated for our gain.[883] That is, they are sanctified and therefore changed in purpose. No longer are they merely an adversity; rather, they are counted as a sacrifice—and sacrifice, we are taught, "brings forth the blessings of heaven."[884] Isaiah said, "And though the Lord give you the bread of adversity, and the water of affliction, yet shall not thy teachers be removed into a corner any more, but thine eyes shall see thy teachers."[885] The Bible footnote for the word "teachers" suggests the Savior. Adversity draws the Savior close.

Therefore, when Zion people suffer, they are ultimately safe in the Covenant. Their affliction will not damage them; it will serve to exalt them: "And we know that all things work together for good to them that love God, to them who are the called according to his purpose [his Covenant]."[886] Whereas a non-covenant person suffers for the purpose of leading him to Christ, a covenant person suffers to lead him closer to Christ or sometimes for "Christ's sake."[887] Among other things, this means that Jesus (because we are bound to him in the Covenant) will stand beside us, suffer with us, and help us to overcome. In the Covenant, Zion people are never left alone. Thus, it is in the Covenant that our afflictions are consecrated for our eternal welfare. Nephi put it this way: "But behold, I say unto you that ye must pray always, and not faint; that ye must not perform any thing unto the Lord save in the first place ye shall pray unto the Father in the name of Christ, *that he will consecrate thy performance unto thee, that thy performance may be for the welfare of thy soul.*"[888]

In a significant way, safety in the Covenant is linked directly to our active and faithful participation in temple worship. It is in the temple that we receive the blessings of the Covenant in their fulness. Heavenly Father will "establish the people that shall worship" in the temple. If we "honorably hold a name and standing in this thy house,"—that is, if we hold and actively and honorably use a temple recommend—we will be blessed now and "to all generations and for eternity." Great blessings of safety follow: "That no weapon formed against them shall prosper; that he who diggeth a pit for them shall fall into the same himself; that no combination of wickedness shall have power to rise up and prevail over thy people upon whom thy name shall be put in this house; and if

---

[881] Alma 30:12.
[882] Alma 30:12–17.
[883] 2 Nephi 2:2.
[884] "Praise to the Man," *Hymns*, no. 27.
[885] Isaiah 30:20.
[886] Romans 8:28.
[887] Alma 4:13; 2 Corinthians 12:10.
[888] 2 Nephi 32:9; emphasis added.

any people shall rise against this people, that thine anger be kindled against them; and if they shall smite this people thou wilt smite them; thou wilt fight for thy people as thou didst in the day of battle, that they may be delivered from the hands of all their enemies."[889]

Speaking of the security derived from the law of consecration, as a significant part of the new and everlasting covenant, the Lord said, "Now, this commandment [Covenant] I give unto my servants for their benefit while they remain, for a manifestation of my blessings upon their heads, and for a reward of their diligence *and for their security; for food and for raiment; for an inheritance; for houses and for lands.*"[890]

Clearly, both collectively and individually, we find safety in the Covenant.

SAFETY THROUGH CONSECRATION IN THE COVENANT

Consider that the work and the glory of God are to raise us to immortality at the highest level, called *eternal life*.[891] To that end the Father provides us the Atonement of his Son. The new and everlasting covenant emerges from the Atonement and makes us partners with Jesus in all things, both the easy and the difficult. By means of the Covenant, we are yoked with the Savior to inseparably face every eventuality. In this relationship, we pledge to each other all that we have and are, and therefore we are entitled to draw upon the resources of the stronger partner for any eventuality. In every way, we are *one* in the Covenant; neither are we divided nor are we alone. Now, because of our covenantal relationship, life's adversities are *consecrated* to the Lord for the welfare of our souls.

Consecration is an inclusive law that requires that we consecrate *everything* to the Lord, which by definition would include our difficulties. Think of it this way: When you marry would you exclude your problems from the vows you make to your spouse? Marriage partners bring everything they have and are to the relationship, and they work through things and make decisions together. Their joint consecration makes them one, and therefore there is no division of resources. They pool everything so that they might face life together. A marriage that does not tolerate the partners' individual problems is not strong and is at risk of failure. But a marriage in which the partners are equally yoked, in which the resources are unselfishly and totally pooled, will survive any storm. So it is with the Lord and us. In the Covenant, we bring all that we have to the relationship, including our problems, and we use the sum of our resources to face life together with the Lord.

That is exactly what the Lord wants. It is by facing difficulties *together* that strong relationships are forged. It is by facing opposition that we discover how deeply loyalties run. As we walk hard roads together, we discover things about each other that we could not learn otherwise. We come to trust and love each other. We find that together we are stronger than when we are apart. We learn to rely on the relationship, and we never want to step away from it. By experience, we discover that in the covenantal relationship, we are absolutely safe. Adversity, therefore, becomes an important solidifying agent for that relationship. By means of adversity, the agreement made at the outset of the Covenant by the baptismal ordinance becomes an unbreakable weld. This could be said of the marriage relationship. The *yes* spoken as a vow to form a marriage is only as good as the *yes* spoken as a vow every day thereafter. A marriage would be of little worth if one spouse were to leave the other or to let him or her down. Just so, the Covenant would be of no worth if God were to abandon us and allow us to face trouble alone. President George Q. Cannon said:

> No matter how serious the trial, how deep the distress, how great the affliction, [God] will never desert us. He never has, and He never will. He cannot do it. It is not His character [to do so]. He is

---

[889] D&C 109:24–28.
[890] D&C 70:15–16.
[891] Moses 1:39.

an unchangeable being; the same yesterday, the same today, and He will be the same throughout the eternal ages to come. We have found that God. We have made Him our friend, by obeying His Gospel; and He will stand by us. We may pass through the fiery furnace; we may pass through deep waters; but we shall not be consumed nor overwhelmed. We shall emerge from all these trials and difficulties the better and purer for them, if we only trust in our God and keep His commandments.[892]

THE GREAT DISCOVERY

One of the monumental discoveries of our taking and abiding in the Covenant is this: *God will take care of us*. The Lord's intention is to exalt us in the Covenant, not to destroy us; he uses adversarial situations to build faith rather than to confuse us. He is an omniscient God of consistency, power, mercy, and love. Therefore, in the Covenant with him we are absolutely safe.

One of the greatest demonstrations of the safety of the Covenant is that of the ancient Israelites.

> This is thy God that brought thee up out of Egypt, and had wrought great provocations; yet thou in thy manifold mercies *forsookest them not* in the wilderness: the pillar of the *cloud departed not* from them by day, to lead them in the way; *neither the pillar of fire* by night, to shew them light, and the way wherein they should go. Thou gavest also thy good spirit to *instruct them,* and withheldest not thy *manna* from their mouth, and gavest them *water* for their thirst. *Yea, forty years didst thou sustain them* in the wilderness, [so that] they *lacked nothing;* their *clothes waxed not old, and their feet swelled not.*[893]

The Lord never forsook them, although they were often weak and rebellious. He was with them both day and night. He constantly instructed them. He provided manna and water to sustain them. For four decades of wandering, they lacked nothing! Amazingly, neither their clothing nor their shoes wore out. Perhaps to teach his obstinate children an invaluable lesson, the Lord showed them unmistakably that he could keep them safe in the Covenant.

At the end of Jesus' life, just before he entered Gethsemane, he reminded his apostles of their early missions when he had purposely placed them in a condition of *lack* to teach them of their safety in the Covenant. He accomplished this lesson by sending them out with neither purse nor scrip. Now, looking back, he asked them: "When I sent you without purse, and scrip, and shoes, lacked ye any thing? And they said, Nothing."[894] As much as the apostles needed firsthand experience with the Covenant's safety, so do we. When we lack, we can go to the Lord, and because we are one with him in the Covenant, he will take care of us. We are safe.

EXAMPLES OF SAFETY IN THE COVENANT

After the Lord clothed Adam and Eve in skins representing the Atonement,[895] he sent them into the lone and dreary world, where they were kept safe in the Covenant.

---

[892] Cannon, *Collected Discourses*, 2:185; emphasis added.
[893] Nehemiah 9:18–21; emphasis added.
[894] Luke 22:35.
[895] McConkie and Ostler, *Revelations of the Restoration*, 223.

Lehi abandoned everything to make an extraordinary journey through the harsh wilderness, and he was kept safe in the Covenant. Does safety mean being free from afflictions and adversity? Of course not. Rather, safety in the Covenant suggests that the Lord never leaves us alone. Like the bridegroom who would never leave his suffering wife's side, the Bridegroom, who is our Savior, never leaves us in times of trial. By covenant, he stands beside us, upholds us, cares for us, and loves us through to our journey's or trial's end. That is true safety that is inherent in the Covenant.

The Brother of Jared found safety in the Covenant. After an arduous journey to the seashore, he committed his people into the safekeeping of God and launched eight vessels toward an unknown destination. For 344 days, they were driven forth by a furious wind upon the water. They were tossed and crushed by mountainous waves, buried in the depths of the sea, and cast about by great and terrible tempests—and yet they were safe in the Covenant they had made. "There was no water that could hurt them." The Lord was ever with them: "When they were encompassed about by many waters they did cry unto the Lord, and he did bring them forth again upon the top of the waters. . . . No monster of the sea could break them, neither whale that could mar them; and they did have light continually." They had made the Covenant and they were safe in it. "And they did sing praises unto the Lord; yea, the brother of Jared did sing praises unto the Lord, and he did thank and praise the Lord all the day long; and when the night came, they did not cease to praise the Lord."[896]

Abraham lay bound upon the altar, but he was safe in the Covenant. The Lord delivered him. His wife was taken from him twice, but she was safe in the Covenant. Abraham prepared to sacrifice Isaac, but he and his son were safe in the Covenant. Even martyrs such as Abinadi and the women and children of Ammonihah were ultimately safe "in the arms of Jesus."[897] Ironically, their safety was defined by martyrdom, which launched them into eternal life. Of course, martyrdom is a manifestation of the sacrifice of all things, which Joseph Smith said was necessary to obtain eternal life.[898] Nevertheless, while they made their sacrifice, they were kept safe in the Covenant. And as we make our sacrifice, the Covenant will keep us safe, too.

Understanding the importance of keeping the Covenant at all costs, Helaman urged the Ammonites to stand firm in their resolve, even when the country was about to be overrun. "But I would not suffer them that they should break this covenant which they had made, supposing that God would strengthen us, insomuch that we should not suffer more because of the fulfilling the oath which they had taken."[899]

Clearly, the best course of action is to keep the Covenant. Mortality is a place of testing and a time to make our sacrifices. But while we are doing so, we gain greater strength and do "not suffer more because of the fulfilling of the oath which [we have] taken."

Lazarus was dead for four days, but he was safe in the Covenant. On that occasion, the Savior focused the attention of Lazarus's sister, Martha, on Jesus' true identity, saying, "I am the resurrection, and the life: he that believeth in me, though he were dead, yet shall he live: *And whosoever liveth and believeth in me shall never die. Believest thou this?*"[900] It is a question that each of us must answer: Do we believe—*really believe*—in this Jesus with whom we have made the Covenant? Will we believe, even with the stark reality of death staring at us, that we are yet safe?

The people of Alma the Elder people escaped their Babylon, made the Covenant with the Lord, and continued to abide in it at every hazard, even when they were in captivity. "And it came to pass that the voice of the Lord came to them in their afflictions, saying: Lift up your heads and be of good comfort, *for I know of the covenant which ye have made unto me; and I will covenant with my people and*

---

[896] Ether 6:5–11.
[897] Mosiah 13:9; Alma 14:11; Mormon 5:11.
[898] Smith, *Lectures on Faith*, 6:7.
[899] Alma 56:8.
[900] John 11:25–26; emphasis added.

deliver them out of bondage."[901] Alma's people had no misgivings; their faith in the Lord and his Covenant were verified. They were, and always had been, safe in the Covenant.

An incident in Jesus' ministry demonstrates safety in the Covenant. The exhausted Lord set out in a boat by night with his disciples. "And there arose a great storm of wind, and the waves beat into the ship, so that it was now full. And he was in the hinder part of the ship, asleep on a pillow: and they awake him, and say unto him, Master, carest thou not that we perish? And he arose, and rebuked the wind, and said unto the sea, Peace, be still. And the wind ceased, and there was a great calm. And he said unto them, Why are ye so fearful? how is it that ye have no faith?"[902] The Lord's question feels like a rebuke. He might have said, "We have entered the Covenant together, haven't we? That means that I am with you—*always!* Why, then, are you afraid? Where is your faith? Don't you know yet who I am and what to expect of me? We are in this together. You are safe in the Covenant!"

Finally, consider the stripling warriors. These were young men who had taken the Covenant and who were suddenly thrust into a new and dangerous environment that required enormous faith. "They never had fought, yet they did not fear death." How had they achieved this level of courage? Helaman described their bravery as the greatest he had ever seen among the Nephites. They had learned it at their mothers' knees. Evidently the concept of safety in the Covenant had been drilled into them so well that they "did not doubt [that] God would deliver them." When Helaman asked them, "What say ye, my sons, will ye go against [the Lamanites] to battle?" they answered, "Father, behold our God is with us, and he will not suffer that we should fall; then let us go forth." They knew who the Lord was, and their faith was in the power and safety of the Covenant: "And they rehearsed unto me the words of their mothers, saying: We do not doubt our mothers knew it." Helaman reported the result: "To my great joy, there had not one soul of them fallen to the earth; yea, and they had fought as if with the strength of God; yea, never were men known to have fought with such miraculous strength."[903] They drew upon the power of God, which was available to them in the Covenant, and they were safe.

For Zion people, the lesson of safety is of ultimate importance. Only faith that the Lord is near and that he will never leave us can provide sufficient confidence for us to leave Babylon behind, as have other people of great faith, and throw ourselves wholly upon the tender mercies of the Lord. Only faith in the Lord and his promises can help us break from telestial law and embrace celestial law, which makes little sense in a telestial world. But if we will have the courage to sever ourselves from Babylon and allow the Covenant to make of us Zion people, we will make the discovery of a lifetime: We are absolutely safe in the Covenant—safer than we have ever been or felt before.

Progressing in the Covenant

Years of service and purifying exertion are required to prepare us to endure the celestial glory that is typical of Zion. No casual effort will allow us to stand shoulder to shoulder with heavenly beings; our effort must include the totality of our heart, might, mind, and strength. The new and everlasting covenant is designed to snatch us from telestial bondage and complacency, introduce us to celestial law, and fit us for celestial glory.

We begin our progression in the Covenant by duty, which is motivation enough to provide us shelter in the Covenant. Then, keeping the Covenant's associated commandments will hold us firmly on the strait and narrow path. Along the way, as we have experience with the Covenant, we begin to be motivated by understanding; that is, we start to comprehend the reasoning behind the Covenant, and we hunger and thirst for more information. In other words, we now have tasted of the fruit, found it to be delicious, and we desire more. Somewhere along the path, we discover that the Covenant is

---

[901] Mosiah 24:13.
[902] Mark 4:37–40.
[903] Alma 56:44–47, 56.

much more than a set of laws, which seems at times to be restrictive; the Covenant, rather, is a relationship. The Covenant is all about love. Knowing that, we begin to be motivated by love. We love God and his Son in return, and our ability to love grows. The more we love God and our fellowmen, the more we become Zion people. Finally, the path of the Covenant that we entered into at baptism leads us carefully along until we can stand in the presence of God. But the Covenant does not stop there; the Covenant is an eternal agreement whereby we become like God, inherit all that he has, do all that he does, and have the right to draw upon his resources forever to build our individual kingdoms.

As we examine the Covenant, we see that it begins with general requirements that progressively become more specific. For example, when we are baptized, we make broad agreements, one of which is to take upon ourselves the name of Jesus Christ. Later, when we receive the covenant of the sacrament, we take upon us his name again—this time more specifically—by partaking of the emblems representing his body and blood. Then, as we progress further in the Covenant and receive the covenant of the priesthood, the Lord once again places upon us his name,[904] which allows us to authoritatively do his works. Later still, when we go to the temple to obtain the revelation of the priesthood,[905] we receive, as Brigham Young said, sacred "key words, signs and tokens"[906] that specifically point to Christ and the power of his name.[907] Finally, when we marry for time and eternity and enter into the patriarchal order of the priesthood, we enter the door of exaltation where we receive our spouse in a way that binds us together with a bond that is symbolically as secure as that by which we are bound to the Father and the Son. Now we have taken an essential step in magnifying our primary priesthood *calling,* the call to eternal life that is stipulated in the oath and covenant of the priesthood.[908] Only by being sealed in marriage can we respond to that call. Only by the marriage covenant can we come to "know the only wise and true God, and Jesus Christ," and experience "eternal lives."[909] Now we have progressed to the point where we can truly begin to become like the Father and the Son.

So it is with all our covenants. Initially, we make broad agreements that require general sacrifice and obedience. Then as we gain understanding about those covenants, we must demonstrate more specific obedience and greater sacrifice. The end result of the process of covenant making is the creation of a celestial person, Zionlike, fully formed in the image of Christ, someone who is willing to be profoundly obedient to every word that proceeds from the mouth of God and to sacrifice anything and everything for him.

Discovering the Relationship through Progression

As we progress in the Covenant, we discover that it is a relationship of equality between two people who love each other. Although this relationship is amazingly *horizontal* rather than *vertical,* we nevertheless covenant to recognize and sustain the lordship of the Savior and the sovereignty of the Father.

Our relationship progresses along lines of intimacy. We enter the Covenant as a servant, we progress to a friend, and we end up as a son or daughter. Joseph Smith set the latter-day example. For example, at the beginning of Joseph's ministry, we hear the Lord referring to him as his servant: "Wherefore, I the Lord, knowing the calamity which should come upon the inhabitants of the earth, called upon *my servant* Joseph Smith, Jun., and spake unto him from heaven, and gave him

---

[904] Abraham 1:18.
[905] D&C 2:1.
[906] Young, *Discourses of Brigham Young,* 416.
[907] Moroni 7:48; 1 John 3:2; D&C 132:24; *Encyclopedia of Mormonism,* 1428.
[908] D&C 84:33.
[909] D&C 132:34.

commandments."[910] Later, we hear the Lord referring to Joseph as his friend: "Verily, I say unto my servant Joseph Smith, Jun., or in other words, I will call you friends, for you are my friends, and ye shall have an inheritance with me."[911] Still later, after Joseph had proved that he would abide in the Covenant at all hazards, we hear the Lord calling him his son: "*My son,* peace be unto thy soul; thine adversity and thine afflictions shall be but a small moment. And then, if thou endure it well, God shall exalt thee on high; thou shalt triumph over all thy foes."[912] Of course, these titles are somewhat intermixed, but the progression we are speaking of seems to be evident in the Doctrine and Covenants, and these examples serve to illustrate the point.

This pattern—*servant-friend-son*—might help us to understand our progression in the Covenant. A servant receives and fulfills the commandments of his Lord. A servant might know his Lord, but not intimately.

A friend, on the other hand, because of his relationship with the Lord, is in a position to ask what he can do for the other person. Friends do not command each other; rather, one friend might request something of the other, knowing that his friend will help. Friends share intimate conversations, they know a great deal about each other, and they have much in common. It is worth noting that servants and friends do not necessarily represent eternal relationships, as does a family. The status of servant or friend can be temporary, but always these relationships are defined by set boundaries. Therefore, if we are to progress from servant or friend to family, something significant in the relationship must change. That brings us to the ultimate stage of the Covenant: *children of God.*

A child—a son or daughter—is part of the most intimate relationship: *family.* A child comes to know everything about his Parent. A child has the right to say to his Parent, "Your name is my name and your work is my work. I am yours forever by covenant; we are linked together by blood; we are bound together by eternal love." While one of the greatest manifestations of love is offering your life for a friend,[913] the ultimate sacrifices are made within family, which is the highest level of friendship. There the greatest loyalties are forged. We enter the Covenant to serve the Lord, become his intimate friend, and become his child to whom he bequeaths all that he has. "Marvel not that all mankind, yea, men and women, all nations, kindreds, tongues and people, must be born again; yea, born of God, changed from their carnal and fallen state, to a state of righteousness, being redeemed of God, *becoming his sons and daughters.*"[914] Zion people walk and talk with their Father and Brother and enjoy their familial relationship.[915]

ORDER IN THE COVENANT

Having received the Covenant, Frederick G. Williams, a close associate of Joseph Smith, relaxed his agreement. The result, as is always the case, was that Satan gained power over him. In a merciful rebuke, the Lord called him back to the safety of the Covenant: "I have commanded you to bring up your children in light and truth. But verily I say unto you, my servant Frederick G. Williams, you have continued under this condemnation; you have not taught your children light and truth, according to the commandments; *and that wicked one hath power, as yet, over you, and this is the cause of your affliction.* And now a commandment I give unto you—*if you will be delivered you shall set in order your own house,* for there are many things that are not right in your house."[916]

---

[910] D&C 1:17; emphasis added.
[911] D&C 93:45; emphasis added; D&C 100:1.
[912] D&C 121:7–8.
[913] John 15:13.
[914] Mosiah 27:25; emphasis added.
[915] Moses 7:21.
[916] D&C 93:40–43; emphasis added.

Zion is defined by order, and order defines the lives of Zion people. As much as the Covenant brings power and safety into our lives, the Covenant also brings order—the order of Zion. The covenant making instances in our lives are like compass points that keep us oriented to true north. By giving strict diligence to the ordinances and covenants, we invite the Lord's order into our lives. Repeatedly, the Lord reminds us that his house is an ordered house: "Behold, mine house is a house of order, saith the Lord God, and not a house of confusion."[917] Therefore, he commands us to organize ourselves against the standard of the Covenant so that we might remain safe and clean: "And I give unto you, who are the first laborers in this last kingdom, a commandment that you assemble yourselves together, *and organize yourselves,* and prepare yourselves, and sanctify yourselves; yea, purify your hearts, and cleanse your hands and your feet before me, that I may make you clean."[918] This quality of order and its associated blessings can be accomplished and found only by and through the Covenant.

ORDER AND ORDINANCES

The words *order, ordain,* and *ordinance* come from the same root. Ordinances give order to the Covenant; ordinances ordain order in our lives. The order of salvation is an order of authorized *ordinances.* Ordinances are the markers that define the path leading to eternal life. Is there any other way to achieve exaltation? No. Jesus said, "My house is a house of order."[919] To Peter and the apostles, he said, "Go ye into all the world, and preach the gospel to every creature. He that believeth and is baptized shall be saved; but he that believeth not shall be damned."[920] Without authorized ordinances there is no possibility of salvation.

This process of ordinances seems like nonsense to many in the world. The Lord uses sacred symbols and rites to teach us about *his* world. To access the powers associated with these ordinances, we must make agreements or covenants with the Lord. When we keep our part of the agreement, he keeps his. Then we progress in an orderly manner, ordinance to ordinance, blessing to blessing, power to power, knowledge to knowledge, until we become like God.

We must receive the ordinances in the correct order; otherwise, they lack power to save. The Apostle Paul was teaching in the province of Ephesus when he met a group of twelve disciples who said they had been baptized. He wondered about this and asked them if they had received the Holy Ghost. They had not. Joseph Smith said you might as well baptize a bag of sand as baptize without conferring the Holy Ghost—one without the other is meaningless.[921] Paul asked these people how they had been baptized, and they said they had received John's baptism. We might speculate on what they meant, but obviously they had not received the ordinances correctly. Paul explained to them that baptisms must be done in the name of Jesus Christ by someone having the authority of Jesus Christ. That is the order of this ordinance. Because Paul had authority to baptize correctly, he baptized them *again* the right way, and then he conferred upon them the gift of the Holy Ghost. Now they were on the ordained path.

What do we learn from this account? Being good is not enough to save us, nor is merely having good intentions. We must be good and do the right thing in the right order if we want to end up in the right place. We should keep in mind that the people whom Paul was teaching were sincere people who were trying to live good lives, but they had a mistaken idea. When Paul, who was authorized by Jesus Christ, performed the ordinance of baptism correctly, these people suddenly received the promised blessings associated with true baptism and the Holy Ghost, and miraculous things began to

---

[917] D&C 132:8, 18; 88:119; 109:8.
[918] D&C 88:74; emphasis added.
[919] D&C 132:8.
[920] Mark 16:15–16.
[921] Smith, *Teachings of the Prophet Joseph Smith,* 314.

happen: "And when Paul had laid [his] hands upon them, the Holy Ghost came on them; and they spake with tongues, and prophesied."[922] Miracles always happen as a result of receiving covenants and ordinances. These miracles are signs that the ordinances are true. Zion people order their lives according to the ordinances; they follow the ordained markers leading to eternal life, and they experience miracle after miracle along the way.

Order and Consecration

The issue of order goes to the heart of the new and everlasting covenant: *the law of consecration*. This culminating law bids us to acknowledge that all things belong to God. We are stewards[923] who are accountable to him for the discharge of our stewardships.[924] What is done with his property is not our prerogative to dictate—it is his. The element of order mandated by consecration insists that we esteem others as ourselves[925] in order that all men and women might be made equal according to their wants, needs, family situations, and access to the Lord's storehouse.[926]

This is the established order of the law of consecration as dictated by the Covenant. When we ignore, rationalize, or modify this order to fit our personal objectives, we step away from the Covenant and become a law unto ourselves.[927] That attitude opens the door for Satan to afflict us. Then we, like Frederick G. Williams, might also receive the Lord's rebuke. But if we will allow the Covenant to help us organize ourselves and set our houses in order, we will reap power, safety, and prosperity in the order of the Covenant.

Abide in the Covenant

We began by quoting the Lord's requirement of those who have received the Covenant: "I have decreed in my heart, saith the Lord, that I will prove you in all things, whether you will abide in my covenant, even unto death, that you may be found worthy. For if ye will not abide in my covenant ye are not worthy of me."[928] Our access to power, our safety, our progression, and our future glory pivot on our abiding (staying put) in the Covenant. The Covenant secures us to Jesus Christ, the *True Vine*, from whom we, the branches, receive life and sustaining nourishment. Jesus taught:

> I am the true vine, and my Father is the husbandman.
> Every branch in me that beareth not fruit he taketh away: and every branch that beareth fruit, he purgeth it, that it may bring forth more fruit.
> Now ye are clean through the word which I have spoken unto you.
> Abide in me, and I in you. As the branch cannot bear fruit of itself, except it abide in the vine; no more can ye, except ye abide in me.
> I am the vine, ye are the branches: He that abideth in me, and I in him, the same bringeth forth much fruit: for without me ye can do nothing.

---

[922] Acts 19:1–7.
[923] D&C 38:17; 104:11–14.
[924] D&C 72:3; 104:13–18.
[925] D&C 38:24–27; 51:3, 9; 70:14; 78:6; 82:17.
[926] D&C 51:3.
[927] D&C 88:21–35.
[928] D&C 98:14–15.

> If a man abide not in me, he is cast forth as a branch, and is withered; and men gather them, and cast them into the fire, and they are burned.
>
> If ye abide in me, and my words abide in you, ye shall ask what ye will, and it shall be done unto you.
>
> Herein is my Father glorified, that ye bear much fruit; so shall ye be my disciples.[929]

Notice that the branches are already producing when the husbandman (God) comes, but he wants to urge them to produce at a higher level. Therefore, he begins to prune, that is, to "purge and purify." With regard to the Covenant made between the Husbandman and the branches, purging and purifying is exactly what each party agreed must happen. The branches (us) agreed to endure (abide) the Husbandman's purging and purifying process with the assurance that they would progressively gain greater strength and produce more fruit. With that goal in mind, the Husbandman begins to cut away from the branches anything that saps their strength. He carefully directs the new growth so that the branches might perform optimally. For a period of time, the branches might appear (and probably feel) pitiful and barren. For a season, they might not produce much fruit. But the Husbandman knows that in time the purging and purifying procedure will cause the branches to mature and bring forth more than they ever have before.

Returning to the Lord's commandment—"abide in my covenant"—we see the two meanings of *abide* represented in the purging and purifying process: (1) the branches must *remain* attached to the True Vine for the duration of the process; (2) the branches must *endure* the husbandman's purging and purifying efforts. Sometimes this procedure is called *chastening*. "For whom the Lord loveth he chasteneth, and scourgeth every son whom he receiveth. If ye endure chastening, God dealeth with you as with sons; for what son is he whom the father chasteneth not?" In this case, to chasten means "to make chaste"[930] or to purify. "Now no chastening for the present seemeth to be joyous, but grievous: nevertheless afterward it yieldeth the peaceable fruit of righteousness unto them which are exercised thereby."[931] "Without sufferings [chastisement]," we are reminded, "[we] could not be made perfect."[932]

ABIDING IN THE COVENANT SUMMONS DIVINE LOVE

Our faithfulness in abiding in the Covenant directly affects our ability to draw upon the Savior's love. Jesus said, "If ye keep my commandments, ye shall abide in my love."[933] The stated reward is remarkable: "Ye shall ask what ye will, and it shall be done unto you."[934] We will never lack for nourishment or strength if we (the branches) abide in Christ (the True Vine), and if we will endure the purging and purifying process. To lack nothing is a central principle of Zion. Our determination to remain unfailingly attached to the True Vine allows us the covenantal right to ask for blessings and to receive accordingly.

Abiding in the Covenant disproportionately rewards the sacrifice that we make to remain and endure. King Benjamin reminded us that God's blessings always exceed our efforts in faithfulness: "If ye should serve him with all your whole souls yet ye would be unprofitable servants."[935] Eternal law

---

[929] John 15:1–8.
[930] *Encyclopedia of Mormonism*, 264.
[931] Hebrews 12:6–7, 11.
[932] JST Hebrews 11:40.
[933] John 15:10.
[934] John 15:8.
[935] Mosiah 2:21.

states that God cannot be in debt or beholden to anyone; we are always in debt to him. King Benjamin illustrated this truism by pointing out that God blesses us with our lives and supports us from moment to moment—indebtedness that we can never repay. Beyond life and support, he has also blessed us with the Atonement and the Covenant. By means of the Covenant, he has blessed us by revealing his lifestyle—his commandments. When we obey his commandments, he rewards us immediately, which creates an even greater imbalance in his favor: "And ye are still indebted unto him, and are, and will be, forever and ever."[936] Hence, by abiding in the Covenant we learn that there is risk neither in trusting him nor in sacrificing to obey him. We are always blessed in excess of our sacrifice.

Beyond receiving abundant blessings, abiding in the Covenant also defines the relationship between us and the Lord, which is founded on love. Blessings flow to us in this covenantal relationship. Just as a loving husband showers his wife with gifts of affection, so God generously and voluntarily showers us with blessings that speak of his love for us—indisputable evidences of his affection.

Blessings are also a means by which God and man are reconciled through the Atonement of Jesus Christ. Moreover, blessings comfort the righteous[937] and lift the hearts of the oppressed.[938] Blessings describe the Lord's devotion to the Covenant and his gratitude for our likewise abiding in it. Blessings reveal the Lord's perfect set of attributes and characteristics, including his power, his awareness, and his love, all of which he consecrates to us in the Covenant. Blessings attest to his nearness and his interest in our welfare. They communicate, "I am aware. I am near. I love you." Blessings anchor us to our hope in Christ, which strengthens us to continue to abide in the Covenant until we have arrived at its exalted destination. Blessings communicate that we are never alone; in the Covenant that would simply be impossible.

ABIDING IN THE COVENANT THROUGH THE SACRAMENT

As mentioned previously, one way that we abide in the Covenant is through the covenant of the sacrament. By means of this singular ordinance, we "retain a remission of sins"[939] and "remember, and always retain in remembrance, the greatness of God."[940]

The sacrament allows us to renew our baptismal covenant by worthily partaking of "the emblems of the flesh and blood of Christ."[941] Once again, we agree to (1) Take upon ourselves the name of Jesus Christ; (2) Always remember him, his Atonement, his teachings, his example, and his love for us; and (3) Keep all the agreements that we made at baptism, including every commandment of God, and "to live by every word that proceedeth forth from the mouth of God."[942] The sacrament is significant in that it assures us a continuing remission of our sins, which is essential for pure-hearted Zion people.

It is by the ordinance of the sacrament that we receive the assurance of our retaining the gift of the Holy Ghost, which we were commanded to receive at baptism. Always having the Lord's Spirit with us is the Lord's sign to us that we are yet retaining a remission of sins by the merits of Jesus Christ.[943] This allows us imperfect beings to progress in the Covenant until we become Zionlike and receive the ultimate promise concerning the sacramental covenant: eternal life. Elder McConkie

---

[936] Mosiah 2:22–24.
[937] Daniel 9:4.
[938] Psalms 74:20–21.
[939] Mosiah 4:12; JST Matthew 26:22–25; JST Mark 14:20–25; JST Luke 22:17–20.
[940] Mosiah 4:12.
[941] D&C 20:40.
[942] McConkie, *Mormon Doctrine*, 660; D&C 84:44.
[943] 2 Nephi 31:19; Moroni 6:4; D&C 3:20.

wrote: "As his part of the contract, the Lord covenants: 1. That such worthy saints shall have his Spirit to be with them; and 2. That in due course they shall inherit eternal life."[944]

Summary and Conclusion

The new and everlasting covenant is the first pillar upon which Zion is built. The Covenant is the most glorious ever revealed. It contains the greatest hope and the most impressive promises of anything found on earth or in heaven. By abiding its terms we can escape Babylon, flee to Zion, and forever abide safely in the embrace of our Eternal Father.

The Father himself created the new and everlasting covenant for the salvation of his children.[945] The purposes of the Covenant are to provide us: (1) knowledge and power for personal salvation, and (2) knowledge, authority, and power to help save other people by offering and administering to them the Covenant. Our ability to become Zion people—and even our entire eternal future—hang upon our diligence in adhering to the terms of the Covenant. The Lord said, "I have decreed in my heart, saith the Lord, that I will prove you in all things, whether you will abide in my covenant, even unto death, that you may be found worthy. For if ye will not abide in my covenant ye are not worthy of me."[946]

The deeper we dig into the doctrine of the Covenant, the more we discover a loving relationship. A caring Father is offering us all that he has and is. Therefore, he reveals to us the laws by which he lives, and the same eternal covenants of progression and exaltation that made him who he is. He offers these to us knowing that the Covenant will help us to grow from dependence to independence, from natural men to gods.

To make our relationship *sure*, and, furthermore, to insure the terms of the Covenant, three distinct offerings must be made: (1) The Father offers to share with us the supernal blessings of the Covenant; (2) the Son offers to cover the infinite expenses of the Covenant that we cannot meet; (3) we offer our hearts. Yielding our hearts to God allows us to be assimilated into the celestial order of the gods. We do this by living the celestial laws of Zion in a telestial world, adopting the Father's work of redemption as our own, and becoming experts at serving and saving his children.

The Covenant contains multiple benefits and powers. For example, because it is the word of God, the Covenant has the inherent power of *leavening*. Its doctrines grow within us until we are totally leavened by them. The doctrines of the Covenant transform us into Zion people.

The Covenant separates us from the world. When we enter into the Covenant by baptism, we are *born again* into a new life.[947] We *die* as to our old life and are *born* again as new beings with a new father, Jesus Christ; we have a new family, the Church of Jesus Christ.[948] Now we are his covenant people. As such, we will be forever separate and unique, the Lord's peculiar treasure.[949]

There is power in the Covenant. As we enter the Covenant through baptism, the Lord places upon us his name, which is a name of power—*Jesus Christ*. Through that name, because we are now in a loving covenantal relationship, we can ask the Father for blessings by the power of the name of Jesus Christ, and God will respond—*because we are family*.

There is safety in the Covenant. Because Babylon is a dangerous condition, we seek the Lord's safety. This can be found only in the Covenant. When we finally garner the courage to abandon the telestial condition and embrace celestial law, which we must do in order to become Zionlike, we will

---

[944] John 6:5–4; McConkie, *Mormon Doctrine*, 660.
[945] 3 Nephi 16:5; 20:12, 25, 27, 29, 46; 21:4, 7; 29:1; Mormon 5:14; 9:47; Ether 4:15; Moroni 10:33; D&C 84:40.
[946] D&C 98:14–15.
[947] Mosiah 27:25; Alma 7:14; Moses 6:59; John 3:3–7.
[948] Moses 5:7.
[949] Exodus 19:5; Psalms 135:4.

make the discovery of a lifetime: We are absolutely safe—safer than we have ever been or felt before! Safety in the Covenant also applies to the afflictions that we suffer in mortality. When we suffer, our afflictions are consecrated for our gain *in the Covenant*.[950] The Lord converts our afflictions from destructive to exalting: "And we know that all things work together for good to them that love God, to them who are the called according to his purpose [his Covenant]."[951]

The Covenant *orders* our lives so that we might progress to eternal life. As order applies to progression, we initially obey the laws of the Covenant out of a sense of duty. Over time, duty progresses to understanding, and ultimately we are motivated to obey because of love. Step by step, as we progress in the Covenant with each higher law and ordinance, general requirements become more specific. Likewise, we progress in the Covenant from servant to friend to a son or daughter of God.

Living within the order of the Covenant protects us from the wicked one, while disorder, or disobedience, gives Satan power to afflict us. Therefore, the Lord commands us to set our houses in order according to the stipulations of the Covenant.

The order available to us through living the laws and ordinances of the Covenant keeps the compass of our lives oriented toward true north. The Lord reminds us that his house is a house of order and not of confusion. We progress to eternal life by following the ordained path. This path has markers or ordinances, which define the order of the Covenant. Each ordinance must be received in its proper order and lived faithfully if eternal life is to be gained. There is no other way. Without authorized ordinances there is no possibility of salvation.

The order of the Covenant and *the law of consecration* go hand in hand. The Lord's claim to the resources of the earth supersedes our claims. This is the covenantal order. No longer can we consider ourselves as owners but rather as accountable stewards of the Lord's property. Moreover, the covenantal order of relationships is one of equality, esteeming all men and women as ourselves and seeking for unity and cooperation. We cannot achieve the necessary faith to live the law of consecration without the ordering power of the priesthood and the Covenant's additional covenants and ordinances. But if we will allow the Covenant to help us to order our houses and lives, we will reap power, safety, and prosperity, according to the order of the Covenant.

"Abide in the Covenant" is the commandment of the Lord. Our ability to access power, find safety, progress, and attain future glory hinge on our abiding (staying put) in the Covenant. The Covenant secures us to Jesus Christ, the *True Vine*, from whom we, the branches, receive life and sustaining nourishment. In the Vine, the Husbandman, by covenant, purges and purifies us to fit us for eternal life.

Our faithfulness in abiding in the Covenant directly affects our ability to use the name of Jesus Christ. By this name of power, which we receive a right to use at baptism, we can approach the Father and ask for and receive blessings. Because the Father and the Son promise to respond, we never need to experience *lack;* sufficiency and abundance are central principles of Zion.

Our receiving the Father's blessings speaks to a covenantal relationship founded on love. His blessings anchor us to our hope in Christ and communicate that we are never alone. Because of God's blessings, we are always indebted to him—an incredible benefit understood only by those who abide faithfully in the Covenant.

These are the blessings of the Covenant and the condition of Zion people.

---

[950] 2 Nephi 2:2.
[951] Romans 8:28.

Section 8

The New and Everlasting Covenant—

The Holy Marriage

Throughout the scriptures, the marriage metaphor is used to describe our covenantal relationship with the Lord. He is the Bridegroom,[952] and the Church is the bride.[953] By extension, we, individually, are his bride: "For as a young man marrieth a virgin, so shall thy sons marry thee: and as the bridegroom rejoiceth over the bride, so shall thy God rejoice over thee."[954] We are to prepare ourselves for the time the Bridegroom comes to receive us: "Wherefore, be faithful, praying always, having your lamps trimmed and burning, and oil with you, that you may be ready at the coming of the Bridegroom—For behold, verily, verily, I say unto you, that I come quickly."[955] We are to become prepared and "beautiful" for him: "adorned as a bride."[956]

That the Lord chose marriage to describe the new and everlasting covenant should summon our solemn contemplation. Marriage is the summit of gospel covenants, the relationship that is the most intimate, most enduring, and the most loving of unions. Marriage is the relationship in which is manifest the power of God to create; children spring from this union; multiplication, replenishment, and fruitfulness become possible. The metaphor of marriage suggests profound loyalty, the abandonment of selfish interests, and complete sacrifice. Marriage requires the consecration of one's time, talents, and resources to his or her companion, the sum of what one is and has. Marriage is a covenantal lifestyle that results in *oneness*, a relationship wherein the partners are no longer "twain, but one flesh," joined together by God and intended to endure beyond man's attempts to put asunder.[957]

---

[952] Matthew 9:15; Mark 2:19; Luke 5:34; John 3:29.
[953] Revelation 21:2, 9–10; 22:17.
[954] Isaiah 62:5.
[955] D&C 33:17; see also D&C 88:92; 133:10, 19.
[956] D&C 109:74.
[957] Matthew 19:6.

If marriage is to be successful, it requires losing one's life in selfless service to and the loving of one's spouse; then, in return, marriage leads to finding one's life in a more exalted purpose.[958] Marriage urges the best of behavior in the partners. Think of what we would say of our "marriage" to the Lord: "and they shall mention the loving kindness of their Lord, and all that he has bestowed upon them according to his goodness, and according to his loving kindness, forever and ever."[959] Marriage is *being yoked* together to ease one another's burdens,[960] and the mutual sharing of each other's challenges: "In all their afflictions he was afflicted . . . ; and in his love, and in his pity, he redeemed them, and bore them, and carried them all the days."[961] By purpose and by design marriage is eternal,[962] the highest order of celestial living,[963] the ultimate source of happiness,[964] and significantly the highest order of the priesthood.[965] Conversely, disloyalty to the marriage covenant is a grievous sin, "most abominable above all sins save it be the shedding of innocent blood or denying the Holy Ghost."[966] Clearly, the Lord takes seriously the new and everlasting covenant and expects us to do the same.

In the foreword of Donna B. Nielsen's excellent work, *The Beloved Bridegroom*, Dr. Robert J. Norman wrote: "The wedding ceremony was a metaphor often used by Christ and the Old Testament authors. A study of the Jewish marriage customs yields a wealth of spiritual understanding and deeper insight into the teachings of Jesus and the Biblical prophets."[967] Donna Nielsen explained: "A knowledge of Biblical marriage imagery can greatly enrich our understanding of how God relates to us through covenants. Biblical covenant marriage imagery encompasses principles as diverse as Sabbath observance, the Atonement, temple worship, and missionary work. It literally begins with Adam and ends with Zion."[968] Let us, therefore, examine the new and everlasting covenant by contrasting it with the Jewish marriage tradition. In advance, we thank Donna B. Nielsen for her generous support in providing access to her research.

BORN TO MARRY

Elder John A. Widtsoe stated that marriage is "the most important event between birth and death,"[969] and certainly the Jewish people agreed. We cannot overstate the importance of marriage in Jewish society. Marriage was clearly linked to the covenant God made with Israel; in fact, we might say that it was understood that children were born with the purpose of marrying. Donna Nielsen stated that an infant male "was often affectionately called 'the little bridegroom.' This reflected one of three great hopes that parents had for their children, namely that their children would study Torah [study the scriptures], be under the wedding canopy [marry in the covenant], and do good deeds [live righteous lives]."[970] Immediately we see the connection between marriage and the new and everlasting covenant. And so with us, if we understand the symbolism, from the moment of birth, our life's purpose should be to learn about and prepare for the Bridegroom, enter into a Covenant with the

---

[958] Matthew 10:39.
[959] D&C 133:52.
[960] Matthew 11:30.
[961] D&C 133:53.
[962] D&C 132:19.
[963] D&C 131:2.
[964] McKay, *Man May Know for Himself*, 235.
[965] McConkie, *Mormon Doctrine*, 559.
[966] Alma 39:5.
[967] Nielsen, *Beloved Bridegroom*, iii.
[968] Nielsen, *Beloved Bridegroom*, 2.
[969] Widtsoe, *Evidences and Reconciliations*, 297.
[970] Nielsen, *Beloved Bridegroom*, 4.

Bridegroom, and do the works of the Bridegroom. As much as Jewish children were born to marry, we are born to enter into the Covenant.

Because marriage was *the* goal of Jewish life, husbands and wives married at an early age. No later than eighteen was the norm, and most often they married years before that. A boy became a Son of the Law by age thirteen, and technically one month later he was considered of marriageable age. Girls were eligible at twelve years and one month.[971] In today's culture, we might have difficulty imagining Joseph and Mary, two teenagers, taking on the heavy responsibility of marriage and caring for the Savior of the world. Also, we might struggle with the concept that Jesus could have been married for twelve to fifteen years and had children before he began his ministry at age thirty. But, according to Jewish custom, this may have been true. Marriage was the focal point of Jewish life, and we might imagine that Joseph and Mary followed the prevailing tradition by marrying in their teens.

THE PARENTS' RESPONSIBILITY AND THE BRIDE'S CHOICE

Marriages were thought to be too important to be left to chance. Fathers and mothers made these decisions for their children. Who else loved the child more? Who else had the child's best interests in mind? Who else wanted the child's happiness more than the parents? Today, we might cringe at this ancient custom, but Jewish children expected their parents to advocate for their happiness. Despite the fact that the parents were expected to prayerfully deliberate, then introduce their child to the intended spouse, the child owned the ultimate choice. Their agency was never violated.

Today, of course, parents do not formally choose their children's mates, but the similarity between the Covenant and the ancient custom is clear: Parents have the responsibility to introduce their children to Christ. Fathers, by virtue of holding the priesthood, have the responsibility to take their children into the waters of baptism and help them to enter into the new and everlasting covenant with Jesus. Now the children are given over or "married" to Christ by Covenant, and, taking upon them his name, they begin a relationship with him that will end up in the mansions of his Father.[972]

Love for each other was expected to be cultivated after the marriage, not necessarily before.[973] We note that after Isaac married Rebekah he grew in his love for her.[974] This reversal of order might seem strange to us, but the implication is intriguing: Covenant people grow together in love as they remain true to each other. When we enter into the new and everlasting covenant, we do so without a full appreciation for or love of the Lord. These things take time. But as we live together in the Covenant and as we have experience with the Lord, we grow to love him more and more. "The Semitic root word for 'love' is *haw* or *hav*. It means 'to warm' or 'to kindle,' 'to set on fire.'"[975] Over time, our love for the Bridegroom grows from an ember to a blazing fire until that love becomes as perfect as the God of love,[976] who "dwells in everlasting burnings."[977]

REQUIREMENTS TO LEGALIZE THE COVENANT

The marriage covenant "had serious implications. There were three parts that were vital to a completed marriage contract in biblical times. These were *money*, *writ*, and *intercourse*. All three of these conditions had to be met for a marriage to be recognized as legal." The groom was expected to pay a *bride price* for his beloved. Then he was to offer her a marriage contract, a *writ* or *ketuba*,

---

[971] Nielsen, *Beloved Bridegroom*, 2.
[972] Enos 1:27; Ether 12:32–37; D&C 59:2; 98:18.
[973] Nielsen, *Beloved Bridegroom*, 13.
[974] Genesis 24:67.
[975] Nielsen, *Beloved Bridegroom*, 13.
[976] 1 John 4:8.
[977] Isaiah 33:14–15.

whereby he consecrated himself to his bride. Finally, the marriage had to be consummated; he must *know* his wife through *sexual relations*. This last condition fulfilled the requirement that blood be shed to complete the covenant.[978]

Thus, in comparing marriage to the new and everlasting covenant, we (the bride) are:

1. "Bought with a price."[979]
2. United by covenant according to the law of consecration, which is "the law of the celestial kingdom."[980]
3. *Known*, or "made perfect through Jesus the mediator of the new covenant, who wrought out this perfect atonement through the shedding of his own blood."[981]

When we consider these conditions, we begin to understand the price that Jesus was willing to pay to draw us to him, redeem us, and secure our eternal affections. Marvin Wilson wrote: "The joining of a man and a woman is a reenactment or replica of God's eternal covenant relation to his chosen. To understand Biblical marriage is to understand the Biblical concept of covenant. In Hebrew 'to make a covenant' is literally 'to cut a covenant.' . . . The shedding of blood [in the sacrifice of an animal] dramatically ratified and sealed the covenant (Genesis 15:9–18; Jeremiah 34:18–20). If one attempted to break the covenant, the blood served as a powerful visual lesson that one's own blood would be shed. In brief, it was a solemn oath to be kept on pain of death. It was thus inviolable and irrevocable."[982]

INITIATING THE MARRIAGE PROPOSAL

The bridegroom initiated the offering of the covenant of marriage to the bride. When we consider this action in light of the new and everlasting covenant, we see something tender and loving about the character of the Savior. We are immediately impressed by the fact that he, not we, invites us into the new and everlasting covenant. Clearly, "we love him, because he first loved us."[983] We often miss the fact that when we are baptized, Jesus is the one who reached out to us and bade us enter into an eternal covenantal relationship with him. We sometimes mistakenly think that we were the ones who instigated the process, but, using the comparisons with the Jewish marriage tradition, that is not true. In advance of every baptism is Jesus' implied invitation. This fact speaks to his adoring love for us. He is the Bridegroom, and we are his potential bride. He is the one who begins the covenant-making process. He does this through the Holy Ghost and through his authorized representatives: fathers, home teachers, bishops, or missionaries.

The marriage proposal often took place at the harvest season, suggesting a bounteous relationship and a fruitful future.[984] Likewise, when we join with the Lord in the Covenant, we glorify both him and his Father and we "bear much fruit" together.[985] The proposal procedure began with the bridegroom going to the house of the bride. He was accompanied by his father or a close friend or friends. We can envision a small entourage, a companionship, two or more witnesses (like missionary companions), on an important mission to convey an invitation of infinite worth to the intended bride. In her presence, the bridegroom would make the covenantal offer while his friends supported him and

---

[978] Nielsen, *Beloved Bridegroom*, 18.
[979] 1 Corinthians 6:20.
[980] D&C 105:4.
[981] D&C 76:69.
[982] Wilson, *Our Father Abraham*, 205.
[983] 1 John 4:19.
[984] Nielsen, *Beloved Bridegroom*, 14.
[985] John 15:8.

bore witness of the event. This was the beginning of a union of holiness, for, truly, upon her acceptance of the marriage covenant, the bride would effectively ascribe holiness unto the lord,[986] her new husband. Donna Nielsen wrote: "The collective term for all that broadly comprises a Jewish marriage is *Kiddushin*, which literally means 'sanctities.' This concept includes the ideas of being *devoted irrevocably*, being *sanctified and set apart*, and being *consecrated*."[987] Clearly, the Jewish marriage is the perfect metaphor for the new and everlasting covenant.

Entering into the Covenant

The Bridegroom's proposal to us includes sacred rituals that *consecrate* him to us (the bride), and our accepting his proposal consecrates us to him. We hear overtures of the law of consecration in this. Other symbolisms of the new and everlasting covenant become evident as the betrothal ceremony unfolds. In the ancient Jewish marriage, the groom offered the bride's father a "bride price"—she was "bought with a price."[988] Then the bridegroom presented his potential bride a written covenant of marriage that he had prepared. He also offered her a "gift of value," which represented a "token" of his promise and an "emblem" of his love. With the token he recited a pledge to irrevocably bind and consecrate (dedicate) himself to her forever. Then, in the presence of two witnesses, he placed before his beloved a cup of wine. If she drank of the cup, the contract of marriage was ratified or sealed, and the betrothal period began. Moreover, by drinking of the cup, she indicated her willingness to take upon herself her husband's name. At that point, the couple, along with their guests, shared a covenantal meal.

Thus, by these rituals that were rich in imagery, the bridegroom and bride entered into the eternal covenant of marriage. When the ceremony was complete, the only question that remained was whether or not the rituals that represented the Covenant would translate into lifelong acts of devotion and consecration. That is, would the covenant become *enduring* by the couple's subsequent loyalty, patience, sacrifice, and love? Or would the covenant remain a set of symbols and a piece of paper upon which promises had been made but never enacted?

Now let us examine the symbolism of laws, rites, and ordinances[989] of the Jewish betrothal period and marriage.

Bought with a Price

When the marriage delegation, which included the groom, his father, his friends, and witnesses, arrived at the bride's home, the proposal ceremony began. First, the young man paid the girl's father a "bride price." There are several important symbolic parallels to our covenant with the Savior that are portrayed in the price that the bridegroom paid for the bride. "It meant a pledge of money given by the man to seal his offer to marry. This was not like buying a slave but was perceived as compensating the father for the great loss of his daughter and her contribution to the household. It recognized the care and diligence required to raise her to be a suitable wife. In addition, it also sealed a bond of alliance between the two families."[990] This relationship of *ownership* is described in the word *segulah*, "which means 'peculiar treasure' or 'treasured relationship.' . . . Truly, the worth of a bride was great in the eyes of her husband."[991]

---

[986] Exodus 39:30.
[987] Nielsen, *Beloved Bridegroom*, 18.
[988] 1 Corinthians 6:20.
[989] Lundwall, *Temples of the Most High*, 87.
[990] Nielsen, *Beloved Bridegroom*, 21.
[991] Nielsen, *Beloved Bridegroom*, 25–26.

Importantly, the bride price "signified the transfer of authority from father to husband."[992] That is, when the bride gave her consent and entered into the covenant, she agreed to fully belong to her husband, not as if she were a slave or property, but that their relationship would be *exclusive* as that of a beloved eternal companion. She was "bought with a price."[993] Now she was expected to shift her loyalty from her father to her husband and follow him in righteousness.

Of great significance was the amount of the bride price. A small amount suggested that her husband held her in low esteem and of little value. But if he paid a great deal for her in money or service, the implication was that he was acquiring something extremely valuable that required cherishing.[994] Thus, a bridegroom consecrating his all to "purchase" his bride would signify both immense sacrifice and unbounded love. It showed that, in his eyes, she was of infinite worth. We recall that Jacob "served seven years for Rachel, and they seemed to him but a few days because of his love for her."[995] When we consider the bride price, we cannot avoid the reference to the Savior who paid for us with his life and offers us all that he is and has. He bought us with "his own blood."[996]

Although the bride's father received the bride price, he returned most of it to his daughter. This became her dowry, which her husband could never access. It was her security, in case her husband died. Effectively, her father gave her *an endowment* so that she might enter her new life with adequate security to face the uncertainties of that life.[997] Thus, her security originated in the sacrifice of her husband and culminated in the generosity of her father.

The Marriage Contract

In Jewish thought, all covenantal relationships were extremely serious. Often, only when they were sealed in blood did they become final and legally binding. The actual terms of the marriage covenant "were spelled out in a formal document called a *ketubah* . . . which stated the bride price . . . the promises and obligations of the groom and listed the rights of the bride. It signified a permanent covenant and an exclusive agreement."[998] The wording of an ancient *ketubah* might be representative:

1. "I will provide you with food, clothing and necessities.
2. "I will redeem you if you are ever taken captive.
3. "I will live with you as a husband according to the universal custom."

Notice that the marriage contract was weighted in the bride's favor. The groom listed "what he would do for *her*, what he would give *her*, and how he would care and provide for *her*."[999] While it is true that we agree "to take upon us the name of [the] Son, and always remember him and keep his commandments,"[1000] it is also true that we sometimes forget how much the new and everlasting covenant is weighted in our favor. If we "receive" Jesus, we also receive all that Jesus inherits from his Father, particularly "[the] Father's kingdom . . . [and] all that my Father hath shall be given unto him."[1001] "They are they into whose hands the Father has given all things."[1002]

---

[992] Nielsen, *Beloved Bridegroom*, 21, referencing John J. Collins, "Marriage, Divorce, and Family in Second Temple Judaism," 104–62.
[993] 1 Corinthians 7:23.
[994] Nielsen, *Beloved Bridegroom*, 22.
[995] Genesis 29:20.
[996] Acts 20:28.
[997] Nielsen, *Beloved Bridegroom*, 23.
[998] Nielsen, *Beloved Bridegroom*, 26, 111.
[999] Nielsen, *Beloved Bridegroom*, 111.
[1000] D&C 20:77.
[1001] D&C 84:38.
[1002] D&C 76:55.

The marriage covenant in ancient times was meant to be one of love, security, and comforting assurance. The bridegroom listed promises to always take care of his wife with food, clothing, necessities, redemption, and affectionate attention.[1003] We would expect the same treatment from our relationship with the Lord in the Covenant. The text of Psalm 37 in the Jewish *Tanakh* reads: "The Lord is concerned for the needs of the blameless [in this case, the bride]; their portion lasts forever; they shall not come to grief in bad times; in famine, they shall eat their fill. . . . I have never seen a righteous man abandoned, or his children seeking bread. [The Lord] is always generous."[1004] By taking some license, we might personalize the promise of continuous caring that Jesus gave to his apostles on both continents:

> And why take ye thought for raiment? Consider the lilies of the field how they grow; they toil not, neither do they spin; and yet I say unto you, that even Solomon, in all his glory, was not arrayed like one of these. Wherefore, if God so clothe the grass of the field, which today is, and tomorrow is cast into the oven, even so will he clothe you, if ye are not of little faith.
> Therefore take no thought, saying, What shall we eat? or, What shall we drink? or, Wherewithal shall we be clothed? For your heavenly Father knoweth that ye have need of all these things. But seek ye first the kingdom of God and his righteousness, and all these things shall be added unto you.[1005]

Another stipulation of the marriage contract was the bridegroom's vow to redeem his wife should she ever be taken captive.[1006] Lehi assured his son Jacob of the surety of the Lord's redemption: "Wherefore, redemption cometh in and through the Holy Messiah; for he is full of grace and truth. Behold, he offereth himself a sacrifice."[1007] All of us have sinned and to one extent or another have been taken captive by the enemy of our souls. Each of us is in need of the Bridegroom's promise of redemption: "and he will take upon him death, that he may loose the bands of death which bind his people."[1008] We are reminded of Abraham, a type of the Savior, who assembled an army to rescue Lot and his household from their enemies when they had been taken captive. "And [Abraham] brought back all the goods, and also brought again his brother Lot, and his goods, and the women also, and the people."[1009] Thus, by covenant the Bridegroom places all that he has and is, including his own life, on the altar of sacrifice to redeem us from our enemies and to clear every obstacle that stands between us and exaltation.

Finally, the bridegroom anciently promised to live with his wife with love and affection. Donna Nielsen wrote: "The third and last promise in the [marriage contract] was the groom's promise to live as a husband with the bride and to give her an opportunity to bear children. In Hebrew 'to bear children' was synonymous with the term 'to bear fruit.' Children were called the 'fruit of the womb' (Luke 1:42)."[1010] To first be married (*oneness*) and to then bear fruit (*fruitfulness*) was considered by the ancients to be the measure of one's creation.[1011] The *oneness* and *fruitfulness* shared by a husband

---

[1003] Nielsen, *Beloved Bridegroom*, 111.
[1004] *Tanakh*, Psalms 37:18–19, 25–26.
[1005] 3 Nephi 13:28–33.
[1006] Nielsen, *Beloved Bridegroom*, 112.
[1007] 2 Nephi 2:6–7.
[1008] Alma 7:12.
[1009] Genesis 14:16.
[1010] Nielsen, *Beloved Bridegroom*, 114.
[1011] Smith, *Restoration of All Things*, 244.

and wife, and compared to our relationship with the Lord, is described by the Savior (the True Vine) in the following verse: "I am the vine, ye are the branches: He that abideth in me, and I in him, the same bringeth forth much fruit: for without me ye can do nothing."[1012] As long as we abide in the Covenant with him, he promises to abide in us, and together our union will be one of abundant fruitfulness.

Moreover, he promises his continuous affection. Nephi called these acts of affection "tender mercies," gentle reminders of his love and awareness; we might consider them "love notes" from the one who knows and adores us most. "Behold, I, Nephi, will show unto you that the tender mercies of the Lord are over all those whom he hath chosen."[1013] These evidences of love flow to us quietly but continually; there are a "multitude of his tender mercies."[1014] When the bride recognizes her husband's constant goodness, she is brought to tears for her good fortune, just as the Jaredites did upon recognizing the Lord's protection on their journey: "And when they had set their feet upon the shores of the promised land they bowed themselves down upon the face of the land, and did humble themselves before the Lord, and did shed tears of joy before the Lord, because of the multitude of his tender mercies over them."[1015]

The marriage contract itself was often elaborately decorated, becoming a piece of art and thus a thing of beauty. It contained the words of a binding and holy agreement, and the bride cherished it. The marriage contract was tangible proof of her future husband's devotion and her immutable rights.[1016] In this we again hear overtones of the new and everlasting covenant. No doctrine is more glorious. We cling to the Covenant because it offers us the Bridegroom's guarantees that he will continually provide for us, keep us safe, redeem us from our enemies, and live with us in loving and fruitful companionship. The Covenant promises us the Bridegroom's name, and it reminds us of the great price that he paid for us. The Covenant guarantees that he will endow us with all that he is and has. It states that we, his bride, are his "great treasure," and the Covenant reminds us that he has given his own blood to seal the covenant. What bride would not cherish such a document, especially if it was backed up by years of verifiable devotion?

The Gift of Value

The presentation of the marriage contract was followed by the bridegroom offering his beloved "a token," that is, "a gift of value." This gift was different from the bride price, which the bridegroom had paid to the young woman's father. In this case, the groom offered the token directly to his intended bride. "The groom's gift was considered to be an extension of himself. . . . It also symbolized his willingness to sacrifice and served as a reminder of his love. A gold ring was frequently used as this token or gift because it represented eternity. Anciently, the ring used was often a link from a gold chain. The chain represented past and future family associations and was seen as symbolically linking the girl to her new family."[1017]

Sometimes the "gift of value" was silver or gold coins. A devoted bride would often make a chain of the coins and attach them "to her veil as an important part of her headdress." In private and in public, she was spoken for, beloved, and ever abiding in the covenant.[1018] If she lost something this valuable, she would view it as a tragedy. Jesus' parable of the lost coin makes more sense in this light; the loss of something so precious could indicate that she had been careless with the token that her

---

[1012] John 15:5.
[1013] 1 Nephi 1:20.
[1014] 1 Nephi 8:8.
[1015] Ether 6:12.
[1016] Nielsen, *Beloved Bridegroom*, 28.
[1017] Nielsen, *Beloved Bridegroom*, 28.
[1018] D&C 98:14; 132:19.

betrothed husband had given her. Clearly, our treatment of the Lord's gifts is an indication of our respect for him and the Covenant that we have entered into. The tokens he gives us are the emblems of his sacrifice,[1019] represented by the emblems of the sacrament.

THE PLEDGE

After the bridegroom had paid the bride price, offered his beloved the covenantal marriage contract, and given her the token or gift of value, he "recited a ritual statement to consecrate himself to his bride."[1020] For example, the biblical prophet, Hosea, speaking for the Lord, pledged, "And I will betroth thee unto me for ever; yea, I will betroth thee unto me in righteousness, and in judgment, and in lovingkindness, and in mercies. I will even betroth thee unto me in faithfulness: and thou shalt know the Lord."[1021]

Donna Nielsen explained that the word "consecrate, wherein the groom consecrated himself to the bride, is used to mean, 'to devote irrevocably.' The groom has no options here—no escape clauses—there is no question ever that he would rescind his invitation to the woman to marry. He cannot break this [covenant] if the woman remains faithful, for he is bound if she fulfills her part of the covenant."[1022]

Just so, Christ consecrates and devotes himself to us irrevocably when he offers us the Covenant. He will absolutely live up to every promise made in the Covenant. The scriptures are replete with such language. For example: "What I the Lord have spoken, I have spoken, and I excuse not myself; and though the heavens and the earth pass away, my word shall not pass away, but shall all be fulfilled."[1023] "Ye know in all your hearts and in all your souls, that not one thing hath failed of all the good things which the Lord your God spake concerning you; all are come to pass unto you, and not one thing hath failed thereof."[1024] "Who am I, saith the Lord, that have promised and have not fulfilled?"[1025]

THE CUP TO SEAL THE COVENANT

Now the bride had before her the marriage covenant, which stated the bride price, and the token or gift of value. She had heard the bridegroom make an irrevocable pledge stating his eternal devotion and indivisible consecration to her. At this point, he placed before her a cup of wine, which represented blood. Donna Nielsen wrote: "The idea was that the *blood* of the covenant superseded all other loyalties." The wine also signified sacrifice and joy. "These three elements [blood, sacrifice, and joy] were intrinsic to the marriage relationship. . . .

"Now came the suspenseful part. At this point, the woman had about thirty seconds to make up her mind. . . . If the woman was willing to receive the man and his proposed condition, she would accept his gift [token] and also drink the cup of wine, which sealed the covenant. This showed that she was willing to take his name upon her."

When the Savior offers us the new and everlasting covenant, we must not vacillate but rather make a firm decision. Our being "lukewarm" only summons the Savior's rebuke.[1026] Elijah became indignant with such indecision: "How long halt ye between two opinions? if the Lord be God, follow

---

[1019] "A Poor Wayfaring Man of Grief," *Hymns*, no. 153, verse 7.
[1020] Nielsen, *Beloved Bridegroom*, 29.
[1021] Hosea 2:19–20.
[1022] Nielsen, *Beloved Bridegroom*, 31.
[1023] D&C 1:38.
[1024] Joshua 23:14.
[1025] D&C 58:31.
[1026] Revelation 3:15–16.

him: but if Baal, then follow him."[1027] However, in the act of the ancient bride's acceptance, we see glimpses of our saying yes to baptism, receiving the sacrament, and consenting to making our temple covenants and ordinances. Drinking of the marriage cup is implied in every covenant-making instance: "But Jesus answered and said, . . . Are ye able to drink of the cup that I shall drink of, and to be baptized with the baptism that I am baptized with? They say unto him, We are able. And he saith unto them, Ye shall drink indeed of my cup, and be baptized with the baptism that I am baptized with."[1028]

The bride's drinking of the cup of wine had to be witnessed by two observers. If and when the bride drank of the cup, the couple was considered betrothed for marriage. "Following the woman's acceptance, the groom, and sometimes the girl's father, recited additional formal statements. . . . To the bride, the groom would speak the words, 'Thou art *set apart* (or consecrated) for me according to the law of Moses and Israel.' Interestingly, the same word for 'set apart,' in the New Testament Greek, '*hagiazo*,' was also used to describe the state of a temple once it was dedicated."[1029] The bride's body was now considered a *temple* for her husband. Likewise, when we enter the Covenant our bodies become temples for the Spirit of the Lord. That idea was suggested by Paul: "Know ye not that your body is the temple of the Holy Ghost which is in you, which ye have of God, and ye are not your own?"[1030] "The temple of God is holy, which temple ye are."[1031]

All of this suggests, of course, that the marriage covenant represented more than mere ritual or the rehearsing of words. To become valid and eternal, those outward ritualistic actions had to become an inward condition of two hearts bound together by love: "But this shall be the covenant that I will make with the house of Israel [the bride]; after those days, saith the Lord, I will put my law in their inward parts, and write it in their hearts; and will be their God, and they shall be my people [my bride]. And they shall teach no more every man his neighbour, and every man his brother, saying, Know the Lord: for they shall all know me, from the least of them unto the greatest of them, saith the Lord."[1032] Most intimately and most completely, we will *know* the Bridegroom, and our love would not permit us to violate our Covenant with him. "This is eternal lives—to know the only wise and true God, and Jesus Christ, whom he hath sent. I am he. Receive ye, therefore, my law."[1033]

THE COVENANTAL FEAST

The betrothal ceremony often ended with a feast at the home of the bride. Included in the feast would be the "breaking of bread." By partaking of the "same loaf at the same table," the participants became bound together as companions. Significantly, the sharing of a meal together *followed* the couple's entering into a covenant.[1034]

We cast our thoughts immediately upon the sacrament table and the Lord's supper,[1035] which among other things reminds us of our previously having entered into the new and everlasting covenant with the Lord through baptism. Additionally, the sacrament reminds us that we are "in waiting," anticipating the time when the Bridegroom will come for us and take us into the place that

---

[1027] 1 Kings 18:21.
[1028] Matthew 20:22–23.
[1029] Nielsen, *Beloved Bridegroom*, 30–31.
[1030] 1 Corinthians 6:19.
[1031] 1 Corinthians 3:17.
[1032] Jeremiah 31:33–34.
[1033] D&C 132:24.
[1034] Nielsen, *Beloved Bridegroom*, 20–21, 32.
[1035] 1 Corinthians 11:20.

he has prepared for us in the mansions of his Father.[1036] We are always in a state of remembrance, obediently preparing and patiently anticipating the Bridegroom.

The sacrament also helps us to hearken back to the day when we accepted the Lord's proposal and made mutual vows to each other in the presence of two witnesses. That was the day when we formalized our covenant with Lord by being immersed in the living waters of baptism, or, in other words, by drinking fully from the cup of his love.[1037] To commemorate the day we entered into the new and everlasting covenant, we eat a covenantal meal containing broken bread from the same loaf. Therefore, by the bread and the cup of wine, we keep in the forefront of our minds our love for and hope in our loving Bridegroom; we hold in sacred remembrance our immutable vows to each other; and we know that he will someday come at an unannounced hour to carry us away to the place that he has prepared for us, our eternal inheritance—our "mansion"—where we will live with him forever in the house of his Father.

THE FATHER'S ANNOUNCEMENT

Immediately after the betrothal ceremony, the bridegroom's father made the first of two announcements of the upcoming marriage of his son. This announcement, or *calling*, is proffered to close friends, family, and others who were invited to the wedding.[1038] The scriptures inform us that "many are called"[1039] to the wedding because of their relationship with the Father and the Son. If the invited people accepted the father's invitation, they were duty-bound, by covenant, to honor their commitment; that is, they must agree to come to the wedding when it was eventually announced, regardless of the inconvenience of the hour. Donna Nielsen explained: "The initial acceptance obliged the guest to respond to the summons at the 'hour of the banquet.' Only those who accepted the first invitation would receive the final invitation when the feast was ready."[1040]

THE BRIDE'S VEIL

Maidens who were not yet spoken for would be seen in public with unveiled faces. But once they had entered the betrothal or engagement period—that is, when they had entered the Covenant—they veiled their faces in public. This custom, of course, is reminiscent of temple worship. Once the young woman had accepted her beloved's proposal of marriage, she was considered set apart, consecrated, and holy. Therefore, she wore the veil as an indication that she belonged only to her husband and that no one else had the right to appreciate her beauty except him.

As a symbol of her consecration, the bride would forevermore "wear a veil over her hair whenever she was in public. This would indicate her status as a betrothed woman and signal that she was not available to anyone else. She would wear a veil over her hair for the remainder of her life as a symbol of her devotion and faithfulness to her husband. Properly understood, her veil hid only that which was too precious for the common, careless gaze." This was not a sign of inferiority, but rather of glory. Her beauty was to be "enjoyed exclusively by her groom. In fact, only those things which were treasured and glorious were veiled."[1041]

Sometimes in scripture Christ becomes the Bride, who beckons us to receive *him*. As the Bride, he also symbolically becomes the "veil,"[1042] as indicated by the author of Hebrews. This term, *veil*, seems to signify that we go through him to return to the Father. In this light, other scriptures

---

[1036] Enos 1:27; Ether 12:32, 34, 37; D&C 98:18.
[1037] Matthew 20:22–23; 3 Nephi 18:8–9.
[1038] Nielsen, *Beloved Bridegroom*, 40.
[1039] D&C 121:40; Matthew 22:14.
[1040] Nielsen, *Beloved Bridegroom*, 41.
[1041] Nielsen, *Beloved Bridegroom*, 16, 31.
[1042] Hebrews 10:20.

connecting Christ and the veil begin to take on added meaning. For example, "Sanctify yourselves that your minds become single to God, and the days will come that you will see him; *for he will unveil his face unto you,* and it shall be in his own time, and in his own way, and according to his own will."[1043] Only the bridegroom was allowed to look upon the bride's beauty that remained hidden behind the veil. Just so, it is our unique honor to part the veil and gaze upon the glory of the Lord: "And again, verily I say unto you that it is your privilege, and a promise I give unto you that have been ordained unto this ministry, that inasmuch as you strip yourselves from jealousies and fears, and humble yourselves before me, for ye are not sufficiently humble, *the veil shall be rent* and you shall see me and know that I am."[1044]

Clearly, that which is most holy is hidden behind the veil. We recall that Moses veiled his face after he returned from speaking with the Lord. His face was filled with so much glory that the people could not endure his presence.[1045] That same idea of veiling that which is most holy was represented in the tabernacle and later in the temple of Solomon: a first veil concealed the inside of the temple, and a second veil concealed the Holy of Holies.[1046] As we have mentioned, in some respects the bride became a temple to her husband; therefore, in symbolism, she wore the veil to indicate that by covenant her beauty and her loyalties belonged exclusively to her husband.

Likewise, by covenant, we "veil ourselves" from the things of the world and allow no unhallowed hand or glance to remove us from the Bridegroom, to whom we give exclusively the beauty of the temple of our souls. By covenant, we "come unto Christ [the Bridegroom] . . . and deny [ourselves] of all ungodliness," and we love him with all our "might, mind and strength."[1047] Symbolically, we hold sacred those things about ourselves that only the Bridegroom might cherish. "Like a temple," wrote Donna Nielsen, "the woman was now 'set apart' for holiness—the greatest holiness of all."[1048]

THE FRIEND OF THE BRIDEGROOM

The bridegroom paid the bride price, offered his beloved the marriage covenant, gave her a token or emblem, consecrated himself to her, and pledged his enduring devotion. Then the bride indicated her agreement to enter into the marriage covenant by drinking the cup of wine in the presence of witnesses. Finally, the two shared a covenantal meal together. Then, at last, the bridegroom left to prepare a place for her in his father's house. The bridegroom and the bride would not have contact with each other again for about a year. Then, on an unspecified night, he would come suddenly for her and whisk her away.

Until then, the friend of the bridegroom, who had been a witness of the couple's covenant, would act "as liaison between the bride-to-be and the groom during the betrothal period. . . . [He would become] the guarantor of the bride's virgin chastity until the consummation took place. . . . [Later he acted as the] governor at the marriage feast, and finally, his last obligation was announcing to the assembled guests that the full marriage was successfully 'completed.'"[1049]

In this tradition, we see obvious symbols of the role of the Holy Ghost, who witnesses our initial covenant-making process. Thereafter, as we wait and prepare for the Lord, the Holy Ghost conveys messages between the Bridegroom and us (the bride). Additionally, he prepares us for the coming of the Bridegroom, encourages us to remain faithful, and, ultimately, when we are finally brought to the wedding, the Holy Ghost justifies us to the Bridegroom and bears testimony of our worthiness. Thus,

---

[1043] D&C 88:68; emphasis added.
[1044] D&C 67:10; emphasis added.
[1045] Exodus 34:29–35.
[1046] Hebrews 9:1–7.
[1047] Moroni 10:32.
[1048] Nielsen, *Beloved Bridegroom*, 31.
[1049] Nielsen, *Beloved Bridegroom*, 19.

he oversees the entire proceedings from start to completion, and in the end he declares the covenantal process is finished. Then the Bridegroom's friend hands us over to the Bridegroom, and the friend's job is completed.

Preparing for Each Other

During the preparation period, which often approached one year, the bridegroom and the bride busied themselves with the primary thing on their minds: their coming wedding. As we have mentioned, the young woman was now considered a bride, so she wore a veil over her hair in public as a token of her new status. Whereas she had belonged to her mother and father, she now belonged to her husband; therefore, she set her relationship with her husband above all other relationships. Her new marriage relationship would define her forevermore: "Therefore shall a man leave his father and his mother, and shall cleave unto his wife: and they shall be one flesh."[1050]

For the bride to be separated from her beloved for a year was an exercise in long-suffering and patience. As she prepared for her wedding, she wondered when her bridegroom would come for her. Not knowing the day or hour is a theme regarding the Second Coming that is widely rehearsed in scripture. For example: "The hour and the day no man knoweth, neither the angels in heaven, nor shall they know until he comes."[1051] Because the bride did not know the time, she had to live her life in constant anticipation and readiness. Her faithfulness is recalled in the parable of the five virgins whose lamps were trimmed and filled with oil when the bridegroom came.[1052] Her example also hearkens to the parable of the chosen few, the handful of faithful Saints among the many who were called to the marriage of the king's son. Only those people who proved themselves worthy were actually allowed to attend the wedding.[1053]

The Apostle Paul used the imagery of a woman who was about to give birth: "For yourselves know perfectly that the day of the Lord so cometh as a thief in the night. For when they shall say, Peace and safety; then sudden destruction cometh upon them, *as travail upon a woman with child*; and they shall not escape. But ye, brethren, are not in darkness, that that day should overtake you as a thief."[1054] Commenting on this image, Elder Bruce R. McConkie wrote:

> Paul's illustration here is perfect. The Second Coming is compared to a woman about to give birth to a child. She does not know the hour or the minute of the child's arrival, but she does know the approximate time. There are signs which precede and presage the promised arrival. And so it is with our Lord's coming. He shall come as a thief in the night, unexpectedly and without warning, to the world, to those who are in spiritual darkness, to those who are not enlightened by the power of the Spirit. But his coming shall not overtake the saints as a thief, for they know and understand the signs of the times.[1055]

On difficult days, the bride might have even despaired, wondering if her bridegroom would ever come. Likewise, we might become discouraged when the Lord "delays his coming" to our aid.

[1050] Genesis 2:24.
[1051] D&C 49:7.
[1052] Matthew 25:1–13; D&C 45:56–59.
[1053] Matthew 22:1–14.
[1054] 1 Thessalonians 5:2–4.
[1055] McConkie, *Doctrinal New Testament Commentary*, 3:54.

Nevertheless, we are counseled to watch, pray, and not faint while waiting.[1056] We are to "seek the face of the Lord always, that in patience ye may possess your souls, and ye shall have eternal life."[1057] In every difficulty, the Lord will eventually come for us. Even if the time is protracted, he will come. The Lord told Isaiah, "Say to them that are of a fearful heart, Be strong, fear not: behold, your God will come . . . ; he will come and save you."[1058] We are assured that "he remembereth every creature of his creating, he will make himself manifest unto all."[1059] "Ye may know of a surety that I, the Lord God, do visit my people in their afflictions."[1060] Most certainly, the Bridegroom will come; it is not a matter of *if* but *when*.

To comfort and help the bride endure his absence, the bridegroom left in her possession reminders of his promise to return—"I go away and come again unto you"[1061]—which symbolize his enduring love for her. These reminders, which she holds close to her heart, are the bride price, the marriage contract, and the token. When he left her, he knew her wait would be difficult. His pledge is reminiscent of his words to us: "Let not your hearts be troubled; for in my Father's house are many mansions, and I have prepared a place for you; and where my Father and I am, there ye shall be also."[1062] And at another time, he said, "I go to prepare a place for you."[1063]

It is important here to realize that during the separation period the bridegroom was also preparing for his bride; she was not preparing alone. Additionally, although he would be physically absent from her, he had arranged to provide for her safety and her comfort. He assigned his trusted friend or "comforter" to watch over her until he returned. We recall that when Jesus announced his imminent departure, he said to the apostles, "I will not leave you comfortless."[1064] As we have mentioned, the Lord's "friend" is the Holy Ghost.

During the protracted betrothal period, the bridegroom spent his time building his beloved a bridal chamber within the confines of his father's house or estate. After the wedding, the chamber would become their home. Donna Nielsen explained, "The new home was built under the direct personal supervision of the groom's father. In that culture, a son is considered to be a representative of his father, and everything that the son does reflects either favorably or unfavorably on the father. . . . With such close identification between a father and his son, the father wanted everything regarding the bride's new home to be as beautiful and perfect as it could be. . . . The father of the groom was the sole judge of when the preparations were complete. . . . When the father determined everything was ready, he gave permission for the son to claim his bride. No one knew when that permission was forthcoming; . . . only the father knew."[1065] The bride would not see her bridegroom until the night he came for her, which time was hidden from her. Thus, the bride spent the betrothal period preparing for the time that her bridegroom, who was also preparing, would finally receive his father's commission, and suddenly appear with little warning to whisk her away to the "mansion" that he had prepared for her.

[1056] Matthew 26:41; Luke 1:18.
[1057] D&C 101:38.
[1058] Isaiah 35:4.
[1059] Mosiah 27:30.
[1060] Mosiah 24:14.
[1061] John 14:28.
[1062] D&C 98:18.
[1063] John 14:2.
[1064] John 14:18.
[1065] Nielsen, *Beloved Bridegroom*, 34–35.

THE SERIOUS NATURE OF PREPARING

The subjects of preparing for the Bridegroom's return and receiving an inheritance in his Father's kingdom occupy chapter 25 of Matthew. This chapter describes who and what we are preparing for, how we must prepare, and how the principle of stewardship assists us to prepare. Here the Lord gives three parables—the parable of the ten virgins, the parable of the talents, and the parable of the sheep and the goats. Kent P. Jackson wrote:

> These allegories seem to form a progression, teaching different aspects of readiness that Jesus encouraged of His listeners and readers. The Joseph Smith translation of verse 1 places the story of the ten virgins clearly in the context of the Second Coming. . . . (Matthew 25:1–13.) Preparation is a necessary precaution because "ye know neither the day nor the hour wherein the Son of Man cometh." This parable . . . ends with the admonition, "Watch!"
>
> In the parable of the Talents (Matthew 25:14–30), the master, traveling to "a far country," leaves different quantities of his goods in the hands of three servants, to each "according to his several ability." Two of the servants doubled their master's resources that had been entrusted to them. The third, however, hid his allotment for safekeeping. To the two who magnified their investment, the master said upon his return, "Well done, good and faithful servant; thou hast been faithful over a few things, I will make thee ruler over many things: enter thou into the joy of thy lord." The final servant returned the master's talent to him, yet he did not receive his lord's praise but rather his condemnation: "Thou wicked and slothful servant." This is not a parable about the uncertain timing of Christ's return but about what we are to do with the gifts He has entrusted to us while we were waiting. As Joseph Smith taught, we should "improve upon all things committed to [our] charge." This parable . . . ends with the unprofitable servant's intense sorrow, "weeping and gnashing of teeth."
>
> The final parable, that of the Sheep and the Goats (see Matthew 25:31–46), again addresses what people do with the blessings entrusted to them—but in a different way. The setting . . . is a judgment scene: "When the Son of Man shall come in his glory . . . and he shall separate them one from another, as a shepherd divideth his sheep from the goats." Those placed on his right hand will receive an inheritance in His kingdom, whereas those on his left hand will be sent off to "everlasting fire." Jesus explained in some detail the criteria for the King's just judgment. Those worthy of an inheritance of glory will be those who fed Him when he was hungry, gave Him drink when he was thirsty, took Him in when He was a stranger, clothed Him when He was naked, visited Him when He was sick, and came to Him when He was in prison. Those who will be

condemned will be the ones who had the same opportunities but did none of those worthy things.[1066]

The burden of stewardship is intrinsically linked to our preparation for the Lord's Second Coming. In this context, we are both the bride and the steward. First, as the bride, we must anticipate the Bridegroom's arrival in an attitude of constant readiness, as a betrothed bride would prepare and watch as she waited for the promised return of her beloved. She would "always remember him."[1067] Just so, during our wait, we are to remain absolutely loyal to the Bridegroom. We are not to divide our affections with another. Our entire attention is to prepare for the coming wedding when we will be *more surely* joined with the Bridegroom and live with him forevermore. The one who helps us to prepare and who comforts us so that we can endure the wait is the Bridegroom's "friend," the Holy Ghost. We are also comforted by holding in our possession the price that the Bridegroom paid for us, the Covenant he made with us, and the tokens (his wounds, as symbolized in the sacrament) that he gave to us.

In our dual roles of bride and steward, we receive from the Lord both gifts and stewardships to help us endure the wait and to prepare: (1) as the "bride," we receive from the Lord gifts to help us remember him and his promise to return; (2) as the "steward," we receive from the Lord stewardships as sacred trusts to manage his property (that which he has given us and those callings he has extended to us) and resources (time, talents, spiritual gifts, etc.) until he returns. As both the bride and the steward, we are to anticipate the Lord's return and actively prepare for it. As the steward, we are to magnify our stewardships during the wait. We do so by using the resources and surpluses of our stewardships to bless the Lord's children. As the steward and the bride, we have covenanted to take upon us his name, and therefore we belong to him. As his bride, his children become our children, and we share in his efforts to take care of them.

Both the loyal bride and the faithful steward are "accounted worthy to inherit the mansions prepared for him of my Father."[1068] But, as both the bride and the steward, if we do not prepare for the Bridegroom, if we do not remain loyal to him, if we do not listen to his *friend*, if we are ashamed of the gifts he has given us or hide or misuse our stewardships or do not use them as he instructed (to bless the lives of others)—if we do any of these things, he will say to us when he comes that he does not know us: "Depart from me." Then, sadly, we will have forfeited the marriage. In that miserable state, we will be cast away to where there is "weeping and gnashing of teeth." We will find ourselves on the Lord's left hand, the place that is called "cursed," and described as "everlasting fire prepared for the devil and his angels."[1069]

Clearly, the Bridegroom expects his bride to hold his name in high regard, always remember him, and remain loyal to their marriage covenant. To the extent that the bride remains faithful, she will have the Bridegroom's friend to attend, comfort, instruct, and prepare her for the Bridegroom's coming and the wedding.

THE BRIDE'S FINAL PREPARATIONS

As we have mentioned, the ancient Jewish bride did not know the exact day and hour of the bridegroom's coming, but her relationship with the bridegroom's friend would have provided her with signs of the bridegroom's coming. As the approximate time approached, she intensified her preparations. She kept herself adorned. She practiced applying wedding make-up, and she paid special

---

[1066] Jackson, "The Olivet Discourse," in Holzapfel and Wayment, *From the Transfiguration through the Triumphant Entry*, 342–43.
[1067] D&C 20:77.
[1068] D&C 72:3–4.
[1069] Matthew 25:12, 30, 41.

THE NEW AND EVERLASTING COVENANT—THE HOLY MARRIAGE

attention to her fingernails, hair, and skin so that she would appear as attractive as possible for her new husband. Also, from the time of the bridegroom's departure, she had kept a lamp burning in her window; she would keep it burning bright until he came for her.[1070]

"As the time of the wedding drew closer, the young girl anxiously awaited her groom's arrival. By custom, it would be sudden, with an element of surprise, and often late at night. She invited her sisters, cousins, and friends to join her vigil and be supportive at this time of joyous anticipation. . . . Night after night, they would strain to hear the shouts of the bridegroom and his friends."[1071]

This custom is illustrated, of course, in Jesus' parable of the ten virgins. We recall that the vigil had gone on a long time, and the bridegroom had "tarried." Then, late in the night, "at midnight there was a cry made, Behold, the bridegroom cometh; go ye out to meet him."[1072] Intrinsic in the new and everlasting covenant is the stipulation that we, the bride, "watch." That is, we must live in a state of happy anticipation and preparation, "for ye know neither the day nor the hour wherein the Son of man cometh."[1073]

In the last days before her wedding, the bride would submit to a ritual washing and anointing, because she was about to become royalty. At her wedding, according to the custom, she would become a queen and would be presented to a king.[1074] In a special pool called a *mikvah*, the bride immersed herself completely in "living waters." "Her life and her body were to be the gift of a living sacrifice to her husband, and to be pure without spot or blemish was a condition required of sacrifices (Ephesians 5:27; Romans 12:1). . . . The Jewish bride did not immerse herself because of uncleanness, but in preparation for holiness, to fulfill God's commandment to be fruitful and multiply. . . . After her immersion in the *mikvah*, the bride's friends would help her anoint herself as part of the preparation for marriage."[1075] This ceremonial immersion in living water symbolized, among other things, "a preparation for holiness." Additionally, "it also represented a separation from an old life to a new life—from life as a single woman to life as a married woman."[1076]

As part of the new and everlasting covenant, we are also to go into a holy place (the temple) "to prepare . . . for the ordinances and endowments, washings and anointing."[1077] The visual image of washing relates to the process of purification, which eliminates impurities, contaminants, and pollutants.[1078] We are washed or purified in preparation to be anointed and thus sanctified. The idea of anointing[1079] speaks to the process of changing the purpose of something or someone.[1080] By ceremonially washing and anointing her body, the bride avowed that she was clean and ready for her life's purpose to change; she was now ready to be endowed with the fulness of the marriage covenant and thus become a queen in Israel. By the rituals of washing (purification) and anointing (sanctification), the bride demonstrated her willingness to become totally consecrated to her husband and yield to the transformation of her life's purpose. Now all was in order for her to join with her husband, who would be her king.[1081]

Iinterestingly, the bridegroom, although it was not required, usually also submitted himself to a washing in the *mikvah* to purify himself in preparation for the wedding. This voluntary washing

---

[1070] Nielsen, *Beloved Bridegroom*, 36, 38.
[1071] Nielsen, *Beloved Bridegroom*, 39.
[1072] Matthew 25:5–6.
[1073] Matthew 25:13.
[1074] Nielsen, *Beloved Bridegroom*, 38.
[1075] Nielsen, *Beloved Bridegroom*, 37–38.
[1076] Nielsen, *Beloved Bridegroom*, 125.
[1077] Smith, *Teachings of the Prophet Joseph Smith*, 308.
[1078] Isaiah 4:4; Psalm 51:2.
[1079] Leviticus 8:10–12.
[1080] D&C 20:77.
[1081] Nielsen, *Beloved Bridegroom*, 44.

reminds us that the Savior submitted to baptism, although he was sinless. His purpose in receiving the ordinance was to enter the new and everlasting covenant and "fulfil all righteousness."[1082] Later, at the end of his life, he also voluntarily sanctified himself so that he might better help others to become sanctified so that they could become *one* with him: "And for their sakes I sanctify myself, that they also might be sanctified through the truth. . . . That they all may be one; as thou, Father, art in me, and I in thee, that they also may be one in us."[1083] Thus we see Jesus submitting to the processes of purification and sanctification to prepare himself to become *one* with those whom he loved. It is said that Jesus Christ is our *Mikvah-Israel*, which means "hope of Israel."[1084]

INVITATION TO THE WEDDING

When the bridegroom completed the "little mansion or bridal chamber"[1085] for his bride, and when the groom's father finally declared that the construction and preparations met with his approval, the father at last gave his son permission to go and claim his bride. Immediately, the bridegroom began to organize a wedding procession by calling and gathering his close associates. In this we remember the reference to the Lord's coming with "all the holy angels with him."[1086]

While the bridegroom was thus engaged, the father sent his servants to make the second announcement or, in other words, "for the last time."[1087] We recall that the first announcement or *calling* happened at the time of betrothal. At that time, the invited guests covenanted to come to the wedding whenever the father announced that the wedding, feast, and festivities were about to commence.[1088] We must keep in mind that the chosen ones had promised that they would remain in readiness and attend the marriage of the son. To reject the invitation now would be nothing short of a monumental insult and a serious offense. Jesus spoke about the second "announcement" and the seriousness of following through on our initial covenant:

> A certain man made a great supper, and bade many:
> And sent his servant at supper time to say to them that were bidden, Come; for all things are now ready.
> And they all with one consent began to make excuse. The first said unto him, I have bought a piece of ground, and I must needs go and see it: I pray thee have me excused.
> And another said, I have bought five yoke of oxen, and I go to prove them: I pray thee have me excused.
> And another said, I have married a wife, and therefore I cannot come.
> So that servant came, and shewed his lord these things. Then the master of the house being angry said to his servant, Go out quickly into the streets and lanes of the city, and bring in hither the poor, and the maimed, and the halt, and the blind.
> And the servant said, Lord, it is done as thou hast commanded, and yet there is room.

[1082] Matthew 3:15.
[1083] John 17:19, 21.
[1084] Nielsen, *Beloved Bridegroom*, 125, quoting a rabbi from the first century.
[1085] Nielsen, *Beloved Bridegroom*, 33.
[1086] Matthew 25:31.
[1087] Jacob 5:62–64; D&C 24:19; 39:17; 43:28; 88:84; 95:4; 112:30.
[1088] Nielsen, *Beloved Bridegroom*, 40.

> And the lord said unto the servant, Go out into the highways and hedges, and compel them to come in, that my house may be filled.
>
> For I say unto you, That none of those men which were bidden shall taste of my supper.[1089]

Notice that the chosen guests who did not attend the wedding used as excuses property, possessions, and family concerns. It is sad but true that many of the chosen ones will step aside from their covenant: "Behold, there are many called, but few are chosen. And why are they not chosen? Because their hearts are set so much upon the things of this world, and aspire to the honors of men."[1090] For an invited guest to place anything above his commitment to attend the wedding, or for an invited guest to be unprepared, as were five of the ten virgins, are insults that will summon the Father's indignation. Not responding to the Bridegroom's invitation at his advent will most certainly result in such individuals being shut out from the wedding and the Bridegroom denying that he knows them.[1091]

THE WEDDING PROCESSIONAL

In the ancient Jewish practice, the bridegroom led a procession to the bride's home to claim her. He was decked out in regal attire, often wearing a crown, dressed in garments "scented with frankincense and myrrh," and appearing in every way like a king. This joyous occasion was one of "singing, dancing and merriment." Now the bridegroom's long-awaited purpose and the object of his sacrifice were about to be realized.[1092] The clamorous late-night procession wound through the streets with their torches beaming and their trumpets blaring, awakening everyone along the way. The scriptures inform us that "the Son of Man shall come, and he shall send his angels before him with the great sound of a trumpet." Those in the procession beckoned others to join them, as the Savior will: "And they shall gather together the remainder of his elect from the four winds, from one end of heaven to the other."[1093]

When the procession neared the bride's home, "a messenger was sent ahead to give the shout, 'The bridegroom cometh!'" At that point, the bride had about half an hour "to make final preparations" before the shout was given again and the bridegroom arrived.[1094] So shall it be at the Savior's second coming: "And he [the angelic messenger] shall sound his trump both long and loud, and all nations shall hear it. *And there shall be silence in heaven for the space of half an hour;* and immediately after shall the curtain of heaven be unfolded, as a scroll is unfolded after it is rolled up, and the face of the Lord shall be unveiled."[1095]

CLAIMING THE BRIDE

The ancient Jewish marriage is filled with the imagery of the new and everlasting covenant. When we entered into the Covenant with the Bridegroom through baptism, we recognized the fact that he had paid a price for us. In the covenantal agreement, he promised to provide for us, redeem us, and to live with us in a loving relationship. Then he presented us with tokens (his wounds) representing his love and devotion. He did all of this in the presence of witnesses. He vowed to prepare a place for us in the

---

[1089] Luke 14:16–24.
[1090] D&C 121:34–35.
[1091] Matthew 25:1–13.
[1092] Nielsen, *Beloved Bridegroom*, 41.
[1093] JS–Matthew 1:37.
[1094] Nielsen, *Beloved Bridegroom*, 42.
[1095] D&C 88:94–95; emphasis added.

mansions of his Father, and he promised to one day return for us: "I will come again, and receive you unto myself; that where I am, there ye may be also."[1096] When at last he would finally come for us, we together would make the marriage complete and he would *seal us his*.[1097] This is an interesting phrase, given our understanding of the temple ordinances. Conversely, if we neglect or reject our covenant with the Lord, "the devil doth seal [us] his."[1098]

The hour had finally come for the loyal and long-suffering bride. Having made all proper preparations, having waited faithfully and patiently for the bridegroom's return, having heard the trumpet and the shout, having gathered everything together during the last half hour, and having heard the final shout, the bride now gave herself willingly to the bridegroom as he burst through the door of her home to claim her. By this action, the bridegroom suddenly elevated his bride to the stature of a queen.

The new and everlasting covenant provides for such regal unity: "[The Bridegroom] hast made us unto our God kings and priests [and queens and priestesses]: and we shall reign on the earth."[1099] Elder Bruce R. McConkie wrote: "This unity among all the saints, and between them and the Father and the Son, is reserved for those who gain exaltation and inherit the fulness of the Father's kingdom. Those who attain it will all know the same things; think the same thoughts; exercise the same powers; do the same acts; respond in the same way to the same circumstances; beget the same kind of offspring; rejoice in the same continuation of the seeds forever; create the same type of worlds; enjoy the same eternal fulness; and glory in the same exaltation."[1100]

Immediately, the bride was lifted up into a special chair—a throne—"and carried to her new home. The four strong men" who conveyed the bride were "given the honorary title, *Giborei Yisrael*, or heroes of Israel."[1101] In this regal setting, the bride appeared stunningly beautiful, without spot or blemish. Moreover, she was beautiful within, having prepared and faithfully endured during the wait. Similarly, the Apostle John saw latter-day Zion "prepared as a bride adorned for her husband."[1102] The psalmist wrote, "The king's daughter is all glorious within: her clothing is of wrought gold. She shall be brought unto the king in raiment of needlework: the virgins her companions that follow her shall be brought unto thee. With gladness and rejoicing shall they be brought: they shall enter into the king's palace."[1103]

Now the bridegroom brought her to the place he had prepared for her. Donna Nielsen explained: "The most important period of the marriage festivities was when the bride entered her new home. The bride and groom were sometimes crowned with real crowns or with garlands or roses, myrtle, or olive leaves. . . . The couple was treated like royalty during this time. The new husband was literally considered a king and priest in his own home, with his wife as queen."[1104] How glorious is the Covenant that exalts us and makes us equal with the King of Heaven!

THE WEDDING

A number of symbolic events occurred when the guests entered into the father's home. These events point to blessings that attend the new and everlasting covenant. For example, each guest had his feet and hands washed; then he was anointed, embraced, and kissed. These gestures were evidences of

---

[1096] John 14:2–3.
[1097] Mosiah 5:15.
[1098] Alma 34:35.
[1099] Revelation 5:10.
[1100] McConkie, *Mormon Doctrine*, 814.
[1101] Nielsen, *Beloved Bridegroom*, 43.
[1102] Revelation 21:2.
[1103] Psalms 45:13–15.
[1104] Nielsen, *Beloved Bridegroom*, 44.

The New and Everlasting Covenant—The Holy Marriage

reconciliation; no hard feelings would be allowed in the father's house on such a joyous occasion. We might expect to be thus treated when we regain the Father's presence.

"Another Jewish custom was to wear a 'wedding garment.'" These garments were supplied to the guests by the bridegroom's father. They were white, "a color associated with royalty." Moreover, the white garments represented light. If someone were found not wearing a garment, such as the guest mentioned in Matthew 22:11, his action would be interpreted as disdain for the father's generosity and he would be cast out.

While the guests were dressing, greeting, and conversing, the bridegroom and the bride dressed in their white wedding clothing, which was symbolic of "purity, forgiveness of sins, and solemn joy."[1105] Isaiah exulted, "I will greatly rejoice in the Lord, my soul shall be joyful in my God; for he hath clothed me with the garments of salvation, he hath covered me with the robe of righteousness, as a bridegroom decketh himself with ornaments, and as a bride adorneth herself with her jewels."[1106]

At this point, the bride would be anointed with sweet olive oil. We remember that this sanctifying act signified her joy and her willingness to transform her life from a single woman to a queen to her husband. This change of status was shared by both the bride and the bridegroom. "Each groom at the time of his wedding and later in his own home was to be considered as a king and a priest." The act of clothing the couple in royal wedding robes signified among other things that they were now consecrated to become fruitful and bear children.[1107] Similarly, the Covenant enables us to clothe ourselves "with the bond of charity, as with a mantle, which is the bond of perfectness and peace."[1108] Our purpose changes from profane to holy, and, joined with the Lord, we become fruitful.[1109]

Now the time of the wedding was at hand. The place of making the covenant was under a canopy, a square piece of cloth held up by four poles. The canopy was open on all sides, reminiscent of the hospitality Abraham and Sarah showed guests in their open tent. The canopy was usually positioned outside so as to be under the stars. Symbolically, it represented, among other things, "God's sheltering love," and also the covenant that God made with Abraham, promising that his children would be as numerous as the stars of the heavens.[1110] Likewise, when we marry in the temple, we are sealed together in the presence of the luminaries of heaven and blessed with all the blessings of Abraham, including "a fulness and a continuation of the seeds forever and ever."[1111]

After the bridegroom had been escorted to the canopy by his parents, the bride was brought to the canopy by hers. At that point, the "officiator faced the couple and read the Psalm of Thanksgiving (Psalm 100). A goblet of wine was raised, and a blessing was said over the wine. This was called the 'Cup of Joy.' Both the bride and the bridegroom drank from the same cup, indicating they would share the joys of life together." Likewise, we are yoked to Jesus in the new and everlasting covenant.[1112] Our Bridegroom has covenanted to share with us all the joys and sorrows of life; by covenant, we will never be left alone.

Then the bridegroom placed a ring, representing eternity, on the bride's right index finger. It was the right hand that was used for making covenants. At that point, the bridegroom "lifted the bride's veil and placed the corner of it on his shoulder. This was a proclamation to everyone present that the government of his bride now rested on his shoulder," an image that Isaiah used to describe the

---

[1105] Nielsen, *Beloved Bridegroom*, 51–54.
[1106] Isaiah 61:10.
[1107] Nielsen, *Beloved Bridegroom*, 52, 54–55.
[1108] D&C 88:125.
[1109] John 15:5–8.
[1110] Nielsen, *Beloved Bridegroom*, 55–56.
[1111] D&C 132:19.
[1112] Matthew 11:29–30.

Savior's relationship to us.[1113] Then the marriage contract was read aloud for all to witness, followed by the officiator reciting blessings. Similarly, the Lord pronounces blessings upon those whom he seals together:

> And again, verily I say unto you, if a man marry a wife by my word, which is my law, and by the new and everlasting covenant, and it is sealed unto them by the Holy Spirit of promise, by him who is anointed, unto whom I have appointed this power and the keys of this priesthood; and it shall be said unto them—Ye shall come forth in the first resurrection . . . and shall inherit thrones, kingdoms, principalities, and powers, dominions, all heights and depths . . . , and if ye abide in my covenant, and commit no murder whereby to shed innocent blood, it shall be done unto them in all things whatsoever my servant hath put upon them, in time, and through all eternity; and shall be of full force when they are out of the world; and they shall pass by the angels, and the gods, which are set there, to their exaltation and glory in all things, as hath been sealed upon their heads, which glory shall be a fulness and a continuation of the seeds forever and ever.
>
> Then shall they be gods, because they have no end; therefore shall they be from everlasting to everlasting, because they continue; then shall they be above all, because all things are subject unto them. Then shall they be gods, because they have all power, and the angels are subject unto them.[1114]

Next, the officiator offered a second cup of wine to the couple. "This cup was called the 'Cup of Sacrifice' and the 'Cup of Salvation.' They would have to share sacrifices in life, but eventually those sacrifices would be a source of salvation for both of them."[1115] Likewise, in the Covenant, the Bridegroom vows to walk the path of life by our side. Against all odds, he drank of the cup of sacrifice for our salvation: "the cup which my Father hath given me, shall I not drink it?"[1116] Our life together is one of mutual sacrifice that most assuredly will lead to our salvation. In the Covenant, we counsel and make decisions together; we love together; we hurt together. What he wants, we want. We share in our hopes, desires, and dreams, and we also share in our sorrows. We are one.

Drinking from the cup of sacrifice or the cup of salvation is vividly described in the Savior's own words: "For behold, I, God, have suffered these things for all, that they might not suffer if they would repent; but if they would not repent they must suffer even as I; which suffering caused myself, even God, the greatest of all, to tremble because of pain, and to bleed at every pore, and to suffer both body and spirit—and would that I might not drink the bitter cup, and shrink—nevertheless, glory be to the Father, and I partook and finished my preparations unto the children of men."[1117]

THE BRIDEGROOM'S PLEA

No doctrine is more glorious than the new and everlasting covenant. Significantly, the Bridegroom initiates the invitation to join with him in a covenantal relationship that is as holy, loving, intimate,

---

[1113] Isaiah 9:6.
[1114] D&C 132:19–20.
[1115] Nielsen, *Beloved Bridegroom*, 57–60.
[1116] John 18:11.
[1117] D&C 19:16–19.

fruitful, trusting, and enduring as an eternal marriage. Equally significant is the fact that in inviting us to enter into a covenant relationship, the Lord essentially pleads with us that we will have mercy *on him* that we might agree to join with him. That is, he desires our steadfast love and loyalty above all else. This is an interesting twist considering the fact that we are ever pleading for *his* mercy, love, and loyalty.

We begin to understand this gospel irony when we note that the Hebrew word for mercy is *hesed*, which "refers to the deep spiritual and emotional bond that exists between two very close people such as husband and wife. Immediately, one perceives that God wants us to be as emotionally and spiritually close to him in thought and action as a devoted husband and wife would be. . . . It is a humbling moment when we realize that such a powerful, loving, and kind God wants this type of a relationship. Such knowledge inspires one to 'grow up' spiritually and to think more about the impact his life has on God."[1118]

That the Lord would literally plead with us to enter into a covenantal relationship with him evokes tender images. At the end of his earthly ministry, we recall that Jesus lamented over proud Jerusalem, the bride whom he had courted for so long, the bride whom he would have gathered to him so many times in protective and loving care, and yet she would not give him her love.[1119] That image evokes the vision of a prospective groom who has loved a woman for a very long time, and finally has managed to gather enough to pay a substantial bride price by sacrificing his all. Now he hands her a document written on fine parchment which contains his covenantal promises: He will provide for her, redeem her, love her, and give her his name. Then he offers her a token or a gift of value, a representation of his promises, and in the presence of witnesses he recites a pledge to irrevocably bind and consecrate himself to her forever. Now he places a cup of wine before her . . . and waits. Will she drink of the cup or will she refuse him?

How we respond to the Bridegroom's invitation will determine our eternal future. A great and potentially divisive decision lies before each of us. Those who neglect or reject the Lord's proposal to enter into the new and everlasting covenant will find themselves on his left hand, symbolically (to the Jewish mind) the hand of disdain. Conversely, those who accept the Lord's proposal and thereafter live faithfully in the Covenant will find themselves on his right hand, the hand of covenant making, the hand on which the bride accepts her husband's ring.[1120] Jesus commented on this reality in words of stark imagery:

> When the Son of man shall come in his glory, and all the holy angels with him, then shall he sit upon the throne of his glory: And before him shall be gathered all nations: and he shall separate them one from another, as a shepherd divideth [his] sheep from the goats: And he shall set the sheep on his right hand, but the goats on the left.
>
> Then shall the King say unto them on his right hand, Come, ye blessed of my Father, inherit the kingdom prepared for you from the foundation of the world. . . . Then shall he say also unto them on the left hand, Depart from me, ye cursed, into everlasting fire, prepared for the devil and his angels.[1121]

[1118] Nielsen, *Beloved Bridegroom*, iv.
[1119] Matthew 23:37.
[1120] Nielsen, *Beloved Bridegroom*, 57.
[1121] Matthew 25:31–34, 41.

May we respond to the Lord's plea and accept his invitation to join him in the new and everlasting covenant. Then may we, like the bride, stand forever on the Bridegroom's right hand and there exult as did Jeremiah: "This is the joy and rejoicing of mine heart: for I am called by thy name, O Lord God of hosts."[1122]

Postlude

The first pillar of Zion is the new and everlasting covenant. It stands as the first and premiere covenant that creates a Zionlike life. To formally accept the Atonement of Jesus Christ, we must enter into the new and everlasting covenant by baptism, and then follow the Covenant to its perfect conclusion. The path we will follow is called the *strait and narrow path*, and it is marked with other covenants that we must take upon us.

The new and everlasting covenant consists of two primary covenants: the covenant of baptism, and the oath and covenant of the priesthood. The priesthood covenant is magnified by (1) ordination for worthy men; (2) temple covenants and ordinances for worthy men and women; (3) the temple sealing covenant, which is called the covenant of exaltation,[1123] for worthy men and women.

In total, these covenants, which emerge from the new and everlasting covenant, cleanse us, separate us from the world, prepare us for coronation, and protect us from Satan. They endow us with keys to the knowledge and power of God, and they establish us in our eternal kingdoms.

The new and everlasting covenant defines the road to becoming a Zion person, and Zion, we have learned, is our ideal and the standard among celestial and celestial-seeking people.[1124] "We ought to have the building up of Zion as our greatest object,"[1125] taught Joseph Smith; and Brigham Young added, "[Zion] commences in the heart of each person."[1126]

If our desire is truly to achieve Zion in our lives, we must enter into this Covenant and make a contract, which is agreed to by each member of the Godhead. Initially, we might perceive the Covenant as a series of laws, but as we spend time in the Covenant, we soon discover that it is a manifestation of love. In a most remarkable way, the Covenant is like a marriage covenant, with love as the foundational motivator. Ultimately, we discover that the Covenant is all about our relationship with God. He invites us into a union that he describes in terms of marriage, the most holy, intimate, fruitful, trusting, and enduring of all relationships.

Thus, we end as we began: To become Zion people and thus ensure our salvation and exaltation, we must enter into the new and everlasting covenant and abide in it forevermore. By this, we witness that we have made a choice between Zion and Babylon. Furthermore, we witness that we agree to follow the Covenant to its perfect conclusion: to be snatched from Babylon, to be singled out, to be purified and to have our hearts sanctified, to be prepared in every way to regain the presence of God, and to obtain our inheritance and our crown. "This is Zion: THE PURE IN HEART."[1127]

[1122] Jeremiah 15:16.

[1123] Nelson, *The Power within Us*, 136; Smith, *Doctrines of Salvation*, 2:58. Note: Elder McConkie stated that men make a covenant of exaltation twice: once upon ordination to the Melchizedek Priesthood and again at the time of the marriage sealing: "Ordination to office in the Melchizedek priesthood and entering into that 'order of the priesthood' named 'the new and everlasting covenant of marriage' are both occasions when men make the covenant of exaltation, being promised through their faithfulness all that the Father hath (D&C 131:1–4; 84:39–41; 132; Num. 25:13)." (McConkie, *Mormon Doctrine*, 167.)

[1124] D&C 105:5.

[1125] Smith, *Teachings of the Prophet Joseph Smith*, 60.

[1126] Young, *Discourses of Brigham Young*, 118.

[1127] D&C 97:21.

BOOK 3:

THE SECOND PILLAR OF ZION—THE OATH AND COVENANT OF THE PRIESTHOOD

Introduction

"We ought to have the building up of Zion as our greatest object."[1128]—Joseph Smith

In this third book of *The Three Pillars of Zion* series, we will examine in depth the second pillar of Zion: *The Oath and Covenant of the Priesthood*. We recall that the "Law of the Church" (D&C 42) states that three covenants are sufficient to establish us as Zion people: "And ye shall hereafter receive church covenants, such as shall be sufficient to establish you, both here and in the New Jerusalem."[1129] These covenants are:

1. The New and Everlasting Covenant (D&C 132:4–7).
2. The Oath and Covenant of the Priesthood (D&C 84:33–44).
3. The Law of Consecration (D&C 82:11–15).

In Book 1, we learned that Zion was our origin and will be our destiny. She is our ideal, and she is also the antithesis of Babylon. Moreover, Zion is the standard among celestial and celestial-seeking people.[1130] Brigham Young said, "[Zion] commences in the heart of each person."[1131] Clearly, the responsibility to become Zion people rests upon each of us individually.

That responsibility begins with formally accepting the Atonement by receiving the new and everlasting covenant by way of baptism. The new and everlasting covenant is the *umbrella covenant*, consisting of two primary covenants: the covenant of baptism, and the oath and covenant of the priesthood. The priesthood covenant is magnified by (1) ordination for worthy men; (2) temple covenants and ordinances for worthy men and women; and (3) the temple sealing covenant, which is called the Covenant of Exaltation,[1132] for worthy men and women.

[1128] Smith, *Teachings of the Prophet Joseph Smith*, 60.
[1129] D&C 42:67.
[1130] D&C 105:5.
[1131] Young, *Discourses of Brigham Young*, 118.
[1132] Nelson, *The Power within Us*, 136; Smith, *Doctrines of Salvation*, 2:58. Note: Elder McConkie stated that men make a covenant of exaltation twice: once upon ordination to the Melchizedek Priesthood and again at the time of the marriage sealing: "Ordination to office in the Melchizedek priesthood and entering into that 'order of the priesthood' named 'the new and everlasting covenant of marriage' are both occasions when men make the covenant of exaltation, being promised through their faithfulness all that the Father hath (D&C 131:1–4; 84:39–41; 132; Num. 25:13)." (*Mormon Doctrine*, 167).

Introduction

The new and everlasting covenant not only provides a way to be cleansed from sin and separated from the world, but it provides us a way to receive God's authority, power, and knowledge—everything we need to become like him and inherit all that he has. This is the essence of the second pillar of Zion—the oath and covenant of the priesthood.

As we will learn, the principles in this book apply to both worthy men and women. The priesthood covenant is received by men at the time of ordination, but its principles are expansive and eventually lead to the temple. There, faithful men and women are endowed with priesthood covenants and ordinances that culminate at a marriage altar. An editorial in the *Improvement Era* noted: "Now, as far as the Church of Christ is concerned, this oath and covenant is made first in baptism, when the Holy Ghost is given, and more especially when the Priesthood is conferred. It is, secondly, repeated by partaking of the Sacrament, and by entering into special covenants in holy places [the temple]."[1133] Elder Bruce R. McConkie said, "This covenant, made when the priesthood is received, is renewed when the recipient enters the order of eternal marriage."[1134] Clearly, both men and women are involved in the doctrines of the priesthood.

In this section, we will examine the history of the priesthood and men who were great examples of righteousness in the priesthood. We will discuss priesthood keys and their importance in the restored church of Jesus Christ. Then we will survey our covenantal agreements and the Father's oath, instructions, and promises. Following those sections, we will examine what President Stephen L Richards called "The Constitution of the Priesthood,"[1135] found in Doctrine and Covenants 121. We will discuss why many are called to eternal life, but few are chosen. We will also study the Lord's instructions and rewards for the chosen few who keep their covenants. In the end, we come to understand that receiving the priesthood is more than an ordination; it is a way of life, and the power to pursue that life. Without the priesthood and its guiding principles, neither a man nor a woman could achieve Zion in his or her life and thus attain the ultimate form of salvation, *exaltation* in the celestial kingdom.

[1133] Editor's Note, "The Bondage of Sin," *Improvement Era*, Feb. 1923.
[1134] McConkie, *A New Witness for the Articles of Faith*, 313.
[1135] Richards, Conference Report, Apr. 1955, 12.

Section 9

The Holy Priesthood after the Order of the Son of God

Note: Because this series is a sequential work, with one concept building upon another, the section numbers pick up where the last book ended. Thus, this book begins with Section 9. We also note that the first time we refer to a covenant or unique doctrine, we may capitalize it to call special attention to it. Thereafter, we will lowercase the name of the covenant or doctrine, with two exceptions: (1) If the name is capitalized in a quotation from another source, we will leave it as found in that source; and (2) if we are referring to the new and everlasting covenant by the shorthand of "the Covenant," we will capitalize it in that setting.

Priesthood is power, said President Marion G. Romney.[1136] To receive that power—the power of God—is to be set apart and authorized as the most honored of God's sons. But we also have the greatest responsibility. We should give diligent heed to learn all we can about this great power.

Nevertheless, despite our best efforts through prayer, study, and faithful performance of our duties, we will not fully comprehend the priesthood in this life. But what we do learn and experience will leave us in awe. Brigham Young said, "The Priesthood of the Son of God . . . is the law by which the worlds are, were, and will continue forever and ever. It is that system which brings worlds into existence and peoples them, gives them their revolutions—their days, weeks, months, years, their seasons and times and by which they are rolled up as a scroll, as it were, and go into a higher state of existence."[1137]

From the days of Adam until Melchizedek, the priesthood was called *The Holy Priesthood after the Order of the Son of God*. "But out of respect or reverence to the name of the Supreme Being, to avoid the too frequent repetition of his name, they, the church, in ancient days, called that priesthood after Melchizedek, or the Melchizedek Priesthood."[1138] As we learned in Book 2, this high priesthood is

---

[1136] Romney, "Priesthood," 43.
[1137] Young, *Discourses of Brigham Young*, 130.
[1138] D&C 107:3–4.

received with the Father's oath and our covenant.[1139] The oath and covenant of the priesthood is the second pillar of Zion. The oath and covenant of the priesthood is also the second of two covenants (baptism being the first) that comprise the Covenant of Mercy.

THE DOCTRINES OF THE PRIESTHOOD AS THEY APPLY TO MEN AND WOMEN

This section will explore the priesthood covenant in depth as it applies to both men and women. Elder James E. Talmage wrote, "It is a precept of the Church that women of the Church share the authority of the Priesthood with their husbands, actual or prospective; and therefore women, whether taking the endowment for themselves or for the dead, are not ordained to specific rank in the Priesthood. Nevertheless there is no grade, rank, or phase of the temple endowment to which women are not eligible on an equality with men. . . . Within the House of the Lord the woman is the equal and the help-meet of the man."[1140]

Previously (in Book 2) we discussed the fact that the priesthood covenant cannot deliver power without our magnifying our calling in the priesthood. As we will explain, that calling is the call to eternal life. We magnify that calling progressively by (1) ordination to the priesthood, (2) receiving temple ordinances, (3) being married in the temple. Because women are included the last two criteria, they are clearly involved in the doctrines of the priesthood.

With that in mind, let us make the following examination.

MELCHIZEDEK, THE TITLE AND THE MAN

Melchizedek, as we discussed in Book 1, is a title as well as a name, which in Hebrew means *King of Righteousness*. The identity of the man who originally bore this title is the subject of conjecture. What we do know about the man Melchizedek is of importance to every man who desires to become a Zion person and thus takes upon himself the high priesthood. Melchizedek "represents the scriptural ideal of one who obtains the power of God through faith, repentance, and sacred ordinances, for the purpose of inspiring and blessing his fellow beings."[1141] Because the man Melchizedek was so righteous and faithful "in the execution of his high priestly duties . . . he became a prototype of Jesus Christ (Heb. 7:15)."[1142]

Men who receive the high priesthood by ordination assume the title of *Melchizedek*. Becoming a part of that order, they are expected to do the works of Melchizedek and of Jesus Christ, the two great exemplars of what a priesthood holder should be. They are to become *kings of righteousness* to their posterity.

In Melchizedek's life we see an example of what we should become. His ministry is a model that we should apply to our own priesthood service. In the first place, because the new and everlasting covenant has been available to all of God's sons and daughters, Melchizedek would have received that Covenant by baptism and thereafter would have made each additional covenant, received every ordinance, and endured in faith until he finally received the ultimate promise of salvation. From the beginning, he would have desired to progress in the Covenant and become a savior to his people in the similitude of the Savior. Therefore, at some point, he would have sought for his ordination to the Holy Priesthood after the Order of the Son of God so that he might administer the blessings of the Covenant to help save his people.

The scripture reads: "Now this Melchizedek was a king over the land of Salem and his people had waxed strong in iniquity and abomination; yea, they had all gone astray; they were full of all manner of wickedness; but Melchizedek having exercised mighty faith, and received the office of the

---

[1139] D&C 84:33–44.
[1140] Talmage, *The House of the Lord*, 79.
[1141] *Encyclopedia of Mormonism*, 879–80.
[1142] *Encyclopedia of Mormonism*, 879–80.

high priesthood according to the holy order of God, did preach repentance unto his people." Like Enoch, Melchizedek was enormously successful, and taught his people the principles of Zion until they, too, became Zion people: "And behold, they did repent; and Melchizedek did establish peace in the land in his days; therefore he was called the prince of peace, for he was the king of Salem; and he did reign under his father."[1143] From this account, we learn that "Melchizedek was a man of faith, who wrought righteousness. . . . And his people wrought righteousness, and obtained heaven, and sought for the city of Enoch [they became Zion people and were likewise translated]."[1144] This is our priesthood model as holders of the Melchizedek Priesthood.

Again, we emphasize the fact that Melchizedek would have progressed in this as we all must do: by baptism, by receiving the high priesthood with an oath and covenant, and by receiving all temple blessings, culminating with eternal marriage, which is the patriarchal order or the highest order of the priesthood.[1145] We know that Melchizedek progressed in this manner because he is described as being both a king and a priest unto God,[1146] meaning that he received a fulness of the priesthood. The titles *king* and *priest* and their associated blessings are possible only by receiving the fulness of temple ordinances.[1147] This is the *fulness* that defines Zion people.

"What was the power of Melchizedek?" asked the Prophet Joseph Smith. "Those holding the fulness of the Melchizedek Priesthood are kings and priests of the Most High God, holding the keys of power and blessings. In fact, that Priesthood is a perfect law of theocracy, and stands as God to give laws to the people, administering endless lives to the sons and daughters of Adam."[1148] Zion marriages, families, and priesthood societies function under the Melchizedek Priesthood, which is the "perfect law of theocracy." Through Melchizedek's righteousness and faith, he received the keys of power and blessings, ruled as a king of righteousness, administered *endless lives* (the covenants and ordinances of eternal life) to his people, and brought them back into the presence of God. This is the power of the Melchizedek Priesthood and the purpose and expectation of our ordination. Everything about the priesthood points to establishing Zion in a life, a marriage, a family, and in a priesthood society.

Because Melchizedek was an authorized servant of the Lord, he had the keys to ordain Abraham to the priesthood. Moreover, Melchizedek administered to Abraham the new and everlasting covenant, tutored him in the doctrine of the priesthood,[1149] and, of great importance, gave him authority to effect the ordinance of eternal marriage and perpetuate the patriarchal order, "a system that would make [Abraham] the Father of the Faithful from that day onward as long as the earth should stand."[1150]

Additionally, Melchizedek kept "the storehouse of God," where the "tithes for the poor" were held,[1151] as is typical of a Zion priesthood society. We read that Melchizedek gave priesthood blessings to individuals such as Abraham[1152]; he preached repentance[1153]; and he administered the ordinances of the new and everlasting covenant to his people "after this manner, that thereby the people might look forward on the Son of God . . . for a remission of their sins, that they might enter into the rest of the Lord."[1154]

[1143] Alma 13:17–18.
[1144] JST Genesis 14:26, 34.
[1145] D&C 131:1–4.
[1146] Alma 13:17–18; JST Hebrews 7:3.
[1147] McConkie, Conference Report, Oct. 1950, 15–16; Smith, *The Words of Joseph Smith*, 304.
[1148] Smith, *Teachings of the Prophet Joseph Smith*, 322.
[1149] D&C 84:14; JST Genesis 14:40.
[1150] McConkie, *A New Witness for the Articles of Faith*, 36.
[1151] JST Genesis 14:37–38.
[1152] JST Genesis 14:18, 25, 37.
[1153] Alma 13:18.
[1154] Alma 13:16; JST Genesis 14:17.

Melchizedek ministered with "extraordinary goodness and power, . . . diligently administered in the office of high priest and 'did preach repentance unto his people. And behold, they did repent; and Melchizedek did establish peace in the land in his days' (Alma 13:18). Consequently, Melchizedek became known as 'the prince of peace' (JST Gen. 14:33; Heb. 7:1–2; Alma 13:18). 'His people wrought righteousness, and obtained heaven' (JST Gen. 14:34)."[1155] Clearly, all of this is indicative of Zion, and, therefore, establishing Zion is the goal and the outcome of the oath and covenant of the priesthood.

Alma noted that it was this "order" of the high priesthood, coupled with faith, "that gave Melchizedek the power and knowledge that influenced his people to repent and become worthy to be with God. . . . Those ordained to this order were to 'have power, by faith,' and, according to 'the will of the Son of God,' to work miracles. Ultimately, those in this order were 'to stand in the presence of God' (JST Gen. 14:30–31). This was accomplished by participating in the ordinances of this order (Alma 13:16; D&C 84:20–22). The result was that 'men having this faith, coming up unto this order of God, were translated and taken up into heaven' (JST Gen. 14:32). Accordingly, the Prophet Joseph Smith taught that the priesthood held by Melchizedek had 'the power of endless lives.'"[1156]

If we ever hope to become Zionlike people, we must follow the example of Melchizedek in our individual lives, marriages, and families, as well as within the realms of our callings. Like Melchizedek, we must enter into the new and everlasting covenant, follow it through to its conclusion, and live worthily so that we might receive a fulness of the priesthood. We must seek the blessings of the priesthood for the purposes of individual salvation and the salvation of those in our stewardships. We must become kings and priests unto God by means of temple ordinances, and "kings of righteousness" to our families and to those in our stewardships. We must function in the priesthood, which is the perfect law of theocracy, to preach repentance, administer endless lives, and bring our charges back into the presence of God. We must set an example of righteousness by exemplifying Jesus Christ, "that thereby the people might look forward on the Son of God . . . for a remission of their sins, that they might enter into the rest of the Lord."[1157] We must become princes of peace by entering the order of the Son of God, and in every way typifying Jesus Christ, whose authority we hold. As Melchizedek Priesthood holders, we take upon ourselves the title of Melchizedek and must become even as Jesus Christ is.[1158] Because Melchizedek was able to achieve Zion by virtue of the priesthood, we, who take upon ourselves the title of Melchizedek and who hold that same authority, strive to achieve Zion in our lives, marriages, families, and stewardships.

King Benjamin, a Type of Melchizedek

If Melchizedek is an ideal of a priesthood holder in the Bible, King Benjamin is an ideal in the Book of Mormon. Both kings used their priesthood to facilitate a spiritual rebirth of their people and managed to bring them into the presence of the Lord.

BYU professor M. Catherine Thomas wrote, "The power to play a saving role is the most sought-after power among righteous priesthood holders in time and eternity. The greater the soul, it seems, the deeper the desire to labor to bring souls to Christ through causing them to take his name upon them."[1159] King Benjamin was such a priesthood holder, a king and a priest after the order of Melchizedek. Because we are likewise kings and priests to our people, whether our people be our personal families, our home teaching families, our quorums, wards, stakes, or otherwise, we can glean

---

[1155] *Encyclopedia of Mormonism*, 879.
[1156] *Encyclopedia of Mormonism*, 879.
[1157] Alma 13:16; JST Genesis 14:17.
[1158] 3 Nephi 27:27; 28:10.
[1159] Thomas, "Benjamin and the Mysteries of God," 279.

priesthood saving principles from the example of King Benjamin and thus learn how to establish the principles of Zion in the lives of those over whom we have stewardship.

One of the first things we learn about King Benjamin is that he followed in the tradition of great priesthood holders before him. What he desired and accomplished for his people was not new. As we learned in Book 1, Adam set the example. The Prophet Joseph Smith taught, "[Adam] wanted to bring [his people] into the presence of God. They looked for a city . . . 'whose builder and maker is God' (Hebrews 11:10)."[1160] Later, Enoch, Noah, and Melchizedek followed this pattern. Now Benjamin, who "held the keys of power and blessing for his community," prayed earnestly for priesthood power to endow his people with spiritual blessings and make them Zionlike people. Of priesthood holders' preparation to enact such a change in their people, Catherine Thomas wrote:

A priesthood holder's office is to sanctify himself and stand as an advocate before God seeking blessings for his community in the manner of the Lord Jesus Christ himself (see John 17:19), whether the community be as small as a family or as large as Benjamin's kingdom. A righteous priesthood holder can work by faith to provide great benefits to his fellow beings (see Mosiah 8:18). He can, in fact, exercise great faith in behalf of others of lesser faith, "filling in" with faith for them; thus a prophet [or any priesthood holder] and a people together can bring down blessings for even a whole community (for example, see Ether 12:14). The Lord seems to be interested not only in individuals but also in groups of people who wish to establish holy cities and unite with heavenly communities. Like the ancients, one who holds the holy priesthood is always trying to establish a holy community, is always "look[ing] for a city" (Hebrews 11:10, 16). So it was with Benjamin.[1161]

Imagine if every priesthood holder would approach his stewardship in this manner: metaphorically always "looking for a city." If such were the case, Zion could begin to more fully be established in families, quorums, wards, and stakes. The Lord said, "The power and authority of the higher, or Melchizedek Priesthood, is to hold the keys of all the spiritual blessings of the church—to have the privilege of receiving the mysteries of the kingdom of heaven, to have the heavens opened unto them, to commune with the general assembly and church of the Firstborn, and to enjoy the communion and presence of God the Father, and Jesus the mediator of the new covenant."[1162] If Melchizedek Priesthood holders do not instigate and disseminate spiritual blessings, those blessings will remain forever unknown and unclaimed.

What did King Benjamin do that is worthy of our emulation? First, he lived a Christlike life, the covenantal obligation of all priesthood holders, having labored ceaselessly in the service of his people and his God.[1163] Next, he prepared his people for the blessings of salvation by fighting for them, waging battles in their behalf, doing all that he could to "triumph over the powers of evil—over 'enemies.'" Catherine Thomas wrote, "This is the pattern: the priesthood holder labors with all his faculties to rout Satan from his loved ones as that enemy is manifested in contention, mental warfare, and physical violence among the people. For any priesthood holder to become a prince of peace, he must in some degree wrest his kingdom, great or small, from the adversary and halt the plans of the destroyer on behalf of his loved ones." Establishing peace is absolutely essential for spiritual progress and "to receive greater spiritual blessings."[1164] Thus, Melchizedek and Abraham were called princes of peace[1165] after the order to Jesus Christ, *the* Prince of Peace.

Another priesthood action of King Benjamin that is worthy of our emulation is that he sanctified himself and prayed earnestly for priesthood power to bring his people into the presence of the Lord.

[1160] Smith, *Teachings of the Prophet Joseph Smith*, 159.
[1161] Thomas, "Benjamin and the Mysteries of God," 281–82.
[1162] D&C 107:18–19.
[1163] Mosiah 2:10–16.
[1164] Thomas, "Benjamin and the Mysteries of God," 282–83; Mosiah 4:14.
[1165] Alma 13:17–18; Abraham 1:2.

We cannot overemphasize this step. As we have discussed in Book 2, the process of sanctification is to purify (eliminate contaminants), and then change the purpose of something. For example, we take common bread and water, sanctify them by the purifying power of the priesthood, and thus change their purpose to become the sacred emblems of the sacrament. King Benjamin sanctified himself to move from king and protector to prophet and priest, or more specifically, to savior in the similitude of the Savior.

In response to his prayer, an angel appeared, giving the king permission to gather the people for the purpose of bestowing upon them a great spiritual endowment, along with instructions for how to do it. "The Lord hath heard thy prayers," the angel said, "and hath judged of thy righteousness, and hath sent me to declare unto thee that thou mayest rejoice; *and that thou mayest declare unto thy people, that they may also be filled with joy.*"[1166] These were "glad tidings of great joy," the very thing that Benjamin had wanted for his people. The message of the angel would distinguish this group of people "above all the people which the Lord hath brought out of the land of Jerusalem."[1167] Catherine Thomas explained, "Perhaps this was the first time among all the people brought out from the land of Jerusalem that a king and priest—in the tradition of Adam, Enoch, and Melchizedek—had succeeded in bringing his people to this point of transformation actually to receive the name of Christ."[1168]

What exactly happened for them to "actually receive the name of Christ"? The process of taking upon ourselves the name of Christ begins at baptism,[1169] and our subsequent partaking of the sacrament indicates our *willingness* to take upon ourselves the name of Jesus Christ,[1170] but to actually do so usually lies in the future. Elder Bruce R. McConkie explained,

Mere compliance with the formality of the ordinance of baptism does not mean that a person has been born again. No one can be born again without baptism, but the immersion in water and the laying on of hands to confer the Holy Ghost do not of themselves guarantee that a person has been or will be born again. The new birth takes place only for those who actually enjoy the gift or companionship of the Holy Ghost, only for those who are fully converted, who have given themselves without restraint to the Lord. Thus Alma addressed himself to his "brethren of the church," and pointedly asked them if they had "spiritually been born of God," received the Lord's image in their countenances, and had the "mighty change" in their hearts which always attends the birth of the Spirit. (Alma 5:14, 31.)[1171]

Beyond the ordinance of baptism and ordination to the priesthood for men, fully taking upon ourselves the name of Christ requires at least three things: (1) intervention by the priesthood (as explained below), (2) receiving all of the temple covenants and ordinances, and (3) living worthily of all that we have received.

King Benjamin understood his priesthood role to act as an advocate for the people and to facilitate a spiritual experience whereby they could receive a greater endowment of the Spirit in a temple setting. We must realize that the responsibility of the priesthood is to bring people to the Holy Ghost, whose responsibility is to bring people to Jesus Christ—whose responsibility is to bring people to the Father. King Benjamin sanctified himself, thus changing his purpose from being king and protector to becoming a savior to his people. The priesthood is the power to facilitate a conversion opportunity for those of one's stewardship, to bring people to Christ so that they might more fully take upon themselves his name, and to unlock the mysteries of the kingdom of heaven that can be learned

---

[1166] Mosiah 3:3–4; emphasis added.
[1167] Mosiah 1:11.
[1168] Thomas, "Benjamin and the Mysteries of God," 290–91.
[1169] 2 Nephi 31:13.
[1170] Moroni 4:3; D&C 20:37.
[1171] McConkie, *Mormon Doctrine*, 101.

only by revelation. This astounding idea links priesthood authority, the name of Christ, and unlocking blessings for those whom we serve.

King Benjamin adhered to this priesthood principle and prayed and received the angel's permission to proceed with the promise that his people might "rejoice with exceedingly great joy,"[1172] and be "filled with joy,"[1173] which terms, according to Catherine Thomas, are synonymous with being born again.[1174] Then he gathered his people to the temple, where he administered to them something akin to the temple endowment. He covered such temple themes as "the creation, fall, Atonement, consecration, and covenant making. Benjamin's last words pertain to being 'sealed' to Christ and receiving eternal life (see Mosiah 5:15)." The result was as astonishing as anything else we read in scripture. These people became Zion people; they "received an endowment of spiritual knowledge and power which took them from being good people to Christlike people—all in a temple setting. What they experienced through the power of the priesthood was a revelation of Christ's nature and the power to be assimilated to his image."[1175] That is, by King Benjamin's priesthood intervention, they fully took upon themselves the name of Jesus Christ and consummated their journey to full rebirth. Now they were Zion people.

The connection of the priesthood, temple, and receiving the name of Christ should not escape us. The scriptures teach us that the temple is a house for "the name" of the Lord.[1176] The Kirtland Temple was a place where "thy name shall be put upon this house."[1177] Clearly, the temple is where we fully receive the name of Jesus Christ through the covenants and ordinances of salvation. Our leaders have taught that when we partake of the sacrament, we indicate our willingness to make our way to the temple to take upon ourselves fully the name of Christ and receive the blessings of exaltation. These include those highest blessings associated with the name of Christ given to those who live righteously against all hazards.[1178]

Priesthood holders are specifically commissioned to help people take upon themselves the name of Christ. Beyond administering the ordinances of baptism and the Holy Ghost, priesthood holders are responsible to get people to the temple, where we take upon us the name of Christ more fully. Then priesthood holders are to teach those exalting covenants and to set an example of righteous covenantal living. The result will make their charges Zion people and eventually gods. Elder Bruce R. McConkie wrote, "God's name is God. To have his name written on a person is to identify that person as a god. How can it be said more plainly? Those who gain eternal life become gods!"[1179] To fully take upon us the name of Jesus Christ, which we do through the endowment, an event that can happen only in a temple, opens the door to be nominated as a candidate for exaltation. For King Benjamin's people, this pivotal experience resulted in a "profound transformation from basic goodness to something that exceeded their ability to even describe. This much did they say, 'The Spirit of the Lord Omnipotent . . . has wrought a mighty change in us, or in our hearts, that we have no more disposition to do evil, but to do good continually' (Mosiah 5:2)."[1180]

Who can underestimate a priesthood holder's power and responsibility to help to establish Zion principles in his people? Catherine Thomas concluded, "It is the privilege and responsibility of a community's priesthood leader, through exercising mighty faith and laboring with his people, to bring

---

[1172] Mosiah 3:13.
[1173] Mosiah 4:3.
[1174] Thomas, "Benjamin and the Mysteries of God," 285–86.
[1175] Thomas, "Benjamin and the Mysteries of God," 292.
[1176] 1 Kings 3:2; 5:5; 8:16–20, 29, 44, 48; 1 Chronicles 22:8–10, 19; 29:16; 2:4; 6:5–10, 20, 34, 38.
[1177] D&C 109:26.
[1178] Oaks, "Taking Upon Us the Name of Jesus Christ," *Ensign*, May 1985, 80–83.
[1179] McConkie, *Doctrinal New Testament Commentary*, 3:459.
[1180] Thomas, "Benjamin and the Mysteries of God," 290.

them to a higher spiritual plane in their quest to return to God. Benjamin had been praying that the Lord would send power to bring to pass a spiritually transforming experience for his people. The Lord sent his angel to declare to the king that power would be given to cause the people to be spiritually reborn, to become sons and daughters of Christ, and to receive the sacred name forever. . . . The people tasted of the glory of God and came to a personal knowledge of him; through the power of the Holy Spirit they experienced the mighty change of heart and the mystery of spiritual rebirth."[1181]

No other priesthood responsibility could take precedence. It has everything to do with establishing Zion in one life or many lives. President Benson said, "When we awake and are born of God, a new day will break and Zion will be redeemed."[1182] That is what Benjamin did with his priesthood—that is what we all must do: awaken the people so that they are born of God; seek for a new day, so that Zion will be redeemed. This is the "city" we look for, the city "whose builder and maker is God."[1183]

This, then, is the priesthood model that draws people toward perfection and the ideal of Zion. This model calls for priesthood holders to sanctify themselves, as did King Benjamin, so that they might have a redeeming effect on the people they serve. This model also calls for the followers of such righteous priesthood holders to take advantage of the conversion opportunity proffered them. Joseph Smith said, "The nearer man approaches perfection, the clearer are his views, and the greater his enjoyments, till he has overcome the evils of his life and lost every desire for sin; and like the ancients, arrives at that point of faith where he is wrapped in the power and glory of his Maker and is caught up to dwell with Him."[1184]

THE RESTORATION OF THE PRIESTHOOD

Joseph Smith said, "All Priesthood is Melchizedek, but there are different portions or degrees of it."[1185] That is, there is but one priesthood, which is Melchizedek, and it is "the highest and holiest priesthood, and is after the order of the Son of God, and all other priesthoods are only parts, ramifications, powers and blessings belonging to the same, and are held, controlled, and directed by it."[1186] The Melchizedek Priesthood has a variety of *orders*, among which are Aaronic, Melchizedek, and Patriarchal.[1187] After the great apostasy, each of these priesthood orders needed to be restored. Because establishing Zion in the life of an individual, a marriage, a family, or a priesthood society is impossible without the Melchizedek Priesthood, and because Zion must be established for the Lord to come,[1188] the priesthood must exist upon the earth.

The earliest recorded reference to priesthood restoration was in 1823, when Moroni appeared to Joseph Smith and prophesied, "I will reveal [restore] unto you the priesthood by the hand of the Elijah."[1189] But to which order of the priesthood was Moroni referring?

The restoration of the priesthood began on May 15, 1829, with the appearance of John the Baptist, who restored the Aaronic Priesthood.[1190] Shortly thereafter, in June 1829, it is assumed, Peter, James, and John restored the Melchizedek Priesthood, including the keys to the kingdom of God.[1191]

[1181] Thomas, "Benjamin and the Mysteries of God," 293.
[1182] Benson, *A Witness and a Warning*, 66.
[1183] Hebrews 11:10.
[1184] Smith, *Teachings of the Prophet Joseph Smith*, 51.
[1185] Smith, *Teachings of the Prophet Joseph Smith*, 180.
[1186] Smith, *Teachings of the Prophet Joseph Smith*, 166–67.
[1187] *Encyclopedia of Mormonism*, 1067–68.
[1188] Whitney, Conference Report, Oct. 1928, 60.
[1189] D&C 2:1.
[1190] D&C 13.
[1191] Benson, "What I Hope You Will Teach Your Children about the Temple," 6–10.

These priesthood and keys authorize men to perform the ordinances of salvation, and give those priesthood holders the right and the commission to preach the gospel of salvation throughout the world.[1192] Now the Aaronic and Melchizedek priesthoods had been restored, but in 1823 Moroni had prophesied that Elijah would come and reveal priesthood. The fact that Elijah had not yet appeared indicates that there was still more of the priesthood to be revealed.

ELIJAH RESTORES THE SEALING KEYS OF THE PATRIARCHAL ORDER OF THE PRIESTHOOD

A few years later, as recorded in Doctrine and Covenants 110, Elijah would return and reveal or restore the sealing keys associated with what is called the *Patriarchal Order of the Priesthood*, which was restored in a preceding vision by Elias. But prior to those events, a temple had to be built. Joseph Smith learned that the patriarchal order could not be restored unless it took place in a temple. Once, while expounding on the various priesthood orders, the Prophet made the following statement: "[This] . . . Priesthood is Patriarchal authority. Go to and finish the temple, and God will fill it with power, and you will then receive more knowledge concerning this priesthood."[1193]

Shortly after the dedication of the Kirtland Temple, on April 3, 1836, Elijah appeared to Joseph Smith and Oliver Cowdery and committed to them the sealing keys associated with the patriarchal order of the priesthood.[1194] This priesthood had power "to turn the hearts of the fathers to the children, and the children to the fathers."[1195] This patriarchal order of the priesthood is entered into by husbands and wives when they are sealed in the temple. "The patriarchal order is, in the words of Elder James E. Talmage 'a condition where 'woman shares with man the blessings of the Priesthood,' where husband and wife minister, 'seeing and understanding alike, and cooperating to the full in the government of their family kingdom.' A man cannot hold this priesthood without a wife, and a woman cannot share the blessings of this priesthood without a husband, sealed in the temple."[1196]

To turn the hearts of parents and children to each other means, according to Joseph Smith, *sealing* their hearts together: "Elijah shall reveal the covenants to *seal* the hearts of the fathers to the children, and the children to the fathers."[1197] To make possible this linkage, Elijah restored the keys that bind 'the covenants of the fathers in relation to the children, and the covenants of the children in relation to the fathers.'"[1198] That is, Elijah restored the sealing keys of the priesthood whereby covenants and ordinances made and performed are bound in earth and in heaven,[1199] and therefore they carry "efficacy, virtue, or force in and after the resurrection of the dead."[1200]

With regard to Zion, the message is clear: Zion is defined by the priesthood, by couples and families gathering to temples to obtain the covenants and ordinances of salvation, by entering into the patriarchal order of the priesthood through h, and by having those marriages and families sealed together forever.

[1192] Mark 16:15; McConkie, *Mormon Doctrine*, 220.
[1193] Smith, *History of the Church*, 5:554–55.
[1194] Tvedtnes, *The Church of the Old Testament*, 34.
[1195] D&C 110:15.
[1196] Talmage, *Young Woman's Journal* 25:602–3; *Encyclopedia of Mormonism*, 1067.
[1197] Smith, *Teachings of the Prophet Joseph Smith*, 323.
[1198] Brown, *The Gate of Heaven*, 215; Roberts, *Comprehensive History of the Church*, 5:530.
[1199] D&C 127:7; 128:8.
[1200] D&C 132:7.

ELIJAH RESTORES THE FULNESS OF THE PRIESTHOOD

Elijah's mission was greater still; Elijah's charge was also to restore the "fulness of the priesthood," which includes the fulness of the temple covenants and the ordinances of the house of the Lord.[1201] Therefore, the Lord commanded the Saints to build a temple for the purpose of endowing them with power from on high: "Yea, verily I say unto you, I gave unto you a commandment that you should build a house, in the which house I design to *endow* those whom I have chosen with *power from on high*."[1202] To endow means to present as a gift of honor; to award, bestow, confer, give, grant.[1203] When a college receives an endowment, the principal is typically placed in a fund where it spins off income perpetually; that is, the endowment is structured to continually give. Just so, God endows us in the temple with knowledge and power that bless us eternally. By drawing upon the Lord's endowment and by growing in our understanding of it, we receive progressively greater power to bless our families and others of God's children.

Of the connection between the ordinances associated with the temple endowment and the fulness of the priesthood, Elder Bruce R. McConkie wrote, "It is *only through the ordinances* of his holy house that the Lord deigns to 'restore again that which was lost unto you, or which he hath taken away, even *the fulness of the priesthood*.'"[1204] And Joseph Smith said: "If a man gets a fulness of the priesthood of God he has to get it in the same way that Jesus Christ obtained it, and that was by keeping all the commandments and obeying all the ordinances of the house of the Lord."[1205]

Again, we see Zion in these descriptions. Zion people are endowed with power from on high; they receive all the ordinances of salvation, which culminates with temple marriage and the fulness of the priesthood. Their eternal standing and blessings are confirmed by revelation and by ordinance.

MOSES RESTORES PRIESTHOOD KEYS OF FAMILY GATHERING

Elijah's appearance in the Kirtland Temple was preceded by the appearances of the Savior, Moses, and Elias. That Moses and Elias came to restore priesthood keys should hold enormous significance for parents in Zion. Moses committed the keys of the gathering of both the dead and the living of the family of Israel. This suggests that individually we now are in possession of priesthood powers to gather our families "from the four parts of the earth."[1206]

For what purpose is the gathering of families? Elder McConkie wrote, "Israel gathers for the purpose of building temples in which the ordinances of salvation and exaltation are performed for the living and the dead."[1207] On an individual level, this statement suggests that Zion people now have power to gather or call their families to the temple to receive the crowning ordinances of salvation.

ELIAS RESTORES PRIESTHOOD KEYS

Elias, whose office is that of forerunner,[1208] appeared after Moses and "committed the dispensation of the gospel of Abraham, saying that in us and our seed all generations after us should be blessed."[1209] President Joseph Fielding Smith said, "Elias came, after Moses had conferred his keys, and brought the

---

[1201] Benson, "What I Hope You Will Teach Your Children About the Temple," 6–10; Smith, *Teachings of the Prophet Joseph Smith*, 308.

[1202] D&C 95:8; emphasis added.

[1203] *American Heritage Dictionary*, s.v. "endow."

[1204] D&C 124:28; 127:8; 128:17; McConkie, *Mormon Doctrine*, 637; emphasis added.

[1205] Smith, *Teachings of the Prophet Joseph Smith*, 308.

[1206] D&C 110:11.

[1207] McConkie, *A New Witness for the Articles of Faith*, 539.

[1208] *Encyclopedia of Mormonism*, 449.

[1209] D&C 110:12.

gospel of the dispensation in which Abraham lived. *Everything that pertains to that dispensation, the blessings that were conferred upon Abraham, the promises that were given to his posterity, all had to be restored, and Elias, who held the keys of that dispensation, came.*"[1210] This is the power to organize families into eternal units.[1211] That is, because of Elias, our children and grandchildren can now be blessed with the gospel of Abraham (the new and everlasting covenant), blessings of which include the rights to receive the priesthood, all gospel blessings, ordinances, and sealings, including the sealing of eternal marriage and the sealing to eternal life. These rights flow to children who are born in the covenant to parents in Zion because those parents, like Abraham, Isaac, and Jacob and their wives, have entered into the new and everlasting covenant and progressed until they entered into the new and everlasting covenant of marriage.[1212] Elder McConkie wrote,

> That same day "Elias appeared, and committed the dispensation of the gospel of Abraham," meaning the great commission given to Abraham that he and his seed had a right to the priesthood, the gospel, and eternal life. Accordingly, Elias promised those upon whom these ancient promises were then renewed that in them and in their seed all generations should be blessed. (D&C 110:12–16.) Thus, through the joint ministry of Elijah, who brought the sealing power, and Elias, who restored the marriage discipline of Abraham, the way was prepared for the planting in the hearts of the children of the promises made to the fathers. (D&C 2:2.) These are the promises of eternal life through the priesthood and the gospel and celestial marriage.[1213]

THE JOINT MISSIONS OF ELIAS AND ELIJAH

Joseph Fielding McConkie wrote, "Simply stated, Elijah was sent to restore the keys of the patriarchal order of priesthood, rights which had not yet been fully operational in this dispensation. Elijah restored the keys whereby families (organized in the patriarchal order through the keys delivered by Elias) could be bound and sealed for eternity."[1214] Why is the patriarchal priesthood important to Zion people? Because patriarchal priesthood is *family* priesthood; entering into this order of the priesthood directly affects and eternally empowers fathers and mothers to do the work of redemption among their posterity. President Joseph Fielding Smith said, "Through the power [keys] of this priesthood which Elijah bestowed, husband and wife may be sealed, or married for eternity; children may be sealed to their parents for eternity; thus the family is made eternal, and death does not separate the members. *This is the great principle that will save the world from utter destruction.*"[1215]

Imagine Moses, Elias, and Elijah laying their hands upon your head to give you a blessing. First, Moses blesses you with the ability to gather with your family to the kingdom of God and the holy temple. Then Elias blesses you and your spouse and children to organize into an eternal family. He offers you the same covenant of the gospel that Abraham received—the new and everlasting covenant. When you agree to its terms, Elias blesses you with everything that was promised to Abraham: you and your posterity will have the eternal "right to the priesthood, the gospel, and eternal life."[1216] Central to those blessings is "the marriage discipline of Abraham,"[1217] meaning the promise

---

[1210] Smith, *Doctrines of Salvation*, 3:127; emphasis added.

[1211] Millet and McConkie, *The Life Beyond*, 96.

[1212] D&C 131:2.

[1213] McConkie, *A New Witness for the Articles of Faith*, 322.

[1214] Robert L. Millet and Joseph Fielding McConkie, The Life Beyond, 96. For other references stating that Elijah restored the sealing keys of the patriarchal priesthood, see Tvedtnes, *The Church of the Old Testament*, 33–35; Smith, *Teachings of the Prophet Joseph Smith*, 172: "Elijah's mission was to "restore the authority and deliver the keys of the priesthood. . . . Why send Elijah? Because he holds the keys of the authority to administer in all the ordinances of the priesthood."

[1215] Smith, *Doctrines of Salvation*, 2:118; emphasis added.

[1216] McConkie, *A New Witness for the Articles of Faith*, 322.

[1217] McConkie, *A New Witness for the Articles of Faith*, 322.

that your marriage will be eternal, through your faithfulness, and that you and your spouse will enjoy the blessing of eternal posterity. Additionally, you are promised, as was Abraham, that you and your posterity will receive a promised land in this world and a promised inheritance in the celestial world to come.

Now that you have entered into the new and everlasting covenant, which includes eternal marriage, Elijah confirms these blessings with a *seal*, a "welding link,"[1218] that cannot be broken. Then, as a final blessing, because you have proven faithful at all hazards, Elijah seals upon you the *fulness of the priesthood*, which in the ultimate sense means that he seals you up unto eternal life; that is, Elijah makes everything with which you have been blessed *more sure*.[1219] Now, because of your righteousness, Elijah extends to you a promise for your children. The promise is this: *As you turn your heart to your children, their hearts will turn to you and the Covenant that you have made.* Elijah's blessing guarantees to you that no matter what happens in time or eternity, these children are yours. Then, when Elias and Elijah finish their blessings upon your head, the Savior steps forward and receives you into his embrace. You are home at last, and your spouse and your children are there with you.

Building One Priesthood Power upon Another

Of the interwoven tapestry of the restoration of the priesthood, Joseph Fielding McConkie wrote,

> Joseph Smith taught that ultimate salvation is found only in the eternal union of man and woman. Every priesthood, grace, power, and authority restored to the Prophet Joseph Smith centers in the salvation of the family. Peter, James, and John restored the Holy Priesthood, thereby authorizing men to perform the ordinances of salvation; Elias restored the ordinance of eternal marriage and the promise of an endless seed; and Elijah restored the sealing power and the fulness of the priesthood by which husband, wife, and children are bound eternally. These doctrines build on the assurance of the Book of Mormon that the resurrection is corporeal and thus that women will be resurrected as women and men as men, the bond of their love ever intact. Thus, as baptism is the gate to the strait and narrow path leading to eternal life, eternal marriage becomes the door through which all who inherit that glory must enter. None enter alone. The man and the woman must stand side by side. Couples in turn must be bound in eternal covenant with their righteous progenitors and with their posterity. In that eternal and restored system we know as The Church of Jesus Christ of Latter-day Saints, salvation is a family affair.[1220]

Rescuing This Generation

Joseph Smith said, "How shall God come to rescue this generation? He will send Elijah the Prophet. . . . *Elijah shall reveal the covenants to seal* the hearts of the fathers to the children, and the children to the fathers."[1221] Achieving Zion is impossible without eternal marriages and families. On a family level, the Lord will rescue *this* generation by sending Elijah the prophet to seal the hearts of the fathers to the

---

[1218] D&C 128:18.
[1219] Smith, *Teachings of the Prophet Joseph Smith*, 337–38.
[1220] McConkie, *Joseph Smith: The Choice Seer*, chapter 20.
[1221] Smith, *Teachings of the Prophet Joseph Smith*, 323.

children, and the children to the fathers. Elijah's sealing power is the crowning blessing of the priesthood.

We see the blessings of the priesthood unfold in the pattern set forth in Doctrine and Covenants 110. First, the Savior comes. He directs the work of salvation and exaltation. His Atonement makes eternal marriage and family possible. Then comes Moses, whose keys gather a couple and a family to the temple. Then comes Elias, whose keys bless a couple and their children with saving and exalting ordinances. Finally, Elijah comes and seals or confirms "more sure" all that has happened. The generation of that couple is rescued, and Zion is established.

Eternal Principle of Power

"Like God himself," taught Elder McConkie, "the Melchizedek Priesthood is eternal and everlasting in nature."[1222] Joseph Smith said, "The priesthood is an everlasting principle, and existed with God from eternity, and will to eternity, without beginning of days or end of years."[1223] That is, the priesthood had no beginning and will have no end. When the authority of God is conferred on a worthy man, he will always possess it as long as he remains true to the covenant associated with the priesthood.

Beyond authority, the priesthood becomes power when a man exercises righteousness. Moses revealed, "[Every man] being ordained after this order and calling should have power, by faith, to break mountains, to divide the seas, to dry up waters, to turn them out of their course; to put at defiance the armies of nations, to divide the earth, to break every band, to stand in the presence of God; to do all things according to his will, according to his command subdue principalities and powers; and this by the will of the Son of God which was from before the foundation of the world."[1224] Clearly, priesthood is power.

What is this ideal Zion like? In the last days, we are told, it will be a place of refuge in a doomed world. "It shall be called the New Jerusalem, a land of peace, a city of refuge, a place of safety for the saints of the Most High God; . . . and the terror of the Lord also shall be there, . . . and it shall be called Zion" (D&C 45:66–67). At that time, "every man that will not take his sword against his neighbor must needs flee unto Zion for safety" (D&C 45:68). And the wicked shall say that Zion is terrible. Terrible because it is indestructible. Her invulnerability makes her an object of awe and terror. As Enoch said, "Surely Zion shall dwell in safety forever. But the Lord said unto Enoch: Zion have I blessed, but the residue of the people have I cursed" (Moses 7:20). So Zion was taken away and the rest destroyed. Zion itself is never in danger; on the contrary, it alone offers safety to the world, "that the gathering together upon the land of Zion, and upon her stakes, may be for a defense, and for a refuge from the storm, and from wrath when it shall be poured out without mixture upon the whole earth" (D&C 115:6). It would seem that Zion enjoys the complete security of a bit of the celestial world and that nothing can touch it as long as it retains the character. But *celestial* order it must be.[1225]

Premortal Qualification for the Priesthood

As a rule, we who strive to live celestial laws and are thus judged worthy to be ordained to the Melchizedek Priesthood were qualified to hold that authority in the premortal life, which Alma calls the "first place."[1226] Quoting Alma and Joseph Smith, Elder McConkie taught that worthy priesthood holders were "'on the same standing with their brethren,' meaning that initially all had equal opportunity to progress through righteousness. But while yet in the eternal worlds, certain of the offspring of God, 'having chosen good, and exercising exceeding great faith,' were as a consequence

---

[1222] McConkie, *Mormon Doctrine*, 475–83.
[1223] Smith, *Teachings of the Prophet Joseph Smith*, 157–58, 323; D&C 84:17; JST Hebrews 7:1–3.
[1224] JST Genesis 14:30–31.
[1225] Nibley, *Approaching Zion*, 6–7.
[1226] Alma 13:3.

'called and prepared from the foundation of the world according to the foreknowledge of God' to enjoy the blessings and powers of the priesthood. These priesthood calls were made 'from the foundation of the world,' or in other words faithful men held priesthood power and authority first in pre-existence and then again on earth. 'Every man who has a calling to minister to the inhabitants of the world was ordained to that very purpose in the Grand Council of heaven before this world was.'"[1227]

Our premortal calling to and preparation in the priesthood, Alma says, was "on account of [our] exceeding faith and good works." Having chosen independently to embrace the good and eschew evil, and to exercise "exceedingly great faith," we received the authority of God, which qualified us for a "preparatory redemption."[1228] That is, in the "first place," we earned the blessings of redemption, which guaranteed that we would be offered those blessings again in the flesh. Unless we chose otherwise in this life, the blessings of redemption would be ours forever.

THE OBLIGATION OF ZION PRIESTHOOD HOLDERS

"Priesthood is the great governing authority in the universe," writes M. Catherine Thomas, assistant professor emeritus of Ancient Scripture at Brigham Young University. "It unlocks spiritual blessings of the eternal world for the heirs of salvation."[1229] The priesthood is always conferred upon us with the understanding that we will minister among God's children, offer them the blessings of the plan of redemption, and bring them to Christ for the purpose of establishing Zion in their lives.[1230] This is modeled in the scriptures by Enoch leaving the land of Cainan to preach the gospel to the people, offer the ordinances of salvation, and bring them to Zion.[1231] Likewise, Melchizedek preached the gospel, administered the ordinances, and achieved Zion: "And his people wrought righteousness, and obtained heaven, and sought for the city of Enoch which God had before taken, separating it from the earth, having reserved it unto the latter days, or the end of the world."[1232]

The Book of Mormon offers another example: "And it came to pass that the thirty and fourth year passed away, and also the thirty and fifth, and behold the disciples of Jesus had formed a church of Christ in all the lands round about. And as many as did come unto them, and did truly repent of their sins, were baptized in the name of Jesus; and they did also receive the Holy Ghost. *And it came to pass in the thirty and sixth year, the people were all converted unto the Lord, upon all the face of the land, both Nephites and Lamanites,* and there were no contentions and disputations among them, and every man did deal justly one with another."[1233]

Catherine Thomas writes, "The power to play a saving role is the most sought-after power among righteous priesthood holders in time or in eternity. The greater the soul, it seems, the deeper the desire to labor to brings souls to Christ. . . . A brief look at the history of the priesthood on the earth reveals that men like [King] Benjamin have stood in this priesthood channel unlocking the blessings of salvation for their people since the days of Adam. Adam, in fact, was the great prototype of priesthood holders who strove to bring their communities and their posterity into at-one-ment with the Lord Jesus Christ. Adam blessed his posterity because, the Prophet Joseph taught, 'he wanted to bring them into the presence of God. They looked for a city . . . 'whose builder and maker is God' (Hebrews 11:10).'"

[1227] McConkie, *Mormon Doctrine*, 475–83; Alma 13:3, 5; Smith, *Teachings of the Prophet Joseph Smith*, 365.
[1228] Alma 13:3.
[1229] Thomas, "Benjamin and the Mysteries of God," 279.
[1230] Eyring, "Faith and the Oath and Covenant of the Priesthood," 61–64.
[1231] Moses 6:41; see Moses 6–7.
[1232] JST Genesis 14:34.
[1233] 4 Nephi 1:1–2; emphasis added.

As we have said, a priesthood holder is under obligation to sanctify himself so that he can advocate for his people, as did Adam, Enoch, Melchizedek, Moses, King Benjamin, and Joseph Smith. As examples, Dr. Thomas explains the duties of a priesthood holder. "A priesthood holder's office is to sanctify himself and stand as an advocate before God seeking blessings for his community in the manner of Jesus Christ (see John 17:19), whether the community be as small as a family or as large as Benjamin's kingdom. A righteous priesthood holder can work by faith to provide great benefits to his fellow beings (see Mosiah 8:18). He can, in fact, exercise great faith in behalf of others of lesser faith, 'filling in' with faith for them. . . . The Lord seems interested not only in individual but in groups of people who wish to establish holy cities and unite with heavenly communities. Like the ancients, one who holds the holy priesthood is always trying to establish a holy community, is always 'look[ing] for a city' (Hebrews 11:10, 16)."[1234]

OUR PRIESTHOOD WORK THEN AND NOW

Our works on earth are an extension of the works we did in the premortal world. Alma explained that our premortal calling to the priesthood set us apart from others in that realm, those who hardened their hearts against the gospel and thus forfeited their privileges: "And thus they [priesthood holders] have been called to this holy calling on account of their faith, while others would reject the Spirit of God on account of the hardness of their hearts and blindness of their minds, while, if it had not been for this they might have had as great privilege as their brethren." Clearly, we distinguished ourselves in premortality by embracing the gospel and the principles of Zion, and therefore we were rewarded in that "first place" with the priesthood: "Thus this holy calling [was] prepared from the foundation of the world for such as would not harden their hearts, being in and through the Atonement of the Only Begotten Son."

Having received the priesthood, we became part of the same order as the Son of God and went about doing his work, the work of Zion: "And thus being called by this holy calling, and ordained unto the high priesthood of the holy order of God, to teach his commandments unto the children of men, that they also might enter into his rest—this high priesthood being after the order of his Son, which order was from the foundation of the world; or in other words, being without beginning of days or end of years, being prepared from eternity to all eternity, according to his foreknowledge of all things—Now they were ordained after this manner—being called with a holy calling, and ordained with a holy ordinance, and taking upon them the high priesthood of the holy order, which calling, and ordinance, and high priesthood, is without beginning or end—thus they become high priests forever, after the order of the Son, the Only Begotten of the Father, who is without beginning of days or end of years, who is full of grace, equity, and truth. And thus it is. Amen."[1235]

Clearly, our past experience with the priesthood will be exceeded only by our glorious future experience. Moreover, our priesthood work now is an extension of our work then; and our work in the priesthood will continue into the eternities: "The faithful elders of this dispensation, when they depart from mortal life, continue their labors in the preaching of the gospel of repentance and redemption, through the sacrifice of the Only Begotten Son of God."[1236]

The work that we assumed so long ago—the work of redemption—is the work that helps to establish Zion in the lives of people. This work is as eternal as is the priesthood. The priesthood vitalizes the plan of redemption and makes possible the establishment of Zion. The priesthood of God is the power by which the foundation of Zion (the Atonement) and the three pillars of Zion function

---

[1234] Thomas, "Benjamin and the Mysteries of God," 280–82.
[1235] Alma 13:4–9.
[1236] D&C 138:57.

together. Upon this sure foundation and its pillars, Zion rises to form "the highest order of priesthood society."[1237]

THE COVENANT OF THE PRIESTHOOD

"When we receive the Melchizedek Priesthood," Elder Bruce R. McConkie testified, "we enter into a covenant with the Lord. It is the covenant of exaltation. . . . There neither is nor can be a covenant more wondrous and great."[1238]

After we receive the new and everlasting covenant by baptism, the Spirit begins to purify us and change our nature; the Spirit also urges us to progress in the Covenant; and our desire migrates from selfish to selfless. The more we become Zionlike, the more we yearn to share the Covenant with others and to invite them to become Zionlike. The only authoritative way to bless other people with the Covenant is to seek the priesthood, as did Abraham, and receive it by covenant. This is the second pillar of Zion—*the oath and covenant of the priesthood*. It emerges from the Covenant of Mercy, which likewise emerges from the new and everlasting covenant.

We seek to enter the priesthood covenant for both personal and universal reasons. The priesthood offers us supernal individual gifts, such as individual salvation, keys to the knowledge and power of God, and eternal marriage, none of which can be obtained in any other manner. But the priesthood is also the "power and authority of God" that allows us "to minister to other beings to bring about their happiness."[1239] Let us examine the priesthood and its covenant that allow us these privileges.

THE LESSER AND GREATER PORTIONS

"All priesthood is Melchizedek," said the Prophet Joseph Smith, "but there are different portions or degrees of it."[1240] The lesser "portion," or the preparatory priesthood, is called the Aaronic or Levitical Priesthood, one of the blessings of which is the keys to the ministering of angels. The higher "portion" of the priesthood is the Melchizedek Priesthood, one of the blessings of which is that righteous men and women have the ability "to speak with God face to face."[1241] This privilege is descriptive of Zion people, with whom the Lord makes his abode.[1242] Elder McConkie taught that these two orders of the priesthood are received by covenant, but only the Melchizedek Priesthood is received with the Father's oath.

The covenant regarding the Aaronic Priesthood, said Elder McConkie, states that a worthy man must promise to forsake the world, magnify his *calling*, minister and give service to others, and obey the commandments. In return, the Lord promises to magnify the priesthood holder in his position and to prepare him in every way to receive the Melchizedek Priesthood.

Elder McConkie continued by saying that the covenant regarding the Melchizedek Priesthood is that a worthy man promises to magnify his *calling*, obey the commandments, be an example of Jesus Christ, serve as the Lord would serve, "live by every word that proceedeth forth from the mouth of

---

[1237] Kimball, *Teachings of Spencer W. Kimball*, 125.

[1238] McConkie, *A New Witness for the Articles of Faith*, 312–13. Note: In *Doctrines of Salvation*, 2:58, Joseph Fielding Smith reminded us that the marriage covenant is also called the covenant of exaltation. "The marriage covenant flows from the covenant of the priesthood; the marriage covenant is the order of the priesthood (Patriarchal) that allows us to become like God. Therefore, in the marriage covenant, all the blessings of exaltation contained in the priesthood covenant are renewed and pronounced upon both the man and the woman."

[1239] Riddle, "The New and Everlasting Covenant," 231.

[1240] Smith, *Teachings of the Prophet Joseph Smith*, 180.

[1241] Smith, *Teachings of the Prophet Joseph Smith*, 180.

[1242] Moses 7:21; Psalm 132:13.

God" (D&C 84:44), and marry in the temple for time and eternity. In return, the Father promises *with an oath* that he will give that man all that the Father has, which is the definition of eternal life. These covenantal blessings comprise the promises of exaltation, godhood, eternal marriage, and endless posterity.[1243]

THE PATRIARCHAL ORDER

In addition to the Aaronic and Melchizedek orders of the priesthood is the patriarchal order. Neither Zion nor Zion people can be established without the patriarchal order of the priesthood. This order is not a separate priesthood, but rather the highest order of the Melchizedek Priesthood.[1244] According to Elder McConkie, this is the Lord's eternal patriarchal order, or the priesthood order of the gods. This order exists only in the highest degree of the celestial kingdom, and it is the priesthood order by which husbands and wives, who have been sealed for time and eternity, may enjoy eternal increase of spirit children in the resurrection.[1245] This is the order of priesthood government that exists in heaven among all glorified fathers and mothers who preside over their vast families.

Elder McConkie wrote: "'This order was instituted in the days of Adam, and came down by lineage.' It was designed 'to be handed down from father to son.' It came down in succession; it is priesthood government; it is the government of God both on earth and in heaven. And even today, it 'rightly belongs to the literal descendants of the chosen seed, to whom the promises were made.' (D&C 107:40–41.) *That it is not now in full operation simply means that fallen men have departed from the ancient ways and are now governing each other as they choose.*"[1246] That is, the patriarchal order of the priesthood presently functions within righteous marriages and families by virtue of the husband and wife's marriage covenant and sealing, but it does not yet function as it did in the beginning as the government of the Church. This form of priesthood government exists in the celestial kingdom.[1247]

DIFFERING PURPOSES AND POWERS

The Aaronic and Melchizedek priesthoods administer different elements of the gospel. The Aaronic Priesthood holds "the keys of the ministering of angels, and to administer in outward ordinances, the letter of the gospel, the baptism of repentance for the remission of sins, agreeable to the covenants and commandments."[1248] This priesthood *cannot* establish Zion, because "Zion is heaven. It is where God lives."[1249] The ideal of Zion people is to enjoy the presence of God: "For without [the ordinances of the Melchizedek Priesthood] no man can see the face of God, even the Father, and live."[1250]

When the Melchizedek Priesthood, its ordinances, and principles of Zion are neglected or rejected by a covenant person, the Lord swears in his wrath that that person risks losing the blessings of eternal life. The Melchizedek Priesthood and its blessings cease to function in such a person. He is left with a preparatory gospel, and he is in danger of losing his blessings altogether, as did the Nephites and Jaredites. The ancient Israelites are an example of losing blessings due to neglect or rejection of the priesthood.

Now this Moses plainly taught to the children of Israel in the wilderness, and sought diligently to sanctify his people that they might behold the face of God; but they hardened their hearts and could not endure his presence; therefore, the Lord in his wrath, for his anger was kindled against them,

---

[1243] McConkie, "The Doctrine of the Priesthood," 32; D&C 131:1–4.
[1244] *Encyclopedia of Mormonism*, 1067.
[1245] McConkie, "The Doctrine of the Priesthood," 32; D&C 131:1–4.
[1246] McConkie, *A New Witness for the Articles of Faith*, 35; emphasis added.
[1247] McConkie, *Mormon Doctrine*, 559.
[1248] D&C 107:20.
[1249] Nibley, *Approaching Zion*, 6–7.
[1250] D&C 84:22.

swore that they should not enter into his rest while in the wilderness, which rest is the fulness of his glory. Therefore, he took Moses out of their midst, and the Holy Priesthood also; and the lesser priesthood continued, which priesthood holdeth the key of the ministering of angels and the preparatory gospel; which gospel is the gospel of repentance and of baptism, and the remission of sins, and the law of carnal commandments, which the Lord in his wrath caused to continue with the house of Aaron among the children of Israel.[1251]

Zion people embrace the Melchizedek Priesthood, which "administereth the gospel and holdeth the key of the mysteries of the kingdom, even the key of the knowledge of God."[1252]

Grand Purposes of the Priesthood

As we can see, the Melchizedek Priesthood has two grand purposes: to administer the gospel (meaning to preside) and the covenants and ordinances of salvation; and to enable its holders to stand in the presence of God, and receive personal revelation directly from him. This eminent level of revelation, which is enjoyed by Zion people, is made possible only by the ordinances of the Melchizedek Priesthood: "Therefore, in the ordinances thereof, the power of godliness [i.e., the power to become Godlike] is manifest. And without the ordinances thereof, and the authority of the priesthood, the power of godliness is not manifest unto men in the flesh; for without this [the power to become Godlike] no man can see the face of God, even the Father, and live."[1253]

This information about the priesthood is of profound significance. To stand in the authority of God, to wield his power, and to stand in his presence are definitive of Zion and of eternal life. Of Zion, Moses wrote: "The Lord came and dwelt with his people, and they dwelt in righteousness." Enoch declared, "Surely Zion shall dwell in safety forever," whereupon the Lord answered, "Zion have I blessed." Moses continued his narrative: "Zion, in the process of time, was taken into heaven. And the Lord said unto Enoch: Behold mine abode forever."[1254]

Priesthood Blessings

If men desire to become Zionlike, they must be ordained to the Melchizedek Priesthood and abide in the covenant of the priesthood. If women desire to become Zionlike, they must also embrace the principles of the covenant of the priesthood by receiving the ordinances of the priesthood, including eternal marriage, thereby entering into the patriarchal order of the priesthood with their husbands. Here, we must keep in mind that Zion is a journey. That single men and women might presently lack temple marriage does not discount their ability to qualify now as Zion people. As with all gospel ideals, it is the direction in which we are headed that qualifies us for blessings. The Lord's grace allows him to reward us *as if* we had met all of the requirements. We simply must do the best we can with present realities.

For men, this process begins with the Father's invitation. He offers them the priesthood by swearing a sacred oath; then they enter into a covenant with him. If they remain faithful to that covenant, it will lead them to eternal life. They progress in the priesthood covenant by ordination, receiving temple covenants and ordinances, and temple marriage, at which time the Father's oath given in the priesthood covenant is renewed.[1255] Only by progressing in this way can men ever hope to obtain the blessings of Zion, stand in the presence of God, receive intelligence and instructions from him, become in every way as God is, and inherit what he has.

And the blessings of the priesthood multiply.

[1251] D&C 84:23–27.
[1252] D&C 84:19.
[1253] D&C 84:20–22.
[1254] Moses 7:16, 20–21.
[1255] McConkie, *A New Witness for the Articles of Faith*, 313.

When men have received the priesthood ordination and the temple covenants and ordinances, they then possess the authority to administer the same to others of God's children. They become saviors on Mount Zion[1256] for both the living and the dead. They are authorized to assist in the eternal redemptive work of God, which is to bring people to Christ so that those people might also receive the blessings of immortal glory and "eternal lives."[1257] Therefore, as we have said, men receive the priesthood for two reasons: "for your sake, and not for your sake only, but for the sake of the whole world."[1258]

The Blessings of Adam

Joseph Smith taught: "The Priesthood was first given to Adam; he obtained the First Presidency, and held the keys of it from generation to generation. The Priesthood is an everlasting principle. The keys have to be brought from heaven whenever the Gospel is sent. When they are revealed from heaven, it is by Adam's authority."[1259] The "Holy Priesthood after the order of the Son of God"[1260] provided for the promises that God made to Adam[1261]—to provide a Savior to redeem him and his children from their fallen condition,[1262] and restore them to a Zionlike condition through the new and everlasting covenant, which includes the oath and covenant of the priesthood. This covenantal relationship forms the foundation to the plan of salvation that God gave to Adam, and this plan was determined from the beginning to be administered by "the order of the Son of God." Adam was first taught by God and angels, and then he taught his children by the authority of the priesthood how to become Zionlike in character and how to regain God's presence.

The holy priesthood offered Adam the greatest promises of personal blessings, but perhaps more importantly it also provided Adam the necessary authority to minister those blessings to his family.[1263] Among those blessings is the establishment of Zion. Adam's righteousness summoned the Lord to establish the foundations of Adam-ondi-Ahman, the first Zion priesthood society.[1264] It was there that Adam eventually succeeded in bringing his faithful posterity back into the presence of the Lord.[1265]

We see in Adam's example the redemptive power of the priesthood and the exalting power of Zionlike principles that are incorporated in the priesthood. It was by means of the power of the priesthood, specifically the power of the ordinances of the Melchizedek Priesthood,[1266] that Adam was able to accomplish these supernal feats. President Benson asked, "How did Adam bring his descendants into the presence of the Lord? The answer: Adam and his descendants entered into the priesthood order of God. Today we would say they went to the House of the Lord and received their blessings."[1267] We may follow the example of Adam by going to the House of the Lord and entering

---

[1256] Obadiah 1:21.
[1257] Smith, *Teachings of the Prophet Joseph Smith*, 322; Moses 1:39.
[1258] D&C 84:48.
[1259] Smith, *History of the Church*, 3:385–86.
[1260] D&C 107:3.
[1261] Moses 5:6–10.
[1262] Alma 13:2.
[1263] Smith, *Teachings of the Prophet Joseph Smith*, 159.
[1264] Bruce R. McConkie wrote, "In our popular Latter-day Saint hymn which begins, 'Glorious things are sung of Zion, Enoch's city seen of old,' we find William W. Phelps preserving the doctrine that 'In Adam-ondi-Ahman, Zion rose where Eden was.' And in another hymn, written by the same author in the days of the Prophet Joseph Smith, we find these expressions; 'We read that Enoch walk'd with God, Above the power of mammon, While Zion spread herself abroad, And Saints and angels sang aloud, In Adam-ondi-Ahman'" (*Mormon Doctrine*, 20).
[1265] D&C 107:53–54.
[1266] D&C 84:19–22.
[1267] Benson, *Teachings of Ezra Taft Benson*, 257.

into "the order of the Son of God" that we, too, might obtain power to bring ourselves, our children, and other people for whom we have responsibilities, into the presence of God.

There is great power in the Melchizedek Priesthood and its ordinances, power to ask for and receive blessings, which is personal revelation at the highest level. Adam and Eve exemplified the pattern of asking and receiving. Finding themselves estranged from God, they offered mighty prayer at an altar. In that sacred setting, they sought for reconciliation and for knowledge and power to return to the Lord's presence. When God determined that they qualified for the blessings that they were seeking, the veil was rent and "an angel of the Lord appeared," providing the promise of a Savior and of deliverance.[1268] Eventually, Adam would receive additional priesthood ordinances so that he might receive the knowledge of God, power to counsel with and ask him questions directly, and power to return to his presence.

This is a priesthood journey that every son or daughter of Adam and Eve must make—the journey out of Babylon to Zion. No power except "the order of the Son of God"—the Melchizedek Priesthood and its ordinances—has the ability to bring us to God and teach us how to ask for and receive revelation so that we might successfully make the journey. President Ezra Taft Benson taught, "To enter into the order of the Son of God is the equivalent today of entering into the fullness of the Melchizedek Priesthood, which is only received in the house of the Lord."[1269] If men and women endure in faith, they can qualify to receive the fulness of the priesthood in the temple, where they also receive the covenants and ordinances of the priesthood and enter into the highest order of the priesthood—eternal marriage. Zion, in the ultimate sense, can be established in no other way, and Adam and Eve are our models.

THE BLESSINGS OF ABRAHAM

Whereas Adam and Eve were the parents of the human race, Abraham and Sarah were the parents of the faithful. Like Adam and Eve, whose faith was so great that they were able to approach God in mighty prayer and receive his assurance of a Savior and the plan of salvation for their family,[1270] Abraham and Sarah also had great faith to approach God in mighty prayer and receive promises of the new and everlasting covenant and the perpetual rights to priesthood for their family. They received the promise that the Savior would come through their lineage and that through the combined ministries of the Savior and their family, all of the children of Adam and Eve could be blessed with the Covenant.

Abraham and Sarah's heritage was Zion, and Zion was what they desired to reestablish as a legacy.[1271] Reading the records of his fathers, Abraham knew that he had a right to the priesthood and therefore was of the heritage of Zion.[1272] For the purpose of placing priesthood power to become Zion into Abraham's hands, the Lord guided him to Melchizedek, whose people were Zionlike.[1273] Later, Melchizedek and his people in Salem were translated and taken from the earth, as had been Enoch and his people. Then, we assume, Abraham and Sarah were left behind as the surviving Zion people on the earth.

As we have learned, the new and everlasting covenant comprises all gospel blessings, including eternal marriage and eternal posterity. The familial right to this Covenant was given to this wonderful couple. Because we are literally their children, or adopted into their family by baptism, we are heirs to their blessings. Abraham received the blessings of the new and everlasting covenant, the priesthood,

---

[1268] Moses 5:6–9.
[1269] Benson, *Teachings of Ezra Taft Benson*, 257.
[1270] Moses 5:6–12.
[1271] Hebrews 11:9, 16.
[1272] Abraham 1:2–3, 31.
[1273] Clark, *The Blessings of Abraham*, 136-41.

temple blessings, and eternal marriage in an unbroken chain from Melchizedek back to Noah, to Enoch, to Adam. Of Abraham, Elder McConkie wrote,

> He was called by the Lord to "be a father of many nations." To him the Lord said: "I will establish my covenant [the gospel covenant] between me and thee and thy seed after thee in their generations for an everlasting covenant, to be a God unto thee and to thy seed after thee." (Genesis 17:4, 7.) "And in thy seed shall all the nations of the earth be blessed" (Genesis 22:18), meaning that all who thereafter believed what Abraham believed and lived as Abraham lived would bless themselves through the everlasting gospel covenant. The Lord promised Abraham, "Thou shalt be a blessing unto thy seed after thee," the Lord promised Abraham, "that in their hands they shall bear this ministry and Priesthood unto all nations." This is the very thing the seed of Abraham is commencing to do in these last days. "I will bless them [all nations] through thy name," the Lord continues, "for as many as receive this Gospel shall be called after thy name, and shall be accounted thy seed, and shall rise up and bless thee, as their father." Even the believing Gentiles shall cleave unto Abraham, account him as their father, and be adopted into his family. "And I will bless them that bless thee," saith the Lord, "and curse them that curse thee; and in thee (that is, in thy Priesthood) and in thy seed (that is, thy Priesthood), for I give unto thee a promise that this right shall continue in thee, and in thy seed after thee (that is to say, the literal seed, or the seed of the body) shall all the families of the earth be blessed, even with the blessings of the Gospel, which are the blessings of salvation, even of life eternal." (Abraham 2:9–11.)[1274]

Has there ever been such a promise? If we are faithful, we, the children or adopted children of Abraham, receive the blessings of Abraham. "The seed of Abraham shall take the gospel and the priesthood to all nations, and those who accept the divine word shall become as though they too were the chosen seed." Abraham's children "have a right to hear the gospel, and if they accept it, to receive the priesthood, to have their own family units continue everlastingly so that they with Abraham shall have eternal life."[1275] When Zion is established by the Lord, as a person, a family, or a priesthood society, it is through the ministry of Abraham's authorized children.

Adam and Eve and Abraham and Sarah are our models. At various points of the temple experience, we see them exemplified. We see them as they seek for and secure blessings for themselves and for us, their children. When we set out on our journey to find redemption, we are like Adam and Eve, who set the example of that experience. When we kneel with our sweethearts at a temple altar to be married for eternity, we assume, then follow, the example of Abraham and Sarah, receiving all the blessings that were given to them in the same culminating temple ordinance. These blessings define and exalt Zion people.

ABRAHAM'S QUALIFICATIONS AND DESIRE

Abraham knew something about the priesthood that we need to know. He knew that achieving the celestial kingdom was not possible unless he took someone with him, and he knew that taking someone with him was not possible without the priesthood. Therefore, he diligently sought the priesthood so that he could bless others: "I sought after the right," he said, "whereunto I should be ordained *to administer the same*."[1276]

Blessing other people, we are taught, results in one of the highest attainments of joy: If we cry repentance, the Lord says, "How great shall be your joy with him in the kingdom of my Father!"[1277]

[1274] McConkie, *A New Witness for the Articles of Faith*, 36.
[1275] McConkie, *A New Witness for the Articles of Faith*, 37.
[1276] Abraham 1:2.
[1277] D&C 18:15.

Abraham knew that the priesthood offered him "greater happiness and peace and rest,"[1278] and *rest*, of course, is the fulness of the glory of the Lord.[1279]

Abraham spared no effort or expense in seeking the blessings of the priesthood. His quest required that he move away from a wicked environment,[1280] a discovery that every Zion person must make. In seeking the priesthood, he listed his qualifications and desires:

- He had been a follower of righteousness.
- He had a desire to become a *greater* follower of righteousness.
- He had a desire for great knowledge.
- He had a desire to possess a *greater* knowledge.
- He had a desire to become a father of many nations (an eternal father).
- He had a desire to become a prince of peace, like Melchizedek and the Savior.
- He had a desire to receive instructions from God.
- He had a desire to keep the highest revealed commandments of God.

Abraham was, by birth, a rightful heir to the priesthood, as we, his children, are. That he had to qualify for his appointment to the priesthood by desire and righteousness should be a lesson for all of us. Abraham's journey to receive the priesthood took him from Ur to Hebron to Salem, where he finally met Melchizedek, the only man on earth who had the keys to confer upon him the holy priesthood and its blessings. Now Abraham's faith, faithfulness, patience, and endurance were rewarded. He was ordained a high priest, and his authoritative ministry began. We, who are Abraham's children, have been commanded to do likewise: "Go ye, therefore, and do the works of Abraham; enter ye into my law and ye shall be saved."[1281]

BLESSINGS OF THE PRIESTHOOD

Now ordained and empowered, having covenanted to be obedient to "every word that proceedeth forth from the mouth of God,"[1282] to sacrifice all things,[1283] and to remain faithful in the Covenant, Abraham received blessings that every worthy priesthood holder might expect to receive: a revelation of the Creation and all the works of God; an endowment of divine knowledge and power; a specially proffered gift; and God's setting him apart for a special commission. Abraham's journey in the priesthood would lead him to coronation; he would become a king and a priest unto God forever, and he would be set in his kingdom by the ordinance of eternal marriage. Because the priesthood temple ordinances are also available to the daughters and adopted daughters of Abraham, worthy women also may qualify to receive these blessings.

This is the priesthood journey of our parents, Adam and Eve and Abraham and Sarah, which journey is symbolized in the sacred setting of the temple. Our journey to celestial glory is like theirs. Every power in the priesthood, every covenant, ordinance, instruction, and honor, even the privilege of eternal marriage and entering into the patriarchal order of the Gods—everything that was given to these, our parents, is offered to us if we, too, desire, qualify, sacrifice, and endure.

In both Adam's and Abraham's examples, we see the ultimate blessing of the priesthood: to stand in the presence of God. Of Adam, it is recorded: "Three years previous to the death of Adam, he called Seth, Enos, Cainan, Mahalaleel, Jared, Enoch, and Methuselah, who were all high priests, with

---

[1278] Abraham 1:2.
[1279] D&C 84:24.
[1280] Abraham 1:1.
[1281] D&C 132:32.
[1282] D&C 84:44.
[1283] Smith, *Lectures on Faith*, 6:7.

the residue of his posterity who were righteous, into the valley of Adam-ondi-Ahman, and there bestowed upon them his last blessing. *And the Lord appeared unto them,* and they rose up and blessed Adam, and called him Michael, the prince, the archangel."[1284] Centuries later, Abraham wrote: "I, Abraham . . . prayed unto the Lord, and the Lord appeared unto me." In that vision, the Lord declared, "I am the Lord thy God; I dwell in heaven; the earth is my footstool; I stretch my hand over the sea, and it obeys my voice; I cause the wind and the fire to be my chariot; I say to the mountains—Depart hence—and behold, they are taken away by a whirlwind, in an instant, suddenly. My name is Jehovah, and I know the end from the beginning; therefore my hand shall be over thee." When the vision had ended, Abraham exclaimed, "Thy servant has sought thee earnestly; now I have found thee."[1285]

THE PRIZE IS WORTH THE PRICE

In our day, the Prophet Joseph Smith recorded a similar experience after he and Sidney Rigdon had seen in vision the Father and the Son. "Great and marvelous are the works of the Lord, and the mysteries of his kingdom which he showed unto us, which surpass all understanding in glory, and in might, and in dominion; which he commanded us we should not write while we were yet in the Spirit, and are not lawful for man to utter; neither is man capable to make them known, for they are only to be seen and understood by the power of the Holy Spirit, which God bestows on those who love him, and purify themselves before him; *to whom he grants this privilege of seeing and knowing for themselves;* that through the power and manifestation of the Spirit, *while in the flesh,* they may be able to bear his presence in the world of glory."[1286]

This is the sum of gospel teaching: God's sons and daughters can return to him *while in the flesh!* And the priesthood is the power that makes it all possible. Zion, indeed!

Here, then, we see the purposes of the new and everlasting covenant and the oath and covenant of the priesthood—the first and second pillars of Zion. The Lord calls us out of the world and places us under covenant to become new people. To that end he begins to purify us of sin and sanctify us for a new and holy purpose. He places upon us his name and authority, then prepares us to receive our kingdom by cleansing (purifying) and anointing (sanctifying) us for coronation. He clothes us in a way that our body becomes a temple, then endows us with the keys of divine knowledge and power, and teaches us how to ask for and receive blessings so that we know how to enter his presence. In the process, we receive from him a special gift or intelligence, and he gives us a commission. Ultimately, he draws us into his kingdom, where we receive from him our eternal kingdom in the patriarchal order of the gods.

Do we appreciate our priesthood blessings? Are we applying the principles of the priesthood to seek the Lord diligently, as did Abraham, so that we, too, might find him? Or are we neglectful, sitting on a plateau, and taking our privileges for granted? President Kimball succinctly stated the purposes of the priesthood: "Priesthood is the means to exaltation. The priesthood is the power and authority of God delegated to man on earth to act in all things pertaining to the salvation of men. It is the means whereby the Lord acts through men to save souls. Without this priesthood power, men are lost. Only through this power does man 'hold the keys of all the spiritual blessings of the church,' enabling him to receive 'the mysteries of the kingdom of heaven, to have the heavens opened' unto him (see D&C 107:18–19), enabling him to enter the new and everlasting covenant of marriage and to have his wife and children bound to him in an everlasting tie, enabling him to become a patriarch to his posterity forever, and enabling him to receive a fullness of the blessings of the Lord."[1287]

[1284] D&C 107:43–53.
[1285] Abraham 2:6–8, 12.
[1286] D&C 76:114–18.
[1287] Kimball, *Teachings of Spencer W. Kimball,* 494.

The quality of Zion cannot be achieved in a person, marriage, family, or society without the priesthood. Elias Higbee asked Joseph Smith, "What is meant by the command in Isaiah, 52nd chapter, 1st verse, which saith: Put on thy strength, O Zion—and what people had Isaiah reference to?" The Prophet answered, "He had reference to those whom God should call in the last days, who should hold the power of priesthood to bring again Zion, and the redemption of Israel; and to put on her strength is to put on the authority of the priesthood, which she, Zion, has a right to by lineage; also to return to that power which she had lost."[1288]

THE AUTHORITY AND KEYS OF THE PRIESTHOOD

The authority of God is God's to give, and then it is conferred by covenant to his worthy sons. The Apostle Paul taught, "No man taketh this honour unto himself but he that is called of God, as was Aaron."[1289] Elder McConkie listed four criteria concerning the doctrine of priesthood authority:

1. There is a God in heaven whose powers and authority are infinite. He is the author and creator of salvation, and he has offered salvation to men on his own terms and on no others.
2. The Lord's house is a house of order. He has given a law unto all things, and all blessings come by obedience to those laws upon which their receipt is predicated.
3. Salvation is available to men through the gospel. The gospel is, in fact, the plan of salvation, and in it are set forth the terms and conditions upon which God offers salvation to men.
4. Deity calls his own prophets, his own ministers, and his own legal administrators to preach his gospel and to administer the affairs of his earthly kingdom, all so that salvation may be made available to his earthly children.[1290]

According to Elder McConkie, the best statement on the doctrine of priesthood authority is found in Doctrine and Covenants 132:7—"All covenants, contracts, bonds, obligations, oaths, vows, performances, connections, associations, or expectations, that are not made and entered into and sealed by the Holy Spirit of promise, of him who is anointed, both as well for time and for all eternity, and that too most holy, by revelation and commandment through the medium of mine anointed, whom I have appointed on the earth to hold this power, . . . are of no efficacy, virtue, or force in and after the resurrection from the dead; for all contracts that are not made unto this end have an end when men are dead."

Elder McConkie adds this statement: "Men can do what they please and make any assumptions they like as to the validity of any of their acts in this life. But as the Lord lives, nothing they do will endure in heaven unless it meets the divine standard here set forth. It must be done in righteousness; it must be approved by the Spirit; and it must be performed and sealed by a legal administrator."[1291]

Becoming a Zion person is impossible without the priesthood and its covenants and ordinances. The priesthood is conferred upon a man for two purposes: (1) his personal salvation; (2) the salvation of others. No man can "presume to be a true minister of salvation unless he is called of God," taught Elder McConkie.[1292] The Lord's house is a house of order and not a house of confusion.[1293] "We believe that a man must be called of God, by prophecy, and by the laying on of hands by those who are in authority, to preach the gospel and administer in the ordinances thereof."[1294] A man's personal

---

[1288] D&C 113:7–8.
[1289] Hebrews 5:4.
[1290] McConkie, *A New Witness for the Articles of Faith*, 306.
[1291] McConkie, *A New Witness for the Articles of Faith*, 307.
[1292] McConkie, *A New Witness for the Articles of Faith*, 305.
[1293] D&C 132:7–8.
[1294] Articles of Faith 1:5.

salvation is tied to his discharge of his priesthood responsibilities: to preach the gospel and to administer the ordinances of salvation to God's children.

All priesthood authority flows to us by means of the delegated *keys of authority* that come directly from the President of the Church, who holds all of the administrative keys. When we are called by prophecy to a responsibility by an authorized priesthood leader who holds the keys of authority, we in turn receive the necessary authority to fulfill our duty. We receive "the right and power to speak for the Lord, to state what he wants stated, to say what he would say if he personally were here!" We receive "divine power, the power to perform the ordinances of salvation. . . . ! Without [priesthood keys and authority], there is no true gospel, no divine church, no salvation for fallen man."[1295]

"The keys of the priesthood," continues Elder McConkie, "are the right and power of presidency. They are the directing, controlling, and governing power. Those who hold them are empowered to direct the manner in which others use their priesthood. Every ministerial act performed by a priesthood holder must be done at the proper time and place and in the proper way. The power of directing these labors constitutes the keys of the priesthood."[1296] When the priesthood society of Zion is established on the earth, it will be under the direction of the President of the Church, who holds the authoritative keys to do so. When Zion is established in the life of an individual, in a marriage or in a family, it is done by the power of the priesthood, which comes from priesthood ordinances and righteousness.

DOCTRINE OF THE PRIESTHOOD

Elder Bruce R. McConkie taught that personal revelation is the only way to know the doctrine of the priesthood.[1297] By charity and virtue, we gain "confidence to stand in the presence of God,"[1298] and "the Father teacheth [us] of the covenant."[1299] The Lord's language in the oath and covenant of the priesthood bears a strict injunction: "For you shall live by every word that proceedeth forth from the mouth of God."[1300] Because this is a covenant, the assumed promise is that God will reveal his word to us. By this covenant priesthood relationship we receive and live by *every* word that proceeds from God, an amazing principle that unlocks the "mystery of godliness"[1301] and those things that "eye has not seen, nor ear heard, nor yet entered into the heart of man."[1302]

The doctrine of the priesthood will "distil" upon our souls "as the dews from heaven," the scripture says.[1303] If we were to walk through dewy grass in the early morning, we would soon be drenched in moisture. Tens of thousands of tiny, almost imperceptible droplets combining together would eventually create a veritable flood. The distillation process of the priesthood settles upon those who love and serve God with all their "heart, might, mind, and strength."[1304] According to Elder McConkie, this process occurs line upon line and precept upon precept by the power of the Holy Ghost. If we are "full of charity towards all men, and to the household of faith" and if virtue garnishes our thoughts unceasingly, the doctrine of the priesthood will distil upon us until we are saturated in it.[1305]

[1295] McConkie, *A New Witness for the Articles of Faith*, 308.
[1296] McConkie, *A New Witness for the Articles of Faith*, 309.
[1297] McConkie, "The Doctrine of the Priesthood," 32.
[1298] D&C 121:45.
[1299] D&C 84:48.
[1300] D&C 84:44.
[1301] D&C 19:10.
[1302] D&C 76:10.
[1303] D&C 121:45.
[1304] D&C 98:12.
[1305] McConkie, "The Doctrine of the Priesthood," 32; D&C 121:45.

What, then, is the doctrine of the priesthood that pivots on charity and virtue? Elder McConkie lists the following:

- The priesthood is the actual power of God, and the actual name of the power of God. It is the power by which he created and creates the heavens, and it is the power by which he governs, sustains, and preserves all things. To become as he is, we must exercise his priesthood, or power, as he does.
- The priesthood is the power of faith—faith is power and power is priesthood. Faith is a true belief or knowledge that is acted upon.[1306] The priesthood is useless unless put into action; thus the combination of faith, truth, virtue, and priesthood results in actual power. By faith, then, priesthood becomes power "to put at defiance the armies of nations, to divide the earth, to break every band, to stand in the presence of God; to do all things according to his will, according to his command, subdue principalities and powers; and this by the will of the Son of God" (JST Genesis 14:31).[1307] To the extent that we act with our priesthood in faith, according to charity and virtue, we become like God, who is the perfection of faith, priesthood, and power. By this means, we can lay hold on eternal life.
- The priesthood is the doctrine that "God lives and is and ever shall be. He is the Everlasting Elohim who dwells in heaven above. He is our Father, the father of our spirits; we are his children, the offspring of his begetting. He has a glorified body of flesh and bones; he lives in the family unit; and he possesses all power, all might, all dominion, and all truth. The name of the kind of life he lives is eternal life [that is, he lives in the family unit]."[1308]
- The priesthood provides us the knowledge that our Heavenly Father enjoys an exalted status of glory, perfection, and power because his faith and his priesthood are perfect and infinite.
- The priesthood of God is *after the order of his Son,* which power, like God himself, is infinite and eternal. We who receive this endowment of power become of that same order.
- The priesthood is a system of orders, the highest of which is named *The New and Everlasting Covenant of Marriage* (see D&C 131:2)[1309] or the patriarchal order. Only in this order can we become like God, creating for ourselves eternal family units patterned after the family of God.
- The doctrine of the priesthood is that we can progress until we obtain the priesthood's *fulness,* which increasingly gives us power by faith to govern and control all temporal and spiritual things, to effect miracles, to help to perfect God's children, to stand in Father's presence, and to become like him, having developed his faith, perfections, and power.
- The priesthood is the power to do all things that are expedient: move mountains, control the elements, cast away evil spirits, defeat every enemy, conquer any adversity, provide protection, cure disease, raise the dead, bind together marriages and families, and ultimately to achieve glorious immortality in the celestial kingdom of God.[1310]

"As My Father Hath Sent Me, Even So Send I You"[1311]

The priesthood separates us for a holy purpose: "for your sake, and not for your sake only, but for the sake of the whole world."[1312] By covenant, when we receive the priesthood, we agree to seek our own

---

[1306] Alma 32:21.
[1307] JST Genesis 14:31.
[1308] McConkie, *A New Witness for the Articles of Faith,* 704.
[1309] D&C 131:2.
[1310] McConkie, "The Doctrine of the Priesthood," 32.
[1311] John 20:21.
[1312] D&C 84:48.

salvation and to seek the salvation of others by bringing people to Christ and becoming to them saviors on Mount Zion.[1313] We have a model. As the Father sent his Son into the world (Babylon) to raise the standard or banner of Zion, set an example, and call people out of the world, so the Son sends us, his sons, back into Babylon to do likewise. For the sons of God, Babylon is what we are to battle, not what we are to embrace; we are to overcome Babylon, not to be overcome by it. Zion is who we are; Zion is what we are to proclaim. We, like Jesus Christ, our spiritual father, are to raise the standard of Zion, set the example of Zion, and call the sons and daughters of God to Zion. We are sent by Jesus Christ into the world to minister to God's children and to declare to them in word, deed, and example that God's kingdom is at hand. We, who hold the priesthood of God and are authorized to act in his name, are commissioned to be living proof that the kingdom of God has indeed come!

During his mortal ministry, Jesus ordained the seventy, gave them power to use his name, and then sent them into the world on missions. Their charge was to provide service with the priesthood in the name of the Lord as a sign that the kingdom of heaven was finally among the people. The seventy were commissioned to be the kingdom's representatives. Jesus instructed the seventy, "Heal the sick therein, and say unto them, The kingdom of heaven is come nigh unto you [i.e., *We have come with power as authorized servants of the kingdom of heaven, and we have authority to use the name of Jesus Christ to bless you*]." When the seventy returned from their missions, they were astonished at the power of the priesthood and the name of Jesus Christ: "And the seventy returned again with joy, saying, Lord, even the devils are subject unto us *through thy name*."[1314]

Neither the priesthood nor its commission has changed since that time. We, the Lord's servants, represent him and the kingdom; we minister, bless, cast out vexing spirits, and call people to Zion in his name. We are Zion!

SUMMARY AND CONCLUSION

Zion is built on the foundation of the Atonement, upon which three pillars stand: The new and everlasting covenant, the oath and covenant of the priesthood, and the law of consecration. Upon this sure foundation and its pillars rises Zion, "the highest order of priesthood society."[1315] Like the other pillars, the oath and covenant of the priesthood has a singular purpose in making Zion possible for each of us, both men and women.

The priesthood is our heritage; it is that authority and power that we qualified for in the "first place" or the premortal world. In this life, we must qualify again to receive the priesthood and its blessings, as did Adam, Melchizedek, Abraham, and others. Like these righteous individuals, we too receive the priesthood by a covenant with the Father.

This covenant is the oath and covenant of the priesthood and is often referred to as the covenant of exaltation. The Father's guarantees are so sacred that he swears to deliver them with an oath, putting his godhood on the line. Likewise, with similar determination, we must swear to him our promise to keep the priesthood covenant. If we meet the conditions of the covenant of the priesthood, exaltation will be ours by virtue of the Father's personal guarantee.

Our primary covenantal promise is to magnify our eternal *calling*, which includes receiving the Melchizedek priesthood; receiving Christ, the Father, and the Father's kingdom; living by every word that proceeds forth from the mouth of God; and marrying for eternity, which is the patriarchal order of the priesthood and places us in the patriarchal order of the Gods. This patriarchal priesthood order provides that we, like Melchizedek, can become kings and priests and queens and priestesses, thereby becoming gods. Only this priesthood order provides us the blessing of eternal lives, which is endless posterity. Because the blessings of the priesthood ultimately involve the temple blessings and the

---

[1313] Obadiah 1:21.
[1314] Luke 10:9, 17; emphasis added.
[1315] Kimball, *Teachings of Spencer W. Kimball*, 125.

marriage covenant, and because both the priesthood and marriage covenants are called the covenant of exaltation, the call to eternal life that we must magnify carries significance for both men and women.

Upon receiving the priesthood, the Lord calls us out of the world and places us under covenant to become new people. He places upon us his name and authority, then prepares us to receive our kingdom by cleansing (purifying) and anointing (sanctifying) us for coronation. He clothes us so that our body becomes a temple; then he endows us with the keys of divine knowledge and power and teaches us how to ask for and receive blessings so that we know how to enter his presence. In the process, we receive from him a special gift or intelligence, and he gives us a commission. Ultimately, he draws us into his kingdom, where we receive from him our eternal kingdom in the patriarchal order of the gods.

The covenant associated with the Melchizedek Priesthood surpasses the privileges of the Aaronic Priesthood. This supernal authority and power is that which allows righteous men and women "to speak with God face to face,"[1316] a privilege that is descriptive of Zion people, with whom the Lord makes his abode.[1317] Adam was the first to receive the oath and covenant of the priesthood, and by applying its principles, he was able to secure for his posterity the blessings of a Savior and the plan of salvation. Likewise, Abraham sought the blessings of the priesthood, and by applying priesthood principles, he was able to secure the Lord's promise that his children would have a right to the blessings of the gospel and priesthood forever. He also received the promise that through us, his children, all of the nations of the earth would be blessed with the gospel and priesthood blessings. As we follow Adam and Eve's and Abraham and Sarah's examples, we too can qualify for their blessings. As we grow in charity and virtue, the doctrine of the priesthood will distil upon our souls, line upon line, until we have power to stand in the presence of God and receive instructions, intelligence, blessings, and, ultimately, coronation.

Beyond the priesthood's personal privileges, the priesthood is the authority and power to bless other souls with the new and everlasting covenant and the blessings of the priesthood. In a great way, our blessing other people is representative of the environment of Zion. Our covenant commission in the priesthood is to become saviors on Mount Zion. If a person neglects his or her responsibility to bring the living and the dead to Christ, that person's priesthood and priesthood blessings cease to function. Therefore, we take upon ourselves the priesthood with a covenant to assume the Lord's work as our own. This work is the eternal work of redemption. This work is not new to us; it is an extension of our premortal work, and it will be our work hereafter and forever. We came from Zion, our earthly heritage is Zion, our immediate aim is Zion, and our eternal future is Zion. And Zion is, and always has been, a product of the priesthood.

[1316] Smith, *Teachings of the Prophet Joseph Smith*, 180.
[1317] Moses 7:21; Psalm 132:13.

Section 10

The Oath and Covenant of the Priesthood:

Our Agreements

The second pillar of Zion is the oath and covenant of the priesthood. Our agreements in the covenant are faithfulness, obtaining the Aaronic Priesthood and Melchizedek Priesthood, and magnifying our *calling* in the priesthood.[1318] Additionally, we agree to receive Christ and his Father and live by every word that proceeds from the mouth of God, both of which we will discuss. Although these initial chapters on the priesthood apply to worthy men, faithful women, as we will see, take part in this covenant with their husbands. Again, faithful single men and women are not exempted from the blessings of Zion. Blessings are predicated on what we are doing with what we have. Blessings are not withheld by what we lack. Therefore, single men *and* women should become conversant with priesthood principles.

Our leaders have said that the purpose of the Melchizedek Priesthood centers on obtaining eternal life. We receive the priesthood by covenant and with the Father's immutable oath. Inasmuch as the covenant of baptism is renewed in the covenant of the sacrament, the covenant of the priesthood is renewed in the temple ceremonies. Failure to make the covenant of the priesthood or neglecting to keep the covenant after we have received it brings severe penalties and tragic consequences. But if we are trying to do our best we need not fear; embedded in the covenant is God's promise that he will sustain us, help us live the covenant, and bless us with success.[1319]

[1318] D&C 84:33.
[1319] Eyring, "Faith and the Oath and Covenant of the Priesthood," 61–64.

The priesthood comes to us by the Father's invitation. We are "called by this holy calling," Alma taught, "and ordained unto the high priesthood of the holy order of God."[1320] The Father offers us the priesthood through his authorized servants. That fact alone is evidence that we have been chosen and called by God. Our responsibility is to qualify by becoming worthy of the honor. The Apostle Paul taught, "No man taketh this honour unto himself but he that is called of God, as was Aaron."[1321] And the fifth Article of Faith declares, "We believe that a man must be called of God, by prophecy, and by the laying on of hands by those who are in authority, to preach the gospel and administer in the ordinances thereof."[1322]

To be chosen and called of God, to receive his authority, power, and name to speak authoritatively as would God, to have the power to do what God would do, and to act in the capacity of the Savior are honors without equal. That the Father seeks us out, chooses and calls us, and offers us the covenant of the priesthood, and then swears his covenantal promise with an oath are indications of his anxiousness to bestow upon us exalted blessings. Moreover, by offering us the priesthood, he is furthering his work: to bring to pass the immortality and eternal life of man.[1323] He knows that the quality of immortality called eternal life can be achieved only by our receiving and living worthily of the oath and covenant of the priesthood. No wonder then that Elder McConkie called the priesthood covenant "the covenant of exaltation."[1324] This is the second pillar of Zion.

The oath and the covenant of the priesthood are set forth in Doctrine and Covenants 84:33–44:

For whoso is faithful unto the obtaining these two priesthoods of which I have spoken, and the magnifying their *calling,* are sanctified by the Spirit unto the renewing of their bodies. They become the sons of Moses and of Aaron and the seed of Abraham, and the church and kingdom, and the elect of God.

And also all they who receive this priesthood receive me, saith the Lord; for he that receiveth my servants receiveth me; and he that receiveth me receiveth my Father; and he that receiveth my Father receiveth my Father's kingdom; therefore all that my Father hath shall be given unto him.

And this is according to the oath and covenant which belongeth to the priesthood. Therefore, all those who receive the priesthood, receive this oath and covenant of my Father, which he cannot break, neither can it be moved. But whoso breaketh this covenant after he hath received it, and altogether turneth therefrom, shall not have forgiveness of sins in this world nor in the world to come. And wo unto all those who come not unto this priesthood which ye have received, which I now confirm upon you who are present this day, by mine own voice out of the heavens; and even I have given the heavenly hosts and mine angels charge concerning you.

And I now give unto you a commandment to beware concerning yourselves, to give diligent heed to the words of eternal life. For you shall live by every word that proceedeth forth from the mouth of God.

This covenant, like all other covenants, contains *if-then* clauses: *If* we fulfill our obligations, *then* the Father will fulfill his oath—guaranteed! Here are our covenantal promises:

IF WE ARE FAITHFUL . . .

Faithfulness or righteousness is the first promise that we make in the oath and covenant of the priesthood. Abraham is a model of faithfulness; he made himself good so that he could do good. Therefore, he worked to make his righteousness equal to his desire to receive the priesthood.[1325]

[1320] Alma 13:6.
[1321] Hebrews 5:4.
[1322] *Articles of Faith* 1:5.
[1323] Moses 1:39.
[1324] McConkie, *A New Witness for the Articles of Faith,* 312–13.
[1325] Abraham 1:2.

Righteousness not only qualifies a man to receive this honor, but it also is the principle upon which the priesthood functions: "The rights of the priesthood ... cannot be controlled nor handled only upon the principles of righteousness." Without righteousness, "the heavens withdraw themselves; the Spirit of the Lord is grieved; and when it is withdrawn, Amen to the priesthood or the authority of that man."[1326]

The requirement of righteousness is self-evident. By receiving the priesthood, we receive the Lord's name,[1327] and therefore we are called to become models of him whose name we bear. As ambassadors of Jesus Christ, said President Joseph Fielding Smith, we are commissioned to represent him. We who hold the holy priesthood must live lives and do all things as the Lord would do them if he were personally present.[1328] Elder McConkie wrote, "[Melchizedek Priesthood holders] pray and minister in the place and stead of their Master."[1329] That is, we become the hands, arms, and voice of Jesus Christ. For example, Edward Partridge was told by the Lord, "I will lay my hand upon you by the hand of my servant Sidney Rigdon."[1330] In a similar manner, priesthood holders are the arms of Jesus Christ: "And their arm shall be my arm."[1331] Likewise, the Lord emphasizes his willingness to support us when we, through the priesthood, minister in his name and thus become his voice: "What I the Lord have spoken, I have spoken, and I excuse not myself; and though the heavens and the earth pass away, my word shall not pass away, but shall all be fulfilled, whether by mine own voice or by the voice of my servants, it is the same."[1332]

Clearly, faithfulness empowers us to fulfill our priesthood commission. That is essential. While priesthood authority is conferred upon us at the time of ordination, priesthood *power* comes only when priesthood *authority* is exercised in righteousness.[1333] Being good precedes doing good.

If We Obtain the Aaronic and the Melchizedek Priesthoods . . .

Following the requirement of righteousness is the requirement of receiving the Aaronic and Melchizedek orders of the priesthood.[1334] As we have noted, both of these two orders of the priesthood are received by covenant, but only the Melchizedek Priesthood is received with the Father's oath.[1335] Also, as we have discussed, the covenant regarding the Aaronic Priesthood is that we promise to forsake the world, magnify our calling, minister to God's children by preaching, teaching, and giving service, and by obeying God's commandments. In return, the Lord promises to magnify us in the Aaronic Priesthood and to prepare us in every way to receive the Melchizedek Priesthood. This is the covenant of the Aaronic or preparatory priesthood.

The covenant regarding the Melchizedek Priesthood is that we promise to live faithfully to the Aaronic and Melchizedek priesthoods' covenants, magnify our *calling,* obey the commandments, be an example of Jesus Christ, serve as the Lord would serve, "live by every word that proceedeth forth from the mouth of God" (D&C 84:44), and marry in the temple for time and eternity. In return, the Father

---

[1326] D&C 121:36–37.
[1327] Abraham 1:18.
[1328] Smith, "Our Responsibility As Priesthood Holders," 49.
[1329] McConkie, *A New Witness for the Articles of Faith,* 379.
[1330] D&C 36:2; emphasis added.
[1331] D&C 35:14.
[1332] D&C 1:38; emphasis added.
[1333] Nelson, "Personal Priesthood Responsibility," 44; emphasis added.
[1334] We note here that the Melchizedek Priesthood encompasses the Aaronic Priesthood. If a man is ordained only to the Melchizedek Priesthood, it is correct to understand that he can also function in the Aaronic Priesthood and enjoy those blessings.
[1335] McConkie, "The Doctrine of the Priesthood," 32; D&C 131:1–4.

promises us *with an oath* that he will give us all that he has, which by definition is eternal life. This is the Lord's promise of exaltation, godhood, eternal marriage, and endless posterity.[1336]

We receive these two priesthoods for various common and some diverse reasons. For example, both priesthoods carry the responsibilities of preaching, teaching, expounding, exhorting, and, in the case of Aaronic Priesthood priests, the responsibilities of baptizing and administering the sacrament—these by delegation of the apostles.[1337] Both priesthoods carry the responsibilities of inviting all people to come unto Christ, and to watch over the Church by visiting, exhorting, and strengthening the members. But only the Melchizedek Priesthood "confirm[s] the church by the laying on of the hands, and the giving of the Holy Ghost; and to take the lead of all meetings."[1338]

The Aaronic Priesthood holds "the keys of the ministering of angels, and to administer in outward ordinances, the letter of the gospel, the baptism of repentance for the remission of sins, agreeable to the covenants and commandments."[1339] This priesthood has the power to prepare us, or a person to whom we are ministering, for the higher, exalting ordinances of the gospel. Both priesthoods are received for the purposes of personal salvation and the salvation of others: "for your sake, and not for your sake only, but for the sake of the whole world."[1340]

The scripture reads, the Melchizedek Priesthood "administereth the gospel and holdeth the key of the mysteries of the kingdom, even the key of the knowledge of God."[1341] That is, the high priesthood has two grand purposes: (1) to administer the gospel, meaning to preside, and to administer the covenants and ordinances of salvation; and (2) to stand in the presence of God, and receive personal revelation directly from him. "Therefore, in the ordinances thereof, the power of godliness [i.e., the power to become Godlike] is manifest. And without the ordinances thereof, and the authority of the priesthood, the power of godliness is not manifest unto men in the flesh; for without this [the power to become Godlike] no man can see the face of God, even the Father, and live."[1342]

Moreover, the high priesthood is the "power and authority of God" that allows us "to minister to other beings to bring about their happiness."[1343] The high priesthood is the power to become saviors on Mount Zion[1344] for both the living and the dead, and to receive and administer the blessings of "endless lives."[1345]

IF WE MAGNIFY OUR CALLING . . .

Possibly the central agreement of the covenant of the priesthood is to magnify our calling. Of interest, the covenant states that we agree to magnify our *calling* rather than our *callings*. There is a difference between the calling *of* the priesthood and callings *in* the priesthood. What, then, is the singular *calling* to which the covenant refers?

A review might be in order. As we have learned, Alma said that our experience with the priesthood began premortally, in the "first place,"[1346] where we were "*called* and prepared from the foundation of the world according to the foreknowledge of God, on account of [our] exceeding faith

---

[1336] McConkie, "The Doctrine of the Priesthood," 32; D&C 131:1–4.

[1337] D&C 20:38–39, 40.

[1338] D&C 20:44. Note: Priests may take the lead in meetings in the absence of an elder (see D&C 20:49).

[1339] D&C 107:20.

[1340] D&C 84:48.

[1341] D&C 84:19.

[1342] D&C 84:20–22.

[1343] Riddle, "The New and Everlasting Covenant," 231.

[1344] Obadiah 1:21.

[1345] Smith, *Teachings of the Prophet Joseph Smith*, 322.

[1346] Alma 13:3.

and good works."[1347] In that premortal setting, we qualified to be *called* and elected (selected) for eternal life. In this life, when we are baptized and enter into the new and everlasting covenant—we are "*called* into the fellowship of Jesus Christ."[1348] Then as we progress in the Covenant and receive the oath and covenant of the priesthood, we are *called* again to eternal life. Therefore, our *calling* in the priesthood is the call to eternal life, or, in other words, to become like God. And therefore, the Lord said, "All they who receive this priesthood receive me, saith the Lord; . . . and he that receiveth me receiveth my Father."[1349]

Magnifying the Calling and Callings

Of course, magnifying our *calling* assumes that we will magnify all of our priesthood *callings*. According to the *Encyclopedia of Mormonism*, we magnify each of our callings by taking our responsibilities seriously, making them honorable in the eyes of God's children, and making them glorious to the Lord.[1350] Additionally, we magnify our callings by functioning faithfully under the guidance of priesthood leadership and the instruction of the Holy Ghost.[1351] Our various priesthood callings—like our singular *calling*—hearkens back to the premortal world: "Every man who has a calling to minister to the inhabitants of the world," said Joseph Smith, "was ordained to that very purpose in the grand council of heaven before this world was."[1352] It is the magnification of our singular *calling* and our various callings that provide the key to our eventual glory; that is, the end-result of our present labors is to become like God.

The seriousness of magnifying our *calling* is set out in Doctrine and Covenants 121:34, 40: "Many are called, but few are chosen." That is, "many are called to the priesthood, but few are chosen for eternal life."[1353] Institute instructor S. Brent Farley taught,

One who magnifies his calling to the priesthood will understand that "the rights of the priesthood are inseparably connected with the powers of heaven, and that the powers of heaven cannot be controlled nor handled only upon the principles of righteousness." He will know that "no power or influence can or ought to be maintained by virtue of the priesthood, only by persuasion, by long-suffering, by gentleness and meekness, and by love unfeigned; by kindness, and pure knowledge, which shall greatly enlarge the soul without hypocrisy, and without guile." (D&C 121:36, 41–42.) One whose service is characterized by those qualities is magnifying his priesthood *calling*, and he has the foundation for success for the various priesthood tasks and offices he may hold throughout his life. He will also use these principles in his home.[1354]

Interestingly, the word *virtue* means both "moral excellence" and "power." The phrase "by virtue of the priesthood" means "by the power of the priesthood," and that power is developed only by virtue of character, or moral excellence. A terrifying chain of events occurs when moral virtue slips. According to Doctrine and Covenants 121, when our hearts are set upon the things of this world and we aspire to the honors of men, we will then attempt to cover our sins, gratify our pride and our vain ambitions, and then we will begin to exercise unrighteous dominion. These conditions result in the heavens withdrawing, the Spirit of the Lord being grieved, and the cessation of priesthood authority and power. The cycle leads to breaking our covenant to magnify our priesthood calling. On the other hand, when our hearts are set on the things of God and we aspire for God's approval, we will repent,

---

[1347] Alma 13:3–5.
[1348] 1 Corinthians 1:9, 26–27; Hebrews 3:1.
[1349] D&C 84:35, 37.
[1350] *Encyclopedia of Mormonism*, 850.
[1351] Riddle, "The New and Everlasting Covenant," 232.
[1352] Smith, *Teachings of the Prophet Joseph Smith*, 365.
[1353] McConkie, *Mormon Doctrine*, 482.
[1354] Farley, "The Oath and Covenant of the Priesthood," 42–43.

seek first for the things of the kingdom of God, and demonstrate charity. These conditions result in the heavens drawing near, the Spirit of the Lord becoming our constant companion, and receiving an increase of priesthood power. Now we are fulfilling our covenant to magnify our priesthood calling.

What does it mean to magnify a calling in the priesthood? Elder McConkie explained:

Now, to magnify as here used means to enlarge or increase, to improve upon, to hold up to honor and dignity, to make the calling noble and respectable in the eyes of all men by performing the mission which appertains to the calling in an admirable and successful manner. So to magnify a calling in the ministry requires brethren first to learn what duties go with their respective offices and callings and then to go to with their might and do the work assigned them. By doing this, which includes within it the requirement to "give diligent heed to the words of eternal life," and to "live by every word that proceedeth forth from the mouth of God" (D. & C. 84:43–44), they are assured of an eventual inheritance of eternal life in the kingdom of God.[1355]

Again we see the connection of our various priesthood *callings* to our singular overriding priesthood *calling*. Our leaders teach us that there are four ways that we magnify our various callings in the priesthood:

- By learning our responsibility and fully accomplishing it.[1356]
- By doing our very best in our assignments.
- By consecrating our time, talents, and resources to the Lord and his work as our leaders request and as the Spirit whispers.[1357]
- By teaching and being an example of the truth.[1358]

The Book of Mormon prophet Jacob described the result of faithfully magnifying a calling in the priesthood: "We did magnify our office unto the Lord, taking upon us the responsibility, . . . [teaching] them the word of God with all diligence; . . . [and] laboring with our might."[1359]

Melchizedek also set an example of magnifying a priesthood calling: "Now this Melchizedek was a king over the land of Salem; and his people had waxed strong in iniquity and abomination; yea, they had all gone astray; they were full of all manner of wickedness; but Melchizedek having exercised mighty faith, and received the office of the high priesthood according to the holy order of God, did preach repentance unto his people. And behold, they did repent; and Melchizedek did establish peace in the land in his days; therefore he was called the prince of peace."[1360] "And his people wrought righteousness, and obtained heaven."[1361]

Because we are of the same order of the priesthood as Melchizedek, and because we take upon ourselves the title *Melchizedek* when we receive the priesthood, we, by covenant, are expected to magnify our *calling* and *callings* as did this "great high priest."[1362]

As the high priesthood pertains to Zion, we note the following item of interest: The priesthood order of Melchizedek is "after the order of Enoch, which was after the order of the Only Begotten Son."[1363] Enoch's order is the order of Zion, which order is also the order of Melchizedek and the order

---

[1355] McConkie, *Mormon Doctrine*, 481.
[1356] D&C 107:99–100.
[1357] Kimball, "Becoming the Pure in Heart," 5.
[1358] Asay, "The Oath and Covenant of the Priesthood," 43.
[1359] Jacob 1:19.
[1360] Alma 13:17–18.
[1361] JST Genesis 14:34.
[1362] D&C 107:2.
[1363] D&C 76:57.

of the Only Begotten Son. We become Zion people by entering into priesthood covenant and magnifying our priesthood *calling,* as did Melchizedek, Enoch, and Jesus Christ.

Three Ways to Magnify Our Calling

President Marion G. Romney explained that magnifying our singular priesthood *calling* consists of at least three steps:

1. Obtaining gospel knowledge.
2. Personal righteousness by compliance with gospel standards.
3. Giving dedicated service.[1364]

Obtaining Gospel Knowledge

We cannot magnify our *calling* without searching the scriptures and the words of the prophets. Especially important is the Book of Mormon, which contains "the fulness of the gospel of Jesus Christ."[1365] The Book of Mormon, said the Prophet Joseph, is "the most correct of any book on earth, and the keystone of our religion, and a man would get nearer to God by abiding by its precepts, than by any other book."[1366] How could we expect to be on the Lord's errand, minister to his people, represent him to the covenant people and the inhabitants of the world, stand in his stead, speak his words, and teach his children the words of eternal life, if we are not conversant with his words?

The Nephite prophet Jacob drew a connection between priesthood power and gospel knowledge: "Wherefore, we search the prophets, and we have many revelations and the spirit of prophecy; and having all these witnesses we obtain a hope, and our faith becometh unshaken, insomuch that *we truly can command in the name of Jesus* and the very trees obey us, or the mountains, or the waves of the sea."[1367] Power in the priesthood, Jacob said, comes by searching "the prophets," that is, by searching the scriptures. By so doing, we become familiar with the voice of the Spirit, we enjoy "many revelations," and we develop the "spirit of prophecy." Jacob stated that "all these witnesses" from the Spirit increase our hope, faith, and spiritual experience, until our confidence in Jesus Christ and his name become "unshaken," and we truly can perform many mighty miracles. Clearly, obtaining and applying gospel knowledge serve to magnify our priesthood *calling.*

Personal Righteousness

We cannot magnify our priesthood *calling* if we "undertake to cover our sins, or to gratify our pride, our vain ambition, or to exercise control or dominion or compulsion upon the souls of the children of men, in any degree of unrighteousness" or to "exercise unrighteous dominion."[1368] How could we expect to represent and exemplify the Lord, as the covenant of the priesthood requires, if our personal lives are contrary to his? We might gain a trivial knowledge of gospel facts, but if we do not live the gospel, "Amen to the priesthood or the authority of that man."[1369]

Personal righteousness describes a Zion person, and personal righteousness consists of pure knowledge, pure actions, and pure motives. Zion is the pure in heart.[1370] "Zion is pure," writes Hugh Nibley, "which means 'not mixed with any impurities, unalloyed'; it is all Zion and nothing else."[1371]

[1364] Romney, "'The Oath and Covenant Which Belongeth to the Priesthood,'" 43.
[1365] D&C 20:9.
[1366] Smith, *History of the Church,* 4:461.
[1367] Jacob 4:6–7; emphasis added.
[1368] D&C 121:37, 39.
[1369] D&C 121:37.
[1370] D&C 97:21.
[1371] Nibley, *Approaching Zion,* 26–27.

The covenantal deportment of a Zionlike priesthood holder is set forth in the scriptures: "No power or influence can or ought to be maintained by virtue of the priesthood, only by persuasion, by longsuffering, by gentleness and meekness, and by love unfeigned; by kindness, and pure knowledge, which shall greatly enlarge the soul without hypocrisy, and without guile—reproving betimes with sharpness, when moved upon by the Holy Ghost; and then showing forth afterwards an increase of love toward him whom thou hast reproved, lest he esteem thee to be his enemy."[1372]

In the oath and covenant of the priesthood, we covenant to "keep the commandments of God, to live by every word that proceedeth forth from the mouth of Deity, and to walk in paths of righteousness and virtue."[1373] These criteria are absolutely essential if we wish to magnify our priesthood *calling*.

To attain to personal righteousness is to exemplify the Master, whom we must come to know and love. We do this by serving him and keeping his commandments[1374]: "If thou lovest me thou shalt serve me and keep all my commandments."[1375] It is a principle with promises: "And unto him that keepeth my commandments I will give the mysteries of my kingdom, and the same shall be in him a well of living water, springing up unto everlasting life."[1376] To attain to personal righteousness leads to receiving the fulness of the priesthood: "And no man receiveth a fulness unless he keepeth his commandments. He that keepeth his commandments receiveth truth and light, until he is glorified in truth and knoweth all things."[1377] Can we not see the essence of Zion in these promises?

As a model for magnifying our *calling* through our personal conduct, President Romney directs us to Doctrine and Covenants 42, "the Law of the Church,"[1378] which comprises the law of Zion. There are at least twenty points made in this revelation that paint a portrait of a Zion person.

1. The Lord's "first commandment" in Doctrine and Covenants 42 is to "go forth in my name." The covenant of the priesthood commissions us and makes it possible for us to lift up our voices, "preaching the gospel . . . with the sound of a trump," declaring the word of God like unto the angels.[1379]
2. Our sights should be set upon becoming Zion people, so that we might become the Lord's people.[1380]
3. We are to accept priesthood assignments and stand in the offices to which we are called.[1381]
4. We are to "observe the covenants and church articles to do them," and use them as our text when teaching, as directed by the Spirit.[1382]
5. We are to strive to receive the Spirit before attempting to teach.[1383]
6. We are to boldly speak and prophesy according to the promptings of the Spirit.[1384]
7. We will not kill, steal, lie, commit adultery, or speak evil—nor will we avoid repentance.[1385]

[1372] D&C 121:41–43.
[1373] McConkie, *Mormon Doctrine*, 480.
[1374] D&C 42:29.
[1375] D&C 42:29.
[1376] D&C 63:23.
[1377] D&C 93:27–28.
[1378] D&C 42, heading.
[1379] D&C 42:4, 6.
[1380] D&C 42:9.
[1381] D&C 42:10.
[1382] D&C 42:13.
[1383] D&C 42:14.
[1384] D&C 42:16–17.
[1385] D&C 42:19–21, 24–25.

8. We will love our wives with all our heart, cleave unto none else, and lust after no other women.[1386]

9. With special regard to Zion, we will "remember the poor, and consecrate [our] properties for their support that which [we] have to impart unto them," agreeing that we are stewards over the Lord's property and accountable for our discharge of our stewardship.[1387]

10. We will consecrate our surplus to the bishop "to administer to the poor and the needy" and for the building up of the Church and the establishment of Zion.[1388]

11. We are to forsake pride and costly apparel, and create beautiful things with our own hands.[1389]

12. We are to do all things in cleanliness before the Lord.[1390]

13. We are to be industrious.[1391]

14. We are to minister in the Lord's name by healing the sick, blessing the afflicted, and nourishing and bearing the infirmities of those who are of weaker faith until they are made whole.[1392]

15. We are to stand in our stewardship and not take anything from a brother without paying him fairly.[1393]

16. We are to ask the Lord for intelligence with the expectation of receiving revelation, knowledge, and the mysteries of the kingdom.[1394]

17. We are to be faithful to everything that the Lord reveals.[1395]

18. We agree to become Zion people by taking upon us the new and everlasting covenant, the oath and covenant of the priesthood, and the law of consecration.[1396]

19. If we lack anything, we are to ask of God, who will give to us liberally.[1397]

20. If someone offends us, we are to "take him or her between him or her and thee alone; and if he or she confess thou shalt be reconciled. . . . And thus ye shall conduct in all things."[1398]

Personal righteousness allows one to be a representative of Zion and therefore a vessel of blessedness. The Beatitudes given by the Lord to his disciples in Jerusalem and later to the Nephites describe this state of blessedness.[1399] President Harold B. Lee called these sermons that contain the Beatitudes "the constitution for a perfect life."[1400] Additionally, President Romney directed us to the instructions for personal conduct given in Doctrine and Covenants 59 and Doctrine and Covenants 88, particularly verses 117–26. These instructions include at least twenty-two points of personal conduct that describe Zionlike righteousness:

1. "Thou shalt love the Lord thy God with all thy heart, with all thy might, mind, and strength."[1401]

[1386] D&C 42:22–23.
[1387] D&C 42:30–32.
[1388] D&C 42:34.
[1389] D&C 42:40.
[1390] D&C 42:41.
[1391] D&C 42:42.
[1392] D&C 42:43–52.
[1393] D&C 42:53–54.
[1394] D&C 42:56, 61–62, 65.
[1395] D&C 42:66.
[1396] D&C 42:67.
[1397] D&C 42:68.
[1398] D&C 42:88–93.
[1399] Matthew 5:1–11; 3 Nephi 12:1–12.
[1400] Lee, *Decisions for Successful Living*, 56–57.
[1401] D&C 59:5.

2. "In the name of Jesus Christ thou shalt serve him."[1402]
3. "Thou shalt love thy neighbor as thyself."[1403]
4. "Thou shalt not steal . . ."[1404]
5. "Neither commit adultery, nor kill, nor do anything like unto it" [i.e., we should avoid any type of sexual sin or anything that approaches the taking of life].[1405]
6. "Thou shalt thank the Lord thy God in all things. . . . And in nothing doth man offend God, or against none is his wrath kindled, save those who confess not his hand in all things, and obey not his commandments."[1406]
7. "Thou shalt offer a sacrifice unto the Lord thy God in righteousness, even that of a broken heart and a contrite spirit."[1407]
8. "And that thou mayest more fully keep thyself unspotted from the world, thou shalt go to the house of prayer and offer up thy sacraments upon my holy day."[1408]
9. "And as all have not faith, seek ye diligently and teach one another words of wisdom; yea, seek ye out of the best books words of wisdom; seek learning, even by study and also by faith."[1409]
10. "Organize yourselves."[1410]
11. "Prepare every needful thing."[1411]
12. "Cease from all your light speeches, from all laughter, from all your lustful desires, from all your pride and light-mindedness, and from all your wicked doings."[1412]
13. "Appoint among yourselves a teacher, and let not all be spokesmen at once; but let one speak at a time and let all listen unto his sayings, that when all have spoken that all may be edified of all, and that every man may have an equal privilege."[1413]
14. "See that ye love one another."[1414]
15. "Cease to be covetous."[1415]
16. "Learn to impart one to another as the gospel requires."[1416]
17. "Cease to be idle."[1417]
18. "Cease to be unclean."[1418]
19. "Cease to find fault one with another."[1419]
20. "Cease to sleep longer than is needful; retire to thy bed early, that ye may not be weary; arise early, that your bodies and your minds may be invigorated."[1420]

[1402] D&C 59:5.
[1403] D&C 59:6.
[1404] D&C 59:6.
[1405] D&C 59:6.
[1406] D&C 59:7, 21.
[1407] D&C 59:8.
[1408] D&C 59:9.
[1409] D&C 88:118.
[1410] D&C 88:119.
[1411] D&C 88:119.
[1412] D&C 88:121.
[1413] D&C 88:122.
[1414] D&C 88:123.
[1415] D&C 88:123.
[1416] D&C 88:123.
[1417] D&C 88:124.
[1418] D&C 88:124.
[1419] D&C 88:124.
[1420] D&C 88:124.

21. "And above all things, clothe yourselves with the bond of charity, as with a mantle, which is the bond of perfectness and peace."[1421]

22. "Pray always, that ye may not faint, until I come."[1422]

The Lord promises that "he who doeth the works of righteousness shall receive his reward, even peace in this world, and eternal life in the world to come."[1423]

Dedicated Service

We cannot magnify our priesthood *calling* without freely offering charitable, selfless service—a central hallmark of a Zion person. The Lord said, "Men should be anxiously engaged in a good cause, and do many things of their own free will, and bring to pass much righteousness; for the power is in them."[1424] While anyone can give charitable service, only men and women of the Covenant can give charitable service *that has the power to save another person*. Such saving service is a priesthood privilege and a priesthood responsibility, according to President Marion G. Romney, which "can be done properly only by men who are magnifying their priesthood—who know the gospel, conform their lives to its standards, and enthusiastically give dedicated service."[1425] Of course, the same could be said of women who are living their covenants.

Service is the lifeblood of Zion. The selfishness of Babylon must give way to the *selflessness* of Zion in order that Zionlike attributes might be established in a covenant person. The spirit of charitable service cannot be mandated; that spirit is a condition of the heart that motivates a person to lift another. It is no wonder, then, that Zion is described as having no poverty of any kind. Zion people can neither tolerate lack nor endure poverty abiding among them. They attack misery wherever they find it. They abolish every form of scarcity, hurt, impairment, injustice, illness, and sorrow. They think of their brethren like unto themselves, and they are familiar with all and free with their substance, that others might be rich like unto themselves.[1426] Therefore, they insist on having "all things common among them; therefore there [are] not rich and poor, bond and free, but they [are] all made free, and partakers of the heavenly gift." Consequently, there never could be a happier people.[1427]

Zion people "love one another and serve one another." They "succor those that stand in need of [their] succor," and they "administer of [their] substance unto him that standeth in need." They "will not suffer that the beggar [put] up his petition to [them] in vain, and turn him out to perish."[1428] Zion people "bear one another's burdens, that they may be light," and they "are willing to mourn with those that mourn; yea, and comfort those that stand in need of comfort."[1429]

King Benjamin pointed out that there are blessings that flow only from dedicated service. These things we must learn if we hope to become Zionlike. For example, service allows us to retain "a remission of [our] sins from day to day, that [we] may walk guiltless before God." Therefore, King Benjamin exhorted us, "I would that ye should impart of your substance to the poor, every man according to that which he hath, such as feeding the hungry, clothing the naked, visiting the sick and

---

[1421] D&C 88:125.
[1422] D&C 88:126.
[1423] D&C 59:23.
[1424] D&C 58:27–28.
[1425] Romney, "'The Oath and Covenant Which Belongeth to the Priesthood,'" 43.
[1426] Jacob 2:17.
[1427] 4 Nephi 1:3, 16.
[1428] Mosiah 4:15–16.
[1429] Mosiah 18:8–9.

administering to their relief, both spiritually and temporally, according to their wants."[1430] And of course, the astonishing statement regarding service: "When ye are in the service of your fellow beings ye are only in the service of your God."[1431]

In Doctrine and Covenants 42, "the law of the Church," we read the following verse: "For inasmuch as ye do it unto the least of these, ye do it unto me."[1432] The implication is intriguing. Because God lacks for nothing and is in no need of our service to him, he passes our desire to serve *him* to serving his children, who *do* need our help. As we transfer our service from him to his children, he does not forget our wanting to express our love to him. He counts our service to his children as service to him, and he rewards us accordingly.

As we have discussed, God is in debt to no one. When we serve him by serving one of his children, he "doth immediately bless [us]; and therefore he hath paid [us]. And [we] are still indebted unto him, and are, and will be, forever and ever."[1433] To arrest any hint of debt or imbalance in the checks and balances of heaven, God quickly erases any claim by immediately blessing us in excess of our service. Therefore, we live forever in his debt. We are always awarded more blessings than we expend in service, and for that reason we are gratefully "unprofitable servants."[1434]

It is upon the principle of service that we progress toward perfection. By receiving grace (the Lord's help) *for* grace (our service and blessings to others), we grow *from* grace (light, truth, power, and perfection) *to* grace (more light, truth, power, and perfection). According to John the Baptist's testimony, Jesus grew in grace (light, truth, power, and perfection) by giving grace (service and blessings to others): "And I, John, saw that he received not of the fulness at first, but received grace *for* grace. And he received not of the fulness at first, but continued from grace *to* grace, until he received a fulness."[1435] Likewise, we progress toward a fulness incrementally—grace *to* grace—by keeping the commandments and giving service, for which the Lord blesses us—grace *for* grace: "For if you keep my commandments you shall receive of his fulness, and be glorified in me as I am in the Father; therefore, I say unto you, you shall receive grace *for* grace."[1436] Clearly giving and receiving grace are central to the priesthood covenant.

GRACE *TO* GRACE BY GRACE *FOR* GRACE

The above definitions of *grace* are in addition to the common definition: the Lord's help, strength, or enabling power.[1437] Jesus' grace is ever evident in the unequalled service that he proffers. Here is a formula for receiving his help or grace: *We come unto Christ in humility and faith, having done all we can do,*[1438] *and then he makes up the difference.* Consequently, we will never lack. In this, we again hear overtones of Zion: *no lack* and *divine help* to accomplish our work.

Pertaining to the concept of *no lack*, we recall again the Lord's abundant grace to the wandering Israelites, as recorded by the prophet Nehemiah:

This is thy God that brought thee up out of Egypt, and had wrought great provocations; yet thou in thy manifold mercies *forsookest them not* in the wilderness: the pillar of the *cloud departed not* from them by day, to lead them in the way; *neither the pillar of fire* by night, to shew them light, and the way wherein they should go. Thou gavest also thy good spirit to *instruct them*, and withheldest not thy

---

[1430] Mosiah 4:26.
[1431] Mosiah 2:17.
[1432] D&C 42:38.
[1433] Mosiah 2:24.
[1434] Mosiah 2:21.
[1435] D&C 93:12–13; emphasis added.
[1436] D&C 93:20; emphasis added.
[1437] LDS Bible Dictionary, s.v. "Grace," 697.
[1438] 2 Nephi 25:23: "for we know that it is by grace that we are saved [helped], after all we can do."

manna from their mouth, and gavest them *water* for their thirst. *Yea, forty years didst thou sustain them in the wilderness,* [so that] *they* lacked nothing; *their* clothes waxed not old, and their feet swelled not.[1439]

The Lord never forsook them. He was with them both day and night. He constantly instructed them. He provided manna and water to sustain them. For four decades of wandering, they lacked nothing! Amazingly, neither their clothing nor their shoes wore out. The Israelites experienced the Lord's grace.

We see these two elements of grace—no lack and divine help—in an incident in the Savior's life. Just before Jesus entered Gethsemane, he reminded his apostles of their early missions when he had purposely placed them in a condition of lack by sending them out with neither purse nor scrip. He had expected them to give grace (service) by means of his grace, that is, by relying completely on him and on nothing else. Now he asked them, "When I sent you without purse, and scrip, and shoes, lacked ye any thing? And they said, Nothing."[1440]

They needed to internalize this lesson in order to fulfill their priesthood assignments. They had learned from that experience that what had initially appeared to be a condition of lack was not one after all; the Lord had provided his grace (divine help) to sustain them in proportion to the grace (service) they proffered to the people. The situation had been carefully orchestrated by the Lord to teach them to trust him while they served. Their service would produce blessings of sustenance for the people, and by serving they (the servants) would never lack. The apostles needed to understand the inherent safety and security that derives from the new and everlasting covenant and the oath and covenant of the priesthood. These covenants contain the Lord's promise of sustaining grace. Therefore, the apostles needed firsthand experience to see if the Lord would be true to his promise. Without his grace, they could neither survive nor gain the necessary power to fulfill their priesthood calling.

Similarly, we need experience with the Lord and the covenants. We need to know that our lack is resolved by service; as we give grace, we receive grace. That is the formula. When we experience a lack of something, we can go to the Lord and he will take care of us in proportion to how we take care of his children. Moreover, because we are under covenant to represent and emulate the Lord, we must demonstrate by word and deed that we, like Jesus, will abide in the new and everlasting covenant and the oath and covenant of the priesthood by giving his children help, strength, and enablement. The Lord is clearly our example of priesthood service, and by covenant we have agreed to do as he would do.

IF ANY OF YOU LACK

James, the Lord's brother, offered a solution for those of us who lack in a specific way: "If any of you lack wisdom, let him ask of God, that giveth to all men liberally, and upbraideth not, and it shall be given him."[1441] Personalized, this scripture could read: "If I lack *anything,* I can ask of God, who will give to me *abundantly,* and he will never chastise me for having asked for his help. Instead, he will help me." This is the promise of grace!

Grace allows our lack to be swallowed up in Christ's abundance. We come unto him in humility and faith, we do all we can do, which must include offering service, and then we have the assurance that he will make up the difference. By living this principle, we never need lack for anything. Our lack might include any physical, emotional, or spiritual deficit. Also, we might experience lack when we minister to the Lord's children. In any of these situations, when we experience lack and attempt to remedy the situation, we almost certainly will come up short; that is the condition of mortality. In some way, we will lack sufficient ability or resources to counter the lack. Both the new and everlasting

---

[1439] Nehemiah 9:18–21; emphasis added.
[1440] Luke 22:35.
[1441] James 1:5; emphasis added.

covenant and the oath and covenant of the priesthood provide that we can draw upon the Savior's resource and power as we minister to his children.

On two remarkable occasions, the apostles experienced the Lord's grace when they came up short in attempting to minister to people who lacked something. These occasions were when Jesus fed the five thousand and later the four thousand.[1442] In each case, hungry people were in immediate need of help, and the apostles could manage only scant resources. Jesus' response was identical in both cases: *Bring all that you have or your best effort to me; I will bless it; you will have enough to feed the people until they are filled. Then, when it is your turn to eat, you will have enough. In fact, you will have more than you started with. Your responsibility is to feed my sheep, not to worry about having enough. Just go forth and minister, and I will multiply your efforts so that you never lack.*

When we go to the Savior for his grace, we will not encounter someone who is lacking in grace. The Savior is *full* of grace.[1443] We can obtain a fulness of grace as the Savior did: by extending grace to others. We grow in our capacity to give grace by covenanting to consecrate our best efforts and resources to the Lord, taking those efforts and resources to the Lord and asking for his blessing and help, and then going forth in faith to feed the Lord's sheep. In return, he multiplies our efforts and resources, thus providing us more grace to give away. It is a formula that applies to other gospel principles: "Blessed are the merciful: for they shall obtain mercy."[1444] We could say, "Blessed are those who extend grace, for they shall obtain more grace." Elder Mark E. Petersen said, "Love and understanding—cooperation and brotherhood—will reproduce themselves in the hearts of others when given willingly and sincerely."[1445]

For instance, if we were given a kernel of corn and ate it, the kernel would be gone forever. But if we were to plant the kernel and nourish it, the kernel would soon grow into a stalk with several ears and many kernels. Then, if we were to eat just a few of the kernels and plant the rest, the kernels would become a field of corn and a huge harvest. And it all began with a single kernel!

As we humbly seek and receive the Lord's grace, then extend that grace to others, the Lord will give us more grace, and the cycle of receiving and giving will continue until we are filled with grace. If we do not stop the cycle by hoarding the Lord's blessings, we will grow from grace to grace by giving grace for the grace until we are perfected by grace. Elder Boyd K. Packer said, "As you give what you have, there is a replacement, with increase!"[1446] Of charitable service, President Gordon B. Hinckley promised that we cannot extend merciful blessings to God's children and not experience a harvest of merciful blessings in return.[1447]

Magnifying Our Priesthood Calling by Bearing Testimony

We cannot overemphasize the fact that God calls us to the priesthood for the express purpose of assisting him in doing his work: to bring to pass the immortality and eternal life of man.[1448] Because this work is the work of God, it requires the authority and power of God, and we must exercise our priesthood to accomplish it. President Wilford Woodruff said, "We [priesthood holders] have a labor laid upon our shoulders . . . and we will be condemned if we do not fulfill it."[1449] He also said, "If we . .

[1442] Mark 6:35–44; 1–9.
[1443] D&C 93:11.
[1444] Matthew 5:7.
[1445] Petersen, Conference Report, Oct. 1967, 67.
[1446] Packer, "The Candle of the Lord," 54–55.
[1447] Hinckley, "Blessed Are the Merciful," 68.
[1448] Moses 1:39.
[1449] Woodruff, *Discourses of Wilford Woodruff*, 102.

. , bearing the priesthood, use that priesthood for any purpose under heaven but to build up the Kingdom of God, . . . our power will fail."[1450]

Part of our priesthood responsibility is bearing testimony of the truth. The following verse lies adjacent to the oath and covenant of the priesthood: "Therefore, go ye into all the world; and unto whatsoever place ye cannot go ye shall send, that the testimony may go from you into all the world unto every creature."[1451] It is our priesthood obligation to raise our voices in testimony.[1452] A testimony is a "declaration made under oath or affirmation by a witness in court to establish a fact—a public avowal . . . to give witness—a firsthand account."[1453] Effectively, we are saying, "I put my character on the line to avow that what I say is true." Therefore, the opposite of testimony would be perjury.

Bearing testimony fulfills the law of witnesses.[1454] Effectively, we are saying, "We add our witness to others that have been given." For example, Alma "began to speak unto [Zeezrom], and to establish the words of Amulek."[1455] And we read: "Moses did not only testify of these things, but also all the holy prophets, from his days even to the days of Abraham."[1456] And to this group we add our testimonies. Clearly, the weight of multiple testimonies serves to establish the truth.

We do God's work by bearing testimony. By covenant, we are to stand as witnesses of God at all times.[1457] To that end, the Lord has placed upon us the "testimony of the covenant."[1458] President Joseph Fielding Smith wrote, "People are converted by their hearts being penetrated by the Spirit of the Lord when they humbly hearken to the testimonies of the Lord's servants."[1459] Zion is established, and we establish ourselves as Zion people by bearing testimony.[1460] On the other hand, those who are "not valiant in the testimony of Jesus" forfeit their celestial inheritance and their "crown over the kingdom of our God."[1461] The terrestrial kingdom is their likely destiny.

The result of our bearing testimony is sanctification and renewal: "Nevertheless, ye are blessed, for the testimony which ye have borne is recorded in heaven for the angels to look upon; and they rejoice over you, and your sins are forgiven you."[1462] That is, our sincere testimony becomes part of the record of heaven and simultaneously purifies the heart! In another place we read, "Whosoever shall confess me before men, him shall the Son of man also confess before the angels of God."[1463] Our testimony of Christ summons his testimony of us! And in still another place, "Whosoever shall confess that Jesus is the Son of God, God dwelleth in him, and he in God."[1464] Our testimony makes us one with God. Clearly, God blesses those who bear testimony in word and example.

Why does God give such honor to sincere testimony? Because bearing testimony is an act of charity; that is, because we love him, we are willing to advocate and endorse him—and if we love our fellowmen, we will want to help them find the truth. Mormon wrote, "If a man be meek and lowly in heart, and confesses by the power of the Holy Ghost that Jesus is the Christ, he must needs have

---

[1450] Woodruff, Conference Report, Apr. 1880, 83.
[1451] D&C 84:62.
[1452] Eyring, "Faith and the Oath and Covenant of the Priesthood," 61–64.
[1453] *American Heritage Dictionary*, s.v. "Testimony."
[1454] Deuteronomy 19:15.
[1455] Alma 12:1.
[1456] Helaman 8:16.
[1457] Mosiah 18:9.
[1458] D&C 109:38.
[1459] Smith, *Church History and Modern Revelation*, 1:36–37.
[1460] D&C 58:13.
[1461] D&C 76:79.
[1462] D&C 62:3.
[1463] Luke 12:8.
[1464] 1 John 4:15.

charity; for if he have not charity he is nothing; wherefore he must needs have charity."[1465] Significantly, the ultimate testimony that we can bear is with our lives.[1466]

The law of increase has impact on the bearing of testimony. By bearing testimony, a testimony grows. Brigham Young said, "A man who wishes to receive light and knowledge, to increase in the faith of the Holy Gospel, and to grow in the knowledge of the truth as it is in Jesus Christ, will find that when he imparts knowledge to others he will also grow and increase. Be not miserly in your feelings, but get knowledge and understanding by freely imparting it to others. . . . Wherever you see an opportunity to do good, do it, for that is the way to increase and grow in the knowledge of the truth."[1467]

Clearly, the bearing of testimony magnifies our priesthood calling, and thus sanctifies and renews us. Our sins are forgiven, our witness is recorded as part of the eternal record of the truth, we are made one with God, and the Lord in turn commends us to the hosts of heaven. Ultimately, the bearing of testimony is an act of love, one in which we unashamedly stand forth, place our character and reputation on the line, and give solemn testimony of God. Bearing testimony is a confession of truth that summons great blessings from God.

THE ULTIMATE MAGNIFICATION OF OUR CALLING

Beyond every calling in the priesthood, the one calling that stands supreme is to become like God. That calling can be accomplished only through the ordinances of the temple. It is by means of these priesthood ordinances that "the power of godliness is manifest." Only these sacred ordinances hold "the key of the mysteries of the kingdom, even the key of the knowledge of God." Without these ordinances, "no man can see the face of God, even the Father, and live [eternal life]."[1468] If we expect to become like God, "overcome" all things, become part of "the church of the Firstborn . . . into whose hands the Father has given all things," become "priests and kings, who have received of his fulness, and of his glory; . . . priests of the Most High, after the order of Melchizedek, which was after the order of Enoch, which was after the order of the Only Begotten Son," and become "gods, even the sons of God," among those of whom it is said, "all things are theirs, whether life or death, or things present, or things to come, all are theirs and they are Christ's, and Christ is God's"[1469]—we must magnify our priesthood *calling*. We do that by going to the temple to receive the holy ordinances, including the endowment of priesthood knowledge and power.[1470] These ordinances culminate with eternal marriage and the fulness of the priesthood.

Elder McConkie said, "In setting forth as much as can, with propriety, be spoken outside of the temple, the Lord says that 'the fulness of the priesthood' is received only in the temple itself. This fulness is received through washings, anointings, solemn assemblies, oracles in holy places, conversations, ordinances, endowments, and sealings. (D&C 124:40.) It is in the temple that we enter into the patriarchal order, the order of priesthood that bears the name 'the new and everlasting covenant of marriage' [D&C 131:2]."[1471] Temple ordinances and eternal marriage lead to the "fulness of the priesthood," and only by receiving that fulness can we ultimately magnify, or enlarge, our *calling* and progress to become like God. This is exactly how Jesus magnified his *calling*. Joseph Smith said, "If a man gets a fulness of the priesthood of God he has to get it in the same way that Jesus Christ

---

[1465] Moroni 7:44.
[1466] D&C 135:1.
[1467] Young, *Discourses of Brigham Young*, 335.
[1468] D&C 84:19–22.
[1469] D&C 76:53–60.
[1470] D&C 95:8.
[1471] McConkie, *A New Witness for the Articles of Faith*, 315.

obtained it, and that was by keeping all the commandments and obeying all the ordinances of the house of the Lord."[1472]

A man might serve faithfully in the Church and have numerous callings, but if he is capable and has the opportunity, and then chooses to neglect (1) to make temple covenants and receive temple ordinances, and (2) to marry for eternity in the temple and thus enter into the patriarchal order of the priesthood, he has *not* magnified his priesthood, and he is violating the terms of the oath and covenant of the priesthood.[1473] Zion is established in the life of an individual by fulfilling these essential priesthood qualifications; because they lead to divine knowledge, power, and an eternal kingdom, they also lead to Zion and eventual exaltation.

THE THREE STAGES OF THE PRIESTHOOD COVENANT

We take upon ourselves the oath and covenant of the priesthood and magnify our calling in three stages:

1. Ordination to the priesthood.
2. Temple endowment.
3. Temple marriage.

Note that two of the three stages involve both worthy men and women. The following information comes from an address given by BYU professor Chauncey Riddle at the Sperry Symposium in 1989:

There are three stages by which one takes upon himself the oath and covenant of the holy priesthood and receives the power and authority of the Son of God [see D&C 68:2–4]. The first stage is to receive the priesthood, which one does by receiving ordination, being set apart to a calling, and by functioning faithfully in that calling under the guidance and instruction of the Holy Spirit. Those who thus function carry out the mind and the will of God. If they do this faithfully, they will be given progressively greater power and responsibility in their stewardships, but this does not necessarily mean church position [see Matthew 25:14–30]. To receive the priesthood does mean that one fully accepts the priesthood authority of The Church of Jesus Christ of Latter-day Saints and that one will be subject to those who preside over him in that priesthood.

The second stage of receiving the oath and covenant of the holy priesthood is to receive one's personal endowment in the holy temple of God. First, the endowment consists of special blessings that are given to the person so that he can bear the power of God in this world without being destroyed by the abundant evil that will confront and oppose his labors to do the work of God in the power of God. Second, the endowment is a set of instructions and understandings that assist the person to understand mortality and his role therein. Third, the endowment involves covenants that the person makes, special promises to bear the burden of the work of the Lord in righteousness and purity. These promises are covenants of the oath and covenant of the priesthood [see D&C 84:39]. The oath is action taken by God, who cannot lie nor sin in any way. Men, who can and do sin and lie, make covenants with God that they might escape sinning altogether and wield the power of God in righteousness, and they do this altogether for the glory of God, as part of their worship of him for his goodness, for his righteousness [see D&C 82:19].

The third part of the oath and covenant of the holy priesthood is to receive the covenant of marriage in the temple. This is God's marriage, eternal marriage, the establishment of a new eternal kingdom in the pattern of godliness, to do the supreme work of godliness eternally. Blessings are

---

[1472] Smith, *Teachings of the Prophet Joseph Smith*, 308.
[1473] D&C 84:41–42.

bestowed, covenants are made, and power and authority to act in the priesthood roles of husband and wife, father and mother, are given [see D&C 131:1–4].[1474]

As we achieve each stage of the oath and covenant of the priesthood, we progressively receive more responsibility and more power. That power speaks to the reasons we entered into the covenant of the priesthood in the first place: (1) to become like Christ, and (2) to have the power to bring people to Christ. These reasons are central to becoming a Zion person.

SUMMARY AND CONCLUSION

The second pillar of Zion is the oath and covenant of the priesthood, the covenant of exaltation. Our agreements in the covenant are faithfulness, obtaining the Aaronic Priesthood and Melchizedek Priesthood, magnifying our *calling*, receiving Christ and his Father, and living by every word that proceeds from the mouth of God. The Father's oath states that he will exalt us and give us all that he has.

The priesthood covenant comes to us by the Father's invitation through his authorized servants. We are "called by this holy calling, and ordained unto the high priesthood of the holy order of God."[1475] To be chosen and called of God, to receive his authority, power, and name to speak authoritatively as would God, to have the power to do what God would do, and to act in the capacity of the Savior, are honors without equal. By offering us the priesthood, he is offering us the opportunity to assume and further his work: to bring to pass the immortality and eternal life of man.[1476]

The oath and covenant of the priesthood contains *if-then* clauses: *If* we fulfill our obligations *then* the Father will fulfill his oath. The covenantal promises are:

If we are faithful—Faithfulness or righteousness is the first promise that we make in the priesthood covenant. By receiving the priesthood, we receive the Lord's name, and therefore we are called to become models of him. Faithfulness empowers us to fulfill our priesthood commission.

If we obtain the Aaronic and the Melchizedek priesthoods—We are required to progress in the priesthood until we receive a fulness of the priesthood. Both the Aaronic and Melchizedek orders of the priesthood are received by covenant, but only the Melchizedek Priesthood is received with the Father's oath.

If we magnify our calling—A central agreement in the oath and covenant of the priesthood is magnifying our singular calling to eternal life, which impacts our various callings in mortality. We received that calling in the premortal world. There, we qualified to be *called* and elected (selected) for eternal life. It is the magnification of our singular calling and our various callings that provide the key to our eventual exaltation. Magnifying our singular priesthood *calling* consists of at least three steps:

1. Obtaining gospel knowledge.
2. Personal righteousness by compliance with gospel standards.
3. Giving dedicated service.[1477]

Magnifying our calling is ultimately dependent upon the principle of giving dedicated service. By giving service we progress toward perfection. However, giving adequate service, which is called *grace* (in one meaning of the word), lies beyond our ability; we need the Lord's help, which is also called *grace*. By receiving the Lord's grace (his help, light, truth, power, and perfecting principles), we grow in grace (ability to help, give light, truth, power, and perfecting principles to others), which enables us to give more grace to other people. In other words: *We come unto Christ in humility and faith, having*

[1474] Riddle, "The New and Everlasting Covenant," 232–33.
[1475] Alma 13:6.
[1476] Moses 1:39.
[1477] Romney, "'The Oath and Covenant Which Belongeth to the Priesthood,'" 43.

done all we can do,[1478] *and then he makes up the difference.* Consequently, we will never lack grace. This is a condition of Zion people—*no lack.* The Lord takes care of us in proportion to how we take care of his children.

One way that we magnify our priesthood calling is by bearing testimony of the Lord. This act serves to sanctify and renew us. By bearing testimony our sins are forgiven, our witness is recorded as part of the eternal record of the truth, we are made one with God, and the Lord in turn bears testimony of us. Ultimately, bearing testimony is an act of love. It is a confession of truth that summons some of God's greatest blessings.

The calling in the priesthood that stands supreme is to become like God. That calling can be accomplished only through the ordinances of the temple, which culminate with eternal marriage and the fulness of the priesthood. We take upon ourselves the priesthood covenant and magnify our calling in three stages:

1. Ordination to the priesthood.
2. Temple endowment.
3. Temple marriage.

Of significance, two of the three stages include worthy women. We enter into the priesthood covenant and receive its blessings to become like Christ and to bring people to Christ. Only by receiving the new and everlasting covenant and thereafter receiving the oath and covenant of the priesthood, the first and second pillars of Zion, can we become Zion people and one day attain to the covenantal priesthood society of Zion.

[1478] 2 Nephi 25:23: "for we know that it is by grace that we are saved [helped], after all we can do."

Section 11

The Oath and Covenant of the Priesthood:

The Father's Oath, Instructions, and Promises

The oath and covenant of the priesthood—the second pillar of Zion—contains a remarkable oath; the Father swears this oath upon a man's ordination to the Melchizedek Priesthood. In the most sacred language, the Father promises us that we will be sanctified by the Spirit unto the renewing of our bodies and that we will become "the sons of Moses and of Aaron and the seed of Abraham, and the church and kingdom, and the elect of God." Our making the covenant of the priesthood signals that we are willing to receive Jesus Christ and the Father; the Father promises in his oath that upon our faithfulness he will give us his kingdom, meaning all that he has, which allows us to become all that he is, which is eternal life. Furthermore, upon our making the priesthood covenant, Jesus assigns the heavenly hosts and his angels charge concerning us.[1479] To assure that we learn the doctrine and workings of the priesthood covenant, the Father personally takes charge of our education concerning it. These promises combined constitute the Father's oath.

[1479] D&C 84:33–38, 42.

In discussing these sublime truths, we run the risk of feeling overwhelmed and unworthy. Such is not the intention of this book. Like ensigns, ideals are set on high mountains, waving loftily in the wind of hope, beckoning us to make the climb. Because no one can ascend without divine help, the Savior wrought the Atonement to clear the obstacles and make the journey possible. Elder McConkie taught that persisting in the strait and narrow path guarantees our arriving at our goal of eternal life.[1480] Therefore, our success is a given, assuming that we persist in faith and faithfulness. Nevertheless, as we mount toward that ideal, we often will feel stretched and weighed down by the reality of our present weaknesses. During such times, we might remember that all gospel blessings derive from a principle of progress referred to as "line upon line" or "from grace to grace." We have been taught repeatedly that the direction we are heading is as important as arriving.

As we have mentioned, faithful women have every reason to become familiar with these principles. Although the priesthood is conferred upon worthy men, both men and women receive all of the blessings of the Father's oath when it is repeated at the time they are married.[1481] Just so, single women have been promised repeatedly by the prophets that they simply need to remain worthy to receive every blessing that they have been denied in this season of their existence. On that occasion, the couple enters into the Patriarchal Order of the Priesthood with all the blessings of Abraham, Isaac, and Jacob. Included in those blessings are the rights to the gospel and priesthood for the couple's posterity. A woman claims these priesthood blessings alongside her husband. Therefore, it is fitting that both the oath and covenant of the priesthood and the covenant of eternal marriage are simultaneously called the covenant of exaltation.[1482]

Therefore, let us examine the Father's oath and the ideal of the oath's associated blessings with the confidence that as we progress in the oath and covenant of the priesthood, we, both men and their wives, will eventually qualify for every reward.

THE FATHER'S TWO OATHS GUARANTEEING US THE BLESSINGS OF ABRAHAM

Because of his righteousness, Abraham received the honor of becoming the "father of the faithful."[1483] The Lord promised Abraham *with an oath* that he would bless and multiply him.[1484] The Lord promised further: "And I will make of thee a great nation, and I will bless thee above measure, and make thy name great among all nations, and thou shalt be a blessing unto thy seed after thee, that in their hands they shall bear this ministry and Priesthood unto all nations; and I will bless them through thy name; for as many as receive this Gospel shall be called after thy name, and shall be accounted thy seed, and shall rise up and bless thee, as their father; and I will bless them that bless thee, and curse them that curse thee; and in thee (that is, in thy Priesthood) and in thy seed (that is, thy Priesthood), for I give unto thee a promise that this right shall continue in thee, and in thy seed after thee (that is to say, the literal seed, or the seed of the body) shall all the families of the earth be blessed, even with the blessings of the Gospel, which are the blessings of salvation, even of life eternal."[1485] Thus we see that Abraham and his children, including those who are adopted into Abraham's family, have a "*right* to the priesthood, to the gospel, and to eternal life."[1486] This is the right and condition of every Zion person.

[1480] McConkie, "The Probationary Test of Mortality," 11.
[1481] McConkie, *A New Witness for the Articles of Faith*, 313.
[1482] McConkie, *Mormon Doctrine*, 167.
[1483] D&C 138:41.
[1484] Hebrews 6:13–15.
[1485] Abraham 2:9–11.
[1486] McConkie, *A New Witness for the Articles of Faith*, 317.

Abraham's blessings, which were renewed with Isaac and Jacob, are the "promises made to the fathers" that Moroni prophesied would be restored in this dispensation.[1487] The fulfillment of that prophecy occurred in the Kirtland Temple on April 3, 1836,[1488] when Moses, Elias, and Elijah appeared and delivered their sacred priesthood keys. The crowning promise given to the fathers was the blessing that the Savior, Jesus Christ, would come through their lineage,[1489] in part to ensure that the terms of the new and everlasting covenant would be set in motion to save the fathers' children—us!

To do the work of salvation, the Savior needed the priesthood. Jesus is our great Exemplar; what he did to obtain the priesthood we must also do. To understand, we must look back to an ancient time.

In the premortal world, Jesus lived in a way to qualify to receive the priesthood. So did we. Of course, the priesthood is inherent in Jesus; nevertheless, in this life, he again was "called of God an high priest after the order of Melchisedec."[1490] Evidently Jesus received the priesthood by covenant and the Father's oath. Elder McConkie explained that this was the first of two oaths concerning the priesthood that the Father swore. The Father swore an oath that his Son would be a "high priest forever."[1491] When we receive the priesthood, the Father swears to us an oath. This is the *second* oath, following the first oath that the Father swore to his Son. The second oath states that we will become priests and kings unto God forever, we will inherit all that the Father has, and we will become all that the Father is, just like his Beloved Son.

The author of Hebrews wrote, "All those who are ordained unto this priesthood are made like unto the Son of God, abiding a priest continually."[1492] And at another time he wrote: "God, willing more abundantly to shew unto the heirs of promise the immutability of his counsel, confirmed it by an oath: That by *two immutable things [two oaths]*, in which it was impossible for God to lie, we might have a strong consolation, who have fled for refuge to lay hold upon the hope set before us."[1493] In other words, the Father gives his word *twice*, first to his Son and then to us, thereby confirming to us, the children of Abraham and heirs of the promise, the immutability of his oath! Elder McConkie taught:

Because the blessings of Abraham exceed anything else on earth or in heaven, Deity uses the most solemn language known to man to confirm their verity. That is, he swears with an oath in his own name that these blessings shall rest upon the faithful forever. . . . When men anciently swore with an oath in the Lord's name to perform an act, they thereby made God their partner; and because God does not fail, they were then bound to perform the act or lay down their lives in the attempt. When God himself swears with an oath, he puts his own Godhood on the line: either what he promises shall come to pass or he ceases to be God. . . . God swore not one oath but two that the promises made to Abraham—that he and his seed had a right to the priesthood, to the gospel, and to eternal life—would surely come to pass.[1494]

Two oaths guaranteeing the promise of eternal life!

[1487] D&C 2:2.
[1488] D&C 110.
[1489] Galatians 3:16.
[1490] Hebrews 5:4–10.
[1491] Hebrews 6:16–20.
[1492] JST Hebrews 7:1–3.
[1493] Hebrews 6:17–18.
[1494] McConkie, *A New Witness for the Articles of Faith*, 317.

Sanctification by the Spirit unto the Renewing of Our Bodies

Zion is the pure in heart,[1495] they who are purified and sanctified. We recall our definition that purification is the process of ridding something of impurities, and sanctification is the process of changing the purpose of something. A Zion person is someone whom the Spirit has purified and whom the Spirit has changed into a new creature[1496] in the similitude of God's Only Begotten Son.[1497] We agree to this process, which is called the baptism of fire, when we enter into the new and everlasting covenant. The purifying and sanctifying process accelerates when we enter into the oath and covenant of the priesthood. It is in the priesthood covenant that the Father promises renewal of our bodies.[1498] This renewal will reach its highest manifestation in the celestial resurrection[1499] when we become gods[1500] and can fully assume the work of the Father.[1501]

The Spirit sanctifies and renews the body in a variety of ways, such as when we undergo adversity or give service, and impressing our minds and hearts with intelligence and peace. The process of sanctification also renews our bodies at covenant-making and covenant-renewing occasions. Baptism, confirmation, partaking of the sacrament, receiving the priesthood, receiving temple ordinances, and eternal marriage are examples. The Father's oath at the time of priesthood conferral heightens the process of sanctification that was set in motion at the time of baptism and confirmation. Now, the Holy Ghost begins to purify "not only the minds of worthy priesthood holders, but also their bodies, until they are enlivened and strengthened to minister among the nations of the earth."[1502] We see in these descriptions the condition and the work of Zion people. Receiving the priesthood carries with it a call for us to minister among God's children and become saviors on Mount Zion. This is the work of God and therefore is beyond our normal capability. In order to accomplish such a work, we must experience sanctification; our bodies must be renewed, reformed, rejuvenated, and empowered. Otherwise, left to our natural fallen condition, we could never achieve success.

In advance of his mission, Moses learned that he would need the sanctifying support of the Spirit to retool his body for the work that he had been called to do. Without the Spirit's sanctifying renewal, he would have been left significantly impotent and weak.[1503]

We deceive ourselves if we suppose that we, without the Spirit, are independently powerful.[1504] It is the doctrine of the anti-Christ that man, of himself, "fare[s] in this life according to the management of the creature . . . prosper[s] according to his genius, and that every man conquer[s] according to his strength."[1505] Jesus clearly tells us that he is the source of life[1506] and the True Vine[1507] from whom we draw sanctifying strength and power. It is through him that our bodies are renewed and fashioned so that we might become instruments in his hands.

Therefore, the hearts of Zion people are purified and sanctified by covenant and the reception of the Holy Ghost. Their bodies are renewed by the Spirit to enable them to engage and persist in the

---

[1495] D&C 97:21.
[1496] 2 Corinthians 5:17.
[1497] Moses 1:6, 13.
[1498] D&C 84:33.
[1499] D&C 88:28–29.
[1500] D&C 132:19–31.
[1501] Moses 1:39.
[1502] *Encyclopedia of Mormonism*, 1019.
[1503] Moses 1:9–11.
[1504] D&C 88:5–13.
[1505] Alma 30:17.
[1506] John 11:25.
[1507] John 15:1; 1 Nephi 15:15; Alma 16:17.

work of God, which otherwise would be beyond their ability. Neither Zion people nor Zion communities can be created in any other way; they must be renewed.

THE PROGRESSION OF THE RENEWING OF OUR BODIES

President Faust taught that renewal or sanctification is linked to our desires and efforts to become holy.[1508] Such desires and efforts invite the Holy Ghost to do his sanctifying work. Sanctification, as we have learned, leads to a change of heart.[1509] According to the Apostle Paul, we prepare our hearts to be changed with "the words of faith and of good doctrine."[1510] These "words" lead us to the covenants and ordinances of the priesthood, which further change our hearts. Thus, King Benjamin taught, "Because of the covenant which ye have made . . . *your hearts are changed through faith on his name.*"[1511] President Faust said that it is the combination of faith, obedience, and adherence to the covenants and ordinances of the gospel that paves the way for the Spirit to purify our hearts and purge us of all that is unholy. The result of this purifying effort is sanctification, or holiness, which, he said, is the soul's true source of strength.[1512]

Sanctification unto the renewing of the body is another manifestation of being born again. The Father's promise—"sanctification by the Spirit unto the renewing of [our] bodies"[1513]—enumerates both the process and the eventual outcome of the Holy Ghost's sanctifying motions. Of course, we are sanctified by degrees. We begin by having faith in Christ, which always leads to repentance. We are motivated because we hope for the blessings of eternal life that we see distantly. By faith and repentance, our hearts are changed; we are *renewed and reborn*, and we seek to enter the kingdom by covenant. Baptism and confirmation are the entrance ordinances. Upon receiving the Holy Ghost, our hearts are further changed; we are *renewed and reborn* to a greater degree, and we begin to feel willing and anxious to sacrifice and consecrate all that we have and are to sustain and defend the kingdom of God. We feel the fallen, natural part of us give way to the saintly man or woman. Now our nature becomes "as a child, submissive, meek, humble, patient, full of love, willing to submit to all things which the Lord seeth fit to inflict upon him."[1514]

Further sanctification and renewal occur when we receive the oath and covenant of the priesthood. This covenant leads us to and includes the sacred ordinances of the temple. Successively, these ordinances cleanse and purify us again; they renew and empower our bodies, member by member, for more exalted purposes. Now, to a greater degree, we are separate from the telestial order of things.[1515] More than ever before, we are Zionlike. We are anointed and consecrated for a holy purpose, which is to become like God. Therefore, our bodies are renewed and thus prepared to receive a kingdom in this life that will span eternity. In every way, our bodies become a temple.

The sanctification and renewal process continues as we receive the more impressive ordinances of the temple, which Moroni indicated was the revelation of the priesthood.[1516] These sacred covenants and ordinances orient us toward eternal life and change our hearts. They serve to instruct us more perfectly "in theory, in principle, and in doctrine"[1517] concerning our relationship to the Father, his plan of salvation, and the celestial system of laws that govern Zion people.

[1508] Faust "Standing in Holy Places," 62.
[1509] Eyring, "Faith and the Oath and Covenant of the Priesthood," 61–64.
[1510] 1 Timothy 4:6.
[1511] Mosiah 5:7; emphasis added.
[1512] Faust, "Standing in Holy Places," 62.
[1513] D&C 84:33.
[1514] Mosiah 3:19.
[1515] 2 Corinthians 6:17; Alma 5:57.
[1516] D&C 2:1.
[1517] D&C 97:14.

Our temple experience renews our bodies by heightening former covenants. *The Encyclopedia of Mormonism* states, "The words set forth eternal principles to be used in solving life's dilemmas, and they mark the way to become more Christlike and progressively qualify to live with God. There, the laws of the new and everlasting covenant are taught—laws of obedience, sacrifice, order, love, chastity, and consecration."[1518] In the temple, we once again, *and more specifically*, promise to exercise strict obedience to all of the commandments,[1519] including obedience to every word that proceeds forth from God's mouth.[1520] We agree to sacrifice anything and everything to sustain and defend the kingdom of God,[1521] which is the vehicle to prepare for the establishment of Zion.[1522] We agree to live a unique celestial lifestyle called *chastity*,[1523] which is to hold sacred, within the bond of legal and lawful matrimony, the power of procreation, which is God's power of "eternal lives."[1524] We agree to consecrate all that we are and have for the building up of God's kingdom on the earth,[1525] which kingdom is the custodian of the priesthood and the new and everlasting covenant,[1526] and we do all of this to promote the cause of Zion in our personal lives, marriages, families, and the Church.

We experience even greater sanctification, renewal, and change by marrying for time and eternity and entering into the Patriarchal Order of the Priesthood. Now the power of procreation is legitimatized, and our bodies are sanctified and renewed to become authorized and empowered life-giving agents in the similitude of God the Father.

Finally, when we have proven that we will abide in our covenants "at all hazards," we experience an extraordinary renewal referred to as making one's "calling and election sure."[1527] Having faithfully kept our covenantal promises, and having overcome all things by faith, we are privileged to receive the Father's personal assurance that we will receive an inheritance in the celestial kingdom. This blessing is described in Doctrine and Covenants 76:58: "Wherefore, as it is written, they are gods, even the sons of God."

POWER GIVEN TO THE RENEWED AND SANCTIFIED

The result of sanctification is power—the renewing strength and capacity to magnify our *calling* and callings in the priesthood, the vitality and vigor associated with Zion. We learn a lesson of renewal and sanctification from Enos, the Book of Mormon prophet. Enos began the process of sanctification by repenting. Then, yearning for the promise of eternal life and knowing that no unclean thing can dwell in God's presence,[1528] he wrestled before God to receive a remission of his sins: "And my soul hungered; and I kneeled down before my Maker, and I cried unto him in mighty prayer and supplication for mine own soul. . . . And there came a voice unto me, saying: Enos, thy sins are forgiven thee, and thou shalt be blessed."[1529]

Notice that coupled with the Lord's assurance of forgiveness was his promise to Enos of future blessings. Now, having achieved a higher level of renewal, Enos immediately began to seek for those promised blessings, which included the ability to obtain priesthood power so that he could engage in

---

[1518] *Encyclopedia of Mormonism*, 1449.
[1519] Moroni 4:3; D&C 20:77.
[1520] D&C 84:44.
[1521] Smith, *Lectures on Faith*, 6:7.
[1522] Roberts, *Seventy's Course of Theology*, 1:10.
[1523] Exodus 20:14; 22:16; Leviticus 18:6–23; Matthew 5:27–28; 3 Nephi 12:27–28; Jacob 2:28, 31–35; Alma 39:5; Moroni 9:9; D&C 42:23–26; 63:16; 76:103.
[1524] Clark, *Messages of the First Presidency*, 6:176.
[1525] D&C 42.
[1526] Smith, *Teachings of the Prophet Joseph Smith*, 271–74.
[1527] Smith, *Teachings of the Prophet Joseph Smith*, 150.
[1528] 3 Nephi 27:19; Moses 6:57.
[1529] Enos 1:5.

THE FATHER'S OATH, INSTRUCTIONS, AND PROMISES

the work of redemption and influence an increasing number of people. Enos had experienced *renewal*; he was stronger in the Spirit than he had ever been. Now he had more confidence to approach the Lord, who had told him: "Whatsoever thing ye shall ask in faith, believing that ye shall receive in the name of Christ, ye shall receive it."[1530]

Enos's renewal and sanctification led him to the point that he now had power to ask the Lord to bless his people: "I began to feel a desire for the welfare of my brethren, the Nephites; wherefore, I did pour out my whole soul unto God for them."[1531] The Lord's subsequent promise to bless Enos's family resulted in Enos experiencing greater sanctification and renewal. Consequently, his power to do the work of God increased. This is an important principle of Zion: *The sanctified gain increasing power to become saviors on Mount Zion for an increasing number of people.*

Now that Enos's faith "began to be unshaken in the Lord,"[1532] he prayed for his enemies—those estranged family members who opposed him: "I prayed unto [God] with many long struggling for my brethren, the Lamanites. And it came to pass that after I had prayed and labored with all diligence, the Lord said unto me: I will grant unto thee according to thy desires, because of thy faith."[1533] The Lord's response to that prayer had eternal implications, which would transcend Enos's mortal life and extend to the coming forth of the Book of Mormon. Such were the renewing blessings that the Spirit laid upon a Zionlike man, who persisted in the sanctification process and gained power through prayer to call down the blessings of the gospel and priesthood upon his troubled family.

This is the same sanctifying and renewing process that Melchizedek employed to draw upon the Spirit and do the work of Zion among his people. These were individuals who "had waxed strong in iniquity and abomination; yea, they had all gone astray; they were full of all manner of wickedness; but Melchizedek having exercised mighty faith, and received the office of the high priesthood according to the holy order of God, did preach repentance unto his people. And behold, they did repent; and Melchizedek did establish peace in the land in his days."[1534]

Similarly, Joseph, who was sold into Egypt, remained true to the priesthood covenant as he was sanctified and renewed by the Spirit during his fourteen-year ordeal in Pharaoh's prison. The result was Joseph's power in the priesthood to bless numerous people. Catherine Thomas wrote, "Our ancestor and patriarch Joseph who was sold into Egypt was the model for us as he sanctified himself to have a sanctifying influence on his very troubled family and, like his Savior, exercised a saving power on his brethren."[1535] We, who are Joseph's children (or otherwise born of or adopted into Israel), enjoy the blessings of Joseph's renewing sanctification. Just so, we who are willing to accept the Spirit's sanctifying motions experience renewal and empowerment so that we might do the redemptive work of Zion, which includes the power to pray for sanctifying blessings for many souls for many generations.

BLESSINGS GIVEN TO THE RENEWED AND SANCTIFIED

In teaching Adam the essentials of the new and everlasting covenant, the Lord revealed that the process of renewal and sanctification follows the pattern of physical birth—water, spirit, and blood. This pattern is repeated at the time of our spiritual birth, when we are *born again* into the kingdom of heaven. The Lord explained that by means of this second birth, which consists of baptism (water), reception of the Holy Ghost (spirit), and the Atonement of Jesus Christ (blood), we emerge cleansed and sanctified of all sin. Now our new life provides that we might "enjoy the words of eternal life in

---

[1530] Enos 1:15.
[1531] Enos 1:9.
[1532] Enos 1:11.
[1533] Enos 1:11–12.
[1534] Alma 13:17–18.
[1535] Thomas, "Alma the Younger, Part 1," n.p.

this world, and eternal life in the world to come, even immortal glory."[1536] The ultimate manifestation of the "words of eternal life" is the "more sure word of prophecy."[1537] This is the Father's pronouncement that our place in his kingdom is *made sure*; that is, our exaltation is sealed upon us[1538] "by revelation and the spirit of prophecy through the power of the Holy Priesthood."[1539]

Because the oath and covenant of the priesthood mandates that we "give diligent heed to the words of eternal life,"[1540] we must understand and submit to the process of sanctification, which renews our bodies. Let us remember here that the sanctified are the pure in heart, the people of Zion, those who have been born again into the kingdom of God through the new and everlasting covenant, and those who strive for a greater level of renewal by entering into the oath and covenant of the priesthood.

The Lord explained to Adam that obedience to the pattern of sanctification—rebirth by water, Spirit, and blood—justify us for the blessings of eternal life. These blessings are available only to those who are renewed by the Spirit and thus sanctified: "For by the water ye keep the commandment; by the Spirit ye are justified, and by the blood ye are sanctified."[1541] In other words, by baptism in water we keep the commandment to pursue a new life in Christ. The Spirit justifies that action and justifies our continuing obedience to God's laws so that we might receive promised blessings. Although the Holy Ghost is the purifying and sanctifying agent, ultimately the blood of Christ makes the sanctification process possible.

But there is more. The Lord taught Adam that his being justified by the Spirit and sanctified by the blood of Christ lead to unequalled blessings: "Therefore it is given to abide in you; the record of heaven; the Comforter; the peaceable things of immortal glory; the truth of all things; that which quickeneth all things, which maketh alive all things; that which knoweth all things, and hath all power according to wisdom, mercy, truth, justice, and judgment."[1542]

This list of blessings describes the effects of spiritual birth by the water, justification by the Spirit, and sanctification by the atoning blood of Christ. Our names are written in the "record of heaven." This event assumes the promise of eternal life delivered by "another comforter . . . even the Holy Spirit of promise."[1543] There could be no greater comfort than to receive this promise. The scripture reads: "Behold, this is pleasing unto your Lord, and the angels rejoice over you; the alms of your prayers have come up into the ears of the Lord of Sabaoth, and are recorded in the book of the names of the sanctified, even them of the celestial world. Wherefore, I now send upon you another Comforter, even upon you my friends, that it may abide in your hearts, even the Holy Spirit of promise; which other Comforter is the same that I promised unto my disciples, as is recorded in the testimony of John. *This Comforter is the promise which I give unto you of eternal life, even the glory of the celestial kingdom.*"[1544]

And the blessings to those whose bodies are renewed multiply: "If thou shalt ask, thou shalt receive revelation upon revelation, knowledge upon knowledge, that thou mayest know the mysteries and peaceable things—that which bringeth joy, that which bringeth life eternal."[1545] Combined, these scriptures give us a glimpse of the Lord's blessings to those who obey the commandment, who are justified by the Spirit, and who are sanctified by the blood of Christ.

[1536] Moses 6:59.
[1537] D&C 131:5.
[1538] McConkie, *Mormon Doctrine*, 217; emphasis added.
[1539] D&C 131:5.
[1540] D&C 84:43.
[1541] Moses 6:60.
[1542] Moses 6:61.
[1543] D&C 88:2–4.
[1544] D&C 88:2–4.
[1545] D&C 42:61.

The Father's Oath, Instructions, and Promises

These blessings correspond with other blessings given to the renewed and sanctified. For example, in Doctrine and Covenants 50, the Lord promises priesthood holders an exalted status among men, provided that we humble ourselves, as did the Savior, and use that exalted status to minister among God's children: "He that is ordained of God and sent forth, the same is appointed to be the greatest, notwithstanding he is the least and the servant of all."[1546] Moreover, the Lord confirms the promises of the oath and covenant of the priesthood on the condition of our striving to be cleansed and purified: "Wherefore, [the priesthood holder] is possessor of all things; for all things are subject unto him, both in heaven and on the earth, the life and the light, the Spirit and the power, sent forth by the will of the Father through Jesus Christ, his Son. But no man is possessor of all things except he be purified and cleansed from all sin."[1547] The result is power given to us to ask for and receive blessings, and, additionally, power over all spirits: "And if ye are purified and cleansed from all sin, ye shall ask whatsoever you will in the name of Jesus and it shall be done. But know this, it shall be given you what you shall ask; and as ye are appointed to the head, the spirits shall be subject unto you."[1548]

As great as are these blessings, could any blessings be greater than those listed in Doctrine and Covenants 76? Here are the promises to those who are "washed and cleansed from all their sins, and receive the Holy Spirit by the laying on of the hands of him who is ordained and sealed unto this power; and who overcome by faith, and are sealed by the Holy Spirit of promise, which the Father sheds forth upon all those who are just and true."[1549]

They are they who are the church of the Firstborn. They are they into whose hands the Father has given all things—They are they who are priests and kings, who have received of his fulness, and of his glory; and are priests of the Most High, after the order of Melchizedek, which was after the order of Enoch, which was after the order of the Only Begotten Son.

Wherefore, as it is written, they are gods, even the sons of God—wherefore, all things are theirs, whether life or death, or things present, or things to come, all are theirs and they are Christ's, and Christ is God's. And they shall overcome all things.

Wherefore, let no man glory in man, but rather let him glory in God, who shall subdue all enemies under his feet.

These shall dwell in the presence of God and his Christ forever and ever. These are they whom he shall bring with him, when he shall come in the clouds of heaven to reign on the earth over his people. These are they who shall have part in the first resurrection. These are they who shall come forth in the resurrection of the just. These are they who are come unto Mount Zion, and unto the city of the living God, the heavenly place, the holiest of all. These are they who have come to an innumerable company of angels, to the general assembly and church of Enoch, and of the Firstborn. These are they whose names are written in heaven, where God and Christ are the judge of all. These are they who are just men made perfect through Jesus the mediator of the new covenant, who wrought out this perfect Atonement through the shedding of his own blood. These are they whose bodies are celestial, whose glory is that of the sun, even the glory of God, the highest of all, whose glory the sun of the firmament is written of as being typical.[1550]

These are the blessings given to those who receive the priesthood unto the renewing of their bodies. This is the pattern that the Lord revealed to Adam. From this pattern, supernal blessings flow. This pattern makes our hearts pure so that we can become Zion people. This pattern contains the essence of the plan of salvation. By this pattern, we may become sons of God. The Lord told Adam:

[1546] D&C 50:26.
[1547] D&C 50:27–28.
[1548] D&C 50:29–30.
[1549] D&C 76:52–53.
[1550] D&C 76:54–70.

And now, behold, I say unto you: This is the plan of salvation unto all men, through the blood of mine Only Begotten, who shall come in the meridian of time. . . .

And thus he [Adam] was baptized, and the Spirit of God descended upon him, and thus he was born of the Spirit, and became quickened in the inner man.

And he heard a voice out of heaven, saying: Thou art baptized with fire, and with the Holy Ghost. This is the record of the Father, and the Son, from henceforth and forever; and thou art after the [priesthood] order of him who was without beginning of days or end of years, from all eternity to all eternity. Behold, thou art one in me, a son of God; and thus may all become my sons. Amen.[1551]

"I Sanctify Myself, That They Also Might Be Sanctified"

A primary purpose of the priesthood is to obtain power to save God's children. As we shall see, Jesus exemplified the fact that our effort to sanctify ourselves has a direct sanctifying effect upon others for whom we are praying or are trying to help. Such a sanctifying effort is Zionlike in nature, and such Zionlike people will be motivated to sanctify themselves to help others by charity, the pure love of Christ.

Sanctification, we have learned, results in a changed and renewed heart. That renewal, in great part, is defined by charity.[1552] Charity is "the end of the commandment,"[1553] and "the crowning virtue"[1554] without which we could not do the Lord's work.[1555] Charity, of course, is one of the hallmarks of Zion. Equality, unity, the abolition of poverty, and Christlike love define Zion people. We understand that charity is not merely love; it is *saving* love—the pure love of Christ; it is the love that characterizes Zion, which never fails and endures forever.[1556]

Without charity, we are useless to God, because the covenant of the priesthood calls for us to care for others.[1557] Moreover, without charity we are useless to ourselves as well—if we are proud, selfish, and without empathy, the scripture tells us, "Except ye have charity ye can in nowise be saved in the kingdom of God."[1558]

Charity, or saving love, is not something we come by naturally. Charity is a spiritual gift that we must first seek and then develop.[1559] Therefore, it is incumbent upon us, who make the covenant of the priesthood, to pursue the covenant's promised renewal of the body to become vessels of charity.

We look to Jesus' example to understand the process and purposes of sanctification and how sanctification renews the body and creates a new heart that is filled with *saving love*. In his great intercessory prayer, the Savior taught us that personal sanctification is *the most important* principle by which one person might save another. Just moments before entering Gethsemane, Jesus made the following statement: "For their sakes I sanctify myself that they also might be sanctified."[1560] In other words, the first action, *personal sanctification*, makes possible the second action, *the saving of another*. We often think of sanctification in the context of being cleansed from sin—and it is certainly that—but here we see Jesus, who had no sin, sanctifying himself for the express purpose of saving others.

[1551] Moses 6:62, 65–68.
[1552] Eyring, "Faith and the Oath and Covenant of the Priesthood," 61–64.
[1553] 1 Timothy 1:5.
[1554] McConkie, *Mormon Doctrine*, 121.
[1555] D&C 12:8; 18:19; see also D&C 4:5.
[1556] 2 Nephi 26:30; Moroni 7:47; 8:25–26.
[1557] Eyring, "Faith and the Oath and Covenant of the Priesthood," 61–64.
[1558] Moroni 10:20–21.
[1559] Moroni 7:48; D&C 121:45; 124:116; 2 Nephi 33:7–9; Alma 7:24; 1 Corinthians 16:14; 1 Timothy 4:12; 2 Timothy 2:22; Titus 2:2; 2 Peter 1:7.
[1560] John 17:19.

So how did Jesus sanctify himself? We learn the answer in the context of the 17th chapter of John. Jesus sanctified himself through strict obedience, partaking of the sacrament, entering into a fast, making a sacrifice, and offering mighty prayer, which might be defined as prayer that is preceded by sacrifice. The result of Jesus' sanctification was that he obtained power to overcome everything that stood between his people and eternal life, including the promise of a glorious resurrection—the ultimate expression of the renewing of the body.

Likewise, we offer *Saviorlike* sacrifice when we enter the temple and perform proxy ordinances for people who could not achieve salvation otherwise. Certainly, by offering these sacred sacrifices, we are indeed acting in a Zionlike way. In the process, we experience a greater degree of sanctification in that we are *offering up* ourselves as a proxy sacrifice in the similitude of Christ. By means of that sacrifice, we, like Jesus, effectively break down obstacles that stand between the deceased and eternal life. When we understand that by pursuing this sanctifying process Jesus gained immeasurable power to ask for and receive blessings, is it any wonder that we, after making a vicarious sacrifice, might also approach the Father with power and, in the precincts of the most sacred location of his house, offer mighty prayer and receive blessings?

Clearly, to symbolically lend our sanctified body, which has been prepared and renewed by the Spirit for this purpose, to someone who is disembodied, to act and speak in the stead of the deceased, to offer our time and effort to someone who has no power to receive saving ordinances in a physical world where these things must be done—to do all of these unselfish acts counts as Christlike sacrifice and love. Sacrificing for someone who is powerless to help himself—that is, standing in the stead of another—is the highest form of love because it is the most Christlike. This is the love that is found in Zion: pure, unselfish, saving love. Zionlike love *lifts us toward the likeness of God and Jesus Christ.*[1561] This is the Savior's pattern of sanctification; it is the renewal of the body for a holy purpose. The Lord stepped into this purpose, as must we. He exercised strict obedience; he partook of the sacrament; he entered into a fast; he made his sacrifice; and he offered mighty prayer. His motivation was love. The result was the renewing of his body. In performing his mission on earth, he conformed himself into the image of the Father to do the Father's will, and he conformed himself into our image, so to speak, so that he could anticipate the entirety of our experience and make a corresponding sacrifice in our behalf. Then he received the ultimate renewal of the body: *celestial resurrection.*

Jesus is our Exemplar, and we must follow his pattern. Unless we seek sanctification and the renewal of the body, we might fall short in our priesthood duties and many of our assignments might go unfinished.[1562] Therefore, the Father makes an oath that faithful priesthood holders will be "sanctified by the Spirit unto the renewing of their bodies." They will be made clean through the power of the Holy Ghost, and then they will be given the Spirit's "operative power giving guidance for life's activities."[1563]

THE SONS OF MOSES AND OF AARON

In the gospel, we enter into a variety of relationships that have reference to family. For example, by birth or adoption we are the children of Abraham, Isaac, and Jacob, and thus we are entitled to the blessings of the gospel and the priesthood.[1564] Additionally, we become sons and daughters of Jesus Christ when we are baptized.[1565] Accepting the Atonement of Jesus Christ makes us, in the fullest sense, the "sons of God."[1566] With the conferral of the Aaronic Priesthood and the Melchizedek

---

[1561] Widtsoe, Conference Report, Apr. 1943, 38; emphasis added.
[1562] Asay, "The Oath and Covenant of the Priesthood," 43.
[1563] Farley, "The Oath and Covenant of the Priesthood," 44.
[1564] Abraham 2:8–11.
[1565] Mosiah 5:7.
[1566] D&C 35:2; 45:8; 76:58.

Priesthood we become the sons of Aaron and of Moses, which relationship, writes LDS scholar S. Brent Farley, "denotes belonging to a family and having certain rights as a member and as an heir." He continues, "Becoming a son implies the acceptance of the person and principles of the one designated as the father. To become a son of Moses and Aaron, then, would imply accepting them and their principles so that we would have a relationship and as heirs, receive certain rights, including the rights of the priesthood."[1567]

According to the oath and covenant of the priesthood, we become sons of these two great priesthood brethren by "obtaining these two priesthoods,"[1568] and by doing the works of Moses and Aaron. What were their works? Farley answers, "Aaron was a spokesman for Moses and an assistant to him, Moses having the greater calling and Aaron the lesser. The lesser, or preparatory, priesthood was named after Aaron. (D&C 84:18, 26–27.) The sons of Aaron today are those who accept the preparatory, or Aaronic, Priesthood and live its principles, thus proving worthy of greater blessings as they enter the Order of the Melchizedek Priesthood. They learn to accept all who are called as spokesmen (those other local and general authorities who help accomplish the Lord's work) under the direction of the prophet. They are also willing themselves to serve as spokesmen in priesthood capacities when called to do so."[1569]

The Aaronic Priesthood also holds the key of "the gospel of repentance, and of baptism by immersion for the remission of sins."[1570] This key punctuates our priesthood covenant to teach and preach the gospel, bring people to Jesus Christ through repentance, initiate them into the kingdom of God by means of baptism and the new and everlasting covenant, all of which set God's children on the path to eternal life. Clearly, receiving the Aaronic Priesthood is a call to serve and the authority to do so.

Moses was called of God as the prophet to gather Israel, lead them from Egyptian bondage, and establish them as an independent and strong people. (Exodus 3:10–17.) He was the prophet, the mouthpiece of the Lord to Israel; by following his inspired direction the people could obtain exaltation. Those who become sons of Moses today are those who accept the mouthpiece of the Lord who has been called to deliver modern Israel from the bondage of worldliness in order to become established as a strong and independent people and be led toward exaltation. They too participate in the gathering of Israel, the keys of which Moses committed to Joseph Smith and Oliver Cowdery in the latter-day restoration (D&C 110:11). The sons of Moses have a right "to the Holy Priesthood," "which priesthood continueth in the church of God in all generations, and is without beginning of days or end of years." (D&C 84:6, 17.) Moses sought diligently to prepare his people for this right to be worthy of the presence of God through the authority, ordinances, and power of the priesthood. (D&C 84:19–23.) The sons of Moses today hearken to the one called of God to guide them in their preparation to behold His presence.

Thus, the sons of Moses and of Aaron today are faithful priesthood holders. In the course of their progress, they will become worthy temple recommend holders. They will "offer an acceptable offering and sacrifice in the house of the Lord" (D&C 84:31) by receiving their own temple endowment and performing work for the dead. "And the sons of Moses and of Aaron shall be filled with the glory of the Lord, upon Mount Zion in the Lord's house, whose sons are ye; and also many whom I have called and sent forth to build up my church." (D&C 84:32).[1571]

A most significant prelude to the oath and covenant of the priesthood references the temple as the focal point of the priesthood. Only through the ordinances of the temple can we "prepare to

---

[1567] Farley, "The Oath and Covenant of the Priesthood," 44.
[1568] D&C 84:14–33.
[1569] Farley, "The Oath and Covenant of the Priesthood," 45.
[1570] D&C 13:1.
[1571] Farley, "The Oath and Covenant of the Priesthood," 44.

achieve the goal sought by Moses for his people: to enter the Lord's presence."[1572] The revelation reads: "Now this [the Melchizedek Priesthood doctrine, covenants, and ordinances] Moses plainly taught to the children of Israel in the wilderness, and sought diligently to sanctify his people that they might behold the face of God."[1573] Elder McConkie noted that "the greatest blessings [of the priesthood covenant] are reserved for those who obtain 'the fulness of the priesthood,' meaning the fullness of the blessings of the priesthood. These blessings are found only in the temples of God."[1574] Every covenant and ordinance received in the temple, the purpose and power of which is to bring us into God's presence, is included in the oath and covenant of the priesthood—the second pillar of Zion.

It is the mission of the latter-day sons of Aaron and Moses to follow in the footsteps of their *fathers*. They support their leaders, serve as spokesmen in priesthood capacities, and watch over the Church. They teach the gospel of repentance, then go forth to gather Israel, preaching and teaching the doctrine of the priesthood. They bring people to Christ to receive their temple blessings, so that the people might be sanctified and enter into the presence of the Lord.[1575] Farley concludes, "The corollary between the mission of Moses in ancient Israel and the mission of the sons of Moses in modern Israel is not coincidental."[1576]

THE SEED OF ABRAHAM

The oath of the priesthood stipulates that our receiving the priesthood fulfills the Father's oath to Abraham, who was promised that the rights to the gospel and priesthood would perpetually belong to him and his seed. Whether we are a blood descendant of Abraham or a person who is adopted into his family, when we receive the covenant of the priesthood, the Father deems us "the seed of Abraham,"[1577] and thus we, by birthright, are entitled to all of the associated blessings.

As we have learned, we, who are of the bloodline of Abraham, qualified premortally to be elected (selected) in this life (1) to receive the blessings of the gospel and priesthood for our own salvation, and (2) to go forth and bless others with these same blessings.[1578] These blessings are the blessings that Abraham sought and received; they include our children's right as "lawful heirs" to be offered the fulness of the gospel and the priesthood "according to the flesh."[1579]

Abraham is our priesthood model. He made himself worthy so that he could qualify to receive the priesthood by covenant; he magnified his calling; he received both Jesus Christ and the Father in the fullest sense; and he gave strict diligence to every word that proceeded forth from the mouth of God. Ultimately, by means of the Melchizedek Priesthood and the temple covenants and ordinances, he entered into the presence of God and eventually achieved godhood.[1580] We are heirs to Abraham's blessings; if we follow his example, we will receive the same blessings. Elder McConkie wrote, "Abraham and his seed (including those adopted into his family) shall have all of the blessings of the gospel, of the priesthood, and of eternal life,"[1581] including eternal increase. The Lord revealed, "This promise is yours also, because ye are of Abraham. . . . Therefore . . . do the works of Abraham."[1582]

[1572] Farley, "The Oath and Covenant of the Priesthood," 45.
[1573] D&C 84:23.
[1574] McConkie, *Mormon Doctrine*, 482.
[1575] D&C 84:2.
[1576] Farley, "The Oath and Covenant of the Priesthood," 45–46.
[1577] D&C 84:34.
[1578] Romans 9:11; 11:5, 7, 28.
[1579] D&C 86:8–11; 113:6.
[1580] D&C 132:37.
[1581] McConkie, *A New Witness for the Articles of Faith*, 505.
[1582] D&C 132:31–32.

"Elder McConkie noted that 'what we say for Abraham, Isaac, and Jacob we say also for Sarah, Rebekah, and Rachel, the wives . . . who with them were true and faithful in all things,' for, as President Joseph Fielding Smith taught, 'the Lord offers to his daughters every spiritual gift and blessing that can be obtained by his sons.'"[1583] The connection of women to the oath and covenant of the priesthood is a subject that we will more fully discuss.

Concerning our being the seed of Abraham and thus entitled to his blessings, Brent Farley taught, "In order to enjoy the full blessings of the oath and covenant of the priesthood, a man must marry for time and eternity in the house of the Lord. Elder McConkie explained that 'this covenant, made when the priesthood is received, is renewed when the recipient enters the order of eternal marriage.' Further, 'when he is married in the temple for time and for all eternity, each worthy member of the Church enters personally into the same covenant the Lord made with Abraham. This is the occasion when the promises of eternal increase are made, and it is then specified that those who keep the covenants made there shall be inheritors of all the blessings of Abraham, Isaac, and Jacob.'"[1584]

THE CHURCH AND KINGDOM OF GOD

The priesthood inseparably links us to The Church of Jesus Christ of Latter-day Saints, which is God's kingdom on earth. Elder McConkie wrote, "The church is a kingdom; it is God's kingdom, the Kingdom of God on earth, and as such is designed to prepare men for an inheritance in the kingdom of God in heaven, which is the celestial kingdom."[1585] As priesthood holders, we represent the Church and kingdom wherever we are. The priesthood makes us bright beacons to draw people to Christ. Jesus taught: "Let your light so shine before men, that they may see your good works, and glorify your Father which is in heaven."[1586] The priesthood is associated with light, the power of light, the light of Christ, which is "the law by which all things are governed."[1587] By virtue of our priesthood calling, the Lord shines his light on us that we might stand as sources of guidance, inspiration, and power. We are the standard bearers of that light to the nations.[1588]

As ministers of Jesus Christ, we are authorized to bless the Father's children in the name of Jesus Christ. The Lord instructed the Seventy, "Heal the sick therein, and say unto them, *The kingdom of heaven is come nigh unto you.*"[1589] That is, "We, who represent the kingdom, are come to bless you." We bearers of the priesthood are *of* the kingdom and, more importantly, we *are* the kingdom. We are the Church and kingdom of God. We magnify our calling in the priesthood, according to President J. Reuben Clark, by building up the kingdom of God, which is done by blessing God's children, and that can only be done by faith in Jesus Christ and the authority of the priesthood.[1590]

THE ELECT OF GOD

Zion people are the elect of God. Elder Bruce R. McConkie explains, "The *elect of God* comprise a very select group, an inner circle of faithful members of The Church of Jesus Christ of Latter-day Saints. These are the portion of church members who are striving with all their hearts to keep the fulness of the gospel law in this life so that they can become inheritors of the fulness of gospel rewards

---

[1583] Farley, "The Oath and Covenant of the Priesthood," 46.

[1584] Farley, "The Oath and Covenant of the Priesthood," 46; McConkie, *A New Witness for the Articles of Faith*, 313, 508; D&C 131:1–3.

[1585] McConkie, *A New Witness for the Articles of Faith*, 335.

[1586] Matthew 5:16.

[1587] D&C 88:13.

[1588] D&C 115:5.

[1589] Luke 10:9; emphasis added.

[1590] Clark, Conference Report, Oct. 1950, 169–71.

in the life to come." Faithful Melchizedek Priesthood holders are among the elect of God. Of this group, Elder McConkie said, they are those who "keep 'the oath and covenant which belongeth to the priesthood,' and are rewarded with the fulness of the Father's kingdom."[1591] The elect of God qualify to enter into the Lord's *rest*, meaning the fulness of his glory.[1592] In the perfection of the term, the elect *receive* the Father and his kingdom, and therefore they receive all that the Father has.[1593] President Marion G. Romney described the elect of God as those who live worthy of every trust; who live by every word of God; who hunger and thirst after righteousness; who make their calling and election sure.[1594]

These descriptions of the elect are those who make covenants, who exhibit profound faithfulness, who overcome the world, and who surmount their fallen condition so that they might be exalted on high; they are wholly Zionlike. These are people who live celestial laws in a telestial setting. They hold up the celestial standard, beckoning all to abandon telestial complacencies and filth and come up to Zion to be saved by the King of Zion. They are Zion people, the pure-hearted, elect of God.

The word *elect* suggests *election* or *selection*. As we have learned, our selection for exaltation began in the premortal world. There we embraced the ideal of Zion. Because of our righteousness, we were both *called* and *elected* for eternal life. The scripture states that we were "*called* and prepared from the foundation of the world according to the foreknowledge of God, on account of [our] exceeding faith and good works."[1595] That is, we were *called* and elected (selected) to receive the priesthood in the premortal world, an ordination that qualified us to receive the priesthood in this life. In the premortal world, we who entered into the holy order of the priesthood "elected to become gods" and to "come to earth and learn the work of redemption in apprenticeship to the Lord Jesus Christ." Therefore, we elected, and were *selected*, to come to mortality as heirs of special blessings, to embrace the ideal of Zion *again*, and to continue to do the work of redemption here so that we would someday "qualify to live with the Gods in the eternal worlds."[1596] This was our premortal calling and election.

Elder McConkie wrote, "If the full blessings of salvation are to follow, the doctrine of election must operate twice. First, righteous spirits are elected or chosen to come to mortality as heirs of special blessings. Then, they must be called and elected again in this life, an occurrence which takes place when they join the true Church. (D&C 53:1.) Finally, in order to reap eternal salvation, they must press forward in obedient devotion to the truth until they make their 'calling and election sure' (2 Pet. 1:10), that is, are 'sealed up unto eternal life.' (D&C 131:5.)"[1597]

In this life, we are called and elected once more. Through baptism, we are *called* into the fellowship of Jesus Christ,[1598] that is, we receive our "calling and election in the church."[1599] That *calling* leads us to our being *called* to receive our *calling* to and in the priesthood. The oath and covenant of the priesthood requires that we magnify that calling, which is to become like God. That goal can be accomplished only by obedience, sacrifice, and living by "every word that proceedeth forth from the mouth of God."[1600] If, after we have lived our covenants at all hazards by persisting in the new and everlasting covenant and the oath and covenant of the priesthood—the first and second pillars of Zion—we will eventually receive the Lord's guarantee of eternal life, and our provisional

---

[1591] McConkie, *Mormon Doctrine*, 217.
[1592] D&C 84:24.
[1593] D&C 84:35–38.
[1594] Romney, Conference Report, Apr. 1974, 116.
[1595] Alma 13:3–5.
[1596] Thomas, "Alma the Younger, Part 1," n.p.
[1597] McConkie, *Mormon Doctrine*, 217.
[1598] 1 Corinthians 1:9, 26–27; Hebrews 3:1.
[1599] D&C 53:1.
[1600] D&C 84:44.

calling and election will now be made *sure*.[1601] Then we are "sealed up unto eternal life"[1602] and become, in the fullest sense, the elect of God, who have been called and *selected* by God's own oath and the promise of the certainty of eternal life. We have fulfilled and magnified our priesthood calling.

Calling and Election Made Sure

Describing the elect of God, Elder McConkie said they are members of the Church who "devote themselves wholly to righteousness."[1603] Joseph Smith explained the journey to becoming the elect, and the ideal description of that term: "After a person has faith in Christ, repents of his sins, and is baptized for the remission of his sins and receives the Holy Ghost, (by the laying on of hands), which is the first Comforter, then let him continue to humble himself before God, hungering and thirsting after righteousness, and living by every word of God, and the Lord will soon say unto him, Son, thou shall be exalted. When the Lord has thoroughly proved him, and finds that the man is determined to serve him at all hazards, then the man will find his calling and election made sure, then it will be his privilege to receive the other Comforter."[1604]

Here the Prophet links the *calling and election made sure* with becoming worthy to come into the presence of the Lord and receive his comfort. Joseph Smith said, "Then it will be [our] privilege to receive the other Comforter. Now what is this other Comforter? It is no more nor less than the Lord Jesus Christ himself; . . . when any man obtains this last Comforter, he will have the personage of Jesus Christ to attend him, or appear unto him from time to time, and even he will manifest the Father unto him, and they will take up their abode with him, and the visions of the heavens will be opened unto him, and the Lord will teach him face to face, and he may have a perfect knowledge of the mysteries of the Kingdom of God."[1605]

Elder McConkie gives the following definition of the calling and election made sure: "To have one's calling and election made sure is to be sealed up unto eternal life; it is to have the unconditional guarantee of exaltation in the highest heaven of the celestial world; it is to receive the assurance of godhood; it is, in effect, to have the day of judgment advanced, so that an inheritance of all the glory and honor of the Father's kingdom is assured prior to the day when the faithful actually enter into the divine presence to sit with Christ in his throne, even as he is 'set down' with his 'Father in his throne.' (Rev. 3:21.) But when the ratifying seal of approval is placed upon someone whose calling and election is thereby made sure—because there are no more conditions to be met by the obedient person—this act of being sealed up unto eternal life is of such transcendent import that of itself it is called being sealed by the Holy Spirit of Promise, which means that in this crowning sense, being so sealed is the same as having one's calling and election made sure."[1606] Obviously, no greater promise can be made by God through the Holy Ghost than the revealed promise of eternal life.

Another term emerges from the scriptures in connection with the calling and election made sure: *the more sure word of prophecy*.[1607] Elder McConkie explains that the elect of God, in the ultimate sense, are those who "receive *the more sure word of prophecy*, which means that the Lord seals their exaltation upon them while they are yet in this life."[1608] The fact that our exaltation is "sealed" upon us suggests a priesthood ordinance by means of the sealing keys. The Doctrine and Covenants describes this term: "The more sure word of prophecy means a man's knowing that he is sealed up

---

[1601] Lee, Conference Report, Oct. 1970, 116; 2 Peter 1:10.
[1602] D&C 131:5.
[1603] McConkie, *Mormon Doctrine*, 217.
[1604] Smith, *Teachings of the Prophet Joseph Smith*, 149–51.
[1605] Smith, *Teachings of the Prophet Joseph Smith*, 150–51; John 14:16:23; D&C 88:3–4; 130:3.
[1606] McConkie, *Doctrinal New Testament Commentary*, 3:336.
[1607] D&C 131:5; 2 Peter 1:19.
[1608] McConkie, *Mormon Doctrine*, 217; emphasis added.

unto eternal life, by revelation and the spirit of prophecy through the power of the Holy Priesthood."[1609] We immediately see the link between the more sure word of prophecy and the oath and covenant of the priesthood, which stipulates that we must "give diligent heed to the words of eternal life."[1610] Clearly, the ultimate manifestation of those *words* of eternal life is the more sure *word* of prophecy that the Father seals upon us through his anointed servant, promising us that we will be called up to his kingdom, and our place in it is made sure.

Elder McConkie expounded: "Those so favored of the Lord are sealed up against all manner of sin and blasphemy except the blasphemy against the Holy Ghost and the shedding of innocent blood. That is, their exaltation is assured; their calling and election is made sure, because they have obeyed the fulness of God's laws and have overcome the world."[1611]

Although having our calling and election made sure stands at the summit of gospel blessings, it is nevertheless remarkably within reach, more so than we might imagine. For example, "on May 16, 1843, Joseph Smith, William Clayton, and company were traveling through Carthage and stopped for the night at the farm of Benjamin F. Johnson in Ramus, Illinois. That evening Joseph instructed the group in detail on the principle of eternal marriage. As Benjamin and his wife listened, the air lavish with the sweet words of life, Joseph put his hand on the knee of William Clayton and promised him: 'Your life is hid with Christ in God, and so are many others. Nothing but the unpardonable sin can prevent you from inheriting eternal life for you are sealed up by the power of the priesthood unto eternal life, having taken the step necessary for that purpose. William Clayton was twenty-eight years old when Joseph avowed to him the irrevocable promise of eternal life. He had been a member of the Church for a little more than five years."[1612]

In an article entitled "The Stripling Exalted," James T. Summerhays, an editor at *BYU Studies*, writes, "A recurring motif in Joseph Smith's discourse is the principle of calling and election. 'There is some grand secret here,' Joseph said, and he wanted to reveal 'the secret and grand key' that would unlock 'the most glorious principle of the Gospel of Jesus Christ.'"[1613]

Continuing, Summerhays says,

In my mind, four words divulge the secret: *Spiritual blessings are timely.* That's it. That's the key. Imagine the absurdity of being given the sword of valor only after you slay the dragon, or being received into a house of refuge only after the storm is passed. Instead, the promise has a more timely purpose: "Having this promise [of eternal life] sealed unto them," spoke Joseph, "it was an anchor to the soul, sure and steadfast. Though the thunders might roll and lightnings flash, and earthquakes bellow, and war gather thick around, yet this hope and knowledge would support the soul in every hour of trial, trouble and tribulation" (*History of the Church*, 5:401).

I see a clear chronology to Joseph's statement: first, the promise is given to make the receiver strong, and then the thunders roll. My instinct tells me that this is why Heber C. Kimball and many others were given the promise so early in life: it was to shore up their courage for the coming storm and fury.

The "calling and election made sure" fulfills a more expedient and satisfying purpose—it was not intended to be only a capstone to a life of faithfulness; nor is it a final prize to be given out after the race of life is already won.

Imagine the peace of mind that would come if we already knew that God had signed our names in the Book of Life. No surprises at Judgment Day, no sudden and everlasting thrusting down to the

---

[1609] D&C 131:5.

[1610] D&C 84:43.

[1611] McConkie, *Mormon Doctrine*, 109–10.

[1612] Summerhays, "The Stripling Elect," Feb. 20, 2009; referencing Allen, *No Toil Nor Labor Fear: The Story of William Clayton*, 129–30.

[1613] Smith, *Teachings of the Prophet Joseph Smith*, 298.

dark abyss. Being able to almost taste salvation, we might become much more light-hearted, jovial, and resilient in the face of trials and sorrows that must come but now seem so trifling in the eternal scheme of things. We could be ablaze with confidence, having internalized the words of Peter which say, "Make your calling and election sure: for if ye do these things, ye shall never fall" (2 Peter 1:10).

Above all, being unshackled with worries over personal salvation, we would feel free and wholly available to give ourselves to the salvation of others. In other words, we will have made a cosmic leap forward in being more like God, who is not too worried about himself but whose whole glory rests upon bringing "to pass the immortality and eternal life of man" (Moses 1:39).[1614]

Clearly, we do not need to have arrived at perfection to experience our calling and election made sure. Rather, this is a step in our progression that makes perfection possible. It comes after the Lord tries our faith and determines that we will remain in the Covenant at all hazards. It becomes the ultimate comfort that provides us strength to face and endure the trials of mortality, providing us knowledge that our future is secure with God.

Blaine Yorgason explained that having our calling and election made sure is both a revelation and an ordinance called the *more sure word of prophecy*. "Scriptural evidence seems to indicate that one's calling and election can be made sure in either of two ways, though it seems likely that both are interrelated. They are (1) receiving the voice of God in a personal revelation wherein the promise of exaltation is given; and (2) receiving by ordinance the fullness of the priesthood through the more sure word of prophecy by 'him who is anointed' (D&C 132:7)."[1615] Evidently, we can receive either the revelation or the ordinance first, but eventually we will receive both. In either case, the revelation and the ordinance deliver the assurance of attaining eternal life.

That said, too many of us flounder because we do not seek this revelation, when in fact the Holy Spirit of Promise may have already set his seal upon us. We may be like the converted Lamanites, who had been "baptized with fire and with the Holy Ghost, and they but knew it not."[1616] We suppose that this blessing comes only to the venerable aged, and then only by ordinance; therefore, we fail to seek the personal revelation from the Holy Ghost, which would provide us strength and comfort to pursue our lives' missions.

Many blessings flow from having our calling and election made sure. To the elect of God, the Lord has promised the ultimate sanctification and renewal of the body: "Ye shall come forth in the first resurrection. . . . They shall pass by the angels, and the gods, which are set there, to their exaltation and glory in all things, as hath been sealed upon their heads, which glory shall be a fulness and a continuation of the seeds forever and ever. Then shall they be gods, because they have no end; therefore shall they be from everlasting to everlasting, because they continue; then shall they be above all, because all things are subject unto them. Then shall they be gods, because they have all power, and the angels are subject unto them."[1617]

The elect of God are Zion people forever in an eternal Zion priesthood society. No wonder, then, that Joseph Smith exhorted the Saints "to go on and continue to call upon God until you make your calling and election sure for yourselves, by obtaining this more sure word of prophecy, and wait patiently for the promise until you obtain it."[1618]

Receiving Christ and the Father

Monte S. Nyman writes: "Through receiving the priesthood, a person is receiving Jesus Christ because the recipient is taking the name of Christ and acting with his authority. And those who receive Jesus

---

[1614] Summerhays, "The Stripling Exalted," Feb. 20, 2009.
[1615] Yorgason, *I Need Thee Every Hour*, 387–88.
[1616] 3 Nephi 9:20.
[1617] D&C 132:19–20.
[1618] Smith, *History of the Church*, 6:365; 5:388–89.

are actually receiving the Father because all that Jesus does is by divine investiture of the Father. Those who receive the Father receive his kingdom; they receive the fullness of the glory of the Father. 'Therefore all that [the] Father hath shall be given unto [them]' (D&C 84:34–38). In short, they shall receive eternal life. All that the Father has was given to Jesus, and he is willing to give the same to the faithful priesthood holder (John 15:16)."[1619]

The language of the oath and covenant of the priesthood has overtones of courtship—a plea from God who loves us to join with him. In the priesthood covenant we hear him yearning that we might choose to love him as he loves us, to give to him our hearts, to take upon us his name (priesthood), and to enter into a marriage-like covenant whereby we fully *receive* him: "And also all they who receive this priesthood receive me, saith the Lord; for he that receiveth my servants receiveth me; and he that receiveth me receiveth my Father."[1620] Notice that the Father endows us with all that he has, just as a husband will endow his bride with all that he possesses or will possess. Both the husband and the Father make that consecration with a solemn *oath*.

The marriage motif continues. Whereas a husband and wife are sealed together as one, so we are invited in the priesthood covenant to become one with the Father as the Father and the Son are one. The vehicle by which we become one with them is entering into their same order of the priesthood. S. Brent Farley writes, "Such unity was the Savior's desire when he prayed: 'Holy Father, keep through thine own name those whom thou hast given me, that they may be one, as we are. . . . Father, I will that they also, whom thou hast given me, be with me where I am; that they may behold my glory, which thou hast given me.' (John 17:11, 24.) The oath and covenant of the priesthood is the means for the fulfillment of that prayer. . . . Herein is the fulfillment of heirship."[1621]

Because the oath and covenant of the priesthood approximates the marriage covenant, and because the oath and covenant of the priesthood is the second pillar of Zion, the condition of Zion is very much like a marriage. As husbands and wives *receive* each other in the covenant of marriage, so, similarly, we *receive* the Father and Jesus Christ. In each relationship, we grow together until we become one. In both relationships, we mature in appreciation and love for our *beloved*, and over time we, together, become more and more like each other.

Joseph Smith explained this process of growing together in love: "And all those who keep his commandments shall grow up from grace to grace, and become heirs of the heavenly kingdom, and joint-heirs with Jesus Christ; possessing the same mind, being transformed into the same image or likeness, even the express image of him who fills all in all; being filled with the fulness of his glory, and become one in him, even as the Father, Son and Holy Spirit are one. . . . A sure reward [is] laid up for them in heaven, even that of partaking of the fullness of the Father and the Son through the spirit. As the Son partakes of the fullness of the Father through the Spirit, so the saints are, by the same Spirit, to be partakers of the same fullness, to enjoy the same glory; for as the Father and the Son are one, so, in like manner, the saints are to be one in them. Through the love of the Father, the mediation of Jesus Christ, and the gift of the Holy Spirit, they are to be heirs of God, and joint heirs with Jesus Christ."[1622]

Our *receiving* God leads to our knowing and seeing God. These privileges are some of the "rights of the priesthood."[1623] As we have learned, only the priesthood ordinances revealed in the temple have the power to provide a man or a woman with these consummate blessings: "For without this [the

---

[1619] Nyman, "Priesthood, Keys, Councils, and Covenants," 125.
[1620] D&C 84:35–37.
[1621] Farley, "The Oath and Covenant of the Priesthood," 46.
[1622] Smith, *Lectures on Faith*, 5:2–3.
[1623] D&C 121:36.

power of godliness that is facilitated through temple ordinances] no man can see the face of God, even the Father, and live."[1624] Elder McConkie wrote:

> What greater personal revelation could anyone receive than to see the face of his Maker? Is not this the crowning blessing of life? . . . There is a true doctrine on these points, a doctrine unknown to many and unbelieved by more, a doctrine that is spelled out as specifically and extensively in the revealed word as are any of the other great revealed truths. There is no need for uncertainty or misunderstanding; and surely, if the Lord reveals a doctrine, we should seek to learn its principles and strive to apply them in our lives. This doctrine is that mortal man, while in the flesh, has it in his power to see the Lord, to stand in his presence, to feel the nail marks in his hands and feet, and to receive from him such blessings as are reserved for those only who keep all his commandments and who are qualified for that eternal life which includes being in his presence forever.[1625]

If we are true and faithful to the oath and covenant of the priesthood, where will it lead us? The focal point of the priesthood, the reason that we enter into this covenant, the motivation that drives us to bring others to Christ, is to regain the presence of God—to *receive* him. Having personally experienced that blessing, Joseph Smith exclaimed, "Great and marvelous are the works of the Lord, and the mysteries of his kingdom which he showed unto us, which surpass all understanding in glory, and in might, and in dominion; which he commanded us we should not write while we were yet in the Spirit, and are not lawful for man to utter; neither is man capable to make them known, for they are only to be seen and understood by the power of the Holy Spirit, which God bestows on those who love him, and purify themselves before him; *to whom he grants this privilege of seeing and knowing for themselves; that through the power and manifestation of the Spirit, while in the flesh, they may be able to bear his presence in the world of glory.*"[1626]

"While in the flesh!" proclaims Elder McConkie. "For those who 'purify themselves before him,' this is the time and the day and the hour when they have power to see their God!"[1627] This "right" of the priesthood is, of course, dependent on our allowing the Holy Ghost to purify our hearts, for only Zion people, the pure in heart, may see and receive God.[1628] This "right" of the priesthood also reminds us of two words in the priesthood covenant that we have discussed: *calling* and *elect*.[1629] Elder McConkie said, "Brethren whose calling and election is made sure always hold the holy Melchizedek Priesthood. Without this delegation of power and authority they cannot be sealed up unto eternal life."[1630]

Ultimately, *receiving* Christ and the Father means receiving the "fulness of the priesthood,"[1631] the ordinance involving the more sure word of prophecy, which we have discussed. Blaine M. Yorgason writes:

> Peter calls this ordinance, which was to be restored to the earth through priesthood authority in the Nauvoo Temple, "the more sure word of prophecy"; Elder McConkie calls it "the fulness of the sealing power"; and the Prophet Joseph Smith referred to it as both "the patriarchal power," and "the keys of knowledge and power." It is all the same—the sealing up of individuals to eternal life through the authorized priesthood ministrations of the Lord's mouthpiece or those he may have appointed. . . . When the president of the Church is instructed "by revelation and commandment" to exercise these keys of sealing power in their fulness in behalf of worthy Church members, his blessings or

---

[1624] D&C 84:22.
[1625] McConkie, *A New Witness for the Articles of Faith*, 492.
[1626] D&C 76:114–18.
[1627] McConkie, *A New Witness for the Articles of Faith*, 495.
[1628] 3 Nephi 12:8; Matthew 5:8.
[1629] D&C 84:33–34.
[1630] McConkie, *The Promised Messiah*, 587.
[1631] D&C 124:28.

pronouncement of fullness of the priesthood is called in the scripture "the more sure word of prophecy"; that is, it is a prophetic declaration as if from the mouth of God that will not fail, for, as the Lord says, "Whether by mine own voice or by the voice of my servants, it is the same." The Lord declares, "The more sure word of prophecy means a man's *knowing* that he is sealed up unto eternal life, by revelation and the spirit of prophecy through the power of the Holy Priesthood." Thus Joseph said, "I anointed [Judge James Adams] to the patriarchal power—to receive the keys of knowledge and power, by revelation to himself."[1632]

All of these blessings are associated with receiving Jesus Christ and the Father. This is both a stipulation and a blessing stated in the oath and covenant of the priesthood. Zion people must understand and embrace this commandment if they are to become one with the Father and Jesus Christ. In a most beautiful way, our receiving them is symbolic of the marriage covenant. "And this is according to the oath and covenant which belongeth to the priesthood."[1633]

"All That My Father Hath"

Our Heavenly Father sets the example of consecration. With no selfish motive, he offers each of us, *indivisibly*, all that he has. Just how much is all that he has? To Moses, who was given a panoramic view of the universe, the Lord said, "And worlds without number have I created . . . innumerable are they unto man; but all things are numbered unto me, for they are mine and I know them. . . . The heavens, they are many, and they cannot be numbered unto man; but they are numbered unto me, for they are mine. And as one earth shall pass away, and the heavens thereof even so shall another come; and there is no end to my works, neither to my words."[1634]

A quantity so vast that it would appear numberless unto man is beyond our comprehension, even with the aid of modern technology. That the Father promises us with an oath that, upon the condition of our faithfulness, he will give us the totality of his kingdom is equally beyond our comprehension. The Father's promise of our eventual exaltation is so expansive and glorious that it defies explanation.[1635]

To attempt to grasp the extent of the Father's creations, let us examine what we know about the heavens. In 1983, before the Hubble telescope and modern computer technology, The National Geographic Society published an article and a map of the known universe.[1636] The editors explained that our solar system has a radius of 150 million kilometers, or .000016 light years. A light year is the distance that light travels (at 186,000 miles per second) for a year: 5,878,625,373,183.61 miles—almost 6 trillion miles per year! Our solar system resides on the outskirts of the Milky Way galaxy in a *neighborhood* of twenty nearby stars. The radius of this neighborhood is twenty light years or 120 trillion miles. This tiny grouping of stars is only a pinpoint in the enormous Milky Way galaxy, which has a radius of 50,000 light years, and, by one estimate, is made up of some 100–200 billion stars like our sun. On a clear night, when we gaze up into the heavens, we see, but we cannot comprehend, the vastness of our galaxy. Traveling at 220 kilometers per second, our sun makes one revolution around the center of our galaxy every 230 million years!

As incomprehensible as are these numbers, the Milky Way galaxy is still only a pinpoint in the ocean of the known universe. Consider this—our galaxy is one of a *cluster* of twenty nearby galaxies of like size. This cluster is called a "Local Group" containing 2 to 4 trillion stars. The radius of our Local

---

[1632] Yorgason, *I Need Thee Every Hour*, 395–98; quoting 2 Peter 1:19; McConkie, *Mormon Doctrine*, 217; Smith, *Teachings of the Prophet Joseph Smith*, 325; D&C 1:38; 131:5; emphasis added; Smith, *Teachings of the Prophet Joseph Smith*, 326.
[1633] D&C 84:39–40.
[1634] Moses 1:33–38.
[1635] Asay, "The Oath and Covenant of the Priesthood," 43.
[1636] "Galaxy Map," *National Geographic Society*, June 1983.

Group is two million light years. But it is only a dot in the universe. Local Groups tend to congregate in "Local Superclusters," which are the largest of celestial formations. Each "Local Supercluster" may be comprised of thousands of member galaxies. The Local Supercluster in which we reside has a radius of 75 million light years. As incredible as these numbers might seem, nothing is more unfathomable than the fact that our Local Supercluster is still a mere speck in the known universe. And there is no visible end to these creations! When this National Geographic article was written in 1983, astronomers could not have imagined that the dots in far reaches of space they were mapping would one day be identified as numerous Superclusters. With the help of advanced technology, astronomers now estimate that the *known* universe is comprised of some 125 billion galaxies, and, as Enoch exclaimed to the Lord, "Thy curtains are stretched out still!"[1637]

If by means of modern telescopes we are able see to this extent, imagine what Moses was able to see by the power of God! And yet God had to limit that vision of his creations in order to keep Moses in the flesh.[1638] Enoch saw this same vision. Within that context, he viewed the eternal resting place of his Zion people, and, in a universal sense, he saw his Zion in relation to all the creations of God. In awe, he exclaimed, "And thou hast taken Zion to thine own bosom, *from all thy creations,* from all eternity to all eternity."[1639]

All of this the Father offers us. Clearly, we who strive to become Zionlike will be richly rewarded for our investment of faithfulness. The scriptures describe our reward as inheriting "thrones, kingdoms, principalities, and powers, dominions, all heights and depths." We will move on from this telestial realm to surmount the heavens and "pass by the angels, and the gods, which are set there, to [our] exaltation and glory in all things, as hath been sealed upon [our] heads, which glory shall be a fulness and a continuation of the seeds forever and ever."[1640] Numberless worlds, innumerable posterity, and eternal, exalted life—such are the blessings of the oath and covenant of the priesthood! Failing to find adequate language to describe these blessings, the apostle Paul conceded, "Eye hath not seen, nor ear heard, neither have entered into the heart of man, the things which God hath prepared for them that love him."[1641]

These are Father's gifts that he guarantees us in his oath. By revelation, the Prophet wrote, "Wherefore, all things are theirs. . . . These shall dwell in the presence of God and his Christ forever and ever. . . . They who dwell in his presence are the church of the Firstborn; . . . and he makes them equal in power, and in might, and in dominion."[1642] This is the condition and destiny of Zion people.

Ministering and Protection of Angels

The oath and covenant of the priesthood contains the Lord's special promise of angelic help, counsel, and protection to accomplish our work upon the earth: "I have given the heavenly hosts and mine angels charge concerning you."[1643] In that same revelation, the Lord adds, "And whoso receiveth you, there I will be also, for I will go before your face. I will be on your right hand and on your left, and my Spirit shall be in your hearts, and mine angels round about you, to bear you up."[1644] Zion people are continually blessed by and become conversant with angels.

[1637] Moses 7:30.
[1638] Moses 1:4.
[1639] Moses 7:31.
[1640] D&C 132:19.
[1641] 1 Corinthians 2:9.
[1642] D&C 76:59, 62, 94–95.
[1643] D&C 84:42.
[1644] D&C 84:88.

The Father's Oath, Instructions, and Promises

Angelic ministrations may come as visitations or promptings, but in any case, these ministrations occur under the direction of the Holy Ghost, for "angels speak by the power of the Holy Ghost."[1645] According to the scriptures, angelic ministrations are for the purposes of:

- Delivering messages.[1646]
- Ministering and prophesying.[1647]
- Teaching doctrines of salvation.[1648]
- Calling us to repentance.[1649]
- Rescuing us from peril.[1650]
- Helping us to fight our battles.[1651]
- Guiding us in the performance of our work.[1652]
- Helping us to find and bless others with the gospel.[1653]
- Helping us to perform all needful things relative to God's work.[1654]
- Comforting us, as the angel comforted Jesus in his Gethsemane.[1655]

The promise of angelic ministration includes several different types of beings, broadly classed as "heavenly hosts."[1656] These beings are members of the Church of the Firstborn, another name for Zion, the heavenly church whose faithful members are prepared by the earthly Church of Jesus Christ of Latter-day Saints,[1657] also another name for Zion, or Zion in process. The Church of the Firstborn is made up of resurrected beings, translated beings, premortal spirits, spirits of the deceased (who are called "just men made perfect"[1658]) and righteous mortal beings. Each being can function as an angel, and each type of being has specific powers. If we are worthy, we will "have the rights of fellowship and communion 'with the general assembly and church of the Firstborn' (D&C 107:19), meaning those faithful members whose names 'are written in heaven' (Hebrews 12:23), referring to Saints on both sides of the veil."[1659] Angels!

Zionlike people, people of the Covenant, they who have received the holy priesthood by covenant, are *never* left alone. And neither are their children. Embedded in Jesus' instructions on ministering to his little ones is the comforting phrase: "In heaven their angels do always behold the face of my Father which is in heaven."[1660] Angels are continually around us, serving, blessing, and protecting us. Joseph Smith taught, "The spirits of the just are exalted to a greater and more glorious work; hence they are blessed in their departure to the world of spirits. Enveloped in flaming fire, they

---

[1645] 2 Nephi 32:3; see also 1 Nephi 17:45.
[1646] Luke 1:11–38.
[1647] Acts 10:1–8, 30–32.
[1648] Mosiah 3.
[1649] Moroni 7:31.
[1650] 1 Nephi 3:29–31; Daniel 6:22.
[1651] 2 Kings 6:15–17.
[1652] Genesis 24:7.
[1653] Matthew 24:31.
[1654] Moroni 7:29–33.
[1655] Luke 22:42-43.
[1656] D&C 84:42.
[1657] McConkie, *Mormon Doctrine*, 139–40.
[1658] D&C 76:69; 129:3; Hebrews 12:23.
[1659] Farley, "The Oath and Covenant of the Priesthood," 50.
[1660] Matthew 18:10.

are not far from us, and know and understand our thoughts, feelings, and motions, and are often pained therewith."[1661]

Who are these ministering angels? Often they are our deceased relatives, friends, and people with whom we have labored in the work of the Lord. President Joseph F. Smith said, "When messengers are sent to minister to the inhabitants of this earth, they are not strangers, but from the ranks of our kindred, friends, and fellow-beings and fellow-servants. . . . Our fathers and mothers, brothers, sisters and friends who have passed away from this earth, having been faithful, and worthy to enjoy these rights and privileges, may have a mission given them to visit their relatives and friends upon the earth again, bringing from the divine Presence messages of love, of warning, or reproof and instruction, to those whom they had learned to love in the flesh."[1662] In President Smith's vision of the spirit world, he declared, "I beheld that the faithful elders [and sisters] of this dispensation, when they depart from mortal life, continue their labors in the preaching of the gospel of repentance and redemption, through the sacrifice of the Only Begotten Son of God, among those who are in darkness and under the bondage of sin in the great world of the spirits of the dead."[1663]

To discount the reality of the constant ministering by angels is to deny one of the supernal blessings of Zion and the restored gospel—a central blessing pertaining to both the Aaronic and Melchizedek priesthoods. As Moroni was closing the Book of Mormon, he quoted his father, Mormon, who exhorted us to believe in miracles and in the ministering of angels: "Wherefore, if these things [miracles and the ministering of angels] have ceased wo be unto the children of men, for it is because of unbelief, and all is vain."[1664] In other words, without heavenly help we are left to ourselves to struggle through life without a shield to deflect the adversary's blows. We are alone, and trying to find meaning in life is vain.

Because we are children of God, we have planted within our souls the innate desire to do the work of God. But in our fallen condition we can do very little. When it comes to redeeming others and bringing them to Zion, we are often limited to loving and exhorting them, praying for them, and bearing testimony—that is, we can only attempt to create an atmosphere in which the Spirit can function. We are not equipped to change a person's heart, provide him a spiritual experience, or rescue him from spiritual death. That is the special work of the Godhead. To achieve any spiritual goal, we must order our lives according to our covenants and petition the Father in the name of Christ for help. His response will come by the Holy Ghost, who may deliver God's messages and blessings to us through the ministering of angels, who are other Zionlike people sent to help us become Zion people.

Of our exhortation to believe in the ministration of angels and expect their help, LDS writer and family life specialist H. Wallace Goddard, wrote,

When we impose mortal constraints on eternal doings, we are surely selling heaven short. As the Prophet Joseph observed, "It is the constitutional disposition of mankind to set up stakes and set bounds to the works and ways of the Almighty." If we limit heaven's doings by our rules and assumptions, we will shortchange Heaven and ourselves. Maybe a set of laws very different from those we know for mortality governs the doings of immortals. My propositions for the laws that govern immortals include the following:

1. Immortals love us and yearn to be a part of our lives. There is nothing they enjoy more than serving the family and friends who literally mean everything to them.

[1661] Burton, *Discourses of the Prophet Joseph Smith*, 128.
[1662] Smith, *Gospel Doctrine*, 435.
[1663] D&C 138:57.
[1664] Moroni 7:37.

2. Those who live in eternity are not everlastingly at odds with time. While those in the spirit world may not be fully free of the constraints of time, surely they do not struggle with time the way we do.

3. Immortals can only participate fully in our lives when we allow them to. They are not allowed to intrude on our lives uninvited but may take part as we appropriately invite them to take part.

4. They will not violate our agency (nor do our chores), but they gladly teach us, love us, reassure us, and guide us according to heavenly wisdom.

5. Though it may take us years to learn to hear their language, they already know us and our language.[1665]

President James E. Faust taught that angelic ministration is the common right and experience of all Zion people in every dispensation. Angels have always appeared or prompted the Saints by giving instruction, warnings, and direction. We underestimate the extent to which they affect our lives. Their ministry has always been an important part of the gospel.[1666]

Our entrance into the new and everlasting covenant through baptism and confirmation blesses us with the gift of the ministering of angels through the gift of the Holy Ghost. These two gifts are inseparable. As we partake of the sacrament and renew the Covenant, the blessing of the Lord's Spirit—the Holy Ghost—to always be with us is renewed and confirmed. This promise of the companionship of the Holy Ghost carries with it the promise of angelic ministration. When worthy men receive the Aaronic Priesthood, the promise of ministering angels is renewed, confirmed, and magnified. This priesthood holds the "keys of the ministering of angels."[1667] This additional promise of angelic ministration now provides us heavenly help to do our priesthood duty.

We receive the promise of angelic help again when we are ordained to the Melchizedek Priesthood. Once more, that promise is renewed, confirmed, and magnified in the oath and covenant of the priesthood. This time we receive the promise of angelic help with the Father's oath.[1668] With the Melchizedek Priesthood, the blessings of angelic ministration multiply. Through the ministering of angels, Melchizedek priesthood holders who are worthy have "the privilege of receiving the mysteries of the kingdom of heaven, to have the heavens opened unto them, to commune with the general assembly and church of the Firstborn, and to enjoy the communion and presence of God the Father, and Jesus the mediator of the new covenant."[1669] These supernal blessings are associated with the oath and covenant of the priesthood, which promise the angelic ministration and continuing help from the hosts of heaven.

Such are the promises given to Zion people—"they who are come unto Mount Zion, and unto the city of the living God, the heavenly place, the holiest of all . . . they who have come to an innumerable company of angels, to the general assembly and church of Enoch, and of the Firstborn."[1670]

THE FATHER'S INSTRUCTIONS: *BE CAREFUL AND BE DILIGENT*

By way of commandment, as stated in the priesthood covenant, the Father charges us to beware—to be careful or to *take care*—concerning our diligence to the words of eternal life. Why? Because the oath and covenant of the priesthood carries the promise of exaltation: "And I now give unto you a commandment to beware [be careful] concerning yourselves, to give diligent heed to the words of

---

[1665] Goddard, "Blessed by Angels"; quoting Smith, *Teachings of the Prophet Joseph Smith*, 320.
[1666] Faust, "A Royal Priesthood," 50–53.
[1667] D&C 13:1.
[1668] D&C 84:39–42.
[1669] D&C 107:18–19.
[1670] D&C 76:66–67.

eternal life."[1671] Carelessness, negligence, or rejection of the priesthood covenant results in the Father's condemnation and the cessation of the priesthood rights and promises.[1672] On the other hand, President Romney said, obedience, or giving careful diligence to the words of eternal life, entitles us to the priesthood covenant's blessings and rewards.

Expounding on the commandment to be careful and give diligent heed to the words of eternal life, S. Brent Farley says, "This verse is a key verse within the oath and covenant of the priesthood. It leads one to an understanding of how to obtain the fulness of the oath and covenant of the priesthood."[1673] This commandment precedes the Father's instruction: "For you shall live by every word that proceedeth forth from the mouth of God."[1674] This instruction suggests that we are obligated to search and learn the revealed word of the Lord. And where are the words of eternal life found? In the scriptures; the teachings of the prophets and apostles; the inspired words of parents, teachers, and local leaders; and direct revelation from the Holy Ghost. In each case, as we search and learn the words of eternal life, the Holy Ghost will confirm them to us by personal revelation.[1675]

Brother Farley says, "How one receives these words is next explained in a chain of logic: 'For the word of the Lord is truth, and whatsoever is truth is light, and whatsoever is light is Spirit, even the Spirit of Jesus Christ. And the Spirit giveth light to every man that cometh into the world; and the Spirit enlighteneth every man through the world, that hearkeneth to the voice of the Spirit.' Elder McConkie explained that the light of Christ 'is the instrumentality and agency by which Deity keeps in touch and communes with all his children, both the righteous and the wicked. It has an edifying, enlightening, and uplifting influence on men. . . . It is the means by which the Lord invites and entices all men to improve their lot and to come unto him and receive his gospel.'"[1676]

Thus, we are commanded to be careful and diligent to the words of eternal life because they are essential to our becoming Zion people. The words of eternal life flow to us by our sincerely searching the scriptures and the prophets, and these words are confirmed to us by testimony of the Holy Ghost. The result of this process is coming unto God, which is the premier purpose of the Melchizedek Priesthood. Quoting Doctrine and Covenants 84:47, S. Brent Farley says, "'And every one that hearkeneth to the voice of the Spirit cometh unto God, even the Father.' Elder McConkie explained: 'By following the light of Christ, men are led to the gospel covenant, to the baptismal covenant, to the church and kingdom. There they receive the Holy Ghost.' Those who are sensitive to the Holy Ghost continue to learn the words of God and direct their lives according to his counsel. Faithful brethren are led by this process to the oath and covenant of the priesthood."[1677] By following this process to its perfect conclusion, being careful and giving diligent heed, Zion people ultimately receive the fulness of the priesthood covenant's promise: *eternal life*.

"AND THE FATHER TEACHETH HIM OF THE COVENANT"

As we have learned, it is with the Father that we make the oath and covenant of the priesthood. He is the one who takes both the responsibility and the initiative to teach us concerning the priesthood covenant. Herein lies the predominant key to learning the covenant's doctrine and scope. The

---

[1671] D&C 84:43.

[1672] D&C 84:41.

[1673] Farley, "The Oath and Covenant of the Priesthood," 51.

[1674] D&C 84:44.

[1675] Asay, "The Oath and Covenant of the Priesthood," 43.

[1676] Farley, "The Oath and Covenant of the Priesthood," 51; quoting McConkie, *A New Witness for the Articles of Faith*, 258, 260.

[1677] Farley, "The Oath and Covenant of the Priesthood," 51; quoting McConkie, *A New Witness for the Articles of Faith*, 258, 260.

Father's promise reads: "And the Father teacheth him of the covenant which he has renewed and confirmed upon you."[1678]

The covenantal promise contained in this clause speaks to the Father's taking direct charge of our priesthood education. Through our faithfulness and by personal revelation, line upon line, distilling intelligence upon us as the dews from heaven, the Father rains priesthood knowledge upon our souls until we are saturated in it. This doctrine is unknown in the world and not widely known in the Church, Elder McConkie taught. The priesthood information that the Father distils upon us cannot fully be learned in the scriptures or even in the teachings of the prophets. God reserves the right to teach the doctrine of the priesthood by the Holy Ghost to those who love and serve him completely.[1679] S. Brent Farley taught, "Sufficient scriptural information is given to place a brother upon the pathway of exaltation, but the printed word in the standard works is not the culmination point. It is an aid in helping one to progress to the point where *revelation is the key* in magnifying a calling and in learning more about the oath and covenant of the priesthood."[1680] The doctrine of the priesthood, therefore, is one of the sublime mysteries of the kingdom that we are entitled to learn by personal revelation by means of the Melchizedek Priesthood ordinances.[1681]

We insert a stipulation and a caution here. It is the Father's prerogative—not ours—to reveal to us the covenant and doctrine of the priesthood. That he may choose to instruct us through his authorized servants in the order of the priesthood is a distinct possibility, but, as Elder McConkie stated, this sacred information is so individualized that it cannot be fully learned even in the scriptures or through the prophets. It is learned by revelation. Therefore, because the Father's revelations are tailor-made to our needs, and because they are his to give, we must be careful how and from whom we choose to receive them. The Father has specifically commanded, "Thou shalt have no other gods before me."[1682] To set another person before God, from whom we would receive this specialized education, is to step into idolatry. Our effort should be to live righteously and hone the essential spiritual skills so as to invite personal revelation. Brigham Young said,

There is one principle that I wish the people would understand and lay to heart. Just as fast as you will prove before your God that you are worthy to receive the mysteries, if you please to call them so, of the Kingdom of heaven—that you are full of confidence in God—that you will never betray a thing that God tells you—that you will never reveal to your neighbor that which ought not to be revealed, as quick as you prepare to be entrusted with the things of God, there is an eternity of them to bestow upon you. Instead of pleading with the Lord to bestow more upon you, plead with yourselves to have confidence in yourselves, to have integrity in yourselves, and know when to speak and what to speak, what to reveal, and how to carry yourselves and walk before the Lord. And just as fast as you prove to him that you will preserve everything secret that ought to be—that you will deal out to your neighbors all which you ought, and no more, and learn how to dispense your knowledge to your families, friends, neighbors, and brethren, the Lord will bestow upon you, and give to you, and bestow upon you, until finally he will say to you, "You shall never fall; your salvation is sealed unto you; you are sealed up unto eternal life and salvation, through your integrity."[1683]

Of retaining integrity to the revelations of God, Alma explained, "It is given unto many to know the mysteries of God; nevertheless they are laid under a strict command that they shall not impart only according to the portion of his word which he doth grant unto the children of men, according to the heed and diligence which they give unto him." Mysteries are things that can be received only by

---

[1678] D&C 84:48.
[1679] McConkie, "The Doctrine of the Priesthood," 32.
[1680] Farley, "The Oath and Covenant of the Priesthood," 52.
[1681] D&C 84:19–22.
[1682] Exodus 20:3.
[1683] Young, *Discourses of Brigham Young*, 93.

revelation. Because they might exceed the general doctrines set forth by prophets and in the scriptures, we are under "strict command" to not impart them, so as not to step in front of our file leaders—and so that we don't share them with those who are not ready. We are only allowed to impart "according to the portion of his word which he doth grant unto the children of men," and then only "according to the heed and diligence which they give unto him." But seek the mysteries we must, for in them lies the Father's instruction on the doctrine of the priesthood. Alma said, "And therefore, he that will harden his heart, the same receiveth the lesser portion of the word; and he that will not harden his heart, to him is given the greater portion of the word, until it is given unto him to know the mysteries of God until he know them in full. And they that will harden their hearts, to them is given the lesser portion of the word until they know nothing concerning his mysteries; and then they are taken captive by the devil, and led by his will down to destruction. Now this is what is meant by the chains of hell."[1684] Clearly, our protection and salvation depend upon our seeking and receiving the Father's instruction.

This level of divine education that the Father provides is not possible, of course, unless we exercise the priesthood properly. Therefore, the Lord directs: "Let thy bowels also be full of charity towards all men, and to the household of faith, and let virtue garnish thy thoughts unceasingly; then shall thy confidence wax strong in the presence of God; *and the doctrine of the priesthood shall distil upon thy soul as the dews from heaven.*"[1685] This instruction is the key that opens the door to the Father's priesthood education, and the means by which we progress within the oath and covenant of the priesthood.

Concerning personal revelation, Joseph Smith taught John Taylor, "If you be true to [the Spirit's] whisperings it will in time become in you a principle of revelation, so that you will know all things."[1686] The Prophet also taught, "A person may profit by noticing the first intimation of the spirit of revelation; for instance, when you feel pure intelligence flowing into you, it may give you sudden strokes of ideas, so that by noticing it, you may find it fulfilled the same day or soon; (i.e.) those things that were presented unto your minds by the Spirit of God, will come to pass; and thus by learning the Spirit of God and understanding it, you may grow unto the principle of revelation, until you become perfect in Christ Jesus."[1687] The Father teaches us the doctrine of the priesthood in this way.

In time, the day will come when we will be able to stand in his presence and receive intelligence from him face to face, which describes Zion people. This ultimate blessing is a right and part of the doctrine of the priesthood. To this end, the Lord commands: "Sanctify yourselves that your minds become single to God, and the days will come that you will see him; *for he will unveil his face unto you*, and it shall be in his own time, and in his own way, and according to his own will."[1688] And again, "And *seek the face of the Lord always*, that in patience ye may possess your souls, and ye shall have eternal life."[1689] Such is the condition of Zion people, for we read: "The Lord came and dwelt with his people, and they dwelt in righteousness."[1690]

THE PROMISE OF ETERNAL LIFE

Over and over, the oath and covenant of the priesthood points us to the promise of eternal life, the outcome of making our calling and election sure. This promise is such a prevalent theme in the priesthood covenant that we are obliged to consider it as the focal point. To accomplish this lofty

---

[1684] Alma 12:9–11.
[1685] D&C 121:45.
[1686] Taylor, *Journal of Discourses*, 19:154.
[1687] Smith, *Teachings of the Prophet Joseph Smith*, 151.
[1688] D&C 88:68; emphasis added.
[1689] D&C 101:38; emphasis added.
[1690] Moses 7:16.

goal, the Lord reveals to us a sacred pattern to follow and endows us with power from on high to pursue that pattern. As we have discussed, sacred revelatory privileges and powers—"keys," as Joseph Smith called them[1691]—are granted to faithful Melchizedek Priesthood holders. The most powerful manifestation of these "keys" is found in the temple ordinances. The scripture reads: "[The Melchizedek Priesthood] holdeth the key of the mysteries of the kingdom, even the key of the knowledge of God. Therefore, in the ordinances thereof, the power of godliness is manifest."[1692] As the Father teaches us the intricacies of the priesthood covenant, he also reveals to us the uses, powers, and blessings of these "keys."

Blaine Yorgason notes that the definition of the word *keys* has somewhat migrated since the early days of the Restoration. "The Lord, His modern prophets, and others who have been closely associated with them frequently refer to the ordinances of the priesthood, as administered in the temple, as 'keys' or 'keys of the priesthood.' In our day, however, such usage has become more narrowly or carefully defined. Now the word 'keys' or the phrase 'keys of the priesthood,' . . . refer specifically to the powers and authority held in fullness by the president of the Church and passed down from him by ordination or setting apart through specific lines of priesthood authority."[1693]

These ordinances, or *keys* (speaking in the earlier sense), are the ordered manner by which we may obtain the power to speak with God in his presence—the ultimate form of revelation. In fact, these keys are the only way to return to God's presence and "enter into his rest, which rest is the fulness of his glory"[1694]—*eternal life*. This quality of *rest* is the condition in which Zion and its people reside. Once again, we encounter the subject of making our calling and election sure in the oath and covenant of the priesthood. This is the revealed promise of our eventual exaltation or the guarantee of eternal life that Elder Romney confirmed comes only by a divine witness.[1695] Our faithful persistence in the priesthood covenant leads to this revelation. To teach this truth, Elder McConkie wrote a fourth verse to the hymn, "Come Listen to a Prophet's Voice." It reads:

Then heed the words of truth and light
That flow from fountains pure.
Yea, keep His law with all thy might
Till thine election's sure,
Till thou shalt hear the holy voice
Assure eternal reign,
While joy and cheer attend thy choice,
As one who shall obtain.[1696]

Alma said it this way: "And whosoever doeth this [repentance and baptism], and keepeth the commandments of God from thenceforth, the same will remember that I say unto him, yea, he will remember that I have said unto him, *he shall have eternal life.*"[1697]

Joseph Smith received the promise of eternal life by revelation: "For I am the Lord thy God, and will be with thee even unto the end of the world, and through all eternity; for verily I seal upon you your exaltation, and prepare a throne for you in the kingdom of my Father, with Abraham your

---

[1691] Smith, *History of the Church*, 4:608; 5:1–2; Smith, *Teachings of the Prophet Joseph Smith*, 226; *Juvenile Instructor*, June 1, 1892, 345; Smith, *The Words of Joseph Smith*, 54, footnote 19.
[1692] D&C 84:19–20.
[1693] Yorgason, *I Need Thee Every Hour*, 367.
[1694] D&C 84:22–24.
[1695] Romney, Conference Report, Oct. 1965, 20.
[1696] McConkie, "Come Listen to a Prophet's Voice," fourth verse, *Hymns*, no. 21.
[1697] Alma 7:16; emphasis added.

father."¹⁶⁹⁸ We recall that the calling and election made sure is both a revelation and an ordinance associated with the more sure word of prophecy. Of the revelation, Blaine Yorgason writes, "Throughout history, even when the blessings of receiving the fullness of the priesthood have not been readily available, righteous men and women who have progressed spiritually to the fullest extent possible have obtained the voice of God declaring their callings and elections to be sure. Thus Moses taught, '[The approval of God] was delivered unto men by *the calling of his own voice,* according to his own will, unto as many as believed on his name' (JST Genesis 14:29)."¹⁶⁹⁹

A survey of the scriptures and historical journals reveals multiple ways whereby this promise of eternal life is delivered. Each communication might be as unique as there are recipients. For example, James T. Summerhays writes:

On June 9, 1830, the newly restored Church held its first conference. About thirty members attended. After singing and prayer, many began to prophesy, when several had the visions of heaven unveiled to them. So overcome were these visionaries that it was necessary to find beds or some location to safely lay them down. One of these, Newel Knight, could not understand why his fellow Saints were making such a fuss to lay him on a bed; his spirit was soaring so high that he did not notice that his body was helpless. As they lay him down, a vision burst upon his view. "He saw heaven opened, and beheld the Lord Jesus Christ, seated at the right hand of the majesty on high," recounts Joseph Smith, "and had it made plain to his understanding that the time would come when he would be admitted into His presence to enjoy His society for ever and ever."

The Colesville Branch of the Church, having lived in the relative civility of New York and Ohio, followed the call to resettle on the frontier in Jackson County, Missouri. At first, the branch had neither tents nor implements to farm with. They had little to eat but some beef and cornmeal made by rubbing ears of corn against an old tin grater. Yet when the Prophet visited them, he found them in a lively mood. Amid what for lesser people would have been a plight of abject misery, the Colesville Branch welcomed their Prophet as had those that once shouted Hosanna at Christ's triumphal entry into Jerusalem; they rejoiced as the ancient Saints had when Paul returned from his long dispersion. Joseph, overcome with their greatness of soul and generosity of heart, gathered them together and did something that caused a considerable stir among those that witnessed it—he sealed up the branch, all present, to Eternal Life.¹⁷⁰⁰

Of his own experience, Heber C. Kimball wrote:

I returned to Far West, April 5th. My family having been gone about two months, during which time I heard nothing from them; our brethren being in prison; death and destruction following us everywhere we went; I felt very sorrowful and lonely. The following words came to my mind, and the Spirit said unto me, 'write,' which I did by taking a piece of paper and writing on my knee as follows: FAR WEST, April 6th, 1839. A word from the Spirit of the Lord to my servant, Heber C. Kimball: Verily I say unto my servant Heber, thou art my son, in whom I am well pleased; for thou art careful to hearken to my words, and not transgress my law, nor rebel against my servant Joseph Smith, for thou hast a respect to the words of mine anointed, even from the least to the greatest of them; *therefore thy name is written in heaven, no more to be blotted out for ever,* because of these things; and this Spirit and blessing shall rest down upon thy posterity for ever and ever; for they shall be called after thy name, for thou shalt have many more sons and daughters, for thy seed shall be as numerous as the sands upon the sea shore; therefore, my servant Heber, be faithful, go forth in my name and I will go with you, and be on your right hand and on your left and my angels shall go before you and raise you up when you are cast down and afflicted; remember that I am always with you, even to the end,

---

¹⁶⁹⁸ D&C 132:49.

¹⁶⁹⁹ Yorgason, *I Need Thee Every Hour,* 387–88.

¹⁷⁰⁰ Summerhays, "The Stripling Exalted," Feb. 20, 2009; quoting Smith, *History of the Church,* 1:85; Jessee, "Joseph Knight's Recollection of Early Mormon History," 39.

therefore be of good cheer, my son, and my spirit shall be in your heart to teach you the peaceable things of the kingdom.[1701]

Notice that the Lord repeated to Elder Kimball the oath given in the covenant of the priesthood. The Lord also confirmed that Elder Kimball would obtain eternal life, as the covenant promises. In this man's case, the Lord revealed the assurance of exaltation directly to Elder Kimball's mind. In the case of Mary Elizabeth Rollins Lightner, Joseph Smith, an authorized servant of God, delivered the revelation to her and others. In an address at Brigham Young University in 1905, she said,

Joseph looked around very solemnly. It was the first time some of them had ever seen him. Said he, "There are enough here to hold a little meeting." They got a board and put it across two chairs to make seats. Martin Harris sat on a little box at Joseph's feet. They sang and prayed. Joseph got up and began to speak to us. As he began to speak very solemnly and very earnestly, all at once his countenance changed and he stood mute. Those who looked at him that day said there was a search light within him, over every part of his body. I never saw anything like it on the earth. I could not take my eyes off him; he got so white that anyone who saw him would have thought he was transparent. I remember I thought I could almost see the cheek bones through the flesh. I have been through many changes since but that is photographed on my brain. I shall remember it and see in my mind's eye as long as I remain upon the earth. He stood some moments. He looked over the congregation as if to pierce every heart. He said, "Do you know who has been in your midst?" One of the Smiths said an angel of the Lord. Martin Harris said, "It was our Lord and Savior, Jesus Christ." Joseph put his hand down on Martin and said: "God revealed that to you. Brethren and sisters, the Spirit of God has been here. The Savior has been in your midst this night and I want you to remember it. There is a veil over your eyes for you could not endure to look upon Him. You must be fed with milk, not with strong meat. I want you to remember this as if it were the last thing that escaped my lips. *He has given all of you to me and has sealed you up to everlasting life that where he is, you may be also.* And if you are tempted of Satan say, 'Get behind me, Satan.'" These words are figured upon my brain and I never took my eye off his countenance. Then he knelt down and prayed. I have never heard anything like it before or since. I felt that he was talking to the Lord and that power rested down upon the congregation. Every soul felt it. The spirit rested upon us in every fiber of our bodies, and we received a sermon from the lips of the representative of God.[1702]

Expounding on the Father's oath and promise of eternal life, S. Brent Farley says, "As the Lord confirmed the priesthood by his own voice out of the heavens to his servants (D&C 84:42), so may he confirm the promise of eternal life [to us], whether in this life or the next. The fulfillment of that promise of eternal life is the grand purpose of the oath and covenant of the priesthood. Every worthy priesthood holder may qualify if he will keep the covenants of the priesthood."[1703]

President Joseph Fielding Smith taught that no promises are more glorious than those given to us in the oath and covenant of the priesthood.[1704] The Father's oath brings to pass the noblest goal of existence: "For behold, this is my work and my glory—to bring to pass the immortality and eternal life of man."[1705]

Penalties for Neglecting or Rejecting the Covenant of the Priesthood

Sobering consequences follow those who take their priesthood covenant lightly or who break it after they have made it. Equally grave penalties await those who refuse to accept the covenant once they have been offered it. The Lord warns: "But whoso breaketh this covenant after he hath received it,

---

[1701] Whitney, *Life of Heber C. Kimball*, 241–242; emphasis added.
[1702] Lightner, Address at Brigham Young University, 1905, 1; emphasis added.
[1703] Farley, "The Oath and Covenant of the Priesthood," 53.
[1704] Smith, Conference Report, Oct. 1970, 92.
[1705] Moses 1:39.

and altogether turneth therefrom, shall not have forgiveness of sins in this world nor in the world to come."[1706] And to those who refuse to enter into the priesthood covenant, the Lord cautions: "And wo unto all those who come not unto this priesthood."[1707] The word *wo* suggests condemnation, distress, misery, and calamity.[1708] Whatever leads to a person's choice for neglecting this covenant, the dire consequence is the same.[1709]

Although this is a solemn declaration, it is not necessarily equated to becoming a son of perdition. Elder McConkie wrote: "This has never been interpreted by the Brethren to mean that those who forsake their priesthood duties, altogether turning therefrom, shall be sons of perdition; rather, the meaning seems to be that they shall be denied the exaltation that otherwise might have been theirs."[1710] S. Brent Farley writes: "President Joseph Fielding Smith explained that there is a chance to repent if a man has not altogether turned from the priesthood. If he does altogether turn from it, however, there is no forgiveness."[1711] The meaning of these two condemnations, said President Smith, is that a man who neglects or rejects the covenant will be denied forever the privilege of exercising the priesthood and thus achieving eternal life. That man will no longer be associated with Zion. He will forfeit Zion's blessings, the holy priesthood, and the privileges that are associated with exaltation—and he will never again be offered those blessings![1712] Brother Farley concludes, "As the priesthood is the only source and channel through which exaltation may be obtained from the Lord, it follows that those who avoid it also avoid their only chance for eternal happiness in the celestial kingdom."[1713]

Summary and Conclusion

We, who strive to become worthy Zionlike men, seek for the Melchizedek Priesthood and its blessings by entering into the oath and covenant of the priesthood. Our primary qualification is to have received and been faithful to the new and everlasting covenant—the first pillar of Zion, which contains the first promise of eternal life. Thereafter, we must have lived worthily to have received the Aaronic Priesthood by covenant. Then, having proven worthy of these two covenants and having prepared ourselves through righteous living, the Father, through his authorized servant, will offer us the Melchizedek Priesthood, the authority of God. We receive this priesthood by means of the oath and covenant of the priesthood—the second pillar of Zion, which contains the second promise of eternal life.

The oath and covenant of the priesthood repeats our previous *calls* and *elections* (selections) to and for eternal life. These we received premortally and when we were baptized. These calls and elections were provisional and needed to be made *sure*. A primary purpose of the oath and covenant of the priesthood is to obtain personal salvation—to make our calling and election *sure*. The second purpose of the priesthood covenant is to do the work of God by bringing people to Christ. We could not accomplish this work without the authority of God. The priesthood obligates and empowers us to raise our voices in testimony, which is a vehicle to convey the Spirit to others, and to bless the Father's children with the covenants, ordinances, and blessings of the new and everlasting covenant.

We enter the oath and covenant of the priesthood by agreeing to faithfulness, obtaining the Aaronic Priesthood and Melchizedek Priesthood, receiving Christ and his Father, living by every word

---

[1706] D&C 84:41.
[1707] D&C 84:42.
[1708] *American Heritage Dictionary*, s.v. "woe."
[1709] Eyring, "Faith and the Oath and Covenant of the Priesthood," 61–64.
[1710] McConkie, *A New Witness for the Articles of Faith*, 232.
[1711] Farley, "The Oath and Covenant of the Priesthood," 50.
[1712] Smith, Conference Report, Oct. 1970, 92.
[1713] Farley, "The Oath and Covenant of the Priesthood," 50.

that proceeds from the mouth of God, and magnifying our singular priesthood *calling*.[1714] Three ways to magnify our calling are:

1. Obtaining gospel knowledge.
2. Personal righteousness by compliance with gospel standards.
3. Giving dedicated service.[1715]

Ultimately, to magnify our priesthood calling means to become like God. To do that we must make temple covenants, receive temple ordinances, and marry for eternity. Then we must endure worthily in these covenants to the end. Zion's purity, ideal, and eternal life can be achieved in no other way.

The Father enters the covenant of the priesthood with us by swearing an oath. In doing so, he places his godhood on the line in warranting that every promise he makes in the priesthood covenant will be fulfilled, contingent on our faithfulness to the covenant. The Father promises us all of the blessings of our fathers: Abraham, Isaac, and Jacob. He promises that the Holy Ghost will sanctify us and renew our bodies so that we might become capable of fulfilling our priesthood calling and callings, and so that we might be made fit for eternal life.

We receive the Melchizedek Priesthood for two reasons: "for your sake, and not for your sake only, but for the sake of the whole world."[1716] As we sanctify ourselves and as the Spirit sanctifies us, we gain power upon power in the priesthood. Then, as we bless others with the blessings that God gives us, we grow from grace *to* grace by giving grace *for* grace. Increasingly, we become more and more like the Savior; we become saviors on Mount Zion[1717] for both the living and the dead, authorized and empowered to assist in the eternal redemptive work of God. We gain heightened ability to bring people to Christ so that they, too, might receive the blessings of immortal glory and "eternal lives."[1718] The process of receiving blessings and giving them away sanctifies, renews, and magnifies us until we become like God, can stand in his presence, receive all that he has, and become all that he is. The Spirit's sanctification renews our heart, so that it is filled with saving love—*charity*: "the end of the commandment"[1719] and "the crowning virtue."[1720]

In the oath and covenant of the priesthood, the Father promises that we will become the sons of Moses and of Aaron, and thus we are eternally identified with these great brethren and authorized to do their works. Moreover, he promises that we will become the seed of Abraham with the reconfirmed assurance that we, and our children through us, will retain and have rights to all of the gospel blessings, including the new and everlasting covenant and the oath and covenant of the priesthood. Additionally, the Father declares that we are his Church and Kingdom. Wherever we go and whatever we do, we represent him and his Church. Because we hold the high priesthood, by which he places upon us his name, we literally are the kingdom of God. As we minister among his children, we, like the Seventy of old, can say to the people with authority, "The kingdom of heaven is come nigh unto you."[1721]

In the priesthood covenant, the Father promises us angelic ministration and protection as we function in the priesthood. He promises that we will become his elect—called and selected on

---

[1714] D&C 84:33.
[1715] Romney, "'The Oath and Covenant Which Belongeth to the Priesthood,'" 43.
[1716] D&C 84:48.
[1717] Obadiah 1:21.
[1718] Smith, *Teachings of the Prophet Joseph Smith*, 322; Moses 1:39.
[1719] 1 Timothy 1:5.
[1720] McConkie, *Mormon Doctrine*, 121.
[1721] Luke 10:9.

account of our good works. Our priesthood calling in the flesh is an extension of the work in which we were engaged in the premortal world: the work of redemption. Now we are once again authorized and empowered to continue that work. As we continue our work, magnify our priesthood calling and callings, and give diligent heed to the words of eternal life, the day will come when the Father, by revelation, will declare our calling and election *sure*. The associated ordinance called the more sure word of prophecy will either precede or follow that revelation. That revelation fulfills his oath, guaranteeing to us all that he has. Moreover, he promises to make us equal to him in might, power, and dominion. In all these supernal blessings, Jesus Christ is our model. As he became the Son of God, so we, by following his example, become the sons of God and joint heirs to the Father's kingdom with him.

  The Father makes these promises to us in the oath and covenant of the priesthood with a charge that we should beware, or be careful, and give diligent heed to the words of eternal life. These words are found in the scriptures, the counsel of the prophets and apostles, the holy temple, and in the language of the priesthood covenant. Moreover, these words are the intelligence that we receive through personal revelation, for we have covenanted to "live by every word that proceedeth forth from the mouth of God."[1722] The Father promises that he will teach us of the priesthood covenant by the gift of the Holy Ghost, pointing us to the day when we can stand in God's presence and receive his instructions and counsel face to face. The Father's warning to be cautious and diligent forebodes harsh penalties that will be suffered by those who neglect or reject the oath and covenant of the priesthood. God will not be mocked; he takes this covenant and our word seriously. The only safe path to eternal life is to make this priesthood covenant and then keep it with all our hearts, might, minds, and strength.

  No greater promise is contained in the oath and covenant of the priesthood than the Father's oath guaranteeing eternal life to those who keep the covenant. If we are faithful, he promises "thrones, kingdoms, principalities, and powers, dominions, all heights and depths." We will "pass by the angels, and the gods, which are set there, to [our] exaltation and glory in all things, as hath been sealed upon [our] heads, which glory shall be a fulness and a continuation of the seeds forever and ever."[1723] "Wherefore, all things are theirs," the Father promises. "These shall dwell in the presence of God and his Christ forever and ever. . . . They who dwell in his presence are the church of the Firstborn; . . . and he makes them equal in power, and in might, and in dominion."[1724]

  Such are the blessings of the oath and covenant of the priesthood—the second pillar of Zion.

[1722] D&C 84:44.
[1723] D&C 132:19.
[1724] D&C 76:59, 62, 94–95.

Section 12

The Constitution of the Priesthood:

Why Many Are Called, but Not Chosen

President Stephen L Richards called Doctrine and Covenants 121:34–46 "The Constitution of the Priesthood."[1725] This is that constitution:

Behold, there are many called, but few are chosen. And why are they not chosen?

Because their hearts are set so much upon the things of this world, and aspire to the honors of men, that they do not learn this one lesson—that the rights of the priesthood are inseparably connected with the powers of heaven, and that the powers of heaven cannot be controlled nor handled only upon the principles of righteousness.

That they may be conferred upon us, it is true; but when we undertake to cover our sins, or to gratify our pride, our vain ambition, or to exercise control or dominion or compulsion upon the souls of the children of men, in any degree of unrighteousness, behold, the heavens withdraw themselves; the Spirit of the Lord is grieved; and when it is withdrawn, Amen to the priesthood or the authority of that man.

We have learned by sad experience that it is the nature and disposition of almost all men, as soon as they get a little authority, as they suppose, they will immediately begin to exercise unrighteous dominion.

Hence many are called, but few are chosen.

No power or influence can or ought to be maintained by virtue of the priesthood, only by persuasion, by long-suffering, by gentleness and meekness, and by love unfeigned; by kindness, and pure knowledge, which shall greatly enlarge the soul without hypocrisy, and without guile—

Reproving betimes with sharpness, when moved upon by the Holy Ghost; and then showing forth afterwards an increase of love toward him whom thou hast reproved, lest he esteem thee to be his enemy; that he may know that thy faithfulness is stronger than the cords of death.

[1725] Richards, *Conference Report*, Apr. 1955, 12.

Let thy bowels also be full of charity towards all men, and to the household of faith, and let virtue garnish thy thoughts unceasingly; then shall thy confidence wax strong in the presence of God; and the doctrine of the priesthood shall distil upon thy soul as the dews from heaven.

The Holy Ghost shall be thy constant companion, and thy scepter an unchanging scepter of righteousness and truth; and thy dominion shall be an everlasting dominion, and without compulsory means it shall flow unto thee forever and ever.

This constitution contains some the greatest blessings and one of the harshest indictments pronounced by the Lord upon priesthood holders. Endowed women are not exempt. The denouncement, "Behold, there are many called, but few are chosen," applies equally to them. Anyone who has entered into the new and everlasting covenant and received the priesthood blessings of the temple should understand the principles contained in the Constitution of the Priesthood. Therefore, as with other sections of this book describing priesthood principles, women can benefit from the discussion.

Two Groups

In the Constitution of the Priesthood, the Lord divides the totality of priesthood holders into two groups: (1) those who respond to the call to eternal life,[1726] magnify their calling to eternal life, and thereafter obtain the promise of exaltation, and (2) those who neglect or reject the call to eternal life, take casually or ignore that calling, and forfeit exaltation. There are only two choices, and each of us, male and female, belongs to one of those two groups. Why would "many" be placed in the second group? The Lord gives us the answer: "Because their hearts are set so much upon the things of this world, and [they] aspire to the honors of men."[1727]

Love of money!

Love of power!

Love of popularity, which is attention, recognition, and influence!

We could divide and define the groups as Zion people and Babylon people. Hugh Nibley taught that these two groups are mutually exclusive; they represent two ways that are heading in opposite directions. We cannot choose to belong to both.[1728] To attempt to do so summons the Lord's ominous denouncement: "Amen to the priesthood or the authority of that man!"[1729] This statement hangs over our heads like a sword. The implication is *amen to the exaltation of that man!*

A Satanic Strategy

Looking forward to our day, Nephi saw a frightening satanic strategy to carefully deceive men and women. Nephi saw Satan lulling us into supposed carnal security and thereby convincing us to abandon our birthright blessings, take our eyes off Zion, and quietly persuade us to sacrifice the promise of eternal life. Satan's strategy was designed to trick us into minimizing our covenants, including the oath and covenant of the priesthood. Satan's tactic is one that he had employed anciently, one that he had taught to Cain. He has successfully used it ever since, convincing untold thousands that they can simultaneously focus on money and Zion. Because it is impossible to serve both God and mammon, Satan knows that he can thereafter dupe us into setting aside and abandoning our priesthood covenant, which will cause us to spiral downward into temporal and spiritual destruction.

[1726] McConkie, *Mormon Doctrine*, 482.
[1727] D&C 121:35.
[1728] Nibley, *Approaching Zion*, 18–19.
[1729] D&C 121:37; emphasis added.

Here is what Nephi foresaw in his words: "And others will he pacify, and lull them away into carnal security, that they will say: All is well in Zion; yea, Zion prospereth, all is well—and thus the devil cheateth their souls, and leadeth them away carefully down to hell."[1730]

Few prophecies are repeated more often by Latter-day Saints. We quote this verse regularly in classes; we trumpet it from the pulpit; and yet many of us will fall into the devil's snare, thinking that the scripture applies to others. If we are not careful, we will fail in our priesthood calling, forfeit Zion, and fall short of eternal life. The chosen few are not those who place the god of money, power, and recognition before the one true God. On the other hand, the prophesied result to the many who were called but not chosen will be "Amen to the priesthood or the authority of that man!"

A Test of Loyalties

President Ezra Taft Benson taught, "When we put God first, all other things fall into their proper place or drop out of our lives. Our love of the Lord will govern the claims of our affection, the demands on our time, the interests we pursue, and the order of our priorities."[1731]

To Moses, the Lord revealed our covenantal relationship to God: "Thou shalt have no other gods before me. Thou shalt not make unto thee any graven image, or any likeness of any thing that is in heaven above, or that is in the earth beneath, or that is in the water under the earth: Thou shalt not bow down thyself to them, nor serve them: for I the LORD thy God am a jealous God. . . . Thou shalt not take the name of the LORD thy God in vain; for the LORD will not hold him guiltless that taketh his name in vain."[1732]

These first three commandments allow no wiggle room; they demand our total allegiance to God. We are allowed no other affections before God—no idolizing, adoring, or worshipping anything or anyone in front of God, and no taking upon us his name and then dishonoring him by placing our loyalties elsewhere. In no uncertain terms, the Lord said we would not be held guiltless for such actions. We cannot suppose that we can enter the priesthood covenant, replace it in our minds and hearts with other affections, and then receive a few stripes at the day of judgment and go on to inherit eternal life. God demands our total loyalty to at least the same degree that a wife demands total loyalty from her husband. "Thou shalt have no other gods before me"

A common hypocrisy is to expect total loyalty from God while not returning total loyalty to him. Mortality is a perfect environment in which to test the depth of these loyalties. A pivotal test is the choice between God and mammon. Hugh Nibley explains that the Hebrew word, *mammon* means "financial activity of any kind."[1733] The Savior warned that we cannot choose both: "Ye cannot serve God and Mammon."[1734] Some people try to simultaneously choose both God and mammon, but that defines them as mammon choosers, which categorizes them among the many who are called but not chosen. Gospel writers Leaun G. Otten and C. Max Caldwell explained: "There are many brethren who are called and given the rights or authority of the priesthood, but few of them are also chosen for an inheritance of eternal life. Those who are to receive eternal lives must first learn and apply the fundamental principles upon which the priesthood must function."[1735] One of the first principles on that list would be fierce loyalty to God.

[1730] 2 Nephi 28:21.
[1731] Benson, *Teachings of Ezra Taft Benson*, 349–50.
[1732] Exodus 20:3–7.
[1733] Nibley, *Approaching Zion*, 20–21.
[1734] Matthew 6:24; 3 Nephi 13:24.
[1735] Otten and Caldwell, *Sacred Truths of the Doctrine and Covenants*, 2:305.

Zion people are classified as the few who are both called and chosen, those who distinguish themselves from the "many" by choosing and serving God over mammon and remaining loyal to the end, enduring in the covenants "at all hazards."[1736]

Restoration of the Constitution of the Priesthood

As we have mentioned, the verses contained in Doctrine and Covenants 121:34–46 have been referred to as the Constitution of the Priesthood. These verses are among the "plain and precious"[1737] parts of the gospel that the Lord restored in the dispensation of the fulness of times. Elder Neal A. Maxwell explained that this section contains an "elaboration [that] is given nowhere else in scripture! It is a significant part of the fulness of the Restoration and includes counsel on how human foibles can keep us from gaining access to the powers of heaven and how power and authority are to be exercised."[1738]

Of the many who are called to eternal life, evidently only a few will distinguish themselves in the priesthood by abiding the principles of the Constitution of the Priesthood and thereby earn their reward.

The Marriage of the King's Son

The "elaboration" mentioned above by Elder Maxwell refers to the Savior's parable of the royal feast found in Matthew 22:1–10. In this parable, "a certain king" sends his servants out to "call them that were bidden to a marriage for his son." Elder James E. Talmage writes, "The invitation of a king to his subjects is equivalent to a command. The marriage feast was no surprise event, for the selected guests had been bidden long aforetime; and, in accordance with oriental custom were notified again on the opening day of the festivities." As we shall see, this parable delineates those who are called from those who are chosen.

According to custom, the select guests who had been invited to the marriage would have included the king's family and close friends. In Jewish custom, such guests are first honored by the king's sending them an invitation and subsequently are more honored when they arrive at the wedding. They comprise the king's inner circle, those whom he knows and loves best. When they arrive at the wedding, the king has them clothed in beautiful wedding garments and treated with great respect. Sadly, in the case of this "certain king," "many of the bidden guests refused to come when formally summoned; and of the tolerant king's later and more pressing message they made light and went their ways, while the most wicked turned upon the servants who brought the royal summons, mistreated them cruelly, and some of them they killed."

The latter-day interpretation of this parable should be obvious. These select guests, who are members of the King's family and his closest friends, are they who have taken upon them his name, and who profess to love him and his Son, and who have a right to attend this most sacred event. They are the Church—*us!* Only those who have covenanted their allegiance to the King could be invited to the marriage of his Beloved Son. Elder Talmage concurs: "The guests who were bidden early, yet who refused to come when the feast was ready, are the covenant people."[1739]

We should note that, according to Elder McConkie, the bride of the Bridegroom is also *us*, "the Church composed of the faithful saints who have watched for his return," the Saints whom the Bridegroom will come to claim. We are the Lord's *bride,* that is, the few who are called and chosen.

The marriage of the supper of the Lamb that is described in this parable is an actual future event. Elder McConkie explained: "The elders of Israel by preaching the message of the restoration are

---

[1736] Smith, *History of the Church*, 3:379, 380.
[1737] 1 Nephi 13:34.
[1738] Maxwell, *Men and Women of Christ*, 123.
[1739] Talmage, *Jesus the Christ*, 499.

inviting men to come to that supper. 'For this cause I have sent you,' the Lord says to his missionaries, 'that a feast of fat things might be prepared for the poor; yea, a feast of fat things, of wine on the lees well refined, that the earth may know that the mouths of the prophets shall not fail; yea, a supper of the house of the Lord, well prepared, unto which all nations shall be invited. First, the rich and the learned, the wise and the noble; and after that cometh the day of my power; then shall the poor, the lame, and the blind, and the deaf, come in unto the marriage of the Lamb, and partake of the supper of the Lord, prepared for the great day to come.' (D. & C. 58:6–11; 65:3.)" Of that event, Elder McConkie also wrote: "Soon the scripture shall be fulfilled which saith: 'The marriage of the Lamb is come, and his wife hath made herself ready. And to her was granted that she should be arrayed in fine linen, clean and white: for the fine linen is the righteousness of saints. And he saith unto me, Write, Blessed are they which are called unto the marriage supper of the Lamb.' (Rev. 19:7–9.)"[1740]

In the parable of the royal feast, we are awed by the honor extended to the "many," who were called to the marriage, and simultaneously we are appalled that so "few" responded. Some of them had actually grown so hardened against the King that they reacted with open rebellion. Of course, only a small number of Latter-day Saints would be in that company. However, the group that should frighten us most is the one that "made light" of the invitation, those who "went their ways, one to his farm, another to his merchandise."[1741] Of this group, Elder Talmage writes, "The turning away by one man to his farm and by another to his merchandise is in part an evidence of their engrossment in material pursuits to the utter disregard of their sovereign's will; but it signifies further an effort to deaden their troubled consciences by some absorbing occupation; and possibly also a premeditated demonstration of the fact that they placed their personal affairs above the call of their king."[1742] Unfortunately, many will belong to this group and thus forfeit their call to the wedding.

Will the King allow his Son's marriage to go unattended? No.

Elder Talmage writes: "Finding the guests who had some claim on the royal invitation to be utterly unworthy, the king sent out his servants again, and these gathered in from the highways and cross-roads, from the byways and the lanes, all they could find, irrespective of rank or station, whether rich or poor, good or bad; 'and the wedding was furnished with guests.'" Elder Talmage concludes, "The children of the covenant will be rejected except they make good their title by godly works; while to the heathen and the sinners the portals of heaven shall open, if by repentance and compliance with the laws and ordinances of the gospel they shall merit salvation."[1743]

Were it not for modern revelation, we might assign this parable solely to the Jews in the meridian of time. But a phrase in this parable links it to us, we who would be the Zion people of the latter-days; that phrase is: "many are called, but few are chosen."[1744] In 1833, the Lord commanded the brethren to attend to their priesthood duties, saying, "There are many who have been ordained among you, whom I have called but few of them are chosen. They who are not chosen have sinned a very grievous sin, in that they are walking in darkness at noon-day. . . . If you keep not my commandments, the love of the Father shall not continue with you, therefore you shall walk in darkness."[1745] That "grievous sin" is a result, in part, from our straying from the ordinances and thus breaking the everlasting covenant: "They seek not the Lord to establish his righteousness, but every man walketh in his own way, and after the image of his own god, whose image is in the likeness of the world, and whose

---

[1740] McConkie, *Mormon Doctrine*, 469.
[1741] Matthew 22:5.
[1742] Talmage, *Jesus the Christ*, 499.
[1743] Talmage, *Jesus the Christ*, 501.
[1744] Matthew 22:14; D&C 121:34.
[1745] D&C 95:5–6, 12.

substance is that of an idol, which waxeth old and shall perish in Babylon, even Babylon the great, which shall fall."[1746]

The marriage of the king's son contains imagery that reminds us of the conflict between Zion and Babylon. The king had called many guests to the wedding. These people were friends and family, those who should have shown the most interest and who should have exhibited the greatest loyalty. Nevertheless, the "many" would not make the time, or they spurned the invitation outright. We see in their actions Babylon captivating the children of Zion and seducing them with idolatry, the love of mammon over the love of God. In the end, only a few of the called actually attended the wedding. How we choose to respond to the King's call will determine our loyalties and identify the group to which we will belong.

"Many Will Say to Me in That Day"

When we examine the parable of the royal feast, we shudder when we read of the guest who tried to enter the marriage without a wedding garment.[1747] Perhaps he was attempting to enter without submitting to the laws governing the wedding; or maybe he had received the garment and then removed or rejected it. In any case, a terrible wo is pronounced upon such people who mock the King: "And [the king] saith unto him, Friend, how camest thou in hither not having a wedding garment? And he was speechless. Then said the king to the servants, Bind him hand and foot, and take him away, and cast him into outer darkness; there shall be weeping and gnashing of teeth. For many are called, but few are chosen."[1748]

There is a lesson here concerning Zion. All are invited to become Zion people and to gain an inheritance in Zion; all are called to eternal life when they receive the new and everlasting covenant. But only they who keep the Covenant have actual claim to the blessings of Zion. No one can enter illegitimately. No citizen of Babylon is welcome. Because a person professes to be part of Zion does not mean that he actually is a Zion person. How he honors his *garment,* which symbolizes his devotion to his Covenant, determines his place at the royal wedding. They who treat the Covenant lightly, who go "their ways, one to his farm, another to his merchandise," will be excluded and replaced. They who refuse to submit to the laws of the wedding and pay homage to other gods rather than to the one true God will be cast out. Sadly, the people who make up these groups seem to be the "many."

Of the "many," they who are invited to the wedding, the Lord says, "Many will say to me in that day, Lord, Lord, have we not prophesied in thy name? and in thy name have cast out devils? and in thy name done many wonderful works? And then will I profess unto them, I never knew you: depart from me, ye that work iniquity."[1749] We should note here that priesthood holders are included in this scripture. We have established the fact that the "many" are they who have been called to eternal life, but have forfeited their calling through neglect or disobedience. In this scripture, they, the "many," will perform all sorts of marvelous works and yet in the end come up short. The Lord says that they have spent their days working iniquity, which is that "grievous sin" which we discussed above. We know that sin so well, for it is common to Babylon: the love of money, power, and popularity. The "many" have attempted to embrace both God and mammon, they have sought power and recognition while professing Zion, and in the process they have abandoned their calling, forfeited the blessings of the priesthood, and will be excluded from the wedding feast.

Their works of iniquity, their grievous sin was idolatry, which places love of God second to love of money, power, and popularity. These things always result in oppressive class distinction and inequality, strife, and persecution; they stand in stark contrast to the unity, equality, peace, and

---

[1746] D&C 1:15–16.
[1747] Matthew 22:11.
[1748] Matthew 22:13–14.
[1749] Matthew 7:22–23.

charity required by the celestial law of Zion.[1750] Therefore, the Lord said, "But it is not given that one man should possess that which is above another, *wherefore the o lieth in sin.*"[1751] Clearly, many of us will forfeit our invitation to the wedding because we "go [our] way" and love our "merchandise" more than we love God and his needy children. Thus, even now, "many" of us are staggering under the weight of the Lord's condemnation. When we treat lightly our covenants and spend our time and effort pursuing vain ambitions, our minds become darkened with unbelief and neglect, and we run the risk of losing our calling. Then when the time of the wedding arrives, "many" of us might find ourselves under condemnation. This condition of darkness is apparently so widespread that the Lord's condemnation "resteth upon the children of Zion, even all."[1752] *The many!* Pray, therefore, that we come to ourselves and strive to become the "few," who are both called and chosen.

CALLED AND CHOSEN FOR ETERNAL LIFE

Zion people are the "few." Zion people are they who live celestial laws in the telestial environment of Babylon. Zion people are the *elect* who are invited to the marriage of the Lamb and who attend joyfully dressed in holy garments. Zion people are the "chosen," meaning "chosen for eternal life."[1753] Zion people fully embrace the oath and covenant of the priesthood, the objective of which is to bring us to the point that we can be "chosen" and receive all the blessings that the Father offers us in that covenant. To be chosen from among those who are called depends upon our magnifying our calling. Then when we have proven faithful, the announcement will come that we have been *elected,* that is *selected* for eternal life.

Joseph of Egypt is an example of someone who was called and then chosen (elected) by embracing the principles of Zion, that is, by worthily living the new and everlasting covenant and the oath and covenant of the priesthood. Commenting, Kent P. Jackson and Robert L. Millet, wrote, "Joseph chose righteousness and the Lord chose him; this redounded to the everlasting blessing of all his literal and spiritual posterity. The far-sighted Pharaoh recognized something in this stalwart slave not found in most ordinary men—i.e., the attributes of godliness. Said he, 'Can we find such a one as this is, a man in whom the spirit of God is?' Without waiting for the answer, he turned to Joseph, 'Thou shalt be over my house, and according unto thy word shall all my people be ruled: only in the throne will I be greater than you.'"[1754] The question posed by Pharaoh concerning Joseph could be asked of us: "Can we find such a one as this is, a man in whom the spirit of God is?"

If we enter into the oath and covenant of the priesthood and keep it in every respect, the priesthood covenant will lead to our eventually being chosen for eternal life. This announcement, as we have discussed, is conveyed in a variety of ways, but it always involves the voice of God through the Holy Ghost. The Lord said: "I speak unto you with my voice, even the voice of my Spirit."[1755] Elder McConkie wrote, "As is well known, many are called to the Lord's work but few are chosen for eternal life. So that those who are chosen may be sealed up unto eternal life, the scripture says: 'It shall be manifest unto my servant, by the voice of the Spirit, those that are chosen; and they shall be sanctified.' (D&C 105:36.) They are chosen by the Lord, but the announcement of their calling and election is delivered by the Spirit."[1756] Therefore, the call goes out to all, a few respond to the call, which distinguishes them from the "many," and eventually, through faithfulness, the announcement of the surety of that calling and *chosenness* (election) will be delivered by the voice of the Spirit.

[1750] D&C 105:5.
[1751] D&C 49:20; emphasis added.
[1752] D&C 84:54–56.
[1753] McConkie, *Mormon Doctrine,* 482.
[1754] Jackson and Millet, *Studies in Scripture,* 3:69; quoting Genesis 41:38, 40.
[1755] D&C 97:1.
[1756] McConkie, *A New Witness for the Articles of Faith,* 270.

Imagine the President of the Church issuing a directive that all the Saints should give diligent heed to become designated as the "few" by striving to make their calling and election sure. And yet such a call was given by the dispensation leaders of both the meridian of time and the dispensation of the fulness of times. Peter admonished the ancient Saints to "give diligence to make your calling and election sure: for if ye do these things, ye shall never fall: For so an entrance [into the celestial kingdom] shall be ministered unto you abundantly into the everlasting kingdom of our Lord and Saviour Jesus Christ."[1757] And Joseph Smith exhorted the Saints, "Oh! I beseech you to go forward, go forward and make your calling and your election sure; and if any man preach any other Gospel than that which I have preached, he shall be cursed."[1758] Because these appeals were universally given by the presidents of the Church, we should perhaps rethink our position and consider the calling and election made sure as an attainable event in our gospel progression, one that is as important as receiving the ordinances of the temple or eternal marriage.

In a landmark article called "What I Hope You Will Teach Your Children about the Temple," President Ezra Taft Benson invoked God's blessings upon us that we would seek and receive every blessing associated with Elijah so that our callings and election could be made sure.[1759] Perhaps we should cease considering this event beyond our mortal reach and begin to study and pursue it with careful diligence. In the final analysis, the "few" who are called and elected to eternal life may well be those who have received the revelation that their calling and election has been made sure, and in a broader sense, these "few" might actually total an even greater number of people, whose salvation has been guaranteed without their having thought to ask if it is so.

Abiding Zion's Celestial Law in Babylon's Telestial Setting

The challenge of convincing those who professed to be Zion people to live the celestial laws of Zion weighed continually upon Joseph Smith's mind. His purpose seemed to be riveted upon creating a Zion people, who would be defined by their overcoming Babylon and ultimately becoming a nation of priests and kings unto God.[1760] In a speech given to the Relief Society in 1842, the Prophet admonished the sisters to live up to their covenants; strive for the unity that is found in Zion; become separate from Babylon; and become virtuous, holy, and thus "select"—*chosen*. The purpose of God, he said, was to make a Zion, as in Enoch's day—a holy kingdom of priests.

All difficulties which might and would cross our way must be surmounted. Though the soul be tried, the heart faint, and the hands hang down, we must not retrace out steps; there must be decision of character, aside from sympathy. When instructed, we must obey that voice, observe the laws of the Kingdom of God, that the blessings of heaven may rest down upon us. All must act in concert, or nothing can be done, and should move according to the ancient Priesthood; hence the Saints should be a select people, separate from all the evils of the world—choice, virtuous, and holy. The Lord was going to make of the Church of Jesus Christ a kingdom of Priests, a holy people, a chosen generation, as in Enoch's day, having all the gifts.[1761]

At another time Joseph said, "I have tried for a number of years to get the minds of the Saints prepared to receive the things of God; but we frequently see some of them, after suffering all they have for the work of God, will fly to pieces like glass as soon as anything comes that is contrary to their traditions: they cannot stand the fire at all. *How many will be able to abide a celestial law, and go through and receive their exaltation, I am unable to say, as many are called, but few are chosen.*"[1762]

[1757] 2 Peter 1:10–11.
[1758] Smith, *Teachings of the Prophet Joseph Smith*, 366.
[1759] Benson, "What I Hope You Will Teach Your Children about the Temple," 6.
[1760] Exodus 19:5–6. Note: Women become priestesses and queens unto their husbands.
[1761] Smith, *Teachings of the Prophet Joseph Smith*, 202.
[1762] Smith, *History of the Church*, 6:184–85; emphasis added.

Decidedly, it is difficult to step away from Babylon and its allurements. "Even if we try to leave Babylon," wrote Elder Maxwell, "some of us endeavor to keep a second residence there, or we commute on weekends."[1763] But leave Babylon, we must. Zion lies in the opposite direction, and soon, straddling the ever-widening gulf between Babylon and Zion will become impossible and we will have to jump to one side or the other. The unavoidable truth is that leaving Babylon is the sacrifice we make and the price we pay for eternal life. Upon this decision we create a broken heart and a contrite spirit.

Former BYU religion instructor, Rodney Turner, writes, "One reason many are called and few are chosen is that *they fail the test—which is to live celestial principles in a telestial setting. Insofar as circumstances permit, we are expected to do the eternally natural thing under unnatural conditions.* . . . However, we can take heart from the fact that those things which call for sacrifice and sheer grit in mortality will be accomplished with ease and unmitigated joy in eternity. But first we must demonstrate our love of righteousness by practicing it in adversity. Doing the easy and the convenient thing proves nothing, for it does not call for effort, self-denial or any strength beyond our own. Only after we have been tried successfully in the refining fires of human weakness and worldly opposition can we abide the eternal burnings of celestial glory—for 'our God is a consuming fire.'"[1764]

THE END-PURPOSE OF OUR CALLING

As we have mentioned, our *calling*, which was first extended to us in the premortal world, has always been the call to eternal life. In this life, we are called to eternal life again when we enter the new and everlasting covenant through baptism.[1765] Then we are called once more to eternal life when we enter into the oath and covenant of the priesthood. S. Brent Farley says, "Alma repeatedly associates the word *called* or *calling* with the priesthood itself (as contrasted with particular priesthood assignments), teaching that men are 'called by this holy calling, and ordained unto the high priesthood of the holy order of God.' (Alma 13:6.)"[1766]

All priesthood *callings* point us toward our being *chosen* for eternal life, but they do not guarantee that reward. That supernal blessing depends upon our giving "diligent heed to the words of eternal life."[1767] President James E. Faust wrote, "We are called when hands are laid upon our heads and we are given the priesthood, but we are not chosen until we demonstrate to God our righteousness, our faithfulness, and our commitment."[1768] Elder Neal A. Maxwell gives an elegant explanation of why many are called but few are chosen: "It makes sense to me that the Lord would choose out of the world those who are (or who could become) different from the world and, therefore, could lead the world to a different outcome. We must be different in order to make a difference."[1769] Zion people comprise the few who are different and they who make a difference.

To that end, we are commanded to magnify our singular calling. Magnification of our calling exceeds obeying the commandments, which are means and not ends to achieving the glory of Zion. President Kimball taught, "The faithful in the priesthood are those who fulfill the covenant by 'magnifying their calling' and living 'by every word that proceedeth forth from the mouth of God.' (D&C 84:33, 44.) Far more seems to be implied in these requirements than token obedience—far more is needed than mere attendance at a few meetings and token fulfillment of assignments. *The perfection of body and spirit are implied, and that includes the kind of service that goes far beyond the normal*

[1763] Maxwell, *A Wonderful Flood of Light*, 47.
[1764] Turner, *Woman and the Priesthood*, 235; emphasis added.
[1765] D&C 55:1.
[1766] Farley, "The Oath and Covenant of the Priesthood," 42–43.
[1767] D&C 84:43.
[1768] Faust and Bell, *In the Strength of the Lord*, 394.
[1769] Maxwell, *Deposition of a Disciple*, 55.

definition of duty. 'Behold, there are many called, but few are chosen.' (D&C 121:34.)"[1770] Ultimately, to magnify our priesthood calling, which is the call to eternal life, is to marry in the temple and thereby enter into the order of the Gods; it is to achieve exaltation and inherit eternal lives.[1771] Clearly, these statements point to the magnificent end-purpose of the priesthood covenant. Those few who respond to their priesthood calling are those who will be chosen for eternal life.

Distinctions between Those Who Are Called and Chosen

Elder Maxwell reminded us that premortal worthiness is simply the first of several tests of worthiness that we must pass in order to obtain eternal life: "Just because we were chosen 'there and then,' surely does not mean we can be indifferent 'here and now.' Whether foreordination for men, or foredesignation for women, those called and prepared must also prove 'chosen and faithful.'"[1772] The difference, he said, between the "many called" and the "few chosen" are faithfulness and submission to the celestial laws that make the priesthood operative. He stated, "One reason for the distinction between being 'called' and being 'chosen' is that the latter can understand this next reality: the powers of heaven are accessed and controlled only upon the principles of righteousness (D&C 121:36)."[1773] The principles of righteousness, which the Lord wishes to call to our attention, are these:

No power or influence can or ought to be maintained by virtue of the priesthood, only by persuasion, by long-suffering, by gentleness and meekness, and by love unfeigned; by kindness, and pure knowledge, which shall greatly enlarge the soul without hypocrisy, and without guile—

Reproving betimes with sharpness, when moved upon by the Holy Ghost; and then showing forth afterwards an increase of love toward him whom thou hast reproved, lest he esteem thee to be his enemy; that he may know that thy faithfulness is stronger than the cords of death.

Let thy bowels also be full of charity towards all men, and to the household of faith, and let virtue garnish thy thoughts unceasingly.[1774]

The inverse of these principles are those that retard or negate priesthood power: *love of money, power, and popularity (attention, recognition, and influence)*. These things are highly destructive. Their common denominator is selfishness, one of Babylon's hallmark attributes. Babylon would use money, power, and influence to compete, suppress, control, dominate, compel, gratify one's pride, and build a personal empire on the shaky foundation of supposed security[1775]—all "vain ambitions," according to the scripture.[1776] On the other hand, Zion would use money, power, and influence for building the kingdom of God, leveling up the poor, thus providing equal esteem to all people, caring for one another's needs, blessing the sick, comforting the afflicted, clothing the naked, feeding the hungry, and establishing peace.

The attitude of Babylon leads to pride, contention, hardened hearts, withdrawing from the core principles of the Church, and promoting behavior that is akin to persecuting the poor and afflicted. It is Satanic thinking and actions, idolatry, idleness and idle talk, envy, strife, self-indulgence, lying, dishonesty, robbery, inappropriate sexual dalliance, murder, and all manner of wickedness. Conversely, the attitude of Zion leads to confidence to be able to stand in the presence of God, priesthood power, a growing knowledge of the doctrine of the priesthood, the constant companionship of the Holy Ghost, and becoming unto God a king and priest, who wields an unchanging scepter of righteousness and truth. The attitude of Zion leads to inheriting everlasting kingdoms, thrones,

---

[1770] Kimball, *Teachings of Spencer W. Kimball*, 496.
[1771] D&C 132:24.
[1772] Maxwell, *The Neal A. Maxwell Quote Book*, 127.
[1773] Maxwell, *But for a Small Moment*, 113.
[1774] D&C 121:41–45.
[1775] Alma 1:20–32.
[1776] D&C 121:37.

principalities, powers, and dominions, the blessings of which will flow to a Zion person forever and ever.[1777]

BUILDING A SURE HOUSE

In a speech entitled "Beware Lest Ye Fall," President George Q. Cannon exhorted us to become identified with the "few" who are "chosen." Our effort will supersede any other individual attainment, he promised, and the benefits of the priesthood will extend to our children. How we fare in becoming one of the "few" will have a direct impact on our descendants and our ability to build for them a "sure house." He said, "The Lord is weeding out His Church continually. The work of selection is going on. 'Many are called,' the Lord has said, 'but few are chosen.' The Lord is choosing the people now. The Lord is pulling up—in fact, they are pulling themselves up—the unfaithful, the transgressor. The work of cleansing the Church is going on perpetually, and it will continue until Christ comes. What an impressive lesson this ought to be to us! Do we desire to live and to be connected with the work of God? Do we desire our children to be numbered with the people of God? The great desire of some of the prophets and mighty men of old was that the Lord would build them a sure house."[1778]

Clearly, how we respond to the priesthood "call" distinguishes the "few" from the "many." Of the latter group the Lord said, "When I called, ye did not answer."[1779] Our response has everything to do with our eventually being "chosen" or *elected*. Joseph Smith was an example. Janne M. Sjodahl and Hyrum M. Smith wrote: "The Prophet Joseph was 'called and chosen' to give to the world the Book of Mormon and to engage in the ministry. God called him, through the Angel, and when he manifested his willingness to obey the call, he was chosen for the work." Then a significant observation, *"The call always precedes the election: 'Give diligence to make your calling and election sure' (2 Peter 1:10). He who is called, is sure of his election if he obeys the call."*[1780]

MORTAL TESTS THAT CHALLENGE OUR CALLING

"We believe in being true," proclaims the thirteenth Article of Faith. To God, to family, to country, to our brethren, to our covenants, and to the cause of Zion, we believe in being true. The "true" are the "few" who are called and chosen. The "true" are contrasted from the "many," they who are also called but *not* chosen because they are distracted by money, power, and popularity; the "many" are they who receive God's power and then misuse it by attempting to dominate and control. In the test of life, the "true" are the "few" who live their covenants despite all hazards; they flee Babylon, as they have been commanded, and they choose Zion over every other consideration. How we choose between Babylon and Zion is a pivotal element in the test of life; that choice separates the *true few* from the *untrue many*. In an article published in the *Improvement Era*, James G. Duffin wrote:

God chooses his own way of testing men and preparing them for the work he designs them to do. "Many are called but few are chosen." The chosen ones are those upon whom he can rely under the most trying conditions. Tests, in themselves apparently trifling, may determine the integrity of those thought of for more important work. It is related of the Prophet Joseph that when he was making up his company to go West, to find a suitable location for his suffering people, where they could worship God without being molested by mob violence, one day he invited a number of brethren to take a horseback ride with him. As the prophet led his little company along the road, he came to a large pool of water, around the edge of which the road made a curve. Without hesitating, the prophet plunged his horse through the water. A number of those with him followed without saying a word, while others followed the road around the pool. It is related that when he made up his company, Joseph selected

---

[1777] D&C 121:45–46.
[1778] Cannon, "Beware Lest Ye Fall," Feb. 16, 1896.
[1779] Isaiah 65:12.
[1780] Smith and Sjodahl, *Doctrine and Covenants Commentary*, 123; emphasis added.

every man who followed him through the pool of water, and not one of the others was chosen. "Blind obedience," says one. *The key is this: intelligent beings moved by the same spirit act in unison.*[1781]

Such is the test and condition of Zion people. Tests bring us to the crucible of choosing. The early Saints reached such a crucible when, impoverished and persecuted, they were commanded to build the Kirtland Temple. The act was a kind one. The Lord knew that the key to their deliverance and the redemption of Zion lay in receiving priesthood ordinances and living the law of the celestial kingdom. The administration of these ordinances and the celestial law could be received only in a temple. Thus, the Saints understood from the outset that Zion must be their goal, and "Zion cannot be built up unless it is by the principles of the law of the celestial kingdom."[1782] When this revelation (D&C 105) was received, "the Kirtland Temple was under construction. The faithful were to receive 'their endowment from on high' in this House of the Lord, for 'the time [had] come for a *day of choosing*' (D&C 105:12, 33, 35). Those 'chosen' for this blessing would be those whose works had manifested their worthiness."[1783] The "few" priesthood holders who would be called and chosen would be those who lived the law of the celestial kingdom and thus become Zion people.

Likewise, our day of choosing and our deliverance center on the temple and the criterion of worthiness to attend the temple. How we choose—and there are only two choices—is our test: Will we or will we not choose to remain true to our covenants? Elijah said it this way: "How long halt ye between two opinions? if the Lord be God, follow him: but if Baal [a god of Babylon], then follow him."[1784] We cannot have it both ways; we must choose. If we choose to keep our covenants and separate ourselves from Babylon, we are promised that we will be "endowed with power from on high,"[1785] which endowment is the power of deliverance, the power of godliness, and the power to bring us back into the presence of God.[1786] If, on the other hand, we choose to neglect or reject our covenants, we will receive the pronouncement: "Amen to the priesthood or authority of that man!" Clearly, our day of choosing is today, and how we choose places us in the camp of the wise or the camp of the foolish, for according to the scriptures, only the "wise virgins" will be ready when comes the day of choosing. "And until that hour there will be foolish virgins among the wise; *and at that hour cometh an entire separation of the righteous and the wicked*; and in that day will I send mine angels to pluck out the wicked and cast them into unquenchable fire."[1787] Thus, "there are many called, but few are chosen."

THE DAUNTING TEST OF RICHES

Jesus sounded a warning against our tendency to step into the snare of the love of money: "For what is a man profited if he shall gain the whole world and lose his own soul?"[1788] Sadly, "many" priesthood holders are wont to rationalize their preoccupation with wealth, and thus they choose to remain in Babylon. When Joseph Smith was incarcerated in Liberty Jail, he issued an epistle warning the Saints about this snare. Parts of that epistle became sections 121 and 122 of the Doctrine and Covenants. Joseph admonished those Saints who would "aspire after their own aggrandizement and seek their own opulence while their brethren are groping in poverty." Care should be given, he wrote, that our

---

[1781] Duffin, "A Character Test," *Improvement Era*, Feb. 1911.
[1782] D&C 105:5.
[1783] Brewster, *Doctrine and Covenants Encyclopedia*, 124.
[1784] 1 Kings 18:21.
[1785] D&C 105:11.
[1786] D&C 84:20–21.
[1787] D&C 63:54; emphasis added.
[1788] Matthew 16:26.

hearts not be open to "such high mindedness." Otherwise a condition would prevail wherein "there are many called but few are chosen."[1789]

As we have discussed, of the "many" who are called to eternal life, only a "few" will ultimately give diligent heed to their priesthood calling and move forward in faith toward Zion. The "few" will become the "chosen." Part of the price of becoming one of the "chosen" is choosing God over mammon, one of the most difficult tests of mortality.

When a wealthy young man went away sorrowing after having received the Lord's answer regarding the price for him to become perfect, Jesus turned to his disciples and said, "A rich man shall *hardly* enter into the kingdom of heaven."[1790] Embedded in the Lord's explanation is an introduction to the law of consecration. This law is our safety net from the preoccupation of wealth, and it is a key to our becoming perfect. To the rich young man, the Lord said, "If thou wilt be perfect, go and sell that thou hast, and give to the poor."[1791] Although the rich man was clearly a good man who had lived the commandments, he could not bring himself to accept the law of consecration, which would have covered him in safety and opened the door to perfection. Truly, it is *hard* for a rich man—or for that matter, a proud, selfish, power-hungry, recognition-seeking man—to lay aside the things of this world and still achieve heaven.

SAFETY AND PERFECTION IN CONSECRATION

We learn several important principles of Zion from the incident of the Savior and the rich young man:

1. Perfection hinges not on living the commandments alone, but on living the law of consecration.

2. The ultimate test of discipleship is the law of consecration.

3. The law of consecration was instituted, in part, for our safety, because pursuing and hoarding wealth can result in the loss of exaltation.

4. The law of consecration is hard to live, but it is harder for a rich man.

5. Only divine intervention can save the rich, who are those who have too much of what they do not need or deserve, but that intervention is not necessarily guaranteed.

6. Consecrating our excess to the poor tends to stockpile treasure in heaven, where treasure is needed.

7. The law of consecration makes us truly safe and secure. The Lord invited the rich young man to "come and follow me," which implies true safety. If we are with the Lord, we are safe.

8. Consecrated sacrifices earn "an hundredfold" return. If that is true, the rich young man would have received hundredfold more blessings than he sacrificed to bless the poor, and as the young man gave, the Lord would have kept him safe; he would have achieved perfection, and he would have earned eternal life.

Thus sang the Psalmist: "Blessed is he that considereth the poor: the Lord will deliver him in time of trouble. The Lord will preserve him, and keep him alive; and he shall be blessed upon the earth: and thou wilt not deliver him unto the will of his enemies. The Lord will strengthen him upon the bed of languishing: thou wilt make all his bed in his sickness."[1792] Deliverance, preservation, safety, blessings, protection, strength, and health—these are the blessings of consecration. But only a few of the many who are called will actually embrace this celestial law of Zion and live within its safety.

[1789] Millet and Jackson, 1:471–72.
[1790] Matthew 19:23.
[1791] Matthew 19:21.
[1792] Psalms 41:1–3.

The Sacrifice of All Things—a "Hard Thing"

Seeking after and clinging to riches can be a difficult test. Obtaining wealth often requires sidestepping the principles of Zion and embracing the principles of Babylon. Letting go of riches, a principle essential to becoming a Zion person, requires our rethinking a core Babylonian philosophy that brought us riches in the first place.

The Book of Mormon prophet, Jacob, stated emphatically that the only legitimate celestial purpose for seeking wealth is to obtain more resources to give away: "to clothe the naked, and to feed the hungry, and to liberate the captive, and administer relief to the sick and the afflicted." He said seeking the kingdom of God takes precedence over seeking riches—first one, then the other. We often try to invert this process. Only by following Jacob's prescribed sequence will we use wealth for its intended purpose, and that purpose is clearly *not* for personal empire building.

If we are to become Zionlike, we can harbor no selfish motive with our time, talents, and *everything* that God has given us. Jacob said, "Think of your brethren like unto yourselves, and be familiar with all and free with your substance, that they may be rich like unto you."[1793] Otherwise, he said, damning pride sets in, which condition God will not justify. Rather, pride condemns its victims with God's harsh judgment. A selfish attitude toward wealth is destructive and wholly Babylonian in nature; it is classified by Jacob as an iniquity and an abomination.[1794] Essentially, he said, we are persecuting and afflicting the poor[1795]; we are advancing inequality and promoting classes of people, which actions are contrary to the culture of Zion in every way. When such conditions exist, we hear the Lord's condemnation: "Amen to the priesthood or the authority of that man!"

Of course, many rich people would not want to hear this. It is a "hard thing"[1796] to reject telestial philosophies that seem so alluring and make so much sense here. With little doubt, it is a hard thing to make the sacrifice of all things, which is the crowning sacrifice required for eternal life.[1797] But that sacrifice becomes much more difficult for a rich person; he has much more to unload, and in the process he must also abandon his telestial attitude of wealth-building. While no prophet has condemned wealth, every prophet has condemned pursuing and hoarding it. Zion is described as a condition of unequalled abundance—there are simply no poor in Zion—but that abundance must be obtained in the right sequence and for the right reasons.

Only the law of consecration can protect us from the snare of wealth and provide us ultimate protection. This celestial law makes little sense in a telestial world, but it is in its application that Zion people realize great abundance and safety.

Safety in the "Royal Law"

Love motivates us to consecrate. Because we love, we are willing to give ourselves and that which we have to building up God's kingdom, promoting the cause of Zion, and taking care of God's children. Consecration can be lived only by love, which James called the "Royal Law," *Thou shalt love thy neighbour as thyself.*[1798]

President Marion G. Romney said we must do an *about-face* and begin to live according to the "royal law." This law is central to the law that governs the celestial kingdom.[1799] Elder Romney taught that Zion people can be established on no other principle. Priesthood holders must fully and

---

[1793] Jacob 2:17–19.
[1794] Jacob 2:13–16.
[1795] Psalms 10:2; 2 Nephi 9:30; 28:13.
[1796] 1 Nephi 3:5.
[1797] Smith, *Lectures on Faith*, 6:7.
[1798] James 2:8.
[1799] D&C 105:4–5.

ungrudgingly yield obedience to the "royal law." The Lord has stated unequivocally that Zion people must become united according to the "union required by the laws of the Celestial Kingdom," which stipulates that we must impart of our substance "as becometh saints, to the poor and afflicted."[1800]

We should insert here that money is not the only item of wealth that we must consecrate. For example, we might be rich in time, talent, or other resources that the Lord has given us. Holding back and not consecrating *any* abundance that God has blessed us with is categorized, as we have said, as persecuting the poor.[1801] Catastrophic consequences follow such self-dealing and selfish intent. Mormon identified ignoring the poor as a central reason for the pre-Christ destruction of the Nephite nation:

"Now this great loss of the Nephites, and the great slaughter which was among them, would not have happened had it not been for their wickedness and their abomination which was among them; *yea, and it was among those also who professed to belong to the church of God. And it was because of the pride of their hearts, because of their exceeding riches, yea, it was because of their oppression to the poor, withholding their food from the hungry, withholding their clothing from the naked,* and smiting their humble brethren upon the cheek, making a mock of that which was sacred, denying the spirit of prophecy and of revelation, murdering, plundering, lying, stealing, committing adultery, rising up in great contentions, and deserting away."[1802]

We must be so very careful. We must be ruled by the "royal law," and exhibit love that is deep enough to consecrate all that we are and have to God, his purposes, and his children. Love vitalizes the priesthood covenant as much as love infuses life into Zion people.

The Dangers of Rationalization and Postponement

Consecration is the ultimate sacrifice, for it involves all that we are and have. That sacrifice, which Joseph Smith described as the "sacrifice of all things," is the *only* sacrifice that has "power sufficient to produce the faith necessary unto life and salvation."[1803] Certainly this sacrifice is daunting, but it is equally certain that we must make it; and when we do, we will make it in a highly individualized way by consecration.

In advance of making this sacrifice, we must first sacrifice the selfish, prideful telestial attitudes that have stood in the way of such a sacrifice. The price of eternal life is total devotion, which can be proven only by the sacrifice of all things. Upon this sacrifice hangs our inheritance in the celestial kingdom; thus it was designed to cause us to stretch.

Because this ultimate sacrifice is extremely difficult, we often shrink from making it; we rationalize all sorts of reasons to set it aside. Sometimes we try to assuage our conscience, as do the "many" who are called but not chosen, by saying that we are doing our best to live the commandments; but then we remember that the rich young man was also living the commandments but would not make the sacrifice and fell short of eternal life. Or perhaps we postpone the sacrifice by saying that we would certainly be willing to live the law of consecration whenever the President of the Church sends down a new program. But the reality is that the law of consecration is neither a new law nor one that is waiting for a program. Again, the Lord told the rich young man that today was the day of obedience and sacrifice; the one thing the young man lacked, *if he would be perfect*, was to sell all that he had and give to the poor *today*, with the immediate promise that he would have treasure in heaven.

As mentioned, the Savior's invitation to the rich young man is the same as his invitation to every man who makes the oath and covenant of the priesthood: "Come and follow me." When the young

---

[1800] Marion G. Romney, "The Royal Law of Love," 95; quoting D&C 105:1–6.
[1801] 2 Nephi 9:30; 13:15; 28:13; Mosiah 4:26; Alma 5:55; Helaman 4:12; Mormon 8:37.
[1802] Helaman 4:11–12.
[1803] Smith, *Lectures on Faith*, 6:7.

man declined the invitation, shrank from the sacrifice, and went away, the Lord noted that a rich man's effort to develop a new attitude toward riches is difficult indeed: "It is easier for a camel to go through the eye of a needle, than for a rich man to enter into the kingdom of God."[1804] Of course, the disciples were as astonished by this doctrine as are we. They wondered aloud, who then could be saved? Jesus answered that such a feat requires God's intervention. But that statement should not be viewed as a comfort or a guarantee. The Joseph Smith Translation of this scripture reads: "It is *impossible* for them who trust in riches, to enter into the kingdom of God; but he who forsaketh the things which are of this world, it is possible with God, that he should enter in."[1805]

Jesus' concluding warning to the disciples should be sobering to every priesthood holder: "But *many* that are first shall be last; and the last shall be first." Again, we see the word "many" and contemplate the implied condemnation: "*many* are called, but *few* are chosen." It is upon the law of consecration that the "few" distinguish themselves from the "many" and make sure their calling to eternal life.

THE LAW OF RESTITUTION—AN *HUNDREDFOLD* REWARD

True safety and prosperity are found only in making the sacrifice of all things through consecration and by following Christ. The incident of the rich young man disturbed the apostles so much that they began to search their souls. Evidently, they wondered if they had fully complied with the laws of sacrifice and consecration so that they might obtain eternal life. Jesus offered them an astonishing promise: "And every one that hath forsaken houses, or brethren, or sisters, or father, or mother, or wife, or children, or lands, for my name's sake, *shall receive an hundredfold, and shall inherit everlasting life.*"[1806] Here the Lord makes two divine promises connected with consecration: (1) an hundredfold return, and (2) the promise of eternal life. The "few" priesthood holders who are called and chosen are blessed a hundred times their sacrifice, and they will inherit exaltation![1807]

The *hundredfold reward* principle is a manifestation of the Law of Restoration,[1808] which flows from the laws of sacrifice and consecration—whatever we give the Lord in priesthood service and personal sacrifice are restored to us "an hundredfold." The apostles had firsthand experience with the hundredfold principle on at least two occasions: first, when Jesus fed the five thousand and, second, when he fed the four thousand.[1809] Each time, Jesus required the apostles to bring (consecrate) *all* that they could to the Lord. Then Jesus blessed their offering, and then the resource multiplied and fed many. Of significance, in each instance, the apostles were instructed to gather up the remaining fragments and take note of the resulting quantity. Five loaves and two fishes had not only fed thousands until they were filled, but the fragments now filled twelve baskets![1810] *An hundredfold return!* Later, seven loaves and a few small fishes had not only fed thousands until they were filled, but the fragments now filled seven baskets![1811] *An hundredfold return!* These are lessons for every priesthood holder.

The law of restoration is a law of faith. When we priesthood holders and women counterparts consecrate our time, talents, and resources to build the kingdom of God, to promote the cause of Zion, and to bless the lives of others, we invoke a celestial law of abundance upon which Zion people and a Zion priesthood society are built. What the Lord said to his disciples, he repeats to us: "Freely ye

---

[1804] Luke 18:25.
[1805] JST Luke 18:27; emphasis added.
[1806] Matthew 19:29.
[1807] Matthew 19:16–30.
[1808] Smith, *Teachings of the Prophet Joseph Smith*, 395.
[1809] Mark 6:35–44; 8:1–9.
[1810] Mark 6:35–44.
[1811] Mark 8:1–9.

have received, freely give"[1812]; "Feed my lambs. . . . Feed my sheep."[1813] Of the "many" priesthood holders who are called to eternal life, only a "few" will actually achieve it, and when they do it will be because they made a consecrated effort, allowing the law of restoration to engage, which triggered the powers of earth and heaven to work together to return to us an hundredfold reward and the promise of eternal life.

Babylon among Us

When priesthood holders make the covenant of consecration and then neglect it or fall back into Babylon, they risk forfeiture of the Lord's blessings and their own salvation. The Mormon pioneers are examples. After they, the "many" who had been called to eternal life, had sacrificed everything to leave Babylon to establish Zion in the tops of the mountains, Brigham Young lamented that they, the "many," had brought Babylon with them.

The cry has come to [us]—"Separate yourselves from sinners and from sin." If we, as a people, had not believed this, we should not have been here this day. "Be not partakers of her sins, lest ye receive of her plagues, for her sins have reached unto heaven, and God hath remembered her iniquities." This we believe, consequently I have to say to the people, we have not come with any new doctrine; we have believed this ever since we were baptized for the remission of sins. Have the people come out from the nations? Yes. Have we separated ourselves from the nations? Yes. And what else have we done? Ask ourselves the question. Have we not brought Babylon with us? Are we not promoting Babylon here in our midst? Are we not fostering the spirit of Babylon that is now abroad on the face of the whole earth? I ask myself this question, and I answer, Yes, yes, to some extent, and there is not a Latter-day Saint but what feels that we have too much of Babylon in our midst. The spirit of Babylon is too prevalent here. What is it? Confusion, discord, strife, animosity, vexation, pride, arrogance, selfwill and the spirit of the world. Are these things in the midst of those called Latter-day Saints? Yes, and we feel this.[1814]

Alma the Younger's people were no different. In the beginning, under the direction of their prophet, Alma the Elder, they were the "many" who been called to eternal life. Later, they had suffered greatly at the hands of their enemies. Then they had experienced deliverance. But safe in Zarahemla, they had abandoned Zion for the charms of Babylon.[1815] Brigham Young noted that the Latter-day Saints were following the same pattern. He then issued a prophecy that is chilling. He foretold that the Saints would become the richest people on earth, but he also forewarned that those same riches would become a terrible trial. That vision caused him to mourn that "many" of us, who are called to eternal life like Alma's people, would fail the test of wealth and risk losing our exaltation. President Young said, "The worst fear that I have about this people is that they will get rich in this country, forget God and his people, wax fat, and kick themselves out of the Church and go to hell. This people will stand mobbing, robbing, poverty, and all manner of persecution, and be true. But my greater fear for them is that they cannot stand wealth; and yet they have to be tried with riches, for they will become the richest people on this earth."[1816]

Like us, Alma's people were divided into the many who were called and the few who were chosen. The first chapter of Alma gives us some helpful descriptions.

The" many" who were called but not chosen exhibited the following characteristics:

- pride

[1812] Matthew 10:8.
[1813] John 21:15–16.
[1814] Young, *Journal of Discourses*, 17:38.
[1815] Alma 1:20–32.
[1816] Nibley, *Brigham Young*, 128.

- contention
- hardened hearts
- distancing or withdrawing from the Church
- persecuting the "few"
- sorceries
- idolatry
- idleness
- babblings (idle talk)
- envy
- strife
- wearing costly apparel
- lying
- thieving
- robbing
- committing whoredoms (sexual sins)
- murdering
- all manner of wickedness

The "few" who were called and chosen exhibited the following characteristics:

- humility
- imparting the word of God, one with another, without money and without price
- remaining steadfast and immovable in keeping the commandments of God
- bearing persecution with patience
- leaving the cares of the world behind to hear the word of God
- not esteeming themselves above each other
- striving for equality
- laboring according to each person's individual strength
- imparting their substance according to each other's needs
- caring for the poor, the needy, the sick and the afflicted
- dressing modestly and avoiding costly apparel
- being neat and comely in appearance[1817]

Interestingly, the "few" who were chosen for eternal life enjoyed an incredible abundance of peace and wealth—even to exceed riches of the "many" who had defected to Babylon. These "few" used their abundance to level up those around them and to bless those who were not members of the Church. They accomplished this feat—becoming Zion people and establishing their Zion—in a matter of months![1818]

And thus they did establish the affairs of the church; and thus they began to have continual peace again, notwithstanding all their persecutions.

And now, because of the steadiness of the church they began to be exceedingly rich, having abundance of all things whatsoever they stood in need—an abundance of flocks and herds, and fatlings of every kind, and also abundance of grain, and of gold, and of silver, and of precious things, and abundance of silk and fine-twined linen, and all manner of good homely cloth.

[1817] Alma 1:20–32.
[1818] Alma 1:23.

And thus, in their prosperous circumstances, they did not send away any who were naked, or that were hungry, or that were athirst, or that were sick, or that had not been nourished; and they did not set their hearts upon riches; therefore they were liberal to all, both old and young, both bond and free, both male and female, whether out of the church or in the church, having no respect to persons as to those who stood in need. And thus they did prosper and become far more wealthy than those who did not belong to their church.[1819]

Walking in Darkness at Noon-day

Regarding the "many" who fail to live up to their premortal and mortal callings, who are unwilling to face and overcome the obstacles that cut off the blessings of the priesthood and hinder them from becoming Zion people, President Harold B. Lee, wrote,

"The Lord requireth the heart and a willing mind; and the willing and obedient shall eat the good of the land of Zion in these last days." (D&C 64:34.) I fear there are many among us who because of their faithfulness in the spirit world were "called" to do a great work here, but like reckless spendthrifts they are exercising their free agency in riotous living and are losing their birthright and the blessings that were theirs had they proved faithful to their calling. Hence as the Lord has said, "there are many called but few are chosen," and then he gives us two reasons as to why his chosen and ordained fail of their blessings: First, because their hearts are set so much upon the things of this world, and second, they aspire so much to the honors of men that they do not learn that "the powers of heaven cannot be controlled nor handled only upon the principles of righteousness." (D&C 121:34–36.) *All these have sinned "a very grievous sin, in that they are walking in darkness at noon-day."* (D&C 95:5–6.)[1820]

They have not sinned ignorantly. They have taken upon them the oath and covenant of the priesthood and the covenant of consecration and they have set them aside. "They are walking in darkness at noonday."

Quoting the scripture, "Many are called, few are chosen," President Wilford Woodruff grieved, "The Almighty has revealed in our day the reasons, but what a mighty host have wrecked their eternal hopes on those fatal reefs—love of the riches of this world, the honors and praises of men, and the exercises of unrighteous dominion."[1821] The "many" know the law and yet they reject the law.

This is the day for choosing between Zion and Babylon. We cannot escape the fact that President Young's prophecy is true: Many priesthood holders are rich by the world's standard, and yet they, who long for and profess to be Zion people, are too much identified with Babylon. They are walking in darkness at noonday, according to President Lee, and their actions constitute a very grievous sin. They have agreed to follow the principles of obedience, sacrifice, and consecration, but they do not do so. President Woodruff warned that their behavior carries severe eternal risks. Their pursuit and love of riches, their selfish attitude regarding their time and talents, their insistence upon gratifying their pride with praise and honor, and their demeaning and unequal treatment of others will have the eventual effect of dashing their eternal hopes on fatal reefs. The priesthood cannot function under such conditions. Unless the priesthood "many" come to their senses and admit that all is *not* well in Zion, the devil will cheat their souls, as prophesied, and lead the "many" carefully down to hell.[1822] Then the priesthood becomes totally inoperative.

[1819] Alma 1:28–31.
[1820] Lee, *Decisions for Successful Living*, 169; emphasis added.
[1821] Clark, *Messages of the First Presidency*, 3:131.
[1822] 2 Nephi 28:21.

THE TEST OF PRAISE

Who does not feel a rush of exhilaration when praise and recognition are lavished upon him? But how many have become intoxicated by the opiate of praise, and then have fallen? Elder Harold B. Lee identified seeking worldly things and aspiring to the honors of men as the primary causes of failure in prominent men and their loss of the highest priesthood possibilities.[1823] Jesus taught that it is impossible to simultaneously serve two masters.[1824] We see evidence of the truth of this principle in the construct of our minds and hearts: We can neither think two thoughts at the same time, nor can we simultaneously set our hearts upon two things. Ultimately, we will "hate the one, and love the other." Therefore, when we are tempted to aspire to the honors of men, we are faced with making a choice between the honors of men and the honor of God. How we choose determines whether we are of Babylon or of Zion, whether we are of the "many" who are called and not chosen or the "few" who will respond to their priesthood calling and be chosen for eternal life.

Seeking acclaim, popularity, attention, and recognition are the ugly sisters of praise-seeking. Any one of them leads to the same disastrous end. It has been observed that nothing good ever comes from seeking praise. Undisciplined, praise can only promote pride in the receiver. Moreover, praise suggests that unequal levels of worth exist among God's children—one standing above the other, with the praised one standing on top. This attitude is not Zionlike and runs contrary to the priesthood, which stipulates that priesthood holders must strive to level up God's children and that we must be the servants to all.[1825]

Seeking and receiving praise sets in motion a destructive cycle that will soon spiral out of control. Self-centeredness almost always follows; self-centeredness is fed by praise. Self-centeredness is the bedfellow of competition, which also loves praise. Winners receive the secondary prize of praise, which they often desire more than the primary prize of their competitive enterprise. Babylon glorifies winners and lavishes upon them the spoils of victory: money, power, popularity, and influence. Winners are set up as heroes; they are superhuman; they are gods. Consequently, winners receive our adoration and our praise. No wonder, then, that praise is a foundational principle of inequality.

We praise the beautiful, the rich, the smart, the talented, and the strong. We often give them more acclaim than we give our God. We set them up as examples. We pay them tribute. We write about them, talk about them, and try to draw near to them. When we praise another so as to exalt and glorify him, and when the person being praised accepts the praise and becomes elevated in his eyes, both the praiser and the praised have sinned. Both have joined the "many" who have broken the priesthood covenant and traded their priesthood calling for a fleeting prize.

Perhaps, one of the reasons that God gives us adversity is to shake us loose from praise. Adversity is a great equalizer. It is at the common denominator of adversity that the proud and the humble, the rich and the poor, the powerful and the weak, the popular and the nobodies, and the praised and the praisers are equal. Perhaps it is by means of adversity that God tries to teach us the principle of equality. When the joy of achievement is measured by praise, when life is a contest in which everyone is constantly comparing himself to others, lives will be ruined and people will become miserable. Unfortunately, this is the sad state of the "many," who "set their hearts upon the things of this world, and aspire to the honors of men," those who compete and "exercise unrighteous dominion," those whose actions grieve the Spirit and thus cause the heavens to withdraw with a sounding *amen* to their priesthood.[1826]

[1823] Lee, Conference Report, Oct. 1965, 128.
[1824] Matthew 6:24.
[1825] Smith, *History of the Church*, 4:492.
[1826] D&C 121:37, 39.

Joseph Fielding McConkie and Robert L. Millet write, "Whenever men of any age value the approval of their fellows more than the approbation of their God, they forfeit the reward that might have been theirs. . . . President Joseph F. Smith warned against three great dangers, which the Saints of God must encounter: false educational ideas, sexual impurity, *and the flattery of prominent men* (see *Gospel Doctrine*, p. 313). To those who seek the applause of mortals, the words of the Master are clear and poignant: 'They have their reward' (Matthew 6:5)."[1827]

To forfeit the wealth of eternity for the transitory riches of this world, and to set aside the everlasting praise of God for the fickle honors of men is shortsighted and foolish. These insanities are nothing more than replays of Esau's selling his birthright for a mess of pottage. Do we really crave praise so much that we would choose it rather than the power and honor of God? If we were to ask parents what is the worst danger their children face, they would likely answer *peer pressure*. And yet many adults do not perceive that danger in their own lives. We crave praise and acceptance, and often we will do whatever it takes to get them. Has history taught us nothing? If Saul, David, and Solomon could fall by aspiring to the honors of men, could not we?

Our desire for praise encroaches on every area of our lives, even our attitude toward Church service. There is a dangerous tendency here: Occasionally, praise-seeking individuals are tempted to mold their callings in such a way that it draws attention to themselves. Idolatry results—the serving of false gods instead of serving the true God and his children. For example, a young woman's leader might be tempted to focus her effort on gaining the honor of her class, and soon, her attempts to teach the gospel will take second place to her basking in her students' admiration and respect. She is doing a good work for the wrong reason; she has her reward—*praise*—but it is the wrong reward. Or a new elders quorum president, whose is rightly held in esteem by his quorum, might feel invigorated and elevated as he notes that his brethren now cling to his every authoritative word. Then rather than feeling humble and dependent upon God, he might feel powerful and important; worse, he might actively seek for more of these feelings by seeking more praise. Now, having lost view of his priesthood calling, he is in great danger of losing his authority altogether. He has "a form of godliness,"[1828] but he denies the principles upon which the priesthood functions. He has the appearance of righteousness, but he is failing the test of praise. He has his reward—the wrong one—but he no longer has priesthood power.

A Zion life cannot be established where there is unholy praise: seeking and receiving acclaim that leads to pride; giving recognition and acclaim to others so as to exalt them.

"Rights of the Priesthood"

The Lord boils everything down to a single lesson, and we must learn that lesson if we hope that the priesthood will become a power and remain functional within us. The lesson is "that the rights of the priesthood are inseparably connected with the powers of heaven, and that the powers of heaven cannot be controlled nor handled only upon the principles of righteousness."[1829]

The priesthood "rights" that the Lord mentions here are not "rites," that is, those sacred ordinances and ceremonies necessary for salvation. Rather, these "rights" are privileges that flow from recognizing the source of priesthood power. This power can be accessed only by obedience to the laws of heaven where the power originates; this power comes by magnifying our priesthood calling and by living a life distinguished by persuasion rather than force, long-suffering rather than impatience, gentleness rather than harshness, meekness rather than pride, love unfeigned (not pretended or insincere) rather than contrived, and kindness rather than abusiveness. Clearly, the priesthood is a lifestyle. The scripture states that if we will assume the true lifestyle of the priesthood, the Holy Ghost

---

[1827] McConkie and Millet, *Doctrinal Commentary on the Book of Mormon*, 1:90; emphasis added.
[1828] 2 Timothy 3:5.
[1829] D&C 121:36.

will distil upon us pure knowledge. It is pure knowledge that has the effect of aligning us, sincerely and with no devious motive, with the character of God.

Now we are in a position to have the right to the *rights* of the priesthood. One of those priesthood rights is the right to occasionally correct people in our stewardships. We exercise that priesthood right by "reproving betimes with sharpness, when moved upon by the Holy Ghost; and then showing forth afterwards an increase of love toward him whom thou hast reproved, lest he esteem thee to be his enemy."[1830] Notice that this right guarantees us the companionship of the Holy Ghost in our stewardships. The influence of the Holy Ghost makes interactions with those in our stewardships experiences of love rather than experiences of discouragement and embarrassment. By exercising this right of the priesthood in occasional loving correction, we will help to increase faith, hope, and repentance in the corrected person. Then our relationship with that person will be strengthened, and we will come to be known by the hallmark priesthood characteristics of virtue and charity.[1831] So it is with all priesthood rights, which have the power to establish Zion in our lives.

"Inseparably Connected"—Righteousness and Priesthood Power

We need only scan the scriptures to glimpse the power of these priesthood rights. For example, these rights have the power to create and control the elements, to heal the sick, to raise the dead, to cast out evil spirits, to teach with the tongue of angels, to know the truth of all things, and to stand in the presence of God. Before we can obtain these rights, as we have mentioned, we must first align our lives with the characteristics of God and the laws of heaven by which these rights are governed. If we should step away from this pattern, we risk severing the cord that binds us to the source of priesthood power. Again, the scripture reads "that the rights of the priesthood are inseparably connected with the powers of heaven, and that the powers of heaven cannot be controlled nor handled only upon the principles of righteousness."[1832]

If we are not experiencing the powers of heaven that flow from these priesthood rights, we might profit by first looking inward and realigning our lives with the Constitution of the Priesthood. Then we must repair the connection between heaven and us.

It should be clear by now that priesthood authority and priesthood power are distinct terms. Priesthood authority is granted upon ordination, but priesthood power is dependent upon our righteousness.[1833] There are causes and effects at play. Unrighteous dominion is the ugly consequence of our undertaking to cover our sins, gratify our pride or vain ambitions, or to exercise control or compulsion upon other people *in any degree of unrighteousness.* Even the slightest inclination toward these evils results in priesthood cessation: "Behold, the heavens withdraw themselves; the Spirit of the Lord is grieved; and when it is withdrawn, Amen to the priesthood or the authority of that man."[1834] Of course, when the heavens withdraw, we can repent and the power of the priesthood will be restored.

Clearly, the priesthood is a way of life that Zion people follow. Taking upon us the oath and covenant of the priesthood demands that we separate from the philosophies of Babylon and exercise strict obedience to the laws that govern God's power. Thus, to the degree that we exhibit righteousness, we place ourselves in a position to have access to the "rights of the priesthood."

[1830] D&C 121:43.
[1831] D&C 121:41–45.
[1832] D&C 121:36.
[1833] Nelson, "Personal Priesthood Responsibility," 44.
[1834] D&C 121:37; emphasis added.

Connecting to the True Vine

To access priesthood power through the rights of the priesthood is to be attached to the True Vine. Before his crucifixion, Jesus taught his apostles concerning their priesthood calling, which, he said, they could not magnify without remaining connected to him. He called himself the *True Vine*, and he delineated them the branches. We must never lose sight of the fact that these men were priesthood holders, and they were receiving a significant priesthood lesson from the Master about the rights of the priesthood. Jesus taught:

I am the true vine, and my Father is the husbandman. Every branch in me that beareth not fruit he taketh away: and every [branch] that beareth fruit, he purgeth it, that it may bring forth more fruit. Now ye are clean through the word which I have spoken unto you. Abide in me, and I in you. As the branch cannot bear fruit of itself, except it abide in the vine; no more can ye, except ye abide in me. I am the vine, ye [are] the branches: He that abideth in me, and I in him, the same bringeth forth much fruit: for without me ye can do nothing. If a man abide not in me, he is cast forth as a branch, and is withered; and men gather them, and cast [them] into the fire, and they are burned. If ye abide in me, and my words abide in you, ye shall ask what ye will, and it shall be done unto you. Herein is my Father glorified, that ye bear much fruit; so shall ye be my disciples.[1835]

This metaphor has a variety of applications. For instance, a man who sanctifies himself has greater power in the priesthood than a man who does not; a man or woman who sanctifies himself or herself by honoring his or her temple covenants has greater power to ask for and receive blessings than a man or woman who does not; a husband and wife who sanctify themselves in the patriarchal order of the priesthood have greater power to bless their family than a couple who does not.

We, the branches, grow from the True Vine and draw our nourishment from it. We note with interest that in Jesus' metaphor the branches are already producing, but the Husbandman (the Father) wants them to produce more. Personalizing this, we might say that through ordination we received priesthood authority and are "producing" to a degree, but the Father wants to seek priesthood power through righteousness so that we can produce more. To that end, God (the Husbandman) begins to prune—to "purge and purify"—us. We, the branches, must endure this purging and purifying process if we hope to gain greater strength in the priesthood and produce more fruit. To that end, the Husbandman cuts from us, the branches, anything that depletes our strength, and he carefully directs the process of growth so that we, the branches, can perform optimally. For a while we, the branches, might look (and probably feel) pitiful and barren. We might not produce much fruit for a season. But the Husbandman knows that in time the purging and purifying procedure will cause us, the branches, to bring forth more than we have or ever could. Therefore, enduring the Husbandman's purging process and remaining attached to Christ, the True Vine, are key elements in obtaining the rights and power of the priesthood.

Christ's promise is this: As long as we, the branches, remain in him and he in us, our nourishment and strength will never fail. "Ye shall ask what ye will, and it shall be done unto you."[1836] Think of the implications! To the degree that we are *in* him and he is *in* us, and to the degree that we submit to the Father's process of purification and sanctification, the Lord promises us that we may draw strength from the True Vine, ask for priesthood power, and receive the blessings associated with the priesthood rights.

[1835] John 15:1–8.
[1836] John 15:8.

AMEN TO THE PRIESTHOOD

Jesus said, "Not every one that saith unto me, Lord, Lord, shall enter into the kingdom of heaven; but he that doeth the will of my Father who is in heaven."[1837] We should note here that no one could authoritatively utter the name of the Lord except those on whom the Lord has placed his name[1838]—Melchizedek Priesthood holders. It should go without saying, however, that just because we have been ordained to the priesthood and are going through the motions does not necessarily mean that we have or are doing so with power. As we have learned, by our actions we can sever ourselves from priesthood rights and power in the same way we can sever ourselves from the True Vine. Then priesthood power comes to an abrupt *amen*.

Hugh Nibley wrote, "Men can confer the powers of the priesthood upon others, it is true (D&C 121:37), but only God can validate that ordination, *which in most cases he does not recognize*: 'Hence many are called, but few are chosen' (D&C 121:40). . . . The exercise of the powers of heaven 'in any degree of unrighteousness' invalidates the priesthood—'Amen to the priesthood or the authority of that man' (D&C 121:37). . . . The moment I even think of my priesthood as a status symbol or a mark of superiority, it becomes a mere hollow pretense. At the slightest hint of gloating or self-congratulation, the priesthood holder is instantly and automatically unfrocked."[1839]

President John Taylor taught, "Do you think that God will give power to any man only to carry out his own contracted or selfish purposes? I tell you he never will, never, no never. . . . There is no priesthood of the Son of God that authorizes one man to oppress another or to intrude upon his rights in any way. There is no such thing in the category; it does not exist."[1840]

The consequences for the poor conduct mentioned in the Constitution of the Priesthood are dire: "behold, the heavens withdraw themselves; the Spirit of the Lord is grieved; and when it is withdrawn, Amen to the priesthood or the authority of that man."[1841] And it gets worse! When the Spirit of the Lord withdraws from a man, "ere he is aware," that is, before he even notices, he will be "left unto himself, to kick against the pricks, to persecute the saints, and to fight against God."[1842] Thus, as if in a spiraling downward circle, that unrepentant man will become increasingly irritated with pure doctrine, he will find fault with those who remain true, and soon he will find himself powerless and on the outside, fighting against the God whom he had once purported to love and serve. It is a sad circumstance, the scripture says, but nevertheless it is "the nature and disposition of almost all men"—the many who are called—"as soon as they get a little authority, as they suppose, they will immediately begin to exercise unrighteous dominion. Hence many are called, but few are chosen."[1843]

An official statement from the First Presidency appeared in 1961:

It is the doctrine that those who hold this power and authority will be chosen for an inheritance of eternal life if they exercise their priesthood upon principles of righteousness; if they walk in the light; if they keep the commandments; if they put first in their lives the things of God's kingdom and let temporal concerns take a secondary place; if they serve in the kingdom with an eye single to the glory of God. It is the doctrine that even though men have the rights of the priesthood conferred upon them, they shall not reap its eternal blessings if they use it for unrighteous purposes; if they commit sin; if the things of this world take preeminence in their lives over the things of the Spirit. It is a

---

[1837] 3 Nephi 14:21; Matthew 7:21.
[1838] Abraham 1:18.
[1839] Nibley, *Temple and Cosmos*, 535–36.
[1840] Taylor, *Journal of Discourses*, 20:262–63.
[1841] D&C 121:37.
[1842] D&C 121:38.
[1843] D&C 121:34–40.

fearful thing to contemplate this priesthood truth: Behold, many are called to the priesthood, and few are chosen for eternal life.[1844]

In an effort to call us away from danger and lift our sights to the glorious "rights of the priesthood," Elder Charles W. Penrose said, "If we would only live up to the things that He has revealed to us; if we would be as pure and virtuous, and honest and upright, and conscientious and patient, and long-suffering and charitable as we are commanded to be in the revelations the Lord has given unto us in these latter times, we would be better prepared for the great things yet to be unfolded. . . . For we are called with a holy calling, and if we do not live up to our professions, it were better we had never made them. *Let us return to the Lord, and the Lord will return to us; his Spirit will be manifested in our midst to a still greater degree, and His gifts and blessings will abound. Our sick will be healed as in times past. We have seen the sick healed instantaneously. The lame have been made to walk, the dumb to speak, the blind to see and the deaf to hear, by the power of God through the administrations of the servants of God. The gifts of tongues, prophecy, dreams, faith, discernment, and every gift and blessing spoken of in the Bible.*"[1845]

SUMMARY AND CONCLUSION

President Stephen L Richards called Doctrine and Covenants 121:34–46 "The Constitution of the Priesthood."[1846] In that significant document, the Lord restores a phrase that he originally gave to his apostles in the parable that is often called the parable of the royal feast. That restored phrase is "many are called but few are chosen." As this phrase applies to the Constitution of the Priesthood, the Lord divides the totality of priesthood holders into two groups: (1) those who respond to the call to eternal life,[1847] magnify their calling to eternal life, and thereafter obtain the promise of exaltation, and (2) those who neglect or reject the call to eternal life, take casually or ignore that calling, and forfeit exaltation. The Lord gives the reason for the "many" being placed in the second group: "Because their hearts are set so much upon the things of this world, and [they] aspire to the honors of men."[1848]

In that denouncing statement, the Lord reveals Satan's latter-day strategy to convince "many" who have been called to eternal life to sell their blessings, as did Esau, for a mess of pottage: *Love of money! Love of power! Love of popularity!* Satan knows that it is impossible for us to simultaneously serve both God and mammon, but he tries to convince us otherwise. When we make the attempt, we automatically step into his snare, which has the purpose of causing us to abandon our priesthood covenant and spiraling us out of control into a downward temporal and spiritual destruction.

At the heart of the issue of being called and chosen is the test of loyalties. Other loves, such as money, power, and popularity, are the equivalents of idolatry—other gods that we worship instead of the true God. The Lord has declared that we will not be held guiltless for shifting our affections. The priesthood covenant demands complete allegiance to God.

In the parable of the royal feast, the king called "many" of his friends and family to the marriage of his son, but "few" of those who should have been loyal responded to the call. We see in this division Babylon's captivating the children of Zion and convincing them to love mammon over God. How we choose to respond to the King's call determines our loyalties and identifies the group to which we belong. Everyone who has entered into the new and everlasting covenant has received the King's call; each person who has received the oath and covenant of the priesthood has received that call again. All are invited to become Zion people and to gain an inheritance in Zion. But only they who keep these covenants have actual claim to the blessings of Zion. No one can enter illegitimately.

[1844] First Presidency Message, *Improvement Era*, Feb. 1961, 115.
[1845] Penrose, *Journal of Discourses*, 20:297–98; emphasis added.
[1846] Richards, Conference Report, Apr. 1955, 12.
[1847] McConkie, *Mormon Doctrine*, 482.
[1848] D&C 121:35.

The "many" who are called to eternal life and yet are not chosen include those who are going through the motions of Church activity but who have not yet made the choice between God and mammon. Of this group, the Lord says that they have spent their days working iniquity or that "grievous sin." That sin, as we have discussed, lies at the foundation of Babylon: the love of money, power, and popularity. These *loves* have always resulted in oppressive class distinction and inequality, strife, and persecution; they stand in stark contrast to unity, equality, peace, and charity required by the celestial law of Zion.[1849] The "many" who seek for these things will be excluded from the wedding feast.

Zion people are the "few" who are both called and chosen for eternal life. They live the celestial laws in a telestial environment. They are the *elect* who are invited to the marriage of the Lamb, joyfully dressed in holy garments. They embrace the oath and covenant of the priesthood, which promises them all that the Father has. To that end, they magnify their priesthood calling, which is the call to eternal life. When they have proven faithful, the announcement will come that we have been *elected* for exaltation.

That announcement is so central to our salvation that the head of the previous dispensation, Peter, as well as of the present one, Joseph Smith, have admonished the Saints to "give diligence to make your calling and election sure."[1850]

Achieving such a lofty goal, the "few" must choose to abide Zion's celestial law in Babylon's telestial setting. With Zion ever on his mind, the Prophet Joseph Smith continually endeavored to establish a Zion people who could overcome Babylon and become a nation of priests and kings unto God.[1851] Thus, the Prophet admonished the Saints to live up to their covenants; strive for the unity that defines Zion; become separate from Babylon; and be virtuous, holy, and thus "select"—*chosen*. To become the chosen "few" depends upon our giving "diligent heed to the words of eternal life."[1852] To that end, we are commanded to magnify our singular calling. Magnification of our calling exceeds obeying the commandments, which are means and not ends to achieving the glory of Zion. President Kimball taught, "The faithful in the priesthood are those who fulfill the covenant by 'magnifying their calling' and living 'by every word that proceedeth forth from the mouth of God.'"[1853] Ultimately, to magnify our priesthood calling is to one day marry in the temple and thereby enter into the order of the Gods; it is to achieve exaltation and inherit eternal lives.[1854]

The Constitution of the Priesthood lists a primary distinction between those who are called and those who are chosen: the powers of heaven are accessed and controlled only upon the principles of righteousness. The inverse of these principles are those that retard or negate priesthood power: *love of money, power, and popularity*. When we abide the principles of righteousness and access the powers of heaven, we build a "sure house," as President George Q. Cannon taught.

To bring us to the crucible of choosing to become one of the "few" often requires mortal testing. These tests challenge our devotion to our covenants. If we choose to keep our covenants and separate ourselves from Babylon, we are promised that we will be "endowed with power from on high,"[1855] which endowment is the power of deliverance, the power of godliness, and the power to bring us back into the presence of God.[1856] If, on the other hand, we choose to neglect or reject our covenants, we will receive the pronouncement: "Amen to the priesthood or authority of that man!"

[1849] D&C 105:5.
[1850] 2 Peter 1:10–11.
[1851] Exodus 19:5–6. Note: Women become priestesses and queens unto their husbands.
[1852] D&C 84:43.
[1853] Kimball, *Teachings of Spencer W. Kimball*, 496.
[1854] D&C 132:24.
[1855] D&C 105:11.
[1856] D&C 84:20–21.

One most difficult tests of mortality is the test of wealth seeking: Will we or will we not choose God over mammon? The Book of Mormon prophet Jacob stated that the only legitimate celestial purpose for seeking wealth is to obtain more resources to give away: "to clothe the naked, and to feed the hungry, and to liberate the captive, and administer relief to the sick and the afflicted." He taught that seeking the kingdom of God takes precedence over seeking riches—first one, and then the other. The law of consecration is our safety net from the preoccupation of wealth, and, as we learn from the Savior's encounter with the rich young man, consecration is a key to our becoming perfect. We learn several important principles of Zion from this incident:

1. Perfection hinges not on living the commandments alone, but on living the law of consecration.
2. The ultimate test of discipleship is the law of consecration.
3. The law of consecration was instituted, in part, for our safety, because pursuing and hoarding wealth can result in the loss of exaltation.
4. The law of consecration is hard to live, but it is harder for a rich man.
5. Only divine intervention can save the rich, who are those who have too much of what they do not need or deserve, but that intervention is not necessarily guaranteed.
6. Consecrating our excess to the poor tends to stockpile treasure in heaven, where treasure is needed.
7. The law of consecration makes us truly safe and secure. The Lord invited the rich young man to "come and follow me," which implies true safety. If we are with the Lord, we are safe.
8. Consecrated sacrifices earn "an hundredfold" return.

The law of consecration is the vehicle for the sacrifice of all things, which Joseph Smith said was necessary to inherit eternal life. Only the law of consecration can protect us from the snare of wealth and provide us ultimate protection. This celestial law makes little sense in a telestial world, but it is in its application that Zion people realize great abundance and safety.

It is especially true that upon the law of consecration the "few" divide out from the "many." To rationalize away or postpone consecration is dangerous to our achieving eternal life. Because consecration and the sacrifice of all things are by definition the most difficult sacrifices, the "many" often shrink from making them; and yet, if they would summon courage and move forward in faith, the Lord will bless them according to the law of restitution with "an *hundredfold*" reward, which includes the promise of eternal life. While we are making our consecrated sacrifice, the Lord will keep us safe, however that safety might be defined.

Safety is also found in the "royal law," which is, *"Thou shalt love thy neighbour as thyself."*[1857] Love motivates us to consecrate. Because we love, we are willing to give ourselves and that which we have to building up God's kingdom, promoting the cause of Zion, and taking care of God's children. Consecration can be lived only by love; therefore, the principle of love is more pronounced in the "few" than in the "many."

The choice to be one of the "many" or the "few" is ever before us. Babylon continues to be the nemesis of Zion, attempting to lure us away with enticements to money, power, and popularity. Brigham Young reminded us that his worst fear was that "we would set our hearts on riches and forget God."[1858] Clearly, we have become some of the most prosperous people on earth, and therein, as President Young prophesied, is our test. The "few" choose to use their abundance to level up those around them, while the "many" exalt themselves. The "many" are walking in darkness at noon-day.

[1857] James 2:8.
[1858] Nibley, *Brigham Young*, 128.

They have agreed to be obedient, to sacrifice, and to consecrate, but they do not do so. President Woodruff warned that their behavior carries severe eternal risks.

For the priesthood to become a power within us, we must remember that priesthood rights originate in heaven and can be accessed only upon our righteousness.[1859] Clearly, the priesthood is a lifestyle. If we will assume the priesthood lifestyle, the Holy Ghost will distil upon us pure knowledge. These rights of the priesthood are the power to create and control the elements, to heal the sick, to raise the dead, to cast out evil spirits, to teach with the tongue of angels, to know the truth of all things, and to stand in the presence of God. Before we can obtain these rights, we must align our lives with the characteristics of God and the laws of heaven by which these rights are governed. If we are not experiencing the powers of heaven that flow from these priesthood rights, we might look inward and realign our lives with the Constitution of the Priesthood. Then we must repair the connection between heaven and us. As long as we, the branches, remain in him through righteousness, our nourishment and priesthood strength will never fail. To the degree that we exhibit righteousness, we place ourselves in a position to access to the "rights of the priesthood."

The Constitution of the Priesthood lays out principles of action, inaction, and evils that divide the "many" who have been called to eternal life from the "few" who are actually chosen for eternal life. The Constitution explains the source of priesthood power and how the priesthood becomes a lifestyle for those who enter into the oath and covenant of the priesthood. That these principles apply to both men and women should be evident. Because women share in the blessings of the priesthood with their husbands, they also share in the obligations of righteous living. If worthy men and women will do so, they will not only be called to the marriage of the King's son, but they will also be among the chosen "few" to actually attend the wedding, clothed in beautiful wedding garments, and blessed to partake of the King's feast.

[1859] D&C 121:36.

Section 13—

The Constitution of the Priesthood:

Instructing the Chosen Few

At each milestone along the path to eternal life, we, both men and women, receive new instructions, covenants, and ordinances that renew our initial calling and election to eternal life. For example, when we are baptized and first enter into the new and everlasting covenant, which is the first pillar of Zion, we receive our first "calling and election." When Sidney Gilbert received baptism and entered into the Covenant, the Lord said, "I have heard your prayers; and you have called upon me that it should be made known unto you, of the Lord your God, *concerning your calling and election in the church,* which I, the Lord, have raised up in these last days." Then the Lord gave Brother Gilbert two charges to help him continue on the path that would lead to his calling and election being made sure. These charges are common to all of us: (1) come out of Babylon, and (2) receive the oath and covenant of the priesthood, which is the second pillar of Zion: "Behold, I, the Lord, who was crucified for the sins of the world, *give unto you a commandment that you shall forsake the world. Take upon you mine ordination,* even that of an elder, to preach faith and repentance and remission of sins, according to my word, and the reception of the Holy Spirit by the laying on of hands."[1860] Only entering into the new and everlasting covenant, forsaking the world, receiving the oath and covenant of the priesthood (priesthood blessings for women), and bringing people to Christ can qualify us for the guarantee of eternal life.

As we have noted, the priesthood is both a way of life and the way to eternal life. The priesthood makes us "different" from the world, Elder Maxwell stated, so that we can "make a difference."[1861] Sadly, "many" who are called to the priesthood do not bother to magnify their calling, as stipulated in the Constitution of the Priesthood,[1862] and therefore they do not qualify to be "chosen" for eternal life.

[1860] D&C 53:1–3.
[1861] Maxwell, *Deposition of a Disciple*, 55.
[1862] Richards, Conference Report, Apr. 1955, 12.

On the other hand, a "few" press forward and experience the blessings of the gospel and priesthood. They will desire that everyone within their influence should escape Babylon, come to Zion, and receive these blessings. The priesthood is our power to partner with God in the work of redemption. If we honor the priesthood, we invite the Spirit, whose light *enlightens* us so that we become *lights* to point people to the *Light*[1863] and show them the way out of darkness.[1864] When they observe us, Elder Maxwell said, they will perceive something bright and "different." But if they detect no difference in us, they will not be drawn to the Light or feel motivated to flee the darkness.

STAGES OF PROGRESSION WITHIN THE COVENANT

From the moment we entered into the new and everlasting covenant, we accepted a trust. At baptism, the Lord gave us his name, and we agreed to "stand as witnesses of God at all times and in all things, and in all places." If we achieve eternal life, it will be because we give diligent effort to keeping this trust.[1865] At the time of our priesthood ordination, the Lord gave us his authority, and again placed upon us his name.[1866] Our obligation to carry that name and become *even as he is*[1867] took a substantial leap forward.

Now our call to eternal life expanded. First, we entered the new and everlasting covenant and agreed to become like the Lord; second, we received the oath and covenant of the priesthood and we agreed to make God's work our work. We agreed that we would never again adopt the behavior or philosophies of Babylon. Now and forever we would be identified with Zion, and we would begin to live according to the celestial order in a telestial world.

To facilitate our ability to adopt this new way of life and to become empowered to do the works of God, the Lord revealed to us the Constitution of the Priesthood. In this document, the Lord offered a list of instructions (D&C 21:41-45) that makes the priesthood functional and sets us apart as the "few" who are both called and chosen. Following that list of instructions, the Lord uses the word *then* to commence the list of promises of priesthood power and exaltation: "*Then* shall thy confidence wax strong in the presence of God; and the doctrine of the priesthood shall distil upon thy soul as the dews from heaven. The Holy Ghost shall be thy constant companion, and thy scepter an unchanging scepter of righteousness and truth; and thy dominion shall be an everlasting dominion, and without compulsory means it shall flow unto thee forever and ever."[1868]

Contrasting Babylon with Zion, let us examine these instructions as they apply to our representing Christ and as they summon power in the priesthood.

NO POWER OR INFLUENCE CAN OR OUGHT TO BE MAINTAINED BY VIRTUE OF THE PRIESTHOOD

At the great council in heaven, Satan proposed a frightening doctrine that would forever differentiate his kingdom, Babylon, from God's kingdom, Zion. That doctrine would also distinguish Satan's *priestcraft* from God's *priesthood*. This doctrine was one of control and force. To become a disciple of Satan and to gain membership in his Great and Abominable Church[1869] would require the sacrifice of personal agency. From that moment until now, control and force, which limits or nullifies agency, has characterized Satan's kingdom, his doctrines, and his power or *priestcraft*.

[1863] 3 Nephi 9:18; John 8:12.
[1864] Matthew 5:14.
[1865] Mosiah 18:9.
[1866] Abraham 1:18.
[1867] 3 Nephi 27:27.
[1868] D&C 121:45–46; emphasis added.
[1869] 1 Nephi 13:5–34; 14:3–17; 22:13–14; 2 Nephi 6:12; 28:18; D&C 29:21.

Any manifestation of priestcraft is dangerous. When Nehor first introduced it among the Nephites, Alma the Elder quickly moved to abolish it lest priestcraft become a cancer and consume the nation. He said, "Behold, this is the first time that priestcraft has been introduced among this people. And behold, thou art not only guilty of priestcraft, but hast endeavored to enforce it by the sword; *and were priestcraft to be enforced among this people it would prove their entire destruction.*"[1870] Satan's church and kingdom, Babylon, can always be detected by its implementation of force; and the worst manifestation of force is seen when it is employed to enrich, expand the influence of or draw attention to its perpetrator. Zion people are expressly forbidden to "exercise control or dominion or compulsion upon the souls of the children of men, in any degree of unrighteousness." When a priesthood holder steps into this territory, even in the smallest degree, he suddenly ceases to represent God. Then the heavens retreat, the Spirit is grieved and withdraws, the man is left unto himself, and finally he is the subject of the pronouncement: "Amen to the priesthood or authority of that man!"[1871] Unfortunately, "it is the nature and disposition of almost all men [the "many"], as soon as they get a little authority, as they suppose, they will immediately begin to exercise unrighteous dominion."[1872]

This is priestcraft; this is Babylon—the appetite for power and influence by means of control and force.

Joseph Fielding McConkie and Robert L. Millet wrote:

The only true antidote to priestcraft is charity (see 2 Nephi 26:30–31). It is interesting to note that the opposite of charity is priestcraft. Whereas priestcrafts oppress the laborer to increase profits (priestcraft is adhered to by their proponents as a religion—"priests" who follow this philosophy), charity elevates the poor. Priestcraft draws attention to self while charity draws attention to Christ. Priestcraft seeks to become a light while charity points to the true light. There is no room in priestcraft for love—only profit: "This is a business decision." Priestcrafts taken to extreme result in murder, thievery, dishonesty, sexual sin, envy, malice, taking God's name in vain. The person who practices these things shall perish, while the laborer in Zion is commanded to avoid priestcrafts and labor for Zion and not for money [riches]. This life becomes the great experiment, for the poor are ever with us. Where is our heart, and what are our eternal desires?[1873]

Zion's Approach to Agency

Zion's approach to power and influence is exactly opposite that of Babylon's. Because of our approach, we Zion people qualify as the chosen "few." Power and influence naturally flow to all Zion people, both priesthood holders and faithful women, because the Lord makes us *lights* in a dark world, and our light draws people to the Light, Jesus Christ. Whereas Babylon would use the resulting power and influence to enrich and exalt herself, Zion would adopt Ammon's philosophy of being "wise, yet harmless."[1874] If the Lord empowers us by means of the priesthood, and if he shines his light on us to garner the attention of others, we must consecrate that power and influence back to him to further his redemptive work. If we will do so, the Lord will increase our power and influence among his children in proportion to our righteousness and our willingness to consecrate and engage in his work.

Being "wise, yet harmless" speaks to honoring another person's agency. As we function within the priesthood, we offer loving instruction and persuasion without force or coercion. We create situations and an environment of choice, giving people opportunities to use their agency to experiment with and embrace gospel principles. When we interact with family, friends, associates, or people within our stewardship, we will honor their agency and stand with God as our partner, never

---

[1870] Alma 1:12.
[1871] D&C 121:37.
[1872] D&C 121:39.
[1873] McConkie and Millet, *Doctrinal Commentary on the Book of Mormon*, 3:5.
[1874] Alma 18:21.

stepping in front of him and always acting as the Holy Ghost directs. We will take Jesus Christ as our example, as President Hugh B. Brown explained: "The Lord himself, though all powerful, refuses to use force to accomplish his purposes. Christ's obedience was always voluntary and love-inspired. He has said that his work and his glory is to bring to pass the immortality and eternal life of man, but this he will not do by force."[1875]

Such a course invites the Spirit, who brings with him the power and influence of the priesthood.

Persuasion vs. Babylon's Counterparts

Babylon will make its argument at all costs. Babylon is always right; she is rigid, inflexible, and unyielding. Babylon's intention is to win; therefore, we can spot the Babylonian tactic by its competitive nature. Babylon will attempt to employ negative campaigning, intimidation, manipulation, domineering speech, bullying, and coercing to beat down and discourage another person until that person surrenders. A goal of Babylon is subjugation, and Babylon will employ her overbearing manner to browbeat until she achieves victory.

Babylon enjoys debating everything. Babylon will contend, bicker, disagree, and oppose until she prevails and succeeds in wearing down her opponent until that person surrenders. Babylon will not relent; her method is loveless, and she engenders distrust, discouragement, and broken relationships. Unfortunately, many of those who are called adopt this philosophy and thereby sacrifice both their right to the companionship of the Spirit and efficacy in the priesthood.

Zion's Patient Persuasion

Conversely, Zion, the "few" who are called and chosen, will entreat another person by means of patient reasoning, gentle urging, and encouragement. Zion attempts to win someone over with love and empathy. Zion is a good listener and seeks to understand the other person's concerns and points of view. Zion seeks common ground without sacrificing her standards. Zion's conversations are harmless and safe: "wise, yet harmless." There is no threat that anything will be used against the other person.

Zion is a leader, who carefully draws the other person forward, attempting to induce, convince, or influence, without using force. If and when another person finally aligns himself with Zion's philosophy, it will be by choice.

Zion's goal is to strengthen relationships, despite differences. In the end, love grows, understanding increases, unity comes into view, equality becomes possible, and mutual respect is achieved. Because Zion represents Christlike attributes, the Holy Ghost finds a home in a Zionlike person, and consequently priesthood power and influence increase in that person.

Patience and Long-suffering

Babylon thinks only of herself. Babylon is impatient and intolerant of delays or opposing opinions. Babylon becomes frustrated, put out, and restless when she feels that she has been imposed upon. Babylon hates being asked to wait for, wait with, or wait upon someone. Babylon is eager to move on and pursue her own desires, and she becomes agitated or irritated when she is asked to sacrifice or change her mind. Babylon despises being bothered. Babylon's time is neither given nor shared without a profitable return: *Time is money!* is her motto. Therefore, Babylon dictates the terms and the disbursement of her time. Too many of the *many who are called and not chosen* are seduced by this doctrine! And too many thereby grieve the Spirit and lose the rights to the priesthood.

Conversely, Zion's time is consecrated for the building up of God's kingdom and the establishment of Zion. Two identifying traits of a Zion person are patience and long-suffering—the

---

[1875] Brown, *Continuing the Quest*, 228–29.

unselfish giving of consecrated time for the blessing of God's children. Only the Zionlike people, the *few who are called and chosen*, will embrace this doctrine and grow in priesthood power and influence.

Let us examine these attributes separately, beginning with patience.

PATIENCE

Priesthood holders are commanded to be patient and long-suffering.[1876] Not only in patience will we possess our souls,[1877] but we will acquire an attribute of Deity. An astute Institute student wrote: "Nothing could be as frightening as an impatient God." Who could believe in a God whose patience wanes or whose love is limited? There is no place for impatience in the priesthood or in Zion.

Because Zion people represent God, they are patient. As patience applies to faith in Jesus Christ, the virtue of patience constitutes waiting and anticipating with "a perfect brightness of hope"[1878] for the Lord's deliverance. Therefore, patience is not waiting with the feeling of impending doom; patience, according to Elder Neal A. Maxwell, is an active principle. It is being willing to submit to God's will and submit to what the scriptures call the "process of time."[1879]

Through righteous waiting we learn Godlike patience.

> Patience is waiting *for* someone.
> Patience is waiting *with* someone.
> Patience is waiting *upon*, or serving, someone.

Patience requires faith, which is often developed by the trial of our patience. Elder Maxwell warned that our trial of patience can turn to our discouragement and turning from God. Impatience, he said, suggests that we think we know better than God knows what is best, and thereby, through our impatience, we question God's omniscience. Thus, when our patience is being tried, our faith is simultaneously being tried. Our challenge, then, is to patiently and gracefully submit to those things that the Lord "seeth fit to inflict upon [us]," as did Alma's people, who submitted "cheerfully and with patience to all the will of the Lord."[1880]

As patience pertains to long-suffering, Elder Maxwell said our course of life is often correct enough, but we need to persist in that course long enough for the desired result. In any case, when we discover that our patience is being tried, we might expect that our faith will also be tried; and when we discover that our capacity for patience is increasing, we might also expect that our faith is increasing. We simply cannot become as is God without having developed the ability to demonstrate infinite patience with perfect faith. Therefore, it should come as no surprise that God would provide us with multiple opportunities to develop patience and faith by having them regularly tried.[1881]

The law of the harvest is a product of patience. This law and the principle of patience are inseparable. *Whatsoever ye sow, that shall ye also reap.*[1882] Between the *sowing* and the *reaping* are *patience* and *long-suffering*. The quality of the harvest is dependent upon our patient actions *after* we sow the seed. Elder Maxwell wrote, "Paul confirms that those who 'inherit the promises' are those who have triumphed 'through faith and patience' (Hebrews 6:12). Abraham 'obtained the promise,' but only 'after he had patiently endured' (Hebrews 6:15). Long-suffering, endurance, and patience are

---

[1876] D&C 121:41.
[1877] D&C 101:38.
[1878] 2 Nephi 31:20.
[1879] Maxwell, "Patience," 28; referencing Moses 7:21.
[1880] Maxwell, "Patience," 28; see also Mosiah 3:19; 24:15.
[1881] Maxwell, *Lord, Increase Our Faith*, 39.
[1882] D&C 6:33.

designed to be constant companions, as are faith, hope, and charity."[1883] The "few" who are called and chosen, who are faith-filled, patient Zion people, cling to the Lord's promise:

Verily I say unto you my friends, fear not, let your hearts be comforted; yea, rejoice evermore, and in everything give thanks; waiting patiently on the Lord, for your prayers have entered into the ears of the Lord of Sabaoth, and are recorded with this seal and testament—the Lord hath sworn and decreed that they shall be granted. Therefore, he giveth this promise unto you, with an immutable covenant that they shall be fulfilled; and all things wherewith you have been afflicted shall work together for your good, and to my name's glory, saith the Lord.[1884]

If patience and faith are companions, Elder Maxwell continued, so are patience and agency. When we lose our patience, we reveal an ugly side of us that is associated with Babylon; this side becomes irritated when it feels that it is being inconvenienced. We must remember that at the first moment of agitated impatience, we cross over into Babylon. On the other hand, Zion people are submissive and forbearing; they do not try to override others or hasten an outcome that would abuse another person's agency.[1885] Neither God nor a Zion person would do that. As always, when we consider these things we are struck with the fact that there are only two ways: Zion's faith and patience or Babylon's selfishness and impatience. There are no other choices, and the consequences for making that choice are exact opposites.

Patience, faith, long-suffering, and endurance are inseparably connected to God's *timing*. "It is in length of patience, and endurance, and forbearance that so much of what is good in mankind and womankind is shown."[1886] The Lord's timetable is proprietary to him.[1887] "My words are sure and shall not fail, but all things must come to pass in their time."[1888]

The fact that patience requires faith in God and his timing brings us to the issue of trust. Do we or do we not trust God and his way of doing things? Do we trust that his timing is as perfect as he is? Or do we think that he is imperfect in this one area and ought to take counsel from us about timing? Elder Maxwell wrote: "The issue for us is trusting God enough to trust also His timing. If we can truly believe He has our welfare at heart, may we not let His plans unfold as He thinks best? The same is true with the second coming and with all those matters wherein our faith needs to include faith in the Lord's timing for us personally, not just in His overall plans and purposes."[1889] Both Elder Maxwell and Elder Oaks concluded that we cannot truly exhibit faith in God without also trusting in his will and timing.[1890]

Priesthood holders, who are classified as the "few," know that time is on their side because God is on their side. God will cause that "all things [will] come to pass in their time."[1891] This attitude of patient, long-suffering speaks to the level of faith that all Zion people develop over years of righteous living; they know that they have never been let down by God, and they know that all good things come to pass with perfect timing. Prefacing the Constitution of the Priesthood, in Doctrine and Covenants 121, the Lord asked rhetorically, "How long can rolling waters remain impure? What power shall stay the heavens?" Then he answers with a profound promise to the patient and long-suffering: "As well might man stretch forth his puny arm to stop the Missouri river in its decreed course, or to turn it up stream, as to hinder the Almighty from pouring down knowledge from heaven

---

[1883] Maxwell, *Lord, Increase Our Faith*, 39.
[1884] D&C 98:2.
[1885] Maxwell, "Patience," 28.
[1886] "Talks to Young Men," *Improvement Era*, Sept. 1903.
[1887] Dallin H. Oaks, "Timing," 11.
[1888] D&C 64:31–32.
[1889] Maxwell, *Even As I Am*, 93.
[1890] Dallin H. Oaks, "Timing," 11.
[1891] D&C 64:31–32.

upon the heads of the Latter-day Saints."[1892] Clearly, our prayers have been heard, blessings are being prepared, eventually those blessings will flow, and our patience will be rewarded.

Priesthood faith, Zion faith, is this: By staying our course in patience and in faith, we facilitate rather than frustrate God's work. Because we have developed the ability to endure in patience, and because we are sufficiently acquainted with God to know that he will not divert from his decreed course, we know that we can persist in confidence with the belief that God has a perfect and a *perfectly* timed plan for us; we are confident that he will enact that plan "in his own time, and in his own way, and according to his own will."[1893] Neither the priesthood nor Zion can function with a belief system that is otherwise placed.

LONG-SUFFERING

Priesthood holders cannot effectively minister among God's children unless they develop the attribute of long-suffering. To suffer long with someone is to suffer [allow] him his right to preserve and exercise his agency. Thus, long-suffering is characteristic of priesthood holders in Zion. To suffer long is to suffer with a person as we watch him suffer the consequences of his actions, even when those consequences do not motivate him to change. To suffer long is to suffer in urgent prayer that perhaps a change of heart might occur and finally drive an errant soul to the Savior, who has suffered for him. For the "few" who are called and chosen, such righteous long-suffering is counted as a sacrifice, and, as we know, it is sacrifice that "brings forth the blessings of heaven."[1894] When we suffer long with and for "one of the least" of God's children, who might be temporarily *least* because of his poor choices, the Lord counts our long-suffering as a sacrificial service to the Savior.[1895] Because the Savior can be in debt to no one, he rewards our sacrifice with an incredible return—"an hundredfold."[1896] Truly, he is the most generous paymaster.

President Kimball, quoting Elder Orson F. Whitney, wrote: "No pain that we suffer, no trial that we experience is wasted. It ministers to our education, to the development of such qualities as patience, faith, fortitude and humility. All that we suffer and all that we endure, especially when we endure it patiently, builds up our characters, purifies our hearts, expands our souls, and makes us more tender and charitable, more worthy to be called the children of God . . . and it is through sorrow and suffering, toil and tribulation, that we gain the education that we come here to acquire and which will make us more like our Father and Mother in heaven." Then President Kimball concluded: "Suffering can make saints of people as they learn patience, long-suffering, and self-mastery. The sufferings of our Savior were part of his education."[1897]

Zion people have suffered long in the heat of the Lord's crucible and emerged as gold. Priesthood holders in Zion exercise their authority as a power by suffering long in the pursuit of righteousness. When our ability to suffer long is tried beyond our apparent limit to endure, and when we search our souls for something more to give, only to find an empty reservoir, we can take comfort in Elder Maxwell's perspective: "The dues of discipleship are high indeed, and how much we can *take* so often determines how much we can then *give!*"[1898] The purpose of long-suffering is growth.

Patience and long-suffering are Christlike traits that both strengthen Zion people and identify us with that holy ideal. By developing these virtues, the purposes of the priesthood find fulfillment. We become better equipped to stand as witnesses and representatives of God at all times and in all places;

[1892] D&C 121:33.
[1893] D&C 88:68.
[1894] "Praise to the Man," *Hymns*, no. 27.
[1895] Matthew 25:40.
[1896] Matthew 19:29.
[1897] Kimball, *Faith Precedes the Miracle*, 98.
[1898] Maxwell, *Notwithstanding My Weakness*, 63.

we provide a sacred precinct for the Holy Ghost to dwell; and our power in the priesthood increases so that we might better do the work of God.

Gentleness and Meekness

Babylon presents itself as intense, loud, wild, nonconforming and untamed. In dealing with people, Babylon is heavy-handed, controlling, competitive and unkind. All these characteristics are opposite Zion's gentility and meekness. To Babylon meek is weak; she is wont to persecute those who possess this attribute.[1899] Babylon flexes her muscle; she is proud, domineering, stubborn, and obstinate; she is unregenerate, meaning unrepentant, unwilling to be spiritually reformed, and loath to be reconciled to change. In her sinful state, Babylon lacks moral restraint and indulges in sensual pleasures and vices. To the degree that a person exhibits any of these traits, he is Babylonian in nature and stands opposite of God. The Spirit flees such a person, and his authority in the priesthood withers, if it does not cease altogether.

On the other hand, Zion people are gentle and meek. Interestingly, the Constitution of the Priesthood combines these attributes in a single phrase: "gentleness and meekness."[1900] That these traits are inseparable cannot be denied. Jesus is our example; he is both gentle and meek.[1901] We see Jesus' gentleness constantly displayed as he ministered among the people. Gently, he would encourage them to raise their sights. To those who were sick and afflicted, he would gently take them aside and work with them to increase their faith. He would use carefully worded conversation in an effort to establish contact with them and raise their confidence. Then he would heal them. He sought no acclaim; he desired only to give freely what he had. Jesus was gentle and meek.

Likewise, a priesthood holder in Zion is expected to be of a considerate and kindly disposition. He is amiable and tender, not harsh or severe. Mild and soft are words that describe him. He is submissive, refined, modest, and polite. Because he holds the priesthood and has been anointed to become a king and priest unto God, a priesthood holder in Zion appears noble and courteous, as did King Benjamin, whose chivalrous and kindly acts endeared him to his people. Moreover, a priesthood holder in Zion is a peacemaker, which is another word associated with gentleness and meekness. In dealing with people and by virtue of his ordination, he can soothe, pacify, and tame the distressed or wild heart. Such a person, as we have pointed out, is like Ammon, "wise yet harmless."[1902] He employs his knowledge and power not to overwhelm, astonish, or subjugate, but to engage, reason, persuade, and testify, all of which create an environment in which the Spirit of the Lord might do his work of conversion.

A priesthood holder in Zion is meek like his Master, and he, like Jesus, "shall inherit the earth."[1903] Meekness is a childlike quality,[1904] which the Savior attributes to himself,[1905] and therefore expects of everyone who enters into his holy order. The meek are not easily incited to anger or annoyed. They are humble, teachable, and willing to listen and learn; they seek for and act upon the whisperings of the Spirit. The meek are childlike in their submission to the Lord, and they place his wisdom above their own.[1906] Clearly, the priesthood would become a power in such people.

[1899] 2 Nephi 9:30; 28:13; Helaman 6:39.
[1900] D&C 121:41.
[1901] Matthew 11:29.
[1902] Alma 18:22.
[1903] 3 Nephi 12:6.
[1904] Mosiah 3:19.
[1905] Matthew 11:29.
[1906] Hinckley, *Stand a Little Taller*, 18.

Taking the Savior as their example, the meek become lowly in heart, which means they prepare themselves "to hear the word of the Lord."[1907] Such priesthood holders in Zion are filled with faith in Christ; they humble themselves, repent, enter into the new and everlasting covenant through baptism, and receive a remission of sins, which "bringeth meekness, and lowliness of heart; and because of meekness and lowliness of heart cometh the visitation of the Holy Ghost, which Comforter filleth with hope and perfect love."[1908]

The "few" who are called and chosen for eternal life, the meek of Zion and the lowly of heart are those who "find rest to their souls."[1909] This *rest* is the glory of the Lord.[1910] Thus, priesthood holders in Zion live so as to feel the love of God and to receive divine confirmation that they are right before their Maker.[1911]

Such Zion people seek to become meek and lowly of heart so that they can obtain exclusive spiritual gifts: faith, hope, and charity. Any other lifestyle is defined as "vain," the scripture says, "for none is acceptable before God, save the meek and lowly in heart."[1912] Moreover, priesthood holders in Zion seek to become meek because that virtue gives them access to the Lord's grace,[1913] which is the principle of heavenly help or strength that comes through Jesus Christ.[1914] Hence, they strive to become gentle, meek, lowly of heart, "humble, patient, full of love, willing to submit to all things which the Lord seeth fit to inflict upon him, even as a child doth submit to his father."[1915] The Lord's promise to such priesthood holders and the faithful women who are their counterpart is that they will gain an eternal inheritance on the earth,[1916] the destiny of which is to become Zion and a celestial kingdom to those who inherit it.[1917] To the "few" who are called and chosen, the gentle and meek people of Zion, the priesthood is a living, vibrant principle of power.

FEIGNED AND UNFEIGNED LOVE

Babylon has a variety of definitions of love, but all are counterfeits, none of which approach the true meaning of the word. Babylon's love is *feigned love,* meaning imagined, pretended, insincere, manipulative, or contrived love. Whereas true love equalizes and unites, false love is selfish, lustful, domineering, and divisive. Babylon's love serves self, while Zion's love serves another. Babylon's love is a foolish and often extravagant passion, a temporary juvenile attraction or an admiration that is unreasoning and short-lived. Worse, Babylon's version of love is wholly ungrounded in any spiritual activity or standard; it has no celestial underpinnings that would allow it to endure. Babylon's love might start as an infatuated dream, but it will end up as a nightmare.

A sad expression of Babylon's love is any form of forbidden sexual dalliance, which Nephi predicted would become epidemic in the last days. In a vision of latter-day Babylon, he may have seen rampant sexual experimentation, everything from inappropriate kissing and touching to out-of-wedlock intercourse, same-sex attraction, and other loathsome sexual perversions. He was so disgusted with the scene that he lumped the whole into a single word—*whoredoms.* Then he pronounced a certain and severe penalty on those who would participate unrepentantly in such

---

[1907] Largey, *Book of Mormon Reference Companion,* 524.
[1908] Moroni 8:26.
[1909] Alma 37:33–34.
[1910] D&C 84:24.
[1911] Smith, *Gospel Doctrine,* 58, 125–26.
[1912] Moroni 7:43–44.
[1913] Ether 12:26–27.
[1914] LDS Bible Dictionary, s.v. "Grace," 697.
[1915] Mosiah 3:19.
[1916] 3 Nephi 12:5.
[1917] D&C 88:17–26; 130:9.

actions: "for whoso doeth them shall perish;"[1918] "wo, wo, wo be unto them, saith the Lord God Almighty, for they shall be thrust down to hell!"[1919] Nephi foresaw that this sexual cancer would spread throughout the world and sicken the whole of humanity; even the "chosen few" of Zion would need to beware. While mourning, he wrote: ". . . because of whoredoms, they have all gone astray save it be a few, who are the humble followers of Christ; nevertheless, they are led, that in many instances they do err because they are taught by the precepts of men."[1920]

The "chosen few" of Zion have been amply warned to beware lest Babylon's counterfeits for love become so alluring that they ensnare the elect and drag them down to hell. Clearly, there is no future in Babylon's love. It is designed to decoy and trap its victims and lead them down to misery. Those who embrace Babylon's love—and may even feel a form of affection for a time—discover soon enough that this love is ultimately destructive and discouraging; it leads to break-ups and disdain for one another. There is no future in it; and there is no future in the priesthood for the person who engages in such actions *in any degree*. The priesthood holder who does so ceases to represent Christ, the Spirit departs, and priesthood power becomes nonexistent.

LOVE UNFEIGNED

Zion's love is called charity. It is "love unfeigned." In other words, it is sincere, genuine, true, unaffected, uncontrived love. Charity has no selfish intent. It is forever giving, patient, sacrificing, loyal, and trustworthy. Zion's love flows from heaven, down through us, to a loved one or to someone we are serving; therefore, charity is forever connected to the True Vine who makes it an eternal principle.

Significantly, this quality of love is unattainable without receiving it as a spiritual endowment. We simply cannot come by it naturally. Charity will always be a spiritual gift delivered and enhanced by the Holy Ghost. It must be sought after as we would seek after any spiritual gift, such as the gift of healing or the gift of testimony.[1921] Mormon exhorted us to "pray unto the Father with all the energy of heart, that ye may be filled with *this* love."[1922] Righteous priesthood holders in Zion who possess this gift will also have priesthood power.

According to President Joseph F. Smith, "Charity . . . is the greatest principle in existence."[1923] Charity is the "pure love of Christ,"[1924] therefore, charity is *saving* love. The Apostle John taught that the man or woman who loves best knows God best: "Beloved, let us love one another: for love is of God; and every one that loveth is born of God, and knoweth God." For emphasis, John rephrased this scripture to read, "He that loveth not knoweth not God; for God is love."[1925] That is, the man or woman who does not love well does not know God well. The more like God we become, the more love we have to give, and the more love we have to give, the more power we have to save others. Priesthood holders in Zion can be identified by this quality of love. Such Zion people who are united in charitable love obtain saving power that is perhaps only exceeded by the saving power of God.

[1918] 2 Nephi 26:10, 14, 32.
[1919] 2 Nephi 28:15.
[1920] 2 Nephi 28:14.
[1921] D&C 46:10–30.
[1922] Moroni 7:48; emphasis added.
[1923] Smith, *Conference Report*, Apr. 1917, 4.
[1924] Moroni 7:47.
[1925] 1 John 4:7–8.

What Is "True Love?"

There is a vast difference between being *in love* and being *loving*. Babylon leans one way, while Zion leans the other. True love—charity—is built on three sets of triplets. The first set is that of charity's essential qualities:

1. Complete loyalty
2. Complete sacrifice
3. Complete trust

The second set has to do with patience:

1. "I will wait *for* you."
2. "I will wait *with* you."
3. "I will wait *upon* you." That is, "I will serve you."

The third set has to do with how love is received, expressed, and given. Referencing Elder Max Caldwell, H. Wallace Goddard observed that charity has three meanings:

1. Love *from* Christ
2. Love *for* Christ
3. Love *like* Christ

The process of loving begins when we feel Jesus reaching after us *(love from Christ)*. Goddard writes: "Somewhere along the path the miracle of His love breaks down our resistance. As we begin to understand His goodness and redemptiveness, we are changed. We are filled with a profound awe and gratitude for Him. We experience the stirrings of hope. Without this conversion, we are nothing spiritually (1 Cor. 13:2; 2 Nephi 26:30; Moroni 7:44, 46; D&C 18:19). As the amazing truth of His unrelenting love pierces our hearts, we are led to the second kind of charity, *love for Christ*. 'We love him, because he first loved us' (1 John 1:19). . . . As soon as we glimpse His love for us we instinctively love Him in return. We fall at His feet and bathe them with tears of gratitude. Why would He do all He has done to love and rescue my flawed soul? Why??? The answer is charity. As we feel the love from Him and for Him, we naturally *love like Him*. We become saviors on Mount Zion with Him. 'Charity is first and foremost the redemptive love that Jesus offers all of us. It is the love from Christ. He is the model of charity—which never faileth.'"[1926] With regard to our loving *like* Christ, our salvation depends on giving charitable service.[1927]

In each of these descriptions of charity, or "love unfeigned," we observe that true love means being *loving*, which is being charitable or "purely" loving as Christ loves.[1928] Charity, then, is more than a feeling; it is a principle of power that allows us to lift and to save another. Therefore, this quality of love is central to our inviting the Spirit into our lives, to becoming Zionlike, and to obtaining power in the priesthood.

[1926] Goddard, *Drawing Heaven into Your Marriage*, 111.
[1927] Jensen, "Living after the Manner of Happiness," 56.
[1928] Moroni 7:47.

To Love First

How does love begin? By someone loving first. "Herein is love, not that we loved God, but that he loved us. . . . We love him, because he first loved us."[1929]

Love grows and endures on the principle of extending love. In that way, Zion's love is different from Babylon's love. Zion people love first, *then* love is returned—first one, then the other. It is an oft-repeated scriptural formula that has many applications. For example, "Blessed are the merciful: for they shall obtain mercy."[1930] Giving away what we have results in blessings returning to us with increase.[1931] Loving quickly and loving first are key qualities of true love.

Love actively seeks love; that is, love is comfortable in the company of love. Love cleaves unto love like light cleaves unto light, the scripture says.[1932] Moreover, as we have noted, true love—Zion's love—is saving love, the kind of love that the scriptures say *never faileth!*[1933] This love lifts another so that both might be exalted. John Greenleaf Whittier said: "I'll lift you, and you lift me, and we'll both ascend together."

Of course, loving in this way is fraught with risk. Love unfeigned, which is love freely given, might not immediately be returned. Edith Hamilton wrote: "When love meets no return the result is suffering and the greater the love the greater the suffering. There can be no greater suffering than to love purely and perfectly one, who is bent upon evil and self-destruction. That was what God endured at the hands of men."[1934] Elder Maxwell explained that the pain we feel in such moments provides us with an appreciation for the Savior, which appreciation we might not otherwise gain.[1935] Nevertheless, love we must, for only love unfeigned has the power to do the redemptive work of the Father and the Son. If we seek to love God's children back to him, which is our covenantal obligation, we must start by loving God better. This effort increases our capacity to love. Then we are in a position to better love someone else.

Loving God so that we can love better is a key to becoming both a Zion person and a priesthood holder who wields priesthood power. *Loving God so that we can love better* requires that we love for the sake of loving and with no selfish intent; that is, we love because we are loving beings and cannot do otherwise. Although we realize that our loving disposition might make us vulnerable (we might extend love to someone before that person returns love to us), we nevertheless love quickly and first. The nature of the true love within us presses us to persist in loving until love breaks down every barrier, softens a hardened heart, embraces that person in an unbreakable bond, and finally urges that person home. Someone has said that a person is never in more need of understanding than when he is nonapproachable, and he is never more in need of love than when he is unlovable.[1936]

Zion people love quickly and first with the pure love of Christ. They love for the same reasons that the Lord loves—to lift, rescue, and redeem. They keep an eye on love's perfect conclusion: to love like God loves. The priesthood flourishes in those who love.

Love Perfected

Being loving to another person is not only an expansive principle, but it is a perfecting one that draws God near. John said, "If we love one another, God dwelleth in us, and his love is perfected in us."[1937]

[1929] 1 John 4:10, 19.
[1930] Matthew 5:7.
[1931] Packer, "The Candle of the Lord," 33.
[1932] D&C 88:40.
[1933] Moroni 7:46; emphasis added.
[1934] Hamilton, *Spokesman for God*, 112.
[1935] Maxwell, "Enduring Well," 7.
[1936] Skidmore, "What Part Should the Teenager Play in a Family?" *Improvement Era*, Jan. 1952.
[1937] 1 John 4:12.

Additionally, by loving acts we are endowed with a greater measure of the Holy Ghost, the vitalizer of priesthood power: "Hereby know we that we dwell in him, and he in us, because he hath given us of his Spirit."[1938] As we abide in the cycle of giving, receiving and giving love again, our love grows until it eventually becomes perfect: "God is love; and he that dwelleth in love dwelleth in God, and God in him. Herein is our love made perfect."[1939] This is the condition of Zion and an essential principle upon which priesthood authority becomes priesthood power.

No Fear in Love

Perhaps one of the greatest benefits of loving is ceasing to be afraid: "There is no fear in love; but perfect love casteth out fear." Here we see an unmistakable contrast in Zion's and Babylon's love. If our circumstance is causing us to fear, we might reexamine the foundation upon which our love is built, "because fear hath torment." There is no future in such supposed love: "He that feareth is not made perfect in love."[1940]

To shift from Babylon's love to Zion's love, we must regroup and become loving as Jesus is loving, and then the love that we give quickly and first will return to us with increase. As love grows, we will feel fear decrease. Neither Zion nor the priesthood can flourish in fear or lack of love.

Love—the Greatest Power

Love—true love, Zion love, perfect love—is the greatest power in the universe. For that reason it is linked inseparably with the priesthood. Love motivates God to do all that he does.[1941] The greatest expression of his love is to give life and to redeem life. Inspired by love, he invites his children to experience his quality of life, for therein is his joy made full.[1942] By following his example—giving life and redeeming life—our joy is also made full.[1943]

Eternal marriage is the ultimate expression of love; eternal marriage is the end-purpose of the new and everlasting covenant and the oath and covenant of the priesthood. There is no truer statement than this: *All the stars in the universe and all the seraphic hosts of heaven can be traced back to two people who fell in love, knelt at an altar, and made an eternal covenant.* Marriage is the perfection and hope of our love. By love, God creates children and places them on earth, and by love unfeigned he works with them and offers them salvation and exaltation.

There can be no greater power than love. By love we exemplify God. By love we pursue his lifestyle so that we might give and redeem life. By love Zion is established. By love the priesthood becomes operative.

Kindness

Babylon is not kind. Because Babylon is self-serving and has little regard for another's feelings, she will only pretend benevolence when she can somehow benefit. Otherwise, Babylon is loath to extend warmhearted nurturing or to act considerately. Babylon insists that her personal needs be met over every other consideration. Babylon is neither humane, sympathetic, generous nor forgiving. Babylon is friendly only when she can profit thereby. Babylon is neither forbearing nor tolerant; rather, she is thoughtless, inconsiderate, mean, merciless, cruel, and pitiless. Whenever one, or any combination, of these traits is exhibited in covenant people, they immediately assume the appearance of the author of

---

[1938] 1 John 4:13.
[1939] 1 John 4:16–17.
[1940] 1 John 4:18.
[1941] Moses 1:39.
[1942] 3 Nephi 17:20.
[1943] Alma 26:11, 16; 3 Nephi 27:31; 28:10.

these characteristics and become Babylonian. Then the Holy Ghost departs from them; they abandon Zion, and their power in the priesthood comes to an abrupt halt.

Zion people, conversely, exemplify the Savior, who is the perfection of kindness. Because Jesus is their true friend,[1944] they strive to likewise be true friends. They are kind, caring, generous, and warm-hearted. When they interact with other people, they are charitable, considerate, forbearing, and tolerant. They are quick to show sympathy and understanding, and they are humane and compassionate. Zion people are solicitous; that is, they are sincerely concerned, anxious to help, and eagerly attentive. They are nurturing and empathetic, unwilling to allow hurt or permit *lack* to exist among them. When they discover poverty in any form, they attack it with mercy, tenderness, pity, and kindness. Their actions qualify them to summon priesthood power from heaven, where perfect kindness governs the authority of God.

PURE KNOWLEDGE VS. FALSE KNOWLEDGE

"Pure knowledge," according the Constitution of the Priesthood, "shall greatly enlarge the soul without hypocrisy, and without guile."[1945] This statement stands in stark contrast to the reality of much of man's knowledge. Telestial knowledge, although valuable, often poses as truth, while it blinds the mind, retards the soul, and holds its captives in ignorance or oppressive traditions. While man fumbles around trying to discover the truth, he would be better served if he appealed to the Source of truth and admitted that all truth has a divine origin.

A reverse reading of the above scripture reveals two devious characteristics of those people who tout man's knowledge as truth: *hypocrisy and guile*. Hypocrisy is that action and "the practice of professing beliefs, feelings, or virtues that one does not hold or possess." Hypocrisy is "falseness."[1946] That is, while knowing that the "knowledge" that he is advancing is not completely sound, the promoter nevertheless presents it as such for sole purpose of personal gain—money, power, popularity, and followers. Such supposed "experts" are highly rewarded by the world for their "knowledge."

The second characteristic, *guile*, enforces the first, *hypocrisy*. Guile is defined as "treacherous cunning, and skillful deceit."[1947] Together, hypocrisy and guile, applied to man's knowledge, are at least risky and often destructive, and that knowledge is frequently advanced for the gain and praise of those who forward their ideas.

In the 123rd section of the Doctrine and Covenants, Joseph Smith condemned such knowledge and the perpetrators of it, and he identified the evil source and strategy. While he was held in Liberty Jail, he penned a letter to the Saints regarding their duty to expose and counter their persecutors. Much of what he said speaks to the issue of ignorance and oppressive traditions that promote guile, hypocrisy, and false knowledge.

It is an imperative duty that we owe to God, to angels, with whom we shall be brought to stand, and also to ourselves, to our wives and children, who have been made to bow down with grief, sorrow, and care, under the most damning hand of murder, tyranny, and oppression, supported and urged on and upheld by the influence of that spirit which hath so strongly riveted the creeds of the fathers, who have inherited lies, upon the hearts of the children, and filled the world with confusion, and has been growing stronger and stronger, and is now the very mainspring of all corruption, and the whole earth groans under the weight of its iniquity.

Satan is that oppressive spirit who has riveted creeds and lies upon the children of men, and the confusion that he has caused is now so strong that it is the "mainspring of all corruption." The world groans under its weight. How successful has Satan been in perpetrating his lies? Apparently so

---

[1944] D&C 104:1.
[1945] D&C 121:42.
[1946] *American Heritage Dictionary*, s.v. "hypocrisy."
[1947] *American Heritage Dictionary*, s.v. "guile."

successful that even he is astonished: "Which dark and blackening deeds are enough to make hell itself shudder, and to stand aghast and pale, and the hands of the very devil to tremble and palsy."

Consider the Prophet's description of this plague: "It is an iron yoke, it is a strong band; they are the very handcuffs, and chains, and shackles, and fetters of hell." As Zion people and as priesthood holders in Zion, what is our duty to dispel falsehoods and promote the truth? The Prophet gave the answer:

Therefore it is an imperative duty that we owe, not only to our own wives and children, but to the widows and fatherless, whose husbands and fathers have been murdered under its iron hand. . . . And also it is an imperative duty that we owe to all the rising generation, *and to all the pure in heart*—For there are many yet on the earth among all sects, parties, and denominations, who are blinded by the subtle craftiness of men, whereby they lie in wait to deceive, and who are only kept from the truth because they know not where to find it—Therefore, that we should waste and wear out our lives in bringing to light all the hidden things of darkness, wherein we know them; and they are truly manifest from heaven—These should then be attended to with great earnestness.

Our children and grandchildren, our fellow Saints, our brothers and sisters who have not yet found the truth—all of these, including the *pure in heart*, depend on us to defend the truth and denounce error. Our future depends on it: "Let no man count them as small things; for there is much which lieth in futurity, pertaining to the saints, which depends upon these things."[1948]

We must be so very careful when weighing man's knowledge against God's knowledge. In the last days, "many" who are called to eternal life will become "foolish virgins,"[1949] and therefore they will find themselves excluded from the marriage of the King's son. Beyond their indifferent attitude toward preparing for the Bridegroom, these "virgins" are also foolish because they have listened to the wrong voices. Jacob warned against such practices: "The wisdom of the learned is foolishness," he taught; "When men are learned they think they are wise."[1950]

Babylon thinks she is very wise. She examines the creations and workings of God and attempts to explain them without adding God to the equation. Consequently, godless teachings and theories abound. They come and go and are embraced as truth for awhile, until finally truth rips through their fabric and they are exposed for what they are—empty theories and falsehoods. But even when that happens, men do not repent; they simply replace the old, godless teaching with another newer, *wiser*, godless teaching.

An example is the present theory of evolution. In a question-and-answer forum, gospel writer and scientist H. Clay Gorton answered a question of a young geology student in South Africa. He wrote to the youth:

You state that the theory of evolution is demonstrable and provable. That may be true only if you accept the *a priori* premises on which it is based, and the methodology and accuracy of the experimental data.

The theory of evolution is based on and is a part of the more general theory of uniformitarianism, which states that changes in the earth's topology have occurred exclusively as the imperceptively slow erosion processes of rain, wind, freezing and thawing, and the counter imperceptively slow mountain uplift from tectonic plate motion. Catastrophism, the counter theory to uniformitarianism, which includes catastrophic flooding, volcanic action, earthquakes, meteoric impact and near misses by planetoids, has much more to commend it than does uniformitarianism. . . . Let me give you an example—

There is one and only one way of dating any geological, anthropological or paleontological event, and that is by the potassium-argon decay rate. Potassium, the most prevalent element in the earth's

---

[1948] D&C 123:7–15.
[1949] D&C 63:54.
[1950] 2 Nephi 9:28.

crust, has a radioisotope, K40, found in a concentration of the order of .01%. The half life of K40 is 1.8 times 10 to the 9th years, and it decays to the stable A40, which is a gas. While any rock is molten, any argon produced from K40 escapes, but if the rock is solid the argon is captured. The only dating process ever used to place a time line on any geological, anthropological or paleontological event is to measure the K40/A40 ratio in a sample of rock taken from the site. In the first place the date thus established does NOT measure the age of the site. It measures the age of the rock found at the site! Secondly, this measurement technique is highly unreliable, but its unreliability is never taken into account since it is the only possible way of dating into the distant past. So the method is accepted without question, as shown by the following experiment—

Two samples of volcanic rock were submitted for dating by the K/A decay method. One sample measured to be 65 million years old and the other, 2.5 billion years old. These two samples were taken from the lava flows from two volcanoes in Hawaii. The eruption from which the first sample was taken occurred in 1800 a.d., and the eruption from which the second sample was taken occurred in 1802 a.d.! When confronted with this data the researchers concluded that the two rocks could not have been part of the lava flow, but were picked up as debris while the flow was yet molten.

This demonstrates the tenacity with which any currently held scientific theory or method is held. Data that are contrary to the currently held theory are merely discarded. In truth, it takes a veritable scientific revolution to change the currently held theories of science. Each of the proponents of the theories of past ages, beginning with the Greeks, knew that they had the ultimate truth. But each was finally proven to be completely wrong and was replaced by the succeeding theory, in the same manner that the theories currently held to be true will also find their way into the dustbins of history.[1951]

"O the foolishness of men!"[1952] our Book of Mormon prophets lament, "for the reward of their pride and their foolishness they shall reap destruction; for because they yield unto the devil and choose works of darkness rather than light, therefore they must go down to hell."[1953]

Babylon is the custodian and promoter of the false, transitory, foolish knowledge that the world accepts as truth and wisdom. The apostle Paul foresaw that the people in the last days would be "ever learning, and never able to come to the knowledge of the truth."[1954] Nephi added, "There shall be many which shall teach after this manner, false and vain and foolish doctrines." He gives the reason: *pride*. People in the latter days "shall be puffed up in their hearts, and shall seek deep to hide their counsels from the Lord; and their works shall be in the dark." These false teachings will be widely accepted: "Yea, they have *all* gone out of the way; they have become corrupted." Why? "Because of pride, and because of false teachers, and false doctrine." Frighteningly, the children of Zion would not be exempt from buying into this counterfeit wisdom: "They have all gone astray save it be a few, who are the humble followers of Christ; nevertheless, they are led, that in many instances they do err because they are taught by the precepts of men." Nephi pronounces the Lord's curse on the wise and learned of Babylon: "O the wise, and the learned, and the rich, that are puffed up in the pride of their hearts, and all those who preach false doctrines, and all those who commit whoredoms, and pervert the right way of the Lord, wo, wo, wo be unto them, saith the Lord God Almighty, for they shall be thrust down to hell!" He pronounces a curse upon those who reject the knowledge of God and embrace the knowledge of man: "Wo unto them that turn aside the just for a thing of naught and revile against that which is good, and say that it is of no worth! For the day shall come that the Lord

---

[1951] Gorton, "My concern is that creation seems to contradict the provable and demonstrable theory of evolution of species," *AskGramps.org*
[1952] 2 Nephi 9:28.
[1953] 2 Nephi 26:10.
[1954] 2 Timothy 3:7.

God will speedily visit the inhabitants of the earth; and in that day that they are fully ripe in iniquity they shall perish."[1955]

Are we really so anxious to accept the wisdom of man when it clearly does not square with the revealed word of God? Can we become Zion people under such delusions? Can there be power in the priesthood when a man professes to embrace the truth on one hand and believe or promote falsehoods on the other?

Reviewing the near-destruction of the Nephite nation prior to the birth of Christ, Mormon described the character of those who embrace Babylon and accept its teachings as truth: "O how foolish, and how vain, and how evil, and devilish, and how quick to do iniquity, and how slow to do good, are the children of men; yea, how quick to hearken unto the words of the evil one, and to set their hearts upon the vain things of the world!"[1956] Gratefully, Babylon will not forever succeed in propagating its falsehoods. The Lord has stated emphatically, "The wisdom of the wise shall perish."[1957]

The message should be clear: to the extent that we believe and promote the wisdom of Babylon, we shut out the Holy Ghost, who is the disseminator of all truth,[1958] and thus we limit our power in the priesthood.

ZION'S APPROACH TO "PURE KNOWLEDGE"

Zion approaches knowledge in a manner that is opposite Babylon's approach. A Zion people are taught that there is a *key* to receiving "pure knowledge." This *key* consists of three elements: (1) priesthood authority, (2) priesthood ordinances, and (3) the power of the Holy Ghost.[1959] When these elements are in place, this *key* becomes functional and can be used to discover the truth in recesses of telestial knowledge and to unlock the library of heaven, or, as Brigham Young said, "to enable us to discern between truth and error, light and darkness, him who is of God, and him who is not of God, and to know how to place everything where it belongs. That is the only way to be a scientific Christian; there is no other method or process which will actually school a person so that he can become a Saint of God, and prepare him for a celestial glory; he must have within him the testimony of the spirit of the Gospel."[1960]

According to Elder Alvin R. Dyer, "pure knowledge" is disseminated in no other way.[1961] By this *key*—priesthood authority, priesthood ordinances, and the power of the Holy Ghost—we are promised that we might "know the truth of all things."[1962]

Priesthood holders in Zion are the "few" who are instructed in the acquisition of "pure knowledge." They are taught that this knowledge comes only through the Spirit. They know that they must receive and retain the gift of the Holy Ghost or forever remain at the mercy of man's knowledge. Because the Holy Ghost is both the agent of "pure knowledge" and priesthood power, the sacrament covenant becomes vitally important to us. The sacrament promises the Spirit's continued companionship on the condition of worthiness. The companionship of the Holy Ghost provides us with spiritual gifts, including the gift of "pure knowledge."[1963] These spiritual gifts include gifts related to priesthood rights and powers, for example, the gift of administration; understanding the operations

---

[1955] 2 Nephi 28:9, 11–12, 14–16.
[1956] Helaman 12:4.
[1957] D&C 76:9.
[1958] Moroni 10:5.
[1959] D&C 84:19–21; Moroni 10:5.
[1960] Young, *Discourses of Brigham Young*, 429.
[1961] Dyer, Conference Report, Oct. 1964, 133–34.
[1962] Moroni 10:5; D&C 124:97; Moses 6:61.
[1963] D&C 46:18.

of spirits; wisdom; faith to heal and be healed; the working of miracles; and the ability to prophesy, discern spirits, and speak with tongues and interpret tongues.[1964]

Significantly, the Holy Ghost disseminates "pure knowledge" to our minds while priesthood ordinances unlock the door to the celestial library of knowledge. As we have demonstrated, there is an inseparable connection between priesthood power and the Holy Ghost. Any action on our part to cause the Spirit to withdraw also causes priesthood power to cease. Hence, we cannot expect to receive "pure knowledge" from the Holy Ghost by means of the priesthood ordinances if we are sinful or unrepentant, or if we are engaging in any of the activities that are prohibited by the Constitution of the Priesthood.

On the other hand, if we are doing all we can to abide in our covenants, honor God's laws, obey his commandments, live by every word that proceeds forth from the mouth of God, and develop the virtues listed in the Constitution of the Priesthood, we may ask for and receive "pure knowledge, which shall greatly enlarge the soul without hypocrisy or guile." This is knowledge that exalts man, taught Elder Alvin R. Dyer.[1965] This knowledge begins as a seed, according to Alma, and must pass four tests to qualify as truth:

1. When the seed of truth is planted in our souls, we feel something positive stirring within us.
2. We feel invigorated, and we are motivated to become a better person.
3. The seed of truth corresponds with, builds upon, and clarifies other ideas that we have had, and it sparks new ideas.
4. The seed of truth feels so good that we want to keep seeking after it and see it through to its perfect conclusion.

"Pure knowledge" is expansive, enlightening, and delicious. It increases faith; it is discernable; it is clearly good. If we do not neglect or reject it, this knowledge will grow into a tree that bears beautiful, delicious fruit, "which is most precious, which is sweet above all that is sweet, and which is white, yea, and pure above all that is pure."[1966]

"Pure knowledge" is manifested to both the mind and the heart; that is, to our intellect and to our emotional center.[1967] Two witnesses! "Pure knowledge" might be presented to us as a new idea, but it will seem reasonable (witness to the mind), and it will evoke a positive emotion (witness to the heart). The witness to the mind and the heart may vary in sequence. The second witness may come in conjunction with the first witness or after much study, fasting and prayer—but it will come. Otherwise, without these two witnesses, we would suspect that the idea is not grounded in truth.

The emotional witness might take any number of forms. For example, the Prophet Joseph Smith once described the manner in which such direct inspiration comes: "Yea, thus saith the still small voice, which whispereth through and pierceth all things, and often times it maketh my bones to quake while it maketh manifest."[1968] The quaking of the body, a burning in the bosom or any other number of physical reactions are indications that "pure knowledge" is being introduced to the soul.

Likewise, the intellect might be acted upon and react in multiple ways when it is being presented with truth. Again, the Prophet taught, "A person may profit by noticing the first intimation of the spirit of revelation; for instance, when you feel pure intelligence flowing into you, it may give you sudden strokes of ideas, so that by noticing it, you may find it fulfilled the same day or soon; (i.e.) those things that were presented unto your minds by the Spirit of God, will come to pass; and thus by

---

[1964] D&C 46:15–17, 19–25.
[1965] Dyer, Conference Report, Oct. 1964, 133–34.
[1966] Alma 32:26–43.
[1967] D&C 8:2.
[1968] D&C 85:6.

learning the Spirit of God and understanding it, you may grow unto the principle of revelation, until you become perfect in Christ Jesus."[1969]

Those who would deny such revelations of God are of Babylon. Moroni wrote: "And again I speak unto you who deny the revelations of God, and say that they are done away, that there are no revelations, nor prophecies, nor gifts, nor healing, nor speaking with tongues, and the interpretation of tongues; Behold I say unto you, he that denieth these things knoweth not the gospel of Christ; yea, he has not read the scriptures; if so, he does not understand them. For do we not read that God is the same yesterday, today, and forever, and in him there is no variableness neither shadow of changing?"[1970]

Because by covenant, priesthood holders agree to "live by every word that proceedeth forth from the mouth of God,"[1971] we must understand the process and obligation to obtaining pure knowledge. Of course, one of the ultimate communications of "pure knowledge" is to receive the divine announcement that our calling and election has been made sure. It is imperative that we strive with all our might to magnify our calling, give diligent heed to the words of the eternal life, and live by every word that proceedeth forth from the mouth of God[1972] so that we might obtain this communication of "pure knowledge." The Lord said, "It is impossible for a man to be saved in ignorance;"[1973] that is, ignorant of our future with God.

Wisdom carries us to this knowledge. Wisdom begins by humbly seeking the Lord: "Let him that is ignorant learn wisdom by humbling himself and calling upon the Lord his God, that his eyes may be opened that he may see, and his ears opened that he may hear."[1974] Gaining pure knowledge and wisdom become our challenge, said Elder Alvin R. Dyer; we are to abide faithfully our covenants and gain wisdom upon wisdom, until we receive pure knowledge from the mouth of God and thus make our calling and election sure.[1975]

WISDOM AND "PURE KNOWLEDGE"

Pure knowledge becomes trivia unless it is acted upon. The combination of knowledge (or belief) and action is the definition of faith; this combination produces wisdom. Wisdom is an understanding of what is true, right, or lasting. Wisdom is insight that leads to common sense and good judgment. Wisdom is selecting truth from the sum of scholarly learning, sages, and prophets, and formulating those truths into a sound outlook on life and a well-reasoned plan or course of action.[1976] Priesthood holders in Zion are expected to be wise.

James, the Lord's brother, explained how we might differentiate between a wise and an unwise priesthood holder: "Who is a wise man and endued [endowed] with knowledge among you? Let him shew out of a good conversation his works with meekness of wisdom. But if ye have bitter envying and strife in your hearts, glory not, and lie not against the truth. This wisdom descendeth not from above, but is earthly, sensual, devilish. For where envying and strife is, there is confusion and every evil work. But the wisdom that is from above is first pure, then peaceable, gentle, and easy to be entreated, full of mercy and good fruits, without partiality, and without hypocrisy. And the fruit of righteousness is sown in peace of them that make peace."[1977]

[1969] Smith, *Teachings of the Prophet Joseph Smith*, 151.
[1970] Mormon 9:7–9.
[1971] D&C 84:44.
[1972] D&C 84:33, 43–44.
[1973] D&C 131:6.
[1974] D&C 136:32.
[1975] Dyer, Conference Report, Oct. 1964, 133–34.
[1976] *American Heritage Dictionary*, s.v. "wisdom."
[1977] James 3:13–18.

The scriptures paint a portrait of a wise man:

- A wise man need not be compelled to do that which is right.[1978]
- A wise man is a humble man, who seeks sound instruction[1979] and hearkens to the wisdom that is imparted.[1980]
- A wise man will pursue wisdom over riches,[1981] and he will treasure up pure knowledge in his bosom.[1982]
- Because the word of wisdom and the word of knowledge are spiritual gifts, which are bestowed only by the Holy Ghost, a wise man will live his life so that he can ask for and receive these gifts.[1983]
- A wise man will judiciously disperse his wisdom to others so that they too might praise the Lord.[1984]
- A wise man's reward is much; his wisdom shall beget more wisdom,[1985] and as wisdom multiplies, it shall become very great.[1986]
- A wise man seeks to receive communication from God[1987] so that he might enter into the joy of the Lord.[1988]
- If a man is wise in mortality, he shall be counted worthy to inherit the mansions of God.[1989]
- A wise man will receive the Lord's seal and blessing, guaranteeing him that in the midst of the Lord's house, he shall become a ruler in the celestial kingdom.[1990]

REPROVING THE LORD'S WAY

The Lord's call to the priesthood holders of the last days is to cry nothing but repentance to this generation.[1991] We must cry repentance the Lord's way. Any person with a stewardship, whether he (or she) is a parent, a missionary, a priesthood or auxiliary leader, an instructor, or a prophet, will find himself in a situation where he must call someone to repentance. In *every* case, the directive is to seek inspiration, and then speak as the Spirit gives utterance. The instruction reads: "Reproving betimes with sharpness, when moved upon by the Holy Ghost; and then showing forth afterwards an increase of love toward him whom thou hast reproved, lest he esteem thee to be his enemy. That he [the reproved person] may know that thy faithfulness is stronger than the cords of death."[1992]

In such situations when reproof must be given, we teeter precariously on the edge of a precipice. Reproving Babylon's way—domineeringly, impatiently, angrily, harshly, proudly, insensitively, or belittlingly, without first seeking the Spirit and without regard to the person's salvation—the reproved one will become discouraged, victimlike, and fearful. Our relationship with him will suffer—and worse, his relationship with God could suffer. Over time, he might develop a low regard for the

---

[1978] D&C 58:26.
[1979] D&C 1:26.
[1980] D&C 50:1.
[1981] D&C 6:7; 11:7.
[1982] D&C 38:30.
[1983] D&C 46:17–18.
[1984] D&C 52:17.
[1985] D&C 88:40.
[1986] D&C 76:9.
[1987] D&C 78:2.
[1988] D&C 51:19.
[1989] D&C 72:4.
[1990] D&C 101:61.
[1991] D&C 6:9; 11:9.
[1992] D&C 121:43–44.

priesthood and the gospel. If we step into that contentious arena in any degree, the Spirit leaves us and priesthood power ceases. And yet, unfortunately, this is a common occurrence among the "many" who are called: "We have learned by sad experience that it is the nature and disposition of almost all men, as soon as they get a little authority, as they suppose, they will immediately begin to exercise unrighteous dominion."[1993]

Significantly, the directive to carefully "reprove" follows the directives of avoiding unrighteous dominion, exercising persuasion, being patient and long-suffering, being gentle, meek, loving, and kind, and seeking pure knowledge from the Spirit so that we do not come across as hypocritical, deceitful, or harmful. If we are such people, then we might reprove as the Spirit directs, but before reproving, we might ponder this proverb: "A soft answer turneth away wrath, but grievous words stir up anger."[1994]

This priesthood instruction regarding reproving and calling a person to repentance is often misunderstood. A quick review of definitions might help us comprehend the Lord's intention.

Reprove means to "voice or convey disapproval of; rebuke . . . admonish. To find fault with."[1995]

Betimes means "In good time; early. . . . Once in a while; on occasion." Or less commonly, "Quickly; soon."[1996]

Sharp or *sharpness* has many definitions, but the one that seems most reasonable in this context is "Clearly and distinctly set forth."[1997] Of interest, a synonym for *sharp* is *harsh*, which is totally out of character with the priesthood.

Therefore, we might recraft "reproving betimes with sharpness" to read: "admonishing in a good time with clarity and love." Nothing about this directive gives us license to explode angrily, demean, or discourage. The entire intent of reproving by the Spirit is to point out errant behavior at the right time—early, if possible—for the purpose of correcting a person's direction, and calling him back to safety. It is redemption—not discipline—that is the goal of admonition. Therefore, the correction must be delivered as the Spirit directs, but softly and accompanied by "pure testimony"[1998] borne in clarity and love.

We cannot magnify the priesthood and avoid reproving. Because our calling contains the commandment to cry repentance, we are obligated to do so or forfeit our authority. To that end, the Lord explains the Zion way to reprove: "then showing forth afterwards an increase of love toward him whom thou hast reproved, lest he esteem thee to be his enemy. That he may know that thy faithfulness is stronger than the cords of death."[1999] Love must *increase*; love must become greater than it was before the reproving!

REPROVING WITH LOVE

Let us review what we have learned about love as it applies to reproof. In the first place, true love is called *charity*, "the pure love of Christ."[2000] Therefore, the Apostle John can be confident when he says, "There is no fear in love, but perfect love casteth out fear." He goes on to say, "If we love one another, God dwelleth in us, and his love is perfected in us. Hereby know we that we dwell in him, and he in us, because he hath given us of his Spirit." That is, when it comes to loving, we must take the initiative. This pattern of loving is modeled by God toward us: "Herein is love, not that we loved

---

[1993] D&C 121:39.
[1994] Proverbs 15:1.
[1995] *American Heritage Dictionary*, s.v. "reprove."
[1996] *American Heritage Dictionary*, s.v. "betimes."
[1997] *American Heritage Dictionary*, s.v. "sharp."
[1998] Alma 4:19.
[1999] D&C 121:43–44.
[2000] Moroni 7:47.

God, but that he loved us. . . . We love him, because he first loved us."[2001] What is the end result of loving Christ's way? It "never faileth!"[2002]

The only proof that a reproved person has that our faithfulness (our love for him and our devotion to God) is greater than the "cords of death" is our showing him "love unfeigned [unpretended]." The phrase "cords of death" evokes the image of the inevitable and unceasing draw of death as it tries to separate us. Because death is any separation, it will attempt to divide us from our spouse, children, and friends—and from God. Death, in any of its forms, is contrary to the priesthood order of Zion, which is unity. A priesthood holder in Zion will show an increase of love after the reproof to counter the "cords of death" that might otherwise separate him from the reproved person.

CORDS OF DEATH AND BONDS OF LOVE

Opposite death is life, the uniting of two or more things to make them *one*. Life is made possible only by the At-one-ment of Jesus Christ, which is ever pulling divided things back into their perfect, unified forms—to make them *at one*. Whereas Babylon is defined by its "cords of death," which pull us apart, Zion is defined by its "bonds of love,"[2003] which pull us together. We always feel the tug of these two forces. We invoke the unifying power of the At-one-ment by means of love that binds, which is stronger than the cords of death. This fact is of great significance to covenant people; it should be, perhaps, of even greater significance to priesthood holders, whose responsibility it is to create the atmosphere of unity so that Zion might be established.

Elder Stephen L Richards said family ties are (or should be) the strongest bonds of love by reason of the sealing power. But next to these bonds are the bonds of the holy priesthood. By revelation, these bonds are "stronger than the cords of death," according to the Constitution of the Priesthood. Because we have made unifying covenants, the loving relationships that we form and enjoy in the Church weld us together more perfectly with each other than do any other relationships.[2004] Therefore, when we serve our family or in the Church, especially when we are impressed by the Spirit to reprove, we must strive for the *oneness* that is characteristic of Zion. The Savior said, "Be one; and if ye are not one ye are not mine."[2005] No one can be happy or effective if he is not one with his family and the Saints of God.[2006]

Admittedly, the instruction to carefully reprove can be challenging for the best of us. The occasions that call for such correcting are often charged with emotion and misunderstanding. But we must remember what is at stake; if we reprove Babylon's way, we risk losing access to the Spirit and ongoing power in the priesthood. The way of Babylon, which is chosen by the "many," leaves us to ourselves, defrocks us of the rights of the priesthood, destroys relationships, and binds us in the cords of death. The way of Zion, which is chosen by the "few," clothes us in the Spirit, empowers us with the rights of the priesthood, enhances relationships with added love, and wraps us in unifying bonds of charity.

CHARITY TOWARD ALL MEN AND THE HOUSEHOLD OF GOD

The Apostle Paul foresaw that the behavior of the people of Babylon in the last days would cause "perilous" conditions to arise:

For men shall be lovers of their own selves, covetous, boasters, proud, blasphemers, disobedient to parents, unthankful, unholy, without natural affection, trucebreakers, false accusers, incontinent,

---

[2001] 1 John 4:10, 13, 18, 19.
[2002] Moroni 7:46.
[2003] D&C 88:133.
[2004] Richards, Conference Report, Oct. 1938, 114.
[2005] D&C 38:27.
[2006] Richards, Conference Report, Oct. 1938, 114.

fierce, despisers of those that are good, traitors, heady, highminded, lovers of pleasures more than lovers of God; having a form of godliness, but denying the power thereof: from such turn away. For of this sort are they which creep into houses, and lead captive silly women laden with sins, led away with divers lusts, ever learning, and never able to come to the knowledge of the truth.[2007]

Interestingly, of all these loathsome characteristics, the first on Paul's list is "lovers of their own selves." The prophet Mormon made a similar list as he contrasted Alma's Zion people to the rest of the Nephite nation. Those who characterized Babylon were selfish, indulgent, devilish, idolatrous, immoral, jealous, and proud.[2008] Again, we see self-indulgence at the top of the list.

Neither the people of Zion nor priesthood holders in Zion are selfish in any way! Zion people have consecrated all that they are and have to building up God's kingdom and establishing Zion. According to Mormon, Zion people were selfless, modest, and steady, and consequently they became rich!—"And thus, in their prosperous circumstances, they did not send away any who were naked, or that were hungry, or that were athirst, or that were sick, or that had not been nourished; and they did not set their hearts upon riches; therefore they were liberal to all, both old and young, both bond and free, both male and female, whether out of the church or in the church, having no respect to persons as to those who stood in need."[2009] These people were living according to the mandate of the Constitution of the Priesthood, which states: "Let thy bowels also be full of charity towards all men, and to the household of faith."[2010]

The "household of faith" constitutes the Saints of God. "All men" is everyone else. According to Alma the Elder, the charity of Zion people causes them to be "liberal to all." He said that their charity compels them to reach down to another and lift him up. Their charity will not allow them to tolerate suffering or depravation of any kind. Wherever there is hurt, they seek to heal; wherever there is want, they apply their abundance; wherever there is need, they labor to satisfy it. They do not think of themselves; they think of others. They worship God by emulating him and caring for his children. Because they love, they are not envious; rather, they rejoice in the accomplishments and stewardships of others. By their charitable actions, they "are willing to bear one another's burdens, that they may be light; yea, and are willing to mourn with those that mourn; yea, and comfort those that stand in need of comfort." Because of their charity, they qualify to be called God's people. Clothed in the mantle of charity, they humbly "stand as witnesses of God at all times and in all things, and in all places that [they] may be in, *even until death*."[2011]

To such Zion people, the power of charity enhances the power of the priesthood; charity magnifies the promises made in the oath and covenant of the priesthood, which are repeated in the Constitution of the Priesthood; and by charity, this power and these promises are made sure.

LET VIRTUE GARNISH THY THOUGHTS UNCEASINGLY

Babylon is characterized by immorality and amorality.

On the one hand Babylon is blatantly depraved, flaunting its wickedness and proudly waving its demonic behavior like a flag. Babylon is carnal, sensual, and devilish by design; that is, it goes out of its way to be worldly, catering to its physical and sexual appetites; it sets aside spiritual and intellectual interests, and it focuses on pampering the physical and sexual senses to provide luxuriant gratification; it is malicious, evil, mischievous, annoying, contemptible, fiendish, excessive, and extreme—in every way, Babylon is characteristic of its father, the devil, whom it worships.

[2007] 2 Timothy 3:2–7.
[2008] Alma 1:22, 32.
[2009] Alma 1:30.
[2010] D&C 121:45.
[2011] Mosiah 18:8–9; emphasis added.

On the other hand, Babylon seeks to appear moral without admitting to moral distinctions or judgments. It lacks sensibility to the traditional standard of morality; it is uncaring about right and wrong; and it is zealously tolerant of shifting values. To be immoral or amoral, to cast off discipline and entertain depraved thoughts or adopt dishonorable behavior *to any degree* results in the Holy Ghost's departure and his taking with him priesthood power.

Zion's virtue is five-fold. First, it is moral excellence, righteousness, and goodness. Second, it is chastity. Third, it is the sum of positive character attributes. Fourth, it is courage and valor. Fifth, it is power.

Moral virtue, taught Elder Gordon B. Hinckley, provides freedom from regret. Virtue is the only way to achieve peace of conscience and to lay hold on the covenantal promises of God. Jesus taught this principle in the form of a covenant: "Blessed are the pure in heart: for they shall see God."[2012] As much as God has the power to fulfill that covenant, he also has the power to fulfill the covenant in the Constitution of the Priesthood: "Let virtue garnish thy thoughts unceasingly" with the promise: "Then shall thy confidence wax strong in the presence of God; and the doctrine of the priesthood shall distil upon thy soul as the dews from heaven. The Holy Ghost shall be thy constant companion, and thy scepter an unchanging scepter of righteousness and truth; and thy dominion shall be an everlasting dominion, and without compulsory means it shall flow unto thee forever and ever."[2013] Elder Hinckley concluded that this promise—and there are few promises that are greater—is extended to every virtuous man *and* woman.[2014] Only to the virtuous person, he said, come the blessings of undreamed of glory, peace, love, trust, and loyalty.[2015] President Heber J. Grant taught similarly: To a very great extent the path to eternal life is maintained by those whose thoughts are garnished by virtue and whose words are gentle and pure.[2016]

Garnishing Our Thoughts with Virtue

To *garnish* is to embellish or adorn; it is to "enhance in appearance by adding decorative touches."[2017] Virtue adds delightful color, flavor, or "trim" to our thoughts, thus inviting the Holy Ghost. The Constitution of the Priesthood instructs us to garnish our thoughts with virtue with the promise that the blessings of eternity will follow.

In Hebrew culture, a newly betrothed young man would spend the better part of a year preparing a bridal chamber for his bride. No effort was too great and no detail of craftsmanship was too insignificant; he was preparing the place that he would one day bring his beloved. Therefore, with "diligent heed," he would garnish the chamber with beautiful items, sweet incense, and delicious food, so that it would be perfect for his bride.[2018]

In a like manner, we carefully and patiently prepare and adorn our minds with virtue so that we might invite the Holy Ghost, our beloved and constant companion, to come and reside with us. As much as the bridegroom would never offend his beloved with unholy behavior or language, and as much as he would never betray her trust in his thoughts, neither would we act, speak, or think anything unworthy that would dishearten our beloved Friend, whom the Savior gave to us as his precious gift. Hence, the mind that is garnished with virtue is the mind wherein the Holy Ghost is willing to comfortably and continually dwell. And where the Holy Ghost dwells, there is priesthood power.

[2012] Matthew 5:8.
[2013] D&C 121:45–46.
[2014] Hinckley, Conference Report, Oct. 1970, 66.
[2015] Hinckley, Conference Report, Oct. 1970, 66.
[2016] Grant, Conference Report, Apr. 1937, 11–12.
[2017] *American Heritage Dictionary*, s.v. "garnish."
[2018] Nielsen, *Beloved Bridegroom*, 35–36.

Then blessings abound (notice the word *then*).

SUMMARY AND CONCLUSION

The Constitution of the Priesthood begins with a sobering declaration: "Behold, there are many called, but few are chosen."[2019] Unless we disbelieve the word of the Lord, we are forced to admit that many who are called to the priesthood and thus to eternal life will struggle or fail in their calling. The stated reasons for their failure are setting their hearts on the things of the world, aspiring to the honors of men, neglecting or rejecting the principles of righteousness, and attempting to dominate and control.

When a priesthood holder violates the oath and covenant of the priesthood "in any degree of unrighteousness, behold, the heavens withdraw themselves; the Spirit of the Lord is grieved; and when it is withdrawn, Amen to the priesthood or the authority of that man."[2020] These are the beginning of his troubles. Beyond losing the Spirit and priesthood power, the man, if he remains unrepentant, will begin to spin out of control, first becoming critical of the Church and its leaders, then persecuting the Saints, and finally fighting against God.[2021]

The Constitution of the Priesthood also sets forth instructions that invite the Holy Ghost into our lives; the presence of the Holy Ghost makes the priesthood functional. A person who lives by these instructions becomes Christlike and therefore powerful in the priesthood, as was Jesus.

Avoiding the behavior of Babylon and embracing the attributes of Zion summons unimaginable rewards. That is the subject we will explore in the next and final chapter on the Constitution of the Priesthood, and the final chapter in this section of the oath and covenant of the priesthood, the second pillar of Zion.

[2019] D&C 121:34.
[2020] D&C 121:37.
[2021] D&C 121:34–38.

Section 14

The Constitution of the Priesthood:

The Rewards for the Chosen Few

Note: This chapter explores some of the most impressive blessings of the gospel that describe the ideal of Zion and the fulness of the priesthood. While it is true that they lie within the reach of every worthy covenant person, it is also true that achieving them might require a lifetime of effort—and that effort might extend after death up until the time of resurrection. We need only recall that both Abraham and Moses had lived to an extended age before they realized the fulness of these blessings. Therefore, this chapter is not designed to discourage, but rather to state the ideal, define terms, lift our sights, and set clear goals. We do not know the Lord's timing, but we do know that every covenant we make, including the oath and covenant of the priesthood, mandates that we persist in righteousness until we obtain these blessings. Zion people, the "few" who are both called and chosen, are characterized by both their pursuit and the achievement of these eternal rewards.

Because the quest for the highest blessings is a commandment, the Lord assumes an obligation to help us fulfill that commandment, provided we put forth the effort. Our obligation is to seek until we find. As long as we move forward on the path to eternal life, we will achieve our goal—guaranteed! We must do so. Our exaltation depends on it. What will happen along the way? Zion becomes our character, priesthood knowledge distils upon our souls, and we are filled with a greater portion of the Spirit.

Then come the blessings of eternity!

Of the many who are called to eternal life by virtue of the priesthood covenant, a few will actually heed the call of Zion, forsake Babylon and its identifying behaviors, as described in the Constitution of the Priesthood, and order their lives accordingly. The blessings for doing so are a restatement of those rewards listed in the oath and covenant of the priesthood: eternal life and exaltation. And lest women feel excluded, we must remember Elder McConkie's reassurance that because the promises contained in the priesthood covenant are repeated at the occasion of temple marriage, they are pertinent to both men and women.[2022]

[2022] McConkie, *A New Witness for the Articles of Faith*, 313.

THE REWARDS

Then shall thy confidence wax strong in the presence of God; and the doctrine of the priesthood shall distil upon thy soul as the dews from heaven. The Holy Ghost shall be thy constant companion, and thy scepter an unchanging scepter of righteousness and truth; and thy dominion shall be an everlasting dominion, and without compulsory means it shall flow unto thee forever and ever.[2023]

Notice that the word "then" prefaces the rewards. After we have qualified, *then* the blessings begin to flow:

- Our confidence grows so that we can obtain the presence of God.
- The doctrine of the priesthood distils upon our souls as the dews from heaven; that is, the Father teaches us of the priesthood covenant.[2024]
- The promise of the constant companionship of the Holy Ghost is once again confirmed and renewed to us—this time, in greater measure.
- We receive a scepter of unchanging righteousness and truth, thus signifying that we are at last true sons (or daughters) of God, kings and priests (queens and priestesses), and like him in every way.
- We receive an everlasting dominion, that is, an inheritance in the celestial world with the promise of eternal increase.
- Our kingdom will flow unto us and expand of its own accord, which is according to celestial law; that is, our *righteous* dominion grows without our compelling it and without force or *unrighteous* dominion.

"THEN SHALL THY CONFIDENCE WAX STRONG IN THE PRESENCE OF GOD"

This promise assumes that we first believe that we actually *can* stand in the presence of God—*in this life*. Such a belief might challenge our paradigm of the gospel and urge us into new territory. Before embarking on this trek, we must resist the temptation to shy away from the more impressive blessings of the gospel. It was this attitude that earned the Israelites forfeiture of Melchizedek Priesthood blessings and thus lost them their opportunity to become Zion people.

We learn that Moses "plainly taught . . . the children of Israel in the wilderness [that] this greater priesthood administereth the gospel and holdeth the key of the mysteries of the kingdom, *even the key of the knowledge of God. Therefore, in the ordinances thereof, the power of godliness is manifest. And without the ordinances thereof, and the authority of the priesthood, the power of godliness is not manifest unto men in the flesh; for without this no man can see the face of God, even the Father, and live.*" Moses held this priesthood and had received its blessings; therefore, to also make his people Zionlike, Moses "sought diligently to sanctify his people that they might behold the face of God; but they hardened their hearts and could not endure his presence; therefore, the Lord in his wrath, for his anger was kindled against them, swore that they should not enter into his rest while in the wilderness, which rest is the fulness of his glory."[2025]

It is hard to imagine a sadder scene. Despite their being the children of the covenant, despite their having been miraculously delivered from bondage, and despite their having been miraculously preserved by the hand of God, the Israelites desired only to live a *comfortable* gospel. They contented themselves to have their prophet see and talk with God and convey to them the Lord's

---

[2023] D&C 121:45–46; emphasis added.
[2024] D&C 84:48.
[2025] D&C 84:19–24.

communication. But when it came time for them individually to pay the price to receive the same privilege, they held back. They perceived the challenge *and the invitation* as being too difficult.

The Lord does not react well to our treating lightly or rejecting his invitations. Because a central purpose of the Melchizedek Priesthood is to bring people into the presence of God, the Lord had no choice except to withdraw it and leave the people with a lesser and more *comfortable* gospel law.[2026] Now without the higher priesthood and its attendant covenants, laws, and ordinances, the Israelites found it impossible to become Zion people. With the lesser priesthood they could become good, but they could never become great.

In our day, the early Latter-day Saints also rejected the higher law that would have made them Zion people and eventually ushered them into the presence of God. Contrary to Moses' time, however, the Lord did not withdraw the Melchizedek Priesthood, but, nevertheless, his wrath was kindled against them. He drove the Saints into the wilderness to prepare for Zion, and we have been preparing ever since. The Lord has given us the covenants, laws, and ordinances that we need to become Zion people if we will simply employ them. The call to forsake Babylon and come unto Christ—to *truly* come unto Christ—continues to be God's invitation. Will we listen this time? If we do not, we risk once again the Lord's wrath.

Now Is the Time

In all our ponderings, duties, and devotions involving the priesthood, we must remember that regaining the presence of God is the consummate event and the pinnacle of priesthood belief. Everything about the new and everlasting covenant and the oath and covenant of the priesthood points to this singular occurrence. Our "calling" in the priesthood invites us to seek to stand in the presence of God *in this life,* and the priesthood empowers us to do so. It is not enough that our prophet stands in God's presence and receives intelligence from him; if we would avoid becoming like Moses' people, we must employ the authority, principles, and powers of the Melchizedek Priesthood to follow the path that leads to the presence of God, and pursue that goal with all our heart, might, mind, and strength. We cannot become the *ideal* of Zion people otherwise. Elder McConkie wrote:

We must not wrest the scriptures and suppose that the promises of seeing the Lord refer to some future day, either a Millennial or a celestial day, days in which, as we all know, the Lord will be present. *The promises apply to this mortal sphere in which we now live.* This is clearly set forth in the Vision of the Degrees of Glory. After Joseph Smith and Sidney Rigdon had seen the Father and the Son, concourses of angels, and the wonders of each kingdom of glory, and after they had written the account thereof, their continuing language says: "Great and marvelous are the works of the Lord, and the mysteries of his kingdom which he showed unto us, which surpass all understanding in glory, and in might, and in dominion; which he commanded us we should not write while we were yet in the Spirit, and are not lawful for man to utter; neither is man capable to make them known, for they are only to be seen and understood by the power of the Holy Spirit, which God bestows on those who love him, and purify themselves before him; to whom he grants this privilege of seeing and knowing for themselves; that through the power and manifestation of the Spirit, *while in the flesh,* they may be able to bear his presence in the world of glory." (D&C 76:114–18.) While in the flesh! For those who "purify themselves before him," this is the time and the day and the hour when they have power to see their God![2027]

[2026] D&C 84:25.
[2027] McConkie, *A New Witness for the Articles of Faith,* 495; emphasis added.

A Change of Paradigm

When we consider that Zion is the pure in heart,[2028] and then when we consider that the pure in heart are they who see God,[2029] we are suddenly faced with the uncomfortable realization that our definition of Zion might be lacking. While it is true that Zion is a land, the Church, a stake, a ward, a sealed marriage, an eternal family, and a covenant person, Zion, *the ideal,* is so much more. If we are not willing to expand the boundaries of our thinking, the most impressive blessings of Zion will remain outside of our reach.

Sometimes we imagine that the ideal of Zion is obtained by our calling and election being made sure, and therefore calling and election is the ultimate gospel experience. But it is not. Coming into the presence of God is the summit gospel peak, and the calling and election made sure is an essential step in getting there. Again, this process and ideal might require a change of thinking. Remember, Zion is the pure in heart, and the pure in heart see God. The Lord gives us instructions for rending the veil: "And again, verily I say unto you that it is your privilege, and a promise I give unto you that have been ordained unto this ministry, that inasmuch as you strip yourselves from jealousies and fears, and humble yourselves before me, for ye are not sufficiently humble, the veil shall be rent and you shall see me and know that I am—not with the carnal neither natural mind, but with the spiritual."

The inverse would also be true: jealousies, fears, arrogance, and pride will hold the veil in place. We must put off the natural man and become Saints of God, capable of being quickened by the Spirit so that we can stand in the presence of God: "For no man has seen God at any time in the flesh, except quickened by the Spirit of God. Neither can any natural man abide the presence of God, neither after the carnal mind."

The Lord is patient with us as we strive toward the goal: "Ye are not able to abide the presence of God now, neither the ministering of angels; wherefore, continue in patience until ye are perfected." But strive we must: "Let not your minds turn back; and when ye are worthy, in mine own due time, ye shall see and know. . . ."[2030]

Elder McConkie listed reasons why even the best of us shrink from the ideal of Zion: "There are, of course, those whose callings and election have been made sure who have never exercised the faith nor exhibited the righteousness which would enable them to commune with the Lord on the promised basis. There are even those who neither believe nor know that it is possible to see the Lord in this day, and they therefore are without the personal incentive that would urge them onward in the pursuit of this consummation so devoutly desired by those with spiritual insight."[2031]

Think of it this way. Having our calling and election made sure is like the final marker on the pathway that leads to a special door, or *veil,* that opens to the presence of the Lord. Behind that door stands the Savior, who is knocking. Listen to Jesus' words: "Behold, I stand at the door, and knock: if any man hear my voice, and open the door, I will come in to him, and will sup with him, and he with me."[2032] The Lord first issued the invitation to enter when we took upon ourselves the new and everlasting covenant; he renewed the invitation when we took upon ourselves the oath and covenant of the priesthood. Will we respond to the Lord's knock?

Turning the Key

How did we arrive at this wonderful door, separated by the thickness of linen from our Lord? The answer should be obvious. We followed the Holy Ghost, who showed us the *markers* on the pathway

---

[2028] D&C 97:21.
[2029] Matthew 5:8; 3 Nephi 12:8.
[2030] D&C 67:10–14.
[2031] McConkie, *The Promised Messiah,* 586.
[2032] Revelation 3:20.

that led to the door. These markers are priesthood markers, which consist of all the covenants and saving ordinances. These markers were laid down by Jesus Christ to guide us along the path, and they are safeguarded by the Church of Jesus Christ, the institution that is the custodian of these sacred things. Combined, these markers constitute the *key* that allows Zion people, who have received the priesthood and priesthood covenants and ordinances, to respond to the Lord's invitation and step through the door. So how did we arrive at the door? By following the priesthood, which brings us to the Holy Ghost, who brings us to Christ, who brings us to the Father.

But we cannot enter the presence of God of our own accord. The law of heaven demands that, first, we must be pronounced pure, clean, true, and faithful by a righteous judge who knows us intimately; and second, that we must be escorted into the presence of the Lord by someone who knows the way. The Holy Ghost, who has always been our companion and who has guided and taught us every step of the way, is our judge, friend, and escort. Now he has brought us to the door, where he helps us respond to the Lord's invitation. He is in the unique position to recommend us to God and state our case. The Holy Ghost stands beside us, supports, prompts, and shows us how to use the *key*. Finally, like a father releasing his daughter into the arms of her new husband, he hands us off to the loving embrace of our Lord.

There are a number of ways to view the symbolism that represents this holy experience, but one way is to recognize all three members of the Godhead in their individual roles. At the outset of our journey to the presence of God—at baptism—each of the Godhead covenanted with us to bring us to the door and usher us into celestial glory. As we stand at the door now, we realize that they have fulfilled their promise. There, at the threshold of eternity, as we anticipate our entrance into the Lord's presence, we look beside us and see at our side the Holy Ghost, our guide and escort; behind the door, we recognize the Father's voice, and we hear him beckoning us to him; before us is the door or *veil*, which we must go through to reach the Father. Paul said that Jesus Christ is the *veil*,[2033] and we must go *through* him to reach God. To qualify to enter, we must be conversant with our covenants; they are the *keys* that open the door. Our faithfulness allows us to ask for a supernal gift, and when we receive it, we will finally we be invited into the embrace and fellowship of God.

Obtaining, at Last, a Perfect Knowledge of the Savior

Coming to Jesus Christ and then to the Father *through* Jesus Christ are experiences like no others. As a reference, we have the account of Nephites, who were invited one by one to experience the individual nature of the Atonement firsthand.[2034] Too often we wonder what part of the Atonement (if any) was uniquely for us, as individuals. Such ponderings betray our ignorance of the Father and the Son's ability to indivisibly extend one hundred percent of their time and attention to *each* of us.

Allow me for a moment to form the following thoughts in first person.

What part of the Atonement was mine? *All of it!* In that tender and supernal, one-on-one experience with the Lord, when I am finally invited to touch each of the wounds in his hands, feet, and side, when I remember the great drops of blood in the Garden, the betrayal, the injustice, the mocking, the beatings, the crown of thorns, the scourging, and the crucifixion—then I will know with a perfect knowledge that he did *all of it* for me.

This universal experience with Jesus is recorded in the Book of Mormon. Listen to the Lord's invitation, and imagine the day when he will extend it to us:

Arise and come forth unto me, that ye may thrust your hands into my side, and also that ye may feel the prints of the nails in my hands and in my feet, that ye may know that I am the God of Israel, and the God of the whole earth, and have been slain for the sins of the world.

[2033] Hebrews 10:20.
[2034] 3 Nephi 11:15.

And it came to pass that the multitude went forth, and thrust their hands into his side, and did feel the prints of the nails in his hands and in his feet; and this they did do, going forth one by one until they had all gone forth, and did see with their eyes and did feel with their hands, and did know of a surety and did bear record, that it was he, of whom it was written by the prophets, that should come.

And when they had all gone forth and had witnessed for themselves, they did cry out with one accord, saying: Hosanna! Blessed be the name of the Most High God! And they did fall down at the feet of Jesus, and did worship him.[2035]

Again, each person who walks the path to Zion will have this experience. Therefore, each Zion person must obtain the *key*, and respond to the knock. To attain to this singular event might require a change of paradigm. But, nevertheless, it is true, and every Zion person can attest that it is true. The prophets, the scriptures, and the temple testify that the end purpose and the power of the Melchizedek Priesthood is to rend the veil and convey a man or woman into the presence of God.

Will we believe it? Will we pursue that blessing once we believe it? Will we thereby become Zion people?

The commandment is clear: "And *seek the face of the Lord always*, that in patience ye may possess your souls, and ye shall have eternal life."[2036] Such is the ideal and condition of Zion people, for we read: "the Lord came and dwelt with his people, and they dwelt in righteousness."[2037]

Receiving the Greatest Comfort

Is the prize worth the price? Joseph Smith assured us that it is. If we are willing to lift our sights, believe the *entirety* of the gospel, and apply the *totality* of the priesthood, the Prophet promised that we would eventually receive the Second Comforter, even the Lord Jesus Christ.

Now what is this other Comforter? It is no more nor less than the Lord Jesus Christ Himself; and this is the sum and substance of the whole matter; that when any man obtains this last Comforter, he will have the personage of Jesus Christ to attend him, or appear unto him from time to time, and even He will manifest the Father unto him, and they will take up their abode with him, and the visions of the heavens will be opened unto him, and the Lord will teach him face to face, and he may have a perfect knowledge of the mysteries of the Kingdom of God.[2038]

Elder McConkie explained that this privilege is the blessing that lies beyond the "door." It is a blessing that exceeds the blessing of having our calling and election made sure, and it is the purpose for which that assurance is given.

After the true saints receive and enjoy the gift of the Holy Ghost; after they know how to attune themselves to the voice of the Spirit; after they mature spiritually so that they see visions, work miracles, and entertain angels; *after they make their calling and election sure and prove themselves worthy of every trust*—after all this and more—it becomes their right and privilege to see the Lord and commune with him face to face. Revelations, visions, angelic visitations, the rending of the heavens, and appearances among men of the Lord himself—all these things are for all of the faithful. They are not reserved for apostles and prophets only. God is no respecter of persons.[2039]

Would not this experience—receiving the Second Comforter—give us the greatest comfort? Should we not pursue this goal by implementing the priesthood for its ultimate intended purpose?

[2035] 3 Nephi 11:14–17.
[2036] D&C 101:38; emphasis added.
[2037] Moses 7:16.
[2038] Smith, *Teachings of the Prophet Joseph Smith*, 150.
[2039] McConkie, *The Promised Messiah*, 575; emphasis added.

REGAINING THE PRESENCE OF GOD—THE END-PURPOSE OF THE PRIESTHOOD

Consider the following sampling among myriad statements and promises on the subject of our regaining God's presence:

If a man love me, he will keep my words: and my Father will love him, *and we will come unto him, and make our abode with him.*[2040]

Sanctify yourselves that your minds become single to God, and the days will come that you will see him; *for he will unveil his face unto you,* and it shall be in his own time, and in his own way, and according to his own will.[2041]

God hath not revealed anything to Joseph [Smith], but what He will make known unto the Twelve, and even the least Saint may know all things as fast as he is able to bear them, for the day must come when no man need say to his neighbor, Know ye the Lord; for all shall know Him (who remain) from the least to the greatest.[2042]

Is our faith strengthened? Will we believe it? Do we understand for what purpose we have received the priesthood and its ordinances, and will we pursue that purpose and become Zion people? Elder McConkie wrote:

All who are now living those laws [the laws of Zion] to the full which will enable them to go where God and Christ are, and there enjoy eternal association with them—that is, all those who are now living in its entirety the law of the celestial kingdom—*are already qualified to see the Lord.* The attainment of such a state of righteousness and perfection is the object and end toward which all of the Lord's people are striving. We seek to see the face of the Lord while we yet dwell in mortality, and we seek to dwell with him everlastingly in the eternal kingdoms that are prepared.[2043]

THE REVEALED PROCESS FOR STANDING IN THE PRESENCE OF GOD

What then should we do? What are the steps? The Lord gave us the simple formula:

Verily, thus saith the Lord: It shall come to pass that every soul who forsaketh his sins and cometh unto me, and calleth on my name, and obeyeth my voice, and keepeth my commandments, shall see my face and know that I am.[2044]

It is a covenant with a promise. (1) Forsake our sins; (2) come unto Christ; (3) call on his name; (4) obey his voice; (5) keep his commandments. *Then* we shall see him. But of the many who are called only a few will follow this pattern, and therefore only a few will "receive" the Lord in this life and enter his presence.

For strait is the gate, and narrow the way that leadeth unto the exaltation and continuation of the lives, and few there be that find it, because ye receive me not in the world neither do ye know me. But if ye receive me in the world, then shall ye know me, and shall receive your exaltation; that where I am ye shall be also.[2045]

We cannot fully receive Christ if we do not know him. That would be like a husband claiming to have wedded or received a wife whom he has never met. On the other hand, Zion people, the bride, know and receive the Bridegroom. They know him because he is the one who claimed them by "separating" them out from all other affections; he is the one who lovingly "received" them, his bride, unto himself.[2046]

[2040] John 14:23; emphasis added.
[2041] D&C 88:68; emphasis added.
[2042] Smith, *Teachings of the Prophet Joseph Smith*, 149.
[2043] McConkie, *The Promised Messiah*, 578.
[2044] D&C 93:1.
[2045] D&C 132:22–23.
[2046] D&C 45:12.

The Priesthood Is the Power to Stand in God's Presence

Clearly, the holy priesthood is the source of confidence and the actual power to stand in the presence of God. Elder McConkie expounds:

The priesthood is the power, authority, and means that prepares men to see their Lord; also, that in the priesthood is found everything that is needed to bring this consummation to pass. Accordingly, it is written: "The power and authority of the higher, or Melchizedek Priesthood, is to hold the keys of all the spiritual blessings of the church—To have the privilege of receiving the mysteries of the kingdom of heaven, to have the heavens opened unto them, to commune with the general assembly and church of the Firstborn, and to enjoy the communion and presence of God the Father, and Jesus the mediator of the new covenant." (D&C 107:18–19). . . . Thus, through the priesthood the door may be opened and the way provided for men [and women] to see the Father and the Son. From all of this it follows, automatically and axiomatically, that if and when the holy priesthood operates to the full in the life of any man [or woman], he will receive its great and full blessings, which are that rending of the heavens and that parting of the veil of which we now speak.[2047]

Joseph Smith asked, "How do men obtain a knowledge of the glory of God, his perfections and attributes?" Then the answer, "By devoting themselves to his service, through prayer and supplication incessantly strengthening their faith in him, until, like Enoch, the brother of Jared, and Moses, they obtain a manifestation of God to themselves."[2048]

Therefore, when we feel the Spirit summoning us to the temple, and when we hear the voice of God "revealing through the heavens the grand Key-words of the Priesthood,"[2049] our hearts should be filled with desire and hope. We raise our eyes and cry out, "O my Father, thou that dwellest in the high and glorious place, when shall I regain thy presence and again behold thy face?"[2050] Our salvation depends upon our giving diligent heed to regaining his presence and again beholding his face. Thus, we devote our lives to living and serving in such a way that we might obtain this knowledge. The Prophet Joseph Smith revealed, "It is impossible for a man to be saved in ignorance."[2051] And on another occasion, "A man is saved no faster than he gets knowledge."[2052] The ultimate knowledge—the knowledge of the surety of our salvation; the knowledge of our origin and destiny; the knowledge that brings us to the ideal of Zion—is the perfect knowledge of the reality of God.

"The Doctrine of the Priesthood Shall Distil upon Thy Soul"

Joseph Smith said, "A man can do nothing for himself unless God directs him in the right way; and *the priesthood is for that purpose.*"[2053]

In examining the rewards listed in the Constitution of the Priesthood, we notice that the Lord bookends these verses (D&C 121:45–46) with promises concerning our glorious destiny. These promises are the ability to stand in the presence of God and receive our coronation. The verses sandwiched between these promises reveal the markers along the path. The first marker has to do with priesthood education: "The doctrine of the priesthood shall distil upon thy soul as the dews from heaven."[2054] This statement hearkens back to the promise made in the oath and covenant of the

---

[2047] McConkie, *The Promised Messiah*, 587–88.
[2048] Smith, *Lectures on Faith*, 2:55.
[2049] Abraham, Facsimile No. 2, Explanation, Figure 7.
[2050] "O My Father," *Hymns*, no. 292.
[2051] D&C 131:6.
[2052] Smith, *History of the Church*, 4:588.
[2053] Smith, *Teachings of the Prophet Joseph Smith*, 364; emphasis added.
[2054] D&C 121:45.

priesthood: "And the Father teacheth [us] of the covenant which he has renewed and confirmed upon [us]."[2055]

As we have discussed, the Father takes both the responsibility and the initiative to teach us concerning the priesthood covenant. By the power of the Holy Ghost, under whom angels minister, the Father will summon all the powers in heaven and earth to distil priesthood knowledge upon us as fast as we are willing to receive it. Here, then, is a key to gaining priesthood understanding and power: *We are taught from on high.* Elder McConkie said this doctrine is unknown in the world and not widely known in the Church. The priesthood information that the Father distils upon us cannot be fully learned in the scriptures or even in the teachings of the prophets, he said. God reserves the right to reveal this doctrine of the priesthood by the gift of the Holy Ghost, which will likely involve the ministering of angels.[2056]

Earlier in this book, we discussed at length the doctrine of the priesthood and how the Father distils priesthood knowledge upon us. By way of review, we qualify for this personal revelation by exemplifying charity and virtue.[2057] The distillation of priesthood doctrine settles upon those who love and serve God with all their "heart, might, mind, and strength,"[2058] and the process occurs line upon line and precept upon precept by the power of the Holy Ghost. Soon, after having walked through the dewy grasses of priesthood doctrine, we find ourselves saturated in it.

What, then, is the doctrine of the priesthood that pivots on charity and virtue? Elder McConkie lists the following:

- The priesthood is the actual power of God, and the actual name of the power of God. It is the power by which he created and creates the heavens, and it is the power by which he governs, sustains and preserves all things. To become as he is, we must exercise his priesthood, or power, as does he.
- The priesthood is the power of faith—*Faith is power and power is priesthood.* Faith is a true belief or knowledge that is acted upon.[2059] The priesthood is useless unless it is put into action; thus the combination of faith, truth, virtue, and priesthood results in actual power. By faith, priesthood becomes power "to put at defiance the armies of nations, to divide the earth, to break every band, to stand in the presence of God; to do all things according to his will, according to his command, subdue principalities and powers; and this by the will of the Son of God."[2060] To the extent that we act with our priesthood in faith, according to charity and virtue, we become like God, who is the perfection of faith, priesthood, and power. By this means, we can lay hold on eternal life.
- The priesthood is the doctrine that "God lives and is and ever shall be. He is the Everlasting Elohim who dwells in heaven above. He is our Father, the father of our spirits; we are his children, the offspring of his begetting. He has a glorified body of flesh and bones; he lives in the family unit; and he possesses all power, all might, all dominion, and all truth. The name of the kind of life he lives is eternal life [that is, he lives in the family unit]."[2061]
- The priesthood is the doctrine or lifestyle that our Heavenly Father enjoys in his exalted status—that of glory, perfection, and power, because his faith and his priesthood are perfect and infinite.

[2055] D&C 84:48.
[2056] McConkie, "The Doctrine of the Priesthood," 32.
[2057] D&C 121:45.
[2058] D&C 98:12.
[2059] Alma 32:21.
[2060] JST Genesis 14:31.
[2061] McConkie, *A New Witness for the Articles of Faith*, 704.

- The priesthood of God is *after the order of his Son,* which power, like God himself, is infinite and eternal. We who receive this endowment of power become part of that same order.
- The priesthood is a system of orders, the highest of which is named the new and everlasting covenant of marriage,[2062] or the patriarchal order. Only in this order can we become like God, creating for ourselves eternal family units patterned after the family of God.
- The doctrine of the priesthood is that we can progress until we obtain the priesthood's *fulness,* which increasingly gives us power by faith to govern and control all temporal and spiritual things, to effect miracles, to help to perfect God's children, to stand in Father's presence, and to become like him, having developed his faith, perfections, and power.
- The priesthood is the power to do all things that are expedient: move mountains, control the elements, cast away evil spirits, defeat every enemy, conquer any adversity, provide protection, cure disease, raise the dead, bind together marriages and families, and ultimately to achieve glorious immortality in the celestial kingdom of God.[2063]

The Rights and the Doctrine of the Priesthood

Having the Father as our instructor might be considered a *right* belonging to the priesthood. These rights, as we have learned, are "inseparably connected with the powers of heaven," and they are made functional upon "the principles of righteousness."[2064] These rights are part of the doctrine of the priesthood that the Father distils upon our souls as the dews from heaven. The Lord describes the glorious rights and blessings that he is willing to impart to us in our priesthood instruction:

For thus saith the Lord—I, the Lord, am merciful and gracious unto those who fear me, and delight to honor those who serve me in righteousness and in truth unto the end. Great shall be their reward and eternal shall be their glory.

And to them will I reveal all mysteries, yea, all the hidden mysteries of my kingdom from days of old, and for ages to come, will I make known unto them the good pleasure of my will concerning all things pertaining to my kingdom. Yea, even the wonders of eternity shall they know, and things to come will I show them, even the things of many generations.

And their wisdom shall be great, and their understanding reach to heaven; and before them the wisdom of the wise shall perish, and the understanding of the prudent shall come to naught. For by my Spirit will I enlighten them, and by my power will I make known unto them the secrets of my will—yea, even those things which eye has not seen, nor ear heard, nor yet entered into the heart of man.[2065]

Clearly, the doctrine of the priesthood is glorious, and few blessings could be as wonderful as receiving these priesthood rights.

The Doctrine of the Priesthood and the Law of Asking

If we desire the doctrine of the priesthood to distil upon our souls, we must take the initiative and ask. Becoming Zionlike and obtaining priesthood understanding is an educational process, and we must become eager students. We open the door to revelation by *asking:* "If thou shalt ask, thou shalt receive revelation upon revelation, knowledge upon knowledge, that thou mayest know the mysteries and peaceable things—that which bringeth joy, that which bringeth life eternal."[2066] We walk through the door by diligent pursuit. Behold, thou shalt observe all these things, and great shall be thy reward; for

---

[2062] D&C 131:2.
[2063] McConkie, "The Doctrine of the Priesthood," 32.
[2064] D&C 121:36.
[2065] D&C 76:5–10.
[2066] D&C 42:61.

unto you it is given to know the mysteries of the kingdom, but unto the world it is not given to know them. Ye shall observe the laws which ye have received and be faithful."[2067]

The principle of asking is common to receiving all gospel blessings. We ask to receive baptism; we ask to receive the priesthood; we ask to enter the temple and receive priesthood covenants and ordinances; we ask for a temple recommend to be sealed to our eternal sweetheart. Why, then, if we desire some of the most impressive blessings of the gospel, do we often neglect to ask? The law of asking is immutable: "Therefore, he that lacketh wisdom, let him ask of me, and I will give him liberally and upbraid him not."[2068] If we desire to receive revelation upon revelation concerning the doctrine of the priesthood, or to receive the ministering of angels, or have our calling and election made sure, or to become part of the general assembly and Church of the Firstborn,[2069] or to become Zion people, or to finally enter into the presence of God and receive the "privilege of seeing and knowing for [ourselves],"[2070] we must ask. But sadly, although asking to receive is a commandment, we do not always obey it: "Behold this is my will; ask and ye shall receive; but men do not always do my will."[2071]

Asking to receive is an eternal law with a promise. Notice the word *shall* indicating a promised answer: "Therefore, ask, and ye *shall* receive; knock, and it *shall* be opened unto you; for he that asketh, receiveth; and unto him that knocketh, it *shall* be opened."[2072]

Asking becomes effectual *after* moving forward in faith, repenting, and seeking: "Behold, I say unto you, go forth as I have commanded you; repent of all your sins; ask and ye shall receive; knock and it shall be opened unto you."[2073] "Draw near unto me and I will draw near unto you; seek me diligently and ye shall find me; ask, and ye shall receive; knock, and it shall be opened unto you."[2074]

The law of asking opens the door to fulness of joy, and, implied in the scripture, today is the time to start: "Hitherto have ye asked nothing in my name: ask, and ye shall receive, that your joy may be full."[2075]

To distinguish ourselves in the priesthood from the "many who are called" and to be identified with the "few who are chosen," to qualify to stand with the prophets, to know what they have known, to see what they have seen, and to receive the mysteries (not the mysterious) of the kingdom in absolute clarity, we must actively and deliberately seek and ask: "Unto you it is given to know the mysteries of the kingdom of God: but to others in parables; that seeing they might not see, and hearing they might not understand."[2076]

The forfeited blessings for our not bothering to ask are great. Although we might be good people, if we do not seek and ask, we might never qualify to receive more than the "lesser portion of the word." Alma taught that we must be constantly reaching heavenward for information and instruction; our complacency is at least dangerous and at worst damning:

And therefore, he that will harden his heart, the same receiveth the lesser portion of the word; and he that will not harden his heart, to him is given the greater portion of the word, until it is given unto him to know the mysteries of God until he know them in full. And they that will harden their hearts, to them is given the lesser portion of the word until they know nothing concerning his

---

[2067] D&C 42:65–66.
[2068] D&C 42:67.
[2069] D&C 76:54, 94; 77:11; 78:21; 88:5; 93:22; 107:19.
[2070] D&C 76:117.
[2071] D&C 103:31.
[2072] 3 Nephi 27:29; see also D&C 4:7; 66:9; 103:35.
[2073] D&C 49:26.
[2074] D&C 88:63.
[2075] John 16:24.
[2076] Luke 8:10.

mysteries; and then they are taken captive by the devil, and led by his will down to destruction. Now this is what is meant by the chains of hell.[2077]

Finally, the priesthood ordinances hold the ultimate power of asking and receiving. These ordinances are sometimes called *keys*,[2078] "by which [we] may ask and receive blessings." We qualify to use these keys to ask and receive by being humble and without guile. Then we "shall receive of [the Lord's] Spirit, even the Comforter, which shall manifest unto [us] the truth of all things."[2079]

Lesser and Greater Portions of the Doctrine of the Priesthood

According to Alma, hardheartedness is the characteristic that results in our receiving the "lesser portion of the word." To harden one's heart is to close it off to receiving what God would give for the asking. Such people are left with the "lesser portion of the word," which consists of the gospel basics, concepts, and principles that are generally known. Of course, we all must understand the lesser portion of the word, but after we have received it, we must immediately begin to reach higher. To remain contented with the lesser portion, Alma taught, puts us at risk of being "taken captive by the devil, and led by his will down to destruction." The "many" who are called but not chosen make up this group; they do not seek the "greater portion of the word."

Conversely, the "few" who are called and chosen do not harden their hearts, and they actively seek the "greater portion of the word." The Lord will answer their request and give them "the greater portion of the word, until it is given unto [them] to know the mysteries of God until he know them in full." As we have noted, these mysteries are not "secrets,"[2080] as Satan reveals; mysteries consist of intelligence that can be learned only by revelation from God. Mysteries distil upon our souls "revelation upon revelation" and include the rights of the priesthood, spiritual gifts, and "peaceable things—that which bringeth joy, that which bringeth life eternal."[2081]

Ultimately, they will see heaven! Surely, these *mysteries* can be known in no other way than by seeking and asking for them by means of the rights, or *keys*, of the priesthood. This privilege caused Paul to exult, "Eye hath not seen, nor ear heard, neither have entered into the heart of man, the things which God hath prepared for them that love him."[2082]

The Necessity and Power of Priesthood Ordinances

A significant right belonging to the priesthood is the Father's taking charge of our priesthood education. The oath and covenant of the priesthood states: "And the Father teacheth him of the covenant."[2083] Knowing who our Teacher is also identifies who distils "the doctrine of the priesthood . . . upon [our] soul[s] as the dews from heaven."[2084] That is not to say that Jesus Christ and the Holy Ghost are not involved; but it does seem to indicate that the Father wants to assure us of the origin of priesthood instruction. Therefore, when we worthily invoke the law of asking in faith and subsequently experience the distillation of priesthood doctrine upon our souls, we can rest assured that the Father is the source of that revelation.

[2077] Alma 12:9–11.
[2078] Smith, *History of the Church*, 4:608; 5:1–2; Smith, *Teachings of the Prophet Joseph Smith*, 226; Smith, *Juvenile Instructor*, June 1, 1892, 345; Smith, *The Words of Joseph Smith*, 54, footnote 19.
[2079] D&C 124:97.
[2080] Moses 5:31, 49.
[2081] D&C 42:61.
[2082] 1 Corinthians 2:9.
[2083] D&C 84:48.
[2084] D&C 121:45.

Distillation of priesthood doctrine must be done in an ordered way,[2085] and that ordered way is by means of *ordinances,* which are another "right" of the priesthood. Elder Dennis Neuenschwander said ordinances mark the progressive order of the kingdom of God, and as we apply the ordinances in our lives, we gain a revelation of the character of God that otherwise would be impossible.[2086] Zion people receive the priesthood temple ordinances, and under the Father's tutelage they learn to use them. One of the most definitive statements in scripture on this subject is found in Doctrine and Covenants 84:19, which precedes the oath and covenant of the priesthood:

And this greater priesthood administereth the gospel and holdeth the key of the mysteries of the kingdom, even the key of the knowledge of God. Therefore, in the ordinances thereof, the power of godliness is manifest. And without the ordinances thereof, and the authority of the priesthood, the power of godliness is not manifest unto men in the flesh; for without this no man can see the face of God, even the Father, and live.[2087]

The powers resident in these temple priesthood ordinances are without peer. Elder A. Theodore Tuttle taught parents that they must teach their children that becoming like God and achieving exaltation are possible only if they receive these ordinances and their attendant covenants.[2088] Earlier, Elder Joseph Fielding Smith had likewise taught that we cannot become Zion people without the temple priesthood ordinances; neither can we achieve exaltation nor obtain "the fullness of the glory of God."[2089]

Joseph Smith said, "The question is frequently asked, 'Can we not be saved without going through with all those ordinances?' I would answer, No, not the fulness of salvation . . . any person who is exalted to the highest mansion has to abide a celestial law, and the whole law too."[2090] And on another occasion, "All men [and women] who become heirs of God and joint heirs with Jesus Christ will have to receive the fulness of the ordinances of his kingdom; and those who will not receive all the ordinances will come short of the fullness of that glory, if they do not lose the whole."[2091]

President Kimball wrote about the necessity of ordinances and their connection to the priesthood: "Men require priesthood for exaltation. No man will ever reach godhood who does not hold the priesthood. You have to be a member of the higher priesthood—an elder, seventy, or high priest—and today is the day to get it and magnify it. Righteousness and ordinances are required. Can you conceive of the vastness of the program? Can you begin to understand it? But remember this: exaltation is available only to righteous members of the Church of Jesus Christ; only to those who accept the gospel; only to those who have their endowments; only to those who have been through the holy temple of God and have been sealed for eternity and who then continue to live righteously throughout their lives."[2092]

The verses (D&C 84:19–22) that we have discussed clearly indicate that "the power of godliness" is manifested "unto men in the flesh" by means of the ordinances of the priesthood. The very experience we are seeking—to "see the face of God, even the Father, and live"—simply cannot happen without these priesthood ordinances. The temple endowment shows us the pattern of how this must be done—the *ordered* way by means of *ordinances.* The ordinances are "the key of the mysteries of the kingdom, even the key of the knowledge of God." Without this *key,* or ordinances, "the power of godliness is not manifest, and no man can see God."

[2085] D&C 132:8, 18.
[2086] Neuenschwander, "Ordinances and Covenants," 20.
[2087] D&C 84:19–22.
[2088] Tuttle, Conference Report, Apr. 1984, 33.
[2089] Smith, "The Duties of the Priesthood in Temple Work," 4.
[2090] Smith, *Teachings of the Prophet Joseph Smith,* 331.
[2091] Smith, *Teachings of the Prophet Joseph Smith,* 309.
[2092] Kimball, *Teachings of Spencer W. Kimball,* 51.

The Doctrine of the Priesthood and Revelatory "Keys"

This right of the priesthood—*ordinances*—is too sacred to discuss outside the temple, except in general terms. By covenant, we guard and protect these things. When we receive information about these ordinances, it is from or under the direction of the Father, for he is our teacher who distils the doctrine of the priesthood upon our souls and guides our education. Under his supervision, we are informed that utilizing the ordinances appropriately opens the revelatory channel between him and us; therefore, we are given both instruction and power whereby we might ask for and receive further light and knowledge. Andrew Ehat and Lyndon Cook write:

> Joseph Smith received a revelation specifically requiring that he teach Hyrum Smith and William Law certain "keys by which they could ask and receive" (D&C 124:95, 97). In the 1879 edition of the Doctrine and Covenants, Orson Pratt indicated that these keys were "the order of God for receiving revelations"—the keys to the oracles of God. . . . Elder Charles C. Rich, a member of the Council of the Twelve, was [a] preserver of Joseph's revelations on the temple ordinances and who obviously was sensitive to the propriety of discussing endowment ordinances. Nevertheless, he publicly gave this very important account of the revelation of these keys of the priesthood, during a stake conference meeting in Idaho in 1878. "It was a long time after the Prophet Joseph Smith had received the keys of the Kingdom of God, and after Hyrum and others had received many blessings, that the Lord gave Joseph a revelation, to show him and others how they could ask for and receive certain blessings. We read in the revelations of St. John, that [of] the white stone [as follows:] 'and in the stone a new name, which no man knoweth save him that receiveth it.' Joseph tells us [in D&C 130:10–11] that this new name is a key-word, which can only be obtained through the endowments. This is one of the keys and blessings that will be bestowed upon the Saints in these last days, for which we should be very thankful" (*Journal of Discourses*, 19:250).[2093]

As we can see, besides being a priesthood right, these ordinances are often referred to as "keys." (Recall, however, that this is a different use of the word *keys* than that which is typical in today's Church.) Their purpose is highly significant to people who would become Zionlike. These keys are the divinely prescribed and ordered manner by which "the power of godliness is manifest," and therefore they open the door to the presence of God: "And without the ordinances thereof [the Melchizedek Priesthood], and the authority of the priesthood, the power of godliness is not manifest unto men in the flesh; for without this no man can see the face of God, even the Father, and live."[2094] In another place, the scriptures say it this way: "[These are] the keys whereby [we] may ask and receive, and be crowned with the same blessing, and glory, and honor, and priesthood, and gifts of the priesthood."[2095]

These ordinances—*keys*—are the only legitimate way to see God, return to his presence, and "enter into his rest, which rest is the fulness of his glory"[2096]—*eternal life*. Therefore, it behooves a Zion person to diligently apply to temple worship and pray earnestly for light and knowledge from God concerning this essential right belonging to the priesthood.

All of the scriptures mentioned herein link our education in priesthood doctrine to the temple. By now, it should be clear that we will not, and should not, learn this doctrine in a Sunday School class or in quorum or Relief Society meetings; furthermore, we will not, and should not, hear the specifics of this doctrine preached from the pulpit. The doctrine of the priesthood is a sacred one-on-one course taught by the Father primarily in the precincts of his holy house, the temple. He expects us to prepare to enter, seek, ask, and use the keys that he has given us to open the door to the "mysteries of the kingdom," "the power of godliness," and "the knowledge of God." Therefore, Zion people are

---

[2093] Smith, *The Words of Joseph Smith*, 53.
[2094] D&C 84:19–22.
[2095] D&C 124:95.
[2096] D&C 84:22–24.

instructed to attend the temple often. There they offer proxy sacrifice and service for deceased persons who cannot receive the covenants and ordinances for themselves; and there they spend time with God as he carefully and constantly distils upon their souls the precious doctrines of the priesthood. Brigham Young said:

> If the Latter-day Saints will walk up to their privileges and exercise faith in the name of Jesus Christ and live in the enjoyment of the fulness of the Holy Ghost constantly day by day, there is nothing on the face of the earth that they could ask for that would not be given to them. The Lord is waiting to be very gracious unto this people and to pour out upon them riches, honor, glory, and power, even that they may possess all things according to the promises He has made through His apostles and prophets.[2097]

"The Holy Ghost Shall Be Thy Constant Companion"

As we have discussed, the new and everlasting covenant adds layer upon layer until gospel principles are enhanced, then perfected. One of these principles is the gift of the Holy Ghost.

Upon receiving baptism, we are confirmed members of the Church, and then we receive the gift of the Holy Ghost, which includes the ministering of angels.[2098] Thereafter, to retain this gift, we make the covenant of the sacrament, which stipulates that our faithfulness to the sacramental covenant ensures that we will "always have his Spirit to be with [us]."[2099] Then when a man receives the oath and covenant of the priesthood, he receives an added portion of the Spirit "unto the renewing of his body," and furthermore, he receives the renewed and enhanced promise of the ministering of angels.[2100] The Constitution of the Priesthood (D&C 121:34–46) renews the promise of the gift of the Holy Ghost: "The Holy Ghost shall be thy constant companion."[2101] That promise is perfected when we live up to the Constitution's terms of righteousness; at that point, we receive the gift of the Holy Ghost in its fulness. President John Taylor said, "Then shall you feel the power of the Holy Ghost resting upon you and its influence penetrating your soul, and then it will grow and spread until its influence extends everywhere; and then will men respect, esteem, and venerate you for your fidelity and for your adherence to the truth."[2102]

In the dedicatory prayer of the Kirtland Temple, Joseph Smith connected the "fulness of the Holy Ghost" to the temple: "And do thou grant, Holy Father, that all those who shall worship in this house . . . may grow up in thee, and receive a fulness of the Holy Ghost."[2103] Then supernal blessings follow. Elder Carlos E. Asay wrote: "We are told that we can speak with the tongue of angels when under the influence of the Holy Ghost (see 2 Nephi 31:13). We read that people are sealed with the Holy Ghost or the Holy Spirit of Promise (see Ephesians 1:13). We know that those who are wise receive the truth and take the Holy Spirit for their guide (see D&C 45:57). Hence, those who go to the temple and partake of its saving ordinances are endowed with power from on high, even the fullness of the Holy Ghost."[2104] Such are the blessings given to priesthood holders and their female counterparts in Zion.

[2097] Young, *Discourses of Brigham Young*, 156.
[2098] D&C 84:26; 107:20.
[2099] D&C 20:77.
[2100] D&C 84:33, 42.
[2101] D&C 121:46.
[2102] Taylor, *Journal of Discourses*, 20:262–63.
[2103] D&C 109:14–15.
[2104] Asay, *Family Pecan Trees*, 220.

The Holy Spirit of Promise

The Holy Ghost has a distinctive title that is most valuable to Zion people: *The Holy Spirit of Promise.* The "promise" is that of exaltation and eternal life. It is the Holy Ghost's office, explains gospel scholar Matthew B. Brown, to "bind certain acts that are performed on earth so that they will be bound in heaven. This seal validates or ratifies all earthly 'covenants, contracts, bonds, obligations, oaths, vows, performances, connections, associations, or expectations' so that they will have 'efficacy, virtue, or force in and after the resurrection from the dead' (D&C 132:7, 18–19, 26). Thus, to have an earthly act sealed by the Holy Spirit of Promise is to receive a promise or assurance that the act so sealed will be valid for eternity."[2105] President Joseph Fielding Smith gave this succinct definition: "The Holy Spirit of Promise is the Holy Ghost who places the stamp of approval upon every ordinance that is done righteously; and when covenants are broken he removes the seal."[2106] His final words echo the Constitution of the Priesthood's ominous indictment: "Amen to the priesthood or authority of that man."[2107]

Zion people seek for the gift of the Holy Ghost and the ultimate expression of that gift—the sealing of the Holy Spirit of Promise. Elder McConkie wrote the following regarding the Holy Ghost: "He is the Comforter, Testator, Revelator, Sanctifier, Holy Spirit, Holy Spirit of Promise, Spirit of Truth, Spirit of the Lord, and Messenger of the Father and the Son, and his companionship is the greatest gift that mortal man can enjoy."[2108] When we consider that the Holy Ghost is the agent that the Father uses to teach us the truth of all things,[2109] including the doctrine of the priesthood, and when we consider that it is the Holy Ghost that seals or makes our covenants *more sure*, then we should also realize that we must seek this gift at every covenant opportunity and thereafter cling to that gift with all our might until we receive its fulness. The Holy Ghost will make priesthood a power; he will purify and sanctify and make us Zion people.

Scepters and Dominions—the Holy Interview

This section of priesthood rewards (D&C 121:45–46) ends as it began: in the presence of God, where we now receive the future promise of coronation in God's eternal kingdom. Notice the word *shall* in the promise: " . . . and thy scepter an unchanging scepter of righteousness and truth; and thy dominion *shall* be an everlasting dominion, and without compulsory means it *shall* flow unto thee forever and ever."[2110] According to Elder Orson Pratt, when we are standing at last in the presence of God, we will not necessarily receive our "crowns of glory" at that time. Coronation does not happen "until after the resurrection."[2111] But we will receive the assurance of that coronation and a view of our eventual scepter and dominion.

Let us review. A central purpose of the priesthood and its ordinances is to prepare, empower, and lead Zionlike men and women into God's presence. Those who see God are the pure in heart,[2112] and the pure in heart are Zion people.[2113] Therefore, our abilities to see God and become the ideal of Zion people are inseparably linked with the priesthood. Unless we change our paradigm regarding the purpose of the priesthood, raise our sights, and follow the road of the priesthood to its intended destination, we will continue to languish in Babylon and remain subject to the laws and conditions of

---

[2105] Brown, *The Gate of Heaven*, 253.
[2106] Smith, *Doctrines of Salvation*, 1:55.
[2107] D&C 121:37.
[2108] McConkie, *Mormon Doctrine*, 359.
[2109] Moroni 10:5; D&C 124:97; Moses 6:61.
[2110] D&C 121:46; emphasis added.
[2111] Pratt, *Times and Seasons*, June 1, 1845.
[2112] Matthew 5:8; 3 Nephi 12:8.
[2113] D&C 97:21.

this benighted kingdom. But if we will look up and harness the power of the covenants and ordinances of the priesthood, the glorious promises of Zion will burst upon us, and we will achieve coronation, scepters, and dominions at our journey's end.

What should we expect when we at last are standing in the presence of God? A thoughtful review of scriptures and the writings of righteous and qualified individuals provides examples and explanations. We must remember that God's dealings with his children are highly individualized. What might occur quickly for one person might stretch into years or even extend into the next life for another person.

One of the blessings we might expect to receive is a vision of God's creations. For example, Abraham stood in the presence of God and said, "And I saw the stars, that they were very great, and that one of them was nearest unto the throne of God; and there were many great ones which were near unto it."[2114] In addition to the stars, he saw all "the intelligences that were organized before the world was," and he saw the creation of the world and of man.[2115] Similarly, Moses saw the creation of the world "and the ends thereof," "the inhabitants thereof," "many lands, and each land was called earth," and their inhabitants, "worlds without number," and the creation of man.[2116] Lehi, Nephi, John the Beloved, Mormon, Moroni, and Joseph Smith recorded similar visions in their interviews with the Lord. Our temple experience foreshadows this future vision.[2117] Therefore, it stands to reason that God would allow us to survey the kingdom that we are about to inherit[2118] and to gain a view of our infinite possibilities as an heir to that kingdom.

Another blessing is to be endowed with the keys to God's knowledge and power, which can be learned only by revelation. The idea of being endowed leads us back to our temple experience. *The Encyclopedia of Mormonism* states: "As he introduced temple ordinances in 1842 at Nauvoo, the Prophet Joseph Smith taught that these were 'of things spiritual, and to be received only by the spiritual minded' (TPJS, p. 237). The Endowment was necessary, he said, to organize the Church fully, that the Saints might be organized according to the laws of God, and, as the dedicatory prayer of the Kirtland Temple petitioned, that they would 'be prepared to obtain every needful thing' (D&C 109:15). The Endowment was designed to give 'a comprehensive view of our condition and true relation to God' (TPJS, p. 324), 'to prepare the disciples for their missions in the world' (p. 274), to prevent being 'overcome by evils' (p. 259), to enable them to 'secure the fulness of those blessings which have been prepared for the Church of the Firstborn' (p. 237)."[2119]

One of the most detailed accounts of the endowment of knowledge is that of the Brother of Jared. "And [the Lord] ministered unto him even as he ministered unto the Nephites; and all this, that this man might know that he was God, because of the many great works which the Lord had showed unto him. And because of the knowledge of this man he could not be kept from beholding within the veil; and he saw the finger of Jesus, which, when he saw, he fell with fear; for he knew that it was the finger of the Lord; and he had faith no longer, for he knew, nothing doubting. Wherefore, having this perfect knowledge of God, he could not be kept from within the veil; therefore he saw Jesus; and he did minister unto him."[2120]

Another blessing that we might expect in our interview with the Lord is our receiving an invitation to ask him for a special gift. For example, the Brother of Jared asked, "Lord, show thyself

---

[2114] Abraham 3:2.
[2115] Abraham 3:22; 4–5.
[2116] Moses 1:8, 27–29, 33–38; 2–3.
[2117] *Encyclopedia of Mormonism*, 455.
[2118] D&C 84:38.
[2119] *Encyclopedia of Mormonism*, 455.
[2120] Ether 3:18–20.

unto me."[2121] Nephi had a similar experience: "And the Spirit said unto me: Behold, what desirest thou? And I said: I desire to behold the things which my father saw."[2122] Nephi's vision expanded to the view of the birth of the Savior, his ministry, and his Atonement, a detailed vision of the land of promise, the rise and fall of Babylon, the restoration of the Church of Jesus Christ, the gathering of Israel, and the establishment of latter-day Zion.[2123] Joseph Smith and Sidney Rigdon stood in the presence of God and received a vision of the resurrections and the various kingdoms of glory.[2124]

Of course, our entire gospel experience is to lead us to the blessings of Abraham. When our great progenitor had his interview with the Lord and received the desire of his heart, the Lord promised him blessings that we all might expect to receive: a promised land (celestial inheritance), the promise of eternal gospel blessings and priesthood power for us and our children, and the promise of eternal increase. The parting statement of the interview states: "Now, after the Lord had withdrawn from speaking to me, and withdrawn his face from me, I said in my heart: Thy servant has sought thee earnestly; now I have found thee."[2125] When these blessings are given to us in our interview, we might utter the same psalm of praise.

Another interesting blessing that we might expect is being "ordained of God and sent forth,"[2126] meaning, we would be instructed and sent back into the world with individualized missions to draw other people out. For example, in his intercessory prayer, Jesus stated the apostles were no longer part of the world, although they continued to live in the world. Then he said, "I pray not that thou shouldest take them out of the world, but that thou shouldest keep them from the evil. They are not of the world, even as I am not of the world." And then he sent them back into the world with divine commissions: "As thou hast sent me into the world, even so have I also sent them into the world."[2127] Similarly, in our interview with the Lord, we will be termed "not of the world," but nevertheless, we will be "ordained of God and sent forth," back into the world with a unique mission to draw out of the world the children of God and deliver them to Christ.

Priests and Kings, Priestesses and Queens

After we have been purified and sanctified by the Holy Ghost to the extent that our calling and election has been made sure, after we have pressed forward in diligently seeking the face of the Lord until finally we are standing in his presence, then we will receive the Lord's sure promise that in the resurrection we will be anointed priests and kings, priestesses and queens.[2128] For Zion people, this priesthood experience is singular. What was once provisional is now made sure by divine proclamation.

"What is it to be kings and priests?" asked Elder Orson Pratt. "It is to have honour, authority, and dominion, having kingdoms to preside over, and subjects to govern, and possessing the ability ever to increase their authority and glory, and extend their dominion."[2129] Elder McConkie wrote: "Those who gain exaltation are ordained kings and queens, priests and priestesses, in which positions they shall exercise power and authority in the Lord's eternal kingdoms forever."[2130] Regarding righteous women as priestesses, he added, "Women who go on to their exaltation, ruling and reigning

---

[2121] Ether 3:10.
[2122] 1 Nephi 11:2–3.
[2123] 1 Nephi 11–15.
[2124] D&C 76.
[2125] Abraham 2:6–12.
[2126] D&C 50:26.
[2127] John 17:11, 15–16, 18.
[2128] McConkie, *Mormon Doctrine*, 425, 613.
[2129] Pratt, *Times and Seasons*, June 1, 1845.
[2130] McConkie, *Mormon Doctrine*, 424; see also Revelation 1:6; 5:10.

with husbands who are kings and priests, will themselves be queens and priestesses. They will hold positions of power, authority, and preferment in eternity."[2131] And as queens, he said, "If righteous men have power through the gospel and its crowning ordinance of celestial marriage to become kings and priests to rule in exaltation forever, it follows that the women by their side (without whom they cannot attain exaltation) will be queens and priestesses. (Rev. 1:6; 5:10.) Exaltation grows out of the eternal union of a man and his wife. Of those whose marriage endures in eternity, the Lord says, 'Then shall they be gods' (D. & C. 132:20); that is, each of them, the man and the woman, will be a god. As such they will rule over their dominions forever."[2132]

Throughout his ministry, Joseph Smith sought to make his people Zionlike, that is, a kingdom of priests through the full ordinances of the temple "as in Paul's day, as in Enoch's day."[2133] The Prophet said, "Those holding the fulness of the Melchizedek Priesthood are kings and priests of the Most High God, holding the keys of power and blessings."[2134] Elder McConkie explained: "Holders of the Melchizedek Priesthood have power to press forward in righteousness, living by every word that proceedeth forth from the mouth of God, magnifying their callings, going from grace to grace, until through the fulness of the ordinances of the temple they receive the fulness of the priesthood and are ordained kings and priests. Those so attaining shall have exaltation and be kings, priests, rulers, and lords in their respective spheres in the eternal kingdoms of the great King who is God our Father (Rev. 1:6; 5:10)."[2135]

We are anointed to become kings, queens, priests, and priestesses now, with the futuristic hope of the surety of that blessing. Blaine Yorgason wrote, "It was ever Joseph's intention that these priests and kings act in their office in communing with God. Speaking to the Twelve on February 23, 1844, Joseph Smith said: 'I want every man that goes [west to explore for a new home for the Saints] to be a king and a priest. When he gets on the mountains [the Lord's temple] he may want to talk with his God' (*History of the Church*, 6:224)."[2136]

Of course we would want to talk with our God as near to his presence as possible, and the priesthood ordinances are the only way to approach his presence and the *key* to doing so. These blessings are no less impressive for women. Elder James E. Talmage wrote:

In the restored Church of Jesus Christ, . . . in accordance with Divine requirement . . . it is not given to woman to exercise the authority of the Priesthood independently; nevertheless, in the sacred endowments associated with the ordinances pertaining to the House of the Lord, woman shares with man the blessings of the Priesthood. When the frailties and imperfections of mortality are left behind, in the glorified state of the blessed hereafter, husband and wife will administer in their respective stations, seeing and understanding alike, and co-operating to the full in the government of their family kingdom. Then shall woman be recompensed in rich measure for all the injustice that womanhood has endured in mortality. Then shall woman reign by Divine right, a queen [and priestess] in the resplendent realm of her glorified state, even as exalted man shall stand, priest and king unto the Most High God. Mortal eye cannot see nor mind comprehend the beauty, glory, and majesty of a righteous woman made perfect in the celestial kingdom of God.[2137]

The two callings—priest (priestess) and king (queen)—suggest the two primary functions of the priesthood: to administer the ordinances of salvation to others and to preside as a prince (princess) of

---

[2131] McConkie, *Mormon Doctrine*, 594.
[2132] McConkie, *Mormon Doctrine*, 613.
[2133] Smith, *The Words of Joseph Smith*, 54–55.
[2134] Smith, *Teachings of the Prophet Joseph Smith*, 322.
[2135] McConkie, *Mormon Doctrine*, 425.
[2136] Yorgason, *I Need Thee Every Hour*, 402–3.
[2137] Talmage, "The Eternity of Sex," 602–3.

peace.[2138] The title *king* or *queen* also suggests *kingdom* as well as *throne*. In the Constitution of the Priesthood (D&C 121:34–46), we who become priests and kings, with our female counterparts, receive God's renewed pronouncement of an inheritance in his kingdom ("everlasting dominion[s]") with the authority to rule and reign forever ("an unchanging scepter of righteousness and truth").[2139] Does not this description suggest the ideal of Zion?

To righteous couples who are sealed by God's authority and who thereafter have that seal confirmed by the Holy Spirit of Promise, the Lord promises "everlasting dominions" and "unchanging scepters of righteousness and truth":

And again, verily I say unto you, if a man marry a wife by my word, which is my law, and by the new and everlasting covenant, and it is sealed unto them by the Holy Spirit of promise, by him who is anointed, unto whom I have appointed this power and the keys of this priesthood; and it shall be said unto them—Ye shall come forth in the first resurrection; and if it be after the first resurrection, in the next resurrection; *and shall inherit thrones, kingdoms, principalities, and powers, dominions, all heights and depths,* . . . and they shall pass by the angels, and the gods, which are set there, to their exaltation and glory in all things, as hath been sealed upon their heads, which glory shall be a fulness and a continuation of the seeds forever and ever. Then shall they be gods, because they have no end; therefore shall they be from everlasting to everlasting, because they continue; then shall they be above all, because all things are subject unto them. Then shall they be gods, because they have all power, and the angels are subject unto them.[2140]

Becoming Members of the Church of the Firstborn

In a remarkable vision of the kingdoms, Joseph Smith recorded the following description of those who receive all of the priesthood ordinances and thereafter strive to live the celestial law of Zion:

And thus we saw the glory of the celestial, which excels in all things—where God, even the Father, reigns upon his throne forever and ever; before whose throne all things bow in humble reverence, and give him glory forever and ever. They who dwell in his presence are the church of the Firstborn; and they see as they are seen, and know as they are known, having received of his fulness and of his grace; and he makes them equal in power, and in might, and in dominion.[2141]

Whereas The Church of Jesus Christ of Latter-day Saints is Christ's church on the earth, the Church of the Firstborn is Christ's church in heaven, "and its members are exalted beings who gain an inheritance in the highest heaven of the celestial world and for whom the family continues in eternity." We enter into the Church of Jesus Christ through the gate defined as baptism and by receiving the Holy Ghost, and we enter into the Church of the Firstborn through the higher ordinances of the priesthood. "To secure the blessings that pertain to the Church of the Firstborn, one must obey the gospel from the heart, receive all of the ordinances that pertain to the house of the Lord, and be sealed by the Holy Spirit of promise in the Celestial Kingdom of God."[2142]

Are Zion people simultaneously members of that heavenly church? Yes. If we have received the ordinances of the temple, including temple marriage, we have entered the gate of the Church of the Firstborn. Elder McConkie said, "Celestial marriage is the gate to membership in the Church of the Firstborn."[2143] Of the organization of that church, the *Encyclopedia of Mormonism* states: "The Church of the Firstborn is the divine patriarchal order in its eternal form. Building the priesthood family order

---

[2138] Abraham 1:2; D&C 84:19.
[2139] D&C 121:46.
[2140] D&C 132:19–20.
[2141] D&C 76:92–95.
[2142] *Encyclopedia of Mormonism*, 1:276; see also D&C 76:67, 71, 94; 77:11; 78:21; 88:1–5.
[2143] McConkie, *Doctrinal New Testament Commentary*, 3:230.

on this earth by receiving sealings in the temple is a preparation and foundation for this blessing in eternity."[2144]

We note here that while temple ordinances and sealings allow us to enter the gate of membership in the Church of the Firstborn, they do not guarantee that we will receive all of the blessings of that church. Only faithfulness can do that. "When persons have proved themselves faithful in all things required by the Lord, it is their privilege to receive covenants and obligations that will enable them to be heirs of God as members of the Church of the Firstborn. They are 'sealed by the Holy Spirit of promise' and are those 'into whose hands the Father has given all things' (D&C 76:51–55). They will be priests and priestesses, kings and queens, receiving the Father's glory, having the fulness of knowledge, wisdom, power, and dominion (D&C 76:56–62; cf. 107:19). At the second coming of Jesus Christ, the 'general assembly of the Church of the Firstborn' will descend with him (Heb. 12:22–23; JST Gen. 9:23; D&C 76:54, 63)."[2145]

All of this has to do with the priesthood—*patriarchal priesthood*. Zion people first become members of Christ's earthly church by priesthood covenants and ordinances; then, as they progress in the gospel and receive the fulness of priesthood covenants and ordinances, culminating with temple marriage, they achieve membership in Christ's heavenly church.[2146] There, in the Church of the Firstborn, Zion and its people exist forever. The heavenly church, which consists of exalted beings in the family unit, continues to function under the administrative keys of the priesthood. Elder McConkie explained:

Members of The Church of Jesus Christ of Latter-day Saints who so devote themselves to righteousness that they receive the higher ordinances of exaltation become members of the Church of the Firstborn . . . [which consists of] the inner circle of faithful saints who are heirs of exaltation and the fulness of the Father's kingdom. (D. & C. 76:54, 67, 71, 94, 102; 77:11; 78:21; 88:1–5; Heb. 12:23.)

The Church of the Firstborn is made up of the sons of God, those who have been adopted into the family of the Lord, those who are destined to be joint-heirs with Christ in receiving all that the Father hath. "If you keep my commandments you shall receive of his fulness, and be glorified in me as I am in the Father; . . . And all those who are begotten through me are partakers of the glory of the same, and are the church of the Firstborn." (D&C 93:20–22; *Doctrines of Salvation*, vol. 2, p. 9, 41–43.)[2147]

Those Zion people, who travel the road leading to the Church of the Firstborn, must face and survive the *ordained* ordeals while remaining faithful. That road is marked by priesthood covenants and ordinances. Brigham Young said, "[No one can] dwell with the Father and the Son, unless they go through those ordeals that are ordained for the Church of the Firstborn. The ordinances of the House of God are expressly for the Church of the Firstborn."[2148]

Because Zion people are members of the Church of the Firstborn, they receive the "inheritance of the Firstborn and become joint-heirs with Christ in receiving all that the Father has. . . . The Lord said, 'If you keep my commandments you shall receive of his fulness, and be glorified in me as I am in the Father; . . . I . . . am the Firstborn; . . . And all those who are begotten through me are partakers of the glory of the same, and are the Church of the Firstborn.'"[2149]

[2144] *Encyclopedia of Mormonism*, 1:276.
[2145] *Encyclopedia of Mormonism*, 1:276.
[2146] McConkie, *Doctrinal New Testament Commentary*, 3:230.
[2147] McConkie, *Mormon Doctrine*, 139.
[2148] Young, *Journal of Discourses*, 8:54.
[2149] *Encyclopedia of Mormonism*, 1:276; quoting Romans 8:14–17; D&C 84:33–38; 93:20–22.

Angelic Ministers from the Church of the Firstborn

As we have discussed, the Aaronic Priesthood holds the keys of the ministration of angels,[2150] who, we would venture, are presided over by the Holy Ghost.[2151] When we are baptized and receive the gift of the Holy Ghost, we automatically receive the gift of the ministering of angels. These two gifts are renewed and enhanced in the oath and covenant of the priesthood[2152] and in the Constitution of the Priesthood.[2153]

The author of the book of Hebrews wrote to a group of Saints who were living a Zionlike life. These Saints had achieved membership in the Church of the Firstborn and thus were enjoying the ministering of angels. Consider the blessings of these Zion people: "But ye are come unto mount Sion, and unto the city of the living God, the heavenly Jerusalem, and to an innumerable company of angels, to the general assembly and church of the firstborn, which are written in heaven, and to God the Judge of all, and to the spirits of just men made perfect, and to Jesus the mediator of the new covenant."[2154] Blaine Yorgason explained, "In other words, the righteous Hebrew Saints had attained the right to the ministry and association of angelic members of Christ's heavenly Church—the general assembly and Church of the Firstborn."[2155]

The angels, who minister to us from the heavenly realms, are members of the Church of the Firstborn. They exist in "grades" or levels, according to President John Taylor;[2156] that is, they are variously resurrected beings,[2157] spirits of individuals made perfect,[2158] and translated beings.[2159] A fourth class, suggests Yorgason, "might be departed members of the Church [of Jesus Christ] who are still 'coming unto Christ' and yet are called, from time to time, to minister to their mortal loved ones."[2160]

Expounding on the situation of the Hebrew Saints, the Prophet Joseph Smith described the organization of angels in the Church of the Firstborn and their ministry to us: "The organization of the spiritual and heavenly worlds, and of spiritual and heavenly beings, was agreeable to the most perfect order and harmony: their limits and bounds were fixed irrevocably." Continuing, the Prophet said that the privilege of angelic ministration is a power connected with the ordinances of the priesthood: "I assure the Saints that truth, in reference to these matters, can and may be known through the revelations of God in the way of His ordinances, and in answer to prayer."

What intelligence might we expect to receive from angels? Joseph Smith explained that if we pursue the course of the Hebrew church and strive to become Zionlike as they did, our privileges would be identical: "What did they learn by coming to the spirits of just men made perfect? Is it written? No. What they learned has not been and could not have been written. What object was gained by this communication with the spirits of the just? It was the established order of the Kingdom of God: The keys of power and knowledge were with them to communicate to the Saints."[2161]

President John Taylor taught that the various types of angels sent to us from the Church of the Firstborn are our watchmen and the "police of heaven." Moreover, they gather, teach, report, and

---

[2150] D&C 13:1.
[2151] 2 Nephi 32:2–3; Moses 5:58; Moroni 7:36.
[2152] D&C 84:42.
[2153] D&C 121:46.
[2154] Hebrews 12:22–24.
[2155] Yorgason, *I Need Thee Every Hour*, 286.
[2156] Taylor, *The Gospel Kingdom*, 31.
[2157] D&C 129:1.
[2158] D&C 129:3.
[2159] D&C 7:6.
[2160] Yorgason, *I Need Thee Every Hour*, 288.
[2161] Smith, *Teachings of the Prophet Joseph Smith*, 325.

help us with our prayers: "But, without going into a particular detail of the offices and duties of the different grades of angels, let us close by saying that the angels gather the elect, and pluck out all that offends. They are the police of heaven and report whatever transpires on earth, and carry the petitions and supplications of men, women, and children to the mansions of remembrance, where they are kept as tokens of obedience by the sanctified, in 'golden vials' labeled 'the prayers of the saints.'"

He continued by stating that their influence upon us often goes unnoticed and unfortunately is widely disbelieved, but nevertheless, their influence is among the greatest realities in our lives: "The action of the angels, or messengers of God, upon our minds, so that the heart can conceive things past, present, and to come, and revelations from the eternal world, is, among a majority of mankind, a greater mystery than all the secrets of philosophy, literature, superstition, and bigotry, put together. Though some men try to deny it, and some try to explain away the meaning, still there is so much testimony in the Bible, and among a respectable portion of the world, that one might as well undertake to throw the water out of this world into the moon with a teaspoon, as to do away with the supervision of angels upon the human mind."[2162]

We who have entered the gate of the Church of the Firstborn, which is the entrance to heavenly Zion, we who have received the temple ordinances and have been sealed to our eternal companion, we who have endured in righteousness—we are members of the heavenly church and therefore privileged to associate with and receive instruction and protection from these, our fellow servants. They may come to us in the form of spirits or translated or resurrected beings—but they come. And when they come, they bless us beyond our ability to recognize or appreciate. These are ministers who, under the direction of the Holy Ghost, speak the words of Christ.[2163] They "interact with mortals and . . . have communion with members of the mortal church—according to their respective stewardships . . . thereby encouraging and giving power and direction"[2164] to us, their associates and charges. Their ministration is a manifestation of the love of Jesus Christ, whose servants they are.

THE ORDER OF THE SON OF GOD

According to Blaine Yorgason, something of significance occurs when our calling and election has been made sure: "We are brought into what is called the order of the Son of God."[2165] Let us first state that an order of the priesthood is a group of like individuals, who are *one* in purpose, heart, mind, and authority. By this definition, therefore, men belonging to the *Order of Aaron* are Aaronic Priesthood holders, and men belonging to the *Order of Melchizedek* are Melchizedek Priesthood holders. Other priesthood orders involve both men and women (not to suggest that women are ordained to the priesthood), for example, the Order of Enoch[2166] and the Patriarchal Order.[2167] These two priesthood orders are not separate priesthoods or offices in the priesthood; rather, the priesthood Order of Enoch is comprised of people who covenant to belong to the same order as the people of Enoch, and the Patriarchal Order of the Priesthood is comprised of sealed husbands and wives (that is, belonging to the same order as the Gods).[2168]

[2162] Taylor, *The Gospel Kingdom*, 31.

[2163] Moroni 7:31; 2 Nephi 32:3.

[2164] Yorgason, *I Need Thee Every Hour*, 288.

[2165] Yorgason, *I Need Thee Every Hour*, 403–6.

[2166] D&C 76:57; McConkie, "The Doctrine of the Priesthood," 32; Harold B. Lee, Conference Report, Oct. 1953, 25.

[2167] Kimball, "The Fruit of Our Welfare Services Labors," 74; McConkie, "The Ten Blessings of the Priesthood," 33.

[2168] McConkie, *Mormon Doctrine*, 548.

Every priesthood order points us to becoming gods! Being part of the order of the Son of God, we receive "an unchanging scepter of righteousness and truth," and we receive "an everlasting dominion."[2169] Elder McConkie wrote:

Those who receive the gospel and join The Church of Jesus Christ of Latter-day Saints have power given them to become the sons of God. (D&C 11:30; 35:2; 39:1–6; 45:8; John 1:12.) Sonship does not come from church membership alone, but admission into the Church opens the door to such high status, if it is followed by continued faith and devotion. (Rom. 8:14–18; Gal. 3:26–29; 4:1–7.) The sons of God are members of his family and, hence, are joint-heirs with Christ, inheriting with him the fulness of the Father. (D&C 93:17–23.) Before gaining entrance to that glorious household, they must receive the higher priesthood (Moses 6:67–68), magnify their callings therein (D&C 84:33–41), enter into the new and everlasting covenant of marriage (D&C 131:1–4; 132), and be obedient in all things. (*Doctrines of Salvation*, vol. 2, pp. 8–9, 37–41, 59, 64–65.) Those who become the sons of God in this life (1 John 3:1–3) are the ones who by enduring in continued righteousness will be gods in eternity. (D&C 76:58.)[2170]

When worthy men are ordained to the Melchizedek Priesthood, they enter into *The Holy Priesthood after the Order of the Son of God*.[2171] Then as men *and women* progress in priesthood principles (temple ordinances and sealings), the order of the Son of God takes on additional significance. President Ezra Taft Benson stated that the order of the Son of God is the equivalent of the fulness of the Melchizedek Priesthood, and therefore requires that we receive *every* saving and exalting ordinance available in the temple.[2172] Thus, worthy men and women can enter into the same order as Jesus Christ.

We credit Alma with having provided us one of best descriptions of the order of the Son of God.

Now, as I said concerning the holy order, or this high priesthood, there were many who were ordained and became high priests of God; and it was on account of their exceeding faith and repentance, and their righteousness before God, they choosing to repent and work righteousness rather than to perish; *therefore they were called after this holy order*, and were sanctified, and their garments were washed white through the blood of the Lamb.

Now they, after being sanctified by the Holy Ghost, having their garments made white, being pure and spotless before God, could not look upon sin save it were with abhorrence; and there were many, exceedingly great many, who were made pure and entered into the rest of the Lord their God.[2173]

We wish that this description applied to every man who is ordained to the high priesthood, but it does not. Alma's representation seems to point to a higher, holier order of the Son of God, *an order within the order*, an order consisting of those whose worthiness elevates them into "the rest of the Lord their God." That *rest*, of course, "is the fulness of his glory."[2174]

When President Benson used the term *fulness of the priesthood*, he referenced the patriarchal order of the priesthood, and faithfulness to the covenants that govern that priesthood order. It is only when men and women are sealed in eternal marriage and thus enter into the patriarchal order of the priesthood that the door to priesthood fulness can be accessed. Only then can the fulness of priesthood blessings begin to flow. This "fulness" is both a doctrine and a right of the priesthood that we learn of and obtain under the Father's tutelage; he distils information upon our souls as the dews

---

[2169] D&C 121:46.
[2170] McConkie, *Mormon Doctrine*, 745.
[2171] D&C 107:3.
[2172] Benson, "What I Hope You Will Teach Your Children about the Temple," 6–10.
[2173] Alma 13:10–12; emphasis added.
[2174] D&C 84:24.

from heaven until we are saturated in priesthood doctrine and fulness. The fulness of the priesthood is a condition that characterizes Zion people.

THE ORDER OF THE SON OF GOD AND MARRIAGE

Another element of the order of the Son of God is its association with the patriarchal order of the priesthood. As we have said, this order of the priesthood is relevant to both men and women, and the doctrine surrounding it provides the clearest statement on receiving our scepter and our everlasting dominion. That statement reads:

It shall be said unto them—Ye shall come forth in the first resurrection; and if it be after the first resurrection, in the next resurrection; and shall inherit thrones, kingdoms, principalities, and powers, dominions, all heights and depths . . . ; and they shall pass by the angels, and the gods, which are set there, to their exaltation and glory in all things, as hath been sealed upon their heads, which glory shall be a fulness and a continuation of the seeds forever and ever.

Then shall they be gods, because they have no end; therefore shall they be from everlasting to everlasting, because they continue; then shall they be above all, because all things are subject unto them. Then shall they be gods, because they have all power, and the angels are subject unto them. Verily, verily, I say unto you, except ye abide my law ye cannot attain to this glory.[2175]

Neither Zion individuals nor Zion marriages nor the priesthood society of Zion can be established without the patriarchal order of the priesthood, which is part of the order of the Son of God. President Benson stated that Adam and Eve made temple covenants and complied with the associated ordinances; then God said to them, "Thou art after the order of him who was without beginning of days or end of years, from all eternity to all eternity."[2176]

The power of this priesthood order, according to President Benson, is sufficient to bring us into the presence of God. And Zion, we recall, is comprised of pure-hearted people who are qualified to see God. Three years before Adam died, our first father called his righteous direct-line descendants, along with others of his righteous posterity, into the valley of Adam-ondi-Ahman. On that occasion, Adam bestowed upon them his last blessing. "And the Lord appeared unto them, and they rose up and blessed Adam, and called him Michael, the prince, the archangel."[2177] Among all the superlative events that happened at that time, we must not overlook the fact that Adam's primary intent—*and the power of his priesthood*—was to bring his family into God's presence.

Of that occasion, Joseph Smith said, "Adam blessed his posterity" because "he wanted to bring them into the presence of God."[2178] Because this event will play out again in the last days at Adam-ondi-Ahman,[2179] we should pay attention to the particulars. Quoting from Doctrine and Covenants 107, President Benson explained how Adam succeeded in bringing himself and his righteous posterity into the presence of God: "The order of this priesthood was confirmed to be handed down from father to son, and rightly belongs to the literal descendants of the chosen seed, to whom the promises were made. This order was instituted in the days of Adam, and came down by lineage [in order] . . . that his posterity should be the chosen of the Lord, and that they should be preserved unto the end of the earth."[2180] That is, Adam received and complied with *all* the temple covenants and ordinances and thereby entered into the *patriarchal* order of the Son of God; then he brought his family into the presence of the Lord.

[2175] D&C 132:19–21.
[2176] Benson, "What I Hope You Will Teach Your Children about the Temple," 6–10; quoting Moses 6:67.
[2177] D&C 107:53–54.
[2178] Smith, *Teachings of the Prophet Joseph Smith*, 159.
[2179] D&C 116:1.
[2180] Benson, "What I Hope You Will Teach Your Children about the Temple," 6–10; quoting D&C 107:40–42; emphasis added.

The patriarchal order of the priesthood governs eternal families. Fathers and mothers preside. If we had more of the revelation of the gathering at Adam-ondi-Ahman, we would likely see Eve playing a prominent role in the gathering and spiritual outpouring. Likewise, fathers and mothers in Zion might draw upon patriarchal priesthood power whereby they, like Adam and Eve, might do the work of God and seek to bring their families into God's presence. By reason of their sealing, parents possess the patriarchal power to do this work. President Benson said that Adam set the example of a righteous patriarch. He entered into the patriarchal order with Eve, his wife, persisted in righteousness until he had received all the blessings of the temple, and thereby he entered into the order of the Son of God. Now Adam had power to bring his posterity into the presence of God.

Because Zion is the pure in heart, and because the pure in heart are qualified to see God, the principles of the patriarchal order of the Son of God become profoundly important. Enoch, who was present at the gathering at Adam-ondi-Ahman, followed Adam's lead to establish Zion principles in the hearts of his people, and thereby he brought them into the presence of God. President Benson said that Noah and Shem also followed this pattern and brought themselves and many people into God's presence. Moses understood the pattern, having achieved the blessing in his life, and attempted to bring his people into the same holy order of the Son of God and thereafter into the presence of God. But, as we have discussed, the Israelites shunned the opportunity, and the Lord withdrew the privilege of entering into his rest, "which rest is the fulness of his glory."[2181]

On that occasion, the Lord told Moses, "I will take away the priesthood out of their midst; *therefore my holy order, and the ordinances thereof shall not go before them; for my presence shall not go up in their midst.*"[2182] In this verse we hear echoes from the denunciation found in the Constitution of the Priesthood: "Behold, the heavens withdraw themselves; the Spirit of the Lord is grieved; and when it is withdrawn, Amen to the priesthood or the authority of that man."[2183]

By obedience to the new and everlasting covenant, by receiving ordination in the Melchizedek Priesthood and becoming part of *The Holy Priesthood after the Order of the Son of God,* by obedience to the oath and covenant of the priesthood and to the Constitution of the Priesthood, we can seek and at last stand before God. Our having received and proven faithful to all the ordinances of salvation and exaltation have qualified us to be members of the sacred priesthood order called the *Order of the Son of God*. This order is associated with the patriarchal order of the priesthood. These orders of the priesthood, along with their attendant powers, are highly relevant to Zion people—for Zion is the pure in heart, and the pure in heart are those who qualify to see God.

THE FULNESS OF THE PRIESTHOOD

When at last we stand in the presence of God, the grand purposes of the priesthood, as they pertain to mortality, are fulfilled. Now unequalled blessings begin to flow. As we have discussed, these blessings might include a vision of the infinite kingdom that God is about to bestow upon us, an endowment of extraordinary knowledge and power, the receipt of a significant gift that corresponds with our request, and a special ordination to be sent back into the world to accomplish a unique mission among God's children.

Perhaps with this divine interview in mind, President Joseph Fielding Smith said when we have lived faithfully and done all that the Lord has required of us, then we will be given the privilege of asking for and receiving *other covenants* and *other obligations* both of which will make of us heirs and members of the Church of the Firstborn: "They are they into whose hands the Father has given all things."[2184] Such Zion people, continued President Smith, will receive of the Father's fulness and of his

---

[2181] D&C 84:23–25.
[2182] JST Exodus 34:1; emphasis mine.
[2183] D&C 121:37.
[2184] D&C 76:55.

glory. Therefore, we should expend every effort to achieve this objective; only obedience and actively seeking this goal will bring us face to face with God, in which setting we will receive wisdom, power, and dominion. President Smith concluded by saying that the temple is where we receive the fulness of these blessings.[2185] It is there that we are taught the exalting principles and receive the essential covenants and ordinances to lay hold on the privileges and powers of the order of the Son of God. It is there that we become Zion people.

POWER IN THE PRIESTHOOD

Standing in the presence of God, being endowed and commissioned to do a singular work, Zion people receive a singular ordination with attendant power. Blaine Yorgason gives examples of righteous individuals who achieved the holy order of the Son of God and were given powers commensurate with their calling from the Lord.

Enoch used this power according to the holy order of the Son of God with great effectiveness. In the writings of Moses as revealed to Joseph Smith we read: "So great was the faith of Enoch, that he led the people of God, and their enemies came to battle against them; and he spake the word of the Lord, and the earth trembled, and the mountains fled, even according to his command; and the rivers of water were turned out of their course; and the roar of the lions was heard out of the wilderness; and all nations feared greatly, so powerful was the word of Enoch, and so great was the power of the language which God had given him" (Moses 7:13).[2186]

Clearly, we might not fully appreciate the power given to Zion people!

Equating the order of the Son of God with the fulness of the patriarchal order of the priesthood, Yorgason continues,

The scriptures contain other accounts of the remarkable powers that accompany the granting of the fulness of this patriarchal order of the priesthood. For instance, we know that the Lord said to Nephi, the son of Helaman: "Behold, thou art Nephi, and I am God. Behold, I declare it unto thee in the presence of mine angels, that ye shall have power over this people, and shall smite the earth with famine, and with pestilence, and destruction, according to the wickedness of this people. Behold, I give unto you power, that whatsoever ye shall seal on earth shall be sealed in heaven; and whatsoever ye shall loose on earth shall be loosed in heaven; and thus shall ye have power among this people. And thus, if ye shall say unto this temple it shall be rent in twain, it shall be done. And if ye shall say unto this mountain, Be thou cast down and become smooth, it shall be done. And behold, if ye shall say that God shall smite this people, it shall come to pass" (Helaman 10:6–10).

Moroni points to the Brother of Jared as one who gained the presence of the Lord and received exceptional power in the priesthood, according to the order of the Son of God: "There were many whose faith was so exceedingly strong, even before Christ came, who could not be kept from within the veil, but truly saw with their eyes the things which they had beheld with an eye of faith, and they were glad. And behold, we have seen in this record that one of these was the brother of Jared; for so great was his faith in God, that when God put forth his finger he could not hide it from the sight of the brother of Jared, because of his word which he had spoken unto him, which word he had obtained by faith. And after the brother of Jared had beheld the finger of the Lord, because of the promise which the brother of Jared had obtained by faith, the Lord could not withhold anything from his sight; wherefore he showed him all things, for he could no longer be kept without the veil" (Ether 12:19–21).

Commenting, Yorgason says: "Thereafter the brother of Jared ordered the mountain Zerin to remove and it was removed (see Ether 12:30). But he was given another power that is even more remarkable and that was almost the envy of the great Moroni, who wrote in prayer: 'Behold, thou hast

---

[2185] Smith, Conference Report, Apr. 1969, 123.
[2186] Yorgason, *I Need Thee Every Hour*, 407–8.

not made us mighty in writing like unto the brother of Jared, for thou madest him that the things which he wrote were mighty even as thou art, unto the overpowering of man to read them' (Ether 12:24)."[2187]

The commission that we received at baptism to be witnesses of God,[2188] which we renew every time we partake of the sacrament, and which we renew again when we receive the oath and covenant of the priesthood, is advanced to a degree that approaches perfection when we now stand in the presence of God. In that holy encounter, we actually see God, which greatly empowers our witness. We consecrate back to him that testimony by carefully imparting it to others for the purpose of bringing them to Christ. Similarly, we consecrate back to him the endowment of knowledge and power and the special gift that he gives us. We recommit to the consecration of our lives by accepting his commission to accomplish a new and special mission in the ministry of Jesus Christ. Now, more than ever before, we have become Zion people.

"Without Compulsory Means It Shall Flow unto Thee Forever"

The Constitution of the Priesthood lists opposites—those things that bring the priesthood to a halt, and those things that bring power and blessings. One set of opposites involves the word *dominion* as it applies to the presence and the absence of compulsion.

The "many" (Babylon people) who are called but not chosen would use force or compulsion in "unrighteous dominion,"[2189] that is, they would focus their influence on insisting that other people would conform their lives to match theirs. To accomplish their objective, they would exert an effort to forcibly draw others into their circle and hold them there. Conversely, the "few" (Zion people) who are called *and* chosen, they who would focus their attention on personal sanctification so that they could better extend charitable service, will receive an "everlasting dominion" that will flow unto them without force—"without compulsory means."[2190]

The dominions of Zion people flow unto them naturally, without having to be compelled. This action is like a river seeking its origin. It is like light, which naturally "cleaveth unto light,"[2191] ultimately seeking the Source of light. A sign that we are succeeding and becoming more Zionlike is that blessings begin to flow to us of their own accord. They seek us out as if they sense a home in us. This is the condition of Zion people and a right of the priesthood: "thy dominion shall be an everlasting dominion, and without compulsory means it shall flow unto thee forever and ever."[2192]

Because the blessings listed in the Constitution of the Priesthood are so exalted, they lie outside the realm of telestial experience, and they surpass our ability to fully envision. Nevertheless, they are true and an important part of the gospel and Zion. That they should be given to us in the flesh is the Father's desire and design. Notice the Lord's deliberate use of language to drive home this point: "He that is ordained of God and sent forth, the same is appointed to be the greatest, notwithstanding he is the least and the servant of all. Wherefore, he *is* possessor of all things; for all things *are* subject unto him, both in heaven and on the earth, the life and the light, the Spirit and the power, sent forth by the will of the Father through Jesus Christ, his Son."[2193]

[2187] Yorgason, *I Need Thee Every Hour*, 407–9.
[2188] Mosiah 18:9.
[2189] D&C 121:39.
[2190] D&C 121:39, 46.
[2191] D&C 88:40.
[2192] D&C 121:46.
[2193] D&C 50:27–26; emphasis added.

SUMMARY AND CONCLUSION

The new and everlasting covenant, the umbrella gospel covenant, is the first pillar of Zion. The oath and covenant of the priesthood is the second pillar of Zion. These essential covenants stand upon the foundation of the Atonement of Jesus Christ.

Our journey to Zion begins with a covenant—the new and everlasting covenant. As we progress in that Covenant and receive all the gospel covenants, including the priesthood and temple covenants, we are following the same ancient and eternal pattern of the creation of gods. President Wilford Woodruff taught that God the Father "had His endowments long ago; it is thousands of millions of years since He received His blessings."[2194] In a temple dedicatory prayer, President Gordon B. Hinckley confirmed that the initiatory ordinances, endowment, and sealings are eternal in nature.[2195] In the same way that the Father became God, in the same way that every god became a god, we too can become gods. Like our eternal Father and Mother, our kingdom begins at an altar in a temple, where we enter into an eternal union with our spouse and make with each other and with God the covenant of exaltation.[2196] Now a new kingdom is established. On that occasion all of the blessings of the oath and covenant of the priesthood are renewed to both the husband and wife.[2197] Now the infinite and eternal purposes of the priesthood begin to come clear and Zion becomes a reality. Former BYU professor of religion Rodney Turner wrote:

Priesthood is the authority and power to organize, sustain, direct, redeem and sanctify. These operations are as valid in terms of the home as they are in terms of a planet or a galaxy. The microcosm is, ultimately, the macrocosm. This is why those who prove faithful over a few things will be made rulers over many things. Many are called and few are chosen to retain the priesthood in eternity because their hearts are set upon the things of the world rather than upon the work and the glory of that God they purport to represent. A true priesthood father is like no other father on earth. His children recognize the difference between him and other men. His priesthood is a light to his family and, therefore to the world. Men and women can provide all of the essential ingredients of good parenthood as defined by social scientists without being members of the Church. Both the gospel and the holy priesthood must make a difference for there to be a difference![2198]

As we said, our journey to Zion begins with a covenant, which is motivated by our realization that only Jesus "can unlock the gate of heaven and let us in."[2199] Therefore, we seek to enter into an agreement of salvation with him. The new and everlasting covenant is that covenant, and exaltation is its end purpose. The Covenant stipulates that we cannot achieve exaltation unless we become like Christ and bring other people to Christ. These two essentials are impossible without the power of Christ. Therefore, to progress in the new and everlasting covenant we seek ordination to the priesthood, whereby we enter into the order of the Son of God. This is also done by covenant—the oath and covenant of the priesthood, which is the first of two instances that is called the covenant of exaltation.[2200]

As we progress in the priesthood covenant, we soon learn that its blessings apply to both men and women. We obtain these priesthood blessings in stages: first, worthy men are ordained; second,

---

[2194] Woodruff, *Journal of Discourses*, 4:192.
[2195] Hinckley, *Church News*, Nov. 8, 1997, 4.
[2196] Smith, *Doctrines of Salvation*, 2:58.
[2197] McConkie, *A New Witness for the Articles of Faith*, 313.
[2198] Turner, *Woman and the Priesthood*, 302.
[2199] "There Is a Green Hill Far Away," *Hymns*, no. 194.
[2200] McConkie, *Mormon Doctrine*, 167: "Ordination to office in the Melchizedek priesthood and entering into that 'order of the priesthood' named 'the new and everlasting covenant of marriage' are both occasions when men make the covenant of exaltation, being promised through their faithfulness all that the Father hath. (D. & C. 131:1–4; 84:39–41; 132; Num. 25:13.)"

worthy men and women are purified and endowed in the temple; third, worthy men and women enter into the highest order of the priesthood—the patriarchal order—the priesthood order of temple marriage which is the second instance called the covenant of exaltation.

Because the "rights of the priesthood are inseparably connected with the powers of heaven," and because the "powers of heaven cannot be controlled nor handled only upon the principles of righteousness," the Lord revealed to us what President Stephen L Richards called the Constitution of the Priesthood.[2201] This Constitution (D&C 121:34–46) enumerates the principles upon which the priesthood fails or functions, and it lists the blessings that flow from obedience. These blessings are offered to the "many" who are called to the priesthood and thus to eternal life, but sadly, these blessings are achieved only by a "few" who persist in priesthood principles and ultimately are chosen for eternal life. The covenantal statement of priesthood blessings is this:

Then shall thy confidence wax strong in the presence of God; and the doctrine of the priesthood shall distil upon thy soul as the dews from heaven. The Holy Ghost shall be thy constant companion, and thy scepter an unchanging scepter of righteousness and truth; and thy dominion shall be an everlasting dominion, and without compulsory means it shall flow unto thee forever and ever.[2202]

These blessings are a clear statement of the ultimate objectives of the priesthood, and the Constitution of the Priesthood is a second witness, so to speak, of the principles and blessings set forth in the oath and covenant of the priesthood. We have discussed at least eight blessings and purposes of the priesthood:

1. To make us like Christ and his Father.
2. To empower us to bring people to Christ.
3. To bring us into the presence of God.
4. To give us a view of our celestial inheritance.
5. To endow us with the knowledge and power of God.
6. To provide us the opportunity to ask for and receive a special gift from God.
7. To give us a personalized commission from God to serve in the cause of Christ.
8. To establish us in our eternal kingdoms.

Thus authorized and empowered, we receive the Lord's guarantee of eternal life and the privilege of becoming part of the order of the Son of God. The highest manifestation of that priesthood order is the patriarchal order of the priesthood, which we enter into when we are sealed to our spouse for time and eternity. Ultimately, the order of the Son of God is the power to prevail with God and at last stand in his presence. In that holy setting, we are given the promise of a scepter and a dominion; that is, we receive the promise that we will become priests and kings (priestesses and queens) with power to administer the blessings of the new and everlasting covenant to others, and we receive the promise that we will inherit dominions and rule and reign in the kingdom of God forever. We are to seek this experience while we are yet in the flesh.

The priesthood is the power to bring us to our journey's end—exaltation. The priesthood is the power to establish Zion in our lives. The priesthood opens the door to our eternal destiny.

Progression in the priesthood attracts magnificent blessings. Great powers become manifested in our lives, and these powers amplify our ability to accomplish our God-given priesthood commission. One of those powers is an increase of the Spirit. The Holy Ghost enlightens us to a greater degree, and the brighter we become the more we are capable of drawing lesser lights to us. The effect of this migration of light begins to create a kingdom that flows to us forever of its own accord. Under the Father's careful supervision, the Holy Ghost distils priesthood knowledge upon our souls until that

---

[2201] Richards, Conference Report, Apr. 1955, 12.
[2202] D&C 121:45–46.

knowledge becomes perfect. It is the Holy Ghost who guides every step of our journey, and it is he who now commends and introduces us to our Heavenly Father.

Standing, finally, in the presence of God, having expended every effort to return to him, to see him, to learn from him, to be blessed by him, we proclaim, as did our father Abraham, the anthem of the priesthood: "Thy servant has sought thee earnestly; now I have found thee!"[2203] This is the consummate blessing of the "few" who are called to the priesthood and to eternal life and who are ultimately chosen for the most supernal blessings.

POSTLUDE

The second pillar of Zion is *the oath and covenant of the priesthood*. It is preceded by the new and everlasting covenant, and it is followed by the law of consecration. According to the "Law of the Church" (D&C 42), these three covenants are sufficient to establish us as Zion people.

Now we have learned that Zion was our origin and will be our destiny. She is our ideal, and she is also the antithesis of Babylon. Moreover, Zion is the standard among celestial and celestial-seeking people.[2204] Brigham Young said, "[Zion] commences in the heart of each person."[2205] Clearly, the responsibility to become Zion people rests upon each of us, individually.

That responsibility begins with formally accepting the Atonement by receiving the new and everlasting covenant by way of baptism. The new and everlasting covenant is the *umbrella covenant*, consisting of two primary covenants: (1) the covenant of baptism, and (2) the oath and covenant of the priesthood. The priesthood covenant is magnified by (1) ordination for worthy men; (2) temple covenants and ordinances for worthy men and women; (3) the temple sealing covenant, which is called the covenant of exaltation,[2206] for worthy men and women.

The new and everlasting covenant not only provides a way to be cleansed from sin and separated from the world, but it provides us a way to receive God's authority, power, and knowledge—everything we need to become like him and inherit all that he has. This is the essence of the second pillar of Zion—the oath and covenant of the priesthood.

As we have seen, this section applies to both worthy men and women. The priesthood covenant is received by men at the time of ordination, but its principles are expansive and eventually lead to the temple. There, faithful men and women are endowed with priesthood covenants and ordinances that culminate at a marriage altar. An editorial in the *Improvement Era* noted: "Now, as far as the Church of Christ is concerned, this oath and covenant is made first in baptism, when the Holy Ghost is given, and more especially when the Priesthood is conferred. It is, secondly, repeated by partaking of the Sacrament, and by entering into special covenants in holy places [the temple]."[2207] Elder Bruce R. McConkie said, "This covenant, made when the priesthood is received, is renewed when the recipient enters the order of eternal marriage."[2208] Clearly, both men and women are involved in the doctrines of the priesthood.

[2203] Abraham 2:12.
[2204] D&C 105:5.
[2205] Young, *Discourses of Brigham Young*, 118.
[2206] Nelson, *The Power within Us*, 136; Smith, *Doctrines of Salvation*, 2:58. Note: Elder McConkie stated that men make a covenant of exaltation twice: once upon ordination to the Melchizedek Priesthood and again at the time of the marriage sealing: "Ordination to office in the Melchizedek priesthood and entering into that 'order of the priesthood' named 'the new and everlasting covenant of marriage' are both occasions when men make the covenant of exaltation, being promised through their faithfulness all that the Father hath (D&C 131:1–4; 84:39–41; 132; Num. 25:13)." (McConkie, *Mormon Doctrine*, 167.)
[2207] Editor's Table, *Improvement Era*, Feb. 1923.
[2208] McConkie, *A New Witness for the Articles of Faith*, 313.

In this section, we have examined the history of the priesthood and men who were great examples. We discussed priesthood keys and their importance in the restored Church of Jesus Christ. Then we surveyed our covenantal agreements and the Father's oath, instructions, and promise. We also examined what President Stephen L Richards called, "The Constitution of the Priesthood," found in Doctrine and Covenants 121. We discussed why many are called to eternal life, but few are chosen. We also studied the Lord's instructions and rewards for the chosen few. In the end, we came to understand that priesthood is more than an ordination; it is a way of life and the power to pursue that life. Without the priesthood and its guiding principles, neither a man nor a woman can achieve Zion in his/her life and thus attain the ultimate form of salvation, *exaltation*.

Book 4:

The Third Pillar of Zion—The Law of Consecration

Introduction

"[Zion] commences in the heart of each person"[2209]
—Brigham Young

In this fourth book of *The Three Pillars of Zion* series, we will examine in depth the third pillar of Zion: *The Law of Consecration*. We recall that the "Law of the Church" (D&C 42) states that three covenants are sufficient to establish us as Zion people: "And ye shall hereafter receive church covenants, such as shall be sufficient to establish you, both here and in the New Jerusalem."[2210] These covenants are:

1. The New and Everlasting Covenant (D&C 132:4–7).
2. The Oath and Covenant of the Priesthood (D&C 84:33–44).
3. The Law of Consecration (D&C 82:11–15).

In Book 1, we learned that Zion was our origin and will be our destiny. She is our ideal, and she is also the antithesis of Babylon. Moreover, Zion is the standard among celestial and celestial-seeking people.[2211] Joseph Smith said, "We ought to have the building up of Zion as our greatest object."[2212] The obligation to become Zion people rests upon each of us individually.

That obligation begins with formally accepting the Atonement by receiving the new and everlasting covenant (Book 2) by way of baptism. The new and everlasting covenant is the *umbrella covenant*, consisting of two primary covenants: the covenant of baptism, and the oath and covenant of

---

[2209] Young, *Discourses of Brigham Young*, 118.
[2210] D&C 42:67.
[2211] D&C 105:5.
[2212] Smith, *Teachings of the Prophet Joseph Smith*, 60.

the priesthood (Book 3). The priesthood covenant is magnified by (1) ordination for worthy men; (2) temple covenants and ordinances for worthy men and women; and (3) the temple sealing covenant, which is called the Covenant of Exaltation,[2213] for worthy men and women.

As we have learned in Book 2, the new and everlasting covenant not only provides a way to be cleansed from sin and separated from the world, but it also provides us a way to receive God's authority, power, and knowledge—everything we need to become like him and inherit all that he has. This is the essence of the second pillar of Zion—the oath and covenant of the priesthood.

As we learned in Book 3, the principles of the priesthood apply to both worthy men and women. The priesthood covenant is received by men at the time of ordination, but its principles are expansive and eventually lead to the temple. There, faithful men and women are endowed with priesthood covenants and ordinances that culminate at a marriage altar. Elder Bruce R. McConkie said, "This covenant, made when the priesthood is received, is renewed when the recipient enters the order of eternal marriage."[2214] Clearly, both men and women are involved in the doctrines of the priesthood.

We discussed the history of the priesthood and men who were great examples. We discussed priesthood keys and their importance in the restored Church of Jesus Christ. Then we surveyed our covenantal agreements and the Father's oath, instructions, and promises. Later we examined "The Constitution of the Priesthood," found in Doctrine and Covenants 121, and we discussed why many are called to eternal life but few are chosen. We also studied the Lord's instructions and rewards for the chosen few. We came to understand that priesthood is more than an ordination; it is a way of life and the power to pursue that life. Without the priesthood and its guiding principles, neither a man nor a woman could achieve Zion in his or her life and thus attain the ultimate form of salvation, *exaltation* in the celestial kingdom.

In this fourth book of the Zion series, we will examine the law of the celestial kingdom,[2215] which is the foundational law of Zion—*The Law of Consecration*. Few laws of God are as misunderstood. We will discuss what the law of consecration is and what it is not. We will demonstrate how this law is a template that can be used (and has been used) in any number of situations. We will also discuss how living the law of consecration results in equality and unity, two foundational characteristics that describe the celestial kingdom. We will study the guiding principles of consecration and contrast them with the condition of Babylon. Then we will discuss the ultimate test during mortality: the decision that we must make between God and mammon.

Finally, we will learn that the law of consecration is an outgrowth of "The Royal Law,"[2216] which is this: "Thou shalt love the Lord thy God with all thy heart, and with all thy soul, and with all thy mind. This is the first and great commandment. And the second is like unto it, Thou shalt love thy neighbour as thyself." The royal law is "the first and great commandment," according to Jesus, and upon it "hang all the law and the prophets."[2217] When all is said and done, we consecrate ourselves and all that we have and are because we love God and we love his children.

[2213] Nelson, *The Power within Us*, 136; Smith, *Doctrines of Salvation*, 2:58. Note: Elder McConkie stated that men make a covenant of exaltation twice: once upon ordination to the Melchizedek Priesthood and again at the time of the marriage sealing: "Ordination to office in the Melchizedek priesthood and entering into that 'order of the priesthood' named 'the new and everlasting covenant of marriage' are both occasions when men make the covenant of exaltation, being promised through their faithfulness all that the Father hath (D&C 131:1–4; 84:39–41; 132; Num. 25:13)." (*Mormon Doctrine*, 167.)

[2214] McConkie, *A New Witness for the Articles of Faith*, 313.
[2215] D&C 105:5.
[2216] James 2:8.
[2217] Matthew 22:36–40.

Section 15

What Is the Law of Consecration?

Note: Because this series is a sequential work, with one concept building upon another, the section numbers pick up where the last book ended. Thus, this book begins with Section 15. We also note that the first time we refer to a covenant or unique doctrine, we may capitalize it to call special attention to it. Thereafter, we will lowercase the name of the covenant or doctrine, with two exceptions: (1) If the name is capitalized in a quotation from another source, we will leave it as found in that source; and (2) if we are referring to the new and everlasting covenant by the shorthand of "the Covenant," we will capitalize it in that setting.

Imagine going into partnership with a benevolent billionaire. You express to him your desire to build a company, and to accommodate your desire he makes you a co-owner in his fortune. Now you have unlimited access to his unlimited resources; you need only ask and report responsibly and the fortune is at your disposal. Your agreement with your benefactor is simple: What is his is yours, and what is yours is his. But there is more. Beyond your having access to your partner's incomprehensible wealth, you also have access to his expertise, his influence, and his name. Now there is no knowledge that you cannot tap, no power beyond your reach, and no door that you cannot enter.

Could you not succeed in such a situation?

In a similar way, assuming we are living the laws that govern the celestial kingdom, we may draw upon the resources of God's higher kingdom to build our eternal kingdoms. Because we are in a covenant relationship with our Heavenly Father, we may invoke the terms of the new and everlasting covenant and gain unrestricted, unlimited, and indivisible rights to the resources of his kingdom, including access to his knowledge and power. Additionally, he gives us his full time and attention, and he puts upon us his name, that same name to which all beings, powers, and principalities in the universe must bow in humble adoration and submission. Finally, he makes us equal to him in every way.

Consecration—The Principle of Exaltation

Heavenly Father lives the law of consecration perfectly. He withholds nothing from us—neither his time, ability, knowledge, power, nor his vast kingdom. He does all of this so that we might become like him—*one* with him—in attributes, honor, glory, power, might, and dominion. This is his stated work and glory.[2218] To accomplish this, he lives the eternal laws that elevated him to the status of God and that makes gods of all other worthy beings of his race. The capstone of these laws is called *consecration*.

The law of consecration provides that greater beings partner with lesser beings in a covenant relationship—a *family* relationship—to allow the lesser beings to rise to a progressively higher stature by giving them the ability to draw upon the resources of the higher kingdom. This covenant relationship has no end, thus ensuring that the emerging god can progress eternally and expand his kingdom infinitely. In return for this incomprehensible gift, the lesser being, by covenant, consecrates his kingdom to the greater being, whereupon the higher kingdom expands, resulting in both beings enjoying infinite and eternal increase. This is exaltation.

Joseph Smith explained it this way: "What did Jesus do? Why; I do the things I saw my Father do when worlds came rolling into existence. My Father worked out his kingdom with fear and trembling, and I must do the same; and when I get my kingdom, I shall present it to my Father, so that he may obtain kingdom upon kingdom, and it will exalt him in glory. He will then take a higher exaltation, and I will take his place, and thereby become exalted myself. So that Jesus treads in the tracks of his Father, and inherits what God did before; and God is thus glorified and exalted in the salvation and exaltation of all his children."[2219]

Considering the covenant relationship that exists between greater and lesser beings, the law of consecration might be better called the *Covenant* of Consecration. When we agree to live the covenant, the Father affixes his signature to it, so to speak, which sets in motion the process of our exaltation. Upon the condition that both parties agree to consecrate to each other their all, we lesser beings obtain license to access the Father's time, abilities, and all that he has and is to establish and grow our personal kingdoms. Then, as Joseph Smith explained, as we consecrate our kingdom back to the Father, essentially assimilating it into the Father's kingdom, his dominion grows and he is further exalted. As he moves up, we take his place, and both of us experience extended and eternal exaltation. In this way, both the Father and we obtain "kingdom upon kingdom," which results in eternal upward movement and increase. All of this is made possible by the covenant we enter into with God: the covenant of *consecration*.

Which brings us to consecration in this life.

If we ever hope to achieve the most profound blessings of the gospel, we must embrace the law of consecration. Because "Zion cannot be built up unless it is by the principles of the law of the celestial kingdom,"[2220] we can never expect to achieve that holy place, abide its glory, and progress from one exaltation to another unless we abide this law.[2221] We have ample opportunities to learn how to live this law of the celestial kingdom here and now. For example, we are commanded to "remember the poor, and consecrate of [our] properties for their support that which [we have] to impart unto them, with a covenant and a deed which cannot be broken."[2222] That is, we prepare to become like God by learning how to reach down and lift up those of lesser means by consecrating our time, talents, and resources to the Lord's work. Thus, by learning to consecrate now we experience an essential principle of exaltation while in the flesh. Perhaps the act of consecration creates and defines Zion's oneness, equality, and pure-heartedness better than anything else.

[2218] Moses 1:39.
[2219] Smith, *Teachings of the Prophet Joseph Smith*, 347; emphasis added.
[2220] D&C 105:5.
[2221] D&C 88:22.
[2222] D&C 42:30.

THE CONDITION OF BABYLON

The world hands the law of consecration a huge challenge. This foundational law of Zion is wholly foreign to everything we see around us. Consecration simply makes no sense in Babylon. Where in this world do we hear the idea that giving away money and possessions is a principle of prosperity, safety, happiness, and security? We simply cannot wrap our minds around the concept. *Less becomes more?* How could that be? The philosophies of men (which often attempt to be legitimized with scripture) teach us that we live in a dog-eat-dog world where only the smartest, fittest, strongest, and most beautiful survive. We had better conform to the realities of life, they say, or we will find ourselves on the outside looking in.

And there seems to be plenty of evidence that Babylon is right.

From our youth, we have been taught that if we don't look out for ourselves, who will? All of us know the "self-made man's" formula of success: *dedicate yourself completely to the accumulation of wealth; never let up, day after day, year after year; let no one get in your way.* We are taught that no goal is as worthy as the pursuit of the good life, and we are bombarded with messages that giving away our time, talents, and assets won't get us there. It all sounds so reasonable. Except for one tiny detail: This philosophy is anti-Zion, and therefore it is anti-celestial.

At the opening of the dispensation of the fulness of times, the Lord told his young prophet, "Behold, the world at this time lieth in sin, and there is none that doeth good, *no not one.* And mine anger is kindling against the inhabitants of the earth to visit them according to this ungodliness."[2223] It is sobering to note that the Lord said the same thing of Sodom and Gomorrah.[2224] What condition could be so prevalent and depraved that it could envelop the entirety of humanity? The Lord gave the answer: "But it is not given that one man should possess that which is above another, wherefore the world lieth in sin."[2225] Like pride, this condition is a universal sin.

Moroni taught the same truth. He ends his record of the Book of Mormon dispensation in the same way our dispensation began, with an ominous view of the future. Foreseeing universal latter-day ungodliness, he said, "And wo be unto the children of men . . . ; for there shall be none that doeth good among you, *no not one.*" Not one person is exempt from this universal sin! How can we escape this woeful condition? Moroni gave the answer: "For if there be one among you that doeth good, he shall work by the power and gifts of God."[2226] Moroni links true goodness with working by the power and gifts of God. In the end, the power and gifts of God are sufficient to help us break free of this universal sin, reject the philosophies of men, release our grasp on the things of this world, and embrace the law of the celestial kingdom.

The solution for protection from this universal sin and establishing a Zionlike life is *consecration*. The Lord restored this celestial law, in part, for our safety and ultimate salvation. Hugh Nibley taught, "God has always commanded his people to give up that way of life [Babylon], come out of the world, and follow his special instructions. *The main purpose of the Doctrine and Covenants, you will find, is to implement the law of consecration.*"[2227]

THE GREATEST DESIRE

What is our greatest desire? Although we might have a variety of answers, we would hope that our greatest desire aligns with the great desire of the prophets, whom we covenant to follow. President

---

[2223] Nibley, *Nibley on the Timely and the Timeless*, 280–81.
[2224] Genesis 18, 19.
[2225] D&C 49:20; emphasis added.
[2226] Moroni 10:25; emphasis added.
[2227] Nibley, *Approaching Zion*, 174.

Lorenzo Snow expressed his "greatest desire," and offered an eloquent list of promised blessings to those whose wish was similar.

> For my greatest desire is to see Zion established according to the revelations of God, to see her inhabitants industrious and self-sustaining, filled with wisdom and the power of God, that around us may be built a wall of defense, a protection against the mighty powers of Babylon; and while the disobedient of our Father's family are contending, and filling up their cup of iniquity, even to the brim, and thus preparing themselves for the burning, we who are the acknowledged children of the kingdom, being filled with the righteousness and knowledge of God, may be like the wise virgins, clothed in our wedding garments, and properly prepared for the coming of our Lord and Savior.[2228]

President Snow's desire was no different from the desire of every other prophet from Adam to the present: the establishment of a Zion people, whose lives are founded upon the law of consecration.

Definition of Consecration

President Ezra Taft Benson made the following statement about consecration's purpose: "We covenant to live the law of consecration. This law is that we consecrate our time, talents, strength, property, and money for the upbuilding of the kingdom of God on this earth and the establishment of Zion. . . . The law of consecration is a celestial law, not an economic experiment."[2229]

The law of consecration was given to the Church in its early days. Because a variety of attempts were either suspended or ultimately failed, many members of the Church believe that the law of consecration is for the future, and that it will emerge again someday as a formal, legally binding economic order. Therefore, they imagine that either the law of consecration does not apply today or, if it does, it applies in a watered-down form. This assumption is completely erroneous. The lesson we should learn from former attempts is this: The principles of consecration constitute a *template* that can be applied successfully to any number of situations, and it can be adapted to the needs of the few or the many. This template is at once individual, familial, societal, economical, temporal, and spiritual.

That we limit consecration in our minds to a certain application is a mistake of monumental proportions. The future most certainly holds a formal application—*or applications*—of the law of consecration; formal application(s) will be administered by the prophets in the Lord's own time. But on no occasion has the Lord repealed the consecration covenant that we make in the temple. This law does not lie in some sort of suspended state, waiting for an announcement for us to live it. Consecration is current and in full force today, and it must be lived actively by each of us who makes the covenant; otherwise, we can neither build up the kingdom of God nor establish the principles of Zion in our lives. The future Zion priesthood society, which will depend wholly upon consecration, will certainly be established by people who live the law of consecration now, and who thus have become Zionlike.[2230]

To consecrate something is to sanctify, purify, and set it apart for a sacred use, to make it holy, to dedicate it solemnly to a special service, or to give it religious sanction, as with an oath or a vow.[2231] Joseph Smith defined consecration this way: "When we consecrate our property to the Lord it is to administer to the wants of the poor and needy, for this is the law of God. . . . Now for a man to consecrate . . . is nothing more nor less than to feed the hungry, clothe the naked, visit the widow and fatherless, the sick and afflicted, and do all he can to administer to their relief in their afflictions, and for him and his house to serve the Lord. In order to do this, he and all his house must be virtuous, and must shun the very appearance of evil."[2232]

[2228] Snow, *The Teachings of Lorenzo Snow*, 180.
[2229] Benson, *The Teachings of Ezra Taft Benson*, 121.
[2230] Gardner, "Becoming a Zion Society," 31.
[2231] *American Heritage Dictionary*, s.v. "consecrate," "sanctify."
[2232] Smith, *Teachings of the Prophet Joseph Smith*, 127.

What Is the Law of Consecration?

Consecration comes down to one thing: *the giving of one's whole self to God*. This giving of self, which encompasses sacrifice, according to President Spencer W. Kimball, "is the giving of one's own time, talents, and means to care for those in need—whether spiritually or temporally—and in building the Lord's kingdom."[2233] That is, we contribute the totality of who we are, what we are, and all that we have or will have—*everything!*[2234] Nothing less than our all will do. Such total sacrifice of self cannot be legislated; it is a free-will offering made from the purity of the heart. Thus, we *choose* to consecrate our all because we value the kingdom of God and Zion more than we value our things.

Could there be any misunderstanding that the law of consecration is a covenant that must be lived today? Hugh Nibley writes, "The law of consecration has no historical development; the issues are perennial. We like to think that we are living under special conditions today."[2235] But we are not. Consecration is an eternal law that does not depend upon man's current economic or social situation. It works in one life or many lives, in poverty or prosperity, in Africa or America, in the days of Adam or the latter days. Consecration simply waits for a covenant person's decision to live it and propel it into action.

The Law We Must Live to Achieve the Celestial Kingdom

The Church welfare plan describes a consecrated person as one who does not seek for worldly riches; who esteems his brother as himself; who, through tithes and offerings, helps to build up the kingdom of God by making his worldly goods, over and above his family's necessities, available for the Lord's work; and who, with his time, talents, and means, takes care of the temporally and spiritually poor. Referring to the Church welfare plan, Elder Bruce R. McConkie wrote, "The practice of the law of consecration is inextricably intertwined with the development of the attributes of godliness in this life and the attainment of eternal life in the world to come. 'The law pertaining to material aid is so formulated that the carrying of it out necessitates practices calculated to root out human traits not in harmony with requirements for living in the celestial kingdom and replacing those inharmonious traits with the virtues and character essential to life in that abode.'"[2236]

Therefore, we are left without excuse. We have made the covenant of consecration in the temple, and the covenant is manifested today as a Church-wide program called the welfare plan. Beyond the global application of the welfare plan, consecration espouses the principle of individual choice in giving time, talents, and resources to sustain the Lord's work and to care for family and the temporally and spiritually poor. If and when consecration takes another form, it will not step away from the divine *template*, but in any case, we are not excused for failing to live our covenant here and now.

Consecrating the Good and the Bad

When the Lord demands that we consecrate everything to him, he expects that we consecrate *all* that we are: both the good and the bad. How else could he transform us into what we must become to inherit the celestial kingdom? When we lay everything on the altar, including our weaknesses, troubles, and sins, he agrees to gladly take those things, reconstitute them into something positive, and help us manage the affairs of our lives. Hence his declaration: "[God] shall consecrate thine afflictions for thy gain."[2237]

[2233] D&C 38:17; 104:11–14; Kimball, *The Teachings of Spencer W. Kimball*, 366.
[2234] D&C 64:34; 82:19; 88:67–68; 98:12–14.
[2235] Nibley, *Approaching Zion*, 463.
[2236] McConkie, *Mormon Doctrine*, 157; quoting Albert E. Bowen, *The Church Welfare Plan*, 6.
[2237] 2 Nephi 2:2.

This remarkable promise corresponds with the Lord's injunction: "Search diligently, pray always, and be believing, and all things shall work together for your good, if ye walk uprightly and remember the covenant wherewith ye have covenanted one with another."[2238] Here we notice that having all things working together for our good is linked to our abiding in the covenant wherewith we have covenanted with each other. That covenant is *consecration*.[2239] Nephi learned the same principle of consecration: "But behold, I say unto you that ye must pray always, and not faint; that ye must not perform any thing unto the Lord save in the first place ye shall pray unto the Father in the name of Christ, that he will consecrate thy performance unto thee, that thy performance may be for the welfare of thy soul."[2240]

When we withhold nothing, God withholds nothing, and thus we experience the miracle of consecration.

Premise of Consecration

To enter into this covenant, we acknowledge that all things belong to the Lord and we are stewards.[2241] President George Q. Cannon said, "God our Eternal Father has placed all these possessions and blessings—that is, the possessions of the earth and the blessings connected with the earth—He has placed them in our hands merely as stewards, and we hold them subject to Him—in other words, in trust for Him—and if He calls upon us to use them in any given direction He may indicate, it is our duty as His children, occupying the relationship that we do to Him and with the hopes in our breasts that we have, to hold them entirely subject to Him."[2242]

Other key principles of consecration are laid out in the scriptures:
- We are to esteem each other as ourselves.[2243]
- We practice this law upon the principle of agency.[2244]
- We are made equal according to our wants, needs, and family situations.[2245]
- We are accountable to the Lord for our stewardships.[2246]

Perhaps King Benjamin described best the premise of the law of consecration: "For behold, are we not all beggars? Do we not all depend upon the same Being, even God, for all the substance which we have, for both food and raiment, and for gold, and for silver, and for all the riches which we have of every kind? . . . And now, if God, who has created you, on whom you are dependent for your lives and for all that ye have and are, doth grant unto you whatsoever ye ask that is right, in faith, believing that ye shall receive, O then, how ye ought to impart of the substance that ye have one to another."[2247]

Consecration Is Nonnegotiable

If we make the covenant, we must live the covenant: "And behold, none are exempt from this law who belong to the church of the living God."[2248] Nevertheless, as Nephi learned, if we will put forth

---

[2238] D&C 90:24.
[2239] D&C 90:23.
[2240] 2 Nephi 32:9.
[2241] Kimball, *The Teachings of Spencer W. Kimball*, 366.
[2242] Cannon, *Gospel Truth*, 275.
[2243] D&C 38:24–27; 51:3, 9; 70:14; 78:6; 82:17.
[2244] D&C 104:17.
[2245] D&C 51:3.
[2246] D&C 72:3; 104:13–18.
[2247] Mosiah 4:19, 21.
[2248] D&C 70:20.

the effort to live this celestial law in a telestial environment, the Lord will help us, as Nephi asserted: "I will go and do the things which the Lord hath commanded, for I know that the Lord giveth no commandments unto the children of men, save he shall prepare a way for them that they may accomplish the thing which he commandeth them."[2249]

Although consecration is described as a celestial law, it is designed so all can live it.[2250] Consecration is an "easy," foundational requirement of Zion. Brigham Young said, "No revelation that was ever given is more easy of comprehension than that of the law of consecration."[2251] Then he lamented, "It was one of the first commandments or revelations given to this people after they had the privilege of organizing themselves as a Church, as a body, as the kingdom of God on the earth. I observed then, and I now think, that it will be one of the last revelations which the people will receive into their hearts and understand, of their own free will and choice, and esteem it as a pleasure, a privilege, and a blessing unto them to observe and keep most holy."[2252]

We risk losing the blessing of eternal life when we postpone or water down the concept of consecration. If we desire exaltation, living this law is nonnegotiable. Earning that supernal gift pivots on our strict adherence to this law that governs the celestial kingdom.

RESTORATION OF THE LAW OF CONSECRATION

As early as 1829, the Lord began to point Joseph Smith toward establishing "the cause of Zion."[2253] This single fact should help us realize that the focal point of the Restoration and its end purpose was Zion. After the Church was organized, the Prophet received revelations to lay the foundation of Zion. On January 2, 1831, a significant revelation (D&C 38) linked latter-day Zion with ancient Zion, and suddenly Enoch literature began to emerge.[2254] The concept of receiving inheritances from the Lord on the condition of living a specific law was introduced: "I . . . deign to give you greater riches," the Lord promised, "even a land of promise . . . and the land of your inheritance, if you seek it with all your hearts." In that same revelation, the Saints learned that these blessings would be available to them only if they made the associated covenant and lived the law that governed that covenant.[2255] The revelation also foretold some of the basic conditions of the law of consecration: "And let every man esteem his brother as himself, and practise virtue and holiness before me. . . . I say unto you, be one; and if ye are not one ye are not mine." Further, the Lord said, "And ye shall look to the poor and the needy, and administer to their relief that they shall not suffer."[2256]

To learn more about Zion and its law, the Prophet was commanded to go to Ohio to receive "the law of the Church,"[2257] which is often called the law of Zion. On February 9th of that year, Joseph Smith received what is now Doctrine and Covenants 42. "This revelation presented the laws of the Church government and moral conduct for members and established the basic principles of consecration."[2258] Shortly thereafter, at the third general conference of the Church, the law of consecration was formally accepted by the membership, and from that moment until now, the law has never been rescinded.

Bruce Van Orden, professor of Church history and doctrine, wrote:

[2249] 1 Nephi 3:7.
[2250] Nibley, *Approaching Zion*, 422; quoting Zechariah 14:17–18.
[2251] Young, *Journal of Discourses*, 2:306.
[2252] Young, *Discourses of Brigham Young*, 179.
[2253] D&C 6:6; 11:6; 14:6.
[2254] D&C 38:4, 32.
[2255] D&C 38:18–19, 32.
[2256] D&C 38:24, 27, 35.
[2257] D&C 42, headnote.
[2258] *Encyclopedia of Mormonism*, 312.

> A historical misunderstanding arose in the church regarding this early economic application of the Law of Consecration. Most Saints have thought that the united order was widely practiced in Ohio and Missouri. Indeed, the phrases order, united order, and order of Enoch frequently appear in the Doctrine and Covenants, thus adding credence to this assumption. In actuality, these are substitute phrases for "united firm," the original words of the revelations for an organization, which was disbanded 23 April 1834 (see D&C 104). The wording was changed so that enemies of the Church and creditors would not use the printed revelations against the Church. . . .
>
> The united firm was a partnership between a handful of Church leaders, no more than twelve at any time, to consolidate the financial resources and organizational and professional talents of these men to generate profits to be used for the personal living expenses as well as the economic needs of the Church. . . . The main reason for the tremendous indebtedness accrued by the united firm was the destruction of the printing press and the closure of Sidney Gilbert's store by mobs in Independence, Missouri, in July 1831. It is important for modern students of the Doctrine and Covenants to realize that the important revelations that seem to speak of a united order (D&C 78, 82, 92, 96) in actuality give directions about the united firm.[2259]

The point we wish to reiterate is that the principles of consecration are a template. In the early days of the Church, this template was applied to a variety of situations and experiments, and this template will likely be applied and adapted for future uses.

A historical example happened in Far West, Missouri, on July 9, 1838, in response to the Prophet's plea, "O, Lord! show unto thy servant how much thou requirest of the properties of thy people for a tithing."[2260] Then the Lord revealed that henceforth, the Saints were to "pay one-tenth of all their interest annually." Thus tithing qualified as a surplus and became a manifestation of economic consecration. According to the revelation, tithing was to be used specifically "for the building of mine house, and for laying the foundation of Zion and for the priesthood, and for the debts of the Presidency of my Church."[2261] Van Orden explained, "The law of tithing, while considered by some commentators in the past as an 'inferior' law to the Law of Consecration, seems to have been merely a new phase of consecration."[2262]

LDS historian Lyndon Cook wrote, "Indeed, many hailed it [the law of tithing] as a markedly improved economic plan for obtaining donations and contributions. Admittedly, this program did not provide for the bishop to redistribute the wealth of the members, nor to allocate specific inheritances or personal stewardships. Yet, significantly, the equalizing effect of the 1838 plan on the members was identical to earlier programs."[2263] Thus, tithes and offerings (D&C 119) became the official law of consecration, and this law has remained unaltered to this day. The resulting "program" maintained all of the driving principles of consecration without mandating a formal law requiring that all properties

---

[2259] Van Orden, "The Law of Consecration," 85; referencing Cook, *Joseph Smith and the Law of Consecration*, 57–70.
[2260] Smith, *History of the Church*, 3:87–89.
[2261] D&C 119:2, 4.
[2262] Van Orden, "The Law of Consecration," 86.
[2263] Cook, *Joseph Smith and the Law of Consecration*, 77.

be donated to the Church. From 1838 to the present, this economic manifestation of the law of consecration has been the Church's official program: the Saints pay tithing, according to a defined amount,[2264] and they pay offerings according to choice and personal revelation. The present welfare plan embraces the 1838 revelation.

Does this mean that another official program or programs relating to economic consecration will never be necessary? It is not our prerogative to say. However, numerous prophets' statements indicate that consecration may take on additional forms to fit circumstances and times. Brother Van Orden explained, "Today . . . paying a full and honest tithing in cash of all we earn has proven to be an efficient and productive means of both living the economic side of the Law of Consecration and also with providing the Church with needed operating funds."[2265] This is the official program, but perhaps even greater blessings flow from practicing consecration in our personal lives: consecrating time, talents, and resources.

Consecrating Tithes and Offerings

The combination of tithes and offerings provides Saints a unique opportunity to (1) build up the kingdom of God on the earth, which is the primary function of tithing, and (2) establish the cause of Zion, which is the primary function of offerings. Whereas the revealed use of tithing is "for the building of mine house, and for laying the foundation of Zion and for the priesthood, and for the debts of the Presidency of my Church,"[2266] offerings establish the economic base of Zion by providing for the poor.[2267]

Together, tithes and offerings allow us to keep the law of consecration and progress in our understanding of that law with ever increasing faith. Because tithing is a defined amount, paying it requires less faith than paying offerings, which are left to our discretion. A person exercises greater faith by yielding to the "enticings of the Holy Spirit"[2268] to determine the amount of his offerings. Thus, the payment of offerings provides a vehicle to increase faith, mature in the gospel, and gain the most impressive blessings of the gospel, which are available only to those who approach the ideal of consecration—giving all that they are and have to the Lord.

Ultimately, every offering that we place on the altar represents the only offering that matters: the heart. "Thou shalt offer a sacrifice unto the Lord thy God in righteousness, even that of a broken heart and a contrite spirit."[2269] Clearly, the greatest opportunity in consecration lies in giving offerings.

Modern Applications of Consecration

The covenant of consecration was fully revealed during the construction of the Nauvoo Temple. Beginning in 1842, Joseph Smith introduced to trusted associates a sacred ritual, the Endowment of the Holy Priesthood. Total commitment in all things was expected. Complete surrender to the Lord's will was required. Now there could be no doubt that consecration was much more than an economic program; consecration was the complete, free-will offering of one's self.

As we have mentioned, the template of consecration has been laid over a variety of programs that were intended to build the kingdom of God in anticipation of Zion. Most recently, the current welfare plan has steadily grown since its inception in 1936, and it now includes "hundreds of projects,

---

[2264] D&C 119:4.
[2265] Van Orden, "The Law of Consecration," 87.
[2266] D&C 119:2, 4.
[2267] Malachi 3:8; Smith, *Gospel Doctrine*, 243; McConkie, *Mormon Doctrine*, 277–78.
[2268] Mosiah 3:19.
[2269] D&C 59:8.

farms, ranches, canneries, and storehouses. This plan, both in theory and in practice, has become the envy of millions of people in public, private, and religious enterprises."[2270]

Furthermore, we see consecration's application in LDS Philanthropies, which "serves as the central coordinating agency for all donations to the Church or one of its institutions—beyond tithing and fast offerings—with the goal of helping members and friends of the Church meet the needs of people worldwide."[2271] We also see consecration principles at the heart of the Perpetual Education Fund, the Missionary Fund, LDS Humanitarian Services, and other funds that rely on consecrated free-will offerings. We see consecration in action when missionaries give two years of their lives to the Lord, and when parents sacrifice to support them. We see the spirit of consecration in the lives of senior missionaries; temple patrons; those people who sacrifice to serve in Church callings; those who visit the poor, the needy, and the oppressed; and those who bless the lives of others beyond the bounds of the Church organization. All of these sacrifices are manifestations of consecration by pure-hearted people, whose intention is to build up the kingdom of God and to establish the cause of Zion.

Learning to Better Live the Law of Consecration

Can we become even more consecrated? Of course. We, the covenant, consecrated Saints of God, must apply this law in ever increasing faith until poverty in each of its ugly forms—temporal, emotional, and spiritual—is abolished from among us. Then, when the promised establishment of the priesthood society of Zion is come, the ideal of consecration will shine forth; we will fully be one, and there will be no poor among us. At that day, the poor who have pled to the Lord for relief will find it in Zion.[2272]

The Lord said that he is preparing "a feast of fat things . . . for the poor" in "the land upon which the Zion of God shall stand."[2273] These humble, impoverished souls, who are being nurtured by the pure-hearted of Zion, will soon join with those who have blessed them and together come to the "marriage of the Lamb."[2274] Safe in Zion, they "shall be provided for,"[2275] and "exalted."[2276] Clearly, the poor have every reason to "rejoice in the Holy One"[2277] and to trust in his Zion.[2278]

What an honor it is to establish the cause of Zion!

Sanctified by Consecration: The Law of the Celestial Kingdom

Clearly, consecration is more than a law; it is a way of life. Consecration is a mindset that impacts the heart in such a way that it finally becomes pure. The attitude that signals a change of heart at baptism—"to bear one another's burdens, that they may be light; yea, and . . . to mourn with those that mourn; yea, and comfort those that stand in need of comfort"[2279]—is later vitalized with power in the oath and covenant of the priesthood and finally formalized and perfected by the covenant of consecration in the temple.

Upon the law of consecration the Lord can establish Zion in the hearts of individuals, families, wards, stakes, and the Church. Moreover, with the law of consecration, sanctification increases. According to Doctrine and Covenants 88, this must happen if we are to be cleansed "from all

---

[2270] Van Orden, "The Law of Consecration," 89.
[2271] See mission statement at www.LDSPhilanthropies.org.
[2272] D&C 38:16.
[2273] D&C 58:8, 7.
[2274] D&C 58:11.
[2275] D&C 83:6.
[2276] D&C 104:16.
[2277] 2 Nephi 27:30.
[2278] Isaiah 14:32.
[2279] Mosiah 18:8–9.

unrighteousness, that [we] may be prepared for the celestial glory." Like the earth, we can fill "the measure of [our] creation" only by abiding the celestial law. Ultimately, by abiding that law, we, like the earth, "shall be crowned with glory, even with the presence of God the Father." Clearly, the stakes are high, and consecration seems to be the pivotal point for us. The Lord said, "And they who are not sanctified through the law which I have given unto you, even the law of Christ, must inherit another kingdom, even that of a terrestrial kingdom, or that of a telestial kingdom. For he who is not able to abide the law of a celestial kingdom cannot abide a celestial glory."[2280]

If Zion is "the highest order of priesthood society,"[2281] and if Zion is founded upon the law of consecration, it behooves us to take seriously this celestial law that governs that priesthood society. Zion can be established in no other way. Inferior choices can result only in inferior blessings and inferior kingdoms. As Elder Neal A. Maxwell reminded us, the terrestrial kingdom will consist of the honorable ones who were not valiant, meaning casually obedient and modestly Christlike. To be valiant is to become like Jesus and to obey him. On the other hand, Elder Maxwell said, consecration helps to create a Christlike character; it is the consecration or surrender of self that defines ultimate victory, because surrender introduces us to God's higher ways.[2282]

The Lord has declared in the language of absolutes that the law we are willing to abide sanctifies us to that degree. President Lorenzo Snow said, "[Consecration] is a perfect law,"[2283] which concurs with the Savior's injunction to the rich young man who came seeking eternal life: "If thou wilt be perfect, go and sell that thou hast, and give to the poor, and thou shalt have treasure in heaven: and come and follow me."[2284] If we ever hope to achieve perfection or Zionlike hearts or an inheritance in the celestial kingdom, we must make and keep the covenant of consecration. President Ezra Taft Benson said, "The law of consecration is a law for an inheritance in the celestial kingdom. God, the Eternal Father, His Son Jesus Christ, and all holy beings abide by this law. It is an eternal law. . . . it will be mandatory for all Saints to live the law in its fulness to receive celestial inheritance."[2285]

Familiarity

There could be no principle as foreign to a telestial world or as opposite to Babylon as the law of consecration. But to covenant people who are striving to become pure in heart, consecration feels familiar. The more effort they make to live it, the more their awareness of the beauty and safety of that law. President Lorenzo Snow said, "[The law of consecration] is something that is natural."[2286]

As we make efforts to live this law, we become comfortable with consecration because we recognize its benefits; inherently, we understand its blessings. Therefore, we simply need to begin to live it and its familiar fruits will become evident. Soon we will feel as if we have come home.

Ultimate Consecration—To Sacrifice a Prepared and Purified Heart

Only the pure in heart are able to live the law of consecration. Obedience, sacrifice, and living the laws and ordinances of the gospel, including the celestial lifestyle called *chastity*, prepare us to live this law and to make this ultimate sacrifice. When we finally succeed in living the law to the extent that we can consecrate ourselves unrestrictedly, we will have truly come unto Christ. Then our hearts will finally have become pure. Indeed, consecration is one of the deciding requirements for coming into the presence of the Lord.

[2280] D&C 88:18–22.
[2281] Kimball, *The Teachings of Spencer W. Kimball*, 125.
[2282] Maxwell, "Consecrate Thy Performance," 36; quoting D&C 76:75, 79; 3 Nephi 27:27; Isaiah 55:9.
[2283] Snow, *The Teachings of Lorenzo Snow*, 183.
[2284] Matthew 19:21.
[2285] Benson, "A Vision and a Hope for the Youth of Zion," 75.
[2286] Snow, *The Teachings of Lorenzo Snow*, 184.

Elder Maxwell taught that consecration is so much more than yielding up our possessions when we are directed; ultimate consecration, he said, is yielding up our whole selves to the Lord by choice. That is, we give to him *everything* that is uniquely ours: *our heart, mind, and soul*. This first great commandment, he said, becomes the last test of discipleship, and that which identifies the pure in heart. Ultimate consecration—the *ideal* of consecration—is complete surrender, the total yielding of our thoughts, feelings, words, and actions. When we keep this law, all that we do and all that happens to us, both the good and the bad, work together for our good[2287] and for the everlasting welfare of our souls.[2288]

Partial consecration could never produce the blessings of eternal reward, and in one respect partial consecration is a contradiction of terms. Hugh Nibley wrote:

> By very definition we cannot pay a partial tithe. . . . And if we cannot pay a partial tithe, neither can we keep the law of chastity in a casual and convenient way. . . . We cannot enjoy optional obedience to the law of God, or place our own limits on the law of sacrifice, or mitigate the charges of righteous conduct connected with the law of the gospel. We cannot be willing to sacrifice only that which is convenient to part with, and then expect a reward. The Atonement is everything; it is not to be had "on the cheap." God is not mocked in these things; we do not make promises and covenants with mental reservations. Unless we live up to every covenant, we are literally in Satan's power—a condition easily recognized by the mist of fraud and deception that has enveloped our whole society. . . . The point of all this is that the Atonement requires of the beneficiary nothing less than willingness to part with his most precious possession. . . . The law of consecration . . . has no limiting "if necessary" clause; we agree to it unconditionally here and now. *It represents our contribution to our salvation.*[2289]

LIVE CONSECRATION OR LOSE ETERNAL LIFE

How serious is the Lord about our living the law of consecration? President Lorenzo Snow had the answer:

> We must dedicate our time, talents, and ability. If we as elders fail to keep the covenants we have made, namely, to use our time, talents, and ability for the upbuilding of the kingdom of God upon the earth, how can we reasonably expect to come forth in the morning of the First Resurrection, identified with the great work of redemption? If we in our manner, habits and dealings, imitate the Gentile world, thereby identifying ourselves with the world, do you think, my brethren, that God will bestow upon us the blessings we desire to inherit? I tell you no, He will not![2290]

[2287] D&C 90:24; 98:3; 105:40.
[2288] Maxwell, "Consecrate Thy Performance," 36; referencing Matthew 22:37; 2 Nephi 32:9.
[2289] Nibley, *Approaching Zion*, 589–92; emphasis added.
[2290] Snow, *The Teachings of Lorenzo Snow*, 44.

President Kimball spoke of the man who chose to build a kingdom to himself rather than build the kingdom of God: "And now, as life is ebbing out gradually, he finds himself standing alone, forsaken, bitter, unloved, and unsung; and with self-pity, he can still think of only one person, himself. He has sought to save for himself his time, talents, and his means. He has lost the abundant life."[2291]

And yet, with all of this prophetic evidence, there are those among us who feel that they are the exception and can have it both ways.

Laying Everything on the Altar

President Kimball explained that consecration is a law that we learn to live by degrees. As we do so, we gain great insights, spiritual maturity, and strength to take consecration to the next level. "We must lay on the altar and sacrifice whatever is required by the Lord. We begin by offering a broken heart and a contrite spirit. We follow this by giving our best effort in our assigned fields of labor and callings. We learn our duty and execute it fully. Finally we consecrate our time, talents, and means as called upon by our file leaders and as prompted by the whisperings of the Spirit. In the Church, as in the welfare system also, we can give expression to every ability, every righteous desire, every thoughtful impulse, and in the end, we learn it was no sacrifice at all."[2292]

The concept of laying our all on the altar is a gospel theme that began with Adam and continues to this day. When we think of totally consecrated sacrifices made on an altar, we automatically think of the sacrifice of Abraham, who truly exemplified sacrifice by consecration. We do not individually build altars for sacrifice today, but worshipping and sacrificing at altars remains a central part of our religion. For example, the sacramental table is like an altar, and, of course we find altars in temples.[2293] Because we are taught that the body is a temple,[2294] we might expect to find an altar therein. Using Abraham as an example, Andrew Skinner explains that the altar of the body is the heart:

> On Moriah Abraham built an altar. The Hebrew word for altar, *mizbeah*, is derived from the word for sacrifice, *zebah*. Thus, "altar" literally means "the place of sacrificing." But where did Abraham's sacrifice of Isaac first occur? In rabbinic and Talmudic times the phrase "building an altar" was used as a metaphor to mean not only the observance of the commandments, but also the total consecration of all one possessed—even the laying down of one's own life—for the sanctification of God's name. Some of the ancient rabbinic sages, therefore, coined expressions like "as if an altar was erected in his heart" to portray those individuals who were willing to do all that God required. Some of them well understood that sacrifice was first made in the mind and heart of the offerer. Their exemplar was Abraham. He had erected an altar long before he reached Moriah. Things are not so different today. We talk about being ready to "lay it all on the altar." We covenant at altars to sacrifice all we possess to the Lord, and in doing so we "build altars in our hearts," as the rabbis said. Our exemplar is also Abraham.[2295]

[2291] Kimball, *The Teachings of Spencer W. Kimball*, 251.
[2292] Kimball, *The Teachings of Spencer W. Kimball*, 364.
[2293] *Encyclopedia of Mormonism*, 36–37.
[2294] John 2:21; 1 Corinthians 6:19.
[2295] Skinner: "Genesis 22: The Paradigm for True Sacrifice in Latter-day Israel," 77–78.

To make the consecrated sacrifice of all that we are and possess on the altar of the heart, the heart itself must first be prepared and purified through obedience, events requiring sacrifice, adherence to the law of the gospel, and living a life of strict chastity. Then we are ready to climb to our Mount Moriah, build an altar in our heart, and offer everything that we are to God.

Consecration and the Atonement

Because the results of consecration are equality and oneness, consecration becomes immediately connected to the Atonement; the purpose of both is to bring separated things back into a state of *oneness*.

We need only survey the condition of Babylon to see that humanity lives in a constant state of *separation*, which is common in a telestial world. Misery always results from separation in its various forms. The continual struggle of telestial residents is to hold together things that want to drift apart. We suffer the effects of separation in relationships, in health, and in finances. We often expend enormous effort and resources to counter the natural tendency of things to wear out, rust, become corrupt, and eventually disintegrate. The telestial world is one of *entropy*, "the tendency for all matter and energy in the universe to evolve toward a state of inert uniformity. Inevitable and steady deterioration."[2296] Whenever we experience entropy or separation, we experience misery, to a lesser or greater degree. We sense that life is out of balance; it is lacking, imperfect, spinning out of control, and beyond our ability to reclaim, and when that happens something inside of us says this condition is neither right nor natural.

On the other hand, the Atonement, which is motivated by love, is ever attempting to draw separated things back into a state of unity and perfection with the resulting happiness and abundance. Thus we feel the powers of Satan and Christ constantly pulling at us: Satan pulls us toward separation and misery, and Christ pulls us toward unification and happiness.

Mormon called for the urgent employment of the Atonement's unifying capability to ward off Satan's efforts to separate us from God through sin and inequality: "And thus we see how great the inequality of man is because of sin and transgression, and the power of the devil, which comes by the cunning plans which he hath devised to ensnare the hearts of men. And thus we see the great call of diligence of men to labor in the vineyards of the Lord; and thus we see the great reason of sorrow, and also of rejoicing—sorrow because of death and destruction among men, and joy because of the light of Christ unto life."[2297]

What does this have to do with consecration and Zion? It is a purpose of the Atonement to correct lack, reverse inequality, bring unequal things back into balance, and unify that which is presently in a state of separation. Therefore, we are called with "a great call of diligence" to labor in the cause of the Atonement. We accomplish that labor through our consecrated effort, which is the giving of who we are and what we have for the purposes of lifting, unifying, equalizing, restoring, and healing whomever or whatever we encounter that is suffering a separated, unequal, or less than perfect state of being.

When we draw people into the Atonement through our consecrated sacrifice, their condition vastly improves. Now they begin to achieve balance, abundance, peace, and joy, all of which are described in the scriptures by the words *full* and *fulness*. Consider these verses as they apply to the unifying power of the Atonement:

"And for this cause ye shall have *fulness* of joy; and ye shall sit down in the kingdom of my Father; yea, your joy shall be *full*, even as the Father hath given me *fulness* of joy; and ye shall be even as I am, and I am even as the Father; and the Father and I are one."[2298]

[2296] *American Heritage Dictionary*, s.v. "entropy."
[2297] Alma 28:13–14.
[2298] 3 Nephi 28:10.

"For man is spirit. The elements are eternal, and spirit and element, inseparably connected, receive a *fulness* of joy; and when separated, man cannot receive a *fulness* of joy."[2299]

"Their sleeping dust was to be restored unto its perfect frame, bone to his bone, and the sinews and the flesh upon them, the spirit and the body to be united never again to be divided, that they might receive a *fulness* of joy."[2300]

For something separated to become *one*, the Atonement must be applied, and the application of the Atonement is always inaugurated by a consecrated effort.

Consecration—A Temporal Law with Spiritual Implications

Although we must consecrate the things that we possess, which is a temporal manifestation of consecration, our consecrated action is a spiritual sacrifice that speaks of who we are. The Lord said, "Wherefore, verily I say unto you that all things unto me are spiritual, and not at any time have I given unto you a law which was temporal; neither any man, nor the children of men; neither Adam, your father, whom I created. Behold, I gave unto him that he should be an agent unto himself; and I gave unto him commandment, but no temporal commandment gave I unto him, for my commandments are spiritual."[2301]

David O. McKay made this astute observation concerning temporal consecration as it applies to the spiritual:

> The development of our spiritual nature should concern us most. Spirituality is the highest acquisition of the soul, the divine in man; "the supreme, crowning gift that makes him king of all created things." It is the consciousness of victory over self and of communion with the infinite. It is spirituality alone which really gives one the best in life. It is something to supply clothing to the scantily clad, to furnish ample food to those whose table is thinly spread, to give activity to those who are fighting desperately the despair that comes from enforced idleness, but after all is said and done, the greatest blessings that will accrue from the Church are spiritual. Outwardly, every act seems to be directed toward the physical: re-making of dresses and suits of clothes, canning fruits and vegetables, storing foodstuffs, choosing of fertile fields for settlement—all seem strictly temporal, but permeating all these acts, inspiring and sanctifying them, is the element of spirituality.[2302]

Clearly, it is *temporal* consecration that accomplishes *spiritual* sanctification, and it is sanctification that creates a pure, Zionlike heart. Helaman portrayed this principle—*temporal consecration leading to spiritual sanctification*—by describing a faithful group of Saints who grew "firmer and firmer in the faith of Christ . . . even to the purifying and the sanctification of their hearts, which sanctification cometh because of their yielding their hearts unto God."[2303] Our willingness to accept and master consecration is central to our becoming sanctified and preparing for the establishment of

---

[2299] D&C 93:34.
[2300] D&C 138:17.
[2301] D&C 29:34–35.
[2302] McKay, *Gospel Ideals*, 202.
[2303] Helaman 3:35.

Zion in our hearts. Ultimately, Zion succeeds or fails in our hearts according to the diligence we give to consecrating our lives to God.[2304]

Addressing the reluctance of some Saints to embrace and implement the law of consecration as it pertained to the newly announced welfare plan, President J. Reuben Clark Jr. made this significant statement: "The Church has found that the whole problem is essentially a question of spirituality, rather than of finance or economics. Where the spirituality has been high, the Plan has succeeded; where the spirituality is low, the Plan has lagged. The Church has proved there is no substitute for the great commandments: 'Thou shalt love the Lord thy God with all thy . . . might, mind, and strength, and thy neighbor as thyself.'"[2305]

Forty-one years later, in 1980, President Marion G. Romney reported that the Church had made great strides in implementing the welfare plan, but the measurement of its success continued to be reflected in spiritual terms. In the end, he said, consecration can only be measured spiritually by the condition of the hearts of both givers and receivers.[2306]

CONSECRATION—A LAW THAT MAKES US INDEPENDENT FROM THE WORLD

A familiar phrase that distinguishes Zion from Babylon is "in the world but not of the world." This phrase implies independence *from* the world. If Zion cohabits with the world or depends upon Babylon in any degree, it ceases to qualify as Zion.

Zion is independent, unalloyed, wholly separate, distinct, and diametrically opposed to Babylon. Zion does not build a bridge to Babylon, and then come and go at will. Zion severs any connection with Babylon and stays on its side of the chasm. In vision, Lehi saw the three classes of members of the Church who started down the path leading to the tree of life. Sadly, only one group arrived and remained. The select few of that group managed to remain at the tree by clinging to the word of God and ignoring the taunts and temptations of the people who resided in what Lehi described as a "great and spacious building." What was the principle of power that the select few implemented to stay out of and remain independent from the great and spacious building, which of course is a symbol for Babylon? Nephi quoted his father, Lehi, as saying, "We heeded them not." Then as if to punctuate the point, Nephi explained that it is lethal to venture into Babylon. His concluding statement is sweeping and inclusive: "For as many as heeded them [the people in the building—Babylon], had fallen away."[2307]

Consecration is one of the culminating principles in the new and everlasting covenant that allows Zion people to reside in the world but not of the world—to be wholly independent from the world. To the children of Zion, the Lord said, "Wherefore, a commandment I give unto you, to prepare and organize yourselves by a bond or everlasting covenant that cannot be broken. . . . Behold, this is the preparation wherewith I prepare you, and the foundation, and the ensample which I give unto you, whereby you may accomplish the commandments which are given you; that through my providence, notwithstanding the tribulation which shall descend upon you, *that the church may stand independent above all other creatures beneath the celestial world.*"[2308] That is to say, the new and everlasting covenant was designed by God to bind us together so that we might more fully keep the commandments. Living the commandments in unison infuses power into our lives. That unifying empowerment prepares us for the tribulation that Babylon always heaps upon Zion. But ultimately the covenant keeps us safe and allows us to stand independent of all other creatures or creations. The *Doctrine and Covenants Encyclopedia* states: "In 1832, God revealed his desire to have the Church

---

[2304] Gardner, "Becoming a Zion Society," 31.
[2305] Clark, *Church Welfare Plan*, 32–33.
[2306] Romney, "Church Welfare—Temporal Service in a Spiritual Setting," 84.
[2307] 1 Nephi 8:19–34.
[2308] D&C 78:11, 13–14; emphasis added.

'stand independent above all other creatures beneath the celestial world.' The term 'creature' is used here in its widest meaning, to signify all that is created, and refers especially to the various organizations in the world, whether ecclesiastical, political, financial, or industrial. The ultimate destiny of the celestial Saints is to stand above all creatures and creations of lower orders."[2309]

The principles that provide the priesthood society of Zion its independence from Babylon are the same principles that afford independence to an individual Zion person. To judge the folly of depending on Babylon, we need only recall that the great and spacious building stood on a foundation of air.[2310] With nothing holding it up except pride, its fall is inevitable. On the other hand, when Zion people build their foundation upon the rock of their Redeemer,[2311] which foundation is "wide as all eternity,"[2312] we are characterized by the Lord as "wise." The Lord's promise to us is that the Zion life we are cultivating in our hearts will neither crumble nor fall.[2313] With that knowledge, we will enjoy the resulting feelings of peace and safety: "If ye are prepared, ye shall not fear."[2314]

How, then, does consecration contribute to our becoming independent from Babylon? Simply put, Zion takes care of her own, both temporally and spiritually. The following is taken from the *Encyclopedia of Mormonism*:

> The term "self-sufficiency" refers to a principle underlying the LDS program of Welfare Services, and to an ideal of social experience. Self-sufficiency is the ability to maintain one's self and relates to women and men being agents for themselves. Independence and self-sufficiency are critical keys to spiritual and temporal growth. A situation that threatens one's ability to be self-sufficient also threatens one's confidence, self-esteem, and freedom. As dependence is increased, the freedom to act is decreased.
>
> Church writings often use the terms self-sufficiency and "self-reliance" interchangeably. Teachings pertaining to Welfare Services emphasize and place considerable importance on both individual and family independence. Six principles form the foundation of the infrastructure of the Welfare program. Three of these principles emphasize responsibility to care for one's own needs: work, self-reliance, and stewardship; the other three focus on responsibility to others: love, service, and consecration (Faust, p. 91).
>
> President Spencer W. Kimball defined Welfare Services as the "essence of the Gospel . . . the Gospel in action" (Kimball, p. 77). Within the context of Welfare, the term self-sufficiency also includes an emphasis on prevention, temporary assistance, and rehabilitation. Self-sufficiency is helping oneself to the point of reliance. Welfare, a program based on self-sufficiency, helps individuals to help themselves. Home industry, gardening, food storage, emergency preparedness, and avoidance of debt reflect the applications of self-sufficiency (*Welfare Services Resource Handbook*, p. 21). . . .

[2309] Brewster, *Doctrine and Covenants Encyclopedia*, 113.
[2310] 1 Nephi 8:26.
[2311] Helaman 5:12.
[2312] Moses 7:41.
[2313] Matthew 7:24–27.
[2314] D&C 38:30.

> As a social ideal, self-sufficiency includes spiritual, intellectual, and emotional dimensions.... Self-sufficiency is central to such interdependence and is necessary for one to be in a position to assist others, beginning with one's own family, neighbors, and ward....
>
> New Testament teachings conceive of liberty as a person's relationship to God and others (Buttrick, p. 121). Christ gave his followers sacred charge and opportunity to serve the poor, needy, sick, and afflicted. Rather than looking on God as the only one able to provide, individuals as self-sufficient beings work together in mutual responsibility, compassion, gentleness, and love.
>
> Perspective on the balance between an individual person's being totally self-sufficient and also needing assistance comes from the understanding that everyone is self-reliant in some areas and dependent in others. Latter-day Saints accept the observation that everyone is flawed and imperfect; everyone experiences human limitation or poverty. Scriptures recognize that poverty resides in both temporal or spiritual matters. In fact, all are "beggars" for a remission of sins (Mosiah 4:20). Nevertheless, a certain equality emerges from human interdependence, noted in the counsel to be equal in both heavenly and earthly things: "For if ye are not equal in earthly things ye cannot be equal in obtaining heavenly things" (D&C 78:6). From one's strengths, each should endeavor to help another; on the other hand, one should accept the help of another. "If a man be overtaken in a fault, ye which are spiritual, restore such an one in the spirit of meekness; ... bear ye one another's burdens, and so fulfill the law of Christ" (Gal. 6:1–2). Interdependence, then, creates the opportunity to participate in the sanctifying experience of giving and receiving (Romney, p. 91).
>
> In a gospel sense, there exists an interdependence between those who have and those who have not. The process of sharing lifts the poor, humbles the rich, and sanctifies both. The poor are released from bondage and limitations of poverty and are able to rise to their full potential, both temporally and spiritually. The rich, by imparting of their surplus, participate in the eternal principle of sharing. A person who is whole or self-sufficient can reach out to others, and the cycle of equality and giving repeats itself.
>
> Without self-sufficiency it is difficult to exercise these innate desires to serve. Food for the hungry cannot come from empty shelves; money to assist the needy cannot come from an empty purse; support and understanding cannot come from the emotionally starved; teaching cannot come from the unlearned. Most important of all, spiritual guidance only comes from the spiritually strong. Indeed, self-sufficiency forms the basis to bear one another's burdens and to live interdependently.[2315]

Clearly, Zion people espouse the principle of independence and achieve it by virtue of the law of consecration. Babylon has no efficient program that provides its citizens with true independence.

[2315] *Encyclopedia of Mormonism*, 1293–94.

Repeatedly, the prophets have counseled us to guard against worldly substitutes to care for ourselves and the poor among us. The prophets go so far as to call these government programs ineffective, misleading, and counterfeit.[2316] President Marion G. Romney quoted one head of state as saying, "We're going to take all the money we think is unnecessarily being spent and take it from the 'haves' and give to the 'have nots' that need it so much."[2317] Then he stated that the difference between taking money from us to administer welfare assistance and voluntarily contributing it out of our love of God and fellowman is the difference between slavery and freedom. On another occasion, he said that no institution that continues to promote forced socialized welfare programs can long endure.[2318]

Conversely, Zion people shoulder an obligation to achieve self-sufficiency through consecrated service and offerings, and we must approach self-sufficiency in this way if we ever expect to attain eternal life. Only Zion offers a true and permanent solution for personal and societal independence.

CONSECRATION—AN ORDER THAT ORDERS OUR LIVES

The new and everlasting covenant transforms an undisciplined telestial life into an ordered celestial life. "My house is a house of order," the Lord said.[2319] Every law that comprises the Covenant orders our lives so that we might conform to the order of life that God enjoys. It should be no surprise, then, that the law of consecration is one of the culminating laws of the Covenant that precedes our receiving an eternal kingdom by means of temple marriage.

Consecration is a way of life—an *ordered* life. Consecration bids us acknowledge that all things belong to God, and we are stewards.[2320] We are accountable to God for the discharge of those stewardships.[2321] Although he allows us custodianship of our property, we recognize that ultimately it is his, and he has final say as to the property's use. That he allows us the freedom to manage his property does not exempt us from being accountable to him. This is the celestial order mandated by consecration. President Benson said, "The basic principle underlying [consecration] is that everything we have belongs to the Lord; and, therefore, the Lord may call upon us for any and all of our property, because it belongs to Him."[2322]

Consecration orders our relationship with God and his children. First, we are to love "the Lord thy God with all thy heart, with all thy might, mind, and strength," and, second, we are to "love thy neighbor as thyself."[2323] First one, and then the other—this is the order. With regard to loving others, we are to assume the attitude of esteeming other people as ourselves.[2324] This attitude reflects the celestially ordered view of relationships that allows for all men and women to be equal according to their wants, needs, family situations, and access to the Lord's resources.[2325] Clearly, at the heart of the celestial order is the law of consecration. When we ignore, rationalize, or modify this order to fit our personal objectives, we step away from the new and everlasting covenant and become a law unto ourselves.[2326]

Consecration is a progressive process that begins with repentance and baptism for the remission of sins, which order our lives in such a way that eventually we can consecrate our hearts. Upon

---

[2316] Kimball, "Becoming the Pure in Heart," 79; Romney, Conference Report, Oct. 1972, 115.
[2317] Romney, "Church Welfare Services' Basic Principles," 120; quoting *Congressional Record*, 1964, 6142.
[2318] Romney, Conference Report, Apr. 1976, 169.
[2319] D&C 132:18.
[2320] D&C 38:17; 104:11–14.
[2321] D&C 72:3; 104:13–18.
[2322] Benson, *The Teachings of Ezra Taft Benson*, 121.
[2323] D&C 59:5–6.
[2324] D&C 38:24–27; 51:3, 9; 70:14; 78:6; 82:17.
[2325] D&C 51:3.
[2326] D&C 88:21–35.

receiving the gift of the Holy Ghost, we begin to experience the ministering of angels, which further help us to order our lives. The promise of angelic ministration is reconfirmed when we enter the order of the priesthood,[2327] which requires a higher standard of righteousness to make the priesthood effectual[2328]—which means more order! The path to eternal life is marked with other covenants and ordinances that prepare and point us to the sacrifice of all things, which is ultimate consecration. Elder Bruce C. Hafen wrote, "When we move on to the more mature stage represented by the blessings of the Melchizedek Priesthood and the temple ordinances, we advance to a higher level of religious life. . . . The contrast with the higher law is staggering: '*Love thy wife* with all thy heart'; and '*Be* ye therefore perfect.' (Matthew 5:48.) The higher law asks not only for new behavior; it asks for a new heart."[2329] President Benson taught that the initial covenants and ordinances prepare us to consecrate our all to the Lord: "Until one abides by the laws of obedience, sacrifice, the gospel, and chastity, he cannot abide the law of consecration, which is the law pertaining to the celestial kingdom. 'For if you will that I give you place in the celestial world, you must prepare yourselves by doing the things which I have commanded you and required of you' (D&C 78:7)."[2330]

Consecration orders everything in our lives, and it focuses everything we do on eternal implications. Our attitudes toward property and toward God and his children are brought into order, as are our devotions. For example, we are told that we are not to seek for riches but for wisdom.[2331] Notice how the celestial order places first things first, exactly opposite to the order of Babylon. The Book of Mormon prophet Jacob taught: "But before ye seek for riches, seek ye for the kingdom of God. And after ye have obtained a hope in Christ ye shall obtain riches, if ye seek them; and ye will seek them for the intent to do good—to clothe the naked, and to feed the hungry, and to liberate the captive, and administer relief to the sick and the afflicted."[2332] Here the celestial sequence is clearly set forth. Nowhere in Babylon would we hear such doctrine; it is not part of that order.

If we would pay the price to live the order of consecration by first loving God and then his children, seeking for the kingdom of God, and hungering for wisdom over every temporal enticement, we would find ourselves aligned with the celestial order. We would achieve an unshakable, faith-filled relationship with God; we would learn to love all of God's creations, including his children;[2333] our wisdom and understanding would become great;[2334] and we would remain safe from the damning preoccupation with wealth.

The result of the ultimate consecrated effort is the "sacrifice of all things," which is required for eternal life.[2335] There is no doubt that this sacrifice is daunting; it is supposed to be. Nevertheless, we are promised that if we will persevere and make this sacrifice, which can be compared to the Savior's comment about losing our lives for his sake, it will lead us to finding our lives.[2336] Again, we see a celestial order provided by the order of consecration: "lose" our lives, first, and then "find" our lives, second. Elder Neal A. Maxwell said, "So many of us are kept from eventual consecration because we mistakenly think that, somehow, by letting our wills be swallowed up in the will of God, we lose our individuality. What we are really worried about, of course, is not giving up self, but selfish things—like our roles, time, pre-eminence, and possessions. No wonder we are instructed by the Savior to lose

---

[2327] D&C 84:42.
[2328] D&C 121:34–46.
[2329] Hafen, *The Broken Heart*, 158.
[2330] Ezra Taft Benson, *The Teachings of Ezra Taft Benson*, 121.
[2331] D&C 6:7.
[2332] Jacob 2:18–19.
[2333] McMullin, "Come to Zion! Come to Zion!" 94.
[2334] D&C 76:2.
[2335] Smith, *Lectures on Faith*, 6:7.
[2336] Matthew 10:39.

ourselves." Then Elder Maxwell added, "It is not a question of one's losing identity but of finding his true identity!"[2337]

In the end, we discover that living the order of consecration has little to do with managing property; consecration has everything to do with managing the condition of the heart.

WHAT CONSECRATION IS NOT

President Ezra Taft Benson drew a distinction between Zion's law of consecration, which he referred to as the united order, and Babylon's counterfeits.

> It has been erroneously concluded by some that the united order is both communal and communistic in theory and practice because the revelations speak of equality. Equality under the united order is not economic and social leveling as advocated by some today. Equality, as described by the Lord, is "equal[ity] according to [a man's] family, according to his circumstances and his wants and needs" (D&C 51:3).
>
> Is the united order a communal system? Emphatically not. It never has been and never will be. It is "intensely individualistic." Does the united order eliminate private ownership of property? No. "The fundamental principle of this system [is] the private ownership of property."[2338]

TEMPORAL AND SPIRITUAL SALVATION

The Lord declared, "[Consecration exists] for the benefit of my church, and for the salvation of men," until the Lord comes.[2339] On another occasion, he said, "And for your salvation I give unto you a commandment, for I have heard your prayers, and the poor have complained before me, and the rich have I made, and all flesh is mine, and I am no respecter of persons."[2340] We enter into the covenant of consecration by agreeing to give our all to the Lord, and in return he covenants to take care of us with his all. By reason of living this covenant, we are protected and saved both temporally and spiritually.

Perhaps the Lord was thinking of consecration's inherent quality of safety when he compared himself to a mother hen under whose wings we children of the Covenant enjoy safety and security: "For, behold, I will gather them as a hen gathereth her chickens under her wings, if they will not harden their hearts."[2341] In this covenantal relationship, the Lord assumes the responsibility to supply our needs and wants, provided that we extend our best effort and invoke the law of asking. Hugh Nibley wrote: "The covenant [of consecration] is made by the individual to the Father in the name of the Son, a private and a personal thing, a covenant with the Lord. He intends it specifically to implement a social order—to save his people as a people, to unite them and make them of one heart and one mind, independent of any power on earth."[2342]

[2337] Maxwell, *If Thou Endure It Well*, 51.

[2338] Benson, *The Teachings of Ezra Taft Benson*, 122; referencing J. Reuben Clark, Jr., Conference Report, Oct. 1942, 57.

[2339] D&C 104:1.

[2340] D&C 38:16.

[2341] D&C 10:65; see also Matthew 23:37; Luke 13:34; 3 Nephi 10:4–6; D&C 29:2; 43:34.

[2342] Nibley, *Approaching Zion*, 468.

Equally important, we are saved spiritually by living the law of consecration. Only by making this sacrifice, the sacrifice of all things, which is required for exaltation,[2343] can we lay hold on the promise of eternal life. Significantly, before we can receive our eternal kingdom by the ordinance of celestial marriage, we must first covenant to consecrate; then, before our marriage is sealed by the Holy Spirit of Promise[2344] and thus *made sure*, we must first accomplish the sacrifice of all things by applying the law of consecration. Consecration, therefore, becomes the point upon which salvation and exaltation are lost or gained. All other covenants and ordinances point us to this singular requirement.

Finally, consecration is the ultimate test of discipleship, the supreme indicator of conversion. President Joseph F. Smith said, "A man who cannot sacrifice his own wishes, who cannot say in his heart, 'Father, Thy will be done, not mine,' is not a truly and thoroughly converted child of God; he is still, to some extent, in the grasp of error and in the shades of darkness that hover around the world, hiding God from the presence of mankind."[2345]

SUMMARY AND CONCLUSION

The law of consecration is the law of the celestial kingdom and thus the law of Zion. This law provides that greater beings partner with lesser beings in a covenantal family relationship to allow the lesser beings to rise to a progressively higher stature by giving them the ability to draw upon the resources of the higher kingdom. Heavenly Father lives the law of consecration perfectly. He withholds nothing from us—neither his time, ability, knowledge, power, nor his vast kingdom. He does all of this so that we might become like him—*one* with him—in attributes, honor, glory, power, might, and dominion. This is his stated work and glory.[2346]

This foundational law of Zion is wholly foreign to Babylon. Hence, the Lord declared to Joseph Smith, "Behold, the world at this time lieth in sin, and there is none that doeth good, *no not one*. And mine anger is kindling against the inhabitants of the earth to visit them according to this ungodliness."[2347] The universal condition known as ungodliness is this: "But it is not given that one man should possess that which is above another, wherefore the world lieth in sin."[2348] Like pride, selfishness and inequality are universal sins. The protective solution is consecration.

The "greatest desire" of prophets "is to see Zion established according to the revelations of God." That desire can happen only upon the principle of consecration. But too many people feel that consecration is a program for the future and that we are living a watered-down version of it today. That assumption is erroneous. The principles of consecration form a *template* that can be applied successfully to any number of situations, and it can be adapted to the needs of the few or the many. The law of consecration does not lie in some kind of suspended state, waiting for an announcement that the time has come to living it. Consecration is current and in full force today, and it must be lived actively by each of us who makes the covenant; otherwise, we can neither build up the kingdom of God nor establish the principles of Zion in our lives.

Joseph Smith gave the following definition of consecration: "When we consecrate our property to the Lord it is to administer to the wants of the poor and needy, for this is the law of God. . . . Now for a man to consecrate . . . is nothing more nor less than to feed the hungry, clothe the naked, visit the widow and fatherless, the sick and afflicted, and do all he can to administer to their relief in their

---

[2343] Joseph Smith, *Lectures on Faith*, 6:7.
[2344] D&C 132:7, 19.
[2345] Smith, *Teachings of Presidents of the Church*, 192.
[2346] Moses 1:39.
[2347] Nibley, *Nibley on the Timely and the Timeless*, 280–81.
[2348] D&C 49:20; emphasis added.

afflictions, and for him and his house to serve the Lord. In order to do this, he and all his house must be virtuous, and must shun the very appearance of evil."[2349]

The present Church welfare plan espouses these principles, both on a Church-wide and a personal basis. This plan describes a consecrated person as someone who does not seek for worldly riches; who esteems his brother as himself; who, through tithes and offerings, helps to build up the kingdom of God by caring for the temporal needs of those General Authorities whom God has called into full-time service; who makes his worldly goods available, over and above his family's necessities, for the Lord's work; and who, with his time, talents, and means, takes care of the temporally and spiritually poor.[2350]

The law of consecration requires that we consecrate everything to God, both the good and the bad. In that way, he can transform us into what we must become to inherit the celestial kingdom. The promise is this: "[God] shall consecrate thine afflictions for thy gain."[2351]

The law of consecration, which is also a covenant, requires that we acknowledge that all things belong to the Lord and we are stewards.[2352] We are to esteem each other as ourselves.[2353] We practice this law upon the principle of free agency.[2354] We are made equal according to our wants, needs, and family situations.[2355] We are accountable to the Lord for our stewardships.[2356] If we make this covenant, we must live the covenant: "And behold, none are exempt from this law who belong to the church of the living God."[2357]

Consecration is designed so all can live it.[2358] According to Brigham Young, the law of consecration is "easy" to understand and to live.[2359] Nevertheless, "it was one of the first commandments or revelations given to this people . . . and I now think, that it will be one of the last revelations which the people will receive into their hearts and understand."[2360]

The restoration of the law of consecration began as early as 1829, when the Lord pointed Joseph Smith toward establishing "the cause of Zion."[2361] After the organization of the Church, the Prophet was commanded to go to Ohio to receive "the law of the Church,"[2362] which is often called the law of Zion. That law is recorded in Doctrine and Covenants 42. Because consecration is a template for living God's law, it was applied to a variety of situations for varying lengths of time, involving either a few people or the entire Church. With regard to the Church, the law of tithes and offerings became the manifestation of the law of consecration that has continued until this day. The combination of tithes and offerings provides for (1) building up the kingdom of God on the earth, which is the primary function of tithing, and (2) establishing the cause of Zion, which is the primary function of offerings. Ultimately, every offering that we place on the altar represents the only offering that matters: the heart. Most recently, the current welfare plan has become a mainstay of the law of consecration. In addition, we enjoy other programs that are built with the template of consecration.

[2349] Smith, *Teachings of the Prophet Joseph Smith*, 127.
[2350] Bowen, *The Church Welfare Plan*, 6.
[2351] 2 Nephi 2:2.
[2352] Kimball, *The Teachings of Spencer W. Kimball*, 366.
[2353] D&C 38:24–27; 51:3, 9; 70:14; 78:6; 82:17.
[2354] D&C 104:17.
[2355] D&C 51:3.
[2356] D&C 72:3; 104:13–18.
[2357] D&C 70:20.
[2358] Nibley, *Approaching Zion*, 422; quoting Zechariah 14:17–18.
[2359] Young, *Journal of Discourses*, 2:306.
[2360] Young, *Discourses of Brigham Young*, 179.
[2361] D&C 6:6; 11:6; 14:6.
[2362] D&C 42, headnote.

Some of these include LDS Philanthropies, the Perpetual Education Fund, the Missionary Fund, and LDS Humanitarian Services. Those of us who are covenant, consecrated Saints of God, must apply this law in ever increasing faith until poverty in each of its ugly forms—temporal, emotional, and spiritual—is abolished from among us.

Consecration is more than a law; it is a way of life that feels familiar to us, or, as President Lorenzo Snow said, "something that is natural."[2363] Consecration is a mindset that impacts the heart in such a way that it finally becomes pure. By living the law of consecration, sanctification increases. If Zion is "the highest order of priesthood society,"[2364] and if Zion is founded upon the law of consecration, it behooves us to take seriously this celestial law that governs that priesthood society. Inferior choices can result only in inferior blessings and inferior kingdoms.

Only the pure in heart are able to live the law of consecration. Obedience, sacrifice, and living the laws and ordinances of gospel, including the celestial lifestyle called *chastity*, prepare us to live this law and to make this ultimate sacrifice. Partial consecration could never produce the blessings of eternal reward. But we need not run faster than we are able. We learn to live a consecrated life by degrees. As we do so, we gain great insights, spiritual maturity, and strength to take our consecration to the next level.

Because the results of consecration are equality and oneness, consecration becomes immediately connected to the Atonement; the purpose of both is to bring separated things back into a state of *oneness*. For something separated to become *one*, the Atonement must be applied, and the application of the Atonement is always inaugurated by a consecrated effort.

Consecration is often manifested as a temporal sacrifice, but our action has immediate spiritual implications. Consecration speaks of who we are inside, and it vitalizes spiritual sanctification, which creates a pure, Zionlike heart. Therefore, consecration is ultimately measured by the condition of the hearts of both givers and receivers.[2365]

Consecration is a law that makes us independent from the world. Our purpose for living in the world is to invite others out of the world and into Zion. Therefore, if we cohabit with the world or depend upon Babylon in any degree, we cease to qualify as Zion people. Zion is independent, unalloyed, wholly separate, distinct, and diametrically opposed to Babylon. Zion people depend upon consecration to remain independent from Babylon. Simply put, Zion people take care of their own, both temporally and spiritually. Zion people do so by espousing the principles of independence that the law of consecration provides. On the other hand, Babylon has no efficient program that can take care of its citizens or truly make them free.

In the end consecration is an *ordered* way of life. Consecration orders our relationships with God and his children. Consecration orders everything in our lives, and it points us toward celestial goals. Our attitudes toward our possessions, our time and talents, and our attitude toward God and his children are brought into order through consecration. This law is the vehicle for our making the essential "sacrifice of all things," which is required for achieving eternal life.[2366]

Consecration is not man-made; it is neither a communal nor a communistic experiment. It is a celestial law that governs celestial beings and allows them eternal progression and the expansion of their kingdoms. In this life, consecration is our best opportunity for both temporal and spiritual salvation.

[2363] Snow, *The Teachings of Lorenzo Snow*, 184,
[2364] Kimball, *The Teachings of Spencer W. Kimball*, 125.
[2365] Romney, "Church Welfare—Temporal Service in a Spiritual Setting," 84.
[2366] Smith, *Lectures on Faith*, 6:7.

Section 16

Consecration Results in Equality and Unity

President Marion G. Romney listed six characteristics of the law of consecration:
1. *We must have a belief in God.*
2. *We must make our freewill offerings voluntarily, and not by legislation.*
3. *We must maintain private ownership and individual management of our property and possessions.*
4. *The program of consecration is nonpolitical.*
5. *The prerequisite to our being able to live this law is righteousness.*
6. *Consecration exalts the poor and humbles the rich.*[2367]

Undergirding this list are two fundamental principles that define Zion: "every man seeking the interest of his neighbor, and doing all things with an eye single to the glory of God."[2368] Contrasted with Babylon, the results of such an attitude are astonishing. Because of our love of God and his children, we voluntarily choose to abase ourselves so that we might succor those in need of succor, impart of our substance to the poor and the needy, feed the hungry, and suffer "all manner of afflictions for Christ's sake."[2369] By so doing, we promote the celestial characteristics of *equality* and *unity*, and thus we our hearts become Zionlike.

Let us examine *equality* and *unity* as they pertain to consecration.

[2367] Romney, "The Purpose of Church Welfare Services," 92.
[2368] D&C 82:19.
[2369] Alma 4:13.

EQUALITY—"IN MINE OWN WAY"

President Joseph F. Smith said, "The principles of the Gospel are calculated to make us unselfish, to broaden our minds, to give breadth to our desires for good, to remove hatred, animosity, envy and anger from our hearts, and make us peaceful, tractable, teachable, and willing to sacrifice our own desires, and perchance our own interests, for the welfare of our fellow-creatures, and for the advancement of the Kingdom of God."[2370] Upon such fertile ground, the seeds of equality can be planted in the heart; then those seeds sprout and blossom into a bouquet of purity required by Zion.

In the world, the subject of equality troubles people and nations. We see Babylon's attempts to equalize society through counterfeit programs such as forced taxation, communism, and other economic experiments. The results inevitably limit freedom of choice, stifle initiative, hamper prosperity, promote divisiveness, and ultimately level down individuals and societies. True equality cannot be legislated, and it can never be achieved in this way. Without the dual motivations of love of God and of mankind, equality will ever need to be mandated rather than chosen, causing both the poor and the rich to feel dissatisfied.

On the other hand, Zionlike equality *levels up* people and societies. Zion exalts the poor by means of the consecrated freewill offerings of the rich, who are those who have excess resources. The Lord said, "And it is my purpose to provide for my saints, for all things are mine. *But it must needs be done in mine own way*; and behold this is the way that I, the Lord, have decreed to provide for my saints, that the poor shall be exalted, in that the rich are made low."[2371]

"To make low" sounds harsh to some people, who interpret this phrase as forced socialism or legislated redistribution of wealth. Actually, "to make low" is not a demeaning event at all; it is a safeguard against pride. Jesus, himself, is described as being "lowly in heart."[2372] Therefore, to be "made low" is to be made like Jesus. We are admonished to become lowly in heart to achieve a state of blessedness, and thus we will find rest to our souls.[2373] It is no wonder, then, that the lowly in heart are also those people who are filled with charity and deemed acceptable to God.[2374] Consequently, a lowly in heart Zion person allows no poor—no monetarily, emotionally, physically, or spiritually poor—within his circle of influence to experience want.[2375] Because he is driven by the love of God and his fellowman, a Zion person will attack lack wherever he encounters it. Therefore, it is the love of the lowly in heart that advances equality in Zion. This is Christ's "own way," the consecrated way.

EQUALITY AND THE LAW OF PROSPERITY

In a telestial world, especially one in which the philosophies of Babylon enjoy almost free rein, we struggle when we are confronted with living celestial laws, such as consecration. We can point to nothing in our environment that suggests these laws will work for us if we attempt to live them. For example, how could giving ten percent of our money to the Lord return to us blessings beyond our ability to receive?[2376] In a telestial world, we can no more make sense of *less is more* than we can of walking on water. So when we survey the laws of Zion, specifically consecration, how do we make sense of giving away progressively more in order to achieve the promised unequalled prosperity of Zion?

[2370] Smith, *Collected Discourses*, vol. 3, Sept. 3, 1892.
[2371] D&C 104:15–16; emphasis added.
[2372] Matthew 11:29.
[2373] Alma 32:8; 37:33–34.
[2374] Moroni 7:44.
[2375] Moses 7:18.
[2376] Malachi 3:10.

We rely on prophets to articulate celestial laws and to urge us to experiment with them. One celestial law is the law of prosperity. King Benjamin summed it up:

> And behold, all that [God] requires of you is to keep his commandments; and he has promised you that if ye would keep his commandments ye should prosper in the land; and he never doth vary from that which he hath said; therefore, if ye do keep his commandments he doth bless you and prosper you. And now, in the first place, he hath created you, and granted unto you your lives, for which ye are indebted unto him. And secondly, he doth require that ye should do as he hath commanded you; for which if ye do, he doth immediately bless you; and therefore he hath paid you. And ye are still indebted unto him, and are, and will be, forever and ever; therefore, of what have ye to boast?[2377]

Clearly, we have nothing to boast about. We are in debt to God and will be forever. But whereas telestial debt is a curse, celestial debt propels us toward blessings. Here is how we might portray the celestial "law of prosperity," as it applies to the law of consecration:

- Our love of God motivates us to seek to serve him.
- Because God is not in need, he immediately asks us to transfer our service to his suffering children, who need our help. That is, he asks us to serve him by serving his children, which we do in a spirit of consecration.
- When we do as he asks, God accepts our sacrifice "unto the least of these" as if we had done it unto God.[2378]
- Our sacrifice creates something akin to a *credit* in our favor, which credit demands payment.
- God assumes this obligation, which is actually an opportunity to bless us. He rewards us for our service: first, because he loves us; second, because we have obeyed the law upon which the blessing is predicated,[2379] and third, because our service has created an implied celestial deficit that needs correcting.
- Because God will not and cannot remain in a real or implied deficit position, "he doth immediately bless [us]; and therefore he hath paid [us]. And [we] are still indebted unto him, and are, and will be, forever and ever."
- Here is where the *hundredfold* principle (discussed earlier in this series) comes in—we are always rewarded beyond our sacrifice. God overpays his obligations, and therefore we find ourselves eternally indebted to him.
- What is the result? Because we are consecrated to God and he is consecrated to us, we live forever in the condition of abundance, the engine of which is driven by celestial debts and credits created and earned by consecrated service and offerings.

NEW MATH

We cannot make sense of the law of prosperity for an obvious reason: *the math doesn't work*. In a telestial world, ten minus one equals nine; but in a celestial world, because we are dealing with a celestial law and celestial math, ten minus one can equal eleven or fifteen or fifty or "an

---

[2377] Mosiah 2:22–24.
[2378] D&C 42:38.
[2379] D&C 130:21.

hundredfold."[2380] But never nine. For instance, we recall the example of the kernel of corn. Given the choice of planting or eating it, we chose to exercise faith and plant. Our faith increased when our seed grew into a stalk with several ears of corn. Then we exercised faith again by planting rather than eating the kernels from some of those ears. The result of our faith and sacrifice was a great harvest—all from a single kernel. Elder Boyd K. Packer said, "As you give what you have, there is a replacement, with increase!"[2381] That is how consecration works.

We do not have to make sense of the celestial law of prosperity; we just need to know that it works. It has to. Because it is God's law, if it ceased working, God would cease to be God.[2382] For now, we must live the law of prosperity by faith, moving forward with the hope that our obedience will always produce an inexplicable miracle that translates into spiritual and temporal abundance. Like the kernel of corn, when that abundance is replanted or consecrated back to the Lord, we experience a harvest of blessings, which allows us to partner with God to "level up" his children.

Esteeming All Flesh in One

Nephi said, "Behold, the Lord esteemeth all flesh in one; he that is righteous is favored of God."[2383] Equality governs God's dealings with his children; and righteous Zion people, who also espouse equality, receive God's greatest blessings. What are the "favored of God" supposed to do with their blessings? Clearly, they are supposed to do that which qualified them to be called "righteous" in the first place: use them to bless God's children.

If we desire to become "righteous" Zionlike people and "the favored of God," we cannot treat God's children differently than he does. Rhetorically, Nephi asked, "Behold, hath the Lord commanded any that they should not partake of his goodness?" Then, answering his own question, he said, "Behold I say unto you, Nay; but all men are privileged the one like unto the other, and none are forbidden. . . . He inviteth them all to come unto him and partake of his goodness; and he denieth none that come unto him, black and white, bond and free, male and female."[2384] Can we expect to become Zionlike if we adopt inequality?

The Lord treats his children equally, but the same is not always true of us. Nevertheless, the law of consecration stipulates that we shoulder the obligation of the covenant to lift others. It is anti-Zion to exalt ourselves while others languish in poverty. The Apostle Paul wrote, "Let no man seek his own, but every man another's good."[2385] What is the divine result of seeking equality? "And the Lord called his people Zion, *because* they were of one heart and one mind, and dwelt in righteousness; and there was no poor among them."[2386] Pay particular attention to the word *because* in this scripture. *Because* pure-hearted people strive to lift their neighbors and esteem all of God's children as themselves, Zion flourishes. Zion is established *because* we make a choice to become Zionlike.[2387] President Gordon B. Hinckley said, "If we are to build that Zion of which the prophets have spoken and of which the Lord has given mighty promise, we must set aside our consuming selfishness. We must rise above our love for comfort and ease, and in the very process of effort and struggle, even in our extremity, we shall become better acquainted with our God."[2388]

[2380] Genesis 26:12; 2 Samuel 24:3; Matthew 13:8–23;19:29; Mark 10:30; Luke 8:8; D&C 98:25; 132:55.
[2381] Packer, "The Candle of the Lord," 51.
[2382] Alma 42:13, 22, 25.
[2383] 1 Nephi 17:35.
[2384] 2 Nephi 26:28, 33.
[2385] JST 1 Corinthians 10:24.
[2386] Moses 7:18; emphasis added.
[2387] McMullin, "Come to Zion! Come to Zion!" 94.
[2388] Hinckley, *Teachings of Gordon B. Hinckley*, 725.

Seven Points of Equality

The virtues of equality and love are inseparable. Without divine love, equality could not exist. Without divine love, no redeeming virtue could exist. Indeed, the totality of the gospel is defined by love.[2389] The *Encyclopedia of Mormonism* lists various points of equality[2390] that flow from consecration and therefore are characterized by divine love. This is the love exemplified by Zion people.

1. **Equal in the sight of God.** All people are equal in the sight of God. He is "no respecter of persons."[2391] Regardless of race, station, or circumstance, each person is as precious as another. "For none of these iniquities come of the Lord; for he doeth that which is good among the children of men; and he doeth nothing save it be plain unto the children of men; and he inviteth them all to come unto him and partake of his goodness; and he denieth none that come unto him, black and white, bond and free, male and female; and he remembereth the heathen; and all are alike unto God, both Jew and Gentile."[2392]

2. **Equal opportunity for eternal life.** God sets the example of equality by evenly offering his children his greatest gift: *eternal life*. "Remember the worth of souls is great in the sight of God; for, behold, the Lord your Redeemer suffered death in the flesh; wherefore he suffered the pain of *all* men, that *all* men might repent and come unto him. And he hath risen again from the dead, that he might bring *all* men unto him, on conditions of repentance."[2393] "But behold, the resurrection of Christ redeemeth mankind, yea, even *all* mankind, and bringeth them back into the presence of the Lord."[2394]

3. **Joint heirs.** Jesus sets the example of equality. Everyone who orders his life in such a way that he qualifies for the celestial kingdom becomes Christ's equal—joint heirs with *the* Heir, possessing all that Christ possesses, which is all that the Father has. Heirs with Christ become equal with him.[2395]

4. **Equality in love.** When we love as God requires us to love—love so great that we would sacrifice our life for another—we become Zionlike in our hearts. Then we start to appreciate the equality and love that exists in heaven. We begin to understand the type of equality that defines relationships in the celestial world. "This is my commandment, That ye love one another, as I have loved you. Greater love hath no man than this, that a man lay down his life for his friends."[2396] "Verily, verily, I say unto you, ye are little children, and ye have not as yet understood how great blessings the Father hath in his own hands and prepared for you; and ye cannot bear all things now; nevertheless, be of good cheer, for I will lead you along. The kingdom is yours and the blessings thereof are yours, and the riches of eternity are yours."[2397]

5. **All things common.** The virtue of equality that is characteristic of Zion allows that the people enjoy "all things common among them."[2398] This statement of equality means equal access to the Lord's resources and to the resources consecrated to the Lord; it does not mean, according to President Marion G. Romney, that the Zion is an economic order characterized

---

[2389] Matthew 22:37–40.
[2390] *Encyclopedia of Mormonism*, 463–64.
[2391] D&C 38:16; see also D&C 1:35.
[2392] 2 Nephi 26:33; see also Alma 26:37.
[2393] D&C 18:10–12; emphasis added.
[2394] Helaman 14:17; emphasis added.
[2395] D&C 88:107.
[2396] John 15:12–13.
[2397] D&C 78:17–18.
[2398] 3 Nephi 26:19; 4 Nephi 1:3.

by commonly owned property.[2399] To Joseph Smith the Lord explained the eternal order of common access: "And you are to be equal, or in other words, *you are to have equal claims on the properties,* for the benefit of managing the concerns of your stewardships, every man according to his wants and his needs, inasmuch as his wants are just—and all this for the benefit of the church of the living God, that every man may improve upon his talent, that every man may gain other talents, yea, even an hundred fold, to be cast into the Lord's storehouse, to become the common property of the whole church—every man seeking the interest of his neighbor, and doing all things with an eye single to the glory of God. This order I have appointed to be an everlasting order unto you."[2400]

6. **Equal opportunities to receive and contribute.** Equality means equal opportunity to receive education, develop talents and abilities, and to engage people in the work of Zion, everyone contributing according to their individual strengths and gifts: "And thus they were all equal, and they did all labor, every man according to his strength."[2401]

7. **Equal in fulfillment of needs and wants.** The equality requisite for inheritance in Zion insists that we receive as equals those things that we need to survive and that contribute to our well-being. The more we pursue this objective, the more our Zion will have "no poor among them."[2402] Does that mean that everyone receives the same amount? No. Zion is neither an economic system of communally held property nor a socialistic program that legislates the redistribution of wealth; rather, Zion promotes private ownership, individuality, and incentive, with each individual receiving equal access to the Lord's storehouse of free-will offerings for his unique needs and wants. Zion anticipates and provides for each person's situation, "appoint[ing] unto this people their portions, every man equal according to his family, according to his circumstances and his wants and needs."[2403] Nevertheless, in providing equally according to needs and wants, there must be accountability, for the Lord said, "[It is] not given that one should possess that which is above another." Otherwise, Zion would be filled with greed and idleness, which would breed inequality, and where there is inequality "the world lieth in sin."[2404] Moreover, "the abundance of the manifestations of the Spirit [would be] withheld."[2405] Therefore, the Lord commanded, "And let every man deal honestly, and be alike among this people, and receive alike, that ye may be one, even as I have commanded you."[2406]

Taking Equal Responsibility for the Cause of Zion

If we are to become equal in receiving and disseminating the blessings of Zion, we must take an equal part in advancing Zion's cause. Joseph Smith taught, "The cause of God is one common cause, in which the Saints are alike all interested; we are all members of the one common body, and all partake of the same spirit, and are baptized into one baptism and possess alike the same glorious hope. The advancement of the cause of God and the building up of Zion is as much one man's business as another's. The only difference is, that one is called to fulfill one duty, and another another duty; . . .

[2399] Romney, "The Purpose of Church Welfare Services," 92.
[2400] D&C 82:17–20; emphasis added.
[2401] Alma 1:26.
[2402] Moses 7:18; 4 Nephi 1:3.
[2403] D&C 51:3; see also verse 8; D&C 42:33.
[2404] D&C 49:20; see also Alma 5:53–54.
[2405] D&C 70:14.
[2406] D&C 51:9.

party feelings, separate interests, exclusive designs should be lost sight of in the one common cause, in the interest of the whole."[2407]

King Benjamin taught his people this principle of taking equal responsibility for the cause of Zion, despite rank and position: "And I, even I, whom ye call your king, am no better than ye yourselves are."[2408] Equality and service, he said, allow us to walk "with a clear conscience before God . . . [and] be found blameless . . . when [we] shall stand to be judged of God."[2409] He reminded his people that protection and prosperity follow such a course of action: "Ye shall prosper in the land, and your enemies shall have no power over you."[2410]

When we embrace consecration and strive for equality, we draw near unto Zion. The Book of Mormon describes the characteristics of such a blessed people:

> And they did impart of their substance, every man according to that which he had, to the poor, and the needy, and the sick, and the afflicted; and they did not wear costly apparel, yet they were neat and comely. And thus they did establish the affairs of the church; and thus they began to have continual peace again, notwithstanding all their persecutions.
>
> And now, because of the steadiness of the church they began to be exceedingly rich, having abundance of all things whatsoever they stood in need—an abundance of flocks and herds, and fatlings of every kind, and also abundance of grain, and of gold, and of silver, and of precious things, and abundance of silk and fine-twined linen, and all manner of good homely cloth.
>
> And thus, in their prosperous circumstances, they did not send away any who were naked, or that were hungry, or that were athirst, or that were sick, or that had not been nourished; and they did not set their hearts upon riches; therefore they were liberal to all, both old and young, both bond and free, both male and female, whether out of the church or in the church, having no respect to persons as to those who stood in need. And thus they did prosper and become far more wealthy than those who did not belong to their church.[2411]

UNITY

President Gordon B. Hinckley observed, "When you are united, your power is limitless. You can accomplish anything you wish to accomplish."[2412]

This remarkable promise speaks to the power of unity, which flows only from a mutually consecrated effort. Such consecration lies on the bedrock of obedience, sacrifice, observing the law of the gospel, and strictly abiding the celestial lifestyle called *chastity*. President Daniel H. Wells, former counselor in the First Presidency, taught: "The principles of the Holy Gospel are calculated in their nature to unite the hearts of the people one with another, and to promote faith, union and love

---

[2407] Smith, *Teachings of the Prophet Joseph Smith*, 231.
[2408] Mosiah 2:26.
[2409] Mosiah 2:27.
[2410] Mosiah 2:31.
[2411] Alma 1:27–31.
[2412] Hinckley, "Your Greatest Challenge, Mother," 97–100.

towards our fellows."[2413] Because we cannot expect the Lord to establish Zion in our hearts without consecrated unity, the Savior commanded us, "I say unto you, be one; and if ye are not one ye are not mine." Prefacing this directive, he made a powerful statement regarding the importance of unity: "It is even as I am."[2414]

After Jesus educated his disciples in Jerusalem regarding the power of unity, he taught the principle anew in this dispensation: "Verily, verily, I say unto you, as I said unto my disciples, where two or three are gathered together in my name, *as touching one thing*, behold, there will I be in the midst of them—even so am I in the midst of you."[2415] We see in this scripture the means by which President Hinckley's promise is realized. Gathering into one in the name of Christ for a common purpose invites the Savior into our circle. Clearly, unity is a celestial law, and when we obey it, we enjoy its blessings.

The Unifying Power of the At-one-ment

Unity—*oneness*—is exemplified throughout the gospel. Perhaps the foremost example is the Godhead, which is comprised of three distinct individuals, whose united purpose makes them *one*.[2416] They should be our model. Central to their oneness is the At-one-ment. We become *at one* with the Godhead through the Atonement of Jesus Christ, and it is through his At-one-ment that we become *one*[2417] with each other and joint-heirs with Christ.[2418]

Oneness is the divinely mandated goal for every covenant relationship; only the Atonement can make and keep such relationships *one*. The highest order of covenant relationships is a Zion relationship. Wherever such a relationship exists there is *oneness*, and consequently there is the Lord: "The Lord came and dwelt with his people, and they dwelt in righteousness."[2419] Individuals who covenant to enter into any Zion relationship (i.e., marriage, family, quorum, Relief Society, ward, stake, Church), are instructed to become of "one heart and one mind," and, remarkably, when they do so, the resulting unified environment has "no poor among them."[2420] Beyond the economic implications, "no poor" also means *no poor in spirit*—that is, no spiritually or emotionally poor. No lack at all! For instance, in the *oneness* of a Zion marriage, where the power of the Atonement has made two people *one*, and where the husband and wife have worked to knit their hearts and minds together as *one*, there is simply no lack.

This is the *oneness* that the Nephites achieved after the visitation of the resurrected Christ. Within a period of only two years, they had managed to reach out to all unbelievers, and soon everyone in the nation was converted to the Lord. Under the umbrella of the Atonement, everyone was unified, and no one lacked for anything. There were no temporally or spiritually poor among them, and all were made *one*. By the power of the righteous Nephites' *oneness*, every unbeliever repented and became *one* with his or her brothers and sisters.[2421] Now notice the language that describes their *oneness*:

> and there were no contentions and disputations among them, and every man did deal justly one with another. And they had all things

---

[2413] Wells, *Journal of Discourses*, 24:314.
[2414] D&C 38:27.
[2415] D&C 6:32; emphasis added; see also Matthew 18:20.
[2416] Hinckley, *Teachings of Gordon B. Hinckley*, 239.
[2417] McConkie, *The Mortal Messiah*, 1:131.
[2418] Romans 8:17.
[2419] Moses 7:16.
[2420] Moses 7:18.
[2421] 4 Nephi 1:1–2; emphasis added.

common among them; therefore there were not rich and poor, bond and free, but they were all made free, and partakers of the heavenly gift. . . . And the Lord did prosper them exceedingly in the land; . . . [they] became an exceedingly fair and delightsome people. And they were married, and given in marriage, and were blessed according to the multitude of the promises which the Lord had made unto them. . . . And it came to pass that there was no contention in the land, because of the love of God which did dwell in the hearts of the people. And there were no envyings, nor strifes, nor tumults, nor whoredoms, nor lyings, nor murders, nor any manner of lasciviousness; and surely there could not be a happier people among all the people who had been created by the hand of God. . . . They were in one, the children of Christ, and heirs to the kingdom of God. And how blessed were they![2422]

Other scriptural accounts describe the power of the Atonement and *oneness*. For example, Alma and Amulek became *one* and converted thousands of wicked Nephites. The sons of Mosiah became *one* and converted tens of thousands of wicked people. Alma's grandsons, Nephi and Lehi, became *one* and converted thousands of wicked people.

The attitude of *oneness* starts by internalizing the Atonement and allowing its sanctifying effect to make of us a "new creature."[2423] That is, Zion begins and flourishes in the heart, and Zion continues as a condition of the heart. Once Zion is firmly rooted there, it wants to find greater expression. Covenant relationships are where Zion thrives. Each time Zion finds a new home, it yields the same unparalleled blessings that the Nephites experienced: unity, happiness, abundance, and conversion power.

Understanding this principle is essential to husbands and wives. At the time of their sealing, they are pronounced *one*. Subsequently, upon their faithfulness, the Holy Spirit of Promise confirms their sealing[2424] and makes their bond *more sure*. Such a marriage is now a celestial marriage, a Zion marriage, and then the blessings of Zion begin to flow: unity, happiness, abundance, and conversion power. President James E. Faust offered one of the clearest statements on the subject: "When the covenant of marriage for time and eternity, the culminating gospel ordinance, is sealed by the Holy Spirit of promise, *it can literally open the windows of heaven for great blessings to flow to a married couple who seek for those blessings.*"[2425]

Because every Zion relationship has inherent unifying and conversion power, those who come in contact with Zion people in those Zion relationships (for example, children of Zionlike parents) are leavened by their inherent *oneness*. Like great suns, they draw people toward them until everyone within their gravitational pull becomes *one* with them. Thus, in the same way that Jesus Christ and Heavenly Father are *one*, which *oneness* enables Jesus to draw all men to him,[2426] so we, by our *oneness* in our covenant relationships, gain power to draw people to us—to Zion—to the At-*one*-ment.

Oneness and Synergy

Oneness has a synergistic effect. *Synergy* refers to the phenomenon in which two or more agents acting together create an effect greater than the sum of the individual agents. For example, if one thread can

---

[2422] 4 Nephi 1:2–3, 7, 10, 11, 15–18.
[2423] 2 Corinthians 5:17.
[2424] D&C 132:19.
[2425] Faust, "The Gift of the Holy Ghost—A Sure Compass," 2; emphasis added.
[2426] 3 Nephi 27:14–15.

hold five pounds before it breaks, two threads woven together might be predicted to hold twice as much—ten pounds. But, because of the effect of synergy, the two threads woven together can now hold four times as much—twenty pounds!

Disturbingly, the opposite of synergy is *antagonism,* where two agents work against each other and achieve *less* in combination than the individuals could achieve separately. Adam and Eve are an example both of synergy and antagonism. When God married them, he made them *one;* but when Satan tempted Eve, she chose to act alone, as if she and Adam were still two. This is *antagonism.* The antagonistic effect greatly weakened both Adam and Eve. Despite Eve's rationale at the moment of temptation, because she was now married and had been made *one* with her husband, everything that she did affected Adam—as though he had also done the deed. Now Adam was faced with the prospect of eternal division—more *antagonism*—because Eve would have been cast out of the Garden and Adam would have been left a lone man there. Therefore, Adam seized the opportunity to change *antagonism* back to *synergy.* He made the decision to remain *one* with his wife, and to that end, he also ate the forbidden fruit. He knew that his action would require a fall, but he also knew that he had to act in a way that would rejoin the two of them as one. Thereafter, we never see Adam and Eve acting separately. We always see them functioning as *one,* and the power of their *oneness* attracted the promise of an atoning Savior.[2427]

Abraham and Sarah are another example of synergy. Their *oneness* drew down the *new and everlasting covenant* upon a degenerate and famished world, and by their synergy they secured for their posterity the eternal right to all gospel blessings. Gospel writer E. Douglas Clark has noted:

> . . . Abraham had been alone in the world, alone against the world, but now [with Sarah] everything changed. . . . Sarah had her work, and Abraham had his, but it was all part of the same cause. From this point on in Abraham's life, to speak of his mission and accomplishments is necessarily to include Sarah also; for as a modern rabbi has observed, she was not merely a strong personality in her own right, but, as Abraham's spouse, was "an important balancing factor in his life. Abraham and Sarah were not just *a married couple* but a team, two people working in harmony," as seen in the Genesis portrayal "of two as one unit" and "as equals"—"as partners, working together for the same goals, walking together along the same path, united in thought, word, and deed." Or, as told by Philo, "Everywhere and always she was at his side, . . . and his true partner in life and life's events, resolved to share alike the good and the ill." Theirs was the priceless unity of heart and mind that is ever the hallmark of Zion.[2428]

President Kimball taught that the Spirit of the Lord cannot help us magnify our efforts without oneness and cooperation in all that we do. Then, quoting Joseph Smith, he said, "The greatest temporal and spiritual blessings which always come from faithfulness and concentrated effort, *never attended individual exertion or enterprise.*"[2429]

[2427] Moses 5.
[2428] Clark, *The Blessings of Abraham,* 60.
[2429] Kimball, "Becoming the Pure in Heart," 79; quoting Smith, *Teachings of the Prophet Joseph Smith,* 183.

Antagonism—The Opposite of Synergy

The Lord commanded us to be one and to share each other's burdens: "And be you afflicted in all his afflictions, ever lifting up your heart unto me in prayer and faith, for his and your deliverance."[2430] Oneness brings deliverance!

Because we live in a fallen world where we are subject to the temptations of Satan, duality and conflict often retard unity and peace. At such times, we must quickly recognize and rectify such conditions. Then synergy can replace antagonism, and unity and strength will reenter the relationship. An antagonistic relationship simply cannot produce the power necessary to create the atmosphere of Zion.

David Whitmer, a close friend of Joseph Smith, related an enlightening experience that happened while the Prophet was translating the gold plates.

> He [Joseph] was a religious and straightforward man. He had to be; for he was illiterate and could do nothing himself. He had to trust in God. He could not translate unless he was humble and possessed the right feelings towards everyone. To illustrate so you can see: One morning when he was getting ready to continue the translation, something went wrong about the house and he was put out about it. Something that Emma, his wife, had done. Oliver and I went upstairs and Joseph came up soon after to continue the translation but he could not do anything. He could not translate a single syllable. He went downstairs, out into the orchard, and made supplication to the Lord; was gone about an hour—came back to the house, and asked Emma's forgiveness and then came upstairs where we were and then the translation went on all right. He could do nothing save he was humble and faithful.[2431]

Joseph Smith endeavored to achieve *oneness* with his wife, with God, and with those of his fellowmen who would purify their hearts in the cause of Zion. Interestingly, in the process of striving for unity, he learned a frightening truth of which every seeker of Zion should become aware. He said, "In relation to the kingdom of God, the devil always sets up his kingdom at the very same time in opposition to God."[2432] Imagine, when we were married in the temple and established a new kingdom, Satan simultaneously established an opposing effort to try to destroy us. We simply cannot take the risk of disunity.

Unity and Prayer

In the presence of six elders, the Prophet Joseph Smith received a revelation (D&C 29) that, in part, speaks of the power of multiple voices united in prayer. The Lord prefaced this revelation by reminding those brethren of his power to gather his people "as a hen gathereth her chickens under her wings, even as many as will hearken to my voice and humble themselves before me, and call upon me in mighty prayer."[2433] That is, to be gathered together in one is dependent upon obedience, humility, and mighty prayer. The Lord goes on to say, "Behold, verily, verily, I say unto you, that at this time

---

[2430] D&C 30:6.
[2431] Roberts, *History of the Church*, 1:131.
[2432] Smith, *Teachings of the Prophet Joseph Smith*, 365.
[2433] D&C 29:2.

your sins are forgiven you, *therefore ye receive these things.*"[2434] Note that the hearts of these brethren were pure and unified, which qualified them to pray for a blessing. This is the power of being gathered into unity as it pertains to praying for blessings.

Because these brethren had gathered in the Lord's name and were united in prayer, the Lord came to them according to celestial law—"where two or three are gathered together in my name, as touching one thing, behold, there will I be in the midst of them."[2435] In that setting, the Lord invited them to ask for a blessing, and gave them instructions for how to do so: "Lift up your hearts and be glad, for *I am in your midst,* and am your advocate with the Father; and it is his good will to give you the kingdom. And, as it is written—Whatsoever ye shall ask in faith, *being united in prayer* according to my command, ye shall receive."[2436] Then the Lord blessed them with what they were praying for because "it is given unto you that ye may understand, *because ye have asked it of me and are agreed.*"[2437]

On December 27, 1832, Joseph Smith received one of the greatest revelations of this dispensation. The Prophet designated it "The Olive Leaf," and in a letter to W. W. Phelps, he said it was "plucked from the Tree of Paradise." The revelation, which is now section 88 of the Doctrine and Covenants, is "the Lord's message of peace to us."[2438] Rich in doctrine, the revelation opens a window into the mysteries of God and provides profound details of the events leading up to the Second Coming, including the fall of Babylon, and of the subsequent thousand years of peace. The episode that paved the way to this revelation is as amazing as the revelation itself.

The Prophet had received a revelation commanding him to organize a "school of the prophets."[2439] Just after Christmas, a group of high priests gathered by special invitation to the Prophet's "translating room" in the Gilbert and Whitney store. According to the revelation, these brethren were to attend the school to prepare to better serve one another through increased knowledge and understanding. On the occasion of the revelation, Joseph said, "To receive revelation and the blessings of heaven it [is] necessary to have our minds on God and exercise faith and become of one heart and mind."[2440] Of note, Zebedee Coltrin, a member of the School of the Prophets, reported that the brethren would typically come fasting and gather in the morning about sunrise. Before the school began, they would wash, put on clean linen, and partake of the sacrament. Then they would gather to pray.[2441] Thus prepared, on the day of the revelation of Doctrine and Covenants 88, the Prophet instructed them "to pray separately and vocally to the Lord for [Him] to reveal His will unto us concerning the upbuilding of Zion and for the benefit of the Saints." The record indicates that each brother "bowed down before the Lord, after which each one arose and spoke in his turn his feelings and determination to keep the commandments of God. And then [Joseph] proceeded to receive a revelation."[2442]

The pattern of the School of the Prophets clearly demonstrates the power of prepared, unified voices asking in the prayer of faith for blessings.

[2434] D&C 29:3; emphasis added.
[2435] D&C 6:32; Matthew 18:20.
[2436] D&C 29:5–6; emphasis added.
[2437] D&C 29:33; emphasis added.
[2438] Smith, *Teachings of the Prophet Joseph Smith,* 18.
[2439] D&C 88:118–41.
[2440] *Kirtland Council Minute Book,* LDS Church Archives, 3–4.
[2441] *Salt Lake School of the Prophets Minutes,* Oct. 3, 1883, 56.
[2442] *Kirtland Council Minute Book,* LDS Church Archives, 3–4.

How We Achieve Unity

President Marion G. Romney taught us that seeking the Lord and his righteousness is the only avenue to unity.[2443] That is, we achieve unity by following the Lord, by learning his will, and by doing what he tells us to do. These are basic but essential principles that we must observe; otherwise we can achieve neither unity nor righteousness. The Lord promised that if we will seek him and seek a sounder understanding of the principles of the gospel, we will come to a state of *oneness* that will strengthen us beyond anything we have ever known. Therefore, humbling ourselves, keeping the commandments, studying the word of the Lord, following the living prophet without hardening our hearts, applying these teachings to our lives, asking the Lord in faith with the belief that we will receive—these basic principles promote unity.

Is becoming unified essential to our preservation? President Romney said that only a unified people, who keep God's commands and live these principles, can expect God's protection.[2444] President Lorenzo Snow also stated that safety lies only in unity: "I tell you, in the name of the Lord God, that the time is coming when there will be no safety only in the principles of union, for therein lies the secret of our temporal and spiritual salvation."[2445]

The End Result of Unity

Moses was given a panoramic vision of the enormity of the universe with its "worlds without number" and its equally numerous inhabitants who reside upon those worlds.[2446] With awe, we, too, gaze into the night sky and wonder about the origin of creation and by what power it is upheld.

The gospel offers us an answer.

All the creations, all the inhabitants, and all the seraphic beings that form and live in this universe can be traced back to two people who made an eternal covenant at a temple altar and unified their hearts in love.

This is the power of *oneness*.

All Things Common among Them

The astonishing blessings associated with equality and unity are exceeded only by a condition that always describes Zion: "They had all things common among them."[2447] Although some gospel authorities and writers have reshaped this phrase as "all things *in* common," it is not scriptural, and it often leads to misunderstandings. Brigham Young University associate professor Clark V. Johnson explained,

> The Lord does not desire his people to have everything the same or all things in common, but to have "all things common among them." (4 Nephi 1:3; see also Moses 7:18.) To have "all things common among them" is to understand that everything a person has is a gift from God, which God has given to bless his children. This attitude does away with superiority complexes and class structure and allows people to reach a level of equality in which there are no "rich and poor, bond and free," but all are "made free, and partakers of the heavenly gift," or life eternal. (4 Nephi 1:3; see also D&C 42:61.) Joseph Smith taught that this same attitude must exist on the part of

---

[2443] 3 Nephi 13:3.
[2444] Romney, "Unity," 17–18.
[2445] Snow, *The Teachings of Lorenzo Snow*, 180.
[2446] Moses 1:29, 33.
[2447] 3 Nephi 26:19; 4 Nephi 1:3; Acts 2:44; 4:32.

the destitute, "He that hath not, and cannot obtain, but saith in his heart, if I had, I would give freely, is accepted as freely as he that gives of his abundance."[2448]

The law of consecration calls for members of the Church to contribute generously to the Lord's storehouse, upon which the members may draw, when necessary, for their temporal welfare. That is, we all have *common access* to the resource, thus assuring that there are no poor among us.[2449] Of course, we do not all descend upon the storehouse and pick from its shelves without prior permission and accountability. It is the bishop's stewardship to manage and provide access to the common storehouse.[2450] Then all things are done in order.

But the law of consecration is also a spiritual law, which demands that we consecrate our time, talents, and other things that the Lord has or will put into our hands for the dual purposes of building the kingdom and establishing Zion.[2451] Because we claim no ownership of these gifts, but rather count them as stewardships, we find ourselves giving service in the Church, bearing one another's burdens that they might be light, mourning with those that mourn, comforting those that stand in need of comfort, and standing as witnesses of God at all times and in all things and in all places "even until death."[2452] In other words, we consecrate what we have and who we are to the common cause of Zion, which in turn provides us with common claim upon the resources of Zion. Thus, we are saved both temporally and spiritually.[2453]

Consecration and the Law of Offense

Offenses put equality and unity at risk. In the early days of the Church, a number of attempts to live the law of consecration failed, due in part to greed and contention. Admittedly, this celestial law, which demands our all, can be difficult to live—especially when we perceive that others might not be as dedicated as we are. Misunderstandings might arise. The Lord provided for this and gave us the Law of Offense, which suggests a hierarchy of judgment. At each level, the directive for judgment is this: "Judge not unrighteously, that ye be not judged; but judge righteous judgment."[2454]

BYU professor Clark V. Johnson described the law of offense this way:

> Recognizing that differences of opinion and personality clashes might occur among Church members, the Lord also revealed the law of offense to his followers. If someone were offended, he was to go to the person who had offended him and settle the differences. If the differences could not be resolved between the two parties, then the matter was to be taken before the elders. Thus, violators of the commandments and covenants were to be tried by the Church, subject to the "law of God." (D&C 42:81.) The principle set forth by the Savior in this situation is this: "And if thy brother or sister offend many, he or she shall be chastened before many. And if any one offend openly, he or she shall be rebuked openly. . . . If any shall

---

[2448] Johnson, "The Law of Consecration," 101.
[2449] Moses 7:18.
[2450] D&C 42:30, 34.
[2451] Benson, *The Teachings of Ezra Taft Benson*, 121.
[2452] Mosiah 18:8–9.
[2453] Romney, "Church Welfare—Temporal Service in a Spiritual Setting," 82; see also Kimball, *The Teachings of Spencer W. Kimball*, 366.
[2454] JST Matthew 7:2; see also JST John 7:24.

offend in secret, he or she shall be rebuked in secret, that he or she
may have opportunity to confess in secret to him or her whom he or
she has offended, and to God, that the church may not speak
reproachfully of him or her." (D&C 42:90–92.)[2455]

LAW OF COMMON CONSENT

To further ensure the equality, unity, and commonality of the Saints, the Lord also provided the Law of Common Consent: "All things shall be done by common consent in the church."[2456] This law allows each member of the Church equal power[2457] in sustaining the governing officers and supporting decisions that leaders make regarding the policies and management of the kingdom. Beyond these factors, common consent seems to imply a covenantal relationship that paves the way for revelation and guidance. For example, when we sustain the bishop, we raise our arm to the square, which is a sign of covenant making.[2458] By that action, we covenant to accept the bishop as the servant of Jesus Christ. Therefore, when we counsel with him and receive his judgments or blessings, it is as though his voice and hands are those of the Lord. This, of course, places a significant burden upon the bishop to live worthily of that trust, and it places a burden on us to accept him as the servant of Christ. When we raise our arm to the square and covenant to sustain the bishop by common consent, we are as obligated to keep that covenant as any other covenant that we make. Then it would seem that the Lord also covenants to reveal his mind and will to us through the bishop, and the Lord also confirms the blessings that his servant pronounces upon us: "Unto him will I confirm all my words, even unto the ends of the earth."[2459] "Verily, if a man be called of my Father, as was Aaron, by mine own voice, and by the voice of him that sent me, and I have endowed him with the keys of the power of this priesthood, *if he do anything in my name, and according to my law and by my word, he will not commit sin, and I will justify him.*"[2460]

Thus, by the covenant of common consent we all enjoy common access to the bishop, the Lord's servant, and we enjoy the totality of the Lord's temporal and spiritual blessings. These are the things that equalize and unify us and make all of the temporal and spiritual resources of the Lord common among us.

CONNECTING CONSECRATION WITH THE LAW OF THE GOSPEL AND THE LAW OF SACRIFICE

Equality and unity are impossible to achieve without the law of consecration. This law stands at the summit of a series of laws to which we must adhere if we expect to conform to and qualify for celestial glory. Hugh Nibley explained: "We have noted that the covenants of the endowment are progressively more binding, in the sense of allowing less and less latitude for personal interpretation as one advances. Thus (1) the law of God is general and mentions no specifics; (2) the law of obedience states that specific orders are to be given and observed; (3) the law of sacrifice still allows a margin of interpretation (this is as far as the old law goes—the Aaronic Priesthood carries out the law of sacrifice and no farther; and it specifies that while sacrifice is a solemn obligation on all, it is up to the individual to decide just how much he will give); (4) the law of chastity, on the other hand, is something else; here at last we have an absolute, bound by a solemn sign; (5) finally the law of

---

[2455] Johnson, "The Law of Consecration," 101.
[2456] D&C 26:2.
[2457] *Encyclopedia of Mormonism*, 463.
[2458] "Abraham's Act of Faith Reflects 'a Soul Like Unto Our Savior,'" *LDS Church News*, Apr. 2, 1994.
[2459] Mormon 9:24–25.
[2460] D&C 132:59.

consecration is equally uncompromising—everything the Lord has given one is to be consecrated. This law is bound by the firmest token of all."[2461]

Although consecration is evident in every gospel covenant, it is most readily connected with the laws of the gospel and of sacrifice. As we have discussed, the Law of the Gospel is really the fulness of the gospel, which the Savior summed up as the gospel of love: "Thou shalt love the Lord thy God with all thy heart, and with all thy soul, and with all thy mind. This is the first and great commandment. And the second is like unto it, Thou shalt love thy neighbour as thyself. On these two commandments hang all the law and the prophets."[2462] This is the higher law, which Jesus came to reveal; it is the law that replaced Moses' preparatory system of lesser sacrifices, laws, performances, and ordinances.

The higher law is characterized by a new heart, one that loves God and his children. To develop such a heart requires preparation, so that eventually it can be sacrificed, that is, "broken"[2463] or offered up to God without reservation. From such a pure and loving heart, righteous actions flow without legislation. Thus, the higher gospel is motivated by love rather than regulated by a system of rules.

Elder Bruce C. Hafen writes, "The gospel of the higher law was so simple and so profound that the Pharisees and other learned people of Christ's day missed it completely. They missed the simple part—the core—and they missed everything."[2464] The "core" of the higher gospel law is love.

This higher law, which produces higher love—*divine love,* or *charity*—is the love that gives God a celestial heart. This is the very attribute that Jesus was trying to reveal to the people about the Father. God is motivated to do what he does because he loves. We can trace his every action, thought, and word back to love. "God is love."[2465]

At a BYU Women's Conference, Sister A. D. Sorensen said, "Divine love [God's love] . . . comprehends and fulfills the whole law of the gospel. . . . First, divine love has for its ultimate aim that humankind avoid death and realize everlasting fulness of life. The achievement of that aim represents, as we have observed, the highest possibility of humankind, their ultimate good, and the final purpose of God. But second, divine love also makes possible, indeed literally constitutes, fulness of life."[2466]

The law of the gospel provides the miracle of a changed heart and beckons us forward to courageously pursue perfection. Then, when we finally become like God, we, too, will be motivated to act and think because of the love within us. At that point, we could legitimately insert our name into the scripture: "God [our name] is love." When we consider that consecration can be lived only by love, and when we consider how consecration lifts and exalts both the giver and receiver, we begin to understand why the law of consecration, the law of sacrifice, and the law of the gospel are connected. President Joseph F. Smith taught, "I would advise that we learn to love each other, and then friendship will be true and sweet. It has been said by one, that 'we may give without loving, but we cannot love without giving.'"[2467]

LOVE LEADS US TO ETERNAL LIFE

True equality and unity are motivated by love. This higher gospel law of love defines the pathway leading to eternal life. Because we love God and we desire eternal life, we make a covenant, knowing that only Heavenly Father, Jesus Christ, and the Holy Ghost know the way. Because these three Gods

---

[2461] Nibley, *Approaching Zion,* 441–42.
[2462] Matthew 22:37–40.
[2463] D&C 59:8.
[2464] Hafen, *The Broken Heart,* 1.
[2465] 1 John 4:8, 16.
[2466] Sorensen, "No Respector of Persons: Equality in the Kingdom," 55.
[2467] Smith, *Teachings of the Presidents of the Church: Joseph F. Smith,* 192.

love us, they covenant to help us achieve our goal. For our part, we agree to adopt a new lifestyle that is conducive to living in the celestial kingdom, where we want to be. As we have learned, this covenant is called the *new and everlasting covenant,* which is another name for the law of the gospel. Motivated by love, each member of the Godhead effectively *signs* his name to the Covenant at the time of our baptism, and they do so with the purpose of leading us to exaltation.

Part of our agreement is to follow the designated path to its perfect conclusion. This path, as we have learned, is marked by authorized *ordinances*; that is, the path is an *ordered* path with authorized *markers* that measure our progress and infuse us along the way with celestial power and knowledge. This marked path is the *only* path that will lead us to our divine destination.

To Peter and the apostles, Jesus said, "Go ye into all the world, and preach the gospel to every creature. He that believeth and is baptized shall be saved; but he that believeth not shall be damned."[2468] In this scripture, damnation suggests restricted blessings. According to Jesus' statement, anyone who rejected his teachings and baptism at the hands of the apostles would be "damned" or unworthy of further blessings. Clearly, without the order of ordinances that we receive along the path leading to eternal life, we would be "damned." This condition is not one of equality, unity, or love.

Is Baptism Sufficient for Exaltation?

No. Baptism and receiving the Holy Ghost only get us on the path. These ordinances can *save* us in the celestial kingdom, but will not exalt us there. Exaltation requires our receiving the authority of God (priesthood ordination);[2469] specific purification and sanctification to prepare us for our future sacred appointment (temple washing and anointing);[2470] protection from Satan, our eternal enemy (the garment of the holy priesthood);[2471] an infusion of heavenly power and knowledge (temple endowment);[2472] acceptance of the law of the celestial kingdom (consecration);[2473] and the promise of an eternal kingdom, given by the Father (celestial marriage).[2474] These covenants and ordinances are the markers along the path leading to exaltation. When we make any of these covenants and receive their associated ordinances by the authority of priesthood keys, we are assured, upon our worthiness, that the terms of that covenant will be fulfilled and will endure eternally. We have God's personal *seal* and guarantee.

Two Purposes of the Law of the Gospel

The two primary purposes of the law of the gospel—the new and everlasting covenant—are: (1) to return us to God, and (2) to help us become like our Heavenly Father and Mother. If we follow the path to its conclusion and abide in the law of the gospel to the end, these are the promises:

> And again, verily I say unto you, if a man marry a wife by my word, which is my law, and by the new and everlasting covenant, and it is sealed unto them by the Holy Spirit of promise, by him who is anointed [the prophet], unto whom I have appointed this power and the keys of this priesthood; and it shall be said unto them—Ye shall come forth in the first resurrection; and if it be after the first resurrection, in the next resurrection; and shall inherit thrones,

---

[2468] Mark 16:15–16.
[2469] D&C 84:33.
[2470] *Encyclopedia of Mormonism,* 1551.
[2471] *Encyclopedia of Mormonism,* 534; Ephesians 6:13; D&C 27:15.
[2472] *Encyclopedia of Mormonism,* 455.
[2473] D&C 42; 105:4–5.
[2474] D&C 132:19–24.

kingdoms, principalities, and powers, dominions, all heights and depths—then shall it be written in the Lamb's Book of Life, that he shall commit no murder whereby to shed innocent blood, and if ye abide in my covenant, and commit no murder whereby to shed innocent blood, it shall be done unto them in all things whatsoever my servant hath put upon them, in time, and through all eternity; and shall be of full force when they are out of the world; and they shall pass by the angels, and the gods, which are set there, to their exaltation and glory in all things, as hath been sealed upon their heads, which glory shall be a fulness and a continuation of the seeds forever and ever.

Then shall they be gods, because they have no end; therefore shall they be from everlasting to everlasting, because they continue; then shall they be above all, because all things are subject unto them. Then shall they be gods, because they have all power, and the angels are subject unto them.[2475]

No Other Way

Can a person obtain these promises in any other way? No. The Lord states, "Verily, verily, I say unto you, except ye abide my law ye cannot attain to this glory. For strait is the gate, and narrow the way that leadeth unto the exaltation and continuation of the lives, and few there be that find it."[2476]

Why do only a few find this path? "Because ye receive me not in the world neither do ye know me."[2477]

Does this mean that God condemns these people? No. It usually means that they have not found him yet, so he will find them. We have to remember that God is our Father and not a condemning judge. No loving parent would withhold the greatest of blessings from his children because of ignorance. We are assured that Heavenly Father will use all his resources and work ceaselessly and relentlessly to offer these blessings to his children. Even if his children do not understand at first, he will continue to try until they understand perfectly and can make an informed choice. This is one of the great works of the Church of Jesus Christ, and it is the essence of the law of the gospel. No single issue is more important than this: God loves his children and he never gives up trying to offer them the blessings provided by this law.

What happens when we desire these blessings with all our heart and put forth the effort to obtain them? Here is the Lord's promise: "But if ye receive me in the world, then shall ye know me, and shall receive your exaltation; that where I am ye shall be also."[2478]

The Interwoven Covenants

As we have learned, the law of sacrifice and the law of the gospel are connected. Each is motivated by love, and each one points to the highest manifestation of love, called *consecration*. We might say that the law of consecration is the perfect outgrowth of the law of the gospel; that is, consecration is the supernal expression of sacrifice that we agree to when we enter the gospel covenant. This sacrifice culminates with giving our all to God, and we make that sacrifice for the purposes of choosing God over mammon, and lifting others and urging them forward toward eternal life. Thus, consecration

---

[2475] D&C 132:19–20.
[2476] D&C 132:22.
[2477] D&C 132:22.
[2478] D&C 132:23.

could have as its mission statement the same that Jesus attached to the gospel itself: "Thou shalt love the Lord thy God with all thy heart, and with all thy soul, and with all thy mind. This is the first and great commandment. And the second is like unto it, Thou shalt love thy neighbour as thyself. On these two commandments hang all the law and the prophets."[2479] Herein is equality and unity achieved and perfected.

Perhaps more than any other law, the law of consecration defines the love of God, love of others, and true discipleship; moreover, consecration is the foundational principle of Zionlike equality and unity. Therefore, a consecrated person, by his own choice, liberally imparts of his substance unto the poor and the needy, "according to the law of [the] gospel."[2480] As we have said, this attitude cannot be legislated. It is lived by love and choice or not at all. Consecration is the law that creates this ultimate change of heart, which is required for an inheritance in the celestial kingdom. No wonder, then, that consecration is the last law that we must agree to live before we can stand in the presence of God. Significantly, it is only after we agree to live the law of consecration that we can pray with enough power (perhaps power that derives from consecration) to approach God and enter his presence. There, in that sacred setting, we see all three members of the Godhead,[2481] the same three that symbolically *signed* their names to the new and everlasting covenant in the first place and agreed to bring us to this point. Now they are here to greet us, as if to signify that they have fulfilled their agreement and are ready to usher us into the presence of God. Equally significant is the fact that it is only after we have agreed to accept this last law, *consecration*, which allows us entrance to celestial glory, that the Father can bless us with our kingdom—*eternal marriage*.

THE LAW OF SACRIFICE

Without the law of sacrifice, we could not achieve equality and unity. Again we emphasize that the law of sacrifice is tied to the law of the gospel in the same way that these two laws are connected with the law of consecration.[2482] The Lord said, "Verily I say unto you, all among them who know their hearts are honest, and are broken, and their spirits contrite, and are willing to observe their covenants by sacrifice—yea, every sacrifice which I, the Lord, shall command—they are accepted of me."[2483]

Sacrifice can appear to be a negative or a painful principle unless we consider that no good thing is ever accomplished without choice and effort. We are willing to choose between bad, good, better, and best alternatives when we want something badly enough.[2484] To implement our choice, we willingly sacrifice all other choices. The same could be said of effort. Once we have made a choice, we are willing to expend effort to achieve that choice; the more essential the choice, the more effort is required. To achieve our most important goals, we are willing to gather around us every available resource, fix our minds on our objective, and summon strength to stay the course. It is in the process of making a choice and expending effort that we prove our loyalty to our goal. We know that a lackluster decision or a mediocre exertion will result in failure. Only dedicated and unrelenting sacrifice will prove our loyalty to our cause and sustain us until we achieve success.

Likewise, we simply cannot prove our loyalty to God, remain obedient to our covenants, and live the law of the gospel without a firm decision and concerted effort—in other words, *sacrifice*. Our willingness to decide once and for all to choose Zion over Babylon—and to confirm that decision by our offering a free-will sacrifice of time, talents, and all that we have and are to God—is consecration.

[2479] Matthew 22:37–40.
[2480] D&C 104:18.
[2481] Note: Hebrews 10:20 states that Christ is the veil.
[2482] McConkie, "Obedience, Consecration, and Sacrifice," 50.
[2483] D&C 97:8.
[2484] Oaks, "Good, Better, Best," 104–8.

This is the ultimate manifestation of the law of sacrifice, which finally proves our loyalty to God, the building up of his kingdom, and the establishment of his Zion.

Sacrifice and Love

We recall that the law of the gospel is simultaneously called the new and everlasting covenant and the Gospel of Love. We also recall that the law of the gospel, coupled with sacrifice and love, sets the stage for equality and unity.

True love stands on a three-legged stool of total loyalty, sacrifice, and trust. With that image in our minds, we begin to understand why the law of sacrifice and the law of the gospel go hand in hand. True love cannot exist when loyalties are divided; neither can love exist when either party is selfish or untrustworthy. True love can flourish only when an eternal decision has been made and when continual, strenuous effort is expended. Then love will grow to its perfect conclusion. Clearly, without sacrifice, there can be no love; where there is no love, there is limited obedience to the law of the gospel; and without these things in place, consecration is nonexistent and eternal life is forfeited.

On the other hand, if we are willing to obey the law of the gospel, we will be filled with love and anxious to sacrifice anything and everything for eternal life. It has been said that sacrifice is giving up something for something better—and it is certainly that. But sacrifice is much more. To a pure-hearted, covenant person, sacrifices are made in the similitude of Christ, and therefore each sacrifice has proxy characteristics—that is, doing something for someone who cannot do that thing alone or for himself. Therefore, a sacrifice made at a higher level is not a sacrifice that we make for our own purposes; rather, this higher sacrifice is made for another person. Consequently, the Lord consecrates our sacrifice for the welfare of our souls.[2485]

Such a consecrated, Christlike sacrifice has a redeeming effect upon the recipient and the giver; both are lifted and exalted. This is the essence of the higher law of the gospel. Together, love of God and neighbor and proxy sacrifice form the mechanism that allows us to become Christlike and causes a state of blessedness and purity of heart.

Sacrifice—Our Contribution to Our Salvation

What price must be paid to save and exalt a soul? Hugh Nibley explained: "The . . . Atonement requires of the beneficiary nothing less than willingness to part with his most precious possession. Joined with the law of sacrifice is the law of consecration, which has no limiting 'if necessary' clause; we agree to it unconditionally here and now. It represents our contribution to our salvation."[2486] The connection between sacrifice and consecration is obvious, and both are necessary for our salvation. President Gordon B. Hinckley concurred. He also taught that total sacrifice is "our contribution to our salvation." But because of our fallen nature, he said, our sacrifice will ultimately fall short of what is needed. The full price of eternal life can be paid only by our sacrificing "everything that we can give and everything that God can give (His Son) and everything that Jesus can give (His life) and everything that the Holy Ghost can give—their full time, ability and resources. God's work and glory demand his all, and we must give our all."[2487]

How much is "our all"? Jesus set the example and described his sacrifice in these words: "How sore you know not, how exquisite you know not, yea, how hard to bear you know not. . . . Which suffering caused myself, even God, the greatest of all, to tremble because of pain, and to bleed at every

---

[2485] 2 Nephi 32:9.
[2486] Nibley, *Approaching Zion*, 590–92.
[2487] Hinckley, *Teachings of Gordon B. Hinckley*, 147.

pore, and to suffer both body and spirit."[2488] If he sacrificed for our salvation to the extent of his ability, we likewise must sacrifice to the extent of our ability.

Of this total kind of sacrifice, Joseph Smith said,

> Let us here observe, that a religion that does not require the sacrifice of all things never has power sufficient to produce the faith necessary unto life and salvation; for, from the first existence of man, the faith necessary unto the enjoyment of life and salvation never could be obtained without the sacrifice of all earthly things. It was through this sacrifice, and this only, that God has ordained that men should enjoy eternal life. . . . Those, then, who make the sacrifice, will have the testimony that their course is pleasing in the sight of God; and those who have this testimony will have faith to lay hold on eternal life, and will be enabled, through faith, to endure unto the end, and receive the crown that is laid up for them that love the appearing of our Lord Jesus Christ. But those who do not make the sacrifice cannot enjoy this faith, because men are dependent upon this sacrifice in order to obtain this faith: therefore, they cannot lay hold upon eternal life.[2489]

To gain exaltation, we must pay the price of exaltation, which is our all. That price is *consecration*—the law of sacrifice in its highest form. Elder Neal A. Maxwell asked, What if Jesus, who performed so many miracles, had stopped short of the miracle of the Atonement? The consequences would have been catastrophic. Just so, we might ask ourselves, What if we live good and decent lives, hoping for exaltation, and yet, when the opportunity presents itself, we shrink when we are faced with the necessary sacrifice for exaltation? We must embrace consecration with faith, Elder Maxwell said. Then our best effort will summon Christ's grace, which is sufficient to make weak things strong. The Lord promises that in the end, we will achieve our hoped-for destination, but in the meantime we have a journey to trek. Along our journey toward eternal life, we will discover that sacrificing our will to God is really not a sacrifice at all. Such a sacrifice leads to receiving all that Father has.[2490]

Clearly, consecration is the ultimate manifestation of the law of sacrifice, the law that prepares and purifies the heart so that it can be consecrated and offered to God. On a rudimentary level, sacrifice is giving up something good for something better; but sacrifice on a higher level is *proxy* sacrifice and therefore Christlike in nature—the giving up of something to bless another person. Such a sacrifice is counted by God as doing it unto him.[2491] This is the essence of consecration, the sacrifice of the heart. All other sacrifices are shadows of this sacrifice, just as such sacrifices were with Jesus. Every sacrifice that he made led him to Gethsemane and Calvary, where he sacrificed the totality of his heart. Like Jesus, our consecrated sacrifice of all things has the power to usher us into the presence of God.

In the end, we learn that the more our hearts are owned by Zion, the more we will desire to give, and the more we give, the more capable we will become to sacrifice and consecrate our hearts.

SUMMARY AND CONCLUSION

According to President Marion G. Romney, six criteria make up the law of consecration:

[2488] D&C 19:15–18.
[2489] Smith, *Lectures on Faith*, 6:7, 10.
[2490] Maxwell, "Consecrate Thy Performance," 36.
[2491] Matthew 25:40.

1. Belief in God
2. Freewill offerings
3. Private ownership and individual management
4. A nonpolitical program
5. Righteousness as the prerequisite
6. Exalts the poor and humbles the rich.[2492]

Moreover, two fundamental principles define Zion: "every man seeking the interest of his neighbor," and "doing all things with an eye single to the glory of God."[2493] This philosophy leads to voluntary unity and equality that is motivated by love of God and his children. The Babylonian counterparts include forced taxation, communism, and other economic experiments. The results inevitably limit freedom of choice, stifle initiative, hamper prosperity, promote divisiveness, and ultimately "level down" individuals and societies. Conversely, Zionlike equality *levels up* people, exalting the poor by means of the consecrated, freewill offerings of the rich. This is the Lord's "own way."[2494]

Equality is a celestial law that provides for the prosperity of all. When we give to one of God's children, our action is counted as though we did it unto God, and, therefore, he recompenses us *"an hundredfold,"* as though he were repaying a debt. Because we are always rewarded beyond our sacrifice, however, we are forever eternally indebted to God.

The law of consecration requires that we, like the Lord, esteem "all flesh in one."[2495] God equally offers us, the "favored of God," access to his blessings, and when we receive them, we must in turn use them to bless others. If we do not, we are anti-Zion; we simply cannot treat God's children differently than he does and expect to become Zion people.

Equality could not exist except by receiving divine love and exhibiting love for others. Love is one of several criteria upon which we can become equal. Other criteria include: equal in the sight of God; equal opportunity for eternal life; joint heirs with Christ; having all things common; equal opportunities to contribute and receive education, to develop talents and abilities, and to engage people in the work of Zion; equality in labor, power, and consent; and equal as to fulfillment of needs and wants. By receiving these gifts, we are to use them to take an equal responsibility for the cause of Zion.

As much as consecration is dependent upon equality, it is also dependent upon unity. Unity infuses power into Zion and its people. President Gordon B. Hinckley said, "When you are united, your power is limitless. You can accomplish anything you wish to accomplish."[2496] An example is unified prayer—multiple voices praying for a common goal. Gathering as one in the name of Christ for a common purpose invites the Savior into our circle. The power to unify is provided only by the At-one-ment, which brings separated things or people back into *oneness,* the divinely mandated goal for every covenant relationship. Wherever there is oneness, there is the Lord, and, consequently, there is power. Scriptural accounts describe the power of the Atonement and *oneness*. The Godhead, Alma and Amulek, the sons of Mosiah, and Alma's grandsons Nephi and Lehi are examples of the power of unity. Whenever unity is achieved, happiness, abundance, and conversion power result.

Unity has a synergistic effect; united people have many times more strength than the sum of their individual strengths. The opposite of synergy is *antagonism*; antagonistic people have less combined strength than the sum strengths of the individuals. President Kimball taught that the Spirit of the

---

[2492] Romney, "The Purpose of Church Welfare Services," 92.
[2493] D&C 82:19.
[2494] D&C 104:15–16; emphasis added.
[2495] 1 Nephi 17:35.
[2496] Hinckley, "Your Greatest Challenge, Mother," 97–100.

Lord cannot help us magnify our efforts without oneness and cooperation in all that we do. We achieve unity only through righteousness; unity is our only safety; unity is the power by which the heavens were made and all the seraphic hosts of heaven were created.

Unity, as a celestial principle, meaning that we have "all things common,"[2497] gives us *common access* to the Lord and his resources. This condition assures that there are no poor among us.[2498] Although this is a temporal manifestation of the law of consecration, it reflects the spiritual aspects of the law. If we are to be truly equal and unified and have all things common among us, we must consecrate our time, talents, and other things that the Lord has or will put into our hands for the dual purposes of building the kingdom and establishing Zion.[2499] We must consecrate our hearts if we are to advance the common cause of Zion and lay claim to the common resources of Zion. Then we are saved both temporally and spiritually.[2500]

The Lord provided a way to handle offenses, which put equality and unity at risk. To counter misunderstandings among the people, the Lord placed major judgments pertaining to the kingdom of God under the auspices of the priesthood. On a day-to-day basis, the Lord gave us a directive and provided the law of offense. The directive is: "Judge not unrighteously, that ye be not judged; but judge righteous judgment."[2501] Before we make judgments, we must first obtain the mind of the Lord, and then act upon his promptings.

To further ensure that equality, unity, and commonality remain intact, the Lord provided the law of common consent. This law allows each member of the Church equal ability to sustain the governing officers, who make decisions that affect the kingdom.

The law of consecration stands at the summit of a series of covenants to which we must adhere if we expect to conform to and qualify for celestial glory. Together, these covenants and laws form the framework of the higher law, which in turn is characterized by each one receiving a new heart, one that loves God and his children. To develop such a heart requires preparation through living the covenants and laws, so that eventually the heart can be sacrificed as a "broken" heart,[2502] or one that is offered up to God without reservation. Love, not a system of rules, motivates a pure and loving heart. Such a heart approaches the quality of God's heart; "God is love." By following the covenants and laws of the gospel, we can experience the miracle of a changed heart and finally become like God.

When we consider that consecration can be lived only by love, and when we consider how consecration lifts and exalts both the giver and receiver, we begin to understand why the law of consecration, the law of sacrifice, and the law of the gospel are connected. The two primary purposes of the law of the gospel—the new and everlasting covenant—are: (1) to return us to God, and (2) to help us become like our Heavenly Father and Mother. The two primary ways to live the law of sacrifice are: (1) to give up something for something better, and (2) to give up something for the sake of helping someone who cannot fully help themselves. Consecration marries these principles by supplying the time, talents, and resources to make this sacrifice, which returns us to God and makes us like him. Moreover, sacrifice is the contribution we make to our own salvation. The full price of eternal life can be paid only by the sacrifice of "everything that we can give and everything that God can give (His Son) and everything that Jesus can give (His life) and everything that the Holy Ghost

---

[2497] 3 Nephi 26:19; 4 Nephi 1:3; Acts 2:44; 4:32.

[2498] Moses 7:18.

[2499] Benson, *The Teachings of Ezra Taft Benson*, 121.

[2500] Romney, "Church Welfare—Temporal Service in a Spiritual Setting," 84; see also Kimball, *The Teachings of Spencer W. Kimball*, 366.

[2501] JST Matthew 7:2; see also JST John 7:24.

[2502] D&C 59:8.

can give—their full time, ability and resources. God's work and glory demand his all, and we must give our all."[2503]

The law of the gospel, the law of sacrifice, and the law of consecration are motivated by love. The law of the gospel is summed up by two laws of love: "Thou shalt love the Lord thy God with all thy heart, and with all thy soul, and with all thy mind. This is the first and great commandment. And the second is like unto it, Thou shalt love thy neighbour as thyself. On these two commandments hang all the law and the prophets."[2504] Herein are equality and unity achieved and perfected; consecration is the law that creates this ultimate change of heart, which allows for equality and unity. No wonder, then, that consecration is the last law that we must agree to live before we can stand in the presence of God. Significantly, it is only after we agree to live the law of consecration that we can pray with enough power to approach God and enter his presence. Moreover, it is only after we covenant to live the law of consecration that we qualify to receive our own eternal kingdom through temple marriage.

By means of the law of the gospel, the law of sacrifice, and the law of consecration, we prove our loyalty to God once and for all. We remain obedient to our covenants with a firm decision and concerted effort, and we are willing to back up that commitment with all that we are and all that we possess. Only by this ultimate manifestation of obedience and sacrifice can we build up God's kingdom and prepare the way for the establishment of Zion.

[2503] Hinckley, *Teachings of Gordon B. Hinckley*, 147.
[2504] Matthew 22:37–40.

Section 17

The Guiding Principles of Consecration

Nearly two years after the organization of the Church, Joseph Smith received a revelation from the Lord instructing him to take the next step in establishing the law of consecration. "For verily I say unto you, the time has come, and is now at hand; and behold, and lo, it must needs be that there be an organization of my people, in regulating and establishing the affairs of the storehouse for the poor of my people, both in this place and in the land of Zion." This "order" was to be considered "a permanent and everlasting establishment and order unto my church, to advance the cause, which ye have espoused, to the salvation of man, and to the glory of your Father who is in heaven." Beyond advancing the cause of Zion and providing a means of salvation for us, this "order" was to make the Saints "equal in the bonds of heavenly things, yea, and earthly things also, for the obtaining of heavenly things." Notice that equality is a constant theme in consecration literature: "For if ye are not equal in earthly things ye cannot be equal in obtaining heavenly things." Obeying the law of consecration cannot be overstated: "For if you will that I give unto you a place in the celestial world, you must prepare yourselves by doing the things which I have commanded you and required of you."[2505]

The Prophet learned that disobeying this law carries dire consequences: disloyalty to the truth, blindness to the Source of our blessings, and perhaps worse, the loss of our standing before God, and subjugation to Satan. The Saints must live this law, the Lord said, "Otherwise, Satan seeketh to turn their hearts away from the truth, that they become blinded and understand not the things which are prepared for them. Wherefore, a commandment I give unto you, to prepare and organize yourselves by a bond or everlasting covenant that cannot be broken. And he who breaketh it shall lose his office and standing in the church, and shall be delivered over to the buffetings of Satan until the day of redemption."[2506]

[2505] D&C 78:7.
[2506] D&C 78:11–12.

Conversely, the "order" of consecration is the key to our temporal and spiritual salvation. Consecration prepares us against the trials of the last days, and sets us apart as independent from this wicked world: "Behold, this is the preparation wherewith I prepare you, and the foundation, and the ensample which I give unto you, whereby you may accomplish the commandments which are given you; that through my providence, notwithstanding the tribulation which shall descend upon you, that the church may stand independent above all other creatures beneath the celestial world."[2507]

Guiding Principles of Consecration

In this section, we have discussed a variety of characteristics of consecration, including equality and unity. In this chapter, we will explore the additional principles of agency, stewardship, accountability, and labor, as they appear in the scriptures and as they apply to consecration.

Agency

President Marion G. Romney defined agency as both the liberty and the capability to choose and act. Beyond the gift of life, he said, agency is our most precious gift from God.[2508] Speaking of agency, President Brigham Young taught: "This is a law which has always existed from all eternity, and will continue to exist throughout all the eternities to come. Every intelligent being must have the power of choice."[2509]

Elder Bruce R. McConkie wrote: "Four great principles must be in force if there is to be agency: 1. Laws must exist, laws ordained by an Omnipotent power, laws which can be obeyed or disobeyed; 2. Opposites must exist—good and evil, virtue and vice, right and wrong—that is, there must be an opposition, one force pulling one way and another pulling the other; 3. A knowledge of good and evil must be had by those who are to enjoy the agency, that is, they must know the difference between the opposites; and 4. An unfettered power of choice must prevail."[2510]

Agency and Truth

The measure of our agency increases as we learn and apply truth. For example, a pilot has more agency than a passenger, and a surgeon has more agency than a patient. We cannot exercise agency without information to act upon. Because consecration is perhaps the highest and most demanding exercise of agency, we must become acquainted with its premise and principles. Knowledge of the laws of life helps us to understand their associated blessings and protective punishments. We make better choices (or should), when we are in the possession of knowledge. The scriptures remind us, "And ye shall know the truth, and the truth shall make you free." But freedom of choice carries an obligation: While we are free to act, we are not free to define right and wrong. Once we are in possession of the truth, we must choose to act upon it correctly if we hope to obtain the blessings.[2511]

Consecration is a choice. That choice can neither be forced upon us nor legislated. However, once we have received light and truth regarding this law, and when we have covenanted to live it, we are faced with an inescapable decision: *Will we consecrate or will we not?* How we choose will determine whether or not we will receive the highest of blessings or the condemnation.[2512] When we become acquainted with this law and covenant to live it, we are still free to consecrate or not, but we are not free to ignore the law, redefine it, or expect that we can achieve celestial glory without abiding

---

[2507] D&C 78:13–14.
[2508] Romney, "Church Welfare Services' Basic Principles," 120.
[2509] Young, *Deseret News*, Oct. 10, 1866, 355.
[2510] McConkie, *Mormon Doctrine*, 26.
[2511] Cannon, "Agency and Accountability," 88–89; quoting John 8:32.
[2512] Matthew 25:14–30.

The Guiding Principles of Consecration

it.[2513] When we consider that consecration is the ultimate sacrifice and test of will, we might say that God gave us our agency, in part, for the purpose of giving us a choice to live this law so that we could achieve eternal life. Because achieving exaltation pivots on our willingness to consecrate our all to God, and because the sacrifice of all things[2514] (defined as a broken heart and a contrite spirit, a sacrifice that answers the end of the law[2515]) is *the* criterion, we must be in possession of the "unfettered power of choice" and the capability to act upon that choice.

Agency—A Gift Assured and Protected by the Savior

He who gave us our agency is God.[2516] He who opposes our agency is the devil. And he who safeguards our right to this gift is the Savior: "And the Messiah cometh in the fulness of time, that he may redeem the children of men from the fall. *And because they are redeemed from the fall they have become free forever, knowing good from evil, to act for themselves.* . . . Wherefore, men are free according to the flesh; and all things are given them which are expedient unto man. And they are free to choose liberty and eternal life, through the great Mediator of all men, or to choose captivity and death, according to the captivity and power of the devil; for he seeketh that all men might be miserable like unto himself."[2517]

Children of God are endowed with the inherent capacity to choose liberty and eternal life or captivity and death—to choose to become a god or a devil. As we have said, without God's gift of agency and the Savior's protection of it, we could not choose to consecrate, which is the singular law that allows us to inherit the celestial kingdom and exaltation.

The Body—The Vehicle for Moral Agency

Just as a pilot (an agent of flight) needs an airplane to give expression to his knowledge, so a spirit (an agent of light) needs a physical body to give ultimate expression to its desires. Think of it this way: A pilot cannot choose to fly without a plane any more than a spirit can choose to act physically without a body.

Together, spirit and body constitute "the soul of man."[2518] To achieve exaltation the soul needs experience in the two major elements that constitute the universe: spirit matter and physical matter. The physical body becomes the great tool of feeling and expression that the spirit can choose to "act upon."[2519] The physical body is like the artist's brush; to a spirit, the physical world is its canvas.

Suddenly, with a body, we can choose from and enjoy infinite possibilities. President John Taylor said, "The body was formed as an agent for the spirit."[2520] With a body, then, we have both the intellect and the vehicle to imagine and reason, then choose to act out our thoughts. With a body we can give expression to our dreams, desires, and hungers. With a body we have the unlimited potential to reach stratospheric godlike heights or plunge to the hellish depths. With a body, we who are the children of God, and thus have infinite potential, are capable of literally anything—"nothing [would] be impossible."[2521] But to become as God, we must learn to control the physical body and discipline it into channels of exalted purposes, the greatest of which, interestingly, are realized only by means of a consecrated effort.

[2513] Cannon, "Agency and Accountability," 88–89.
[2514] Smith, *Lectures on Faith*, 6:7.
[2515] 2 Nephi 2:7.
[2516] Moses 7:32.
[2517] 2 Nephi 2:26–27; emphasis added.
[2518] D&C 88:15.
[2519] 2 Nephi 2:13.
[2520] Taylor, "The Government of God," in *Teachings of the Latter-day Prophets*, 15:77–79.
[2521] Luke 1:37.

Controlling the body is no small feat. By descending to this planet to take up a fallen, telestial body made of fallen, telestial material, we become "by nature . . . carnal, sensual, and devilish."[2522] Consequently, we become subject to the devil.[2523] This fallen condition has a name, *natural man*, which by definition is "an enemy to God." In order to progress toward exaltation, we need to experience a spiritual awakening and press the body to be enticed by "the Holy Spirit and [put] off the natural man and [become] a saint through the Atonement of Christ the Lord." This transformation is preceded by a choice, which means we need our agency. Therefore, to qualify for eternal life, we must choose to suppress our innate carnal, sensual, and devilish natures and become childlike, "submissive, meek, humble, patient, full of love, willing to submit to all things which the Lord seeth fit to inflict upon [us], even as a child doth submit to his father."[2524]

Thus, earth life is designed to be a test consisting of choices made possible by our God-given agency. Our mortal test—choosing between the physical and spiritual and between Satan and God—involves learning to "act as an independent being . . . to see what we will do, . . . to be righteous in the dark—to be the friend of God."[2525] Our test is to exercise our agency and choose to be faithful, even if our circumstances become "darker than 10,000 midnights."[2526]

Our Eternal Destiny Lies within Our Body

With agency and a body, every experience is heightened—we can fall lower or rise higher than anything we had previously known. We can feel more fully, hurt more completely, love more deeply, and, because we now are a complete *soul* comprised of the two building blocks of the universe, we have the potential to "receive a fulness of joy."[2527] Clearly, our destiny lies within the potential of our bodies.

Satan would expend every effort to persuade us to misuse our bodies. He knows, for example, that with a body we suddenly have the power to reproduce ourselves by procreating other carnate children of God—a powerful and sometimes frightening idea. Satan eagerly zeroes in on this God-defining power and relentlessly tries to influence us to misuse our bodies by experimenting with the sacred powers of procreation. Once we choose badly, we lose agency and give it up to him. Another Satanic ploy is to use ignorance as a tool to destroy us—ignorance about who we really are, where we came from, why we are here, and what could be our glorious future. By keeping us ignorant, Satan can more easily tempt us to choose to disobey God. He knows that disobedience cuts a wide gash in the soul and causes us to hemorrhage light and truth.[2528] Once that happens, we become weakened and disempowered. We lose agency incrementally; then Satan can gain control over us.[2529]

On the other hand, the body, when properly used and understood, according to Joseph Smith, can put us beyond Satan and all of our enemies.[2530] He said, "All beings who have bodies have power over those who have not. The devil has no power over us only as we permit him. The moment we revolt at anything which comes from God, the devil takes power."[2531] Therefore, "Satan's power over

---

[2522] Alma 42:10.
[2523] Mosiah 16:3.
[2524] Mosiah 3:19.
[2525] Maxwell, *That Ye May Believe*, 194–95.
[2526] Young, *Journal of Discourses*, 3:207.
[2527] D&C 93:33–34.
[2528] D&C 93:39.
[2529] Mosiah 16:3–5.
[2530] Smith, *The Words of Joseph Smith*, 208.
[2531] Smith, *Teachings of the Prophet Joseph Smith*, 181.

us *always* hinges upon our obedience or disobedience—our willingness or unwillingness to submit to the mind and will of the Father."[2532]

The body is designed to be the "tabernacle of God,"[2533] a holy, walled fortress to hold the spirit and shield it.[2534] We must not forget that the spirit, the actual offspring of God that animates the body, is a powerful being. Our spirit is made of the substance called *truth*, which is also referred to as spirit, light, light of truth, intelligence, glory, power, and, interestingly, "law."[2535] Because the body is carnal, sensual, and devilish by nature, it might not perceive the entity of light and truth that resides within it; but the spirit knows who it is. By nature, the spirit is truth-discerning, constructed and instructed so that it can perceive both truth and error.[2536] Beyond our limited five physical senses, an ocean of truth exists around us, and although we might try stubbornly to deny it, we are nevertheless drenched in truth.[2537] Therefore, within the construct of our souls resides all the necessary tools to allow us to learn and to choose. We are clearly beings of agency.

AGENCY AND AGENTS

Agents are people who have the power and authority to act.[2538] Therefore, agents have agency, which is the ability to "act for themselves,"[2539] or the ability to act for themselves with respect to a given responsibility or obligation. Moreover, agents have the capacity to be accountable for their actions. Whereas *freedom* is the power and privilege to exercise our will and act upon it, *agency* is the power, independence of mind, and individual will to choose to act. *Moral agency* describes our ability to act upon and be accountable for spiritual matters.[2540] Zion people exercise their God-given agency to choose to make and keep covenants and to reject the enticements of Babylon.

And choose we must.

Posing the choice between Jehovah and Baal, Elijah asked, "How long halt ye between two opinions? if the Lord be God, follow him: but if Baal, then follow him."[2541] In our day, he would have been asking us to choose between Zion and Babylon. Remaining lukewarm on celestial issues is not acceptable: "I know thy works, that thou art neither cold nor hot," the Lord said. "I would thou wert cold or hot. So then because thou art lukewarm, and neither cold nor hot, I will spue thee out of my mouth."[2542] Consecration is not a lukewarm issue. Everything of eternal consequence rides on our choosing to obey this law. Because we are agents of choice, we have the capacity to choose one way or another. But there is no middle ground when it comes to consecration; either we consecrate or we do not.

When the Lord began to establish his people in the land of Zion, he instructed the Saints to consecrate their money for the cause: "And let all the moneys which can be spared, it mattereth not unto me whether it be little or much, be sent up unto the land of Zion."[2543] Notice that it did not matter how much the Saints gave as long as they exercised their agency and chose to give all that they could spare. There is an unspoken assumption here that concerns the principle of grace: When we do

---

[2532] Yorgason, *I Need Thee Every Hour*, 348.
[2533] D&C 93:35.
[2534] Young, *Journal of Discourses*, 9:139–40.
[2535] D&C 93:23–29, 36; 88:6–13.
[2536] 2 Nephi 2:5.
[2537] Alma 32:28.
[2538] *American Heritage Dictionary*, s.v. "agent."
[2539] 2 Nephi 2:26.
[2540] D&C 29:35.
[2541] 1 Kings 18:21.
[2542] Revelation 3:15–16.
[2543] D&C 63:40.

all we can do, the Lord will make up the difference. As we know, the Lord can take a consecration as small as five loaves and two fishes and bless it so that it can feed thousands.[2544] Addressing Newel K. Whitney, the Lord said, "Let him impart all the money which he can impart, to be sent up unto the land of Zion. Behold, these things are in his own hands, let him do according to ,m."[2545] Again, we encounter the principle of choice: "These things are in his own hands, let him do according to wisdom." Brother Whitney and the Saints had received a commandment to consecrate, but the choice and the amount were left up to them. They were agents.

Agency and Self-reliance

The Lord intends that man is to be "an agent unto himself."[2546] But it is impossible to be an independent agent if we are not temporally and spiritually self-reliant. When circumstances jeopardize our self-reliance, our agency is also jeopardized. Likewise, the more we are dependent, ignorant, or impoverished, the less we can exercise our agency. According to President Marion G. Romney, our independence and agency to act are inexorably linked to our self-reliance, making self-reliance a critical key to our spiritual development.

Spiritual self-reliance depends on our ability, understanding, and willingness to exercise our agency and keep God's commandments. Invariably, the commandments demand that we choose to serve. Without our keeping the commandments, which leads to self-reliance, President Romney said, our ability to serve is limited. We cannot give from empty shelves; we cannot comfort if we are emotionally impoverished; we cannot instruct if we are ignorant; we cannot show others the way if we are spiritually deficient.

As we become more self-reliant, our agency increases; then we can better choose to serve and to help other people to become more self-reliant. President Romney went on to say that there is an interdependence between the rich and the poor. In the process of giving, both parties are sanctified: the impoverished person is freed from poverty and becomes self-reliant, whereupon as a free man he is free to rise to his full temporal and spiritual potential; the self-reliant rich person is blessed and multiplied by fulfilling the celestial law of giving. Keep in mind that wealth and poverty are defined in terms of things financial, emotional, educational, physical, and spiritual. A miracle occurs when we rescue an impoverished person. Now he is self-reliant and free to use his agency to rescue others. This is the cycle of Zion, which constantly repeats itself, rescuing, sanctifying, and exalting its participants.[2547]

But self-reliance is only the beginning of the blessings of Zion. On an elementary level, self-reliance allows us to take care of our own, but our agency to serve an increasing number of people is limited. As we have discussed elsewhere, Zion people practice giving with the assurance that the Lord will subsequently bless them "an hundredfold."[2548] If the Zion people will advance the process by giving again of the Lord's blessings, abundance will ensue, resulting in enough for Zion people to remain self-sufficient while they help others to become self-sufficient. This process is the Lord's "own way,"[2549] and the way he expects us to manage our stewardships.[2550]

Therefore, our agency (freedom and ability to choose) is proportional to our self-reliance. When we, who have a greater resource, reach down to lift an impoverished person to a higher degree of self-reliance, that person is then in a position to reach down and lift someone else. In each case,

---

[2544] Matthew 14:13–21.
[2545] D&C 63:43–44.
[2546] D&C 29:35.
[2547] Romney, "The Celestial Nature of Self-reliance," 61–65.
[2548] Matthew 19:29.
[2549] D&C 104:16.
[2550] Gardner, "Becoming a Zion Society," 31.

abundance results: the impoverished person is made whole, and we are rewarded "an hundredfold." Thus the ever-repeating cycle of Zion exalts its people, increases their agency, ensures their self-reliance, and prospers them. And it all begins with a choice.

AGENCY FUELED BY OPPOSITES

Opposition and opposites are the fuel of agency: "And it must needs be that the devil should tempt the children of men, or they could not be agents unto themselves; for if they never should have bitter they could not know the sweet."[2551] Therefore, we are free to choose our destiny—we can choose Zion's principles to our salvation, or we can choose Babylon's lack of principles to our condemnation. God provides us enough information to choose between the opposites: "Behold, here is the agency of man, and here is the condemnation of man; because that which was from the beginning is plainly manifest unto them, and they receive not the light."[2552]

Agency and freedom flourish in a Zionlike environment. "If the Son therefore shall make you free, ye shall be free indeed."[2553] Zion people enjoy the highest degree of both agency and freedom. "And because that they are redeemed from the fall they have become free forever, knowing good from evil; to act for themselves and not to be acted upon."[2554]

Whereas agency and freedom exist at their highest levels in a Zionlike environment, they decrease to abysmal levels in Babylon: "And the whole world [Babylon] lieth in sin, and groaneth under darkness and under the bondage of sin."[2555] Choosing Babylonian principles always results in fewer choices and less freedom; choosing Zion principles always results in limitless choices and unequalled freedom. If we ever hope to become Zionlike in this life and achieve the celestial kingdom in the life to come, we must exercise our God-given agency and choose to covenant and obey the law—consecration—upon which Zion lives are founded.

STEWARDSHIP

In the vocabulary of *consecration*, an agent is a steward.[2556] The trust extended to a steward is a stewardship, which, according to the *Encyclopedia of Mormonism*, is a "responsibility given through the Lord to act in behalf of others." The concept of stewardship reminds us of the principle that "all things ultimately belong to the Lord, whether property, time, talents, families, or capacity for service within the Church organization. An individual acts in a Church calling as a trustee for the Lord, not out of personal ownership or privilege." When we receive a stewardship, whether as a calling, a trust, or an inheritance, we are "expected to sacrifice time and talent in the service of others," which builds "a sense of community. When all serve, all may partake of the blessings of service. The ideal attitude toward stewardship suggests that it is not the position held but how well the work is done that counts."[2557] One can readily see why stewardship is central to Zion and the law of consecration.

THE RICHES OF THE EARTH ARE THE LORD'S

When a Zion person exercises his agency to live the law of consecration, he makes a conscious choice to become a steward of the Lord's property. His approach to ownership is that "the earth is the Lord's, and the fulness thereof."[2558] Elder Bruce R. McConkie said, "Underlying this principle of stewardship

---

[2551] D&C 29:39.
[2552] D&C 93:31.
[2553] John 8:36.
[2554] 2 Nephi 2:26.
[2555] D&C 84:49–50.
[2556] D&C 104:17.
[2557] *Encyclopedia of Mormonism*, 1418.
[2558] Psalm 24:1.

is the eternal gospel truth that all things belong to the Lord. 'I, the Lord, stretched out the heavens, and built the earth, my very handiwork; and all things therein are mine. . . . Behold, all these properties are mine. . . . And if the properties are mine, then ye are stewards; otherwise ye are no stewards.'"[2559] There can be no mistake about who owns what; the Lord states emphatically, "the riches of the earth are mine."[2560]

Even in a telestial setting, we encounter the concept of stewardship constantly. For example, a business owner will enter into an agreement to hand over the management of his company to a trusted employee, provided the employee gives his best effort, pursues the mission of the company, is committed to increasing the company's profitability, and is accountable to his employer. In return, the employer pays the employee a fair wage, with which the employee takes care of his family. The employee has no right to divide his attention with another interest, change the purpose of the company, use its resources outside his employer's desire, or take the profits for himself. We might ask ourselves, If we understand these principles on a telestial level, why can we not apply them to a celestial situation?

Let us examine the law of consecration in this light. By agreeing to take upon us this covenant, we agree that everything belongs to the Lord and we are stewards. From that point forward, we cease to lay claim to our time, talents, and possessions. Rather, we essentially enter into a *management agreement* with the Lord, in which we agree to give him our best and undivided effort as we administer the affairs of the stewardship that he places in our hands. We agree to pursue the ordained purpose of that stewardship, the core issue of which is always to assist in bringing to pass the immortality (the *quality* of immortality, whether telestial, terrestrial, or celestial) and the eternal life of man.[2561] Moreover, we agree to use and disseminate the stewardship's resources as the stewardship's Owner directs. We agree to magnify the stewardship, to take no more of the surplus than we are entitled to, and to be accountable to the Owner for our management of his resources. For the Lord's part, he agrees to allow us our agency in managing his resources, and he agrees to take care of us and keep us safe while we are on his errand.

In no uncertain terms, we are expressly forbidden to hoard the Lord's property or claim it as our own. Martin Harris learned this lesson: "I command thee that thou shalt not covet thine own property, but impart it freely to the printing of the Book of Mormon."[2562] At another time, the Lord commanded William E. McLellin to focus on proclaiming the gospel and to "think not of thy property."[2563] Clearly, a Zion person's claim to his property is subordinate to the Lord's claim. But if we view our property as our own and not as a stewardship, we break the law of consecration and step into sin: "Let them repent of all their sins, and of all their covetous desires, before me, saith the Lord; for what is property unto me?"[2564] Who can lay claim to property or tempt the Lord with it, especially when we know that everything belongs to him in the first place? We recall that Satan tried to entice Jesus with property and was soundly condemned: "Again, the devil taketh him up into an exceeding high mountain, and sheweth him all the kingdoms of the world, and the glory of them; and saith unto him, All these things will I give thee, if thou wilt fall down and worship me. Then saith Jesus unto him, Get thee hence, Satan."[2565]

On the other hand, as Martin Harris and William E. McLellin learned, our property is a stewardship that must be consecrated for the building up of the kingdom of God and the

---

[2559] McConkie, *Mormon Doctrine*, 767; quoting D&C 104:14, 55–56.
[2560] D&C 38:39.
[2561] Moses 1:39.
[2562] D&C 19:26.
[2563] D&C 66:6.
[2564] D&C 117:4.
[2565] Matthew 4:8–10.

establishment of Zion. The law of consecration provides that no poor should exist among us. Ultimately we will be held accountable for the diligence we pay to living this law and for the discharge of our stewardships.[2566]

God Becomes Our Paymaster

An early attempt to implement the law of consecration required members to deed over their property to the Church.[2567] Today, we are asked to figuratively deed over our hearts. We recognize that ultimately our time, talents, and property belong to the Lord, and we are stewards assigned to manage his resources under his direction. To appropriately fulfill our assignment, we agree to "live by every word that proceedeth forth from the mouth of God."[2568] Furthermore, we agree to become "submissive, meek, humble, patient, full of love," and "willing to submit" to the Lord.[2569] Then a remarkable thing happens: God helps us to depart from Babylon, and he becomes our Paymaster in Zion. Of course, this miracle is individualized for each person, but it occurs nevertheless.

The Lord takes care of those in his household; he supports the stewards in his employ, and "the laborer is worthy of his hire."[2570] What the Lord said to Warren A. Cowdery could be said to every steward in Zion: "[My steward shall] devote his whole time to this high and holy calling, which I now give unto him, seeking diligently the kingdom of heaven and its righteousness, *and all things necessary shall be added thereunto.*"[2571]

Now that the steward has been extracted and insulated from Babylon, he resides in the safety of his Lord, allowing him to devote his entire effort to his stewardships. In the transition, he ceases to labor for the cause of money and he begins to labor for the cause of Zion: "But the laborer in Zion shall labor for Zion; for if they labor for money they shall perish."[2572] This does not mean that the steward does not need money or to receive monetary compensation for his labor; rather, it means that the cause of Zion and managing his stewardship are his focus. The moment he views the stewardship as his own or attempts to accumulate the resources of the stewardship to himself, he is in conflict with the interests of his Paymaster. Even in Babylon, such an employee would be considered dishonest and an extortionist; he would be summarily dismissed and cast out. Any employee knows that the surpluses derived from his labor belong to the owner to do with as he pleases. The employee errs when he judges the employer's use and distribution of profits.

The righteous steward discovers that his Lord is a very generous Paymaster. What Elder Carlos E. Asay said of missionaries' meriting blessings for their labor could be said of any steward:

> The word merit is defined as "reward . . . just deserts" (*Webster's Third New International Dictionary*). Such a definition often turns our minds to temporal gains received for service rendered. It also suggests a dollar return on a dollar invested and nothing more. Another definition, however, refers to merit as "spiritual credit or stored moral surplusage regarded as earned by performance of righteous acts and as ensuring future benefits" (ibid.). This latter definition appeals to me and seems to apply to missionary service because the process of sharing the gospel with others is centered in "righteous acts" and

---

[2566] D&C 51:19; 72:3–4; 78:22, 82:3, 11; Matthew 25:14–30; Luke 16:2; 19:17.
[2567] D&C 42:30.
[2568] D&C 84:44.
[2569] Mosiah 3:19.
[2570] D&C 84:79.
[2571] D&C 106:3; emphasis added.
[2572] 2 Nephi 26:31.

carries "future benefits" for both the giver and the receiver. In fact, the list of spiritual credits or by-products received by those who seek to save souls is endless. *Those who engage in missionary service soon learn that God is a very generous paymaster. We can never place him in our debt* (see Mosiah 2:22–24).[2573]

Righteous stewards earn temporal and spiritual credits, which may be redeemed in the storehouse of their most generous Paymaster for many times their original value.

Never Turn Back

We must become a righteous steward. Once the Lord has separated us from Babylon, as is exemplified in the temple initiatory ordinances, and when he has placed within our care a stewardship in his kingdom, we must discharge our duty faithfully and never turn back.

Peter taught, "For if after they have escaped the pollutions of the world through the knowledge of the Lord and Saviour Jesus Christ, they are again entangled therein, and overcome, *the latter end is worse with them than the beginning*. For it had been better for them not to have known the way of righteousness, than, after they have known it, to turn from the holy commandment delivered unto them."[2574] The implications are sobering. If we have cried unto the Lord to help us escape Babylon, and then he rescues us and gives us a stewardship and *employment* in his kingdom—if, after all that, we weaken and return to Babylon and again become entangled in its charms, our situation will be worse than the first. We will find ourselves left alone with no further claim on the Lord's resources or on him as our Paymaster.

Nephi explained that the journey from Babylon to Zion is the most significant journey in time or eternity. Nothing could be more important than arriving at the tree of life and partaking of its fruit, both of which are symbolic of the love of God.[2575] When we finally reach our destination, we must stay. Otherwise, according to Nephi, every person who arrived at the tree and thereafter gave heed to Babylon "had fallen away."[2576] Here, then, is the safety and the condemnation of the law of stewardship.

The Law of Stewardship and the Oath and Covenant of the Priesthood

When righteous men (and later righteous men and women at the time of temple marriage) take upon them the oath and covenant of the priesthood, they agree to receive the blessings and obligations of the priesthood "for your sakes, and not for your sakes only, but for the sake of the world."[2577] That is, we are under covenant to exercise the priesthood to gain our salvation by helping to save others. Therefore, to fulfill this part of the priesthood covenant, we approach our stewardships with the attitude of caring for our families, caring for others, and caring for the Lord's purposes. Consider the Lord's admonition to the elders, who had taken upon them the oath and covenant of the priesthood:

> And behold, thou wilt remember the poor, and consecrate of thy properties for their support that which thou hast to impart unto them. . . . And inasmuch as ye impart of your substance unto the poor, ye will do it unto me; . . . every man shall be made accountable unto me, a steward over his own property, or that which he has

---

[2573] Asay, *The Seven M's of Missionary Service*, 9; emphasis added.
[2574] 2 Peter 2:20–21; emphasis added.
[2575] 1 Nephi 11:21–23.
[2576] 1 Nephi 8:34.
[2577] D&C 84:48.

received by consecration, as much as is sufficient for himself and family. And again, if there shall be properties in the hands of the church, or any individuals of it, more than is necessary for their support after this first consecration, which is a residue to be consecrated unto the bishop, it shall be kept to administer to those who have not, from time to time, that every man who has need may be amply supplied and receive according to his wants. Therefore, the residue shall be kept in my storehouse, to administer to the poor and the needy, . . . that my covenant people may be gathered in one in that day when I shall come to my temple. And this I do for the salvation of my people. . . . For inasmuch as ye do it unto the least of these, ye do it unto me. For it shall come to pass, that which I spake by the mouths of my prophets shall be fulfilled; for I will consecrate of the riches of those who embrace my gospel among the Gentiles unto the poor of my people who are of the house of Israel.[2578]

Stewardship and Equality

The law of stewardship is the law upon which Zion's equality is achieved. As we have mentioned, equality is defined as having equal access.[2579] In Zion, each person must have equal opportunity to receive a stewardship, to develop it, and to have equal access to the Lord and the Lord's resources. To qualify for the celestial kingdom, we must live the foundational law of stewardship,[2580] which stipulates that "every man [must be made] equal according to his family, according to his circumstances and his wants and needs."[2581]

Inequality is wholly telestial in nature; inequality cannot exist in a celestial atmosphere. As we recall, the Lord has stated emphatically that we must become "equal in the bonds of heavenly things, yea, and earthly things also, for the obtaining of heavenly things. For if ye are not equal in earthly things ye cannot be equal in obtaining heavenly things; for if you will that I give unto you a place in the celestial world, you must prepare yourselves by doing the things which I have commanded you and required of you."[2582]

Failing to live the law of stewardship and turning a blind eye to inequality are classified as sins: "But it is not given that one man should possess that which is above another, wherefore the world lieth in sin."[2583] We need only look at the world condition to see the consequences of selfishness, greed, and using the resources entrusted to us without accountability to God: "And the whole world lieth in sin, and groaneth under darkness and under the bondage of sin." How can we escape this darkness and bondage? The answer separates righteous Zion people from the wicked people of Babylon: "And by this you may know they [the people of Babylon] are under the bondage of sin, *because they come not unto me. For whoso cometh not unto me is under the bondage of sin. And whoso receiveth not my voice is not acquainted with my voice, and is not of me. And by this you may know the righteous from the wicked,* and that the whole world groaneth under sin and darkness even now."[2584]

[2578] D&C 42:30–39.
[2579] D&C 82:17.
[2580] D&C 101:5.
[2581] D&C 51:3.
[2582] D&C 78:3–5.
[2583] D&C 49:20.
[2584] D&C 84:50–53.

We might ask ourselves this question: Could it be possible to make the covenant of consecration, then ignore the law of stewardship with its injunction to equalize people—and still claim that we are acquainted with the voice of the Lord and that we have come unto him?

Zion people come unto Christ and hearken to his voice by seeking to purify their hearts; by seeking to equalize the condition of the Lord's children through the giving of their means; by striving to heal the Lord's children, bolster their faith, and love them. The *pure in heart* view themselves as stewards rather than owners, and they seek to bless the Lord's children with their stewardships, which is the sum of everything that they have and are.

STEWARDSHIPS IN THE SCRIPTURES

As we study the standard works, we discover the concept of stewardship throughout. Stewardships are also referred to as callings, trusts, charges, responsibilities, and inheritances or portions.[2585] Some stewardships are classified as spiritual while others are temporal.[2586] For example, a Church calling is a spiritual stewardship, while an individual's business and holdings are a temporal stewardship. Of course, even temporal things are spiritual unto the Lord.[2587]

In the early days of the Church, stewardships were also called inheritances or "portions." BYU professor Clark V. Johnson explained that the Lord "required the bishop of the Church to give every man an inheritance. [The Lord] explained that Church members were equal according to their family, circumstances, wants, and needs (D&C 51:4)." Here we see the principles of stewardship and accountability as they apply to an inheritance. We note that it is the bishop who assigns inheritances in Zion, and he is also the one who, in behalf of the Lord, receives an account of their management. Receiving and reporting on Church callings and tithing settlement are manifestations of these principles. With regard to the management of their stewardships, "the Lord reminded members of the Church that when they had enough to satisfy their needs, they were to give the surplus to the storehouse. Excess gained in the operation of the stewardship was to be used to administer to those who were in need (D&C 42:33–34). The bishop kept all surplus donated from the stewardships in a storehouse he organized (D&C 51:13)."[2588]

Even today we might expect to render accountings of our various stewardships to the bishop. For example, we make such an accounting to him when he interviews us for a temple recommend, and from time to time, when we counsel with him, we also make an accounting of our lives. Because the law of consecration requires that we consecrate our time, talents, and all that we have and are to the kingdom of God, the bulk of our stewardships usually lie outside the Church organization. Nevertheless, we are accountable for them to the Lord and to his servant, the bishop. Perhaps more blessings would flow to us if we lived the law of stewardship more faithfully and felt more accountability on each point of the law.

We would expect that our actual inheritances in priesthood society of Zion would follow the pattern described in Doctrine and Covenants 58: "This is a law unto every man that cometh unto this land to receive an inheritance; and he shall do with his moneys according as the law [of consecration] directs."[2589] Although we privately own our inheritances, we must consider them as consecrated

---

[2585] Genesis 26:5; Exodus 6:13; Numbers 4:4; 27:23; Matthew 18:23; 20:8; 21:33; 24:45; 25:21; Luke 12:42; 12:48; 16:2; 19:17; 1 Corinthians 4:2; 1 Timothy 4:14; Titus 1:7; 1 Peter 4:10; Jacob 1:19; 2:2; Alma 35:16; D&C 42:32, 70; 51:19; 64:40; 69:5; 70:4, 9; 72:3; 78:22; 82:3, 11; 101:90; 104:11, 55; 124:14; 136:27; JS–H 1:59; see also Genesis 48:22; Deuteronomy 32:9; Psalm 16:5; Isaiah 53:12; Zechariah 2:12; Luke 12:46; D&C 19:34; 51:3; 78:21; 104:18; 132:39.
[2586] D&C 42:33, 71.
[2587] D&C 29:34–35.
[2588] Johnson, "The Law of Consecration," 100.
[2589] D&C 58:36.

stewardships, and thus we are accountable to the Lord for them according to the law of accountability.[2590] If we live the law of stewardship, we are promised safety, for our consecrated effort is "to prepare [us] against the day of vengeance and burning."[2591] If we do not live this law, we run the risk of suffering the consequences: "If any man shall take of the abundance which I have made, and impart not his portion, according to the law of my gospel, unto the poor and the needy, he shall, with the wicked, lift up his eyes in hell, being in torment."[2592]

Understanding the Order of the Law of Stewardship

In section 104 of the Doctrine and Covenants, the Lord revealed the order by which inheritances (stewardships) are apportioned from the Lord's resources to us, the stewards. We are reminded that "the sacred things" which are "delivered into the treasury" are the Lord's, "and no man among you shall call it his own, or any part of it, for it shall belong to you *all* with one accord." The surplus derived from the management of the stewardship rightly belongs to Lord and must be placed in his sacred repository for the common good: "And thus shall ye preserve the avails of the sacred things in the treasury, for sacred and holy purposes. And this shall be called the sacred treasury of the Lord; and a seal shall be kept upon it that it may be holy and consecrated unto the Lord."[2593] The Lord's servant, the bishop, manages the treasury and the Lord's resources. This is the order of the law of stewardship.

In our day, we would call this sacred treasury the bishop's storehouse. Of course, the Church maintains other treasuries—for instance, monetary funds, warehouses of supplies, and service departments. We also read of sacred treasuries in heaven. For example, "Lay up for yourselves a treasure in heaven, yea, which is eternal, and which fadeth not away; yea, that ye may have that precious gift of eternal life."[2594] To access that heavenly treasury, we must sacrifice our personal treasures in this world: "Now when Jesus heard these things, he said unto [the rich young man], Yet lackest thou one thing: sell all that thou hast, and distribute unto the poor, and thou shalt have treasure in heaven: and come, follow me."[2595]

One definition of "treasure" is anything that is good. Under this definition, even our testimonies could be considered stewardships. We know that the law of consecration requires that every good thing that we receive from the Lord must be returned to him with increase. Interestingly, when we bear sincere testimony, our testimony grows,[2596] and that allows us to fulfill the law and return our testimony to the Lord with increase. Our bearing witness of the truth is much like casting our testimony into the treasury of heaven; in return, great blessings are unleashed: "Nevertheless, ye are blessed, for the testimony which ye have borne is recorded in heaven for the angels to look upon; and they rejoice over you, and your sins are forgiven you."[2597] "Also I say unto you, Whosoever shall confess me before men, him shall the Son of man also confess before the angels of God."[2598] Again, these blessings flow from the order of the law of stewardships.

Upon what principle do consecrated properties flow into the sacred treasuries? "Joseph Smith taught that the consecration of properties must be done by mutual consent. The bishop could not dictate in matters of consecration or he would have 'more power than a king.' The Prophet further

---

[2590] D&C 42:32.
[2591] D&C 85:3.
[2592] D&C 104:18.
[2593] D&C 104:64–66.
[2594] Helaman 5:8.
[2595] Luke 18:22.
[2596] Young, *Discourses of Brigham Young*, 335.
[2597] D&C 62:3.
[2598] Luke 12:8.

explained that there must be a balance of power between the bishop and the people in order to preserve 'harmony and good-will.'"[2599] Therefore, the bishop, who is the Lord's steward, is authorized to extend stewardships to his people; the people accept the stewardship and manage and account for it by their free-will choice; the people sustain the bishop in his calling. That sustaining is done by mutual covenant: the people agree to accept the bishop as the voice of the Lord, and he agrees to receive their accountings and judge them righteously in the Lord's name. In his office, the bishop is entrusted to receive free-will offerings from the surpluses of the stewards' stewardships, and he places those offerings in the common treasury. Then the stewards, who have common access to the treasury, may draw upon it, with the bishop's permission, for their needs and wants.

Clearly, the interaction between the stewards and the bishop is one of common consent. The bishop manages the treasury, assigns stewardships, and takes accountings, and the people sustain his actions, and through his ministry gain access to the Lord's treasury. Such transactions are to be done "only by the voice of the order, or by commandment. . . . And there shall not any part of it [the treasury's resource] be used, or taken out of the treasury, only by the voice and common consent of the order."[2600]

We see this law in action in every ward in the Church today. One of the highest manifestations of this law is that the steward receives access to the Lord's resources for the purpose of growing and managing his stewardship: "And this shall be the voice and common consent of the order—that any man among you say to the treasurer: I have need of this to help me in my stewardship."[2601] In whatever form the law of consecration and the law of stewardship exist, the order that governs those laws will always apply. By common consent, the bishop, who is sustained by the voice of the people, will always apportion, aid in, judge, and take accounting of all stewardships pertaining to the kingdom of God. This is the order of the law of consecration.

Spiritual Gifts Are Stewardships to Bless Others

The stewardships that the Lord places in our trust are our time, talents and abilities, and everything else that we are or possess. Some of these stewardships are listed in Doctrine and Covenants 46 and are called *spiritual gifts*. These gifts include:

- The gift of knowing—"that Jesus Christ is the Son of God, and that he was crucified for the sins of the world."
- The gift of believing—"on their words, that they also might have eternal life if they continue faithful."
- The gift of administration—"the differences of administration."
- The gift of "the diversities of operations, whether they be of God, that the manifestations of the Spirit may be given to every man to profit withal."
- The gift of "the word of wisdom."
- The gift of "the word of knowledge, that all may be taught to be wise and to have knowledge."
- The gift to have "faith to be healed."
- The gift to have "faith to heal."
- The gift of "the working of miracles."
- The gift of the ability "to prophesy."
- The gift of "discerning of spirits."

[2599] Johnson, "The Law of Consecration," 100; quoting Joseph Smith, *Teachings of the Prophet Joseph Smith*, 23.

[2600] D&C 104:64, 71.

[2601] D&C 104:72–73.

- The gift of speaking "with tongues."
- The gift of "the interpretation of tongues."[2602]

Why does the Lord give us these gifts as stewardships? The answer echoes the language in the priesthood covenant. We receive gifts from the Lord "for [our] sakes, and not for [our] sakes only, but for the sake of the world."[2603] The Lord said, "All these gifts come from God, for the benefit of the children of God."[2604] When we consider the Lord's answer, we recall other scriptural injunctions to consecrate our resources for the purpose of blessing other people: "For of him unto whom much is given much is required."[2605] "Freely ye have received, freely give."[2606] Clearly, we cannot achieve celestial glory without blessing others.

Significantly, Doctrine and Covenants 46 mirrors many of the principles stated in the parable of the talents,[2607] signaling to us the parable's latter-day relevance. Talents are gifts and therefore stewardships, and thus are to be used to bless the Lord's children. Because every person receives a gift or gifts from God, we are treated equally—a characteristic of Zion. Thus, the Lord says, "And you are to be equal, or in other words, you are to have equal claims on the properties, for the benefit of managing the concerns of your stewardships, every man according to his wants and his needs, inasmuch as his wants are just—*and all this for the benefit of the church of the living God, that every man may improve upon his talent, that every man may gain other talents, yea, even an hundred fold, to be cast into the Lord's storehouse, to become the common property of the whole church*—every man seeking the interest of his neighbor, and doing all things with an eye single to the glory of God."[2608]

These gifts, or talents, prepare us for the Lord's return; they "are suited to the gifts and needs of the individual to give him or her the maximum opportunity for growth in the Kingdom of God."[2609] How we manage our talents determines our eventual inheritance in the celestial kingdom. Joseph Smith taught: "Many of our brethren are wise in . . . their labors, and have rid their garments of the blood of this generation and are approved before the Lord."[2610]

Profitable and Unprofitable Servants

Jesus first introduced the idea of profitable and unprofitable servants in the parable of the talents.[2611] Over a century earlier, King Benjamin discussed the concept of serving profitably.[2612] Although our present mortal circumstances greatly hamper us from being profitable to the Lord, nevertheless, we must make the attempt, because profitability is central to our eternal progression and thus to the ever-expanding kingdom of God. When the Lord gives us a trust, we are to magnify it on our watch. Otherwise, as the parable of the talents states, the unprofitable servant is cast into outer darkness, where "there shall be weeping and gnashing of teeth."[2613]

[2602] D&C 46:13–25.
[2603] D&C 84:48.
[2604] D&C 46:13–25.
[2605] D&C 82:3.
[2606] Matthew 10:8.
[2607] Matthew 25:14–30.
[2608] D&C 82:17–19; emphasis added.
[2609] Johnson, "The Law of Consecration," 100.
[2610] Smith, *Evening and Morning Star*, July 1833.
[2611] Matthew 25:14–30.
[2612] Mosiah 2:20–21.
[2613] Matthew 25:30.

At least two criteria lead to profitability: (1) our being "anxiously engaged in a good cause, do[ing] many things of [our] own free will, and bring[ing] to pass much righteousness,"[2614] and (2) yielding our hearts and wills to God.[2615] Because we are agents with agency, we are endowed with the power of choice and the capability to magnify our stewardships. The goal of our creative effort is to "bring to pass much righteousness."

We also learn that the greater the profitability of the stewardship, the greater the trusts that God will eventually place in our care. Commenting on the teachings of Joseph Smith, Orson Hyde wrote:

> The most eminent and distinguished prophets who have laid down their lives for their testimony (Jesus among the rest), will be crowned at the head of the largest kingdoms under the Father, and will be one with Christ as Christ is one with his Father; for their kingdoms are all joined together, and such as do the will of the Father, the same are his mothers, sisters, and brothers. He that has been faithful over a few things, will be made ruler over many things; he that has been faithful over ten talents, shall have dominion over ten cities, and he that has been faithful over five talents, shall have dominion over five cities, and to every man will be given a kingdom and a dominion, according to his merit, powers, and abilities to govern and control. . . . There are kingdoms of all sizes, an infinite variety to suit all grades of merit and ability. The chosen vessels unto God are the kings and priests that are placed at the head of these kingdoms. These have received their washings and anointings in the temple of God on this earth; they have been chosen, ordained, and anointed kings and priests, to reign as such in the resurrection of the just.[2616]

For the present, our maximum effort will not generate the maximum *profits* that our stewardship is capable of producing. For that to happen, we must draw upon the principle of grace; we must humbly yield our wills to God, submit to his counsel, and allow him to do for us what we cannot do for ourselves. Only by such a partnership can the stewardship reach the summit of its potential. We are greatly benefitted by such a relationship. Elder Neal A. Maxwell taught that we enhance our individuality by yielding our wills to God; that is, as we are stretched and molded by him, we become more capable of receiving "all that the Father hath."[2617] He concluded by saying we simply could not be entrusted with God's "all" until our wills more closely corresponded to God's will.

Profitable servants improve upon that with which they have been entrusted; they employ sound management principles by reducing waste and insisting that invested resources generate an appropriate return; they are tireless workers and represent well the person to whom they are accountable: "O ye that embark in the service of God, see that ye serve him with all your heart, might, mind and strength."[2618] Then, when profits are produced over and above that which the servant needs to care for his family and himself, the servant releases that surplus to the Lord, to whom the surplus rightly belongs: "Nevertheless, inasmuch as they receive more than is needful for their necessities and their wants, it shall be given into my storehouse; and the benefits shall be consecrated

---

[2614] D&C 58:27.
[2615] Helaman 3:35.
[2616] Smith, *The Words of Joseph Smith*, 299.
[2617] D&C 84:38.
[2618] D&C 4:2.

unto the inhabitants of Zion, and unto their generations, inasmuch as they become heirs according to the laws of the kingdom. Behold, this is what the Lord requires of every man in his stewardship, even as I, the Lord, have appointed or shall hereafter appoint unto any man. And behold, none are exempt from this law who belong to the church of the living God."[2619]

How happy are the profitable servants who can report to God that they have accomplished everything that they were charged to do. They will hear: "Well done, thou good and faithful servant: thou hast been faithful over a few things, I will make thee ruler over many things."[2620]

Stewardships Prepare Us for Eternal Life

Because the law of consecration is the law of the celestial kingdom,[2621] we might expect to receive, develop, and account for stewardships there.[2622] This assumption is evidenced in the Lord's promise to righteous couples who are sealed in the temple and keep their marriage covenant. He promises that they "shall inherit thrones, kingdoms, principalities, and powers, dominions, all heights and depths."[2623] The fact that this list contains diverse stations stated in the plural suggests that our celestial assignments and inheritances might shift and expand throughout the eternities, as we progress in our Father's kingdom. We also might expect that we will receive these stewardships by consecration, and that we will be held accountable for them. To develop our celestial stewardships, we might expect that we would draw upon the Father's vast resources to improve and manage our stewardships, and, in turn, we would consecrate the resources thereof back to his higher kingdom to which we belong. If that is the case, if we intend to achieve that exalted state and live in that priesthood society, we must first learn to live the laws of consecration and stewardship here and now.

The Lord said, "And whoso is found a faithful, a just, and a wise steward shall enter into the joy of his Lord, and shall inherit eternal life."[2624] And Elder McConkie added, "It is by the wise use of one's stewardship that eternal life is won."[2625]

Accountability

As always, Jesus Christ sets the example for stewardship and accountability. We are taught that he is the steward as Creator under the Father's direction.[2626] The Father creates everything spiritually; then Jesus creates everything physically as an exact duplicate of the spiritual.[2627] Upon completion, he returns to the Father, gives his report, and the Father pronounces his approval. Just so, it behooves every steward to strive to discover the Father's spiritual creation of his stewardship, duplicate it according to the Father's vision, then return to the Father and report. We could receive no greater confirmation from the Father's commendation that we were good and faithful servants.[2628]

We see in Jesus' example all of the guiding principles of consecration. He exercises his agency to do the Father's will; he is given a stewardship in which he duplicates the Father's spiritual creation; he gives accountings to the Father of his management of his stewardship; and he brings to the stewardship his concerted labor. For this, Jesus is exalted on high and receives his Father's throne.

[2619] D&C 70:8–10.
[2620] Matthew 25:21.
[2621] D&C 105:4–5.
[2622] D&C 88:107.
[2623] D&C 132:19.
[2624] D&C 51:19.
[2625] McConkie, *Mormon Doctrine*, 767.
[2626] Moses 7:29; John 1:1–3; Colossians 1:16–17; Hebrews 1:1–3; D&C 38:1–4; 76:22–24; Abraham 3:22–24.
[2627] McConkie, *Mormon Doctrine*, 170.
[2628] Matthew 25:21, 23.

Accounting in Time and Eternity

All stewards ultimately receive their stewardships from the Father, and they must account for their stewardships to him. The Father delegates the giving of stewardships and the receiving of accountings to Jesus Christ, who is the Father's representative. It is Jesus Christ who will judge our efforts.[2629]

In addition to our being accountable to the Father and the Son, we are also accountable to the Lord's representative, the bishop. Clark V. Johnson wrote, "The Lord reminded his prophet, who subsequently reminded Church members, that they were the Lord's stewards and therefore, had to account for their stewardship 'both in time and in eternity.' (D&C 72:3; see also 70:4, 9.) The accounting procedures were quite clear. First, members accounted to the bishop for their stewardship as well as for their personal conduct. (D&C 72:5, 16–17; 104:12–13.) And second, they will ultimately account to their Father in heaven."[2630] The scripture states: "And an account of this stewardship will I require of them in the day of judgment."[2631]

At the time of accounting, at least three things are certain in both time and eternity:

1. Diligence in lesser stewardships results in receiving greater stewardships: "And he that is a faithful and wise steward shall inherit all things."[2632] "For he who is faithful and wise in time is accounted worthy to inherit the mansions prepared for him of my Father."[2633]
2. The greater the stewardship, the greater the accountability: "To whom much is given, much is required."[2634]
3. While the faithful and wise steward is rewarded, the unjust or slothful steward gains but little, and may even lose what he has: "Take therefore the talent from him, and give it unto him which hath ten talents."[2635] The stewardship continues, but the slothful steward loses the opportunity to work with it.

A stewardship that is extended through a Church calling is reported to the Lord's representative, who is the steward's immediate superior.[2636] "For example, a ward Relief Society president reports to the bishop of her ward. A bishop reports to his stake president."[2637] Zion people are under covenant to account for their earthly stewardships to the Lord's servant, the bishop: "Verily I say unto you, the elders of the church in this part of my vineyard shall render an account of their stewardship unto the bishop, who shall be appointed of me in this part of my vineyard. These things shall be had on record, to be handed over unto the bishop in Zion."[2638] For this reason, we report our financial stewardship regarding our tithes and offerings to the bishop each year.

On the day of judgment, each of us will be required to render our report to Jesus Christ, who will give a report to the Father: "The primary accounting is with the Lord. He knows a person's heart, intentions, and talents."[2639]

[2629] Luke 16:2; 19:17.
[2630] Johnson, "The Law of Consecration," 100.
[2631] D&C 70:4.
[2632] D&C 78:22.
[2633] D&C 72:3–4.
[2634] Luke 12:48; D&C 82:3.
[2635] Matthew 25:28.
[2636] Clarke, "Successful Welfare Stewardship," 81.
[2637] *Encyclopedia of Mormonism*, 1418.
[2638] D&C 72:5–6.
[2639] *Encyclopedia of Mormonism*, 1418.

Accountability and Agency

In Galatians we read, "Be not deceived; God is not mocked: for whatsoever a man soweth, that shall he also reap."[2640] That is, we are free to choose, but we are responsible for how we choose, and because our agency is a stewardship, we are accountable to God for our use of this gift.[2641]

The principle of agency applies to how we manage the resources that the Lord places in our hands. Mormon foresaw the latter-day abandonment of the concept of stewardship, our contrary choices with regard to the Lord's resources, and our present abysmal lack of accountability: "Why do ye adorn yourselves with that which hath no life, and yet suffer the hungry, and the needy, and the naked, and the sick and the afflicted to pass by you, and notice them not? Yea, why do ye . . . cause that widows should mourn before the Lord, and also orphans to mourn before the Lord?"[2642]

Our freedom to choose is a stewardship that carries accountability that we cannot escape. When we receive any stewardship from the Lord, whether it be in the form of time, talents, resources, property, or any other good thing, we will render an accounting both in time and eternity. How we report will determine our receiving additional trusts, and our report will determine whether we qualify to receive all that the Father has or instead will forfeit our stewardship and inherit little to nothing.

Labor

Consecration demands all that we have and are, including our effort. When we are given a stewardship from God, we magnify it by our labor. Elder Bruce R. McConkie wrote, "Work is the great basic principle which makes all things possible both in time and in eternity. Men, spirits, angels, and Gods use their physical and mental powers in work."[2643]

Work, like other principles, exists in degrees ranging from telestial to celestial. Adam was commanded to work to support his family in this telestial world.[2644] He made his labor a celestial endeavor by his attitude toward his work. He clearly understood that he was to use his stewardship to support his family and to support the kingdom of God for the establishment of Zion. He was not to use his stewardship, as did Cain, for empire building, plundering, extorting, leveraging, competing, augmenting his balance sheet, or amassing personal wealth on the backs of the poor, all of which are telestial approaches to labor. Rather, Adam worked to create the first Zionlike society upon the earth: Adam-ondi-Ahman. W. W. Phelps captures that idea in his hymn: "And men did live a holy race and worship Jesus face to face in Adam-ondi-Ahman."[2645] There he labored to sustain his immediate family and to bless the lives of others.

Likewise, Enoch labored to support his family and to establish Zion, as did Melchizedek. Nephi is another example: "And it came to pass that I, Nephi, did cause my people to be industrious, and to labor with their hands."[2646] Nephi's people worked together for the benefit of all. They labored to establish righteousness. They worked in unity to raise crops, smelt ore to create weapons for defense, and fashion objects of beauty. Together, they built buildings and a temple. Because of their celestial level of labor they were blessed with prosperity and familial strength: "And it came to pass that we began to prosper exceedingly, and to multiply in the land."[2647] Things began to fall apart when the Nephites became selfish and began to work on a telestial level. Jacob chastised them for searching "for gold, and for silver, and for all manner of precious ores" for the purpose of obtaining riches "more abundantly than that of your brethren," causing some errant Nephites to be "lifted up in the pride of

---

[2640] Galatians 6:7.
[2641] Cannon, "Agency and Accountability," 88–89.
[2642] Mormon 8:39–40.
[2643] McConkie, *Mormon Doctrine*, 847.
[2644] Genesis 3:19.
[2645] Phelps, "Adam-ondi-Ahman," *Hymns*, no. 49.
[2646] 2 Nephi 5:17.
[2647] 2 Nephi 5:10–16.

your hearts, and . . . suppose that ye are better than they."[2648] This kind of labor is not justified in Zion; it is condemned. President Kimball said, "As I understand these matters, Zion can be established only by those who are pure in heart, and who labor for Zion, for the 'laborer in Zion shall labor for Zion; for if they labor for money [riches] they shall perish.'"[2649]

Jacob taught the celestial law of labor and its underlying motivation: "Think of your brethren like unto yourselves, and be familiar with all and free with your substance, that they may be rich like unto you. But before ye seek for riches, seek ye for the kingdom of God. And after ye have obtained a hope in Christ ye shall obtain riches, if ye seek them; and ye will seek them for the intent to do good—to clothe the naked, and to feed the hungry, and to liberate the captive, and administer relief to the sick and the afflicted."[2650] Clearly, we must work, but what we work for determines whether the work is telestial or celestial.

IDLENESS CONDEMNED

"Idleness has no place [in Zion]," said President Benson, "and greed, selfishness, and covetousness are condemned. [Zion] may therefore operate only with a righteous people."[2651]

When the Lord revealed the law of the Church (D&C 42), which sets forth the law of consecration, he condemned the idler—both the poor and the rich idlers: "Thou shalt not be idle; for he that is idle shall not eat the bread nor wear the garments of the laborer."[2652] The Lord insists that Zion be founded upon the principle of industry and thrift: "Behold, they have been sent to preach my gospel among the congregations of the wicked; wherefore, I give unto them a commandment, thus: Thou shalt not idle away thy time, neither shalt thou bury thy talent that it may not be known."[2653]

THE IDLE POOR

The Lord denounces wanton idleness, its attendant pride, and the attitude of entitlement: "Wo unto you poor men, whose hearts are not broken, whose spirits are not contrite, and whose bellies are not satisfied, and whose hands are not stayed from laying hold upon other men's goods, whose eyes are full of greediness, and who will not labor with your own hands!"[2654]

On the other hand, the Lord opens his storehouse to the poor who are trying their best.[2655] Beyond his agreeing to help the poor in their present circumstance, he promises to compensate them for their suffering with rich abundance in the future: "But blessed are the poor who are pure in heart, whose hearts are broken, and whose spirits are contrite, for they shall see the kingdom of God coming in power and great glory unto their deliverance; for the fatness of the earth shall be theirs. For behold, the Lord shall come, and his recompense shall be with him, and he shall reward every man, and the poor shall rejoice."[2656]

On the other hand, the idle poor need to beware. To shirk one's familial duties or to approach a stewardship apathetically is akin to apostasy: "But if any provide not for his own, and specially for those of his own house, he hath denied the faith, and is worse than an infidel." Such people tend to

---

[2648] Jacob 2:12–14.
[2649] Kimball, *The Teachings of Spencer W. Kimball*, 363.
[2650] Jacob 2:17–19.
[2651] Benson, "A Vision and a Hope for the Youth of Zion," 74.
[2652] D&C 42:42.
[2653] D&C 60:13.
[2654] D&C 56:17.
[2655] Deuteronomy 15:7–11; 24:19; 2 Thessalonians 3:10.
[2656] D&C 56:18–19.

perfect the skill of idleness by roaming here and there, and preying on the goodhearted laborers: "And withal they learn [to be] idle, wandering about from house to house."[2657]

The Lord warns that such idleness sets a bad example that will condemn the idlers and spill over into the next generation: "And the inhabitants of Zion also shall remember their labors, inasmuch as they are appointed to labor, in all faithfulness; for the idler shall be had in remembrance before the Lord. Now, I, the Lord, am not well pleased with the inhabitants of Zion, for there are idlers among them; and their children are also growing up in wickedness; they also seek not earnestly the riches of eternity, but their eyes are full of greediness. These things ought not to be, and must be done away from among them."[2658]

Our mandate is to cease to be idle and expend exerted effort in all our stewardships—family, Church callings, time, talents, and everything that the Lord has given and all that we are. Our eternal salvation depends upon how well we labor: "Behold, I say unto you that it is my will that you should go forth and not tarry, neither be idle but labor with your might. . . . And again, verily I say unto you, that every man who is obliged to provide for his own family, let him provide, and he shall in nowise lose his crown; and let him labor. . . . Let every man be diligent in all things. And the idler shall not have place in the church, except he repent and mend his ways."[2659]

However, when the legitimate poor need help, the Lord has provided a means of assistance. The Lord's stewards are to use the resources and surpluses of their stewardships to help the poor become self-reliant and independent as much as possible. Often, this aid comes through the bishop. The Lord has revealed a hierarchy of aid to the poor. When a person has done all he can temporally and spiritually, he should go first to his family for help and then the Church.[2660] It makes sense. Both the family and the Church are Zion organizations charged with helping the poor.

But help does not stop there. Because we are "agents," who are commanded to "be anxiously engaged in a good cause, and do many things of [our] own free will, and bring to pass much righteousness,"[2661] we must attack poverty and suffering wherever we encounter them, stretching forth a helping hand, lifting up the impoverished person, and placing him in a situation where his labor will sustain him.

THE IDLE RICH

The rich, who hold people in poverty, living a life of luxury and idleness from the efforts of the poor people's labor, are also condemned by the Lord. An article in the 1936 *Improvement Era* reads: "'Suspended animation' is the prerogative of no man. . . . The fact that the man of comparative wealth needs no food or comfort or service does not excuse him from producing needful goods or services for those who are in want."[2662]

Hugh Nibley offered this insight regarding the scripture about the idler: "'The idler shall not eat the bread of the laborer,' which means that the idle rich shall not eat the bread of the laboring poor. That's the way it has been throughout history; the poor have been ground down supporting the rich. Brigham said, 'Man has become so perverted as to debar his fellows as much as possible from these blessings, and constrain them by physical force or circumstances to contribute the proceeds of their labor to sustain the favored few.'"[2663]

[2657] 1 Timothy 5:8, 13.
[2658] D&C 68:30–32.
[2659] D&C 75:3, 28–29.
[2660] "Statement of the Presiding Bishopric," 20.
[2661] D&C 58:27–28.
[2662] Editorial, "The Right to Labor," *Improvement Era*, Sept. 1936.
[2663] Nibley, *Teachings of the Book of Mormon*, Semester 1, 233; quoting Brigham Young, *Millennial Star* 17:673–74.

Hugh Nibley defined idlers as those persons who neglect laboring for Zion. He also denounced wealthy people whose riches allow them a life of pleasure, while the poor suffer:

> An idler in the Lord's book is one who is not working for the building up of the kingdom of God on earth and the establishment of Zion, no matter how hard he may be working to satisfy his own greed. Latter-day Saints prefer to ignore that distinction as they repeat a favorite maxim of their own invention, that the idler shall not eat the bread or wear the clothing of the laborer. And what an ingenious argument they make of it! The director of a Latter-day Saint Institute was recently astounded when this writer pointed out to him that the ancient teaching that the idler shall not eat the bread of the laborer has always meant that the idle rich shall not eat the bread of the laboring poor, as they always have. "To serve the classes that are living on them," Brigham Young reports from England, "the poor, the laboring men and women are toiling, working their lives out to earn that which will keep a little life in them. Is this equality? No! What is going to be done? The Latter-day Saints will never accomplish their mission until this inequality shall cease on the earth." But the institute director was amazed, because he had always been taught that the idle poor should not eat the bread of the laboring rich, because it is perfectly obvious that a poor man has not worked as hard as a rich man. With the same lucid logic my Latter-day Saint students tell me that there were no poor in the Zion of Enoch because only the well-to-do were admitted to the city.[2664]

Clearly, the rich people in Zion are to labor alongside the poor for the cause of Zion. The rich are to lift the poor rather than suppress or ignore them. They are to increase their stewardships for the Lord's purposes and not their own, and those purposes, according to the covenant of consecration, are for the building up of God's kingdom on the earth and the establishment of Zion. Beyond these points, an idler is anyone, poor or rich, who is under covenant to advance the cause of Zion and does not.

THE VIRTUE OF LABOR

President David O. McKay said, "Work brings happiness, and that happiness is doubled to him who initiates the work."[2665] President Spencer W. Kimball concurred: "Work brings happiness, self-esteem, and prosperity. It is the means of all accomplishment; it is the opposite of idleness. We are commanded to work. Attempts to obtain our temporal, social, emotional, or spiritual well-being by means of a dole violate the divine mandate that we should work for what we receive. Work should be the ruling principle in the lives of our Church membership."[2666]

On the day the Church was organized, the Lord linked labor with significant rewards. He declared, "I will bless all those who labor in my vineyard with a mighty blessing."[2667] Later he said to Amos Davies the same thing he would say to each of us: "Let him . . . labor with his own hands that he may obtain the confidence of men."[2668] Clearly, to qualify for double happiness, as President

---

[2664] Nibley, *Approaching Zion*, 240–41.
[2665] McKay, *Gospel Ideals*, 204.
[2666] Kimball, "Welfare Services," 76; referencing Genesis 3:19; D&C 42:42; 56:17; 68:30–32; 75:29.
[2667] D&C 21:9.
[2668] D&C 124:112.

The Guiding Principles of Consecration

McKay said, along with self-respect, prosperity, gaining the confidence of our fellowmen, and receiving the Lord's mighty blessing, we must labor and consecrate that labor to the Lord.

Labor for What?

An intriguing verse concerning labor is found in 2 Nephi 26:31: "But the laborer in Zion shall labor for Zion; for if they labor for money they shall perish."[2669] Obviously, we cannot be compensated with money for laboring in our Church callings. But this verse could also mean that laboring for money as a priority is unacceptable to Zion people. As we consider the hierarchy of compensation in a Zion person's life against the hierarchy of compensation that exists in Babylon, we realize that we might want to change our priorities. For example, a father in Zion must selflessly labor to support his family, provide for the education of his children, save for a rainy day, and build up the kingdom of God, but he is forbidden to step into Babylon and selfishly accumulate wealth for himself. The Lord has warned us: "Thou shalt not covet thine own property."[2670]

Achieving balance can be challenging.

We are taught that laboring for money is strictly prohibited as we fulfill Church callings, but it is allowed when we labor to support our family and provide for their future needs. When we begin to view our responsibilities as stewardships, we begin to see where the delineation comes between providing for and selfishly accumulating. Stewards are under covenant to manage their stewardships and receive fair compensation according to the rules that govern the stewardships. As a test, we might ask ourselves if we recognize that everything we have belongs to the Lord and that we are stewards over our property. Are we doing with his money and resources what he has mandated, or do we seldom discuss with him his desires concerning them?

Speaking of labor in Zion, Hugh Nibley said:

> The whole emphasis in the holy writ is not on whether one works or not, but what one works for: "The laborer in Zion shall labor for Zion; for if they labor for money they shall perish" (2 Nephi 26:31). "The people of the church began to wax proud, because of their exceeding riches . . . precious things, which they had obtained by their industry" (Alma 4:6) and which proved their undoing, for all their hard work. *In Zion you labor, to be sure, but not for money, and not for yourself.*

Then, quoting Brigham Young, Brother Nibley said,

> "If we lust . . . for the riches of the world, and spare no pains [hard work] to obtain and retain them, and feel 'these are mine,' then the spirit of the anti-Christ comes upon us. This is the danger . . . [we] are in." Admirable and indispensable in themselves, hard work, ingenuity, and enterprise become an evil when they are misdirected, meaning directed to personal aggrandizement: "A man says, 'I am going to make iron, and I will have the credit of making the first iron in the Territory. I will have the credit of knowing how to flux the ore that is found in these regions, and bringing out the metal in abundance, or no other man shall.' Now, the beauty and glory of this kind of proceeding is the blackest of darkness, and its

---

[2669] 2 Nephi 26:31.
[2670] Gardner, "Becoming a Zion Society," 31; quoting D&C 19:26.

comeliness as deformity." An act, good in itself, becomes a monstrous deformity when thus misdirected.[2671]

Building up the kingdom of God for the establishment of Zion should be the one and only reason why a covenant Zion person labors. When he sees his family, career, time, talents, interests, Church callings, and everything good through the lens of Zion, he is approaching his labor according to the covenant of consecration. As Zion people, we must exert as much effort as possible in the cause of Zion; this is our calling and our stewardship: "Therefore, O ye that embark in the service of God, see that ye serve him with all your heart, might, mind and strength, that ye may stand blameless before God at the last day."[2672]

A Zion person, who has entered the new and everlasting covenant by baptism, who has thereafter been charged by the holy commission of the priesthood to draw out from Babylon the Lord's children, who has been washed clean and separated from the world, who has been anointed to receive a kingdom and a crown, who has been endowed with keys of knowledge and power, and who, finally, has been placed in an eternal kingdom—such a person can never again return to Babylon and labor as do the people of the world, laboring for the sake of money and claiming it as his own. To the laborers in Zion, the Lord said, "I give unto you a commandment, that every man, both elder, priest, teacher, and also member, go to with his might, with the labor of his hands, to prepare and accomplish the things which I have commanded."[2673] What has he commanded? To labor to build up the kingdom of God for the establishment of Zion.

Augmenting the Effect of Labor

Perhaps one of the greatest discoveries that we make in this life is that we can do very little of ourselves. What we might label genius or extraordinary ability was given to us as a stewardship by God. He is the one who gave us what we have. He is the one who created us, who preserves us, who lends us breath, and who makes it possible for us to live and move and do according to our will from moment to moment.[2674] He is our Paymaster. Should he ever withdraw his Spirit from us, our fortunes would simultaneously collapse. Therefore, if we hope to support ourselves or prosper, we must always give thanks to God, obey him, and live according to his laws that govern consecration and stewardship. By doing so, we will augment the effects, effectiveness, and the rewards of our labor.

Jacob gave us the doctrine and the priorities of labor: "Think of your brethren like unto yourselves, and be familiar with all and free with your substance, that they may be rich like unto you. But before ye seek for riches, seek ye for the kingdom of God. And after ye have obtained a hope in Christ ye shall obtain riches, if ye seek them; and ye will seek them for the intent to do good—to clothe the naked, and to feed the hungry, and to liberate the captive, and administer relief to the sick and the afflicted."[2675] That is, when we labor within the stipulations of the laws of consecration and stewardship, we place ourselves in a position to call upon the Lord to help us augment our labor to bless the lives of others, which is our covenant. In return, the Lord will answer our sincere petition and give us the resources to help us fulfill our consecration covenant.

An example of partnering with the Lord to augment our labor is the law of tithes and offerings. This law prospers, protects, and exalts its adherents. Malachi lists the stipulations and blessings of this law:

[2671] Nibley, *Approaching Zion*, 48–49; emphasis added.
[2672] D&C 4:2.
[2673] D&C 38:40.
[2674] Mosiah 2:21.
[2675] Jacob 2:17–19.

Prosperity. From the fruits of our labors, we are to "bring . . . all the tithes into the storehouse, that there may be meat in mine house, and prove me now herewith, saith the Lord of hosts, if I will not open you the windows of heaven, and pour you out a blessing, that there shall not be room enough to receive it."

Protection. "And I will rebuke the devourer for your sakes, and he shall not destroy the fruits of your ground; neither shall your vine cast her fruit before the time in the field, saith the Lord of hosts."

Exaltation. "And all nations shall call you blessed: for ye shall be a delightsome land, saith the Lord of hosts."[2676]

Because tithes and offerings are part of the law of consecration, and because stewardships are tithed, we may rely on the Lord's promises. He will augment our labors for our support, prosperity, protection, and exaltation. Then we are to use those blessings for the Lord's purposes: to bless our families and to bless the children of God.

LABOR AND JUDGMENT

We read in the Doctrine and Covenants that we will give accountings to and receive rewards from the Lord in the day of judgment: "[When the Lord comes he will] recompense unto every man according to his work."[2677] We determine our eternal status by our attitude toward labor and how we prioritize our efforts with regard to our stewardships.

Brigham Young said our achieving the celestial or a lower kingdom and our becoming a god or a servant will depend upon the quality of and our attitude toward labor. President Young compared many Saints in his day to the Savior's parable of the unprofitable servant: "'How shall I get this or that; how rich can I get; or, how much can I get out of this brother or from that brother?' and dicker and work, and take advantage here and there—no such man ever can magnify the priesthood nor enter the celestial kingdom. Now, remember, they will not enter that kingdom; and if they happen to go there, it will be because somebody takes them by the hand, saying, 'I want you for a servant'; or, 'Master, will you let this man pass in my service?' 'Yes, he may go into your service; but he is not fit for a lord, nor a master, nor fit to be crowned'; and if such men get there, it will be because somebody takes them in as servants."[2678]

"President Marion G. Romney taught that our salvation depends on our laboring to do all we can, whereupon we receive the Lord's grace to make up the difference. Further, he said, we cannot expect to achieve exaltation on the work of someone else." Exerting our own labor is the key to achieving exaltation, as long as our labor is consistent with the laws of the celestial kingdom. From the days of Adam, the Lord has said that individual effort is the foundation of his spiritual and temporal economy. That economy demands "that the poor shall be exalted, in that the rich are made low."[2679] By adhering to the Lord's economy, both the poor and the rich labor and both are blessed: the poor are exalted by the rich and helped to become self-reliant, assuming that the poor are doing all they can do; the rich are made low (lowly in heart) when they help the poor by living the second commandment—"Thou shalt love thy neighbour as thyself"[2680]—and impart of their substance "according to the law of [the] gospel, unto the poor and the needy."[2681] If we will prioritize our labor according to the law of consecration and strive with all our "heart, might, mind and strength" to labor for Zion and not for money, we will be able to "stand blameless before God at the last day."[2682]

[2676] Malachi 3:10–12.
[2677] D&C 1:10; see also D&C 112:34.
[2678] Young, *Journal of Discourses,* 11:297.
[2679] D&C 104:16.
[2680] Matthew 22:39.
[2681] D&C 104:18; see Romney, "'In Mine Own Way,'" 123.
[2682] D&C 4:2.

Summary and Conclusion

The guiding principles of the law of consecration are agency, stewardship, accountability, and labor. By abiding by these principles, we achieve equality, which is a characteristic of the celestial kingdom. That is, we are given equal access to the stewardships, inheritances, and resources of the Lord. The "order" that this celestial system creates is to be considered "a permanent and everlasting establishment and order unto my church, to advance the cause, which ye have espoused, to the salvation of man, and to the glory of your Father who is in heaven."[2683] Additionally, these guiding principles of consecration prepare us for the trials of the last days and the coming of the Savior.

Agency, stewardship, accountability, and labor form an unbreakable foundation upon which consecration thrives. God gives us both the liberty and the capability to choose and to act. By exercising our agency, we choose to escape Babylon and flee to the safety of Zion and its covenants. There, we choose to enter into the new and everlasting covenant and follow the path to exaltation by receiving the oath and covenant of the priesthood, then the temple covenants and ordinances, which culminate with the law of consecration, one of the final covenants that we must make in order to enter into God's presence and thereafter receive our eternal kingdom.

Now we are a Zion person. Now we choose to view everything that we have and are as a stewardship, and thus we qualify to approach God so that he might make us independent and self-reliant, both temporally and spiritually. Now we are accountable stewards. As such, we have (1) freedom to use the proceeds of our stewardship to provide for our personal needs, and (2) the charge to consecrate the surplus of our stewardship to bless God's needy children. Moreover, we stewards agree to apply our diligent labor to our stewardship, striving always to create a physical manifestation of our stewardship according to what God has already created spiritually.

As we discharge our stewardship righteously, we enter into a system of celestial compensation; God becomes our Paymaster. However our living is provided, we trace the source back to God.

The law of consecration stipulates that we be given agency to choose and act, but that we then consecrate our agency back to God in the form of a broken heart and a contrite spirit, allowing our will to be swallowed up in the will of the Father. In return, God agrees to take care of us and guide us as we manage the affairs of our stewardship. Furthermore, we agree to "live by every word that proceedeth forth from the mouth of God"[2684] and become "submissive, meek, humble, patient, full of love," and "willing to submit" to the Lord.[2685] Our effort allows him to bless us, "every man according to his wants and his needs, inasmuch as his wants are just—and all this for the benefit of the church of the living God, that every man may improve upon his talent, that every man may gain other talents, yea, even an hundred fold, to be cast into the Lord's storehouse, to become the common property of the whole church—every man seeking the interest of his neighbor, and doing all things with an eye single to the glory of God."[2686] By doing these things, we are called profitable and just stewards.

Through choosing to live the covenant of consecration, we gain valuable skills that will benefit us in the celestial kingdom. There we "shall inherit thrones, kingdoms, principalities, and powers, dominions, all heights and depths."[2687] Clearly, our celestial stewardships within our Father's kingdom will be vast; therefore we must choose to learn and live the principles of stewardship here and now. This is the promise: "And whoso is found a faithful, a just, and a wise steward shall enter into the joy of his Lord, and shall inherit eternal life."[2688]

[2683] D&C 78:4.
[2684] D&C 84:44.
[2685] Mosiah 3:19.
[2686] D&C 82:17–19; emphasis added.
[2687] D&C 132:19.
[2688] D&C 51:19.

Because all stewardships originate with the Lord, we are accountable to him both in time and in eternity for our performance. While we are free to choose how we manage the Lord's resources, we are not free from being accountable to him. How we choose to handle our stewardships will determine our receiving additional trusts. Our eventually receiving all things or forfeiting our stewardship and inheriting nothing pivot on that choice.

Stewardships are invigorated by our labor. Upon the principle of labor we have another accountable choice: We can either choose to labor and build up the Lord's stewardship to ourselves, pillage its resources for our selfish benefit, claim the property as our own, and take credit for its performance—or we can choose to build up our stewardship for the support of the kingdom of God and the establishment of Zion, use the surplus resources to bless the lives of his children, acknowledge that our stewardship and all we have and are belong to the Lord, and give him all the glory. The question before us is always this: Are we laboring for ourselves or for God? For Babylon or for Zion?

Labor augments our stewardship. "Work is the great basic principle which makes all things possible both in time and in eternity. Men, spirits, angels, and Gods use their physical and mental powers in work."[2689] To achieve the celestial kingdom our labor must mirror the celestial law of labor and its underlying motivation: "Think of your brethren like unto yourselves, and be familiar with all and free with your substance, that they may be rich like unto you. But before ye seek for riches, seek ye for the kingdom of God. And after ye have obtained a hope in Christ ye shall obtain riches, if ye seek them; and ye will seek them for the intent to do good—to clothe the naked, and to feed the hungry, and to liberate the captive, and administer relief to the sick and the afflicted."[2690] Furthermore, we can augment our labor and improve our stewardship by the principle of grace: we do all we can do, then draw upon the Lord's help. The law of tithes and offerings is just such an augmenting principle: by giving a little and doing our best, this law returns us "an hundredfold" of prosperity, protection, and exaltation.

Building up the kingdom of God for the establishment of Zion is the one and only reason that a covenant Zion person labors. Seen through the lens of Zion, this attitude permeates every manifestation of labor.

Idleness cannot land us in the celestial realm: "Thou shalt not be idle; for he that is idle shall not eat the bread nor wear the garments of the laborer."[2691] The idle poor have no claim upon the Lord's resources; the idle rich are rebuked when they live from the efforts of the working poor. Any covenant person who does not labor for Zion is termed "idle," and thus is under condemnation. Only a celestial effort and attitude toward labor will transport us to where we want to be.

These guiding principles of the law of consecration prepare us for the final judgment. "[When the Lord comes he will] recompense unto every man according to his work."[2692] Within the law of consecration, God has given us all that we need to qualify for the highest reward. Our agency allows us to choose and to act; our stewardship provides us a means of self-reliance and a way to fulfill our obligation to care for the Lord's children; our accountability gives us means to progress within the Lord's kingdom, and to gain trust after trust, until we obtain exaltation; our labor bestows upon us double happiness, self-respect, prosperity, the confidence of our fellowmen, and the Lord's mighty blessing. Such is the genius of the law of consecration and its guiding principles.

[2689] McConkie, *Mormon Doctrine*, 847.
[2690] Jacob 2:17–19.
[2691] D&C 42:42.
[2692] D&C 1:10; see also D&C 112:34.

Section 18

The Ultimate Test: God or Mammon

Jesus said we cannot serve God and mammon.[2693] *Mammon* is "the standard Hebrew word for any kind of financial dealing."[2694] Mammon is defined as riches,[2695] or, we would say, love of riches. Serving both God and mammon is as impossible as simultaneously walking east and west.[2696] The two are polar opposites, like love and hate. To the degree that we give our affection to one, we withhold our affection from the other: "Either [we] will hate the one, and love the other; or else [we] will hold to the one, and despise the other."[2697] Neither can we choose to participate in both God's and Satan's economies: Zion and mammon. According to Hugh Nibley, "Every step in the direction of increasing one's personal holdings is a step away from Zion."[2698]

The harshness and absoluteness of these statements are troubling. Of necessity, these statements spawn difficult questions. We hope that the sincere questioners will pursue answers until they discover the principles upon which a Zion life is built. We are saddened when other questioners disbelieve the statements, rationalize their mammon-seeking, or say that present-day realities discount the practicality of avoiding mammon. Almost all of us struggle with how to live this law. The quick answer, as we shall see, centers on the condition and the priorities of our hearts. There is no sin in wealth; there is sin only in setting our hearts on it and seeking it before seeking the kingdom of God; there is sin only in hoarding it rather than regarding it as a stewardship and disseminating it as the law of stewardship demands: to build up the kingdom of God for the establishment of Zion and to bless God's children. When we see wealth through the filter of Zion, we set ourselves up to become very prosperous, for Zion is always described as a place and condition of no lack and exceeding abundance. But that prosperity comes only when we have the right heart, the right motivations.

[2693] Matthew 6:24; Luke 16:13; 3 Nephi 13:24.
[2694] Nibley, *Approaching Zion*, 37.
[2695] LDS Bible Dictionary, "Mammon," 728.
[2696] Hunter, Conference Report, Apr. 1964, 35.
[2697] Matthew 6:24.
[2698] Nibley, *Approaching Zion*, 37.

The Test of Riches

The harsh reality is this: life is a test. At the center of that test is money. Our attitude toward our financial dealings proves the condition of our hearts, as well as our loyalty, character, willingness to sacrifice, and trustworthiness. We can no more avoid this financial test than we can avoid choosing between the relentless opposing forces that try to influence our financial dealings. But choose we must. If we fool ourselves into believing that we can succeed in choosing *both* God and mammon, we are deceived. But that has not deterred many people from trying. Most of humanity has attempted to combine God and mammon, but not one person has ever succeeded—and we will not be the first. From the first moment that we make the attempt, we have already chosen Satan and his economy. Jesus' words are perennially true: "No man can serve two masters."[2699]

So what should we do? Should we take the concept to extremes, take a vow of poverty, shun money, and live lean like medieval monks? Of course not. "You always do have to handle things," Hugh Nibley says. "But in what spirit do we do it? Not . . . by renunciation, for example. . . . If you refuse to be concerned with these things at all, and say, 'I'm above all that,' that's as great a fault. The things of the world have got to be administered; they must be taken care of, they are to be considered. We have to keep things clean, and in order. That's required of us. This is a test by which we are being proven. This is the way by which we prepare, always showing that these things will never captivate our hearts, that they will never become our principal concern. That takes a bit of doing, and that is why we have the formula 'with an eye single to his glory' (Mormon 8:15). Keep first your eye on the star, then on all the other considerations of the ship. You will have all sorts of problems on the ship, but unless you steer by the star, forget the ship. Sink it. You won't go anywhere."[2700]

The test of wealth determines whether or not we can be trusted with God's resources—those things that he has placed in our hands for safekeeping and prudent management. As accountable stewards, some pointed questions are always before us: Will we choose to remain within the guidelines of stewardship? Will we manage the stewardship according to God's desires, or will we "cheat" the Lord?[2701] Will we redefine the terms of stewardship, claim ownership of the Lord's property, then enlarge and indulge ourselves with the proceeds rather than use the surplus for its intended use, which is to take care of God's children and build up the kingdom of God for the establishment of Zion? Our answers to these questions determine our passing or failing the mortal test of riches.

Only the Pure in Heart Can Pass This Test

Without divine intervention, we could not have the power to choose God over mammon. Babylon simply has too great a hold on the hearts of men. Consequently, only the pure in heart who receive a spiritual endowment can make this choice and thereafter live the law of consecration. The pure in heart alone receive the spiritual help to view money for what it is and put it in its proper place. They are children of Zion who do not venture into Babylon and partake of its philosophies. Rather, they enter the temple and make an informed, resolute covenant to receive and manage the Lord's property in an ordered way; then they return to the world and implement that covenant as the Lord directs. Clearly, this test is too hard for the natural man. Only those who know and love God can do it. Hence, *God or mammon* is the ultimate test that determines the condition of the heart and lands us in or out of the celestial kingdom. Nibley writes:

> God has always given his people the same choice of either living
> up to the covenants made with him or being in Satan's power; there

---

[2699] Romney, Conference Report, Oct. 1962, 94; quoting Matthew 6:24.
[2700] Nibley, *Approaching Zion*, 336.
[2701] Nibley, *Approaching Zion*, 426.

is no middle ground (Moses 4:4). True, we spend this time of probation in a no-man's-land between the two camps of salvation and damnation, but at every moment of the day and night we must be moving toward the one or the other. Progressive testing takes place along the way in either direction; the same tests in every dispensation and generation mark the progress of the people of God.

(1) Do you, first of all, agree to do things his way rather than your way—to follow the law of God? (2) If so, will you be obedient to him, no matter what he asks of you? (3) Will you, specifically, be willing to sacrifice anything he asks you for? (4) Will you at all times behave morally and soberly? (5) Finally, if God asks you to part with your worldly possessions by consecrating them all to his work, will you give his own back to him to be distributed as he sees fit, not as you think wise?

That last test has been by far the hardest of all, and few indeed have chosen that strait and narrow way. The rich young man was careful and correct in observing every point of the law—up to that one; but that was too much for him, and the Savior, who refused to compromise or make a deal, could only send him off sorrowing, observing to the apostles that passing that test was so difficult to those possessing the things of the world that only a special dispensation from God could get them by.[2702]

THE LORD'S WILLINGNESS TO BE TESTED

Perhaps because this test requires so much faith, the Lord both promises and offers evidence that if we will live the law of consecration, he will take care of us and even prosper us. The law of tithing, as we have observed, is one of his proofs: "Bring ye all the tithes into the storehouse, that there may be meat in mine house, *and prove me now herewith,* saith the Lord of hosts, if I will not open you the windows of heaven, and pour you out a blessing, that there shall not be room enough to receive it."[2703] Paying tithing is always an act of faith. The math doesn't make sense. Ten minus one is supposed to equal nine, but somehow when we pay our tithing the product is always more than ten. Clearly, celestial math is baffling in a telestial setting, and only faith can urge us on. But if we will persevere and apply the principle of tithing, then experience the pouring out of blessings, we will be prepared to employ that principle in other consecrated offerings, which will require even greater faith.

Alma taught that faith grows like a seed.[2704] First, faith takes root in our hearts by hearing the word of God.[2705] Then it sprouts and blossoms by continual nourishing, which we are willing to do because we observe incremental proofs that the plant is growing.[2706] Over time, the seed becomes a great, fruit-bearing tree.[2707] Tithing is such a tree, and it provides us a way to test the Lord on the principle of consecration; tithing allows us and the Lord to get to know each other. Once we discover that the Lord will not let us down and that he will prosper us, we are willing to take the next step and pay offerings. Once again we discover the Lord's care and abundance, and, as we do, we grow in our

---

[2702] Nibley, *Approaching Zion,* 342.
[2703] Malachi 3:10; emphasis added.
[2704] Alma 32:28.
[2705] Romans 10:17.
[2706] Alma 32:28–37.
[2707] Alma 32:37–42.

appreciation of the principle of consecration until we can live the law according to its ideal. But every step of the way, between initial tithing and eventual total consecration, requires our venturing into the darkness of uncertainty, hoping and anticipating that the light will appear. Each step demands giving before we receive, and every time we take another step, it will make absolutely no mathematical sense. The laws in Babylon that govern finance will scream at us to hold back: "It won't work!" Only our testimony of the celestial laws of tithing and consecrated offerings can provide us the confidence that all will be well and that the outcome will result in safety and abundance. Nibley wrote:

> In giving his children the law, God repeatedly specifies that he is placing before them two ways, the ways of life and death, light and darkness. For parallel to the one law runs another. It is part of the plan that Satan should be allowed to try us and to tempt us to see whether we would prove faithful in all things: Who does not live up to every covenant made with the Lord will be in his power (cf. Moses 4:4, 5:23). So we find ourselves drawn in two directions (Moroni 7:11–13). *Thus this life becomes a special test of probation set before us in this world—it is an economic one. If the law of consecration is the supreme test of virtue—the final one—money is to be the supreme temptation to vice;* sex runs a poor second, but on both counts, this is the time and place for us to meet the challenge of the flesh. It is the weakness of the flesh in both cases to prove our spirits stronger than the pull of matter, to assert our command over the new medium of physical bodies before proceeding onward to another state of existence. As Brigham Young often repeats, "God has given us the things of this world to see what we will do with them." The test will be whether we will set our hearts on the four things that lead to destruction. Whoever seeks for (1) wealth, (2) power, (3) popularity, and (4) the pleasures of the flesh—anyone who seeks those will be destroyed, says the Book of Mormon (1 Nephi 22:23; 3 Nephi 6:15). Need we point out that those four things compose the whole substance of success in the present-day world. They are the things that money will get you.[2708]

Tithing, therefore, is the *preparation* to become Zionlike; offerings are the *opportunity* to become Zionlike. In each case, God is willing to be put to the test. The only question remaining is, *Are we?* Do we really want to become Zion people or not?

Consecration Is All about Love

Certainly, the test of life centers on money, but it has more to do with proving the heart. Consecration is all about relationship: either we love God or we love mammon. If we give God our hearts, giving him our money is easy.

Think of a marriage. All lesser sacrifices are simple if we have offered our spouse our heart. But if we are selfish in any way, the marriage will be damaged and possibly fail. We recall that Ananias and Sapphira held back a portion of their consecration and lost their lives as a consequence of their selfishness.[2709] Our covenant relationship with Christ is like a marriage. He is the Bridegroom, and we

---

[2708] Nibley, *Approaching Zion*, 434–35; emphasis added.
[2709] Acts 5:1–5.

are his *bride*.[2710] If both parties do not place their all on the altar and agree to live thereafter as *one*, meaning complete sacrifice, loyalty, and trust, the relationship will crumble, leaving the two with hollow words and pitiful, surface-level acts of devotion. A husband who will not share his money with his wife is selfish and abusive; if he cannot give his wife his money, he cannot give his wife his heart. The same could be said of a wife who selfishly withholds anything from her husband. Just so, the sacrifice of our money for the purposes of God provides singular *proof* that we love God above every other consideration. Consecration is how we prove our love for God and his children.

A Change of Orders

At the outset of the Doctrine and Covenants, the great Jehovah declared that the order of Babylon, which has oppressed God's people for millennia, was all but used up. "The Lord insists that the whole history of the world is about to turn on its hinges," said Hugh Nibley. "It will change; this is not an order with which he is pleased."[2711] Now a new order—*Zion*—is about to burst upon the stage of human history. Zion's advent will be an act of mercy for the salvation of all mankind.[2712]

From the moment of the First Vision, Christ drew a line in the sand: Babylon on one side, and Zion on the other. His call for the Saints to flee Babylon is the same call that he has issued in past dispensations: "Come out of her, my people, that ye be not partakers of her sins, and that ye receive not of her plagues."[2713] Once escaped from Babylon, we are not to turn back; rather, we are to embrace a new way of life: "Ye shall not live after the manner of the world."[2714] Forevermore, mammon-seeking is strictly forbidden in Zion: "Touch not the evil gift, nor the unclean thing."[2715] From the moment we make that decision, we will feel like and be viewed as "strangers"[2716] in the earth. But that should not be a concern for Zion people. The world as it presently exists is not our home; someday Babylon and its citizenry will fall,[2717] and we, the children of Zion, will inherit the earth.[2718] Until then, we are to live among the people of Babylon with the charge to call as many of them out as possible. But in no case are we to be absorbed by them; rather, we are to be the "light of the world" as our ruler, the King of Zion,[2719] is *the* Light of the world.[2720]

A first step toward Zion is to recognize where we live. When Adam and Eve "found" themselves in the lone and dreary world—a discovery all of us must make—they immediately sought heavenly help to get back home.[2721] This world is not our home, and we must not set up camp here. Our movement should be away and up, and, in the process of going, we must take with us as many people as possible.

Love of Money Is the Root of All Evil

Few statements are as sweeping as Paul's denunciation of covetousness: "For the love of money is the root of all evil."[2722] In one sentence he identifies the origin of all sin: *"the love of money."* The

---

[2710] Isaiah 61:10; 62:5; Jeremiah 7:34; 16:9; 25:10; 33:11; Joel 2:16; John 3:29; Revelation 18:23.
[2711] Nibley, *Approaching Zion*, 331.
[2712] D&C 1.
[2713] Revelation 18:4.
[2714] D&C 95:13.
[2715] Moroni 10:30.
[2716] D&C 45:13.
[2717] Revelation 18:2.
[2718] Matthew 5:5; 3 Nephi 12:5; D&C 59:2.
[2719] Moses 7:53.
[2720] Matthew 5:14; John 8:12.
[2721] Moses 5:4–12.
[2722] 1 Timothy 6:10.

implications of this statement are huge. Lying, sexual transgression, taking God's name in vain, breaking the Sabbath day, pride—every transgression that grows on the tree of sin can be traced to its root cause: a covetous attitude about money and possessions. Those who embrace this attitude are caught in Satan's snare, from which there is little hope of escape: "But they that will be rich fall into temptation and a snare, and into many foolish and hurtful lusts, which drown men in destruction and perdition." Paul warns that those who persist in pursuing wealth "have erred from the faith, and pierced themselves through with many sorrows." This condition is one from which we must run: "But thou, O man of God, flee these things; and follow after righteousness, godliness, faith, love, patience, meekness." In the economy of God, Paul explains, "great gain" is defined as "godliness with contentment."[2723]

The Book of Mormon prophet Jacob listed the love of money as one of the foremost offenses against God. Hugh Nibley wrote:

> It is at the climax of his great discourse on the Atonement that Jacob cries out, "But wo unto the rich, who are rich as to the things of the world. For because they are rich they despise the poor." This is a very important statement, setting down as a general principle that the rich as a matter of course despise the poor, for "their hearts are upon their treasures; wherefore, their treasure is their God. And behold, their treasure shall perish with them also" (2 Nephi 9:30). Why does Jacob make this number one in his explicit list of offenses against God? Because it is the number-one device among the enticings of "that cunning one" (2 Nephi 9:39), who knows that riches are his most effective weapon in leading men astray. You must choose between being at one with God or with Mammon, not both; the one promises everything in this world for money, the other a place in the kingdom after you have "endured the crosses of the world, and despised the shame of it," for only so can you "inherit the kingdom of God, which was prepared for them from the foundation of the world," and where your "joy shall be full forever" (2 Nephi 9:18). Need we point out that the main reason for having money is precisely to avoid "the crosses of the world, and . . . the shame of it"?[2724]

The counsel given by President Anthon H. Lund in 1903 is applicable today:

> The Lord, in one of His revelations given very early in the Church, says: "Seek not for riches, but for wisdom and, behold, the mysteries of God shall be unfolded unto you, and then shall you be made rich; behold he that hath eternal life is rich." The riches of eternal life we ought to seek, not the riches of the world. There is a raging thirst for riches in this land. The love of money is growing, even in our midst. We do not look upon wealth in itself as a curse. We believe that those who can handle means rightly can do much to bless their fellows. But he who is ruled by the love of money is tempted to commit sin. The love of money is the root of all evil.

[2723] 1 Timothy 6:6–11.
[2724] Nibley, *Approaching Zion*, 592–93.

There is hardly a commandment but is violated through this seeking for riches.[2725]

COVETOUSNESS—THE LAST LAW

"Thou shalt not covet," Jehovah commanded Israel.[2726] This was the last law given in the Ten Commandments. In our day, the Lord repeated the injunction: "I command thee that thou shalt not covet thy neighbor's wife. . . . I command thee that thou shalt not covet thine own property, but impart it freely [for the building up of the kingdom of God]."[2727] Joseph Smith expanded on the subject of the last law: "God cursed the children of Israel because they would not receive the last law from Moses. . . . The Israelites prayed that God would speak to Moses and not to them; in consequence of which he cursed them with a carnal law." The Prophet then went on to apparently connect the law of covetousness with the fulness of the priesthood: "Abraham gave a tenth part of all his spoils and then received a blessing under the hands of Melchizedek *even the last law or a fulness of the law or priesthood* which constituted him a king and priest after the order of Melchizedek or an endless life."[2728]

Whether or not the Prophet intended a dual meaning here is not known, but the noticeable connection is sobering. A review of history substantiates that the Israelites rejected the last law—*Thou shalt not covet*—and simultaneously they rejected the last law "or a fulness of the law" of the priesthood, which would have made them kings and priests after the order of Melchizedek, which same order would have brought them to an endless life: "Now this Moses plainly taught to the children of Israel in the wilderness, and sought diligently to sanctify his people that they might behold the face of God; but they hardened their hearts and could not endure his presence; therefore, the Lord in his wrath, for his anger was kindled against them, swore that they should not enter into his rest while in the wilderness, which rest is the fulness of his glory. Therefore, he took Moses out of their midst, and the Holy Priesthood also."[2729] We simply cannot break this last law, *avoiding covetousness,* and expect to receive the fulness of the priesthood, along with its attendant blessings.

As the prohibition against covetousness was the last law given in the lesser law, the law of consecration is the last law given in the higher law. Consecration protects us from covetousness and idolatry by prescribing the usage of our surpluses. If we keep this last law, we will prosper and experience abundance beyond any telestial effort that we might make to enrich ourselves.

THE HIGHER AND LOWER LAWS OF PROSPERITY

Mormon describes the two systems of prosperity. Beginning with the higher law, he said:

> And now, because of the steadiness of the church they began to be exceedingly rich, having abundance of all things whatsoever they stood in need—an abundance of flocks and herds, and fatlings of every kind, and also abundance of grain, and of gold, and of silver, and of precious things, and abundance of silk and fine-twined linen, and all manner of good homely cloth.
>
> And thus, in their prosperous circumstances, they did not send away any who were naked, or that were hungry, or that were athirst,

---

[2725] Lund, Conference Report, Apr. 1903, 97.
[2726] Exodus 20:17.
[2727] D&C 19:25–26.
[2728] Smith, *Words of Joseph Smith,* 245–46; emphasis added.
[2729] D&C 84:23–25.

or that were sick, or that had not been nourished; and they did not set their hearts upon riches; therefore they were liberal to all, both old and young, both bond and free, both male and female, whether out of the church or in the church, having no respect to persons as to those who stood in need.

And thus they did prosper and become far more wealthy than those who did not belong to their church.

For those who did not belong to their church did indulge themselves in sorceries, and in idolatry or idleness, and in babblings, and in envyings and strife; wearing costly apparel; being lifted up in the pride of their own eyes; persecuting, lying, thieving, robbing, committing whoredoms, and murdering, and all manner of wickedness.[2730]

When the Lord determines to enrich us, we become rich indeed. But when we attempt to enrich ourselves, our abundance will subsist only for a season, and in the end we will be left impoverished, temporally, emotionally, and spiritually.

The More Weighty Matters

The Lord's invitation to us is always the same: renounce mammon and choose God; flee Babylon and come to Zion. We hear his voice crying, "Therefore, come up hither unto the land of my people, even Zion." Our success in arriving in Zion depends upon our attitude toward money: "Let them repent of all their sins, and of all their covetous desires, before me, saith the Lord; for what is property unto me? saith the Lord." That is, the things of the world are but a drop in the vast ocean of possible blessings—"the weighty matters"—and those weighty blessings await those who will make the effort: "Is there not room enough on the mountains of Adam-ondi-Ahman, and on the plains of Olaha Shinehah, or the land where Adam dwelt, that you should covet that which is but the drop, and neglect the more weighty matters?"[2731] Obviously, weighty blessings flow from our attending to weighty matters and not from coveting "the drop."

Those who insist on remaining in Babylon or trying to keep one foot there and the other in Zion may expect the Lord's cursing: "Ye are cursed because of your riches, and also are your riches cursed because ye have set your hearts upon them, and have not hearkened unto the words of him who gave them unto you." This condition is despicable evidence of breaking our oath of obedience; it is a manifestation of disloyalty to God and the abandonment of our lawful affections. We are under covenant to always remember the Lord,[2732] his gifts,[2733] and the poor,[2734] but we, rather, too often remember and love our riches: "Ye do not remember the Lord your God in the things with which he hath blessed you, but ye do always remember your riches, not to thank the Lord your God for them; yea, your hearts are not drawn out unto the Lord, but they do swell with great pride, unto boasting, and unto great swelling, envyings, strifes, malice, persecutions, and murders, and all manner of iniquities." In this condition, we sometimes wonder why we are not receiving the Lord's favor. His answer is an indictment of our covetous behavior: "For this cause hath the Lord God caused that a curse should come upon the land, and also upon your riches, and this because of your iniquities."[2735]

[2730] Alma 1:29–32; emphasis added.
[2731] D&C 117:4, 8.
[2732] D&C 20:77, 79.
[2733] D&C 46:10.
[2734] D&C 42:30; 52:40.
[2735] Helaman 13:21–23.

Who could blame him? Our affections are elsewhere, and we hardly give him a second thought. Clearly, covetousness is akin to adultery.

Trying to Mix Mammon and Zion

With an eye on our day, Mormon apparently dug through Nephite history to find a parallel story to describe the consequences of the latter-day epidemic of wealth-seeking. He discovered a perfect example in the Zoramites. Nibley wrote about the Zoramites' sin of combining God and mammon:

> Alma found them [the Zoramites] to be the wickedest people in the world. He couldn't believe that people could be so evil. . . . With all their [supposed] virtues, they set their hearts upon riches (Alma 31:24–38). Alma couldn't stand it. He couldn't look at it anymore. It hurt too much. How could people be so wicked? This is what was wrong: "Behold, O my God, their costly apparel, and their ringlets, and their bracelets, and their ornaments of gold, and all their precious things which they are ornamented with; and behold, their hearts are set upon them, and yet they cry unto thee and say—We thank thee, O God, for we are a chosen people unto thee, while others shall perish" (Alma 31:28). "O, how long, O Lord, wilt thou suffer that thy servants shall dwell here below in the flesh, to behold such gross wickedness among the children of men? Behold, O God, they cry unto thee, and yet their hearts are swallowed up in their pride. Behold, O God, they cry unto thee with their mouths" (Alma 31:26–27). Remember, they went to church once a week, and they bore their testimony, and they were very strict in dress regulations, and so forth. They were brave and courageous and enterprising and prosperous and all those other things—but this was what was wrong: . . . "They cry unto thee with their mouths, while they are puffed up, even to greatness, . . . [with] their ringlets; . . . and behold, their hearts are set upon them, and yet they cry unto thee and say [at the same time], We thank thee, O God, for we are a chosen people unto thee" (Alma 31:27–28). And that was what the great crime was. *Don't try to combine the two.*[2736]

The Zoramites had fallen into a snare. In order to justify laying claim to their wealth, they pointed to their pretended piety, "supposing gain is godliness."[2737] Of course, we are taught that true godliness is tied to the covenants and ordinances of the temple, not to money.[2738] Suddenly, in this account, the two economies become clear: On the one hand, we see hypocrites, the worst of sinners according to Jesus, they who insist "on proper dress and grooming, their careful observance of all the rules, their precious concern for status symbols, their strict legality, their pious patriotism,"[2739] they who appear to be good and blessed because they are rich,[2740] all the while turning a blind eye to the poor; and on the other hand, we see the penitent, meek folk, who are poor in heart, seeking the word

---

[2736] Nibley, *Approaching Zion*, 103–4; emphasis added.
[2737] 1 Timothy 6:5.
[2738] D&C 84:20–21.
[2739] Nibley, *Approaching Zion*, xvi.
[2740] Nibley, *Approaching Zion*, xxi.

of God, and ultimately being pronounced by the prophet as "blessed."[2741] Some of the greatest teachings found in the Book of Mormon were given to these humble followers of Christ, and, as we know, they finally received as a reward an inheritance in a land of promise,[2742] symbolizing that they had achieved Zion.

In this dispensation, the early Saints' attempt to mix Zion with mammon broke Joseph Smith's heart. Speaking to the Saints in Far West, Missouri, concerning covetousness, he said:

> Brethren, we are gathering to this beautiful land to build up Zion; Zion, which is the pure in heart. But since I have been here I have perceived the spirit of selfishness. Covetousness exists in the hearts of the Saints which is not becoming to those who have received the gospel. Here are those who begin to spread out buying up all the land they are able to [get] to the exclusion of the poor ones who are not so much blessed with this world's goods, thinking to lay foundations for themselves, only looking to their own individual families and those who are to follow them. *Now I want to tell you that Zion cannot be built up in any such way.* We are called out from this world to learn God's ways, to become one, looking each to his brother's interest and his welfare, the widow, the fatherless, and poor without distinction. I see signs put out, beer signs, speculative schemes are being introduced. This is the way of the world, Babylon indeed, and I tell you in the name of the God of Israel, if there is not repentance with this people and a turning from ungodliness, covetousness, and self-will, you will be broken up and scattered from this choice land to the four winds of heaven. For the Lord will have a people who will serve him and keep his commandments humbly, each one seeking his neighbor's welfare, to preach the gospel, gather the poor, and aid them, and build up a holy city unto our God.[2743]

Covetousness broke the heart of Brigham Young, too.

> What does the Lord want of us up here in the tops of these mountains? He wishes us to build up Zion. What are the people doing? They are merchandizing, trafficking and trading . . . making [the merchants] immensely rich. We all have our pursuits, our different ways of supplying ourselves with the common necessaries of life and also its luxuries. This is right and the possession of earthly wealth is right, if we follow our varied pursuits, and amass the wealth of this life for the purpose of advancing righteousness and building up the kingdom of God on earth. But how easy it is to wander from the path of righteousness. We toil days and months to attain a certain degree of perfection, a certain victory over a failing or weakness, and in an unguarded moment slide back again to our former state. How quickly we become darkened in our minds when we neglect our

---

[2741] Alma 32:2–8.
[2742] Alma 35:9.
[2743] Stevenson, *Life and History of Elder Edward Stevenson*, 40–41; emphasis added.

duties to God and each other, and forget the great objects of our lives."[2744]

And on another occasion, he said:

> [The Saints] do not know what to do with the revelations, commandments and blessings of God. Talking, for instance about everyday things, how many do we see here that know what to do with money and property when they get it? Are their eyes single to the building up of the kingdom of God? No; they are single to the building up of themselves. . . . There are few who understand the principles of the kingdom and whose eyes are single to the building of it up in all respects; but their eyes are like the fool's eye—looking to the ends of the earth. They want this and that, and they do not know what to do; they lack wisdom. By-and-by, perhaps, their wealth will depart from them, and when left poor and penniless, they will humble themselves before the Lord that they may be saved.[2745]

Warnings against Compromise

We cannot embrace Zion and mammon simultaneously. Hugh Nibley wrote: "Brigham Young and Joseph often warned the Saints about subsiding into this telestial order. Even though the Lord said that Zion could not be built up unless it is in the principle of the law (otherwise I cannot receive her unto myself), the Latter-day Saints still wanted to compromise and say, 'We will not go up unto Zion, and will keep our moneys' (D&C 105:8). But as long as that was their plan, there could be no Zion, they were told."[2746]

The Lord asks rhetorically, "For shall the children of the kingdom pollute my holy land?" Then, answering his own question, he said, "Verily, I say unto you, Nay."[2747] We have a clear choice to make if we truly desire Zion over all other affections: either we forsake the world and come to the Lord's marriage or we languish in Babylon to tend our property and peddle our merchandise; but we cannot do both.[2748] "'Israel, Israel, God is calling,' we often sing, 'Babylon the great is falling,' But we have taken our stand between them; Brigham Young speaks of Latter-day Saints who want to take Babylon by one hand and Zion by the other—it won't work."[2749]

Making Mammon Holy

We try to legitimize our desiring mammon by trying to find something holy about pursuing it. Brigham Young describes such people: "Elders of Israel are greedy after the things of this world. If you ask them if they are ready to build up the kingdom of God, their answer is prompt—'Why, to be sure we are, with our whole souls; but we want first to get so much gold, speculate and get rich, and then we can help the Church considerably. We will go to California and get gold, go and buy goods and get rich, trade with the emigrants, build a mill, make a farm, get a large herd of cattle, and then we can do a

---

[2744] Young, *Journal of Discourses*, 12:155.
[2745] Young, *Journal of Discourses*, 11:325.
[2746] Nibley, *Approaching Zion*, 331.
[2747] D&C 84:59.
[2748] Matthew 22:2–14.
[2749] Nibley, *Approaching Zion*, 279.

great deal for Israel.' When will you be ready to do it? 'In a few years, Brother Brigham, if you do not disturb us.'"[2750]

In our desperation to continue to seek mammon while still retaining our standing in Zion, we sometimes grasp for scriptural comfort. Often we point to the parable of the talents.[2751] We say to ourselves, "Surely we are to increase our holdings if we are to be nominated as good stewards." But, according to the scriptures, there is a vast difference between expanding our stewardship for the kingdom's sake and expanding it for the sake of personal wealth. Jacob gives us the key: "But before ye seek for riches, seek ye for the kingdom of God." First the kingdom, then riches! "And *after* ye have obtained a hope in Christ (notice the sequence) ye shall obtain riches, if ye seek them; and ye will seek them for the intent to do good—to clothe the naked, and to feed the hungry, and to liberate the captive, and administer relief to the sick and the afflicted."[2752] Clearly, we are not justified in seeking riches *before* we seek (or even *simultaneously* seek) the kingdom of God; but *after* we obtain a hope in Christ (and not before), we may ask for riches with the intent to "level people up." Jacob says, "Think of your brethren like unto yourselves, and be familiar with all and free with your substance, that they may be rich like unto you."[2753] It is this attitude toward money that brings us to a hope in Christ, and it is this attitude that now places us in a position to make a request for more resources to bless more people.

We can become rich by following either Zion's way or Babylon's way. But before we decide which way to go, we ought to at least know where the two ways end. The Zion way will land us in heaven, while the Babylon way will land us elsewhere, but not in heaven. We might try to convince ourselves otherwise, but in the end it will not make a difference. We can no more make mammon holy than we can possess it and Zion, too. We cannot have it both ways.

Mormon's View of the Last Days

Few condemnations of mammon are harsher than Moroni's. Understanding our day perhaps better than we do, the last Nephite prophet described a latter-day scene of unequalled depravity, rivaling the days of Noah.[2754] "Behold, I speak unto you as if ye were present, and yet ye are not. But behold, Jesus Christ hath shown you unto me, and I know your doing. And I know that ye do walk in the pride of your hearts; and there are none save a few only who do not lift themselves up in the pride of their hearts, unto the wearing of very fine apparel, unto envying, and strifes, and malice, and persecutions, and all manner of iniquities; and your churches, yea, even every one, have become polluted because of the pride of your hearts. *For behold, ye do love money, and your substance, and your fine apparel, and the adorning of your churches, more than ye love the poor and the needy, the sick and the afflicted.*"[2755]

We often read these verses and congratulate ourselves that we are not part of that wretched group . . . until Moroni points his finger at the hypocritical Saints who have polluted the holy church of God: "O ye pollutions, ye hypocrites, ye teachers, who sell yourselves for that which will canker, why have ye polluted the holy church of God? Why are ye ashamed to take upon you the name of Christ? Why do ye not think that greater is the value of an endless happiness than that misery which never dies—because of the praise of the world? Why do ye adorn yourselves with that which hath no life, and yet suffer the hungry, and the needy, and the naked, and the sick and the afflicted to pass by you, and notice them not?"[2756]

[2750] Young, *Journal of Discourses*, 1:164–65.
[2751] Matthew 25:14–30.
[2752] Jacob 2:18–19; emphasis added.
[2753] Jacob 2:17.
[2754] Joseph Smith–Matthew 1:41.
[2755] Mormon 8:35–37; emphasis added.
[2756] Mormon 8:38–39.

Moroni's question hangs answerless. We have no excuse. The prophet saw us as we really are. Our actions indict us. They are, and always have been, in open prophetic view.

The First Commandments of This Dispensation

A full year before the organization of the Church, the Lord gave Joseph Smith and Oliver Cowdery the first two commandments pertaining to his latter-day kingdom: (1) "Seek to bring forth and establish the cause of Zion"; (2) "Seek not for riches but for wisdom." The promised blessings would eclipse anything that Babylon could offer: "And behold, the mysteries of God shall be unfolded unto you, and then shall you be made rich. Behold, he that hath eternal life is rich."[2757] Then, one month later, as if to accomplish the law of witnesses,[2758] the Lord repeated these commandments verbatim to Hyrum Smith.[2759] Thus, the initial witnesses of the Restoration (Joseph and Oliver) and ultimate witnesses (Joseph and Hyrum), two of whom would seal their testimony with blood, were given the first two commandments that would define all commandments that would follow.

These first commandments stand in stark contrast to Satan's first commandment: *Everything shall have a price.* "Satan's first article of faithlessness has been repeated with creedal clarity since the beginning: One can buy anything in this world for money. It is a hellish philosophy, and those who operate in harmony with it sell that which is priceless for a paltry sum."[2760] From the earliest moment in the Garden of Eden, Hugh Nibley wrote:

> [Satan] flares up in his pride and announces what his program for the economic and political order of the new world is going to be. He will take the resources of the earth, and with precious metals as a medium of exchange he will buy up military and naval might, or rather those who control it, and so will govern the earth—for he is the prince of this world. He does rule: he is king. Here at the outset is the clearest possible statement of a military-industrial complex ruling the earth with violence and ruin. But as we are told, this cannot lead to anything but war, because it has been programmed to do that. It was conceived in the mind of Satan in his determination 'to destroy the world' (Moses 4:6). The whole purpose of the program is to produce blood and horror on this earth.[2761]

The central issue contained in these first two commandments concerns the definition and use of treasure. Consider the results of the two philosophies:

Zion: "Lay not up for yourselves treasures upon earth, where moth and rust doth corrupt, and where thieves break through and steal: But lay up for yourselves treasures in heaven, where neither moth nor rust doth corrupt, and where thieves do not break through nor steal: For where your treasure is, there will your heart be also."[2762]

Babylon: "But wo unto the rich, who are rich as to the things of the world. For because they are rich they despise the poor, and they persecute the meek, and their hearts are upon their treasures; wherefore, their treasure is their God. And behold, their treasure shall perish with them also."[2763]

[2757] D&C 6:6–7.
[2758] Deuteronomy 19:15.
[2759] D&C 11:6–7.
[2760] McConkie and Millet, *Doctrinal Commentary on the Book of Mormon*, 1:302.
[2761] Nibley, *Approaching Zion*, 92.
[2762] Matthew 6:19–21.
[2763] 2 Nephi 9:30.

No Security in Mammon

The quest for riches is a powerful opiate and Satan's most "deadly and effective" weapon.[2764] Seeking security in mammon was detected by Nephi as a latter-day Satanic strategy to destroy the Latter-day Saints: "And others will he pacify, and lull them away into carnal security, that they will say: All is well in Zion; yea, Zion prospereth, all is well—and thus the devil cheateth their souls, and leadeth them away carefully down to hell."[2765] President Spencer W. Kimball drew a distinction between the economies of Babylon and Zion: "Zion can be built up only among those who are the pure in heart, not a people torn by covetousness or greed, but a pure and selfless people. Not a people who are pure in appearance, rather a people who are pure in heart. Zion is to be in the world and not of the world, not dulled by a sense of carnal security, nor paralyzed by materialism. No, Zion is not things of the lower, but of the higher order, things that exalt the mind and sanctify the heart."[2766] Seeking mammon and attempting to find security in it is an illusion and a cheap trick of the devil.

Brigham Young had much to say against worshiping mammon for security: "I would as soon see a man worshipping a little god made of brass or of wood as see him worship his property. . . . Does this congregation understand what idolatry is? The New Testament says that covetousness is idolatry; therefore, a covetous people is an idolatrous people."[2767] President Young focused the last year of his life on preaching against the folly of idolatry: "We wish the wealth or things of the world; we think about them morning, noon and night; they are first in our minds when we awake in the morning, and the last thing before we go to sleep at night."[2768] And at another time he said: "One man has his eye on a gold mine, another is for a silver mine, another is for marketing his flour or his wheat, another for selling his cattle, another to raise cattle, another to get a farm, or building here and there, and trading and trafficking with each other, just like Babylon. . . . Babylon is here, and we are following in the footsteps of the inhabitants of the earth, who are in a perfect sea of confusion. Do you know this? You ought to, for there are none of you but what see it daily. . . . The Latter-day Saints [are] trying to take advantage of their brethren. There are Elders in this Church who would take the widow's last cow, for five dollars, and then kneel down and thank God for the fine bargain they had made."[2769]

At one point the Lord allowed the Saints in wisdom to associate prudently with mammon: "And now, verily I say unto you, and this is wisdom, make unto yourselves friends with the mammon of unrighteousness, and they will not destroy you."[2770] So that we do not see in this scripture a ticket to depart Zion and enter Babylon, Hugh Nibley clarifies, "This was only to save their lives in an emergency."[2771] Wisdom demands that when we read this verse, we cross-reference it with Zenos's allegory of the olive tree. We recall that the tree's natural branches temporarily needed crucial nourishing from the wild trees, but only to preserve them for a season. Their destiny was always to be grafted back into their mother tree, and the destiny of the wild branches was always to be clipped and burned.[2772]

[2764] Nibley, *Approaching Zion*, 39, 332.
[2765] 2 Nephi 28:21.
[2766] Kimball, *The Teachings of Spencer W. Kimball*, 363.
[2767] Young, *Journal of Discourses*, 6:196–97.
[2768] Young, *Journal of Discourses*, 18:239.
[2769] Young, *Journal of Discourses*, 17:41–42.
[2770] D&C 82:22.
[2771] Nibley, *Approaching Zion*, 20.
[2772] Jacob 5.

SLIPPERY TREASURES

There is no security in mammon. Riches are hard to hold and manage—they are "slippery." They can collapse with the whim of financial markets, a dishonest or incompetent partner, or one bad personal decision. Riches are built on the same foundation as the great and spacious building—a foundation of air.[2773] Helaman warned his people of the folly of seeking security in mammon:

> And behold, the time cometh that he curseth your riches, that they become slippery, that ye cannot hold them; and in the days of your poverty ye cannot retain them. And in the days of your poverty ye shall cry unto the Lord; and in vain shall ye cry, for your desolation is already come upon you, and your destruction is made sure; and then shall ye weep and howl in that day, saith the Lord of Hosts.
>
> And then shall ye lament, and say: O that I had repented, and had not killed the prophets, and stoned them, and cast them out. Yea, in that day ye shall say: O that we had remembered the Lord our God in the day that he gave us our riches, and then they would not have become slippery that we should lose them; for behold, our riches are gone from us. Behold, we lay a tool here and on the morrow it is gone; and behold, our swords are taken from us in the day we have sought them for battle. Yea, we have hid up our treasures and they have slipped away from us, because of the curse of the land. O that we had repented in the day that the word of the Lord came unto us; for behold the land is cursed, and all things are become slippery, and we cannot hold them. Behold, we are surrounded by demons, yea, we are encircled about by the angels of him who hath sought to destroy our souls. Behold, our iniquities are great. O Lord, canst thou not turn away thine anger from us? And this shall be your language in those days.
>
> But behold, your days of probation are past; ye have procrastinated the day of your salvation until it is everlastingly too late, and your destruction is made sure; yea, for ye have sought all the days of your lives for that which ye could not obtain; and ye have sought for happiness in doing iniquity, which thing is contrary to the nature of that righteousness which is in our great and Eternal Head.
>
> O ye people of the land, that ye would hear my words! And I pray that the anger of the Lord be turned away from you, and that ye would repent and be saved.[2774]

Cursed are they who set their hearts on mammon and trust in its security; their riches are programmed to become slippery. Nevertheless, despite the Lord's warning, these people will try to hoard their riches; but they *hide* them in vain. One day these people will awaken, and that which they loved so much will be gone. Then they will mourn, to no avail. They will be faced with the stark reality that they chose mammon over God; they rejected the words of the true prophets, and they honored flatterers as if they were prophets. Then Satan and his angels will rejoice.

[2773] 1 Nephi 8:26.
[2774] Helaman 13:31–39.

On the other hand, Zion people are commanded to hide their treasures unto the Lord: "For I will, saith the Lord, that they shall hide up their treasures unto me; and cursed be they who hide not up their treasures unto me; for none hideth up their treasures unto me save it be the righteous; and he that hideth not up his treasures unto me, cursed is he, and also the treasure, and none shall redeem it because of the curse of the land."[2775] The only reasons to hide a treasure are to safeguard it from an enemy and to preserve it for its intended purpose. Therefore, a Zion person might say that he hides or *consecrates* his treasure unto the Lord to keep it safe from unholy hands and to preserve it for its sacred purpose.

LAZARUS AND THE RICH MAN

The tragedy of choosing God over mammon and thus sacrificing one's soul is stated powerfully in Jesus' parable of the rich man and Lazarus.

> There was a certain rich man, which was clothed in purple and fine linen, and fared sumptuously every day: And there was a certain beggar named Lazarus, which was laid at his gate, full of sores, and desiring to be fed with the crumbs which fell from the rich man's table: moreover the dogs came and licked his sores.
> And it came to pass, that the beggar died, and was carried by the angels into Abraham's bosom: the rich man also died, and was buried; and in hell he lift up his eyes, being in torments, and seeth Abraham afar off, and Lazarus in his bosom. And he cried and said, Father Abraham, have mercy on me, and send Lazarus, that he may dip the tip of his finger in water, and cool my tongue; for I am tormented in this flame.
> But Abraham said, Son, remember that thou in thy lifetime receivedst thy good things, and likewise Lazarus evil things: but now he is comforted, and thou art tormented. And beside all this, between us and you there is a great gulf fixed: so that they which would pass from hence to you cannot; neither can they pass to us, that would come from thence.
> Then he said, I pray thee therefore, father, that thou wouldest send him to my father's house: For I have five brethren; that he may testify unto them, lest they also come into this place of torment.
> Abraham saith unto him, They have Moses and the prophets; let them hear them.
> And he said, Nay, father Abraham: but if one went unto them from the dead, they will repent.
> And he said unto him, If they hear not Moses and the prophets, neither will they be persuaded, though one rose from the dead.[2776]

The parable is indeed frightful. A dramatic change of status might be awaiting the righteous poor and the selfish rich. Then the once-selfish rich will look up and cry out to the once-humble poor and cry out for relief as the poor had once cried out for help and found none. James, the Lord's brother, expounded on this subject by saying that the poor who are faithful in this life are destined to become

---

[2775] Helaman 13:19.
[2776] Luke 16:19–31.

heirs of celestial glory.[2777] Then the tables will be turned, and the rich will be the ones to cry out for relief and find none. They will cry out to the poor as the poor had once cried out to them. They will neither enjoy the sweet association of the blessed nor be at rest; rather, they will be in torment with a great gulf dividing them from the righteous.

It is telling that the rich man in the parable was in agony; he pled that Abraham would send Lazarus to his brothers who were still on earth, hoping, we suppose, that there might be the tiniest chance that they could escape his fate. But Abraham knew the lure of mammon. Such people who are taken in that snare, he said, would no more respond to an angel than they would to the prophets, who constantly warn about such behavior.

Nothing Compares to the Danger

"Wealth is a pleasant and heady narcotic that gives the addict an exhilarating sense of power accompanied by a growing deadening of feeling for anything of real value," wrote Hugh Nibley. "Wealth is a jealous mistress: she will not tolerate any competition; rulers of business are openly contemptuous of all other vocations; and all those 'how-to-get-rich' books by rich men virtuously assure us that the first and foremost prerequisite for acquiring wealth is to think of nothing else—the aspirant who is guilty even of a momentary lapse in his loyalty, they tell us, does not deserve the wealth he seeks."[2778]

Mammon is a decoy, a trap, a lure, a snare; it is bait to capture our attention long enough to grasp us in its jaws and devour us. Quoting Brigham Young, Hugh Nibley said, "[Material things] 'decoy . . . [our] minds' away from the real values of things." Then Nibley added: "They are irresistible. The merchants do research: they know what we'll take and what we'll not. They know what will sell, and they know the line that nobody can resist. This is the very real thing we are being tempted by. By these deceptions—through public relations, the skill of advertising, and people who devote their lives to nothing else than trying to entice—the devil tries to entice and tempt us, 'by sorceries and witchcraft that deceive the nations' (cf. Revelation 18:23)."[2779]

On a number of occasions, Brigham Young expressed his fears concerning the Saints' pursuit of wealth over seeking the things of God: "I am more afraid of covetousness in our Elders than I am of the hordes of hell. . . . Those who are covetous and greedy, anxious to grasp the whole world, are all the time uneasy, and are constantly laying their plans and contriving how to obtain this, that, and the other. . . . [But] riches of themselves cannot produce permanent happiness; only the Spirit that comes from above can do that. . . . How the Devil will play with a man who so worships gain!"[2780]

As we have discussed, Jesus was once confronted by a rich young man who asked him concerning eternal life. "Keep the commandments" was the Lord's reply. When the rich man said that he had done this, he asked the Lord what else he lacked. "Now when Jesus heard these things, he said unto him, Yet lackest thou one thing: sell all that thou hast, and distribute unto the poor, and thou shalt have treasure in heaven: and come, follow me. And when he heard this, he was very sorrowful: for he was very rich. And when Jesus saw that he was very sorrowful, he said, How hardly shall they that have riches enter into the kingdom of God!" It is *hard* for a rich man to enter into heaven: "It is easier for a camel to go through a needle's eye, than for a rich man to enter into the kingdom of God." It requires special intervention from heaven: "The things which are impossible with men are possible with God."[2781]

[2777] James 2:5.
[2778] Nibley, *Approaching Zion*, 39–40.
[2779] Nibley, *Approaching Zion*, 330–31.
[2780] Young, *Discourses of Brigham Young*, 306.
[2781] Luke 18:18–27.

The Ultimate Test: God or Mammon

We would have to be blind to miss the point: We cannot achieve eternal life as long as our heart is set upon mammon. It is dangerous to think otherwise. Mammon and Zion do not mix. We cannot have them both. If we hold to one, we will despise the other. If we love one, we hate the other. The message is clear and scriptural: We must give up mammon to obtain God. Joseph Smith said eternal life is bought with a price: the sacrifice of all things.[2782] That is the essence of consecration. Only then are we truly safe.

When someone tried to lure Jesus into a conversation about money, he rebuked him soundly. "Man, who made me a judge or a divider over you?"[2783] The Savior's mission had nothing to do with mammon. Satan had once tried and failed to draw him into the distraction of wealth.[2784] Now here was another person expecting the Lord to take an interest in financial affairs: "Master, speak to my brother, that he divide the inheritance with me." It was an insult, and Jesus told him as much: "Take heed, and beware of covetousness: for a man's life consisteth not in the abundance of the things which he possesseth."[2785] The parable that followed spoke plainly of the folly of building up possessions on earth only to end up destitute in the next life.

> And he spake a parable unto them, saying, The ground of a certain rich man brought forth plentifully: And he thought within himself, saying, What shall I do, because I have no room where to bestow my fruits? And he said, This will I do: I will pull down my barns, and build greater; and there will I bestow all my fruits and my goods. And I will say to my soul, Soul, thou hast much goods laid up for many years; take thine ease, eat, drink, and be merry.
>
> But God said unto him, Thou fool, this night thy soul shall be required of thee: then whose shall those things be, which thou hast provided? So is he that layeth up treasure for himself, and is not rich toward God.[2786]

We are ever moving in the direction of our treasure, and we are investing in that treasure right now. Should we concentrate on filling our barns, we will most certainly abandon God and his children in the process. Jesus asks each of us two questions when we contemplate our loyalties: "For what shall it profit a man, if he shall gain the whole world, and lose his own soul? Or what shall a man give in exchange for his soul?"[2787]

Lessons in the Scriptures Concerning Wealth

The mantra of Babylon might be summed up by one scripture: "Money answereth all things."[2788] But in no uncertain terms the Lord forbids wealth-seeking: "Seek not after riches nor the vain things of this world; for behold, you cannot carry them with you."[2789] Wealth is a fleeting fancy that does not make a good eternal investment: "Riches are not forever."[2790] Satan is he who tempts us to seek for riches, knowing their inherent danger: "Now the cause of this iniquity of the people was this—Satan

---

[2782] Smith, *Lectures on Faith*, 6:7.
[2783] Luke 12:14.
[2784] JST Luke 4:5–8.
[2785] Luke 12:13, 15.
[2786] Luke 16:16–21.
[2787] Mark 8:36–37.
[2788] Ecclesiastes 10:19.
[2789] Alma 39:14.
[2790] Proverbs 27:24.

had great power, unto the stirring up of the people to do all manner of iniquity, and to the puffing them up with pride, tempting them to seek for power, and authority, and riches, and the vain things of the world."[2791]

The scriptures contain many descriptions, cautions, and denunciations concerning our attitude toward wealth. We are clearly warned that "he that trusteth in riches shall fall."[2792] How we obtain riches is even more damning: "He that oppresseth the poor to increase his riches shall surely come to want."[2793]

Seeking and withholding riches blights the soul with a terminal spiritual disease: "Wo unto you rich men, that will not give your substance to the poor, for your riches will canker your souls; and this shall be your lamentation in the day of visitation, and of judgment, and of indignation: The harvest is past, the summer is ended, and my soul is not saved!"[2794]

As evidenced in the scriptures below, when people begin to prosper, the bells of Hades begin to ring, and consequently the Church starts to fail. Notice in each of these scriptures the downward sequence of events:

- "But they grew proud, being lifted up in their hearts, because of their exceedingly great riches; therefore they grew rich in their own eyes, and would not give heed to their words, to walk uprightly before God."[2795]
- "And it came to pass that the fifty and second year ended in peace also, save it were the exceedingly great pride which had gotten into the hearts of the people; and it was because of their exceedingly great riches and their prosperity in the land; and it did grow upon them from day to day."[2796]
- "Now this great loss of the Nephites, and the great slaughter which was among them, would not have happened had it not been for their wickedness and their abomination which was among them; yea, and it was among those also who professed to belong to the church of God. And it was because of the pride of their hearts, because of their exceeding riches, yea, it was because of their oppression to the poor, withholding their food from the hungry, withholding their clothing from the naked, and smiting their humble brethren upon the cheek, making a mock of that which was sacred, denying the spirit of prophecy and of revelation, murdering, plundering, lying, stealing, committing adultery, rising up in great contentions, and deserting away into the land of Nephi, among the Lamanites—and because of this their great wickedness, and their boastings in their own strength, they were left in their own strength; therefore they did not prosper, but were afflicted and smitten, and driven before the Lamanites, until they had lost possession of almost all their lands."[2797]
- "And in the commencement of the sixty and seventh year the people began to grow exceedingly wicked again. For behold, the Lord had blessed them so long with the riches of the world that they had not been stirred up to anger, to wars, nor to bloodshed; therefore they began to set their hearts upon their riches; yea, they began to seek to get gain that they might

---

[2791] 3 Nephi 6:15.
[2792] Proverbs 11:28.
[2793] Proverbs 22:16.
[2794] D&C 56:16.
[2795] Alma 45:24.
[2796] Helaman 3:36.
[2797] Helaman 4:11–13.

The Ultimate Test: God or Mammon

be lifted up one above another; therefore they began to commit secret murders, and to rob and to plunder, that they might get gain."[2798]

Clearly, the scriptures are replete with warnings about mammon-seeking. If we think that we are somehow exempt or that we have a special dispensation to receive other than the universal and eternal reward for mammon-seeking, we are deceived and are destined to become sorely disappointed.

Scriptural Description of the Last Days

Quoting Isaiah, Nephi paints a picture of latter-day idolatry that is chilling: "Their land also is full of silver and gold, neither is there any end of their treasures; their land is also full of horses, neither is there any end of their chariots. Their land is also full of idols; they worship the work of their own hands, that which their own fingers have made." Isaiah foresaw that the resulting pride and lack of humility would challenge the Lord's forgiveness and would be answered with a harsh turn of events: "And the mean man boweth not down, and the great man humbleth himself not, therefore, forgive him not. O ye wicked ones, enter into the rock, and hide thee in the dust, for the fear of the Lord and the glory of his majesty shall smite thee. And it shall come to pass that the lofty looks of man shall be humbled, and the haughtiness of men shall be bowed down, and the Lord alone shall be exalted in that day."[2799]

In the latter days, the Lord prescribed an antidote for such spiritual sickness: "See that ye love one another; cease to be covetous; learn to impart one to another as the gospel requires."[2800]

Scriptures about Idolatry and Wealth

The scriptures have much to say about the ugly sisters, *covetousness* and *idolatry*, which seem to define the last days. Covetousness is idolatry, Paul taught.[2801] A "wo" is pronounced upon those whose "eyes are full of greediness."[2802] It is through greediness and idolatry that many people break "the covenant through covetousness."[2803]

Alma was faced with an idolatrous, selfish people who were ripening for destruction. His words to them could be just as well delivered today as a sermon at general conference:

> And also the Spirit saith unto me, yea, crieth unto me with a mighty voice, saying: Go forth and say unto this people—Repent, for except ye repent ye can in nowise inherit the kingdom of heaven. And again I say unto you, the Spirit saith: Behold, the ax is laid at the root of the tree; therefore every tree that bringeth not forth good fruit shall be hewn down and cast into the fire, yea, a fire which cannot be consumed, even an unquenchable fire. Behold, and remember, the Holy One hath spoken it.
>
> And now my beloved brethren, I say unto you, can ye withstand these sayings; yea, can ye lay aside these things, and trample the Holy One under your feet; yea, can ye be puffed up in the pride of your

---

[2798] Helaman 6:16–17.
[2799] 2 Nephi 12:7–11.
[2800] D&C 88:123.
[2801] Colossians 3:5.
[2802] D&C 56:17.
[2803] D&C 104:4, 52.

hearts; yea, will ye still persist in the wearing of costly apparel and setting your hearts upon the vain things of the world, upon your riches? Yea, will ye persist in supposing that ye are better one than another; yea, will ye persist in the persecution of your brethren, who humble themselves and do walk after the holy order of God, wherewith they have been brought into this church, having been sanctified by the Holy Spirit, and they do bring forth works which are meet for repentance—*yea, and will you persist in turning your backs upon the poor, and the needy, and in withholding your substance from them?*

And finally, all ye that will persist in your wickedness, I say unto you that these are they who shall be hewn down and cast into the fire except they speedily repent.[2804]

SCRIPTURES ABOUT SEEKING WEALTH AND FORGETTING GOD

Seeking wealth and becoming idolatrous are so very dangerous because they cause us to forget God. In the process of pursuing wealth, mammon becomes our god.

Nephi, the son of Helaman, described the downward spiral of sins that result from setting our hearts on mammon and thus forgetting God. Nephi challenged his people: "O, how could you have forgotten your God in the very day that he has delivered you? But behold, it is to get gain, to be praised of men, yea, and that ye might get gold and silver. And ye have set your hearts upon the riches and the vain things of this world, for the which ye do murder, and plunder, and steal, and bear false witness against your neighbor, and do all manner of iniquity. And for this cause wo shall come unto you except ye shall repent."[2805]

Centuries earlier, Moses struggled with his people who had forgotten the God who had preserved them. Moses found them boasting in their own strength and worshipping their riches. Moses denounced them and promised destruction for their haughty attitude: "Who led thee through that great and terrible wilderness, wherein were fiery serpents, and scorpions, and drought, where there was no water; who brought thee forth water out of the rock of flint; who fed thee in the wilderness with manna, which thy fathers knew not, that he might humble thee, and that he might prove thee, to do thee good at thy latter end; *and thou say in thine heart, My power and the might of mine hand hath gotten me this wealth. But thou shalt remember the Lord thy God: for it is he that giveth thee power to get wealth,* that he may establish his covenant which he sware unto thy fathers, as it is this day. And it shall be, if thou do at all forget the Lord thy God, and walk after other gods, and serve them, and worship them, I testify against you this day that ye shall surely perish."[2806]

Clearly, if we seek mammon, we risk forgetting God.

SCRIPTURES ABOUT MAMMON, INEQUALITY, AND DIVISIVENESS

No redeeming quality comes from seeking mammon. Satan programs this process to cause widespread misery: for the poor man, misery occurs by the rich man's unwillingness to part with his goods to help provide for the poor man's necessities and the opportunity to rise above the condition of poverty; for the rich man, misery happens by losing his soul to mammon-seeking and hoarding. In Third Nephi, Mormon chronicles the cycle of misery:

[2804] Alma 5:51–56; emphasis added.
[2805] Helaman 7:20–22.
[2806] Deuteronomy 8:8–19; emphasis added.

> And thus passed away the twenty and eighth year, and the people had continual peace. But it came to pass in the twenty and ninth year there began to be some disputings among the people; and some were lifted up unto pride and boastings because of their exceedingly great riches, yea, even unto great persecutions; for there were many merchants in the land, and also many lawyers, and many officers. And the people began to be distinguished by ranks, according to their riches and their chances for learning; yea, some were ignorant because of their poverty, and others did receive great learning because of their riches. Some were lifted up in pride, and others were exceedingly humble; some did return railing for railing, while others would receive railing and persecution and all manner of afflictions, and would not turn and revile again, but were humble and penitent before God.

Take note of Mormon's description of the perils of mammon-seeking:

- Within a short period of time, peace can devolve to disputations driven by pride;
- Then riches lead to more pride, boasting, and persecution;
- Then merchandising becomes prominent as a distinguishing element of society;
- Then riches define rank and opportunity.
- The resulting oppression of the poor shackles them to their low station.

Frighteningly, only a few righteous people manage to remain uninfected by the growing sickness.

Mormon explained that these conditions lead to inequality and divisiveness, the offspring of Babylon and the antithesis of Zion. The sickness that had infected the Nephite nation, he said, quickly infiltrated the Church, and soon the Saints were crushed under the weight of mammon-seeking. Only a small number managed to climb to high ground and remain safe from the tsunami that was about to drown the nation. Mormon reports: "And thus there became a great inequality in all the land, insomuch that the church began to be broken up; yea, insomuch that in the thirtieth year the church was broken up in all the land save it were among a few of the Lamanites who were converted unto the true faith; and they would not depart from it, for they were firm, and steadfast, and immovable, willing with all diligence to keep the commandments of the Lord."

How had this insanity happened? Mormon had the answer: "Now the cause of this iniquity of the people was this—Satan had great power, unto the stirring up of the people to do all manner of iniquity, and to the puffing them up with pride, tempting them to seek for power, and authority, and riches, and the vain things of the world. And thus Satan did lead away the hearts of the people to do all manner of iniquity; therefore they had enjoyed peace but a few years."

If that news were not bad enough, the subsequent scene was even worse: "And thus, in the commencement of the thirtieth year—the people having been delivered up for the space of a long time to be carried about by the temptations of the devil whithersoever he desired to carry them, and to do whatsoever iniquity he desired they should—and thus in the commencement of this, the thirtieth year, they were in a state of awful wickedness. *Now they did not sin ignorantly, for they knew the will of God concerning them, for it had been taught unto them; therefore they did wilfully rebel against God.*"[2807]

[2807] 3 Nephi 6:9–18; emphasis added.

They knew better! The members of the Church had been warned against seeking wealth by every prophet, including Nephi and Moses, all the way back to Adam, and they did it anyway. They thought they could serve both God and mammon, but in the end they ended up hating God, just as Jesus had predicted: "No man can serve two masters: for either he will hate the one, and love the other; or else he will hold to the one, and despise the other."[2808] The Nephites were living proof.

Scriptural Evidence That the Lord Despises the Selfish Rich

Our ability to access the Lord and receive his blessings is linked to our attitude toward money. Jacob distinguishes between those to whom the Lord responds and those whom he despises: "And whoso knocketh, to him will he open; and the wise, and the learned, and they that are rich, who are puffed up because of their learning, and their wisdom, and their riches—yea, they are they whom he despiseth; and save they shall cast these things away, and consider themselves fools before God, and come down in the depths of humility, he will not open unto them."[2809]

Nephi ends his book with a scathing rebuke, pronouncing three woes upon the prideful rich: "O the wise, and the learned, and the rich, that are puffed up in the pride of their hearts, and all those who preach false doctrines, and all those who commit whoredoms, and pervert the right way of the Lord, wo, wo, wo be unto them, saith the Lord God Almighty, for they shall be thrust down to hell!"[2810] The Lord adds another woe: "Wo unto you rich men, that will not give your substance to the poor."[2811] Another woe is pronounced by King Benjamin, who reminds us that we can lay no legitimate claim on our wealth, and if we attempt to do so, our withholding will cement our condemnation.

> And now, if God, who has created you, on whom you are dependent for your lives and for all that ye have and are, doth grant unto you whatsoever ye ask that is right, in faith, believing that ye shall receive, O then, how ye ought to impart of the substance that ye have one to another. And if ye judge the man who putteth up his petition to you for your substance that he perish not, and condemn him, how much more just will be your condemnation for withholding your substance, which doth not belong to you but to God, to whom also your life belongeth; and yet ye put up no petition, nor repent of the thing which thou hast done. I say unto you, wo be unto that man, for his substance shall perish with him; and now, I say these things unto those who are rich as pertaining to the things of this world.[2812]

Few things could cause the Lord to despise someone. But seeking and hoarding wealth, assuming ownership of that which is rightfully the Lord's, and selfishly holding back when God's children are in need will most certainly summon divine anger and trigger heavenly disgust. Choosing mammon over God is always listed among the darkest of deeds. Moreover, choosing mammon over God is to abandon covenantal loyalty, shift affection, totally disregard sacred covenants, and forget the One who gave us our blessings in the first place. By choosing mammon, we are sending God a message that we despise and hate him, and that we have found another love to serve and adore. Again, "No man can serve two masters: for either he will hate the one, and love the other; or else he will hold to the

---

[2808] Matthew 6:24.
[2809] 2 Nephi 9:42.
[2810] 2 Nephi 28:15.
[2811] D&C 56:16.
[2812] Mosiah 4:21–23.

one, and despise the other. Ye cannot serve God and mammon."[2813] According to King Benjamin, one significant way to love and serve God and to obtain eternal life is to serve God's children: "When ye are in the service of your fellow beings ye are only in the service of your God."[2814]

Persecuting the Poor

Poverty takes many forms—temporal, emotional, spiritual—but in the end, poverty always is defined by a lack. Every prophet has looked upon the condition of the poor, who are oppressed by Babylon, and grieved. In his day, Ezekiel mourned, "The people of the land have used oppression, and exercised robbery, and have vexed the poor and needy: yea, they have oppressed the stranger wrongfully."[2815] Mistreating the poor has always been indicative of the most depraved people: "Behold, this was the iniquity of thy sister Sodom, pride, fulness of bread, and abundance of idleness was in her and in her daughters, *neither did she strengthen the hand of the poor and needy.*"[2816]

The human tendency toward meanness is beyond comprehension. A disfigured child, whose condition should invite pity, is often teased, taunted, and otherwise cruelly mistreated by his peers. Likewise, the Psalmist laments of the poor, "The wicked in his pride doth persecute the poor."[2817] To persecute is to "systematically subject a race or group of people to cruel or unfair treatment; to make somebody the victim of continual pestering or harassment."[2818] The scriptures use extreme language when describing our turning away from impoverished souls. Consider the verbs *persecute, rob, hate, pollute, despise*. Sadly, the poor often search in vain for mercy: "The poor is hated even of his own neighbor."[2819] If we turn our backs on one of God's children, he takes it personally: "Whoso mocketh the poor reproacheth his Maker."[2820] Such a person cannot be classified as a follower of Christ: "And remember in all things the poor and the needy, the sick and the afflicted, for he that doeth not these things, the same is not my disciple."[2821]

On the other hand, the Lord loves and generously recompenses those who care for his disadvantaged children: "He that hath pity upon the poor lendeth unto the Lord; and that which he hath given will he pay him again."[2822]

Wo unto the Rich Who Despise the Poor

Nephi, speaking prophetically, pronounced ten woes on those to whom the Atonement is proffered and who neglect or reject the Savior who wrought it. As we shall see, these woes eventually settle on the issue of mammon-seeking.

The first of these woes condemns an attitude of disregard for and rebellion against the laws of God. A careful reading reveals the troubling fact that Nephi was speaking to members of the Church, those who have received "all the laws of God." Nephi said, "But wo unto him that has the law given, yea, that has all the commandments of God, like unto us, and that transgresseth them, and that wasteth the days of his probation, for awful is his state!" This depraved condition is inspired by Satan and embraced by vain, foolish, and spiritually frail individuals: "O that cunning plan of the evil one! O the vainness, and the frailties, and the foolishness of men! When they are learned they think they

---

[2813] Matthew 6:24.
[2814] Mosiah 2:17.
[2815] Ezekiel 22:29.
[2816] Ezekiel 16:49; emphasis added.
[2817] Psalm 10:2.
[2818] *Encarta Dictionary*, s.v. "persecute."
[2819] Proverbs 14:20.
[2820] Proverbs 17:5.
[2821] D&C 52:40.
[2822] Proverbs 19:17.

are wise, and they hearken not unto the counsel of God, for they set it aside, supposing they know of themselves, wherefore, their wisdom is foolishness and it profiteth them not. And they shall perish."

We might ask ourselves, What could cause a situation so awful that even the covenant people would perish? Nephi answered by listing his set of woes, and, significantly, he began with mammon and its impact on the poor: "But wo unto the rich, who are rich as to the things of the world. For because they are rich they despise the poor, and they persecute the meek, and their hearts are upon their treasures; wherefore, their treasure is their God. And behold, their treasure shall perish with them also."[2823]

We hear echoes of idolatry in these verses. Treasure had captured the hearts of the Saints. They worshipped their treasure adoringly, as if it were their god, and they were paying for their treasure with their souls.

They Rob the Poor

Elsewhere Nephi continues to use the imagery of worship to describe our latter-day adulation of money. In the following verse, he accuses people in the latter days of robbing the poor by using the *Lord's* money for our personal luxuries and building "sanctuaries," that is, "shrines" or "temples" wherein our god can reside: "They rob the poor because of their fine sanctuaries; they rob the poor because of their fine clothing; and they persecute the meek and the poor in heart, because in their pride they are puffed up."[2824] While Nephi may have been referencing actual places of worship, he might also have been speaking metaphorically of places or things that are not of God, which places and things we worship. Do we consider such places and things as "holy," because they represent to us that which we hold most sacred?

Such "sanctuaries" could take all sorts of forms: elegant homes, expensive cars, excessive leisure, "fine clothing," and other luxuries—anything that we worship, anything that we can point to as evidence of our industry, ingenuity, and genius. When it comes to devotion, we are devout worshipers; we are completely loyal to our false *god*. We can always be found in our "sanctuary" paying homage to the deity of mammon. And in the shadows of our sanctuaries, the poor languish and suffer.

Nephi's choice of phrase, "they rob the poor," links our withholding assistance to the poor with thievery. A person can be robbed only of something that rightfully belongs to him. We have no right to cling to or withhold that which does not rightfully belong to us. "The riches of the earth are mine to give," the Lord states emphatically. And to whom does he intend to give those riches as an inheritance? "The poor and the needy." For what purpose? To "administer to their relief that they shall not suffer."[2825] We are stewards of the Lord's property, not owners. We are under covenant to do with the Lord's money as he has directed. But if we claim or hoard the resources of our stewardship, pamper ourselves with the Lord's goods, and withhold these things from the poor, whom the goods could help, we are thieves.

Building Sanctuaries

Moroni scolded the people of the latter-days: "Ye love money more than ye love the poor. For behold, ye do love money, and your substance, and your fine apparel, and the adorning of your churches [sanctuaries], more than ye love the poor and the needy, the sick and the afflicted." Once again we hear the reference to money being used to pamper and adorn rather than helping the Lord's impoverished children. Once again we see money being wrongfully claimed and used in an unordained manner; and once again we see the poor being robbed and suffering for it. Moroni couldn't stand it.

[2823] 2 Nephi 9:27–28, 30.
[2824] 2 Nephi 28:13.
[2825] D&C 38:39, 35.

Again we read: "O ye pollutions, ye hypocrites, ye teachers, who sell yourselves for that which will canker, why have ye polluted the holy church of God? Why are ye ashamed to take upon you the name of Christ? Why do ye not think that greater is the value of an endless happiness than that misery which never dies—because of the praise of the world? Our eternal happiness is at stake, and certain misery is looming if we do not change our attitude toward the poor.

Moroni continued by asking us questions as if he were our judge. We note here that the rich neither have answers for these questions now nor will they have answers at the day of judgment: "Why do ye adorn yourselves with that which hath no life, and yet suffer the hungry, and the needy, and the naked, and the sick and the afflicted to pass by you, and notice them not? Yea, why do ye build up your secret abominations to get gain, and cause that widows should mourn before the Lord, and also orphans to mourn before the Lord, and also the blood of their fathers and their husbands to cry unto the Lord from the ground, for vengeance upon your heads?"[2826] Divine retaliation is the only answer to personal pampering with the Lord's resources and neglect and abuse of the needy.

WEALTH-SEEKING—THE SIN THAT HINDERS AND DESTROYS THE CHURCH

Alma's experience with the plague of wealth-seeking set him on a mission of reclamation.

Alma, "seeing all their inequality, began to be very sorrowful."[2827] The people whom he had loved so much were waxing "proud because of their exceeding riches, and their fine silks, and their fine-twined linen, and because of their many flocks and herds, and their gold and their silver, and all manner of precious things, which they had obtained by their industry; and in all these things were they lifted up in the pride of their eyes, for they began to wear very costly apparel."[2828] The prophet knew where this condition would lead; therefore, he relinquished the judgment seat into capable hands so that "he might preach the word of God unto them, to stir them up in remembrance of their duty, and that he might pull down, by the word of God, all the pride and craftiness and all the contentions which were among the people."[2829] The call of a prophet is to warn the people, cry repentance, and declare the truth.

Alma's task was daunting. The Nephites had enjoyed a season of peace and abundance. Many people had joined the Church, and the people had now grown prosperous. As we so often learn in the Book of Mormon, prosperity is a trial that few people can handle. Now Alma and his companions "saw and beheld with great sorrow that the people of the church began to be lifted up in the pride of their eyes, and to set their hearts upon riches and upon the vain things of the world, that they began to be scornful, one towards another, and they began to persecute those that did not believe according to their own will and pleasure."

The results of this condition were serious and included "great contentions among the people of the church; yea, there were envyings, and strife, and malice, and persecutions, and pride, even to exceed the pride of those who did not belong to the church of God." Moreover, the work of the Church had all but stopped because of the bad example of the members: "The wickedness of the church was a great stumbling-block to those who did not belong to the church; and thus the church began to fail in its progress." Alma knew that this situation could only lead to a disastrous end: "Alma saw the wickedness of the church, and he saw also that the example of the church began to lead those who were unbelievers on from one piece of iniquity to another, thus bringing on the destruction of the people."[2830]

[2826] Mormon 8:37–40.
[2827] Alma 4:15.
[2828] Alma 4:6.
[2829] Alma 4:19.
[2830] Alma 4:8–11.

THE UGLINESS OF INEQUALITY CONTRASTED WITH THE BEAUTIFUL WORK OF ANGELS

The scene worsens: "Yea, [Alma] saw great inequality among the people, some lifting themselves up with their pride, despising others, turning their backs upon the needy and the naked and those who were hungry, and those who were athirst, and those who were sick and afflicted." Where there had been happiness, prosperity, and peace, there was now misery: "Now this was a great cause for lamentations among the people." Only a few members of the Church had remained true to their covenants. Alma found these few humble, faithful souls doing the right things: "abasing themselves, succoring those who stood in need of their succor, such as imparting their substance to the poor and the needy, feeding the hungry, and suffering all manner of afflictions, for Christ's sake, who should come according to the spirit of prophecy; looking forward to that day, thus retaining a remission of their sins; being filled with great joy because of the resurrection of the dead, according to the will and power and deliverance of Jesus Christ from the bands of death." Here we note with interest that these humble followers of Christ, who were administering to the poor, were "retaining a remission of their sins."[2831]

The Lord never intended for inequality to exist among his children: "And again I say unto you, let every man esteem his brother as himself. For what man among you having twelve sons, and is no respecter of them, and they serve him obediently, and he saith unto the one: Be thou clothed in robes and sit thou here; and to the other: Be thou clothed in rags and sit thou there—and looketh upon his sons and saith I am just? Behold, this I have given unto you as a parable, and it is even as I am. I say unto you, be one; and if ye are not one ye are not mine."[2832]

Commenting on this parable, Brigham Young said, "Now the object is to improve the minds of the inhabitants of the earth, until we learn what we are here for, and become one before the Lord, that we may rejoice together and be equal. Not to make all poor, no. The whole world is before us. The earth is here, and the fulness thereof is here. It was made for man; and one man was not made to trample his fellow man under his feet, and enjoy all his heart desires, while the thousands suffer."[2833]

God created the earth to support his children equitably: "For the earth is full, and there is enough and to spare." There is enough as long as we do not hoard! "Therefore, if any man shall take of the abundance which I have made, and impart not his portion, according to the law of my gospel, unto the poor and the needy, he shall, with the wicked, lift up his eyes in hell, being in torment."[2834] President Young added, "The course pursued by men of business in the world has a tendency to make a few rich, and to sink the masses of the people in poverty and degradation. Too many of the Elders of Israel take this course. No matter what comes they are for gain—for gathering around them riches; and when they get rich how are those riches used? Spent on the lusts of the flesh, wasted as a thing of nought."[2835]

How rather should we be applying our efforts? "Take the men that can travel the earth over, preach the Gospel without purse or scrip, and then go to and lay their plans to gather the Saints. *That looks like the work of angels.*"[2836]

[2831] Alma 4:12–14.
[2832] D&C 38:25–27.
[2833] Young, *Discourses of Brigham Young*, 286.
[2834] D&C 104:17–18.
[2835] Young, *Journal of Discourses*, 11:349.
[2836] Young, *Journal of Discourses*, 8:353–54; emphasis added.

Withholding from and Judging the Poor Harshly

Some ninety years before Alma, King Benjamin laid down constitutional laws mirroring those established by Moses. Central to King Benjamin's law was the condition of our hearts and our treatment of the unfortunate: "And also, ye yourselves will succor those that stand in need of your succor; ye will administer of your substance unto him that standeth in need; and ye will not suffer that the beggar putteth up his petition to you in vain, and turn him out to perish." Harsh judgment of the poor, he said, serves only to compound our sin against these people, and we put our inheritance in the celestial kingdom at risk: "Perhaps thou shalt say: The man has brought upon himself his misery; therefore I will stay my hand, and will not give unto him of my food, nor impart unto him of my substance that he may not suffer, for his punishments are just—but I say unto you, O man, whosoever doeth this the same hath great cause to repent; and except he repenteth of that which he hath done he perisheth forever, and hath no interest in the kingdom of God."

A terrible condemnation awaits those who judge a poor person and withhold that which does not belong to them (the withholder), but to God: "And if ye judge the man who putteth up his petition to you for your substance that he perish not, and condemn him, how much more just will be your condemnation for withholding your substance, which doth not belong to you but to God, to whom also your life belongeth; and yet ye put up no petition, nor repent of the thing which thou hast done. I say unto you, wo be unto that man, for his substance shall perish with him; and now, I say these things unto those who are rich as pertaining to the things of this world."[2837]

The Evil of the Age: Life for Money

"He that oppresseth the poor to increase his riches, and he that giveth to the rich, shall surely come to want."[2838] Could there be any sin more disgusting than viewing human beings as property, their only value being that which they can produce for their owners or employers? At its worst, this attitude leads to slavery. To a lesser degree, this attitude defines the common philosophy of business: profit is more important than people—profit at all costs. Is this philosophy ethical? For Babylon, yes; for Zion, no. Often business ethics smack of the ethics advanced by Korihor, the anti-Christ: "Every man fared in this life according to the management of the creature; therefore every man prospered according to his genius, and . . . every man conquered according to his strength; and whatsoever a man did was no crime."[2839] One need only scan the horizon of modern-day business ethics to see its parallel in our times: Except in a few instances, employees are valued and compensated according to their profitability to their employer, and in the end that valuation will determine the employee's prosperity or his poverty.

Hugh Nibley traced oppression of the poor back to Cain. It was Satan, he said, who taught Cain "a special course to make him prosperous in all things: the Mahan technique, the great secret of converting life into property. Later Lamech graduates with the same degree—'Master Mahan, master of that great secret' (Moses 5:49). He glories in what he has done; it becomes the normal world economy. Nearly all the posterity of Adam, we are told, entered into business, and all Adam and Eve could do about it was to mourn before the Lord (Moses 5:27). Everyone went off following the Cainites. And Cain did it all, we are told, for the sake of getting gain (Moses 5:31). He was not ashamed; he 'gloried in that which he had done.' He said, 'I am free; surely the flocks of my brother falleth into my hands' (Moses 5:33)."[2840]

[2837] Mosiah 4:16–18, 22–23.
[2838] Proverbs 22:16.
[2839] Alma 30:17.
[2840] Nibley, *Approaching Zion*, 93–94.

"Particularly reprehensible in Nibley's view is the common practice of some employers who, in the spirit of the perverse 'work ethic,' withhold from laborers the necessities of life in exchange for services—'life in exchange for profits.' 'To make merchandise of another's necessity is an offense to human dignity.' 'The prevailing evil of the age' is 'that men withhold God's gifts from each other in a power game.'"[2841] King Benjamin denounced such dealings: "And ye will not have a mind to injure one another, but to live peaceably, and to render to every man according to that which is his due."[2842] Fair is fair. "Therefore all things whatsoever ye would that men should do to you, do ye even so to them."[2843] If the tables were turned, the rich man would be the first to cry, "Foul!"

The author of Ecclesiastes speaks of accumulating wealth and withholding one's substance from the poor as vain, or, worse, the symptoms of an "evil disease" that can result only in loneliness, sorrow, and misery: "There is a sore evil which I have seen under the sun, namely riches kept for the owners thereof to their hurt. . . . All his days also he eateth in darkness, and he hath much sorrow and wrath with his sickness. . . . There is an evil which I have seen under the sun, and it is common among men: A man to whom God hath given riches, wealth, and honour, so that he wanteth nothing for his soul of all that he desireth, yet God giveth him not power to eat thereof, but a stranger eateth it: this is vanity, and it is an evil disease."[2844]

Clearly, beyond the sins of ignoring, withholding from, and harshly judging the poor is the sin of using a poor man's labor to enrich one's self. This sin runs contrary to the Lord's law of fair pay: "The laborer is worthy of his hire."[2845] And as we have said, this sin is commonplace and defining for the last days.

A Curse on the Daughters of Zion

Isaiah prophesied that the Lord, along with the righteous fathers, kings, and prophets, will pronounce harsh judgment upon those who consume what rightfully belongs to the poor: "The Lord will enter into judgment with the ancients of his people and the princes thereof; for ye have eaten up the vineyard and the spoil of the poor in your houses."

Under such an indictment, we might cry, "Certainly you cannot mean us! What have we done to deserve such a denunciation?"

Then the Lord will answer, "Ye beat my people to pieces, and grind the faces of the poor."

We cannot believe that we are guilty of such a crime. After all, we are the chosen ones, the children of Zion. We would never stoop to such an abysmal level.

But, according to Isaiah, the Lord was adamant, and he pronounced a curse, which interestingly was directed in this case at his latter-day daughters, who would go about proudly, constantly wanting this and that, and who would be consumed by fashion:

> Because the daughters of Zion are haughty, and walk with stretched-forth necks and wanton eyes, walking and mincing as they go, and making a tinkling with their feet—therefore the Lord will smite with a scab the crown of the head of the daughters of Zion, and the Lord will discover their secret parts. In that day the Lord will take away the bravery of their tinkling ornaments, and cauls, and round tires like the moon; the chains and the bracelets, and the mufflers; the bonnets, and the ornaments of the legs, and the

---

[2841] Nibley, *Approaching Zion*, xv.
[2842] Mosiah 4:13.
[2843] Matthew 7:12.
[2844] Ecclesiastes 5:12–17; 6:1–2.
[2845] Luke 10:7; D&C 31:5; 70:12; 84:79; 106:3.

headbands, and the tablets, and the ear-rings; the rings, and nose jewels; the changeable suits of apparel, and the mantles, and the wimples, and the crisping-pins; the glasses, and the fine linen, and hoods, and the veils. And it shall come to pass, instead of sweet smell there shall be stink; and instead of a girdle, a rent; and instead of well set hair, baldness; and instead of a stomacher, a girding of sackcloth; burning instead of beauty.[2846]

Clearly, our directing money toward self-indulgence and fashion rather than dedicating it to bless the poor is an affront to God.

Blessings for Those Who Rescue the Poor

From the beginning, the Lord has pled with us to step outside ourselves and help his impoverished children. The law of Moses mandated mercy and hospitality: "If there be among you a poor man of one of thy brethren within any of thy gates in thy land which the Lord thy God giveth thee, thou shalt not harden thine heart, nor shut thine hand from thy poor brother: But thou shalt open thine hand wide unto him, and shalt surely lend him sufficient for his need, in that which he wanteth."[2847]

Other evidences of kindheartedness can be found in the law. For example, the Lord forbade charging interest on a loan to a poor man.[2848] The temple priests were to be sensitive to the poor man, who was doing his best to comply with the law of sacrifice but who could not manage the price.[2849] During the harvest, land owners were not to completely clear their fields, but leave the corners and the gleanings for the poor.[2850] The people's attitude toward giving was as important as their gift; they were to give because they wanted to and not begrudgingly: "Thou shalt surely give him, and thine heart shall not be grieved when thou givest unto him."[2851]

The law reminded the people that the poor would ever be with them, and that their efforts to rescue the poor would not only bless the poor but the generous giver: "For this thing the Lord thy God shall bless thee in all thy works, and in all that thou puttest thine hand unto. For the poor shall never cease out of the land: therefore I command thee, saying, Thou shalt open thine hand wide unto thy brother, to thy poor, and to thy needy, in thy land."[2852]

When we read these verses, we should keep in mind that the law of Moses was the lesser or preparatory law that required less of us than the higher law of Zion that was revealed by Jesus. We are under covenant to live the higher law: "Bring the poor that are cast out to thy house."[2853] In our day, he told the elders that they had a special priesthood assignment to provide for the poor: "And if any man shall give unto any of you a coat, or a suit, take the old and cast it unto the poor, and go on your way rejoicing."[2854] Because this particular commandment is listed in the same section as the oath and covenant of the priesthood, elders might consider this mandate as part of their priesthood responsibility. Likewise, in that same section, bishops are charged to "search after the poor to administer to their wants by humbling the rich and the proud."[2855] What the prophet Micah said to

---

[2846] 2 Nephi 13:14–24.
[2847] Deuteronomy 15:7–8.
[2848] Exodus 22:25.
[2849] Leviticus 14:21.
[2850] Leviticus 19:10.
[2851] Deuteronomy 15:10.
[2852] Deuteronomy 15:11.
[2853] Isaiah 58:7.
[2854] D&C 84:105.
[2855] D&C 84:112.

the Church in his day continues to be the Lord's call to the elders of the Church today: "I will consecrate their gain unto the Lord, and their substance unto the Lord of the whole earth."[2856]

Great blessings await those who will live the higher law and bless the poor with the Lord's resources: "Blessed is he that considereth the poor."[2857] The book of Proverbs promises happiness and financial security for such generosity: "He that hath mercy on the poor, happy is he."[2858] Prosperity follows the man who digs deeply into his pocket to succor the poor: "He that maketh himself poor shall have great riches."[2859] Security is another blessing: "He that giveth unto the poor shall not lack."[2860]

The scriptures contain many evidences of righteous people who consecrated their all to save impoverished souls temporally, emotionally, or spiritually, and in the process they experienced the Lord's security. An example is Elijah, who was fed by ravens and drank from a brook until the brook dried up. Then the Lord provided for him by sending him to a poor widow, whose food had dwindled to "an handful of meal in a barrel, and a little oil in a cruse." At that point, Elijah applied the Lord's law of abundance to save the poor widow and her son. Acting in the name of the Lord, Elijah asked the widow to make him "a little cake." She was to first "bring it unto [Elijah] and after make for [herself] and for [her] son." By faith, the widow fulfilled the law. When she consecrated what she had to the poor prophet, her security was assured. In return, Elijah, representing the Lord, gave her a blessing: "For thus saith the Lord God of Israel, The barrel of meal shall not waste, neither shall the cruse of oil fail, until the day [that] the Lord sendeth rain upon the earth." And the widow's blessings did not stop there. When her son fell ill and died, Elijah blessed him and brought him back to life.[2861] We would assume that her attitude of faith and her giving spirit saved her and her son. Clearly, faith in the Lord's promises and giving to bless others will result in security on every front for our families.

Another example of blessings for those who aid the needy is Zacchaeus, a rich man who loved the Lord and gave generously to the poor. When Jesus drew near, "Zacchaeus stood, and said unto the Lord; Behold, Lord, the half of my goods I give to the poor; and if I have taken anything from any man by false accusation, I restore him fourfold. And Jesus said unto him, This day is salvation come to this house."[2862] The same could be announced to anyone who qualifies by righteous living and strives to bless the poor: "This day is salvation come to this house."

THE POOR OF THE LORD'S PEOPLE SHALL TRUST IN ZION

The scriptures are replete with hope for the poor who are among the people of Zion. In the first place, the Lord hears the cries of the poor for relief: "I have heard your prayers, and the poor have complained before me."[2863] In fact, as a response to the cries of the poor, the Lord is motivated to establish Zion, a condition that they can finally trust: "The Lord hath founded Zion, and the poor of his people shall trust in it."[2864] Now Zion becomes their place of refuge.[2865] In Zion, they will never again be treated badly. Zion is their rescue, their deliverance. The Lord "raiseth up the poor out of the dust."[2866]

[2856] Micah 4:13.
[2857] Psalm 41:1.
[2858] Proverbs 14:21.
[2859] Proverbs 13:7.
[2860] Proverbs 28:27.
[2861] 1 Kings 17:1–24.
[2862] Luke 19:8–9.
[2863] D&C 38:16.
[2864] Isaiah 14:32.
[2865] 2 Nephi 14:6.
[2866] 1 Samuel 2:7.

Because of their great relief, "the poor among men shall rejoice in the Holy One of Israel."[2867] There, the people of Zion will administer to their needs.[2868] In Zion, the poor will find that their brothers and sisters have consecrated their properties to care for the poor.[2869] Consequently, in Zion there are no poor; it is like nowhere else on earth.[2870] In Zion, the rich make themselves low so that the poor might be exalted.[2871] No more will the poor mourn, for in Zion they receive equally from the Lord's storehouse, which exists to protect and sustain them.[2872] In every way, they will be provided for.[2873] The Lord has promised, "I will satisfy the poor with bread."[2874] Bread is only the beginning of their blessings. In Zion, the poor will discover that the Lord has prepared a bounteous feast for them.[2875]

Finally, the poor, as equals with their brothers and sisters, will be invited to the marriage of the Lamb.[2876] And after their long oppression, the poor shall inherit the earth.[2877]

CONSEQUENCES OF SEEKING WEALTH AND PERSECUTING THE POOR

Ironically, on the basis of eternal salvation alone, poverty and persecution serve us better than wealth and acceptance. Brigham Young said, "When I see this people grow and spread and prosper, I feel that there is more danger than when they are in poverty. *Being driven from city to city or into the mountains is nothing compared to the danger of our becoming rich* and being hailed by outsiders as a first-class community. I am afraid of only one thing. What is that? That we will not live our religion, and that we will partially slide a little from the path of rectitude, and go part of the way to meet our friends [the people of Babylon]."[2878]

Mormon, who is famous for stepping aside to comment while narrating a story, offers this scathing rebuke of the Nephites, who once again were saved and prospered by the Lord, only to abandon all their noble intentions for the pursuit of wealth:

> And thus we can behold how false, and also the unsteadiness of the hearts of the children of men; yea, we can see that the Lord in his great infinite goodness doth bless and prosper those who put their trust in him. Yea, and we may see at the very time when he doth prosper his people, yea, in the increase of their fields, their flocks and their herds, and in gold, and in silver, and in all manner of precious things of every kind and art; sparing their lives, and delivering them out of the hands of their enemies; softening the hearts of their enemies that they should not declare wars against them; yea, and in fine, doing all things for the welfare and happiness of his people; *yea, then is the time that they do harden their hearts, and do forget the Lord*

[2867] 2 Nephi 27:30.
[2868] D&C 38:35.
[2869] D&C 42:30–31, 34, 39; 44:6; 51:5; 52:40; 72:12; 105:3.
[2870] Moses 7:18.
[2871] D&C 104:16.
[2872] D&C 78:3; 82:11–12.
[2873] D&C 83:6.
[2874] Psalm 132:15.
[2875] D&C 56:8–11.
[2876] D&C 58:11.
[2877] D&C 88:17.
[2878] Young, *Discourses of Brigham Young*, 434; emphasis added.

their God, and do trample under their feet the Holy One—yea, and this because of their ease, and their exceedingly great prosperity.[2879]

The list of consequences for such actions is sobering, as detailed below.

Loss of the Providences of Heaven

Elder Joseph B. Wirthlin taught if we perceive that our prayers are not being answered, we ought to ask ourselves if we are answering the cries of the poor, the sick, the hungry, and the afflicted within our influence.[2880]

Brigham Young explained the consequences when we participate in wealth-seeking: "The Latter-day Saints who turn their attention to money-making soon become cold in their feelings toward the ordinances of the house of God. They neglect their prayers, become unwilling to pay any donations; the law of tithing gets too great a task for them; and they finally forsake their God, and the providences of heaven seem to be shut from them—all in consequence of this lust after the things of this world."[2881]

Loss of Priesthood Power and Exaltation

To tempt us, said Hugh Nibley, Satan would "use the strongest, the most powerful pitch he could use, the most irresistible weapon in his arsenal, the one that is tried and true"[2882]—lust for riches. President Young said if a man attempts to "call around him property, be he a merchant, tradesman, or farmer, with his mind continually occupied with: 'How shall I get this or that; how rich can I get; or, how much can I get out of this brother or from that brother?' and dicker and work, and take advantage here and there—no such man ever can magnify the priesthood nor enter the celestial kingdom. Now, remember, they will not enter that kingdom."[2883]

Loss of the Spirit

Joseph Smith spoke of the incompatibility of seeking simultaneously wealth and the Holy Ghost. We must be careful not to "grieve the Holy Spirit," he said. Rather, we must become "properly affected one toward another, and are careful by all means to remember, those who are in bondage, and in heaviness, and in deep affliction for your sakes." Then the caution: "And if there are any among you who aspire after their own aggrandizement, and seek their own opulence, while their brethren are groaning in poverty, and are under sore trials and temptations, they cannot be benefited by the intercession of the Holy Spirit."[2884]

Loss of Revelation

Amulek taught that the heavens withdraw "if ye turn away the needy, and the naked, and visit not the sick and afflicted, and impart of your substance, if ye have, to those who stand in need." Then he pronounces the curse: "I say unto you, if ye do not any of these things, behold, your prayer is vain, and availeth you nothing, and ye are as hypocrites who do deny the faith."[2885]

We live beneath our privileges, declared Brigham Young. "To get . . . revelation it is necessary that the people live so that their spirits are as pure and clean as a piece of blank paper . . . ready to

---

[2879] Helaman 12:1–2.
[2880] Wirthlin, "The Law of the Fast," 73.
[2881] Young, *Discourses of Brigham Young*, 315.
[2882] Nibley, *Approaching Zion*, 332.
[2883] Young, *Journal of Discourses*, 11:297.
[2884] Smith, *Teachings of the Prophet Joseph Smith*, 141.
[2885] Alma 34:28.

THE ULTIMATE TEST: GOD OR MAMMON

receive any mark the writer may make upon it. When you see the Latter-day Saints greedy, and covetous of the things of this world, do you think their minds are in a fit condition to be written upon by the pen of revelation?"[2886] Joseph Smith earlier taught the same principle: "God had often sealed up the heavens because of covetousness in the Church."[2887]

We recall the parable of the sower. Jesus explained that the person who "received seed among the thorns is he that heareth the word,"[2888] "and the cares of this world, and the deceitfulness of riches, and the lusts of other things entering in, choke the word, and it becometh unfruitful."[2889] That is, because of the deceitfulness of riches, the word of God can "bring no fruit to perfection."[2890] Where there is no Spirit there is no life.

Loss of Happy Family Life and Spiritual Commitment

President Kimball added the risks of losing happy family life and spiritual decline to the dangers of pursuing wealth and withholding from the poor: "It is hard to satisfy us. The more we have, the more we want. Why another farm, another herd of sheep, another bunch of cattle, another ranch? Why another hotel, another cafe, another store, another shop? Why another plant, another office, another service, another business? Why another of anything if one has that already which provides the necessities and reasonable luxuries? *Why continue to expand and increase holdings, especially when those increased responsibilities draw one's interests away from proper family and spiritual commitments, and from those things to which the Lord would have us give precedence in our lives?* Why must we always be expanding to the point where our interests are divided and our attentions and thoughts are upon the things of the world? Certainly when one's temporal possessions become great, it is very difficult for one to give proper attention to the spiritual things."[2891]

Loss of the Lord's Help

"Whoso stoppeth his ears at the cry of the poor, he also shall cry himself, but shall not be heard."[2892] Divine deafness is a terrible curse that the Lord imposes on the proud, the selfish and the insensitive. When we stop listening to the poor, the Lord stops listening to us, and when he stops listening, he stops helping.

The Nephite king Limhi knew why his people had suffered severely without the Lord's rescue. "Therefore, who wondereth that they are in bondage, and that they are smitten with sore afflictions? For behold, the Lord hath said: I will not succor my people in the day of their transgression; but I will hedge up their ways that they prosper not; and their doings shall be as a stumbling block before them."[2893] When we stop our ears at the cries of the poor, we commit transgression. The Lord ceases to listen to us, and when he stops helping, our prosperity turns to poverty. Suddenly, we find ourselves in bondage with no relief and we wonder why.

Loss of True Worship

President Young chastised the Saints for shifting their worship from the true God to the god of mammon: "Many professing to be Saints seem to have no knowledge, no light, to see anything beyond a dollar, or a pleasant time, a comfortable house, a fine farm, &c., &c. O fools, and slow of heart to

---

[2886] Young, *Journal of Discourses*, 11:240–41.
[2887] Smith, *Teachings of the Prophet Joseph Smith*, 9.
[2888] Matthew 13:22.
[2889] Mark 4:19.
[2890] Luke 8:14.
[2891] Kimball, *The Teachings of Spencer W. Kimball*, 354.
[2892] Proverbs 21:13.
[2893] Mosiah 7:28–29.

understand the purposes of God and his handiwork among the people."[2894] And at another time: "Go to the child, and what does its joy consist in? Toys, we may call them, something that produces, as they think, pleasure; and so it is with our youth, our young boys and girls; they are thinking too much of this world; and the middle-aged are striving and struggling to obtain the good things of this life, and their hearts are too much upon them. So it is with the aged. Is not this the condition of the Latter-day Saints? It is. . . . *The Latter-day Saints are drifting as fast as they can into idolatry*, drifting into the spirit of the world and into pride and vanity."[2895]

Failure in Our Mission

Our missions in life fail when we set our hearts upon riches. Again, Brigham Young said, "If the Lord ever revealed anything to me, he has shown me that the Elders of Israel must let speculation alone and attend to the duties of their calling, otherwise they will have little or no power in their missions."[2896] Elder Bruce R. McConkie explained it this way:

> The children of Zion fail in their great mission for two reasons: (1) Oftentimes they set their hearts upon temporal things and are more concerned with amassing the things that moth and rust corrupt, and that thieves break through and steal, than in laying up for themselves treasures in heaven. Hence the divine direction: "But the laborer in Zion shall labor for Zion; for if they labor for money they shall perish." (2 Nephi 26:31.) (2) Others fail to live by the high standards of belief and conduct imposed by the gospel. Of them the divine word says: 'Your minds in times past have been darkened because of unbelief, and because you have treated lightly the things you have received—which vanity and unbelief have brought the whole church under condemnation. And this condemnation resteth upon the children of Zion, even all. And they shall remain under this condemnation until they repent and remember the new covenant, even the Book of Mormon and the former commandments which I have given them, not only to say, but to do according to that which I have written—that they may bring forth fruit meet for their Father's kingdom; otherwise there remaineth a scourge and judgment to be poured out upon the children of Zion." (D&C 84:54–58.)[2897]

Loss of Peace

Peace is forfeited when we seek wealth over the things of God, and turn a deaf ear to those in need. Brigham Young did not mince words on this subject: "What is the matter with them? The god of this world has blinded their minds, they give way to selfishness, covetousness, and divers other kinds of wickedness, suffer the allurements of this world to decoy them from the paths of truth, forget their God, their religion, their covenants, and the blessings they have received, and become like beasts, made to be taken and destroyed at the will of the destroyer. This is the situation, not only of the great majority of the world, but of many of the inhabitants of these valleys; they have no correct idea of the day of destruction, the day of calamity; they have no realization of the day of sorrow and retribution.

[2894] Young, *Journal of Discourses*, 8:63.
[2895] Young, *Journal of Discourses*, 18:239; emphasis added.
[2896] Young, *Discourses of Brigham Young*, 315.
[2897] McConkie, *A New Witness for the Articles of Faith*, 580.

They put these things far away and do not wish to think about them, but say, 'Let us eat, drink, and lay down and sleep, and that is all we desire'; then like the brutes they are happy. *It never enters the hearts of the mass of mankind that they are preparing for the day of calamity and slaughter.*"[2898]

The Doctrine and Covenants is filled with such warnings. Hugh Nibley offers the following list:

> Almost the first words spoken by the Lord himself to the boy Joseph in his first vision were, "Behold the world lieth in sin at this time and none doeth good no not one, they have turned aside [sic] from the Gospel and keep not my commandments they draw near to me with their lips while their hearts are far from me and mine anger is kindling against the inhabitants of the earth to visit them acording [sic] to this ungodliness." The preface to the Doctrine and Covenants repeats this: "They seek not the Lord, . . . but every man walketh in his own way . . . in Babylon, even Babylon the great, which shall fall" (D&C 1:16). And so on down: "Behold, the world is ripening in iniquity" (D&C 18:6). "The hour is nigh and the day soon at hand when the earth is ripe; and all the proud and they that do wickedly shall be as stubble; . . . I will take vengeance upon the wicked, for they will not repent; for the cup of mine indignation is full" (D&C 29:9, 17). "All flesh is corrupted before me; and the powers of darkness prevail upon the earth, . . . and all eternity is pained, and the angels are waiting. . . . The enemy is combined" (D&C 38:11–12). (Do such words mean nothing to us?) "Behold, the day has come, when the cup of the wrath of mine indignation is full. . . . Wherefore, labor ye; . . . for the adversary spreadeth his dominions, and darkness reigneth; and the anger of God kindleth against the inhabitants of the earth; and none doeth good, for all have gone out of the way" (D&C 43:26, 28; 82:5–6). "Darkness covereth the earth, and gross darkness the minds of the people, and all flesh has become corrupt before my face. Behold, vengeance cometh speedily . . . upon all the face of the earth. . . . And upon my house shall it begin, . . . first among . . . you . . . who have professed to know my name and have not known me" (D&C 112:23–26).
>
> So the word of the Lord is that Babylon is to remain in Babylon until the day of destruction. Things have not improved since Joseph Smith wrote of "the most damning hand of murder, tyranny, and oppressions, supported and urged on and upheld by the influence of that spirit which has so strongly riveted the creeds of the fathers, who have inherited lies, upon the hearts of the children, and filled the world with confusion, and has been growing stronger and stronger, and is now the very mainspring of all corruption, and the whole earth groans under the weight of its iniquity" (D&C 123:7). "Some may have cried peace," he wrote (and no man ever loved peace more than he), "but the Saints and the world will have little peace from henceforth." "*Destruction,* to the eye of the spiritual beholder, seems to be written by the finger of an invisible hand, in large capitals, upon almost every thing we behold." "There is a spirit that prompts the

---

[2898] Young, *Journal of Discourses,* 3:273.

nations to prepare for war, desolation, and bloodshed—to waste each other away," said Brigham twenty years later. "Do they realize it? No. . . . Is it not a mystery?" "When the nations have for years turned much of their attention to manufacturing instruments of death, they have sooner or later used those instruments. . . . [They] will be used until the people are wasted away, and there is no help for it."[2899]

What is the chief cause of this wickedness? As Nibley said, the Lord opened the Doctrine and Covenants with the answer: "They seek not the Lord to establish his righteousness, but every man walketh in his own way, and after the image of his own god, whose image is in the likeness of the world, and whose substance is that of an idol."[2900] The Lord will tolerate this condition only for so long. Brigham Young makes the following prophetic statement: "You will see that the wisdom of the wise among the nations will perish and be taken from them. They will fall into difficulties, and they will not be able to tell the reason, nor point a way to avert them any more than they can now in this land. They can fight, quarrel, contend and destroy each other, but they do not know how to make peace. So it will be with the inhabitants of the earth."[2901]

Loss of National Security

Commenting on the global implications of wealth-seeking, Joseph Fielding McConkie and Robert Millet offer this insight: "A civilization that wastes its strength in the pursuit of either wealth or glory will not stand. A nation that fosters or encourages selfishness, that allows greed and lust to go unchecked, will sink under its own weight. Babylon will fall because its citizenry will come in time to shun and hate and destroy all that oppose them. Zion will arise and shine forth as an ensign to the nations because its municipals seek the interest of their neighbors and do all things with an eye single to the glory of God (D&C 82:19)."[2902]

The poor are the victims of individual and national selfishness. Hugh Nibley writes: "A community which can at tolerable expense eliminate human distress but refrains from doing so either must believe that it benefits from unemployment or poverty, or that the poor and unemployed are bad people, or that other more important values will be impaired by attempts to help the lower orders—or all of these statements." Quoting a well-known economist Daniel Yergin, Nibley points out the poverty of the 1970s "could have been eliminated at a modest shift of $10–15 billion to the poor from the rest of the community. 15 billion is less than 1.5% of the GNP, about the size of one of the cheaper weapons systems."[2903]

Imagine, now, the law of consecration as a solution for the world's woes. How would life appear if love motivated the actions of governments and citizenry? We need not look beyond The Church of Jesus Christ of Latter-day Saints for an answer. Perhaps better than any other organization, the Saints voluntarily take care of each other by their consecrations, which are motivated by the pure purpose of love. No wonder, then, that President George Q. Cannon called for a change of heart and putting first things first: "We must serve God with all our hearts, our love and affections reaching after Him, and the things of this world must be looked upon by us as secondary considerations. They are good enough in their place; right enough to be attended to; but subordinate always to the love of God."[2904]

[2899] Nibley, *Approaching Zion*, 44–45; quoting Smith, *Teachings of the Prophet Joseph Smith*, 160, 15; Young, *Journal of Discourses*, 8:174–75, 157.

[2900] D&C 1:16.

[2901] Young, *Journal of Discourses*, 10:315.

[2902] McConkie and Millet, *Doctrinal Commentary on the Book of Mormon*, 3:5.

[2903] Nibley, *Approaching Zion*, 515.

[2904] Cannon, *Journal of Discourses*, 22:288–89.

WHO SHALL ENTER?

The Savior's parable of the sheep and goats lays out the criteria for "everlasting punishment" or "eternal life." First, to the sheep, who represent the righteous: "Then shall the King say unto them on his right hand, Come, ye blessed of my Father, inherit the kingdom prepared for you from the foundation of the world: For I was an hungered, and ye gave me meat: I was thirsty, and ye gave me drink: I was a stranger, and ye took me in: Naked, and ye clothed me: I was sick, and ye visited me: I was in prison, and ye came unto me."

Then to the goats, who represent the unrighteous: "Then shall he say also unto them on the left hand, Depart from me, ye cursed, into everlasting fire, prepared for the devil and his angels: For I was an hungered, and ye gave me no meat: I was thirsty, and ye gave me no drink: I was a stranger, and ye took me not in: naked, and ye clothed me not: sick, and in prison, and ye visited me not."[2905]

Gospel writer Matthew B. Brown asks:

> How should Latter-day Saints prepare themselves to be counted among the sheep instead of the goats during the Final Judgment? The way is pointed out in simplicity within the text of the parable itself. According to the Son of God, true Saints who are prepared will (1) give food to the hungry and water to the thirsty, (2) provide shelter and clothing to the needy, and (3) minister to the sick and imprisoned.
>
> The Lord considers such charitable service for the benefit of His brethren as if it were being done for Him. As aptly stated in the Book of Mormon, those who are in the service of their fellow beings are considered to be in the service of God (see Mosiah 2:17). And the reward for engaging in freewill service is to be "blessed" by the Creator of heaven and earth with a blessing with eternal ramifications. Those who fail to act in mortality with a benevolent heart will also receive recompense for which they qualify. . . . To be counted among the sheep when the Lord comes and plumbs the depths of mortal souls will require a sincere effort to bless the lives of others.[2906]

WHAT DOTH IT PROFIT?

Jesus' brother James had much to say about the attitude of the rich concerning their wealth and their treatment of the poor. He peppered his epistle with prophetic counsel that should give us cause to reflect. As an example, he wrote, "For the sun is no sooner risen with a burning heat, but it withereth the grass, and the flower thereof falleth, and the grace of the fashion of it perisheth: so also shall the rich man fade away in his ways."[2907] That is, the rich man might prosper for a season, but his status is fleeting. As sure as the grass will wither in the heat of the sun or petals will one day fall from a flower, so will a rich man's affluence also fade.

James continued by stating that we often hold to an attitude that the Lord finds totally abhorrent, favoring the rich while oppressing the poor: "For if there come unto your assembly a man with a gold ring, in goodly apparel, and there come in also a poor man in vile raiment; and ye have

---

[2905] Matthew 25:31–46.
[2906] Brown, *Prophecies—Signs of the Times*, 129–30.
[2907] James 1:11.

respect to him that weareth the gay clothing, and say unto him, Sit thou here in a good place; and say to the poor, Stand thou there, or sit here under my footstool, Are ye not then partial in yourselves, and are become judges of evil thoughts?" This is an ugly practice: "If ye have respect to persons, ye commit sin."[2908]

"What doth it profit?' James asked. "If a brother or sister be naked, and destitute of daily food, and one of you say unto them, Depart in peace, be ye warmed and filled; notwithstanding ye give them not those things which are needful to the body; what doth it profit?"[2909] That is, when we see someone in need, do we pat them on the head, and send them away only with hollow words of comfort that will neither warm nor fill? When a coat is needed, words will not provide warmth; when food is needed, distant sympathy will not fill an empty belly.

James was indignant with those who pray and ask God to add to their prosperity. Is there not hypocrisy in a prayer that solicits personal needs, when the underlying intent is to gain more for ourselves? Are we justified in asking God whether or not we should purchase things that accrue to our lusts? God will not answer such prayers: "Ye ask, and receive not, because ye ask amiss, that ye may consume it upon your lusts."[2910] This brand of hypocrisy incensed Brigham Young: "I have seen [men] who, when they had a chance to buy a widow's cow for ten cents on the dollar of her real value in cash, would make the purchase, and then thank the Lord that he has so blessed them."[2911] James called such people enemies of God: "Know ye not that the friendship of the world is enmity with God? whosoever therefore will be a friend of the world is the enemy of God."

Are we really willing to act this way? This is not the gospel of Jesus Christ. James gave us a definition: "Pure religion and undefiled before God and the Father is this, To visit the fatherless and widows in their affliction, and to keep himself unspotted from the world."[2912] The essence of the gospel is to help the helpless and to remain separate from Babylon and her ways.

James pronounced woes upon the selfish rich: "Go to now, ye rich men, weep and howl for your miseries that shall come upon you. Your riches are corrupted, and your garments are moth-eaten. Your gold and silver is cankered; and the rust of them shall be a witness against you, and shall eat your flesh as it were fire. Ye have heaped treasure together for the last days." He condemned the businessman, who oppresses the hirelings and enriches himself on their labor: "Behold, the hire of the labourers who have reaped down your fields, which is of you kept back by fraud, crieth: and the cries of them which have reaped are entered into the ears of the Lord of Sabaoth. Ye have lived in pleasure on the earth, and been wanton; ye have nourished your hearts, as in a day of slaughter."[2913]

Throughout James's epistle, his question haunts us: *What doth it profit?* Jesus posed the same question to his disciples: "For what doth it profit a man if he gain the whole world . . . and he lose his own soul, and he himself be a castaway?"[2914] And yet we persist.

THE VOICE OF SEVEN THUNDERS

Brigham Young could not stand the ever-growing tendency toward covetousness, and he continually taught against it. In the last speech he ever gave, he cried: "Now those that can see the spiritual atmosphere can see that many of the Saints are still glued to this earth and lusting and longing after the things of this world, in which there is no profit. . . . According to the present feelings of many of our brethren, they would arrogate to themselves this world and all that pertains to it. . . . Where are

---

[2908] James 2:2–4, 9.
[2909] James 2:15–16.
[2910] James 4:4.
[2911] Young, *Journal of Discourses*, 17:362.
[2912] James 1:27.
[2913] James 5:1–5.
[2914] JST Luke 9:25.

the eyes and the hearts of this people? . . . All the angels in heaven are looking at this little handful of people, and stimulating them to the salvation of the human family. So also are the devils in hell looking at this people, too, and trying to overthrow us, *and the people are still shaking hands with the servants of the devil, instead of sanctifying themselves.*"

He appealed to us to imagine what wisdom our forefathers would impart to us: "What do you suppose the fathers would say if they could speak from the dead? . . . What would they whisper in our ears? Why, if they had the power the very thunders of heaven would be in our ears, if we could but realize the importance of the work we are engaged in. . . . *When I think upon this subject, I want the tongues of seven thunders to wake up the people.*"[2915]

Choosing God over Mammon

As we have said, the Lord gave us the law of consecration, in part, for our safety, security, and salvation. This law provides the *only* way to pass the mortal test of money and arrive in the celestial kingdom. That lofty goal requires that we must be willing to choose consecration as a way of life over the way of Babylon. We must consider everything we are and have as belonging to God; we must view ourselves as stewards rather than owners; we must agree to be accountable to God and his servants for the things that God places in our safekeeping; and we must labor for the cause of Zion and not for selfish reasons or for the sake of making and accumulating money. In other words, the law of consecration requires that we give God our hearts, our all, and that we dedicate ourselves to his work and his children.

Our eventual placement in a kingdom of glory depends upon our adherence to the law of consecration and our living its principles out of love. According to John Tvedtnes, this law is illustrated in Doctrine and Covenants 76, the revelation that describes the various resurrections. He concludes, "Only those who obey the Lord's commandments out of love and a simple desire to do good will inherit the celestial kingdom. Those who obey out of fear of punishment or hope of reward, while good people, will inherit the terrestrial kingdom."[2916] And we would add that telestial people are those who must be constrained to obey. These people have lived with scant desire to do good. They have rejected and despised God, and a worse group still, the sons of Perdition, have hated him.

How, then, might we choose God over mammon, cease compromising, and stop trying to marry the two? We return to Jacob's formula for the answer: "Think of your brethren like unto yourselves, and be familiar with all and free with your substance, that they may be rich like unto you."[2917] We must start with love—love for God and his children. "Therefore all things whatsoever ye would that men should do to you, do ye even so to them."[2918] If we truly love, we cannot stand to see suffering or lack of any kind. We attack these situations and smother conditions of lack with kindness and charity until they cease to exist among us. Then, because charity is the "pure love of Christ,"[2919] love expands with each charitable act until our love approaches the Savior's love, which is infinite and "broad as eternity."[2920] When we encounter more suffering, we feel more empathy, which causes our capacity to love to grow. When that happens, we yearn for more resources so that we might alleviate more misery. That yearning conveys us to God, who is the source of all good things. To him we make our request, for that is the eternal law; we must ask to receive: "And whatsoever ye shall ask the

---

[2915] Young, *Journal of Discourses*, 18:305.
[2916] Tvedtnes, "They Have Their Reward," Feb. 21, 2007.
[2917] Jacob 2:18.
[2918] Matthew 7:12.
[2919] Moroni 7:47.
[2920] Moses 7:53.

Father in my name, which is right, believing that ye shall receive, behold it shall be given unto you."[2921]

At this point, Jacob makes an interjection: "But before ye seek for riches, seek ye for the kingdom of God."[2922] The kingdom of God is defined by the new and everlasting covenant, which includes the covenant of baptism and the oath and covenant of the priesthood. Hence, Jesus ordained and commissioned the Seventy, saying in part, "And heal the sick that are therein, and say unto them, The kingdom of God is come nigh unto you."[2923] That is, "We, the ordained servants of God, who are preaching the gospel and administering its covenants and ordinances, have come to you." When we have received the new and everlasting covenant by baptism (men and women), then the ordination of the priesthood (men), followed by the temple blessings associated with the priesthood (men and women), we, by covenant, are clearly of the kingdom of God. We have the right to ask the Lord for his help and for resources in another's behalf.

OBTAINING A HOPE IN CHRIST

We enhance our ability to ask by taking the next step stated by Jacob: "obtain a hope in Christ."[2924] It is one thing to believe that Christ exists, but it is quite another to believe *who* he is. Therein lies hope. When we understand that he, like his Father, knows our past, present, and future in detail, has all power in heaven and on earth, is perfectly consistent, and loves us completely, we have obtained a hope in him. In *Lectures on Faith*, the Prophet Joseph Smith stated that our faith pivots on our hope and belief that God possesses certain attributes and characteristics in absolute perfection. We would say the same of the Savior. In times of urgency, we *hope* that he has the power to help, we *hope* that he is aware of us, and we *hope* that he loves us enough to rush to our rescue. Because of our hope in him, we are willing to reach out to him and plead for his help. We make this effort because we hope that he has both the ability and the disposition to grant our request. Therefore, when we search our faith and find it lacking, we might ask, "Which of these characteristics do I believe that God does not possess?" Our hope in Christ provides the answer: The Savior lacks neither the perfection of godlike attributes nor divine characteristics.

Personalized, the *Lectures on Faith* might read as follows:

POWERFUL. God is all-powerful. Otherwise, how could we believe that he could help us if we imagined that something was beyond his ability? Nothing is too hard for him. He can do anything, in any situation, at any time, in our behalf.

KNOWLEDGEABLE. God possesses all knowledge about everything, including past, present, and future events. Otherwise, how could we believe that he could anticipate and solve our problems if there was something that he didn't know, or if his attention was momentarily diverted away from us, or if we thought he had forgotten us? He intimately knows and "foreknows" us and is constantly aware of our thoughts and our circumstances.

LOVING. We are God's children. We have all of his attention all of the time. He loves us completely. He is merciful, compassionate, kind, comforting, patient, gracious, and abundant in goodness. Otherwise, how could we seek his help to face unbearable situations or to take the difficult steps of change if anything we were going through or had done could distance us from his love? His love for us is unconditional and continual and is the consistent motivating force in his interactions with us.

[2921] 3 Nephi 18:20.
[2922] Jacob 2:18.
[2923] Luke 10:9.
[2924] Jacob 2:19.

The Ultimate Test: God or Mammon

CONSISTENT. God is perfectly unchangeable. What he did yesterday he will be doing today and tomorrow. Otherwise, how could we anticipate the whims or circumstances that could change his mercy for us to reproach or his love for us to hatred?

JUST. God is perfectly equitable and no respecter of persons. Otherwise, how could we believe in him if we thought that he played favorites? If God's laws specify blessings and consequences, we can count on his justice prevailing and his judgment to be correct.

TRUTHFUL. God cannot lie. He does not make promises casually. Otherwise, how could we believe that our future with him is secure if we thought that he didn't mean what he said, or might seek an out, or might change his mind? He will keep his word in his own way and in his own time.[2925]

Ultimately, our faith in the Father and the Son is strengthened or injured according to our trusting in their divine attributes of character. Faith and trust are synonyms. There are only three reasons for not trusting someone: (1) *I don't know you well enough;* (2) *My past experience with you was disappointing or inconsistent;* (3) *I don't think you can help me.* We might ask ourselves which of these reasons retards our trusting Christ, as we should. Clearly, the deficit is ours alone.

Jacob said if we can push through and obtain a hope in Christ, "ye shall obtain riches, if ye seek them; and ye will seek them for the intent to do good—to clothe the naked, and to feed the hungry, and to liberate the captive, and administer relief to the sick and the afflicted."[2926] The act of administering to the needy is the testimony that we have received a hope in Christ.

FREELY YE HAVE RECEIVED, FREELY GIVE

And administer we must.

Jesus admonished the Seventy, "Freely ye have received, freely give."[2927] By baptism and ordination, the Seventy had embarked on a new path leading to eternal life. Along the way, they would freely receive covenants and ordinances, *gifts* "without price."[2928] Because the *only* way to arrive in the celestial kingdom is to "freely give" of what we have received to alleviate misery, the Seventy went forth distributing their gifts freely so as to bring people to Christ, who heal them. From this point forward, the Seventy were called the "salt of the earth," the "light of the world,"[2929] and "saviors on Mount Zion,"[2930] representing in every way *the* Savior and doing things as he would do them. Jesus commanded them: "Heal the sick, cleanse the lepers, raise the dead, cast out devils."[2931]

Representing Jesus is a weighty responsibility. In a remarkable manner, we become to Jesus what he is to his Father: "As my Father hath sent me, even so send I you."[2932] Given these truths, could we justify ourselves in dividing our affections from the One who had entrusted and endowed us? Could we receive the Lord's goods, then hoard them and ignore his children—the very ones whom he has sent us into the world to save? The Seventy knew better. They fulfilled their commission and returned rejoicing, absolutely astonished at the power of the gifts the Lord had given them: "And the seventy returned again with joy, saying, Lord, even the devils are subject unto us through thy name."[2933]

[2925] This list is a partial adaptation from *Lectures on Faith*.
[2926] Jacob 2:19.
[2927] Matthew 10:8.
[2928] 2 Nephi 9:50; 26:25; Alma 1:20; Isaiah 55:1.
[2929] Matthew 5:13–14.
[2930] Obadiah 1:21.
[2931] Matthew 10:8.
[2932] John 20:21.
[2933] Luke 10:17.

Feeding the Lord's Lambs

To become Zion people and represent the Savior, we must become like him. That is the burden of baptism, according to Alma.[2934] The Israelites, who desired to enter into the new and everlasting covenant and make such a transformation, asked John the Baptist, "What shall we do then? He answereth and saith unto them, He that hath two coats, let him impart to him that hath none; and he that hath meat, let him do likewise."[2935] Change begins with that simple formula: quit being selfish; step outside of yourself and help someone.

Peter took seriously his giving freely of what he had been given. When a lame man begged alms of him, he replied, "Silver and gold have I none; but such as I have give I thee: In the name of Jesus Christ of Nazareth rise up and walk."[2936] Peter had previously given away all his silver and gold in the service of the Savior, but that did not stop him from continuing to minister. Such as he had, he gave freely. He had evidently learned this lesson on two special occasions when he had participated in feeding the five thousand and later the four thousand.[2937] In each giving experience, Jesus had commanded Peter and the apostles to gather up the fragments, which, to their amazement, filled their baskets. Peter must have learned at least two lessons on these occasions: (1) *My job is to feed the Lord's sheep; Jesus' job is to bless my meager offering so that it becomes enough to feed many. He is my perfect partner.* (2) *When it is my turn to eat, I will always have enough; in fact, I will have more than I started with.*

By giving away our goods will we end up with less? No. As Peter learned, we are not really giving away our goods or money; we are planting them with the hope of an abundant harvest. Our offering is an act of faith in the Lord of the Harvest—faith that he will keep his promise and that we will reap untold blessings. This is Zion's celestial law of prosperity, the law that guarantees incredible returns, "an hundredfold."[2938] Our covenant relationship with the Lord ensures our safety while we are giving. This is also called the manna principle, which supplies our daily bread,[2939] that which is sufficient for our needs. But to obtain these blessings requires that we put first things first: "Seek ye first the kingdom of God, and his righteousness; and all these things shall be added unto you."[2940] Then we can be assured that while we are feeding the Lord's lambs, he will take care of us. That is the promise of security enjoyed by Zion people.

Choosing God's Marvelous Work over Babylon's Charms

To live this way calls for a new way of thinking. While Babylon shouts, "Gather about you property for your security," Zion counters with "Man shall not live by bread alone, but by every word that proceedeth out of the mouth of God."[2941] Our choice should be clear. When we took upon us the new and everlasting covenant and thereafter received the blessings of the priesthood, we agreed to come out of Babylon and choose God over mammon forevermore.

Choosing God over mammon also suggests that we also choose to do his marvelous work, as stated in Doctrine and Covenants 4: "Now behold, a marvelous work is about to come forth among the children of men. Therefore, O ye that embark in the service of God, see that ye serve him with all your heart, might, mind and strength, that ye may stand blameless before God at the last day." By

---

[2934] Mosiah 18:8–10.
[2935] Luke 3:10–11.
[2936] Acts 3:6.
[2937] Mark 6:35–44; 8:1–9.
[2938] Luke 8:8; Matthew 19:29.
[2939] Matthew 6:11.
[2940] Matthew 6:33.
[2941] Matthew 4:4.

taking upon us the new and everlasting covenant and receiving the priesthood, we signal our desire to choose and serve God over mammon, therefore we are "called to the work."

The work we have to do is as daunting as Peter's feeding of the five thousand with five loaves and two fishes: "For behold the field is white already to harvest." Only the Lord of the Harvest could increase our meager effort to reap such a harvest. Nevertheless, if we will courageously thrust in our sickle with our might, the Lord assures us of success and salvation to our soul.

While Babylon would qualify her servants with gold, silver, intellect, and flattering words, Zion would qualify her servants with "faith, hope, charity and love, with an eye single to the glory of God," and additionally, "faith, virtue, knowledge, temperance, patience, brotherly kindness, godliness, charity, humility, diligence." Admittedly, Zion is a far cry from Babylon. But if we will embrace such a Zionlike lifestyle, the Lord promises us the key to his abundance: "Ask, and ye shall receive; knock, and it shall be opened unto you."[2942]

It is interesting to note that the humble servants of Zion are often referred to as the "weak things,"[2943] whom the Lord makes strong through his grace.[2944]

INVOKING THE LAW OF ASKING TO RECEIVE

Feeding the Lord's lambs with scanty resource is a monumental act of faith. Only with love, driven by a determined desire to serve and trust in the Lord, could we accomplish such a feat. This act of donating the widow's mite to help another person is a clear indication that we have chosen God over mammon. The Lord helps us by giving us the Law of Asking.

The law of asking provides that we may draw upon the Lord's vast resources to feed his sheep with the promise that as we do, we will always have enough to feed ourselves. Asking is an act of faith: we recognize the sovereignty of God; we acknowledge that he has infinite resources that he is willing to give us; and we concede that he has the power to make and keep promises, and to do anything for or give anything to us. By asking, we acknowledge that we share with him a child-to-parent relationship—a covenant bond that makes us *partners* in his work.

Asking is an eternal principle; our eternal progression depends upon the law of asking. Throughout eternity, we will surely go to God countless times to ask permission to draw resources from his higher kingdom so that we might grow and manage the affairs of our emerging kingdoms.

In this life, by invoking the law of asking, we *receive* the Holy Ghost;[2945] husbands and wives *receive* each other as gifts from God; worthy men *receive* the priesthood and thus *receive* the Lord;[2946] and ultimately, by continuing to ask to receive, we obtain the promise: "he that *receiveth* my Father *receiveth* my Father's kingdom; therefore all that my Father hath shall be given unto him."[2947] To receive any good thing from God, we must first ask.

This is the doctrine of Zion that provides for the abundant life that Jesus promised.[2948] This is a reward for those who choose God over mammon.

SUMMARY AND CONCLUSION

Among the tests of life, one test stands supreme: the choice between God and mammon. Because we cannot serve both, we are forced to choose. The test of wealth determines if we can we be trusted with God's resources. Therefore, in part, the Lord gave us the law of consecration to keep us safely on

---

[2942] D&C 4:1–7.
[2943] D&C 1:19; 35:13; 124:1; 133:59.
[2944] Ether 12:27.
[2945] John 20:22.
[2946] D&C 84:35.
[2947] D&C 84:38; emphasis added.
[2948] John 10:10.

his side and free from the destructive nature of mammon-seeking. We are to manage our stewardship according to God's desires and use the surplus for its intended use: to take care of God's children and build up the kingdom of God for the establishment of Zion. Because the choice between God and mammon is difficult and the stakes are high, only the pure in heart can pass the test. Without divine intervention, we could not have the power to choose God over mammon.

To give us sufficient faith to make this choice, the Lord makes us an offer to be tested on the principles of consecration. That is, as we choose him over mammon, he gives us evidence that he will take care of us and even prosper us. The law that God offers to be tested upon is the law of tithes and offerings. Because this law is a celestial law, the math never makes sense in a telestial setting, so we are forced to live it on faith alone. That we always end up with more than we donate is a truism, but we are hard-pressed to explain how that can be. As we live this manifestation of consecration, we discover that tithing *prepares* us to become Zionlike, and offerings are the *opportunity* to become Zionlike. While tithing is a defined amount, offerings are not; offerings, therefore, are more a condition of the heart than tithing, and thus offerings require more faith to donate. In the end, consecration is about love, the proving of the heart. Consecration is about relationship: either we love God or we love mammon. If we give God our heart, giving him our money is easy.

The restoration of the gospel marked the beginning of a change of orders in the world. The order of Babylon, which has oppressed God's people for millennia, will collapse and a new order—Zion—will burst upon the stage of human history. Zion's advent will be an act of mercy for the salvation of all mankind.[2949] Until then, we are to choose God over mammon while living among the people of Babylon, calling as many of them as possible out of Babylon and into Zion.

In one sentence, the Apostle James identifies the origin of all sin: *"the love of money."* President Anthon H. Lund said, "There is hardly a commandment but is violated through this seeking for riches."[2950] The love of money violates the last of the Ten Commandments, which directs us to not covet. This broken law results in the loss of the "fulness of the law" of the priesthood, which would enable men to become kings and priests after the order of Melchizedek, or an endless life. The same could be said of women, who would become queens and priestesses. We cannot break this last law, *covetousness*, and expect to receive the fulness of the priesthood, along with its attendant blessings.

As covetousness was the last law given in the lesser law, the law of consecration is the last law given in the higher law. Consecration protects us from covetousness and idolatry by defining the usage of our surpluses. If we keep this last law, we will prosper and experience abundance beyond any telestial effort that we might make to enrich ourselves.

Choosing between God and mammon is a "weighty matter." Our success in arriving in Zion depends upon our attitude toward money: "Let them repent of all their sins, and of all their covetous desires, before me, saith the Lord; for what is property unto me? saith the Lord." The things of the world are but a drop in an ocean of blessings. Therefore, why would we choose to "covet that which is but the drop, and neglect the more weighty matters?"[2951] The Zoramites chose the drop over the weighty matters and lost their blessings. To rationalize their choice, they defined gain as godliness.[2952] They tried to make mammon holy. They saw themselves as good, and thus their wealth-seeking must be good. When the original premise is wrong, all points that stem from the premise are wrong. Joseph Smith observed that the Saints, like the Zoramites, were trying to mix mammon with Zion and were rationalizing their actions with supposed pious purposes. The Prophet cried, "Now I want to tell you that Zion cannot be built up in any such way."[2953]

[2949] D&C 1.
[2950] Lund, Conference Report, Apr. 1903, 97.
[2951] D&C 117:4, 8.
[2952] 1 Timothy 6:5.
[2953] Stevenson, *Life and History of Elder Edward Stevenson*, 40–41; emphasis added.

We have been warned repeatedly against compromise. Despite our imaginations, we simply cannot embrace Zion and mammon simultaneously. "Zion cannot be built up unless it is by the principles of the law of the celestial kingdom." Nevertheless, the Latter-day Saints still try to compromise: "We will not go up unto Zion, and will keep our moneys."[2954] But it is not possible.

Whereas mammon is unholy, consecrated wealth is holy; but it must be acquired for the purposes and in the order the Lord prescribed. Jacob said, "But before ye seek for riches, seek ye for the kingdom of God." First things first. "And *after* ye have obtained a hope in Christ, ye shall obtain riches, if ye seek them; and ye will seek them for the intent to do good—to clothe the naked, and to feed the hungry, and to liberate the captive, and administer relief to the sick and the afflicted."[2955] We are not justified in seeking riches *before* we seek the kingdom of God; but *after* we obtain a hope in Christ, we may ask for riches with the intent to level people up. "Think of your brethren like unto yourselves, and be familiar with all and free with your substance, that they may be rich like unto you."[2956] It is this attitude toward money that brings us to a hope in Christ, and it is this attitude that now places us in a position to make a request for more resources to bless more people.

Moroni foresaw the condition of the last days and condemned mammon choosers. He said, "Behold, I speak unto you as if ye were present. . . . Ye do love money, and your substance, and your fine apparel, and the adorning of your churches, more than ye love the poor and the needy, the sick and the afflicted."[2957]

From the outset of the dispensation of the fulness of times, the Lord commanded us against mammon-seeking. The first two commandments were: (1) "Seek to bring forth and establish the cause of Zion," and (2) "Seek not for riches but for wisdom." The promised blessings distinguished Zion from Babylon: "And behold, the mysteries of God shall be unfolded unto you, and then shall you be made rich. Behold, he that hath eternal life is rich."[2958]

There is no security in mammon. Conversely, the quest for riches is a powerful opiate and Satan's most "deadly and effective" weapon.[2959] Seeking security in mammon was detected by Nephi as a latter-day Satanic strategy to destroy the Latter-day Saints: "And others will he pacify, and lull them away into carnal security, that they will say: All is well in Zion; yea, Zion prospereth, all is well—and thus the devil cheateth their souls, and leadeth them away carefully down to hell."[2960] There is a curse placed on mammon: it becomes "slippery treasures" when we "hide" those treasures unto ourselves instead on "hiding" them unto God, or in other words, consecrating them to God. But if we insist on hiding our treasures unto ourselves, we, as Jesus explained, will suffer an abrupt change of status in the spirit world, where the righteous poor are exalted and the selfish rich are made low. Then the former rich will look up and cry out to the poor for relief as the poor once cried out to the rich.[2961]

Nothing compares to the danger of choosing mammon over God. Brigham Young said, "I am more afraid of covetousness in our Elders than I am of the hordes of hell."[2962] The scriptures are filled with lessons concerning wealth-seeking. In each case, the Lord forbids such a focus: "Seek not after riches nor the vain things of this world; for behold, you cannot carry them with you."[2963] Choosing

---

[2954] D&C 105:5, 8.
[2955] Jacob 2:18–19; emphasis added.
[2956] Jacob 2:17.
[2957] Mormon 8:35–37; emphasis added.
[2958] D&C 6:6–7.
[2959] Nibley, *Approaching Zion*, 39, 332.
[2960] 2 Nephi 28:21.
[2961] Luke 16:19–31.
[2962] Young, *Discourses of Brigham Young*, 306.
[2963] Alma 39:14.

mammon over God is the equivalent of idolatry, and it leads to forgetting God, inequality, and divisiveness. Mormon described the perils of mammon-seeking:

- Within a short period of time, peace can devolve to disputations driven by pride;
- Then riches lead to more pride, boasting, and persecution;
- Then merchandising becomes prominent as a distinguishing element of society;
- Then riches define rank and opportunity.
- The resulting oppression of the poor shackles them to their low station.

Because we are not ignorant of the law, we do not sin ignorantly, "for," as Mormon explained of the Nephites, "they knew the will of God concerning them, for it had been taught unto them; therefore they did wilfully rebel against God."[2964] Every prophet since Adam has warned against this dangerous practice, and yet people still insist on trying to serve both God and mammon. But, as Jesus predicted, they only succeed in hating God.[2965]

The Lord despises selfish people; when they knock, "he will not open unto them."[2966] The selfish mammon-seekers persecute the poor, temporally, emotionally, and spiritually. "They rob the poor because of their fine sanctuaries; they rob the poor because of their fine clothing; and they persecute the meek and the poor in heart, because in their pride they are puffed up."[2967] In this sense, sanctuaries are places that we build to ourselves to hold our treasures, that which we worship the most. But if we claim or hoard the resources of our stewardship, pamper ourselves with the Lord's goods, and withhold these things from the poor, whom the goods could help, we are thieves.

Mammon-seeking is a sin that hinders and destroys the Church. It promotes the ugliness of inequality, it keeps the masses in poverty, and it lavishes the rich with lusts of the flesh. Brigham Young said, "The course pursued by men of business in the world has a tendency to make a few rich, and to sink the masses of the people in poverty and degradation. Too many of the Elders of Israel take this course. No matter what comes they are for gain—for gathering around them riches; and when they get rich how are those riches used? Spent on the lusts of the flesh, wasted as a thing of nought."[2968] Rather, choosing God over mammon applies a different set of criteria: "Take the men that can travel the earth over, preach the Gospel without purse or scrip, and then go to and lay their plans to gather the Saints. *That looks like the work of angels.*"[2969]

The sin of withholding from poor is often coupled with the sin of harshly judging or looking down on the poor for the circumstances of their condition. Such a despicable treatment puts at stake our inheritance in the celestial kingdom. A terrible condemnation awaits those who judge a poor person and withhold that which does not belong to them, but to God. This attitude lends to the evil of the age: exchanging life for money. Few sins are more disgusting than viewing human beings as property, their only value being that which they can produce for their owners or employers. This attitude defines the common philosophy of business: profit is more important than people, profit at all costs. Hugh Nibley traced oppression of the poor back to Cain. It was Satan, he said, who taught Cain "a special course to make him prosperous in all things: the Mahan technique, the great secret of converting life into property. Later Lamech graduates with the same degree—'Master Mahan, master of that great secret.'" Beyond the sins of ignoring, withholding from, and harshly judging the poor is

---

[2964] 3 Nephi 6:9–18.
[2965] Matthew 6:24.
[2966] 2 Nephi 9:42.
[2967] 2 Nephi 28:13.
[2968] Young, *Journal of Discourses*, 11:349.
[2969] Young, *Journal of Discourses*, 8:353–54; emphasis added.

the sin of using a poor man's labor to enrich one's self: "converting life into property."[2970] This sin runs contrary to the Lord's law of fair pay: "The laborer is worthy of his hire."[2971]

Perhaps because self-indulgence and fashion-seeking run contrary to the true nature of covenantal womanhood, a curse is placed upon the daughters of Zion when they engage in these offenses. Too many women fall into this trap, and because they are so self-absorbed, they look down on or neglect the poor rather than using their money, talents, and time to selflessly bless the poor and serve the purposes of God. On the other hand, the Lord promises an abundance of blessings for those who rescue the poor.

From the beginning, the Lord has pled with us to step outside ourselves and help his impoverished children. Hallmarks of the law of Moses were mercy and hospitality. Just so, the higher law of Zion promises great blessings to those who bless the poor with the Lord's resources: "Blessed is he that considereth the poor."[2972] Therefore, Zion becomes the consummate hope for the Lord's poor. Because the poor have complained before [the Lord],"[2973] the Lord is motivated to establish Zion, a condition that they can finally trust.

The Lord has decreed stiff consequences for seeking wealth and persecuting the poor. Some of these consequences include:

- Loss of the providences of heaven
- Loss of priesthood power and exaltation
- Loss of the Spirit
- Loss of revelation
- Loss of happy family life and spiritual commitment
- Loss of the Lord's help
- Loss of true worship
- Failure in our mission
- Loss of peace
- Loss of national security

The Savior's parable of the sheep and goats lays out the criteria for "everlasting punishment" or "eternal life." First, to the sheep, who represent the righteous: "Then shall the King say unto them on his right hand, Come, ye blessed of my Father, inherit the kingdom prepared for you from the foundation of the world: For I was an hungered, and ye gave me meat: I was thirsty, and ye gave me drink: I was a stranger, and ye took me in: Naked, and ye clothed me: I was sick, and ye visited me: I was in prison, and ye came unto me." Then to the goats, who represent the unrighteous: "Then shall he say also unto them on the left hand, Depart from me, ye cursed, into everlasting fire, prepared for the devil and his angels: For I was an hungered, and ye gave me no meat: I was thirsty, and ye gave me no drink: I was a stranger, and ye took me not in: naked, and ye clothed me not: sick, and in prison, and ye visited me not."[2974]

Jesus asked the question, "For what doth it profit a man if he gain the whole world . . . and he lose his own soul, and he himself be a castaway?"[2975] James, the Lord's brother, asked the same question, "What doth it profit?" Expounding, he said, "If a brother or sister be naked, and destitute of daily food, and one of you say unto them, Depart in peace, be ye warmed and filled; notwithstanding

---

[2970] Nibley, *Approaching Zion*, xv.
[2971] Luke 10:7; D&C 31:5; 70:12; 84:79; 106:3.
[2972] Psalm 41:1.
[2973] D&C 38:16.
[2974] Matthew 25:31–46.
[2975] JST Luke 9:25.

ye give them not those things which are needful to the body; what doth it profit?"[2976] Brigham Young wanted to cry against mammon-choosing with "the voice of seven thunders." Seeing the ever-growing tendency toward covetousness, he continually taught against it, and in the last speech he ever made, he said, "The people are still shaking hands with the servants of the devil, instead of sanctifying themselves." He appealed to the Saints to imagine what wisdom their forefathers would say to them: "What do you suppose the fathers would say if they could speak from the dead? . . . What would they whisper in our ears? Why, if they had the power the very thunders of heaven would be in our ears, if we could but realize the importance of the work we are engaged in. . . . *When I think upon this subject, I want the tongues of seven thunders to wake up the people.*"[2977]

The Lord gave us the law of consecration, in part, for our safety, security and salvation. This law provides the *only* way to pass the mortal test of money and arrive in the celestial kingdom. That lofty goal requires that we must be willing to choose consecration as a way of life over the way of Babylon. We must consider everything we are and have as belonging to God; we must view ourselves as stewards rather than owners; we must agree to be accountable to God and his servants for the things that God places in our safekeeping; and we must labor for the cause of Zion and not for selfish reasons or for the sake of making and accumulating money. In other words, the law of consecration requires that we give God our hearts, our all, and that we dedicate ourselves to his work and his children. Our eventual placement in a kingdom of glory depends upon our adherence to the law of consecration and our living its principles out of love.

How do we choose God over mammon, cease compromising, and stop trying to marry the two? Jacob's answer was this: "Think of your brethren like unto yourselves, and be familiar with all and free with your substance, that they may be rich like unto you."[2978] Love for God and his children is the answer. "Therefore all things whatsoever ye would that men should do to you, do ye even so to them."[2979] If we truly love, we cannot stand to see suffering or lack of any kind, and our covenants give us the power to attack lack. Now we have the right to ask the Lord for his help and for resources in another's behalf. Our ability to ask for the Lord's help is dependent upon "obtain[ing] a hope in Christ."[2980] Jacob said if we can persevere and obtain a hope in Christ, "ye shall obtain riches, if ye seek them; and ye will seek them for the intent to do good—to clothe the naked, and to feed the hungry, and to liberate the captive, and administer relief to the sick and the afflicted."[2981] The act of administering to the needy is the testimony that we have received a hope in Christ.

Because we have received freely, we must freely give. In the process of feeding the Lord's lambs, we learn that we are in partnership with the Lord: (1) We bring to the Lord the extent of our consecrated resource, he blesses it, and the resource becomes enough to feed many. (2) When it is our turn to eat, we will always have enough; in fact, we will have more than we started with. This is Zion's celestial law of prosperity, the law that guarantees incredible returns, "an hundredfold."[2982] Our covenant relationship with the Lord ensures our safety while we are giving. This is also called the manna principle, which supplies our daily bread,[2983] that which is sufficient for our needs. But to obtain these blessings requires that we put first things first: "Seek ye first the kingdom of God, and his righteousness; and all these things shall be added unto you."[2984] Then we can be assured that while

---

[2976] James 2:15–16.
[2977] Young, *Journal of Discourses,* 18:305.
[2978] Jacob 2:18.
[2979] Matthew 7:12.
[2980] Jacob 2:19.
[2981] Jacob 2:19.
[2982] Luke 8:8; Matthew 19:29.
[2983] Matthew 6:11.
[2984] Matthew 6:33.

we are feeding the Lord's lambs, he will take care of us. That is the promise of security enjoyed by Zion people.

To live this way calls for a new way of thinking. While Babylon shouts, "Gather about you property for your security," Zion counters with "Man shall not live by bread alone, but by every word that proceedeth out of the mouth of God."[2985] Zion is the polar opposite of Babylon. But if we will embrace such a Zionlike lifestyle, the Lord promises us the key to his abundance: "Ask, and ye shall receive; knock, and it shall be opened unto you."[2986]

Feeding the Lord's lambs with scanty resources is a monumental act of faith. Only with love driven by a determined desire to serve and trust in the Lord could we accomplish such a feat. This act of donating the widow's mite to help another person is a clear indication that we have chosen God over mammon. The Lord helps us by giving us the law of asking. The law of asking provides that we may draw upon the Lord's vast resources to feed his sheep, with the promise that as we do, we will always have enough to feed ourselves. Asking is an act of faith: we recognize the sovereignty of God; we acknowledge that he has infinite resources that he is willing to give us; and we concede that he has the power to make and keep promises, to do anything for us or give anything to us. By asking, we acknowledge that we share with him a child-to-parent relationship—a covenant bond that makes us *partners* in his work. Asking is an eternal principle; our eternal progression depends upon the law of asking. Throughout eternity, we surely will go to God countless times to ask permission to draw resources from his higher kingdom so that we might grow and manage the affairs of our emerging kingdoms. To receive any good thing from God, we must first ask.

This doctrine of Zion provides safety, security, and abundance for both the giver and the receiver.[2987] This is the essence of the law of consecration, and these blessings are given as a reward to those who choose God over mammon.

[2985] Matthew 4:4.
[2986] D&C 4:1–7.
[2987] John 10:10.

Section 19

The Royal Law

Beyond all other considerations, the law or covenant of consecration is a law of love. James called it the royal law:[2988] "Thou shalt love the Lord thy God with all thy heart, and with all thy soul, and with all thy mind. This is the first and great commandment. And the second is like unto it, Thou shalt love thy neighbour as thyself." The royal law is "the first and great commandment," according to Jesus, and upon it "hang all the law and the prophets."[2989] When all is said and done, we consecrate ourselves and all that we have and are because we love God and we love his children.

As we have mentioned throughout this series, the covenant of consecration is very much like the covenant of marriage. In Hebrew culture, a bridegroom and a bride consecrate themselves to each other in symbolic rituals. First, the groom offers the bride's father a bride price—she is "bought with a price."[2990] Then the bridegroom offers his bride a written covenant of marriage, which, when she agrees to the terms, he and his bride sign. In the betrothal ceremony, he gives his bride a "gift of value," which represents a "token" of his promise and an "emblem" of his love, whereupon he recites a pledge to irrevocably bind and consecrate himself to her forever. Then, in the presence of two witnesses, the bride drinks a cup of wine to ratify or seal the marriage covenant. By this action, she indicates her willingness to take upon herself her husband's name. At that point, the couple, along with their guests, shares a covenantal meal.

Thus, by these elaborate rituals the bridegroom and bride consecrate themselves to each other with rites rich in symbolism, all of which represent giving their hearts to each other. When the ceremony is complete, the only question that remains is will the ritual of consecration translate into lifelong acts of consecration? That is, will the covenant of consecration become *royal* by the couple's subsequent loyalty, patience, sacrifice, and love? Or will the covenant remain a set of symbols and a piece of paper upon which promises were made but never enacted?

[2988] James 2:8.
[2989] Matthew 22:36–40.
[2990] 1 Corinthians 6:20.

THE ROYAL LAW EXPLAINS THE PRINCIPLES OF CONSECRATION

When we view consecration through the lens of an eternal marriage built on love, the principles of this law begin to become clear. President James E. Faust reminded us that in order for a temple marriage to be sealed by the Holy Spirit of Promise and thus transcend its initial provisional promises and become more sure, the couple must faithfully abide the marriage covenant that they made with God and keep the promises that they made with each other.[2991] When God joins a man and a woman together, the two then embark on a new consecrated life in which they are no more separate but one, pursuing in tandem a single life with a singular purpose that is greater than the sum of their individual parts. To accomplish such unity, the husband and wife make covenants of obedience to live the laws, rites, and ordinances pertaining this new and everlasting covenant of marriage.[2992] They agree to sacrifice anything and everything to sustain and defend their new kingdom, even to the sacrifice of their lives, placing their marriage above any personal concern or agenda. They agree to live the totality of the gospel, which defines their new life, protects them as they journey toward their promised land, and ensures their safe arrival. They agree to live a celestial lifestyle called chastity, in which they agree to never divide their affections or to be disloyal in any way. They agree to give themselves totally to their beloved—that is, they unrestrictedly give the fulness of their hearts: all that they have and are. They promise to withhold nothing from their spouse—neither their time nor their abilities nor anything that they possess. These are evidences of true, consecrated, eternal love.

From the time of their sealing, throughout the remainder of their lives and forever, the husband and wife are equals. Although they have different personalities and fill diverse roles in the marriage, they are nevertheless one. Their equality becomes evident when we see them sacrificing for and serving each other without thought for themselves. They possess things jointly and enjoy equal and common access to the marriage's resources. One spouse is not poor while the other is rich; one does not go without while the other enjoys luxuries—they are equal, and there are "no poor among them."[2993] To maintain their unity and equality, they order their lives so that they love God first. They know that their eternal destiny lies with him, and they show their love for God by keeping their covenants and loving each other.

Their marriage is marked by agency, stewardship, accountability, and labor. By the exercise of agency, they chose to enter into the marriage covenant, and thereafter by the exercise of agency, they continue to choose to live it. At the marriage altar, they abandoned their claims to individual ownership of assets; now, they abide in the covenant by pooling their resources, dividing out fairly familial responsibilities, and jointly managing their resources by agreement. They agree to discuss with and account to each other for the discharge of their responsibilities. They agree to work hard for the marriage and not for selfish interests. Such an ordered and structured marriage will one day be sealed by the Holy Spirit of Promise and receive the unconditional guarantee of eternal duration. This marriage will become royal, "inheriting thrones, kingdoms, principalities, and powers, dominions, all heights and depths."[2994] Such a marriage is welded together by the highest manifestation of love—consecrated love.

Royal love grows. When a husband and wife love God, they can better love each other; when a husband and wife truly love each other, they desire to love children into existence and rear those children in love. Because love begets love, love will increase with each act of love. Soon the couple discovers that they have love to spare. Now their love wants an outlet and looks beyond the marriage and family. When love sees someone who is impoverished, love spills over and becomes the act of

---

[2991] Faust, "The Gift of the Holy Ghost—A Sure Compass," 2; emphasis added.
[2992] D&C 131:2.
[2993] Moses 7:18.
[2994] D&C 132:19.

serving a child of God; then love multiplies and suddenly is "not content with blessing his family alone, but ranges through the whole world, anxious to bless the whole human race."[2995]

Each time a couple gives love away to a child of God, they apply the same loving principles of consecration that apply to love in their marriage. For example, they first choose to exercise their agency and choose to extend loving service; they consider all people as equals and draw them by love into a unifying bond; knowing that they are stewards of the Lord's resources, they ask for and receive the Lord's resources so that they are better equipped to serve his children; they are willing to work hard at loving other people, and they accept the responsibility to account to God for their service. When we see the law of consecration through the lens of a loving marriage, we begin to understand both the purpose and the power of this law. We see meaning behind the symbols, tokens, and the contractual language. We discover that the single, driving principle of consecration is love—the royal law.

DOCTRINE AND COVENANTS 42—THE CORNERSTONES OF THE LAW OF CONSECRATION

At the beginning of 1831, "the Lord revealed to the Prophet Joseph Smith in Fayette, New York, that anciently he had taken the Zion of Enoch to himself and then commanded him to go to Ohio to receive the law [of Zion]."[2996] A month later, February 9, 1831, the Lord revealed to the Prophet "the law," or the *law of Zion*, which the Prophet specified as "embracing the law of the Church."[2997] This law became known as section 42 of the Doctrine and Covenants. The revelation listed a variety of commandments, such as teach by the Spirit; preach the gospel as contained in the New Testament and the Book of Mormon; do not kill, steal, lie, commit adultery or lust, or speak evil of others; beware of pride; and avoid idleness.[2998] Moreover, the revelation defined the four cornerstones of the law of consecration:

1. *Mutual assistance*—the Lord expects his disciples to sustain and help one another.
2. *Proper use of priesthood*—the priesthood is to be used to benefit those who are physically and spiritually ill or needy.
3. *The need for faith*—according to God's will, a person can be healed [physically, emotionally and spiritually] by the power of the priesthood, if that individual has faith in Jesus Christ and if he is "not appointed unto death." This revelatory information is provided through the priesthood to give a person hope, knowing that the Lord is with him and that the Lord will give him time to work out his exaltation.
4. *Reciprocal love*—the Lord expects his disciples to love one another and to become one.[2999]

MUTUAL ASSISTANCE

The cornerstone of mutual assistance is something that we immediately identify with Zion. Because we love God and our neighbor, we do not send away any who are naked, hungry, athirst, sick, or who have not been nourished. We do not set our hearts upon riches; rather, we are "liberal to all, both old and young, both bond and free, both male and female, whether out of the church or in the church, having no respect to persons as to those who [stand] in need."[3000] To assist another person, we appeal

---

[2995] Smith, *History of the Church*, 4:227.
[2996] *Encyclopedia of Mormonism*, 312.
[2997] D&C 42, headnote.
[2998] D&C 42:4–5, 7–8, 12, 18–29, 41–42, 74–93.
[2999] Johnson, "The Law of Consecration," 99.
[3000] Alma 1:30.

THE ROYAL LAW

to God for a stewardship or an increase in our stewardship. We do this because we recognize that everything we have and are belongs to God, and we are stewards.[3001] We recognize that the underlying purpose of any stewardship is to assist God in his work to bring to pass the immortality and eternal life of man.[3002] Therefore, we assist God and his children with the resources of our stewardship, and we receive assistance from the stewardships of others.

Faith and the Proper Use of the Priesthood

At first glance, the next two cornerstones of the law of Zion—proper use of the priesthood and the need for faith—might seem misplaced in a revelation describing consecration. But when we remember that we cannot achieve exaltation without serving others,[3003] which is a stipulation of the priesthood covenant,[3004] the message begins to come clear. Consecration demands that by faith we give all that we are and have to God. This action increases faith. Faith vitalizes the priesthood and transforms priesthood authority into priesthood power. By faith, we consecrate all that we have received from God for the purpose of ministering to God's children, bringing them the announcement of the proximity of the kingdom of heaven, and blessing them so that they might come to Christ, take upon them his name, and achieve salvation. This is the proper use of the priesthood, and central to the priesthood's proper use is the authority to administer to the sick and afflicted—the poor.

The first latter-day mention of an actual priesthood ordinance to heal the sick is sandwiched in the language of the law of the Church—the law of Zion. It is in this amazing section (D&C 42) that the Lord fulfills his promise to give the Saints information that will endow them with power from on high.[3005] It is in this section that the law of consecration is revealed, and embedded in that law is the ordinance of healing the sick. Two previous revelations had alluded to the miracle of healing[3006] and to the need for faith on both the elders' and the recipients' parts, but apparently the actual ordinance was not revealed until this revelation was received on February 9, 1831.

Why would it be so important that the law of consecration should reference healing the sick? A hint might be found in the fact that consecration is a lifestyle that defines the kingdom of heaven with its attendant powers and miracles. We recall that after Jesus ordained the Seventy in his day, he sent them on missions, saying, "Heal the sick therein, and say unto them, The kingdom of heaven is come nigh unto you."[3007] Notice that Jesus connected evidence that the kingdom of heaven had come with the healing distressed souls. Apparently, the Seventy, as authorized representatives of the kingdom of heaven, were to go out to the people, announce that the kingdom of heaven had come, and provide undeniable proof that the kingdom had the power to save. Thus, the ordinance of healing the sick became evidence that the kingdom of heaven had come.

The priesthood is the authority to use the name of Jesus Christ; more pointedly, the priesthood is the name of Jesus Christ,[3008] for its name is "the Holy Priesthood, after the Order of the Son of God."[3009] Keep in mind that the name *Jesus Christ* is both the name of the Savior and the *keyword* that makes the priesthood operative: "Behold, *Jesus Christ is the name* which is given of the Father, and there is none other *name* given whereby man can be saved [both temporally or spiritually]."[3010] Thus,

---

[3001] D&C 38:17; 104:11–14.
[3002] Moses 1:39.
[3003] Holland and Holland, "However Long and Hard the Road," n.p.
[3004] D&C 84:33, 48.
[3005] D&C 38:32.
[3006] D&C 24:13–14; 35:9.
[3007] Luke 10:9.
[3008] John 10:41.
[3009] D&C 107:3.
[3010] D&C 18:21, 23; emphasis added.

the Lord told Abraham, "Behold, I will lead thee by my hand, and I will take thee, to put upon thee *my name, even the Priesthood.*"[3011]

The name and authority of Jesus Christ allow his servants to duplicate his works, which is one of the great miracles of the kingdom of heaven. To duplicate the works of Jesus, the Seventy needed both the Lord's authority *and his name.* Now they could authoritatively represent the kingdom of God and provide evidence to the people that the kingdom was indeed upon the earth. In a great way, the proof in their duplicating the signature miracles of the Savior lay in their healing the sick and casting out devils by the power and in the name of Jesus Christ. "And the seventy returned again with joy, saying, Lord, even the devils are subject unto us *through thy name.*"[3012]

Likewise, we exercise proper use of the priesthood by using Jesus' name and authority to duplicate his works and by representing and announcing the kingdom of heaven.

Announcing the Kingdom of Heaven through Administrations

Previous to Jesus' commissioning the Seventy, he gave the Twelve a similar charge on the occasion of their missions: "And as ye go, preach, saying, The kingdom of heaven is at hand. Heal the sick, cleanse the lepers, raise the dead, cast out devils: freely ye have received, freely give."[3013] We observe here the abundance that the Lord wishes his servants to bestow on the people: freely give of the gift of power that you have been given. Remarkably, the closer we come to the ideal of Zion, the more healings we will experience among us. To ancient Israel the Lord offered the promises of cessation of illness and eternal increase if they would apply to the ideal of Zion: "Thou shalt be blessed above all people: there shall not be male or female barren among you, or among your cattle. And the Lord will take away from thee all sickness."[3014]

Imagine! In the ideal of Zion there is simply no sickness! "No poor among them!"[3015] No lack of any kind!

Significantly, we prepare for the establishment of Zion in the same way that the kingdom of heaven is announced: by first experiencing the miracle of healing through the priesthood. A model is found in the Savior's visit to the Nephites. Before Jesus instituted Zion among the people, he called them to him and healed each sick person. He said, "I see that your faith is sufficient that I should heal you. And it came to pass that when he had thus spoken, all the multitude, with one accord, did go forth with their sick and their afflicted, and their lame, and with their blind, and with their dumb, and with all them that were afflicted in any manner; and he did heal them every one as they were brought forth unto him. And they did all, both they who had been healed and they who were whole, bow down at his feet, and did worship him; and as many as could come for the multitude did kiss his feet, insomuch that they did bathe his feet with their tears."[3016]

Evidently, the essential step of healing precedes the establishment of the ideal of Zion. Until that ideal is realized, the administration ordinance announces that the kingdom of heaven is at hand and that its purpose for being is to prepare the people for the establishment of Zion.

Consecrating a Sickness and a Life to the Lord

The concept of consecration permeates gospel principles. Healing the sick is one example. The administration ordinance effectively consecrates or *reconsecrates* a life to the Lord. To consecrate is to set something apart as holy. Thus, the administration ordinance consecrates or *sets apart* the illness for

---

[3011] Abraham 1:18; emphasis added.
[3012] Luke 10:17; emphasis added.
[3013] Matthew 10:7–8.
[3014] Deuteronomy 7:14–15.
[3015] Moses 7:18.
[3016] 3 Nephi 17:10.

a holy purpose, and that purpose is always the welfare of the afflicted person's soul—whether the expression of that purpose is spoken or unspoken in the ordinance.[3017] The ordinance also consecrates the person's healed and saved life to the Lord. When considered in this light, every affliction is an opportunity to bring a person to Christ, who will heal the afflicted both spirit and body. Therefore, our being saved from sickness and affliction by the power of the priesthood might be viewed as symbolic of Christ's power to deliver us from all our enemies,[3018] including spiritual and physical death. Joseph Fielding McConkie and Robert L. Millet wrote: "It may be that all of the miraculous healings performed by Jesus were but tangible symbols of the greatest healing that he alone could perform—the healing of sick spirits and the cleansing of sin-stained souls."[3019]

A sickness or affliction reminds a person of his fallen state, and it drives him to recognize his helplessness and his need for the Lord's intervention.[3020] That is, because of the Fall, a sick person finds himself in a weakened situation, but he knows that Christ has overcome the Fall and can help him. In the context of Zion, that person finds himself afflicted by the world and desperately seeks deliverance into the health and safety of Zion. When a person is sick or afflicted, he places his hope in the Savior and the Lord's saving power. Then the sick and afflicted person humbly beseeches the Lord for help, which motivates him to call for the Lord's authorized priesthood representatives. The sick and afflicted person recognizes the Lord's servants as having the authority of Jesus Christ, to use his name and answer the person's request.[3021] The elders come in response to that request. Preceding the administration ordinance, the sick person (or a friend, loved one, or the elders[3022]) should offer a sincere prayer of faith in which the person humbly declares his testimony of the Lord. In the prayer of faith, he expresses his belief that the Lord, through His servants, can heal him from the specific effects of the Fall that he is suffering, and he asks the Lord to heal him.[3023] At that point, the elders authoritatively perform the ordinance of administration through the power and in the name of Jesus Christ.[3024] Because the administration is *sealed*, it is recognized in heaven and on earth,[3025] and the Lord promises to confirm or validate it.[3026]

By means of the administration ordinance, powers on earth and in heaven are set in motion, and now the Lord begins to direct the process of healing, both spiritually and physically. When the healing process is completed, the Fall symbolically has been overcome, and the once-afflicted person is now in a position to bear heightened testimony of the reality of the Savior, the Lord's power to deliver, and the certainty of the restoration of the gospel and priesthood. Throughout the process of healing, the person has rededicated and reconsecrated his life to the Lord. No wonder then that the person, through his illness and healing, is brought closer to the Lord and the ideal of Zion. Such a person becomes a witness, someone who can bear testimony of the power that is resident in Zion and the quality of salvation that can be found there.

Administration and Forgiveness of Sins

Consecrating a life to the Lord by means of healing is borne out in James's instruction: "Is any sick among you? let him call for the elders of the church; and let them pray over him, anointing him with

---

[3017] 2 Nephi 32:9.
[3018] Mosiah 29:22; D&C 49:6; 58:22.
[3019] McConkie and Millet, *Doctrinal Commentary on the Book of Mormon*, 4:41.
[3020] Alma 26:12; Moses 1:9–10.
[3021] Alma 15:5–11.
[3022] James 1:14.
[3023] Alma 15:5–11.
[3024] McConkie, *Mormon Doctrine*, 21–22.
[3025] D&C 128:8, 10.
[3026] Mormon 9:24–25; D&C 132:59.

oil in the name of the Lord: And the prayer of faith shall save the sick, and the Lord shall raise him up; *and if he have committed sins, they shall be forgiven him.*"[3027] Whether a person is healed immediately by the administration or subsequent to the administration, the resulting healing carries with it the promise of both physical and spiritual renewal. The healed person's body becomes a sanctified receptacle where the Holy Ghost can reside. Therefore, because Zion people are those who are purified and sanctified, the ordinance of administration is essential to their salvation and their spiritual progress.

Perhaps for the purposes of purification and consecration, we anoint a sick person with consecrated olive oil before we seal the anointing and before the blessing is pronounced. Elder Gerald N. Lund said, "Olive oil is a symbol of the Holy Ghost and its power to provide peace and to purify."[3028] Apparently, the anointing literally infuses the sick person with the power of the Holy Ghost, who, according to President James E. Faust, is the Great Physician's agent of healing.[3029] Elder Lund wrote, "'The olive tree from the earliest times has been the emblem of peace and purity.' (*Doctrines of Salvation*, 3:180) Also, in the Parable of the Ten Virgins, the wise were prepared with oil. (See Matt. 25:1–13.) Modern revelation equates that preparation (having olive oil) with taking 'the Holy Spirit for their guide.' (D&C 45:55–57.) To touch with oil suggests the effect of the Spirit on the same organs of living and acting that had previously been cleansed by the blood of Christ. Thus, every aspect of the candidate's life was purified and sanctified by both the Atonement and the Holy Ghost."[3030]

Remarkably, during the healing process, the Lord restores the person both spirit and body: "and the Lord shall raise him up; and if he have committed sins, they shall be forgiven him."[3031] The Lord's healing brings remission of sins; the entire soul is healed, both body and spirit. Symbolically, the rescued person is snatched from the grasp of Babylon and delivered into Zion.

Consecration Requires Faith

Whether we are consecrating our property or our lives to the Lord, we need to immerse ourselves in faith. The Lord requires faith for receiving, performing, or participating in a miracle. As we have discussed, the miracle of being delivered from Babylon and being placed in the safety of Zion is represented in the administration ordinance. When we are delivered from illness or affliction, we are cognizant that deliverance came as an act of faith. As much as healings come by faith, just so, no one can truly live the law of consecration without faith.

Embedded in the law of the Church (D&C 42) are the Lord's instructions concerning the administration ordinance: "And the elders of the church, two or more, shall be called, and shall pray for and lay their hands upon them in my name; and if they die they shall die unto me, and if they live they shall live unto me . . . And again, it shall come to pass that he that hath faith in me to be healed, and is not appointed unto death, *shall be healed*. He who hath faith to see *shall see*. He who hath faith to hear *shall hear*. The lame who hath faith to leap *shall leap*."[3032] Again, we note the need for faith, and we also note the sweeping language that describes the result. Of course, we are aware that not every administration is followed by a healing miracle[3033]—the phrase, "Thy will be done," is either said or implied in every administration—but in the vast number of cases a customized healing is prescribed and directed by the Lord.

[3027] James 5:14–15.
[3028] Lund, "Old Testament Types and Symbols," 184–86; emphasis added.
[3029] Faust, "He Healeth the Broken Heart," 2–7.
[3030] Lund, *Jesus Christ, Key to the Plan of Salvation*, 61.
[3031] James 5:14–15.
[3032] D&C 42:43, 48–51.
[3033] Oaks, "He Heals the Heavy Laden," 6–9.

Clearly, the administration ordinance exemplifies the healing power of the priesthood that is resident in the kingdom of heaven (Zion), and also resident in the law of consecration. For example, an afflicted person, who is sick from the effects of the Fall, cries out to the Lord for deliverance from the effects of this telestial condition. In response, the Lord sends his authorized servants to use his name and power to answer the sick person's prayer. The elders come as angels, clothed with authority, representing the kingdom of God. That which these angels (elders) have received from the Lord, they consecrate and now give freely to lift up and save the *impoverished* person. The elders stand in proxy for Jesus Christ, authorized to *consecrate* both the sick person's life and his affliction to the Lord. To that end, the elders anoint the sick person with *consecrated* oil, which anointing is thereafter sealed so that it is recognized and validated both on earth and in heaven. By this means, the process of healing begins that will restore the person both spirit and body. During that process, the administration ordinance cleanses the afflicted person from sin and attempts to draw him out of the world, making him separate and sanctifying him for a holy purpose. Now his consecrated life belongs to the Lord, who saved him, and the person's faith is now such that he can bear witness of the saving power of Jesus Christ. As the healed person brings other people to the Lord for healing, he becomes to them a savior in the similitude of the Savior, and the cycle of Zion repeats—each saved person consecrating his healing to the Lord so that others might likewise be saved. Freely they have received, and in return, freely they must give.

Reciprocal Love

To truly live the law of consecration and thus be endowed with power from on high,[3034] we must enjoin mutual assistance, employ the priesthood for its intended purpose, and exercise great faith in the Lord and his promises. Only then are we fully able to love one another and become *one*. The law of the Church (D&C 42) simply states: "Thou shalt live together in love."[3035] That is, we must be willing to give and receive love—true love is reciprocal. We must love both God and his children, and in turn we must receive love from them. This is the "the first and great commandment,"[3036] the royal law.[3037]

If we were limited to use only one word to define Zion, that word would be *love*; likewise, if we were limited to use only one word to describe the power of Zion, it would be *love*. Significantly, of all the words John could have used to portray God, he chose *love*.[3038] President Gordon B. Hinckley wrote: "This principle of love is the basic essence of the gospel of Jesus Christ. Without love of God and love of neighbor there is little else to commend the gospel to us as a way of life."[3039] Therefore, for the pure purpose of love we live the law of Zion by caring for the poor and the sick "with all tenderness."[3040] Elder John A. Widtsoe taught:

> The full and essential nature of love we may not understand. But there are tests by which it may be recognized. Love is always founded in truth. . . . Lies and deceit, or any other violation of the moral law, are proofs of love's absence. Love perishes in the midst of untruth. Thus . . . [he] who falsifies to his loved one, or offers her any act contrary to truth, does not really love her. Further, love does not

---

[3034] D&C 38:32.
[3035] D&C 42:45.
[3036] Matthew 22:36–40.
[3037] James 2:8.
[3038] 1 John 4:8.
[3039] Hinckley, *Faith: The Essence of True Religion*, 49.
[3040] D&C 42:43.

offend or hurt or injure the loved one. . . . Cruelty is as absent from love . . . as truth is from untruth. . . . Love is a positive active force. It helps the loved one. If there is need, love tries to supply it. If there is weakness, love supplants it with strength. . . . Love that does not help is a faked or transient love. Good as these tests are, there is a greater one. True love sacrifices for the loved one. . . . That is the final test. Christ gave of Himself, gave His life, for us, and thereby proclaimed the reality of his love for his mortal brethren and sisters.[3041]

Reciprocal love is the grand key of happiness and glory, wrote Elder Joseph B. Wirthlin. Jesus taught his disciples this "new commandment," to "love one another; as I have loved you."[3042] His quality of love is the model, and we are to love likewise. Reciprocal love—freely giving and freely receiving love—should be our primary focus, if we desire to be disciples of Jesus Christ. Improvement comes more readily to the soul filled with love than any other trait of character.[3043] Neither can the law of consecration be lived nor Zion be established in our lives upon any other principle.

CHARITY—THE PURE LOVE OF CHRIST

True love—unconditional love—is called *charity*. This quality of love encompasses the two laws upon which hang all the law and the prophets—(1) "Thou shalt love the Lord thy God with all thy heart, with all thy might, mind, and strength; and in the name of Jesus Christ thou shalt serve him," and (2) "Thou shalt love thy neighbor as thyself."[3044] Charity, then, not the outward rites of the law of Moses, is the driving force of Jesus' higher gospel law. Charity is the "new commandment"[3045] that Jesus attached to the higher law—*new* because it replaced the gospel motivation linked to the old law of rites and performances with the gospel motivation centered on the condition of the heart. Charity refers more to what we *do* than what we *feel*. There is a vast difference between being *loving* and feeling *in love*. Charity is saving love; charity lifts and rescues; charity forgives from enormous distances. As we experience the giving and receiving of charity, we eventually discover that we cannot escape its loving embrace: "charity endureth forever."[3046]

We have two witnesses—Paul and Mormon—whose testimonies anchor the principles of Zionlike charity in our souls:

- Charity suffers long (endures hardship in faith or endures in faith with someone during his/her hardship)
- Charity is kind
- Charity does not envy
- Charity is not vaunted up (does not boast)
- Charity is not puffed up (is not proud)
- Charity does not behave unseemly (act inappropriately)
- Charity seeks not her own (is not selfish)
- Charity is not easily provoked (keeps anger under control)
- Charity thinks no evil (tries to focus on the good)

[3041] Widtsoe, *An Understandable Religion*, 72.
[3042] John 13:34.
[3043] Wirthlin, "The Great Commandment," 28–31.
[3044] Matthew 22:40.
[3045] John 13:34.
[3046] Moroni 7:47.

- Charity does not rejoice in iniquity but rejoices in the truth (does not enjoy the evil things of the fallen world but rather the true things of God)
- Charity bears all things (bears up under the weight of problems)
- Charity believes all things (recognizes and follows truth)
- Charity hopes all things (knows that ultimately God is in charge)
- Charity endures all things (is willing to make the necessary sacrifices in order to win the prize).[3047]

Without charity, Paul says, we are nothing. Although we might accomplish many good works, speak with the tongue of angels, enjoy incredible spiritual gifts, bestow all our goods to feed the poor, and give our lives as martyrs, if we have not charity our good deeds profit us nothing.[3048] In other words, we might go through the motions of Christian living, but without charity our actions are hollow, and Zion will remain a distant ideal.

The lesser law of Moses was constructed on the bedrock of rites and performances, but the higher law of Jesus Christ is built on the condition of the heart. Consequently, Mormon notes, "charity never faileth." This "pure love of Christ" endures forever and transcends a world in which everything is programmed to fail. Therefore, charity stands above every other virtue and "is the greatest of all."[3049] We could never live the highest of gospel laws—consecration—without having cultivated the highest of gospel virtues—charity.

CHARITY EMERGES FROM FAITH AND HOPE

Having listed the characteristics of charity, Paul submits a roadmap to achieve this quality of love: "And now abideth faith, hope, charity, these three; but the greatest of these is charity."[3050] *Faith, hope, charity*—Christianity's quintessential virtues. Mormon expands our understanding by adding *hope* to the front of the list: *Hope, faith, hope, charity*. "And again, my beloved brethren, I would speak unto you concerning hope. How is it that ye can attain unto faith, save ye shall have hope? . . . Wherefore, if a man have faith he must needs have hope."[3051] The fact that hope is repeated is significant. Hoping that a principle is true leads us to experiment or act upon the principle. When we notice a desirable result from our action, hope increases. This cycle of faith and hope increases our charity, because the action of faith inevitably and by design leads to reconciliation with God, as well as service to him and his children.

Alma takes the formula one step further by adding *desire* to the process of developing charity. He says, hearing the word of God starts us down this path. When we hear the word of God, we desire to know more; we desire to see if the principle will work in our lives; we begin to hunger and thirst for righteousness. Alma informs us that the word of God, which develops into charity, is delivered to us by angels: "And now, [God] imparteth his word by angels unto men."[3052] Nephi informs us that angels are both mortal and immortal beings who "speak the words of Christ" "by the power of the Holy Ghost."[3053] Somewhere along the path, we begin to understand that charity is dissimilar from the substitute forms of love produced by the world; charity's uniqueness lies in the fact that it is a spiritual gift.

[3047] 1 Corinthians 13:4–8; commentary added; see also Moroni 7:45.
[3048] 1 Corinthians 13:1–3.
[3049] Moroni 7:46–47.
[3050] 1 Corinthians 13:13.
[3051] Moroni 7:40, 42.
[3052] Alma 32:23.
[3053] 2 Nephi 32:3.

Alma continues by explaining that the word of God, which is delivered by angels under the direction of the Holy Ghost, is structured so that once it is planted in the soul, it will stir desire and hope: "And now my beloved brethren, as ye have *desired* to know of me what ye shall do. . . ."[3054] That is, upon hearing the word, we begin to experience hunger pangs for light and truth—we are filled with *desire*. At some point, desire and hope motivate us to take a spiritual risk and experiment with the word of God. Now by faith we summon courage to try an "experiment" with the word; we want to see if the desired result actually happens. The action of experimenting is not only an act of faith, but it is also a manifestation of our agency; it is the action of our hope. The moment that action is applied to hope, hope becomes faith; and Alma explained that even a "particle of faith"—the smallest of actions—has the effect of the seed of faith to take root in our souls.

Alma explained that at that point something marvelous begins to happen. Beyond our consciousness, stirring occurs beneath the surface; roots have ruptured through the hull of the seed, and an independent life has begun. If we will hang on and tend the spot of ground where the seed has been planted, the new life will soon burst into open view. One day a tender plant will erupt through the soil; it will have changed from a seed of hope to a seedling of faith like a caterpillar transforms into a butterfly. As the seedling matures with measurable "swelling motions,"[3055] we start to recognize that our experiment with the seed of faith was "good." Alma said, "It beginneth to enlarge my soul."

The evidence of growth leads us to hope more—hope is confirmable expectation. That is, we allow ourselves to imagine the harvest that might come from the seed; more importantly, we *expect* an abundant harvest. Beyond all other products of the harvest, the common product is charity. Charity is always a product of hope and faith.

Alma explained that the trueness of the seed is confirmed by four tests:

1. We feel something positive stirring within us.
2. We feel invigorated, and we are motivated to become a better person.
3. The idea corresponds with, builds upon, and clarifies other ideas that we have had, and now it sparks new ideas.
4. The idea feels so good that we want to keep seeking after it to follow it to its perfect conclusion.

The "seed," or the word of God, is expansive, enlightening, and delicious. It increases faith; it is discernible; it is clearly good. If we do not neglect or reject it, the seed will grow into a tree that bears the beautiful fruit of charity, the love of God,[3056] "which is most precious, which is sweet above all that is sweet, and which it white, yea, and pure above all that is pure."[3057]

Charity Transforms the Heart

Charity grows from the word of God. If nurtured, this word, or *seed*, which carries the genotype of divinity, will transform its host into the image of God. With every swelling motion toward maturity, the word that was planted in our souls by angels will change our heart until it resembles the heart of Jesus Christ. The more the seed of faith grows, the more we talk, act, serve, and love like the Savior. We are filled with charity, and more importantly we *become* charity, the "pure love of Christ."[3058] As

---

[3054] Alma 32:24; emphasis added.
[3055] Alma 32:28.
[3056] 1 Nephi 11:22.
[3057] Alma 32:26–43.
[3058] Moroni 7:47.

much as "God is love,"[3059] so we become "this love."[3060] Now we can consecrate; now we can become Zion people.

We commence on the road to charity by hearing the word of God from angels. It tastes *delicious* to us; we desire for more and we hope that what we have heard and encountered is true. Desire and hope motivate us to exercise our agency and try an experiment. On faith alone, we nurture the seed of the word of God in our souls. As we care for the seed, it takes root and soon sprouts. Now our experiment of faith experiences its first reward, and we are obligated to recognize the seed as good. That event causes us to hope for a bountiful harvest. For that to occur, we will need our hope to become strengthened hope so that we might remain determined and endure in faith until the time of harvest.

As the growing season continues and the seedling matures, we note that both the seed and now the plant have passed the tests of truth, which realization further validates our hope and fortifies our faith. With that infusion of hope, we are willing to continue in faith, nourishing the plant to the end. Miraculously, the more the plant grows, the more we grow into its image. By the time of the harvest, the plant and we are *one*. By planting and tending the plant of charity, we have become charity.

The glory of Zion is first to obtain charity and then to duplicate the process in others. Now we become the angels, who plant the word of God; now we become God's servants, who help another hope-filled experimenter nourish his tender plant; now we become saviors in Zion, who encourage, strengthen, and hold up the grower when the hot sun scorches his plant and when all seems lost; now we become God's friends, who finally share in his harvest. We are *charity*! We are those whose countenances reflect that of the Lord of the Harvest;[3061] we are the ones who have loved with the pure love of Christ until we have brought our fellow beings into the full image of Christ.

This process never falls short or breaks down: "Charity *never* faileth!" If charity can never fail, Zion can never fail, because Zion is built upon charity, "the greatest of all," the celestial quality of love that "endureth forever."[3062] Clearly, charity is the quintessential virtue, "the end of the commandment,"[3063] the power that invigorates and propels the law of consecration and the establishment of Zion.

CHARITY DEFINES DISCIPLESHIP

Zion people order their lives exactly opposite from the people of Babylon. Zion people "seek . . . first the kingdom of God and his righteousness,"[3064] and they exemplify the defining characteristic of Deity that comprehends all righteousness: *charity*.[3065] They do this by consecrating themselves to the Lord and extending loving service to God and his children. In every way, they are disciples of Jesus Christ and do his works.

Beyond every other virtue, charity defines discipleship. The measure of our belief is how much we love. Therefore, the Lord lists charity as being a central qualification for the ministers of Jesus Christ.[3066] We simply cannot assist the Lord in his work without charity;[3067] therefore, as Elder

---

[3059] 1 John 4:8.
[3060] Moroni 7:48.
[3061] Alma 5:14.
[3062] Moroni 7:46–47.
[3063] 1 Timothy 1:5.
[3064] Matthew 6:33; 3 Nephi 13:33.
[3065] Matthew 22:36–40.
[3066] D&C 4:5.
[3067] D&C 12:8; 18:19.

McConkie reminded us, "The saints of God are commanded to seek and attain it."[3068] Why? Because we cannot give something we do not have. We must first receive love from God, who is the Source of love,[3069] and then we must give that love to God's children. Otherwise, all that was given to us will be lost.

Charity not only defines the pathway of discipleship, but it marks every point along the way. Charity transforms a natural man into a sanctified Saint, someone who by nature seeks to comfort the downtrodden; charity counsels the oppressed in faith, heals the sick and the afflicted, and consoles the brokenhearted. Charity is the light that guides us through valleys of darkness, and ultimately charity leads us to the magnificence of eternal life.[3070]

If charity is the defining characteristic of Jesus Christ, it is also the defining characteristic of his servants. A number of people have wondered how Joseph Smith was able to attract and retain so many followers. His answer epitomizes the connection between charity and consecration: "It is because I possess the principle of love. All I can offer the world is a good heart and a good hand."[3071] The Prophet gave all that he had and was to help others. He did not do these things to fulfill a commandment; rather he did what he did because he was filled with love. When he encountered need, he confronted it; he would not allow lack and suffering to exist in his presence.

KEEPING AND FEEDING—THE TWO TESTS OF CHARITY

Jesus gave us two tests of charity:

1. "If ye love me, *keep* my commandments."[3072]
2. "If ye love me *feed* my sheep."[3073]

Clearly, charity—*Christlike love*—is defined by *action*. A declaration of love is meaningless unless it is demonstrated by remaining faithful and proffering service: *keeping* and *feeding*. The person who professes love but is disloyal is a liar; the person who proclaims love but who is selfish and nonsacrificing is a hypocrite.

Conversely, charity keeps its vows and goes out to find and nourish others; charity heals on every front, physically, mentally, morally, and spiritually. Elder Marvin J. Ashton taught that the *keeping* element of charity centers on keeping the commandments, most specifically the first and great commandment,[3074] the royal law: "Thou shalt love the Lord thy God with all thy heart, and with all thy soul, and with all thy mind. . . . Thou shalt love thy neighbour as thyself."[3075] We show our love for the Lord by obeying the first and great commandment—to go out to find and feed his sheep. Keeping this commandment motivates us to care for, share with, uplift, extend sympathy and kindness, and provide for the comfort of God's children. *Keeping* and *feeding* are to stand proxy for the Savior and do as he would do if he were present. Therefore, to the extent that we *keep* the Lord's commandments, we show our love for him; and to the proportion that we *feed* the Lord's sheep, we *keep* the first and great commandment.

[3068] McConkie, *Mormon Doctrine*, 121–22; see also 1 Corinthians 16:14; 1 Timothy 4:12; 2 Timothy 2:22; Titus 2:2; 2 Peter 1:7; 2 Nephi 33:7–9; Alma 7:24; D&C 121:45; 124:116.
[3069] 1 John 4:19.
[3070] Wirthlin, "The Great Commandment," 28–31.
[3071] Smith, *Teachings of the Prophet Joseph Smith*, 313.
[3072] John 14:15; emphasis added.
[3073] Paraphrased from John 21:16; emphasis added.
[3074] Ashton, "Love Takes Time," 108.
[3075] Matthew 22:36–40.

Feeding and keeping are embedded in King Benjamin's teachings concerning charity. Blaine Yorgason points out: "Benjamin then instructed his people to (1) live peaceably and kindly with each other; (2) give diligent attention to the spiritual and temporal needs of their children; (3) teach their children the peaceable way of Christ; (4) impart freely of their substance to any who stood in need of it, 'every man according to that which he hath, such as feeding the hungry, clothing the naked, visiting the sick and administering to their relief, both spiritually and temporally, according to their wants'; (5) never take advantage of another by borrowing and not returning; (6) always watch their thoughts, words, and deeds, observing the commandments of God, and 'continue in the faith of what ye have heard concerning . . . our Lord, even unto the end of your lives' (Mosiah 4:13–30)."[3076]

CHARITY—THE LIFE BLOOD OF ZION

Most certainly, charity is love in action, and that action always involves sacrifice. Without the action of charitable sacrifice, Zion could not be established in the life of an individual, or in a marriage, a family, a ward, or a society. It is by consecrated sacrifice that we *keep* the commandments and hold true to our covenants.[3077] It is by sacrifice that we *feed* the Lord's sheep. It is by sacrifice that we love God. President Gordon B. Hinckley wrote: "Without sacrifice there is no true worship of God. 'The Father gave his Son, and the Son gave his life,' and we do not worship unless we give—give of our substance, . . . our time, . . . strength, . . . talent, . . . faith, . . . [and] testimonies."[3078]

Helping, giving, and loving always require selfless sacrifice. It is sacrifice, we sing, that "brings forth the blessings of heaven."[3079] As we have mentioned, charitable service creates a positive imbalance that demands correcting. This is the *hundredfold* law,[3080] which President Thomas S. Monson described this way: "It is an immutable law that the more you give away, the more you receive." Then, referencing a quote attributed to Winston Churchill, he said, "'You make a living by what you get, but you make a life by what you give.'"[3081] This "immutable law"—the *hundredfold law*—drives Zion's cycle of abundance and makes Zion people exceedingly prosperous.[3082] In accordance with this law, we give what we have and are, and the Lord rewards us beyond our sacrifice. As long as we do not stop the cycle by keeping what we receive, we will become *vessels of help*; the Lord will pour down blessings through us to his needy children, and in the process our prosperity will increase until it approaches the infinite abundance of the kingdom of heaven. Thus, charity is the lifeblood of Zion, and consecrated sacrifice is the principle that propels Zion's prosperity.

Charity is the principle upon which Zion people achieve equality and unity: "And above all things, clothe yourselves with the bond of charity, as with a mantle, which is the bond of perfectness and peace."[3083] When Zion people give and receive charity, they cease to be afraid: "perfect love casteth out all fear."[3084] Therefore, in the life of a Zion person *all* things are to be done in charity. According to Peter, we are to array ourselves in "fervent charity." Over time, this "pure love of Christ" becomes an integral part of our natures.[3085] Elder McConkie taught: "Charity is more than love, far more; it is everlasting love, perfect love, the pure love of Christ which endureth forever. It is

---

[3076] Yorgason, *I Need Thee Every Hour*, 213.
[3077] D&C 97:8.
[3078] Hinckley, *The Teachings of Gordon B. Hinckley*, 565.
[3079] Phelps, "Praise to the Man," *Hymns*, no. 27.
[3080] Genesis 26:12; 2 Samuel 24:3; Matthew 13:8–23; 19:29; Mark 10:30; Luke 8:8; D&C 98:25; 132:55.
[3081] Monson, "In Quest of the Abundant Life," 2.
[3082] 4 Nephi 1:7.
[3083] D&C 88:125; see also Colossians 3:14.
[3084] Moroni 8:16.
[3085] 1 Peter 4:8.

love so centered in righteousness that the possessor has no aim or desire except for the eternal welfare of his own soul and for the souls of those around him."[3086]

When charity, the love exemplified by Zion people, is planted in the hearts of a few people, it acts as leaven "until the whole [of humanity is] leavened."[3087] Again we recall the words of Joseph Smith: "A man filled with the love of God is not content with blessing his family alone, but ranges through the whole world, anxious to bless the whole human race."[3088] It is charity that infuses Zion people with power. According to Elder Ashton, charity is the crowning principle that makes possible eternal joy and progression.[3089]

Charity Is Defined by Service

President Hinckley called love "the lodestar of life." Citing the Savior's reference to the Final Judgment, President Hinckley reminded us that Jesus will say to those on his right hand that they shall inherit his kingdom because they effectively "fed, clothed, and visited Him" by blessing his children. President Hinckley wrote: "One of the greatest challenges we face in our hurried, self-centered lives is to follow this counsel of the Master, to take the time and make the effort to care for others, to develop and exercise the one quality that would enable us to change the lives of others—what the scriptures call charity. . . . Best defined, charity is that pure love exemplified by Jesus Christ. It embraces kindness, a reaching out to lift and help, the sharing of one's bread, if need be."[3090]

We become angels to the poor and afflicted. We are taught that there are "angels round about [us], to bear [us] up."[3091] As much as angels are instruments in the Lord's hands to sustain us and help to carry our heavy burdens, so we, by our charitable service, are angels to God's children and instruments in the Lord's hands to steady the weak and to heft their weighty load.[3092] Often in our lives, angels are the charitable people around us, people who love us, people who yield their hearts to God that they might be instruments in his hands. President Spencer W. Kimball said, "God does notice us, and he watches over us. But it is usually through another person that he meets our needs. Therefore, it is vital that we serve each other in the kingdom."[3093]

President Kimball gave other essential counsel concerning charitable service:

- *Abundant life.* "One has hardly proved his life abundant until he has built up a crumbling wall, paid off a heavy debt, enticed a disbeliever to his knees, filled an empty stomach, influenced a soul to wash in the blood of the lamb, turned fear and frustration into peace and sureness, led one to be 'born again.' One is measuring up to his opportunity potential when he has saved a crumbling marriage, transformed the weak into the strong, changed a civil to a proper temple marriage, brought enemies from the cesspool of hate to the garden of love, made a child trust and love him, changed a scoffer into a worshiper, melted a stony heart into one of flesh and muscle."[3094]
- *To become like Christ, give yourselves away.* "Christ's life is the epitome of service. *Give yourselves away.* That's the life of the Savior of this world. He gave himself away when he personally went to the house of Peter and blessed his mother-in-law 'who was sick of a fever.'

[3086] McConkie, *Mormon Doctrine*, 121; quoting 2 Nephi 26:30; Moroni 7:47; 8:25–26.
[3087] Matthew 13:33; Luke 13:21.
[3088] Smith, *History of the Church*, 4:227.
[3089] Ashton, "Be a Quality Person," 64.
[3090] Hinckley, *Standing for Something*, 6.
[3091] D&C 84:88.
[3092] Tanner, "All Things Shall Work Together for Your Good," 104.
[3093] Kimball, *The Teachings of Spencer W. Kimball*, 252.
[3094] Kimball, *The Teachings of Spencer W. Kimball*, 249.

He gave himself away when he stood on the mount and preached for hours 'the way of salvation' to the multitude. He gave himself away when he walked long, dusty, tortuous miles to Bethany to bring comfort and even life back to Lazarus, and to Mary and Martha, the sisters who were grieving. He gave himself away when he healed the sick and opened the blind eyes and cleared the stopped hearing and gave strength to the sick. He gave much of himself in every blessing. When the woman reached forth to touch the hem of his garment, he felt that power had gone out of him. He gave that power and part of himself willingly, and after three years of spectacular ministry, he voluntarily walked back into the trap set for him, announced his approaching fate, walked out of Gethsemane into the hands of mobsters and to the courts of politicians and to the cross and gave himself for all mankind."[3095]

- *Perfect service by practicing service.* "A striking personality and good character is achieved by practice, not merely by thinking it. Just as a pianist masters the intricacies of music through hours and weeks of practice, so mastery of life is achieved by the ceaseless practice of mechanics which make up the art of living. *Daily unselfish service to others is one of the rudimentary mechanics of the successful life.* 'For whosoever will save his life,' the Galilean said, 'shall lose it, and whosoever will lose his life for my sake shall find it.' (Matthew 16:25.) What a strange paradox this! And yet one needs only to analyze it to be convinced of its truth."[3096]

- *The divine paradox of service.* "Only when you lift a burden, God will lift your burden. Divine paradox this! The man who staggers and falls because his burden is too great can lighten that burden by taking on the weight of another's burden. *You get by giving, but your part of giving must be given first.*"[3097]

- *Glorious rewards from small charitable acts.* "So often, our acts of service consist of simple encouragement or of giving mundane help with mundane tasks—*but what glorious consequences can flow from mundane acts and from small but deliberate deeds!*"[3098]

- *Most essential quality.* "[This is] perhaps the most essential godlike quality: *compassion and love*—compassion shown forth in service to others, unselfishness, that ultimate expression of concern for others we call love."[3099]

- *Service is the next step in spiritual growth.* "Let us not shrink from the next steps in our spiritual growth, brothers and sisters, by holding back, or sidestepping our *fresh opportunities for service* to our families and our fellowmen."[3100]

- *Difficulties are opportunities for service.* "Let us trust the Lord and take the next steps in our individual lives. . . . Sometimes the solution is not to change our circumstance, but to change our attitude about that circumstance; *difficulties are often opportunities for service.*"[3101]

- *Service is a testimony.* "The most vital thing we can do is to *express our testimonies through service,* which will, in turn, produce spiritual growth, greater commitment, and a greater capacity to keep the commandments."[3102]

- *Service puts problems in perspective.* "When we are engaged in the service of our fellowmen, not only do our deeds assist them, but we put our own problems in a fresher perspective. When we concern ourselves more with others, there is less time to be concerned with ourselves. In the midst of the miracle of serving, there is the promise of Jesus, that by losing ourselves, we

---

[3095] Kimball, *The Teachings of Spencer W. Kimball*, 250.
[3096] Kimball, *The Teachings of Spencer W. Kimball*, 250.
[3097] Kimball, *The Teachings of Spencer W. Kimball*, 251.
[3098] Kimball, *The Teachings of Spencer W. Kimball*, 252.
[3099] Kimball, *The Teachings of Spencer W. Kimball*, 253.
[3100] Kimball, *The Teachings of Spencer W. Kimball*, 253.
[3101] Kimball, *The Teachings of Spencer W. Kimball*, 254.
[3102] Kimball, *The Teachings of Spencer W. Kimball*, 254.

find ourselves. Not only do we 'find' ourselves in terms of acknowledging guidance in our lives, but *the more we serve our fellowmen in appropriate ways, the more substance there is to our souls.*"[3103]
- *Antidote for loneliness.* "Perhaps you could take a loaf of bread or a covered dish to someone in need. Uncompensated service is one answer, one good answer to overcome loneliness."[3104]

CHARITABLE SERVICE SAVES AND EXALTS

It is a gospel verity that charity saves the lives of both the giver and the receiver. What the Lord said to missionaries could be said of anyone who is willing to enter the field of need and thrust in his sickle: "For behold the field is white already to harvest; and lo, he that thrusteth in his sickle with his might, the same layeth up in store that he perisheth not, *but bringeth salvation to his soul.*"[3105] Clearly, there is so much need, and the Lord has placed within our reach the spiritual power to supply that need. A joyful and bounteous harvest awaits those who give charitable service to the Lord's poor: "And if it so be that you should labor all your days in crying repentance unto this people, and bring, save it be one soul unto me, how great shall be your joy with him in the kingdom of my Father! And now, if your joy will be great with one soul that you have brought unto me into the kingdom of my Father, how great will be your joy if you should bring many souls unto me!"[3106]

Charity is sometimes a handout, but it is always a hand up. Salvation comes to our souls when we lift another and give of ourselves and our means for the purest and highest of motivations—*love.* President Joseph F. Smith said, "I would advise that we learn to love each other, and then friendship will be true and sweet. It has been said by one, that 'we may give without loving, but we cannot love without giving.'"[3107] We note with interest that it was only when the people of Limhi repented, unified, and began to practice a form of consecration to care for the widows and orphans that deliverance from bondage came.[3108] Likewise, it was the Mormon Battalion whose men consecrated their earnings and service, thereby saving the Church from financial ruin and providing the necessary capital to equip the impoverished Saints for their westward trek.

MORONI'S PRAYER FOR LATTER-DAY CHARITY

Salvation, or the forfeiture of it, swings on the hinge of charity. Moroni looked into the future with the eyes of a seer and saw the woeful latter-day lack of charitable service. He mourned that our salvation would be at risk: "If the Gentiles have not charity, because of our weakness, . . . thou wilt prove them, and take away their talent, yea, even that which they have received, and give unto them who shall have more abundantly." At that point, Moroni offered a prayer that we might receive the gift of charity for our own salvation. At least to a degree, we might trace the level of charity that we presently enjoy back to Moroni's prayer: "And it came to pass that I prayed unto the Lord that he would give unto the Gentiles grace, that they might have charity."[3109]

During Moroni's prayer, Jesus promised his prophet that he would provide us "Gentiles" of the last days with his grace so that we might receive and exhibit charity, which virtue would open the door to our salvation: "I will show unto them that faith, hope and charity bringeth [souls] unto me." Moroni understood the foundation and importance of charity, and he bore his testimony concerning

---

[3103] Kimball, *The Teachings of Spencer W. Kimball,* 254.
[3104] Kimball, *The Teachings of Spencer W. Kimball,* 256.
[3105] D&C 4:4; emphasis added.
[3106] D&C 18:15–16.
[3107] Smith, *Teachings of Presidents of the Church: Joseph F. Smith,* 192.
[3108] Mosiah 21:16–18.
[3109] Ether 12:35–36.

it: "I remember that thou hast said that thou hast loved the world, even unto the laying down of thy life for the world, that thou mightest take it again to prepare a place for the children of men. And now I know that this love which thou hast had for the children of men is charity; wherefore, except men shall have charity they cannot inherit that place which thou hast prepared in the mansions of thy Father."[3110] Salvation is simply not possible without charity. This virtue is the prerequisite for our entering into the kingdom of heaven. Moroni concludes with these words: "Except ye have charity ye can in nowise be saved in the kingdom of God."[3111]

When the Lord comes in his glory, he will divide out the sheep from the goats. To the sheep on his right hand he will say, "Come, ye blessed of my Father, inherit the kingdom prepared for you from the foundation of the world." The criteria for their salvation will be three-fold: (1) They gave food and drink to those in need; (2) They used their time, talents, and resources for the poor; and (3) They ministered to the sick and the imprisoned. In all their ministrations, they saw in each impoverished soul the image of Jesus Christ, whose child the impoverished, sick, or captive person was.[3112] For what they did and who they became, through the grace of Christ they earned their exaltation.

Charitable Service Protects the Giver

Cain first stated the motto of Babylon in the form of a question: "Am I my brother's keeper?"[3113] That self-centered statement became the foundation of the anti-Christ doctrine that was advanced by Korihor:

1. Hope and faith in Christ are foolish and vain.
2. Those who believe in Christ and his coming are not free, but rather in bondage.
3. There is no such thing as prophecy and revelation.
4. The words of the prophets are foolish traditions.
5. Seeing is believing; reality is only measurable by applying scientific methods.
6. The concept of sin against God's laws and remission of sin based on repentance are evidences of a frenzied, deranged mind that is held captive by false traditions.
7. An atonement for sin is unnecessary and impossible.
8. In this dog-eat-dog world, men get by according to their individual management; they prosper according to their genius, and they conquer according to their strength. Everything depends on me; everything revolves around me.
9. Men legislate the standards of morality. Because God does not exist, men are not accountable to him, and whatsoever they do is not a crime against God.
10. Wickedness brings happiness.
11. Live for today, because when we die, it is the end.
12. The servants of God operate by intrigue. They pretend to receive visions and revelations to keep their people in ignorance. They do this so that they might usurp power and authority over the people, keep them in bondage, and profiteer on the labor and offerings of the people.
13. Lest the people should offend their leaders and forfeit their place in the Church, the people are coerced into consecrating their goods.[3114]

[3110] Ether 12:28–34.
[3111] Moroni 10:21.
[3112] Matthew 25:34–40.
[3113] Genesis 4:9.
[3114] Alma 30:12–28.

None of these statements is Zionlike. The entire anti-Christ philosophy is faithless, immoral, destructive, and selfish. In no way does it draw us to Christ, encourage us to depend on him, shelter us from the consequences of sin, provide for the poor, or make us our brother's keeper. To Cain's selfish motto—"Am I my brother's keeper?"—The Lord countered with the doctrine of Zion that carries promises: "Blessed is he that considereth the poor: the Lord will deliver him in time of trouble. The Lord will preserve him, and keep him alive; and he shall be blessed upon the earth: and thou wilt not deliver him unto the will of his enemies. The Lord will strengthen him."[3115]

The mantra of Zion is a way of life. President Heber J. Grant said, "Make a motto in life: always try and assist someone else to carry his burden."[3116] The prophet of Ecclesiastes stated that when we plant seeds of service to bless God's children, we save our own souls, "for thou knowest not what evil shall be upon the earth." Our safety is on the line. When evil attempts to overwhelm us, when terrifying storms gather above us, when temptations fell trees all about us, charity will protect us— "there [our safety] shall be." The prophet said we do not understand how God transforms our charitable acts into cloaks of safety; we only know that it happens. Therefore, we are to go about liberally planting the seeds of charitable service: "In the morning sow thy seed, and in the evening withhold not thine hand." We do not know which seeds of charity will take root and how they will prosper.[3117] We only know that by sowing and nourishing charitable acts, many people are blessed by our actions and we will be kept safe.

Charitable Service Prospers the Giver

The promise of charitable service is that of an abundant return. President Marion G. Romney taught the following truth: "You cannot give yourself poor in this work; you can only give yourself rich."[3118] His statement is a confirmation of the ancient prophet's teaching: "Cast thy bread upon the waters: for thou shalt find it after many days."[3119] This suggests both a boomerang effect and a germination period. Bread that is cast upon the water will most certainly float back to land on the tide or a current; that is, our charitable actions will always return to bless us. Moreover, the seed that makes the bread that is cast upon the water will eventually find land, set down roots, sprout, and grow; that is, charitable acts carry the potential of life within them; charitable acts might take time to find ground and take root, but in time, those acts will become a beautiful and fruitful tree. We cannot be impoverished by casting the seeds of our charity upon the water. We cannot consecrate ourselves poor.

We recall our discussion about abundance flowing to us as we manifest charity: We grow from grace *to* grace by giving grace *for* grace. We also have learned that it is upon the principle of service that we progress toward perfection. Therefore, by receiving grace (the Lord's help) *for* grace (our service), we grow *from* grace (light, truth, power, and perfection) *to* grace (more light, truth, power, and perfection). According to John the Baptist's testimony, Jesus grew in grace (light, truth, power, and perfection) by giving grace (service): "And I, John, saw that he received not of the fulness at the first, but received grace *for* grace. And he received not of the fulness at first, but continued from grace *to* grace, until he received a fulness."[3120] Likewise, we progress incrementally from grace *to* grace to a fulness of glory by keeping the commandments and giving service, whereupon the Lord blesses us by granting us grace for our having given grace to another: "For if you keep my commandments you shall

---

[3115] Psalm 41:1–2.
[3116] Grant, *Teachings of Presidents of the Church: Heber J. Grant*, 139.
[3117] Ecclesiastes 11:2–6.
[3118] Romney, "Welfare Services: The Savior's Program," 92.
[3119] Ecclesiastes 11:1.
[3120] D&C 93:12–13; emphasis added.

receive of his fulness, and be glorified in me as I am in the Father; therefore, I say unto you, you shall receive grace *for* grace."[3121]

The *hundredfold* principle applies.[3122] When we receive the seed of *grace* from God or a charitable person, we should plant rather than hoard that seed of charity by giving charity to another person. The replanting of the seed will urge a stalk to grow, which contains many seeds. If we will plant again, this time with a great number of seeds that will cover an expansive swath of ground, we will realize a marvelous harvest. Thus, ever repeating the cycle of planting and harvesting constitutes the mystery of Zion's prosperity. It is the Zion principle of giving and receiving in return with increase.[3123]

Therefore, should we be concerned about keeping the commandment to consecrate? Do we really believe that we will end up with less? President Kimball refuted the idea and challenged our faith: "What are we to fear when the Lord is with us? Can we not take the Lord at his word and exercise a particle of faith in him? Our assignment is affirmative: to forsake the things of the world as ends in themselves; to leave off idolatry and press forward in faith; to carry the gospel to our enemies, that they might no longer be our enemies. We must leave off the worship of modern-day idols and a reliance on the 'arm of flesh,' for the Lord has said to all the world in our day, 'I will not spare any that remain in Babylon.'"[3124] Clearly, our ultimate safety is found only in extending charity and consecrating our lives, property, time, and talents for the building up of God's kingdom and the establishment of Zion.

PATIENCE AND CHARITY

President Heber J. Grant explained that charity is often characterized by patience: "The gospel of Christ is a gospel of love and peace, of patience and long suffering, of forbearance and forgiveness, of kindness and good deeds, of charity and brotherly love. Greed, avarice, base ambition, thirst for power, and unrighteous dominion over our fellow men, can have no place in the hearts of Latter-day Saints nor of God-fearing men everywhere."[3125] Our leaders have offered insight into the relationship between patience and charity. Of the thirteen elements of charity listed by Mormon, four of them relate to patience:

1. charity suffereth long
2. is not easily provoked
3. beareth all things
4. endureth all things

We can no more achieve a Christlike character without patience than we can achieve personal value without charity, for if we "have not charity, [we] are nothing."[3126]

Patience means to wait:

"I will wait *for* you."
"I will wait *with* you."
"I will wait *upon* you." In other words, "I will serve you."

[3121] D&C 93:20; emphasis added.
[3122] Matthew 19:29; Mark 10:30.
[3123] Packer, "The Candle of the Lord," 54–55.
[3124] Kimball, *The Teachings of Spencer W. Kimball*, 417; quoting D&C 64:24.
[3125] Grant, *Teachings of Presidents of the Church: Heber J. Grant*, 139.
[3126] Oaks, "The Power of Patience," 15–17; quoting Moroni 7:44–46.

It is the virtue of charity that perfects the virtue of patience, and it is patience that perfects all other virtues. Patience finishes the process of perfection and moves us forward to completion and abundance: "But let patience have her perfect work, that ye may be perfect and entire, wanting nothing."[3127] It is by means of patience that we both manifest and receive charity. Moreover, it is by means of patience that we consecrate ourselves in faith, because we cannot see the end of our consecration from our present vantage point. In patience we suffer or *allow* adversity for a long time, while waiting in faith for the Lord's deliverance. In patience we restrain from giving offense. In patience we forgive multiple times. In patience we show kindness when kindness is not returned. In patience we offer brotherly love over an extended period. Clearly, in patience we wait *for, with,* and *upon* the Lord and his children.

Charity and Virtue—Essential Elements of Priesthood Power

We have learned that we demonstrate our love for God by keeping his commandments and feeding his sheep. We have also have learned that showing love to others is requisite for the doctrine of the priesthood to distill upon our souls as the dews from heaven.[3128] With confidence, then, we might point to charity as the preeminent virtue that transforms priesthood authority into priesthood power. Without charity, priesthood fails, and if priesthood fails, so does Zion.

In addition to all other considerations, charity transforms those who are *called* into those who are *chosen*. Such people are the products of a new and purified heart. They operate "by persuasion, by long-suffering, by gentleness and meekness, and by love unfeigned . . . by kindness, and pure knowledge." Such people are filled with "charity towards all men, and to the household of faith," and virtue garnishes their thoughts unceasingly. Their charitable service and virtue summon the greatest of priesthood blessings: "Then shall thy confidence wax strong in the presence of God; and the doctrine of the priesthood shall distil upon thy soul as the dews from heaven. The Holy Ghost shall be thy constant companion, and thy scepter an unchanging scepter of righteousness and truth; and thy dominion shall be an everlasting dominion, and without compulsory means it shall flow unto thee forever and ever."[3129] Clearly, priesthood power depends on a consecrated heart, virtue, and charitable service. Then when priesthood power is in place, it prepares the way for the establishment of Zion.

Charity Draws the Lord Near

Things that are alike attract: "For intelligence cleaveth unto intelligence; wisdom receiveth wisdom; truth embraceth truth; virtue loveth virtue; light cleaveth unto light; mercy hath compassion on mercy and claimeth her own; justice continueth its course and claimeth its own; judgment goeth before the face of him who sitteth upon the throne and governeth and executeth all things."[3130] The Charitable One draws near when we manifest charity.

Conversely, when we fail to exhibit charity, we sense distance between the Lord and us. President Marion G. Romney suggested that we can close the gap by extending charity. To demonstrate this point, he used the example of the law of the fast, as explained in Isaiah 58:3–12. Often we wonder, why is that our fast seems to go unnoticed by the Lord? "Wherefore have we fasted . . . and thou seest not?" Isaiah gave the Lord's answer. It is because we do not understand and keep the true law of the fast. We accomplish only two of the three criteria of that law (prayer and humility), but we neglect the third criterion: dealing our bread to the hungry, providing for the poor,

---

[3127] James 1:4.
[3128] D&C 121:45.
[3129] D&C 121:40–46.
[3130] D&C 88:40.

and covering the naked. According to Isaiah, a fast without extending charity yields no more blessings than shedding a few extra pounds.

On the other hand, a fast that would "loose the bands of wickedness," "undo the heavy burdens," "let the oppressed go free," and "break every yoke" requires that we must extend charity to the needy, including the hurting members of our family; and from our lives we must eliminate strife, debate, anger, and contention: "Is not this the fast that I have chosen? . . . Is it not to deal thy bread to the hungry, and that thou bring the poor that are cast out to thy house? when thou seest the naked, that thou cover him; and that thou hide not thyself from thine own flesh [family]?"

The law of the fast serves as model for other laws of God. The principle of charity is woven into the fabric of each of them. If we would obtain the promised blessing for any obeyed law, we must extend charitable service to our family and to others of the children of God; we must not allow strife, debate, anger, or contention to invade our lives in any degree. Otherwise, the desired blessings for living the law will be forfeited, and the distance between the Lord and us will remain unaltered.

But, if we will live the laws of God, eliminate strife, debate, anger, and contention from our lives, and give generous charitable service, then the Lord will draw near: "Then shalt thou call, and the Lord shall answer; thou shalt cry, and he shall say, Here I am." The Lord always draws near to those who follow such a course, and when he comes, he always brings blessings with him:

> Then shall thy light break forth as the morning, and thine health shall spring forth speedily: and thy righteousness shall go before thee; the glory of the Lord shall be thy rereward [protector]. . .
> . And if thou draw out thy soul to the hungry, and satisfy the afflicted soul; then shall thy light rise in obscurity, and thy darkness be as the noonday: and the Lord shall guide thee continually, and satisfy thy soul in drought, and make fat thy bones: and thou shalt be like a watered garden, and like a spring of water, whose waters fail not. And they that shall be of thee [your posterity] shall build the old waste places: thou shalt raise up the foundations of many generations; and thou shalt be called, The repairer of the breach, The restorer of paths to dwell in.[3131]

Consider the blessings of combining charity with obedience! Answers to prayers; light bursting upon the soul, dispelling darkness; restoration of health; increase of righteousness and righteous influence; divine protection and guidance; relief and deliverance; sustenance; abundance; a constant flow of blessings; power; redemption; exaltation; a healing of our generations; multiplication of righteous posterity; and, finally, a savior to our family and to others.

President Romney stated that extending charitable service to the needy is the primary purpose and a fixed requirement of *The Royal Law*. For example, Amulek taught the people that the law of prayer, like the law of the fast, requires charitable giving to be effective: " . . . after ye have done all these things, if ye turn away the needy, and the naked, and visit not the sick and afflicted, and impart of your substance, if ye have, to those who stand in need—I say unto you, if ye do not any of these things, *behold, your prayer is vain, and availeth you nothing, and ye are as hypocrites who do deny the faith.*"[3132] This is the proper way to pray. If we pray and do not extend charitable service, we have not fulfilled the law that governs prayer, and, therefore, we cannot expect our prayers to be answered.

Neither fasting nor prayer nor substantially any other law of God becomes valid or a principle of power without charity. Neither can our testimony be a declaration of the truth unless our lives are

---

[3131] Isaiah 58:8–12.
[3132] Romney, "The Royal Law of Love," 95; quoting Alma 34:28.

filled with charity. Mormon said, "If a man be meek and lowly in heart, and confesses by the power of the Holy Ghost that Jesus is the Christ, he must needs have charity; for if he have not charity he is nothing; wherefore he must needs have charity."[3133] Clearly, without charity, we are nothing.

Charity Is an Absolute

Few scriptural absolutes are as stunning as those describing charity:

- "If ye have not charity, ye are nothing."
- "Charity never faileth."
- "Charity . . . is the greatest of all."
- "Charity . . . endureth forever.[3134]

In a world where everything fails, only those things that are built upon the foundation of charity will not fail. When we seek charity first, as exemplified by our seeking the kingdom of God and his righteousness first, we are promised that all else will fall into place and be added unto us.[3135] Because of charity, the blessings of the priesthood will flow to us forever without compulsory means.[3136]

Charity Is a Gift—the Greatest Gift

Despite our best efforts, we never will obtain charity or know its power in our lives unless the Holy Ghost delivers it to us. Charity is a spiritual gift that must be sought. Like the principle that states that we are saved by grace only after all we can do,[3137] we receive charity as a gift only after we do all we can to obtain it. Therefore, because salvation is impossible without charity and because charity is delivered to us as a gift of the Spirit, Mormon pleads with us to "pray unto the Father with all the energy of heart, that ye may be filled with this love, which he hath bestowed upon all who are true followers of his Son, Jesus Christ."

When charity finally enters our souls, Mormon continues, this love becomes the vehicle to make of us "sons of God." Charity has the power to make us "like him." Ultimately, upon the principle of charity, we will become "as he is." This is our "hope; that we [through our charity] may be purified even as he is pure."[3138] This is the principal aim and the ultimate destination of the royal law, the celestial law of love. It is this quality of love that propels the law of consecration and fulfills the first and second commandments: "Thou shalt love the Lord thy God with all thy heart, and with all thy soul, and with all thy mind. This is the first and great commandment. And the second is like unto it, Thou shalt love thy neighbour as thyself." Upon these commandments, said Jesus, "hang all the law and the prophets."[3139] We consecrate because we love.

Summary and Conclusion

The law of consecration is the last and most difficult law to live. Only by our agreeing to obey this law and abide its precepts can we qualify for celestial glory and become like God. Consecration cannot be lived without charity; consecration is the natural outgrowth of charity.

[3133] Moroni 7:44.
[3134] Moroni 7:46–47.
[3135] 3 Nephi 13:33.
[3136] D&C 121:46.
[3137] 2 Nephi 25:23.
[3138] Moroni 7:48.
[3139] Matthew 22:36–40.

THE ROYAL LAW

This quality of love—"the pure love of Christ"—has the capacity to lift and to save others; therefore, it is unlike any other type of love, and it is completely foreign to the natural man. Only a fervent effort on our part can summon the Holy Ghost to infuse us with this spiritual gift. Once we have it, charity will provide us with the motivation and the power to live a consecrated life. The evidence of charity and consecration is our yielding our hearts to God and our giving him the totality of who we are and what we have.

When we make the decision to yield our hearts to God and to consecrate our lives to him, we signal our desire that the Holy Ghost will come and perform in our lives the miracles of purification and sanctification.[3140] We understand that only by our submitting to this process can we obtain the highest degree of salvation, which is *exaltation*. We also understand that only the virtue of charity can convey us there. It is charity that saturates us with the necessary courage to consecrate our lives and to change the nature of our hearts.

Our leaders have taught us that the Final Judgment will be more an accounting of what we have become than a tally of our good and bad actions. Unfortunately, many of us go through the motions of gospel living as if we were making deposits into a heavenly account that we hope will save us. But going through the motions of keeping the commandments, ordinances, and covenants does not have power to save us. *Becoming* is the key to obtaining eternal life; the more we become as God is, the more we embrace his lifestyle; and fundamental to his lifestyle is the law of consecration.

Therefore, we must allow the Holy Ghost to purify and change our hearts, or we will come up short.[3141] Our actions must be motivated not by regulations, rites, and performances, but by a purified and consecrated heart that holds nothing back from God and his children, a heart that wants to be transformed into the similitude of the heart of its Maker, who is describes as love.[3142] As much as God is love, God is also a consecrated being.

Consecration flows from "the first and great commandment," upon which hangs "all the law and the prophets."[3143] James calls this law the royal law, which is the law of saving, Christlike love.[3144] Jesus stated it thus: "Thou shalt love the Lord thy God with all thy heart, and with all thy soul, and with all thy mind. This is the first and great commandment. And the second is like unto it, Thou shalt love thy neighbour as thyself."[3145] Because we love God and his children, we consecrate ourselves: our time, abilities, all that we have, and all that we are. We do this for the purpose of building up the kingdom of God, which prepares the way for the establishment of Zion.

Zion and consecration are as inseparable as consecration and charity, or charity and unity and equality. Because we love, we unite and esteem all people as equals. We gather with them and insist that they receive equal treatment and equal access to the blessings of the Lord. This is consecration; this is the love of Zion.

Consecration is also characterized by agency, stewardship, accountability, and labor.

By our agency, we choose to love, and we also choose to give of ourselves and the goods in our stewardship to help others. Because we choose to live the order of consecration, we abandon our claims of ownership, and we consider all that we have and are as belonging to the Lord. Forevermore, we are stewards, not owners, of the Lord's resources, and as stewards, we use the resources under our management for the Owner's intended purpose: to facilitate the highest possible quality of immortality for God's children with the goal of their achieving eternal life.[3146] The law of stewardship provides us

---

[3140] Helaman 3:35.
[3141] Oaks, "The Challenge to Become," 32–34.
[3142] 1 John 4:8.
[3143] Matthew 22:38–40.
[3144] James 2:8.
[3145] Matthew 22:37–40.
[3146] Moses 1:39.

with the highest level of safety and security. God becomes our Paymaster. As we faithfully manage the stewardship he has given us, laboring honestly and hard for him, God allows us to receive sufficient for our wants and needs. We agree to be accountable to God and his servant, the bishop, for the management of our stewardship. Presently, we account to the bishop during tithing settlement and when we seek a temple recommend. We also account whenever he feels or we feel the need. Beyond those occasions of accounting, our leaders have instructed us that we should account to God daily in our evening prayers.[3147]

The law of consecration is further characterized by four cornerstones that are listed in the law of the Church (D&C 42). These cornerstones are: (1) *Mutual assistance*, (2) *Proper use of priesthood*, (3) *The need for faith*, and (4) *Reciprocal love*.[3148]

Concerning reciprocal love—*true love, unconditional Christlike love*—we learn that this love, which is *charity*, defines and drives the higher law of the gospel, including the highest law of that higher law, which is the law of consecration. Charity is the only love that can save both the giver and the receiver. This saving love has the ability to lift, forgive, and rescue from enormous distances. This saving love "never faileth."[3149] Charity emerges from desire, faith, and hope. As we have said, all gospel actions are profitless without charity, and Paul reminds us that we too are nothing if we have not cultivated this God-defining .[3150] Charity is the very definition of discipleship. Charity is the primary motivating factor that inspires true disciples of Jesus Christ to live obediently, sacrifice, hold to the law of the gospel, embrace the celestial lifestyle called *Chastity*, and consecrate all that they are and have to God. Clearly, charity vitalizes consecration and provides the lifeblood of Zion.

By means of charitable consecration, the immutable law of abundance is set in motion: that which we give returns to us with increase—an hundredfold. When the principles of charity and consecration are anchored on the earth, they act as leaven "until the whole [of humanity is] leavened."[3151] Then we, who give charitable service, become angels to the poor and the afflicted; we go about attacking poverty of every kind with the sword of charity. We slice away at suffering by consecrating our time, talents, and means. Wherever we encounter lack, we apply the remedy of love. We, the saviors on Mount Zion, do as the Savior would do: lift, heal, console, save, and exalt. And we doggedly keep at it until there are no poor among us.[3152] While we go about extending charitable consecrated service, the Lord protects us in our labors. Our motto is that of Zion: "Always try and assist someone else to carry his burden."[3153]

By giving charitable consecrated service, we prosper. We grow from one *grace* to another by giving *grace*—grace *to* grace by grace *for* grace. By seeking for the kingdom of God first, we become a conduit through which God can funnel blessings to the poor. Instructing us in the celestial law of obtaining wealth, Jacob said: "But before ye seek for riches, seek ye for the kingdom of God. And after ye have obtained a hope in Christ ye shall obtain riches, if ye seek them; and ye will seek them for the intent to do good—to clothe the naked, and to feed the hungry, and to liberate the captive, and administer relief to the sick and the afflicted."[3154]

Charity is inseparably connected to the virtue of patience, which perfects charity, consecration, and every other gospel principle; patience perfects our lives.[3155] By applying patience, we learn to

---

[3147] Bednar, "Pray Always," 41–44.
[3148] Johnson, "The Law of Consecration," 99.
[3149] Moroni 7:47.
[3150] 1 Corinthians 13:1–3.
[3151] Matthew 13:33; Luke 13:21.
[3152] Moses 7:18.
[3153] Grant, *Teachings of Presidents of the Church: Heber J. Grant*, 139.
[3154] Jacob 2:18–19.
[3155] James 1:4.

trust in God's timing. We are willing to wait *with* God and his children; we also wait *for* them; and we wait *upon* them—that is to say, we serve them. We cannot live the law of consecration, exhibit charity, or become perfected without patience.

Patience is also essential to obtaining power in the priesthood. By patience and charity we minister among God's children, dispensing the gifts he has given us through consecrated service. Priesthood power depends upon charity, which we manifest by keeping his commandments—the greatest commandment being loving God and our neighbor, which includes feeding the Lord's sheep. When we do that, the doctrine of the priesthood will distill upon our souls as the dews from heaven,[3156] and we who were once *called* to eternal life will become those who are *chosen* for eternal life.[3157] There, in that glorious setting, we will finally experience the perfection of consecration: In love, we will give all that we are and have to God, and, in return, we will receive "all that the Father hath."[3158] Then, forevermore, we will receive and increase our stewardships in his kingdom according to this law, and eternally we will never lack. By means of consecration and charity, we will become *one* with our Father, and he will give us liberal and equal access to the resources of his infinite kingdom. We will labor in his kingdom forever as we build our kingdoms, and we will offer accountings to him.

In the meantime, we struggle with celestial laws in a telestial setting. By faith alone, we must accept eternal laws and try to live them, but usually we do so without a full understanding of their eternal import. Therefore, in our weakness, we cry unto the Lord for strength and for the spiritual gift of charity so that we can be obedient, willing to sacrifice, devoted to the law of the gospel, loyal, and faithful, and so that we can have the courage to consecrate. As we extend ourselves and provide charitable service to others, God will hear our prayers and respond. Our sincere effort to give service draws him near, and when he comes, he answers our cries and brings blessings of light, health, righteousness, glory, protection, sustenance, relief, deliverance, guidance, abundance, power, redemption, and exaltation.[3159]

Such are the blessings of charity; such are the blessings of consecration; such are the blessings of Zion.

Postlude

The third pillar of Zion is the *law of consecration*. This law emerges from the new and everlasting covenant and is introduced to us in a temple setting as an outgrowth of the oath and covenant of the priesthood. Now the three pillars of Zion are complete. They stand on the foundation of the Atonement, and according to the "law of the church" (D&C 42), they are sufficient to establish us as Zion people.

The law of consecration is the foundational law of the celestial kingdom,[3160] and consequently it is the foundational law of Zion. Although it is often associated with Church programs from earlier times, consecration is a template, the guiding principles of which can be used (and have been used) in any number of situations. Nevertheless, in the final analysis, consecration describes a celestial lifestyle and a condition of the heart.

Any individual or group of individuals who live this law will achieve the celestial condition of equality and unity. Nevertheless, these characteristics, along with other benefits of Zion, are wholly foreign to the world we live in. In Babylon, competition and selfishness rule and ruin lives. Therefore, when we introduced to the law of consecration or any other celestial law, we will not be able to make

---

[3156] D&C 121:45.
[3157] D&C 121:40.
[3158] D&C 84:38.
[3159] Isaiah 58:3–9.
[3160] D&C 105:5.

much sense of it in a telestial environment. Ultimately, celestial laws must be lived by faith, but their rewards are astounding.

Finally, we learn that the law of consecration is an outgrowth of "the royal law,"[3161] which is love: "Thou shalt love the Lord thy God with all thy heart, and with all thy soul, and with all thy mind. This is the first and great commandment. And the second is like unto it, Thou shalt love thy neighbour as thyself."[3162] Clearly, love is the greatest power and motivator in the universe. Ultimately, we consecrate ourselves and all that we have and are because we love God and we love his children.

[3161] James 2:8.
[3162] Matthew 22:36–40.

BOOK 5:

THE PURE IN HEART

Introduction

"[Zion] commences in the heart of each person."[3163]—Brigham Young

In this fifth book of *The Three Pillars of Zion* series, we will examine the journey that leads to Zion and discover along the way what it means to be pure in heart.

By way of review, we learned in Book 1 that Zion was our origin and will be our destiny. She is our ideal, and she is also the antithesis of Babylon. Moreover, Zion is the standard among celestial and celestial-seeking people.[3164] Joseph Smith said, "We ought to have the building up of Zion as our greatest object."[3165] The obligation to become Zion people rests upon each of us individually.

We recall that the "Law of the Church" (D&C 42) states that three covenants are sufficient to establish us as Zion people: "And ye shall hereafter receive church covenants, such as shall be sufficient to establish you, both here and in the New Jerusalem."[3166] These covenants are:

1. The New and Everlasting Covenant (D&C 132:4–7)
2. The Oath and Covenant of the Priesthood (D&C 84:33–44)
3. The Law of Consecration (D&C 82:11–15)

These covenants flow from the Atonement of Jesus Christ. In Book 2, we learned that we accept the Atonement by the formality of receiving the new and everlasting covenant by baptism. The new and everlasting covenant is the first pillar of Zion and the *umbrella covenant* of the gospel. It consists of two primary covenants: (1) the covenant of baptism, and (2) the oath and covenant of the priesthood. The priesthood covenant is magnified by (1) ordination for worthy men; (2) temple covenants and ordinances for worthy men and women; (3) the temple sealing covenant, which is called the covenant

---

[3163] Young, *Discourses of Brigham Young*, 118.
[3164] D&C 105:5.
[3165] Smith, *Teachings of the Prophet Joseph Smith*, 60.
[3166] D&C 42:67.

INTRODUCTION

of exaltation,[3167] for worthy men and women. The new and everlasting covenant provides a way to be cleansed from sin and separated from the world.

As mentioned, the new and everlasting covenant leads to the second pillar of Zion, the oath and covenant of the priesthood. The priesthood covenant provides us a way to receive God's authority, power, and knowledge—everything we need to become like him and inherit all he has.

The principles of the priesthood apply to both worthy men and women. The priesthood covenant is received by men at the time of ordination, but its principles are expansive and eventually lead to the temple. There, faithful men and women are endowed with priesthood covenants and ordinances that culminate at a marriage altar. Elder Bruce R. McConkie said, "This covenant, made when the priesthood is received, is renewed when the recipient enters the order of eternal marriage."[3168] Plainly, both men and women are involved in the doctrines of the priesthood.

We discussed the history of the priesthood and men who were great examples of priesthood worthiness and power. We discussed priesthood keys and their importance in the restored Church of Jesus Christ. Then we surveyed our covenantal agreements and the Father's oath, instructions, and promises. Later we examined "The Constitution of the Priesthood," found in Doctrine and Covenants 121, and we discussed why many are called to eternal life, but few are chosen. We also studied the Lord's instructions and rewards for the chosen few. We came to understand that priesthood is more than an ordination; it is a way of life, and the power to pursue that life. Without the priesthood and its guiding principles, neither a man nor a woman could achieve Zion in his or her life and thus attain *exaltation*, the ultimate form of salvation

In the fourth book of the *Three Pillars of Zion* series, we examined the law of the celestial kingdom,[3169] which is the foundational law of Zion—*the law of consecration*. This is the third pillar of Zion. We demonstrated that this law is a *template* that can be used (and has been used) in a number of situations. Our living the guiding principles of the law of consecration results in equality and unity, two foundational characteristics that describe the celestial kingdom. To live this law, we must make a choice between God and mammon, which is the ultimate test of mortality. In the end, we learned that the law of consecration is all about love. It is a manifestation of "The Royal Law,"[3170] which is this: "Thou shalt love the Lord thy God with all thy heart, and with all thy soul, and with all thy mind. This is the first and great commandment. And the second is like unto it, Thou shalt love thy neighbour as thyself." The royal law is "the first and great commandment," according to Jesus, and upon it "hang all the law and the prophets."[3171] When all is said and done, we consecrate ourselves and all that we have and are because we love God and we love his children.

Now armed with the three pillars of Zion, we embark on the journey to Zion, and in the process we will become pure in heart. The journey necessitates our *falling* into this lone and dreary world. Here we encounter the wilderness of sin, which we enter when we sin and fall away from the Lord, followed by the Lord's wilderness, into which the Lord takes us to purify and sanctify us. To escape the wilderness of sin, we must awaken to our awful situation and cry unto the Lord for deliverance.

[3167] Nelson, *The Power within Us*, 136; Smith, *Doctrines of Salvation*, 2:58. Note: Elder McConkie stated that men make a covenant of exaltation twice: once upon ordination to the Melchizedek Priesthood and again at the time of the marriage sealing: "Ordination to office in the Melchizedek priesthood and entering into that 'order of the priesthood' named 'the new and everlasting covenant of marriage' are both occasions when men make the covenant of exaltation, being promised through their faithfulness all that the Father hath (D&C 131:1–4; 84:39–41; 132; Num. 25:13)." (*Mormon Doctrine*, 167.)

[3168] McConkie, *A New Witness for the Articles of Faith*, 313.

[3169] D&C 105:5.

[3170] James 2:8.

[3171] Matthew 22:36–40.

Rescue comes by making and keeping covenants, and thus we begin our transforming journey that will end up in our own personal land of promise: *Zion*.

The journey is one of purification, elimination of contaminants, and sanctification, to change our purpose in life. To come forth as gold, we must submit to "crucible" periods, which are essentially times when we are thrown into the furnace of affliction. The purpose of these times is to change our nature and our disposition for sin. Only by submitting to this process can we one day be in a position for the Lord to perform our ultimate deliverance and usher us into his presence. Other purposes of crucibles are to weld us into the Covenant with the Lord, to teach us to have faith and to trust him, and to prove us trustworthy of the blessings of eternity.

To navigate the Lord's wilderness involves hard work, traveling by revelation, and journeying exactly as the Lord directs. We discover that angels attend us, and, despite the odds, we always enjoy the Lord's safety and security. To solidify this idea in our minds, and to prepare us for the ultimate day of deliverance, the Lord delivers us multiple times from seemingly impossible situations. Occasionally, the Lord brings us, as he did Lehi, to our own Bountifuls, or places of reprieve. We use these reprieves as Sabbaths: to commune with the Lord, to enter into his rest, and to prepare us for the final and most difficult part of our journey, which becomes our ultimate test of faith.

Somewhere along the way we are confronted by Satan. Once and for all, we must choose between Satan and God. In some cases, this confrontation is also coupled with the equally necessary Abrahamic test. Overcoming Satan and sacrificing all things bring us to the point where we can fully take upon us the name of Jesus Christ, the ultimate manifestation of being born again. Now we are pure in heart and qualify to be ushered into the presence of the Lord. This wilderness journey is how we come to Zion and to Christ. The wilderness journey is the "adventure of discipleship, [the] trek of treks,"[3172] and the end of the path that is called "strait and narrow."

We become pure in heart by increments. Ultimately, however, the ideal of being pure in heart is to qualify to see God.

Indeed, we are commanded to seek the face of the Lord.

This is a process that involves knowing and living the higher law, receiving power from on high, and seeking more doctrine from the Lord. These things make us progressively more holy. To arrive at this point, we strive to become Zion people:

- Above all, pure in heart.
- Separate from Babylon.
- Of one heart and mind—unified with God and our fellowmen.
- Equal in opportunity for and access to God's blessings.
- Stewards, not owners, who are accountable to God.
- Those who have chosen God over mammon.
- Striving to labor for Zion and not to amass personal wealth.
- Those who have completely consecrated ourselves: our time, talents, and all that we have and are for the upbuilding of the kingdom of God and the establishment of Zion.

Now is the day of decision. President Lorenzo Snow said, "It is high time to establish Zion."[3173] If we were to apply ourselves, said Brigham Young, we could qualify for the establishment of Zion in our lives, marriages, and families in as little as one year.[3174] To do so, we must eliminate contention and

---

[3172] Maxwell, *The Promise of Discipleship*, i.
[3173] Snow, *The Teachings of Lorenzo Snow*, 181.
[3174] Young, *Journal of Discourses*, 11:300.

anger and bring into our lives the other principles discussed in this series. The book of Third Nephi is our latter-day guide to establishing Zion.

The account in Third Nephi describes the ultimate reward for becoming pure in heart. Diligent striving to sanctify ourselves carries the promise that one day we—*all of us*—will return to the presence of the Lord and behold his face: "And blessed are *all* the pure in heart, for they *shall* see God."[3175] Seeing him is only the beginning of blessings for the pure in heart. We read that the Lord bade the Nephites to come to him *one by one* and experience for themselves the reality of the Atonement and the sacrifice that he had made *in each person's behalf*. From that account, we learn that many blessings accompany this experience for each of us. For example, as we worship the Lord, rejoice, and bear testimony in his presence, we receive a greater endowment of knowledge and we are healed of all our sicknesses and afflictions. Moreover, we hear him pray for us, and we are encircled about by angels. In his presence, we partake of the Lord's Supper and receive a greater endowment of the Holy Ghost. He wipes away all tears, recompensing and multiplying our blessings in proportion to our sacrifices and service, and compensating us for our sufferings, sorrows, and pain. The Lord also gives us greater revelations, prophecies, explanations, and commandments. When we are in his presence, he offers us the privilege of asking for and receiving a special, personalized gift, which we will consecrate back to him in the form of service to his children.

In the end, what we learn from our journey to Zion and our experience with the Lord is that *Zion is beautiful!* Whether Zion is found within an individual, a marriage, a family, or a priesthood community, Zion is "the perfection of beauty," where "God hath shined."[3176] The interpretation of a baffling scripture has been hotly debated for centuries:[3177] "How beautiful upon the mountains are the feet of him that bringeth good tidings."[3178] Now we can answer the question of the ages: Who were the beautiful ones? We know the answer: the beautiful ones are the pure in heart—*Zion people*.

The blessings that the beautiful ones receive are without equal: "And surely there could not be a happier people among all the people who had been created by the hand of God."[3179] Happiness describes Zion and its people. Joseph Smith said, "Happiness is the object and design of our existence; and will be the end thereof, if we pursue the path that leads to it." Then the Prophet defined the path: "This path is virtue, uprightness, faithfulness, holiness."[3180] The path to happiness is also the path to Zion and the end-goal of our journey: "Happiness is the end of our existence."[3181]

[3175] 3 Nephi 12:8; emphasis added.
[3176] Psalm 50:2.
[3177] Ludlow, *A Companion to Your Study of the Book of Mormon*, 186.
[3178] Isaiah 52:7–10.
[3179] 4 Nephi 1:16.
[3180] Smith, *Teachings of the Prophet Joseph Smith*, 255–56.
[3181] McKay, *Pathways to Happiness*, 208.

Section 20

Come to Zion: The Universal Journey to the Land of Promise

Note: Because this series is a sequential work, one concept building upon another, the section numbers pick up where the last book ended. Thus, this book begins with Section 20.

Eternal life is not easily won. It requires our entering into the covenant of salvation—the new and everlasting covenant—living by faith and obedience, sacrificing all things, and consecrating the entirety of ourselves and our possessions to God. Premortally, when we anticipated the journey to eternal life, we shouted for joy.[3182] But we might imagine, as the reality of mortality set in, even the strongest of spirits possibly shuddered with feelings of inadequacy. Without a doubt, the journey to eternal life is not for the faint-hearted. Only by grace could we succeed "after all we can do."[3183] If we did not keep *arrival* as our goal, we would certainly come up short and lose the prize.

Now that we are here in mortality, we realize that the grandest prize is Zion, with its promise of eternal life. Zion is the glorious land or condition of promise that lies at the end of a well-defined path called the *strait and narrow*.[3184] The word *strait* means confined, restricted, strict, or exacting.[3185] There is no wiggle room on this narrow path. Thus, the route to Zion is ordered or *ordained* with specific markers called *ordinances*, which are gifts of God that are received by covenant. Only by following this strict path and reaching the markers along the way can we hope to arrive in Zion and partake of eternal life.

[3182] Job 38:7.
[3183] 2 Nephi 25:23.
[3184] McConkie, Conference Report, Oct. 1955, 12.
[3185] *Webster's New World Dictionary*, s.v. "strait."

From the outset of our journey, we realize that the path is going to be difficult and rugged. Everything along the way seems to be programmed to distract and oppose us. At times, we feel that we are running the most challenging gauntlet of our existence. As we travel, our true character and desires emerge. Elder Bruce R. McConkie promised that if we would step onto the path and gather the courage to hold faithfully to it until death, we would achieve our goal. Then, when we finally entered the next life, our calling and election would be assured.[3186]

The scriptures are replete with stories of journeys to lands of promise, all of which are representative of the journey to Zion. Moses' and Lehi's journeys dominate the Bible and Book of Mormon. There are other "journey" stories: Abraham, Joseph of Egypt, Elijah, the brother of Jared, Alma the Elder and Alma the Younger, Limhi, and even Jesus. Moreover, the parable of the prodigal son is a journey story that describes flight from sin and the journey home. In the latter days, we remember the journey story of the Mormon pioneers. The goal of these physical or spiritual treks is always the same: "Come unto Mount Zion, and unto the city of the living God, the heavenly Jerusalem, and to an innumerable company of angels; to the general assembly and Church of the Firstborn, which are written in heaven, and to God the judge of all, and to the spirits of just men made perfect, and to Jesus the Mediator of the new covenant."[3187]

Significantly, each of these journeys was tailor-made to the people involved and to their circumstances. Just so, our own individual journey stories will be unique; nevertheless, we will arrive at the same destination. Examining scriptural journeys, we see a pattern emerge, a pattern that we might expect to encounter as we travel toward Zion. In this chapter, we will explore some of the identifying milestones and conditions of the journey to Zion.

ZION IS OUR HERITAGE

The condition of Zion is consistent with our heavenly home, that which we might call the "land of our first inheritance."[3188] We were in the beginning with the Father.[3189] At some point, our spirits were literally begotten by God and experienced a literal birth of the spirit. Our new spirit bodies carried the genotype of our exalted parents. Our spirit birth provided us a new and expanded identity: as sons and daughters of God, our spirit bodies contained seeds of divinity, with the potential to become exactly like our Heavenly Parents.[3190] What remained to become like them was our choosing to walk the same path they had walked and to gain the same experience.

As much as the condition of Zion existed in our first heavenly home, the condition of Zion also existed in our first earthly home. Most certainly, the Garden of Eden was a Zionlike environment. After the Fall, too, Adam patterned his government after the government of heaven. Adam called upon the Lord, and "the Holy One of Zion . . . established the foundations of Adam-ondi-Ahman."[3191] The fact that human life and the first government began this way accentuates and perpetuates an understanding of the reality of our noble heritage. Clearly, we descend from royalty: Our Heavenly Parents, the progenitors of our spirits, are the King and Queen of Heaven, and our earthly progenitors, Adam and Eve, are also royalty. Adam is the archangel Michael, our "prince forever."[3192]

Many of the scriptural journey stories contain references to a royal beginning. For example, Moses was the adopted son of Pharaoh; the sons of Mosiah were sons of the king, and Alma was the

---

[3186] McConkie, "The Probationary Test of Mortality," 11.
[3187] Smith, *Teachings of the Prophet Joseph Smith*, 12; see also Hebrews 12:22–24.
[3188] Alma 54:12.
[3189] D&C 93:21–23.
[3190] McConkie, *Mormon Doctrine*, 750–51.
[3191] D&C 78:15.
[3192] D&C 107:54–55.

son of a prophet. The "certain man" who was the father of the prodigal son was obviously a prominent, wealthy man.[3193] Likewise, we had a regal beginning. Our heritage is royal; our genesis was in the environment of Zion. William Wordsworth wrote:

> Our birth is but a sleep and a forgetting:
> The Soul that rises with us, our life's Star,
> Hath had elsewhere its setting,
> And cometh from afar:
> Not in entire forgetfulness,
> And not in utter nakedness,
> But trailing clouds of glory do we come
> From God, who is our home:
> Heaven lies about us in our infancy![3194]

In the same way that the genes of an infant's physical body hold in them the child's potential and destiny, spiritual genes that are carried in our spiritual bodies contain our divine prospects and future. Therefore, if our heavenly and earthly parents were kings and queens, we, their progeny, contain the programming to become like them. If they are Zionlike and exist in a Zionlike environment, then we, their children, have the potential to become Zionlike and live in Zion. We are products of Zion parents; our origin and our destiny is Zion.

God begot or created us for a specific purpose: *happiness*. Lehi said, "Men are that they might have joy."[3195] Joseph Smith explained it this way: "Happiness is the object and design of our existence; and will be the end thereof, if we pursue the path that leads to it." Then the Prophet defined the path: "This path is virtue, uprightness, faithfulness, holiness."[3196] In the same way that physical genes are programmed to determine the color of eyes, texture of hair, and height, spiritual genes are programmed to determine our happiness. Because we are children of God, we are creations of joy; "happiness is the end of our existence."[3197] Happiness describes Zion, the end-goal of our journey: "And surely there could not be a happier people among all the people who had been created by the hand of God."[3198]

Perfect happiness involves inheriting God's crown. By entitlement of birthright, that crown is rightfully ours. But we cannot obtain it without making the journey, and we cannot make the journey without help. When Adam and Eve scanned the distance between them, happiness, and the crown, they rejoiced that Heavenly Father had provided them a Savior to help them achieve their purpose.

> And in that day the Holy Ghost fell upon Adam, which beareth record of the Father and the Son, saying: I am the Only Begotten of the Father from the beginning, henceforth and forever, that as thou hast fallen thou mayest be redeemed, and all mankind, even as many as will.
>
> And in that day Adam blessed God and was filled, and began to prophesy concerning all the families of the earth, saying: Blessed be the name of God, for because of my transgression my eyes are

---

[3193] Luke 15:11–32.
[3194] Wordsworth, "Ode on Intimations of Immortality," in *Narcissism and the Text*, 116–29.
[3195] 2 Nephi 2:25.
[3196] Smith, *Teachings of the Prophet Joseph Smith*, 255–56.
[3197] McKay, *Pathways to Happiness*, 208.
[3198] 4 Nephi 1:16.

opened, *and in this life I shall have joy,* and again in the flesh I shall see God.

And Eve, his wife, heard all these things and was glad, saying: Were it not for our transgression we never should have had seed, and never should have known good and evil, *and the joy of our redemption,* and the eternal life which God giveth unto all the obedient.[3199]

Adam and Eve could not hold back from telling their children the good news. "And Adam and Eve blessed the name of God, and they made all things known unto their sons and their daughters."[3200] Suddenly, life had a defined purpose—*happiness*; a defined inheritance—*a crown*; and a defined destination—*Zion*. Adam and Eve told their children that if they would enter the path that led to happiness, their children could experience redemption and achieve happiness. Moreover, their children could progress to the point that they could see God, their Heavenly Progenitor, and eventually return home to the place of their origin, Zion, and there receive their crown.

Ironically, the pathway to happiness leads through sorrow and adversity. Lehi explained that it is impossible to experience one principle without experiencing its opposite.[3201] This law of opposition, or opposites, is central to our existence; without opposites, all things would be a "compound in one." That sameness would bring everything to an abrupt halt. In the way that an engine is propelled by electricity alternating between positive and negative poles, the purpose of existence is driven by harnessing the power of opposites. Hence, to ascend up on high we must descend below all things, so that we might comprehend all things, and thereby gain the ability to become as the Gods, who are above and in all and through all things.[3202] For reasons that we do not completely understand, employing the power of the law of opposites is the only way to become exalted.

Happiness, therefore, seems to be a by-product of adversity. That is, by learning to channel the power of adversity we achieve happiness. Heavenly Father constantly deals with heartfelt sorrow for his sinful children, and yet he describes his life as a "fulness of joy."[3203] We can gain an appreciation for this principle through consecration. When we give him our complete selves, including our sorrows, weaknesses, sins, and challenges, he "shall consecrate [our] afflictions for [our] gain."[3204] He knows how to do it. He has the ability to use negatives for positive purposes, and that is the way he launches us toward the end-purpose of our creation: *happiness*. And happiness is a primary descriptor of Zion.[3205]

THE FALL

Earth life is a journey, not a destination. To arrive at our desired destination, we must *fall* into the lone and dreary world[3206] and make our way through it by faith. Suddenly we are in a foreign environment. The author of the book of Hebrews names a number of righteous individuals who fell into this environment and successfully traveled the path that we are on now. These individuals might speak for us: "These [righteous individuals saw their promises] afar off, and . . . confessed that they were strangers and pilgrims on the earth." As we traverse the lone and dreary strait and narrow path, a troubling thought seems to nag at us, saying that things in this telestial environment are not "as they

---

[3199] Moses 5:9–11; emphasis added.
[3200] Moses 5:12.
[3201] 2 Nephi 2:11–12.
[3202] D&C 88:6.
[3203] 3 Nephi 28:10.
[3204] 2 Nephi 2:2.
[3205] 4 Nephi 4:16.
[3206] McConkie and Millet, *Doctrinal Commentary on the Book of Mormon,* 3:276.

really are."[3207] This is a contrived condition that we never have or will experience again. We are strangers here; we are seeking a better country, "that is, an heavenly [country]: wherefore God is not ashamed to be called [our] God: for he hath prepared for [us] a city."[3208] That "city" is Zion, and we need to be constantly moving toward it.

The word *fall* is appropriate. We cannot comprehend the distance or the depth of the Fall precipitated by Adam. We fell physically, spiritually, and emotionally into a condition described by President Joseph F. Smith as "below all things."[3209] We had, in effect, stood upon the safe ledge of the brilliant celestial kingdom and looked downward upon the dangerous darkness, knowing that once we stepped off, we would forfeit our memory and power and become helpless, completely incapable of making it on our own. Worse, we would have no immediate comprehension that we had descended into a fallen world. Unless we were taught differently and gained a testimony of our true identity and heritage, we would be consigned to the belief that this mortal existence is all there is, and worse, that the conditions here are *normal.* Tragically, for a time, we might even embrace the luring dangers that permeate telestial life.

In her "Alma the Younger" series, Brigham Young University religion professor Catherine Thomas stated that in this mortal existence we "would begin to make choices before we had much knowledge or judgment or ability to choose right over wrong consistently and would inevitably make mistakes and sin. . . . As we grew in a fallen environment, we would form wrong opinions and make false assumptions, by which we would then govern our lives, and would unwittingly be programmed by many precepts of men. We would make many choices before we had grasped the significance of even the Light that we had. Many would reach an advanced age before they really saw the Light. Some would never see it in this life."[3210]

We cannot fathom the range of emotions that must have barraged our psyches as we contemplated our descent into this lone and dreary world. Nevertheless, we had vigorously defended the Father's plan in the great war in heaven; we had dedicated our lives to Christ, who was to become our Savior and the central figure in the plan of salvation; we had hoped and prepared in every way for this moment; and yet, we must have been horrified to imagine that we, who stood with the noble and great ones, would come here and succumb to sin. In Catherine Thomas's words, "The period of descent was surely seen by the righteous premortal spirits as a great sacrifice. The most righteous did not want to sin. They knew the truth about sin. A veil was necessary so that they would make the descent . . . into spiritual darkness."[3211] Only profound faith in Christ could have given us the strength to voluntarily fall from our Zion home.

Nevertheless, knowing that falling was the only way to obtain a physical body, make covenants, and gain an eternal kingdom, and armed with the light of Christ, we stepped off the celestial ledge and plummeted into this dark telestial world. Imagine our courage, for because of agency no one would have been compelled to come; imagine our hope, for the transcendent possibilities of eternity lay before us. We knew the risks. We also knew that eternal life would be won only by our entering and keeping our second estate.[3212] Therefore, we willingly *fell* into the unnatural condition of mortality, away from Zion, to rediscover the principles of Zion and make our way back to Zion.

[3207] Jacob 4:13.
[3208] Hebrews 11:13–16.
[3209] Smith, *Gospel Doctrine*, 13.
[3210] Thomas, "Alma the Younger, Part 1," n.p.
[3211] Thomas, "Alma the Younger, Part 1," n.p.
[3212] Abraham 3:26.

The Wilderness of Sin

In this fallen state, we encounter at least two experiences that the scriptures refer to as the *wilderness*. In both wildernesses, the primary purpose is to give us experience so that we can discern and choose between good and evil. One of the wildernesses is the wilderness of the Lord, which we will discuss shortly; we enter that wilderness by the Lord's design. The other wilderness is the wilderness of sin,[3213] which, like a prison, people are consigned to as a consequence of their errant actions or which they choose, as did the prodigal son, by their sinful wanderings from the Lord.

In the parable of the prodigal son, the wilderness of sin is described as a "far country," in which there is famine, disloyalty, and widespread want. This is descriptive of Babylon, where neither it nor its citizens will ultimately support us. When we choose to go to the far country, we are left to ourselves to suffer the harsh realities of our choices. The prodigal entered this wilderness because he had chosen "riotous living," wantonness, gross sin, and wastefulness.[3214] In this wilderness, the idea of being of royal heritage is a thing of naught, and inheritances are sold for a mess of pottage.[3215]

On the other hand, the Lord cast Paul into the wilderness of sin when the resurrected Savior abruptly appeared and intervened in Paul's life. Paul's wilderness experience was compacted into three days of spiritual suffering and physical blindness: "And [Paul] arose from the earth; and when his eyes were opened, he saw no man: but they led him by the hand, and brought him into Damascus. And he was three days without sight, and neither did eat nor drink."[3216] Then he was healed, and he devoted the rest of his life to the Lord.

Likewise, by the act of an angel, Alma was thrust into the wilderness of sin for three hellish days. His description of this wilderness is perhaps the most vivid in scripture:

> And it came to pass that I fell to the earth; and it was for the space of three days and three nights that I could not open my mouth, neither had I the use of my limbs. . . . But I was racked with eternal torment, for my soul was harrowed up to the greatest degree and racked with all my sins.
>
> Yea, I did remember all my sins and iniquities, for which I was tormented with the pains of hell; yea, I saw that I had rebelled against my God, and that I had not kept his holy commandments.
>
> Yea, and I had murdered many of his children, or rather led them away unto destruction; yea, and in fine so great had been my iniquities, that the very thought of coming into the presence of my God did rack my soul with inexpressible horror.
>
> Oh, thought I, that I could be banished and become extinct both soul and body, that I might not be brought to stand in the presence of my God, to be judged of my deeds.
>
> And now, for three days and for three nights was I racked, even with the pains of a damned soul.[3217]

The wilderness of sin is designed to reclaim us. There we suffer the buffetings of Satan, which are so severe that we will eventually cry out for relief. Only the Lord's redemption can rescue us from this

---

[3213] Exodus 16:1.
[3214] Luke 15:13–16.
[3215] Genesis 25:29–34.
[3216] Acts 9:8–9.
[3217] Alma 36:10–16.

fate: "Inasmuch as ye are cut off for transgression, ye cannot escape the buffetings of Satan until the day of redemption."[3218]

Satan knows the secret of sin, and if he can convince us to sin, he can torture us until we become as miserable as he is.[3219] Because Satan is the exact opposite of God, whose life is marked by a "fulness of joy,"[3220] Satan must be the most miserable being in the universe. In an effort to make us equally miserable, he seeks to enter and take over our bodies so that he can transform us into beings like himself. Because "light and truth forsake the evil one,"[3221] he seeks to empty us of light and truth. He does this by persistent temptation. If he can persuade us to sin, he can cause a rupture in our spiritual system that hemorrhages light and truth: "That wicked one cometh and taketh away light and truth, through disobedience."[3222]

The devil's tactic is terrifying: "And thus he flattereth them, and leadeth them along until he draggeth their souls down to hell; and thus he causeth them to catch themselves in their own snare."[3223] Once he gains entrance to our souls by tempting us to sin, he can drain us of light and truth to the point that he can convince us, almost without restraint, to do anything and to follow him down to hell. Then he has what he wanted so much in the beginning—our agency—and we have hardly put up a fight to protect and retain it. The scriptures reveal his strategy:

- "The temptations of the devil . . . blindeth the eyes, and hardeneth the hearts of the children of men, and leadeth them away into broad roads, that they perish and are lost."[3224]
- "[The devil] is the founder of all these things; yea, the founder of murder, and works of darkness; yea, and he leadeth them by the neck with a flaxen cord, until he bindeth them with his strong cords forever."[3225]
- "And others will he pacify, and lull them away into carnal security, that they will say: All is well in Zion; yea, Zion prospereth, all is well—and thus the devil cheateth their souls, and leadeth them away carefully down to hell."[3226]

THE AWAKENING

The prodigal son wandered in the wilderness of sin until, fully miserable, "he came to himself."[3227] When we have had enough, we also come to ourselves, and turn back. We find ourselves miserable in the wilderness of sin, and, as we have learned, misery is contrary to our nature: "Happiness is the object and design of our existence."[3228] We can stand sin and misery for only so long. When we awaken and find ourselves in Babylon, we cry out for help to get back to Zion.

Often, we must be stirred up to repentance: "For the kingdom of the devil must shake, and they which belong to it must needs be stirred up unto repentance, or the devil will grasp them with his everlasting chains, and they . . . perish."[3229] Being stirred up to repentance is the Lord's way of calling

---

[3218] D&C 104:9; see also D&C 78:12; 82:21; 132:26.
[3219] 2 Nephi 2:27.
[3220] 3 Nephi 28:10.
[3221] D&C 93:37.
[3222] D&C 93:39.
[3223] D&C 10:26.
[3224] 1 Nephi 12:17.
[3225] 2 Nephi 26:22.
[3226] 2 Nephi 28:21.
[3227] Luke 15:17.
[3228] Smith, *Teachings of the Prophet Joseph Smith*, 255–56.
[3229] 2 Nephi 28:19.

us home: "And after their temptations, and much tribulation, behold, I, the Lord, will feel after them, and if they harden not their hearts, and stiffen not their necks against me, they shall be converted, and I will heal them."[3230] But, as we have noted, before the healing we often must experience the Lord's chastisement, which is more than scolding; it is punishment with the Lord's rod: "Therefore I command you to repent—repent, lest I smite you by the rod of my mouth, and by my wrath, and by my anger, and your sufferings be sore—how sore you know not, how exquisite you know not, yea, how hard to bear you know not."[3231] As we shall see, in the process of conversion the Lord also uses chastisement and the rod in a refining rather than a punishing sense.

Alma was chastised and stirred up to repentance in the wilderness of sin. He described his awakening this way: "And it came to pass that as I was thus racked with torment, while I was harrowed up by the memory of my many sins. . . ."[3232] To be "racked with torment" summons images of medieval torture, whereby the body is violently stretched, pulling apart vertebrae and tearing limbs from sockets. To be "harrowed up" recalls the image of a plow cutting deeply into the soil, unearthing roots and weeds, and exposing the dark things that are underground to sudden bright light. Only by embracing the light can one be delivered from the rack and the harrow and escape the wilderness of sin.

Like Paul and Alma, we also are stirred up and awakened from our dire situation. As we have noted, "stirring up" can happen "by [the Lord] allowing financial reversals to occur, bringing loss of homes, cars, boats, and incomes; personal or corporate bankruptcy; and so forth. We might also experience a severe loss of health or death of a loved one, which can do the same thing by making worldly things [and sin] unattractive and meaningless."[3233] We are awakened because of the seriousness of our situation. In desperation, we seek a way out, and, when we finally realize that nothing or no one can save us, we finally reach out to the Savior.

Alma recorded: "I remembered also to have heard my father prophesy unto the people concerning the coming of one Jesus Christ, a Son of God, to atone for the sins of the world. Now, as my mind caught hold upon this thought, I cried within my heart: O Jesus, thou Son of God, have mercy on me, who am in the gall of bitterness, and am encircled about by the everlasting chains of death. And now, behold, when I thought this, I could remember my pains no more; yea, I was harrowed up by the memory of my sins no more. And oh, what joy, and what marvelous light I did behold; yea, my soul was filled with joy as exceeding as was my pain!"[3234] He had turned from Babylon and begun the journey back to Zion.

The Cry for Help

The Lord often allows us to linger in the wilderness of sin so that we can internalize lessons that can be learned only there. One of the best examples of the awakening and the cry for help happened among Limhi's people. These people had been languishing in the wilderness of sin because of their transgressions. Finally, after being crushed by the weight of their afflictions, they awakened from their wretched condition and cried out for deliverance: "And they did humble themselves even in the depths of humility; and they did cry mightily to God; yea, even all the day long did they cry unto their God that he would deliver them out of their afflictions."

Their situation was miserable and hopeless. Despite their repeated efforts and their having risked everything, they still could not deliver themselves. This is a universal lesson that everyone in the wilderness of sin must learn: Only the Savior can deliver us. We are helpless without him. Evidently,

---

[3230] D&C 112:13.
[3231] D&C 19:15.
[3232] Alma 36:17.
[3233] Yorgason, *I Need Thee Every Hour*, 206.
[3234] Alma 36:17–20.

Limhi's people needed to learn this lesson completely so that they would never depart from it and subsequently yield to sin. Therefore, "the Lord was slow to hear their cry because of their iniquity."

Of course, the Lord had every right to chastise them. As every parent knows, punishing a child for misconduct is secondary to helping the child internalize a lesson. Therefore, to briefly chastise and then immediately reinstate is not always the wise course. Sometimes wrongdoing requires a season of punishment to help the child rethink the attitude that resulted in his bad behavior. Such was the case of Limhi's people. Mormon informed us that the Lord indeed "did hear their cries," but the Lord temporarily withheld deliverance in an act of mercy that is beyond the ability or maturity level of most parents. The Lord used the natural consequences of sin to create an atmosphere in which he could help Limhi's people learn to trust and obey him. Then, as they learned their lessons, the Lord delivered them by degrees. That is, he eased their burdens in proportion to their repentance; but for the present, "the Lord did not see fit to deliver them out of bondage."[3235]

The approach worked. The next thing we read is that the people drew together in love and adopted a form of consecration to take care of the widows and orphans.[3236] They were discovering the principles of Zion and becoming Zionlike. That change of heart qualified them for deliverance, which miraculously occurred a short time later—and was a testimony of the Lord's intervention. Mormon told us plainly: "There was no way they could deliver themselves . . . , [they were surrounded] on every side."[3237]

Alma the Younger's cry for help is one of the most poignant: "O Jesus, thou Son of God, have mercy on me, who am in the gall of bitterness, and am encircled about by the everlasting chains of death."[3238] Likewise, when we awaken to our awful situation[3239] and cry out, "O Jesus, thou Son of God, have mercy on me," he will respond and, in time, he will deliver us.

To make our way out of the wilderness of sin requires our making or renewing the new and everlasting covenant, which is the covenant of deliverance. After Christ's resurrection, Peter was teaching people who were in the wilderness of sin. His message pierced them by the Spirit, and suddenly they awakened to their awful state and cried out for help: "Now when they heard this, they were pricked in their heart, and said unto Peter and to the rest of the apostles, Men and brethren, what shall we do? Then Peter said unto them, Repent, and be baptized every one of you in the name of Jesus Christ for the remission of sins, and ye shall receive the gift of the Holy Ghost."[3240]

Only the new and everlasting covenant, the covenant of deliverance, offers relief and safety: "Whosoever believeth in [Christ] should not perish."[3241] A man cannot escape the wilderness of sin without being born of the water and of the Spirit. Jesus said, "Verily, verily, I say unto thee, Except a man be born of water and of the Spirit, he cannot enter into the kingdom of God."[3242] As we have discussed, the new and everlasting covenant calls for us to live a new life; if we will do, we receive in return the guarantee of deliverance. Hence, the Lord said, "Ye must be born again."[3243] We are symbolically born again by baptism, then by the sacrament, and finally by the temple ordinances. Agreeing to live a new life is the price we pay for deliverance from the wilderness of sin. When we pay this price and indicate our willingness to remain firm in this decision, the Lord takes us out of the condition of Babylon and points us toward Zion.

[3235] Mosiah 21:1–15.
[3236] Mosiah 21:16–17.
[3237] Mosiah 21:5.
[3238] Alma 36:18.
[3239] Ether 8:24.
[3240] Acts 2:37–38.
[3241] John 3:16.
[3242] John 3:5.
[3243] John 3:6–7.

The Lord's Wilderness

Interpreted broadly, mortality is a wilderness experience. But in mortality we experience specifically the wilderness of sin and the Lord's wilderness. We leave the first wilderness only when we enter the second. Perhaps Lehi was describing the transition we all must make from one wilderness to the other: "Methought I saw in my dream, a dark and dreary wilderness [the wilderness of sin]. And it came to pass that I saw a man, and he was dressed in a white robe; and he came and stood before me. And it came to pass that he spake unto me, and bade me follow him. And it came to pass that as I followed him I beheld myself that I was in a dark and dreary waste [the Lord's wilderness]."[3244] We might call this second "waste" that Lehi had just entered the Lord's wilderness, because within that wilderness was the tree of life.[3245]

The purpose of the Lord's wilderness, which is traveled by means of the strait and narrow path, is not to reclaim, but rather to:

1. Purify (eliminate impurities and cause the spirit to become contrite)
2. Sanctify (change the purpose of the soul's journey by causing the heart to be broken and pliable)
3. Deliver us into the presence of the Lord, where we will receive a crown.

We enter the Lord's wilderness to make our way to Zion. Faith and repentance prepare us to enter this wilderness. Marking the entrance of the Lord's wilderness is a gate, which is distinguished by two ordinances: baptism and confirmation. "For the gate by which ye should enter is repentance and baptism by water; and then cometh a remission of your sins by fire and by the Holy Ghost. And then are ye in this strait and narrow path which leads to eternal life."[3246]

It is vitally important to understand that we are clean when we enter the Lord's wilderness. We are not here in His wilderness to become clean; we are here to become Zionlike and to prepare to return to the presence of the Lord and receive eternal life. Therefore, when we encounter the refining environment of the Lord's wilderness, we must not allow ourselves to be deceived by Satan and imagine that we are being punished. The process of becoming perfected requires that a clean person submit to the Holy Ghost, who will make that person pure and sanctified. "Clean hands and a pure heart" is a description of the process, not just a list of virtues.[3247] Job understood the process and declared, "He that hath clean hands shall be stronger and stronger."[3248] We remain clean by doing all we can do (obeying the commandments, constantly repenting, worthily partaking of the sacrament, having humility, performing charitable service, and so forth), but we become pure in heart by the refining motions of the Holy Ghost in the Lord's wilderness.

Experiencing Opposites

In some ways, the Lord's wilderness can be a harsher environment than the wilderness of sin. Of course, both have similarities. For example, in each wilderness the Lord allows us to experience opposites and opposition in their extremes. However, in the Lord's wilderness, we must prove our worth by descending below all things in order to gain the power to rise above all things.[3249] President Joseph F. Smith taught, "Had we not known before we came the necessity of our coming, the

---

[3244] 1 Nephi 8:5–7.
[3245] 1 Nephi 8:10.
[3246] 2 Nephi 31:17–18.
[3247] Psalm 24:4.
[3248] Job 17:9.
[3249] D&C 88:6.

importance of obtaining tabernacles, the glory to be achieved in posterity, the grand object to be attained by being tried and tested—weighed in the balance, in the exercise of the divine attributes, god-like powers and free agency with which we are endowed; whereby, after descending below all things, Christ-like, we might ascend above all things, and become like our Father, Mother and Elder Brother, Almighty and Eternal!—we never would have come; that is, if we could have stayed away."[3250]

At the outset of his wilderness experience, Moses discovered the highs and lows of universal powers. What began as a remarkable face-to-face vision of the Lord suddenly turned to Moses being left to himself and face-to-face with Satan. When Moses detected and overcame the devil by the power of the name of Jesus Christ, he came full circle back into the presence of the Lord. This cycle of *blessing-descent-to-blessing* or *revelation-to-testing-to greater revelation* is a cycle that wilderness wanderers experience time and again. With each cycle, we grow to know the Savior more intimately, and each time eternal life comes into finer focus. Also, with each cycle, we learn to discern between Babylon and Zion, and that enhanced ability to discern gives us greater power to make exalted choices.

Strangers and Pilgrims

In the Lord's wilderness, we find ourselves in a lone and dreary world—a major discovery!—and we long to go home to Zion. We feel like strangers and pilgrims in a hostile land. Soon a dawning of realization settles upon us: This place is not home. It is a contrived, fallen condition that in no way resembles home or "things as they really are."[3251]

Adults look back upon their school days as foreign to the realities of adult life, and yet in their youth they needed that schooling to help prepare them for life. Just so, the school of mortality is a foreign atmosphere to us as compared to our heavenly home; but mortality is necessary for what lies ahead. Any school environment is temporary, controlled, set apart from real-world conditions, and strict. In school, we are relegated to a place that is not home and that does not even resemble home. But when we complete our schooling, life will never be the same again. The Lord's wilderness is no different. Here in the wilderness, we experience the extremes of joys and difficulties, but the common experience is education.

Lehi described how foreign and weighed down he felt in his wilderness travels: "And after I had traveled for the space of many hours in darkness, I began to pray unto the Lord that he would have mercy on me, according to the multitude of his tender mercies."[3252] This place was not Lehi's home, and he knew it. He was a stranger and a foreigner here. This stark realization caused him to set his sights entirely on getting through the wilderness and going home to where he belonged. He knew that he could not do it alone. He had neither a compass to guide him nor adequate power to persevere. Therefore, he cried out to the Lord for help.

Separation from Babylon

A purpose of the Lord's wilderness is to separate us from Babylon. The call to leave Babylon is accompanied by deliverance from the wilderness of sin. During our sojourn in the Lord's wilderness, we will experience deliverance from time to time, and those experiences will prepare us for the ultimate deliverance: entering into our promised land. Our personalized *promised land* is always symbolic of Zion. From the moment we enter the Lord's wilderness, until we are delivered, we hear the Lord's voice beckoning us to come to him and behold his face, an event which attends ultimate deliverance.

[3250] Smith, *Gospel Doctrine*, 13.
[3251] Jacob 4:13.
[3252] 1 Nephi 8:8.

> Behold, that which you hear is as the voice of one crying in the wilderness—in the wilderness, because you cannot see him—my voice, because my voice is Spirit; my Spirit is truth; truth abideth and hath no end; and if it be in you it shall abound. And if your eye be single to my glory, your whole bodies shall be filled with light, and there shall be no darkness in you; and that body which is filled with light comprehendeth all things. Therefore, sanctify yourselves that your minds become single to God, and the days will come that you shall see him; for he will unveil his face unto you, and it shall be in his own time, and in his own way, and according to his own will.[3253]

No tragedy could be worse than being delivered from the wilderness of sin and entering the Lord's wilderness—only to turn back. The possibility is as real as it is potent. The lure of Babylon permeates our environment and is ever present. Nephi reported, "And it came to pass that as we journeyed in the wilderness, behold Laman and Lemuel, and two of the daughters of Ishmael, and the two sons of Ishmael and their families, did rebel against us; yea, against me, Nephi, and Sam, and their father, Ishmael, and his wife, and his three other daughters. And it came to pass in the which rebellion, they were desirous to return unto the land of Jerusalem."[3254] This dangerous condition caused Nephi to grieve; the entire expedition was suddenly at risk because of Laman and Lemuel's persistently trying to mix Babylon and Zion.

Likewise, if we, who have been delivered from Babylon and the wilderness of sin, look back and return to it, our condition will be worse than it was before we were delivered. Peter taught, "For if after they have escaped the pollutions of the world through the knowledge of the Lord and Saviour Jesus Christ, they are again entangled therein, and overcome, *the latter end is worse with them than the beginning. For it had been better for them not to have known the way of righteousness, than, after they have known it, to turn from the holy commandment delivered unto them.*"[3255]

The conditions of the Lord's wilderness require rejecting Babylon completely, trusting in the Lord absolutely, being willing to exist day to day by the grace of Jesus Christ, surrendering our hearts to him, and traveling as the Lord directs. Upon entering the Lord's wilderness, our source of security shifts from the world to the Lord, and, in the process, our faith is sometimes sorely tried. No wonder, then, that we often look back and long for the life that Babylon offered. No wonder, then, that the Lord continually calls us away from Babylon: "Go ye out from among the nations, even from Babylon, from the midst of wickedness, which is spiritual Babylon."[3256] He pleads with us to stay focused on the journey: "After a person has faith in Christ, repents of his sins, and is baptized for the remission of his sins and receives the Holy Ghost, (by the laying on of hands), which is the first Comforter, then let him continue to humble himself before God, hungering and thirsting after righteousness, and living by every word of God, and the Lord will soon say unto him, Son, thou shalt be exalted."[3257]

When we separate ourselves from Babylon and enter the Lord's wilderness, we figuratively, and sometimes literally, leave behind everything associated with Babylon. We simply cannot take anything of Babylon with us as we travel toward Zion. Lehi and his family literally left everything behind: "And it came to pass that he departed into the wilderness. And he left his house, and the land of his inheritance, and his gold, and his silver, and his precious things, and took nothing with him, save it

---

[3253] D&C 88:66–68.
[3254] 1 Nephi 7:6–7.
[3255] 2 Peter 2:20–21.
[3256] D&C 133:14.
[3257] Smith, *Teachings of the Prophet Joseph Smith*, 150.

were his family, and provisions, and tents, and departed into the wilderness."[3258] We learn that Limhi and his people "did depart by night into the wilderness with [nothing but] their flocks and herds."[3259] Likewise, Alma's people took only their flocks and grain "and departed into the wilderness,"[3260] and later, when they had built the beautiful city of Helam, they left everything again and fled into the Lord's wilderness with only their flocks.[3261] These people's flights are reminiscent of the Latter-day Saints leaving Ohio, Missouri, then Nauvoo, to cross the wilderness with nothing except what they could carry in a wagon or on a cart.

Separation is a sacrifice, and it can be painful. Jesus said, "He that loveth father or mother more than me is not worthy of me: and he that loveth son or daughter more than me is not worthy of me. And he that taketh not his cross, and followeth after me, is not worthy of me."[3262] We separate from Babylon and enter the Lord's wilderness as a test of our loyalty to the Lord and to the new and everlasting covenant: "For if ye will not abide in my covenant ye are not worthy of me."[3263] The Lord allows no excuses; despite the difficulty of the sacrifice, he requires that we come out of Babylon completely and never turn back: "Behold, I, the Lord, who was crucified for the sins of the world, give unto you a commandment that you shall forsake the world."[3264]

Fleeing for Safety

We flee Babylon into the Lord's wilderness for our own safety. Lehi fled to save his life; the Israelites fled to escape Pharaoh; the brother of Jared fled to preserve the individuality of his people and their language. Abraham, who was faced with losing his life and the prospect of a devastating famine, received the following commandment from the Lord: "Get thee out of thy country, and from thy kindred, and from thy father's house, unto a land that I will show thee."[3265] The "land" to which we are called is always our Zion.

Hugh Nibley wrote: "Babylon's time is all but used up, and the only thing for the Saints to do is to get out of her."[3266] Her destiny and the destiny of her people is complete and utter collapse, the extent of which the world has not experienced since the Flood and the annihilation of the nations of the Jaredites, Nephites, and the Jews: "And there followed another angel, saying, Babylon is fallen, is fallen, that great city, because she made all nations drink of the wine of the wrath of her fornication."[3267]

Both Alma the Elder and his son, Alma the Younger, were told to get their people out of their respective Babylons. To the elder Alma the Lord said, "Haste thee and get thou and this people out of this land."[3268] To the younger Alma he said, "Get this people out of this land, that they perish not; for Satan has great hold on the hearts of the Amalekites, who do stir up the Lamanites to anger against their brethren to slay them; therefore get thee out of this land; and blessed are this people in this generation, for I will preserve them."[3269] No matter how persuasive Babylon's propaganda, our

---

[3258] 1 Nephi 2:4.
[3259] Mosiah 22:11.
[3260] Mosiah 23:1.
[3261] Mosiah 24:18–20.
[3262] Matthew 10:37–38.
[3263] D&C 98:15.
[3264] D&C 53:2.
[3265] Abraham 2:3.
[3266] Nibley, *Approaching Zion*, 31.
[3267] Revelation 14:8.
[3268] Mosiah 24:23.
[3269] Alma 27:12.

remaining within her spiritual and physical precincts is deadly. In our individual and collective lives, we must escape Babylon and flee to the Lord's wilderness for safety. Blaine Yorgason wrote:

> For those who would enter the wilderness of the Lord, a separation of sorts must occur as they leave behind those who do not wish, for whatever reasons, to travel where they are going. In our day this separation will usually be more spiritual and emotional than physical, but it will be just as real and difficult as a physical separation might be. It will usually mean that world-oriented loved ones will have less and less in common with the wilderness travelers, conversations about things of the Spirit will decrease as the wilderness travelers' knowledge concerning the things of God increases, and the wilderness sojourners' increasing sense of responsibility for the spiritual welfare of their loved ones will often be unappreciated.
>
> Wilderness travelers must look forward to a certain amount of loneliness. If they talk of their experiences with others who are not fellow travelers (and truthfully there never seem to be many), they will either be misunderstood or, worse, maligned and mocked. One or two such encounters, and they soon learn to keep their mouths closed and to lean wholly upon the strength of the Lord for companionship. Thus does their journey become private and even occasionally secret.[3270]

While our departure from Babylon into the Lord's wilderness might be without fanfare, the 54 will nevertheless save our spiritual and physical lives. Hugh Nibley wrote:

> "He leadeth away the righteous into precious lands, and the wicked he destroyeth, and curseth the land unto them" (1 Nephi 17:38). Such was always the Lord's way. When he brought Lehi out of Jerusalem, "no one knew about it save it were himself and those whom he brought out of the land." Exactly so did the Lord bring Moses and the people in secret out of the wicked land of Egypt, and Abraham fled by night and secretly from Ur of the Chaldees as Lot did from Sodom and Gomorrah, and so was the city of Enoch removed suddenly to an inaccessible place. And in every case, the wicked world thus left behind is soon to be destroyed, so that those who leave the flesh-pots and the "precious things" behind and lose all for a life of hardship are actually losing their lives to save them.[3271]

THE CRUCIBLE

The Lord's wilderness is temporary, but its duration is tailor-made to each person. The commonality of the Lord's wilderness for each of us is that it always results in deliverance for its travelers. In some cases, the Lord's wilderness leads to deliverance in the form of death. Perhaps that is why an extreme,

---

[3270] Yorgason, *I Need Thee Every Hour*, 248.
[3271] Nibley, *An Approach to the Book of Mormon*, 139.

sanctifying trial often precedes death, as if that trial were a final preparation for the promise of eternal life.

Both the duration of the wilderness experience and the distance traveled are punctuated by *crucible* periods. A crucible is a container that receives raw ore and is placed by a metallurgist in a furnace. When the ore becomes molten, the properties of the ore separate, and the metallurgist can divide the pure from the unpure. The result is steel, silver, gold, or some other unalloyed metal. Job entered the Lord's wilderness and submitted to his crucible. At a point of intense heat, he cried out his allegiance and testified: "When [God] hath tried me, I shall come forth as gold."[3272] The transformation of the raw natural man to the purified Saint requires that he, like Job, must submit to the refining process so that he can emerge as a new creature[3273] in the image of God.[3274] The scripture reads: "And [the Lord] shall sit as a refiner and purifier of silver; and he shall purify the sons of Levi, and purge them as gold and silver, that they may offer unto the Lord an offering in righteousness."[3275]

Any number of conditions can qualify as a crucible: relationship challenges, spiritual tests, financial setbacks, illnesses, caring for a sick or afflicted person, or any combination of these things. A crucible can also come in the form of persecution, when the world rejects, hates, and fights against us.[3276] Job's crucible involved the loss of family, fortune, health, and honor. He lost the loyalty of his friends, and the relationship with his wife was strained. At one point his spirituality seems to have taken a beating.

Sometimes crucibles are called *trying* or *chastisement*, and we are required to endure the process or forfeit our eternal inheritance: "My people must be tried in all things, that they may be prepared to receive the glory that I have for them, even the glory of Zion; and he that will not bear chastisement is not worthy of my kingdom."[3277]

During the crucible periods of our lives, we are not only thrown into the furnace to burn out impurities, but we are also straitened by the Lord's rod.[3278] As we have learned, to straiten is to confine or restrict by strict and exacting measures.[3279] A rod is a straight stick used to punish, which is how it is used in the wilderness of sin. A rod is also a staff or scepter that is carried as a symbol of office, rank, or power. Additionally, a rod is used to measure.[3280]

It is easy to see why the Lord would use the terms *straiten* and *rod* in connection with the crucible experience. Because he is the Purifier, he places us in a temporary, confined environment where he can extract from us all impurities. He accomplishes this by strictness and chastisement, and he measures our worth by how we submit to the process. He does all of this in love, of course; punishment occurs only in the 54 of sin. Straitening by the rod has a different purpose in the Lord's wilderness; that purpose is to chasten, which in the Lord's wilderness means, among other things, "to make chaste,"[3281] or in other words, to make us "pure in thought and act."[3282] The author of Hebrews says, "For whom the Lord loveth he chasteneth, and scourgeth every son whom he receiveth. If ye endure chastening, God dealeth with you as with sons; for what son is he whom the father

---

[3272] Job 23:10.
[3273] JST 2 Corinthians 5:17.
[3274] Alma 5:19.
[3275] 3 Nephi 24:3; D&C 128:24.
[3276] Kimball, "A Gift of Gratitude," 1.
[3277] D&C 136:31.
[3278] 1 Nephi 17:41.
[3279] *Webster's New World Dictionary*, s.v. "strait."
[3280] *Webster's New World Dictionary*, s.v. "rod."
[3281] *Encyclopedia of Mormonism*, 264.
[3282] *Merriam-Webster Collegiate Dictionary*, s.v., "chaste."

chasteneth not?" Knowing that we are being *loved* into the image of God might make the purifying experience bearable but it does not necessarily make it easier: "Now no chastening for the present seemeth to be joyous, but grievous: nevertheless afterward it yieldeth the peaceable fruit of righteousness unto them which are exercised thereby."[3283]

Thus, in the Lord's wilderness, straitening by the rod leads to loving chastisement, which makes us *chaste* (pure in thought and act). The process increases our level of righteousness until we approach perfection. This is the purpose of the Lord's wilderness: to purify, sanctify, and perfect us until we "come forth as gold."[3284] Joseph Smith's translation of Hebrews 11:40 reads: "God having provided some better things for them through their sufferings, for without sufferings they could not be made perfect."

In the Gethsemanes—a word meaning "olive press"—of our lives, we are crushed and pressed until impurities are bled from us. Often, at critical moments, we call for the Lord's servants, the elders, to bless us by means of the sacred ordinance of administration.[3285] Perhaps the tears and perspiration that flow during crucible experiences act like a sacred washing, which prepares us to be anointed with oil while we are administered to. Then the elders, who act in the name of Jesus Christ, bless us with healing, instruction, and comfort. It is no wonder, then, that when we are delivered from a physical malady by means of the administration ordinance, we are also delivered spiritually, and, remarkably, our sins are forgiven.[3286]

Something of eternal value is being forged if we will endure the pain of the crucible: "Ye cannot behold with your natural eyes, for the present time, the design of your God concerning those things which shall come hereafter, and the glory which shall follow after much tribulation."[3287] The greatest miracle in time or eternity is about to take place: a god is about to emerge from the ashes of a natural man! But, if we had not been willing to enter the Lord's wilderness and endure its crucible—the straitening, the rod, and the chastisement—we simply would not have been able to accomplish our missions in life or achieve the apex of our potential. Abraham, Job, Nephi, Alma, and Joseph Smith are all examples of individuals who entered the Lord's wilderness, submitted to the fire of the crucible, and came forth as gold.

As we have said, the Lord's 54 and its crucible periods are temporary; nevertheless, they are individualized and of indeterminate length. Nephi traveled eight years in the wilderness before he reached Bountiful. The Israelites wandered forty years before they crossed the Jordan River into the promised land. We often see fourteen years as a common wilderness measurement. For example, the sons of Mosiah served fourteen years among the Lamanites. From the time Ishmael was born, Sarah waited fourteen years for her promised Isaac. Jacob served fourteen years for the privilege to wed Rachel. Joseph of Egypt was imprisoned fourteen years before he was released. Joseph Smith's ministry was fourteen years long (1830–1844) and ended with his death. Once we enter the Lord's wilderness or begin a crucible experience within the wilderness, the Lord will keep us there until the purifying and sanctifying work is complete. Then, when we are pure and sanctified, he will deliver us from his wilderness into Zion, and we will come forth as gold.

When we take into account the purpose of the Lord's wilderness and the crucible periods, we gain insight into a possible reason why some health blessings are delayed. It might be that the Lord's timetable calls for more time for the purification process to reach its goal. If we fail to understand the Lord's crucibles, we might become discouraged and confused when healing is not forthcoming. How do we square that delay with scriptures that state unequivocally that the sick and afflicted "shall be

---

[3283] Hebrews 12:6–7, 11.
[3284] Job 23:10.
[3285] James 5:14; D&C 42:43–52.
[3286] James 5:15.
[3287] D&C 58:3.

healed" unless they are "appointed unto death"?[3288] Unmistakably, we need to broaden our view. Beyond the issue of faith is the issue of the crucible, which perhaps takes precedence. In the meantime, the administration ordinance is absolutely valid, and the healing will take place according to individual needs and the timing and methods of the Lord.[3289] Elder James E. Talmage wrote: "Not always are the administrations of the elders followed by immediate healings; the afflicted may be permitted to suffer in body, perhaps for the accomplishment of good purposes."[3290] The point is this: We cannot and should not attempt to remove people from the Lord's wilderness or its crucibles. We can, however, bless them and place their delivery under the direction of the priesthood; then we can labor to ease their burdens while they endure the heat of the purification process. We are told that during the Savior's crucible experience in Gethsemane an angel came to strengthen him.[3291] The angel did not remove the Savior's burden, but he did strengthen him. We can be angels to people who are working through their crucible experiences.

The Lord's wilderness with its attendant crucibles has defined boundaries. Beyond these boundaries lies a promised land; the Lord's deliverance ushers us there. We will not have to endure chastening one moment longer than is necessary to claim the blessings. When we emerge, we will come forth from the fiery furnace as did the three Hebrew youths: without even the "smell of fire."[3292] We will be infinitely valuable, like pure gold,[3293] having "become holy, without spot."[3294] This is the condition of Zion people.

THE TRAGEDY OF MURMURING

The wilderness and its crucibles are demanding. Occasionally, we encounter periods of extreme difficulty, "emotional trauma and turmoil," wrote Blaine Yorgason, "the despair of believing that all [is] hopeless and that there could be no positive end to the experience." Paradoxically, our fighting through these trials by means of a cheerful attitude is a key to our deliverance. Our resisting and complaining about the lessons of the 54 only prolongs the process. "Both Lehi and Sariah found some of the trials of the wilderness to be almost more than they could bear. They each murmured, repented, and then bore powerful testimonies as to the goodness of God in allowing them to enter their wilderness (see 1 Nephi 5:1–3, 16:20)."[3295]

Murmuring is more than complaining; it is complaining against God. By murmuring, we are criticizing his way of handling things. Essentially, we are accusing him of being unaware of our situation, or lacking power to change things, or being indifferent to our plight. By murmuring, we charge him with not loving us enough to do something about our situation. The irony of murmuring is that while we are accusing God, we are simultaneously acknowledging that he exists, that he is aware of us, and that he has the power to reverse things. The moment we murmur, we halt the process of purification and sanctification, and we become God's enemies rather than his students. Judging from what happened when Laman and Lemuel murmured, the result is tragic.

Conversely, the dual miracles of sanctification and deliverance materialize from a positive attitude: "Therefore, dearly beloved brethren, let us cheerfully do all things that lie in our power; and then may we stand still, with the utmost assurance, to see the salvation of God, and for his arm to be

---

[3288] D&C 42:48.
[3289] Oaks, "He Heals the Heavy Laden," 6–9.
[3290] Talmage, *Articles of Faith*, 205.
[3291] Luke 22:43.
[3292] Daniel 3:19–27.
[3293] Job 23:10.
[3294] Moroni 10:33.
[3295] Yorgason, *I Need Thee Every Hour*, 257.

revealed."[3296] Unless cheerfulness in the midst of adversity is grounded in absolute trust in the Lord, that cheerfulness will appear fake, and it will not have power to sustain or deliver us. Such feigned cheerfulness cannot be maintained. True cheerfulness is a product of faith in Jesus Christ and the safety guaranteed by the new and everlasting covenant.

The result of true cheerfulness is peace, which is a gift of the Spirit that cannot be duplicated. The peace that Jesus offers us is unlike the peace offered by the world. The Lord's peace emerges from our relationship with him; it calms the troubled heart, jettisons fear,[3297] and allows us to relax and move forward with cheerful confidence. The Lord's wilderness experience teaches us that even in our darkest moments, God never leaves us and he always comes to our rescue. Nephi sought to remain cheerful and rejected peace from any other source than the Lord. He rejoiced, saying, "O Lord, I have trusted in thee, and I will trust in thee forever. I will not put my trust in the arm of flesh; for I know that cursed is he that putteth his trust in the arm of flesh. Yea, cursed is he that putteth his trust in man or maketh flesh his arm."[3298]

Finding Joy in the Journey

A challenge that we face in the Lord's wilderness is finding joy amidst our trials. Nevertheless, finding joy is possible. We recall that God created us with his genotype, which made beings with the potential for true happiness. Happiness is one of the predominant characteristics of our nature. We recall that Joseph Smith said, "Happiness is the object and design of our existence and will be the end thereof, if we pursue the path that leads to it."[3299] Zion is a condition or environment of matchless happiness: "Surely there could not be a happier people among all the people who had been created by the hand of God."[3300]

In Nephi's wilderness journey, he continually used the word "delight." He wrote of delighting "in the things of the Lord," "in the scriptures," and "in the great and eternal plan" of our Father in Heaven.[3301] Former general Young Women's president Susan W. Tanner noted that in times of great trial, Nephi was quick to remember the sources of his delight, which empowered him to focus on things of eternal consequence. Delighting in the Lord and his blessings allows us to "lift" our hearts in the midst of affliction and cause to "rejoice."[3302]

Often we wonder how happiness can be achieved when conditions are so difficult. We find our answer in yet another gospel irony called "affliction brings joy." Former general Relief Society president Barbara W. Winder gave this explanation of joy:

> Joy, it seems, is not only happiness, *but the resultant feeling of the Holy Ghost manifested within us.* How can we provide a climate in our lives to foster the presence of the Holy Ghost, that our lives may be more joyful? Just as a reservoir stores water to bring relief and replenish the thirsty land, so we can store experiences, knowledge, and desires to replenish and fortify our spiritual needs. Four ways may be helpful in developing reservoirs of righteousness and spiritual self-reliance. We prepare by—

[3296] D&C 123:17.
[3297] John 14:27.
[3298] 2 Nephi 4:34.
[3299] Smith, *Teachings of the Prophet Joseph Smith*, 255.
[3300] 4 Nephi 1:16.
[3301] 2 Nephi 4:15–16; 11:2–8.
[3302] Tanner, "My Soul Delighteth in the Things of the Lord," 81–83.

1. Developing a cheerful disposition wherein the Spirit can dwell.

2. Learning the Savior's will for us, that we may know our divine potential.

3. Understanding and accepting his atoning sacrifice and repenting of our sins.

4. Keeping his commandments and having a firm determination to serve him."[3303]

Joy, like peace, is a gift of the Spirit. We cannot conjure it up, and Satan cannot duplicate it.[3304] Only the Holy Ghost can produce joy, and, amazingly, he produces it from the seedbed of affliction. Prefacing his report on the mission of the sons of Mosiah, Mormon hinted at the connection between affliction and joy: "And this is the account of Ammon and his brethren, their journeyings in the land of Nephi, their sufferings in the land, their sorrows, *and their afflictions, and their incomprehensible joy*."[3305] Elder Bruce C. Hafen explained that Adam and Eve could never have experienced joy without experiencing affliction:

> Lehi taught his children that if Adam and Eve had not transgressed, they would have remained in the Garden of Eden. Had that happened, Adam and Eve "*would have had no children; wherefore they would have remained in a state of innocence, having no joy, for they knew no misery; doing no good, for they knew no sin*. . . . Adam fell that men might be; and men are, that they might have joy" (2 Nephi 2:23–25; italics added). . . . Without being expelled from the innocent comfort of Eden into the turbulence of mortality, Adam and Eve would not only have had no children, and no misery, but they would never have found joy; *hence, the very meaning of life would have been lost on them*. There really is a deep connection between the hard things of life and the best things of life.[3306]

Remarkably, through the power of the Atonement, the Lord has the power to "consecrate [our] afflictions for [our] gain"[3307] and turn misery into joy. Elder Hafen wrote: "Because they received the Atonement of Jesus Christ, Adam and Eve were able to learn from their experience without being condemned by it."[3308]

Coupled with this idea is the probability that finding joy in the journey contributes to our deliverance. For example, when Paul and Silas were imprisoned and beaten, they reacted joyfully by praying and singing praises: "And suddenly there was a great earthquake, so that the foundations of the prison were shaken: and immediately all the doors were opened, and every one's bands were loosed."[3309] The Jaredites followed a similar course of action: "And they did sing praises unto the Lord; yea, the brother of Jared did sing praises unto the Lord, and he did thank and praise the Lord all

---

[3303] Winder, "Finding Joy in Life," 95; emphasis added.

[3304] Cannon, *Journal of Discourses*, 15:375–76; see also Dew, "Living on the Lord's Side of the Line," Brigham Young University devotional, Mar. 21, 2000.

[3305] Alma 28:8; emphasis added.

[3306] Hafen, *Covenant Hearts*, 65–66; emphasis added.

[3307] 2 Nephi 2:2.

[3308] Hafen, *Covenant Hearts*, 66.

[3309] Acts 16:26.

the day long; and when the night came, they did not cease to praise the Lord. And thus they were driven forth; and no monster of the sea could break them, neither whale that could mar them; and they did have light continually, whether it was above the water or under the water."[3310] And, as we have mentioned, to the suffering Latter-day Saints, the Prophet wrote, "Therefore, dearly beloved brethren, let us cheerfully do all things that lie in our power; and then may we stand still, with the utmost assurance, to see the salvation of God, and for his arm to be revealed."[3311]

Elder Hafen reminded us that the condition of the Lord's wilderness is not one of punishment, but one of discovery and experience: "Through sometimes bitter experience, they [Adam and Eve, who are the models for all married couples] could come to really understand life and meaning and joy. 'They taste the bitter,' the Lord explained to Adam, 'that they might know to prize the good' (Moses 6:55). In fact, He said, 'If they [Adam and Eve] never should have bitter [experiences] they *could not know the sweet*' (D&C 29:39; italics added). In other words, sometimes the twists and turns of life *are* the straight and narrow path."[3312]

Here, then, is the ironic connection between affliction and joy: God created man to have joy, which we all want, but joy can be realized only by experiencing its opposite, *affliction*, which we do not want. Moreover—and this is another irony—if joy is a gift of God, so is affliction. Spiritually mature people develop both the capacity and the perspective to express gratitude for their joys *and* their afflictions. They are not necessarily trying to be noble, nor are they in denial; rather, they have learned something that the Gods know: *without affliction there can be no joy*.

With this understanding, we begin to appreciate the Lord's wilderness as a condition of love, not one of condemnation. The 54 is a condition of the Fall, which "introduced the process by which we can *learn from our experience, which is the central meaning of existence. . . . Learning from hard things is what life is all about*."[3313] Despite present difficulties, the Lord's promise of joy is always before us, and we are expected to discover it. And we will. Because God is a God of truth who cannot lie,[3314] we are assured that his promise will be fulfilled: "After much tribulation come the blessings [joy]."[3315] Ultimately, afflictions will result in joy, and will help rather than injure us.

Consider the example of Nephi. After all he had suffered, he was still able to say that he lived after the manner of happiness.[3316] Somewhere along the journey to the promised land, we too must discover the great plan of happiness,[3317] and when we do, we must cling to it in the midst of afflictions. Then we will discover the invaluable connection between affliction and joy, as we see how the Savior sanctifies our afflictions for our eternal gain.[3318] As we experience the Lord's sustaining and transforming miracles, our relationship with him will solidify, and eventually our relationship will lead us to a "fulness of joy."[3319] Therefore, as we survey the Lord's wilderness and summon courage to take the first step into it, we need to understand that joy through adversity will be the discovery, and fulness of joy will be the end result.

[3310] Ether 6:9–10.
[3311] D&C 123:17.
[3312] Hafen, *Covenant Hearts*, 66.
[3313] Hafen, *Covenant Hearts*, 71–72; emphasis added.
[3314] Ether 3:12.
[3315] D&C 58:4.
[3316] 2 Nephi 5:27.
[3317] Alma 42:8.
[3318] 2 Nephi 2:2.
[3319] 3 Nephi 28:10.

Conditions of the Lord's Wilderness

The wilderness experience has specific purposes and conditions. As we have mentioned, if we were viewing the Lord's wilderness from an eternal perspective, it would surely appear contrived. The condition of Zion is much more natural to us (meaning our innocent spirits) than the condition of mortality. Telestial life is often described as a school; we are to be "in the world but not of the world."[3320] Here, we temporarily set aside "things as they really are,"[3321] and enter into an educational environment.

Joseph Smith explained that the things of men are so dissimilar from "the conditions of God's kingdom . . . that all who are made partakers of that glory, are under the necessity of learning something respecting it previous to their entering into it." That process takes time, he said. "No man ever arrived in a moment: he must have been instructed in the government and laws of that kingdom by proper degrees, until his mind is capable in some measure of comprehending the propriety, justice, equality, and consistency of the same." To that end, the Lord enrolls us in his wilderness school. For example, Joseph Smith said the Lord found Jacob "in a desert land, and in the waste, howling 54; He led him about, He instructed him, He kept him as the apple of His eye, etc.; which will show the force of the last item advanced, that it is necessary for men to receive an understanding concerning the laws of the heavenly kingdom, before they are permitted to enter it: we mean the celestial glory."[3322]

No one who wishes to attain to Zion and enter the celestial kingdom can avoid the Lord's wilderness school. Blaine Yorgason wrote: "Jesus went fasting into the wilderness for forty days so He could learn directly from the Father; Moses did the same. Adam called his wilderness experience being driven into the lone and dreary world, and Lehi called his experience the wilderness of his affliction. Both Ether and Moroni were well acquainted with wilderness schooling, and John the Baptist received his preparation there. The Lord has always required of those who desire to be His people a withdrawal from the world and its telestial ways. If we so desire, we can have the same sanctifying experience."[3323]

Living by Manna

Achieving a Zionlike life is possible only if we learn to trust God implicitly and consecrate our hearts to him. To facilitate those goals and point us toward Zion, the Lord mercifully gave us what we might call the *manna principle*. Wilderness travelers share the common experience of living by the Lord's grace from day to day. The manna principle states that we can gather only enough manna to last for one day; nevertheless, manna will always be there when we need it.

The manna principle persuades us to surrender our will to God as it brings us to the point where we will ask him to manage the affairs of our lives. To accomplish that goal, God often creates a situation that renders us temporarily powerless. Then, when we give our will to him, he provides us manna in return. Elder Maxwell said, "The submission of one's will is placing on God's altar the only uniquely personal thing one has to place there. The many other things we 'give' are actually the things He has already given or loaned to us. However, when we finally submit ourselves by letting our individual wills be swallowed up in God's will, we will really be giving something to Him! It is the only possession which is truly ours to give. Consecration thus constitutes the only unconditional surrender which is also a total victory."[3324]

[3320] McKay, *Gospel Ideals*, 399.
[3321] Jacob 4:13.
[3322] Smith, *Teachings of the Prophet Joseph Smith*, 51.
[3323] Yorgason, *I Need Thee Every Hour*, 215.
[3324] Maxwell, *If Thou Endure It Well*, 54.

The manna principle also allows that we will have sufficient for our needs, but not excess. In other words, the Lord gives us enough of what we need, but no more. Moreover, the manna principle causes our vision to become restricted: when we attempt to look into the future, we see little except for uncertainty. The conditions of having *sufficient but not excess* and *limited vision* are apparently designed to drive us to our knees, where, by necessity, we must continually plead to the Lord for help to get through the day. Of course the Lord does help, but, according to plan, he often sends his help at the very last minute, and then as a miracle. As uncomfortable as this process feels at times, it nevertheless multiplies our hope and faith. What happens after we have experienced a number of these miracles? We begin to expect them. Over time, we learn about the personality and discover the characteristics of the Giver of miracles. We learn that he is aware of us, he has great power, he loves us, he is consistent, and he treats us uniquely but just as well as he does any another person. That discovery is essential to our forging a trusting relationship with him, which is paramount to establishing Zion in our lives.

Despite the length of our 54 journey and the harshness of its occasional crucible experiences, we will emerge from it recognizing that we were always cared for. To the Israelites, Moses said, "For the Lord thy God hath blessed thee in all the works of thy hand: he knoweth thy walking through this great wilderness: these forty years the Lord thy God hath been with thee; *thou hast lacked nothing*."[3325] The absence of lack and the presence of abundance are characteristics of Zion. Although the journey to Zion is rigorous, we will be fed by manna, and we will lack for nothing.

Hard Work

The Lord's wilderness is an experience of hard work, and it is hard work that propels us toward a Zionlike life. Kirtland, Jackson County, Far West, Nauvoo, Salt Lake City—the Mormon pioneers were forever building homes, neighborhoods, cities, and temples by the sweat of their face, which is the law of the mortal existence.[3326] The Lord told the brother of Jared, "Go to work and build, after the manner of barges which ye have hitherto built. And it came to pass that the brother of Jared did go to work, and also his brethren, and built barges after the manner which they had built, according to the instructions of the Lord."[3327] Similarly, Joseph of Egypt instructed his people to labor for seven years to store provisions against the coming famine.[3328] Noah was told to labor and build an ark,[3329] and Nephi was commanded to create tools and build a ship by his labor.[3330]

Significantly, these people were called upon to labor in situations that were foreign to them: temples, cities, massive storage projects, seaworthy submarines and ships. Such projects would have been impossible without the Lord laboring beside them. We learn a lesson from their accounts: Labor we must, but we are divinely helped in proportion to our effort. Only by partnering with the Lord is success made possible. It is by faith in Jesus Christ and receiving his grace (Jesus making up the difference after we do all we can do) that we survive the wilderness and go forward to our own personal promised land of Zion.

Partnering with the Lord is the Zion way to labor. Our motivation, goals, and results become different from the way we labor in Babylon. Working hard in the Zion way presents us with the ongoing opportunity to see the Lord's hand in our lives, and by continually partnering with him, we grow to count on him, love him, and trust him.

[3325] Deuteronomy 2:7; emphasis added.
[3326] Genesis 3:19.
[3327] Ether 2:16.
[3328] Genesis 41:46–49.
[3329] Genesis 5:13–16.
[3330] 1 Nephi 17:8, 10–11, 16.

Zion work is cooperative and exalting, whereas Babylon work focuses on selfishness, independence from God, and self-congratulation. Babylon work advances the philosophy of the anti-Christ: succeeding in life according to personal management, prospering according to one's genius, conquering according to one's strength, and setting personal interpretations on ethics.[3331] On the other hand, Elder McConkie wrote, "Work is the great basic principle which makes all things possible both in time and in eternity. Men, spirits, angels, and Gods use their physical and mental powers in work. 'My Father worketh hitherto, and I work,' Jesus announced. (John 5:17.) Also: 'I must work the works of him that sent me, while it is day.' (John 9:4.)"[3332]

In either environment, Zion or Babylon, we are required to work hard. But there are questions that determine in which camp we are laboring. *With what attitude are we approaching our work?* And, *For what motivation are we working?*

Traveling by Revelation

By scanning the scriptural record, we discover that people entered the Lord's wilderness and journeyed toward their Zion by revelation; that is, they traversed the wilderness as the Lord directed. As we study the accounts of righteous wilderness travelers, the purpose of dependency begins to come clear: The Lord's wilderness is designed to teach us to recognize and respond to the voice of the Lord. Only by revelation and absolute obedience to it can we survive the experience and arrive safely home in the embrace of God. Elder Maxwell wrote: "He cannot fully receive us until we fully follow Him."[3333] Upon this principle our eternal salvation and ultimate safety pivot. Joseph Smith said, "A man is saved no faster than he gets knowledge [from God], for if he does not get knowledge [from God], he will be brought into captivity by some evil power in the other world, as evil spirits will have more knowledge, and consequently more power than many men who are on the earth. Hence [we need] revelation to assist us, and give us knowledge of the things of God."[3334]

Blaine Yorgason stated: "What the Lord is asking from wilderness wanderers is nothing less than absolute trust, absolute faith, absolute obedience. And why is that? Because in this way only can we gain godly, godlike knowledge."[3335] To survive the wilderness and gain its blessings, we must "feast upon the words of Christ; for, behold, the words of Christ will tell [us] *all* things what [we] should do."[3336] Elder Maxwell explained, "What the Lord is asking us to do is to see with His eyes, to think with His mind, and to feel with His heart. Those in the City of Enoch made their mark in this regard (see Moses 7:18). Though we cannot really do that to anything approaching a full degree, we can further trust Him by letting our will be further 'swallowed up' in His."[3337] We cannot achieve Zion in our lives or do the Lord's will unless we learn the Lord's will; otherwise, our efforts are guesswork.

Often, the Lord gives us a physical object to help us with the spiritual process of receiving revelation. For example, Abraham, the brother of Jared, Aaron, King Mosiah, and Joseph Smith each received a Urim and Thummim to assist them in obtaining revelation.[3338] Lehi received the Liahona, an object that was both a compass and a revelation device.[3339] Today, we have the Book of Mormon, our Liahona,[3340] which Joseph Smith called "the most correct of any book on earth, and the keystone

---

[3331] Alma 30:17.
[3332] McConkie, *Mormon Doctrine*, 847.
[3333] Maxwell, *Even as I Am*, 33.
[3334] Smith, *Teachings of the Prophet Joseph Smith*, 217.
[3335] Yorgason, *I Need Thee Every Hour*, 234.
[3336] 2 Nephi 32:3.
[3337] Maxwell, *That Ye May Believe*, 119.
[3338] Abraham 3:1; Ether 3:21–28; Exodus 28:30; Mosiah 8:13–19; JS–H 1:35.
[3339] 1 Nephi 16:10, 26–29; Alma 37:38.
[3340] Dellenbach, "Hour of Conversion," 41.

of our religion." Pertaining to its revelatory power, the Prophet said "a man would get nearer to God by abiding by its precepts than by any other book."[3341]

Upon entering the Lord's wilderness, we are given the gift of the Holy Ghost, who is our Guide, our Purifier, and our Revelator. Joseph Smith said, "You have received the Holy Ghost. Follow its teachings. Sometimes it will seem to you as though it was hardly the right way. No matter, follow its teachings, and it will always lead you right, and if you do so it will, by and by, become to you a principle of revelation, so that you will know all things."[3342] Beyond the Spirit's ability to guide, comfort, purify, and protect, the Holy Ghost reveals the Father and the Son. Specifically, what are we to learn about them? Joseph Smith had the answer: "First, the idea that [God] actually exists. Secondly, a correct idea of his character, perfections, and attributes. Thirdly, an actual knowledge that the course of life which he is pursuing is according to his will. For without an acquaintance with these three important facts, the faith of every rational being must be imperfect and unproductive; but with this understanding it can become perfect and fruitful, abounding in righteousness, unto the praise and glory of God the Father, and the Lord Jesus Christ."[3343]

With some degree of certainty, we could state that every experience related to the Lord's wilderness is calculated to draw us to him; reveal his character, perfections, and attributes; bring our lives in line with his; and forge an eternal relationship. Blaine Yorgason wrote: "The course of study we have entered into, then, is designed by God to assist us in growing into the principle of revelation, this in order that Christ can communicate to us a correct and ultimately perfect understanding of who He is, His 'character, perfections, and attributes,' as well as an understandable witness that our own life is moving in appropriate ways toward our being like Him. In short, his school teaches us how to become gods and goddesses."[3344]

Journeying According to the Lord's Will

Of necessity, the Lord's wilderness is fraught with risks, twists, turns, and dangers. To negotiate the wilderness safely, we must learn to travel exactly as the Lord directs. To Abraham, the Lord said, "Behold, I will lead thee by my hand."[3345] We read that the Jaredites "did travel in the wilderness, and did build barges, in which they did cross many waters, being directed continually by the hand of the Lord."[3346]

Blaine Yorgason expounded on the journey of the Israelites: "Moses, who led the recalcitrant children of Israel into their wilderness experience, said: 'We turned, and took our journey into the wilderness by the way of the Red Sea, as the Lord spake unto me' (Deuteronomy 2:1; see also Exodus 13:17–18). Later, the Lord directed that they circle a certain mountain again and again until a particular lesson had been learned. Only then would He allow them to proceed along their very specific course (see Deuteronomy 2:1–7)."[3347]

Likewise, as we traverse the Lord's wilderness, we must do so by revelations, and at each junction of decision, we will encounter the issues of obedience, faith, truth, and dependency.

Angels Attend Us

Our present consciousness does not permit us to calculate the immensity of the impact of the fall of Adam and Eve. Its effects were so devastating and long-lasting that only a God could remedy the

---

[3341] Smith, *Teachings of the Prophet Joseph Smith*, 294.
[3342] Smith, *Journal of Discourses*, 26:131–32.
[3343] Smith, *Lectures on Faith*, 3:3.
[3344] Yorgason, *I Need Thee Every Hour*, 218.
[3345] Abraham 1:18.
[3346] Ether 2:6.
[3347] Yorgason, *I Need Thee Every Hour*, 233.

situation by the sacrifice of his life. Evidently, according to one apocryphal source, the prospect of sending his Well-beloved Son to rescue Adam and his posterity caused even God the Father to pause. In a conference address in April 2000, Elder Russell M. Nelson cited a passage from a fourth-century A.D. document known as the *Discourse on Abbaton*. This text contains a passage in which the narrator rehearses a conversation between the Father and the Son:

> He . . . made Adam according to Our image and likeness, and he left him lying for forty days and forty nights without putting breath into him. And He heaved sighs over him, saying, "If I put breath into this [man], he must suffer many pains." And I said unto My Father, "Put breath into him; I will be an advocate for him." And My Father said unto Me, "If I put breath into him, My beloved Son, Thou wilt be obliged to go down into the world, and to suffer many pains for him before Thou shalt have redeemed him, and made him to come back to his primal state." And I said unto My Father, "Put breath into him; I will be his advocate, and I will go down into the world, and will fulfil Thy command."[3348]

In this text, Jesus described his willingness to come to this benighted telestial world in an effort to save us. Here in the Lord's wilderness we are to learn the same lessons that our first parents learned in order to survive and achieve deliverance from the wilderness, and in order to go on to Zion and gain our exaltation. For these reasons, and for every other consideration that emerges from the wilderness, we need heavenly help. Blaine Yorgason explained:

> Adam's quest to obtain messengers, once he had entered the lone and dreary world of his wilderness experience, is no idle tale. Beginning with him, all who entered the Lord's wilderness anciently, if they wished to understand the gospel thoroughly, sought for such visitations. And if they remained faithful in gospel study, strict obedience, mighty prayer, and the proper attitude during both the hard times and the Bountifuls, they grew stronger in the Spirit and closer to the Lord until they were blessed with the ministering of angels. Thus, after Adam's profound personal anguish and diligent prayer, an angel finally appeared to him (can his relief even be imagined?) and instructed him in the law of sacrifice and obedience (see Moses 5:6–7).[3349]

The ministering of angels, seen or unseen, mortal or immortal, is common to the wilderness experience. Upon leaving the safety of the Garden of Eden, Adam and Eve literally *fell* into the Lord's wilderness and immediately sought angelic help. This is a pattern that we must follow if we too would merit protection, instructions, comfort, and deliverance. Blaine Yorgason reminded us that Abraham was rescued from the sacrificial altar by an angel.[3350] "Jacob obtained his endowment and new name (Israel) from an angel."[3351] Nephi and his brothers were instructed and encouraged by an angel.[3352]

[3348] *Discourse on Abbaton*, folios 11b–12a, in Budge, *Coptic Martyrdoms*, 482.
[3349] Yorgason, *I Need Thee Every Hour*, 283.
[3350] Abraham 1:15.
[3351] Genesis 32:24–30.
[3352] 1 Nephi 3:29–30.

Later, Nephi received a panoramic vision of the earth's history from an angel and from Christ.[3353] King Benjamin was visited by an angel, who gave him the text of his final sermon.[3354] An angel visited Amulek to prepare the way for Alma.[3355] Helaman's son, Nephi, was ministered to by angels daily.[3356] "Many of King Lamoni's people saw angels."[3357]

We need only survey the Doctrine and Covenants and the journals of our faithful forebears to read about angels consistently ministering to the Saints. With little doubt, we believe in the ministering of angels,[3358] and we have evidence that from the days of Adam to the present that angels have helped righteous people traverse and survive the Lord's wilderness and safely arrive in the condition of Zion.

Safety and Security

We are faced with at least two facts when we exit Babylon and enter the Lord's wilderness: (1) Choosing Zion, we become enemies of Babylon. Babylon will no longer support us. We can expect an all-out war, and attacks might be waged against our finances, our health, and our relationships. (2) Babylon is destined to fall. If we have anchored our safety and security there, we will become part of the fallout. Hence, a curse is placed upon wilderness travelers who attempt to place their trust in the "arm of flesh" rather than trusting in the arm of the Lord.[3359]

The transition from Babylon to Zion is daunting and can be frightening. We might ask ourselves, "What will become of us if we attempt to step away from Babylon and fully embrace the laws and principles of Zion?" The answer is always the same: "Seek ye first the kingdom of God and his righteousness, *and all these things shall be added unto you.*"[3360] The guarantees of safety and security are embedded in the new and everlasting covenant: the Lord will support us, sustain us, stand beside us, and keep us safe. Enoch said, "Surely Zion [the people] shall dwell in safety forever."[3361] Safe in the Covenant, we no longer need worry as we did in Babylon. What Jesus said to his apostles could apply to anyone in the Covenant: "Therefore take no thought, saying, What shall we eat? or, What shall we drink? or, Wherewithal shall we be clothed? For your heavenly Father knoweth that ye have need of all these things."[3362] Again we quote President Kimball, who said, "What are we to fear when the Lord is with us? Can we not take the Lord at his word and exercise a particle of faith in him? Our assignment is affirmative: to forsake the things of the world as ends in themselves; to leave off idolatry and press forward in faith; to carry the gospel to our enemies, that they might no longer be our enemies. We must leave off the worship of modern-day idols and a reliance on the 'arm of flesh,' for the Lord has said to all the world in our day, 'I will not spare any that remain in Babylon.'"[3363]

Consider the example of Nephi. After having traversed the wilderness and arrived in his promised land (his land of Zion), he was able to say that he had lived after the manner of happiness,[3364] a remarkable statement considering all that he had suffered. This quality of life,

---

[3353] 1 Nephi 11:14.
[3354] Mosiah 3:2–27.
[3355] Alma 10:7.
[3356] 3 Nephi 7:18.
[3357] Yorgason, *I Need Thee Every Hour*, 284; Alma 19:34.
[3358] D&C 107:20.
[3359] 2 Nephi 4:34; 28:31.
[3360] Matthew 6:33; emphasis added; see also 3 Nephi 13:33.
[3361] Moses 7:20.
[3362] 3 Nephi 13:31–32.
[3363] Kimball, The Teachings of Spencer W. Kimball, 417; quoting D&C 64:24.
[3364] 2 Nephi 5:27.

happiness, President Faust explained, is a product of absolute faith in Jesus Christ.[3365] Because the Lord is who he is and because he and we are bound together in the Covenant, we are absolutely safe. Gospel writer Ted L. Gibbons describes our safety as being "on belay."[3366] As rock climbers scale dangerous mountains, the one leading the way anchors the rope so that it is secure; then he calls to the climber below: "You are on belay." That is, "You are safe to proceed and follow me; I've got the rope and you are secure." The Savior has us safely on belay. Therefore, could we not exercise a particle of faith in him? Although we might slip and crash into the sides of the mountain from time to time, we cannot fall. We are tethered to Jesus by the seal of the new and everlasting covenant. When we understand the power, safety, and security resident in that Covenant, we, like Nephi, can feel at peace in the eye of the storm and live after the manner of happiness.

The assurance that the Lord is in control is the agent by which all Saints, from Adam to the present day, have been able to experience peace and happiness while enduring the wilderness and its crucibles. The Lord is our shadow by day and our pillar by night,[3367] just as he was for the Israelites; that is, he protects us from the scorching sun and the dark of night; he is our "place of refuge, and . . . a covert from storm and from rain."[3368] Moreover, the Lord's Zion, which is foremost a condition of the heart, is "a land of peace, a city of refuge, a place of safety for the saints of the Most High God."[3369]

The Lord's wilderness is designed to build faith rather than destroy it. Thus, the Lord has no intention of letting us down. That would confuse us and shatter our faith. The reality of his perfect attributes of character and the power of the Covenant hold us on belay, and, despite our occasional feelings to the contrary, we are absolutely safe.

Deliverance Experiences

By definition, deliverance is necessary only when conditions exceed our ability to cope, when we stand in desperate need of help from a greater power. What the Lord said to Nephi he could say to every wilderness traveler: "I will also be your light in the wilderness; and I will prepare the way before you, if it so be that ye shall keep my commandments; wherefore, inasmuch as ye shall keep my commandments ye shall be led towards the promised land; *and ye shall know that it is by me that ye are led. . . . After ye have arrived in the promised land, ye shall know that I, the Lord, am God; and that I, the Lord, did deliver you from destruction; yea, that I did bring you out.*"[3370]

The Lord's wilderness is to prepare us for ultimate deliverance by allowing us to experience periodic deliverances. For example, we recall that angels came to push the handcarts before ultimate deliverance came to the Martin and Willie companies.[3371] Seagulls came to devour the plague of crickets before the Saints could establish a stronghold in the tops of the mountains.[3372] Abraham's wife, Sarah, was spared twice from the clutches of Pharaoh and the king of Gerar[3373] before she experienced her true "deliverance," the birth of Isaac. Before Nephi was delivered into his promised land, he was delivered by an angel from a severe beating.[3374] He was delivered from starvation

---

[3365] Faust, "Standing in Holy Places," 62.
[3366] Gibbons, *Be Not Afraid*, 142–43.
[3367] Exodus 13:21–22; Isaiah 4:6.
[3368] Isaiah 4:6.
[3369] D&C 45:66.
[3370] 1 Nephi 17:13–14; emphasis added.
[3371] Hinckley, "Our Mission of Saving," 54.
[3372] Pratt, *Journal of Discourses*, 21:277–78.
[3373] Genesis 12:14–20; 20:1–13.
[3374] 1 Nephi 3:28–30.

following the breaking of his bow,[3375] and he was delivered from being bound with strong cords onboard ship.[3376] Plainly, the Lord's periodic deliverances prepare us for our ultimate deliverance, which we equate with deliverance into Zion, meaning the condition of a purified heart.

The ancient Israelites are examples of successive deliverance experiences that prepared them for their ultimate deliverance. The angel of death passed over them in Egypt.[3377] They were delivered from Pharaoh's army, first by a column of fire and later as they passed through the Red Sea.[3378] In the wilderness, when they had no water, the Lord delivered them by healing the bitter waters[3379] and later by drawing water from a rock.[3380] When they were hungry, the Lord delivered them by providing manna from heaven.[3381] When they were faced with an overwhelming foe, the Lord delivered them by helping to defeat their enemy.[3382] When they were bitten by poisonous serpents, the Lord delivered them with the miracle of the brazen serpent, which was an agent of healing.[3383] Then when the day of ultimate deliverance finally came, the Lord delivered them by parting the waters of the Jordan River, allowing them to cross over on dry ground to their effectual Zion—their promised land.[3384]

Like these and other wilderness travelers, we will also be delivered from time to time until the Lord effects our ultimate deliverance. Then we, like Alma, will able to testify: "I have been supported under trials and troubles of every kind, yea, and in all manner of afflictions; yea, God has delivered me from prison, and from bonds, and from death; yea, and I do put my trust in him, *and he will still deliver me*."[3385]

THE FOURTH WATCH

The timing of our deliverance is an important condition of the wilderness. Late one dark night when the Lord was absent, his apostles found themselves in a crucible experience.

> And when even was come, the ship was in the midst of the sea, and he alone on the land. And he saw them toiling in rowing; for the wind was contrary unto them: and about the fourth watch of the night he cometh unto them, walking upon the sea, and would have passed by them. But when they saw him walking upon the sea, they supposed it had been a spirit, and cried out: For they all saw him, and were troubled. And immediately he talked with them, and saith unto them, Be of good cheer: it is I; be not afraid. And he went up unto them into the ship; and the wind ceased: and they were sore amazed in themselves beyond measure, and wondered.[3386]

[3375] 1 Nephi 16:18–25.
[3376] 1 Nephi 18:11–22.
[3377] Exodus 13:14.
[3378] Exodus 14:13–31.
[3379] Exodus 15:23–27.
[3380] Exodus 17:1–6.
[3381] Exodus 16:2–4.
[3382] Exodus 17:8–13.
[3383] Numbers 21:6–9.
[3384] Joshua 3:14–17.
[3385] Alma 36:27; emphasis added.
[3386] Mark 6:47–51.

The Lord will always come—even if he has to cross the sea on foot, he will come. But very often he will come in the "fourth watch," the very last minute, the darkest time of night just before the dawn. Because he is who he is, his motive for waiting is not a cruel one. As we have noted, everything about the wilderness experience is calculated to engender, not to destroy, faith and trust. During the fourth watch, the question should never be, *Will he come?* Rather, the question is, *Will we endure in faith until he comes?*

The Lord came in the fourth watch when young Abraham was ready to be sacrificed by the wicked priest.[3387] Similarly, the Lord came in the fourth watch when Isaac was bound on an altar and ready to be sacrificed.[3388] The Lord came to Sarah, who conceived at age ninety, beyond the time any rational being would say a woman could bear a child.[3389] In the fourth watch, Limhi's people and Alma's people were miraculously delivered. To drive home the point, Mormon reminded us three times that "none could deliver them but the Lord their God."[3390] In the fourth watch, the Lord saved Daniel's companions from a fiery furnace and later Daniel himself from the lions.[3391]

Each of us wilderness travelers could add our stories to these. Time and again, we have seen the Lord come to our rescue when all other options have failed, when the only view before us was imminent disaster. Such last-minute deliverance experiences seem to have a purpose. At the least they help us be resolved on the issues of the Lord's existence and his character. Could another method of timing better convince us that he is real, aware, loving, and powerful? Moreover, could another experience better demonstrate that he takes seriously the new and everlasting covenant that we made with him?

While we do not know the mind of the Lord, we nevertheless come to know by experience that he abides the terms of the Covenant that he made with us, which stipulate that he will stand beside us in times of trouble. Thus, in the crucibles of the Lord's wilderness, we, not he, are being proven. The question is always: Will we abide in the Covenant by waiting for his certain deliverance?

Lessons to Be Learned in the Lord's Wilderness

As ironic as it might seem, the Lord's wilderness is a place of spiritual refreshment, a place where spiritual giants have retreated to find and commune with God and to be nourished by him. Jesus sought the wilderness before embarking on his ministry. Likewise, the brother of Jared, Abraham, Moses, King David, Lehi, Helaman and his stripling warriors, John the Baptist, Brigham Young, and many others sought God in the wilderness.

In the Lord's wilderness, our spirits receive what the world cannot supply them: solitude, quiet, serenity, and dependency. These things the spirit craves and Babylon despises. In the wilderness, we are forced to look up toward heaven and continually realign our settings to the Polar Star for direction.[3392] Finally, when we emerge from the wilderness, we are filled with spiritual power, as were these mighty individuals. We know better who we are, and we know our God better. Therefore, what the Lord said of the Church as a whole could be said of us individually: "Before the great day of the Lord shall come, [we] shall flourish in the wilderness."[3393] We will come out "clear as the moon, and fair as the sun, and terrible as an army with banners."[3394]

[3387] Abraham 1:15.
[3388] Genesis 22:10–12.
[3389] Genesis 21:2.
[3390] Mosiah 23:23; 24:21; Alma 36:2.
[3391] Daniel 3:19–27; 6:16–22.
[3392] Hinckley, "Till We Meet Again," 89.
[3393] D&C 49:24.
[3394] D&C 5:14.

Preparation to Live the Higher Law

The Lord's wilderness urges us to grow beyond the level of the schoolmaster law, and it prepares us that we might live the higher law of Zion.

Elder McConkie wrote: "Though the newly called saints of the nineteenth century failed to build their promised Zion, yet they retained the glorious gospel, with all its hopes and promises. They were left in that state which now exists among us. What we now have is a schoolmaster to prepare us for that which is yet to be. We are now seeking to build Zion in our hearts by faith and personal righteousness as we prepare for the day when we will have power to build the city whence the law will go forth when He rules whose right it is." The Lord has been merciful to the latter-day children of Israel. When our ancient Israelite forefathers rejected the fulness of the gospel, and when Moses pled with them "to sanctify [your]selves and receive the fulness of his glory while in the wilderness," only a few "gained wondrous gifts and power, but the generality of the people, obeying only in part, rose no higher in spiritual stature than provided for in the lesser law. And yet in that law, always and everlastingly, there was a call to higher things. The very law itself was a schoolmaster to prepare the people for the fulness of the gospel."[3395]

On the other hand, the Lord has given us the totality of the everlasting gospel, and all of its blessings are within reach. Elder McConkie referred to the Beatitudes, as they define the higher law of Zion, explaining, "If the . . . saints overcome anger; if they are reconciled with their brethren; if they rise above lewd and lascivious thoughts and commit no adultery in their hearts; if they cast away their sins, as though severing an offending hand; if their every spoken word is true as though sworn with an oath; if they do not retaliate when others offend them; if they turn the other cheek and resist not evil impositions; if they love their enemies, bless those who curse them, and pray for those who despitefully use them and persecute them—if they do all these things, they will become perfect even as their Eternal Father is perfect."[3396]

Zion is more than a destination; Zion is a condition of the heart and a way of life. In the Lord's wilderness school, taught Joseph Smith, we "receive an understanding concerning the laws of the heavenly kingdom, *before* [we] are permitted to enter it."[3397] As evidence that this is true, we recall that the Lord first extended only his *promise* of lands of promise to Abraham, Moses, Lehi, the Jaredites, and the early Latter-day Saints; then, to achieve that goal, those people were required to travel through his wilderness to obtain the promise. In the process of traveling through the wilderness, they prepared for their future blessings by shedding sins and developing spiritual skills, until at last they were finally ready to receive their *Zion*.

This is the pattern.

As we travel through the Lord's wilderness, our experiences will enlarge us by "proper degrees," taught Joseph Smith, and this will happen "in proportion to the heed and diligence given to the light communicated from heaven to the intellect." The journey will either make or break us; the family of Lehi is an example. But if we will allow the wilderness experience to do its work, it will refine us and prepare us to live the higher law and embrace its blessings. In the process, an amazing transformation will take place. The Prophet continued by saying, "The nearer man approaches perfection, the clearer are his views, and the greater his enjoyments, till he has overcome the evils of his life and lost every desire for sin; and like the ancients, arrives at that point of faith where he is wrapped in the power and glory of his Maker and is caught up to dwell with Him."[3398] Thus, the Lord's wilderness prepares us to become gods and gain an eternal "land of promise"—our Zion—in our Father's kingdom.

[3395] McConkie, *A New Witness for the Articles of Faith*, 611.
[3396] McConkie, *The Mortal Messiah*, 2:143.
[3397] Smith, *Teachings of the Prophet Joseph Smith*, 51.
[3398] Smith, *Teachings of the Prophet Joseph Smith*, 51.

Putting Off the Natural Man

As we have noted, marriage symbolizes many elements of the new and everlasting covenant. One element is that of death and rebirth. At the altar, the husband and wife *die* as to their former lives, then arise together *alive* as one. Just so, we enter the Lord's wilderness to *die* as to the former natural man; then, when we give ourselves to Christ in the new and everlasting covenant, we begin the process of coming *alive* in Christ. When we emerge from the wilderness, we will be completely the Lord's, having forged an eternal relationship with him.

King Benjamin spoke of the necessity of the *death* of the natural man and the renewal of life: "For the natural man is an enemy to God, and has been from the fall of Adam, and will be, forever and ever unless he yields to the enticings of the Holy Spirit, and putteth off the natural man and becometh a saint." How is the transformation to take place? "Through the atonement of Christ the Lord." What will be the characteristics of this reborn Saint? "[He] becometh as a child, submissive, meek, humble, patient, full of love, willing to submit to all things which the Lord seeth fit to inflict upon him, even as a child doth submit to his father."[3399] No more willfulness, assertiveness, pride, impatience, contention, complaining, or resistance—the natural man is dead, and the Saint is alive in Christ.

We need only compare the lives of people who entered and later departed the wilderness to see this remarkable conversion. These people were never the same again. The people called Anti-Nephi-Lehies are examples. Once they had repented and taken upon themselves the gospel covenant, they entered the Lord's wilderness and experienced God's chastening hand transforming them. Then, when they finally were delivered from the wilderness and gained their land of promise—their Zion—they had no semblance of the natural man remaining.[3400] Their example of faithfulness became the standard of excellence for the Nephite nation for generations, and we have no record that they ever departed from that standard.

Another example is the Nephites who survived the destruction accompanying Christ's death. Initially, they were unable to enter his presence. Evidently they entered the Lord's wilderness to prepare by putting off the natural man, because about a year later,[3401] the Lord appeared to them at the temple in Bountiful. There he taught them the higher law and delivered them into Zion.[3402] Whereas the Lord had chastised them twelve months earlier,[3403] now he blessed them with abundance. Their remarkable transformation caused Mormon to exult: "And it came to pass that there was no contention in the land, because of the love of God which did dwell in the hearts of the people. And there were no envyings, nor strifes, nor tumults, nor whoredoms, nor lyings, nor murders, nor any manner of lasciviousness; and surely there could not be a happier people among all the people who had been created by the hand of God."[3404]

Even the greatest of souls is tempered and prepared in the wilderness. The brother of Jared was divinely corrected when he failed to call upon God for four years.[3405] Nephi came face to face with his own natural man when he apparently became angry while dealing with his older brothers in the land of promise.[3406] Blaine Yorgason wrote: "All of these wilderness travelers discovered—to their sorrow—that despite their desires to remain free from sin, they were continually beset by it. Thus,

---

[3399] Mosiah 3:19.
[3400] Alma 23–25, 27.
[3401] 3 Nephi 10:8:5; 10:18.
[3402] 3 Nephi 11:8–11.
[3403] 3 Nephi 9:13, 22.
[3404] 4 Nephi 1:15–16.
[3405] Ether 2:14–15.
[3406] 2 Nephi 4:27.

they seemed to need an inordinate amount of time on their knees repenting, and even more time on their feet as they went about their daily tasks castigating themselves and feeling godly sorrow that they were such weak servants of the Lord."[3407]

Face to face with his own natural man, Nephi cried, "O wretched man that I am! Yea, my heart sorroweth because of my flesh; my soul grieveth because of mine iniquities. I am encompassed about, because of the temptations and the sins which do so easily beset me."[3408] Then Nephi asked himself some hard questions, "most certainly paralleling the questions other wilderness sojourners have been plagued with. Why do we continue in sin, even when we know better?"[3409] "O then, if I have seen so great things," Nephi said, "if the Lord in his condescension unto the children of men hath visited men in so much mercy, why should my heart weep and my soul linger in the valley of sorrow, and my flesh waste away, and my strength slacken, because of mine afflictions? And why should I yield to sin, because of my flesh? Yea, why should I give way to temptations, that the evil one have place in my heart to destroy my peace and afflict my soul? Why am I angry because of mine enemy?"[3410]

Referring to the writings of Alma, Elder McConkie wrote, "Mortal man is by nature carnal, sensual, and devilish (Alma 42:10), meaning that he has an inherent and earthly inclination to succumb to the lusts and passions of the flesh. This life is the appointed probationary estate in which it is being determined whether he will fall captive to temptations or rise above the allurement of worldly things so as to merit the riches of eternity."[3411] Yorgason added:

> To Moroni the Lord declared: "If men come unto me I will show unto them their weakness. I give unto men weakness that they may be humble" (Ether 12:27). Note that the word "weakness" is not plural here and so cannot refer to the multitude of sins we all struggle with. Being singular, it must refer to the aspect of mortality that is also called "the natural man" (see 1 Corinthians 2:14; Mosiah 3:19; Alma 26:21; D&C 67:12) or our "carnal nature" (see D&C 67:12; Mosiah 16:5; Alma 42:10).
>
> Because of this mortal weakness, we all have an inherent tendency to commit sin. That tendency, according to what the Lord told Moroni, was intentionally "given" to us by God. How was it given? Through genetic traits, conditions under which we are raised, the tormentings of Satan and his evil horde, circumstances we are forced to live through, and so forth. And why was it given? To help keep us humble, penitent, and filled with faith.[3412]

In the makeup of our nature, then, we find the seeds both of our education and of our deliverance. As we come face to face with our natural man and mourn, as did Nephi, for the inherent weakness in our souls, we seek the Lord in humility and plead with him to strengthen and help us overcome by his grace—his enabling power. Partnering with the Lord assists us in rising above our fallen state, and over time it forges a relationship with him that cannot be broken. We enter the Lord's wilderness as a natural man, but we are delivered from it as a new creature, that is, a Saint, a Zion person.

[3407] Yorgason, *I Need Thee Every Hour*, 271–72.
[3408] 2 Nephi 4:17–18.
[3409] Yorgason, *I Need Thee Every Hour*, 273.
[3410] 2 Nephi 4:26–27.
[3411] McConkie, *Doctrinal New Testament Commentary*, 3:249.
[3412] Yorgason, *I Need Thee Every Hour*, 273–74.

Learning the Formula of Obedience

Learning the formula of obedience is a fundamental lesson of the Lord's wilderness. A child takes a huge step forward in maturity when he ceases being obedient because rules are in place and begins to be obedient because he understands the benefits of those rules. Wisdom comes when he finally comprehends that rules are instruments of power by which great works can be accomplished and marvelous blessings gained. To become holy like God is the preeminent goal of obedience. President James E. Faust taught: "Holiness is the strength of the soul. It comes by faith and through obedience to God's laws and ordinances. God then purifies the heart by faith, and the heart becomes purged from that which is profane and unworthy."[3413]

Once we enter into the new and everlasting covenant, we must be obedient to the Covenant, exhibiting as much diligence as did the Savior: "even unto death, that you may be found worthy."[3414] The terms of the Covenant require that we apply the formula of obedience to God's commandments, which will lead us to become perfect as God is perfect.[3415] That is, we must keep all of God's commandments as he does, and if we do so, we will receive, as he did, a "fulness," and we will become an heir of God and a joint-heir with Jesus Christ.[3416]

God places enormous weight on obedience. Elder McConkie called it "the first law of heaven."[3417] We recall that in the beginning, God created a *master* law to which all other *specific* laws are dependent: "There is a [master] law, irrevocably decreed in heaven before the foundations of this world, upon which all [specific] blessings are predicated—And when we obtain any [specific] blessing from God, it is by obedience to that [specific] law upon which it [the specific blessing] is predicated."[3418] That is, the master law of heaven stipulates that each law of God must be comprised of set consequences and blessings. With that in mind, here is one of the most definitive statements on the formula of obedience: "For all who will have a blessing at my hands shall abide the [specific] law which was appointed for that [specific] blessing, and the conditions thereof, as were instituted from before the foundation of the world."[3419] If we are obedient, these blessings are guaranteed, according to the terms of the master law of heaven. God is a God of truth and cannot lie.[3420] He said, "What I the Lord have spoken, I have spoken, and I excuse not myself; and though the heavens and the earth pass away, my word shall not pass away, but shall all be fulfilled, whether by mine own voice or by the voice of my servants, it is the same."[3421] That is, the Lord binds himself to deliver the promised blessings associated with every obeyed law: "I, the Lord, am bound when ye do what I say; but when ye do not what I say, ye have no promise."[3422]

Therefore, the formula of obedience is this: (1) God creates eternal laws with set and eternal consequences and blessings; (2) when we obey one of his laws, God obligates himself to deliver the promised blessing.

Nephi learned the formula of obedience early: "I will go and do the things which the Lord hath commanded, for I know that the Lord giveth no commandments unto the children of men, save he

---

[3413] Faust, "Standing in Holy Places," 62.
[3414] D&C 98:14.
[3415] Matthew 5:48.
[3416] Smith, *Teachings of the Prophet Joseph Smith*, 308–9.
[3417] McConkie, *Mormon Doctrine*, 539.
[3418] D&C 130:20–21.
[3419] D&C 132:5.
[3420] Ether 3:12.
[3421] D&C 1:38.
[3422] D&C 82:10.

shall prepare a way for them that they may accomplish the thing which he commandeth them."[3423] That is, as we obediently get up and get going, a way will open before us—it is guaranteed. Like Nephi, we wilderness travelers are wholly dependent upon the Lord; like Nephi, we cannot access the Lord's power unless we go and do as the Lord commands. This is according to the formula of obedience.

When the Lord commanded Nephi to build a ship, the first words out of the prophet's mouth were, "Lord, whither shall I go that I may find ore to molten?"[3424] Nephi had learned the formula of obedience well. Once again, at the Lord's command, Nephi was ready to go and do, and he expected to be able to surmount the obstacles before him. Likewise, Adam was obedient and offered sacrifice, although he did not have a complete understanding of the ordinance's significance or power.[3425] Eventually, Adam's obedience resulted in the guaranteed blessing. Abraham followed suit. From the outset of his record, he explained that his exercising obedience would be the key that would open the door to the supernal blessings that he desired: happiness, peace and rest, the rights to the priesthood, great knowledge, becoming the father of many nations, the prince of peace, and receiving instructions from God.[3426]

These great individuals are our models. We who are sojourners in the Lord's wilderness must mature in the principle of obedience and apply its formula in order to make it a principle of power in our lives. Our very survival and our success in accomplishing the purposes of the wilderness depend upon our learning this formula.

As much as blessings are guaranteed for obedience to God's laws, so are consequences guaranteed for disobedience. The penalty for disobedience is always weighty: "Therefore I command you to repent—repent, lest I smite you by the rod of my mouth, and by my wrath, and by my anger, and your sufferings be sore—how sore you know not, how exquisite you know not, yea, how hard to bear you know not. . . . Which suffering caused myself, even God, the greatest of all, to tremble because of pain, and to bleed at every pore, and to suffer both body and spirit—and would that I might not drink the bitter cup, and shrink."[3427] In a way, if we return to sin and suffer the consequences of disobedience while we are in *the Lord's* wilderness, this is a tragedy that sends us back to the dire conditions of the wilderness *of sin*, where we were buffeted by Satan. Joseph Smith said, "The devil has no power over us only as we permit him. The moment we revolt at anything which comes from God, the devil takes power."[3428] Satan encircles us "about by the bands of death, and the chains of hell, [with] an everlasting destruction . . . await[ing] [us]."[3429] Yorgason explained, "Satan's power over us *always* hinges upon our obedience or disobedience—our willingness or unwillingness to submit to the mind and will of the Father."[3430]

Significantly, obedience is always accomplished by sacrifice: "Verily I say unto you, all among them who know their hearts are honest, and are broken, and their spirits contrite, and are willing *to observe their covenants by sacrifice—yea, every sacrifice which I, the Lord, shall command*—they are accepted of me."[3431] The disposition to be obedient through sacrifice has the power to sanctify a person, and it is sanctification that is the key to our gaining great power. Therefore, obedience through sacrifice results in sanctification, which results in power.

[3423] 1 Nephi 3:7.
[3424] 1 Nephi 17:9.
[3425] Moses 5:5–8.
[3426] Abraham 1:2.
[3427] D&C 19:15, 18.
[3428] Smith, *Teachings of the Prophet Joseph Smith*, 181.
[3429] Alma 5:7.
[3430] Yorgason, *I Need Thee Every Hour*, 348.
[3431] D&C 97:8; emphasis added.

Our effort to obey is always worth the price. Adam discovered that obedience results in greater knowledge and understanding of God and his purposes.[3432] We are told that those who are willing to live the law of obedience and apply its formula will "have glory added upon their heads for ever and ever."[3433] Obedience results in "liberty and eternal life,"[3434] the very blessings we seek in the Lord's wilderness. Mother Eve taught us that eternal life is the gift "which God giveth unto all the obedient."[3435] The discipline of obedience requires "the heart and a willing mind," but if we will apply to it, we shall receive the promised blessing: "the willing and obedient shall eat the good of the land of Zion in these last days."[3436]

LEARNING TO TRUST GOD: THE UNIVERSAL LESSON

Perhaps no lesson is as common to wilderness travelers as learning to trust God. Why trust is *the* central issue in mortality can be an enigma. To learn to trust God almost always requires that we first be reduced to a powerless situation in which we must trust God to sustain and rescue us. A gospel irony is this: power forms from our becoming powerless and our admitting to it. Only then can our dependency on God and our trusting him graft us into the True Vine[3437] from which we can draw nourishment. This results in self-sufficiency (*sufficiency in God*) and independence (*dependency on God*).

Like so many other things, Babylon distorts the terms *self-sufficiency* and *independence*; Babylon twists the meanings and methods so much that they finally become exactly opposite from celestial law and its purpose. Are we supposed to become self-sufficient and independent? Of course. But not Babylon's way. The very anti-Christ philosophy that we are trying to shed in the Lord's wilderness is that: (1) reliance on Christ is unnecessary; (2) every man fares in this life according to his individual management; (3) every man prospers according to his genius; (4) every man conquers according to his strength.[3438] To root out any semblance of the anti-Christ philosophy from our souls, the Lord is willing to render us helpless and powerless so that we might learn humility, dependency, and trust. Then we will be filled with faith, self-reliance, and independence from the world *in him*; we will learn to become trusting and trustworthy.

Trust is always developed and tested at the limits of our capability. To the spiritually immature, the Lord's allowing us to be pushed to the edge before rescuing us might seem cruel. Nevertheless, for a divine purpose, he consistently brings us to the point where no earthy solution could help. Then, and only then, he delivers us. As much as we might dislike this procedure, it nevertheless serves a purpose. In the process of being delivered time and again, we recognize a pattern emerging:

- Difficulty arises.
- We attempt solutions.
- Difficulty increases.
- We try more options.
- The difficult becomes the impossible.
- No options remain.
- Christ delivers us at the last moment.

[3432] Moses 5:5–12.
[3433] Abraham 3:26.
[3434] 2 Nephi 2:27.
[3435] Moses 5:11.
[3436] D&C 64:34.
[3437] John 15:1.
[3438] Alma 30:17.

This is part of the reason, perhaps, why the Lord is called the Deliverer.[3439] Obviously, we do not need deliverance from *possible* situations; we need deliverance only from *impossible* circumstances that require unearthly intervention.

As we have noted, it is because the Lord's purposes are best served by this method (and because the Lord's deliverance is always miraculous and cannot be duplicated) that we are "cursed" when we look elsewhere for deliverance.[3440] Not only will all other methods fall short, but the Lord's objectives for us will be frustrated. Nephi understood the pattern of deliverance so well that he shuddered at the idea of placing his trust elsewhere: "O Lord, I have trusted in thee, and I will trust in thee forever. I will not put my trust in the arm of flesh; for I know that cursed is he that putteth his trust in the arm of flesh. Yea, cursed is he that putteth his trust in man or maketh flesh his arm."[3441]

That is not to say that we sit back and wait for the Lord to deliver us. Our best effort is always required to summon the Lord's blessings. Moreover, our deliverance will often come by means of other people. As we have noted, President Kimball said, "God does notice us, and he watches over us. But it is usually through another person that he meets our needs. Therefore, it is vital that we serve each other in the kingdom."[3442]

The writer of Proverbs gave us the formula for trust, with its divinely mandated promise: "Trust in the Lord with all thine heart; and lean not unto thine own understanding. In all thy ways acknowledge him, and he shall direct thy paths."[3443] The heart represents the most holy part of the soul. If the body is the temple of God,[3444] the heart surely must be the altar, the center and most sacred place, the holy location where sacrifices and covenants are made, and where two people are bound together for eternity. To purify the heart so that the soul might regain the presence of God is the purpose of the wilderness. When we trust God with all our heart, we submit our will to his with the complete confidence that he will not forsake us. That assurance supersedes our need to place our trust elsewhere, frantically darting about searching for solutions or pridefully clinging to our own genius or self-sufficiency. How easy it is to expect that another person's understanding is greater or more accessible than God's. But if we truly trust God—who he is and what he is—we do not go searching for a "second opinion," and we will not be disappointed. Our truly trusting him bids us acknowledge that he most certainly is involved in every facet of our lives, "in the details," as Elder Maxwell taught us.[3445] When we truly trust him, when we stop inappropriately depending on outside understanding, when we acknowledge his hand in all areas of our lives, we qualify for his help to lead us carefully through the wilderness and to our promised land.

To cement the concept of trust in our souls, multiple deliverances will happen along our journey. Alma taught his son Shiblon that deliverance comes in proportion to our trust in God: "And now my son, Shiblon, I would that ye should remember, that as much as ye shall put your trust in God even so much ye shall be delivered out of your trials, and your troubles, and your afflictions, and ye shall be lifted up at the last day."[3446] The more we trust, the more—perhaps the *faster*—are we delivered.

The Lord never lets us down; that fact serves to forge a trusting relationship with him. Because the wilderness forces us to live by faith from day to day, as we constantly encounter opposition and occasionally experience crucibles, we find ourselves continually being driven to our knees. In those moments, we learn at least three essential lessons of trust: (1) We discover the character, attributes,

---

[3439] D&C 138:23.
[3440] 2 Nephi 4:34; 28:31.
[3441] 2 Nephi 4:34.
[3442] Kimball, *The Teachings of Spencer W. Kimball*, 252.
[3443] Proverbs 3:5.
[3444] John 2:21; 1 Corinthians 6:19.
[3445] Maxwell, *One More Strain of Praise*, 103–4.
[3446] Alma 38:5.

and perfections of God, those things that make him trustworthy; (2) we see that God takes our covenant relationship seriously—hence, we are absolutely safe with him in the Covenant; (3) we need to discover that we, too, are trustworthy. Before Abraham made his sacrifice, God already knew what Abraham would do. What remained was for Abraham to know, too. Therefore, God gave Abraham a way to make this discovery about himself by asking him to sacrifice Isaac. Only through this experience could Abraham know for certain that he was truly trustworthy—that he had the faith necessary to do whatever the Lord would require of him.

As we have discussed, there are three primary reasons not to trust someone: *(1) I don't know you well enough; (2) My past experience with you was disappointing or inconsistent; (3) I don't think you can help me.* Ultimately, our faith in the Lord is strengthened or weakened based on our trust in his divine attributes of character and our belief in the efficacy of our mutual covenant relationship. Moreover, if we personally are not trustworthy, it is difficult to imagine trustworthiness in someone else, especially God, whom we cannot see.

Trust requires that we are willing to be led as if we were blind. Limited vision is the fertile ground into which the seed of trust is planted. In the wilderness, we are allowed to see only today, and we are obliged to hand over tomorrow to God. Except that we know that the outcome will eventually be positive, we are otherwise given little information about our present situation. We know neither the duration of time nor the twists and turns nor the extent of the difficulties that we might face. We are absolutely blind, and we must extend our hand to the only One who knows the way and can help us. Until the day of our deliverance, we will enjoy scant understanding and perspective. In the wilderness we are forced to hope for things that are not seen; vision returns and perspective becomes clear only after the trial of our faith.[3447] And that requires trust.

Trusting God is not limited to mortality. Often we give lip service to our desire to become part of his kingdom without thinking about what that decision will entail. As we have discussed, consecration is the governing law of the celestial kingdom. Under that law we will be given eternal stewardships—*trusts*—for which we will be held accountable. These *trusts* are severally denominated as "kingdoms, thrones, kingdoms, principalities, and powers, dominions, all heights and depths,"[3448] and mansions of many sizes.[3449] Evidently, these lesser kingdoms within the greater kingdom are overseen by the Church of the Firstborn, the heavenly church.[3450] Perhaps in a similar way that we are given family and ecclesiastical stewardships in The Church of Jesus Christ of Latter-day Saints (the earthly kingdom of God), we will be given family and ecclesiastical stewardships in the Church of the Firstborn (the kingdom of heaven).

Almost certainly the same principles that need to be manifest in stewardships here (unity, equality, agency, stewardship, accountability, labor, etc.) will apply there—and framing the foundational relationships that govern our stewardships will be the overriding issue of trust. Our sustaining the prophet is our model and our training in this life. In other words, will we, without reservation, accept God as the one and only sovereign and governor of the kingdom of heaven and trust the way he rules—just as we accept the prophet as our governor on earth? Will we accept Jesus Christ as the one and only head of the Church of the Firstborn—just as we accept the prophet as our leader on earth? Will we rear our eternal families and serve obediently and trustworthily forever in the kingdom of heaven and the Church of the Firstborn—just as we faithfully rear our families and serve on earth? Clearly, our training in the Lord's wilderness prepares us for the responsibilities, opportunities, and trusts of eternal life.

[3447] Ether 12:6.
[3448] D&C 132:19.
[3449] D&C 98:18.
[3450] D&C 88:5; 93:22; 107:19.

We must learn the lessons of trusting in God and becoming trustworthy well enough that these lessons will endure eternally. Therefore, we, like Abraham and Isaac, are often brought to the point of the knife to learn these lessons. "In the wilderness," Blaine Yorgason explained, "our temporal needs are strictly incidental to our spiritual needs. Like the widow who fed Elijah, our temporal needs will be met only after our faith has been tried sufficiently for spiritual growth to have occurred."[3451] It is during the trying of our trust in God and the simultaneous trying of our trustworthiness that we proclaim our allegiance to God when we cry to him for relief: "Nevertheless not my will, but thine, be done."[3452] The three Hebrew youths cried their allegiance at the mouth of the fiery furnace: "If it be so, our God whom we serve is able to deliver us from the burning fiery furnace, and he will deliver us out of thine hand, O king. *But if not*, be it known unto thee, O king, that we will not serve thy gods, nor worship the golden image which thou hast set up."[3453] In the midst of his crucible, Job declared his allegiance: "Though he slay me, yet will I trust in him."[3454] Each of these people trusted God and proved their trust at the point of the knife. Here is the principle of power: To be able to cry allegiance and continue to trust in the Lord when all options have failed summons the Lord's deliverance.

The Lord urged Lehi's family to become trustworthy, and he guaranteed his own trustworthiness: "And I will also be your light in the wilderness; and I will prepare the way before you, if it so be that ye shall keep my commandments; wherefore, inasmuch as ye shall keep my commandments ye shall be led towards the promised land; and ye shall know that it is by me that ye are led. Yea, and the Lord said also that: After ye have arrived in the promised land, ye shall know that I, the Lord, am God; and that I, the Lord, did deliver you from destruction."[3455]

In an episode from the New Testament, Jairus's daughter was dying; all of his options had failed. The account seems to suggest that when Jairus heard that Jesus was coming, he sat on the seashore all night anticipating the Lord's arrival. When Jesus stepped from the boat Jairus "besought him greatly, saying, My little daughter lieth at the point of death: I pray thee, come and lay thy hands on her, that she may be healed; and she shall live." Jesus obliged. As they were going to Jairus's house, "there came from the ruler of the synagogue's house certain which said, Thy daughter is dead: why troublest thou the Master any further? As soon as Jesus heard the word that was spoken, he saith unto the ruler of the synagogue, Be not afraid, only believe."[3456] Notice that, when the negative voices began to trumpet doom, Jesus immediately focused Jairus's attention on the issue of trust. Jesus bade Jairus not to listen to the voices and to trust him. When all seems lost, *trust*! We know the outcome. Jesus restored the child to life and once again proved himself trustworthy.

Jesus gave the same, never-too-late message of his trustworthiness to grieving Martha, who was inconsolable at the death of her brother Lazarus: "Jesus said unto her, I am the resurrection, and the life: he that believeth in me, *though he were dead, yet shall he live*."[3457] Imagine—even then, even though Lazarus had lain in the grave for four days, even when all evidence pointed to Lazarus's complete and unalterable demise, Jesus asked Martha to trust him. And Martha rose to the occasion! Although she was distraught, she trusted the Savior and his saving power: "But I know, that even now, whatsoever thou wilt ask of God, God will give it thee." Jesus confirmed her trust in him: "[He] saith unto her, Thy brother shall rise again."[3458] And Lazarus did rise again. Jesus "cried with a loud

---

[3451] Yorgason, *I Need Thee Every Hour*, 270.
[3452] Luke 22:42.
[3453] Daniel 3:17–18.
[3454] Job 13:15.
[3455] 1 Nephi 17:13–14.
[3456] Mark 5:21–24, 35–43.
[3457] John 11:25; emphasis added.
[3458] John 11:22–23.

voice, Lazarus, come forth. And he that was dead came forth, bound hand and foot with graveclothes: and his face was bound with a napkin. Jesus saith unto them, Loose him, and let him go."[3459]

If trust is *the* most crucial universal issue in the Lord's wilderness, the Lord will not disappoint us. We can expect him to give us multiple opportunities to learn this essential lesson. As we have said, he is not in the business of confusing us or destroying our faith in him. He does not start us down the path to eternal life only to lead us over a cliff. If his purpose is to build our faith and trust in him, we can rely on him to always come to our rescue, fight our battles, feed us manna, quench our thirst, clothe us, stand beside us, teach us, and love us. He will always keep his promises, and he will never let us down.

We need to learn these lessons thoroughly, because, as the scriptural accounts of wilderness travelers attest, deliverance is always preceded by an extraordinary test of faith; our survival and deliverance depend on our being good pupils. We must trust the Lord enough to pass that test. It is vitally important to our deliverance that we are trustworthy and obedient to his instructions. Our arrival in the promised land—our Zion—pivots on our ability to trust the Lord with all our hearts. We must never listen to the alternative voices or imagine that it is too late. We must believe that at any moment, anywhere, and in any situation, the Savior can call to us, as he did to Lazarus, and we will emerge whole. We might be decaying in the bowels of the tomb, bound with the grave clothes, and we will hear the Savior say, *Loose him, and let him go.* The Lord is absolutely trustworthy—this is the universal lesson—and we must internalize that lesson so well that it lasts eternally.

BOUNTIFUL—A REPRIEVE

The Lord grants us places and times of rest from the sometimes exhausting journey through his wilderness. During the eight years that Lehi and his family traveled in the wilderness, they "suffered many afflictions and much difficulty." The land Bountiful was a welcome relief. Whereas they had been living day to day by their skill as hunters, now they "did come to the land which we called Bountiful, because of its much fruit and also wild honey; and all these things were prepared of the Lord that we might not perish." It is no wonder, then, that they "were exceedingly rejoiced."[3460]

After the persecutions and sufferings in Missouri, the Lord granted the Saints a temporary reprieve in Nauvoo. For a season, they recovered, experienced peace, grew in faith. and prospered. Likewise, Moroni recorded that the Jaredites also found reprieve in the land of Moriancumer, another bountiful place: "Behold, it came to pass that the Lord did bring Jared and his brethren forth even to that great sea which divideth the lands. And as they came to the sea they pitched their tents; and they called the name of the place Moriancumer; and they dwelt in tents, and dwelt in tents upon the seashore for the space of four years."[3461]

Interestingly, the lands of Moriancumer and Bountiful were located on the shores of the great seas that the people would need to cross. We learn a lesson here: The reprieves that the Lord allows us are places to regroup, grow in spiritual stature, and prepare to cross over to the land of promise. But we must use these reprieves for the right reasons, as did Nephi, who took full advantage of Bountiful by communing often with the Lord and by building a ship to complete the journey.[3462] On the other hand, the brother of Jared temporarily sat back, relaxed, and ceased to pray, as if he were setting up permanent camp in Moriancumer. We recall that the Lord chastised the brother of Jared, and, to his credit, he repented.[3463] Bountiful is not Zion; it is a reprieve, a place to prepare to become Zionlike. Bountiful is not where we become spiritually lax; Bountiful is a place to prepare to go to Zion and

---

[3459] John 11:43–44.
[3460] 1 Nephi 17:5–6.
[3461] Ether 2:13.
[3462] 1 Nephi 17:7–8.
[3463] Ether 2:13–15; 1 Nephi 17:17–55.

enter into the rest of the Lord.[3464] Bountiful is like a Sabbath experience, a place to rest in the Lord and prepare for the coming week. Bountiful is where "the intensity of the wilderness schooling will be eased. During those times, we are expected to prepare for further wilderness experiences by taking advantage of all the Lord gives us. We are also expected, as were Nephi and the brother of Jared, to use that time of respite to draw ever nearer to the Lord through fasting and mighty prayer."[3465]

Abraham experienced at least two significant reprieves. The first was in Haran, the place to which he escaped "from the terrible famine that pervaded his wilderness experience." When the famine abated, "he left Haran and made his way toward the land of Egypt, for though the famine was everywhere else, in Egypt there was plenty, and Abraham prospered there."[3466] In each place, Haran and Egypt, he built altars, communed with God, grew spiritually stronger, and prepared for the next leg of his wilderness experience, which would end in a temple setting at an altar atop Mount Moriah.

We note from Abraham's story that reprieves are also places of refuge. For example, Alma and his people escaped captivity and "departed into the wilderness; and when they had traveled all day they pitched their tents in a valley, and they called the valley Alma, because he led their way in the wilderness." Notice that they used their reprieve correctly: "Yea, and in the valley of Alma they poured out their thanks to God because he had been merciful unto them, and eased their burdens, and had delivered them out of bondage; for they were in bondage, and none could deliver them except it were the Lord their God. And they gave thanks to God, yea, all their men and all their women and all their children that could speak lifted their voices in the praises of their God." But their reprieve was to be short-lived. "And now the Lord said unto Alma: Haste thee and get thou and this people out of this land, for the Lamanites have awakened and do pursue thee; therefore get thee out of this land, and I will stop the Lamanites in this valley that they come no further in pursuit of this people."[3467]

The valley of Alma was much like the reprieves in our lives, a place with set boundaries beyond which our enemies or afflictions cannot pass. For example, we might experience such a reprieve by emerging from financial distress, away from the reach of creditors. Or we might experience healing after a season of sickness and feel the freedom of having distanced ourselves from the illness. From such reprieves, we regroup and move forward to our land of promise: "And it came to pass that they departed out of the valley, and took their journey into the wilderness. And after they had been in the wilderness twelve days they arrived in the land of Zarahemla; and king Mosiah did also receive them with joy."[3468]

Confronting Satan

At some time during our wilderness journey, we must confront Satan. In the cases of Jesus and Moses, the wilderness experience itself served as a preparation to confront the adversary.[3469] By means of these confrontations, we decide once and for all where our loyalties lie. Moreover, the confrontations with Satan prepare us to be delivered from the wilderness. They also prepare us to reenter it as an emissary of the Lord for the purpose of aiding other people along their way or helping to deliver them. Jesus, Moses, and Joseph Smith are examples of people who confronted Satan, then reentered the wilderness to help other travelers.

The confrontation with Satan could occur in any combination of temptations, demands, threats, or afflictions—for example, temptations to self-indulge, pamper the appetite, seek honor, power, or

---

[3464] D&C 84:24.
[3465] Yorgason, *I Need Thee Every Hour*, 280.
[3466] Yorgason, *I Need Thee Every Hour*, 279–80; see also Abraham 2:4–5, 21.
[3467] Mosiah 24:20–23.
[3468] Mosiah 24:24–25.
[3469] Matthew 4:3–11; Moses 1:12–22.

money; demands for our loyalty; or attempts to destroy us. In these confrontational situations, we are forced to make a concrete decision about whom we will follow and worship. If we choose God, we so indicate by calling upon him to help us defeat and cast away our enemy, and he will not disappoint us. Often, exercising the priesthood is the means by which the confrontation ends.

The confrontation with Satan provides us with an essential key to being delivered from the Lord's wilderness. When Jesus, Moses, and Joseph Smith had confronted and overcome Satan, they experienced an unbelievable outpouring of the Spirit—a type of deliverance. Consider the accounts of their deliverance.

- *Jesus:* "Then the devil leaveth him, and, behold, angels came and ministered unto him."[3470]
- *Moses:* "And it came to pass that when Satan had departed from the presence of Moses, that Moses lifted up his eyes unto heaven, being filled with the Holy Ghost, which beareth record of the Father and the Son; and calling upon the name of God, he beheld his glory again, for it was upon him; and he heard a voice, saying: Blessed art thou, Moses, for I, the Almighty, have chosen thee, and thou shalt be made stronger than many waters; for they shall obey thy command as if thou wert God."[3471]
- *Joseph Smith:* "Just at this moment of great alarm, I saw a pillar of light exactly over my head, above the brightness of the sun, which descended gradually until it fell upon me. It no sooner appeared than I found myself delivered from the enemy which held me bound. When the light rested upon me I saw two Personages, whose brightness and glory defy all description, standing above me in the air. One of them spake unto me, calling me by name and said, pointing to the other—*This is My Beloved Son. Hear Him!*"[3472]

Blaine Yorgason explained that we cannot successfully confront Satan unless we comprehend him.

> Oliver Cowdery wrote that after Joseph had tried to take the plates and couldn't and then prayerfully repented, the angel Moroni "said, 'Look!' and as he thus spake [Joseph] beheld the prince of darkness, surrounded by his innumerable train of associates. All this passed before him, and the heavenly messenger said, 'All this is shown, the good and the evil, the holy and impure, the glory of God and the power of darkness, that you may know hereafter the two powers and never be influenced or overcome by that wicked one. Behold, whatever entices and leads to good and to do good, is of God, and whatever does not is of that wicked one: *It is he that fills the hearts of men with evil, to walk in darkness and blaspheme God*; and you may learn from henceforth, that his ways are to destruction, but the way of holiness is peace and rest. . . . You have now behold the power of God manifested and the power of Satan: You see that there is nothing that is desirable in the works of darkness; that they cannot bring happiness; that those who are overcome therewith are miserable, while on the other hand the righteous are blessed with a place in the Kingdom of God where joy unspeakable surrounds them'" (*The Papers of Joseph Smith*, edited by Dean C. Jessee [Salt Lake City: Deseret Book Company, 1989], 1:87–88).

[3470] Matthew 4:11.
[3471] Moses 1:24–25.
[3472] JS-H 1:16–17.

> Part of our comprehending Satan is accomplished through the ordinances of the holy temple. As Brigham Young stated, "The Spirit of the Lord and the keys of the priesthood, hold power over all animated beings" (Nibley, *Nibley on the Timely and the Timeless*, p. 88). Joseph Smith discussed this power over all animated beings when he said, "I preached in the grove on the keys of the kingdom, charity, etc. The keys are certain signs and words by which false spirits and personages may be detected from true, which cannot be revealed to the elders till the temple is completed. . . . There are signs in heaven, earth and hell; the elders must know them all, to be endowed with power, to finish their work and prevent imposition' (*Discourses of the Prophet Joseph Smith*, p. 152)."[3473]

THE ABRAHAMIC TEST

The prize of eternal life is won by the sacrifice of all things—that is, we place all that we have and are on the altar as a consecration to God. This sacrifice forms the foundation of the law of consecration. Often we call this sacrifice the *Abrahamic Test,* because it is reminiscent of Abraham being willing to offer Isaac as a sacrifice, which in turn is in similitude of the Father's willingness to sacrifice his Beloved Son. Just as Abraham climbed Mount Moriah and built an altar of sacrifice, so must we climb our own figurative Mount Moriahs and build altars of faith. Then, holding back nothing and of our own free will, we must lay our all on the altar and offer it to God. Joseph Smith taught:

> Let us here observe, that a religion that does not require the sacrifice of all things never has power sufficient to produce the faith necessary unto life and salvation; for, from the first existence of man, the faith necessary unto the enjoyment of life and salvation never could be obtained without the sacrifice of all earthly things. It was through this sacrifice, and this only, that God has ordained that men should enjoy eternal life; and it is through the medium of the sacrifice of all earthly things that men do actually know that they are doing the things that are well pleasing in the sight of God. When a man has offered in sacrifice all that he has for the truth's sake, not even withholding his life, and believing before God that he has been called to make this sacrifice because he seeks to do his will, he does know, most assuredly, that God does and will accept his sacrifice and offering, and that he has not, nor will not seek his face in vain. Under these circumstances, then, he can obtain the faith necessary for him to lay hold on eternal life.[3474]

Any number of situations could qualify as an Abrahamic test: health problems, financial reversals, loss of a loved one, giving extended service, or anything else or any combination of things that the Lord requires.

Abraham's particular test consisted of at least four elements:

1. He was required to give up someone (something) that he loved very much.

[3473] Yorgason, *I Need Thee Every Hour*, 342–43.
[3474] Smith, *Lectures on Faith*, 6:7.

2. He was required to do something that he did not want to do.
3. He was required to do something that he did not fully understand.
4. He was required to do something that was thick with irony.

The Lord explains that we must "be chastened and tried, even as Abraham, who was commanded to offer up his only son. For all those who will not endure chastening, but deny me, cannot be sanctified."[3475] We recall that *chastening,* as the term is used in this instance, means "to make chaste" or "pure in thought and act." The sacrifice that we make of all things seems to be connected to our being chastened and tried. Additionally, we will make our sacrifice in full view of God and all his holy angels. These holy beings are more than observers; they are participants who cheer, encourage, and help us, and record our actions and our prayers: "Behold, this is pleasing unto your Lord, and the angels rejoice over you; the alms of your prayers have come up into the ears of the Lord of Sabaoth, and are recorded in the book of the names of the sanctified, even them of the celestial world."[3476]

The results of the sacrifice of all things include the fulfillment of the Lord's promises of deliverance and inheritance, promises he now seals, or makes *more sure.* Another result is that the Lord makes right or restores any losses that we have suffered to make our sacrifice: "Verily I say unto you my friends, fear not, let your hearts be comforted; yea, rejoice evermore, and in everything give thanks; waiting patiently on the Lord, for your prayers have entered into the ears of the Lord of Sabaoth, and are recorded with this seal and testament—the Lord hath sworn and decreed that they shall be granted. Therefore, he giveth this promise unto you, with an immutable covenant that they shall be fulfilled; and all things wherewith you have been afflicted shall work together for your good, and to my name's glory, saith the Lord."[3477] A discovery that we make at the end of the sacrifice of all things is that it was not a sacrifice after all; rather, it was the instrument that provided us the greatest of all blessings.

We who submit to the Abrahamic test by traveling the Lord's wilderness, climbing our Mount Moriah, building an altar of faith, and making a free-will sacrifice will receive the blessings of Abraham: (1) our posterity will have the right to receive all the blessings of the gospel and priesthood; (2) we will receive an inheritance in Zion both now and in eternity; (3) we will be blessed with "eternal lives,"[3478] meaning that our eternal marriage will be blessed to produce endless posterity. If our desire is to claim these blessings of Abraham, we must "do the works of Abraham."[3479]

Lehi "did the works of Abraham" and offered the sacrifice of all things and, like Abraham, was blessed with a promised land.[3480] The brother of Jared did the same by climbing a mountain into a temple setting to present his offering to the Lord.[3481] The Lord rewarded his sacrifice by giving him a land of promise. The Anti-Nephi-Lehies sacrificed everything, even to giving their lives rather than reject their covenant.[3482] Their king set the example by saying, "I will give up all that I possess, yea, I will forsake my kingdom, that I may receive this great joy."[3483] These people were blessed with a land of promise in Jershon, which became their Zion.[3484] Joseph Smith sacrificed all things, including his

---

[3475] D&C 101:4–5.
[3476] D&C 88:2.
[3477] D&C 98:1–3.
[3478] D&C 132:24.
[3479] D&C 132:32.
[3480] 1 Nephi 2:4, 20.
[3481] Ether 3:1–5.
[3482] Alma 24:17–19.
[3483] Alma 22:15.
[3484] Alma 27:22–27; 28:1.

life, and obtained a celestial inheritance.[3485] The Latter-day Saints followed suit, gaining a land of promise in the tops of the mountains,[3486] and will yet obtain the land of Zion.[3487]

All blessings follow testing: "I would show unto the world that faith is things which are hoped for and not seen; wherefore, dispute not because ye see not, for ye receive no witness until after the trial of your faith."[3488] During the trial of our faith we hope but we cannot see the outcome. Nevertheless, by the immutable promise of the Lord the day of testing will someday end, he will deliver us, and our sacrifice will be recorded in "the book of the names of the sanctified, even them of the celestial world."[3489] Then we, like Joseph of Egypt, will be exalted from prisoner to prince and attain our eternal inheritance.

Taking upon Us the Name of Jesus Christ

The greatest wilderness experience—that which takes place at the summit of our mountain—is to come face to face with Christ. The necessary preparation for this supernal event is the sum of the experiences described above. All of these experiences have served to create a new and pure heart, a heart that has "no more disposition to do evil, but to do good continually."[3490] There remains but one essential step to attain this consummate experience—taking upon us *fully* the name of Jesus Christ. By fully taking upon us the Lord's name we approach the ideal of Zion.

The Book of Mormon contains several Zion accounts. The most obvious is found in Third Nephi. There we are introduced to people who initially were unprepared for Zion, but who diligently changed their lives so that the Lord could come and establish Zion among them. But there is another account that begs our attention: the account of the people of King Benjamin. These people *were* prepared for the establishment of Zion; they had been diligently keeping the commandments of the Lord,[3491] and they were ready to ascend to a higher level of spirituality. As we have discussed in the oath and covenant of the priesthood section, King Benjamin used his priesthood to facilitate a spiritual experience that took them to that higher level. This *level* is where the ideal of Zion becomes possible in a person's life; it is this *level* where preparations are finally complete so that we can come into the presence of the Lord. This *level* is marked by fully taking upon us the name of Jesus Christ.

To fully take upon us the name of Christ requires at least three things: (1) intervention by the priesthood, (2) receiving all of the temple covenants and ordinances, and (3) living worthily of all that we have received. Elder David B. Haight taught us of the responsibility and the opportunity of a priesthood holder to bring those of his stewardship to a point where they can fully take upon them the name of Jesus Christ. Referring to "a sacred experience in which he viewed the Savior's ministry and came to a greater understanding of the power of the priesthood,"[3492] he said, "During those days of unconsciousness [brought on by illness] I was given, by the gift of the Holy Ghost, a more perfect knowledge of His mission. *I was also given a more complete understanding of what it means to exercise, in His name, the authority to unlock the mysteries of the kingdom of heaven for the salvation of all who are faithful.*"[3493]

King Benjamin understood his priesthood role to act as an advocate for the people and "to unlock the mysteries of the kingdom for [their] salvation." By the authority of the priesthood, he

---

[3485] D&C 135:1–7.
[3486] Isaiah 2:2.
[3487] D&C 101:43; 103:15–18; 105:9, 13.
[3488] Ether 12:6.
[3489] D&C 88:2.
[3490] Mosiah 5:2.
[3491] Mosiah 1:11.
[3492] Thomas, "Benjamin and the Mysteries of God," 281.
[3493] Haight, "The Sacrament—and the Sacrifice," 59; emphasis added.

facilitated a spiritual experience whereby his people received a greater endowment of the Spirit in a temple setting. We must remember that the responsibility of the priesthood is to bring people to the Holy Ghost, whose responsibility is to bring people to Jesus Christ—whose responsibility is to bring people to the Father. King Benjamin sanctified himself, thus changing his purpose from being king and protector to becoming a savior to his people. The priesthood is the power to facilitate a conversion opportunity for those of one's stewardship, to bring people to Christ so that they might more fully take upon themselves his name, and to unlock the mysteries of the kingdom of heaven that can be learned only by revelation. This astounding idea links priesthood authority, the name of Christ, and unlocking blessings for those whom we serve.

Taking upon Us the Name of Christ through Baptism and the Sacrament

To review, the process of taking upon ourselves the name of Christ begins at baptism,[3494] and it continues by our subsequently partaking of the sacrament, in which we indicate our *willingness* to take upon ourselves the name of Jesus Christ.[3495] In both cases, however, our ability to fully take upon ourselves the name of Christ, which is sometimes termed being *born again* or being *born of God*, is usually something that happens later. Elder Bruce R. McConkie explained:

> Mere compliance with the formality of the ordinance of baptism does not mean that a person has been born again. No one can be born again without baptism, but the immersion in water and the laying on of hands to confer the Holy Ghost do not of themselves guarantee that a person has been or will be born again. The new birth takes place only for those who actually enjoy the gift or companionship of the Holy Ghost, only for those who are fully converted, who have given themselves without restraint to the Lord. Thus Alma addressed himself to his "brethren of the church," and pointedly asked them if they had "spiritually been born of God," received the Lord's image in their countenances, and had the "mighty change" in their hearts which always attends the birth of the Spirit. (Alma 5:14, 31.)[3496]

Beyond the ordinance of baptism and ordination to the priesthood for men, to fully take upon us the name of Christ requires at least three things:

1. The intervention or assistance of the priesthood.
2. Receiving all of the temple covenants and ordinances.
3. Living worthily of all that we have received.

Common Ways of Taking upon Ourselves the Name of Christ

There are several ways we commonly take upon ourselves the name of Christ.

One way that we take upon ourselves his name is to accept him as the father or head of the earthly church to which we belong, the Church that bears his name: *The Church of Jesus Christ of*

[3494] 2 Nephi 31:13.
[3495] Moroni 4:3; D&C 20:37.
[3496] McConkie, *Mormon Doctrine*, 101.

Latter-day Saints.[3497] Our acceptance of him in this role transcends this world, for it is in the next world that we, having taken upon ourselves his name, will more fully see and accept him as the "Mighty God, the Everlasting Father,"[3498] the eternal head of the *heavenly* church to which we will belong: *The Church of the Firstborn.*[3499]

Another way that we take upon ourselves his name is by taking upon ourselves his priesthood. The Lord said to Abraham, "Behold, I will lead thee by my hand, and I will take thee, to put upon thee my name, even the Priesthood of thy father, and my power shall be over thee."[3500]

Moreover, we take upon ourselves the name of Jesus Christ when we bear testimony of him. Testimony bearing and taking upon ourselves Christ's name are linked in the latter-day commandment: "Take upon you the name of Christ, and speak the truth in soberness."[3501] Peter said, "Sanctify the Lord God in your hearts: and be ready always to give an answer to every man that asketh you a reason of the hope that is in you."[3502] Bearing witness of the Lord is to commend him to others and to testify of his reality, his ability, and his works.[3503] This recommendation and witness qualify as a form of taking upon us the name of Christ.

We take upon ourselves the name of Jesus Christ by assuming his work. Significantly, the Twelve Apostles are "special witnesses of the name of Christ in all the world."[3504] By delegation, we take our part in the work of the Twelve, and thus we take upon us the work and name of Christ.

Born of God—The Mystery of Spiritual Rebirth

But there is another way of taking upon ourselves the name of Jesus Christ. This way speaks of a future event that is foreshadowed each time we partake of the sacrament and witness our *willingness* to take upon ourselves his name in this ultimate way. M. Catherine Thomas refers to this future event as "the mystery of spiritual rebirth."[3505]

The idea of spiritual rebirth was introduced to Nicodemus by Jesus: "Ye must be born again."[3506] The concept of birth invokes the image of parents or progenitors. When we are born again by baptism, we agree to accept Jesus as our spiritual father and give ourselves to being adopted into his family, which is his Church. Hence, forevermore, we are called by the name of our adopted father—*Jesus Christ*—which is also the name of our new family. We accept Jesus as our adopted father in the sense that he becomes the father or the progenitor of our salvation; that is, our salvation is born of him. King Benjamin said, "Because of the covenant ye have made ye shall be called the children of Christ, his sons and daughters; for behold, this day he hath spiritually begotten you."[3507] Elder McConkie wrote:

> Those who are born again not only live a new life, but they also have a new father. Their new life is one of righteousness, and their new father is God. They become the sons of God; or, more particularly, they become the sons and daughters of Jesus Christ.

[3497] D&C 115:4; 3 Nephi 27:7–8.
[3498] Isaiah 9:6; 2 Nephi 19:6.
[3499] D&C 76:54, 71, 76, 94; 93:22; 107:19.
[3500] Abraham 1:18.
[3501] Oaks, "Taking Upon Us the Name of Jesus Christ," 80; quoting D&C 18:21.
[3502] 1 Peter 3:15.
[3503] Ether 12:41.
[3504] D&C 107:23.
[3505] Thomas, "Benjamin and the Mysteries of God," 277.
[3506] John 3:7.
[3507] Mosiah 5:7; see also Alma 5:14; 36:23–26.

> They bear, ever thereafter, the name of their new parent; that is, they take upon themselves the name of Christ and become Christians, not only in word but in very deed. They become by adoption the seed or offspring of Christ, the children in his family, the members of his household which is the perfect household of perfect faith.[3508]

That is not to say that we abandon our Heavenly Father, who is the Progenitor of our spirit bodies, in favor of Jesus Christ, who is our elder brother. Conversely, Heavenly Father initiates the mandate that we take upon us the name of his son, Jesus Christ, by our entering in the waters of baptism. Moreover, as we have said, each time we partake of the sacrament, we witness unto the Father our willingness to take upon ourselves the name of Jesus Christ, that is, to prepare ourselves and look forward to the day when we fully take upon ourselves the name of Jesus Christ.

It should be clear by now that taking upon ourselves the name of Jesus Christ is the central issue and objective of the gospel. Possibly nothing is more important to our salvation and eventual exaltation than taking upon ourselves this holy name.

Fully Taking upon Us the Name of Jesus Christ

This brings us to the account of King Benjamin and how he used his priesthood to facilitate a spiritual experience by which his people could fully take upon themselves the name of Jesus Christ—"the mystery of spiritual rebirth."

We recall that the prophet-king sanctified himself and thus fully took upon himself the name of Christ. Now he was in a position to help others. Jesus set the example for this process. In his great intercessory prayer, he said to the Father, "And for their sakes [the apostles] I sanctify myself, that they also might be sanctified."[3509] That is to say, he was about to magnify or increase his purpose through his atoning sacrifice so that he could fully become the Savior. He said that he was going to do this so that he could facilitate a sanctifying opportunity for his apostles, "that they also might be sanctified." Likewise, King Benjamin sanctified himself, fully took upon himself the name of Christ, and then prayed earnestly for priesthood power to bring his people into the presence of the Lord. The process moved him from being a great king and protector to being a great prophet and priest, or more specifically, a savior to his people.

In response to King Benjamin's prayer, an angel appeared, granting him permission to gather the people for the purpose of giving them an endowment that would cause them to "rejoice with exceedingly great joy"[3510] and be "filled with joy."[3511] These terms are connected with being born again.[3512] The central message of the angel involved King Benjamin's giving the people "a name, that thereby they may be distinguished above all the people which the Lord God hath brought out of the land of Jerusalem." Without a doubt, these people were righteous and highly favored. But what had they done to deserve the honor of being granted this "name"? King Benjamin explained that it was because "they have been a diligent people in keeping the commandments of the Lord." For that reason, they would be blessed with "a name that never shall be blotted out, except it be through transgression."[3513]

[3508] McConkie, A New Witness for the Articles of Faith, 284.
[3509] John 17:19.
[3510] Mosiah 3:13.
[3511] Mosiah 4:3.
[3512] Thomas, "Benjamin and the Mysteries of God," 285–86.
[3513] Mosiah 1:11–12.

From that point forward, the king's entire effort—gathering them to the temple, administering to them a sermon that was structured like the temple endowment,[3514] making references to their being "sealed" to Christ in order to receive eternal life[3515]—focused on helping his people fully take upon themselves the name of Jesus Christ.

It is worth emphasizing that these people were righteous people who had been diligent in keeping the commandments, which we may assume would mean that they had received baptism and so had already taken upon themselves the name of Christ. Now King Benjamin, through his priesthood, served as an advocate with God to provide these good people a new and fuller experience with the name of Christ. Obviously, they had never before taken upon themselves the name of Christ to this degree. What happened when they did so? Catherine Thomas said they attained to "a higher spiritual plain in their quest to return to God. . . . The people tasted of the glory of God and came to a personal knowledge of him; through the power of the Holy Spirit they experienced the mighty change of heart and the mystery of spiritual rebirth."[3516] This astonishing experience resulted in a "profound transformation from basic goodness to something that exceeded their ability to even describe. This much did they say, 'The Spirit of the Lord Omnipotent . . . has wrought a mighty change in us, or in our hearts, that we have no more disposition to do evil, but to do good continually' (Mosiah 5:2)."[3517]

President Joseph F. Smith explained the result of taking upon ourselves the name of Jesus Christ and experiencing the mighty change of heart: "If our hearts are fixed with proper intent upon serving God and keeping His commandments, what will be the fruits of it? What will be the result? . . . Men will be full of the spirit of forgiveness, of charity, of mercy, of love unfeigned. They will not seek occasion against each other; nor will they take advantage of the weak, the unwary, or the ignorant; but they will regard the rights of the ignorant, of the weak, of those who are dependent and at their mercy, as they do their very own; they will hold the liberties of their fellow-men as sacred as their own liberties; they will prize the virtue, honor and integrity of their neighbors and brothers just as they would appreciate and prize and hold sacred their own."[3518] Zion indeed!

The Temple and the Name of Christ

The key to understanding "the mystery of spiritual rebirth" is in the fact that King Benjamin's people fully took upon themselves the name of Christ in a temple setting. We cannot overstate the significance of this fact. The temple is a house dedicated to "the name" of the Lord.[3519] The Lord's "name shall be put upon this house."[3520] When we partake of the sacrament, we implicitly indicate our willingness to go to the temple to fully take upon ourselves the name of Christ and receive the blessings of exaltation.[3521] Expounding on our receiving the fulness of the name of Christ, Elder Bruce R. McConkie wrote, "God's name is God. To have his name written on a person is to identify that person as a god. How can it be said more plainly? Those who gain eternal life become gods!"[3522] Thus, it is in the temple that we fully receive the name of Jesus Christ through the covenants and ordinances of salvation.

[3514] Thomas, "Benjamin and the Mysteries of God," 292.
[3515] Mosiah 5:15.
[3516] Thomas, "Benjamin and the Mysteries of God," 293.
[3517] Thomas, "Benjamin and the Mysteries of God," 290.
[3518] Smith, *Teachings of Presidents of the Church: Joseph F. Smith*, 425.
[3519] 1 Kings 3:2; 5:5; 8:16–20, 29, 44, 48; 1 Chronicles 22:8–10, 19; 29:16; 2 Chronicles 2:4; 6:5–10, 20, 34, 38.
[3520] D&C 109:26.
[3521] Oaks, "Taking Upon Us the Name of Jesus Christ," 80.
[3522] McConkie, Doctrinal New Testament Commentary, 3:459.

In the temple we are purified, sanctified, and anointed to become kings and priests, queens and priestesses, in the similitude of Jesus Christ.[3523] It is in the temple that we receive the keys of his knowledge and power. It is in the temple that we make successive covenants that define a Christlike lifestyle.[3524] It is in the temple that we are transformed into saviors on Mount Zion, with his "name written always in [our] hearts,"[3525] and it is there that the price he paid for each of us becomes very real. We recall that the Nephites had something like a temple experience when the Savior invited them, one by one, to step forward and touch his wounds and thus come in contact with the reality of the Atonement on an individual basis.[3526] As they effectively *received* the marks of the Atonement, they were transformed into saviors in the similitude of the Savior; that is, their ability to perform a saving service in behalf of others greatly increased, as evidenced in the beginning verses of Fourth Nephi. In that encounter with the resurrected Savior, in a very literal way, they took upon themselves the name of Christ, whereas previously they had received his name symbolically.

It is in the temple that we are bound to Jesus with a seal that cannot be broken—except by our own sin. There we symbolically ascend to where he is, to become what he is, and to achieve oneness with him as he is one with the Father. It is in the temple that we receive by marriage a kingdom within his Kingdom. Everything about the temple experience points to fully taking upon ourselves the name of Jesus Christ.

The Name of Christ and Coronation

Moreover, everything about the temple experience points to our coronation in God's kingdom.[3527] What we do in the temple symbolically, we will one day do literally.[3528] We recall that the kings of the Nephites typically received a new name when they ascended to the throne. At first, that name was *Nephi*.[3529] Just so, when we ascend to our throne we are given a new name—a coronation name. That royal name is *Jesus Christ*; we become joint heirs with him. Thus, to fully take upon us the name of Jesus Christ opens the door to be nominated a candidate for a throne and exaltation.

The prophet Jeremiah rejoiced when he read, understood, and internalized the import of the word of the Lord as it applied to taking upon himself the name of Jesus Christ: "Thy words were found, and I did eat them; and thy word was unto me the joy and rejoicing of mine heart: for I am called by thy name, O Lord God of hosts."[3530] Elder McConkie taught,

> We have the ability and the capacity and the power to attain unto that status [sons and daughters of God] after we accept the Lord with all our hearts (see D&C 39:1–6). Now the ordinances that are performed in the temples are the ordinances of exaltation; they open the door to us to an inheritance of sonship; they open the door to us so that we may become sons and daughters, members of the household of God in eternity . . . if we thereafter continue faithful, to receive eventually the fullness of the Father. The temple ordinances open the door to gaining all power and all wisdom and all knowledge. Temple ordinances open up the way to membership in the Church of

---

[3523] Smith, Teachings of Presidents of the Church: Joseph Smith, 22.
[3524] Encyclopedia of Mormonism, 454–56.
[3525] Mosiah 5:12.
[3526] 3 Nephi 11:14–17.
[3527] *Encyclopedia of Mormonism*, 1464; McConkie, Conference Report, Oct. 1955, 13.
[3528] D&C 76:55–58.
[3529] *Encyclopedia of Mormonism*, 191.
[3530] Jeremiah 15:16.

the Firstborn. They open the door to becoming kings and priests and inheriting all things.[3531]

Catherine Thomas concluded, "King Benjamin's people received an endowment of spiritual knowledge and power which took them from being good people to Christlike people—all in a temple setting. What they experienced through the power of the priesthood was a revelation of Christ's nature and the power to be assimilated to his image."[3532] Plainly, those who fully take upon themselves the name of Jesus Christ qualify to come into his presence, receive their exaltation, and become gods. This is "the mystery of spiritual rebirth."[3533]

Coming to Christ

Taking upon ourselves the name of Jesus Christ brings us to Christ and then into his presence. Of course, as we have discussed, we come to Christ and take upon us his name by degrees. Our progress is measured by how much we have become like him, how much we want what he wants, and how much we assume his work as our own.

Enos, in his wilderness experience, wrestled in the spirit to come to Christ, and in the process he experienced a mighty change of heart. From his account, we learn that the closer a person comes to Christ, the more his heart expands and wants to bring an increasing number of people into its embrace. A pure heart is continually reaching out, trying to save and bring people to Christ. Joseph Smith taught: "A man filled with the love of God is not content with blessing his family alone, but ranges through the whole world, anxious to bless the whole human race."[3534] When we strive to become fully like the Lord, keep his commandments, want what he wants, and assume his work as our own, we will fully come to him, and then we will see him. The new heart that was given to us by the Lord, a heart resembling his heart, now bids us to seek and cleave unto him.

The brother of Jared, in his wilderness experience, discovered that in every difficulty there is an opportunity to come to Christ. The challenge of lighting their vessels became the miracle of lighting a life.[3535] Joseph Smith's dilemma of finding the true church became the miracle of finding the true God. The famine that drove Abraham from Ur to Haran became the harvest of blessings known as the Abrahamic covenant, which the Lord gave to the patriarch in a face-to-face encounter. That event culminated a long wilderness search and caused Abraham to say in his heart, "Thy servant has sought thee earnestly; now I have found thee."[3536]

The Lord's wilderness is intended to prepare us to find the Lord. The "keys" for such a discovery are given to us in the temple: "And this greater priesthood administereth the gospel and holdeth the key of the mysteries of the kingdom, even the key of the knowledge of God. Therefore, in the ordinances thereof, the power of godliness is manifest. And without the ordinances thereof, and the authority of the priesthood, the power of godliness is not manifest unto men in the flesh; for without this no man can see the face of God, even the Father, and live."[3537] Blaine Yorgason explained:

> The temple is the doorway through which all wilderness travelers must pass to reenter the presence of the Lord. Having lost that presence through birth and our own carnal ways of living, still

---

[3531] McConkie, Conference Report, Oct. 1955, 13.
[3532] Thomas, "Benjamin and the Mysteries of God," 292.
[3533] Thomas, "Benjamin and the Mysteries of God," 277.
[3534] Smith, *History of the Church*, 4:227.
[3535] Ether 3:1–16.
[3536] Abraham 2:12.
[3537] D&C 84:19–22.

we yearn after the perfect love we once felt. Thus we are drawn to the temple, where by sacred ordinances the Lord seals His children to Himself and brings them back into His presence. Adam, cast out into the lone and dreary world, searched relentlessly until he found the keys that would open the narrow doorway behind which the Lord was waiting. Abraham, seeking all the blessings of the fathers, embarked on the same quest. . . .

Isaac and Jacob at their sacred altars, Moses on Mount Horeb, Lehi at the Tree, Nephi on the mountaintop, Moriancumer on the mount Shelem—all these wilderness travelers conducted the search that is outlined and empowered for each of us in the temple, gradually increasing the hold, the seal, between themselves and their Lord, until in reality they were brought back into His presence. That was the very quest for which they had sought and obtained a remission of their sins and for which they had entered the Lord's wilderness—to rend the veil of unbelief, stand in the Lord's presence (see JST Genesis 14:30–31; D&C 84:19; 107:19), and be encircled eternally in the arms of His love (see D&C 6:20; 2 Nephi 1:15).[3538]

Nephi's wilderness experience often beckoned him "into the mount," where he "did pray oft unto the Lord," and the Lord showed him "great things."[3539] Speaking of Nephi and others who went into the mount to find and commune with God, Blaine Yorgason commented: "And what sorts of 'great things' were shown these ancient sojourners in their lofty, cloud-shrouded temples? The exact things we can see and learn today."[3540] Elder John A. Widtsoe said, "The Temple endowment relates the story of man's eternal journey; sets forth the conditions upon which progress in the eternal journey depends; requires covenants or agreements of those participating, to accept and use the laws of progress; gives tests by which our willingness and fitness for righteousness may be known, and finally points out the ultimate destiny of those who love truth and live by it."[3541]

Since the days of Adam to the present, faithful wilderness travelers have come face to face with their God in a temple setting that is most holy. Blaine Yorgason continued by saying, "All this is much more real than most of us realize. As the scripture says of the brother of Jared, 'The Lord showed himself unto him, and said: Because thou knowest these things ye are redeemed from the fall; therefore ye are brought back into my presence; therefore I show myself unto you' (Ether 3:13). Therefore, what Mahonri Moriancumer had beheld for so long with the eye of faith was now visually confirmed. He had rent 'the veil of unbelief' (Ether 4:15) with his persistent efforts, and now he had beheld the face of the Lord. Rather than seeing in order to believe, which is the way of the world, he had believed in order to see, and so on the mountain of the Lord's temple, God rewarded his righteous faith and efforts."[3542]

The end result of the Lord's wilderness is to enter his presence and experience his ultimate deliverance. The Lord's promises are sure: "Verily, thus saith the Lord: It shall come to pass that every

---

[3538] Yorgason, *Spiritual Progression in the Last Days*, 193–94.
[3539] 1 Nephi 18:3.
[3540] Yorgason, *I Need Thee Every Hour*, 358.
[3541] Widtsoe, *Priesthood and Church Government*, 333.
[3542] Yorgason, *I Need Thee Every Hour*, 360; Joseph Smith revealed that Mahonri Moriancumr was the name of the brother of Jared (see Reynolds, "The Jaredites," 282).

soul who forsaketh his sins and cometh unto me, and calleth on my name, and obeyeth my voice, and keepeth my commandments, shall see my face and know that I am."[3543]

Deliverance

The Lord's wilderness provides us ample instances of deliverance. As we have mentioned, each deliverance event is meant to increase our faith and prepare us for our ultimate deliverance. As with the Israelites who wandered in the wilderness for forty years, every aspect of our own journey points to our becoming something new and holy, which is an important goal of deliverance. Once we are refined and sanctified, we are ready for the Lord to come to us, defeat our enemies, and establish Zion in our lives.

Looking back, we will realize that everything about our wilderness experience has prepared us for deliverance.

- We separated from Babylon. We have put off the natural man.
- We learned to live by faith and to trust God.
- We made the sacrifice of all things.
- We confronted and overcame Satan.
- We fully took upon ourselves the name of Christ.
- We fully came to him.

Now we are ready to "cross over," as did the Israelites, Jaredites, and Nephites, and inherit our own promised land. *This is deliverance!*

We take with us other lessons that we have learned in the Lord's wilderness. For example, the wilderness experience has shaped us so that we are now much more like Jesus, who has guided us through his wilderness. From the outset of our journey, he invited us to yoke ourselves to him and stride alongside him—with the promise that he would help us shoulder the weight. We discovered that his is an "easy" yoke.[3544] Along the way, he and we have conversed and shared bonding experiences; for our part, we became acquainted with his character, attributes, and perfections. Now, when he speaks, we recognize his voice, and because we have been delivered by him multiple times, we recognize that he has power to deliver us again. These are just a few of the discoveries and the level of righteousness that we have gained.

The people of Enoch, Melchizedek, Nephi, and others achieved this level of righteousness, which allowed the Lord to establish Zion among them. Then the Lord raised up these Zion people, both literally and figuratively, and took them into his bosom.[3545] They had qualified for these blessings by enduring to the end of their wilderness experiences in faithfulness, and, having been true to their covenants, they became eligible for the Lord's deliverance.

What we learn from their accounts is that ultimate deliverance is often preceded by the most difficult test of faith so far. Both Nephi and the brother of Jared had to build boats, leave behind beautiful environs, cast off into the stormy sea, and commit themselves into the hands of the Lord. Sarah was required to wait ninety years to bear a son. Abraham was required to be willing to sacrifice Isaac. The ancient Israelites were required to walk into the overflowing Jordan River with faith that the Lord would part the waters. The scriptures record the result. The waters rolled back "and the priests that bare the ark of the covenant of the Lord stood firm on dry ground in the midst of Jordan, and all the Israelites passed over on dry ground, until all the people were passed clean over

---

[3543] D&C 93:1.
[3544] Matthew 11:29–30.
[3545] D&C 38:4; Moses 7:31, 69.

Jordan."[3546] Likewise, when the moment of our deliverance is at hand, the Lord will part the waters so we can "cross over," and we will do so, as it were, on dry ground.

Ultimately, deliverance comes after all we can do. Limhi's people tried and tried to deliver themselves, but could not.[3547] That is not the way it works in the Lord's wilderness. Only God can deliver us. After we have tried repeatedly, we finally come to the conclusion that we are helpless without him. It is usually then that we cease looking to ourselves or to others for solutions, and we urgently look to God. It is usually then that we begin to pray another way—we pray in faith. That is, we move from simply listing our requests to truly communing with and crying unto the Lord. We supplicate, plead, beg, beseech, implore, appeal, and importune. Why? Evidently so that we can cement in our souls the lessons of the wilderness and solidify our relationship with the Lord; now it is second nature to know that his deliverance is forthcoming. That instinct of faith seems to be essential to deliverance.

Perhaps deliverance is delayed to allow us to persevere in mighty supplication so that we can completely internalize the concept that there is power and safety in the Covenant. We need to know—*really know*—that the Lord interacts with and delivers us by the pure motivation of compassion and love. Maybe deliverance is postponed to give us the opportunity to develop the essential virtues of mighty faith and unwavering trust in the Lord, which are developed only by waiting in humble anticipation. Thus, to allow us time to learn valuable lessons, the Lord often withholds deliverance or waits until the very last minute. But the education is worth the wait. Moroni tells us that "the Lord did hear the brother of Jared, and had compassion upon him, and said unto him: . . . I will go before thee into a land which is choice above all the lands of the earth. And there will I bless thee and thy seed, and raise up unto me of thy seed, and of the seed of thy brother, and they who shall go with thee, a great nation. And there shall be none greater than the nation which I will raise up unto me of thy seed, upon all the face of the earth. *And this I will do unto thee because this long time ye have cried unto me.*"[3548]

Giving Ourselves Free

Interestingly, ultimate deliverance seems to pivot on our willingness to shed selfishness and summon the courage to give and extend charity. The people of Limhi tried every conceivable way to deliver themselves and could not. It appears that it was only when they began to take care of the widows and orphans that the Lord's deliverance came.[3549]

This powerful principle—*charity opens the door to deliverance*—is so simple that we often miss it. As we have mentioned, giving time, talents, and resources can be manifested telestially, terrestrially, and celestially. A telestial person might not give unless he is forced to or unless he can receive something in return. A terrestrial person will give if he already has something to give. A celestial person gives, not because he is forced to or expects something in return or because he has wherewithal to give, but because he loves God and his children more than he considers his inconvenience. A celestial person gives despite his present circumstances because he knows that the Lord will compensate him *"an hundredfold,"*[3550] which will provide him more so that he can give again. This level and attitude of charitable giving has the power to break the bonds of captivity. Armed only with the unselfish motivation of pure love, we can literally *give* ourselves into freedom!

[3546] Joshua 3:17.
[3547] Mosiah 21:1–15.
[3548] Ether 1:40–43.
[3549] Mosiah 21:17.
[3550] Matthew 19:29.

We recall that despite a lifetime of extending charity,[3551] Job was required to give yet one more time in the darkest hour of his life; he extended charity to his accusatory friends and the result liberated him: "And the Lord turned the captivity of Job, when he prayed for his friends."[3552] Most certainly, Job's past acts of giving contributed to his deliverance, but they did not carry as much weight as the present opportunity to give. Hence, after all that Job had suffered, the single thing that stood between him and deliverance was one last charitable act. Then, when Job was able to reach deeply within himself and find the strength to give one more time, he was set free.

When the widow chose to give to Elijah rather than to give to her son and herself, she obtained deliverance from the famine, and later she experienced another type of deliverance when the Lord mercifully restored her son from the jaws of death.[3553] Likewise, we are set free when we choose to give one last time or to place another's needs before our own.

Mortality provides us ample opportunities to go to the Lord and plead for deliverance. But, according to Amulek, prayer without giving charitable service is hypocritical; moreover, such a prayer is powerless to yield blessings: "And now behold, my beloved brethren, I say unto you, do not suppose that this is all; for after ye have done all these things, if ye turn away the needy, and the naked, and visit not the sick and afflicted, and impart of your substance, if ye have, to those who stand in need—I say unto you, if ye do not any of these things, behold, your prayer is vain, and availeth you nothing, and ye are as hypocrites who do deny the faith. Therefore, if ye do not remember to be charitable, ye are as dross, which the refiners do cast out."[3554] Prayer without extending charity is just words.

Likewise, we often fast to obtain deliverance. We should fast to "loose the bands of wickedness, to undo the heavy burdens, and to let the oppressed go free, and that ye break every yoke." According to Isaiah, our fast counts for nothing more than going hungry unless we "deal [our] bread to the hungry, and . . . bring the poor that are cast out to [our] house," and when we see "the naked, that [we] cover him." It is only *after* we give charitable service that deliverance comes. Notice that Isaiah's promises begin with the word *then*:

> *Then* shall thy light break forth as the morning, and thine health shall spring forth speedily: and thy righteousness shall go before thee; the glory of the Lord shall be thy rereward [protector]. *Then* shalt thou call, and the Lord shall answer; thou shalt cry, and he shall say, Here I am. . . . And if thou draw out thy soul to the hungry, and satisfy the afflicted soul; *then* shall thy light rise in obscurity, and thy darkness be as the noonday: And the Lord shall guide thee continually, and satisfy thy soul in drought, and make fat thy bones: and thou shalt be like a watered garden, and like a spring of water, whose waters fail not. And they that shall be of thee [your family] shall build the old waste places: thou shalt raise up the foundations of many generations; and thou shalt be called, The repairer of the breach, The restorer of paths to dwell in.[3555]

Clearly, prayer and fasting are powerless to deliver without charity.

[3551] Job 31:6, 16–23.
[3552] Job 42:10.
[3553] 1 Kings 17:10–24.
[3554] Alma 34:28–29.
[3555] Isaiah 58:5–12; emphasis added.

Throughout our shared wilderness journey with the Lord, we have learned to love him by emulating him, and in the process we have become what he is: *love*.[3556] If the pure love of Christ is called charity, then we, like Christ whom we love, are *charity*. Charity is not an act but what we become.[3557] And what we have now become holds sufficient power to deliver us. When people learn to extend charity, they become *Zion*. While the world seeks safety with armies and treaties, while it looks for security in rising markets and fat portfolios, and while it tries untold numbers of options to obtain deliverance, Zion people simply keep God's commandments and apply acts of charity. As easy as it was for the Israelites to look upon Moses' brazen serpent to obtain healing, it is likewise easy for us to invoke the simple principle of giving to experience the Lord's safety, security, and deliverance.

Restoration and Exaltation

The land of promise—Zion—is a place or condition where or in which the Lord dwells with his people in righteousness.[3558] When we arrive in our promised land, we will have come full-circle back to our beginning and our heritage. This process of falling, being snatched out of the world, traveling through the Lord's wilderness, being delivered, and crossing over into the land of promise is accomplished both by individuals and by groups of people. For example, collectively the Latter-day Saints will be delivered from the wilderness and return to their first Zion home, Adam-ondi-Ahman.[3559] Then they will return to the place of the earth's first Zion, Jackson County, Missouri, the location of the Garden of Eden.[3560]

Just so, we individually must fall, experience being snatched out of the world, travel the Lord's wilderness, exit by the Lord's intervention, and enter our personal lands of promise. These "promised lands" could take any number of forms: restoration of health, a healed marriage, a child rescued from certain ruin, a return to financial stability, or even moving to a new location. But in one way or another, we are restored, healed, rescued, and stabilized, and we feel as though we have returned home.

Collectively and individually, we are restored to Zion in a similar manner. This restoration will be played out in dramatic fashion after the Saints have completed their collective wilderness experience. Then select righteous individuals will gather at Adam-ondi-Ahman, and there, those people will witness the crowning of their King.[3561] At that point, the King, having taken the reins of government, will accelerate the process of redeeming Zion by commissioning the building of a temple and a holy temple city. When these are completed, the King will visit his people in his temple.[3562] Afterward, the City of Enoch will descend and join with the earthly Zion, and heaven and earth will literally meet and become one.[3563] Then the King will overthrow the wicked, cleanse the earth, and restore this planet to its original paradisiacal glory.[3564] We will enter a time of unimaginable joy. This will be our collective restoration to Zion.

Individually, after we are delivered from the wilderness, the Lord judges us worthy of a crown.[3565] Essentially, our day of judgment is advanced.[3566] Keep in mind that these events are

---

[3556] 1 John 4:8.
[3557] Oaks, "The Challenge to Become," 32–33.
[3558] Moses 7:17.
[3559] D&C 116:1.
[3560] McConkie, *Mormon Doctrine*, 20; see also Kimball, *Journal of Discourses*, 10:235; Cannon, *Journal of Discourses*, 11:336–37.
[3561] McConkie, *A New Witness for the Articles of Faith*, 640.
[3562] McConkie, *A New Witness for the Articles of Faith*, 601.
[3563] McConkie, *A New Witness for the Articles of Faith*, 588.
[3564] McConkie, *A New Witness for the Articles of Faith*, 563–64.
[3565] McConkie, *Mormon Doctrine*, 173.

always described as taking place in connection with a temple. Significantly, the Lord commands us individually to purify and sanctify ourselves so that we might become a holy temple,[3567] and, as we have learned, it is in the temple where we receive the coronation rites and ordinances. Deliverance from the wilderness launches us into a land of promise, which is symbolic of Zion and also means membership in the Church of the Firstborn, the heavenly church.[3568] Deliverance renders us *one* with the members of that church. Now we rise to a level of righteousness enjoyed by former Zion peoples, whose existence was paradisiacal,[3569] a level of increased power and joy. Now we enter a time of extended happiness.

Our deliverance lands us in new surroundings or conditions that do not resemble the wilderness. Whereas we once were required to walk by faith, we now enjoy ready access to the Lord.[3570] We recall that Zion, whether it is a place or a condition, is the Lord's habitation.[3571] Zion is a place or situation of beauty and holiness.[3572] There, we are no longer separated from God, but rather *at one* with him through the *at-one-ment* of Jesus Christ. Being *at one* is the condition of unity that leads to "one heart," which all Zion people achieve.[3573] As much as the lands of promise of the brother of Jared, the Israelites, Lehi, Alma, and the Anti-Nephi-Lehies were different from their wilderness environments, so the city of New Jerusalem and its Zion stakes will be different from the collective wilderness experience of the Latter-day Saints. Equally important, and on an individual basis, every promised land for each wilderness traveler is a vastly different environment from their former experiences.

The elect of God qualify for this quality of deliverance that results in complete restoration and exaltation. Elder McConkie explained:

> The elect of God comprise a very select group, an inner circle of faithful members of The Church of Jesus Christ of Latter-day Saints. They are the portion of church members who are striving with all their hearts to keep the fulness of the gospel law in this life so that they can become inheritors of the fulness of gospel rewards in the life to come.... To gain this elect status they must be endowed in the temple of the Lord (D&C 95:8), enter into that "order of the priesthood" named "the new and everlasting covenant of marriage" (D&C 131:1–4), and overcome by faith until, as the sons of God, they merit membership in the Church of the Firstborn. (D&C 76:50–70, 94–96.) The elect of God are the chosen of God; and he has said: "There are many who have been ordained among you, whom I have called but few of them are chosen." (D&C 95:5; 121:34–40).[3574]

May we strive to become the elect of God, the restored and exalted of Zion.

[3566] McConkie, *Mormon Doctrine*, 109–10.
[3567] 1 Corinthians 6:19.
[3568] McConkie, *A New Witness for the Articles of Faith*, 337.
[3569] Young, *Discourses of Brigham Young*, 438.
[3570] Moses 7:16.
[3571] Psalm 132:13.
[3572] D&C 82:14; Psalm 50:2.
[3573] Moses 7:18.
[3574] McConkie, *Mormon Doctrine*, 217.

Sent Back as an Emissary of Zion

Now delivered, restored, and, to a degree, exalted in their Zion, the elect of God are commissioned by the Lord to return (1) to the wilderness of sin to call people out, and (2) to the Lord's wilderness to help others until the Lord also delivers them. This is Zion at its finest: imparting of our "substance to the poor, . . . feeding the hungry, clothing the naked, visiting the sick and administering to their relief, both spiritually and temporally, according to their wants."[3575] That is not to say that we should not have been living this way all along, but now, for a heightened purpose, the Lord sends us back as his emissaries of Zion.

We recall that when Jesus pronounced his apostles separate from the world,[3576] he then sent them back to bring out others: "Then said Jesus to them again, Peace be unto you: as my Father hath sent me, even so send I you."[3577] Blaine Yorgason explained:

> The Lord invariably expects His successfully graduated wilderness students to carry the things they have learned back to others. That is as it should be, for the closer the wilderness travelers draw to the Lord, the more filled with charity or pure love they become, and the more anxious they are to share their joyous knowledge. Of the repentant sons of Mosiah the record states: "They were desirous that salvation should be declared to every creature, for they could not bear that any human soul should perish; yea, even the very thoughts that any soul should endure endless torment did cause them to quake and tremble. And thus did the Spirit of the Lord work upon them" (Mosiah 28:3–4).
>
> Both Jesus and Moses eagerly returned to teach the very people they were originally led away from, and Enos and Alma left vivid descriptions of their lifelong efforts to bring the message of Christ to the people they called enemies—those they loved who had chosen the things of Babylon over the things of God. Alma declared concerning the success of his life's work: "The Lord doth give me exceedingly great joy in the fruit of my labors; for because of the word which he has imparted unto me, behold, many have been born of God, and have tasted as I have tasted, and have seen eye to eye as I have seen; therefore they do know of these things of which I have spoken, as I do know; and the knowledge which I have is of God. And I have been supported under trials and troubles of every kind, yea, and in all manner of afflictions; yea, God has delivered me from prison, and from bonds, and from death; yea, and I do put my trust in him, and he will still deliver me. And I know that he will raise me up at the last day, to dwell with him in glory; yea, and I will praise him forever" (Alma 36:25–28).[3578]

Summary and Conclusion

This, then, forms the pattern of our universal journey to Zion, our origin, heritage, and destiny.

[3575] Mosiah 4:26.
[3576] John 17:6–16.
[3577] John 17:6–16.
[3578] Yorgason, *I Need Thee Every Hour*, 249–50.

To become like God necessitated our experiencing the highs and lows of mortal life. That is, we had to fall; we had to descend below all things, as did the Savior, and this to gain the ability to ascend above all things.

Our fall from Zion landed us in a "dark and dreary waste," which inevitably led us into the wilderness of sin. Because we were created for the purpose of becoming consummately happy, and finally realizing that wickedness never could result in happiness, we awoke to our awful situation and cried out for the Lord's deliverance.

The process of deliverance required that we make a covenant with the Lord by which he agreed to rescue us on the condition that we would change—not just stop sinning, but actually change our natural disposition to want to sin. Upon attempting such a feat, we immediately understood that our desire to change would fall short of our ability to effect such a transformation. Therefore, we called upon the Lord to help us; we placed our lives in his hands and agreed to abide with him in the Covenant while he guided us through the difficult process of purification and sanctification. Only by our submitting to this process could we place ourselves in a position for the Lord to one day perform the ultimate deliverance and take us into our own personal land of promise—our Zion. Now, with the new and everlasting covenant in place, we fled or were delivered from the wilderness of sin, rendering us safe in the Lord from that situation, and forever after, we agreed to remain separate from the world, which is Babylon.

The place or condition in which our covenantal transformation took place was another wilderness: the Lord's wilderness. Having been baptized and blessed with the Holy Ghost, we could now discern between good and evil; therefore, we began to judge and choose between GHSW and celestial things. Consequently, we began to feel like strangers and pilgrims in a foreign land. The Lord's wilderness was not home; it was simply *the way* home.

To accelerate and punctuate our progress in the wilderness, we encountered extremely difficult periods called *crucibles*. Their purposes were to weld us into our Covenant with the Lord, teach us to have faith and to trust him, and prove us trustworthy of the blessings of eternity. In the face of these trying times, our challenge was to avoid murmuring against the Lord and to find joy in the journey. Significantly, our achieving cheerfulness in the face of adversity actually empowered us to endure to the end.

We soon discovered that the conditions of the Lord's wilderness involved hard work, traveling by revelation, and journeying exactly as the Lord directed. We also discovered that angels attended us. Despite the odds, we realized that we had always enjoyed the Lord's safety and security. We realized something else that was important: To prepare us for the ultimate day of deliverance, the Lord had delivered us multiple times from seemingly impossible situations.

Somewhere along the way, we were confronted by Satan. This necessary experience forced us to choose once and for all between Satan and God. In some cases, this confrontation was also coupled with the equally necessary Abrahamic test. Armed with little information, and in the face of irony, we were required to climb our own Mount Moriahs, build altars of faith, cry our allegiance to God, and make our sacrifice of all things. Overcoming Satan and sacrificing all things brought us to the point where we fully took upon ourselves the name of Jesus Christ, the ultimate manifestation of being born again. Then we were ushered into the presence of the Lord.

We learned invaluable lessons in the Lord's wilderness, lessons that prepared us to live the higher law. Little by little, we felt our natural man give way to the Saint that wanted to emerge. Occasionally, the Lord brought us to our own Bountifuls, or places of reprieve. We used these reprieves as Sabbaths: to commune with the Lord, to enter into his rest, and to prepare us for the final and most difficult part of our journey, which became our ultimate test of faith. By miraculous means, the Lord delivered us from his wilderness and returned us home to Zion, our promised land.

This wilderness journey is how we come to Zion and to Christ. The wilderness journey is the "adventure of discipleship, [the] trek of treks,"[3579] and the end of the path called the strait and narrow.

[3579] Maxwell, *The Promise of Discipleship*, i.

SECTION 21

THE PURE IN HEART

In the final analysis, Zion people are defined by a single phrase: "the pure in heart."[3580] This simple but powerful statement carries with it the further definition that the pure in heart are those who see God.[3581] Joseph Smith corrected the promise in the gospel of Matthew to read: "And blessed are *all* the pure in heart; for they *shall* see God."[3582] It stands to reason, then, that the pure in heart are all those who seek to qualify to see God and who are working toward that future privilege. Until then, the promise stands: "they *shall* see God."

This event differs from the global viewing of the Savior when he comes again in glory. The pure in heart qualify to see Christ personally, *as he is*, because they have become like him. What, therefore, is the determining factor that makes a person pure in heart? Moroni gave the answer: *charity*. He taught, "Wherefore, my beloved brethren, pray unto the Father with all the energy of heart, that ye may be filled with *this love,* which he hath bestowed upon all who are true followers of his Son, Jesus Christ; that ye may become the sons of God; *that when he shall appear we shall be like him, for we shall see him as he is*; that we may have this hope; that we may be purified even as he is pure."[3583] Charity, then, is the deciding virtue that leads to our becoming pure in heart, pure "even as he is pure."

Where will the pure in heart see their God? The temple is the likely location: "Yea, and my presence shall be there [in the temple], for I will come into it, and all the pure in heart that shall come into it shall see God."[3584] "My name shall be here [in the temple]; and I will manifest myself to my people in mercy in this house. Yea, I will appear unto my servants, and speak unto them with mine own voice, if my people will keep my commandments."[3585]

BLESSINGS FOR THE PURE IN HEART

The Book of Mormon prophet Jacob offered counsel to the pure in heart: "But behold, I, Jacob, would speak unto you that are pure in heart. Look unto God with firmness of mind, and pray unto him with

---

[3580] D&C 97:21.
[3581] Matthew 5:8; 3 Nephi 12:8.
[3582] JST Matthew 5:10; emphasis added.
[3583] Moroni 7:48; emphasis added.
[3584] D&C 97:16.
[3585] D&C 110:7–8.

exceeding faith. . . . O all ye that are pure in heart, lift up your heads and receive the pleasing word of God, and feast upon his love." His counsel was coupled with promises: "And he will console you in your afflictions, and he will plead your cause, and send down justice upon those who seek your destruction." And then came the ultimate promise: "For ye may [receive the pleasing word of God and feast upon his love], if your minds are firm, forever."

On the other hand, Jacob pronounced woes upon those who are not pure in heart: "But, wo, wo, unto you that are not pure in heart, that are filthy this day before God; for except ye repent the land is cursed for your sakes; and [your enemies] . . . shall scourge you even unto destruction."[3586]

The Lord further defines the pure in heart as those who have broken hearts and contrite spirits. The Lord promises these people deliverance and abundance: "But blessed are the poor who are pure in heart, whose hearts are broken, and whose spirits are contrite, for they shall see the kingdom of God coming in power and great glory unto their deliverance; for the fatness of the earth shall be theirs."[3587]

The pure in heart experience life in a vastly different manner than do the people of Babylon. As Babylon self-destructs, Zion rises from the ashes: "Therefore, verily, thus saith the Lord, let Zion rejoice, for this is Zion—THE PURE IN HEART; therefore, let Zion rejoice, while all the wicked shall mourn."[3588] We would venture that all the pure in heart will spiritually survive the destructions of the last days, and many will temporally and physically survive. Then, with their families who are sealed to them, they will go forth and help to lay the foundation of latter-day Zion, where they will receive an eternal inheritance in the celestial kingdom of God: "They that remain, and are pure in heart, shall return, and come to their inheritances, they and their children, with songs of everlasting joy, to build up the waste places of Zion."[3589]

Commanded to Seek the Lord's Face

Elder Jeffrey R. Holland said, "My desire today is for *all* of us—not just those who are 'poor in spirit' but *all* of us—to have more straightforward personal experience with the Savior's example. Sometimes we seek heaven too obliquely, focusing on programs or history or the experience of others. Those are important but not as important as personal experience, true discipleship, and the strength that comes from experiencing firsthand the majesty of His touch."[3590]

Something dire happens when we fail to obey the Lord's commands and live up to our privileges. Consider the Israelites, who lost the Melchizedek Priesthood and its blessings when they rejected Moses' offer to bring them into the presence of the Lord: "Now *this* [meaning the Melchizedek Priesthood and its ordinances, which are the power to see God] Moses plainly taught to the children of Israel in the wilderness, and sought diligently to sanctify his people that they might behold the face of God; but they hardened their hearts and could not endure his presence; therefore, the Lord in his wrath, for his anger was kindled against them, swore that they should not enter into his rest while in the wilderness, which rest is the fulness of his glory. Therefore, he took Moses out of their midst, and the Holy Priesthood also; and the lesser priesthood continued."[3591] That the Melchizedek Priesthood has been restored carries the injunction to apply that power and earnestly seek the face of God.

The Lord extends the invitation to all the pure in heart: "Call upon me while I am near—Draw near unto me and I will draw near unto you; seek me diligently and ye shall find me; ask, and ye shall

---

[3586] Jacob 3:1–3.
[3587] D&C 56:18.
[3588] D&C 97:21.
[3589] D&C 101:18.
[3590] Holland, "Broken Things to Mend," 69–71.
[3591] D&C 84:23–26; emphasis added.

receive; knock, and it shall be opened unto you."[3592] Commenting on this passage, Elder McConkie wrote: "Surely, this is what we must do if we ever expect to see his face. He is there waiting our call, anxious to have us seek his face, awaiting our importuning pleas to rend the veil so that we can see the things of the Spirit."[3593]

Purification

We are commanded most literally to seek the Lord's face *while in the flesh* by loving God and purifying ourselves. Purification, as we recall, is to draw out contaminations, whereas sanctification is to change the purpose of something after it has been purified. Combined, purification and sanctification form the process of becoming like God.

Concerning purification as a requirement to see God, the Lord said, "But great and marvelous are the works of the Lord, and the mysteries of his kingdom which he showed unto us, which surpass all understanding in glory, and in might, and in dominion; . . . they are only to be seen and understood by the power of the Holy Spirit, which God bestows on those who love him, and *purify themselves* before him; to whom he grants this privilege of seeing and knowing for themselves; that through the power and manifestation of the Spirit, *while in the flesh,* they may be able to bear his presence in the world of glory."[3594] Elder McConkie wrote:

> There is a true doctrine on these points, a doctrine unknown to many and unbelieved by more, a doctrine that is spelled out as specifically and extensively in the revealed word as are any of the other great revealed truths. There is no need for uncertainty or misunderstanding; and surely, if the Lord reveals a doctrine, we should seek to learn its principles and strive to apply them in our lives. This doctrine is that mortal man, *while in the flesh,* has it in his power to see the Lord, to stand in his presence, to feel the nail marks in his hands and feet, and to receive from him such blessings as are reserved for those only who keep all his commandments and who are qualified for that eternal life which includes being in his presence forever.[3595]

Sanctification

The Lord is ever beckoning us to sanctify ourselves so that we might return to his presence and see him. Again, to *sanctify* is to make holy, to change the purpose of something, to set it apart for another use; for example, we bless common bread by the authority of the priesthood and thereby change its purpose so that the common bread now becomes a sanctified sacramental emblem.[3596] In a similar manner, the Lord bids us to sanctify ourselves and change our purpose (to experience the mighty change of heart) by fully taking upon ourselves his name so that we might enter into his presence:

> Behold, that which you hear is as the voice of one crying in the wilderness—in the wilderness, because you cannot see him—my voice, because my voice is Spirit; my Spirit is truth; truth abideth and

---

[3592] D&C 88:62.
[3593] McConkie, *The Promised Messiah*, 582.
[3594] D&C 76:114–18; emphasis added.
[3595] McConkie, *A New Witness for the Articles of Faith*, 492.
[3596] D&C 20:77.

> hath no end; and if it be in you it shall abound. And if your eye be single to my glory, your whole bodies shall be filled with light, and there shall be no darkness in you; and that body which is filled with light comprehendeth all things.
>
> Therefore, *sanctify yourselves* that your minds become single to God, and the days will come that you shall see him; for he will unveil his face unto you, and it shall be in his own time, and in his own way, and according to his own will.

Then pleadingly he adds: "Remember the great and last promise which I have made unto you."[3597] The great and last promise is his vow to reveal himself to us.

WHO MAY SEEK THE LORD'S FACE?

The Lord gave the following instructions to those who would be pure in heart and seek his face: "Verily, thus saith the Lord: It shall come to pass that every soul who forsaketh his sins and cometh unto me, and calleth on my name, and obeyeth my voice, and keepeth my commandments, shall see my face and know that I am."[3598] Notice the inclusive language: *every soul*. Jesus offered his disciples the same universal promise, stating that anyone who exercises obedience and loves him qualifies to enjoy the presence of the Father and the Son: "If a man love me, he will keep my words: and my Father will love him, and we will come unto him, and make our abode with him."[3599] Of that all-encompassing promise, Elder McConkie commented:

> After the true saints receive and enjoy the gift of the Holy Ghost; after they know how to attune themselves to the voice of the Spirit; after they mature spiritually so that they see visions, work miracles, and entertain angels; after they make their calling and election sure and prove themselves worthy of every trust—after all this and more—it becomes their right and privilege to see the Lord and commune with him face to face. Revelations, visions, angelic visitations, the rending of the heavens, and appearances among men of the Lord himself—all these things are for all of the faithful. They are not reserved for apostles and prophets only. God is no respecter of persons. They are not reserved for one age only, or for a select lineage or people. We are all our Father's children. All men are welcome. "And he inviteth them all to come unto him and partake of his goodness; and he denieth none that come unto him, black and white, bond and free, male and female; and he remembereth the heathen; and all are alike unto God, both Jew and Gentile" (2 Ne. 26:33).[3600]

Brigham Young taught, "We live far beneath our privileges."[3601] The pure in heart must raise their sights and pursue with vigor the promised blessings that are ever within their reach.

[3597] D&C 88:67–69; emphasis added.
[3598] D&C 93:1.
[3599] John 14:23.
[3600] McConkie, *The Promised Messiah*, 575.
[3601] Young, *Discourses of Brigham Young*, 32.

How Do We Come into the Presence of the Lord?

In Doctrine and Covenants 88, which the Prophet Joseph Smith called the "olive leaf... plucked from the Tree of Paradise, the Lord's message of peace to us,"[3602] the Lord gave a parable that reveals his management of and personal attention to all of the lesser kingdoms that comprise his universal kingdom.[3603] Of significance, he indicated that "each man," like each of the individual kingdoms, shall have his hour with the Lord: "And thus they all received the light of the countenance of their lord, every man in his hour, and in his time, and in his season."[3604] Unmistakably, each individual who is pure in heart may expect this special one-on-one experience with the Lord. Of that event and the various ways it might happen, Nephi prophesied that the Lord "shall manifest himself unto [us] in word, and also in power, in very deed."[3605]

We do not rush into the presence of the Lord. We must work our way there by continually purifying and sanctifying ourselves. For example, we must continually exercise faith in Jesus Christ, repent, make and recommit to our covenants, and constantly follow the voice of the Holy Ghost. This is the process of progression that leads to perfection: "Therefore, *not* leaving the principles of the doctrine of Christ, let us go on unto perfection."[3606]

There are three requirements to become pure in heart so that we might see God: (1) know and live the correct process, (2) know and live the higher law and its principles of progression, and (3) receive power from on high.

Knowing and Living the Correct Process

In 2 Nephi 31, we learn the process of coming into God's presence: faith, repentance, baptism, receiving the Holy Ghost, feasting on the word of Christ, and enduring to the end. Nephi declared, "This is the way; and there is none other way..., behold, this is the doctrine of Christ."[3607] The doctrine of Christ, which is synonymous with the process of coming into God's presence, is described and verified in the "words of Christ," which are delivered to us by the Holy Ghost, who "will show unto [us] all things what [we] should do."[3608] Thus, the Holy Ghost imparts to us the words of Christ, which reveal the process of coming into the presence of the Lord. That process is a continuous cycle of faith in Jesus Christ, repentance, making and recommitting to covenants, feasting on the word of Christ, and enduring to the end.

The inclusive language in the above scriptures is impressive. Without exception, the process, the words of Christ, and the Holy Ghost will lead us to every truth, law, principle, and perfection, and ultimately they will lead us into the presence of the Lord.

Knowing and Living the Higher Law and Its Principles of Progression

Revealed in the Sermon on the Mount and the Sermon at the Nephite Temple are the higher law and its principles of progression and perfection.[3609] President Harold B. Lee called these teachings (the Beatitudes) the "constitution for a perfect life."[3610] These two sermons provide us a description of the personality and celestial lifestyle of God, and, by living the laws and principles contained therein, we

---

[3602] Smith, *Teachings of the Prophet Joseph Smith*, 18.
[3603] D&C 88:46–61.
[3604] D&C 88:58.
[3605] 1 Nephi 14:1.
[3606] JST Hebrews 6:1; emphasis added.
[3607] 2 Nephi 31:21.
[3608] 2 Nephi 32:3, 5.
[3609] Matthew 5–7; 3 Nephi 12–14.
[3610] Lee, *Stand Ye in Holy Places*, 342–43.

become ready to see the face of the Lord. Both sermons state definitively: "Blessed are all the pure in heart, for they shall see God."[3611]

Receiving Power from on High

Finally, the temple covenants and ordinances endow us with "power from on high."[3612] This power is necessary so that we can transcend this fallen existence and literally come into the presence of Jesus Christ.

The account of the Savior's appearance in Third Nephi is proof that following the correct process, accepting and internalizing the higher law, and being endowed with power from on high are sufficient to usher us into the presence of the Lord. This account also proves that once we are face to face with the Lord, we will receive incredible blessings, greater knowledge, doctrine, understanding, and even higher commandments.

Receiving More Doctrine

Nephi declared that faith, repentance, baptism, receiving the Holy Ghost, feasting on the word of Christ, and enduring to the end are "the doctrine of Christ." Then he made an intriguing statement: "And there will be no more doctrine given until after he shall manifest himself unto you in the flesh."[3613] At first glance, we would interpret this scripture as meaning that Christ would reveal doctrine beyond the first principles of the gospel, and that would certainly serve as an accurate interpretation. But perhaps there is a deeper meaning. We have learned that these principles lead us to perfection,[3614] so what doctrine could be greater?

For a possible answer, we refer to Abraham, who was not content with living the gospel superficially, but desired to be "a greater follower of righteousness, desiring also to be one who possessed great knowledge, and to be a greater follower of righteousness, and to possess a greater knowledge, and to be a father of many nations, a prince of peace, and desiring to receive [greater] instructions, and to keep the [greater] commandments of God."[3615] We are commanded to "do the works of Abraham,"[3616] so what did he do? He entered into the law of Christ,[3617] which is the new and everlasting covenant[3618] that culminates with the new and everlasting covenant of marriage.[3619] Thereafter, he abode in the Covenant in faithfulness, and diligently sought the face of the Lord. Then, after Abraham had *found* the Lord, who manifested himself unto Abraham[3620] "in the flesh,"[3621] Abraham received more doctrine and commandments, as the book of Abraham testifies. The fact does not escape us that all of this plays out in a temple setting. The greater doctrine and commandments are temple doctrine and commandments, which lead us to see him, whereupon we would receive more doctrine and commandments.

When we consider that commandments are really revelations of the pattern of the divine lifestyle, and when we further remember that obedience to commandments unlocks the door to

---

[3611] Matthew 5:8; 3 Nephi 12:8.
[3612] D&C 95:8; 105:11.
[3613] 2 Nephi 32:6.
[3614] JST Hebrews 6:1.
[3615] Abraham 1:2.
[3616] D&C 132:32.
[3617] D&C 132:32.
[3618] D&C 132:4–7.
[3619] D&C 131:2.
[3620] Abraham 2:12.
[3621] 2 Nephi 32:6.

The Pure in Heart

blessings, we realize that it is no wonder that Abraham and other noble people actively sought to receive greater commandments and more doctrine. Such revelations are events of great joy. Ammon exulted, "I know that which the Lord hath commanded me, and I glory in it. I do not glory of myself, but *I glory in that which the Lord hath commanded me*; yea, and this is my glory, that perhaps I may be an instrument in the hands of God to bring some soul to repentance; and this is my joy."[3622] Zion people are they who qualify to receive more doctrine and greater commandments: "Yea, blessed are they whose feet stand upon the land of Zion, who have obeyed my gospel; for they shall receive for their reward the good things of the earth, and it shall bring forth in its strength. And they shall also be crowned with blessings from above, *yea, and with commandments not a few*, and with revelations in their time—they that are faithful and diligent before me."[3623]

Nephi revealed what will happen when the Lord manifests himself unto us in the flesh: "And when he shall manifest himself unto you in the flesh, *the things which he shall say unto you* shall ye observe to do."[3624] On that occasion, Jesus will reveal to us much more of his doctrine, and he will ask us to do some things for him that will stretch us and bless us. Until then, he will work with us, and when he knows that we will do everything that he will command and that we will not retreat from the things that he will tell us, he will manifest himself unto us "in the flesh."

Receiving More Doctrine by Choice

The pure in heart begin their quest to seek the face of the Lord by first making a choice; that choice is to abandon the telestial and embrace the celestial, even when the celestial does not make immediate sense. The choice is formalized at an altar in a temple setting where covenants are made, ordinances are given, and tokens are exchanged. Altars are the only place where legitimizing our choice can take place. Altars are where we make sacrifices and exchange gifts—the more the better. Such sacrifices and gifts are intended to be the best that we have to give.

At the altar we sacrifice the life of our natural man (the wild, untamed part of us) to the Lord, and in return, the Lord sacrifices his life for us. At the altar we give him the gift of our heart and he gives us the gift of his atonement. From that point forward, our covenant relationship with the Lord is defined by a broken heart: "not my will"; and a contrite spirit: "but thine be done."[3625]

Brigham Young taught that our choice to become Zionlike and to seek the face of the Lord colors everything in our lives: "If you want to make Zion in your families and be happy in your homes, you must retain the Spirit of the Lord in your own hearts; and let it be the first and the last, the Alpha and Omega of your lives. *Then you will have Zion*; and the little difficulties, losses, crosses, and changing scenes of this mortal life will not disturb the equanimity of your lives; but they will appear frivolous things of no moment."[3626]

Receiving More Doctrine by Desire

Our choice to seek the Lord's face emerges from our desire. Alma noted that our longing summons the Lord's "unalterable decree," his absolute promise that we shall obtain our wish: "For I know that he granteth unto men according to their desire, . . . yea, I know that he allotteth unto men, yea, *decreeth unto them decrees which are unalterable, according to their wills*."[3627]

[3622] Alma 29:9.
[3623] D&C 59:3–4; emphasis added.
[3624] 2 Nephi 32:6; emphasis added.
[3625] Luke 22:42.
[3626] Young, *Millennial Star* 16:674–75.
[3627] Alma 29:4; emphasis added.

Receiving More Doctrine by Faith

Our desire motivates us to obey the Lord and follow him on faith alone. This attitude is essential to our progress, because usually in this telestial world we do not immediately comprehend celestial laws and their principles. President Boyd K. Packer wrote, "Somewhere in your quest for spiritual knowledge, there is that 'leap of faith,' as the philosophers call it. It is the moment when you have gone to the edge of the light and step into the darkness to discover that the way is lighted ahead for just a footstep or two."[3628] The process of faith is also the process of receiving more doctrine. We are required to travel the path to the presence of the Lord by conviction and trust, and by allowing him "from time to time . . . to unfold the mysteries of the kingdom,"[3629] as if he were carefully opening up the petals of a beautiful flower until it is fully displayed.

Receiving More Doctrine by Persistence and Improvement

Our experiment with faith in the word of God always yields a harvest of blessings. The evidence of growth encourages us to persevere. Blaine Yorgason wrote:

> To obtain the ultimate blessing of seeing the face of Christ and partaking of His divine love and approbation, righteous individuals must progress steadily forward in the spirit, clinging steadfastly to every word that proceeds forth from the mouth of God, and fulfilling the other requirements outlined by the Lord: "Strip yourselves from jealousies and fears, and humble yourselves before me, . . . let[ting] not your minds turn back" (D&C 67:10, 14); "seek the face of the Lord always, that in patience ye may possess your souls, and ye shall have eternal life" (D&C 101:38). Then, "in mine own due time, . . ." the Lord promises, "the veil shall be rent and you shall see me and know that I am" (D&C 64:114, 10).[3630]

Receiving More Doctrine by Service

Joseph Smith asked, "How do men obtain a knowledge of the glory of God, his perfections and attributes?" Then, answering the question, he said, "By devoting themselves to his service, through prayer and supplication incessantly strengthening their faith in him, until, like Enoch, the brother of Jared, and Moses, they obtain a manifestation of God to themselves."[3631] Without service, we have learned prayers are just words[3632] and fasts are just going hungry.[3633]

Receiving More Doctrine by Seeking

Blaine Yorgason wrote, "Diligent seeking . . . permits qualified, pure-hearted men and women to 'have the privilege of receiving the mysteries of the kingdom of heaven, to have the heavens opened unto them, to commune with the general assembly and church of the Firstborn, and to enjoy the communion and presence of God the Father, and Jesus the mediator of the new covenant' (D&C 107:19)."[3634]

[3628] Packer, *That All May Be Edified*, 340.
[3629] D&C 90:14.
[3630] Yorgason, *I Need Thee Every Hour*, 431.
[3631] Smith, *Lectures on Faith*, 2:55.
[3632] Alma 34:28.
[3633] Isaiah 58:7, 10.
[3634] Yorgason, *I Need Thee Every Hour*, 432.

Elder McConkie taught similarly: "The attainment of such a state of righteousness and perfection is the object and end toward which all of the Lord's people are striving. We seek to see the face of the Lord while we yet dwell in mortality, and we seek to dwell with him everlastingly in the eternal kingdoms that are prepared."[3635] Of these and other promises, we might apply the Lord's counsel, "Treasure up these words in thy heart."[3636]

Receiving More Doctrine by Treasuring Up

The Lord has repeatedly commanded that we "treasure up in [our] minds continually the words of life."[3637] "Wherefore, ye shall treasure up the things which ye have seen and heard."[3638] To treasure up is like finding something valuable and placing it in a safe and secure place so that we never lose it.

In this world, we "enjoy the words of eternal life" and treasure them up so that one day we might achieve "eternal life in the world to come, even immortal glory."[3639] For now, we are to treasure up and "give diligent heed to the words of eternal life."[3640]

When a great division came among the disciples of Jesus, and many who had once believed now abandoned him, he turned to his apostles and asked poignantly, "Will ye also go away? Then Simon Peter answered him, Lord, to whom shall we go? thou hast the words of eternal life. And we believe and are sure that thou art that Christ, the Son of the living God."[3641] Peter answered for all of us: there is nowhere else to go. Only through the Word of God can we receive the words of God; and only by treasuring them up can we obtain eternal life. "Therefore treasure up these words in thy heart."[3642]

So much depends on our desiring, seeking, and treasuring up more doctrine. The Lord piqued our interest when he revealed, "Now, as touching the law of the priesthood, there are many things pertaining thereunto."[3643] Upon the foundation of the atonement stands the doctrine of Zion, which comprises three pillars: (1) The New and Everlasting Covenant; (2) The Oath and Covenant of the Priesthood; and (3) The Law of Consecration.[3644] Beyond receiving these covenants, we must seek to understand the doctrine so that we might better live it. Therein lies our opportunity to become Zion people.

The Significance of the Temple Recommend

How do we know we are on track? President Gordon B. Hinckley suggested that our temple recommend is a good indicator. If the temple represents heaven on earth and most literally the house and presence of God, if it is in the temple that we are taught how to come into the presence of the Lord, and if it is in the temple that the pure in heart at last see God, then our temple recommend should be tangible proof—if our lives are absolutely square with the temple recommend questions—that we are living up to the basic requirements of the gospel and doing what the Lord expects of us.[3645]

[3635] McConkie, *The Promised Messiah*, 578.
[3636] D&C 6:20.
[3637] D&C 84:85.
[3638] Ether 3:21.
[3639] Moses 6:59.
[3640] D&C 84:43.
[3641] John 6:67–69.
[3642] D&C 6:20.
[3643] D&C 132:58.
[3644] D&C 42:67.
[3645] Hinckley, speech given at the BYU Center for Near Eastern Studies in Jerusalem, Mar. 21, 1999.

Where do our efforts to live up to our covenants and to the requirements of the temple recommend lead us? If our hearts are right, if our private devotions, devotedness, yearnings, and consecrations are right before God, the day will come when we will see him. Could there be a greater blessing than finally beholding the face of the Lord? Elder McConkie exclaimed: "What greater personal revelation could anyone receive than to see the face of his Maker? Is not this the crowning blessing of life? Can all the wealth of the earth, all of the powers of the world, and all of the honors of men compare with it? And is it an unseemly or unrighteous desire on man's part to hope and live and pray, all in such a way as to qualify for so great a manifestation?"[3646]

Such are the promised blessings for all the pure in heart.

BY WHAT POWER MIGHT WE SEEK THE LORD'S FACE?

No man casually approaches the Lord and suddenly finds himself face to face with Deity. The common aim of fallen men who seek to become pure in heart is to return to their God and stand again in his presence. But by what means might we attain to such a lofty goal? The Lord himself gave the answer: "And this greater priesthood administereth the gospel and holdeth the key of the mysteries of the kingdom, *even the key of the knowledge of God*. Therefore, in the ordinances thereof, the power of godliness is manifest. And without the ordinances thereof, and the authority of the priesthood, the power of godliness is not manifest unto men in the flesh; *for without this no man can see the face of God, even the Father, and live*."[3647]

Thus, it is this "power of godliness"—which flows from the Melchizedek Priesthood and its ordinances—that provides us the capacity to "see the face of God."

According to Joseph Smith, the "key of the knowledge of God"[3648] is synonymous with "the keys of this [Melchizedek] priesthood," which resulted in Noah "obtaining the voice of Jehovah that He talked with him [Noah] in a familiar and friendly manner, that He continued to him the keys, the covenants, the power and the glory, with which He blessed Adam at the beginning."[3649] That is, the Melchizedek Priesthood *keys* have always been the source of power that righteous individuals have employed to see and talk with God. (Note: The word *key(s)* in this instance does not mean administrative powers, but rather revelatory powers.[3650])

The power to see God has always resided in the revelatory *keys* of the Melchizedek Priesthood. What are the priesthood *keys* that yield such a magnificent revelation? According to the scripture above, the "key to the knowledge of God" is synonymous with the "ordinances thereof," meaning the ordinances of the Melchizedek Priesthood. Thus, these *keys* are the temple ordinances that comprise the endowment of "power from on high."[3651] The Prophet explained, "Now the great and grand secret of the whole matter, and the *summum bonum* of the whole subject that is lying before us, consists in obtaining the powers of the Holy Priesthood. For him to whom these keys are given there is no difficulty in obtaining a knowledge of facts in relation to the salvation of the children of men, both as well for the dead as for the living."[3652]

What "facts" and whose "salvation"?

Obviously, these are the facts of eternal life relevant to our salvation related to us by the Lord. Elder McConkie explained:

[3646] McConkie, *A New Witness for the Articles of Faith*, 492.
[3647] D&C 84:19–22; emphasis added.
[3648] D&C 84:19.
[3649] Smith, *Teachings of the Prophet Joseph Smith*, 172.
[3650] D&C 142:27–28, 34; see Smith, *History of the Church*, 4:608; 5:1–2; Smith, *Teachings of the Prophet Joseph Smith*, 226.
[3651] D&C 38:32, 38; 95:8; 105:11.
[3652] D&C 128:11.

> The priesthood is the power, authority, and means that prepares men to see their Lord; also, . . . in the priesthood is found everything that is needed to bring this consummation to pass. Accordingly, it is written: "The power and authority of the higher, or Melchizedek Priesthood, is to hold the keys of all the spiritual blessings of the church—To have the privilege of receiving the mysteries of the kingdom of heaven, to have the heavens opened unto them, to commune with the general assembly and church of the Firstborn, and to enjoy the communion and presence of God the Father, and Jesus the mediator of the new covenant" (D&C 107:18–19).[3653]

Only when the priesthood operates fully in our lives—ordination for men and the endowment for men and women—can we qualify for the supernal event of standing in the presence of God. Elder McConkie wrote: "Thus, through the priesthood the door may be opened and the way provided for men to see the Father and the Son. From all of this it follows, automatically and axiomatically, that if and when the holy priesthood operates to the full in the life of any man [or woman], he will receive its great and full blessings, which are that rending of the heavens and that parting of the veil of which we now speak. . . . *The purpose of the endowment in the house of the Lord is to prepare and sanctify his saints so they will be able to see his face, here and now, as well as to bear the glory of his presence in the eternal worlds.*"[3654]

How does the priesthood operate fully in our lives? The Lord says, "Sanctify yourselves; yea, purify your hearts, and cleanse your hands and your feet before me, that I may make you clean; that I may testify unto your Father, and your God, and my God, that you are clean from the blood of this wicked generation."[3655]

Then comes the Lord's "great and last promise"— ". . . the days will come that you shall see him; for he will unveil his face unto you, and it shall be in his own time, and in his own way, and according to his own will."[3656]

Andrew Ehat and Lyndon Cook commented, "These keys of access to God (D&C 128:10–11), held in all their fulness by the President of the Church, enable the 'least member' in the Church to have power in his priesthood (see *Teachings of the Prophet Joseph Smith*, p. 137). It was not enough to Joseph Smith to be a king and a priest unto the Most High, but he insisted that his people be a society of priests 'as in Paul's day, as in Enoch's day' through the ordinances of the temple. . . . Throughout the remainder of his Nauvoo experience, Joseph Smith taught and emphasized the importance of the temple ordinances, ordinances that would bestow upon members of the Church the knowledge and power he foreshadows in this discourse [on the priesthood]."[3657]

Blaine Yorgason expounded, "This experience, of course, is true worship, and according to Moses, it occurs when calling upon God through the name of His Only Begotten in mighty prayer (Moses 1:17), which for the pure in heart is accomplished with greatest effectiveness through worship in God's holy temples."[3658] As Paul said, "Eye hath not seen, nor ear heard, neither have entered into the heart of man, the things which God hath prepared for them that love him."[3659]

[3653] McConkie, *The Promised Messiah*, 587.
[3654] McConkie, *The Promised Messiah*, 588; emphasis added.
[3655] D&C 88:74–75.
[3656] D&C 88:68.
[3657] Smith, *The Words of Joseph Smith*, 54–55.
[3658] Yorgason, *I Need Thee Every Hour*, 433.
[3659] 1 Corinthians 2:9.

HOLINESS TO THE LORD

Why must Zion people actively seek to purify and sanctify themselves so that they might see the face of the Lord? One of the reasons is that the priesthood society of Zion is described as a place where God dwells with his people.[3660] Ultimately, the ideal of Zion and seeing the Lord are synonymous. Of course, that level of purification and sanctification occurs line upon line and step by step—growing from one "grace" to another by giving "grace for grace."[3661]

We become Zionlike by degrees. At times, we might not even perceive that we are progressing. Imagine a man who stands up in an airplane and begins to stride toward the stewardess. From his point of view, each step covers only a few feet; but from an outsider's point of view, because of the movement of the airplane the man has spanned thousands of feet. Just so, from our point of view we might perceive that our progress is minuscule, whereas God might perceive our advancement as extensive. Small, consistent efforts to purify the heart, a characteristic of Zion people, transform a life. These concerted daily efforts include seeking out and gathering in the elect of God, genealogical work, temple worship and service, covenant renewal, welfare and compassionate service, and striving better to live the law of consecration by the generous payment of fast offerings, donations and by giving our time, talents, and means to help the less fortunate.[3662] Each of these might appear to us as small steps, but in fact they cover enormous ground toward the goal of holiness.

A marvelous transformation takes place in the lives of those who strive to become pure in heart. As the prophet Zachariah said, *Holiness to the Lord* is written in their hearts and in all aspects of their lives.[3663] This attitude is so prevalent in Zion that "even upon the bells of the horses shall be written *Holiness to the Lord.*"[3664]

Of Zion as a pervasive theme, Brigham Young said, "Let there be an hallowed influence go from us over all things over which we have any power; over the soil we cultivate, over the houses we build, and over everything we possess." Such is the condition of Zion. Continuing, he said,

> I have Zion in my view constantly. We are not going to wait for angels, or for Enoch and his company to come and build up Zion, but we are going to build it. We will raise our wheat, build our houses, fence our farms, plant our vineyards and orchards, and produce everything that will make our bodies comfortable and happy, and in this manner we intend to build up Zion on the earth and purify it and cleanse it from all pollutions. . . . If we cease to hold fellowship with that which is corrupt and establish the Zion of God in our hearts, in our own houses, in our cities, and throughout our country, we shall ultimately overcome the earth, for we are the lords of the earth; and, instead of thorns and thistles, every useful plant that is good for the food of man and to beautify and adorn will spring from its bosom.[3665]

This condition would truly be *Holiness to the Lord.*

[3660] Moses 7:16, 21.
[3661] D&C 93:12, 20; Helaman 12:24.
[3662] Gardner, "Becoming a Zion Society," 31.
[3663] Zechariah 14:20.
[3664] Smith, *History of the Church,* 2:357–58.
[3665] Young, *Discourses of Brigham Young,* 443.

On a personal level, *Holiness to the Lord* requires a mighty change of heart,[3666] the conversion experience or experiences that transform a natural man into a Zion person. President James E. Faust connected holiness to spiritual strength. Becoming holy, he said, is a process that involves receiving the covenants and ordinances, then trusting God as he purifies and purges our hearts.[3667] The resulting mighty change is common to Zion people. As we are purified and cleansed from sin, we progressively receive more light. Holiness is achieved by humbling ourselves, seeking the priesthood and its blessings, and desiring to relentlessly bring people to Christ. Moreover, holiness comes by persistently trying to rise above the telestial world and seeking for the celestial in all things. Holiness transforms priesthood authority into priesthood power. Holiness increases our confidence to ask for and receive blessings in the name of Jesus Christ.[3668] Ultimately, holiness allows us to literally stand in the presence of the Father and the Son and enjoy their association.[3669]

The ability to become holy is within our reach. Absolutely everything that we need to achieve a mighty change of heart and attain *Holiness to the Lord*—every principle, truth, power, covenant, and ordinance—has been revealed in the latter days. We need only understand what we have and live it.

A New Commitment

To become Zion people, we must make a decision. Once and for all, we must commit to both believe and live what we have received. It is not enough to go through the motions of being a Latter-day Saint. We must thoroughly study and understand the new and everlasting covenant, which is the offspring of the Atonement. Receiving, committing to, studying, and living the Covenant are the vehicles that allow us to *become* Zion people. In the final analysis, it is what we have become that will determine our eternal possibilities.[3670]

If we are to become Zion people, what will be our characteristics?

- Above all, pure in heart.
- Separate from Babylon.
- Of one heart and mind—unified with God and our fellowmen.
- Equal in opportunity for and access to God's blessings.
- Stewards, not owners, who are accountable to God.
- Having chosen God over mammon.
- Striving to labor for Zion and not to amass personal wealth.
- Having completely consecrated ourselves: our time, talents, and all that we have and are for the upbuilding of the kingdom of God and the establishment of Zion.

If Zion is our aspiration, this description is what we must become. And it all starts with making a commitment. Well did Elijah challenge his contemporaries: "How long halt ye between two opinions? if the Lord be God, follow him: but if Baal, then follow him."[3671] As long as our commitment waits, Zion's blessings remain unclaimed.

In a conference address entitled "Becoming the Pure in Heart," President Spencer W. Kimball taught that we should keep uppermost in our minds the vision of who we are and what we are about. He said, "For many years we have been taught that one important end result of our labors, hopes, and

---

[3666] Alma 5:13.
[3667] Faust, "Standing in Holy Places," 62.
[3668] D&C 50:24–29.
[3669] John 14:15–23.
[3670] Oaks, "The Challenge to Become," 32–34.
[3671] 1 Kings 18:21.

aspirations in this work is the building of a latter-day Zion, a Zion characterized by love, harmony, and peace—a Zion in which the Lord's children are as one." Then he quoted Doctrine and Covenants 48, in which the Lord gives us a glimpse of the latter-day Zion:

> Ye cannot behold with your natural eyes, for the present time, the design of your God concerning those things which shall come hereafter, and the glory which shall follow after much tribulation. For after much tribulation come the blessings. Wherefore the day cometh that ye shall be crowned with much glory; the hour is not yet, but is nigh at hand. . . .
>
> Behold, verily I say unto you, for this cause I have sent you—that you might be obedient, and that your hearts might be prepared to bear testimony of the things which are to come; and also that you might be honored in laying the foundation, and in bearing record of the land upon which the Zion of God shall stand.
>
> And after that cometh the day of my power; then shall the poor, the lame, and the blind, and the deaf, come in unto the marriage of the Lamb, and partake of the supper of the Lord, prepared for the great day to come. Behold, I, the Lord, have spoken it.[3672]

With the gift of seership, President Kimball proclaimed that this scripture will be fulfilled. The day of Zion will surely come, and it is our destiny to cause it to happen. Then he asked if these promises do not inspire us to lengthen our stride and quicken our pace to do our part in this marvelous latter-day work. At that point he mourned that many of us are still mired in Babylon, uncommitted and floundering between two divergent philosophies. He said,

> Unfortunately we live in a world that largely rejects the values of Zion. Babylon has not and never will comprehend Zion. . . . Zion can be built up only among those who are the pure in heart, not a people torn by covetousness or greed, but a pure and selfless people. Not a people who are pure in appearance, rather a people who are pure in heart. Zion is to be in the world and not of the world, not dulled by a sense of carnal security, nor paralyzed by materialism. No, Zion is not things of the lower, but of the higher order, things that exalt the mind and sanctify the heart. Zion is "every man seeking the interest of his neighbor, and doing all things with an eye single to the glory of God." (D&C 82:19.) As I understand these matters, Zion can be established only by those who are pure in heart, and who labor for Zion, for "the laborer in Zion shall labor for Zion; for if they labor for money they shall perish." (2 Nephi 26:31).[3673]

Our duty and our opportunity are clear. We need only to commit.

"IT IS HIGH TIME TO ESTABLISH ZION"

In an address given to the Saints on May 2, 1842, Joseph Smith rejoiced in the coming day of Zion, which assumes that some individuals within the Church will have prepared themselves to become the

---

[3672] D&C 58:3–12.
[3673] Kimball, *The Teachings of Spencer W. Kimball*, 362–63.

pure in heart: "The building up of Zion is a cause that has interested the people of God in every age; it is a theme upon which prophets, priests and kings have dwelt with peculiar delight; they have looked forward with joyful anticipation to the day in which we live; and fired with heavenly and joyful anticipations they have sung and written and prophesied of this our day; but they died without the sight; we are the favored people that God has made choice of to bring about the latter-day glory; it is left for us to see, participate in and help to roll forward the latter-day glory."

Continuing, the Prophet announced that three great gatherings will take place in "the dispensation of the fulness of times." First, "the Saints of God will be gathered in one from every nation, and kindred, and people, and tongue." Second, "the Jews will be gathered together into one." And third, "the wicked will also be gathered together to be destroyed." The polarization that will result from these gatherings will be felt by all people: "The Spirit of God will also dwell with His people, and be withdrawn from the rest of the nations."

Joseph taught that the effects of the outpouring of the Spirit of God and the gathering will result in an astounding *oneness* among the people of God, a oneness which is unique to the dispensation of the fulness of times. He said, "[The Lord will draw together] all things whether in heaven or on earth, [and all things] will be in one, even in Christ." Moreover, "the heavenly Priesthood will unite with the earthly, to bring about those great purposes." Being "thus united in one common cause, to roll forth the kingdom of God, the heavenly Priesthood [will not be] idle spectators." Rather, "the Spirit of God will be showered down from above, and it will dwell in our midst. The blessings of the Most High will rest upon our tabernacles, and our name will be handed down to future ages; our children will rise up and call us blessed; and generations yet unborn will dwell with peculiar delight upon the scenes that we have passed through, the privations that we have endured; the untiring zeal that we have manifested; the all but insurmountable difficulties that we have overcome in laying the foundation of a work that brought about the glory and blessing which they will realize." Clearly, we will enjoy the ministering of angels as we go forth in our individual missions and stewardships.

Finally, the Prophet taught that the establishment of Zion is "a work that God and angels have contemplated with delight for generations past; that fired the souls of the ancient patriarchs and prophets; a work that is destined to bring about the destruction of the powers of darkness, the renovation of the earth, the glory of God, and the salvation of the human family."[3674]

To establish Zion, whether in the heart of an individual, a marriage, a family, or in a priesthood community of Saints, President Lorenzo Snow admonished us to cease the destructive practice of competition and the selfish building up of our own kingdoms. We must resolve now, he said, to center our efforts on the building of God's kingdom for the establishment of Zion: "It is high time to establish Zion. Let us try to build up Zion. Zion is the pure in heart. Zion cannot be built up except on the principles of union required by the celestial law. It is high time for us to enter into these things. It is more pleasant and agreeable for the Latter-day Saints to enter into this work and build up Zion, than to build up ourselves and have this great competition which is destroying us." Again, calling for us to prepare for the establishment of Zion today and simultaneously denouncing the competitive practices that prohibit Zion, President Snow said, "What a lovely thing it would be if there was a Zion now, as in the days of Enoch, that there would be peace in our midst and no necessity for a man to contend and tread upon the toes of another to attain a better position, and advance himself ahead of his neighbor! And there should be no unjust competition in matters that belong to the Latter-day Saints. That which creates division among us pertaining to our temporal interests should not be."[3675]

Let us state here that Zion, meaning the ideal of Zion, is the perfection of sanctification. That is our aim and the reason that we submit to the transforming process of being sanctified by the Holy Ghost. If Zion is the pure in heart, then we must become pure—that is to say, unalloyed, unmixed,

---

[3674] Smith, *Teachings of the Prophet Joseph Smith*, 231.
[3675] Snow, *The Teachings of Lorenzo Snow*, 181.

uncontaminated, uncorrupted, unsullied—if we truly desire to qualify for the ultimate blessings of Zion. President Snow ended with this definitive statement: "So long as unrighteous acts are suffered in the Church, it cannot be sanctified, neither can Zion be redeemed."[3676] Our call to become Zion people is a call to act now and begin to embrace the principles of Zion, "or else," the Lord warns, our "faith is vain."[3677]

An editorial written by Bishop Newel K. Whitney and his counselors in the *Messenger and Advocate* sums up the urgency to become Zion people now: "Whatever is glorious. Whatever is desirable—Whatever pertains to salvation, either temporal or spiritual. Our hopes, our expectations, our glory and our reward, all depend on our building up Zion according to the testimony of the prophets. For unless Zion is built: our hopes perish, our expectations fail, our prospects are blasted, our salvation withers, and God will come and smite the whole earth with a curse."[3678]

Priesthood Holders Must Set the Example

Although all members of the Church are called to become Zion people, President Lorenzo Snow pointed to priesthood holders specifically as those who are called to promote the cause of Zion: "We are told that the priesthood is not called to work for money, but to establish Zion."[3679] President Snow further stipulated that priesthood brethren must decide once and for all to embrace the principles of Zion by setting a proper example and living the law of consecration: "I will assure you, my brethren, that you and I will never be selected and called to go to Jackson County until it is evident that we are willing to abide that law [consecration]. It is a perfect law. Had the people in Jackson County observed it, it would have united them together, made them immensely rich, and they could have accomplished all that the Lord desired."[3680]

Elders have the specific responsibility to call people out of Babylon and into Zion by extending Christlike service that exemplifies Zion. By fulfilling their responsibility, Joseph Smith taught, priesthood holders can rid their garments of the blood and sins of this generation: "Every Elder that can, after providing for his family (if he has any) and paying his debts, must go forth and clear his skirts from the blood of this generation. . . . Let every one labor to prepare himself for the vineyard, sparing a little time to comfort the mourners, to bind up the broken-hearted, to reclaim the backslider, to bring back the wanderer, to re-invite into the kingdom such as have been cut off, by encouraging them to lay to while the day lasts, and work righteousness, and, with one heart and one mind, prepare to help to redeem Zion, that goodly land of promise, where the willing and obedient shall be blessed."[3681]

According to our several abilities and standing in our callings, we must all do our part, said the Prophet: "The advancement of the cause of God and the building up of Zion is as much one man's business as another's. The only difference is, that one is called to fulfill one duty, and another another duty; 'but if one member suffers, all the members suffer with it, and if one member is honored all the rest rejoice with it, and the eye cannot say to the ear, I have no need of thee, nor the head to the foot, I have no need of thee;' party feelings, separate interests, exclusive designs should be lost sight of in the one common cause, in the interest of the whole."[3682]

The duty of the priesthood is to gather "the elect of the Lord out of every nation on earth, and [bring] them to the place of the Lord of Hosts, when the city of righteousness shall be built, and

---

[3676] Smith, *History of the Church*, 2:146.
[3677] D&C 104:54–55.
[3678] Whitney, Cahoon, and Knight, *Messenger and Advocate* 3 (Sept. 1837): 563.
[3679] Snow, *The Teachings of Lorenzo Snow*, 181.
[3680] Snow, *The Teachings of Lorenzo Snow*, 183.
[3681] Smith, *History of the Church*, 2:228–29.
[3682] Smith, *Teachings of the Prophet Joseph Smith*, 231.

where the people shall be of one heart and one mind, when the Savior comes: yea, where the people shall walk with God like Enoch, and be free from sin."[3683] According to the Prophet, this work is described in the scriptures as "righteousness and truth sweeping the earth as with a flood."[3684] "And now, I ask, how righteousness and truth are going to sweep the earth as with a flood? I will answer. *Men and angels are to be co-workers in bringing to pass this great work*, and Zion is to be prepared, even a new Jerusalem, for the elect that are to be gathered from the four quarters of the earth, and to be established an holy city, for the tabernacle of the Lord shall be with them."[3685] To accomplish an endeavor that involves heavenly partnering, elders must truly be pure in heart.

A Few Could Form the Foundation of Zion

If we accept the Book of Mormon to be our latter-day guide, we also accept the account in Third Nephi to be our model for the latter-day establishment of Zion. In surveying that account, we are immediately struck by the fact that even a few pure-in-heart people could anchor the principles of Zion to the earth. Mormon makes the point that only 2,500 Nephites made up the initial group of Zion people. According to the Third Nephi model, the small group of the pure-in-heart people act as leaven by setting an example and encouraging others to become pure in heart and join with them under the organizational leadership of the priesthood. We note with interest that within a few years, the entire Nephite population had become pure in heart and was assimilated into Zion.[3686]

Are we willing to be counted among the few who have the courage to embrace the principles of Zion in our lives? Hugh Nibley quoted Brigham Young, who issued the following warning: "If we are not faithful, others will take our place." Zion is our opportunity, but we can lose it through apathy or carelessness. President Young said that though individuals might fail, nevertheless the Church will succeed: "We may fail, if we are not faithful; but God will not fail in accomplishing his work, whether we abide it or not." Obviously, our individual inaction will have little impact on the Lord's global plans for Zion. His purposes will roll forth, and the prophecies and promises concerning Zion will all be fulfilled: "If we do not wake up and cease to long after the things of this earth, we will find that we as individuals will go down to hell, although the Lord will preserve a people unto himself."

Then President Young asked, "Shall we do this in our present condition as a people? No; for we must be pure and holy." Continuing, he said, "If my brethren and sisters do not walk up to the principles of the holy Gospel . . . they will be removed out of their places, and others will be called to occupy them." To the uncommitted, he stated that the unifying principles of Zion can be divisive and troublesome: "Of the great many who have been baptized into this Church, but few have been able to abide the word of the Lord; they have fallen out on the right and on the left . . . and a few have gathered together."

Joseph Smith also lamented about the Saints' lack of commitment to the cause of Zion: "I have tried for a number of years to get the minds of the Saints prepared to receive the things of God; but we frequently see some of them, after suffering all they have for the work of God, will fly to pieces like glass as soon as anything comes that is contrary to their traditions: they cannot stand the fire at all. How many will be able to abide a celestial law, and go through and receive their exaltation, I am unable to say, as many are called, but few are chosen."[3687]

The first latter-day opportunity to build up Zion evaporated with the contentions and jealousies of the early Saints. That will not happen again. Most certainly, the Lord, through his prophet, will call

---

[3683] Smith, *Teachings of the Prophet Joseph Smith*, 93.

[3684] Moses 7:62.

[3685] Smith, *Teachings of the Prophet Joseph Smith*, 84; emphasis added.

[3686] 3 Nephi 17:25; 19:1–5; 4 Nephi 1:2.

[3687] Nibley, "Educating the Saints—a Brigham Young Mosaic," 85; quoting Young, *Journal of Discourses*, 8:144, 183; 18:304; 8:144; 16:26; 11:324; Smith, *Teachings of the Prophet Joseph Smith*, 331.

a "select" few, "who are worthy to be called" to form the foundation of latter-day Zion, and when that happens, Babylon's fate is sealed. Elder McConkie wrote:

> "There has been a day of calling," a day in which all the elders of the kingdom were invited to come forward and build the New Jerusalem, "but the time has come for a day of choosing." The response of his early Latter-day Saints having been inadequate, the Lord will now choose, when he will, those who are to accomplish the great work. "And let those be chosen that are worthy." When the day comes, none but those who qualify by obedience and righteousness will participate in the work. "And it shall be manifest unto my servant"—the President of the Church who then governs the kingdom—"by the voice of the Spirit, those that are chosen; and they shall be sanctified; and inasmuch as they follow the counsel which they receive, they shall have power after many days to accomplish all things pertaining to Zion." (D&C 105:14–37.) After many days, a designated period in which we still live, those who are called, chosen, selected, appointed, and sent forth by the voice of the Spirit, as it speaks to the President of the Church, shall build the New Jerusalem and the holy temple to which the Lord Jesus Christ shall come in power and glory as the great Millennium is ushered in. In the meantime, our work as a people is to keep the commandments and sanctify ourselves so that if the call comes in our day, we shall be worthy to respond.[3688]

If we are waiting to become Zion people when we hear the announcement of the priesthood society of Zion, we will be sorely disappointed. Zion is a condition of the heart. Hence, we no more wait for an announcement to become Zionlike than we wait for an announcement to live the law of consecration. When it comes to living the laws and principles of Zion in our individual lives, nothing waits. We have covenanted and we are expected to strive to become Zion people today.

According to Revelation

Regarding the future priesthood society of Zion, we cannot overemphasize the fact that we must not step in front of the Lord or his authorized servants. Zion is "the highest order of priesthood society";[3689] therefore, Zion must be established under the direction of the priesthood and not by some alternative movement or individual initiative. Joseph Smith taught:

> In regard to the building up of Zion, it has to be done by the counsel of Jehovah, by the revelations of heaven; and we should feel to say, "If the Lord go not with us, carry us not up hence." We would say to the Saints that come here, we have laid the foundation for the gathering of God's people to this place, and they expect that when the Saints do come, they will be under the counsel that God has appointed. The Twelve are set apart to counsel the Saints pertaining to this matter; and we expect that those who come here will send before them their wise men according to revelation; or if not

---

[3688] McConkie, *A New Witness for the Articles of Faith*, 619.
[3689] Kimball, *The Teachings of Spencer W. Kimball*, 125.

practicable, be subject to the counsel that God has given, or they cannot receive an inheritance among the Saints, or be considered as God's people, and they will be dealt with as transgressors of the laws of God. We are trying here to gird up our loins, and purge from our midst the workers of iniquity; and we hope that when our brethren arrive from abroad, they will assist us to roll forth this good work, and to accomplish this great design, that "Zion may be built up in righteousness; and all nations flock to her standard;" that as God's people, under His direction, and obedient to His law, we may grow up in righteousness and truth; that when His purposes shall be accomplished, we may receive an inheritance among those that are sanctified.[3690]

While the priesthood society of Zion can be established only under the direction of the President of the Church, Zion people are most definitely established by their own initiative, facilitated by their priesthood leaders. Zion people, of course, are those who will one day make up the priesthood society of Zion.

We are assured that the Lord, who sees the "end from the beginning,"[3691] has a master plan for the establishment of the priesthood society of Zion. He knows both the timing and how that holy society will be established. Robert Millet wrote:

> As Zion has grown, so has our understanding of Zion. And a part of that understanding is an appreciation for the patient maturity required for the regeneration of a people and the renovation of a society, an awareness that Zion is established "in process of time." (Moses 7:21.) Neither spiritual marathons nor excessive zeal are required; rather, the peaceful plodding that characterizes those who have a "steadfastness in Christ" (2 Nephi 31:20) will result in purity of heart and achievement of the prophetic ideal. "Let our anxiety be centred upon this one thing," President Brigham Young counseled, "the sanctification of our own hearts, the purifying of our own affections, the preparing of ourselves for the approach of the events that are hastening upon us." And then in a manner that has particular relevance to those of us who grow impatient with the Lord's timetable, President Young added: "Be satisfied to let the Lord have his own time and way, and be patient. Seek to have the Spirit of Christ, that we may . . . prepare ourselves for the times that are coming. This is our duty."[3692]

OUR DUTY TO INDIVIDUALLY BECOME ZION

Our preparation for "the upbuilding of an 'holy city' which shall be called Zion" is plainly an individual effort that centers on our attempts to purify our hearts. Joseph Smith said, "All who build thereon [the foundation of Zion] are to worship the true and living God, and all believe in one

---

[3690] Smith, *Teachings of the Prophet Joseph Smith*, 254.
[3691] Abraham 2:8.
[3692] Millet, *Quest for the City of God*, 169–70.

doctrine, even the doctrine of our Lord and Savior Jesus Christ."[3693] To this end, President Lorenzo Snow counseled, "Then let us practice honesty and diligence in our various callings, seeking unity and to cultivate the spirit of brotherhood financially as well as spiritually, that we may be in readiness, upon call, to go forth and build up the center stake of Zion and prepare a house in which to meet the Lord our Savior and Redeemer."[3694] Until the prophetic call to Zion comes, said Joseph Smith, "the Lord wants the wheat and tares to grow together; for Zion must be redeemed with judgment, and her converts with righteousness."[3695]

What, then, must we be about? The Prophet Joseph Smith answered, "We ought to have the building up of Zion as our greatest object."[3696] Repeatedly the Lord has commanded us to "seek to bring forth and establish the cause of Zion."[3697] Therefore, we are to "arise and shine forth, that [our] light may be a standard for the nations." Our safety and the safety of other good-hearted people are at stake. Only in Zion will there be temporal and spiritual protection: "And that the gathering together upon the land of Zion, and upon her stakes, may be for a defense, and for a refuge from the storm, and from wrath when it shall be poured out without mixture upon the whole earth."[3698] Our unique latter-day calling is to prepare the earth for the coming of Christ, the great Millennium, and the vanquishing of Satan.[3699]

How shall we begin to become individual Zion persons? President Kimball offered three steps: "First, we must eliminate the individual tendency to selfishness that snares the soul, shrinks the heart, and darkens the mind. . . . Second, we must cooperate completely and work in harmony one with the other. . . . Third, we must lay on the altar and sacrifice whatever is required by the Lord."[3700] The result of living these steps, he said, is charity. Everything about Zion comes down to love. If we are filled with charity, we will be selfless, cooperative, and willing to sacrifice all that we have and are; we truly will be Zion people. It is interesting to note that Enoch established a city called Zion *after* his people had been denominated *Zion* by the Lord.[3701] The society *of* Zion is comprised of people who have first qualified *as* Zion in their hearts.

Third Nephi—Latter-day Guide to Establishing Zion

The Lord renewed with Noah the same promise that he had made with Enoch, Noah's great-grandfather. That promise concerned the advent of latter-day Zion. The Lord vowed, "When men should keep all my commandments, Zion should again come on the earth."[3702] Understanding the process, Brigham Young said, "[Zion] commences in the heart of each person."[3703] He prefaced this statement by saying, "The length of time required 'to accomplish all things pertaining to Zion' is strictly up to us and how we live."[3704] At another time President Young suggested an intriguing time frame for the establishment of Zion in our lives: " . . . which we might have received in one year."[3705]

[3693] Smith, *Teachings of the Prophet Joseph Smith*, 79.
[3694] Snow, *The Teachings of Lorenzo Snow*, 185.
[3695] Smith, *History of the Church*, 2:228.
[3696] Smith, *Teachings of the Prophet Joseph Smith*, 160.
[3697] D&C 6:6; 11:6; 12:6; 14:6.
[3698] D&C 115:5–6.
[3699] Moses 7:60–65; D&C 43:28–35.
[3700] Kimball, *The Teachings of Spencer W. Kimball*, 364.
[3701] Moses 7:18–19.
[3702] JST Genesis 9:21.
[3703] Young, *Journal of Discourses*, 9:284.
[3704] Young, *Journal of Discourses*, 9:283.
[3705] Young, *Journal of Discourses*, 11:300.

If it were not for the account in Third Nephi, we might discount President Young's preparatory "year" as optimistically short. Nevertheless, as we shall see, the Nephites, who were very much like us, qualified in about a year to become pure in heart so they could see God and achieve Zion. The account in Third Nephi, then, becomes our model for how individuals and a people prepare to become Zion and to enter into the presence of the Lord. But let us first examine the parallels between the Nephites and ourselves as conditions and events lead to the destruction of the wicked and the establishment of Zion.

The book of Third Nephi begins with a spectacular sign of the Savior's birth. This sign served to save the believers from certain death. We are struck with the fact that the Savior was saving his people from the moment of his birth! We read that as the sun set, the sky remained as bright as noonday—a phenomenon that had never occurred. The people responded with a combination of fear and awe that pierced every heart. The prophet Mormon recounted that "*all* the people upon the face of the *whole* earth from the west to the east, both in the land north and the land south, were so exceedingly astonished that they fell to the earth."[3706] This powerful heavenly display was given to the people as a sign of the Savior's coming. Likewise, we are told that the Lord's *second* coming will be announced by celestial manifestations: "The stars shall fall from heaven, and there shall be greater signs in heaven above."[3707]

In the case of the Nephites, the signs fell on many who were weak in faith and could not retain the impact of the miracle in their hearts. Therefore, when Satan sent forth "lyings and deceivings" among the people to harden their hearts,[3708] "the people began to forget those signs and wonders which they had heard, and began to be less and less astonished at a sign or a wonder from heaven, insomuch that they began to be hard in their hearts, and blind in their minds, and began to disbelieve all which they had heard and seen—imagining up some vain thing in their hearts, that it was wrought by men and by the power of the devil, to lead away and deceive the hearts of the people; and thus did Satan get possession of the hearts of the people again, insomuch that he did blind their eyes and lead them away to believe that the doctrine of Christ was a foolish and a vain thing."[3709]

In the last days, we might expect that we will experience a variety of signs that signal the imminent coming of the Lord. We might also expect that as astonishing as these signs might be, they will be widely dismissed. To the wicked or the weak in faith, signs do not carry conversion power; only the Holy Ghost can convert. Rather, signs are designed to warn the wicked and call them to repentance, and to confirm the faith of the righteous, not produce it: "Faith cometh not by signs, but signs follow those that believe."[3710]

We learn from the Nephite account that if people do not respond to the signs and if they persist in their evil ways, they will become vulnerable to Satan's attacks, and soon they will explain away the signs with their own version of the truth. Then, horrifyingly, their wickedness becomes worse than it was before, causing an ever-widening rift between themselves and the righteous. Thus Mormon reported, "And it came to pass that the people began to wax strong in wickedness and abominations; and they did not believe that there should be any more signs or wonders given; and Satan did go about, leading away the hearts of the people, tempting them and causing them that they should do great wickedness in the land."[3711]

[3706] 3 Nephi 1:17; emphasis added.
[3707] D&C 29:14.
[3708] 3 Nephi 1:22.
[3709] 3 Nephi 2:1–2.
[3710] D&C 63:9.
[3711] 3 Nephi 2:3.

We need only review the modern-day response to signs and catastrophic events to note that people initially reach out to God when they are frightened, but after they catch their breath they are quick to return to wickedness, which results in greater evil and further decline.

Although the Nephite prophets made a concerted effort to reclaim the people with "much preaching and prophesying which was sent among them," their effort made little difference. "The people did still remain in wickedness." Then the society began to deteriorate rapidly: "There began to be wars and contentions throughout all the land." We will shortly discuss *contention*, which Jesus says is a major deterrent to the establishment of Zion. Contention can devolve until it spawns secret combinations, such as the ancient terrorists that gained a foothold in the Nephite society. They soon became "so numerous" that they "did slay so many of the people, and did lay waste so many cities, and did spread so much death and carnage throughout the land, that it became expedient that *all* the people . . . should take up arms against them." Interestingly, during this time when the Nephite Babylon was crumbling, missionary work flourished, and the people who were converted "did unite with their brethren." Nevertheless, the people as a whole were threatened with the loss of rights, freedom, and liberty, including the ability to worship God. Soon war erupted in their own land and became "exceedingly sore." Now the entire Nephite people "were threatened with utter destruction."[3712]

It requires little imagination to see the parallels between the Nephite civilization and ours today. From the moment that the signs were given, only nine years elapsed before the Nephites found themselves awash in wickedness and caught in a life-and-death struggle.[3713] Within seventeen years, the Nephites had surrendered their lands to the terrorists and supporters of secret combinations, and finally they were obligated to gather into one body to preserve themselves.[3714] Do we not have similar prophecies of rapid decline, threats to freedoms, external and internal wars, polarization of the righteous and the wicked, and the necessity of gathering for safety? And do we not have prophecies of astounding missionary success in the midst of worldwide chaos?[3715]

When God delivered the embattled Nephites from their enemies, the people repented, and peace and prosperity abounded for about twelve years. Mormon told us straight out: "And now there was nothing in all the land to hinder the people from prospering continually, except they should fall into transgression." But peace was not to last. Once again, contention became the culprit: "There began to be some disputings among the people." Suddenly, we hear "the bells of Hades" tolling. Having now read over four hundred pages in the Book of Mormon, we know what contention and pride can do to crush a people. We should be so versed in the subject at this point that we can predict where the downward cycle of destruction will lead. Any time we encounter statements such as, "some were lifted up unto pride and boastings because of their exceedingly great riches, yea, even unto great persecutions,"[3716] we know that we soon will be reading about yet another war.

Why would Mormon have included these accounts if they were not important? No one in his generation benefitted from reading his book. The Book of Mormon was written only for us. Mormon's task was not to recount history; it was to draw parallels from his history to warn and instruct us. With little doubt, our generation has been more anticipated and prepared for than any other. Ours is the generation that must prepare for the establishment of Zion and the second coming of the Lord. If we overlook the parallels and messages of the Book of Mormon, we dismiss the single most significant book that has power to help us accomplish our mission; it is a book that can save and protect us.

[3712] 3 Nephi 2:10–13.
[3713] 3 Nephi 2:8.
[3714] 3 Nephi 3:22.
[3715] Hinckley, "The Stone Cut Out of the Mountain," 83–86.
[3716] 3 Nephi 6:5, 10.

Let us look at Mormon's deliberately mirroring language. He explained that the Nephite nation, at the time of the first coming of Christ, was much like ours today: "There were many merchants in the land, and also many lawyers, and many officers." Then with a voice of warning, he said that a terrible stratification began to occur, primarily because of affluence and the disparity of educational opportunities: "And the people began to be distinguished by ranks, according to their riches and their chances for learning; yea, some were ignorant because of their poverty, and others did receive great learning because of their riches. Some were lifted up in pride, and others were exceedingly humble; some did return railing for railing, while others would receive railing and persecution and all manner of afflictions, and would not turn and revile again, but were humble and penitent before God." We should pay particular attention to the fact that even the Saints were caught up in this insanity: "And thus there became a great inequality in all the land, insomuch that the church began to be broken up."[3717] Mormon traced this sad state of affairs to wanton and deliberate wickedness:

> Now the cause of this iniquity of the people was this—Satan had great power, unto the stirring up of the people to do all manner of iniquity, and to the puffing them up with pride, tempting them to seek for power, and authority, and riches, and the vain things of the world. And thus Satan did lead away the hearts of the people to do all manner of iniquity; therefore they had enjoyed peace but a few years.
>
> And thus, in the commencement of the thirtieth year—the people having been delivered up for the space of a long time to be carried about by the temptations of the devil whithersoever he desired to carry them, and to do whatsoever iniquity he desired they should—and thus in the commencement of this, the thirtieth year, they were in a state of awful wickedness.
>
> *Now they did not sin ignorantly, for they knew the will of God concerning them, for it had been taught unto them; therefore they did wilfully rebel against God.*[3718]

This last sentence is perhaps the most frightening. The only people who could not sin ignorantly and who would unmistakably know the will of God concerning them would be the members of the Church. Was Mormon sending us a warning?

Continuing, we read that when the Lord increased his efforts to recover the wayward Nephites, *anger*, *contention*'s ugly sister, surfaced: "Now there were many of the people who were exceedingly angry. . . . And they did set at defiance the law and the rights of their country."[3719] Note that a secret combination formed and became so powerful that it was able to infiltrate the inner circles of leadership and finally succeeded in murdering the chief judge and overthrowing the government.

Then the unthinkable happened, something that had never occurred in all the history of the Nephites: they divided into tribes. Mormon wrote: "And the people were divided one against another; and they did separate one from another into tribes, every man according to his family and his kindred and friends; and thus they did destroy the government of the land . . . *and all this iniquity had come upon the people because they did yield themselves unto the power of Satan*. And the regulations of the government were destroyed, because of the secret combination of the friends and kindreds of those who murdered the prophets. *And they did cause a great contention in the land*, insomuch that the more

---

[3717] 3 Nephi 6:11–14.
[3718] 3 Nephi 6:15–18; emphasis added.
[3719] 3 Nephi 6:21, 30.

righteous part of the people had nearly all become wicked; yea, there were but few righteous men among them."

Mormon could not contain his disgust: "And thus six years had not passed away since the more part of the people had turned from their righteousness, like the dog to his vomit, or like the sow to her wallowing in the mire."[3720] Mormon noted that the current prophet, whose name was Nephi, had success in turning some people back to Christ, but the majority remained wicked.[3721]

Reviewing this scene, do we not see a template emerge for the latter days? Knowing what happens next, we are left to wonder how the Lord was able to establish Zion in the midst of such wickedness.

"Which We Might Have Received in One Year"[3722]

We recall that at the crucifixion of Jesus Christ, the wicked Nephites and Lamanites were all destroyed. Such will be the case at the Lord's second coming: the wicked will be destroyed "with the brightness of his coming."[3723] From the darkness and ashes of that cataclysmic event in their time, the surviving Nephites heard the voice of the Lord declaring that they who had been spared were alive only because they had been more righteous. There is little comfort in those words. The Lord told them that they still had a great spiritual distance to travel, and unless they repented and came to him with full purpose of heart, "the places of your dwellings shall become desolate." In other words, they would suffer the same fate as had the wicked. Then the Lord reminded the Nephites of his long-term effort to gather them into the Covenant, but "ye would not."[3724] This scathing rebuke is something that we ought to take to heart. How many times has the Lord tried to gather us to him with the hope that we will learn of and embrace the Covenant, and we would not?

Mormon made the point that the destruction and the three days of darkness happened at the beginning of the Nephite year, "in the thirty and fourth year, *in the first month, on the fourth day of the month.*"[3725] Later, Mormon stated that he was going to leap ahead and pick up his narrative at "the *ending* of the thirty and fourth year"[3726]—nearly *one year* later. At that point, he said that he would give us an account of the coming of the resurrected Lord, who would show his glorified body to a group of Nephites, minister unto them, and bless them with great favors and blessings.[3727]

By carefully following the chronology of events, we discover the astonishing fact that Jesus was able to establish Zion among a people who only one year earlier had been rebuked by the Lord, even though they had been righteous enough to avoid destruction. These were the same people whom the Savior had tried repeatedly to gather without total success. These were the ones whom he had told to repent and come to him with full purpose of heart or else they would suffer the same fate as the wicked. We are left to wonder what miraculous transformation had happened in these people's lives during that pivotal year. What had taken place in twelve months that qualified them for such supernal blessings as coming into the presence of the Lord, having the individual experience of touching the nail marks in his hands and feet, thrusting their hands into the spear wound in his side, and being healed from every infirmity? The scriptures are silent as to what happened during that preparatory year, but Mormon gave us a few hints.

[3720] 3 Nephi 7:2–8; emphasis added.
[3721] 3 Nephi 7:21–26.
[3722] Young, *Journal of Discourses*, 11:300.
[3723] 2 Thessalonians 2:8.
[3724] 3 Nephi 9:13; 10:4–7.
[3725] 3 Nephi 8:4, 23; emphasis added.
[3726] 3 Nephi 10:18.
[3727] 3 Nephi 10:18–19.

The Pure in Heart

In the first place, we suspect that the Nephites took to heart Jesus' admonition to repent—*really repent*—and come to him with full—*not partial*—purpose of heart. Alma described this process as being "born of the spirit."[3728] King Benjamin's people called it the "mighty change" in which they had "no more disposition to do evil, but to do good continually."[3729] In examining various scriptural accounts of those who attempted to describe the transformation that had occurred in their hearts—often within a short period of time—Blaine Yorgason listed ten significant aspects of this mighty change:

> 1. The birth of the Spirit, being born again, most often occurs after we have been stirred up to complete repentance of all our sins, usually through uncomfortable circumstances of some sort. . . .
>
> 2. We must be taught of Christ's Atonement prior to the experience and have a sincere desire to believe in it.
>
> 3. We must show godly sorrow for our sins, manifested as a broken heart and a contrite spirit.
>
> 4. The birth of the spirit occurs only after crying out to God for mercy in mighty prayer, which is exercising faith in Christ unto repentance.
>
> 5. As the experience concludes, we feel our guilt swept away as we receive a remission of sins through the power of the Holy Ghost. This is the baptism of fire, which some in modern times have described as a sensation of warmth that sweeps over their body in a cleansing action that is otherwise indescribable. Others describe it as being filled with an overwhelming feeling of love, which lingers for an indeterminate period of time and is absolutely indescribable. This is certainly a manifestation of Christ's charity or Christ's pure love.
>
> 6. Knowing that our sins have been remitted, we feel complete peace of conscience for all our past sins. This feeling is so wonderful that all sin becomes abhorrent to us, we have no more disposition to do evil, and we resolve to never sin intentionally again. However, this does not mean that we will never sin again—only that we will do everything in our power to avoid sinning intentionally. Nor does it mean that we will forget our sins; it seems that memory is left until the resurrection so that learning will occur. . . . However, with guilt swept away through the Atonement of Christ, the memory is no longer painful, and it will ever after be useful for instruction of self and others. That is why Benjamin said to "remember and perish not" (Mosiah 4:30).
>
> 7. Once the experience is over, we are filled with an amazing heightened sense of love for our fellow beings, which is a further manifestation of charity, or the pure love of Christ. This love will be manifested by long-suffering, kindness, lack of envy, loss of pride, selflessness, being not easily provoked to anger, thinking only good rather than evil, rejoicing not in iniquity but only in the truth, and being perfectly willing to bear all things, believe all things, hope all things, and endure all things (Moroni 7:45).

[3728] Mosiah 27:24.
[3729] Mosiah 5:2.

> 8. Consumed with this love, we are also filled with the burning desire to acquaint all others with what we have discovered concerning Christ and His power to deliver from sin—this that they might enjoy the same peace and happiness we have found.
>
> 9. From this time forward, we will strive for a closer relationship with God and His Son. We will do this through intense study, humble living, constant repentance, earnest keeping of the commandments, and diligent service to those around us. With the light of heaven resting upon us, the course we are to pursue is now lighted plainly. In exactly following this course, we will be manifesting the image of Christ in our countenances.
>
> 10. Through this process, we have received a witness from the Father that Christ's suffering and dying have been gifts of God and that those gifts have wrought an at-one-ment in our lives, making us one with, or bringing us into the family of, the Lord Jesus Christ.[3730]

Another thing that the Nephites must have overcome during their year of preparation was to rid themselves of contention and disputations. When the Savior appeared to them, he said, "And there shall be no disputations among you, *as there have hitherto been*; neither shall there be disputations among you concerning the points of my doctrine, *as there have hitherto been*. For verily, verily I say unto you, he that hath the spirit of contention is not of me, but is of the devil, who is the father of contention, and he stirreth up the hearts of men to contend with anger, one with another. Behold, this is not my doctrine, to stir up the hearts of men with anger, one against another; but this is my doctrine, that such things should be done away."[3731]

Contentions and disputations had always been the common denominators of Nephite decline, apostasy, and war.[3732] Contentions had also brought down the Jaredite civilization,[3733] and later contention had nearly destroyed the Nephites after the birth of Christ.[3734] Jesus seemed to be reminding and warning them about contentions and disputations with the commandment to abandon such behavior once and for all. His teaching against contention was a central theme of the Sermon on the Plain.[3735] Joseph Smith translated a key passage from that sermon to read, "And unto him who smiteth thee on the cheek, offer also the other; *or in other words, it is better to offer the other, than to revile again*. And him who taketh away thy cloak, forbid not to take thy coat also. *For it is better that thou suffer thine enemy to take these things, than to contend with him*. Verily I say unto you, Your heavenly Father who seeth in secret, shall bring that wicked one into judgment."[3736] Evidently contention is so dangerous and so damning that it must be avoided with extraordinary actions and care. Contention is the specific evil that Mormon names as standing between us and the establishment of Zion.[3737]

A cursing is pronounced upon those who contend,[3738] and prophets and great leaders have sought to teach equalizing and unifying principles to help us avoid contention.[3739] King Benjamin

---

[3730] Yorgason, *I Need Thee Every Hour*, 171–74.

[3731] 3 Nephi 11:28–30; emphasis added.

[3732] 1 Nephi 9:4; 12:3; 19:4; 2 Nephi 26:2, 32; 28:4; Omni 1:17; Words of Mormon 1:12; Mosiah 9:13; Alma 2:5; 4:9; 50:25; 51:9; Helaman 16:22; 3 Nephi 2:11.

[3733] Ether 11:7.

[3734] 3 Nephi 2:11.

[3735] "Sermon Given to Different People," *LDS Church News*, Feb. 18, 1995.

[3736] JST Luke 6:29–30.

[3737] 3 Nephi 11:28–30.

[3738] Ether 4:8.

warned, "But, O my people, beware lest there shall arise contentions among you, and ye list to obey the evil spirit. . . . For behold, there is a wo pronounced upon him who listeth to obey that spirit; for if he listeth to obey him, and remaineth and dieth in his sins, the same drinketh damnation to his own soul; for he receiveth for his wages an everlasting punishment, having transgressed the law of God contrary to his own knowledge."[3740] Later, Alma commanded the members of the Church "that there should be no contention one with another, but that . . . their hearts [should be] knit together in unity and in love one towards another."[3741] Looking out across the generations of his children, Nephi sadly prophesied that contention would define his people's history and eventually cause their downfall: "For behold, I say unto you that I have beheld that many generations shall pass away, and there shall be great wars and contentions among my people."[3742]

When the resurrected Jesus appeared to the Nephites, he commanded them never again to contend or dispute with each other. If they would obey this command, he said, they would also to a great degree eliminate envy, strife, tumult, sexual sin, lying, murder, lasciviousness, secret combinations, and economic and social distinctions.[3743] We know that the people obeyed the Lord, because the next time we read about them, we discover that "there was no contention in the land, because of the love of God which did dwell in the hearts of the people. . . . And surely there could not be a happier people among all the people who had been created by the hand of God."[3744] What a difference a year of intense preparation can make!

Perhaps the greatest change the Nephites made during that preparatory year was developing faith—*true and vibrant faith*—in Christ. Moroni indicated as much: "For it was by faith that Christ showed himself unto our fathers, after he had risen from the dead; *and he showed not himself unto them until after they had faith in him.*" Evidently, not everyone was able to immediately achieve the faith necessary to enter into the presence of the Lord. For the time being, the nation would need to rely on the initial 2,500 chosen few to anchor Zion to the earth: "Wherefore, it must needs be that *some* had faith in him, for he showed himself not unto the world." Then Moroni offered us the same privilege if we would strive to develop faith in Christ: "Wherefore, ye may also have hope, and be partakers of the gift, if ye will but have faith." However, this miracle, as with all miracles, will lie forever outside our reach "until after [our] faith. Wherefore," Moroni said of the Nephites, "they first believed in the Son of God." From the days of Adam to the present day, this promise is universal to every Zion seeker: "And there were many whose faith was so exceedingly strong, even before Christ came, who could not be kept from within the veil, but truly saw with their eyes the things which they had beheld with an eye of faith, and they were glad."[3745]

Therefore, we might conjecture that if we would diligently strive to exercise an elevated level of faith in Christ, repent, and come to him with full purpose of heart, and rid our lives of contentions and disputations, we too might qualify in a short period of time, even in as little as one year, as the Nephite record and Brigham Young suggest, for the Lord to come to us and establish us as individual Zion people.

[3739] Mosiah 29:7.
[3740] Mosiah 2:32–33.
[3741] Mosiah 18:21.
[3742] 2 Nephi 26:2.
[3743] 4 Nephi 1:24–25.
[3744] 4 Nephi 1:15–18; emphasis added.
[3745] Ether 12:7, 9, 18–19; emphasis added.

The Pure in Heart *Shall* See God

The account in Third Nephi describes the ultimate reward for the pure in heart. Diligent striving to sanctify ourselves carries the promise that one day we—*all of us*—will return to the presence of the Lord and behold him: "And blessed are *all* the pure in heart, for they *shall* see God."[3746]

Once again, we pause to note that the Book of Mormon was written as a guide for our day. From the outset of his record, Nephi gives us permission to liken the scriptures to our individual lives and circumstances.[3747] If we were not to keep in mind this *likening,* we might peruse the account of the Savior's appearance to the Nephite believers and miss the point that we are reading about a universal experience that will happen to each of us who endeavors to become pure in heart. Therefore, by likening the account in Third Nephi to ourselves, we can extract a list of events and blessings that each of us can expect during our eventual face-to-face encounter with the Lord.

The Father's Testimony

First, we are told that the Father himself introduced his Son and commanded the people that they should hear and obey Jesus: "Behold my Beloved Son, in whom I am well pleased, in whom I have glorified my name—hear ye him."[3748] This is the ultimate testimony of Jesus Christ—and once we receive it we must obey what we hear.

Failure to hear has always characterized the disobedient: "They hear thy words, but they will not do them."[3749] On the other hand, hearing with the intent of acting on that which is said summons great blessings: "Unto you that hear shall more be given."[3750] The Ten Commandments begin with the mandate to hear and obey: "Hear, O Israel: The Lord our God is one Lord."[3751] We must live so as to anticipate and merit the Father's testimony: "If [the Lord] call thee, that thou shalt say, Speak, Lord; for thy servant heareth."[3752] Therefore, to the end that we might warrant the experience of seeing and hearing for ourselves, Jesus instructs, "He that hath ears to hear let him hear."[3753] The greatest message we will ever hear is the Father's testimony of his Son.

The Savior's Testimony

After Jesus appeared to the Nephites, he declared his true identity: "Behold, I am Jesus Christ, whom the prophets testified shall come into the world. And behold, I am the light and the life of the world; and I have drunk out of that bitter cup which the Father hath given me, and have glorified the Father in taking upon me the sins of the world, in the which I have suffered the will of the Father in all things from the beginning."[3754]

Again, we must remember that Jesus' appearance to the Nephites is a model of his appearance to each of us individually. On that private occasion, we might expect the Savior to bear similar testimony to us. A survey of the revelations verifies that Jesus often bears testimony of his identity and mission. For example: "Thus saith the Lord your God, even Jesus Christ, the Great I AM, Alpha and Omega, the beginning and the end, the same which looked upon the wide expanse of eternity, and all the seraphic hosts of heaven, before the world was made; the same which knoweth all things, for all

---

[3746] 3 Nephi 12:8; emphasis added.
[3747] 1 Nephi 19:23.
[3748] 3 Nephi 11:7.
[3749] Ezekiel 33:31.
[3750] Mark 4:24.
[3751] Deuteronomy 6:4.
[3752] 1 Samuel 3:9.
[3753] Mark 4:9.
[3754] 3 Nephi 11:10–11.

things are present before mine eyes; I am the same which spake, and the world was made, and all things came by me."[3755]

The Father's testimony of the Son and the Son's testimony of himself fulfill the law of witnesses.[3756] These two testimonies establish the truth concerning the identity of the Savior and his mission as it pertains to each person who receives these testimonies. But there are other testimonies that are borne either at the moment of visitation or borne previously with the purpose of bringing us to this experience; these are the testimonies of the Holy Ghost and the prophets. Notice the voices of the testifiers (the Holy Ghost who bore witness to the prophets, who then bear witness to us) in the following verses: "And now, after the many testimonies which have been given of him, this is the testimony, last of all, which we give of him: That he lives! For we saw him, even on the right hand of God; and we heard the voice bearing record that he is the Only Begotten of the Father—That by him, and through him, and of him, the worlds are and were created, and the inhabitants thereof are begotten sons and daughters unto God."[3757]

As we shall see, all these testimonies summon from us our own personal declaration of the reality of the Savior.

COMING FORTH TO SEE AND KNOW

We read that the Lord beckoned the Nephites to come to him *one by one* and experience for themselves the reality of the Atonement and the sacrifice that the Savior had made *in each person's behalf*:

> Arise and come forth unto me, that ye may thrust your hands into my side, and also that ye may feel the prints of the nails in my hands and in my feet, that ye may know that I am the God of Israel, and the God of the whole earth, and have been slain for the sins of the world. And it came to pass that the multitude went forth, and thrust their hands into his side, and did feel the prints of the nails in his hands and in his feet; and this they did do, going forth one by one until they had all gone forth, and did see with their eyes and did feel with their hands, and did know of a surety and did bear record, that it was he, of whom it was written by the prophets, that should come.[3758]

That each individual was invited to touch the Savior's wounds reminds us of the Lord's promise that each of us shall have our "hour" with the Lord.[3759] Could there be a greater evidence of the reality of and the price he paid for our individual redemption than to come to the Lord and touch his wounds?

When that happens to us, we are placed in a position to bear testimony with greater surety. This is evidenced by the fact that every Nephite "witnessed for themselves."[3760] Now we add our testimony to that of the Father, the Son, the Holy Ghost, and the prophets.
Rejoicing, Worshipping, and Bearing Testimony

[3755] D&C 38:1–3.
[3756] Deuteronomy 19:15.
[3757] D&C 76:22–24.
[3758] 3 Nephi 11:14–15.
[3759] D&C 88:58.
[3760] 3 Nephi 11:16.

Our testimony is accompanied by worshipping and rejoicing. "With one accord," the people, both as a group and as individuals, rejoiced in their salvation, worshipped the Savior, and testified of him in his presence: "Hosanna! Blessed be the name of the Most High God! And they did fall down at the feet of Jesus, and did worship him."[3761] *Hosanna* means: *Save now!* Or *Save I pray thee.*[3762] This is a fitting exclamation in that it simultaneously recognizes Jesus as the Savior and bears testimony of him.

We remember that others have testified of Christ in his presence. For example, Nathanael, upon first meeting the Lord, declared, "Thou art the Son of God; thou art the King of Israel."[3763] Also, when Jesus calmed the sea and saved his frightened disciples, they cried, "Of a truth thou art the Son of God."[3764] And to the Lord's question, "But whom say ye that I am? . . . Simon Peter answered and said, Thou art the Christ, the Son of the living God."[3765] Hence, we might expect our interaction with the Lord to evoke from us a shout of praise and an expression of testimony.

Receiving an Endowment of Knowledge

When the Lord appeared to the Nephites, he gave them a new revelation or an endowment of knowledge.[3766] We recall that Abraham began his journey into the Lord's presence by desiring "greater knowledge."[3767] When Enoch and Moses stood before the Lord, they were endowed with great knowledge concerning God's creations and their place in them.[3768] Likewise, the brother of Jared, John the Revelator, Nephi, Mormon, Moroni, Joseph Smith, and a host of other righteous people received "greater knowledge" when they stood in the presence of the Lord. In the case of the Nephites, they received the higher law of the gospel. This expanded their vision of the things of eternity and gave them additional tools to continue on and achieve celestial glory.

In our case, the "greater knowledge" we might receive could include anything that is recorded in the visions of the prophets or anything that the Lord deems to tell us during our "hour" with him. We cannot overemphasize that this experience is highly personalized, both in the method and the content of the manifestation. Nevertheless, we might expect this model of similarities to be followed.

Healing

The next gift that the Nephites received was a gift that is very tender, a gift that speaks of the Savior's individual concern for each of us. That gift was the blessing of *healing*. A scan of the scriptures shows that whenever the Savior is among his people, he heals them. Healing is a sign of his divinity and his ability to save us from anything, including death and sin. Healing is also a condition of the ideal of Zion. The Lord promised ancient Israel: "Thou shalt be blessed above all people: there shall not be male or female barren among you, or among your cattle. *And the Lord will take away from thee all sickness.*"[3769] We recall that in addition to overcoming sin and death, the Lord's Atonement involved "suffering pains and afflictions and temptations of every kind; and this that the word might be fulfilled which saith he will take upon him the pains and the sicknesses of his people."[3770] We might conclude, therefore, that unless the Savior had a reason that we should continue with an affliction, our face-to-face interview with him would include the blessing of healing.

[3761] 3 Nephi 11:17.
[3762] *Easton Illustrated Bible Dictionary*, s.v. "Hosanna."
[3763] John 1:49.
[3764] Matthew 14:33.
[3765] Matthew 16:15–16.
[3766] 3 Nephi 12–16.
[3767] Abraham 1:2.
[3768] Moses 1–8.
[3769] Deuteronomy 7:14–15; emphasis added
[3770] Alma 7:11.

We look to the experience of the Nephites as an example:

> And he said unto them: Behold, my bowels are filled with compassion towards you. Have ye any that are sick among you? Bring them hither. Have ye any that are lame, or blind, or halt, or maimed, or leprous, or that are withered, or that are deaf, or that are afflicted in any manner? Bring them hither and I will heal them, for I have compassion upon you; my bowels are filled with mercy. For I perceive that ye desire that I should show unto you what I have done unto your brethren at Jerusalem, for I see that your faith is sufficient that I should heal you.
>
> And it came to pass that when he had thus spoken, all the multitude, with one accord, did go forth with their sick and their afflicted, and their lame, and with their blind, and with their dumb, and with all them that were afflicted in any manner; and he did heal them every one as they were brought forth unto him. And they did all, both they who had been healed and they who were whole, bow down at his feet, and did worship him; and as many as could come for the multitude did kiss his feet, insomuch that they did bathe his feet with their tears.[3771]

THE SAVIOR'S PRAYER FOR US AND OUR PRAYER TO HIM

Another tender blessing that we might expect in our experience with the Lord is to have him pray for us while we are in his presence. Imagine how the Nephites felt when the Savior prayed for them, when they discovered firsthand what actually happens when the Savior pleads our case to the Father and advocates for mercy in our behalf:

> And it came to pass that when they had all been brought, and Jesus stood in the midst, he commanded the multitude that they should kneel down upon the ground. And it came to pass that when they had knelt upon the ground, Jesus groaned within himself, and said: Father, I am troubled because of the wickedness of the people of the house of Israel. And when he had said these words, he himself also knelt upon the earth; and behold he prayed unto the Father, and the things which he prayed cannot be written, and the multitude did bear record who heard him.
>
> And after this manner do they bear record: The eye hath never seen, neither hath the ear heard, before, so great and marvelous things as we saw and heard Jesus speak unto the Father; and no tongue can speak, neither can there be written by any man, neither can the hearts of men conceive so great and marvelous things as we both saw and heard Jesus speak; and no one can conceive of the joy which filled our souls at the time we heard him pray for us unto the Father.[3772]

[3771] 3 Nephi 17:6–10.
[3772] 3 Nephi 17:13–17.

From these verses, we gain a glimpse into what the Savior might ask the Father in our behalf. Undoubtedly, he would be troubled by the wickedness that surrounds us and he would seek to protect us as much as we would be willing to accept.

Notice that when the Savior prayed once again for the Nephite people, he spoke of choosing them out and separating them from the world: "It is because of their belief in me that I have chosen them out of the world."[3773] The word *chosen* reminds us of the chosen few, who are among the many who are called to eternal life. These chosen few are the truly pure in heart, they who are "full of charity towards all men, and to the household of faith." It is to such people that the Lord commanded, "Let virtue garnish thy thoughts unceasingly." They mature spiritually to the point that their "confidence [waxes] strong in the presence of God; and the doctrine of the priesthood distil[s] upon [their] souls as the dews from heaven." These chosen few enjoy the Holy Ghost as their "constant companion." They are promised that their "scepter" shall be "an unchanging scepter of righteousness and truth; and [their] dominion shall be an everlasting dominion, and without compulsory means it shall flow unto [them] forever and ever."[3774]

We might expect that after the Lord defines us as one of the "chosen few," he would send us back into the world, as he sent out his initial Nephite disciples,[3775] to become his emissaries, that is, to invite people out of the world and to bring them to Christ. A result of this gathering is to achieve *oneness* among the pure in heart and the Father and the Son: "Father, I pray thee that thou wilt give the Holy Ghost *unto all them that shall believe in their words*. . . . And now Father, I pray unto thee for them, *and also for all those who shall believe on their words,* that they may believe in me, that I may be in them as thou, Father, art in me, that we may be one."[3776]

Notice that when we are in the presence of the Savior, it is proper to pray to him as he prays for us: "They did pray unto Jesus, calling him their Lord and their God." Then Jesus prayed, "Father, . . . they pray unto me because I am with them."[3777] Standing before the Lord, our prayers intensify, now being guided by the Holy Ghost. Our confidence waxes strong in his presence,[3778] and we are consumed with desire: "Behold, they did still continue, without ceasing, to pray unto him; and they did not multiply many words, for it was given unto them what they should pray, and they were filled with desire." Then came the Lord's blessing: "And it came to pass that Jesus blessed them as they did pray unto him."[3779]

At that point, something remarkable happened: "His countenance did smile upon them."[3780] That is, Jesus was *pleased*. This is an understatement, of course. Human vocabulary fails when we attempt to explain what occurs when we merit divine approval. Somehow, in the way that Heavenly Father is "well pleased"[3781] with his Beloved Son, the Beloved Son is also well pleased with us,[3782] and thus the Lord's countenance "smiles" upon us. We are filled with light, power, and glory: "And the light of his countenance did shine upon them, and behold they were as white as the countenance and also the garments of Jesus; and behold the whiteness thereof did exceed all the whiteness, yea,

---

[3773] 3 Nephi 19:20.
[3774] D&C 121:45–46.
[3775] 3 Nephi 19:2–3.
[3776] 3 Nephi 19:20–21, 23.
[3777] 3 Nephi 19:18, 22.
[3778] D&C 121:45.
[3779] 3 Nephi 19:24–25.
[3780] 3 Nephi 19:25.
[3781] Matthew 3:17; 3 Nephi 11:7.
[3782] D&C 1:30; 38:10; 50:37; 51:3; 61:35; 84:3; 97:3; 124:1, 12.

even there could be nothing upon earth so white as the whiteness thereof."[3783] We become more than we were. We are transformed into the image of his countenance.[3784]

When we stand in the presence of the Lord, we, too, will experience this transformation that the Savior has prayed for in our behalf. What will happen is summed up in two words: (1) *purification*, which indicates that all impurities have been separated from our souls, and (2) *sanctification*, which signifies that our purpose has changed to that of the Savior's. Notice that Jesus prayed, "Father, I thank thee that thou hast purified those whom I have chosen." Then he indicated that their purification had led to their sanctification; their purpose had changed, and now they had become saviors on Mount Zion, who would continue the Savior's work: "Because of their faith, . . . I pray for them, *and also for them who shall believe on their words*, that they [the people of the world] may be purified in me, through faith on their [my disciples'] words, even as they [my disciples] are purified in me."[3785]

It is through this process—divine approval, purification, and sanctification—that we can fully assume the work of God[3786] and become one with him: "Father, I pray . . . for those whom thou hast given me out of the world, because of their faith, that they may be purified in me, that I may be in them as thou, Father, art in me, that we may be one, that I may be glorified in them."[3787]

Elements of the prayer that the Savior would offer for us while we are in his presence would most likely be beyond our ability to comprehend, let alone record: "And tongue cannot speak the words which he prayed, neither can be written by man the words which he prayed. And the multitude did hear and do bear record; and their hearts were open and they did understand in their hearts the words which he prayed. Nevertheless, so great and marvelous were the words which he prayed that they cannot be written, neither can they be uttered by man."[3788]

Encircled about by Angels

We are taught that the pure in heart, who receive and keep the oath and covenant of the priesthood, are entitled to the ministering of angels: "I have given the heavenly hosts and mine angels charge concerning you."[3789] Because every faithful man and woman receives the Melchizedek Priesthood ordinances in the House of the Lord, and because the oath and covenant of the priesthood "is renewed when the recipient enters the order of eternal marriage,"[3790] the ministration of angels is available to each worthy individual. This promise is articulated in section 107 of the Doctrine and Covenants, where we learn that righteousness coupled with the Melchizedek Priesthood and its ordinances qualify both men and women "to hold the keys of all the spiritual blessings of the church—To have the privilege of receiving the mysteries of the kingdom of heaven, to have the heavens opened unto them, to commune with the general assembly and church of the Firstborn, and to enjoy the communion and presence of God the Father, and Jesus the mediator of the new covenant."[3791]

Like the Nephite children, who beheld the Savior's face and who were surrounded and blessed by angels, we too will be encircled about and ministered to by angels, which will likely include our loved ones, friends, and co-workers in the heavenly Church of the Firstborn: "And as they looked to behold they cast their eyes towards heaven, and they saw the heavens open, and they saw angels descending

---

[3783] 3 Nephi 19:25.
[3784] Alma 5:14.
[3785] 3 Nephi 19:28–29.
[3786] Moses 1:39.
[3787] 3 Nephi 19:29.
[3788] 3 Nephi 19:32–24.
[3789] D&C 84:42.
[3790] McConkie, *A New Witness for the Articles of Faith*, 313.
[3791] D&C 107:18–19.

out of heaven as it were in the midst of fire; and they came down and encircled those little ones about, and they were encircled about with fire; and the angels did minister unto them."[3792] Standing in the presence of the Lord, we might also expect to enjoy the ministering of angels and commune with the heavenly hosts.

Partaking of the Lord's Supper in His Presence

Both Jesus' disciples in Jerusalem and in America partook of the sacrament while the Lord was in attendance (and saw him actually administer it).[3793] At some point, in the presence of the Lord, each person who is pure in heart, who strives to lay the foundation of Zion in his life, will be invited to "a supper of the house of the Lord."[3794] This "supper" corresponds with "the marriage of the Lamb," when he will receive his bride: *us!*[3795] On that beautiful occasion, we will "partake of the supper of the Lord, prepared for the great day to come."[3796] As we then literally "internalize"—take into our own bodies—the Atonement, we will understand, perhaps better than we ever have, the significance of the emblems, the personal nature of Christ's sacrifice for us, and why he holds us as dear as a bride is to her husband.

Receiving a Greater Endowment of the Holy Ghost

It is interesting that even though the Nephites were in the presence of the Lord, they longed for the Holy Ghost. Thus we read that they prayed "for that which they most desired"—the Holy Ghost.[3797] Remarkably, of all the things that they might have wanted, the Holy Ghost was preeminent on their list. Once bestowed, that supernal gift unlocked amazing blessings: "The Holy Ghost did fall upon them, and they were filled with the Holy Ghost and with fire. And behold, they were encircled about as if it were by fire; and it came down from heaven, and the multitude did witness it, and did bear record; and angels did come down out of heaven and did minister unto them. And it came to pass that while the angels were ministering unto the disciples, behold, Jesus came and stood in the midst and ministered unto them."[3798]

The command to receive the Holy Ghost is given at the time of baptism and confirmation, but the fulness of this gift is not automatic. The enjoyment of the gift of the Holy Ghost comes to us incrementally by asking and by righteous living. Nephi said that the Holy Ghost "is the gift of God unto all those who diligently seek him."[3799] Thus, we might expect that when we become the pure in heart who see the Lord, we will desire a greater endowment of the Holy Ghost, as did the Nephites, and we will desire that gift so that our knowledge, power, affections, and perfections might approach those of God. The Holy Ghost is the only way to obtain these supernal blessings.[3800]

[3792] 3 Nephi 17:24.
[3793] Matthew 26:26–28; 3 Nephi 18:1–10.
[3794] D&C 58:9.
[3795] Revelation 21:2, 9; Isaiah 62:5.
[3796] D&C 58:7–11.
[3797] 3 Nephi 19:9.
[3798] 3 Nephi 19:13–15.
[3799] 1 Nephi 10:17.
[3800] Moroni 10:5.

THE HUNDREDFOLD LAW

Essential to and indicative of Zion is the principle of abundance. To both the disciples in Jerusalem and the Nephites, the Lord demonstrated this principle of abundance, the *hundredfold law*, by multiplying a small resource so that it fed a multitude.[3801]
In each of our lives, we experience this principle of returned abundance when we pay tithes and offerings or when we give service. When we are in the presence of the Lord, we might expect him to multiply our blessings in proportion to our sacrifices and service, and to compensate us for our sufferings, sorrows, and pain[3802] "an hundredfold."[3803]

REVELATIONS, PROPHECIES, AND EXPLANATIONS

Some of the most remarkable blessings that the Savior gave the Nephites while in his presence were new revelations, doctrines, principles, laws, and prophecies regarding them personally and their children.[3804] These revelations had profound implications. For example, the Sermon at the Temple,[3805] which is the Book of Mormon equivalent of the Sermon on the Mount,[3806] prepared the Nephite faithful to enter the Father's presence by teaching them how they should live to become pure in heart and by revealing the celestial laws that make the Father who he is.

To the Nephites, who were in the Lord's presence, Jesus, the consummate prophet, seer, and revelator, became the perfect teacher. He expounded all things pertaining to the gospel; he paid close attention to detail, so that the people would not misunderstand the new revelations, doctrines, principles, laws, and prophecies: "And now it came to pass that when Jesus had told these things he expounded them unto the multitude; and he did expound all things unto them, both great and small. . . . And now there cannot be written in this book even a hundredth part of the things which Jesus did truly teach unto the people."[3807]

When we stand before Christ, we might expect him to expand our minds, too, with revelations, prophecies, and insights that we have not previously known. This level of teaching, explained by Joseph Smith, often involves the privilege of receiving the Second Comforter:

> Now what is this other Comforter? It is no more nor less than the Lord Jesus Christ Himself; and this is the sum and substance of the whole matter; that when any man obtains this last Comforter, he will have the personage of Jesus Christ to attend him, or appear unto him from time to time, and even He will manifest the Father unto him, and they will take up their abode with him, and the visions of the heavens will be opened unto him, and the Lord will teach him face to face, and he may have a perfect knowledge of the mysteries of the Kingdom of God; and this is the state and place the ancient Saints arrived at when they had such glorious visions—Isaiah, Ezekiel, John upon the Isle of Patmos, St. Paul in the three heavens,

---

[3801] Mark 6:35–44; 8:1–9; 3 Nephi 20:6–9.
[3802] Revelation 21:4.
[3803] Genesis 26:12; 2 Samuel 24:3; Matthew 13:8–23; 19:29; Mark 10:30; Luke 8:8; D&C 98:25; 132:55.
[3804] 3 Nephi 12–16, 18, 20–27.
[3805] 3 Nephi 12–14.
[3806] Matthew 5–7.
[3807] 3 Nephi 26:1, 6.

and all the Saints who held communion with the general assembly and Church of the Firstborn."[3808]

The caveat that the Lord held out to the Nephites was this: if they were willing to receive the "lesser part of the things which [Jesus] taught," they would qualify to receive "greater things." Likewise, Mormon promised the pure in heart of the latter days: "And when they shall have received this, which is expedient that they should have first, to try their faith, and if it shall so be that they shall believe these things then shall the greater things be made manifest unto them."[3809]

Of immediate interest, the "greater things" would include the writings of the brother of Jared—"they reveal all things from the foundation of the world unto the end thereof."[3810] The Lord told Moroni: "There never were greater things made manifest than those which were made manifest unto the brother of Jared. . . . And in that day [the latter days] that they shall exercise faith in me, saith the Lord, even as the brother of Jared did, that they may become sanctified in me, then will I manifest unto them the things which the brother of Jared saw, even to the unfolding unto them all my revelations, saith Jesus Christ, the Son of God, the Father of the heavens and of the earth, and all things that in them are."[3811]

We might speculate that one definition of the "day of faith" that Moroni refers to is the day when we individually stand in the presence of the Lord and partake of his revelations, prophecies, and detailed explanations.

Greater Commandments

Greater commandments accompany greater revelations. We realize the importance of receiving greater commandments when we read that Elder Orson F. Whitney referred to commandments as "sacred patterns,"[3812] or, in other words, what we might call God's revelation of his celestial lifestyle. We recall that one of the crowning blessings of becoming Zion people is to receive "commandments not a few."[3813] In the presence of Christ, the pure in heart seek and receive greater commandments that are calculated to align our lives with that of God and those who live in the celestial kingdom.

As we have learned, Abraham desired to become like God and to receive greater revelations and privileges. Therefore, to that end he sought for the higher commandments, which are associated with the Melchizedek Priesthood and which yield those results. These greater commandments helped to conduct Abraham, a "follower of righteousness," into the Lord's presence.[3814] Likewise, when the Nephites stood in the presence of the Lord, they received greater commandments that had to do with celestial living.[3815] Their account becomes our model.

The Greater Commandment to Pray Always

Of the many commandments that the Lord gave to the Nephites on the occasion of his appearance, we will single out three that directly produce a Zionlike life. The first is the commandment to pray always. Jesus "commanded them that they should not cease to pray in their hearts."[3816]

[3808] Smith, *Teachings of the Prophet Joseph Smith*, 151.
[3809] 3 Nephi 26:8–10.
[3810] 2 Nephi 27:10; see verses 7–11.
[3811] Ether 4:4, 7.
[3812] Whitney, *Saturday Night Thoughts*, 133–34; Whitney, *Gospel Themes*, 115.
[3813] D&C 59:4.
[3814] Abraham 1:2, 15–19.
[3815] See, for example, 3 Nephi 12–14.
[3816] 3 Nephi 20:1.

THE PURE IN HEART

At a minimum, praying always would mean that we should assume a reverent, prayerful attitude while we go about our daily activities. This would include continual communication, worship, awareness, gratitude, accountability to God for our actions, and recognizing our total dependence on the Lord. This prayerful attitude is the engine that drives humility and the purification of the heart; this attitude raises the antenna of revelation and flags opportunities to serve.

Continual prayer forms a shield of protection against the adversary, whose attacks are as persistent as should be our prayers. To the Nephites, Jesus said, "Verily, verily, I say unto you, ye must watch and pray always, lest ye be tempted by the devil, and ye be led away captive by him. . . . Behold, verily, verily, I say unto you, ye must watch and pray always lest ye enter into temptation; for Satan desireth to have you, that he may sift you as wheat. Therefore ye must always pray unto the Father in my name."[3817]

Then Jesus raised the issue of *light* as a reason to pray. As much as he was *the* Light and had set a bright example, so his disciples must become lights themselves, for the purpose of drawing people to the Light by means of their prayers and actions: "Behold I am the light; I have set an example for you. . . . Therefore, hold up your light that it may shine unto the world. Behold I am the light which ye shall hold up—that which ye have seen me do. Behold ye see that I have prayed unto the Father, and ye all have witnessed. And ye see that I have commanded that none of you should go away, but rather have commanded that ye should come unto me, that ye might feel and see; *even so shall ye do unto the world.*" We must personalize and live this commandment; but if we neglect to live it, we will lose the protection of prayer and become vulnerable to the attacks of Satan: "And whosoever breaketh this commandment suffereth himself to be led into temptation."[3818]

Constant prayer helps us to retain *light*. As we know, light[3819] is synonymous with truth,[3820] spirit,[3821] intelligence,[3822] power,[3823] law,[3824] life,[3825] agency,[3826] and glory,[3827] to name a few things. Whereas a celestially resurrected body "shall be filled with light, and there shall be no darkness in [it],"[3828] a telestial body must receive ongoing transfusions of light in order to progress spiritually: That which is of God is light; and that light growth brighter and brighter until the perfect day."[3829]

The Lord has told us how we can infuse light into our systems. A few transfusion methods are participating in scripture study, partaking of the sacrament, being anointed with oil, performing charitable service, participating in temple worship, and, of course, praying. The more our bodies are filled with light, the more we can comprehend all things.[3830] Therefore, we should pray always.

Continual prayer facilitates the creation of Zion people by offering them an avenue of communication with God. But there is more. Continual prayer provides Zion people access to God's protection and power of discernment. Continual prayer gives them a way to infuse light into their beings, thus increasing their capacity to assimilate or enjoy truth, spirit, intelligence, power, celestial

---

[3817] 3 Nephi 18:15, 18–19.
[3818] 3 Nephi 18:16, 24–25; emphasis added.
[3819] D&C 88:7–13.
[3820] 1 John 5:6; D&C 84:45; 88:66.
[3821] D&C 84:45.
[3822] D&C 93:29.
[3823] D&C 88:7–10, 13.
[3824] D&C 88:13.
[3825] John 1:4.
[3826] D&C 93:30–31.
[3827] D&C 93:36.
[3828] D&C 88:67.
[3829] D&C 50:23–24.
[3830] D&C 88:67.

law, spiritual life, and glory, and agency. Once *lighted* through constant prayer, a Zion person is commanded to *light* other people and bring them to *the Light*, even Jesus Christ.

Prayer fulfills the law of asking and receiving.[3831] The simple act of praying is a powerful agent to access God and draw upon his goodness, abilities, and resources. As we have discussed, asking the Father in the name of Jesus Christ for those things that we need is central to the law of consecration. Once we have covenanted to live that law—and indeed are striving to live it—we are forevermore entitled to ask for those things that we need and want from the higher kingdom so that we might build ours. And what is the eternal kingdom that we are striving to build by asking and receiving? *Our families*. Therefore, the Lord instructed, "Pray in your families unto the Father, always in my name, that your wives and your children may be blessed."[3832] Continual prayer is the vehicle to ask and receive, and sincere prayer carries the Lord's absolute promise: "And whatsoever ye shall ask the Father in my name, which is right, believing that ye shall receive, *behold it shall be given unto you*."[3833]

From all indications, it seems that once the Nephites, in their interaction with the resurrected Lord, had experienced the power of prayer, they never returned to offering casual prayers. Surely they recognized prayer's inherent power to make them Zion people, and obviously they employed it. If we wish to become Zion people with the ability to ask for and receive blessings, we must follow this same pattern.

The Greater Commandment to Have All Things in Common

Almost as an aside, Mormon noted that after the Savior's visit, the Nephites experienced a cultural transformation that was as extraordinary as the mighty change that they had experienced in their hearts. Mormon wrote: "And they taught, and did minister one to another; and they had all things common among them, every man dealing justly, one with another."[3834]

It is difficult to overstate the significance of this occurrence. The cultural change that had happened among the converted Nephites was the polar opposite to life as they had known it. Once they had made a covenant to assume this new way of life, they determined to live that new way without external legislation. That is, they managed to live a new way by individual *choice*. Because of the new condition of their hearts, they determined to become stewards who were accountable to God; no longer would they see themselves as owners of the Lord's property. Forevermore, they would labor to build up the Church and their Zion instead of selfishly pursuing individual wealth-building enterprises. They would fully embrace the *Royal Law* of the gospel: "Thou shalt love the Lord thy God with all thy heart, and with all thy soul, and with all thy mind. This is the first and great commandment. And the second is like unto it, Thou shalt love thy neighbour as thyself."[3835] The result of their transformation was that they became *one* and had all things in common.

Their faith in living this new cultural *experiment* paid off with unbelievable and unanticipated blessings. Mormon recorded that contentions and disputations ceased; "and every man did deal justly one with another;" poverty, servitude, and social stratification were eradicated; the people became equal; peace prevailed; and great and marvelous miracles became the norm. Moreover, the people experienced unequalled prosperity. Now unified, they built great cities, and "did wax strong, and did multiply exceedingly fast, and became an exceedingly fair and delightsome people." They married within the Covenant, "and were blessed according to the multitude of the promises which the Lord had made unto them." They became strictly obedient and "did walk after the commandments which they had received from their Lord and their God, continuing in fasting and prayer, and in meeting

---

[3831] John 16:24; 3 Nephi 27:29; D&C 4:7; 49:26; 88:63; 103:31.
[3832] 3 Nephi 18:21.
[3833] 3 Nephi 18:20; emphasis added.
[3834] 3 Nephi 26:19.
[3835] Matthew 22:37–39.

together oft both to pray and to hear the word of the Lord." The love of God dwelt in the hearts of the people. "And there were no envyings, nor strifes, nor tumults, nor whoredoms, nor lyings, nor murders, nor any manner of lasciviousness; and surely there could not be a happier people among all the people who had been created by the hand of God. There were no robbers, nor murderers, neither were there Lamanites, nor any manner of -ites; but they were in one, the children of Christ, and heirs to the kingdom of God. And how blessed were they! For the Lord did bless them in all their doings."[3836]

We might expect that our initial attempts to implement the law of Zion so that commonality could prevail would feel like a temporary cultural shock, causing us to rethink our priorities. But if we can summon courage and push through the learning curve, incredible blessings await us, which will more than compensate for the effort.

THE GREATER COMMANDMENT TO BE "EVEN AS THE LORD IS"

For the commandments to pray always and have all things in common, Jesus is our Exemplar. When he prayed for the Nephites he focused their attention on his example: "Behold ye see that I have prayed unto the Father, and ye have all witnessed."[3837] Jesus is our model of a celestial lifestyle: "I have set an example for you."[3838] Pertaining to the law of consecration, which produces commonality among all people, the Lord said that this law is "even as I am." If we were to choose one word to describe Jesus' relationship with the Father and the relationship to which we must aspire if we hope to become even as he is, that word would be *oneness*: "I say unto you, be one; and if ye are not one ye are not mine."[3839]

If we are commanded to become like him, we might ask ourselves, *What are the Father and the Son like?* Perhaps Joseph Smith offered the best description: "God is the only supreme governor and independent being in whom all fullness and perfection dwell; who is omnipotent, omnipresent, and omniscient; without beginning of days or end of life; and that in him every good gift and every good principle dwell; and that he is the Father of lights; in him the principle of faith dwells independently."[3840] Of course, at this stage of our existence, we can only appreciate these divine traits; for now, these traits are beyond our reach. Therefore, our efforts should be centered on developing these divine traits. As we continue to progress, we rely on the Lord's promise that our journey will lead us to inheriting all that God has and become all that he is.[3841]

As we strive to become even as the Father and the Son are, we remember that we have in common with them our *co-eternalness*; that is, our origin is the same; likewise, because we are literal children of God, our potential destiny can be the same. Our challenge, therefore, is to become co-equal with the Father and the Son,[3842] and that is accomplished by following their example and developing their traits and their level of oneness.

To become like God is to internalize his lifestyle so completely that we will not depart from it. Describing God, Joseph Smith said that he was the same before the creation as he is today: "He changes not, neither is there variableness with him; but that he is the same from everlasting to everlasting, being the same yesterday, to-day, and for ever; and that his course is one eternal round, without variation." For us to become even as the Father and the Son are, we must strive for a consistency of righteousness.

[3836] 4 Nephi 1:3–18.
[3837] 3 Nephi 18:24.
[3838] 3 Nephi 18:16.
[3839] D&C 38:27.
[3840] Smith, *Lectures on Faith*, 2:2.
[3841] D&C 84:35–39; 132:19–24.
[3842] Smith, *Teachings of the Prophet Joseph Smith*, 395.

The Prophet continued to list a set of characteristics and attributes that the Father and the Son possess in perfection. We must develop these traits if we are to become like them. The Prophet began with the characteristics of mercy and graciousness ("indulgent, generous, displaying divine grace and compassion"). Continuing, the Prophet said that God is "slow to anger" and "abundant in goodness." Moreover, "He is a God of truth and cannot lie"; "He is no respecter of persons"; that is, if we work righteousness, he is obliged to accept and bless us, just as he accepted and blessed Adam, Enoch, Noah, Abraham, Joseph Smith, and all who sought his face—and if we do wickedly, he is obliged to send consequences, regardless of our previous favor. Finally, "he is love."[3843]

The Prophet went on to say that God's character is a set of perfect attributes; that is, he possesses the following qualities in totality. These are:

> *Knowledge*—He knows all things past, present, and future.
> *Faith or power*—He is all powerful.
> *Justice*—He is completely fair and equitable.
> *Judgment*—He is perfect in both his reasoning and his rulings.
> *Mercy*—His grace, compassion, long-suffering, pity, clemency, forgiveness, kindness, sympathy, understanding, leniency, and benevolence are infinite and unending.
> *Truth*—Beyond being incapable of lying, he deals with things as they really are; he is accurate, genuine, precise; he is honest, loyal, devoted, and sincere; his integrity is impeccable; he deals with unimpeachable facts and certainties.[3844]

When the Lord commands us to become like him, he expects us to aim for these characteristics and attributes. Our eventual goal is to become like him: that is, celestial governors in our own right; independent beings in whom all fulness and perfection dwell; gods like the supreme God, who is omnipotent, omnipresent, and omniscient, without beginning of days or end of life; beings who possess every good gift and in whom every good principle dwells; celestial fathers and mothers of lights, in whom the principles of faith dwell independently.[3845]

These are samples of greater commandments—to pray always, to have all things in common, and to be even as Jesus Christ is—that have power to help us become the pure in heart and to qualify to stand in the presence of God.

Receiving a Special Gift

Face to face with the Savior, the pure in heart are apparently offered the privilege of asking for or receiving a special, individualized gift—*an endowment* of some kind. Three of the Nephite disciples asked for the gift of being translated,[3846] as did the Apostle John.[3847] Enoch received the promise that the earth would be saved both temporally and spiritually through his great-grandson, Noah, through whose descendants the Savior would be born.[3848] The Lord also promised Enoch that his Zion city would return in the last days to join with the latter-day Zion and become the Lord's eternal abode. The Lord renewed that promise with Noah and established the rainbow as a token of that covenant.[3849] Abraham received the gift of the rights to the gospel and the priesthood through his posterity.

[3843] Smith, *Lectures on Faith*, 3:13–18.
[3844] Smith, *Lectures on Faith*, 4:5–10.
[3845] Smith, *Lectures on Faith*, 2:2.
[3846] 3 Nephi 28:2.
[3847] John 21:21–23; D&C 7:1–8.
[3848] Moses 7:21, 42–47; JST Genesis 9:21.
[3849] Moses 7:62–64.

Likewise, our hoped-for conversation with the Lord, which might precede our receiving a special gift, could resemble the conversation Jesus had with his Nephite disciples *individually*:

> And it came to pass when Jesus had said these words, he spake unto his disciples, *one by one,* saying unto them: What is it that ye desire of me, after that I am gone to the Father?
>
> And they all spake, save it were three, saying: We desire that after we have lived unto the age of man, that our ministry, wherein thou hast called us, may have an end, that we may speedily come unto thee in thy kingdom.
>
> And he said unto them: Blessed are ye because ye desired this thing of me; therefore, after that ye are seventy and two years old ye shall come unto me in my kingdom; and with me ye shall find rest.
>
> And when he had spoken unto them, he turned himself unto the three, and said unto them: What will ye that I should do unto you, when I am gone unto the Father?
>
> And they sorrowed in their hearts, for they durst not speak unto him the thing which they desired.
>
> And he said unto them: Behold, I know your thoughts, and ye have desired the thing which John, my beloved, who was with me in my ministry, before that I was lifted up by the Jews, desired of me. Therefore, more blessed are ye, for ye shall never taste of death; but ye shall live to behold all the doings of the Father unto the children of men, even until all things shall be fulfilled according to the will of the Father, when I shall come in my glory with the powers of heaven.[3850]

Because Jesus Christ, like his Father, is no respecter of persons, we might expect that when we stand in his presence, he will grant us the privilege of asking for and receiving a special gift from him. The endowment that we might receive from him is prefigured in the temple endowment—which is our guide to understanding the steps for such an experience. Propriety does not allow us to discuss these sacred proceedings in detail, but the General Authorities have given us appropriate language to describe these things, and we will not attempt to exceed their descriptions.[3851]

Let it suffice to say that we might expect to receive, like prophets of old, a vision of that which we will eventually inherit; this vision could include a view of the vastness of God's creations.[3852] We might expect to be shown our genesis, that is, our individual creation.[3853] Then we might expect to be shown our unique placement on the earth and the realities of our fallen situation,[3854] or, as Joseph Smith said, "a comprehensive view of our condition and true relation to God."[3855] Now, fully understanding that we are in a telestial state, and desiring to receive from the Lord intelligence to

---

[3850] 3 Nephi 28:1–7.
[3851] See, for example, Talmage, *The House of the Lord*, 99–101; *Encyclopedia of Mormonism*, 454–56; McConkie, *Mormon Doctrine*, 226–28.
[3852] D&C 84:38; Moses 1:27–38; Abraham 3:21.
[3853] Abraham 3:22–23.
[3854] Moses 1:6–10; 4:1–31.
[3855] Smith, *Teachings of the Prophet Joseph Smith*, 237.

transcend this sphere and to return home to celestial glory, we might expect to be tutored in the plan of salvation and our place in it.[3856]

Our temple experience will have prepared us to receive this ultimate endowment when we at last stand in the presence of the Lord. We will have received the essential covenants and ordinances, which will have prepared us to "obtain every needful thing,"[3857] prevented us from being "overcome by . . . evils,"[3858] prepared us for our "missions in the world,"[3859] helped us to seek "the fulness of the Holy Ghost,"[3860] secured for us "the blessings which have been prepared for the Church of the Firstborn,"[3861] and which would have empowered us with "power from on high"[3862] so that we might approach the Lord with greater efficacy.

It is in the temple that we see in clear detail the end-purpose of the priesthood: to come into the presence of the Lord and receive "all that [the] Father hath."[3863] Now we see the various levels of ministry that have prepared us for this consummate event. The ministry of the priesthood is to bring us to the Holy Ghost. The ministry of the Holy Ghost is to mentor, purify, justify, sanctify, and bring us to Christ. The ministry of Christ is to bring us to the Father, who endows us with all that he has. The endowment that we will receive when we at last stand worthily in the presence of God will certainly include the promise of all that the Father has. But, additionally, we might be invited, as were the Jerusalem Twelve and the Nephite Twelve, to request a gift or endowment of a special nature, perhaps a special mission to bring people to Christ. We recall that after such an experience, Enoch, Abraham, Moses, Joseph Smith, and others were sent back into the world by the Lord to perform a significant mission.

Considering these beautiful promises that are foreshadowed by our temple worship experience, we might ask ourselves: Is it worth the effort? Should we not pay the price to become pure in heart so that we might qualify to return to God and see him as he is? Are we willing to work diligently so that we might be transformed in as little as one year, as Brigham Young suggested, to qualify for our hour with the Lord and for an eternity with the Father?

Beautiful Zion

We sing of Zion's beauty in the beloved hymn:

> Zion, Zion, lovely Zion;
> Beautiful Zion;
> Zion, city of our God![3864]

What we could say of Zion, the priesthood society, we could say of Zion, the people: *Zion is beautiful!* Whether Zion is an individual, a marriage, a family, or a priesthood community, Zion is "the perfection of beauty," where "God hath shined."[3865]

An example of irony in the Book of Mormon is the account of Abinadi, who, with his life hanging in the balance, was questioned by King Noah's wicked priests concerning, of all things, the identity of those whom the Lord had called *beautiful,* or those whose beautiful feet bring the gospel message. This, of course, was a satanic trick, an effort to trap and convict him. A similar ploy was later

---

[3856] Moses 5:6–12; Talmage, *The House of the Lord,* 83–84.
[3857] D&C 109:15.
[3858] Smith, *Teachings of the Prophet Joseph Smith,* 259.
[3859] Smith, *Teachings of the Prophet Joseph Smith,* 274.
[3860] D&C 109:15.
[3861] Smith, *Teachings of the Prophet Joseph Smith,* 237.
[3862] D&C 105:11.
[3863] D&C 84:38.
[3864] Gill, "Beautiful Zion, Built Above," *Hymns,* no. 44.
[3865] Psalm 50:2.

attempted by a lawyer, who tempted Jesus with a supposedly unanswerable question: "Which is the great commandment in the law?" Jesus' answer—to love God and to love your neighbor—put to rest the issue once and for all.[3866] In the case of Abinadi, the wicked priests challenged the prophet to interpret Isaiah's scripture: "How beautiful upon the mountains are the feet of him that bringeth good tidings."[3867] The interpretation had been hotly debated for centuries.[3868] Who were the beautiful ones? The so-called scriptural scholars had never agreed; so to pose the question to this supposed madman seemed an easy way to gain a quick indictment. But Abinadi's powerful answer, like the Savior's, silenced his critics. In the end, the wicked accusers on both continents had no evidence to indict their captors, so they executed them for their testimonies. Abinadi testified that "God himself should come down among the children of men,"[3869] and Jesus testified that he was "the Son of God."[3870]

To the question, *Who are the beautiful ones?* Abinadi offered an answer that framed a sermon which converted a future prophet, Alma, set the doctrinal foundation for the Nephite church, and eventually changed a nation.[3871] Abinadi gave his life, in part, for the testimony of the beautiful ones.

That Mormon would place such weight on this incident should signal to us its significance as it pertains to Zion. Consider Mormon's account of Abinadi's experience:

> And it came to pass that one of them said unto him: What meaneth the words which are written, and which have been taught by our fathers, saying:
>
> How beautiful upon the mountains are the feet of him that bringeth good tidings; that publisheth peace; that bringeth good tidings of good; that publisheth salvation; that saith unto Zion, Thy God reigneth;
>
> Thy watchmen shall lift up the voice; with the voice together shall they sing; for they shall see eye to eye when the Lord shall bring again Zion;
>
> Break forth into joy; sing together ye waste places of Jerusalem; for the Lord hath comforted his people, he hath redeemed Jerusalem;
>
> The Lord hath made bare his holy arm in the eyes of all the nations, and all the ends of the earth shall see the salvation of our God?[3872]

Kent P. Jackson explained: "Abinadi did not answer the question immediately, but after his scathing rebuke of the priests for their wickedness, he taught them about the coming of the Savior as the Suffering Servant, reading them Isaiah 53 in its entirety. He interpreted chapter 53 that 'God himself should come down among the children of men' (Mosiah 17:8)—the teaching for which Abinadi would be put to death."[3873] All of the preceding was building like a grand crescendo toward the answer.

[3866] Matthew 22:36–40.
[3867] Isaiah 52:7–10.
[3868] Ludlow, *A Companion to Your Study of the Book of Mormon*, 186.
[3869] Mosiah 17:8.
[3870] John 19:7.
[3871] Mosiah 17–18.
[3872] Mosiah 12:20–24.
[3873] Jackson, *Studies in Scripture*, 4:150.

Suddenly, Abinadi turned the tables and asked the wicked priests the question that Isaiah had once posed, *the question of questions,* the question that each of us must answer as a testimony, the question that helps to define the beautiful ones: "And now I say unto you, who shall declare his generation?"[3874] That is to say, Who is capable of discovering the origin of Jesus? Is he really the Son of God, *generated* by the Father, himself, or was Jesus simply a great teacher and religious leader? Elder Bruce R. McConkie wrote:

> It is a true principle that 'no man can say [or, rather, know—see JST 1 Corinthians 12:3] that Jesus is the Lord, but by the Holy Ghost.' (1 Cor. 12:3.) The testimony of Jesus, which is also the spirit of prophecy, is to know by personal revelation that Jesus Christ is the Son of the living God. In the full and complete sense of the word no one ever knows that Jesus is Lord of all except by personal revelation; and all persons to whom that testimony or revelation comes are then able to declare His generation, to assert from a standpoint of personal knowledge that they know that Mary is his mother and God is his Father. And so, in the final analysis it is the faithful saints, those who have testimonies of the truth and divinity of this great latter-day work, who declare our Lord's generation to the world. Their testimony is that Mary's son is God's Son; that he was conceived and begotten in the normal way; that he took upon himself mortality by the natural birth processes; that he inherited the power of mortality from his mother and the power of immortality from his Father—in consequence of all of which he was able to work out the infinite and eternal Atonement. This is their testimony as to his generation and mission.[3875]

Do we believe in Jesus Christ and who he really is or do we not? Believers are the "beautiful ones," they who keep his commandments, give heed to his prophets, and follow his testator, the Holy Ghost. Beyond being called *beautiful,* such people are called "his seed."

Who, therefore, can declare the reality of Jesus Christ, the mission of Joseph Smith, the truthfulness of the Book of Mormon, the actuality of the restoration of the Church of Jesus Christ, or any other essential doctrine? Only those who receive this knowledge by revelation from the Holy Ghost. Who are they? Abinadi said that Christ's "seed" are they who receive this witness. These are they whom the Savior saw and suffered for, both the righteous whom he saw in the spirit world after the Atonement and the righteous whom he saw and sees from his heavenly vantage point.

Clearly, Jesus saw us and atoned for us. How might we come to know this? By the witness of the Holy Ghost. Then, we, "his seed," having received this witness, become the ones who bear record that Jesus is indeed the Christ, our adopted spiritual Father and personal Savior, and the Redeemer of the entire world.

Building toward the answer concerning the beautiful ones, Abinadi continued, "And who shall be his seed?" Then responding to his own question, he said, "Behold I say unto you, that whosoever has heard the words of the prophets, yea, all the holy prophets who have prophesied concerning the coming of the Lord—I say unto you, that all those who have hearkened unto their words, and believed that the Lord would redeem his people, and have looked forward to that day for a remission of their sins, I say unto you, that these are his seed, or they are the heirs of the kingdom of God. For

---

[3874] Mosiah 15:10; Isaiah 53:8.
[3875] McConkie, *The Promised Messiah,* 472.

these are they whose sins he has borne; these are they for whom he has died, to redeem them from their transgressions. And now, are they not his seed?"[3876]

That is, by obtaining the testimony that Jesus is the Christ, we are numbered among his seed; and if we bear that testimony to others, in one sense we are numbered among the prophets, "for the testimony of Jesus is the spirit of prophecy."[3877] The holy prophets are also numbered among the seed of Christ. In the words of Abinadi: "Are not the prophets, every one that has opened his mouth to prophesy, that has not fallen into transgression, I mean all the holy prophets ever since the world began? I say unto you that they are his seed."

And what do we do as prophets?

Abinadi answered, "And these are they who have published peace, who have brought good tidings of good, who have published salvation; and said unto Zion: Thy God reigneth!"[3878] The seed of Christ—we, who to one degree or another might be among those whom Abinadi called "prophets"—are they who proclaim the peace of the Prince of Peace; we bring to the world the good news of the gospel; we testify of the Author and Plan of Salvation; and we rejoice with all the pure in heart that the God of heaven lives; he works among his children; and he controls the affairs of nations.

And then comes Abinadi's answer to the priests' question: "And O how beautiful upon the mountains were their feet! And again, how beautiful upon the mountains are the feet of those that are still publishing peace! And again, how beautiful upon the mountains are the feet of those who shall hereafter publish peace, yea, from this time henceforth and forever!"[3879] Anyone who qualifies as the seed of Christ and as a prophet by their publishing peace and testifying of Christ—that person is a beautiful one. That person is a true Zion person. We can be those whose feet are beautiful upon the mountains!

Blessings for the Beautiful Ones

What are the blessings for the beautiful ones? President Charles W. Penrose of the First Presidency prophesied:

> And the time will come when the Lord shall have established his Church perfectly upon the earth, and all things move in their proper course, that God will find a place adapted to every person, in which each will have more joy than in any other place and be able to do more good to the community than in any other. . . . Now, my brethren, there are privileges and powers pertaining to these callings [of the priesthood]. . . . The powers of the Aaronic priesthood reach out a great way, for we are told that that priesthood holds the keys of the ministration of angels. . . . But we read that the Melchisedec priesthood contains greater powers than that. It not only holds the keys of the ministration of angels, but of communion with the heavenly Jerusalem, the general assembly and church of the first-born with Jesus Christ the Mediator of the new covenant and God the highest and holiest of all. And the time will come when under this priesthood to those who hold this authority and calling, and have the spirit of it and minister in that spirit and obtain the power thereof,

---

[3876] Mosiah 15:11–12.
[3877] Revelation 19:10.
[3878] Mosiah 15:14.
[3879] Mosiah 15:15–17.

the Lord will unveil his face and they shall gaze upon his glory. That time will come, for there is no word of the Lord revealed but what will come to pass. . . . The time will come when the servants of the living God will purify themselves before him until they will be fit to receive these blessings. When that holy temple is built in Zion, God will take away the veil from the eyes of his servants; and the day is yet to dawn when the sons of Moses and Aaron, having become sanctified to the renewing of their bodies, will administer in that holy house, and the veil will be taken away, and they will gaze upon the glories of that world now unseen, and upon the faces of beings now to them invisible; but it will be when they have purified themselves from the evils of this world, and are really the servants of the living God, and temples of the Holy Ghost.[3880]

President Lorenzo Snow likewise prophesied that in the Lord's time "many of you will be living in Jackson County, and there you will be assisting in building the temple; and if you will not have seen the Lord Jesus at that time you may expect Him very soon, to see Him, to eat and drink with Him, to shake hands with Him and to invite Him to your houses as He was invited when He was here before. I am saying things to you now of which I know something of the truth of them."[3881]

Certainly, Zion and its people are beautiful. Nephi gloried, "And blessed are they who shall seek to bring forth my Zion at that day, for they shall have the gift and the power of the Holy Ghost; and if they endure unto the end they shall be lifted up at the last day, and shall be saved in the everlasting kingdom of the Lamb; and whoso shall publish peace, yea, tidings of great joy, how beautiful upon the mountains shall they be."[3882]

Summary and Conclusion—The Three Pillars of Zion

The new and everlasting covenant is the greatest revelation that God has ever proffered his children. It is the ultimate message of peace and the fulness of the gospel of Jesus Christ, which encompasses all the knowledge, rites, covenants, and ordinances necessary for salvation and exaltation. The Covenant simultaneously cleanses and removes us from the blood and sins of this world and sets us on a course that leads to the presence of God. The Covenant provides the way to become what God is, to know what he knows, to have what he has, and to possess his power, perfections, and attributes of character. By means of the Covenant, our belief gives way to knowledge, "for they shall all know me, from the least of them unto the greatest of them, saith the Lord."[3883]

The Covenant is designed to usher us into the vast celestial kingdom of God and set us and our eternal companions in our personal kingdoms, where we together will become gods in our own right. There, we will be resurrected, immortal, celestial beings, who will inherit "thrones, kingdoms, principalities, and powers, dominions, all heights and depths . . . pass[ing] by the angels, and the gods, which are set there, to [our] exaltation and glory in all things, as hath been sealed upon [our] heads, which glory shall be a fulness and a continuation of the seeds forever and ever."[3884]

The Covenant fastens us to the Father securely, "as a nail in a sure place," as Isaiah said.[3885] That is, the Covenant binds us to God as surely as Christ was bound to the cross—a very sacred

---

[3880] Penrose, *Journal of Discourses*, 21:49–50.
[3881] Snow, *The Teachings of Lorenzo Snow*, 186.
[3882] 1 Nephi 13:37.
[3883] Jeremiah 31:34.
[3884] D&C 132:19.
[3885] Isaiah 22:23.

reference. The tokens of Christ's atoning experience—the marks that Jesus still carries in his body—are tokens that we may receive symbolically in our bodies that bind us to him and make us *one*. This is the purpose of the Covenant: to help us to fully take upon ourselves the name of Jesus Christ and to obtain his presence.

Is the Covenant not the most wonderful of all revelations? We should rejoice in it continually and write its precepts in our hearts! Jeremiah proclaimed, "But this shall be the covenant that I will make with the house of Israel; After those days, saith the Lord, I will put my law in their inward parts, and write it in their hearts; and will be their God, and they shall be my people."[3886]

A few times in history, most notably during the eras of Enoch and the Nephites at the time of Christ, the people sanctified themselves so that their bodies truly became temples.[3887] Having thus prepared themselves, the Lord engraved the Covenant upon the altars of their hearts. Paul described this as "the epistle of Christ ministered by us, written not with ink, but with the Spirit of the living God; not in tablets of stone, but in fleshy tables of the heart."[3888] Thus, Zion people are they who take upon them the Covenant, follow it through to its perfect conclusion, and thus become pure in heart. Upon their hearts the Covenant is inscribed forever. Zion people are they who treasure up in their hearts the testimony of Jesus and the sacred covenants and ordinances that comprise the new and everlasting covenant. Zion people are they who have experienced a mighty change of heart and now have no disposition to do evil.[3889]

The Covenant is a product of the Atonement. By means of the Covenant, Zion people receive a new identity, that is, a new name, even that of *Jesus Christ*. The covenant of baptism, the first of two primary covenants that make up the new and everlasting covenant, gives them this new name in the first instance, and the accompanying ordinance of confirmation legalizes their adoption into the Lord's family. Now, with Christ as their father, they have familial rights, including the right to have access to the Father, so that they might gain intelligence from him and progress to become like him.

Through the Covenant, Zion people have access to the Atonement and receive a remission of their sins, a remission that is so comprehensive that the Father and the Son "remember [our sins] no more."[3890] That is, without violating their ability to know everything, they choose to file away the recollection of our sins in a nether region of their minds so that the events are as though they never happened and therefore have no power to carry a memory. The Atonement makes this possible. Thus, by the Covenant that emerges from the Atonement, Zion people can grow from life's experiences without being condemned by them.

The Covenant provides us with the gift of the Holy Ghost, entitling us, through worthy living, to the constant companionship of this member of the Godhead. The Holy Ghost is essential to our obtaining all the benefits of the Covenant and is charged with leading us through all the steps that guide us back to God. The benefits are enormous. The Holy Ghost "witnesses of the Father and the Son."[3891] He reveals and "teaches the truth of all things."[3892] He "will show [us] all things what [we] should do."[3893] He helps us remember all things that Christ has taught.[3894] He blesses us with special and otherwise unattainable spiritual gifts.[3895] As the Comforter, the Holy Ghost blesses us with divine

---

[3886] Jeremiah 31:33.
[3887] 1 Corinthians 6:19.
[3888] 2 Corinthians 3:3.
[3889] Mosiah 5:2.
[3890] D&C 58:42.
[3891] 2 Nephi 31:18.
[3892] Moroni 10:5.
[3893] 2 Nephi 32:1–5.
[3894] John 14:26.
[3895] D&C 46:9–11.

peace, which calms our troubled hearts and displaces fear.[3896] He fills us "with hope and perfect love"[3897] and will "teach [us] the peaceable things of the kingdom."[3898] He helps us discern good from evil.[3899] He is the Sanctifier and Purifier who purges us of all sin so that we might be fit for exaltation in the celestial kingdom.[3900] In his unique calling, he baptizes us "with fire"[3901] to burn out paralyzing impurities. He is the Holy Spirit of Promise, who confirms and ratifies our sacred covenants and ordinances.[3902] Without the Holy Ghost, the new and everlasting covenant could not be entered into, followed, verified, or ratified. There could be no justification for righteous deeds redounding to eternal blessings.

One brief statement located in the "Law of the Church" delineates how Zion can be established in the life of an individual, a marriage, a family, or a group of those who would become pure in heart: "And ye shall hereafter receive church covenants, such as shall be sufficient to establish you, both here and in the New Jerusalem."[3903] The references in the footnotes to Doctrine and Covenants 42:67 lead to: (1) *The New and Everlasting Covenant*,[3904] (2) *The Oath and Covenant of the Priesthood*,[3905] and (3) *The Law of Consecration*.[3906] These three covenants—*The Three Pillars of Zion*—are sufficient to establish us as Zion people! We have everything that is necessary to become Zion people. We only need to understand what we have been given and live up to our privileges.[3907]

The New and Everlasting Covenant is the key to our becoming Zion people. As we have noted, the Covenant is comprised of two primary covenants. The first is the covenant of baptism, which sets us on the path to becoming Zionlike and thus to eternal life. The second covenant is the oath and covenant of the priesthood, which leads us to the other priesthood covenants and their associated ordinances, which are received in the temple. Combined, these covenants and ordinances cleanse, purify, sanctify, protect, endow us with "power from on high,"[3908] and set us in our eternal kingdoms.

The Melchizedek Priesthood is received by ordination with an oath and a covenant. Thereby the Lord puts upon us his name[3909] or authority. When this takes place, worthy men can act in the name of Jesus Christ and Jesus Christ will confirm their actions as if they themselves were the Lord. For the priesthood covenant to become valid, we must magnify our calling, receive the Father, and live by every word that proceeds from the mouth of God. Although magnifying one's *calling* could have a variety of meanings, the ultimate meaning of "calling" is the call to eternal life. When we magnify *that* calling, we will achieve the calling's greatest blessings, and we will finally come into total compliance with that covenantal calling and fully "receive" the Father and "all that the Father hath."[3910] Beyond all other priesthood callings that we must magnify, the call to eternal life should be preeminent.

The Oath and Covenant of the Priesthood is the covenant that draws Zion people—both men and women—to the temple, where their priesthood experience continues. There they are ceremonially

---

[3896] John 14:26–27.
[3897] Moroni 8:26.
[3898] D&C 36:2.
[3899] Moroni 7:13–16.
[3900] Mosiah 5:1–6; 3 Nephi 27:20; Moses 6:64–68.
[3901] D&C 33:11.
[3902] D&C 132:7, 18–19, 26.
[3903] D&C 42:67.
[3904] D&C 132:4–7.
[3905] D&C 84:39.
[3906] D&C 82:11–15.
[3907] Young, *Discourses of Brigham Young*, 32.
[3908] D&C 38:32, 38; 95:8; 105:11.
[3909] Abraham 1:18.
[3910] D&C 84:33–44.

washed and anointed,[3911] and sanctified—or set apart—for a holy purpose. That purpose is to become "kings and queens, priests and priestesses"[3912] to God forever. In what is obviously a coronation event, we are endowed with *keys* that give us access to the knowledge and power of God. It is in the temple, said President Hinckley, that we learn "the answers of eternity"; we also learn "the eternal principles to be used in solving life's dilemmas, [that] mark the way to become more Christlike and progressively qualify to live with God. There [in the temple], the laws of the new and everlasting covenant are taught—laws of obedience, sacrifice, order, love, chastity, and consecration. In the temple, one learns the sacred roles of men and women in the eternal plan of God the Father and toward each other."[3913]

The Law of Consecration, given and received in the temple, grows out of the priesthood covenant. We learn that all preceding covenants lead us to the law of consecration. This covenant is the "law of the celestial kingdom,"[3914] the law that makes the Lord as he is.[3915] Now, having been introduced to this foundational law of the celestial kingdom—the kingdom we are to inherit—having been taught and empowered to have access to God, having been justified to approach him, and having heard his voice, received his gift, and been invited into his presence, we lack but one thing to fully receive the Father and become all that he is, to inherit all that he has, and to truly become Zion people. Now we must enter into his *order*—we must marry for eternity.

The New and Everlasting Covenant of Marriage[3916] is the culminating covenant of the new and everlasting covenant and the end purpose of the oath and covenant of the priesthood. This crowning covenant sets husbands and wives in the patriarchal order of the priesthood,[3917] that is, the order of the gods into whose patriarchal chain we are to be welded.[3918] Like the covenant of baptism, the covenant of marriage is called the covenant of exaltation.[3919] Only by entering into this covenant and worthily abiding in it can husbands and wives achieve the highest degree of the celestial kingdom.[3920] Having done so, we are now ready to become like God and live his life—*eternal life*.[3921]

Our eternal kingdoms begin at a most sacred place in the temple: an altar. There, husbands and wives kneel at that which is symbolically the throne of God.[3922] Before God, angels, and witnesses, we enter into the new and everlasting covenant of marriage, whereby we make eternal covenants with each other and with the Father. Then he who represents God seals us together for time and eternity. He seals upon us the blessings of a glorious resurrection filled with infinite power—God's power—and the possibility of endless posterity.[3923] He seals upon us—both the man and the woman[3924]—the promise contained in the oath and covenant of the priesthood: "all that [the] Father hath."[3925] This promise includes the blessings mentioned in Doctrine and Covenants 132:19: "thrones, kingdoms, principalities, powers, dominions, [and] exaltation." He further blesses us with "the promises made to

---

[3911] D&C 124:39.
[3912] McConkie, *Mormon Doctrine*, 424.
[3913] *Encyclopedia of Mormonism*, 1449; quoting Hinckley, "Why These Temples?" 37.
[3914] D&C 105:4–5.
[3915] D&C 38:27.
[3916] D&C 131:2.
[3917] Smith, *History of the Church*, 5:554–55; McConkie, *A New Witness for the Articles of Faith*, 312.
[3918] D&C 128:18.
[3919] Smith, *Doctrines of Salvation*, 2:58; McConkie, *Mormon Doctrine*, 13.
[3920] D&C 131:1–2.
[3921] D&C 132:34.
[3922] Clarke, *Clarke's Commentary on the Bible*, 1:133.
[3923] D&C 132:19–20.
[3924] McConkie, *A New Witness for the Articles of Faith*, 313.
[3925] D&C 84:38.

the fathers,"[3926] even the fulness of the new and everlasting covenant as given to our progenitors, Abraham, Isaac, and Jacob.[3927]

By faithfully abiding in the new and everlasting covenant and living true to all of our covenants, the kingdom that we establish here on earth will become part of God's vast Kingdom, which functions and progresses upon the principles of the law of consecration. Therefore, these three covenants or *pillars*—the New and Everlasting Covenant, the Oath and Covenant of the Priesthood, and the Law of Consecration—are sufficient to establish us now and in eternity as Zion people who qualify to live in a Zion condition. These three pillars are sufficient to instruct and empower us so that we might live with God, obtain his power, know what he knows, do what he does, inherit all that he has, and become like him.

Zion, then, should be the ultimate aim of human existence. Zion is our origin and our destiny. Before we entered this existence, we lived in Zion, and there we were prepared to establish it again, first in our hearts, and second among others who were also pure in heart. Lorenzo Snow said, "Establish the principles of Zion in your hearts, and then you will be worthy to receive Zion outside."[3928]

Will we do it? Will we live up to our latter-day calling and privileges?

Joseph Smith taught, "We ought to have the building up of Zion as our greatest object."[3929] Then, exhorting us to take courage, the Prophet reminded us that the prize is worth the price: "Let us realize that we are not to live to ourselves, but to God; by so doing the greatest blessings will rest upon us both in time and in eternity."[3930]

Should his words not fan the fire of the Covenant in our souls? Consider the following account from Church history:

> By September 1846, most of the Saints had crossed Iowa at a terrible price and were preparing to winter at Winter Quarters. (Before that winter was over, about six hundred died at Winter Quarters.) On September 25, Brigham Young received word of the Battle of Nauvoo from a group who had just come from Nauvoo. The last ones still in the city were the poor, the widowed, and the orphans who had not been able to find a way to leave. Mobs finally came in and drove them out, picking up the men and throwing them in the river, driving the women and children with bayonets, threatening to kill them if they crossed back over the river. When Brigham Young received word of that, even though the rest of the Saints were in the most destitute and terrible of conditions themselves, he gathered the brethren and said: "The poor brethren and sisters, widows and orphans, sick and destitute, are now lying on the west bank of the Mississippi, waiting for teams and wagons and means to remove them. Now is the time for labor. *Let the fire of the covenant, which you made in the house of the Lord, burn in your hearts like flame unquenchable.*"[3931]

[3926] D&C 2:2.
[3927] D&C 132:1–14, 19–24.
[3928] Snow, *The Teachings of Lorenzo Snow*, 181.
[3929] Smith, *Teachings of the Prophet Joseph Smith*, 160.
[3930] Smith, *Teachings of the Prophet Joseph Smith*, 179.
[3931] Anderson, Dalton, and Green, *Every Good Thing*, 275–76; emphasis added.

Commenting on this incident, Susan Easton Black and William G. Hartley wrote: "Brigham Young didn't talk to them [just] about the suffering of those poor people. He called to their minds the covenants they had made with God in the house of the Lord. He went on: '[I want every man who is able to] rise up with his teams and go straightway. . . . This is a day of action and not of argument.' Before too many days had passed, almost a hundred wagons were moving east to go and rescue the poor. I love that phrase, 'the fire of the covenant,' because that is what drove these people. That is why they did what they did."[3932]

May we feel the fire of the Covenant in our souls. May we rise to our destiny and establish Zion in our lives upon the three pillars that stand on the foundation of the Atonement of Jesus Christ. "This is Zion: THE PURE IN HEART."[3933] There could be no greater cause in time or eternity.

[3932] Young, *Journal History*, Sept. 28, 1846, as cited in Black and Hartley, *The Iowa Mormon Trail*, 163.
[3933] D&C 97:21.

BIBLIOGRAPHY

The Three Pillars of Zion

American Heritage Dictionary. Boston, MA: Houghton Mifflin, 2000.

Anderson, Dawn Hall, Green, Susette Fletcher and Dalton, Dlora Hall, eds. *Clothed with Charity: Talks from the 1996 Women's Conference.* Salt Lake City, UT: Deseret Book, 1997.

Asay, Carlos E. "The Oath and Covenant of the Priesthood." Salt Lake City, UT: *Ensign*, November 1985.

—*Family Pecan Trees: Planting a Legacy of Faith at Home.* Salt Lake City, UT: Deseret Book, 1992.

—*The Seven M's of Missionary Service: Proclaiming the Gospel as a Member or Full-time Missionary.* Salt Lake City, UT: Bookcraft, 1996.

Ashton, Marvin J. "Be a Quality Person." Salt Lake City, UT: *Ensign*, February 1993.

—"Love Takes Time." Salt Lake City, UT: *Ensign*, November 1975.

Bednar, David A. "Pray Always." Salt Lake City, UT: *Ensign*, November 2008.

Benson, Ezra Taft. "A Vision and a Hope for the Youth of Zion," *Devotional Speeches of the Year.* Provo, UT: Brigham Young University Press, 1978.

—*A Witness and a Warning: A Modern-Day Prophet Testifies of the Book of Mormon.* Salt Lake City, UT: Deseret Book, 1988.

—"Beware of Pride," Salt Lake City, UT: *Ensign*, May 1989.

—*Devotional Speeches of the Year.* Provo, UT: Brigham Young University Press, 1978.

—*God, Family, Country: Our Three Great Loyalties.* Salt Lake City, UT: Deseret Book, 1975.

—"In His Steps," Salt Lake City, UT: *Ensign*, September 1988.

—"Jesus Christ—Gifts and Expectations." Salt Lake City, UT: *New Era*, May 1975.

—*The Teachings of Ezra Taft Benson.* Salt Lake City, UT: Deseret Book, 1988.

—"What I Hope You Will Teach Your Children about the Temple," Salt Lake City, UT: *Ensign*, August 1985.

Bible Dictionary. Salt Lake City, UT: The Church of Jesus Christ of Latter-day Saints, 1989.

Black, Susan Easton, et al. *Doctrines for Exaltation: The 1989 Sperry Symposium on the Doctrine and Covenants.* Salt Lake City, UT: Deseret Book, 1989.

—*The Iowa Mormon Trail: Legacy of Faith and Courage.* Orem, UT: Helix Publishing, 1997.

Bowen, Albert E. *The Church Welfare Plan.* Salt Lake City, UT: The Church of Jesus Christ of Latter-day Saints, 1946.

Brown, Hugh B. *Continuing the Quest.* Salt Lake City, UT: Bookcraft, 1961.

Brown, Matthew B. *Prophecies. The Gate of Heaven.* American Fork, UT: Covenant Communications, 1999.

—*Signs of the Times, Second Coming, Millenium.* American Fork, UT: Covenant communications, 2006.

Brewster, Hoyt W. Jr. *Doctrine and Covenants Encyclopedia.* Salt Lake City, UT: Bookcraft, 1988.

Budge, Ernest A. Wallis. *Coptic Martyrdoms Discourse on Abbaton.* London: British Museum, 1914.

Burton, Alma P. ed., *Discourses of the Prophet Joseph Smith.* Salt Lake City, UT: Deseret Book, 1956.

Cannon, Donald Q. *Teachings of the Latter-day Prophets.* Salt Lake City, UT: Bookcraft, 1998.

Cannon, Elaine. "Agency and Accountability." Salt Lake City, *Ensign*, November 1983.

Cannon, George Q. "Beware Lest Ye Fall." Discourse delivered at the Morgan Stake Conference, Sunday, February 16, 1896.

—*Gospel Truth: Discourses and Writings of President George Q. Cannon.* Salt Lake City, UT: Deseret Book, 1974.

Cannon, Joseph A. *Mormon Times.* Salt Lake City, UT: *Deseret News*, June 12, 2008

Clark, E. Douglas. *The Blessings of Abraham—Becoming a Zion People*. American Fork, UT: Covenant Communications, 2005.

Clark, J. Reuben. *Church Welfare Plan: A Discussion*. Salt Lake, City, UT General Church Welfare Committee, 1939.

Clark, James R. comp. *Messages of the First Presidency of The Church of Jesus Christ of Latter-day Saints*. Salt Lake City: Bookcraft, 1965-75.

Clarke, Adam. *Clarke's Commentary on the Bible*. Baker Book House: Grand Rapids, MI, 1967.

Clarke, J. Richard "Successful Welfare Stewardship." Salt Lake City, UT: *Ensign*, November 1978.

Conference Report. Salt Lake City, UT: The Church of Jesus Christ of Latter-day Saints, 1897-2009.

Cook, Lyndon. *Joseph Smith and the Law of Consecration*. Provo, UT: Keepsake Books, 1991.

Cowley, Matthew. *Matthew Cowley speaks: Discourses of Elder Matthew Cowley of the Quorum of the Twelve of the Church of Jesus Christ of Latter-day Saints*. Salt Lake City, UT: Deseret Book Company, 1954.

Dalrymple, G. Brent. *The Age of the Earth*. Stanford, CA: Stanford University Press, 1991.

Dellenbach, Robert K. "Hour of Conversion." Salt Lake City, UT: *New Era*, June 2002.

DeMille, Cecil B. *BYU Speeches of the Year*. Provo, UT: Brigham Young University Press, May 1957.

Draper, Richard D. ed., Lund, Gerald N. "Old Testament Types and Symbols," *A Witness of Jesus Christ: The 1989 Sperry Symposium on the Old Testament*. Salt Lake City, UT: Deseret Book, 1990.

Durham, G. Homer, ed. *The Gospel Kingdom: Selections from the Writings and Discourses of John Taylor, Third President of The Church of Jesus Christ of Latter-day Saints*. Salt Lake City, UT: Bookcraft, 1943.

—*Gospel Ideals: Selections from the Discourses of David O. McKay*. Salt Lake City, UT: Improvement Era, 1953.

Cook, Gene R. "Home and Family: A Divine Eternal Pattern." Salt Lake City, UT: *Ensign*, May 1984.

— "The Seat Next to You." Salt Lake City, UT: *New Era*, October 1983.

Dibble, Philo. "Recollections of the Prophet Joseph Smith." Salt Lake City, UT: *Juvenile Instructor*, June 1892.

Duffin, James G. "A Character Test." Salt Lake City, UT: *Improvement Era*, February 1911.

Easton, M.G. *Illustrated Bible Dictionary*. Nashville: TN: Thomas Nelson, 1897.

Editors Table, "The Bondage of Sin." Salt Lake City, UT: *Improvement Era*, February 1923.

Ehat, Andrew F. and Cook, Lyndon W. *The Words of Joseph Smith: The Contemporary Accounts of the Nauvoo Discourses of the Prophet Joseph*. Provo, UT: Religious Studies Center Brigham Young University, 1980.

Encarta World English Dictionary. New York, NY: St. Martins Press, 1999.

Eyring, Henry B. "Faith and the Oath and Covenant of the Priesthood." Salt Lake City, UT: *Ensign*, May 2008.

Farley, S. Brent. "The Oath and Covenant of the Priesthood." *Sperry Symposium on the Doctrine and Covenants*. Salt Lake City: Deseret Book, 1989.

First Presidency, "What is the Doctrine of the Priesthood?" Salt Lake City, UT: *Improvement Era*, February 1961.

Faust, James E. "A Royal Priesthood." Salt Lake City, UT: *Ensign*, May 2006.

—*In the Strength of the Lord: The Life and Teachings of James E. Faust*. Salt Lake City, UT: Deseret Book, 1999.

—"He Healeth the Broken Heart." Salt Lake City, UT: *Ensign* July 2005.

—"Standing in Holy Places." Salt Lake City, UT: *Ensign*, May 2005.

—"The Devil's Throat." Salt Lake City, UT: *Ensign*, May 2003.

—"The Gift of the Holy Ghost—A Sure Compass." Salt Lake City, UT: *Ensign*, April 1996.

—"The Shield of Faith." Salt Lake City, UT: *Ensign*, May 2000.

"Galaxy Map." Washington D.C.: The National Geographic Society, June 1983.

Galbraith, David B., Ogden, D. Kelly, and Skinner, Andrew C. *Jerusalem—The Eternal City*. Salt Lake City, UT: Deseret Book, 1996.

Gardner, R. Quinn. "Becoming a Zion Society." Salt Lake City, UT: *Ensign*, February 1979.

—"I Have a Question." Salt Lake City, UT: *Ensign*, March 1978.

Gibbons, Ted L. *Be Not Afraid*, Springville, UT: Cedar Fort, Inc., 2009.

Goddard, Wallace H. "Blessed by Angels." . Fairfax, VA: *MeridianMagazine.com*, July 27, 2009.

—*Drawing Heaven into Your Marriage*. Fairfax, VA: Meridian Publishing, 2007.

Grant, Heber J. *Teachings of Presidents of the Church.* Salt Lake City, UT: The Church of Jesus Christ of Latter-day Saints, 2002.

Guralnik, David B. ed. *Webster's New World Dictionary, 2nd College Edition.* New York City, NY: The New World Publishing Company, 1970.

First Presidency, "What is the Doctrine of the Priesthood?" Salt Lake City, UT: *Improvement Era*, February 1961.

Hafen, Bruce C. *The Broken Heart: Applying the Atonement to Life's Experiences.* Salt Lake City, UT: Deseret Book, 1989.

Haight, David B. "The Sacrament and the Sacrifice." Salt Lake City, UT: *Ensign*, November 1989.

Hamilton, Edith. *Spokesman for God.* New York, NY: Norton and Company, 1977.

Hinckley, Gordon B. "Blessed Are the Merciful." Salt Lake City, UT: *Ensign*, May 1990.

—*Faith: The Essence of True Religion.* Salt Lake City, UT: Deseret Book, 1989.

—"Our Mission of Saving." Salt Lake City, UT: *Ensign*, November 1991.

—"Priesthood: The Power of Godliness." Salt Lake City, UT: *Improvement Era*, December 1970.

—*Stand a Little Taller.* Salt Lake City, UT: Eagle Gate, 2000.

—*Standing for Something.* New York, NY: Three Rivers Press, 2000.

—*Teachings of Gordon B. Hinckley.* Salt Lake City, UT: Deseret Book, 2002.

—"The Dawning of a Brighter Day." Salt Lake City, UT: *Ensign*, May 2004.

—"The Stone Cut Out of the Mountain." Salt Lake City, UT: *Ensign*, 2007.

—"Till We Meet Again." Salt Lake City, UT: *Ensign*, November 2001.

—"We Thank Thee for This Sacred Structure." Salt Lake City, UT: *Church News*, 8 November 1997.

— "Your Greatest Challenge, Mother." Salt Lake City, UT: *Ensign*, November 2000.

Holland, Jeffrey R. "Broken Things to Mend." Salt Lake City, UT: *Ensign*, May 2006.

—"However Long and Hard the Road." Salt Lake City, UT: *Ensign*, September 2002.

—*On Earth As It Is In Heaven.* Salt Lake City, UT: Deseret Book, 1989.

Holzapfel, Richard Neitzel and Wayment, Thomas A., eds. *The Life and Teachings of Jesus Christ: From the Transfiguration through the Triumphant Entry.* Salt Lake City, UT: Deseret Book, 2006.

Horton, George A. "Abraham's Act of Faith Reflects 'a Soul Like Unto Our Savior." Salt Lake City, UT: *LDS Church News*, April 2, 1994.

"'Hymn of the Pearl': an Ancient Counterpart To 'O My Father.'" Provo, UT: BYU Studies, vol. 36, 1996-97.

Hymns of the Church of Jesus Christ of Latter-day Saints. Salt Lake City, UT: The Church of Jesus Christ of Latter-day Saints, 1985.

Jackson, Kent P. and Millet, Robert L. eds., *Studies in Scripture.* Salt Lake City, UT: Deseret Book 1989.

Jensen, Marlin K. "Living after the Manner of Happiness." Salt Lake City, UT: *Ensign*, December 2002.

Jenson, Andrew, *Historical Record: A Monthly Periodical.* Salt Lake City, UT: Deseret News, 1886—1890.

Jessee, Dean. "Joseph Knight's Recollection of Early Mormon History." Provo, UT: BYU Studies 17, no. 1, 1976.

Johnson, Clark V. *Doctrines for Exaltation: The 1989 Sperry Symposium on the Doctrine and Covenants.* Salt Lake City, UT: Deseret Book, 1989.

Josephus. *Complete Works.* William Whiston, trans. Grand Rapids, MI: Kregal Publications, 1960.

Kimball, Spencer W. "A Gift of Gratitude." Salt Lake City, UT: *Tambuli*, December 1977.

—"Becoming the Pure in Heart." Salt Lake City, UT: *Ensign*, May 1978.

—*Faith Precedes the Miracle: Based on Discourses of Spencer W. Kimball.* Salt Lake City, UT: Deseret Book, 1972.

—"The Fruit of Our Welfare Services Labors." Salt Lake City, UT: *Ensign*, November 1978.

—"The Role of Righteous Women." Salt Lake City, UT: *Ensign*, November 1979.

—*The Teachings of Spencer W. Kimball.* Salt Lake City, UT: Bookcraft, 1982.

—"Welfare Services: The Gospel in Action." Salt Lake City, UT: *Ensign*, November 1977.

—"Young Women Fireside 1981—In Love and Power and without Fear." Salt Lake City, UT: *New Era*, July 1981.

Kirchhoff, Frederick. "Reconstruction of Self in Wordsworth's "Ode on Intimations of Immortality from Recollections of Early Childhood." *Narcissism and the Text.* New York, NY: New York University Press, 1986.

Kirtland Council Minute Book. Salt Lake City, UT: Collier's, 1996.

Largey, Dennis L. *Book of Mormon Reference Companion.* Salt Lake City, UT: Deseret Book, 2003.

Larsen, Dean L. "A Royal Generation." Salt Lake City, UT: *Ensign,* May 1983.

Larson, Stan "The King Follett Discourse: a Newly Amalgamated Text." Provo, UT: *BYU Studies,* 1978.

Layton, Lynne and Schapiro, Barbara A.. *Narcissism and the Text: Studies in Literature and the Psychology of Self.* New York, NY: New York University Press, 1986.

Lee, Harold B. *Decisions for Successful Living.* Salt Lake City, UT: Deseret Book, 1973.

—"Stand Ye in Holy Places." Salt Lake City, UT: *Ensign,* July 1973.

—*The Teachings of Harold B. Lee.* Salt Lake City, UT: Deseret Book, 1974.

Lightner, Mary. Address to Brigham Young University. Provo, UT: *BYU Archives and Manuscripts, Writings of Early Latter-day Saints,* 1905.

Ludlow, Daniel H. *A Companion to Your Study of the Book of Mormon.* Salt Lake City, UT: Deseret Book, 1976.

—*Encyclopedia of Mormonism.* New York City, NY: Macmillan Publishing, 1992.

Lund, Gerald N. *Jesus Christ, Key to the Plan of Salvation.* Salt Lake City, UT: Deseret Book, 1991.

Lundquist, John M. and Ricks, Stephen D. eds., *By Study and Also by Faith: Essays in Honor of Hugh W. Nibley on the Occasion of His Eightieth Birthday.* Provo, UT: Maxwell Institute, 1992.

Lundwall, N. B. *Temples of the Most High.* Salt Lake City, UT: Bookcraft, 1965.

"Map: Old Testament Stories: Part Two." Salt Lake City, UT: *Deseret News.* Jan. 8, 1994.

Maxwell, Cory H., ed. *The Neal A. Maxwell Quote Book.* Salt Lake City, UT: Bookcraft, 1997.

Maxwell, Neal A. *A Wonderful Flood of Light.* Salt Lake City, UT: Deseret Book, 1991.

—*But for a Small Moment.* Salt Lake City, UT: Bookcraft, 1987.

—"Consecrate Thy Performance." *Ensign,* May 2002.

—*Disposition of a Disciple.* Salt Lake City, UT: Deseret Book, 1976.

—"Enduring Well." Salt Lake City, UT: *Ensign,* Apr 1997.

—*Even As I Am.* Salt Lake City, UT: Deseret Book, 1991.

—*If Thou Endure It Well.* Salt Lake City, UT: Bookcraft, 2002.

—*Lord, Increase Our Faith.* Salt Lake City, UT: Bookcraft, 1994.

—*Men and Women of Christ.* Salt Lake City, UT: Deseret Book, 1991.

—*Notwithstanding My Weakness.* Salt Lake City, UT: Deseret Book, 1981.

—*One More Strain of Praise.* Salt Lake City, UT: Deseret Book, 2003.

—"Patience."Salt Lake City, UT: *Ensign,* October 1980.

—*That Ye May Believe.* Salt Lake City, UT: Bookcraft, 1994.

—*The Promise of Discipleship.* Salt Lake City, UT: Deseret Book, 2001.

—"These Are Your Days." Salt Lake City, UT: *New Era,* January 1985.

McConkie. Bruce R. *A New Witness for the Articles of Faith.* Salt Lake City, UT: Deseret Book, 1985.

—*Doctrinal New Testament Commentary.* Salt Lake City, UT: Deseret Book, 1972.

—*Doctrines of Salvation: Sermons and Writings of Joseph Fielding Smith,* Salt Lake City, UT: Bookcraft, 1954-1956.

—*Mormon Doctrine.* Salt Lake City, UT: Bookcraft: 1966.

—"Obedience, Consecration, and Sacrifice." Salt Lake City, UT: *Ensign,* May 1975.

—"The Doctrine of the Priesthood." Salt Lake City, UT: *Ensign,* May 1982.

—*The Mortal Messiah: From Bethlehem to Calvary.* Salt Lake City, UT: Deseret Book, 1981.

—"The Probationary Test of Mortality." Address delivered at the University of Utah Institute, January 10, 1982.

—*The Promised Messiah: The First Coming of Christ.* Salt Lake City, UT: Deseret Book, 1981.

—"The Ten Blessings of the Priesthood." Salt Lake City, UT: *Ensign,* November 1977.

McConkie, Joseph Fielding and Millet, Robert L. *Doctrinal Commentary on the Book of Mormon.* Salt Lake City, UT: Deseret Book, 1987-1993.

—*Joseph Smith: The Choice Seer.* Salt Lake City, UT: Bookcraft, 1996.

—*Revelations of the Restoration.* Salt Lake City, UT: Deseret Book, 2000.

McKay, David O. Gospel Ideals: Selections from the Discourses of David O. McKay. Salt Lake City, UT: Deseret Book, 1993.

—*Pathways to Happiness.* Salt Lake City, UT: Bookcraft 1957.

McMullin, Keith B. "Come to Zion! Come to Zion!" Salt Lake City, UT:*Ensign*, November 2002.

Merriam Webster's New World Dictionary, Third Edition. New York, NY: Simon and Schuster, 1998.

Middlemiss, Clare. *Man May Know for Himself: Teachings of President David O. McKay.* Salt Lake City, UT: Deseret Book, 1967.

Millet, Robert L. "Quest for the City of God: The Doctrine Of Zion In Modern Revelation," *1989 Sperry Symposium on the Doctrine and Covenants.* Salt Lake City, UT: Desert Book, 1989.

—*The Capstone of Our Religion: Insights into the Doctrine and Covenants.* Salt Lake City, UT: Deseret Book, 1989.

—*The Life Beyond.* Salt Lake City, UT: Deseret Book, 1986.

—*The Power of the Word: Saving Doctrines from the Book of Mormon.* Salt Lake City, UT: Deseret Book, 2000.

Monson, Thomas S. "In Quest of the Abundant Life."Salt Lake City, UT: *Ensign*, March 1988.

Nelson, Russell M. "Personal Priesthood Responsibility." Salt Lake City, UT: *Ensign*, October 2005.

—*The Power within Us.* Salt Lake City, UT: Deseret Book, 1989.

Nelson, William O. "Enoch and His Message for Latter Days." Salt Lake City, UT: *Deseret News.* Feb. 5, 1994.

Neuenschwander, Dennis. "Ordinances and Covenants." Salt Lake City, UT: *Ensign*, August 2001.

Nibley, Hugh. *Abraham in Egypt.* Salt Lake City, UT and Provo, UT: Deseret Book and FARMS, 2000.

—*An Approach to the Book of Mormon.* Salt Lake City, UT: Deseret Book, 1988.

—*Approaching Zion.* Salt Lake City, UT: Deseret Book, 1989.

—"Educating the Saints—a Brigham Young Mosaic." Provo, UT: *BYU Studies*, Autumn 1970.

—*Nibley on the Timely and the Timeless.* Provo, UT: Religious Studies Center, Brigham Young University, 2004.

—*Teachings of the Book of Mormon.* Provo, UT: Covenant Communications, 2004.

—*Temple and Cosmos: Beyond This Ignorant Present.* Salt Lake City, UT: Deseret Book, 1992.

Nibley, Preston. *Brigham Young: The Man and His Work*, 4th ed. Salt Lake City, UT: Deseret Book, 1960.

Nielsen, Donna B. *Beloved Bridegroom.* Salt Lake City, UT: Onyx Press, 1999.

Nyman, Monte S. and Tate, Charles D. Jr., eds. *Fourth Nephi through Moroni: From Zion to Destruction.* Salt Lake City, UT: Bookcraft, 1992.

—*The Capstone of Our Religion: Insights into the Doctrine and Covenants.* Salt Lake City, UT: Bookcraft, 1989.

Oaks, Dallin H. "Good, Better, Best." Salt Lake City, UT: *Ensign*, November 2007.

—"He Heals the Heavy Laden," *Ensign*, Nov. 2006

— "Preparation for the Second Coming." Salt Lake City, UT: *Ensign*, November 2004.

—"Taking Upon Us the Name of Jesus Christ." Salt Lake City, UT: *Ensign*, May 1985.

—"The Challenge to Become." Salt Lake City, UT: *Ensign*, November 2000.

—"Timing." Salt Lake City, UT: *Ensign*, October 2003.

Oaks, Robert C. "The Power of Patience." Salt Lake City, UT: *Ensign*, November 2006.

Otten, L. G. and Caldwell, C. M. *Sacred Truths of the Doctrine and Covenants.* Salt Lake City, UT: Deseret Book, 1982-1983.

Pack, Frederick J. "Was the Earth Created in Six Days of Twenty-Four Hours Each?" Salt Lake City, UT: *Improvement Era*, October 1930.

Packer, Boyd K. "Personal Revelation: The Gift, the Test, and the Promise." Salt Lake City, UT: *Ensign*, November 1994.

—"Restoration," First Worldwide Leadership Training Meeting. Salt Lake City, UT: The Church of Jesus Christ of Latter-day Saints, January 2003.

—*That All May Be Edified*, Salt Lake City, UT: Bookcraft, 1982.

—"The Candle of the Lord." Salt Lake City, UT: Ensign, January 1983.

—"The One Pure Defense (An Evening with President Boyd K. Packer)." Salt Lake City, UT: Intellectual Reserve, 2004.

Parry, Donald W. ed., *Temples of the Ancient World: Ritual and Symbolism.* Salt Lake City, UT and Provo, UT: Deseret and FARMS, 1994.

—*Understanding the Book of Revelation,* Salt Lake City, UT: Deseret Book, 1998.

Peterson, H. Burke. "Your Special Purpose." Salt Lake City, UT: *New Era,* October 2001.

Pratt, Orson. *Times and Seasons,* Vol. 6. no. 10, 1 June 1845.

Riddle, Chauncey C. "The New and Everlasting Covenant," 1989 *Sperry Symposium on the Doctrine and Covenants.* Salt Lake City: Desert Book, 1989.

Roberts, B.H. *Comprehensive History of the Church of Jesus Christ of Latter-day Saints.* Salt Lake City, UT: Church of Jesus Christ of Latter-day Saints, 1930.

—*Seventy's Course of Theology.* Salt Lake City, UT: Deseret Book, 1931.

Romney, Marion G. "Church Welfare Services' Basic Principles." Salt Lake City, UT: *Ensign,* May 1976.

—"Church Welfare—Temporal Service in a Spiritual Setting." Salt Lake City, UT:*Ensign,* May 1980—"Priesthood." Salt Lake City, UT: *Ensign,* May 1982.

—"'In Mine Own Way'." Salt Lake City, UT: *Ensign,* November 1976.

—"The Celestial Nature of Self-reliance." Salt Lake City, UT: *Ensign,* November 1982.

—"The Oath and Covenant Which Belongeth to the Priesthood." Salt Lake City, UT: *Ensign,* November 1980.

—"The Purpose of Church Welfare Services." Salt Lake City, UT: *Ensign,* May 1977.

—"The Royal Law of Love." Salt Lake City, UT: *Ensign,* May 1978.

—"Unity." *Ensign,* Salt Lake City, UT May 1983.

—"Welfare Services: The Savior's Program." Salt Lake City, UT: *Ensign,* October 1980.

Salt Lake School of the Prophets Minutes. Salt Lake City, UT: The Church of Jesus Christ of Latter-day Saints, 1899.

"Sermon Given to Different People." Salt Lake City, UT: *LDS Church News,* Feb. 18, 1995.

Skidmore, Rex A. "What Part Should a Teenager Play in a Family?" Salt Lake City, UT: *Improvement Era* 1952.

Skinner, Andrew C. *Temple Worship: 20 Truths That Will Bless Your Life.* Salt Lake City, UT: Deseret Book, 2008.

—*The Old Testament and the Latter-Day Saints.* Salt Lake City, UT: Deseret Book, 2005.

Smith, Hyrum M. and Sjodahl, Janne M. *Doctrine and Covenants Commentary.* Salt Lake City, UT: Deseret Book, 1960.

Smith, Joseph. *Evening and Morning Star,* July, 1833.

—*History of The Church of Jesus Christ of Latter-day Saints.* Salt Lake City, UT: Deseret Book, 1980.

—*Lectures on Faith.* Salt Lake City, UT: Deseret Book, 1993.

Smith, Joseph F. *Gospel Doctrine: Selections from the Sermons and Writings of Joseph F. Smith.* Deseret News Press, 1919.

—*Teachings of Presidents of the Church.* Salt Lake City, UT: *The Church of Jesus Christ of Latter-day Saints,* 1998.

Smith, Joseph Fielding. *Church History and Modern Revelation.* Salt Lake City, UT: The Church of Jesus Christ of Latter-day Saints, 1946.

—"Our responsibility as Priesthood Holders." Salt Lake City, UT: *Ensign,* June 1971.

—*Teachings of the Prophet Joseph Smith.* Salt Lake City, UT: Deseret Book, 1938.

—"The Duties of the Priesthood in Temple Work." Salt Lake City, UT: *The Utah Genealogical and Historical Magazine.* Vol. 30, no. 1, January 1939.

—*The Restoration of All Things.* Salt Lake City, UT: Deseret News Press, 1945.

Snow, Lorenzo. *The Teachings of Lorenzo Snow,* Salt Lake City, UT: Bookcraft, 1984.

Sorensen, A. D. *As Women of Faith: Talks Selected from the BYU Women's Conferences.* Salt Lake City, UT: Deseret Book, 1989.

Stevenson, Edward. "Life and History of Elder Edward Stevenson." Provo, UT: Special Collections, Harold B. Lee Library, Brigham Young University, n.d.

Stoval, Mary E., ed. *As Women of Faith: Talks Selected from the BYU Women's Conferences.* Salt Lake City, UT: Deseret Book, 1989.

Stuy, Brian H., comp., *Collected Discourses.* Burbank, CA: B.H.S. Publishing, 1988.

Summerhays, James T. "The Stripling Elect." Fairfax, VA: *MeridianMagazine.com*, February 20, 2009.

Talmage, James E. *Articles of Faith*. Salt Lake City, UT: Deseret Book, 1984.

—*Jesus the Christ*. Salt Lake City: Deseret News Press, 1915.

—"The Eternity of Sex." Salt Lake City, UT: *Young Woman's Journal*, October 1914.

—*The House of the Lord*. Salt Lake City, UT: Bookcraft, 1962.

Tanakh: A New Translation of the Holy Scriptures According to the Traditional Hebrew Text. Philadelphia, PA: Jewish Publication Society of America, November 1985.

Tanner, Susan W. "All Things Shall Work Together for Your Good." Salt Lake City, UT: *Ensign*, May 2004.

—"My Soul Delighteth in the Things of the Lord." Salt Lake City, UT: *Ensign*, 2008.

Taylor, John. *Teachings of the Latter-day Prophets*. Salt Lake City, UT: Bookcraft, 1998.

Times and Seasons, Vol. 6. no. 10, 1 June 1845.

Thomas, M. Catherine. "Alma the Younger, Part 1," Provo, UT: Neal A. Maxwell Institute for Religious Scholarship, 1996.

—"Alma the Younger, Part 2," Provo, UT: Neal A. Maxwell Institute for Religious Scholarship, 1996.

—"Benjamin and the Mysteries of God," *King Benjamin's Speech*. Provo, UT: Foundation for Ancient Research and Mormon Studies, 1998.

Turner, Rodney. *Woman and the Priesthood*. Salt Lake City, UT: Deseret Book, 1972.

Tvedtnes, John A. *The Church of the Old Testament*. Salt Lake City, UT: Deseret Book, 1967.

—"They Have Their Reward." Fairfax, VA: *MeridianMagazine.com*, February 21, 2007.

Research and Mormon Studies, 1998.

Van Orden, Bruce A. and Top, Brent L. "*Doctrines of the Book of Mormon: The 1991 Sperry Symposium*," Provo, UT: Maxwell Institute, 1993.

Watt, George D., ed. *Journal of Discourses*. Liverpool, England: F.D. Richards, et al., 1854-1886.

Whitney, Newell K. *Messenger and Advocate*. Kirtland, OH: The Church of Jesus Christ of Latter-day Saints, September 3, 1837.

Whitney, Orson F. *Gospel Themes*. Salt Lake City, UT: n.p., 1914.

—*Life of Heber C. Kimball*. Salt Lake City, UT: Bookcraft, 1975.

—*Saturday Night Thoughts*. Salt Lake City, UT: Deseret News, 1927.

Wickman, Lance B. "Today." Salt Lake City, UT: *Ensign*, May 2008.

Widtsoe, John A. *An Understandable Religion*. Salt Lake City, UT: The Church of Jesus Christ of Latter-day Saints, 1944.

—*Priesthood and Church Government*. Salt Lake City, UT: Deseret Book, 1939.

—*Utah Genealogical and Historical Magazine*. Salt Lake City, UT: October 1934.

Williams, Clyde J. *The Teachings of Lorenzo Snow, Fifth President of the Church of Jesus Christ of Latter-day Saints*. Salt Lake City, UT: Bookcraft, 1984.

Wilson, Marvin. *Our Father Abraham*, Grand Rapids, MI: Eerdmans Publishing Co., 1989.

Winder, Barbara W. "Finding Joy in Life." Salt Lake City, UT: *Ensign*, Nov 1987.

Wirthlin, Joseph B. "The Great Commandment."Salt Lake City, UT: *Ensign*, Nov. 2007.

—"The Law of the Fast." Salt Lake City, UT: *Ensign*, May 2001.

Woodruff, Wilford. *The Discourses of Wilford Woodruff*. Salt Lake City, UT: Bookcraft, 1946.

Yarn, David H. *The Gospel: God, Man, and Truth*. Salt Lake City, UT: Deseret Book, 1965.

Yorgason, Blaine M. *I Need Thee Every Hour*. Salt Lake City, UT: Deseret Book, 2003.

—*Spiritual Progression in the Last Days*. Salt Lake City, UT: Deseret Book, 1994.

Young, Brigham.*Deseret News*, Oct. 10, 1866.

—*Discourses of Brigham Young*. Salt Lake City, UT: Deseret Book, 1926.

—*Journal History*. Sept. 28, 1846.

—*Millennial Star*, Vol. 16. Salt Lake City, UT: The Church of Jesus Christ of Latter-day Saints, 1840-1970.

Concordance

adultery, 48, 51, 68, 130, 210, 212, 270, 427, 437, 471, 530

adversity, 117, 131, 134, 135, 137, 140, 200, 225, 264, 275, 318, 489, 504, 518, 520, 558

afflicted, 25, 69, 77, 148, 211, 251, 265, 269, 270, 273, 282, 289, 291, 347, 361, 363, 365, 374, 378, 410, 411, 415, 418, 430, 437, 442, 443, 444, 445, 451, 460, 464, 467, 472, 473, 474, 476, 481, 483, 490, 493, 515, 516, 543, 554, 590

affluence, 72, 87, 456, 582

agency, 21, 36, 54, 94, 95, 96, 100, 103, 112, 113, 118, 149, 246, 247, 274, 285, 286, 289, 290, 349, 353, 366, 393, 394, 395, 396, 397, 398, 399, 407, 408, 410, 417, 418, 470, 471, 479, 480, 492, 505, 507, 511, 537, 596, 597

agnostic, 70

all things common, 26, 28, 44, 213, 372, 376, 380, 389, 390, 597

Almighty, 60, 245, 274, 289, 293, 299, 441, 511, 541

altar, 11, 105, 106, 122, 123, 129, 137, 153, 174, 194, 195, 296, 337, 339, 343, 348, 352, 356, 357, 366, 380, 423, 470, 498, 521, 525, 529, 531, 536, 540, 542, 543, 566, 579, 608

Amulek, 47, 69, 132, 217, 376, 389, 451, 490, 526, 554

angel, 11, 24, 33, 55, 79, 80, 180, 181, 182, 194, 244, 252, 435, 506, 513, 517, 525, 527, 528, 541, 547

anger, 18, 51, 57, 65, 73, 74, 79, 82, 83, 135, 191, 291, 304, 310, 346, 365, 369, 425, 433, 437, 441, 454, 477, 490, 499, 508, 513, 530, 534, 561, 582, 584, 585, 599

anoint, 106, 163, 475, 476

anti-Christ, 20, 32, 44, 45, 46, 54, 68, 71, 72, 85, 86, 134, 225, 414, 446, 486, 487, 523, 535

apostasy, 25, 31, 53, 59, 182, 411, 585

apostle, 52, 79, 104, 243, 299

Atonement, xiii, 12, 13, 21, 22, 38, 40, 42, 58, 61, 90, 92, 95, 97, 98, 103, 104, 105, 106, 108, 109, 110, 111, 112, 113, 114, 115, 116, 118, 119, 120, 121, 122, 127, 135, 136, 144, 148, 170, 173, 181, 187, 189, 201, 223, 228, 230, 232, 313, 326, 337, 339, 342, 355, 357, 358, 367, 375, 376, 387, 388, 389, 395, 424, 442, 475, 494, 497, 499, 519, 549, 572, 584, 588, 589, 593, 603, 606, 610, 613

Babel, 47, 48, 54, 65, 85

Baptism, viii, xiv, xvii, 34, 107, 116, 119, 120, 130, 225, 226, 384, 545

Beatitudes, 27, 211, 530, 564

beggar, 22, 213, 434, 446

Beloved Son, 42, 224, 259, 541, 542, 587, 591

Bible, 35, 43, 47, 48, 49, 55, 70, 104, 113, 120, 134, 178, 214, 280, 292, 331, 419, 502, 589, 608, 611, 612

bishop, 17, 122, 211, 351, 381, 382, 402, 403, 404, 405, 409, 412, 493

Blaine Yorgason, v, 32, 45, 65, 66, 84, 239, 250, 251, 327, 330, 331, 335, 482, 514, 517, 521, 523, 524, 525, 531, 538, 541, 550, 551, 557, 567, 570, 584

blasphemy, 52, 238

Book of Mormon, 3, 6, 13, 17, 28, 31, 34, 54, 57, 59, 61, 67, 87, 104, 132, 178, 186, 188, 208, 209, 227, 228, 245, 266, 269, 276, 282, 286, 292, 299, 313, 346, 363, 374, 399, 412, 422, 424, 428, 431, 444, 453, 455, 456, 471, 474, 500, 502, 504, 514, 523, 544, 560, 576, 581, 587, 594, 601, 602, 603, 611, 614, 615, 617

Bridegroom, ix, 65, 72, 137, 147, 148, 149, 150, 151, 152, 153, 154, 155, 156, 157, 158, 160, 161, 162, 163, 164, 165, 166, 167, 168, 169, 170, 259, 298, 307, 315, 422, 615

Brigham Young, 5, 6, 7, 13, 35, 36, 39, 41, 76, 88, 90, 139, 170, 173, 175, 188, 218, 248, 252, 272, 282, 300, 323, 329, 339, 342, 350, 366, 380, 393, 404, 412, 413, 414, 416, 422, 428, 429, 432, 435, 445, 450, 451, 453, 455, 457, 464, 465, 467, 497, 499, 505, 519, 529, 542, 556, 563, 566, 571, 576, 578, 579, 586, 601, 607, 609, 610, 611, 612, 614, 615, 616, 617

Brother of Jared, 13, 137, 325, 335

Bruce R. McConkie, 11, 41, 90, 159, 166, 174, 180, 181, 184, 190, 193, 199, 235, 339, 343, 348, 393, 398, 410, 453, 498, 502, 545, 548, 603

business, 32, 47, 65, 68, 131, 286, 373, 399, 403, 435, 445, 446, 452, 465, 539, 575

Cain, vii, 13, 45, 46, 47, 48, 54, 60, 62, 64, 66, 68, 76, 85, 257, 410, 446, 465, 486, 487

calling and election made sure, 237, 238, 239, 251, 263, 312, 314, 319

captivate, 45, 420

carnal, 18, 22, 52, 54, 61, 75, 76, 86, 96, 109, 110, 113, 117, 140, 192, 257, 258, 306, 312, 395, 396, 425, 432, 464, 507, 532, 550, 573

Catherine Thomas, 36, 38, 40, 48, 124, 178, 179, 180, 181, 188, 228, 505, 546, 548, 550

celestial kingdom, 43, 101, 102, 103, 104, 105, 107, 112, 120, 150, 174, 191, 195, 200, 227, 229, 235, 253, 263, 267, 269, 270, 292, 303, 315, 318, 327, 343, 344, 345, 346, 348, 350, 354, 363, 365, 366, 372, 384, 386, 394, 398, 402, 406, 408, 416, 417, 418, 420, 446, 451, 458, 460, 464, 465, 467, 494, 498, 505, 521, 537, 561, 595, 605, 607, 608

charity, 23, 25, 66, 67, 69, 105, 123, 167, 199, 200, 202, 208, 213, 217, 231, 249, 254, 257, 262, 265, 277, 281, 286, 289, 292, 293, 294, 304, 305, 306, 317, 369, 383, 458, 462, 477, 478, 479, 480, 481, 482, 483, 485, 487, 488, 489, 490, 491, 492, 493, 494, 542, 548, 553, 554, 555, 557, 560, 579, 584, 591

chaste, 94, 108, 143, 515, 516, 543

Chauncey Riddle, 94, 111, 113, 219

Christ, iii, vii, xi, xvi, xvii, xviii, 3, 4, 5, 7, 9, 12, 13, 21, 22, 24, 26, 28, 30, 33, 36, 38, 39, 40, 41, 42, 43, 44, 45, 54, 57, 58, 59, 64, 66, 73, 75, 77, 80, 81, 83, 85, 90, 92, 94, 95, 97, 99, 101, 102, 103, 104, 105, 106, 108, 110, 111, 112, 113, 115, 116, 117, 118, 119, 120, 121, 123, 124, 125, 126, 127, 130, 132, 133, 134, 139, 141, 142, 143, 144, 145, 146, 148, 149, 155, 156, 157, 158, 161, 164, 170, 174, 176, 178, 179, 180, 181, 182, 184, 186, 188, 189, 190, 193, 201, 202, 203, 205, 206, 207, 209, 212, 214, 215, 217, 218, 219, 220, 221, 222, 224, 226, 228, 229, 230, 231, 232, 233, 234, 235, 236, 237, 238, 239, 240, 241, 242, 243, 244, 245, 247, 249, 251, 252, 253, 254, 255, 259, 260, 263, 266, 270, 271, 278, 284, 285, 286, 287, 288, 292, 293, 294, 295, 299, 300, 302, 304, 305, 311, 313, 314, 315, 320, 321, 323, 326, 327, 328, 329, 330, 331, 332, 335, 336, 337, 338, 339, 340, 343, 349, 354, 357, 358, 361, 363, 368, 369, 372, 375, 376, 382, 383, 385, 386, 387, 388, 389, 395, 401, 403, 405, 407, 408, 409, 411, 415, 418, 422, 423, 428, 430, 442, 444, 445, 455, 457, 458, 459, 460, 461, 464, 467, 471, 472, 473, 474, 475, 476, 477, 478, 479, 480, 481, 482, 483, 486, 487, 488, 491, 492, 493, 497, 498, 499, 505, 508, 509, 511, 512, 516, 518, 519, 522, 523, 524, 526, 527, 531, 533, 535, 537, 544, 545, 546, 547, 548, 549, 550, 552, 555, 556, 557, 558, 559, 560, 564, 565, 567, 568, 572, 574, 577, 578, 579, 580, 582, 583, 584, 585, 586, 587, 589, 591, 593, 594, 595, 597, 598, 599, 600, 601, 603, 604, 605, 606, 607, 610, 611, 612, 613, 614, 615, 616, 617, 635

Church, iii, vii, xi, xiii, xv, 4, 5, 6, 9, 17, 18, 19, 21, 25, 26, 29, 31, 32, 34, 38, 39, 42, 50, 51, 54, 55, 56, 66, 70, 73, 86, 88, 90, 92, 109, 115, 117, 119, 120, 123, 124, 125, 130, 132, 145, 147, 173, 174, 176, 183, 185, 186, 191, 193, 199, 206, 209, 210, 211, 214, 217, 219, 227, 234, 235, 236, 237, 238, 239, 241, 244, 248, 250, 251, 254, 259, 263, 265, 266, 270, 272, 273, 275, 276, 281, 285, 305, 308, 312, 313, 316, 317, 319, 320, 321, 322, 323, 325, 326, 327, 328, 329, 330, 331, 332, 334, 337, 339, 340, 342, 343, 347, 348, 350, 351, 352, 353, 356, 358, 359, 360, 362, 365, 366, 367, 368, 373, 375, 378, 379, 381, 382, 383, 385, 389, 390, 392, 393, 398, 400, 403, 404, 405, 409, 411, 412, 413, 414, 415, 424, 429, 431, 432, 437, 440, 441, 442, 444, 445, 449, 452, 455, 465, 471, 472, 475, 476, 483, 485, 486, 487, 488, 493, 494, 497, 498, 502, 529, 537, 545, 546, 548, 549, 550, 551, 556, 569, 570, 571, 573, 575, 576, 577, 578, 579, 582, 585, 586, 592, 595, 597, 601, 603, 604, 607, 608, 609, 611, 612, 613, 615, 616, 617

City of Enoch, 16, 523, 555

combinations, 31, 44, 53, 54, 56, 77, 78, 82, 84, 581, 586

comforter, 120, 160, 229

commandment, 3, 25, 29, 31, 33, 62, 64, 92, 99, 100, 135, 140, 141, 143, 144, 146, 163, 184, 198, 204, 210, 229, 231, 241, 242, 246, 247, 254, 284, 304, 309, 314, 319, 343, 355, 358, 359, 364, 372, 383, 386, 391, 392, 397, 401, 405, 411, 415, 416, 425, 431, 448, 463, 469, 476, 477, 480, 481, 488, 491, 492, 494, 495, 498, 512, 513, 546, 585, 595, 596, 597, 602

commerce, 65, 67

Concordance

compete, 68, 75, 265, 275

consecrate, 82, 106, 122, 134, 135, 151, 155, 169, 211, 216, 226, 227, 269, 270, 271, 282, 283, 286, 336, 343, 345, 347, 348, 349, 354, 356, 358, 362, 365, 366, 381, 388, 390, 393, 394, 396, 401, 403, 406, 408, 414, 417, 449, 469, 472, 473, 476, 480, 487, 488, 489, 491, 492, 493, 494, 495, 498, 500, 504, 519, 521

contention, 19, 20, 22, 27, 57, 59, 68, 73, 75, 86, 179, 265, 273, 376, 381, 490, 499, 531, 581, 582, 585, 586

cooperate, 95, 97, 579

coronation, 91, 97, 170, 196, 197, 202, 316, 324, 325, 549, 556, 608

corrupt, 49, 57, 73, 74, 76, 78, 85, 87, 357, 431, 453, 454, 571

covenant, 6, 7, 9, 11, 15, 16, 17, 18, 20, 23, 24, 29, 32, 33, 34, 38, 39, 60, 65, 66, 86, 88, 90, 91, 92, 93, 94, 95, 96, 97, 98, 99, 100, 101, 102, 103, 105, 106, 108, 111, 112, 113, 114, 115, 116, 117, 118, 119, 120, 121, 123, 124, 126, 128, 129, 130, 131, 132, 133, 134, 137, 139, 140, 141, 142, 143, 144, 145, 146, 148, 149, 150, 151, 152, 153, 154, 155, 156, 157, 158, 162, 163, 164, 165, 166, 167, 168, 169, 170, 173, 174, 175, 176, 177, 179, 181, 185, 186, 187, 190, 191, 192, 194, 195, 196, 197, 198, 199, 200, 201, 202, 203, 204, 205, 206, 207, 208, 209, 210, 213, 214, 215, 217, 219, 220, 221, 222, 223, 224, 225, 226, 227, 228, 229, 230, 231, 233, 234, 235, 236, 240, 241, 242, 244, 246, 247, 248, 249, 250, 252, 253, 254, 255, 257, 258, 259, 260, 262, 264, 270, 272, 274, 275, 280, 281, 284, 289, 296, 300, 302, 305, 307, 309, 310, 312, 315, 316, 317, 320, 322, 323, 324, 330, 331, 337, 339, 342, 343, 344, 345, 346, 347, 348, 349, 350, 352, 353, 354, 355, 356, 359, 364, 365, 366, 367, 371, 375, 376, 380, 382, 383, 384, 385, 387, 389, 391, 392, 393, 398, 399, 401, 402, 403, 405, 406, 408, 409, 413, 414, 415, 417, 418, 420, 422, 426, 438, 439, 443, 448, 453, 459, 461, 462, 467, 468, 469, 470, 472, 497, 498, 501, 502, 509, 513, 531, 537, 543, 546, 550, 552, 558, 565, 566, 567, 570, 571, 572, 592, 597, 599, 604, 606, 607, 608, 609, 610

covet, 23, 61, 399, 414, 425, 426, 463

Creator, 50, 85, 93, 408, 456

criticize, 75

crown, 9, 88, 91, 165, 170, 217, 313, 388, 412, 415, 447, 503, 504, 510, 555

curse, 53, 61, 62, 72, 82, 83, 131, 195, 223, 299, 370, 424, 426, 433, 434, 447, 451, 452, 464, 466, 526, 530, 575

deceive, 55, 56, 63, 73, 83, 85, 87, 225, 257, 298, 435, 580

Deity, 42, 125, 198, 210, 224, 247, 288, 480, 569

deliver, 46, 60, 132, 133, 138, 176, 185, 201, 233, 239, 245, 268, 326, 474, 487, 508, 509, 516, 518, 527, 528, 529, 533, 536, 538, 540, 544, 552, 553, 554, 555, 557, 585

devil, 20, 22, 39, 42, 46, 47, 53, 54, 55, 56, 57, 60, 61, 63, 72, 73, 76, 78, 85, 86, 112, 116, 130, 162, 166, 169, 249, 258, 274, 298, 299, 306, 320, 357, 378, 394, 395, 398, 399, 432, 435, 440, 456, 458, 464, 466, 467, 507, 511, 534, 541, 580, 582, 585, 596

disputations, 28, 44, 51, 188, 375, 440, 465, 585, 586, 597

economic, 51, 67, 82, 347, 348, 351, 352, 364, 369, 372, 373, 375, 389, 422, 431, 586

elect, 51, 55, 72, 85, 87, 125, 129, 165, 204, 222, 235, 236, 237, 239, 241, 254, 262, 281, 293, 331, 556, 557, 571, 575

Elijah, ix, x, 29, 155, 182, 183, 184, 185, 186, 187, 224, 263, 267, 396, 449, 502, 538, 554, 572

elitists, 58

Eliza R. Snow, 31

endow, 29, 91, 94, 97, 154, 170, 179, 184, 240, 338, 472, 565, 607

enemies, 20, 33, 39, 62, 64, 72, 74, 82, 84, 95, 99, 111, 117, 122, 131, 132, 135, 153, 154, 179, 228, 230, 268, 272, 335, 351, 374, 395, 450, 457, 474, 483, 487, 488, 517, 526, 530, 540, 552, 557, 561, 581

Enoch, vi, 4, 5, 7, 14, 15, 16, 18, 30, 33, 49, 51, 64, 74, 75, 87, 99, 177, 179, 180, 187, 188, 189, 192, 193, 194, 195, 196, 208, 218, 230, 243, 246, 263, 316, 327, 331, 334, 335, 350, 351, 410, 413, 471, 514, 526, 552, 567, 570, 571, 574, 576, 579, 589, 599, 601, 606, 615

equal, 25, 37, 51, 57, 74, 100, 142, 166, 176, 187, 204, 212, 220, 243, 255, 265, 275, 328, 344, 349, 361, 362, 364, 366, 370, 372, 373, 374, 382, 389, 390, 392, 402, 403, 406, 417, 421, 445, 470, 492, 494, 500, 597, 598

exalt, 90, 97, 116, 117, 127, 134, 136, 140, 195, 220, 275, 276, 282, 286, 345, 371, 384, 387, 432, 493, 573 excess, 17, 81, 84, 144, 214, 268, 282, 369, 522, 635

Exemplar, 35, 224, 232, 598

Ezra Taft Benson, 8, 23, 37, 54, 59, 193, 194, 258, 263, 332, 347, 354, 362, 363, 364, 381, 390, 611

faith, 14, 15, 17, 18, 19, 24, 33, 36, 38, 45, 53, 54, 57, 58, 59, 61, 69, 70, 71, 76, 81, 99, 102, 104, 106, 112, 113, 116, 118, 119, 121, 122, 123, 125, 126, 131, 132, 136, 138, 146, 153, 176, 177, 178, 179, 181, 182, 187, 188, 189, 194, 196, 199, 200, 206, 208, 209, 211, 212, 214, 215, 216, 218, 220, 223, 226, 227, 228, 230, 235, 236, 237, 239, 249, 257, 265, 268, 270, 271, 277, 280, 282, 284, 288, 289, 290, 291, 292, 301, 302, 306, 312, 315, 316, 317, 318, 319, 320, 323, 325, 332, 335, 349, 352, 353, 358, 363, 367, 371, 374, 378, 379, 380, 388, 403, 405, 411, 421, 424, 440, 441, 449, 451, 459, 460, 461, 462, 463, 468, 471, 472, 473, 474, 475, 476, 477, 478, 479, 480, 481, 482, 485, 486, 488, 489, 490, 493, 494, 495, 499, 501, 504, 505, 512, 517, 518, 522, 523, 524, 526, 527, 529, 530, 532, 533, 535, 536, 537, 538, 539, 542, 543, 544, 547, 551, 552, 553, 554, 556, 558, 561, 564, 565, 567, 575, 580, 584, 586, 590, 591, 592, 595, 597, 598, 599

families, 4, 5, 11, 17, 22, 30, 38, 67, 74, 75, 88, 123, 129, 151, 177, 178, 179, 183, 184, 185, 186, 191, 195, 200, 223, 227, 248, 318, 334, 353, 398, 401, 416, 428, 449, 484, 499, 503, 512, 537, 561, 566, 597

Father in Heaven, 518

fathers, 18, 26, 32, 41, 55, 70, 77, 83, 116, 150, 183, 185, 186, 191, 194, 224, 234, 245, 254, 297, 298, 334, 439, 444, 447, 454, 458, 467, 551, 586, 599, 602, 609

fear, 22, 32, 34, 36, 47, 50, 56, 72, 79, 80, 82, 138, 160, 203, 272, 274, 282, 289, 296, 304, 318, 325, 345, 360, 438, 458, 482, 483, 488, 518, 526, 543, 580, 607

female, 26, 49, 52, 257, 274, 306, 323, 328, 371, 372, 374, 426, 471, 473, 563, 589

filth, 72, 87, 236

financial, 32, 82, 85, 258, 351, 360, 397, 409, 419, 420, 433, 436, 449, 485, 508, 515, 540, 542, 555

Firstborn, xiii, 99, 105, 126, 179, 218, 230, 243, 244, 246, 255, 316, 319, 325, 328, 329, 330, 331, 334, 502, 537, 546, 550, 556, 567, 570, 592, 595, 601

flatter, 63, 81

forgive, 122, 123, 438, 489, 493

fornication, 50, 51, 52, 65, 68, 79, 130, 513

Gadianton robbers, 82

gain, 5, 9, 22, 25, 28, 31, 34, 35, 39, 41, 44, 46, 47, 52, 53, 60, 63, 66, 68, 72, 75, 77, 78, 101, 103, 104, 116, 118, 134, 137, 139, 143, 146, 166, 181, 199, 209, 215, 228, 254, 261, 267, 278, 280, 285, 290, 292, 295, 297, 302, 321, 325, 326, 328, 344, 348, 352, 356, 366, 367, 373, 376, 388, 395, 401, 405, 406, 417, 418, 424, 427, 435, 436, 437, 439, 444, 445, 446, 449, 457, 463, 465, 466, 502, 504, 505, 510, 516, 519, 520, 523, 525, 530, 548, 556, 558, 591, 602, 606

Garden of Eden, 13, 66, 431, 502, 519, 525, 555

generosity, 92, 152, 167, 251, 449

godliness, 18, 29, 45, 57, 76, 134, 192, 199, 206, 218, 219, 241, 250, 262, 267, 276, 281, 306, 310, 321, 322, 348, 424, 427, 462, 463, 550, 569

gold, 25, 44, 46, 51, 52, 55, 66, 81, 107, 108, 154, 166, 273, 290, 349, 374, 378, 410, 425, 427, 429, 432, 438, 439, 444, 450, 456, 457, 461, 462, 498, 512, 515, 516, 517

goods, 23, 50, 60, 130, 153, 161, 348, 366, 411, 412, 428, 429, 436, 439, 443, 449, 460, 461, 465, 478, 486, 492

Gordon B. Hinckley, 8, 112, 216, 307, 337, 371, 374, 375, 387, 389, 391, 476, 482, 568, 613

grace, 5, 7, 11, 12, 26, 38, 93, 103, 104, 105, 106, 108, 110, 113, 119, 121, 125, 127, 153, 186, 189, 192, 214, 215, 216, 220, 221, 223, 240, 254, 292, 327, 328, 388, 396, 407, 416, 418, 456, 462, 485, 486, 487, 488, 491, 493, 501, 512, 521, 522, 532, 571, 599

happy, 13, 129, 163, 305, 408, 449, 452, 454, 466, 558, 566, 571

Harold B. Lee, 27, 70, 211, 274, 275, 331, 564, 614, 616

heal, 3, 4, 41, 277, 283, 291, 301, 306, 403, 405, 459, 460, 472, 473, 474, 493, 508, 590

health, 10, 65, 77, 85, 109, 113, 268, 357, 474, 490, 494, 508, 515, 516, 526, 542, 554, 555

CONCORDANCE

heart, 3, 4, 5, 6, 7, 13, 14, 24, 26, 27, 31, 35, 41, 42, 43, 58, 59, 74, 79, 81, 84, 85, 86, 88, 90, 97, 100, 105, 107, 108, 111, 112, 113, 122, 123, 128, 129, 131, 138, 142, 145, 160, 170, 173, 182, 186, 199, 211, 212, 213, 217, 226, 231, 243, 245, 248, 249, 251, 252, 254, 263, 264, 274, 280, 286, 289, 290, 291, 292, 293, 295, 301, 311, 312, 317, 318, 319, 320, 324, 326, 328, 331, 334, 339, 342, 343, 348, 352, 353, 355, 356, 357, 358, 362, 363, 364, 365, 366, 367, 369, 371, 375, 376, 377, 378, 379, 381, 383, 385, 386, 387, 388, 390, 391, 394, 407, 409, 415, 416, 417, 419, 420, 422, 427, 428, 431, 432, 436, 439, 443, 445, 448, 452, 455, 456, 461, 463, 465, 469, 477, 478, 479, 481, 483, 489, 491, 492, 494, 495, 497, 498, 499, 508, 509, 510, 518, 523, 527, 528, 530, 532, 533, 535, 536, 544, 548, 549, 550, 556, 560, 561, 562, 566, 568, 570, 571, 572, 573, 574, 575, 576, 577, 578, 579, 580, 583, 584, 586, 587, 596, 597, 606

Heber C. Kimball, 238, 251, 252, 617

heir, 12, 47, 85, 196, 233, 325, 533

hell, 42, 55, 60, 61, 63, 64, 85, 86, 111, 249, 258, 272, 274, 293, 298, 299, 320, 404, 432, 434, 435, 441, 445, 458, 464, 506, 507, 534, 542, 576

heresies, 51, 131

homosexuality, 50

hope, 13, 21, 36, 45, 61, 101, 102, 114, 126, 134, 144, 145, 146, 157, 164, 178, 192, 209, 213, 223, 224, 226, 238, 276, 277, 278, 288, 289, 292, 294, 296, 316, 327, 345, 346, 354, 363, 371, 373, 393, 398, 411, 415, 418, 419, 424, 430, 449, 458, 459, 460, 461, 462, 464, 466, 467, 471, 474, 478, 479, 480, 485, 491, 492, 493, 501, 505, 522, 537, 544, 546, 560, 569, 578, 583, 584, 586, 598, 607

Hugh Nibley, 6, 8, 9, 31, 45, 46, 49, 51, 61, 62, 65, 66, 67, 68, 69, 76, 78, 79, 209, 257, 258, 279, 346, 348, 355, 364, 382, 387, 412, 413, 414, 419, 420, 423, 424, 429, 431, 432, 435, 446, 451, 454, 455, 465, 513, 514, 576

humble, 21, 22, 31, 36, 37, 45, 58, 102, 134, 154, 158, 226, 230, 237, 270, 275, 276, 291, 292, 293, 299, 303, 312, 320, 328, 344, 353, 378, 395, 400, 417, 428, 429, 434, 437, 439, 440, 445, 462, 508, 512, 531, 532, 553, 567, 582, 585

hundredfold, 110, 111, 112, 113, 268, 271, 272, 282, 290, 370, 371, 389, 397, 398, 418, 461, 467, 482, 488, 493, 553, 594

hunger, 73, 110, 129, 138, 236, 478, 479

husband, 109, 144, 151, 152, 153, 154, 155, 156, 157, 158, 159, 163, 166, 167, 169, 183, 185, 186, 191, 220, 223, 240, 258, 278, 313, 315, 327, 337, 375, 377, 423, 469, 470, 531, 593

hypocrisy, 68, 69, 123, 207, 210, 256, 258, 265, 297, 301, 302, 457

idleness, 26, 50, 265, 273, 358, 373, 411, 412, 413, 426, 442, 471

idolatrous, 48, 75, 134, 306, 432, 438, 439

immoral, 52, 61, 65, 74, 306, 307, 487

inequality, 73, 261, 269, 275, 281, 357, 365, 371, 373, 402, 413, 440, 444, 445, 465, 582

inherit, 51, 62, 95, 101, 103, 110, 121, 139, 145, 162, 166, 168, 169, 174, 186, 192, 224, 258, 265, 271, 281, 282, 288, 291, 292, 303, 325, 328, 333, 338, 339, 343, 348, 354, 355, 366, 384, 394, 408, 409, 410, 417, 423, 424, 438, 450, 456, 458, 466, 483, 486, 498, 552, 600, 605, 608, 609

Israel, 17, 18, 27, 30, 33, 38, 39, 41, 42, 57, 85, 101, 148, 156, 163, 164, 166, 184, 191, 198, 228, 233, 234, 259, 310, 313, 326, 356, 402, 425, 428, 429, 445, 449, 450, 453, 465, 473, 524, 525, 530, 561, 587, 588, 589, 590, 606

J. Reuben Clark, 40, 235, 359, 364

James E. Faust, 71, 246, 264, 376, 470, 475, 533, 572, 612

Jehovah, 17, 197, 396, 423, 425, 569, 577

Jerusalem, 4, 10, 15, 30, 33, 42, 48, 49, 54, 65, 67, 88, 90, 92, 132, 169, 173, 180, 187, 211, 251, 330, 342, 375, 497, 502, 512, 514, 547, 556, 568, 576, 577, 590, 593, 594, 601, 602, 604, 607, 612

Jesus, iii, xvii, xviii, 3, 4, 5, 7, 8, 10, 12, 13, 21, 22, 24, 26, 27, 28, 31, 36, 38, 40, 41, 42, 43, 44, 45, 47, 51, 52, 57, 62, 63, 64, 69, 72, 73, 77, 80, 81, 87, 90, 92, 95, 97, 98, 99, 102, 103, 104, 105, 106, 108, 110, 111, 112, 113, 115, 116, 117, 118, 119, 120, 121, 123, 124, 125, 126, 127, 129, 130, 131, 133, 134, 135, 136, 137, 138, 139, 141, 142, 143, 144, 145, 146, 148, 149, 150, 152, 153, 154, 156, 160, 161, 163, 164, 167, 169, 170, 174, 176, 178, 179, 180, 181, 184, 186, 188, 189, 190, 201, 205, 207, 209, 212, 214, 215, 216, 217, 218, 219, 222, 224, 225, 228, 230, 231, 232, 233, 234, 235, 236, 237, 238, 239, 240, 242, 244, 246, 247, 249, 251, 252, 255, 259, 260, 263, 267, 268, 271, 275, 278, 279, 286, 287, 288, 291, 292, 294, 296, 297, 302, 305, 307, 308, 312, 313, 314, 316, 320, 321, 323, 325, 326, 327, 328, 329, 330, 331, 332, 336, 337, 340, 343, 345, 354, 369, 372, 375, 376, 382, 383, 384, 385, 386, 387, 388, 390, 399, 401, 404, 405, 406, 407, 408,

409, 410, 420, 427, 430, 434, 435, 436, 441, 445, 448, 449, 452, 455, 456, 457, 459, 460, 461, 462, 464, 465, 466, 469, 471, 472, 473, 474, 475, 476, 477, 478, 479, 480, 481, 483, 484, 485, 486, 487, 491, 492, 493, 497, 498, 499, 502, 508, 509, 511, 512, 513, 516, 518, 519, 521, 522, 523, 524, 525, 526, 527, 529, 533, 537, 538, 540, 541, 544, 545, 546, 547, 548, 549, 550, 552, 556, 557, 558, 560, 563, 564, 565, 566, 567, 568, 570, 572, 577, 579, 581, 583, 584, 585, 586, 587, 589, 590, 591, 592, 593, 594, 595, 596, 597, 598, 599, 600, 602, 603, 604, 605, 606, 607, 610, 611, 612, 613, 614, 615, 616, 617, 635

John A. Widtsoe, 8, 40, 54, 148, 476, 551

Joseph Fielding Smith, 14, 69, 184, 185, 190, 205, 217, 235, 252, 253, 321, 324, 334, 614

Joseph Smith, vi, 4, 5, 6, 15, 24, 29, 30, 37, 40, 41, 43, 57, 59, 63, 76, 80, 87, 88, 90, 92, 93, 95, 98, 102, 108, 109, 110, 111, 112, 124, 127, 131, 137, 139, 140, 141, 161, 163, 170, 173, 177, 178, 179, 182, 183, 184, 185, 186, 187, 188, 189, 190, 193, 197, 198, 202, 206, 207, 218, 219, 227, 233, 237, 238, 239, 240, 241, 242, 244, 245, 246, 249, 250, 251, 252, 254, 263, 266, 267, 270, 271, 281, 282, 297, 301, 302, 311, 314, 315, 316, 320, 321, 322, 323, 325, 326, 327, 328, 330, 333, 335, 342, 345, 347, 350, 351, 352, 365, 366, 373, 374, 377, 378, 379, 380, 388, 392, 395, 404, 405, 406, 407, 425, 428, 430, 431, 436, 451, 452, 454, 455, 459, 463, 471, 481, 483, 497, 500, 502, 503, 507, 512, 516, 518, 521, 523, 524, 530, 533, 534, 540, 541, 542, 543, 549, 550, 551, 560, 564, 567, 569, 570, 573, 574, 575, 576, 577, 578, 579, 585, 589, 594, 595, 598, 599, 600, 601, 603, 609, 611, 612, 614, 616

journey, 4, 5, 7, 12, 22, 43, 132, 137, 154, 181, 192, 194, 195, 196, 223, 237, 313, 325, 337, 338, 339, 388, 401, 470, 497, 498, 499, 500, 501, 502, 503, 504, 508, 510, 512, 514, 518, 519, 520, 522, 524, 530, 536, 539, 540, 551, 552, 555, 557, 558, 559, 589, 598

joy, 8, 11, 13, 15, 21, 22, 23, 24, 33, 36, 44, 62, 85, 93, 96, 108, 109, 110, 129, 131, 133, 138, 154, 155, 161, 167, 170, 180, 181, 195, 201, 229, 250, 264, 275, 296, 303, 318, 319, 320, 357, 358, 395, 408, 417, 424, 445, 453, 460, 473, 483, 485, 501, 503, 504, 507, 508, 518, 519, 520, 540, 541, 543, 547, 549, 555, 556, 557, 558, 561, 566, 590, 602, 604, 605

justice, 20, 25, 50, 57, 58, 63, 81, 94, 95, 97, 98, 100, 101, 102, 103, 104, 108, 112, 113, 114, 118, 119, 229, 460, 489, 521, 561

justified, 69, 94, 95, 98, 100, 102, 104, 113, 117, 118, 229, 411, 430, 457, 464, 608

key, 4, 14, 18, 74, 86, 88, 113, 139, 192, 206, 207, 218, 220, 233, 238, 247, 248, 249, 250, 267, 268, 278, 282, 295, 300, 310, 313, 314, 317, 321, 322, 327, 349, 393, 397, 416, 430, 462, 468, 477, 492, 517, 534, 541, 548, 550, 569, 585, 607

kind, 9, 22, 25, 32, 49, 51, 55, 70, 109, 132, 166, 169, 200, 213, 258, 264, 267, 273, 294, 295, 296, 297, 304, 306, 317, 349, 365, 374, 388, 411, 414, 419, 425, 450, 458, 459, 467, 473, 477, 493, 528, 557, 589, 599

King, vi, ix, xi, 9, 13, 15, 18, 19, 20, 21, 22, 23, 24, 25, 96, 98, 143, 161, 166, 169, 176, 178, 179, 180, 181, 182, 188, 189, 213, 226, 236, 259, 260, 261, 280, 283, 291, 298, 327, 349, 370, 374, 406, 423, 441, 442, 446, 447, 456, 466, 482, 502, 523, 526, 529, 531, 544, 546, 547, 548, 550, 555, 584, 585, 589, 601, 614, 617

King Benjamin, vi, ix, 18, 19, 20, 21, 22, 23, 24, 25, 96, 143, 178, 179, 180, 181, 182, 189, 213, 226, 291, 349, 370, 374, 406, 441, 442, 446, 447, 482, 526, 531, 544, 546, 547, 548, 550, 584, 585, 617

kingdom, 5, 6, 9, 11, 18, 22, 27, 30, 33, 36, 40, 44, 46, 47, 48, 51, 58, 62, 72, 78, 85, 88, 93, 98, 101, 102, 103, 108, 119, 122, 125, 126, 129, 130, 133, 141, 152, 153, 161, 166, 169, 179, 180, 182, 183, 185, 189, 192, 195, 196, 197, 198, 201, 202, 204, 206, 208, 210, 211, 217, 218, 219, 222, 226, 227, 228, 229, 231, 233, 235, 236, 237, 238, 240, 241, 242, 246, 247, 248, 250, 252, 254, 255, 263, 265, 267, 268, 269, 271, 279, 282, 285, 286, 287, 306, 310, 311, 316, 318, 319, 321, 322, 324, 325, 327, 328, 329, 334, 337, 338, 343, 344, 345, 347, 348, 350, 352, 353, 354, 355, 356, 357, 362, 363, 365, 366, 372, 376, 378, 379, 381, 382, 384, 386, 387, 390, 391, 399, 400, 401, 403, 405, 406, 407, 408, 410, 411, 413, 414, 415, 416, 417, 418, 419, 420, 424, 425, 428, 429, 430, 431, 435, 438, 446, 451, 453, 456, 458, 459, 461, 462, 463, 464, 466, 467, 468, 470, 472, 473, 476, 480, 482, 483, 485, 486, 488, 491, 492, 493, 494, 498, 499, 505, 507, 509, 515, 521, 526, 530, 536, 537, 542, 543, 544, 549, 550, 561, 562, 564, 567, 569, 570, 572, 574, 575, 577, 592, 597, 598, 600, 603, 605, 607, 608, 609

kings, 52, 65, 79, 99, 124, 127, 166, 176, 177, 178, 201, 218, 224, 230, 263, 281, 310, 326, 327, 328, 329, 338, 407, 425, 447, 463, 503, 549, 550, 574, 608

Kirtland, 30, 31, 32, 92, 181, 183, 184, 224, 267, 323, 325, 379, 522, 614, 617

Korihor, 45, 68, 446, 486

labor, 19, 22, 25, 28, 38, 71, 121, 178, 188, 216, 286, 306, 356, 357, 373, 389, 393, 400, 408, 410, 411, 412, 413, 414, 415, 416, 417, 418, 447, 453, 454, 457, 458, 466, 467, 470, 485, 486, 492, 494, 499, 517, 522, 537, 572, 573, 575, 597, 609

lack, 8, 13, 34, 58, 78, 109, 110, 111, 136, 141, 143, 146, 192, 203, 211, 213, 214, 215, 216, 221, 296, 297, 357, 369, 375, 398, 410, 419, 429, 438, 442, 449, 458, 467, 473, 481, 485, 493, 494, 522, 576, 584, 608

CONCORDANCE

Laman, 86, 512, 517

Lamb, 54, 56, 110, 131, 259, 262, 281, 332, 353, 385, 450, 573, 593, 605

law, iii, 4, 7, 17, 18, 19, 20, 22, 26, 27, 29, 30, 32, 33, 34, 35, 66, 68, 88, 92, 94, 95, 97, 98, 100, 101, 102, 104, 109, 110, 111, 112, 113, 118, 119, 121, 122, 128, 131, 133, 135, 138, 142, 143, 145, 146, 150, 151, 156, 168, 175, 177, 178, 192, 196, 198, 녔201, 210, 211, 214, 217, 218, 235, 250, 251, 262, 263, 267, 268, 269, 270, 271, 274, 281, 282, 288, 310, 311, 313, 315, 319, 320, 321, 328, 333, 339, 343, 344, 345, 346, 347, 348, 349, 350, 351, 352, 353, 354, 355, 356, 357, 358, 359, 361, 362, 363, 364, 365, 366, 367, 368, 370, 371, 374, 375, 379, 381, 382, 383, 384, 385, 386, 387, 388, 389, 390, 391, 392, 393, 394, 396, 397, 398, 399, 400, 401, 402, 403, 404, 405, 408, 411, 415, 416, 417, 418, 419, 420, 421, 422, 425, 429, 431, 442, 445, 446, 447, 448, 449, 451, 455, 458, 461, 462, 463, 464, 465, 466, 467, 468, 469, 470, 471, 472, 475, 476, 477, 478, 480, 481, 482, 483, 489, 490, 491, 492, 493, 494, 495, 498, 499, 504, 522, 525, 530, 531, 533, 535, 537, 542, 556, 558, 564, 565, 568, 571, 574, 575, 576, 577, 578, 582, 586, 588, 589, 594, 596, 597, 598, 602, 606, 608, 609

lawyers, 73, 77, 440, 582

Lehi, 56, 64, 80, 132, 137, 153, 325, 359, 376, 389, 499, 502, 503, 504, 510, 511, 512, 513, 514, 517, 519, 521, 523, 529, 530, 538, 539, 543, 551, 556

liberties, 117, 548

lies, 10, 17, 21, 46, 55, 63, 105, 169, 180, 217, 220, 247, 249, 264, 281, 297, 314, 352, 374, 380, 395, 454, 459, 470, 478, 501, 503, 511, 517, 568

lifestyle, 12, 58, 70, 73, 81, 84, 87, 94, 98, 116, 118, 134, 144, 147, 227, 276, 283, 292, 296, 317, 354, 367, 374, 384, 462, 468, 470, 472, 492, 493, 494, 549, 564, 565, 595, 598

Lorenzo Snow, 67, 347, 354, 355, 367, 380, 499, 574, 575, 579, 605, 609, 616, 617

love, xiv, 19, 21, 22, 25, 27, 28, 31, 32, 38, 44, 56, 57, 61, 62, 65, 68, 73, 74, 76, 77, 84, 92, 93, 105, 111, 121, 123, 126, 131, 134, 135, 136, 139, 140, 143, 144, 146, 148, 149, 150, 151, 152, 153, 154, 156, 157, 158, 160, 165, 167, 168, 169, 170, 186, 197, 199, 207, 210, 211, 212, 213, 214, 217, 218, 221, 226, 227, 231, 232, 240, 241, 243, 245, 246, 248, 254, 256, 258, 259, 260, 261, 264, 265, 267, 269, 270, 274, 275, 276, 277, 279, 280, 281, 282, 286, 287, 288, 292, 293, 294, 295, 296, 303, 304, 305, 306, 307, 311, 315, 317, 320, 331, 343, 357, 359, 360, 361, 362, 363, 368, 369, 370, 371, 372, 374, 376, 380, 383, 384, 385, 386, 387, 388, 389, 390, 391, 395, 400, 401, 403, 416, 417, 419, 420, 422, 423, 424, 426, 430, 436, 438, 441, 443, 455, 458, 459, 460, 462, 463, 464, 467, 468, 469, 470, 471, 476, 477, 478, 479, 480, 481, 482, 483, 484, 485, 486, 488, 489, 491, 492, 493, 494, 495, 498, 509, 515, 520, 522, 530, 531, 539, 548, 550, 551, 553, 555, 557, 560, 561, 562, 563, 567, 570, 573, 579, 584, 585, 586, 597, 598, 599, 602, 607, 608, 610

Lucifer, 11

Mahan, 46, 60, 68, 446, 465

Maker, 43, 182, 227, 241, 292, 442, 492, 530, 569

mammon, 31, 32, 62, 193, 257, 258, 259, 261, 268, 280, 281, 282, 343, 385, 419, 420, 422, 423, 426, 427, 428, 429, 430, 432, 433, 434, 435, 436, 438, 439, 440, 441, 442, 443, 452, 458, 461, 462, 463, 464, 465, 467, 468, 498, 499, 572

mansions, 65, 149, 157, 160, 162, 166, 303, 331, 409, 486, 537

marriage, 7, 16, 30, 34, 36, 72, 74, 77, 87, 90, 91, 94, 97, 116, 117, 118, 123, 125, 135, 139, 147, 148, 149, 150, 151, 152, 153, 154, 155, 156, 157, 158, 159, 160, 162, 163, 164, 165, 166, 168, 169, 170, 173, 174, 177, 182, 184, 185, 186, 187, 190, 191, 192, 194, 196, 197, 198, 199, 202, 206, 218, 219, 221, 223, 225, 235, 238, 240, 242, 259, 260, 261, 262, 263, 280, 281, 283, 296, 298, 309, 312, 318, 327, 328, 329, 332, 337, 338, 339, 342, 343, 353, 362, 365, 375, 376, 384, 386, 391, 401, 408, 422, 429, 450, 469, 470, 471, 482, 483, 497, 498, 500, 531, 543, 549, 555, 556, 565, 573, 574, 592, 593, 601, 607, 608

martyrdom, 31, 137

materialism, 55, 56, 60, 86, 432, 573

Matthew Cowley, 7, 41, 612

meek, 21, 58, 102, 217, 226, 291, 292, 304, 395, 400, 417, 427, 431, 443, 465, 491, 531

Melchizedek, vi, ix, x, 5, 15, 16, 17, 18, 26, 29, 90, 97, 99, 107, 123, 124, 125, 127, 170, 173, 175, 176, 177, 178, 179, 180, 182, 187, 188, 189, 190, 191, 192, 193, 194, 195, 196, 201, 202, 203, 205, 206, 208, 218, 220, 222, 228, 230, 232, 233, 234, 236, 241, 245, 246, 247, 248, 250, 253, 254, 279, 310, 311, 314, 316, 322, 327, 331, 332, 334, 337, 339, 342, 363, 410, 425, 463, 497, 552, 561, 569, 570, 592, 595, 607

Melchizedek Priesthood, x, 16, 17, 18, 26, 29, 90, 97, 107, 123, 124, 125, 127, 170, 173, 175, 177, 178, 179, 182, 187, 190, 191, 192, 193, 194, 202, 203, 205, 206, 220, 222, 233, 234, 236, 241, 246, 247, 248, 250, 253, 254, 279, 310, 311, 314, 316, 322, 327, 331, 332, 334, 339, 342, 363, 497, 561, 569, 570, 592, 595, 607

merchandise, 25, 66, 79, 260, 261, 262, 429, 447

merciful, 79, 80, 93, 95, 103, 110, 113, 129, 140, 216, 295, 318, 459, 530, 540

miracle, 24, 28, 58, 142, 294, 349, 371, 383, 388, 390, 397, 400, 472, 473, 475, 484, 516, 522, 528, 550, 580, 586

miserable, 44, 45, 46, 53, 66, 67, 97, 103, 162, 275, 394, 507, 508, 541

moral, 45, 70, 71, 207, 291, 307, 350, 400, 476

Moroni, vii, xvi, 3, 29, 54, 60, 77, 78, 87, 104, 106, 113, 120, 121, 128, 139, 144, 145, 158, 180, 182, 183, 218, 224, 226, 227, 231, 244, 245, 292, 293, 294, 295, 300, 302, 304, 305, 324, 325, 330, 331, 335, 346, 369, 422, 423, 430, 431, 443, 444, 458, 464, 477, 478, 479, 480, 482, 483, 485, 486, 488, 491, 493, 517, 521, 532, 539, 541, 545, 553, 560, 584, 586, 589, 593, 595, 606, 607, 615

mortal, 33, 36, 37, 38, 42, 52, 107, 108, 133, 134, 189, 201, 228, 241, 244, 245, 263, 274, 281, 311, 324, 330, 331, 395, 406, 420, 456, 458, 467, 477, 478, 505, 522, 525, 532, 558, 562, 566

Moses, vi, x, xi, 4, 8, 10, 11, 12, 13, 14, 15, 17, 18, 22, 26, 29, 31, 44, 46, 47, 49, 59, 60, 62, 64, 67, 68, 74, 75, 96, 100, 103, 107, 108, 112, 120, 123, 128, 129, 130, 135, 140, 145, 156, 158, 184, 185, 187, 188, 189, 190, 191, 192, 193, 194, 202, 204, 216, 217, 220, 222, 224, 225, 227, 229, 231, 232, 233, 234, 239, 242, 243, 249, 251, 252, 254, 258, 288, 296, 300, 309, 310, 311, 314, 316, 320, 324, 325, 330, 332, 333, 334, 335, 345, 360, 365, 369, 371, 373, 375, 377, 380, 381, 383, 390, 394, 399, 408, 421, 422, 423, 425, 431, 434, 439, 441, 446, 448, 450, 458, 466, 470, 472, 473, 474, 477, 478, 492, 493, 502, 504, 511, 514, 520, 521, 522, 523, 524, 525, 526, 529, 530, 534, 535, 540, 541, 551, 552, 555, 556, 557, 561, 567, 568, 570, 571, 576, 578, 579, 589, 592, 599, 600, 601, 605, 607

mother, 41, 54, 110, 131, 159, 220, 271, 364, 432, 483, 513, 603

murder, 45, 47, 53, 55, 60, 68, 77, 86, 87, 168, 265, 286, 297, 385, 439, 454, 507, 586

murmur, 108, 517

mysteries, 18, 54, 126, 179, 180, 192, 197, 206, 210, 211, 218, 229, 237, 241, 246, 248, 250, 310, 311, 314, 316, 318, 319, 320, 321, 322, 379, 424, 431, 464, 544, 550, 562, 567, 569, 570, 592, 594

natural man, 21, 67, 106, 312, 395, 481, 515, 531, 532, 558, 566, 572

Neal A. Maxwell, 13, 36, 259, 264, 265, 288, 354, 363, 388, 407, 614, 617

needy, 4, 19, 23, 25, 50, 69, 77, 211, 262, 273, 347, 350, 353, 361, 365, 368, 374, 386, 402, 404, 410, 416, 417, 430, 439, 442, 443, 444, 445, 448, 449, 451, 456, 460, 464, 467, 471, 482, 490, 554

Nehor, 25, 71, 72, 286

neighbor, 19, 27, 58, 187, 212, 248, 315, 359, 362, 368, 373, 387, 389, 406, 417, 425, 428, 439, 442, 471, 476, 477, 494, 573, 574, 602

new and everlasting covenant, 7, 8, 9, 11, 16, 26, 28, 29, 30, 34, 39, 42, 43, 53, 64, 86, 88, 90, 91, 92, 94, 95, 96, 97, 103, 104, 106, 107, 108, 109, 110, 113, 114, 115, 116, 117, 118, 119, 120, 121, 125, 126, 127, 128, 130, 135, 138, 142, 145, 147, 148, 149, 150, 151, 152, 154, 155, 156, 157, 163, 164, 165, 166, 167, 168, 169, 170, 173, 175, 176, 177, 178, 185, 186, 190, 193, 194, 197, 201, 202, 207, 211, 215, 216, 218, 221, 224, 225, 227, 228, 229, 233, 236, 246, 253, 254, 257, 261, 262, 264, 280, 284, 285, 292, 296, 311, 312, 318, 323, 328, 332, 334, 337, 338, 339, 342, 343, 344, 359, 362, 377, 384, 386, 387, 390, 415, 417, 459, 461, 462, 470, 494, 497, 498, 501, 509, 513, 518, 526, 527, 529, 531, 533, 556, 558, 565, 572, 605, 606, 607, 608, 609

Nimrod, vii, 45, 47, 48, 49, 51, 54, 85

Noah, vi, vii, 14, 15, 16, 18, 33, 47, 49, 73, 74, 85, 87, 179, 195, 334, 430, 522, 569, 579, 599, 601

oath and covenant of the priesthood, 7, 30, 90, 97, 118, 119, 128, 139, 170, 173, 174, 176, 178, 190, 193, 197, 199, 201, 202, 203, 204, 207, 210, 211, 215, 216, 217, 219, 220, 221, 222, 223, 225, 226, 229, 230, 233, 235, 236, 238, 240, 241, 242, 243, 246, 247, 248, 249, 250, 252, 253, 254, 255, 257, 262, 264, 270, 274, 277, 280, 281, 283, 284, 285, 296, 306, 308, 309, 311, 312, 317, 320, 321, 323, 330, 334, 336, 337, 338, 339, 342, 343, 353, 401, 417, 448, 459, 494, 497, 498, 544, 592, 607, 608

Obedience, xvii, 118, 119, 120, 121, 122, 124, 125, 354, 367, 386, 533, 535, 614

offence, 64

CONCORDANCE

offering, 38, 43, 46, 72, 106, 107, 108, 111, 122, 128, 129, 140, 145, 150, 154, 204, 213, 215, 220, 232, 233, 271, 348, 352, 356, 366, 372, 386, 461, 515, 542, 543, 596, 597

Omnipotent, 21, 23, 24, 181, 393, 548

oneness, 13, 44, 78, 108, 109, 110, 112, 113, 129, 147, 153, 305, 345, 357, 367, 375, 376, 377, 378, 380, 389, 390, 549, 574, 591, 598

opposition, 30, 33, 48, 59, 61, 105, 111, 135, 264, 378, 393, 504, 510, 536

oppress, 279, 286

ordain, 16, 124, 141, 177

ordinance, 7, 11, 29, 46, 113, 115, 117, 119, 120, 121, 127, 133, 135, 141, 144, 146, 164, 176, 177, 180, 184, 186, 189, 195, 196, 234, 237, 239, 241, 251, 255, 324, 327, 332, 365, 376, 472, 473, 474, 475, 476, 516, 517, 534, 545, 572, 606

parent, 38, 41, 303, 385, 462, 468, 509, 547

patience, 22, 25, 64, 108, 151, 159, 160, 196, 249, 273, 287, 288, 289, 290, 294, 312, 314, 424, 462, 469, 488, 489, 493, 494, 567

patriarchal, 16, 29, 30, 123, 125, 139, 177, 183, 185, 191, 192, 196, 197, 200, 201, 202, 218, 219, 241, 278, 318, 328, 329, 332, 333, 334, 335, 338, 608

Paul, v, vii, 37, 51, 52, 61, 64, 75, 76, 77, 87, 111, 141, 156, 159, 198, 204, 226, 243, 251, 288, 299, 305, 306, 313, 320, 327, 371, 423, 438, 477, 478, 493, 506, 508, 519, 570, 594, 606

Paymaster, xiv, 17, 400, 401, 415, 417, 493

peace, 10, 15, 22, 23, 25, 28, 41, 75, 96, 109, 122, 131, 140, 167, 177, 178, 179, 187, 196, 208, 213, 225, 228, 238, 261, 265, 273, 281, 302, 307, 328, 357, 360, 374, 378, 379, 437, 440, 444, 445, 454, 455, 457, 465, 466, 475, 482, 483, 488, 518, 519, 527, 532, 534, 539, 541, 564, 565, 573, 574, 581, 582, 584, 585, 597, 602, 604, 605, 607

persecute, 54, 58, 72, 77, 279, 291, 431, 442, 443, 444, 465, 530

philosophers, 70, 567

plague, 70, 298, 444, 527

pollute, 33, 72, 87, 429, 442

poor, 4, 14, 17, 22, 23, 25, 26, 27, 28, 44, 50, 52, 53, 54, 58, 61, 68, 77, 78, 112, 164, 177, 211, 213, 260, 265, 268, 269, 270, 273, 275, 279, 282, 286, 290, 345, 347, 348, 350, 352, 353, 354, 361, 362, 364, 365, 366, 368, 369, 371, 373, 374, 375, 376, 380, 넛381, 386, 389, 390, 392, 397, 400, 401, 404, 410, 411, 412, 413, 416, 418, 422, 424, 426, 427, 428, 429, 430, 431, 434, 435, 437, 439, 440, 441, 442, 443, 445, 446, 447, 448, 449, 450, 451, 452, 455, 456, 464, 465, 466, 470, 472, 473, 476, 478, 483, 485, 486, 487, 489, 490, 493, 554, 557, 561, 573, 609, 610

popular, 14, 58, 69, 71, 72, 74, 193, 275

possession, 17, 46, 160, 162, 184, 355, 387, 393, 394, 428, 437, 521, 580

praise, 19, 25, 55, 63, 77, 137, 161, 274, 275, 276, 297, 303, 326, 430, 444, 519, 524, 557, 589

pray, 69, 72, 83, 101, 106, 134, 160, 164, 205, 228, 293, 322, 326, 349, 379, 386, 391, 433, 434, 457, 474, 475, 490, 491, 500, 511, 530, 538, 539, 551, 553, 560, 569, 589, 590, 591, 592, 595, 596, 598, 599

pride, 20, 23, 26, 31, 44, 46, 50, 52, 53, 54, 56, 58, 59, 60, 73, 77, 81, 84, 85, 86, 123, 207, 209, 211, 212, 256, 265, 269, 270, 272, 274, 275, 276, 277, 299, 312, 346, 360, 365, 369, 410, 411, 424, 426, 427, 430, 431, 437, 438, 440, 441, 442, 443, 444, 445, 넛453, 465, 471, 531, 581, 582, 584

priest, 16, 17, 25, 71, 106, 124, 166, 167, 177, 178, 180, 196, 208, 224, 265, 291, 321, 327, 415, 425, 529, 547, 570

priestcraft, 25, 46, 47, 54, 59, 71, 73, 285, 286

priesthood, 4, 5, 6, 7, 12, 14, 15, 16, 17, 18, 29, 30, 40, 41, 42, 43, 45, 46, 47, 48, 54, 73, 79, 86, 88, 90, 95, 97, 106, 111, 114, 116, 117, 118, 123, 124, 125, 126, 127, 134, 139, 146, 148, 149, 168, 170, 173, 174, 175, 176, 177, 178, 179, 180, 181, 182, 183, 184, 185, 186, 187, 188, 189, 190, 191, 192, 193, 194, 195, 196, 197, 198, 199, 200, 201, 202, 203, 204, 205, 206, 207, 208, 209, 210, 213, 214, 215, 216, 217, 218, 219, 220, 221, 222, 223, 224, 225, 226, 227, 228, 229, 230, 231, 232, 233, 234, 235, 236, 237, 238, 239, 240, 241, 242, 244, 246, 247, 248, 249, 250, 251, 252, 253, 254, 255, 256, 257, 258, 259, 260, 261, 262, 264, 265, 266, 267, 268, 269, 270, 271, 272, 274, 275, 276, 277, 278, 279, 280, 281, 283, 284, 285, 286, 287, 288, 290, 291, 292, 293, 294, 295, 296, 297, 298, 300, 301, 302, 303, 304, 305, 306, 307, 308, 309, 310, 311, 313, 314, 315, 316, 317, 318, 319, 320, 321, 322, 323, 324, 326, 327, 328, 329, 330, 331, 332, 333, 334, 335,

336, 337, 338, 339, 340, 342, 343, 347, 351, 352, 353, 354, 360, 363, 367, 382, 384, 390, 401, 403, 406, 408, 415, 416, 425, 448, 451, 459, 461, 462, 463, 466, 471, 472, 473, 474, 476, 489, 491, 493, 494, 497, 498, 500, 517, 534, 541, 542, 543, 544, 545, 546, 547, 548, 550, 556, 561, 562, 568, 569, 570, 571, 572, 574, 575, 576, 577, 578, 591, 592, 599, 601, 604, 607, 608

priesthood society, 5, 6, 7, 12, 14, 41, 177, 182, 190, 193, 195, 199, 201, 221, 239, 271, 333, 347, 353, 354, 360, 367, 403, 408, 571, 577, 578, 601

Prince of Peace, 179, 604

princess, 41, 327

principle, 19, 20, 23, 41, 51, 61, 68, 69, 88, 90, 94, 108, 118, 124, 143, 161, 181, 185, 187, 193, 199, 205, 210, 214, 215, 220, 223, 226, 228, 231, 238, 248, 249, 269, 271, 275, 282, 288, 292, 293, 294, 295, 302, 307, 319, 345, 346, 348, 349, 354, 358, 359, 360, 361, 362, 364, 365, 366, 370, 374, 375, 376, 381, 386, 390, 396, 398, 404, 407, 410, 411, 413, 418, 421, 424, 429, 452, 461, 462, 467, 468, 471, 476, 477, 478, 481, 482, 483, 487, 488, 490, 491, 493, 504, 521, 522, 523, 524, 534, 538, 553, 555, 564, 572, 594, 598, 599, 603

prison, 75, 132, 133, 161, 228, 251, 456, 466, 506, 519, 528, 557

probation, 38, 83, 111, 421, 422, 433, 442

properties, 107, 211, 345, 351, 373, 399, 401, 404, 406, 450, 515

Prophecies, xix, 83, 456, 594, 611

prosper, 20, 26, 28, 45, 122, 134, 225, 274, 370, 374, 376, 410, 415, 421, 425, 426, 437, 450, 452, 456, 463, 486, 487, 493

publicans, 69

punish, 108, 515

pure in heart, 4, 5, 7, 8, 9, 12, 15, 18, 23, 30, 41, 43, 104, 209, 225, 229, 241, 298, 307, 312, 324, 334, 354, 355, 367, 403, 411, 420, 428, 432, 463, 497, 498, 499, 500, 510, 560, 561, 563, 564, 565, 566, 568, 569, 570, 571, 572, 573, 574, 576, 580, 587, 591, 592, 593, 594, 595, 599, 601, 604, 606, 607, 609

purification, 104, 105, 106, 163, 164, 225, 278, 384, 475, 492, 498, 516, 517, 558, 562, 571, 592, 596

queen, 79, 163, 166, 167, 327

rainbow, 15, 599

redeem, 41, 59, 121, 150, 152, 153, 154, 165, 169, 193, 295, 296, 337, 394, 434, 575, 603

Redeemer, 19, 57, 93, 98, 116, 360, 372, 579, 603

relationship, 43, 54, 93, 128, 129, 133, 135, 139, 140, 144, 145, 146, 147, 149, 150, 151, 152, 153, 154, 155, 157, 159, 162, 165, 168, 169, 170, 193, 199, 226, 233, 240, 258, 277, 303, 344, 345, 349, 361, 362, 363, 364, 365, 375, 376, 378, 382, 389, 407, 422, 461, 462, 463, 467, 468, 488, 515, 518, 520, 522, 524, 531, 532, 536, 537, 553, 566, 585, 598

repent, 4, 11, 14, 15, 22, 61, 77, 83, 84, 94, 95, 103, 105, 118, 119, 168, 177, 178, 188, 207, 208, 228, 253, 277, 292, 298, 319, 332, 372, 399, 412, 426, 433, 434, 438, 439, 441, 446, 453, 454, 463, 508, 534, 561, 564, 583, 584, 586

resurrected, 13, 26, 57, 73, 80, 101, 110, 186, 244, 330, 331, 375, 506, 549, 583, 586, 596, 597, 605

reveal, 29, 92, 97, 112, 118, 128, 144, 182, 183, 186, 199, 238, 248, 289, 316, 317, 318, 379, 382, 383, 507, 524, 563, 564, 565, 566, 595

rich, 23, 25, 28, 32, 44, 50, 58, 60, 61, 65, 69, 71, 73, 76, 77, 78, 79, 151, 213, 260, 268, 269, 270, 271, 272, 273, 274, 275, 282, 299, 306, 327, 354, 361, 364, 368, 369, 374, 376, 380, 389, 397, 404, 411, 412, 413, 415, 416, 418, 421, 424, 425, 426, 427, 428, 429, 430, 431, 434, 435, 436, 437, 439, 441, 443, 444, 445, 446, 447, 448, 449, 450, 451, 456, 457, 458, 464, 465, 467, 469, 470, 487, 575

rob, 58, 438, 442, 443, 465

Sabbath, viii, 34, 121, 122, 123, 131, 148, 424, 540

sacrament, 27, 101, 106, 120, 121, 122, 123, 124, 139, 144, 155, 156, 157, 162, 180, 181, 203, 206, 225, 232, 246, 300, 323, 336, 379, 509, 510, 545, 546, 547, 548, 593, 596

sacrifice, 11, 17, 19, 36, 94, 98, 100, 104, 105, 108, 111, 118, 121, 122, 123, 131, 133, 134, 137, 139, 143, 147, 150, 151, 152, 153, 154, 155, 163, 165, 168, 189, 196, 212, 226, 227, 232, 233, 236, 245, 257, 264, 269, 270, 271, 274, 282, 283, 285, 287, 290, 294, 323, 348, 352, 353, 354, 355, 356, 357, 358, 363, 365, 367, 369, 370, 371, 372, 374, 382, 383, 385,

CONCORDANCE

386, 387, 388, 389, 390, 391, 394, 398, 404, 420, 421, 423, 436, 448, 469, 470, 482, 493, 494, 499, 505, 513, 519, 525, 534, 537, 542, 543, 544, 547, 552, 558, 566, 579, 588, 593, 608

safe, 24, 80, 82, 129, 133, 134, 135, 136, 137, 138, 141, 146, 154, 161, 255, 268, 272, 282, 287, 359, 363, 399, 420, 434, 436, 440, 458, 467, 470, 487, 505, 526, 527, 537, 558, 568

Salem, 10, 15, 16, 176, 194, 196, 208

salvation, 9, 11, 16, 21, 22, 24, 33, 36, 41, 42, 43, 45, 83, 88, 91, 93, 95, 97, 104, 108, 115, 116, 120, 123, 125, 128, 129, 134, 141, 145, 146, 167, 168, 170, 174, 176, 178, 179, 181, 183, 184, 186, 187, 188, 190, 192, 193, 194, 195, 197, 198, 199, 201, 202, 206, 223, 224, 226, 230, 231, 232, 234, 236, 239, 244, 248, 249, 253, 260, 263, 270, 272, 276, 281, 294, 296, 303, 316, 321, 327, 334, 337, 340, 343, 345, 346, 355, 364, 365, 367, 380, 387, 388, 390, 392, 393, 398, 401, 402, 412, 416, 417, 421, 423, 433, 449, 450, 458, 462, 463, 467, 472, 474, 475, 484, 485, 486, 491, 492, 498, 501, 505, 517, 520, 523, 542, 544, 546, 547, 548, 557, 569, 574, 575, 589, 601, 602, 604, 605

sanctification, 104, 106, 107, 163, 164, 180, 217, 225, 226, 227, 228, 229, 231, 232, 239, 254, 278, 336, 353, 356, 358, 367, 384, 492, 498, 517, 534, 558, 562, 571, 574, 578, 592

sanctuaries, 58, 443, 465

Satan, xvii, 8, 13, 20, 21, 31, 39, 40, 44, 45, 46, 47, 48, 49, 51, 52, 53, 54, 55, 56, 57, 58, 59, 60, 61, 63, 64, 66, 67, 68, 69, 71, 72, 73, 74, 76, 83, 85, 86, 91, 93, 96, 97, 100, 103, 111, 113, 130, 131, 140, 142, 146, 170, 179, 252, 257, 280, 285, 286, 297, 320, 355, 357, 377, 378, 384, 392, 395, 399, 419, 420, 422, 424, 431, 432, 433, 436, 439, 440, 442, 446, 451, 464, 465, 499, 506, 507, 510, 511, 513, 519, 532, 534, 540, 541, 542, 552, 558, 579, 580, 582, 596

Savior, xii, xiv, xviii, 3, 4, 12, 13, 18, 21, 26, 27, 35, 36, 37, 38, 57, 62, 72, 73, 80, 84, 95, 96, 97, 101, 103, 104, 105, 106, 109, 111, 113, 118, 119, 122, 129, 134, 135, 137, 139, 143, 149, 150, 151, 152, 153, 154, 155, 164, 165, 168, 176, 180, 184, 186, 187, 193, 194, 196, 202, 204, 215, 216, 220, 223, 224, 228, 230, 231, 232, 240, 252, 254, 258, 259, 268, 270, 282, 290, 291, 292, 295, 297, 305, 307, 312, 313, 326, 347, 354, 363, 375, 377, 381, 382, 383, 389, 394, 416, 417, 421, 436, 442, 456, 458, 459, 460, 461, 466, 472, 473, 474, 476, 479, 481, 483, 487, 493, 503, 505, 506, 508, 511, 517, 519, 520, 527, 533, 538, 539, 544, 547, 549, 558, 560, 561, 565, 576, 579, 580, 583, 585, 587, 588, 589, 590, 591, 592, 594, 597, 599, 602, 603, 613, 616

saviors on Mount Zion, 38, 116, 123, 193, 201, 202, 206, 225, 228, 254, 294, 460, 493, 549, 592

science, 51, 69, 71, 101, 299

seal, 24, 109, 151, 154, 166, 183, 186, 237, 239, 250, 289, 303, 324, 328, 335, 384, 404, 431, 469, 475, 527, 543, 549, 551

selfish, 52, 64, 75, 77, 82, 105, 116, 147, 190, 231, 242, 268, 269, 270, 274, 279, 292, 293, 295, 306, 363, 387, 410, 418, 422, 434, 438, 452, 457, 458, 461, 464, 465, 467, 470, 477, 481, 487, 574

selfless, 23, 27, 94, 116, 148, 190, 213, 306, 432, 482, 573, 579

Sermon on the Mount, 27, 104, 564, 594

servant, 16, 25, 117, 139, 140, 146, 161, 164, 165, 168, 177, 197, 205, 230, 238, 251, 252, 253, 262, 326, 336, 339, 351, 382, 385, 403, 404, 406, 407, 408, 409, 416, 493, 550, 577, 587

serve, 19, 22, 27, 31, 32, 47, 54, 64, 77, 91, 97, 103, 119, 123, 131, 134, 140, 143, 181, 182, 190, 199, 205, 209, 210, 212, 213, 214, 217, 219, 221, 226, 233, 234, 237, 248, 257, 258, 275, 279, 280, 292, 294, 305, 317, 318, 338, 347, 353, 361, 366, 370, 379, 397, 398, 407, 413, 415, 419, 420, 428, 439, 441, 445, 446, 450, 455, 461, 462, 465, 466, 468, 471, 477, 479, 483, 485, 488, 490, 494, 519, 535, 536, 537, 538, 545, 565, 596

sex, 51, 58, 65, 292, 422

sin, 19, 22, 36, 37, 42, 48, 49, 55, 56, 58, 59, 60, 61, 62, 63, 73, 76, 78, 79, 100, 102, 104, 105, 106, 110, 113, 119, 148, 173, 182, 197, 212, 219, 228, 230, 231, 238, 245, 260, 261, 272, 274, 279, 281, 286, 332, 339, 343, 346, 357, 365, 373, 382, 398, 399, 402, 419, 423, 424, 427, 440, 446, 447, 454, 457, 463, 465, 474, 476, 486, 487, 497, 498, 502, 505, 506, 507, 508, 509, 510, 511, 512, 515, 519, 530, 531, 532, 534, 549, 557, 558, 572, 576, 582, 584, 585, 586, 589, 607

single women, 223

slave, 50, 151, 152, 262

slippery treasures, 464

snare, 61, 63, 258, 267, 269, 280, 282, 424, 427, 435, 507

Sodom, vii, 3, 48, 49, 50, 74, 80, 85, 87, 346, 442, 514

Son, ix, xi, xiii, 11, 12, 22, 36, 37, 40, 46, 54, 73, 87, 91, 92, 93, 95, 97, 98, 99, 108, 112, 114, 116, 117, 124, 126, 127, 129, 131, 135, 139, 145, 146, 149, 152, 157, 161, 163, 165, 166, 169, 175, 176, 177, 178, 182, 187, 189, 193, 194, 197, 200, 201, 208, 217, 218, 219, 224, 225, 230, 231, 237, 240, 245, 255, 259, 260, 279, 295, 311, 313, 316, 317, 318, 324, 329, 331, 332, 333, 334, 335, 336, 337, 338, 354, 364, 387, 390, 398, 404, 405, 409, 434, 456, 460, 472, 482, 491, 503, 508, 509, 512, 524, 525, 541, 560, 563, 568, 570, 572, 585, 586, 587, 588, 589, 591, 595, 598, 599, 602, 603, 606

sorrow, 31, 33, 55, 79, 86, 161, 213, 290, 297, 357, 444, 447, 453, 504, 531, 532, 584

soul, 19, 20, 26, 53, 66, 96, 105, 111, 122, 123, 130, 134, 138, 140, 167, 178, 188, 207, 210, 226, 227, 228, 238, 249, 251, 252, 256, 257, 263, 265, 267, 285, 290, 294, 297, 301, 307, 310, 315, 316, 320, 323, 338, 343, 349, 355, 358, 383, 386, 387, 391, 394, 395, 434, 436, 437, 439, 447, 457, 462, 466, 469, 474, 475, 477, 479, 481, 483, 485, 486, 489, 490, 491, 492, 495, 498, 506, 508, 510, 532, 533, 536, 552, 554, 557, 563, 566, 579, 586, 597

Spencer W. Kimball, 5, 8, 34, 49, 72, 190, 197, 201, 265, 281, 321, 348, 349, 354, 356, 360, 366, 367, 381, 390, 411, 413, 432, 452, 483, 484, 485, 488, 526, 536, 572, 573, 577, 579, 613

storehouse, 17, 142, 177, 373, 381, 392, 401, 402, 403, 404, 406, 407, 411, 416, 417, 421, 450

strategically, 8, 37, 41

submission, 68, 265, 291, 344, 521

sufficiency, 71, 146, 360, 361, 362, 535, 536

surplus, 17, 211, 351, 361, 399, 403, 404, 407, 417, 418, 420, 463

survival, 66, 534, 539

talents, 101, 147, 161, 162, 208, 269, 271, 274, 345, 346, 347, 348, 351, 352, 355, 356, 366, 367, 373, 381, 386, 389, 390, 398, 399, 400, 403, 405, 406, 407, 409, 410, 412, 415, 417, 430, 466, 486, 488, 493, 499, 553, 571, 572

teacher, 69, 71, 212, 322, 415, 594, 603

telestial, 5, 7, 8, 11, 17, 27, 35, 36, 42, 58, 68, 88, 101, 102, 108, 129, 138, 145, 226, 236, 243, 262, 264, 269, 270, 281, 282, 285, 300, 336, 350, 354, 357, 362, 369, 370, 395, 399, 402, 410, 411, 421, 425, 429, 458, 463, 476, 494, 495, 504, 505, 521, 525, 553, 566, 567, 572, 596, 600

temple, 14, 16, 17, 18, 29, 30, 32, 40, 48, 54, 56, 85, 86, 90, 97, 116, 118, 123, 125, 133, 134, 139, 148, 156, 157, 158, 163, 166, 167, 170, 173, 174, 176, 177, 178, 180, 181, 183, 184, 185, 187, 191, 192, 193, 194, 195, 196, 197, 201, 202, 203, 205, 218, 219, 221, 225, 226, 227, 232, 233, 234, 235, 240, 250, 254, 255, 257, 263, 265, 267, 278, 281, 309, 314, 316, 319, 321, 322, 323, 325, 327, 328, 329, 331, 332, 333, 334, 335, 337, 338, 339, 342, 343, 347, 348, 353, 356, 362, 363, 378, 380, 384, 391, 401, 402, 403, 407, 408, 410, 417, 420, 427, 448, 459, 470, 483, 493, 494, 497, 498, 509, 531, 536, 540, 542, 543, 544, 545, 548, 549, 550, 551, 555, 556, 560, 565, 566, 568, 569, 570, 571, 577, 596, 600, 601, 605, 607, 608

temptation, 61, 310, 377, 422, 424, 507, 596

Ten Commandments, 102, 425, 463, 587

Ten Virgins, 72, 87, 475

terrestrial, 5, 7, 8, 101, 217, 354, 399, 458, 553

testimonies, 45, 217, 404, 477, 482, 484, 517, 588, 602, 603

theories, 58, 298, 299

tithes, 17, 34, 177, 348, 351, 352, 366, 409, 415, 416, 418, 421, 463, 594

tolerance, 70, 77

tradition, 83, 148, 149, 150, 158, 179, 180

treasure, 27, 61, 82, 130, 145, 151, 154, 268, 270, 282, 303, 354, 404, 424, 431, 434, 435, 436, 443, 457, 568, 606

trial, 39, 135, 137, 238, 272, 288, 290, 444, 515, 518, 537, 544

truth, 5, 8, 11, 15, 22, 23, 33, 36, 37, 51, 54, 55, 56, 57, 63, 64, 69, 70, 71, 76, 77, 84, 85, 87, 94, 95, 96, 105, 120, 124, 140, 153, 164, 189, 200, 208, 210, 214, 217, 218, 220, 221, 229, 236, 247, 250, 257, 264, 265, 275, 277, 280, 283, 285, 294, 297, 298, 299, 300, 301, 302, 306, 307, 310, 317, 318, 320, 323, 324, 328, 330, 332, 338, 346, 378, 392, 393, 395, 396, 399, 404, 444, 453, 476, 478, 479, 480, 484, 487, 489, 490, 505, 507, 512, 520, 524, 533, 542, 546, 551, 562, 564, 572, 576, 578, 580, 584, 588, 589, 591, 596, 599, 603, 605, 606

unite, 46, 179, 189, 364, 374, 492, 574, 581

Concordance

vain, 56, 58, 61, 69, 73, 82, 83, 123, 207, 209, 213, 245, 256, 258, 262, 265, 277, 286, 292, 299, 300, 424, 433, 436, 439, 440, 442, 444, 446, 447, 451, 464, 486, 490, 542, 554, 575, 580, 582

veil, 36, 49, 154, 157, 158, 159, 167, 194, 244, 252, 312, 313, 314, 316, 325, 335, 386, 505, 551, 562, 567, 570, 586, 605

violence, 14, 33, 74, 79, 81, 179, 266, 431

virtue, 42, 62, 70, 75, 76, 124, 125, 149, 178, 183, 191, 198, 199, 200, 201, 202, 207, 210, 231, 235, 249, 254, 256, 257, 265, 277, 288, 291, 292, 307, 309, 317, 324, 350, 361, 372, 393, 422, 462, 478, 480, 485, 489, 492, 493, 500, 503, 548, 560, 591

vision, 14, 38, 39, 54, 77, 131, 169, 183, 197, 243, 245, 251, 272, 292, 325, 326, 328, 334, 359, 380, 408, 454, 511, 522, 526, 537, 572, 589, 600

wailing, 79

war, 14, 38, 39, 49, 55, 61, 67, 68, 72, 73, 78, 87, 112, 178, 179, 238, 353, 431, 455, 505, 526, 581, 585

warn, 80, 435, 444, 580, 581

wealth, 17, 25, 31, 47, 50, 52, 54, 55, 56, 59, 61, 62, 72, 76, 78, 79, 81, 84, 86, 130, 148, 267, 268, 269, 270, 272, 273, 276, 282, 344, 346, 351, 363, 369, 373, 397, 410, 412, 414, 419, 420, 422, 424, 427, 428, 429, 430, 432, 435, 436, 437, 439, 441, 444, 447, 450, 451, 452, 453, 455, 456, 462, 463, 464, 466, 493, 499, 569, 572, 597

weapon, 51, 62, 134, 424, 432, 451, 464

weighty, 27, 39, 65, 73, 426, 460, 463, 483, 534

whore, 52, 54, 78, 84, 86

wicked, 3, 13, 14, 15, 17, 25, 33, 48, 50, 54, 73, 74, 76, 78, 79, 80, 82, 83, 110, 130, 132, 140, 146, 161, 187, 196, 212, 247, 259, 267, 376, 393, 402, 404, 411, 427, 437, 438, 442, 445, 454, 507, 514, 529, 541, 555, 561, 570, 574, 580, 581, 583, 585, 601, 603

widow, 79, 347, 365, 428, 432, 449, 457, 462, 468, 538, 554

wife, v, 11, 31, 54, 109, 110, 137, 144, 150, 151, 153, 159, 164, 166, 168, 169, 183, 185, 186, 191, 197, 220, 238, 240, 258, 260, 271, 278, 315, 327, 328, 334, 337, 363, 375, 377, 378, 384, 423, 425, 470, 504, 512, 515, 527, 531, 635

wilderness, 17, 18, 132, 136, 137, 191, 214, 234, 310, 311, 335, 425, 439, 498, 499, 506, 507, 508, 509, 510, 511, 512, 513, 514, 515, 516, 517, 518, 520, 521, 522, 523, 524, 525, 526, 527, 528, 529, 530, 531, 532, 533, 534, 535, 536, 537, 538, 539, 540, 541, 543, 544, 550, 551, 552, 553, 555, 556, 557, 558, 559, 561, 562

Wilford Woodruff, 36, 216, 274, 337, 617

wilfully, 73, 440, 465, 582

wisdom, 22, 23, 24, 29, 31, 35, 52, 53, 56, 57, 67, 71, 83, 86, 127, 212, 215, 229, 246, 291, 298, 299, 300, 301, 302, 303, 318, 319, 329, 335, 347, 363, 397, 405, 424, 429, 431, 432, 441, 443, 455, 458, 464, 467, 489, 549

woman, 40, 52, 54, 123, 150, 154, 155, 156, 157, 158, 159, 163, 167, 169, 174, 176, 183, 186, 190, 223, 226, 240, 276, 278, 293, 307, 314, 316, 327, 340, 343, 470, 484, 498, 529, 570, 592, 608

world, 4, 7, 8, 11, 12, 13, 14, 17, 25, 31, 32, 33, 35, 36, 37, 38, 39, 40, 41, 42, 44, 45, 46, 47, 48, 49, 50, 51, 52, 53, 54, 55, 56, 58, 59, 61, 62, 64, 65, 66, 67, 68, 72, 73, 74, 77, 79, 80, 81, 84, 85, 86, 87, 91, 93, 95, 97, 98, 101, 103, 108, 109, 111, 119, 121, 122, 123, 124, 125, 129, 130, 131, 136, 138, 141, 145, 149, 158, 159, 165, 168, 169, 170, 173, 183, 185, 186, 187, 188, 189, 190, 193, 197, 200, 201, 202, 204, 205, 206, 207, 209, 212, 213, 217, 219, 220, 224, 229, 232, 236, 237, 238, 241, 244, 245, 246, 247, 248, 250, 253, 254, 255, 256, 257, 260, 263, 264, 266, 267, 268, 269, 271, 272, 273, 274, 275, 276, 279, 280, 282, 284, 285, 286, 293, 297, 299, 300, 308, 310, 311, 313, 315, 317, 319, 325, 326, 328, 331, 334, 337, 339, 343, 346, 348, 354, 355, 357, 359, 363, 365, 367, 369, 370, 372, 373, 377, 378, 384, 385, 392, 393, 394, 398, 399, 401, 402, 404, 405, 406, 410, 414, 415, 420, 421, 422, 423, 424, 426, 427, 428, 429, 430, 431, 432, 435, 436, 437, 439, 440, 441, 443, 444, 445, 446, 451, 452, 453, 454, 455, 456, 457, 460, 463, 464, 465, 466, 471, 474, 476, 478, 481, 483, 486, 488, 491, 494, 497, 498, 504, 505, 508, 511, 512, 513, 514, 515, 518, 521, 523, 525, 526, 529, 533, 535, 543, 544, 546, 550, 551, 555, 557, 558, 562, 567, 568, 569, 572, 573, 582, 586, 587, 588, 591, 592, 595, 596, 601, 603, 604, 605

yoke, 55, 86, 164, 298, 490, 552, 554

About the Author

Larry Barkdull is a longtime publisher and writer of books, music, art, and magazines. For nine years, he owned Sonos Music Resources and published the Tabernacle Choir Performance Library. He was also the owner and publisher of Keepsake Books. Over the past thirty years, he published about six hundred products for numerous authors, composers, and artists. He founded two nonprofit organizations: The Latter-day Foundation for the Arts, Education and Humanity (to promote LDS arts), and Gospel Ideals International (to promote the gospel of Jesus Christ on the Internet).

His books have sold in excess of 300,000 copies, and they have been translated into Japanese, Korean, Italian, and Hebrew. He is the recipient of the American Family Literary Award; the Benjamin Franklin Book Award; and *Foreword Magazine's* GOLD Book of the Year Award for best fiction. His most recent books are *Priesthood Power—Blessing the Sick and the Afflicted; Rescuing Wayward Children;* and *The Shepherd Song.* He also has created Facebook groups called "Rescuing Wayward Children" and "Three Pillars of Zion—Becoming a Zion Person."

He and his wife, Elizabeth, have ten children and a growing number of grandchildren. They live in Orem, Utah. Visit him at www.LarryBarkdull.com.